# QUANTITATIVE
# FINANCIAL
# ECONOMICS

# QUANTITATIVE FINANCIAL ECONOMICS

## STOCKS, BONDS AND FOREIGN EXCHANGE

Second Edition

KEITH CUTHBERTSON

AND

DIRK NITZSCHE

John Wiley & Sons, Ltd

Copyright © 2004     John Wiley & Sons Ltd, The Atrium, Southern Gate, Chichester,
West Sussex PO19 8SQ, England

Telephone (+44) 1243 779777

Email (for orders and customer service enquiries): cs-books@wiley.co.uk
Visit our Home Page on www.wileyeurope.com or www.wiley.com

Reprinted March 2005

*Other Wiley Editorial Offices*

John Wiley & Sons Inc., 111 River Street, Hoboken, NJ 07030, USA

Jossey-Bass, 989 Market Street, San Francisco, CA 94103-1741, USA

Wiley-VCH Verlag GmbH, Boschstr. 12, D-69469 Weinheim, Germany

John Wiley & Sons Australia Ltd, 33 Park Road, Milton, Queensland 4064, Australia

John Wiley & Sons (Asia) Pte Ltd, 2 Clementi Loop #02-01, Jin Xing Distripark, Singapore 129809

John Wiley & Sons Canada Ltd, 22 Worcester Road, Etobicoke, Ontario, Canada M9W 1L1

Wiley also publishes its books in a variety of electronic formats. Some content that appears
in print may not be available in electronic books.

*Library of Congress Cataloging-in-Publication Data*

Cuthbertson, Keith.
  Quantitative financial economics : stocks, bonds and foreign exchange /
Keith Cuthbertson and Dirk Nitzsche. – 2nd ed.
    p. cm.
  Includes bibliographical references and index.
  ISBN 0-470-09171-1 (pbk. : alk. paper)
  1. Investments – Mathematical models. 2. Capital assets pricing model. 3.
Stocks – Mathematical models. 4. Bonds – Mathematical models. 5. Foreign
exchange – Mathematical models. I. Nitzsche, Dirk. II. Title.
  HG4515.2.C87 2005
  332.6 – dc22
2004018706

*British Library Cataloguing in Publication Data*

A catalogue record for this book is available from the British Library

ISBN-10 0470-09171-1(P/B)
ISBN-13 978-0470-09171-5(P/B)

Typeset in 10/13pt Times by Laserwords Private Limited, Chennai, India
Printed and bound in Great Britain by Antony Rowe Ltd, Chippenham, Wiltshire
This book is printed on acid-free paper responsibly manufactured from sustainable forestry
in which at least two trees are planted for each one used for paper production.

To all our students who have done well enough to be in a position to hire finance consultants

# CONTENTS

# PREFACE

Numerous emails and the fact that the first edition sold out suggests that many found it a positive NPV investment. This is encouraging, as unless these things are turned into a major motion picture, the cash rewards to the author are not great. My wife currently believes that the direct return per hour of effort is less than that of a competent plumber – and she's right. But she has yet to factor in positive externalities and real options theory – that's my counter argument anyway. Nevertheless, being risk averse and with time-varying long-term net liabilities, I do not intend giving up my day job(s).

When invited to dinner, accompanied by the finest wines someone else can buy, and asked to produce a second edition, there comes a critical point late in the evening when you invariably say, 'Yes'. This is a mistake. The reason is obvious. Were it not for electronic copies, the mass of 'stuff' in this area that has appeared over the last 10 years would fill the Albert Hall. The research and first draft were great, subsequent drafts less so and by the end it was agony – Groundhog Day. For me this could have easily been 'A Book Too Far'. But fortuitously, for the second edition, I was able to engage an excellent forensic co-author in Dirk Nitzsche.

For those of you who bought the first edition, a glance at the 'blurb' on the cover tells you that the second edition is about 65% new material and the 'old material' has also been revamped. We hope we have chosen a coherent, interesting and varied range of topics. For those who illegally photocopied the first edition and maybe also got me to sign it – the photocopy that is – I admire your dedication to the cause of involuntary personal contributions to foreign aid. But I hope you think that for this much-improved second edition, you could 'Show Me The Money'.

# Who's it for?

The book is aimed at students on quantitative MSc's in finance and financial economics and should also be useful on PhD programmes. All you need as a pre-requisite is a basic undergraduate course in theory of finance (with the accompanying math) and something on modern time-series econometrics. Any finance practitioners who want to 'get a handle' on whether there is any practical value in all that academic stuff (answer, 'Yes there is – sometimes'), should also dip in at appropriate points. At least, you will then be able to spot whether the poor Emperor, as he emerges from his ivory tower and saunters into the market place, is looking sartorially challenged.

In the book, we cover the main theoretical ideas in the pricing of (spot) assets and the determination of strategic investment decisions (using discrete time analysis), as well as analysing specific trading strategies. Illustrative empirical results are provided, although these are by no means exhaustive (or we hope exhausting). The emphasis is on the intuition behind the finance and economic concepts and the math and stats we need to analyse these ideas in a rigorous fashion. We feel that the material allows 'entry' into recent research work in these areas and we hope it also encourages the reader to move on to explore derivatives pricing, financial engineering and risk management.

We hope you enjoy the book and it leads you to untold riches – who knows, maybe this could be the beginning of a beautiful friendship. Anyway, make the most of it, as after all our past efforts, our goal from now on is to understand everything and publish nothing. Whether this will increase social welfare, only time and you can tell.

Keith Cuthbertson
Dirk Nitzsche
October 2004

# ACKNOWLEDGEMENTS

Special thanks go to our colleagues at CASS Business School, London, for practical insights into many of the topics in the book and also to our colleagues at Tanaka Business School, Imperial College, London. The MSc and PhD students at the above institutions and at the University of Bordeaux-IV, UNAM in Mexico City and the Freie University, Berlin, have also been excellent, critical and attentive 'guinea pigs'.

In particular, we should like to thank the following people for reading draft chapters: Mike Artis, Don Bredin, Francis Breedon, Ian Buckley, Alec Chrystal, David Barr, Lara Cathcart, Ales Cerny, Lina El-Jahel, Luis Galindo, Stephen Hall, Richard Harris, Simon Hayes, Stuart Hyde, Turalay Kenc, David Miles, Michael Moore, Kerry Patterson, Mark Salmon, Lucio Sarno, Peter Smith, Mark Taylor, Dylan Thomas and Mike Wickens.

Also, Tom Engsted at the University of Aarhus and Richard Harris at the University of Exeter kindly provided some corrections to the first edition, which we hope have been accurately incorporated into the second edition. In addition, Niall O'Sullivan has given permission to use part of his PhD material on mutual fund performance in Chapter 9 and Ales Cerny allowed us early access to the drafts of his book *Mathematical Techniques in Finance* (Princeton University Press 2004).

Many thanks to Yvonne Doyle at Imperial College, who expertly typed numerous drafts and is now well on her way to becoming an expert in Greek.

# 1

# BASIC CONCEPTS IN FINANCE

## Aims

- To consider different methods of measuring returns for pure discount bonds, coupon-paying bonds and stocks.
- Use discounted present value techniques, DPV, to price assets.
- Show how utility functions can be used to incorporate risk aversion, and derive asset demand functions from one-period utility maximisation.
- Illustrate the optimal level of physical investment and consumption for a two-period horizon problem.

The aim of this chapter is to quickly run through some of the basic tools of analysis used in finance literature. The topics covered are not exhaustive and they are discussed at a fairly intuitive level.

## 1.1 Returns on Stocks, Bonds and Real Assets

Much of the theoretical work in finance is conducted in terms of compound rates of return or interest rates, even though rates quoted in the market use 'simple interest'. For example, an interest rate of 5 percent payable every six months will be quoted as a simple interest rate of 10 percent per annum in the market. However, if an investor rolled over two six-month bills and the interest rate remained constant, he could actually earn a 'compound' or 'true' or 'effective' annual rate of $(1.05)^2 = 1.1025$ or 10.25 percent. The effective annual rate of return exceeds the simple rate because in the former case the investor earns 'interest-on-interest'.

We now examine how we calculate the terminal value of an investment when the frequency with which interest rates are compounded alters. Clearly, a quoted interest rate of 10 percent per annum when interest is calculated monthly will amount to more at the end of the year than if interest accrues only at the end of the year.

Consider an amount $\$A$ invested for $n$ years at a rate of $R$ per annum (where $R$ is expressed as a decimal). If compounding takes place only at the end of the year, the future value after $n$ years is $FV_n$, where

$$FV_n = \$A(1 + R)^n \tag{1}$$

However, if interest is paid $m$ times per annum, then the terminal value at the end of $n$ years is

$$FV_n^m = \$A(1 + R/m)^{mn} \tag{2}$$

$R/m$ is often referred to as the periodic interest rate. As $m$, the frequency of compounding, increases, the rate becomes 'continuously compounded', and it may be shown that the investment accrues to

$$FV_n^c = \$Ae^{R_c n} \tag{3}$$

where $R_c$ = the continuously compounded rate per annum. For example, if the quoted (simple) interest rate is 10 percent per annum, then the value of $\$100$ at the end of one year ($n = 1$) for different values of $m$ is given in Table 1. For *daily* compounding, with $R = 10\%$ p.a., the terminal value after one year using (2) is $\$110.5155$. Assuming $R_c = 10\%$ gives $FV_n^c = \$100e^{0.10(1)} = \$100.5171$. So, daily compounding is almost equivalent to using a continuously compounded rate (see the last two entries in Table 1).

We now consider how to switch between simple interest rates, periodic rates, effective annual rates and continuously compounded rates. Suppose an investment pays a periodic interest rate of 2 percent each quarter. This will usually be quoted in the market as 8 percent per annum, that is, as a simple annual rate. At the end of the year, $\$A = \$100$ accrues to

$$\$A(1 + R/m)^m = 100(1 + 0.08/4)^4 = \$108.24 \tag{4}$$

The effective annual rate $R_e$ is 8.24% since $\$100(1 + R_e) = 108.24$. $R_e$ exceeds the simple rate because of the payment of interest-on-interest. The relationship between

**Table 1**  Compounding frequency

| Compounding Frequency | Value of $100 at End of Year ($R = 10\%$ p.a.) |
|---|---|
| Annually ($m = 1$) | 110.00 |
| Quarterly ($m = 4$) | 110.38 |
| Weekly ($m = 52$) | 110.51 |
| Daily ($m = 365$) | 110.5155 |
| Continuous ($n = 1$) | 110.5171 |

the quoted simple rate $R$ with payments $m$ times per year and the *effective annual rate* $R_e$ is

$$(1 + R_e) = (1 + R/m)^m \tag{5}$$

We can use (5) to move from periodic interest rates to effective rates and vice versa. For example, an interest rate with quarterly payments that would produce an effective annual rate of 12 percent is given by $1.12 = (1 + R/4)^4$, and hence,

$$R = [(1.12)^{1/4} - 1]4 = 0.0287(4) = 11.48\% \tag{6}$$

So, with interest compounded quarterly, a simple interest rate of 11.48 percent per annum is equivalent to a 12 percent effective rate.

We can use a similar procedure to switch between a simple interest rate $R$, which applies to compounding that takes place over $m$ periods, and an equivalent continuously compounded rate $R_c$. One reason for doing this calculation is that much of the advanced theory of bond pricing (and the pricing of futures and options) uses continuously compounded rates.

Suppose we wish to calculate a value for $R_c$ when we know the $m$-period rate $R$. Since the terminal value after $n$ years of an investment of $\$A$ must be equal when using either interest rate we have

$$Ae^{R_c n} = A(1 + R/m)^{mn} \tag{7}$$

and therefore,

$$R_c = m \ln[1 + R/m] \tag{8}$$

Also, if we are given the continuously compounded rate $R_c$, we can use the above equation to calculate the simple rate $R$, which applies when interest is calculated $m$ times per year:

$$R = m(e^{R_c/m} - 1) \tag{9}$$

We can perhaps best summarise the above array of alternative interest rates by using one final illustrative example. Suppose an investment pays a periodic interest rate of 5 percent every six months ($m = 2$, $R/2 = 0.05$). In the market, this might be quoted as a 'simple rate' of 10 percent per annum. An investment of $\$100$ would yield $100[1 + (0.10/2)]^2 = \$110.25$ after one year (using equation 2). Clearly, the effective annual rate is 10.25% p.a. Suppose we wish to convert the simple annual rate of $R = 0.10$ to an equivalent continuously compounded rate. Using (8), with $m = 2$, we see that this is given by $R_c = 2 \ln(1 + 0.10/2) = 0.09758$ (9.758% p.a.). Of course, if interest is continuously compounded at an annual rate of 9.758 percent, then $\$100$ invested today would accrue to $100 \, e^{R_c \cdot n} = \$110.25$ in $n = 1$ year's time.

## Arithmetic and Geometric Averages

Suppose prices in successive periods are $P_0 = 1$, $P_1 = 0.7$ and $P_2 = 1$, which correspond to (periodic) returns of $R_1 = -0.30$ ($-30\%$) and $R_2 = 0.42857$ (42.857%). The *arithmetic average* return is $\overline{R} = (R_1 + R_2)/2 = 6.4285\%$. However, it would be incorrect to assume that if you have an initial wealth $W_0 = \$100$, then your final wealth after 2 periods will be $W_2 = (1 + \overline{R})W_0 = \$106.4285$. Looking at the price series it is clear that your wealth is unchanged between $t = 0$ and $t = 2$:

$$W_2 = W_0[(1 + R_1)(1 + R_2)] = \$100 \ (0.70)(1.42857) = \$100$$

Now define the *geometric average* return as

$$(1 + \overline{R}_g)^2 = (1 + R_1)(1 + R_2) = 1$$

Here $\overline{R}_g = 0$, and it correctly indicates that the return on your 'wealth portfolio' $R_w(0 \to 2) = (W_2/W_0) - 1 = 0$ between $t = 0$ and $t = 2$. Generalising, the geometric average return is defined as

$$(1 + \overline{R}_g)^n = (1 + R_1)(1 + R_2) \cdots (1 + R_n) \qquad (10)$$

and we can always write

$$W_n = W_0(1 + \overline{R}_g)^n$$

Unless (periodic) returns $R_t$ are constant, the geometric average return is always less than the arithmetic average return. For example, using one-year returns $R_t$, the geometric average return on a US equity value weighted index over the period 1802–1997 is 7% p.a., considerably lower than the arithmetic average of 8.5% p.a. (Siegel 1998).

If returns are serially uncorrelated, $R_t = \mu + \varepsilon_t$ with $\varepsilon_t \sim iid(0, \sigma^2)$, then the arithmetic average is the best return forecast for any *randomly selected* future year. Over long holding periods, the best *forecast* would also use the arithmetic average return compounded, that is, $(1 + \overline{R})^n$. Unfortunately, the latter clear simple result does not apply in practice over long horizons, since stock returns are not *iid*.

In our simple example, if the sequence is repeated, returns are negatively serially correlated (i.e. $-30\%$, $+42.8\%$, alternating in each period). In this case, forecasting over long horizons requires the use of the geometric average return compounded, $(1 + \overline{R}_g)^n$. There is evidence that over long horizons stock returns are 'mildly' mean reverting (i.e. exhibit some negative serial correlation) so that the arithmetic average overstates *expected* future returns, and it may be better to use the geometric average as a *forecast* of future average returns.

## Long Horizons

The (periodic) return is $(1 + R_1) = P_1/P_0$. In intertemporal models, we often require an expression for terminal wealth:

$$W_n = W_0(1 + R_1)(1 + R_2) \cdots (1 + R_n)$$

Alternatively, this can be expressed as

$$\ln(W_n/W_0) = \ln(1 + R_1) + \ln(1 + R_2) + \cdots + \ln(1 + R_n)$$
$$= (R_{c1} + R_{c2} + \cdots + R_{cn}) = \ln(P_n/P_0)$$

where $R_{ct} \equiv \ln(1 + R_t)$ are the continuously compounded rates. Note that the term in parentheses is equal to $\ln(P_n/P_0)$. It follows that

$$W_n = W_0 \exp(R_{c1} + R_{c2} + \cdots + R_{cn}) = W_0(P_n/P_0)$$

Continuously compounded rates are additive, so we can *define* the (total continuously compounded) return over the whole period from $t = 0$ to $t = n$ as

$$R_c(0 \rightarrow n) \equiv (R_{c1} + R_{c2} + \cdots + R_{cn})$$

$$W_n = W_0 \exp[R_c(0 \rightarrow n)]$$

Let us now 'connect' the continuously compounded returns to the geometric average return. It follows from (10) that

$$\ln(1 + \overline{R}_g)^n = (R_{c1} + R_{c2} + \cdots + R_{cn}) \equiv R_c(0 \rightarrow n)$$

Hence

$$W_n = W_0 \exp[\ln(1 + \overline{R}_g)^n] = W_0(1 + \overline{R}_g)^n$$

as we found earlier.

## Nominal and Real Returns

A number of asset pricing models focus on real rather than nominal returns. The real return is the (percent) rate of return from an investment, in terms of the purchasing power over goods and services. A real return of, say, 3% p.a. implies that your initial investment allows you to purchase 3% more of a fixed basket of domestic goods (e.g. Harrod's Hamper for a UK resident) at the end of the year.

If at $t = 0$ you have a nominal wealth $W_0$, then your real wealth is $W_0^r = W_0/P_o^g$, where $P^g$ = price index for goods and services. If $R$ = nominal (proportionate) return on your wealth, then at the end of year-1 you have nominal wealth of $W_0(1 + R)$ and real wealth of

$$W_1^r \equiv \frac{W_1}{P_1^g} = \frac{(W_0^r P_o^g)(1 + R)}{P_1^g}$$

Hence, the increase in your real wealth or, equivalently, your (proportionate) real return is

$$(1 + R^r) \equiv W_1^r / W_0^r = (1 + R)/(1 + \pi) \tag{11}$$

$$R^r \equiv \frac{\Delta W_1^r}{W_0^r} = \frac{R - \pi}{1 + \pi} \approx R - \pi \tag{12}$$

where $1 + \pi \equiv (P_1^g/P_0^g)$. The proportionate change in real wealth is your real return $R^r$, which is *approximately* equal to the nominal return $R$ minus the rate of goods price inflation, $\pi$. In terms of continuously compounded returns,

$$\ln(W_1^r / W_0^r) \equiv R_c^r = \ln(1 + R) - \ln(P_1^g/P_o^g) = R_c - \pi_c \tag{13}$$

where $R_c =$ (continuously compounded) nominal return and $\pi_c =$ continuously compounded rate of inflation. Using continuously compounded returns has the advantage that the log real return over a horizon $t = 0$ to $t = n$ is additive:

$$R_c^r(0 \to n) = (R_{c1} - \pi_{c1}) + (R_{c2} - \pi_{c2}) + \cdots + (R_{cn} - \pi_{cn})$$

$$= (R_{c1}^r + R_{c2}^r + \cdots + R_{cn}^r) \tag{14}$$

Using the above, if initial real wealth is $W_0^r$, then the level of real wealth at $t = n$ is $W_n^r = W_0^r e^{R_c^n(0 \to n)} = W_0^r e^{(R_{c1}^r + R_{c2}^r + \cdots + R_{cn}^r)}$. Alternatively, if we use proportionate changes, then

$$W_n^r = W_0^r (1 + R_1^r)(1 + R_2^r) \cdots (1 + R_n^r) \tag{15}$$

and the *annual average geometric real return* from $t = 0$ to $t = n$, denoted $\overline{R}_{r,g}$ is given by

$$(1 + \overline{R}_{r,g}) = \sqrt[n]{(1 + R_1^r)(1 + R_2^r) \cdots (1 + R_n)^r}$$

and $W_n^r = W_0^r (1 + \overline{R}_{r,g})^n$

## Foreign Investment

Suppose you are considering investing abroad. The nominal *return measured in terms of your domestic currency* can be shown to equal the foreign currency return (sometimes called the *local currency return*) plus the appreciation in the foreign currency. By investing abroad, you can gain (or lose) either from holding the foreign asset or from changes in the exchange rate. For example, consider a UK resident with initial nominal wealth $W_0$ who exchanges (the UK pound) sterling for USDs at a rate $S_0$ (£s per $) and invests in the United States with a nominal (proportionate) return $R^{us}$. Nominal wealth in Sterling at $t = 1$ is

$$W_1 = \frac{W_0(1 + R^{us})S_1}{S_0} \tag{16}$$

Hence, using $S_1 = S_0 + \Delta S_1$, the (proportionate) nominal return to foreign investment for a UK investor is

$$R(UK \to US) \equiv (W_1/W_0) - 1 = R^{us} + \Delta S_1/S_0 + R^{us}(\Delta S_1/S_0) \approx R^{US} + R^{FX} \tag{17}$$

where $R^{FX} = \Delta S_1/S_0$ is the (proportionate) appreciation of FX rate of the USD against sterling, and we have assumed that $R^{us}(\Delta S_1/S_0)$ is negligible. The nominal return to foreign investment is obviously

Nominal return(UK resident) = local currency(US)return + appreciation of USD

In terms of continuously compound returns, the equation is exact:

$$R_c(UK \to US) \equiv \ln(W_1/W_0) = R_c^{us} + \Delta s \tag{18}$$

where $R_c^{us} \equiv \ln(1 + R^{us})$ and $\Delta s \equiv \ln(S_1/S_0)$. Now suppose you are concerned about the *real* return of your foreign investment, in terms of purchasing power *over domestic goods*. The real return to foreign investment is just the nominal return less the domestic rate of price inflation. To demonstrate this, take a UK resident investing in the United States, but ultimately using any profits to spend on UK goods. Real wealth at $t = 1$, in terms of purchasing power over UK goods is

$$W_1^r = \frac{(W_0^r P_o^g)(1 + R^{us})S_1}{P_1^g S_0} \tag{19}$$

It follows that the continuously compounded and proportionate real return to foreign investment is

$$R_c^r(UK \rightarrow US) \equiv \ln(W_1^r/W_0^r) = R_c^{us} + \Delta s - \pi_c^{uk} \tag{20}$$

$$R^r(UK \rightarrow US) \equiv \Delta W_1^r/W_0^r \approx R^{us} + R^{FX} - \pi^{uk} \tag{21}$$

where $\Delta s = \ln(S_1/S_0)$. Hence, the real return $R^r(UK \rightarrow US)$ to a UK resident in terms of UK purchasing power from a round-trip investment in US assets is

Real return (UK resident) = nominal 'local currency' return in US

+ appreciation of USD − inflation in UK

From (20) it is interesting to note that the *real* return to foreign investment for a UK resident $R_c^r(UK \rightarrow US)$ would equal the real return to a US resident investing in the US, $(R_c^{us} - \pi_c^{us})$ if

$$\pi_c^{uk} - \pi_c^{us} = \Delta s \tag{22}$$

As we shall see in Chapter 24, equation (22) is the relative purchasing power parity (PPP) condition. Hence, if relative PPP holds, the *real* return to foreign investment is equal to the real local currency return $R_c^{us} - \pi_c^{us}$, and the change in the exchange rate is immaterial. This is because, under relative PPP, the exchange rate alters to just offset the differential inflation rate between the two countries. As relative PPP holds only over horizons of 5–10 years, the real return to foreign investment over shorter horizons will depend on exchange rate changes.

## 1.2 Discounted Present Value, DPV

Let the quoted annual rate of interest on a completely safe investment over $n$ years be denoted as $r_n$. The future value of $\$A$ in $n$ years' time with interest calculated annually is

$$FV_n = \$A(1 + r_n)^n \tag{23}$$

It follows that if you were given the opportunity to receive with certainty $\$FV_n$ in $n$ years' time, then you would be willing to give up $\$A$ today. The value *today* of a certain payment of $FV_n$ in $n$ years' time is $A. In a more technical language, the *discounted present value* DPV of $FV_n$ is

$$DPV = FV_n/(1 + r_n)^n \qquad (24)$$

We now make the assumption that the safe interest rate applicable to $1, 2, 3, \ldots, n$ year horizons is *constant* and equal to $r$. We are assuming that the term structure of interest rates is flat. The DPV of a *stream* of receipts $FV_i$ ($i = 1$ to $n$) that carry no default risk is then given by

$$DPV = \sum_{i=1}^{n} FV_i/(1 + r)^i \qquad (25)$$

## Annuities

If the future payments are *constant* in each year ($FV_i = \$C$) and the first payment is at the end of the first year, then we have an *ordinary annuity*. The DPV of these payments is

$$DPV = C \sum_{i=1}^{n} 1/(1 + r)^i \qquad (26)$$

Using the formula for the sum of a geometric progression, we can write the DPV of an ordinary annuity as

$$DPV = C \cdot A_{n,r} \quad \text{where } A_{n,r} = (1/r)[1 - 1/(1 + r)^n] \qquad (27)$$

and    $DPV = C/r$    as $n \to \infty$

The term $A_{n,r}$ is called the *annuity factor*, and its numerical value is given in annuity tables for various values of $n$ and $r$. A special case of the annuity formula is when $n$ approaches infinity, then $A_{n,r} = 1/r$ and $DPV = C/r$. This formula is used to price a bond called a perpetuity or console, which pays a coupon $C (but is never redeemed by the issuers). The annuity formula can be used in calculations involving constant payments such as mortgages, pensions and for pricing a coupon-paying bond (see below).

## Physical Investment Project

Consider a physical investment project such as building a new factory, which has a set of prospective net receipts (profits) of $FV_i$. Suppose the capital cost of the project which we assume all accrues today (i.e. at time $t = 0$) is $KC. Then the entrepreneur should invest in the project if

$$DPV \geq KC \qquad (28)$$

or, equivalently, if the net present value NPV satisfies

$$NPV = DPV - KC \geq 0 \qquad (29)$$

If $NPV = 0$, then it can be shown that the net receipts (profits) from the investment project are just sufficient to pay back both the principal ($KC$) and the interest on the

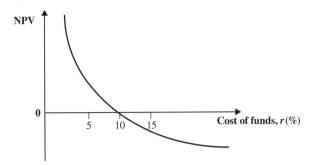

**Figure 1**  NPV and the discount rate

loan, which was taken out to finance the project. If $NPV > 0$, then there are surplus funds available even after these loan repayments.

As the cost of funds $r$ increases, then the NPV falls for any given stream of profits $FV_i$ from the project (Figure 1). There is a value of $r$ ($= 10\%$ in Figure 1) for which the $NPV = 0$. This value of $r$ is known as the internal rate of return IRR of the investment project. Given a stream of net receipts $FV_i$ and the capital cost $KC$ for a project, one can always calculate a project's IRR. It is that constant value of $y$ for which

$$KC = \sum_{i=1}^{n} FV_i/(1+y)^i \qquad (30)$$

An equivalent investment rule to the NPV condition (28) is to invest in the project if

$$IRR(= y) \geq \text{cost of borrowing } (= r) \qquad (31)$$

There are some technical problems with IRR (which luckily are often not problematic in practice). First, a meaningful solution for IRR assumes all the $FV_i > 0$, and hence do not alternate in sign, because otherwise there may be more than one solution for the IRR. Second, the IRR should not be used to compare two projects as it may not give the same decision rule as NPV (see Cuthbertson and Nitzsche 2001a).

We will use these investment rules throughout the book, beginning in this chapter, with the derivation of the yield on bills and bonds and the optimal scale of physical investment projects for the economy. Note that in the calculation of the DPV, we assumed that the interest rate used for discounting the future receipts $FV_i$ was constant for all horizons. Suppose that 'one-year money' carries an interest rate of $r_1$, two-year money costs $r_2$, and so on, then the DPV is given by

$$DPV = FV_1/(1+r_1) + FV_2/(1+r_2)^2 + \cdots + FV_n/(1+r_n)^n = \sum \delta_i FV_i \quad (32)$$

where $\delta_i = 1/(1+r_i)^i$. The $r_i$ are known as *spot rates* of interest since they are the rates that apply to money that you lend over the periods $r_1 = 0$ to 1 year, $r_2 = 0$ to 2 years, and so on (expressed as annual compound rates). At any point in time, the relationship between the spot rates, $r_i$, on default-free assets and their maturity is known as the yield curve. For example, if $r_1 < r_2 < r_3$ and so on, then the yield curve is said to be upward sloping. The relationship between changes in short rates over time and changes in long rates is the subject of the term structure of interest rates.

The DPV formula can also be expressed in real terms. In this case, future receipts $FV_i$ are deflated by the aggregate goods price index and the discount factors are calculated using real rates of interest.

In general, physical investment projects are not riskless since the future receipts are uncertain. There are a number of alternative methods of dealing with uncertainty in the DPV calculation. Perhaps, the simplest method, and the one we shall adopt, has the discount rate $\delta_i$ consisting of the risk-free spot rate $r_i$ plus a risk premium $rp_i$.

$$\delta_i = (1 + r_i + rp_i)^{-1} \tag{33}$$

Equation (33) is an identity and is not operational until we have a model of the risk premium. We examine alternative models for risk premia in Chapter 3.

## Stocks

The difficulty with direct application of the DPV concept to stocks is that future dividends are uncertain and the discount factor may be time varying. It can be shown (see Chapter 4) that the *fundamental value* $V_t$ is the expected DPV of future dividends:

$$V_t = E_t \left[ \frac{D_{t+1}}{(1 + q_1)} + \frac{D_{t+2}}{(1 + q_1)(1 + q_2)} + \cdots \right] \tag{34}$$

where $q_i$ is the one-period return between time period $t + i - 1$ and $t + i$. If there are to be no systematic profitable opportunities to be made from buying and selling shares between well-informed rational traders, then the actual market price of the stock $P_t$ must equal the fundamental value $V_i$. For example, if $P_t < V_t$, then investors should purchase the undervalued stock and hence make a capital gain as $P_t$ rises towards $V_t$. In an efficient market, such profitable opportunities should be immediately eliminated.

Clearly, one cannot directly calculate $V_t$ to see if it does equal $P_t$ because expected dividends (and discount rates) are unobservable. However, in later chapters, we discuss methods for overcoming this problem and examine whether the stock market is efficient in the sense that $P_t = V_t$. If we add some simplifying assumptions to the DPV formula (e.g. future dividends are expected to grow at a constant rate $g$ and the discount rate $q = R$ is constant each period), then (34) becomes

$$V_0 = D_o(1 + g)/(R - g) \tag{35}$$

which is known as the *Gordon Growth Model*. Using this equation, we can calculate the 'fair value' of the stock and compare it to the quoted market price $P_0$ to see whether the share is over- or undervalued. These models are usually referred to as dividend valuation models and are dealt with in Chapter 10.

## Pure Discount Bonds and Spot Yields

Instead of a physical investment project, consider investing in a pure discount bond (zero coupon bond). In the market, these are usually referred to as 'zeros'. A pure discount bond has a fixed redemption price $M$, a known maturity period and pays no coupons. The yield on the bond if held to maturity is determined by the fact that it is purchased at a market price $P_t$ below its redemption price $M$. For a one-year bond, it seems sensible to calculate the yield or interest rate as

$$r_{1t} = (M_1 - P_{1t})/P_{1t} \tag{36}$$

where $r_{1t}$ is measured as a proportion. However, when viewing the problem in terms of DPV, we see that the one-year bond promises a future payment of $M_1$ at the end of the year in exchange for a capital cost of $P_{1t}$ paid out today. Hence the IRR, $y_{1t}$, of the bond can be calculated from

$$P_{1t} = M_1/(1 + y_{1t}) \tag{37}$$

But on rearrangement, we have $y_{1t} = (M_1 - P_{1t})/P_{1t}$, and hence the one-year spot yield $r_{1t}$ is simply the IRR of the bill. Applying the above principle to a two-year bill with redemption price $M_2$, the annual (compound) interest rate $r_{2t}$ on the bill is the solution to

$$P_{2t} = M_2/(1 + r_{2t})^2 \tag{38}$$

which implies

$$r_{2t} = (M_2/P_{2t})^{1/2} - 1 \tag{39}$$

If spot rates are continuously compounded, then

$$P_{nt} = M_n e^{-r_{nt} n} \tag{40}$$

where $r_{nt}$ is now the continuously compounded rate for a bond of maturity $n$ at time $t$. We now see how we can, in principle, calculate a set of (compound) spot rates at $t$ for different maturities from the market prices at time $t$ of pure discount bonds (bills).

## Coupon-Paying Bonds

A *level coupon* (non-callable) bond pays a fixed coupon $\$C$ at known fixed intervals (which we take to be every year) and has a fixed redemption price $M_n$ payable when the bond matures in year $n$. For a bond with $n$ years left to maturity, the current market price is $P_{nt}$. The question is how do we measure the return on the bond if it is held to maturity?

The bond is analogous to our physical investment project with the capital outlay today being $P_{nt}$ and the future receipts being $\$C$ each year (plus the redemption price). The internal rate of return on the bond, which is called the yield to maturity $y_t$, can be calculated from

$$P_{nt} = C/(1 + y_t) + C/(1 + y_t)^2 + \cdots + (C + M_n)/(1 + y_t)^n \tag{41}$$

The yield to maturity is that *constant* rate of discount that at a point in time equates the DPV of future payments with the current market price. Since $P_{nt}$, $M_n$ and $C$ are the known values in the market, (41) has to be solved to give the quoted rate for the yield to maturity $y_t$. There is a subscript 't' on $y_t$ because as the market price falls, the yield to maturity rises (and vice versa) as a matter of 'actuarial arithmetic'. Although widely used in the market and in the financial press, there are some theoretical/conceptual problems in using the yield to maturity as an unambiguous measure of the return on a bond even when it is held to maturity. We deal with some of these issues in Part III.

In the market, coupon payments $C$ are usually paid every six months and the interest rate from (41) is then the periodic six-month rate. If this periodic yield to maturity is calculated as, say, 6 percent, then in the market the quoted yield to maturity will be the simple annual rate of 12 percent per annum (known as the bond-equivalent yield in the United States).

A *perpetuity* is a level coupon bond that is never redeemed by the primary issuer (i.e. $n \to \infty$). If the coupon is $\$C$ per annum and the current market price of the bond is $P_{\infty,t}$, then from (41) the yield to maturity on a perpetuity is

$$y_{\infty,t} = C/P_{\infty,t} \tag{42}$$

It is immediately obvious from (42) that for small changes, the percentage change in the price of a perpetuity equals the percentage change in the yield to maturity. The flat yield or interest yield or running yield $y_{rt} = (C/P_{nt})100$ and is quoted in the financial press, but it is not a particularly theoretically useful concept in analysing the pricing and return on bonds.

Although compound rates of interest (or yields) are quoted in the markets, we often find it more convenient to express bond prices in terms of continuously compounded spot interest rates/yields. If the continuously compounded spot yield is $r_{nt}$, then a coupon-paying bond may be considered as a portfolio of 'zeros', and the price is (see Cuthbertson and Nitzsche 2001a)

$$P_{nt} = \sum_{k=1}^{n} C_k e^{-r_{kt}k} + M_n e^{-r_{nt}n} = \sum_{k=1}^{n} P_{kt}^* + P_{nt}^* \tag{43}$$

where $P_k^* = C_k e^{-r_k k}$ and $P_n^*$ are the prices of zero coupon bonds paying $C_k$ at time $t+k$ and $M_n$ at time $t+n$, respectively.

## Holding Period Return

Much empirical work on stocks deals with the one-period holding period return $H_{t+1}$, which is defined as

$$H_{t+1} = \frac{P_{t+1} - P_t}{P_t} + \frac{D_{t+1}}{P_t} \tag{44}$$

The first term is the proportionate capital gain or loss (over one period) and the second term is the (proportionate) dividend yield. $H_{t+1}$ can be calculated *ex-post* but, of course, viewed from time $t$, $P_{t+1}$ and (perhaps) $D_{t+1}$ are uncertain, and investors can only try and forecast these elements. It also follows that

$$1 + H_{t+i+1} = [(P_{t+i+1} + D_{t+i+1})/P_{t+i}] \tag{45}$$

where $H_{t+i}$ is the one-period return between $t + i$ and $t + i + 1$. Hence ex-post if $\$A$ is invested in the stock (and all dividend payments are reinvested in the stock), then the $\$Y$ payout after $n$ periods is

$$Y = A[1 + H_{t+1}][1 + H_{t+2}] \cdots [1 + H_{t+n}] \qquad (46)$$

The continuously compounded holding period return (or 'log-return') is defined as

$$h_{t+1} = \ln(P_{t+1}/P_t) = p_{t+1} - p_t \qquad (47)$$

The continuously compounded return over period $t$ to $t + n$ is

$$h_{t+n} = p_{t+n} - p_t = h_t + h_{t+1} + \cdots + h_{t+n} \qquad (48)$$

Throughout the book, we will demonstrate how expected one-period returns $H_{t+1}$ can be directly related to the DPV formula. Much of the early empirical work on whether the stock market is efficient centres on trying to establish whether one-period returns $H_{t+1}$ are predictable. Later empirical work concentrated on whether the stock price equalled the DPV of future dividends, and the most recent empirical work brings together these two strands in the literature.

With slight modifications, the one-period holding period return can be defined for any asset. For a coupon-paying bond with initial maturity of $n$ periods and coupon payment of $C$, we have

$$H_{n,t+1} = [(P_{n-1,t+1} - P_{n,t})/P_{n,t}] + C/P_{n,t} \qquad (49)$$

and is also often referred to as the (one-period) holding period yield HPY. Note that the $n$-period bond becomes an $n - 1$ period bond at $t + 1$. The first term is the capital gain on the bond and the second is the coupon (or running) yield. For a zero coupon bond, $C = 0$. In models of the term structure, we usually use *continuously compounded* returns on *zero coupon* bonds, and hence $h_{t+1}$ is given by

$$h_{t+1} = p_{n-1,t} - p_{n,t} \qquad (50)$$

Often, we can apply the same type of economic model to explain movements in holding period returns for both stock and bonds (and other speculative assets), and we begin this analysis with the Capital Asset Pricing Model (CAPM) in the next chapter.

## 1.3    Utility and Indifference Curves

In this section, we briefly discuss the concept of utility but only to a level such that the reader can follow the subsequent material on portfolio choice and stochastic discount factor (SDF) models. Economists frequently set up portfolio models in which the individual chooses a set of assets in order to maximise some function of terminal wealth or portfolio return or consumption. For example, a certain level of wealth will imply a certain level of satisfaction for the individual as he contemplates the goods and services he could purchase with the wealth. If we double his wealth, we may not double his level of satisfaction. Also, for example, if the individual consumes one bottle of wine per night, the additional satisfaction from consuming an extra bottle may not be as great as from the first. This is the assumption of diminishing marginal utility. Utility theory can also be applied to decisions involving uncertain (strictly 'risky') outcomes. In fact, we can classify investors as 'risk averters', 'risk lovers' or 'risk neutral' in terms of the shape of their utility function. Finally, we can also examine how individuals might evaluate 'utility', which arises at different points in time, that is, the concept of discounted utility in a multiperiod or intertemporal framework.

## Fair Lottery

A fair lottery (game) is defined as one that has an expected value of zero (e.g. tossing a coin with $1 for a win (heads) and −$1 for a loss (tails)). Risk aversion implies that the individual would not accept a 'fair' lottery, and it can be shown that this implies a concave utility function over wealth. Consider the random payoff $x$:

$$x = \begin{cases} k_1 \text{ with probability } p \\ k_2 \text{ with probability } 1 - p \end{cases} \tag{51}$$

A fair lottery must have an expected value of zero

$$E(x) = pk_1 + (1 - p)k_2 = 0 \tag{52}$$

which implies $k_1/k_2 = -(1 - p)/p$ or $p = -k_2/(k_1 - k_2)$. For our 'coin toss', $p = 1/2, k_1 = -k_2 = \$1$.

## Expected Utility

Suppose a random variable end-of-period wealth $W$ can have $n$ possible values $W_i$ with probability $p_i$ $\left(\sum_{i=1}^{n} p_i = 1\right)$. The utility from any wealth outcome $W_i$ is denoted $U(W_i)$, and the expected utility from the risky outcomes is

$$E[U(W)] = \sum_{i=1}^{n} p_i U(W_i) \tag{53}$$

## Uncertainty and Risk

The first restriction placed on utility functions is that more is always preferred to less so that $U'(W) > 0$, where $U'(W) = \partial U(W)/\partial W$. Now, consider a simple gamble of receiving $16 for a 'head' on the toss of a coin and $4 for tails. Given a fair coin, the probability of a head is $p = 1/2$ and the expected monetary value of the risky outcome is $10:

$$EW = pW_H + (1 - p)W_T = (1/2)16 + (1/2)4 = \$10 \tag{54}$$

We can see that the game is a fair bet when it costs $c = \$10$ to enter, because then $E(x) = EW - c = 0$. How much would an individual pay to play this game? This depends on the individual's attitude to risk. If the individual is willing to pay $10 to play the game, so that she accepts a fair bet, we say she is *risk neutral*. If you dislike risky outcomes, then you would prefer to keep your $10 rather than gamble on a fair game (with *expected value* of $10) – you are then said to be *risk averse*. A risk lover would pay more than $10 to play the game.

Risk aversion implies that the second derivative of the utility function is negative, $U''(W) < 0$. To see this, note that the utility from keeping your $10 and not gambling is $U(10)$ and this must exceed the expected utility from the gamble:

$$U(10) > 0.5U(16) + 0.5U(4) \quad \text{or} \quad U(10) - U(4) > U(16) - U(10) \qquad (55)$$

so that the utility function has the concave shape, marked 'risk averter', as given in Figure 2. An example of a utility function for a risk-averse person is $U(W) = W^{1/2}$. Note that the above example fits into our earlier notation of a fair bet if $x$ is the risky outcome with $k_1 = W_H - c = 6$ and $k_2 = W_T - c = -6$, because then $E(x) = 0$.

We can demonstrate the concavity proposition in reverse, namely, that concavity implies an unwillingness to accept a fair bet. If $z$ is a random variable and $U(z)$ is concave, then from Jensen's inequality:

$$E\{U(z)\} < U[E(z)] \qquad (56)$$

Let $z = W + x$ where $W$ is now the *initial* wealth, then for a fair gamble, $E(x) = 0$ so that

$$E\{U(W + x)\} < U[E(W + x)] = U(W) \qquad (57)$$

and hence you would not accept the fair bet.

It is easy to deduce that for a risk lover the utility function over wealth is convex (e.g. $U = W^2$), while for a risk-neutral investor who is just indifferent between the gamble or the certain outcome, the utility function is linear (i.e. $U(W) = bW$, with $b > 0$). Hence, we have

$$U''(W) < 0 \text{ risk averse;} \ U''(W) = 0 \text{ risk neutral;} \ U''(W) > 0 \text{ risk lover}$$

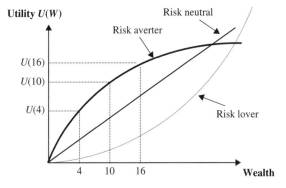

**Figure 2** Utility functions

A risk-averse investor is also said to have diminishing marginal utility of wealth: each additional unit of wealth adds less to utility, the higher the initial level of wealth (i.e. $U''(W) < 0$). The degree of risk aversion is given by the concavity of the utility function in Figure 2 and equivalently by the absolute size of $U''(W)$. Note that the degree of risk aversion even for a specific individual may depend on initial wealth and on the size of the bet. An individual may be risk-neutral for the small bet above and would be willing to pay $10 to play the game. However, a bet of $1 million for 'heads' and $0 for tails has an expected value of $500,000, but this same individual may not be prepared to pay $499,000 to avoid the bet, even though the game is in his or her favour – this same person is risk-averse over large gambles. Of course, if the person we are talking about is Bill Gates of Microsoft, who has rather a lot of initial wealth, he may be willing to pay up to $500,000 to take on the second gamble.

Risk aversion implies concavity of the utility function, over-risky gambles. But how do we quantify this risk aversion in monetary terms, rather than in terms of utility? The answer lies in Figure 3, where the distance $\pi$ is the *known* maximum amount you would be willing to pay to avoid a fair bet. If you pay $\pi$, then you will receive the *expected value* of the bet of $10 for certain and end up with $(10 - \pi)$. Suppose the utility function of our risk-averse investor is $U(W) = W^{1/2}$. The expected utility from the gamble is

$$E[U(W)] = 0.5U(W_{\mathrm{H}}) + 0.5U(W_{\mathrm{T}}) = 0.5(16)^{1/2} + 0.5(4)^{1/2} = 3$$

Note that the expected utility from the gamble $E[U(W)]$ is less than the utility from the certain outcome of not playing the game $U(EW) = 10^{1/2} = 3.162$. Would our risk-averse investor be willing to pay $\pi = \$0.75$ to avoid playing the game? If she does so, then her certain utility would be $U = (10 - 0.75)^{1/2} = 3.04$, which exceeds the expected utility from the bet $E[U(W)] = 3$, so she would pay $0.75 to avoid playing. What is the maximum insurance premium $\pi$ that she would pay? This occurs when the certain utility $U(W - \pi)$ from her lower wealth $(W - \pi)$ just equals $E[U(W)] = 3$, the expected utility from the gamble:

$$U(W - \pi) = (10 - \pi)^{1/2} = E[U(W)] = 3$$

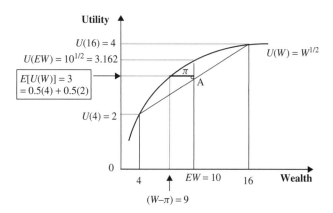

**Figure 3**   Monetary risk premium

which gives the maximum amount $\pi = \$1$ that you would pay to avoid playing the game. The amount of money $\pi$ is known as the risk premium and is the maximum insurance payment you would make to avoid the bet (note that 'risk premium' has another meaning in finance, which we meet later – namely, the expected return on a risky asset in excess of the risk-free rate). A *fair bet* of plus or minus $\$x = 6$ gives you expected utility at point A. If your wealth is reduced to $(W - \pi)$, then the level of utility is $U(W - \pi)$. The risk premium $\pi$ is therefore defined as

$$U(W - \pi) = E\{U(W + x)\} \tag{58}$$

where $W$ is *initial* wealth. To see how $\pi$ is related to the curvature of the utility function, take a Taylor series approximation of (58) around the point $x = 0$ (i.e. the probability density is concentrated around the mean of zero) and the point $\pi = 0$:

$$U(W - \pi) \approx U(W) - \pi U'(W)$$

$$= E\{U(W + x)\} \approx E\{U(W) + xU'(W) + (1/2)x^2 U''(W)\}$$

$$= U(W) + (1/2)\sigma_x^2 U''(W) \tag{59}$$

Because $E(x) = 0$, we require three terms in the expansion of $U(W + x)$. From (59), the risk premium is

$$\pi = -\frac{1}{2}\sigma_x^2 \frac{U''(W)}{U'(W)} = \frac{1}{2}\sigma_x^2 R_A(W) \tag{60}$$

where $R_A(W) = -U''(W)/U'(W)$ is the Arrow (1970)–Pratt (1964) measure of absolute (local) risk aversion. The measure of risk aversion is 'local' because it is a function of the initial level of wealth.

Since $\sigma_x^2$ and $U'(W)$ are positive, $U''(W) < 0$ implies that $\pi$ is positive. Note that the amount you will pay to avoid a fair bet depends on the riskiness of the outcome $\sigma_x^2$ as well as *both* $U''(W)$ and $U'(W)$. For example, you may be very risk-averse ($-U''(W)$ is large) but you may not be willing to pay a high premium $\pi$, if you are also very poor, because then $U'(W)$ will also be high. In fact, two measures of the degree of risk aversion are commonly used:

$$R_A(W) = -U''(W)/U'(W) \tag{61}$$

$$R_R(W) = R_A(W)W \tag{62}$$

$R_A(W)$ is the Arrow–Pratt measure of (local) absolute risk aversion, the larger $R_A(W)$ is, the greater the degree of risk aversion. $R_R(W)$ is the coefficient of relative risk aversion. $R_A$ and $R_R$ are measures of how the investor's risk preferences change with a change in wealth around the initial ('local') level of wealth.

Different mathematical functions give rise to different implications for the form of risk aversion. For example, the function $U(W) = \ln(W)$ exhibits diminishing absolute risk aversion and constant relative risk aversion (see below). Now, we list some of the 'standard' utility functions that are often used in the asset pricing and portfolio literature.

## Power (Constant Relative Risk Aversion)

With an initial (safe) level of wealth $W_0$, a utility function, which relative to the starting point has the property $U(W)/U(W_0) = f(W/W_0)$ so that utility reacts to the *relative* difference in wealth, is of the relative risk aversion type. The latter condition is met by power utility, where the response of utility to $W/W_0$ is constant, hence the equivalent term *constant relative risk aversion CRRA* utility function:

$$U(W) = \frac{W^{(1-\gamma)}}{1 - \gamma} \quad \gamma > 0, \gamma \neq 1$$

$$U'(W) = W^{-\gamma} \qquad U''(W) = -\gamma W^{-\gamma-1}$$

$$R_A(W) = \gamma/W \quad \text{and} \quad R_R(W) = \gamma \text{(a constant)} \qquad (63)$$

Since $\ln[U'(W)] = -\gamma \ln W$, then $\gamma$ is also the elasticity of *marginal* utility with respect to wealth.

## Logarithmic

As $\gamma \to 1$ in (63), it can be shown that the limiting case of power utility is logarithmic.

$$U(W) = \ln(W) \quad \text{and} \quad R_R(W) = 1 \qquad (64)$$

This has the nice simple intuitive property that your satisfaction (utility) doubles each time you double your wealth.

## Quadratic

$$U(W) = W - \frac{b}{2} W^2 \qquad b > 0$$

$$U'(W) = 1 - bW \qquad U''(W) = -b$$

$$R_A(W) = b/(1 - bW) \quad \text{and} \quad R_R(W) = bW/(1 - bW) \qquad (65)$$

Since $U'(W)$ must be positive, the quadratic is only defined for $W < 1/b$, which is known as the 'bliss point'. Marginal utility is linear in wealth and this can sometimes be a useful property. Note that both $R_R$ and $R_A$ are not constant but functions of wealth.

## Negative Exponential (Constant Absolute Risk Aversion)

With an initial (safe) level of wealth $W_0$, a utility function, which relative to the starting point has the property $U(W)/U(W_0) = f(W - W_0)$ so that utility reacts to the *absolute* difference in wealth, is of the absolute risk aversion type. The only (acceptable) function meeting this requirement is the (negative) exponential, where the response of utility to changes in $W - W_0$ is constant, hence the term *constant absolute risk aversion CARA* utility function:

$$U(W) = a - be^{-cW} \quad c > 0$$

$$R_A(W) = c \quad \text{and} \quad R_R(W) = cW \tag{66}$$

It can be shown that the negative exponential utility function plus the assumption of normally distributed asset returns allows one to reduce the problem of maximising expected utility to a problem involving only the maximisation of *a linear function* of expected portfolio return $ER_p$ and risk, that is (unambiguously) represented by the variance $\sigma_p^2$. Then, maximising the above CARA utility function $E[U(W)]$ is equivalent to maximising

$$ER_p - (c/2)\sigma_p^2 \tag{67}$$

where $c =$ the constant coefficient of absolute risk aversion. Equation (67) depends only on the mean and variance of the return on the portfolio: hence the term mean-variance criterion. However, the reader should note that, in general, maximising $E[U(W)]$ cannot be reduced to a maximisation problem in terms of a *general function* $ER_p$ and $\sigma_p^2$ only (see Appendix), and only for the negative exponential can it be reduced to maximising a *linear* function. Some portfolio models assume at the outset that investors are only concerned with the mean-variance maximand and they, therefore, discard any direct link with a specific utility function.

## HARA (Hyperbolic Absolute Risk Aversion)

$$U(W) = \frac{1-\gamma}{\gamma}\left(\frac{\alpha W}{1-\gamma} + \beta\right)^\gamma \tag{68}$$

$$R_A(W) = \left(\frac{W}{1-\gamma} + \frac{\beta}{\alpha}\right)^{-1} \tag{69}$$

$$R_A(W) > 0 \quad \text{when} \quad \gamma > 1, \beta > 0$$

The restrictions are $\gamma \neq 1$, $[\alpha W/(1-\gamma)] + \beta > 0$, and $\alpha > 0$. Also $\beta = 1$ if $\gamma = -\infty$. HARA (Hyperbolic Absolute Risk Aversion) is of interest because it nests constant absolute risk aversion ($\beta = 1, \gamma = -\infty$), constant relative risk aversion ($\gamma < 1, \beta = 0$) and quadratic ($\gamma = 2$), but it is usually these special cases that are used in the literature.

# 1.4 Asset Demands

Frequently, we want to know what determines the optimal demand for stocks, bonds and other assets, in investors' portfolios. Not surprisingly, the answer depends on how we set up the maximisation problem and the constraints facing the investor. Here we concentrate on one-period models with relatively simple solutions – later chapters deal with more complex cases.

## Mean-Variance Optimisation

The simplest model is to assume investors care only about one-period expected portfolio returns and the standard deviation (risk) of these portfolio returns. Let $\alpha$ = proportion of initial wealth $W_0$ held in the *single* risky asset with return $R$ and $(1-\alpha)$ = amount held in the risk-free asset with return $r$. The budget constraint (with zero labour income) is

$$W_1 = (\alpha W_0)(1+R) + [(1-\alpha)W_0](1+r)$$

and therefore the return and variance of the portfolio are

$$R_p \equiv \frac{W_1}{W_0} - 1 = \alpha(R-r) + r$$
$$\sigma_p = \alpha \sigma_R$$

where $\sigma_R$ is the standard deviation of the only stochastic variable $R$. Investors are assumed to maximise

$$\max_{\alpha} \theta = ER_p - \frac{c}{2}\sigma_p^2$$

where $c > 0$ is a measure of risk aversion (more precisely, the trade-off between expected portfolio return and the variance of portfolio returns). The first-order condition FOC is

$$ER - r - \alpha c \sigma_R = 0$$

so that the optimal share of the risky asset is independent of wealth:

$$\alpha^* = \frac{(ER-r)}{c\sigma_R}$$

Hence, the *absolute* (dollar) amount held in the risky asset $A_0 = \alpha^* W_0$ is proportional to initial wealth, and is positively related to the excess return on the risky asset and inversely related to the degree of risk aversion and the volatility of the risky asset. The share of the risk-free asset is simply $(1-\alpha^*) \equiv A_{of}/W_0$. The above is Tobin's (1956) mean-variance model of asset demands, and the reason for the simple closed form solution is that the maximand is quadratic in $\alpha$ (because $\sigma_p^2 = \alpha^2 \sigma_R^2$). If we had included *known* non-stochastic labour income $y$ in the budget constraint, this would not alter the solution. This one-period model is sometimes used in the theoretical literature because it is linear in expected returns, which provides analytic tractability.

The mean-variance approach is easily extended to $n$-risky assets $R = (R_1, R_2, \ldots, R_n)'$, and the maximand is

$$\max_{\alpha} \theta = \alpha'(R - r.e) + r - \frac{c}{2}\alpha' \Omega \alpha$$

where $\alpha = (\alpha_1, \alpha_2, \ldots, \alpha_n)'$, $e$ is an $n \times 1$ column vector of ones and $\Omega = (n \times n)$ variance–covariance matrix of returns. The FOCs give

$$\alpha^* = (c\Omega)^{-1}(ER - r.e)$$

and the share of the risk-free asset is $\alpha_f^* = 1 - \sum_{i=1}^{n} \alpha_i^*$. For two risky assets,

$$\Omega^{-1} = (\sigma_{11}\sigma_{22} - \sigma_{12}\sigma_{21})^{-1} \begin{pmatrix} \sigma_{22} & -\sigma_{21} \\ -\sigma_{12} & \sigma_{11} \end{pmatrix}$$

and therefore the relative weights attached to the expected returns $(ER_1 - r)$ and $(ER_2 - r)$ depend on the individual elements of the variance–covariance matrix of returns. The second-order conditions guarantee that $\partial\alpha_i^*/\partial ER_i > 0$ $(i = 1 \text{ or } 2)$.

## Negative Exponential Utility

It is worth noting that the maximand $\theta$ does not, in general, arise from a second-order Taylor series expansion of an arbitrary utility function depending only on terminal wealth $U(W_1)$. The latter usually gives rise to a *non-linear function* $EU(W) = U(ER_p) + \frac{1}{2}\sigma_p^2 U''(ER_p)$, whereas the mean-variance approach is *linear* in expected return and variance. However, there is one (very special) case where the maximand $\theta$ can be directly linked to a specific utility function, namely,

$$\max_{\alpha} E[U(W)] = -E\{\exp(-bW_1)\} = -E\{\exp(-bW_0(1 + R_p))\}$$

$$\text{subject to } R_p \equiv (W_1/W_0) - 1 = \alpha'(R - r.e) + r$$

where $b$ is the constant coefficient of *absolute* risk aversion. Thus, the utility function must be the negative exponential (in end-of-period wealth, $W_1$), and as we see below, asset returns must also be multivariate normal. If a random variable $x$ is normally distributed, $x \sim N(\mu, \sigma^2)$, then $z = \exp(x)$ is lognormal. The expected value of $z$ is

$$Ez = \exp\left(\mu + \frac{1}{2}\sigma^2\right)$$

In our case, $\mu \equiv R_p$ and $\sigma^2 \equiv \text{var}(R_p)$. The maximand is monotonic in its exponent, therefore, $\max E[U(W)]$ is equivalent to

$$\max_{\alpha} E[U(W_1)] = \alpha'(ER - r.e) - \frac{1}{2}bW_0\alpha'\Omega\alpha$$

where we have discarded the non-stochastic term $\exp(-bW_0)$. The maximand is now linearly related to expected portfolio return and variance. The solution to the FOCs is

$$\alpha^* = (bW_0\Omega)^{-1}(ER - r.e)$$

This is the same form of solution as for the mean-variance case and is equivalent if $c = bW_0$. Note, however, that the asset demand functions derived from the negative exponential utility function imply that the absolute dollar amount $A = \alpha^* W_0$ invested in the risky asset is independent of initial wealth. Therefore, if an individual obtains additional wealth next period, then she will put all of the extra wealth into the risk-free asset – a somewhat implausible result.

## Quadratic Utility

In this section, we will outline how asset shares can be derived when the utility function is quadratic – the math gets rather messy (but not difficult) and therefore we simplify the notation (as in Cerny 2004). We assume one risky asset and a risk-free asset. The budget constraint is

$$W = \tilde{\alpha} W_0 R^* + (1 - \tilde{\alpha}) W_0 R_f^* + y$$

where $\tilde{\alpha} = A/W_0$ is the risky asset share, $y$ is the known labour income and $R^* = 1 + R$ is the *gross* return on the risky asset. The risk-free asset share is $\tilde{\alpha}_f = 1 - \tilde{\alpha}$. After some rearrangement, the budget constraint becomes

$$W = W_{\text{safe}}(1 + \alpha X)$$

where    $W_{\text{safe}} \equiv R_f^* W_0 + y$, $X = R - R_f$ and $\alpha = \tilde{\alpha} W_0 / W_{\text{safe}}$

Hence, $\alpha$ is just a scaled version of $\tilde{\alpha}$. The utility function is quadratic with a fixed 'bliss level' of wealth $W_{\text{bliss}}$:

$$U(W) = -\frac{1}{2}(W - W_{\text{bliss}})^2 = -\frac{1}{2}(W^2 - 2WW_{\text{bliss}} + W_{\text{bliss}}^2)$$

We assume investors are always below the bliss point. It is easy to see from the above that $E[U(W)]$ depends on $\alpha$, $\alpha^2$, $EX$ and $E(X^2)$. The FOCs will therefore be linear in $\alpha$. In addition, $E(X^2) \equiv \text{var}(X) - (EX)^2$ so that the optimal $\alpha$ will depend only on expected excess returns $EX$ and the variance of returns on the risky assets (but the relationship is not linear). Substituting the budget constraint in $E[U(W)]$ and solving the FOC with respect to $\alpha$ gives (after tedious algebra)

$$\alpha^* = q_k \frac{EX}{E(X^2)}$$

where $q_k = 2k(1-k)/2k^2$ and $k = W_{\text{safe}}/W_{\text{bliss}}$.

Note that no *explicit* measure of risk aversion appears in the equation for $\alpha^*$ but it is implicit in the squared term '2' in the utility function, and is therefore a scaling factor in the solution for $\alpha^*$. (Also see below for the solution with power utility that collapses to quadratic utility for $\gamma = -1$.)

In order that we do not exceed the bliss point, we require $k \ll 1$ and to simplify the algebra, take $k = 1/2$ so that $q_k = 1$ (Equation 3.53, p. 68 in Cerny 2004). Hence,

$$\alpha^* = \frac{EX}{E(X^2)} = \frac{\mu_x}{\sigma_x^2 + \mu_x^2} = \frac{1}{\mu_x(1 + 1/SR_x^2)}$$

where $SR_x = \mu_x/\sigma_x$ is known as the Sharpe ratio, and appears through the book as a measure of return per unit of risk (reward-to-risk ratio). Here the optimal $\alpha$ (and $\tilde{\alpha}$) is directly related to the Sharpe ratio. It can be shown that $\alpha^*$ for quadratic utility (and for $W(\alpha^*) < W_{\text{bliss}}$) is also that value that gives the maximum Sharpe ratio (and this generalises when there are many risky assets, (see Cerny 2004, Chapter 4)).

Choosing a portfolio (i.e. $\alpha = (\alpha_1, \alpha_2, \ldots, \alpha_n)$) to maximise the Sharpe ratio can therefore be directly linked to maximising expected quadratic utility (for $W(\alpha^*) < W_{\text{bliss}}$) – although the Sharpe ratio criterion would not be valid if the optimal $\alpha$ implies that $W(\alpha^*) > W_{\text{bliss}}$. The link between the (basic) Sharpe ratio and utility cannot be established for other types of utility function. Nevertheless, the Sharpe ratio is often used in practice to rank alternative risky portfolios without trying to link the decision to any specific utility function – as we see in later chapters. Also, if the 'basic' Sharpe ratio above can be generalised to link it to a constant CARA utility function, then it can be referred to as the *Hodges ratio* (see Cerny 2004, Hodges 1998).

## Power Utility

A closed form solution for asset shares for most utility functions is not possible. We then have to use numerical techniques. We demonstrate this outcome for power utility over (one period) final wealth for one risky and one risk-free asset. The budget constraint is

$$W(\tilde{\alpha}) = \tilde{\alpha} W_0 R^* + (1 - \tilde{\alpha}) W_0 R_f^* + y = W_{\text{safe}}(1 + \alpha X)$$

Suppose we have a simple set-up where $R_u^* = 1.20$ and $R_D^* = 0.90$ so that the risky asset has only two possible outcomes, up or down (i.e. 20% or $-10\%$), with equal probability of 1/2. Let $\gamma = 5, r = 0.03, W_0 = \$1\,m$ and $y = \$200,000$. The maximisation problem with power utility is then

$$\max_{\alpha} \theta = E\left[\frac{W^{1-\gamma}}{(1-\gamma)}\right] = \left\{\frac{1}{2}\frac{W_u^{1-\gamma}}{(1-\gamma)} + \frac{1}{2}\frac{W_D^{1-\gamma}}{(1-\gamma)}\right\}$$

$$= W_{\text{safe}}^{1-\gamma}\left\{\frac{1}{2}\frac{(1+\alpha X_u)}{(1-\gamma)} + \frac{1}{2}\frac{(1+\alpha X_u)^{1-\gamma}}{(1-\gamma)}\right\}$$

Everything in $\theta$ is known except for $\alpha$. Actually, an analytic solution for this case is possible. We would set $\partial\theta/\partial\alpha = 0$, and the resulting equation is solved for $\alpha^*$ and then for $\tilde{\alpha}^* = \alpha^* W_{\text{safe}}/W_0 = 0.3323$ (see Cerny 2004, p. 60). Alternatively, any numerical optimiser would also directly give the solution. Having obtained $\alpha^*$, we can substitute this in the above equation to give the expected utility at the optimum.

$$\theta^* = E[U[W(\alpha^*)]] = -1.110397(10^{-25})$$

The certainty equivalent level of wealth $W_{\text{cert}}$ can be calculated from

$$U(W_{\text{cert}}) = E\{U[W(\alpha^*)]\} \quad \text{that is,} \quad \frac{W_{\text{cert}}^{1-\gamma}}{1-\gamma} = -1.110397(10^{-25})$$

which for $(\gamma = 5)$ gives $W_{\text{cert}} = \$1,224,942$. We have $W_{\text{safe}} = R_f^* W_0 + y = \$1,220,000$, so the investor is better off by $\$4,942$ compared to holding only the risk-free asset.

The above is easily extended to the case where we still have only one risky asset but there are $m$ possible outcomes ('states') for the risky asset excess return $X$ with probabilities $p_i$. The maximand $\theta$ summed over all states is

$$\theta = \max_{\alpha} \sum_{i=1}^{m} p_i U(W_i)$$

where $U(W_i) = W_i^{1-\gamma}/(1-\gamma)$ and $W_i = W_{\text{safe}}(1 + \alpha X_i)$. Again, the only unknown in $\theta$ is the risky asset share $\alpha$ (or $\tilde{\alpha}$), and the optimal $\alpha$ can be obtained from a numerical optimiser (or 'by hand' if you have numerous sheets of paper).

Now let us be a little more adventurous and assume we choose a set of risky assets $\alpha = (\alpha_1, \alpha_2, \ldots, \alpha_n)'$, but for the moment assume there are only $m = 4$ states of nature for each excess return with an associated *joint* probability distribution:

$$X^{(i)} = (X_1^{(i)}, \ldots, X_n^{(i)})' \qquad (n \times 1)$$
$$W_i = W_{\text{safe}}(1 + \alpha' X^{(i)}) \qquad (i = 1 - 4)$$
$$p_i = (p_1, p_2, p_3, p_4) \qquad (1 \times 4)$$

$W_i$ is a scalar, and each outcome for the $n$-vector $X^{(i)}$ has an associated joint probability $p_i$. There are only four possible outcomes for the four vectors $X^{(i)}$ with probabilities $p_i$ and hence four outcomes for $W_i$ and $U(W_i)$. So, $\theta$ contains a sum over four states and is easily calculated but it now depends on the $n$ values of $\alpha_i$. The FOCs are $\partial\theta/\partial\alpha_i = 0$ (for $i = 1, 2, \ldots, n$) and, in general, these non-linear equations cannot be solved analytically and hence an optimiser must be used to obtain the $\alpha_i^*$ ($i = 1, 2, \ldots, n$), which maximises $\theta$.

## Continuous Distribution

Suppose we have $n$ assets but the distribution of returns $R$ is continuous and for expositional purposes, assume the $(n \times 1)$ vector $X = R - r.e$ (where $e = n \times 1$ vector of ones) is multivariate normal with conditional density $f(x|\Lambda)$, where $\Lambda$ is information at $t - 1$ or earlier. We have

$$W = W_{\text{safe}}(1 + \alpha' X)$$
$$U(W) = W^{1-\gamma}/(1-\gamma)$$

Hence:

$$\theta = E\{U[W(\alpha)]\} = \frac{W_{\text{safe}}^{1-\gamma}}{(1-\gamma)} \cdot \int_{-\infty}^{\infty} (1 + \alpha' x)^{1-\gamma} f(x/\Lambda)\, dx$$

For illustrative purposes, assume $n = 2$ and $X|\Lambda \sim N(\mu, \Omega)$, then

$$f(x) = \frac{1}{(2\pi)^n |\det \Omega|} \exp\left[-\frac{1}{2}(x - \mu)\Omega^{-1}(x - \mu)\right]$$

The conditional mean and covariance matrix are assumed 'known' (i.e. estimated by a statistician from historic data), and the term in square brackets is a scalar function of

$x$. In the simplest case where each $x_{it}$ is *iid* over time but there is cross-correlation at time $t$

$$x_i = \mu + \varepsilon_i \quad \Omega = E(\varepsilon' \varepsilon)$$

and the conditional and unconditional moments are equal. The (multiple) integral may be solvable analytically, but usually has to be evaluated numerically. In effect, the optimiser chooses alternative trial values for $\alpha = (\alpha_1, \alpha_2, \ldots, \alpha_n)$, calculates $\theta(\alpha)$ and chooses that value $\alpha = \alpha^*$ that achieves the largest value of $\theta(\alpha^*)$. A clear exposition of optimisation, including some useful GAUSS programmes, can be seen in Chapter 4 of Cerny (2004).

## Risk Aversion and Portfolio Choice

When investors have a one-period horizon and maximise $U(W)$, there is a little more we can say about the response of the demands for risky assets to a change in initial wealth. For simplicity, we assume only one risky asset. We state these results without proof, but they are based on an analysis of the FOC, for any concave utility function:

$$E[U'(W)(R - R_f)] = 0$$

where $W = W_0(1 + R_f) + A(R - R_f)$ and $W_0 = $ initial wealth, $A = $ \$-amount invested in the risky asset (and $(W_0 - A)$ is invested in the risk-free asset). Our first result is easily seen from the FOC. If $ER = R_f$, then $A = 0$ satisfies the FOC, $W = W_0(1 + R_f)$ is non-stochastic, so $E[U'(W)(R - R_f)] = U'(W)E(R - R_f) = 0$. Hence, a risk-averse individual would not accept a fair gamble, namely, $ER - R_f = 0$, since the latter implies $A = 0$. Other results for any concave utility function are:

(i) If $ER > R_f$, then $A > 0$, the investor holds a *positive* amount of the risky asset – she is willing to accept a small gamble with positive expected return.

(ii) Declining *absolute* risk aversion (i.e. $\partial R_A / \partial W_0 < 0$, where $R_A$ is the coefficient of absolute risk aversion) implies that $\partial A / \partial W_0 > 0$, that is, the individual invests more 'dollars' in the risky asset if initial wealth is higher (and vice versa).

(iii) If the coefficient of *relative* risk aversion $R_R$ is decreasing in wealth (i.e. $\partial R_R / \partial W_0 < 0$), then $(\partial A / A_0)/(\partial W / W_0) > 1$, so the individual invests a greater *proportion* in the risky asset as wealth increases. The opposite applies for an investor with a coefficient of relative risk aversion that increases in wealth.

The above complement our earlier results that for *constant* absolute risk aversion, CARA (e.g. negative exponential), $\partial A / \partial W_0 = 0$ and for *constant* relative risk aversion, $\partial A / A = \partial W / W$, so optimal asset *shares* remain constant.

## 1.5  Indifference Curves and Intertemporal Utility

Although it is only the case under somewhat restrictive circumstances, let us assume that the utility function in Figure 2 for the risk averter can be represented solely in terms of the expected return and the variance of the return on the portfolio. The link between end-of-period wealth $W$ and investment in a portfolio of assets yielding an expected return $ER_p$ is $W = (1 + ER_p)W_0$, where $W_0$ is initial wealth. However, we now do assume that the utility function can be represented as

$$U = U(ER_p, \sigma_p^2) \qquad U_1 > 0, U_2 < 0, U_{11}, U_{22} < 0 \tag{70}$$

The sign of the first-order partial derivatives $(U_1, U_2)$ imply that expected return adds to utility, while more 'risk' reduces utility. The second-order partial derivatives indicate diminishing marginal utility to additional expected 'returns' and increasing marginal disutility with respect to additional risk. The indifference curves for the above utility function are shown in Figure 4.

At a point like A on indifference curve $I_1$, the individual requires a higher expected return (A‴–A″) as compensation for a higher level of risk (A–A″) if he is to maintain the level of satisfaction (utility) pertaining at A: the indifference curves have a positive slope in risk–return space. The indifference curves are convex to the 'risk axis', indicating that at higher levels of risk, say at C, the individual requires a higher expected return (C‴–C″ > A‴–A″) for each additional increment to the risk he undertakes, than he did at A: the individual is 'risk-averse'. The indifference curves in risk–return space will be used when analysing portfolio choice in a simple mean-variance model.

## Intertemporal Utility

A number of economic models of individual behaviour assume that investors obtain utility solely from consumption goods. At any point in time, utility depends positively on consumption and exhibits diminishing marginal utility

$$U = U(C_t) \qquad U'(C_t) > 0, U''(C_t) < 0 \tag{71}$$

The utility function, therefore, has the same slope as the 'risk averter' in Figure 2 (with $C$ replacing $W$). The only other issue is how we deal with consumption that accrues at different points in time. The most general form of such an intertemporal lifetime utility function is

$$U_N = U(C_t, C_{t+1}, C_{t+2}, \ldots, C_{t+N}) \tag{72}$$

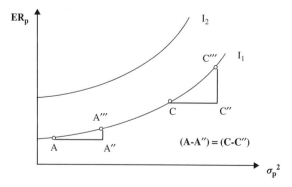

**Figure 4**   Risk–return: indifference curves

However, to make the mathematics tractable, some restrictions are usually placed on the form of U, the most common being additive separability with a constant subjective rate of discount, $0 < \theta < 1$:

$$U_N = U(C_t) + \theta U(C_{t+1}) + \theta^2 U(C_{t+2}) + \cdots + \theta^N U(C_{t+N}) \qquad (73)$$

The lifetime utility function can be truncated at a finite value for $N$, or if $N \to \infty$, then the model is said to be an overlapping generations model since an individual's consumption stream is bequeathed to future generations.

The discount rate used in (73) depends on the 'tastes' of the individual between present and future consumption. If we define $\theta = 1/(1 + d)$, then $d$ is known as the subjective *rate of time preference*. It is the rate at which the individual will swap utility at time $t + j$ for utility at time $t + j + 1$ and still keep lifetime utility constant. The additive separability in (73) implies that the marginal utility from extra consumption in year $t$ is independent of the marginal utility obtained from extra consumption in any other year (suitably discounted).

For the two-period case, we can draw the indifference curves that follow from a simple utility function (e.g. $U = C_0^{\alpha_1} C_1^{\alpha_2}, 0 < \alpha_1, \alpha_2 < 1$) and these are given in Figure 5. Point A is on a higher indifference curve than point B since at A the individual has the same level of consumption in period 1, $C_1$ as at B, but at A, he has more consumption in period zero, $C_0$. At point H, if you reduce $C_0$ by $x_0$ units, then for the individual to maintain a constant level of lifetime utility he must be compensated by $y_0$ extra units of consumption in period 1, so he is then indifferent between points H and E. Diminishing marginal utility arises because at F, if you take away $x_0$ units of $C_0$, then he requires $y_1$ ($> y_0$) extra units of $C_1$ to compensate him. This is because at F he starts off with a lower initial level of $C_0$ than at H, so each unit of $C_0$ he gives up is relatively more valuable and requires more compensation in terms of extra $C_1$.

The intertemporal indifference curves in Figure 5 will be used in discussing investment decisions under certainty in the next section and again when discussing the consumption – CAPM model of portfolio choice and equilibrium asset returns under uncertainty.

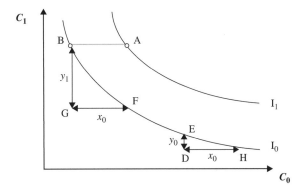

**Figure 5**    Intertemporal consumption: indifference curves

# 1.6   Investment Decisions and Optimal Consumption

Under conditions of certainty about future receipts, our investment decision rules indicate that managers should rank physical investment projects according to either their NPV or IRR. Investment projects should be undertaken until the NPV of the last project undertaken equals zero or equivalently if $IRR = r$, the risk-free rate of interest. Under these circumstances, the marginal (last) investment project undertaken just earns enough net returns (profits) to cover the loan interest and repayment of principal. For the economy as a whole, undertaking real investment requires a sacrifice in terms of lost current consumption output. Labour skills, man-hours and machines are, at $t = 0$, devoted to producing new machines or increased labour skills that will add to output and consumption but only in future periods. The consumption profile (i.e. less consumption goods today and more in the future) that results from the decisions of producers may not coincide with the consumption profile desired by individual consumers. For example, a high level of physical investment will drastically reduce resources available for current consumption and this may be viewed as undesirable by consumers who prefer at the margin, consumption today rather than tomorrow.

How can financial markets, through facilitating borrowing and lending, ensure that entrepreneurs produce the optimal level of physical investment (i.e. which yields high levels of future consumption goods) and also allow individuals to spread their consumption over time according to their preferences? Do the entrepreneurs have to know the preferences of individual consumers in order to choose the optimum level of physical investment? How can the consumers acting as shareholders ensure that the managers of firms undertake the 'correct' physical investment decisions, and can we assume that the financial markets (e.g. stock markets) ensure that funds are channelled to the most efficient investment projects?

Questions of the interaction between 'finance' and real investment decisions lie at the heart of the market system. The full answer to these questions involves complex issues. However, we can gain some useful insights if we consider a simple two-period model of the investment decision in which all outcomes are certain (i.e. riskless) in real terms (i.e. we assume zero price inflation). We shall see that under these assumptions, a *separation principle* applies. If managers ignore the preferences of individuals and simply invest in projects until the $NPV = 0$ or $IRR = r$, that is, maximise the value of the firm, then this policy will, given a capital market, allow each consumer to choose his desired consumption profile, namely, that which maximises his individual welfare. There is therefore a two-stage process or separation of decisions; yet, this still allows consumers to maximise their welfare by distributing their consumption over time according to their preferences. In step one, entrepreneurs decide the optimal level of physical investment, disregarding the preferences of consumers. In step two, consumers borrow or lend in the capital market to rearrange the time profile of their consumption to suit their individual preferences. In explaining this separation principle, we first deal with the production decision and then the consumers' decision before combining these two into the complete model.

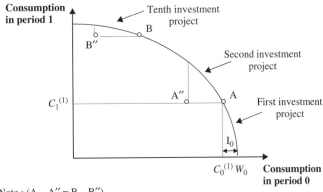

Note : (A – A″ = B – B″).

**Figure 6**    Production possibility curve

All output is either consumed or used for physical investment. The entrepreneur has an initial endowment $W_0$ at $t = 0$. He ranks projects in order of decreasing NPV, using the risk-free interest rate $r$ as the discount factor. By abstaining from consumption of $C_0^{(1)}$, he obtains resources for his first investment project $I_0 = W_0 - C_0^{(1)}$. The physical investment in that project, which has the highest NPV (or IRR), yields consumption output at $t = 1$ of $C_1^{(1)}$, where $C_1^{(1)} > C_0^{(1)}$ (see Figure 6). The IRR of this project (in terms of consumption goods) is

$$1 + IRR^{(1)} = C_1^{(1)}/C_0^{(1)} \tag{74}$$

As he devotes more of his initial endowment $W_0$ to other investment projects with lower NPVs, the IRR $(C_1/C_0)$ falls, which gives rise to the production opportunity curve with the shape given in Figure 6. The first and the most productive investment project has an NPV of

$$NPV^{(1)} = C_1^{(1)}/(1+r) - I_0 > 0 \tag{75}$$

and

$$IRR^{(1)} = C_1^{(1)}/C_0^{(1)} > r \tag{76}$$

Let us now turn to the financing problem. In the capital market, any two consumption streams $C_0$ and $C_1$ have a present value $PV$ given by

$$PV = C_0 + C_1/(1+r) \tag{77a}$$

and hence,

$$C_1 = PV(1+r) - (1+r)C_0 \tag{77b}$$

For a given value of $PV$, this gives a straight line in Figure 7 with a slope equal to $-(1+r)$. The above equation is referred to as the 'money market line' since it

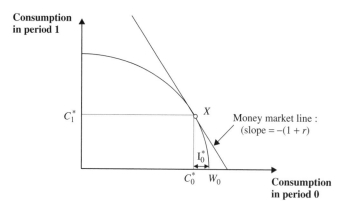

**Figure 7**   Money market line

represents the rate of return on lending and borrowing money. If you lend an amount $C_0$ today, you will receive $C_1 = (1 + r) C_0$ tomorrow.

Our entrepreneur, with an initial endowment of $W_0$, will continue to invest in physical assets until the IRR on the $n$th project just equals the risk-free interest rate

$$IRR^{(n)} = r$$

which occurs at point $(C_0^*, C_1^*)$. Hence, the investment strategy that maximises the (net present) value of the firm involves an investment of

$$I_0^* = W_0 - C_0^*$$

Current consumption is $C_0^*$ and consumption at $t = 1$ is $C_1^*$ (Figure 7). At any point to the right of X, the slope of the investment opportunity curve ($= $ IRR) exceeds the market interest rate ($= r$) and at points to the left of X, the opposite applies. However, the optimal levels of consumption $(C_0^*, C_1^*)$ from the production decision may not conform to those desired by an individual consumer's preferences. We now leave the production decision and turn exclusively to the consumer's decision.

Suppose the consumer has income accruing in both periods and this income stream has a present value of PV. The consumption possibilities that fully exhaust this income (after two periods) are given by (77a). Assume that lifetime utility (satisfaction) of the consumer depends on $C_0$ and $C_1$

$$U = U(C_0, C_1)$$

and there is diminishing marginal utility in both $C_0$ and $C_1$ (i.e. $\partial U/\partial C > 0$, $\partial^2 U/\partial C^2 < 0$). The indifference curves are shown in Figure 8. To give up one unit of $C_0$, the consumer must be compensated with additional units of $C_1$ if he is to maintain his initial level of utility. The consumer wishes to choose $C_0$ and $C_1$ to maximise lifetime utility, subject to his budget constraint. Given his endowment PV, his optimal consumption in the two periods is $(C_0^{**}, C_1^{**})$ – Figure 8. In general, the optimal production or physical investment plan that yields consumption $(C_0^*, C_1^*)$ will not equal

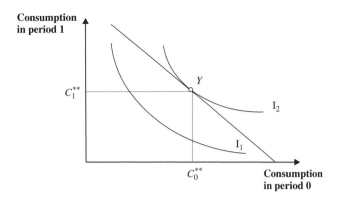

**Figure 8**   Consumer's maximisation

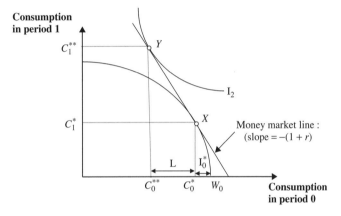

**Figure 9**   Maximisation with capital market

the consumer's optimal consumption profile $(C_0^{**}, C_1^{**})$. However, the existence of a capital market ensures that the consumer's optimal point can be attained. To see this, consider Figure 9.

The entrepreneur has produced a consumption profile $(C_0^*, C_1^*)$ that maximises the value of the firm – Figure 9. We can envisage this consumption profile as being paid out to the owners of the firm in the form of (dividend) income. The present value of this 'cash flow' is PV*, where

$$PV^* = C_0^* + C_1^*/(1+r) \tag{78}$$

This is, of course, the 'income' given to our individual consumer as owner of the firm. But, under conditions of certainty, the consumer can 'swap' this amount PV* for any combination of consumption that satisfies

$$PV^* = C_0 + C_1/(1+r) \tag{79}$$

Given PV* and his indifference curve $I_2$ in Figure 9, he can then borrow or lend in the capital market at the riskless rate $r$ to achieve that combination $(C_0^{**}, C_1^{**})$ that maximises his utility.

Thus, there is a separation of investment and financing (borrowing and lending) decisions. Optimal borrowing and lending take place independently of the physical investment decision. If the entrepreneur and consumer are the same person(s), the separation principle still applies. The investor (as we now call him) first decides how much of his own initial endowment $W_0$ to invest in physical assets, and this decision is independent of his own (subjective) preferences and tastes. This first-stage decision is an objective calculation based on comparing the IRR of his investment projects with the risk-free interest rate. His second-stage decision involves how much to borrow or lend in the capital market to 'smooth out' his desired consumption pattern over time. The latter decision is based on his preferences or tastes, at the margin, for consumption today versus (more) consumption tomorrow.

Much of the rest of this book is concerned with how financing decisions are taken when we have a risky environment. The issue of how shareholders ensure that managers act in the best interest of the shareholders, by maximising the value of the firm, comes under the heading of corporate control mechanisms (e.g. mergers, takeovers). The analysis of corporate control is not directly covered in this book. We only consider whether market prices provide correct signals for resource allocation (i.e. physical investment), but we do not look closely at issues involving the incentive structure within the firm based on these market signals: this is the principal–agent problem in corporate finance.

We can draw a parallel between the above results under certainty with those we shall be developing under a risky environment.

(i) In a risky environment, a somewhat different separation principle applies. Each investor, when choosing his portfolio of risky marketable assets (e.g. shares, bonds), will hold risky assets in the same proportion as all other investors, regardless of his preferences of risk versus return. Having undertaken this first-stage decision, each investor then decides how much to borrow or lend in the money market at the risk-free interest rate – it is at this point that his preferences influence the split between the risky assets and the risk-free asset. This separation principle is the basis of the mean-variance model of optimal portfolio choice and of the CAPM of equilibrium asset returns.

(ii) The optimal amount of borrowing and lending in the money market in the riskless case occurs where the individual's subjective marginal rate of substitution of future for current consumption [i.e. $(\partial C_1 / \partial C_0)_u$] equals $-(1 + r)$, where $r$ is the 'price' or opportunity cost of money. Under uncertainty, an analogous condition applies, namely, that the individual's *subjective* trade-off between expected return and risk is equal to the market price of risk.

## 1.7    Summary

We have developed some basic tools for analysing behaviour in financial markets. There are many nuances on the topics discussed that we have not had time to elaborate in detail, and in future chapters, these omissions will be rectified. The main conclusions to emerge are:

- Market participants generally quote 'simple' annual interest rates but these can always be converted to effective annual (compound) rates or to continuously compounded rates.

- The concepts of DPV and IRR can be used to analyse physical investment projects and to calculate the fair price of bills, bonds and stocks.

- Theoretical models of asset demands and asset prices often use utility functions as their objective function. Utility functions and their associated indifference curves can be used to represent risk aversion, risk lovers and risk-neutral investors.

- Under conditions of certainty, a type of separation principle applies when deciding on (physical) investment projects. Managers can choose investment projects to maximise the value of the firm and disregard investor's preferences. Then, investors are able to borrow and lend to allocate consumption between 'today' and 'tomorrow' in order to maximise their utility.

- One-period models in which utility is assumed to depend only on expected portfolio return and the variance of return give rise to asset shares that depend on expected excess returns, the covariance matrix of returns and 'risk aversion' of the investor.

- One-period models that depend on the expected utility of end-of-period wealth generally do not give closed-form solutions. The exceptions are quadratic utility or negative exponential utility plus multivariate normally distributed returns, where asset demands are linear in expected excess returns. For many other utility functions, the optimal solution for asset demands has to be calculated numerically.

## Appendix: Mean-Variance Model and Utility Functions

If an investor maximises expected utility of end-of-period portfolio wealth, then it can be shown that this is equivalent to maximising *a function* of expected portfolio returns and portfolio variance providing

(a) either utility is quadratic, or

(b) portfolio returns are normally distributed (and utility is concave).

If initial wealth is $W_0$ and the stochastic portfolio return is $R_p$, then end-of-period wealth and utility are

$$W = W_0(1 + R_p) \tag{A1}$$

$$U(W) = U[W_0(1 + R_p)] \tag{A2}$$

Expanding $U(R_p)$ in a Taylor series around the mean of $R_p(=\mu_p)$ gives

$$U(R_p) = U(\mu_p) + (R_p - \mu_p)U'(\mu_p) + (1/2)(R_p - \mu_p)^2 U''(\mu_p)$$
$$+ \text{ higher order terms} \qquad (A3)$$

Since $E(R_p - \mu_p) = 0$, and $E(R_p - \mu_p)^2 = \sigma_p^2$, taking expectations of (A3):

$$E[U(R_p)] = U(\mu_p) + \frac{1}{2}\sigma_p^2 U''(\mu_p) + E(\text{higher} - \text{order terms}) \qquad (A4)$$

If utility is quadratic, then higher-order terms other than $U''$ are zero. If returns are normally distributed, then $E[(R_p - \mu_p)^n] = 0$ for $n$ odd, and $E[(R_p - \mu_p)^n]$ for $n$ even is a function only of the variance $\sigma_p^2$. Hence for cases (a) and (b), $E[U(R_p)]$ is *a function* of only the mean $\mu_p$ and the variance $\sigma_p^2$. This result is moderately useful; for example, it can be shown that if utility is defined only in terms of $\mu_p$ and $\sigma_p$ and is concave, then indifference curves in $(\mu_p, \sigma_p)$ space are convex, as assumed in the text (see Figure 4). However, until we specify a specific utility function, we do not know the functional relationship between $E[U(R_p)]$ and $(\mu_p, \sigma_p)$ and hence we cannot determine whether there is an analytic closed-form solution for asset demands.

Using quadratic utility has the problem that marginal utility is negative for levels of wealth above the bliss point. Assuming normality for returns may not be an accurate representation and also prices may become negative. Continuous time models assume returns that are *instantaneously* normally distributed, and this provides considerable tractability (see Cuthbertson and Nitzsche 2001a), which is widely used in derivatives pricing. Again, the empirical validity of normality even at high frequencies (e.g. tick-data) is debatable, but the usefulness of results depends on the problem at hand (e.g. it seems reasonable when pricing stock index options).

# 2

# BASIC STATISTICS IN FINANCE

## Aims

- Examine the lognormal distribution and Jensen's inequality.

- Discuss the relationship between unit roots, random walk and cointegration.

- Demonstrate the use of Monte Carlo Simulation (MCS) and bootstrapping.

- Indicate how Bayes' rule can be used to combine prior information and data estimates to give an optimal forecast for parameters of interest.

The reader is assumed to have a good knowledge of basic undergraduate statistics and econometrics, and the material in this chapter provides a brief résumé of a few selected topics that are of key importance in understanding modern empirical work in financial economics.

## 2.1 Lognormality and Jensen's Inequality

Suppose $Z$ has a lognormal distribution $z = \ln Z \sim N(\mu_z, \sigma_z^2)$, where $\mu_z = E(\ln Z)$, $\sigma_z^2 = E(\ln Z - E(\ln Z))^2$. Then, the expected value of $Z$ is given by

$$EZ = Ee^z = e^{\mu_z + (1/2)\sigma_z^2} \qquad (1)$$

Equation (1) is a special case of *Jensen's inequality* that applies to expectations of non-linear functions:

$$E[f(Z)] \neq f(EZ) \qquad (2)$$

Here, $Z = \exp(z)$ but $EZ \neq \exp(Ez) = \exp(\mu_z)$. To illustrate this, suppose the $k$-period forward rate is an unbiased predictor of the expected future exchange rate, $k$-periods ahead:

$$E_t S_{t+k} = F_t^k \tag{3}$$

Assume the spot rate is *conditionally* lognormally distributed:

$$\ln S_{t+k} \equiv s_{t+k} \tag{4a}$$

$$s_{t+k}|\Omega_t \sim N[E_t s_{t+k}, \text{var}_t(s_{t+k})] \tag{4b}$$

where $\Omega_t$ is the information set at time $t$. It follows from (1)

$$E_t S_{t+k} = E_t[\exp(s_{t+k})] = \exp[E_t s_{t+k} + (1/2)\text{var}_t(s_{t+k})] \tag{5a}$$

$$\ln(E_t S_{t+k}) = E_t s_{t+k} + (1/2)\text{var}_t(s_{t+k}) \tag{5b}$$

Using (5b) in (3), we have

$$f_t^k = E_t s_{t+k} + (1/2)\text{var}_t(s_{t+k}) \tag{6}$$

where $f_t^k = \ln(F_t^k)$. Hence, the log of the forward rate is *not* an unbiased predictor of the expected value of the (log of the) future spot rate, when the spot rate is conditionally lognormal. The additional variance term in (6) is often referred to as the *Jensen inequality term*. This becomes of relevance when discussing forward rate unbiasedness and other issues in later chapters.

Exchange rates can be measured either as *domestic per unit of foreign currency $S_t$* or vice versa, so that

$$S_{t+1}^* = \frac{1}{S_{t+1}} \tag{7}$$

where $S_{t+1}^*$ is measured as foreign per unit of domestic currency. However, because (7) is a non-linear transformation,

$$E_t S_{t+1}^* = E_t(1/S_{t+1}) \neq 1/E_t(S_{t+1}) \tag{8}$$

so that $E_t(1/S_{t+1}) \neq 1/E_t(S_{t+1})$ – this special case of Jensen's inequality is known as *Siegel's paradox*. However, for the *logarithm* of the exchange rate $s_{t+1} = \ln S_{t+1}$, it is true that

$$E_t(s_{t+1}) = -E_t(-s_{t+1}) \tag{9}$$

## 2.2   Unit Roots, Random Walk and Cointegration

A random walk with drift $(= \mu)$ is an individual stochastic series $x_t$ that behaves as

$$x_t = \mu + x_{t-1} + \varepsilon_t \qquad \varepsilon_t \sim \text{iid}(0, \sigma_\varepsilon^2) \tag{10a}$$

where iid stands for 'identical and independently distributed'. Standard econometric tests are based on the assumption that variables are stationary (i.e. broadly speaking, a constant unconditional population mean and variance and autocorrelations that depend only on the time lag between the series). The series $x_t$ in (10) is non-stationary (i.e. wanders off in an upward or downward direction and rarely re-crosses its starting point) and is said to have a unit root (i.e. $(1 - \rho L)x_t = \varepsilon_t$ where $\rho = 1$). This unit root gives rise to a stochastic trend since from (10a)

$$x_{t+T} = T\mu + x_t + v_t \tag{10b}$$

$$E_t x_{t+T} = T\mu \tag{10c}$$

$$\text{var}_t(x_{t+T}) = T\sigma_\varepsilon^2 \tag{10d}$$

where $v_t = \varepsilon_{t+1} + \varepsilon_{t+2} + \cdots + \varepsilon_{t+T}$. Even when $\mu = 0$ (i.e. no drift), the $x_t$ series 'wanders' further from its starting point and as $T \to \infty$, its variance increases with 'T' – this is the stochastic trend. The first difference of $x_t$, that is, $\Delta x_t = \mu + \varepsilon_t$, is stationary (since $\varepsilon_t$ is stationary) and has a constant mean. A test for stationarity of an individual series $x_t$ can be obtained by running the Augmented Dickey–Fuller, or ADF, test, which is based on the OLS (maintained) regression

$$\Delta x_t = \mu + \gamma x_{t-1} + \sum_{i=1}^{m} \delta_i \Delta x_{t-i} + \varepsilon_t \tag{11}$$

where $\varepsilon_t$ is normally distributed and iid – usually written niid or $N(0, \sigma_\varepsilon^2)$. The null of non-stationarity is

$$H_0 : \gamma = 0$$

and the alternative of stationarity is $H_a : \gamma < 0$ (on a one-tail test). The OLS 't-statistic' for $H_0 : \gamma = 0$ is

$$\hat{\tau}_\mu = \hat{\gamma}/se(\hat{\gamma}) \tag{12}$$

where the subscript $\mu$ indicates that the data generation process (DGP) or 'true' model is (10a). Under the null, $\hat{\tau}_\mu$ is not distributed as a Student's $t$-distribution, hence its 5% critical value has to be determined using MCS (see below) and depends on the 'true' value of $\mu$ in the DGP and on sample size, $n$. For example, for $\mu = 0$, $n = 50$ (and the lag length in (11) is $m = 0$), the 5% (one-tail) critical value is $-2.92$, whereas for $\mu = 0.25$, it is $-2.63$ (Patterson 2000, Table 6, p. 232). For $\mu \neq 0$, the distribution of $\hat{\tau}_\mu$ is *asymptotically* normal, with a 5% critical value of $-1.65$, but rarely do we have enough data points to warrant using the asymptotic value. For $\mu = 0$ in the DGP and $n = 50$, and given a value of $\hat{\tau}_\mu < -2.92$, one would reject the null of non-stationarity. There are many variants on the above test but all follow the same general principle set out above (see Patterson 2000 for an excellent overview of these issues).

Testing for the null of a unit root against a stationary alternative is somewhat 'severe'. If you do not reject the null, you are accepting that the series can 'wander off' to plus or minus infinity (i.e. has an unconditional variance that is proportional to 'time') and 'shocks' have a permanent effect. But if you reject the null, the series is covariance stationary and does not 'explode'. An alternative to this rather extreme dichotomy is the idea of fractional integration. Here, a univariate series is assumed to follow a process $(1 - L)^d x_t = \varepsilon_t$, where $\varepsilon_t$ is stationary (but not necessarily white noise). If $d \geq 0.5$, then this implies non-stationarity but not necessarily explosive behaviour. As $d$ approaches 1, this indicates increasing non-stationarity, until $d = 1$ when $x_t$ has a unit root. If $d \in [0.5, 1)$, then $x_t$ is covariance non-stationary but mean reverting, so an innovation has no permanent effect on $x_t$. Hence, we can test (Robinson 1994) for various values of $d$ to get some idea of the degree of non-stationarity in the series and whether it is explosive or not. However, this approach is not so prevalent in the literature. This is because the implications of cointegration between variables that are shown to be I(1) (rather than fractionally cointegrated) have allowed useful multivariate approaches to testing economic theories (see below).

It is worth noting that most tests for the order of integration of a univariate series have very low power against alternatives that are 'near' unit roots – which occurs for many time series of interest in finance. Hence, one must use one's judgement when interpreting the many 'statistical results' in this area.

## Cointegration

Any series $x_t$ that can be differenced to give a stationary series, with a minimum of $d$ differences, is said to be 'integrated of order-$d$' or 'I($d$)' for short. The random walk is an I(1) series. (Note that not all series that are non-stationary can be differenced to make them stationary.)

If two series $x_t$ and $y_t$ are both I(1), say, then a linear combination of $x_t$ and $y_t$ will generally also be I(1):

$$y_t - \beta x_t = z_t \tag{13}$$

However, it is possible that the (stochastic) trend in $x_t$ is 'offset' by the trend in $y_t$ such that the linear combination is stationary (with constant $\beta$). If this 'special case' holds, then $x_t$ and $y_t$ are said to be cointegrated. A simple test for cointegration is to run the OLS regression

$$y_t = \hat{\alpha} + \hat{\beta} x_t + e_t \tag{14}$$

and test the residuals for stationarity using $e_t$ (in place of $x_t$) in (11) (although the critical values from MCS, for $H_0 : \gamma = 0$ will differ from those given above).

## Engle–Granger Representation Theorem

Engle and Granger (1987) show that if two (or more) I(1) series are cointegrated, then there exists a dynamic error correction model (ECM), whereby the linear combination $(y - \beta x)_{t-1}$ helps predict either $\Delta x_t$ or $\Delta y_t$ or both. To demonstrate this in the simplest possible case, suppose $(x_t, y_t)$ are both I(1) but cointegrated, so that $(y - \beta x)_t$

is stationary. Then $(y - \beta x)_t$ must have a stationary autoregressive moving average (ARMA) representation

$$(y_t - \beta x_t) = \rho_1(y - \beta x)_{t-1} + \rho_2(y - \beta x)_{t-2} + v_t \qquad (15a)$$

$$\Delta x_t = \varepsilon_t \qquad (15b)$$

where we have assumed an AR(2) process for $(y - \beta x)_t$, that $x_t$ is a random walk (with zero drift) and $v_t$ and $\varepsilon_t$ are white noise processes.

From (15a) and (15b), it is straightforward to derive the error correction model ECM

$$\Delta y_t = \delta_1 \Delta y_{t-1} + \delta_2 \Delta x_{t-1} + \lambda_y (y - \beta x)_{t-1} + w_t \qquad (16)$$

where $\delta_1 = -\rho_2$, $\delta_2 = \rho_2 \beta$, $\lambda_y = (\rho_1 + \rho_2 - 1)$ and $w_t = v_t + \beta \varepsilon_t$. Since $(y - \beta x)_t$ is stationary, then $\rho_1 + \rho_2 < 1$ so that $\lambda_y < 0$. Hence, if $y_{t-1} > \beta x_{t-1}$, then next period $\Delta y_t < 0$ (ceteris paribus), and $y$ moves back towards its long run equilibrium $y^* = \beta x$.

If the process for $\Delta x_t$ had been an ARMA process, then the $\Delta x_t$ could also be represented as an error correction model like (15a) with *the same* cointegration term $(y - \beta x)_{t-1}$ but with a different coefficient $\lambda_x$. The two ECM equations, one for $\Delta y_t$ and the other for $\Delta x_t$, are together known as a *bivariate vector ECM* (VECM). It then becomes an empirical question whether $\lambda_x$ or $\lambda_y$ are both non-zero, or only one is non-zero. If $y_t$ and $x_t$ are cointegrated, then at least one of $\lambda_x$ or $\lambda_y$ must be non-zero. The Engle–Granger theorem also implies the converse, namely, if there is an error correction representation for either $\Delta x_t$ or $\Delta y_t$ (or both), then $x_t$ and $y_t$ are cointegrated.

Establishing that two (or more) series are I(1) and then invoking the Engle–Granger theorem to infer predictability has been widely used where one (or more) of the series is an asset price (e.g. stock, bond or price of foreign exchange). This establishes predictability in at least one direction, and the VECM model is used to establish one- or two-way causation. It is worth noting that establishing predictability of stock returns (via cointegration and VECMs) does imply that in repeated gambles, you can earn positive profits, but it does not necessarily imply that these profits are sufficient to cover transactions costs and the risks underlying your repeated gambles – this issue of 'efficient markets' is taken up in much of the rest of the book.

If there are $n > 2$, I(1) variables, then there are at most $(n - 1)$ cointegrating vectors, and these cointegrating vectors are not unique for $n > 2$. *In principle*, these $n - 1$ cointegrating vectors can all appear in *each* of the ECMs for the $n$–variables. The Johansen (1988) procedure allows one to test for the number of cointegrating vectors in the VECM system and also to test restrictions on the parameters of the error correction terms $\beta$ (where $\beta$ is now a vector for each of the distinct cointegrating vectors).

The small sample properties of many test statistics used in the cointegration literature have to be established using Monte Carlo simulation or bootstrapping (e.g. Psaradakis 2001), and often their power properties are poor if the alternative is a near unit root (see the web site for programmes that demonstrate this).

## 2.3   Monte Carlo Simulation (MCS) and Bootstrapping

It is often the case in econometrics that we have asymptotic analytic results for the properties of estimators and their statistical distribution but we do not know what properties the estimator has in small samples. This is where MCS can be useful.

### Dickey–Fuller Test

To start the ball rolling, consider how the critical value for $\hat{\tau}_\mu = \hat{\gamma}/se(\hat{\gamma})$, the Dickey–Fuller 't-statistic' for $H_0 : \gamma = 0$ is obtained using MCS. The subscript $\mu$ indicates that the data generation process, DGP, or 'true' model is (10a). Suppose we draw a random sample of $n = 50$ observations (say) of $\varepsilon_t \sim N(0, 1)$. Set $\mu = 0.25$, $x_0 = 0$ in (10a) and with the 50 random values of $\varepsilon_t$, generate a simulated data series for $x_t$ under the null. Use these 50 simulated observations on $x_t$ and run the Dickey–Fuller OLS regression $\Delta x_t = \hat{\mu} + \hat{\gamma} x_{t-1} + \hat{v}_t$ and retain the value for $\hat{\tau}_\mu = \hat{\gamma}/se(\hat{\gamma})$. This is the first run of the MCS. We now repeat the above with a different set of random draws of $\varepsilon_t$ $(t = 1, 2, \ldots, 50)$ and obtain a large number (say 20,000) values of $\hat{\tau}_\mu$ (under the null $\gamma = 0$), which can be plotted in a histogram. A well-known result is that $\hat{\gamma}$ is biased downwards, and therefore $\hat{\tau}_\mu$ will not be centred on 0 (as it is under the null). We now find the cut-off point in the histogram for $\hat{\tau}_\mu$, which leaves 5% of the area of the simulated distribution in the left tail. This value, as we noted above, is $\hat{\tau}_\mu = -2.63$ (for $\mu = 0.25$, $n = 50$), which is the critical value for a one-tail test. We can then repeat the MCS for alternative sample lengths, alternative values of $\mu$ in the DGP and alternative lag-lengths (see (11)) in the regression and obtain critical values for these alternative scenarios (these alternative critical values can often be represented in terms of a simple formula where the critical value depends on sample size, the value of $\mu$, etc. – this is known as a *response surface*).

### Return Regressions

Next, let us examine a very well known problem in financial econometrics that can be represented:

$$y_t = \alpha + \beta x_{t-1} + u_t \tag{17a}$$

$$x_t = \theta + \rho x_{t-1} + v_t \tag{17b}$$

where $|\rho| < 1$, and $u_t$, $v_t$ are contemporaneously correlated, $\sigma_{uv} \neq O$. However, each error term is normally and independently distributed over time (i.e. no heteroscedasticity or serial correlation in either error term). Assume the two error terms are bivariate normal and the covariance matrix of the errors is

$$\sum = \begin{bmatrix} \sigma_u^2 & \sigma_{uv} \\ \sigma_{uv} & \sigma_v^2 \end{bmatrix} \tag{18}$$

$y_t$ can be taken to be the *change in price* (i.e. return) on an asset during period $t$, and $x_{t-1}$ is a variable known at the end of period $t - 1$. If $y_t$ is the (one-period) return on equity, then $x_{t-1}$ might be the dividend–price ratio (i.e. dividend yield) or book-to-market value or the yield spread. In bond markets, $y_t$ might be the holding period return or the change in the bond yield and $x_{t-1}$ the yield spread. In the FX market, $y_t$ could be the (one-period) change in the spot-FX rate and $x_{t-1}$ is the forward premium. We will meet all of these cases later in the book, usually under the heading of testing the efficient markets hypothesis.

Here, we confine our analysis to that where $y_t$ is a one-period return. The same problems ensue when we examine multiperiod returns. For example, if we have over-lapping data (e.g. monthly data and $y_t$ is the annual price change) then $u_t$ is serially correlated, and similar results to those discussed below apply to the standard estimators (e.g. GMM). It can be shown that the OLS estimator of $\beta$ in (17a) is consistent but biased and the source of the bias is the correlation between $u_t$ and $v_t$. The intuition behind this is as follows. Suppose $u_t > 0$, and $\sigma_{uv} > 0$, then on average, $v_t$ will also be greater than 0. The increase in $v_t$ leads to an increase in $x_t$, so although $v_t$, and hence $u_t$, is uncorrelated with $x_{t-1}$, in (17a), $u_t$ is correlated with $x_t$, and it is the latter that causes the OLS-$\hat{\beta}$ to be biased.

The standard assumption used to prove that the OLS estimator $\hat{\beta}$ in (17a) is BLUE is

$$E\{u_t | \ldots x_{t-2}, x_{t-1}, x_t, x_{t+1}, x_{t+2}, \ldots\} = 0 \qquad (19)$$

So, $u_t$ is assumed to be uncorrelated with $x_t$ *at all leads and lags*. However, when we consider $E(u_t | x_t, x_{t+1}, x_{t+2}, \ldots)$, then as shown above, this expectation is not 0, and the standard OLS results no longer hold. It can be shown that *asymptotically*, $\hat{\beta}$ is consistent and

$$t = \frac{\hat{\beta} - \beta}{se(\hat{\beta})} \sim N(0, 1) \qquad (20)$$

Hence, hypothesis tests on $\beta$ are 'standard' in large samples. Note that for $n \to \infty$, this (pseudo) 't-statistic' is distributed N(0,1). However, in *small samples*, the OLS estimator $\hat{\beta}$ is biased, the OLS formula for $\hat{\sigma}_u^2$ and se($\hat{\beta}$) are also biased and the 't-statistic' in (20) is not distributed as Student's-$t$ (or even normally distributed). If we use the asymptotic result in (20) when we only have a finite sample, then we may draw the wrong inferences. How can we investigate the small sample distribution for the OLS, $\hat{\beta}$? Suppose the null hypothesis we are trying to test is $\beta = 1$ (we choose this for convenience) and $y_t =$ monthly (excess) return on S&P500 and $x_{t-1}$ is the dividend yield at the end of the previous month (this is usually measured as dividends paid from $t - 12$ to $t - 1$ divided by the S&P500 price level at end $t - 1$).

Suppose an OLS regression of (17a) on real data using annual observations and sample size $n = 50$ years gives $\hat{\beta}_d = 2.2$ and se($\hat{\beta}_d$) $= 0.2$. Using the asymptotic 't-statistic' in (20) for $H_0 : \beta = 1$ gives

$$t_d = (2.2 - 1)/0.2 = 6 \qquad (21)$$

On a two-tail test at a 5% significance level, $H_0$ is clearly rejected (since the critical value $= \pm 1.96$) with the $p$-value for $t_d = 6$ being less than 0.001. In order to investigate the small sample properties of the OLS statistics *under the null* $H_0 : \beta = 1$, we undertake a MCS and generate simulated data on $x$ and $y$. To do this, we need to know the parameters $\alpha$, $\beta$, $\theta$, $\rho$ and the elements of $\Sigma$.

As a first approximation, we can use the 'OLS' estimates of these parameters (which are consistent) by running regressions (17a) and (17b) together on the 'real' data set (i.e. SURE estimators). These estimators will be biased in finite samples, but they may provide a reasonable 'ball park' starting point for our Monte Carlo analysis. (We can always see how sensitive our conclusions are to changes in these parameters at a later date.)

Suppose we find that our OLS estimates are $\alpha = 0.2, \theta = 0.1$ and $\rho = 0.98$, where the latter is consistent with the observed persistence (or smoothness) in the dividend–price ratio. We also have our OLS estimates of the elements of $\Sigma$, based on the residuals from (17a) and (17b).

The parameters $\{\alpha, \theta, \rho$ and $\Sigma\}$ are held fixed throughout the MCS, and $\beta = 1$ is fixed at its chosen 'true value' (usually given by economic theory). The MCS consists of the following steps.

(i) Draw $(n_1 + n)$ values of $u_t$ and $v_t$ from a bivariate normal distribution with covariance matrix $\Sigma$.

(ii) Generate the series $x_t$ recursively, starting with $x_o = 4\%$ (the average dividend–price ratio in the data).

(iii) Use the generated $x$-series and the random errors $u_t$ to generate $(n_1 + n)$ values for $y_t$.

(iv) Discard the first $n_1$ values of $x$ and $y$, so you are left with $n$-values.

(v) Calculate the OLS estimator $\tilde{\beta}^{(1)}$ and other statistics of interest such as the asymptotic OLS standard error, $se(\tilde{\beta}^{(1)})$.

(vi) Repeat (i)–(v), for $m = 10{,}000$ times, obtaining $10{,}000$ values for $\tilde{\beta}^{(i)}\{i = 1, 2, \ldots, m\}$ and $se(\tilde{\beta}^{(i)})$.

We discard the first $n_1$ data points so that our generated data is independent of the starting value $x_0$ (usually $n_1 = 150$ is adequate). The fixed sample of 'length' $n = 50$ is crucial as this represents the size of our 'small sample' with the real world data. The number of 'runs' of the MCS ($m = 10{,}000$) does not affect the properties of the estimator and must be large enough to obtain a reasonably precise estimate of the distribution of the $\tilde{\beta}^{(i)}$ – see Figure 1. Calculate the mean value of the $10{,}000$ values of $\tilde{\beta}^{(i)}$

$$mean\,(\tilde{\beta}) = \sum_{i=1}^{m} \beta^{(i)}/m = 2.6\,(say) \tag{22}$$

Thus, when we know that $\beta = 1$ in (17a), we find that the mean of the OLS estimator for $\beta$ in the MCS of sample size $n = 50$ is 2.6. (We make this difference 'large' to make the point, although as we shall see, such a large difference occurs when testing

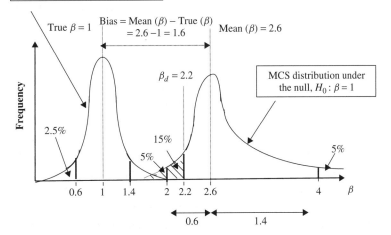

**Figure 1**  Asymptotic and MC distribution

the expectations hypothesis of the term structure of interest rates – Bekaert, Hodrick and Marshall 1997.) It follows that the small sample OLS bias for $\beta$ is

$$bias\,(\hat{\beta}_{\text{OLS}}) = mean\,(\tilde{\beta}) - true(\beta) = 2.6 - 1 = 1.6 \qquad (23)$$

Using real data, our 'one-shot' OLS estimate was $\hat{\beta}_d = 2.2$. But '1.6' of this is accounted for by the bias, and hence a more accurate finite sample estimate of $\beta$ in the real data would be

$$adj\,(\hat{\beta}_d) = \hat{\beta}_d - bias\,(\hat{\beta}_{\text{OLS}}) = 2.2 - 1.6 = 0.6 \qquad (24)$$

The bias-adjusted value $adj\,(\hat{\beta}_d) = 0.6$ is now much closer to the theoretical value of unity, and we are now more likely (ceteris paribus) to accept the null. The 'distance' between the small sample $adj\,(\hat{\beta}_d)$ and the null hypothesis $\beta = 1$ is now only 0.4 (in absolute value):

$$Distance = adj\,(\hat{\beta}_d) - \beta = 0.6 - 1 = -0.4 \qquad (25)$$

We might now be tempted to undertake the following '$t$-test' of $H_0 : \beta = 1$

$$adj\text{-}t = \frac{adj\,(\hat{\beta}_d) - \beta}{\text{se}(\hat{\beta}_d)} = \frac{0.6 - 1}{0.2} = -2 \qquad (26)$$

which is just rejected at the 5% significance level (two-tail test), since from the normal distribution, the (asymptotic) critical value is $-1.96$. But even this result could be misleading because we have used the biased OLS formula to calculate $\text{se}(\hat{\beta}_d)$. We have also assumed that '$adj\text{-}t$' is distributed as N(0,1), in *a finite* sample, and this may not be the case. Can we improve on this using our MCS results?

Figure 1 shows the distribution of the 10,000 values of $\tilde{\beta}^{(i)}$ from the MCS, when we know that $\beta = 1$ and the variance–covariance matrix (of the error terms) $\Sigma$ is representative of that found using the real data. Purely for pedagogic purposes, we assume that the distribution of $\tilde{\beta}^{(i)}$ is not symmetric and, therefore, the mean is not an unambiguous measure of central tendency. We could use the median value in place of $mean(\tilde{\beta})$ instead in (23) and (24) as a sensitivity test of our conclusions. But we will stick with the mean as our measure of central tendency.

In Figure 1, we see that the 'empirical distribution' of $\tilde{\beta}^{(i)}$ is more dispersed (around $mean(\tilde{\beta})$) than in the asymptotic distribution. Indeed, we can calculate the standard *deviation* of $\tilde{\beta}^{(i)}$ from our MCS:

$$mean(\tilde{\beta}) = \sum_{i=1}^{m} \tilde{\beta}^{(i)}/m \tag{27a}$$

$$stdv(\tilde{\beta}) = \left[\sum_{i=1}^{m}\{\tilde{\beta}^{(i)} - mean(\tilde{\beta})\}^2/(m-1)\right]^{1/2} = 0.4\,(say) \tag{27b}$$

which is twice the standard error of the *asymptotic* distribution of the OLS estimator of 0.2.

Often, these MCS standard deviations are reported in place of the analytic asymptotic values because in small samples, the former are thought to be more representative of the true values; although note that if the empirical distribution is not symmetric, the standard deviation may not be a useful measure of the dispersion of our estimate of $\beta$.

If $stdv(\tilde{\beta}) = 0.4$, then using this in (26) would give $adj$-$t = 1$ and hence accepting the asymptotic normality assumption would imply we now do not reject $H_0 : \beta = 1$. But we have the obvious problem that the finite sample distribution of $\tilde{\beta}^{(i)}$ from the MCS is *not* normal and hence we cannot use critical values from the normal distribution when testing for $H_0 : \beta = 1$. What we can do is compare our estimate of beta using the real data $\hat{\beta}_d = 2.2$, with its $p$-value taken from the *empirical distribution*.

From Figure 1, we see that when the true $\beta = 1$ then $mean(\tilde{\beta}) = 2.6$. Hence, we should measure 'how far' the OLS estimate using real data $\hat{\beta}_d = 2.2$ is from $mean(\tilde{\beta}) = 2.6$, in statistical terms. (Note that $2.6 - 2.2 = 0.4$ is the same as the 'Distance' in (25).)

One useful 'statistical measure' of $\hat{\beta}_d = 2.2$ is the proportion of the $\tilde{\beta}^{(i)}$ in the MCS that have values less than 2.2, which is 15% (Figure 1). Hence, the Monte Carlo distribution (which embodies the OLS small sample bias) implies that under the null ($\beta = 1$), the $p$-value (on a one-tail test), given $\hat{\beta}_d = 2.2$, is 15%, suggesting we do not reject $\beta = 1$.

The above is equivalent to moving the empirical distribution to the left (Figure 1) so its mean is centred on $\beta = 1$, but it retains the same standard deviation and shape as the MC distribution. The bias adjusted estimate based on real data is $adj\,(\hat{\beta}_d) = 0.6$ and this would also have a $p$-value of 15% (after moving the MC distribution to the left).

However, it is easier to work with the actual empirical distribution in Figure 1, and here we can calculate the 5th and 95th percentiles as $\beta_L = 2$ and $\beta_u = 4$. Note that these are not symmetric around $mean(\tilde{\beta}) = 2.6$ because we have assumed that the

Monte Carlo distribution is not symmetric. With 90% confidence, we can say that if the $true(\beta) = 1$, then in a finite sample, an OLS value for $\beta$ between 2 and 4 on any real data set (of $n$-observations) does not reject the null that $\beta = 1$. So, if the $true(\beta) = 1$, then an OLS estimate on real data of $\beta_d \leq 1.99$ say would be observed less than 5% of the time. Put another way, given an OLS estimate of 1.99, then for $H_0 : \beta = 1$, the empirical (lower tail) $p$-value is 0.05.

Although we have conducted the above analysis wholly in terms of the MC distribution of $\beta$, we could equally have plotted the MC distribution of the 't-statistic' $\tau^{(i)} = (\tilde{\beta}^{(i)} - 1)/se(\tilde{\beta}^{(i)})$ for $m = 10,000$ runs of the MCS (where the estimators $\hat{\beta}$ and $se(\hat{\beta})$ are consistent). We can then obtain the upper and lower 2.5% tail critical values for the MC distribution of $\tau^{(i)}$, which might be $+2$ and $+6.2$ (say). The t-statistic using the real data is $t_d = (2.2 - 1)/0.2 = 6$, and hence we would not reject the null $\beta = 1$ on the basis of the MC distribution of the 't-statistic', in a finite sample. The distribution of the 't-statistic' is often preferred in MCS (and bootstrapping, see below), to the distribution of $\hat{\beta}$ itself as the former has better statistical properties. The t-statistic is said to be 'pivotal', which means that its distribution does not depend on 'nuisance parameters' such as the variance of the error term.

## Analytic Expressions

In some cases, it is possible (after much effort) to work out an analytic expression for the bias, standard error and $p$-values (under the null) for a particular estimator (e.g. OLS), given a particular model. In the case of (17a) and (17b), the OLS bias is,

$$E\hat{\beta} - \beta = \frac{\sigma_{uv}}{\sigma_v^2}[E\hat{\rho} - \rho] \tag{28}$$

where approximately

$$E\hat{\rho} - \rho \approx -(1 + 3\rho)/n \tag{29}$$

Hence, using $\sigma_{uv} = \rho_{uv}\sigma_u\sigma_v$ where $\rho_{uv}$ is the correlation coefficient between $u$ and $v$

$$E\hat{\beta} - \beta = -\frac{\rho_{uv}\sigma_u}{\sigma_v}\left(\frac{1 + 3\rho}{n}\right) \tag{30}$$

The OLS estimator of $\beta$ is biased upwards (downwards) for $\rho_{uv} < 0 \, (>0)$. The bias is 0 if $\rho_{uv} = 0$ (the standard OLS case), and the bias disappears in large samples ($n \to \infty$). The bias is greater the greater is $\rho$ (i.e. the persistence or autocorrelation in $x_t$) and the larger is $\sigma_u$ relative to $\sigma_v$.

## Bootstrapping

In a MCS, we assume we know the joint distribution of the error terms (e.g. multivariate normal). However, the residuals using the real data might be far from normal, although it is also worth noting that the residuals may be biased estimates of the true errors, since the OLS $\hat{\beta}$ and $\hat{\rho}$ are biased in small samples. Nevertheless, the residuals using the real data are all we have to guide us. Suppose the residuals are iid but not normally distributed. We can then repeat the whole of our MCS using random draws (with replacement) from our set of residuals (in place of the generated multivariate normal errors in the MCS). This is called *bootstrapping*. For each run of the bootstrap, we obtain an OLS estimate of $\tilde{\beta}^{(i)}$ and $\tau^{(i)}$ and their *empirical* (bootstrap) distributions. For example, if the residuals have fat tails (compared to the normal distribution), we might find that the empirical distributions of $\tilde{\beta}^{(i)}$ and $\tau^{(i)}$ under the bootstrap have fatter tails than under the MCS using multivariate normal errors. Again, the bootstrap distribution of $\tau^{(i)}$ is usually used for inference because it is 'better behaved' than that for $\tilde{\beta}^{(i)}$ (i.e. is 'pivotal').

In the bootstrap, we draw $n$ residuals, $(\hat{u}_t, \hat{v}_t)$ in (17a) and (17b) in pairs. This preserves any contemporaneous correlation in the residuals, if $\text{cov}(\hat{u}_t, \hat{v}_t) \neq 0$. The time series of simulated or 'bootstrapped' data for $x_t$ and $y_t$ will not be the same for each run of the bootstrap for two reasons. First, *the order* in which you draw the $n$ values of $\hat{v}_t$ determines $x_t$ (recursively), and this ordering will differ for each run of the bootstrap. Second, since we 'draw with replacement', a particular residual pair, say $(\hat{u}_{10}, \hat{v}_{10})$, from the real data set can be drawn more than once, in any run of the bootstrap.

If the residuals $\hat{u}_t$ or $\hat{v}_t$ are not iid, then the bootstrap has to be modified. For example, if the residuals $\hat{u}_t$ were MA(1), then each 'bootstrap draw' of $\hat{u}_t$ would involve adjacent pairs $(\hat{u}_t, \hat{u}_{t-1})$, together with the corresponding pair of values for $(\hat{v}_t, \hat{v}_{t-1})$ to preserve the contemporaneous correlation *across* equations (Politis and Romano 1994). If $u_t$ were AR(1), the residuals could be randomly chosen in 'blocks' to adequately represent this autocorrelation pattern (not surprisingly, this is called a *block bootstrap* – Li and Maddala 1997). Alternatively, (17b) could be re-estimated with a Cochrane–Orrcutt transformation and then the 'new' residuals would not be autocorrelated and could be bootstrapped in the usual way (this is the basic idea behind the 'sieve bootstrap' – Buhlmann 1997). In general, with some ingenuity, one can devise a bootstrap method of generating repeated samples of the residuals so that the generated residuals 'match' those found in the real data.

The obvious limitations of MCS and bootstrapping are that the results hold for a specific model, null hypothesis and sample size. However, sensitivity analysis provides results for alternative scenarios (e.g. assuming the process for $x_t$ has a unit root), and 'response surfaces' give critical values for alternative sample sizes (and for alternative values of 'nuisance parameters' such as $\mu$ in the ADF test). Increased computing power has led to a major increase in the use of these techniques when testing economic models.

Another use of MCS (and to a less extent bootstrapping) is to set up a theoretical model, calibrate the model using 'reasonable' parameter estimates and then generate artificial data by drawing random samples from the error terms of the model, assuming a known distribution (e.g. multivariate normal). The generated artificial data are therefore consistent with a known theoretical model. By repeatedly generating artificial data from the theory model, we can then examine the statistical properties of key variables (e.g. asset returns, consumption, etc.). Statistical properties might include means, standard deviation, skewness, kurtosis, autocorrelations, cross-correlations and regressions between 'simulated' data series. If the 'moments' of the simulated data broadly match those found in the real data, it shows that the theoretical model is consistent with the 'stylised facts'. This method of validating theoretical models is often referred to as *calibration*, and we will meet numerous examples of this in later chapters.

## 2.4  Bayesian Learning

There is a wide range of alternative methods investors could use to learn about the parameters of a particular stochastic process (e.g. returns $R_{t+1}$ depend linearly on the current level of the dividend–price ratio $(D/P)_t$ so that $R_{t+1} = \alpha + \beta(D/P)_t + \varepsilon_{t+1}$). Under rational expectations, we assume investors know the parameters $\theta = (\alpha, \beta)$ exactly and base their forecasts of $R_{t+1}$ assuming $\theta$ is known with certainty. This is clearly a strong assumption to make. An alternative is to assume investors update their views about the parameters $\theta$ as more data arrives and hence they recognise the uncertainty in their current knowledge about $\theta$. A Bayesian assumes investors have a *prior* estimate of the parameters $\theta$ (e.g. from economic theory), and they update this estimate as more sample data arrives, to give a *posterior* estimate of $\theta$. A number of models we meet in later chapters invoke Bayesian learning and, therefore, we outline the main features of this approach.

The simplest case is to consider a single parameter distribution, which we take to be Poisson. After noting the new organisational changes for London Underground (Metro), suppose you are sitting at home and you think that the mean arrival times of London Underground trains on a busy route will now be either $\lambda = 2$ (minutes) or 4 (minutes). Assume these beliefs are held with prior probabilities

$$P(\lambda = 2) = 0.8 \quad \text{and} \quad P(\lambda = 4) = 0.2$$

Hence, given your prior views, $\lambda = 2$ has 4 times as much chance of being correct as $\lambda = 4$. You now go along to your local Metro stop, and the train arrives after $X = 6$ minutes. Intuition tells you that $\lambda = 4$ seems more likely than $\lambda = 2$, after you have observed $X = 6$. That is, your posterior probability differs from the prior probabilities. The probability density function (p.d.f.) for the Poisson distribution is

$$f(\lambda, x) = \frac{e^{-\lambda}\lambda^x}{x!} \tag{31}$$

Therefore

$$P(X = 6|\lambda = 2) = 0.012 \tag{32a}$$

$$P(X = 6|\lambda = 4) = 0.104 \tag{32b}$$

The posterior probability for $\lambda = 2$, given $X = 6$, is

$$
\begin{aligned}
P(\lambda = 2 | X = 6) &= \frac{P(\lambda = 2, X = 6)}{P(X = 6)} \\
&= \frac{P(\lambda = 2)P(X = 6 | \lambda = 2)}{P(\lambda = 2)P(X = 6 | \lambda = 2) + P(\lambda = 4)P(X = 6 | \lambda = 4)} \\
&= \frac{0.8(0.012)}{0.8(0.012) + 0.2(0.104)} = 0.316
\end{aligned}
\tag{33}
$$

and similarly

$$
P(\lambda = 4 | X = 6) = 0.684
$$

So, after observing $X = 6$, the prior probability $P(\lambda = 2) = 0.8$ has decreased to a posterior probability $P(\lambda = 2 | X = 6) = 0.316$, while the prior probability $P(\lambda = 4) = 0.2$ has increased to $P(\lambda = 4 | X = 6) = 0.684$.

If $\theta = \lambda$ can take more than two values, a Bayesian must assign a *prior p.d.f.* $h(\theta)$ to all possible prior values for the parameter(s) $\theta$. Also, we usually have more than one observation on which to calculate the posterior probabilities. Suppose $Y$ is a statistic for the parameter $\theta$ with p.d.f. $g(y|\theta)$ where $Y$ could be the *mean* $\overline{X}$ of the data sample $X = (X_1, X_2, \ldots, X_n)$ and $g(y|\theta)$ could be the normal distribution (see below). Then the joint p.d.f. $k(y, \theta)$ of the statistic $Y$ and the parameter $\theta$ is

$$
k(y, \theta) = g(y|\theta)h(\theta)
\tag{34}
$$

The marginal p.d.f. of $Y$ is

$$
k_m(y) = \int_{-\infty}^{\infty} h(\theta)g(y|\theta)\, d\theta
\tag{35}
$$

The conditional p.d.f. of the parameter $\theta$, given $Y = y$, is known as the *posterior p.d.f.* of $\theta$, denoted $k(\theta|y)$:

$$
k(\theta|y) = \frac{k(y, \theta)}{k_m(y)} = \frac{g(y|\theta)h(\theta)}{k_m(y)}
\tag{36}
$$

The posterior p.d.f. for $\theta$ depends only on the observed data $Y$. Note that if $h(\theta)$ is a constant, so that the prior p.d.f. is the uniform distribution, then this is referred to as a *noninformative* prior. Bayesians consider $\theta$ as a random variable, and their best forecast (guess) for $\theta$ depends on their loss function. For example, if $Z$ is a random variable and '$b$' is a guess for $Z$ and the loss function is $E[(Z - b)^2]$, this is minimised for $b = EZ$. So if the loss function for a guess $w(y)$ for $\theta$ is $E[\theta - w(y)]^2$, the best (Bayes) estimate for $\theta$ is the conditional mean

$$
w(y) = \int_{-\infty}^{\infty} \theta k(\theta|y)\, d\theta
\tag{37}
$$

Similarly, if the loss function is the *absolute* value of the error $|\theta - w(y)|$, then the *median* of the posterior distribution would be the Bayes estimate for $\theta$.

Perhaps a simple example will provide a slightly more intuitive interpretation of Bayes theorem. Suppose $Y = \bar{x}$ is the *mean* of a random sample of size-$n$, so $x = \{x_1, x_2, \ldots, x_n\}$ where

$$x_i \sim N(\theta, \sigma^2)$$

and we assume $\sigma^2$ is known with certainty. (Therefore, we do not need to use Bayesian updating for $\sigma^2$.) A standard statistical result is that $g(y \equiv \bar{x}|\theta)$ has a p.d.f.

$$g(y \equiv \bar{x}|\theta) = N(\theta, \sigma^2/n) \tag{38}$$

Suppose we assign prior guesses to $\theta$, using the prior p.d.f. $h(\theta)$, which we take to be normal:

$$h(\theta) = N(\theta_0, \sigma_0^2) \tag{39}$$

Then the posterior p.d.f. $k(\theta|y)$ is

$$k(\theta|y) \propto \frac{1}{\sqrt{2\pi}(\sigma/\sqrt{n})} \frac{1}{\sqrt{2\pi}(\sigma_0)} \exp\left[\frac{-(y-\theta)^2}{2(\sigma^2/n)} - \frac{(\theta - \theta_0)^2}{2\sigma_0^2}\right] \tag{40}$$

Now eliminate all constant terms not involving $\theta$ (i.e. including terms involving $y$ only):

$$k(\theta|y) \propto \exp\left[-\frac{(\sigma_0^2 + \sigma/n)\theta^2 - 2(y\sigma_0^2 + \theta_0\sigma^2/n)\theta}{2(\sigma^2/n)\sigma_0^2}\right] \tag{41}$$

After completing the square (and eliminating elements not involving $\theta$), this becomes

$$k(\theta|y) \propto \exp\left[-\frac{(\theta - m)^2}{\text{var}}\right] \tag{42}$$

where

$$m = \frac{y\sigma_o^2 + \theta_0(\sigma^2/n)}{(\sigma_0^2 + \sigma^2/n)} = \left[\frac{\sigma_0^2}{\sigma_0^2 + (\sigma^2/n)}\right]y + \left[\frac{\sigma^2/n}{\sigma_0^2 + (\sigma^2/n)}\right]\theta_0 \tag{43a}$$

$$\text{var} = \frac{(\sigma^2/n)\sigma_0^2}{[\sigma_0^2 + (\sigma^2/n)]} \tag{43b}$$

Hence, the posterior p.d.f. is normal with mean $= m$ and variance $=$ var. If we assume a square error loss function, the Bayes estimate of $\theta$ is the posterior *mean*, given by (43a). The posterior mean is a weighted average of the sample mean $y = \bar{x}$ and the prior mean $\theta_0$, where the weights depend on the relative size of the prior variance $\sigma_0^2$ and the sample variance $\sigma^2/n$ (for $\sigma^2$ known). The prior estimate $\theta_0$ is therefore 'shrunk' towards the sample estimate $\bar{x}$ and as $n$ increases, the posterior mean gets closer to the maximum likelihood estimate, $\bar{x}$. If the loss function in the above had been $|w(y) - \theta|$, then the Bayes estimate would have been the *median* of the posterior distribution given by $k(\theta|y)$.

In the above example, we assumed we knew the conditional distribution $g(y \equiv \bar{x}|\theta)$, as this is a standard statistical result (i.e. the sample mean is the maximum likelihood estimate of the population mean with variance $\sigma^2/n$). In general, we would not necessarily know this result, and hence, given sample observations $\{x_1, x_2, \ldots, x_n\}$, we replace $g(y|\theta)$ by the likelihood function

$$L(\theta) = f(x_1|\theta)f(x_2|\theta)\cdots f(x_n|\theta)$$

which is the joint p.d.f. of $\{x_1, x_2, \ldots, x_n\}$ given $\theta$. Then the posterior p.d.f. is

$$k(\theta|x_1, x_2, \ldots, x_n) \propto h(\theta)L(\theta) \tag{44}$$

The Bayesian estimate of $\theta$, say, $w(x_1, x_2, \ldots, x_n)$, is then some characteristic of the above *posterior* distribution, such as the mean or median. (For an excellent introduction to basic statistics and Bayes theorem, see Hogg and Tanis (1993), from which this section draws heavily.)

Note that Bayes theorem is not the only way we could mimic learning behaviour. For example, if we are willing to assume that agents have no priors about the parameters, then they may use a relatively simple updating procedure such as recursive OLS. If the true population parameters are constant, then the recursive OLS estimates would eventually converge towards the true parameters as more data becomes available. If the true parameters are themselves time varying and we know the stochastic properties of this time variation (e.g. the parameters follow a random walk), then more complex optimal updating of the parameters is often possible (e.g. using the Kalman filter) as more data becomes available. An alternative to time-varying parameters that vary continuously is to assume the true parameters are constant *within* any regime (e.g. high-inflation or low-inflation regimes), but they are different in different regimes. The investor is then faced with a filtering problem since she has to work out the probability of being in a specific regime before she can make forecasts. Where the transition between regimes follows a Markov process, this problem can be solved using the Hamilton (1994) filter. All of the above methods have been used to mimic learning behaviour, as we shall see in future chapters.

## 2.5   Summary

- Jensen's inequality implies that the expectation of a non-linear function of a random variable does not equal the function of the expected value $E[f(Z)] \neq f(EZ)$. For certain distributions, for example, the lognormal $\ln Z \sim N(\mu(\ln Z), \sigma^2(\ln Z))$, we can obtain an explicit expression for the expected value: $EZ = \exp(\mu + (1/2)\sigma^2)$.

- When data series have a unit root, the properties of some statistical tests are 'non-standard'. If two or more series have a unit root, then a linear combination may be stationary – the series are then said to be cointegrated. Cointegrated series are stationary and hence 'standard' statistical results apply. If two (or more) series are cointegrated, then at least one of the variables is 'Granger caused' by the error correction term (i.e. the lagged cointegrating vector).

- MCS and bootstrapping can be used to determine the critical values of test statistics in finite samples, where analytic solutions are not available. Stochastic simulation of theoretical models generates artificial data whose properties can be compared with the real data, in order to validate the model. This is *calibration*.

- Bayes theorem can be used to optimally combine prior information about parameters with the sample estimates of the parameters. This gives a posterior distribution for the parameters that depends only on the data observed and the prior guesses. As more data arrives, the mean of this posterior distribution is determined relatively more by the sample of data, and the prior guesses carry less weight. Hence, Bayes theorem can be used to model a 'rational' learning process by investors when they try and update their views about unknown parameter values as new data arrives.

# 3

# EFFICIENT MARKETS HYPOTHESIS

## Aims

- Show that the EMH (efficient markets hypothesis) implies that no abnormal profits can be made (on average) by trading in risky financial assets.

- Demonstrate the implications of the EMH for investment analysts, mergers and takeovers, capital adequacy and the cost of capital.

- Introduce the concepts of fair game, martingale and a random walk, within the context of the EMH.

- Outline alternative empirical tests of the EMH.

In the United Kingdom, there used to be a TV programme called 'The Price is Right', in which contestants had to try and guess the correct market price of a consumer durable. A shorthand for the EMH could well be 'The Price is Right', where here the price is that of a risky asset. The fair value of the asset represents the DPV (discounted present value) of future receipts from the asset and in an 'efficient market', the market price should always equal this 'fair value'.

In general, when economists speak of capital markets as being *efficient*, they usually consider asset prices and returns as being determined as the outcome of supply and demand in a competitive market, peopled by rational traders. These rational traders rapidly assimilate any information that is relevant to the determination of asset prices or returns (e.g. future dividend prospects) and adjust prices accordingly. Hence, individuals do not have different comparative advantages in the acquisition of information. It follows that, in such a world, there should be no opportunities for making a return on a stock that is in excess of a fair payment for the riskiness of that stock. In short, abnormal profits from trading should be zero. Thus, agents process information efficiently and immediately incorporate this information into stock prices. If current and past information is immediately incorporated into current prices, then only new information or 'news' should cause changes in prices. Since news is by definition unforecastable, then price changes (or returns) should be unforecastable: no information at time $t$ or earlier should help improve the forecast of returns (or equivalently to reduce the forecast error made by the individual). This independence of forecast errors from previous information is known as the *orthogonality property* and it is a widely used concept in testing the efficient markets hypothesis.

## 3.1 Overview

Under the EMH, the stock *price* $P_t$ already incorporates all relevant information, and, the only reason for prices to change between time $t$ and time $t+1$ is the arrival of 'news' or unanticipated events. Forecast errors, that is, $\varepsilon_{t+1} = P_{t+1} - E_t P_{t+1}$ should therefore be zero on average and should be uncorrelated with any information $\Omega_t$ that was available at the time the forecast was made. The latter is often referred to as the *rational expectations* RE element of the EMH and may be represented as:

$$P_{t+1} = E_t P_{t+1} + \varepsilon_{t+1} \tag{1a}$$

$$E_t(P_{t+1} - E_t P_{t+1}) = E_t \varepsilon_{t+1} = 0 \tag{1b}$$

An implication of $E_t \varepsilon_{t+1} = 0$ is that the forecast of $P_{t+1}$ is unbiased (i.e. on *average*, actual price equals the expected price). Note that $\varepsilon_{t+1}$ could also be (loosely) described as the *unexpected* profit (or loss) on holding the stock between $t$ and $t+1$. Under the EMH, unexpected profits must be zero on average and this is represented by (1b).

The statement that 'the forecast error must be independent of any information $\Omega_t$ available at time $t$ (or earlier)' is known as the *orthogonality property*. It may be shown that if $\varepsilon_t$ is serially correlated, then the orthogonality property is violated. An example of a serially correlated error term is the first-order autoregressive process, AR(1):

$$\varepsilon_{t+1} = \rho \varepsilon_t + v_{t+1} \tag{2}$$

where $v_{t+1}$ is a (white noise) random element (and by assumption is independent of information at time $t$, $\Omega_t$). The forecast error $\varepsilon_t = P_t - E_{t-1} P_t$ is known at time $t$ and hence forms part of $\Omega_t$. Equation (2) implies that this period's forecast error $\varepsilon_t$ has a *predictable effect* on next period's error $\varepsilon_{t+1}$ but the latter, according to (1), would be useful in forecasting future prices. This violates the EMH.

We can see more directly why serial correlation in $\varepsilon_t$ implies that information at time $t$ helps to forecast $P_{t+1}$ as follows. Lag equation (1a) one period and multiply it by $\rho$:

$$\rho P_t = \rho(E_{t-1} P_t) + \rho \varepsilon_t \tag{3}$$

Subtract (3) from (1a), and use $v_{t+1} = \varepsilon_{t+1} - \rho\varepsilon_t$:

$$P_{t+1} = \rho P_t + (E_t P_{t+1} - \rho E_{t-1} P_t) + v_{t+1} \tag{4}$$

We can see from (4) that when $\varepsilon$ is serially correlated, tomorrow's price depends upon today's price and is, therefore, (partly) forecastable from the information available today. (Note that the term in brackets being a *change* in expectations is not fore-castable.) Therefore, the assumption of 'no serial correlation' in $\varepsilon$ is really subsumed under the EMH assumption that information available today should be of no use in forecasting tomorrow's stock price (i.e. the orthogonality property).

Note that the EMH/RE assumption places no restrictions on the form of the second and higher moments of the distribution of $\varepsilon_t$. For example, the variance of $\varepsilon_{t+1}$ (denoted $\sigma_{t+1}^2$) may be related to its past value, $\sigma_t^2$ without violating RE. (This is an ARCH process.) RE places restrictions only on the behaviour of the first moment (i.e. expected value) of $\varepsilon_t$.

The efficient markets hypothesis is often applied to the *return* on stocks $R_t$ and implies that one cannot earn abnormal profits by buying and selling stocks. Thus, an equation similar to (1) applies to stock returns. Actual returns $R_{t+1}$ will sometimes be above and sometimes below expected returns, but *on average, unexpected* returns or the forecast errors $\varepsilon_{t+1}$ are zero:

$$\varepsilon_{t+1} = R_{t+1} - E_t R_{t+1} \tag{5}$$

where $E_t \varepsilon_{t+1} = 0$. To test the EMH, we need a model of how investors determine *expected (or required)* returns. This model should be based on rational behaviour (somehow defined). For the moment, assume a very simple model where

(i) stocks pay no dividends, so that the expected return is the expected capital gain due to price changes

(ii) investors are willing to hold stocks as long as expected (required) returns are constant,

Hence,

$$R_{t+1} = k + \varepsilon_{t+1} \tag{6}$$

where $\varepsilon_{t+1}$ is white noise and independent of $\Omega_t$. We may think of the required rate of return $k$ on the risky asset as consisting of a risk-free rate $r$ and a risk premium $rp$ (i.e. $k = r + rp$) and in (6) we assume both are constant over time. Since for a non-dividend paying stock, $R_{t+1} = (P_{t+1} - P_t)/P_t \approx \ln(P_{t+1}/P_t)$, equation (6) implies:

$$\ln P_{t+1} = k + \ln P_t + \varepsilon_{t+1} \tag{7}$$

Equation (7) is a random walk in the logarithm of $P$ with drift term $k$. Note that (the logarithm of) stock prices will only follow a random walk under the EMH if the risk-free rate $r$ and the risk premium $rp$ are constant and dividends are zero. Often, in empirical work, the 'price' at $t + 1$ is adjusted to include dividends paid between $t$ and $t + 1$, and when it is stated that 'stock prices follow a random walk', this usually applies to 'prices inclusive of dividends'. In some empirical work, researchers may take the view that the stock return is dominated by capital gains (and losses) and hence will use quoted prices excluding dividends.

For *daily changes* in stock prices over a period of relative tranquillity (e.g. excluding 'crash periods' like October 1987 and 2000–2003), it may appear a reasonable assumption that the risk premium is a constant. However, when daily changes in stock prices are examined, it is usually found that the error term is serially correlated and that the return varies on different days of the week. In particular, prices tend to fall between Friday and Monday. This is known as the *weekend effect*. It has also been found for some stocks, that daily price changes in the month of January are different from those in other months. 'Weekends' and 'January' are clearly predictable events! Therefore, returns on stocks depend in a predictable way upon information readily available, (e.g. what day of the week it is). This is a violation of the EMH under the assumption of a constant risk premium since returns are, in part, predictable. However, in the 'real world' it may *not* be the case that this predictability implies that investors can earn supernormal profits since transactions costs need to be taken into account.

It should be clear from the above discussion that, in order to test the EMH, we require an economic model of the determination of equilibrium (or required) returns. Our tests of whether agents use information efficiently is conditional on our having chosen the *correct* model to explain expected returns. Rejection of the efficient markets hypothesis could be either because we have the wrong equilibrium 'pricing model' or because agents genuinely do not use information efficiently.

As noted above, another way of describing the EMH is to say that in an efficient market it is impossible for investors to make supernormal profits. Under the EMH, investors make a return on each security that covers the riskiness of that security and any transactions costs. However, under the EMH there must be no opportunities for making *abnormal* profits by dealing in stocks. The latter is often referred to as the 'fair game' property.

## 3.2   Implications of the EMH

The view that equity returns are determined by the action of rational agents in a competitive market, and that equilibrium returns reflect all available public information, is probably quite a widely held view amongst financial economists. The slightly stronger assertion, namely that stock prices also reflect their fundamental value (i.e. the DPV of future dividends), is also widely held. What then are the implications of the EMH applied to the stock market?

As far as a risk-averse investor is concerned the EMH means that she should adopt a 'buy and hold' policy. She should spread her risks and hold the market portfolio (or the 30 or so shares that mimic the market portfolio). Andrew Carnegie's advice to "put all your eggs in one basket and watch the basket" should be avoided. The role for the investment analyst, if the EMH is correct, is very limited and would, for example, include:

(a) advising on the choice of the 30 or so shares that mimic the market portfolio;

(b) altering the proportion of wealth held in each asset to reflect the market share portfolio weights, which will alter over time;

(c) changing the portfolio as taxes change (e.g. if dividends are more highly taxed than capital gains then for high-rate income tax payers it may be optimal, at the margin, to move to shares that have low dividends and high expected capital gains);

(d) 'shopping-around' in order to minimise transactions costs of buying and selling.

Under the EMH, investment analysts cannot 'pick winners' by using publicly available information and therefore 'active' investment managers are wasteful. We can go even further: the individual investor should simply buy a 'passive' *index fund* (e.g. mutual fund or unit trust), which tracks a particular market index such as the S&P500 and has low transactions costs (e.g. less than 1% pa). Practitioners such as investment managers do not take kindly to the assertion that their skills are largely redundant, given a competitive efficient market. However, they often support the view that the market is 'efficient'. But their use of the word 'efficient' is usually the assertion that the stock market should be free of government intervention (e.g. zero stamp duty, minimal regulations on trading positions and capital adequacy). Paradoxically, *active* managers do help ensure that information is rapidly assimilated in prices, so even though they may not earn excess returns (corrected for risk) they do help make the market efficient by their trading activities (Grossman and Stiglitz 1980).

It is worth noting that most individuals and institutions do not hold anything like the 'market portfolio' of all marketable assets. Except for residents of the United States of America, this would require most investors to hold predominantly *foreign securities* (i.e. most corporations would be owned by foreigners). Also, most mutual funds and unit trusts *specialise* and sell funds in particular sectors (e.g. banks) or specific geographical areas (e.g. Japanese stocks). There is a marketing reason for this. If an investment bank operates a number of alternative funds, then it will usually have at least one fund it can boast of as having 'beaten the market' (or its rivals).

## Takeovers, Conglomerates and Financial Institutions

Let us turn now to some public policy issues. The stock market is supposed to provide the 'correct' signals for the allocation of real resources (i.e. fixed investment). Only a small proportion of corporate investment is financed from new issues (e.g. about 4 percent on a gross basis in the UK), nevertheless, the average rate of return of a quoted company on the stock market may provide a reasonable measure of the 'cost of equity funds' corrected for risk. The latter can be used in discounting future expected profits from a physical investment project (i.e. in investment appraisal) for an all-equity firm. However, if the share price does not reflect *fundamentals* but is influenced by whim or fads of 'irrational' investors then this link is broken. An abnormally low share price, which reflects ill-informed extraneous factors (e.g. irrational market prejudice), will then inhibit a firm from raising equity finance and embarking on what (on a rational calculation) is a viable investment project.

The above analysis also applies to takeovers. If the stock market is myopic, that is, only considers profits and dividends that accrue in the *near* future, then managers, fearful of a takeover, may distribute more in current dividends rather than using the retained profits to undertake profitable real investment say on R&D expenditure. This strategy will then boost the share price. This is generally known as 'short-termism'. A possible response by government to such short-termism might be to forbid hostile takeovers (e.g. as in Japan).

The opposite view to the above, namely that hostile takeovers are welfare-enhancing (i.e. in terms of the output and profits of the merged firms), requires the assumption that markets are efficient and that takeovers enable 'bad' incumbent managers to be replaced. In this scenario, the hostile bidder recognises that the incumbent 'bad' management has led shareholders to mark down the firm's share price. The hostile bidder pays a price in excess of the existing share price. After replacing the 'bad' managers and reorganising the firm, the ensuing higher future profits are just sufficient to compensate for the higher price paid by the acquirer. If there are genuine synergy benefits of the merger, then this provides an additional return to the shareholders of the combined firm.

In the 1960s and 1970s, there was a wave of conglomerate formation followed in the 1980s by leveraged buyouts and conglomerate breakups (e.g. 'asset stripping'). Conglomerate mergers were sometimes justified on the grounds that the acquisition of unrelated firms by 'firm-A', reduced risk to the shareholder who held A's shares since the 'conglomerate' constituted a diversified portfolio of firms. Since diversification is easily accomplished by individuals altering *their own* portfolio of stocks, then the above reason for the formation of conglomerates is invalid. (Of course it carries more weight if, for some reason, risk-averse individuals do not diversify their share holdings.)

If share prices do reflect fundamentals but 'news' occurs frequently and is expected to make a substantial impact on a firm's future performance, then one would still expect to observe *highly volatile* share prices, even if the market is efficient. However, if the market is inefficient and prices are subject to longer-term 'irrational swings', then stock price volatility may be greater than that predicted from the efficient markets hypothesis. Here, a *prima facie* case for financial institutions to have enough resources (reserves) to weather such storms seems stronger. This is one argument for general capital adequacy rules applied to the market risk of financial institutions (e.g. under the Basle market risk directives). If there are also systemic risks (i.e. a form of externality), then, in principle, government action is required to ensure that the level of capital reflects the marginal *social* costs of the systemic risk rather than the marginal private costs (for any individual financial institution). Systemic risk would also support Central Bank intervention in organising a rescue package for financial institutions, which might otherwise precipitate other bank failures (e.g. Long-Term Capital Management, LTCM, for which the Federal Reserve Board organised a rescue by a consortium of US banks in 1998).

What are the implications of market efficiency in stock and bond markets for issues in corporate finance? If the market is efficient, then there is no point in delaying a physical investment project in the hope that 'financing conditions will improve' (i.e. that the share price will be higher): under the EMH the current price is the correct price and reflects expected future earnings from the project. Also, under the EMH the firm's cost of capital cannot be lowered by altering the *mix* of debt and equity finance. The Modigliani–Miller theorem (in the absence of taxes and bankruptcy) suggests that in an efficient market, the cost of capital is independent of capital structure (i.e. debt–equity ratio – see Cuthbertson and Nitzsche 2001a). The issue of capital-mix can also be applied to the maturity (term) structure of debt. Since rates on long and short corporate bonds fully reflect available information, the proportion of long-debt to short-dated debt will also not alter the cost of capital to the firm. For example, under the expectations hypothesis, low long-term rates of interest and *high current* short rates, simply reflect expectations of *lower future* short rates. So there is no advantage *ex ante*, to financing an investment project by issuing long bonds rather than 'rolling over' a series of short bonds.

It follows from the above arguments that under the EMH, the role of the Corporate Treasurer as an 'active manager,' either as regards the choice of the appropriate 'mix' of different sources of finance or in analysing the optimum time to float new stock or bond issues, is futile. Of course, if the market is *not* efficient, the Corporate Treasurer has scope to alter the stock market valuation of the firm by his chosen dividend policy or by share repurchase schemes and so on.

As one might imagine, the issue economists find hard to evaluate is what are the precise implications for public policy and the behaviour of firms if markets are *not fully* efficient (i.e. a so-called 'second-best' policy). If markets are efficient, there is a presumption that government intervention is not required. If markets are inefficient, there is a *prima facie* case for government intervention. However, given uncertainty about the impact of any government policies on the behaviour of economic agents, the government should only intervene if, on balance, it feels the expected return from its policies outweigh the risks attached to such policies. Any model of market *inefficiency* needs to ascertain how far from 'efficiency' the market is on average and what implications government policy has for economic welfare in general. This is a rather difficult task.

## 3.3   Expectations, Martingales and Fair Game

The EMH can be formally stated in a number of different ways. We do not wish to get unduly embroiled in the finer points of these alternatives, since our main concern is to see how the hypothesis may be tested and used in understanding the behaviour of asset prices and rates of return. However, some formal definitions are required. To this end, we begin with some properties of conditional *mathematical* expectations, we then state the basic axioms of rational expectations such as unbiasedness, orthogonality and the chain rule of forecasting. Next we introduce the concepts of a martingale and a fair game. We then have the basic tools to examine alternative representations and tests of the EMH.

## Mathematical Expectations

If $X$ is a random variable (e.g. heights of males in the UK), which can take discrete values $X_1, X_2, X_3, \ldots$ with probabilities $\pi_i$, then the expected value of $X$, denoted $EX$ is *defined* as

$$E(X) = \sum_{i=1}^{\infty} \pi_i X_i \tag{8}$$

If $X$ is a continuous random variable $(-\infty < X < \infty)$ with a continuous probability distribution $f(X)$ (e.g. normal distribution), then

$$EX = \int_{-\infty}^{\infty} Xf(X) \, dX \tag{9}$$

*Conditional* probability distributions are used extensively in the RE literature. For example, a fair die has a probability of (1/6)th of landing on any number from 1 to 6. However, suppose a friend lets you know that the die to be used is biased and lands on the number '6' for half the time and on the other numbers equally for the remaining throws. Conditional on the information from your friend, you would then alter your probabilities to (1/2) for a '6' and (1/10) for the remaining five numbers. Your conditional expected value would therefore be different from the expected value from an unbiased die since the associated probabilities (or probability density function) are different. The *conditional expectation* based on the information set (denoted) $\Omega_t$ is defined as

$$E(X_t|\Omega_t) = \int_{-\infty}^{\infty} X_t f(X_t|\Omega_t) \, dX_t \tag{10}$$

where $f(X_t|\Omega_t)$ is the *conditional* density function. A conditional expectation may be viewed as an optimal forecast of the random variable $X_t$, based on all relevant information $\Omega_t$. The conditional forecast error is defined as:

$$\varepsilon_{t+1} = X_{t+1} - E(X_{t+1}|\Omega_t) \tag{11}$$

and is always zero on average:

$$E(\varepsilon_{t+1}|\Omega_t) = E(X_{t+1}|\Omega_t) - E(X_{t+1}|\Omega_t) = 0 \tag{12}$$

Rearranging (11):

$$X_{t+1} = E(X_{t+1}|\Omega_t) + \varepsilon_{t+1} \tag{13}$$

We can reinterpret (13) as stating that the conditional expectation is an unbiased forecast of the out-turn value. Another property of conditional mathematical expectations is that the forecast error is uncorrelated with all information at time $t$ or earlier:

$$E(\varepsilon_{t+1}\,\Omega_t|\Omega_t) = 0 \tag{14}$$

This is known as the *orthogonality property* of conditional expectations. The intuitive reason why (14) holds is that, if $\Omega_t$ could be used to reduce the forecast error $\varepsilon_{t+1}$, then it could be used to improve the forecast: hence, all relevant information could not have been used in forecasting $X_{t+1}$. It also follows that an optimal conditional forecast is one in which subsequent forecast errors are unpredictable.

Note that an optimal forecast need not necessarily predict $X_{t+1}$ accurately. Each $\varepsilon_{t+1}$ can be large and the conditional expectations $E_t X_{t+1}$ may only explain a small part of the variation in actual $X_{t+1}$. What is important is that the optimal forecast cannot be improved upon (in the sense of using $\Omega_t$ to reduce the forecast errors, $\varepsilon_{t+1}$). It is also worth noting that it is only the behaviour of the *mean* of the forecast error that we have restricted in (14). The variance of the conditional forecast error denoted $E(\varepsilon_t^2|\Omega_t)$ need not be constant and indeed may in part be predictable.

Consider for a moment making a forecast in January (at time $t$) as to what your forecast will be in February ($t + 1$), about the outcome of the variable $X$ in March (i.e. $X_{t+2}$). For example, $X_t$ could be the temperature. Mathematically, the forecast may be represented as:

$$E_t[E_{t+1}(X_{t+2})] \tag{15}$$

If information $\Omega_t$ at time $t$ is used efficiently, then you cannot predict today *how you will change* your forecast in the future, hence,

$$E_t[E_{t+1}(X_{t+2})] = E_t(X_{t+2}) \tag{16}$$

where $E_t(X_{t+1})$ is equivalent to $[E(X_{t+1}|\Omega_t)]$. This is the rule of *iterated expectations*.

The three properties discussed here, unbiasedness, orthogonality and iterated expectations, all hold for conditional mathematical expectations (as a matter of mathematical 'logic'). What rational expectations does is to assume that individual agents' *subjective expectations* equal the conditional mathematical expectations, based on the true probability distribution of outcomes. Economic agents are therefore assumed to behave *as if* they form their subjective expectations equal to the mathematical expectations of the true model of the economy. (This is often referred to as 'Muth-RE', Muth 1961.)

To get a feel for what this entails, consider a simple supply and demand model for, say, wheat. The supply and demand curves are subject to random shocks (e.g. changes in the weather on the supply side and changes in 'tastes' on the demand side for wheat-based products such as cookies). Conceptually, the 'rational' farmer has to determine his supply of wheat at each price and the expected supplies of wheat of all other farmers (based on known factors such as technology, prices of inputs etc.). He makes a similar calculation of the known factors influencing demand, such as income, $x_t^d$. He then solves for the *expected* equilibrium price by setting the demand and supply shocks to their expected values of zero. Thus, under (Muth) RE, the farmers behave *as if* they use a competitive stochastic model. The difference between the equilibrium (or expected) price and the out-turn price is a random unforecastable 'error' due to random shocks to the supply and demand functions. No additional information available to the farmer can reduce such errors any further (i.e. the RE orthogonality property holds). The stochastic reduced form is

$$P_{t+1} = P_{t+1}^e + \varepsilon_{t+1} = f(x_t^d, x_t^s) + \varepsilon_{t+1} \tag{17}$$

where $P_{t+1}^e = f(x_t^d, x_t^s)$ is the equilibrium price based on the known factors $x_t^i$, which influence supply and demand. The forecast error is the random variable $\varepsilon_{t+1}$. Hence, under RE, the uncertainty or randomness in the economy (e.g. the weather or new product innovations) gives rise to agents' forecast errors.

To test whether agent's actual *subjective* expectations obey the axioms of mathematical conditional expectations, either we need an accurate measure of individual's subjective expectations or we need to know the form of the true model of the economy used by all agents. Survey data on expectations can provide a 'noisy' proxy variable for each agent's subjective expectations. If we are to test whether actual forecast errors have the properties of conditional mathematical expectations via the second method (i.e. using the true model of the economy), the researcher has to choose a particular model from among the many available on the 'economist's shelf' (e.g. Keynesian, monetarist, real business cycle etc.). Clearly, a failure of the forecast errors from such a model to obey the RE axioms, could be due to the researcher taking the wrong model 'off the shelf'. (That is, agents in the real world, actually use a different model.) The latter can provide a convenient alibi for a supporter of RE, since she can always claim that failure to conform to the axioms is not due to agents being 'non-rational' but because the 'wrong' economic model was used.

## Martingale and Fair Game Properties

Suppose we have a stochastic variable $X_t$, which has the property:

$$E(X_{t+1}|\Omega_t) = X_t \qquad (18)$$

then $X_t$ is said to be a martingale. Given (18) the best forecast of all future values of $X_{t+j}$ ($j \geq 1$) is the current value $X_t$. No other information in $\Omega_t$ helps to improve the forecast once the agent knows $X_t$. A stochastic process $y_t$ is a *fair game* if:

$$E(y_{t+1}|\Omega_t) = 0 \qquad (19)$$

Thus, a fair game has the property that the expected 'return' is zero, given $\Omega_t$. It follows trivially that if $X_t$ is a martingale $y_{t+1} = X_{t+1} - X_t$ is a fair game. A fair game is therefore sometimes referred to as a martingale *difference*. An example of a fair game is tossing an unbiased coin, with a payout of $1 for a head and minus $1 for a tail. The fair game property implies that the 'return' to the random variable $y_t$ is zero on average, even though the agent uses all available information $\Omega_t$, in making his forecast.

One definition of the EMH is that it embodies the fair game property for *unexpected stock returns* $y_{t+1} = R_{t+1} - E_t R_{t+1}$, where $E_t R_{t+1}$ is *the equilibrium expected return* given by some economic model. The fair game property implies that *on average* the abnormal return is zero. Thus, an investor may experience large gains and losses (relative to the equilibrium expected return $E_t R_{t+1}$) in specific periods, but these average out to zero over a series of 'bets'. If we assume equilibrium-required returns by investors are constant ($= k$), then the fair game property implies:

$$E[(R_{t+1} - k)|\Omega_t] = 0 \qquad (20)$$

A straightforward test of whether returns violate the fair game property under the assumption of constant equilibrium returns is to see if returns can be predicted from past data, $\Omega_t$. Assuming a linear regression:

$$R_{t+1} = \alpha + \beta'\Omega_t + \varepsilon_{t+1} \qquad (21)$$

then if $\beta' \neq 0$ (or $\varepsilon_{t+1}$ is serially correlated), the fair game property is violated. Here, the test of the fair game property is equivalent to the orthogonality test for RE.

Samuelson (1965) points out that the fair game result under constant required returns, can be derived under certain (restrictive) assumptions about investor preferences. All investors would have to have a common and constant time preference rate, have homogeneous expectations and be risk-neutral. Investors then prefer to hold whichever asset has the highest expected return, regardless of risk. All returns would therefore be equalised, and the required (real) rate of return equals the real interest rate, which in turn equals the *constant* rate of time preference.

## Martingales and Random Walks

A stochastic variable $X_t$ is said to follow a random walk with drift parameter $\delta$ if

$$X_{t+1} = \delta + X_t + \varepsilon_{t+1} \qquad (22)$$

where $\varepsilon_{t+1}$ is an identically and independently distributed *iid* random variable with:

$$E_t \varepsilon_{t+1} = 0 \qquad E_t(\varepsilon_m \varepsilon_s | X_t) = \begin{pmatrix} \sigma^2 \\ 0 \end{pmatrix} \qquad \text{for} \begin{cases} m = s \\ m \neq s \end{cases} \qquad (23)$$

A random walk without drift has $\delta = 0$. Clearly, $X_{t+1}$ is a martingale and $\Delta X_{t+1} = X_{t+1} - X_t$ is a fair game (for $\delta = 0$). As the $\varepsilon_t$ are *independent* random variables, the joint density function $f(\varepsilon_m, \varepsilon_s) = f(\varepsilon_m)f(\varepsilon_s)$ for $m \neq s$, and this rules out *any* dependence between $\varepsilon_s$ and $\varepsilon_m$, whether linear or non-linear. A martingale is less restrictive than the random walk, since for a martingale $\varepsilon_s$ and $\varepsilon_t$ need only be uncorrelated (i.e. not *linearly* related). Also, the random walk is more restrictive than a martingale since a martingale does not restrict the higher conditional moments (e.g. $\sigma^2$) to be statistically independent. For example, if the price of a stock (including any dividend payments) is a martingale then successive price changes are unpredictable, but a martingale process would allow the conditional variance of the price changes $E(\varepsilon_{t+1}^2 | X_t)$ to be predictable from past variances. But, time-varying conditional variances are not allowable if prices follow a random walk.

## Formal Definition of the EMH

Suppose that at any point in time all relevant (current and past) information for predicting returns is denoted $\Omega_t$, while market participants $p$ have an information set $\Omega_t^p$ (assumed to be available without cost). In an efficient market, agents are assumed to know all relevant information (i.e. $\Omega_t^p = \Omega_t$) and they know the complete (true) probability density function of the possible outcomes for returns

$$f^p(R_{t+n}|\Omega_t^p) = f(R_{t+n}|\Omega_t) \tag{24}$$

Hence, under the EMH, investors *know* the true economic model that generates future returns and use all relevant information to form their 'best' forecast of the expected return. This is the *rational expectations* element of the EMH.

*Ex-post*, agents will see that they have made forecast errors and this will involve *ex-post* profits or losses

$$\eta_{t+1}^p = R_{t+1} - E^p(R_{t+1}|\Omega_t^p) \tag{25}$$

where the superscript p indicates that the expectations and forecast errors are conditional on the equilibrium model of returns used by investors. The expected or equilibrium return will include an element to compensate for any (systemic) risk in the market and to enable investors to earn normal profits. (Exactly what determines this risk premium depends on the valuation model assumed.) The EMH assumes that excess returns (or forecast errors) only change in response to news so that $\eta_{t+1}^p$ are innovations with respect to the information available (i.e. the orthogonality property of RE holds).

For empirical testing, we need a definition of what constitutes 'relevant information', and three broad types have been distinguished.

- **Weak Form:**  The information set consists only of information contained in past prices (returns).

- **Semi-Strong Form:**  The information set incorporates all *publicly available* information (which also includes past prices and returns).

- **Strong Form:**  Prices reflect *all* information that can possibly be known, including 'inside information' (e.g. such as an impending announcement of a takeover or merger).

In empirical work, tests of the EMH are usually considered to be of the semi-strong form. We can now sum up basic ideas that constitute the EMH.

(i)  All agents act as if they have an equilibrium (valuation) model of returns (or price determination).

(ii)  Agents process all relevant information in the same way, in order to determine equilibrium returns (or fundamental value). Forecast errors are unpredictable from information available at the time the forecast is made.

(iii)  Agents cannot make abnormal profits over a series of 'bets'.

Conditional on the researcher having the true economic model used by agents, tests in (ii) reduce to tests of the axioms of rational expectations (e.g. unbiasedness, orthogonality) and are generally referred to as tests of *informational efficiency*. Tests based on (iii) are slightly different. Excess returns may be predictable but whether one can make abnormal profits depends on correctly adjusting returns, for risk and transactions costs. Perhaps (iii) is best expressed by Jensen (1978)

"A market is efficient with respect to an information set $\Omega_t$ if it is impossible to make economic profits by trading on the basis of $\Omega_t$. By economic profits we mean the risk adjusted rate of return, net of all costs".

## 3.4    Testing the EMH

In this section, we provide an overview of some of the test procedures used in assessing the EMH. It is useful to break these down into the following types:

(i) Tests of whether excess (abnormal) returns $\eta_{t+1}^{\mathrm{p}} = R_{it+1} - E_t^{\mathrm{p}} R_{it+1}$ are independent of information $\Omega_t$ available at time $t$ or earlier. To test this proposition consider:

$$R_{it+1} = E_t^{\mathrm{p}} R_{it+1} + \gamma' \Omega_t + w_{t+1} \qquad (26)$$

where $E_t^{\mathrm{p}} R_{it+1}$ = equilibrium expected returns. If information $\Omega_t$ adds any *additional* explanatory power then $R_{it+1} - E_t^{\mathrm{p}} R_{it+1}$ is forecastable. This is a test of *informational efficiency* and it requires an explicit representation of the equilibrium asset-pricing model used by agents.

(ii) Tests of whether actual 'trading rules' (e.g. 'active' strategies such as buy low cap stocks, short-sell high cap stocks) can earn abnormal profits after taking account of transaction costs and the (systematic) risk of the 'active' strategy. Abnormal profits are usually measured relative to a benchmark passive strategy (e.g. holding the S&P500): These tests mimic possible investor behaviour and include explicit trading rules (e.g. value-growth), active strategies based on regression equations and so-called 'anomalies'.

(iii) Tests of whether market prices always equal fundamental value. These tests use past data to calculate fundamental value (or the variance of fundamental value) of stocks, using some form of dividend discount model (RVF). We then test whether the variation in actual prices is consistent with that given by the variability in fundamentals (e.g. Shiller volatility tests).

In principle, the above tests are not mutually exclusive but in practice, they may give different inferences. In fact, in one particular case, namely that of rational bubbles, tests of type (i), even if supportive of the EMH, can, nevertheless, (as a matter of principle) be contradicted by those of type (iii). This is because if rational bubbles are present in the market, expectations are formed rationally and forecast errors are independent of $\Omega_t$ but price *does not equal* fundamental value.

## 3.5  Using Survey Data

Suppose we have accurate survey data that provide a time series of an individual's subjective expectations. We can then, without having to choose a particular model, see if these forecasts obey the axioms of rational expectations. We therefore reduce our joint hypothesis to a test only of the informational efficiency assumptions. Our results will be valid regardless of the equilibrium model actually used by agents. Although tests using survey data appear to avoid a key problem area in testing the EMH (i.e. which equilibrium model to use), such tests, nevertheless, have their own in-built difficulties.

Survey data are sometimes available on an individual agent's expectations of economic variables (e.g. of future inflation, exchange rates or interest rates). This may be in the form of *quantitative* information collected on the individual's expectations, for example, he may reply that "interest rates will be 10 percent this time next year". This information for each individual-i provides a time series of his expectations $Z_{it+j}^e$. Using past data we can directly calculate the forecast error $\varepsilon_{it+j} = Z_{it+j} - Z_{it+j}^e$ for each individual, over all time periods. We do not need to know the precise model the individual uses to forecast $Z_{it+j}$, yet we can test for informational efficiency by running the regression:

$$Z_{it+j} = \beta_0 + \beta_1 Z_{it+j}^e + \beta_2' \Lambda_t + \varepsilon_{it+j} \tag{27}$$

and testing the null $H_0: \beta_0 = \beta_2 = 0$ and $\beta_1 = 1$. If $H_0$ is not rejected, then from (27) the forecast error is zero on average

$$E(Z_{it+j} - Z_{it+j}^e)|\Omega_t) = E(\varepsilon_{it+j}|\Omega_t) = 0 \tag{28}$$

and is independent of information $\Lambda_t$ available at time $t$. The limited information set $\Lambda_t \subset \Omega_t$ consists of any variables known at time $t$ or earlier (e.g. past interest rates, stock returns). For the forecast error $\varepsilon_{it+j}$ to be independent of information at time $t$, we also require $\varepsilon_{it+j}$ to be serially uncorrelated (which only applies for $j = 1$).

Frequently, survey data on expectations are only available 'in aggregate', that is, for a sample of individuals (i.e. the figures are for the average forecast for any period $t + j$ for *all* participants in the survey), and clearly this makes the interpretation of the results more problematic. For example, if only *one* person in a small sample of individuals exhibits behaviour that violates the information efficiency assumptions, this might result in a rejection of the RE axioms. However, under the latter circumstances, most people would argue that the information efficiency was largely upheld.

Indeed, even when we have survey data on *individuals'* expectations, they may have little incentive to reveal their true expectations, that is the forecasts they would have made in an actual real world situation (e.g. by backing their hunch with a large $ investment). In other words, our survey data might reject the information efficiency assumption of RE because participants in the survey had little *incentive* to reveal their true forecasts, since they lose nothing if such forecasts are erroneous. Another problem is that participants in a survey may not be typical of those in the market who are actually doing the trades and 'making the market' (i.e. those who are 'on the margin' rather than intra-marginal). Finally, although there are econometric techniques available (such as instrumental variables estimation) to correct for random errors of measurement in the survey data, such methods cannot deal with mismeasurement on the basis of an individual's systematic inaccurate reporting of their true expectations.

Even more problems arise in these kinds of tests when the survey data is *qualitative* or categorical. In this case, participants respond to questions such as, 'Will interest rates in one year's time be (a) higher, (b) lower, (c) same, as they are at present? Such responses have to be 'transformed' into quantitative data and all the methods currently available require one to impose some restrictive assumptions, which may invalidate the tests under consideration.

The applied work in this area is voluminous, but because of the difficulties discussed above, this avenue of research has not been extensive over the last 10 years. Surveys of empirical work on direct tests of the RE assumptions of unbiasedness and informational efficiency using survey data (e.g. Pesaran 1987, Sheffrin 1983, Taylor 1988) tend to frequently reject the RE axioms (also see *inter alia* Batchelor and Dua 1987, Cavaglia, Verschoor and Wolf 1993, Ito 1990, Frankel and Froot 1988). At this point the reader may feel that it is not worth proceeding with the RE assumption. If expectations are not rational, why go on to discuss models of asset prices that assume rationality? One answer to this question is to note that tests based on survey data are not definitive and they have their limitations as outlined above. Indirect tests of RE based on data on returns or prices that are actually generated by 'real world' trades in the market might therefore provide useful complementary information to direct tests on the basis of survey data.

## Orthogonality and Cross-Equation Restrictions

If survey data are not available, the null hypothesis of efficiency may still be tested but only under the additional assumption that the equilibrium pricing model chosen by the researcher is the one actually used by *market participants* and is therefore the 'true' model. To illustrate orthogonality tests and RE cross-equation restrictions in the simplest possible way, let us assume that an equilibrium pricing model for $Z_{t+1}$ may be represented as:

$$E_t^p Z_{t+1} = \gamma_0 + \gamma' x_t \tag{29}$$

where $x_t$ is a set of variables suggested by the equilibrium-pricing model. A test of information efficiency (or orthogonality), conditional on the chosen equilibrium model, involves a regression

$$Z_{t+1} = \gamma_0 + \gamma' x_t + \beta' \Lambda_t + \varepsilon_{t+1} \tag{30}$$

The orthogonality test is $H_0: \beta' = 0$. One can also test any restrictions on $(\gamma_0, \gamma')$ suggested by the pricing model chosen. The test for $\beta' = 0$ is a test that the determinants

$x_t$ of the equilibrium pricing model fully explain the behaviour of $E_t Z_{t+1}$. Of course, informational efficiency may be tested using alternative equilibrium pricing models.

Note that in all of the tests discussed above, $\varepsilon_{t+1}$ must be serially uncorrelated (since $\varepsilon_t \subset \Omega_t$ the full information set). However, $\varepsilon_{t+1}$ need not be homoscedastic and the *variance* of $\varepsilon_{t+1}$ may vary over time or may depend on other economic variables, without violating informational efficiency. This is because informational efficiency depends only on the first moment of the distribution, namely the expected value of $\varepsilon_{t+1}$.

## Cross-Equation Restrictions

There are stronger tests of 'informational efficiency' that involve cross-equation restrictions. A simple example will suffice at this point and will serve as a useful introduction to the more complex cross-equation restrictions that arise in the vector autoregressive VAR models in later chapters. We keep the algebraic manipulations to a minimum here (but see the appendix for a full derivation). Consider a stock that simply pays an uncertain dividend at the end of period $t+1$ (this could also include a known redemption value for the stock at $t+1$). The 'rational' equilibrium price is:

$$P_t = \delta E_t D_{t+1} \qquad (31)$$

where $\delta$ is a constant discount factor. Now assume an *expectations generating equation* for dividends on the basis of the limited information set $\Lambda_t = (D_t, D_{t-1})$:

$$D_{t+1} = \gamma_1 D_t + \gamma_2 D_{t-1} + v_{t+1} \qquad (32)$$

with $E(v_{t+1}|\Lambda_t) = 0$, under RE. We can now demonstrate that the equilibrium pricing model (31) *plus* the assumed explicit expectations generating equation (32) *plus* the assumption of RE, in short the EMH, implies certain restrictions between the parameters. To see this, note that from (32) under RE

$$E_t D_{t+1} = \gamma_1 D_t + \gamma_2 D_{t-1} \qquad (33)$$

and substituting in (31):
$$P_t = \delta\gamma_1 D_t + \delta\gamma_2 D_{t-1} \qquad (34)$$

We can rewrite (34) as:
$$P_t = \pi_1 D_t + \pi_2 D_{t-1} \qquad (35)$$

where $\pi_1 = \delta\gamma_1$, $\pi_2 = \delta\gamma_2$. A regression of $P_t$ on $(D_t, D_{t-1})$ will yield coefficient estimates $\pi_1$ and $\pi_2$. Similarly, the regression equation (32) will yield *estimates* $\pi_3$ and $\pi_4$:
$$D_{t+1} = \pi_3 D_t + \pi_4 D_{t-1} + v_{t+1} \qquad (36)$$

SECTION 3.5 / USING SURVEY DATA

where $\pi_3 = \gamma_1$ and $\pi_4 = \gamma_2$. However, if (31) and (32) are true, then this implies (34). Hence, from the *regression equations* (35–36), the EMH implies:

$$\pi_1/\pi_3 = \pi_2/\pi_4 = \delta \tag{37}$$

The values of $(\gamma_1, \gamma_2)$ can be directly obtained from the estimated values of $\pi_3$ and $\pi_4$ while from (37), $\delta$ can be obtained either from $\pi_1/\pi_3$ or $\pi_2/\pi_4$. Hence, in general, we obtain two different values for $\delta$ (i.e. the system is 'overidentified').

We have four estimated coefficients (i.e. $\pi_1$ to $\pi_4$) and only three underlying parameters in the model $(\delta, \gamma_1, \gamma_2)$. Therefore, there is *one* restriction amongst the $\pi$'s given in (37), which involves the *estimated* parameters in two distinct equations. Hence, (37) constitutes a non-linear *cross-equation* restriction and is an implication of the pricing model plus RE. (Note that when we impose this restriction we only obtain one value for $\delta$.)

An intuitive interpretation of the cross-equation restrictions is possible. These restrictions do nothing more than ensure that no abnormal profits are earned *on average* and that errors in forecasting dividends are independent of information at time $t$ or earlier. First, consider the profits that can be earned by using our estimated equations (35) and (36). The best forecast of the fair value is given by $V_t = \delta E_t D_{t+1}$ and using (36) gives

$$V_t = \delta(\pi_3 D_t + \pi_4 D_{t-1}) \tag{38}$$

Usually, the realised price will be different from the fundamental value given by (38) because the researcher has less information than the agent operating in the market (i.e. $\Lambda_t \subset \Omega_t$). The price is given by (35) and hence profits are given by:

$$P_t - V_t = (\pi_1 D_t + \pi_2 D_{t-1}) - \delta(\pi_3 D_t + \pi_4 D_{t-1}) = (\pi_1 - \delta\pi_3)D_t + (\pi_2 - \delta\pi_4)D_{t-1} \tag{39}$$

Hence, for all values of $(D_t, D_{t-1})$, profit will be zero only if:

$$\delta = \pi_1/\pi_3 = \pi_2/\pi_4$$

but this is exactly the value of $\delta$, which is imposed in the cross-equation restrictions (37). Now consider the error in forecasting dividends:

$$D_{t+1} - E_t D_{t+1} = (\pi_3 D_t + \pi_4 D_{t-1} + v_{t+1}) - (1/\delta)P_t \tag{40}$$

where we have used (36) and the equilibrium model (31) Substituting for $P_t$ from (35) we have:

$$D_{t+1} - E_t D_{t+1} = (\pi_3 - \pi_1/\delta)D_t + (\pi_4 - \pi_2/\delta)D_{t-1} + v_{t+1} \tag{41}$$

Hence, the forecast error can only be independent of information at time $t$ (i.e. $D_t$ and $D_{t-1}$) if $\delta = \pi_1/\pi_3 = \pi_2/\pi_4$. Tests of cross-equation restrictions are very prevalent in the EMH/RE literature and are usually more complex than the simple example above. However, no matter how complex, such restrictions merely ensure that no abnormal profits are earned on average and that forecast errors are orthogonal to the information set assumed.

One additional problem with the above test procedure is that it is conditional on the *specific* expectations generating equation chosen for $D_{t+1}$. If this is an incorrect representation of how agents form expectations, the estimated parameters $(\pi_3, \pi_4)$ are likely to be biased estimates of the true parameters. Hence, the cross-equation restrictions based on these *estimated* parameters may not hold, even though in a 'true model' they do hold. This is the usual mis-specification bias in econometrics.

## Interpretation of Tests of Market Efficiency

The EMH assumes information is available at zero cost or that the movement in market prices is determined *as if* this were the case. The assumption that the acquisition and processing of information as well as the time involved in acting on such information is costless is a very strong one. If prices 'always reflect all available relevant information', which is also costless to acquire, then why would anyone invest resources in acquiring information? Anyone who did so, would clearly earn a lower return than those who costlessly observed current prices, which under the EMH contain all relevant information. As Grossman and Stiglitz (1980) point out, if information is costly, prices *cannot* perfectly reflect the information available. Stiglitz (1983) also makes the point that speculative markets cannot be completely efficient at all points in time. The profits derived from speculation are the result of being faster in the acquisition and correct interpretation of existing and new information. Thus, one might expect the market to move towards efficiency as the 'well informed' make profits relative to the less well informed. In so doing, the 'smart-money' sells when the actual price is above fundamental value and this moves the price closer to its fundamental value. However, this process may take some time, particularly if agents are unsure of the true model generating fundamentals (e.g. dividends). If, in addition, agents have different endowments of wealth, then some may have a disproportionate influence on prices. Also, irrational or 'noise' traders might be present and then the rational traders have to take account of the behaviour of the noise traders. It is, therefore, possible that prices might deviate from fundamental value for substantial periods. Recently, much research has taken place on learning by agents, on the nature of sequential trading and the behaviour of noise traders. These issues are discussed in later chapters.

# 3.6   Summary

We have considered the basic ideas that underlie the EMH in both intuitive and mathematical terms and our main conclusions are:

- The EMH is important in assessing public policy issues such as the desirability of mergers and takeovers, short-termism and regulation of financial markets and institutions.

- The EMH implies that (unexpected) returns are a fair game.

- Tests of informational efficiency (RE) can be undertaken using survey data on expectations.

- In general, tests of the EMH require an explicit model of equilibrium expected returns. Conditional on the equilibrium model, returns should not be predictable from known data.

- The EMH assumes investors process information efficiently so that persistent abnormal profits cannot be made by trading in financial assets. Cross-equation restrictions are tests of informational efficiency (RE) and zero abnormal profits.

- Failure of the EMH in empirical tests may be due to a failure of informational efficiency (RE), or an inappropriate choice of the model for equilibrium returns, or simply that the EMH does not hold in the 'real world'.

## Appendix: Cross-Equation Restrictions

There are some rather subtle issues in developing these cross-equation restrictions and, in the text, we presented a simplified account. A more complete derivation of the issues is given below. The researcher is unlikely to have the full information set that is available to market participants, $\Lambda_t \subset \Omega_t$. This implies that equation (34) in the text has an error term, which reflects the difference in the informational sets available that is $\omega_{t+1} = [E(D_{t+1}|\Omega_t) - E(D_{t+1}|\Lambda_t)]$. To see this note that the stock price is determined by the full information set available to agents

$$P_t = \delta E(D_{t+1}|\Omega_t) \tag{A1}$$

The econometrician uses a subset $\Lambda_t = (D_t, D_{t-1})$ of the full information set to forecast dividends:

$$D_{t+1} = \gamma_1 D_t + \gamma_2 D_{t-1} + v_{t+1} \tag{A2}$$

We then employ the identity:

$$E(D_{t+1}|\Omega_t) = E(D_{t+1}|\Lambda_t) + \{E(D_{t+1}|\Omega_t) - E(D_{t+1}|\Lambda_t)\}$$
$$= E(D_{t+1}|\Lambda_t) + \omega_{t+1} \tag{A3}$$

where

$$\omega_{t+1} = [(D_{t+1} - E(D_{t+1}|\Lambda_t)] - [D_{t+1} - E(D_{t+1}|\Omega_t)] = v_{t+1} - \eta_{t+1} \tag{A4}$$

and $\eta_{t+1}$ is the true RE forecast error made by agents when using the full information set, $\Omega_t$. Note that $E(\omega_{t+1}|\Lambda_t) = 0$. To derive the correct expression for (34) we use (A1), (A2) and (A3):

$$P_t = \delta E_t(D_{t+1}|\Omega_t) = \delta E_t(D_{t+1}|\Lambda_t) + \delta \omega_{t+1}$$
$$= \delta \gamma_1 D_t + \delta \gamma_2 D_{t-1} + \varepsilon_{t+1} = \pi_1 D_t + \pi_2 D_{t-1} + \varepsilon_{t+1} \tag{A5}$$

where $\varepsilon_{t+1} = \delta\omega_{t+1}$. The complete derivation of the 'no-profit' condition (39) in the text has agents using the full information set to determine $V_t$:

$$V_t = \delta E(D_{t+1}|\Omega_t) = \delta E(D_{t+1}|\Lambda_t) + \delta\omega_{t+1} \tag{A6}$$

Hence, using (A5) and (A6)):

$$P_t - V_t = (\pi_1 D_t + \pi_2 D_{t-1} + \delta\omega_{t+1}) - \delta(\pi_3 D_t + \pi_4 D_{t-1} + \omega_{t+1})$$
$$= (\pi_1 - \delta\pi_3)D_t + (\pi_2 - \delta\pi_4)D_{t-1} \tag{A7}$$

which is equation (39) in the text. The forecast for dividends is based on the full information set available to agents (although not to the econometrician) and using (A2) and (A1) is given by:

$$D_{t+1} - E(D_{t+1}|\Omega_t) = (\pi_3 D_t + \pi_4 D_{t-1} + v_{t+1}) - (1/\delta)P_t \tag{A8}$$

However, substituting for $P_t$ from (A5) and noting that $\omega_{t+1} = v_{t+1} - \eta_{t+1}$, we have:

$$D_{t+1} - E(D_{t+1}|\Omega_t) = (\pi_3 - \pi_1/\delta)D_t + (\pi_4 - \pi_2/\delta)D_{t-1} + \eta_{t+1} \tag{A9}$$

Hence, equation (A9) above, rather than equation (41) in the text, is the correct expression. However, derivation of (41) in the text is less complex and provides the intuition we require at this point in the book.

# 4

# ARE STOCK RETURNS PREDICTABLE?

## Aims

- Examine returns on stocks, bonds and T-bills over the last century.

- Provide a set of alternative tests to ascertain whether stock returns are forecastable over different horizons.

- Introduce univariate tests, including the correlogram (autocorrelations) of returns, a variance-ratio statistic and multivariate tests such as cointegration and error correction models (ECM).

- Use Monte Carlo simulations (MCS) to assess the 'power' of univariate tests of randomness.

- Assess non-linear and regime-switching models applied to stock returns.

- Examine the profitability of 'active' trading strategies (market timing) on the basis of forecasts from regression equations.

## 4.1 A Century of Returns

Figure 1 shows the US monthly *real* S&P500 index from January 1915 to April 2004. The real index is simply the nominal index divided by an aggregate price index (e.g. wholesale or consumer price index) and shows the changing purchasing power (over goods and services) of holding a diversified portfolio of stocks that mimics the S&P500 index. The 1930s crash and the recent crash of 2000–2003 are clearly visible as well as the major long-run rise in the index in the 1990s. The stock index is non-stationary

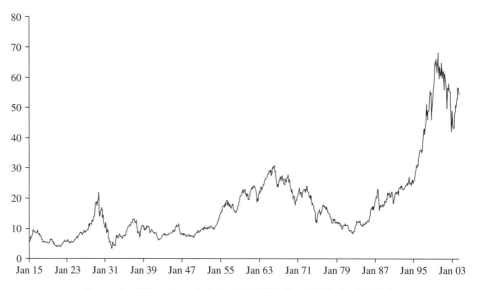

**Figure 1**   US real stock index S&P500 (Jan 1915–April 2004)

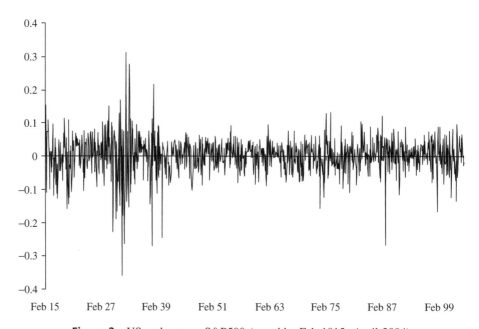

**Figure 2**   US real returns S&P500 (monthly, Feb 1915–April 2004)

(or integrated of order one, I(1)) since its mean level is not constant and rises over time. The monthly return on the index (excluding dividend payments) in Figure 2 appears to be stationary (i.e. I(0)) with a constant (unconditional) mean and variance. The relatively large proportion of 'outliers' in Figure 2 (i.e. very large or very small returns) probably implies that the unconditional returns are non-normal with fat tails and the distribution may be asymmetric, as there are more large negative returns than there are positive returns, which indicates non-normality. This is confirmed in the

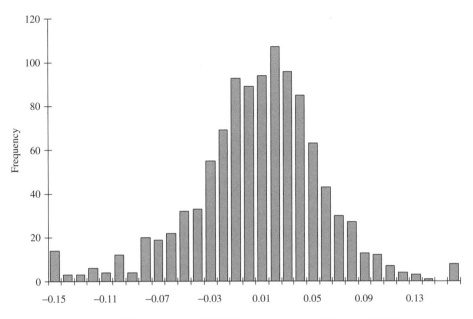

**Figure 3**   US real returns S&P500 (monthly, Feb 1915–April 2004)

histogram of returns, where the fat tails and the negative skew are clearly visible (Figure 3).

Returning to Figure 2, it is evident that the *volatility* in the monthly returns goes through periods of calm (e.g. the 1950s and 1960s) and turbulence (e.g. 1930s, 1970s and at the turn of the 20th century). Once returns become highly volatile, they tend to stay volatile for some time, and similarly, when returns are relatively small (either positive or negative), they tend to stay small for some time. Hence, volatility is *conditionally* autoregressive. As volatility in econometrics is known as *heteroscedasticity*, the behaviour of volatility in Figure 2 is said to follow an autoregressive conditional heteroscedasticity (ARCH) process. A special case of this class of models is the so-called GARCH(1,1) model (see Chapter 29), which when fitted to the data in Figure 2 over the sample period February 1915 to April 2004, gives the following result.

$$R_{t+1} = 0.00315 + \varepsilon_{t+1} \qquad \varepsilon_{t+1}|\Omega_t \sim N(0, h_{t+1})$$
$$[2.09]$$

$$h_{t+1} = 0.00071 + 0.8791\,h_t + 0.0967\,\varepsilon_t^2$$
$$[2.21] \qquad [33.0] \qquad [4.45]$$

t-statistics in parentheses

where $h_{t+1}$ is the conditional variance of returns. The mean (real) return is 0.315% per month (3.85% p.a.). The GARCH equation for the conditional variance $h_{t+1}$ is typical of results using stock returns where volatility at time $t + 1$, $h_{t+1}$ is conditional on volatility at time $t$, $h_t$ and the squared 'surprise' in returns $\varepsilon_t^2$. The relatively large coefficient on the lagged $h_t$ term of 0.8791 implies that if volatility is high (low), it stays

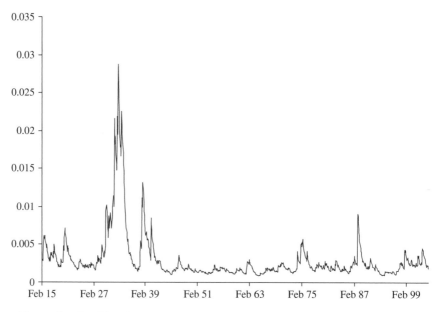

**Figure 4**    Conditional variance, GARCH(1,1) model (US, Feb 1915–April 2004)

high (low) for some time – that is, it is autoregressive. The unconditional volatility is $\sigma^2 = 0.00071/(1-0.8791-0.0967) = 0.0007276$, which implies a standard deviation of 0.02697 (2.697% per month). The time series of $h_{t+1}$ using the above equation is shown in Figure 4, in which the persistence in volatility is evident. It may be worth noting at this point that GARCH-type persistence effects in conditional volatility are found in daily, weekly and monthly returns but returns at lower frequencies (e.g. for returns at horizons greater than three months) generally do not exhibit GARCH effects (but see Engle, Lilien and Robins (1987) for an example of ARCH effect in quarterly term structure data). In other words, volatility is persistent for short-horizon returns but not for long-horizon returns.

Now let us take a look at *average annual* returns and volatility for stocks, bonds and bills using a long data series for the period 1900–2000 (Table 1 – Dimson, Marsh and Staunton 2002). The arithmetic mean returns $\overline{R}$ (in real terms) for stocks in the United Kingdom, in the United States and for a world index (including the USA) are between 7.2% and 8.7% p.a. (Table 1A). The standard deviation of these (arithmetic) returns is around 20% p.a., indicating the high risk attached to holding stocks *in any particular year*. If (log) returns are normally distributed, then $\overline{R} - \overline{R}_g = (1/2)\sigma^2$. For the United States, $\overline{R} - \overline{R}_g = 2.0$ and $(1/2)\sigma^2 = 2.04\%$, which is close, indicating that annual returns are approximately lognormal.

The high volatility of stock returns also means that *ex-post* measures of *average* returns are sensitive to a run of good or bad years. A return in only 1 year out of 100, that was two standard deviations (i.e. 40%) above the average, would raise the average by 40 basis points (0.4% p.a.). This demonstrates the uncertainty attached to our estimate of $\overline{R}$. Put somewhat differently, note that if returns are *niid* (i.e. homoscedastic and not serially correlated), then the standard error in estimating

**Table 1**  Real returns: 1900–2000

**Panel A: Real Stock Returns (% p.a.)**

| | Inflation | | Real Return | | | | | |
|---|---|---|---|---|---|---|---|---|
| | Arith. | Geom. | Arithmetic Mean | Standard Deviation | Standard Error | Geometric Mean | Minimum Return | Maximum Return |
| UK | 4.3 | 4.1 | 7.6 | 20.0 | 2.0 | 5.8 | −57 (in 1974) | +97 (in 1975) |
| USA | 3.3 | 3.2 | 8.7 | 20.2 | 2.0 | 6.7 | −38 (in 1931) | +57 (in 1933) |
| World (incl. USA) | n.a. | n.a. | 7.2 | 17.0 | 1.7 | 6.8 | n.a. | n.a. |

**Panel B: Real Bond Returns (% p.a.)**

| | Inflation | | Real Return | | | |
|---|---|---|---|---|---|---|
| | Arith. | Geom. | Arithmetic Mean | Standard Deviation | Standard Error | Geometric Mean |
| UK | 4.3 | 4.1 | 2.3 | 14.5 | 1.4 | n.a. |
| USA | 3.3 | 3.2 | 2.1 | 10.0 | 1.0 | 1.6 |
| World (incl. USA) | n.a. | n.a. | 1.7 | 10.3 | 1.0 | 1.2 |

**Panel C: Real Returns on Bills (% p.a.)**

| | Inflation | | Real Return | | |
|---|---|---|---|---|---|
| | Arith. | Geom. | Arithmetic Mean | Standard Deviation | Standard Error |
| UK | 4.3 | 4.1 | 1.2 | 6.6 | 0.7 |
| USA | 3.3 | 3.2 | 1.0 | 4.7 | 0.5 |

Notes:
(1) Annual averages taken over 1900–2000. 'World' comprises 16 developed countries including USA, Canada, South Africa, Australia, Japan and European countries.
(2) The real return $= (R_t - \pi_t)/(1 + \pi_t)$, where $R_t =$ nominal return and $\pi_t =$ inflation rate and therefore the average real return does not equal the average nominal return minus the average inflation rate (the latter is an approximation, valid only for low inflation rates).
(3) The standard error has been calculated as $\sigma/\sqrt{T}$.
Figures are extracted from Dimson, Marsh and Staunton (2002).

the mean return is $\sigma_{\overline{R}} = \sigma/\sqrt{n} = 20/\sqrt{101} = 2\%$ p.a., and therefore we can be 95% certain that the mean return (for the USA) lies approximately in the range $\overline{R} \pm 2\sigma_{\overline{R}} = 8.7 \pm 4 = \{4.7, 12.7\}$ – this is quite a wide range of possible outcomes for the mean return. Of course, in any one year taken at random, the actual return has a standard deviation of around 20% p.a., and Table 1 shows a fall as great as 57% (in 1974 in the UK) and a rise of 96.7% (in the UK in 1975). The US stock market also had an average return-per-unit of risk $\overline{R}/\sigma$ of 0.43 and a Sharpe ratio (i.e. the *excess* return-per-unit of risk) of $SR = (\overline{R} - \overline{r})/\sigma$ of around 0.5.

**Table 2**   Equity premium (% p.a.): 1900–2000

|  | Over Bills | | | Over Bonds | |
| --- | --- | --- | --- | --- | --- |
|  | Arith. | Geom. | Standard Error | Arith. | Geom. |
| UK | 6.5 | 4.8 | 2.0 | 5.6 | 4.4 |
| USA | 7.7 | 5.8 | 2.0 | 7.0 | 5.0 |
| World (incl. USA) | 6.2 | 4.9 | 1.6 | 5.6 | 4.6 |

Notes: See Table 1.

The average (real) return on government long-term bonds (Table 1B) is around 2% p.a. with lower volatility than stocks of around 10 to 14% p.a., which gives a return-per-unit of risk for the United States of 0.21, much lower than for stocks. T-bills (Table 1C) have a lower average (real) return than bonds of around 1% p.a. with an even lower volatility than bonds of $\sigma \approx 5$ to 6% p.a. The *relative* returns on equities, bonds and bills and their volatilities in the 14 other countries studied by Dimson, Marsh and Staunton (2002) follow the above pattern noted for the United States and United Kingdom.

The equity premium is the *excess* return of stocks over bonds or bills (Table 2). The arithmetic average equity premium over bills is higher than over bonds, and for the United States, these figures are 7.7% (over bills) and 7% p.a. (over bonds). The standard error of the mean equity premium is $\sigma_{\overline{R}} = 2\%$ p.a.; therefore, the mean equity premium is measured with substantial error, reflecting the high volatility of stock returns noted above. The 95% confidence interval for the arithmetic mean US equity premium is 7.7% ± 4%, which again covers quite a wide range.

The above averages for the equity risk premium calculated by Dimson, Marsh and Staunton (2002) are about 1.5% higher than in some earlier studies (Ibbotson Associates 2001, Barclays Capital 2003, Goetzmann and Jorion 1999). This is due to different time periods and country coverage and different computational methods (e.g. whether dividends as well as price changes are included in measured returns for all countries).

## Risk, Return and the Sharpe Ratio

Clearly, if one's private or state pension contributions are to be invested in risky assets such as stocks, we need to carefully assess the return we might obtain and the risk we are taking on. High average stock returns in the United States cannot be merely due to high productivity of the US economy or impatience (time preference) by consumers, otherwise real returns on bonds would also be high. The reward for saving in government *index-linked* bonds is not high (at around 3% p.a. in real terms), so what high stock returns imply is a high reward for bearing *stock market risk*. As we have seen above, this risk is substantial, giving a range of 12.7 to 4.7% p.a. for $\overline{R}$ in the United States (with 95% confidence). The US equity premium of 7.7% (over bills) is the reward for holding this stock market risk.

Using the CRSP database, Figure 5 demonstrates *the first law of finance*, namely, a higher average return implies a high-level of risk (i.e. standard deviation). The *ex-post* Sharpe ratio $(\overline{R} - \overline{r})/\sigma$, that is, the *excess* return per unit of risk, for *all* the size-sorted

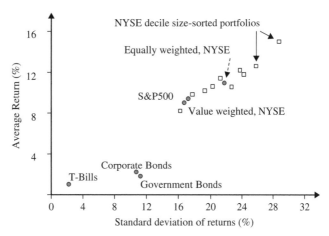

**Figure 5**  Mean and standard deviation: annual averages, US real returns (post-1947)

decile stock portfolios in Figure 5, is around 0.5. Clearly, it is relatively easy to obtain high average returns – you simply take on more risk. Figure 5 also demonstrates that the Sharpe ratio in the post-WWII period for US government and corporate *bonds* is very low at around 0.1 – this is part of the argument for moving some of social security (i.e. state) pension fund contributions into stocks.

It is better to compare the performance of different asset classes using the Sharpe ratio rather than just average returns because it 'corrects for risk' and is also invariant to leverage. For example, suppose a stock is currently priced at $100 and its average return is $\overline{R} = 10\%$, with a standard deviation of 20% and $r = 2\%$. If you invest all your own funds of $100 in the stock, the excess return is 8% and the Sharpe ratio is 0.4. If you borrow 10% (= $10) of the funds at $r = 2\%$ to purchase the stock and use 90% ($90) of your own funds, the return on your levered stock portfolio is $R_p = (100/90)R \approx 11\%$ – you have 'levered' up your (average) return by borrowing to invest in the stock. This levered (expected) return can be increased simply by borrowing more cash and using less of your own funds to invest in the risky assets. The return net of interest cost is

$$R_p \approx 1.1R - 0.1r$$

The *excess* return and standard deviation (remember $\sigma_r = 0$) of the levered portfolio are

$$R_p - r = 1.1(R - r) \qquad \sigma_p = 1.1\sigma_R$$

The Sharpe ratio of the levered portfolio is

$$SR_p = \frac{R_p - r}{\sigma_p} = \frac{(R - r)}{\sigma_R}$$

which is equal to that of the unlevered portfolio and hence is unaffected by leverage.

## Importance of Equity Returns

For investors, the forward-looking equity premium is important because it provides an estimate of the future value of any funds invested in the stock market relative to the risk-free return. This is particularly important for pension funds that invest (a proportion of) their assets in equities. For defined contribution pension schemes, the individual saver receives at retirement a 'pot of money' that she usually then invests (all or part) in an annuity. The equity part of this 'pot of money' is extremely sensitive to the mean return on stocks. For example, for the USA, using $\overline{R}_g = 6.7\%$ p.a., \$100 invested at $t = 0$ accumulates to $\$100 \, (1.067)^{30} = \$700$ after 30 years, whereas if the mean equity return is one standard deviation lower (i.e. $R_g = 4.7\%$ p.a.), then the \$100 accumulates to about \$400 after 30 years. These are real returns, so the higher equity return increases wealth by a factor of 7 but the lower return by a factor of only 4. For a defined benefit pension scheme (i.e. pension is based on final salary), the forward-looking equity return is important for the solvency of the pension scheme. The liabilities of the pension fund are existing and future (final salary) pensions, which the fund is contracted to honour. Clearly, the liabilities are somewhat uncertain (e.g. depending on the growth of real earnings, retirement patterns and longevity). To cover these liabilities we have the reasonably certain pension contributions of individuals and employers (based on salary). A major uncertainty is what these contributions will earn (in real terms) over many years, if invested in equities. After the equity market crash of 2000–2003, a number of defined benefit pension fund trustees took the view that future stock market returns were insufficient to adequately cover future pension liabilities. This led to such schemes being limited to existing members, while new employees had to join a defined *benefit* scheme (so the stock market risk is then shared amongst employees rather than employers *and* employees). Also, firms with a defined benefit scheme that was actuarially in deficit (because of lower expected equity returns) would have to raise contribution levels for employees or employers or both. The closing of defined benefit schemes to new members and the existence of deficits in such funds became a major issue, particularly in the United Kingdom after the crash of 2000–2003.

The historic real (geometric) return on equities of 6.8% for the world index demonstrates that over the last 100 years, a world index *tracker fund* (or even a US or UK fund) would have performed very well (even after deduction of annual fees of around 1% p.a.). An 'actively managed' fund would involve management fees of around 3 to 5%, and so historically would have done reasonably well even if it had only performed as well as a 'tracker' (which the 'average' active fund seems just about to manage to do – see Chapter 9). However, if you believe that the forward-looking real equity return is closer to, say, 4% (see below), then the active fund looks much less attractive, with its high management fees. You would be better off with index-linked bonds, with a real return of around 3% p.a. (e.g. John Ralfe switched all of Boots the Chemists' pension fund into bonds in 2001).

For companies, a key input to calculating the cost of equity capital is a forward-looking measure of the equity premium (adjusted by the company's beta). Historically, the US/UK equity premium has been high at around 7% p.a. (arithmetic mean) which, with a beta of unity and an average real interest rate of 3% p.a. (say), gives a (real) cost of equity capital for the firm of 10% p.a. This may be the hurdle rate used by the firm (i.e. internal rate of return of the investment project must exceed 10% p.a.). But if the forward-looking required return on equity is lower than 10%, then clearly the firm should lower its hurdle rate, otherwise value-enhancing investment projects may be rejected.

Because of their market power, state or privatised utilities are often subject to price caps (e.g. prices can rise no faster than the consumer price index less $x\%$) or 'rate of return regulation' (i.e. the rate of return on capital cannot exceed $y\%$ p.a.). In the case of the latter, a forward-looking required rate of return is required, and if the forecast equity premium is lower, the regulator should ensure that the public utility earns a lower return on its capital (e.g. by lowering its prices). Hence, the forecast equity premium is important for institutional investors like pension funds, for individual's investments in active or passive mutual funds and for the hurdle rate for corporate investment projects.

## Forecasts of the Equity Risk Premium

Needless to say, forecasts of the equity premium are subject to wide margins of error. Welch (2000, 2001) asked 226 financial economists to forecast the average equity premium over the next 30 years for the United States, and the (arithmetic) mean was 7.1% with a standard deviation of around 2%. This forecast is a little lower than the 101-year historic US equity premium of 7.7% (Table 1), but the standard error of respondents' replies is about the same as the historic standard error of 2% (Table 1). Respondents seem fairly closely 'anchored' to the historic premium when forming their view of the future premium (see the psychological biases noted in Chapter 18).

Dimson, Marsh and Staunton (2002) adjust the *ex-post* historic risk premium for the impact of unanticipated higher earnings at the end of the 1990s, for the fact that increased international diversification may have lowered the required return, as might diminished investment risk (e.g. because of the ending of the Cold War, progress in multilateral trade talks, etc.) and because of reduced risk aversion of the marginal investor. They suggest a *forecast equity premium* of 5.4% for the United States, 3.7% for the United Kingdom and 4% for the world index (arithmetic averages, with geometric averages about 1% lower). Campbell (2001), using a variety of methods, suggests a forecast US equity real return of 6.5 to 7% (arithmetic) and 5 to 5.5% (geometric) with a forecast real interest rate of 3 to 3.5%. This implies a forecast range for the equity premium of 3 to 4% (arithmetic) for the United States. Historic returns imply the *ex-post average* equity return is

$$\overline{R}_t \equiv \overline{\left(\frac{D_t}{P_{t-1}}\right)} + \overline{\left(\frac{\Delta P_t}{P_{t-1}}\right)}$$

As well as measuring the equity premium directly from historic returns data, one can try and measure long-run *expected* capital gains using 'price ratios'. If a variable $(X/P)_t$ is stationary (mean reverting), then over the long run, $\overline{(\Delta X_t/X_{t-1})} = \overline{(\Delta P_t/P_{t-1})}$, and the $X$-variable provides an alternative estimate of the average capital gain, to use in the above equation (in place of the actual capital gain). The most obvious candidates for $X_t$ are dividends $D_t$ or earnings $E_t$. Earnings figures are invariant to share repurchases, whereas share repurchases are often employed in lieu of dividend payments, which may distort the dividend growth figures. On the other hand, earnings are more volatile than dividends, which implies their mean value is estimated with greater uncertainty. Dividend–price and earnings–price ratios move in very long slow swings and appear to be stationary variables (see below). It would be somewhat counterintuitive to believe that these ratios moved in the long run to plus or minus infinity since this would imply either that dividend growth or future expected returns are non-stationary (see Chapters 12 and 23).

Fama and French (2002) use average dividend growth and average earnings growth as an estimate of future expected capital gains. (Using dividend growth is equivalent to invoking the Gordon growth model – see Chapter 10.) They find that the (unconditional) real equity premium for 1872–2000 using the dividend growth model is 3.54% p.a., whereas using the historic average stock return, the equity premium is much higher at 5.57% p.a. The difference between the two is due mainly to the last 50 years, since the dividend growth model gives an equity premium of 2.55% p.a. for 1951–2002, whereas the estimate using the average stock return is 7.43% p.a. For 1951–2000, the earnings growth model gives an estimate of the equity premium of 4.32% p.a., which is larger than that from the dividend growth model but still well below the historic average of returns data of 7.43% p.a.

Fama and French note that dividend and earnings price ratios can forecast either future dividend growth or future *expected* returns (see Chapters 12 and 23). But the dividend–price ratio has hardly any explanatory power for the future growth in dividends. Hence, they suggest that the rising price–dividend ratio throughout the 1950–2000 period is mainly due to changes in *expected* returns. They therefore argue that much of the high historic equity return over the 1951–2000 period comprises an *unexpected* capital gain due to a decline in discount rates. The consensus therefore appears to be that the equity premium is forecast to be below its historic average, with the implications noted above (see also Jagannathan, McGatten and Scherbina, 2001).

## 4.2 Simple Models

The main aim in this chapter is to present a range of tests examining the predictability of stock returns. You can if you wish, just think of the regression models as a 'data description' or the 'stylised facts'. However, under constant expected returns, 'predictability' violates informational efficiency and if abnormal profits in excess of transition costs and after correcting for risk are persistent, then this also violates the Efficient Markets Hypothesis (EMH). Tests of the EMH require an equilibrium model of asset returns. We can think of the equilibrium expected return on a risky asset as consisting of a risk-free rate $r_t$ (e.g. on Treasury Bills) and a risk premium, $rp_t$

$$E_t R_{t+1} \equiv r_t + rp_t \qquad (1)$$

At present, we make no sharp distinction between nominal and real variables, and equation (1) could be expressed in either form. Equation (1) is an identity until we have an economic model of the risk premium. Many (early) empirical tests of the EMH assume $rp_t$ and $r_t$ are constant and consider the regression

$$R_{t+1} = k + \gamma' \Omega_t + \varepsilon_{t+1} \qquad (2)$$

where $\Omega_t = $ information available at time $t$. Alternatively, we can use *excess* returns $R_{t+1} - r_t$ in (2). A test of $\gamma' = 0$ provides evidence on the 'informational efficiency' element of the EMH. These regression tests vary, depending on the information assumed:

 (i) data on past returns $R_{t-j}$ $(j = 0, 1, 2, \ldots, m)$

 (ii) data on past forecast errors $\varepsilon_{t-j}$ $(j = 0, 1, \ldots, m)$

(iii) data on variables such as the dividend–price ratio, the earnings–price ratio, interest rates, etc.

When (i) and (ii) are examined together, this gives rise to Autoregressive Moving Average (ARMA) models, for example, the ARMA (1,1) model:

$$R_{t+1} = k + \gamma_1 R_t + \varepsilon_{t+1} - \gamma_2 \varepsilon_t \qquad (3)$$

If one is only concerned with weak-form efficiency, the autocorrelation coefficients between $R_{t+1}$ and $R_{t-j}$ $(j = 0, 1, \ldots, m)$ can be examined to see if they are non-zero. The EMH applies over all holding periods: a day, week, month or even over many years. Hence, we may find violations of the EMH at some horizons but not at others.

Suppose the above tests show that informational efficiency does not hold, so information at time $t$ can be used to help predict future returns. Nevertheless, it may be highly risky for an investor to bet on the outcomes predicted by a regression equation that has a high standard error or low R-squared. It is therefore worth investigating whether such predictability really does allow one to make abnormal profits in actual trading, after taking account of transaction costs. Thus, there are two approaches when testing the EMH, one is informational efficiency and the other is the ability to make abnormal profits (i.e. profits after transaction costs and correcting for *ex-ante risk*).

## Smart Money and Noise Traders

Before discussing the details of the various tests on predictability, it is worth briefly discussing the implications for stock returns and prices of there being some non-rational or noise traders in the market. This enables us to introduce the concepts of mean reversion and excess volatility in a fairly simple way. We assume that the market contains a particular type of noise trader, namely, a positive feedback trader whose demand for stocks increases after there has been a price rise. To simplify matters, we assume the rational traders or smart money believe that expected equilibrium returns are constant, $1 + E_t R_{t+1} = k^*$, or equivalently:

$$E_t[(P_{t+1} + D_{t+1})/P_t = k^* \qquad (4)$$

If only the smart money (fundamentals' traders) is present in the market, prices only respond to new information or news. Price changes are random, and past returns cannot be used to predict future returns. Now consider introducing positive feedback traders into the market. After any good news about dividends, positive feedback traders purchase the stock, increasing its price above fundamental value. If the rational traders recognise this mispricing, they short-sell the overvalued stock, and the price moves back towards its fundamental value. Prices are therefore mean-reverting.

Two things are immediately obvious. First, prices have *overreacted* to fundamentals (i.e. news about dividends). Second, prices are more volatile than would be predicted by changes in fundamentals. It follows that prices are *excessively volatile* compared to what they would be if there are only rational traders in the market. Volatility tests based on the early work of Shiller (1989) and LeRoy and Porter (1981) attempt to measure this excess volatility in a precise way.

As positive feedback traders purchase the stock, then over short horizons, returns are positively serially correlated: positive returns are followed by further positive returns. Conversely, after 'bad news', negative returns are followed by further negative returns. But over *long horizons*, returns are negatively serially correlated as the rational traders move prices back to their fundamental value. Thus, in the presence of feedback traders, short-horizon returns are positively serially correlated, while long-horizon returns are negatively serially correlated. This pattern of serial correlation over different horizons implies that buying recent 'winners' will tend to yield winners next period – this is a *momentum strategy*. Over long horizons (say, 3–5 years), the negative serial correlation implies you should buy low price stocks – this is a *value-growth strategy*. Also, the above scenario implies that returns are likely to be correlated with changes in dividends and the dividend–price ratio, so regressions of $R_{t+1}$ on $(D/P)_t$ have often been interpreted as evidence for the presence of noise traders in the market.

One can also see why feedback traders may cause changes in the variance of returns over *different return horizons*. Suppose the variance of *annual* returns is 15% p.a. If expected returns are constant so that returns are *iid*, then after two years, the variance of returns would be 30%. However, with mean reversion, the variance of returns over two years will be less than twice the variance over one year. This is because prices overshoot their fundamental value in the short run but not in the long run (see the variance-ratio test below).

It may be too difficult to infer whether a given observed path for returns is consistent with market efficiency or with the presence of noise traders. This arises because tests of the EMH are based on a specific model of equilibrium returns, and if the latter is incorrect, the EMH will be rejected by the data. However, another model of equilibrium returns might conceivably support the EMH. Also, predictability *per se* does not refute the EMH if *expected* returns vary over time, since then actual returns will be correlated with variables known at time $t$. We need to look very carefully at alternative models of equilibrium returns before we conclude that 'predictability' refutes the EMH. There are enumerable tests of stock return predictability, and we provide illustrative results below (for a comprehensive bibliography, see Campbell 2000).

## 4.3 Univariate Tests

Over short horizons such as a day, one would expect equilibrium expected returns to be constant. Hence, actual returns probably provide a good approximation to daily *abnormal* returns. Fortune (1991) provides an illustrative statistical analysis of the returns using over 2,700 *daily observations* on the S&P500 share index (closing prices, January 2, 1980, to September 21, 1990). Stock returns are measured as $R_t = \Delta \ln P_t$. A typical regression is

$$R_t = 0.0007 + 0.054\,\varepsilon_{t-1} - 0.037\,\varepsilon_{t-2} - 0.019\varepsilon_{t-3} - 0.054\varepsilon_{t-4} + 0.051\varepsilon_{t-5}$$
$$(2.8) \quad (2.8) \qquad (1.9) \qquad\quad (1.0) \qquad\quad (2.8) \qquad\quad (2.7)$$

$$-0.0017\,\text{WE} + 0.0006\,\text{HOL} + 0.0006\,\text{JAN} + \varepsilon_t \qquad\qquad (5)$$
$$(3.2) \qquad\qquad (0.2) \qquad\qquad (0.82)$$

$$R^2 = 0.0119, \ \text{SEE} = 0.0108, \ (.) = \text{t-statistic}$$

The variable WE = 1 if the trading day is a Monday and 0 otherwise, HOL = 1 if the current trading day is preceded by a one-day holiday (0 otherwise) and JAN = 1 for trading days in January (0 otherwise). The only statistically significant dummy variable (for this data spanning the 1980s) is for the 'weekend effect', which implies that price returns are negative on Mondays. The January effect is not statistically significant in the above regression for the 'aggregate' S&P500 index (but it could still be important for stocks of small companies). The error term is serially correlated with the MA(1), MA(4) and MA(5) terms being statistically significant. Since previous periods forecast errors $\varepsilon_{t-j}$ are known (at time $t$), this is a violation of informational efficiency, under the null of constant equilibrium returns. The MA pattern might not be picked up by longer-term weekly or monthly data, which might therefore have white noise errors and hence be supportive of the EMH.

However, the above data might not indicate a failure of the EMH where the latter is defined as the inability to persistently make abnormal profits. Only about 1 percent (R-squared = 0.01) of the variability in daily stock returns is explained by the regression: hence, potential profitable arbitrage possibilities are likely to involve substantial risk. A strategy to beat the market based on (5) might involve repeatedly short-selling stocks on Friday and re-purchasing these stocks on a Monday, which yields a predictable return on average of 0.17 of 1%. But if the portfolio consists of the 25–30 stocks required to mimic the S&P500 index, this might involve high transactions costs that might well outweigh any profits from these strategies. However, one could mitigate this problem by using stock index futures. Since the coefficients in equation (5) are in a sense averages over the sample data, one would have to be pretty confident that these 'average effects' would persist in the future. Of course, if the coefficient on WE remains negative, the repeated strategy will earn profits (ignoring transactions costs). But at a minimum, one would wish to test the temporal stability of coefficients before embarking on such a set of repeated gambles. In addition, one would probably need a substantial amount of financial resources as the investor may be unlucky in the first few weeks of this strategy and may initially lose a considerable amount of money. Whether the latter is a problem for 'big players' such as pension fund managers depends on how often their performance is evaluated. An R-squared of around 0.01 implies that you are taking on a 51/49 bet, which does not look good if transactions costs are involved. To adequately test the 'supernormal profits' view of the EMH, one needs to examine 'real world' strategies, trading specific stocks within the portfolio, taking account of all transactions costs, bid–ask spreads, managerial and dealers' time and effort and the riskiness of the strategy. In short, if the predictability indicated by regression tests cannot yield risk-adjusted abnormal profits in the real world, one may legitimately treat the statistically significant 'information' in the regression equation as being of no economic significance.

The above regression provides an example of calendar effects in stock returns of which there are many varieties. Here, we have examined these effects in a *single* study using conventional test statistics and 5% critical values. A question arises as to whether those (possibly large numbers of) studies that find calendar effects, do so because they 'trawl' over a large number of alternative calendar effects (e.g. January effects, day-of-the-week effects, weekend effects) and alternative data periods, and hence they bias our judgement in favour of calendar effects – this is discussed in later chapters and is known as *data snooping bias*.

Technical trading rules (e.g. chartists, filter rules, support and resistance levels, neural networks, genetic algorithms) are also used to try and 'beat the market' over short horizons (e.g. daily and intra-day trading), and we discuss these in later chapters both for stocks and for foreign exchange.

## Risk and Investment Horizon

There is a 'rule of thumb' often quoted, that the proportion of stocks an investor should hold in her portfolio of 'stocks plus bonds' should equal '100 minus their age'. So, a 20-year-old should hold 20% in bonds and 80% in stocks, whereas a 70-year old should hold 30% in stocks and 70% in bonds. Is there any logic to this rule of thumb?

Suppose your decision to hold risky assets such as stocks depends only on expected excess return and the variance of your portfolio return (we discuss this 'mean-variance' approach in detail in the next chapter and in Chapters 15 and 16). Are stocks riskier in the short run than in the long run? Does the higher expected return in the long run compensate for the higher risk incurred? Let us take the 'baseline' case where we assume that continuously compounded returns are *iid* (normality is not required here). Then, the mean return and variance of return both scale with horizon, that is, $E_0 R_{0 \to k} = k\mu$ and $\sigma_{0 \to k}^2 = k\sigma^2$ where $k =$ horizon in years (say), $\mu$ is the *annual* expected return (continuously compounded) and $\sigma$ the annual standard deviation. Yes, variance increases with horizon but so does expected return hence, the return (or excess return) per unit of variance is the same for any horizon. Hence, with *iid* returns, one might expect two investors (with the same degree of risk tolerance) to invest the same proportion in risky assets, regardless of horizon (see Chapters 15 and 16 for a formal analysis).

Note it is true that for $\mu > 0$ and *niid* returns, the *probability* that one loses money in the stock market falls with horizon (i.e. we require the probability that $R_n < 0$, where $R_n$ is the return over $n$ years). This 'shortfall probability' for *niid* returns and a horizon of $n$ years is given by the probability that the standard normal variable $z_n$ is less than $-n\mu/\sqrt{n}\sigma = -\sqrt{n}\mu/\sigma$, and this probability declines as $n$ increases. However, even if the shortfall probability is rather small over say, 10 or 20 years, this is surely not *sufficient* to make you invest heavily in the stock market, since you might still end up with little or no increase in your real wealth, and you might have been better holding riskless index government bonds. While it may be mildly reassuring to know that you at least 'get your money back' with high probability, this single consideration is unlikely to dominate your portfolio choice. However, that is not to say that mean and variance are necessarily the only inputs to your investment decision either. Different objectives (e.g. potential losses 'hurt' much more than equal gains, minimising the probability of very bad monetary outcomes) will give different investment choices – as we see later in the book.

An allied (but different) concept to the shortfall probability is (*percent*) *value at risk* (VaR). This is the maximum you *expect* to lose over a given horizon (e.g. 1 year), which will occur 5% of the time (e.g. 1 year in 20). If the mean annual equity return is $\mu$ (%) with standard deviation $\sigma$ (%) and returns are *niid*, then the percent VaR is $(\mu - 1.65\sigma)$, where 1.65 is the 5% left tail cut-off point for the normal distribution. For example, for $\mu = 6\%$ p.a. and $\sigma = 20\%$ p.a., the maximum you expect to lose 1 year out of every 20 is 27% (and in 19 years out of 20, you expect to lose less than this). Of course, the amount you actually lose in any one year is unknown – mere mortals can only make probability statements, only God is omniscient.

## Long-Horizon Returns

Above, we discussed the 'baseline' case of *iid* returns and its implication for portfolio choice. What is the evidence that returns are *iid*? Or are long-horizon stock returns mean-reverting, that is, higher than average returns are followed by lower returns in the future? Fama and French (1988b) and Poterba and Summers (1988) find evidence of mean reversion in stock returns over long horizons (i.e. in excess of two years). Fama and French estimate an autoregression where the return over the interval $t-k$ to $t$, call this $R_{t-k,t}$, is correlated with $R_{t,t+k}$

$$R_{t,t+k} = \alpha_k + \beta_k R_{t-k,t} + \varepsilon_{t+k} \tag{6}$$

Fama and French using monthly returns on an aggregate US stock index consider return horizons $k = 1$ to 10 years, using a long data set covering most of the 1900s. They found little or no predictability, except for holding periods of between $k = 2$ and $k = 7$ years for which $\beta$ is less than 0. There was a peak at $k = 5$ years when $\beta = -0.5$, indicating that a 10 percent negative return over 5 years is, on average, followed by a 5 percent positive return over the next 5 years. The R-squared in the regressions for the three- to five-year horizons are about 0.35. Such mean reversion is consistent with that from the 'anomalies literature', where a 'buy low–sell high', value-growth strategy yields positive profits (see Chapter 18).

Poterba and Summers (1988) investigate mean reversion by looking at variances of holding period returns over different horizons. If stock returns are random *iid*, then variances of holding period returns should increase in proportion to the length of the holding period. To see this, assume the *expected* (log) return is constant $E_t h_{t+1} \equiv E_t p_{t+1} - p_t = \mu$. Under RE, this implies the (log) random walk model of stock prices, and the return over $k$-periods is

$$h_{t,t+k} = (p_{t+k} - p_t) = k\mu + (\varepsilon_{t+1} + \varepsilon_{t+2} + \cdots + \varepsilon_{t+k}) \tag{7}$$

Under RE, the forecast errors $\varepsilon_t$ are *iid* with zero mean, hence

$$E_t h_{t,t+k} = k\mu \text{ and } \mathrm{Var}(h_{t,t+k}) = k\sigma^2 \tag{8}$$

Alternatively and more directly, if log returns are *iid*, then

$$\mathrm{var}(h_{t,t+k}) = \mathrm{var}(h_{t+1} + h_{t+2} + \cdots + h_{t+k}) = k\,\mathrm{var}(h_{t+1}) \tag{9}$$

The variance-ratio statistic is defined as

$$VR_k = \left(\frac{1}{k}\right) \frac{\mathrm{var}(h_{t,t+k})}{\mathrm{var}(h_{t+1})} \approx 1 + \frac{2}{k} \sum_{j=1}^{k-1} (k-j)\rho_j \tag{10}$$

which should be unity if returns are *iid* and less than unity under mean reversion (i.e negative autocorrelation coefficients $\rho_j$). With *iid* returns, the 'adjusted' Sharpe ratio is

$$SR_{t,t+k}/\sqrt{k} = E_t h_{t,t+k}/stdv(h_{t,t+k}) = \mu/\sigma \tag{11}$$

which should be constant for all horizons, $k$. If stock returns are mean reverting, then they are 'safer in the long run than in the short run', as the variance of long-horizon returns rises at a rate less than $k$. The Fama–French regressions, the VR-statistic and the Sharpe ratio are different ways of measuring the same phenomenon, namely mean reversion. Indeed, a sequence of small negative autocorrelations in returns can give rise to long-horizon mean reversion, and it can be shown that $VR_k$ (see (10)) and $\beta_k$ (see (6)) can be written in terms of the *sum* of these negative autocorrelations (see Cochrane 2001, p. 1373).

Using a long span of US data, Poterba and Summers (1988) find that the variance ratio is greater than unity for lags of less than one year and less than unity for lags in excess of one year, which implies that returns are mean reverting (for $8 > k > 1$ years). This conclusion is generally upheld when using a number of alternative aggregate stock price indexes, although the power of the tests is low when detecting persistent yet transitory returns. Work since Fama and French (1988b) has shown that the results using $VR_k$ and $\beta_k$ statistics are not very robust (Cochrane 2001). For example, for some periods (e.g. US 1947–1996 using aggregate stock indices), the $\beta_k$ coefficients for 3–5-year horizons are positive; nevertheless, the 'adjusted' Sharpe ratio remains constant as $k$ increases (indicating *iid* returns), while $VR_k$ is usually consistently less than unity (indicating mean reversion). However, for *individual* stock returns, the evidence for mean reversion is somewhat stronger. So, for aggregate US stock indexes, the different statistics used to measure mean reversion give different inferences in small samples, although there does appear to be some rather weak evidence of mean reversion at long horizons.

Under the null that returns are *niid*, the limiting distribution of $\theta(k) = VR_k - 1$ (Lo and MacKinlay 1988) for non-overlapping (log) returns is:

$$\sqrt{T}\theta(k) \sim N(0, 2k)$$

and for overlapping (log) returns

$$\sqrt{T}\theta(k) \sim N\left(0, \frac{2(2k-1)(k-1)}{3k}\right)$$

where $T$ = number of observations used and $n = k/12$ where $n$ = number of years and $k$ = number of months used in calculating $VR_k$. However, these statistics are not valid in small samples, and $VR_k$ is biased away from unity even when returns (i.e. price changes) are *iid*. Using 1000 MCS from an *niid* series calibrated to historic monthly returns, it can be shown that the median value of $VR_k$ for a 10-year horizon (overlapping monthly data) is 0.810 rather than unity, when using around 900 months (75 years) of data (Table 3, bottom of panel A). Hence, a point estimate of $VR_k < 1$ at a 10-year horizon does not necessarily signify mean reversion.

**Table 3**  Variance-ratio equity returns (excluding dividends)

| Country | 1 Year | 3 Years | 5 Years | 10 Years |
|---|---|---|---|---|
| **Panel A: Monthly data January 1921–December 1996** | | | | |
| US | 1.0 | 0.994 | 0.990 | 0.828 |
| UK | 1.0 | 1.008 | 0.964 | 0.817 |
| Global | 1.0 | 1.211 | 1.309 | 1.238 |
| Asymptotic test statistic 5%, 1-sided | – | 0.712 | 0.571 | 0.314 |
| **MCS (Normality)** | | | | |
| (a) Median VR | – | 0.960 | 0.916 | 0.810 |
| (b) 5th percentile | – | 0.731 | 0.598 | 0.398 |
| **Panel B: Monthly data January 1915–April 2004 (Dow Jones Industrial Average)** | | | | |
| US | 1.0 | 1.198 | 0.886 | 0.549 |
| **MCS (Normality)** | | | | |
| (a) Median VR | – | 1.178 | 0.860 | 0.499 |
| (b) 5th percentile | – | 0.690 | 0.432 | 0.168 |

Source: Author's calculations Panel B, Jorion (2003), Panel A.

Jorion (2003) using *aggregate* stock market indices on 30 different countries over 1921–1996 (Goetzmann and Jorion 1999) finds no evidence of mean reversion in real returns over 1–10 year horizons based on the MCS distributions for $VR_k$ (at 5% left tail significance level) for any of the 30 countries studied. In Table 3, the variance-ratio statistics for the United Kingdom and United States decline with horizon, but not very quickly. This result appears to be invariant to the inclusion or otherwise of dividends, when measuring returns. For markets that were interrupted (e.g. Russia, Germany, Japan), there tends to be mean *aversion* (i.e. $VR_k > 1$) – which means that the *global index* also shows mean aversion (Table 3, panel A, (a) and (b)). The asymptotic test statistics and the 5%, one-sided critical value from the MCS under the normality assumption (Table 3, panel A, (a) and (b)) indicate that the variance-ratio statistics reject the null of mean reversion.

We have incorporated more recent data than Jorion for the United States by using the Dow Jones index (industry average, monthly non-overlapping end-of-period data from January 1915 to April 2004) and find broadly similar results (Table 3, panel B). There is evidence of slightly greater mean reversion at 5- and 10-year horizons than in the Jorion data. Again the median $VR_k$ statistic is biased downwards under the null of no mean reversion (and normality), but the $VR_k$ statistics on the real data are larger than their 5% one-sided critical values from the MCS, thus confirming that statistically we can reject mean reversion at long horizons.

In terms of the absolute level of volatility, many markets are more risky than the US stock market, at most horizons. For the five-year horizon some of the volatilities (log price changes) found in the Jorion study are the United States 59.7%, Austria 82%, Finland 86%, Italy 78%, Japan 89%, Germany 94%, Portugal 155%, Philippines 212%, Brazil 228%, Chile 250%, Columbia 100% and Mexico 187%.

Using the *actual* empirical distribution of US real returns (rather than assuming normally distributed returns), Jorion (2003) finds that the probability of a loss for US stocks at horizons of 1, 5 and 10 years falls only slightly from 36.6% to 34.3% to 33.7% respectively when using price changes (i.e. capital gains) to measure returns (Table 4). When we include the average 3.8% dividend yield and repeat the calculation based on total returns (i.e. capital gains plus dividends) then as expected, these shortfall probabilities fall to 30.8%, 20.7% and 15.5% at 1-, 5- and 10-year horizons, respectively.

Which of these sets of figures is more representative of long-term risks? The figures that include dividends are from stock markets that were not closed down at some point, and hence there is a survivorship bias of around 150 basis points in the returns series. The shortfall probabilities do not take into account the fact that one can always invest in bills or bonds, and therefore it might be better to measure shortfall probabilities in terms of *excess* returns. Given a small positive real return on bills (or bonds) of, say, 1% p.a., this would offset some of the dividend yield and increase the shortfall probabilities for excess returns (relative to those for the 'raw' equity total returns).

We must also consider transactions costs and management fees. For index (tracker) funds, the management fees (currently) are around 50–100 basis points, and your chosen fund may of course underperform the index (by an average of 40–50 basis points for the S&P500 index funds according to Frino and Gallagher (2001) and therefore possibly by more for foreign index funds). For managed (mutual) funds, the transactions

**Table 4** Long-horizon risk and return: 1920–1996

|  | Probability of Loss | | | Value at Risk (5% Left Tail) | | |
|---|---|---|---|---|---|---|
|  | 1 Year | 5 Years | 10 Years | 1 Year | 5 Years | 10 Years |
| US (price change) | 36.6 | 34.3 | 33.7 | −27.8 | −45.5 | −51.2 |
| US (total return) | 30.8 | 20.7 | 15.5 | −24.5 | −33.7 | −22.3 |
| UK (price change) | 40.3 | 32.5 | 45.2 | −24.5 | −54.8 | −50.8 |
| UK (total return) | 30.1 | 22.1 | 30.8 | −24.9 | −47.8 | −45.1 |
| Median (price change) – 30 countries | 48.2 | 46.8 | 48.2 | −31.0 | −60.3 | −65.4 |
| Median (total return) – 15 countries | 36.1 | 26.9 | 19.9 | −24.7 | −39.9 | −34.8 |
| Global index (price change) | 37.8 | 35.4 | 35.2 | −20.8 | −40.4 | −41.1 |
| Global index (total return) | 30.2 | 18.2 | 12.0 | −16.7 | −19.8 | −11.2 |

Notes:

(1) The global index uses GDP weights.
(2) Total return is the % price change plus the % dividend yield.
(3) Statistics are calculated from the empirical distribution of returns.
(4) The median price change using total returns has less coverage as data is only available on dividends for 15 countries.

costs may be in the range 300–500 basis points and on average managed funds may not outperform index funds (see Chapter 9 for evidence on mutual fund performance). Hence, these transactions costs may partly or wholly cancel out the 3.8% dividend yield, so the shortfall probabilities after transactions costs may be closer to the figures using only the capital returns.

One must also be aware that the worst loss over any 5- or 10-year horizon in the United States was −56.4% (ending September 1934) and −60.7% (ending August 1982) respectively – these are 'big-hits' to take over such long horizons, and this is arguably the best-performing stock market in the world. The 5% lower tail, VaR figures (i.e. the maximum *expected loss*, which occurs 5% of the time – see Table 4 and Chapter 28) for US stocks using capital gains (total returns) are for a one-year horizon 27.8% (24.5%), for a five-year horizon 45.5% (33.7%) and for a 10-year horizon 51.2% (22.3%) (Jorion 2003). When we include our more recent data using the Dow Jones index (January 1915 to April 2004), the VaR figures are similar to those found by Jorion, so the recent crash has not had a major effect on the possible size of large losses on stocks over long horizons. This evidence clearly demonstrates that US stocks are very risky, *even over long horizons.* The 29 non-US economies taken together are even more risky (which is reflected in the 'median figures' in Table 4).

If we accept that risk does not attenuate over long horizons; it implies that young investors who trade off expected return against risk (standard deviation) should not hold a greater proportion of their assets in stocks than do older investors. (Of course, there may be other reasons why younger investors should hold more in stocks than older investors – see Chapter 16.)

There is some consolation, however – but not very much. The timing of the worst losses in the 30 different geographical markets is not perfectly synchronised. Some of the worst losses occurred around the 1930s, the second World War, the crash of 1974 and, for some developing countries, in the inflationary 1980s and latterly in the recent crash of 2000–2003. Hence, the global return index (using capital gains only) has volatility at one-year horizon of 16.1% (US = 20.89%). However, at longer 5- and 10-year horizons, the volatility of the global index at 52.87% (US = 59.74%) and 80.73% (US = 81.79) is not too different from the US figures. The probabilities of loss at the 5- and 10-year horizons for the global index are 35.4% (US = 34.3%) and 35.2% (US = 33.7%) respectively, about the same as the US figures, while the VaR for the global index at 5- and 10-year horizons is 40.4% and 41.1% respectively, which are slightly lower than the comparable US figures (Table 4). So, global diversification has slight benefits for a US investor and possibly greater benefits for non-US investors.

Although the evidence in favour of mean reversion is somewhat uncertain, this does not necessarily rule out predictability. $VR_k$ and $\beta_k$ are *univariate* tests of predictability and even if $R_{t,t+k}$ is not forecastable on the basis of any $R_{t-k,t}$, it may be influenced by other variables (e.g. dividend–price ratio, interest rates) in a *multivariate* regression. Cochrane (2001) cleverly shows how a plausible vector auto regressive (VAR) model in which there is a slow-moving *expected* return $h_{t+1}$, determined by a slow-moving dividend–price ratio, can imply very low *univariate*, mean reversion. The VAR gives rise to a univariate moving average representation of the form

$$h_t = \frac{(1 - \gamma L)}{1 - bL} v_t \tag{12}$$

$$= v_t - (\gamma - b)v_{t-1} - b(\gamma - b)v_{t-2} - b^2(\gamma - b)v_{t-3} + \cdots$$

If $\gamma > b$, then a positive shock $v_t$ sets off a string of negative returns, which give rise to mean reversion in the univariate return series. But this ultimately derives from a slow-moving variable affecting *expected* returns and is therefore not a violation of the EMH. Cochrane's VAR is

$$h_{t+1} = x_t + \varepsilon_{ht+1} \tag{13a}$$

$$x_{t+1} = bx_t + \varepsilon_{xt+1} \tag{13b}$$

$$\Delta d_{t+1} = \varepsilon_{dt+1} \tag{13c}$$

where $x_t$ is the slow-moving ($b > 0.95$) forecast variable (e.g. the log dividend–price ratio), $h_{t+1}$ is the return, and dividend growth is not forecastable. Cochrane shows that when $x_t$ determines $E_t h_{t+1}$, and there is zero correlation between dividend growth shocks $\varepsilon_{dt}$ and expected return shocks $\varepsilon_{ht}$, then $(1 - \gamma)/(1 - b) = 0.7$ in (12), which is in the ball-park of the actual long-run mean reversion found in the data. Hence, 'strong' multivariate predictability and low *univariate* mean reversion are not mutually exclusive.

## Power of Tests

It is always possible that in a sample of data, a particular test statistic fails to reject the null hypothesis of randomness even when the true model has returns that really are predictable. The 'power of a test' is the probability of rejecting a false null. Poterba and Summers (1988) provide a nice, simple pedagogic example of how to evaluate 'power'. To evaluate the power properties of the statistics $\rho_k$, $VR_k$ and $\beta_k$ Poterba–Summers set up a *true model* where stock returns *are* correlated. A MCS is used to generate artificial returns, and the test statistics for randomness are calculated. If these 'statistics' are powerful, they should reject the null of randomness in most cases. The true model has stock returns following an ARIMA(1,1) process. The logarithm of actual prices $p_t$ is assumed to comprise a permanent component $p_t^*$ and a transitory component $u_t$, and the permanent component follows a random walk:

$$p_t = p_t^* + u_t \tag{14a}$$

$$p_t^* = p_{t-1}^* + \varepsilon_t \tag{14b}$$

The transitory component $u_t$ is persistent.

$$u_t = \rho u_{t-1} + v_t \tag{14c}$$

where $u_t$, $\varepsilon_t$ and $v_t$ are not contemporaneously correlated. Poterba–Summers set $\rho = 0.98$, implying that innovations in the transitory price component have a half-life of 2.9 years (if the basic time interval is considered to be monthly). From the above three equations, we obtain

$$\Delta p_t = \rho \Delta p_{t-1} + [(\varepsilon_t - \rho \varepsilon_{t-1}) + (v_t - v_{t-1})] \tag{15}$$

Therefore, the model implies that log returns follow an ARMA(1,1) process. They then generate data on $p_t$, taking random drawings for the errors, with the relative share of the variance of $\Delta p_t$ determined by the relative sizes of $\sigma_\varepsilon^2$ and $\sigma_v^2$. They then calculate the statistics $\rho_k$, $VR_k$ and $\beta_k$ from a sample of the generated data of 720 observations (i.e. the same 'length' as that for which they have historic data on returns). They repeat the experiment 25,000 times and obtain the frequency distributions of the three statistics of interest. They find that all three test statistics have little power to distinguish the random walk model (i.e. the false 'null') from the above 'true model', which has a highly persistent yet transitory component.

## Autoregressive Moving Average (ARMA)

If weak-form efficiency does not hold, then actual returns $R_{t+1}$ might not only depend upon past returns but could also depend on past forecast errors (see (15) above) as in a general ARMA($p, q$) model:

$$R_{t+1} = k + \gamma(L)R_t + \theta(L)\varepsilon_{t+1} \tag{16}$$

where $\gamma(L)$ and $\theta(L)$ are polynomials in the lag operator; for example: $\gamma(L) = 1 + \gamma_1 L + \gamma_2 L^2 + \cdots + \gamma_p L^p$ and $L^n R_t = R_{t-n}$. Under the EMH, we expect all parameters in $\gamma(L)$ and $\theta(L)$ to be zero. Regressions based on ARMA models are often used to test the informational efficiency assumption of the EMH. In fact, Poterba and Summers (1988) attempt to fit an ARMA(1,1) model to their generated data on stock returns which, of course, should fit this data by construction. However, in their estimated equations, they find $\gamma_1 = 0.98$ and $\theta_1 = 1$, and because $\rho$ and $\theta$ are 'close to' each other, the estimation package often could not 'separate out' (identify) and successfully estimate statistically distinct values for $\rho$ and $\theta$. When Poterba and Summers do succeed in obtaining estimates, less than 10% of the regressions have parameters that are close to the (known) true values. This is another example of an estimated model failing to mimic the true model in a finite sample.

Cecchetti, Lam and Mark (1990) take up the last point and question whether the results of Poterba and Summers (1988) and Fama and French (1988b) that stock prices are mean-reverting should be interpreted in terms of the presence of noise traders. They note that serial correlation of returns does not in itself imply a violation of efficiency. Cecchetti et al. go on to demonstrate that empirical findings on mean reversion are consistent with data that could have been generated by an *equilibrium* model with time-varying expected returns. They take a specific parameterisation of the Consumption-CAPM (see Chapter 13) as their representative equilibrium model and use Monte Carlo methods to generate artificial data sets. They then subject the artificial data sets to the variance-ratio tests of Poterba–Summers and the long-horizon return regressions of Fama–French. They find that measures of mean reversion in stock prices calculated from historic returns data nearly always lie within a 60% confidence interval of the median of the Monte Carlo distributions implied by the equilibrium consumption-CAPM. Like all Monte Carlo studies, the results are specific to the parameters chosen for the equilibrium model. Cecchetti et al. note that in the Lucas (1978) equilibrium model, consumption equals output, which equals dividends, and their Monte Carlo study investigates all three alternative 'fundamental variables'. Taking dividends as an example, the Monte Carlo simulations assume

$$\ln D_t = \ln D_{t-1} + (\alpha_0 + \alpha_1 S_{t-1}) + \varepsilon_t$$

The term $S_{t-1}$ is a Markov switching variable (see section 7 and Hamilton 1989) that has transition probabilities

$$\Pr(S_t = 1|S_{t-1}) = p \qquad \Pr(S_t = 0|S_{t-1} = 1) = 1 - p$$
$$\Pr(S_t = 0|S_{t-1} = 0) = q \qquad \Pr(S_t = 1|S_{t-1} = 0) = 1 - q$$

Since $\alpha_1$ is restricted to be negative, $S_t = 0$ is a 'high growth' state, $E_t \Delta \ln D_{t+1} = \alpha_0$ and $S_t = 1$ is a low growth state, $E_t \Delta \ln D_{t+1} = \alpha_0 + \alpha_1$ (with $\alpha_1 < 0$). Therefore, $\ln D_t$ is a random walk with a stochastic drift $(\alpha_0 + \alpha_1 S_{t-1})$. The parameters of the dividend process are estimated by maximum likelihood and then used to generate the artificial series for dividends.

The Euler equation for the C-CAPM (with dividends replacing consumption-see Chapter 13) is

$$P_t U'(D_t) = \delta E_t[U'(D_{t+1})(P_{t+1} + D_{t+1})]$$

with preferences given by a power utility function $U(D) = (1 + \gamma)^{-1} D^{1-\gamma}$ with $-\infty < \gamma \leq 0$, the constant coefficient of relative risk aversion (CRRA). The Euler equation can then be written:

$$P_t D_t^\gamma = \delta E_t P_{t+1} D_{t+1}^\gamma + \delta E_t D_{t+1}^{\gamma+1}$$

which when iterated forward gives the solution

$$P_t = D_t^{-\gamma} \sum_{i=1}^{\infty} \delta^i E_t D_{t+i}^{1+\gamma}$$

Simplifying somewhat, the artificial series for dividends when used in the above equation (with representative values for $\delta$ and $\gamma$ the CRRA) gives a generated series for prices, which satisfies the C-CAPM general equilibrium model. Generated data on returns $R_{t+1} = [(P_{t+1} + D_{t+1})/D_t] - 1$ are then used to calculate the Monte Carlo distributions for the Poterba–Summers variance-ratio statistic and the Fama–French long-horizon return regressions.

Essentially, the Cecchetti et al. results demonstrate that with the available 116 annual observations of historic data on US stock returns, one cannot have great faith in return regressions based on, say, returns over a five-year horizon, since there are only about 23 non-overlapping observations. The historic data is therefore too short to make a clear-cut choice between an equilibrium model and a 'noise-trader' model. The Cecchetti et al. results do make one far more circumspect in interpreting weak-form tests of efficiency (which use only data on lagged returns), as signalling the presence of noise traders.

## 4.4 Multivariate Tests

The Fama–French and Poterba–Summers results are univariate tests. However, a number of variables other than past returns have also been found to help predict current returns. Early studies, for example, Keim and Stamburgh (1986), using monthly excess returns on US common stocks (over the T-bill rate) for the period from about 1930 to 1978 find that for a number of portfolios (based on size), the following (somewhat arbitrary) variables are usually statistically significant: (a) the difference in the yield between low-grade corporate bonds and the yield on one-month Treasury bills; (b) the deviation of last periods (real) S&P index from its average over the past 4–5 years and (c) the level of the stock price index based only on 'small stocks'.

They also find a 'pure' January effect in that the impact of (a)–(c) is different in January from other months. (They also find that the above variables influence the monthly rates of return on other assets such as government long-term bonds and high-grade long-term corporate bonds.) However, it should be noted that for monthly return data on stocks, the regressions only explain about 0.6–2% of the actual excess return.

Fama and French (1988b) examine the relationship between (nominal and real) returns and the dividend yield, $D/P$.

$$R_{t,t+k} = a + b(D/P)_t + \varepsilon_{t+k} \tag{17}$$

The equation is run for monthly and quarterly returns and for return horizons of 1–4 years, using the NYSE index. They also test the robustness of the equation by running it over various sub-periods. For monthly and quarterly data, the dividend yield is often statistically significant (and $\beta > 0$) but only explains about 5% of the variability in actual returns. For longer horizons, the explanatory power increases. For example, for nominal returns over the 1941–1986 period the explanatory power for 1-, 2-, 3- and 4-year return horizons are 12, 17, 29 and 49 percent respectively. The longer return horizon regressions are also found to be useful in forecasting 'out-of-sample'.

## Predictability and Market Timing

More recently, Cochrane (2001) using Shiller's data on *excess* stock returns, on US data 1947–1996, for a one-year horizon finds $b \approx 5$ (s.e. = 2) and $R$-squared = 0.15, while for a five-year horizon $b \approx 33$ (s.e. = 5.8) and $R$-squared = 0.60. We have used Shiller's US data from 1947–2002, and the actual and predicted (within sample) annual and five-year excess returns are shown in Figures 6 and 7 for data ending in 2002.

Clearly, the one-year returns are highly volatile, and the dividend–price ratio explains little of the variability in returns. At first glance, the five-year returns appear to fit the data better. The price–dividend ratio (Figure 8) is a slow-moving (persistent) variable that crosses its mean value about once every 20 years, and over the last 10 years (to 2002), has risen to unprecedentedly high values of around 70.

Returning to one-year returns (Figure 9), one can see that this equation in 1998 and 1999 was predicting a negative return (within sample), but these years experienced large price rises (partly due to the telecoms boom). Had you used this model to time the market, you would have missed two years of substantial price rises and also a very large price rise in 1995 (and may have been fired if you were a professional trader). By 2001 and 2002, the equation is 'back on track'.

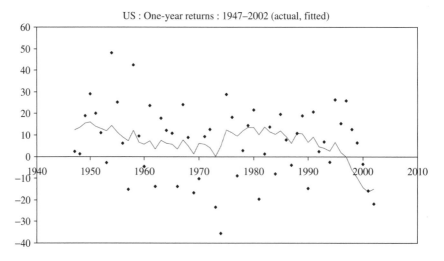

**Figure 6**  One-year excess returns

US : Five-year returns : 1947–2002 (actual, fitted)

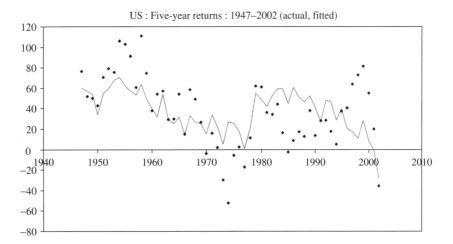

**Figure 7**   Five-year excess returns

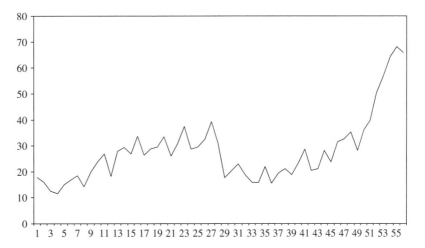

**Figure 8**   Price–dividend ratio: USA (1947–2002)

Outside-sample predictions may well be worse than the in-sample performance discussed above. Indeed, Cochrane (1997) estimates this returns equation up to 1996 (the latest data he had), as well as an AR(1) equation to predict the price–dividend ratio $(P/D)$:

$$R_{t+1} = a + b(P/D)_t + \varepsilon_{t+1} \quad b < 0$$

$$(P/D)_{t+1} = \mu + \rho(P/D)_t + v_{t+1}$$

Using the second equation to predict $(P/D)_{1997} = \mu + \rho(P/D)_{1996}$ and then $\hat{R}_{1998} = a + b(P/D)_{1997}$ etc., Cochrane finds that the equation predicts a $-8\%$ excess return for 1997, and after 10 years, the forecast is still $-5\%$ p.a. Clearly, Figure 9 shows that these forecasts are badly wrong for 1998 and 1999, which experienced rather high returns, but the 'outside-sample' forecasts come 'back on track' for 2000–2002.

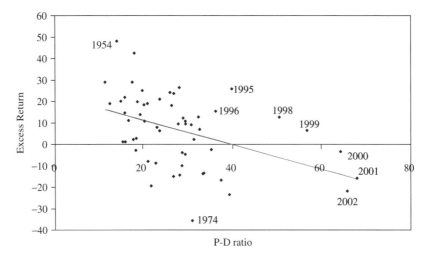

**Figure 9**   One-year excess returns and P–D ratio annual US data (1947–2002)

Certainly, given that the price–dividend ratio in the late 1990s is way above its historic mean value and given the slow movement in the dividend–price ratio in this data (i.e. the autocorrelation coefficient $\rho > 0.95$), the returns equation will predict negative returns for many years to come. But Figures 8 and 9 illustrate the problems of assessing return predictability. Remember that $\rho$ is biased and measured with error, so the persistence in the price–dividend ratio may be less than given by the point estimate. If the price–dividend ratio were not persistent at all (clearly not a truthful statement!), then it would return to its mean very quickly, and any *predicted* negative returns would last for only one period.

There is the possibility that the linear AR model for the price–dividend ratio is incorrect and a non-linear model is appropriate, so that the price–dividend ratio moves faster towards its mean value, if it is currently a long way from its mean. (We assume most of this move to its long-run equilibrium level will be due to price changes rather than dividend changes – since it has been found that the dividend–price ratio has little or no predictability for future dividend changes, Cochrane 2001.) Here we are positing a non-linear dynamic response of the price–dividend ratio, which we discuss in the next section. This implies fewer years of negative returns after 2002.

On the other hand, maybe from now on, the average long-run price–dividend ratio will be higher than its historic average (e.g. because of increased productivity due to the 'new' economy, which may have permanently raised future profits and hence prices relative to *current* dividends). This would also imply that future returns would not fall so drastically, as the price–dividend ratio would then have less distance to fall before it reaches its new higher mean value.

When we look at the return regression (Figure 9), it is possible that there may be a non-linear relationship between $R_{t+1}$ and $(P/D)_t$, and a better fit might ensue if the 'straight-line' actually flattened out at the extreme right-hand side (i.e. data points 2000–2002). If that were the case, then this new equation would predict a much smaller fall in prices in the future. To emphasise the fragility of these results, it is worth noting that Ang and Bekaert (2001), in a study of stock markets across the world, find that the dividend–price ratio has little or no forecasting power for stock returns when data for the late 1990s is included in the sample and the short-rate then becomes the most robust predictor of stock returns (also see Goyal and Welch 1999). All in all, this evidence should alert you to the fact that 'market timing' is a hazardous and risky occupation.

You should also be wary of statistics indicating 'strong predictability' at long horizons that could be misleading for two reasons. First, 'b' is biased (Stamburgh 1999). Second, where the forecasting variable $(D/P)$ is persistent, then as a matter of logic, if short-horizon returns are *very slightly* predictable with a 'small' coefficient, then longer-horizon returns regressions will have increasing values of 'b' and larger $R$-squareds. To see the former, consider

$$R_{t+1} = bx_t + \varepsilon_{t+1} \tag{18a}$$

$$x_t = \rho x_{t-1} + v_t \tag{18b}$$

where $x_t$ is very persistent (i.e. $\rho > 0.9$) and $x_t$ represents the forecasting variable (e.g. $x_t \equiv \ln(D/P)_t$). Then three-period (continuously compounded) returns, for example, are

$$(R_{t+1} + R_{t+2} + R_{t+3}) = b(1 + \rho + \rho^2)x_t + b(1 + \rho)v_{t+1} + bv_{t+2} + \sum_{i=1}^{3} \varepsilon_{t+i} \tag{19}$$

Hence, for $\rho = 0.9$ and $b > 0$, the coefficient on $x_t$ rises with horizon (as does $R$-squared – not shown here). The rising $R$-squared with horizon is a little illusory and mainly demonstrates that periods when the dividend–price ratio is high for long periods (i.e. prices are low) tend to be followed by high returns over the next five years or so. But the overlapping data problem when using annual data and a return over five years means that we really only have one-fifth of the observations we think we have, so predictability is a more contentious issue than it looks by just examining the usual statistics.

What is important is the temporal stability of any estimated coefficients. Certainly, you do not have to look far to find studies that show that return forecasting variables such as the dividend (earnings)–price ratio, the (detrended) T-bill rate, the yield spread, the default spread (i.e. corporate less T-bill yield) and the consumption–wealth ratio, have all been found useful at some time or other in 'explaining' the time-series behaviour of returns (over different horizons) – but the coefficients on these variables are not particularly stable (e.g. see Lettau and Ludvigson 2001a, Pesaran and Timmermann 2000). This means we have to be very careful in interpreting 'predictability' where there has been substantial search over alternative variables and specifications (i.e. data-mining). Clearly 'out-of-sample' forecast tests are useful here, to see whether the regression really does provide a 'market timing' advantage.

The EMH implies that abnormal returns are unpredictable, not that actual returns are unpredictable. Several studies find 'predictability', but as they do not incorporate a reasonably sophisticated model of equilibrium returns, we do not know if the EMH would be rejected in a more general model. For example, the finding that $b > 0$ in (17) could be interpreted within the EMH by asserting that $(D/P)$ is a proxy for changes in *equilibrium* expected returns (and there is some theoretical backing for this – see Chapters 12 and 13). To take another example, if, as in Keim and Stamburgh, an increase in the yield on low-grade bonds reflects an increase in investors' general perception of 'riskiness', we would expect a change in both equilibrium and actual returns. Here, predictability could conceivably be consistent with the EMH, although without a coherent theoretical model of equilibrium returns, such *ex-post* explanations can be a little feeble.

## 4.5   Cointegration and Error Correction Models (ECM)

As we shall see in a later chapter, stock prices $P$ are determined by the present value of expected future dividends $D$ and discount rates (i.e. one-period future returns). Hence, the dividend–price ratio should either predict future dividends or future returns or both. If *expected* future returns are not constant, then there is some theoretical justification for believing that the dividend–price ratio might predict future returns.

Suppose in long-run (static) equilibrium, $p = \ln P$ is proportional to $d = \ln D$, so the dividend–price ratio is constant $(= k)$. Deviations of $(p - d)$ from $k$ might then result in *changes* in the price. This is the basis of the ECM. We assume that the speed and direction of future change in prices depends on the disequilibrium in the 'long-run' price–dividend ratio. If the 'long-run' (log) price–dividend ratio $z = (p - d)$ is assumed to be constant, the 'standard' error correction model ECM is

$$\Delta p_t = \beta_1(L)\Delta d_{t-1} + \beta_2(L)\Delta p_{t-1} - \alpha(z - k)_{t-1} + \varepsilon_t \qquad \alpha > 0 \qquad (20)$$

where $\beta_i(L)$ is a polynomial in the lag operator $(i = 1, 2)$, and $k$ is the long-run equilibrium value of the (log) price–dividend ratio ($P/D$ is around 20 for annual data). When prices are high (relative to 'long-run' dividends), $(p - d) > k$, then $\Delta p_t$ is negative and prices fall next period, bringing $(p - d)$ back towards its equilibrium value. If $p_t$ and $d_t$ are non-stationary I(1) but are cointegrated, then $(p - d)_{t-1}$ should Granger-cause either $\Delta p_t$ or $\Delta d_t$. This is the *statistical* basis for forecasting equations like (20).

MacDonald and Power (1995) estimate an ECM like (20) using US annual data 1871–1987. They have to include the retention ratio (= retained earnings/total earnings) as well as dividends to obtain a stationary cointegrating vector. They find evidence of predictability within sample and obtain reasonable outside-sample forecasts (1976–1987) – although the latter may be due to the inclusion of a *contemporaneous* $\Delta d_t$ term. Similarly, Clare, O'Brien, Thomas and Wickens (1993) provide an ECM based on the gilt-equity yield ratio (*GEYR*). The *GEYR* is widely used by market analysts to predict stock returns (e.g. Hoare Govett 1991). The $GEYR_t = (C/B_t)/(D/P_t)$, where $C$ = coupon on a consol/perpetuity, $B_t$ = bond price, $D$ = dividends, $P_t$ = stock price (of the FT All-Share Index). It is argued that UK pension funds, which are big players in the market, are concerned about income flows rather than capital gains, in the short run. Hence, when $(D/P)$ is low relative to $(C/B)$, they sell equity (and buy bonds). Hence, a high *GEYR* implies a fall in stock prices, next period. Broadly speaking, the rule of thumb used by market analysts is that if *GEYR* > 2.4, then sell equity while for *GEYR* < 2, buy more equity and if $2 \leq GEYR \leq 2.4$, then 'hold' an unchanged position. A simple model that encapsulates the above is

$$\Delta \ln P_t = \alpha_0 + \beta GEYR_{t-1} + \sum_{i=1}^{3} \alpha_i \Delta GEYR_{t-i} + \varepsilon_t$$

In static equilibrium, the long-run *GEYR* is $-\alpha_0/\beta$ and Clare et al. (using quarterly data) find this to be equal to 2.4. For every 0.1 that the *GEYR* exceeds 2.4, then the estimated equation predicts that the FT All-Share Index will fall 5%:

$$\Delta \ln P_t = 122.1 - 50.1 \; GEYR_{t-1} + 48.1\Delta \; GEYR_{t-1} + 6.5\Delta \; GEYR_{t-2}$$
$$(3.7) \qquad (3.4) \qquad\qquad (2.4) \qquad\qquad\qquad (3.4)$$

$$+ \; 32.6\Delta \; GEYR_{t-3} + [\text{dummy variables for } 73(3), 73(4), 75(1), 87(4)]$$
$$(2.8)$$

$$1969(1) - 1992(2), \overline{R}^2 = 0.47$$

They use recursive estimates of the above equation to forecast over 1990(1) – 1993(3) and assume investors' trading rule is to hold equity if the forecast capital gain exceeds the three-month Treasury bill rate (otherwise hold Treasury bills). This strategy, using the above estimated equation, gives a higher *ex-post* capital gain of 12.3% per annum and lower standard deviation ($\sigma = 23.3$) than the simpler analysts' 'rule of thumb' noted above (where the return is 0.4% per annum and $\sigma = 39.9$). The study thus provides some prima facie evidence against weak-form efficiency; although, note that capital gains rather than returns are used in the analysis and transactions costs are not considered. However, it seems unlikely that these two factors would undermine their conclusions.

The above analysis has been replicated and extended by Harris and Sanchez-Valle (2000a, b) for the United States and United Kingdom using monthly data ending around 1997, and the above *GEYR* trading rule generates returns that exceed a buy-and-hold strategy (even after allowing for transactions costs) by around 1–3% p.a., but there is no correction for *ex-ante* risk. Clare, Priestly and Thomas (1997) use the UK *GEYR* to forecast returns on the FTSE100 but find no outside-sample predictability. The evidence is therefore rather weak that the *GEYR* can be used by 'market timers' to beat the market corrected for risk.

Cointegration and the Engle–Granger theorem has led to thousands of empirical studies that (a) seek to establish a set of cointegrating vectors (i.e. maximum of $n-1$), from a set of $(n \times 1)$, non-stationary I(1) variables, **x** (b) use the single equation ECM (or Johansen's (1988), VAR) or multivariate VECMs to demonstrate predictability for some or all of the **x** variables (i.e. Granger causality). Here, the scope for data-mining is vast, and one's faith in such results depends in part on a good statistical analysis (e.g. appropriate diagnostics, out-of-sample performance, etc.) and also on one's view of the 'theoretical' model behind such regressions.

For example, in the finance area alone, there are many studies that examine the predictability of spot FX-rates on the basis of either deviations from purchasing power parity, forward premia or uncovered interest party. Many studies of stock price predictability are based on cointegration between stock prices and dividends (or earnings), which then leads to a VECM where one of the equations 'explains' stock returns. Other studies are based on cointegration between different stock market indices (e.g. does the US stock market Granger-cause the Brazilian stock market, or vice versa) or on cointegration between stock indices and stock index futures prices or on the relationship between other macro variables such as inflation, interest rates and consumption–wealth ratios. The list is endless.

These are usually purely statistical relationships with rather weak (or very simple) theoretical underpinnings. It is as well to remind the reader that such predictability may not apply *ex-ante* and that allowing for transactions costs and the riskiness of trading strategies is of crucial importance. Unfortunately, the literature is so voluminous that one cannot draw general conclusions. But it is likely that any 'free lunches' discovered in the data may turn out to be rather more expensive than the investor bargained for when she uses the equation for *ex-ante* predictions. Later, we examine some 'market timing' strategies that have been carefully undertaken, including outside-sample forecasting performance.

## Cointegration and Persistence

Does the evidence that $P_t$ and $D_t$ often appear to be *not* cointegrated imply that the rational valuation formula (RVF) for stock prices is incorrect? Here, we use a Monte Carlo simulation to investigate this issue. If there is a *constant* discount factor, then stock prices are determined by $P_t = kD_t$ – this is the RVF (see Chapter 10). If $P_t$ and $D_t$ are I(1), then the RVF implies that $P_t$ and $D_t$ should be cointegrated. Empirical studies often find that neither $(P_t, D_t)$ nor $(\ln P_t, \ln D_t)$ are cointegrated, which rejects the RVF but only if expected returns are constant. Using MCS in a model in which dividends and expected returns vary over time and the RVF holds by construction, we can see why $P$ and $D$ might appear to be *not* cointegrated in a finite sample of data. If in our artificial data, standard tests indicate that $P$ and $D$ are not cointegrated, then time-varying returns provide one possible explanation of the non-cointegration found in the actual data even though the RVF holds. Reasonable data-generation processes for dividends and returns are

$$\ln D_t = \mu + \ln D_{t-1} + \varepsilon_{dt} \quad \varepsilon_{dt} \sim niid(0, \sigma_d^2) \tag{21}$$

$$(R_t - \overline{R}) = \rho(R_{t-1} - \overline{R}) + \varepsilon_{rt} \quad \varepsilon_{rt} \sim niid(0, \sigma_R^2) \tag{22}$$

Hence, $E_t D_{t+m} = \exp[m(\mu + \sigma_d^2/2)]$, and after some linearisation around $\overline{R}$ (Poterba and Summers 1986), the 'RE-price' is determined by the following general function.

$$\hat{P}_t = f(g, \overline{R}, \rho, R_t - \overline{R})D_t \tag{23}$$

where $g = \exp(\mu + \sigma_d^2/2) - 1$. Timmermann (1996) undertakes a MCS on (21) and (22), where he generates $\hat{P}_t$ using (23) and then tests for cointegration between either $(\hat{P}_t, D_t)$ or $(\ln \hat{P}_t, \ln D_t)$. He finds that when there is strong persistence in expected returns (i.e. $\rho$ greater than 0.6) but the RVF holds (by construction), then cointegration is frequently rejected (for almost any reasonable values of the volatility of dividends). Hence, rejection of cointegration does not necessarily imply rejection of the RVF, if expected returns are time-varying.

## 4.6  Non-Linear Models

In ECM models above, the effects of the disequilibrium $(d\text{-}p\text{-}k)$ on $\Delta p_t$ is symmetric and independent of the size of the disequilibrium. Non-linear models relax these assumptions. They often tend to be rather ad hoc in the sense that economic theory plays a role only in defining the long-run static equilibrium and the dynamics are determined by some non-linear response to this long-run equilibrium. Other non-linear models include chaos models that form a class of their own, in that they are deterministic, but the non-linearity produces a response that appears random. ARCH and GARCH models are non-linear in the second moment (i.e. variances and covariances) – see Chapter 29. Here, we concentrate on a popular set of ad hoc approaches that model the non-linear *dynamics*.

These non-linear models aim to relax the restrictions on dynamic behaviour found in the symmetric and proportionate response to disequilibrium in the above ECM model (while retaining the long-run equilibrium relationship). We begin with three forms of non-linearity commonly employed in empirical work: a threshold model, a spline model and the (quadratic) smooth transition autoregressive (STAR) model. These models are becoming increasingly popular in applied work, although it is worth remembering that they only deal with alternative dynamics and take the long-run equilibrium as given. They are stylised descriptions of the data, usually with fairly simple long-run equilibrium relationships (e.g. $p\text{-}d$ is constant in the long run).

### Threshold (asymmetric) model

This model is based on a 'switching' dummy variable, depending on whether the disequilibrium term $z_{t-1}$ is above or below some threshold value:

$$\Delta p_t = \beta_1(L)\Delta d_{t-1} + \beta_2(L)\Delta p_{t-1} \tag{24}$$

$$+ \alpha_1(DV_1 = 1, z_{t-1} > c_1)z_{t-1} - \alpha_2(DV_2 = 1, z_{t-1} < c_2)z_{t-1} + \varepsilon_t$$

where $DV_i$ are indicator variables taking the value 1 when the condition on $z_{t-1}$ is satisfied (and 0 otherwise). If $c_1 \neq c_2$, then for $z_{t-1}$ lying between $c_1$ and $c_2$, no adjustment occurs. The model can be estimated by OLS, conditional on a grid search over $c_1$ and $c_2$. Clearly, this model has symmetric effects if $\alpha_1 = \alpha_2$.

### Spline model

This model is a special case of (24) where we set $c_1 = c_2 = 0$, so there is no threshold but possible asymmetry of adjustment:

$$\Delta p_t = \beta_1(L)\Delta d_{t-1} + \beta_2(L)\Delta p_{t-1}$$
$$- \alpha_1(DV_1 = 1, z_{t-1} > 0)z_{t-1} - \alpha_2(DV_2 = 1, z_{t-1} < 0)z_{t-1} + \varepsilon_t \quad (25)$$

### STAR model

In this variant, the adjustment can have different speeds ($\alpha_1 \neq \alpha_2$), but the response to positive and negative disequilibria is symmetric:

$$\Delta p_t = \beta_1(L)\Delta d_{t-1} + \beta_2(L)\Delta p_{t-1} - \alpha_1 z_{t-1}[1 - F(z_{t-1})] - \alpha_2 z_{t-1}[F(z_{t-1})] + \varepsilon_t$$

$$(26a)$$

$$F(z_{t-1}) = [1 + \exp\{-\gamma(z_{t-1} - c_1)(z_{t-1} - c_2)\}/\sigma_z^2]^{-1} \quad \gamma > 0 \qquad (26b)$$

If $\gamma = 0$, the model is linear and as $\gamma \to \infty$, the model approaches the threshold model. For intermediate values of $\gamma$, the adjustment to disequilibrium is smooth.

### ESTAR model

A simpler version of the above model (assuming an AR(1) process) is the *exponential-STAR* model:

$$z_t = (\pi_o + \pi_1 z_{t-1}) + (\pi_1^* z_{t-1})F(z_{t-j}) + \varepsilon_t \qquad (27)$$

where $F(z_{t-j}) = 1 - \exp[-\gamma(z_{t-j} - c)^2/\sigma_z^2]$.

The term $\sigma_z^2$ is usually fixed at its sample mean value. $F(z_{t-1})$ is 'U-shaped' and bounded between zero and unity. If $z_{t-j} = c$, then $F = 0$, and (24) becomes a linear AR(1) model. As $(z_{t-j} - c) \to \infty$, the disequilibrium is very large and $F = 1$, so (27) becomes a different AR(1) model with the coefficient on $z_{t-1}$ being $(\pi_1 + \pi_1^*)$.

Essentially, the ESTAR models allow the adjustment speed to be different the further $z_{t-1} - c$ is from 0. Intuitively, one might expect adjustment to be faster, the larger (in absolute value) is $z_{t-1} - c$. For stocks, if one believes that $z = d - p$ adjusts mainly through changes in prices, then this would constitute the so-called *risky arbitrage hypothesis* (Chiang, Davidson and Okunev 1997). An alternative would be that the adjustment is slower when $z_{t-1} - c$ is large, because traders may have lost so much money while waiting for earlier mispricing to be reversed that they have fewer (borrowed) funds with which to arbitrage away large disequilibria (Shleifer and Vishny 1997) – this is the *limits to arbitrage* hypothesis. These two hypotheses are represented by

$$\pi_1 + \pi_1^* < \pi_1 \text{ 'risky arbitrage' and } \pi_1 + \pi_1^* > \pi_1 \text{ 'limits to arbitrage'} \qquad (28)$$

When estimating this type of model, there are several practical issues that arise:

(i) How do we determine if there are non-linearities of any kind in the data?

(ii) Choosing the lag lengths in the dynamics (i.e. $\Delta$ terms) and the single lag length for $F(y_{t-j})$

(iii) Estimation and convergence

(iv) Evaluating and testing the models

There are several pre-testing procedures to determine general non-linearity such as the BDS-test, the Ramsey reset test and several other tests (see Granger and Terasvirta 1993, Lin and Terasvirta 1994). Popular methods are to approximate the non-linearity in $z_t$ using a Taylor series approximation of some kind. For example, given the ESTAR model (24), we would pre-test using

$$z_t = \pi_o + \pi_1 z_{t-1} + \pi_2 z_{t-1} z_{t-j} + \pi_3 z_{t-1} z_{t-j}^2 + \pi_4 z_{t-1} z_{t-j}^3 + \varepsilon_t \qquad (29)$$

Then a test of linearity versus non-linearity is a test of $\pi_i = 0$ (for $i = 2 - 4$). The Ramsey reset test is similar in that $\hat{z}_t$, the *predictions* from the *linear* model are regressed on higher powers of $\hat{z}_t^q (q = 2, 3, \ldots)$ and the statistical significance of these terms assessed using standard Wald or LR tests. The above is not exhaustive – for example, one could fit a neural network to $z_t$ and then test for linearity (Lee, White and Granger 1993) and Chen (2003) provides a test (which has good power properties for $T > 100$) to discriminate between alternative STAR models (e.g. between LSTAR and ESTAR). Lag lengths are usually found by trial and error (e.g. using the partial autocorrelation function for $z_t$).

Estimation of the above models is usually by NLLS, although convergence problems can sometimes arise. Testing for cointegration (e.g. between $p$ and $d$) and hypothesis testing in the STAR models is not straightforward, but Monte Carlo simulation under the null of non-linearity is used to establish critical values (e.g. Corradi, Swanson and White 2000).

These non-linear dynamic models can easily be applied to any problem where there is a fairly straightforward equation for long-run equilibrium (e.g. purchasing power parity, expectations hypothesis of the term structure) but here we illustrate with the dividend–price ratio. As we know, the (log) dividend–price ratio is a very persistent variable with large deviations around its sample mean value. The ESTAR model can be used to examine whether adjustment of $z_t = (d - p)_t$ is faster, the larger are these deviations. Gallagher and Taylor (2001), using quarterly US data 1926–1997, find the AR(1)-ESTAR model (with $c = 0$, $j = 5$ in the F-function) has $R^2 = 0.70$ with a statistically significant $\gamma = -0.36$ ($t = 3.3$) and the risky arbitrage proposition holds – see (27) and (28). As the authors note, the linear model has an $R^2$ of 0.68, so the improvement here is not large. But the model does imply that the greater the distance $(d - p)$ is from its mean value, the faster the dividend–price ratio moves back to equilibrium. However, the model is agnostic on whether it is $\Delta p$ or $\Delta d$ that is doing most of the adjusting, since the dependent variable in their ESTAR model is $\Delta(d - p)_t$.

Clearly, the danger with these non-linear models containing variables that are highly persistent (i.e. borderline stationary–non-stationary) is that the non-linear results are generated by a few outliers or regime shifts in the data. For example, we know that after the crashes of 1929, the 1940s, 1974/5 and to a lesser extent 1987, stock prices rose quite *fast* and hence so did the price–dividend ratio. It would therefore be interesting to know how sensitive the 'whole-sample' results of such models are to these 'special periods'. One further caveat. It is well known that the mean of the dividend–price ratio was higher in the 1926–1950 period than in the 1950–1997 period and the non-linear effect found in the ESTAR model (which assumes a constant mean) may be the result of a 'regime shift' (see below) but in a *linear* dynamic model. Further work is needed on these models, although one's 'gut feeling' is that there are periods and situations where non-linear adjustment could be present.

## 4.7  Markov Switching Models

Markov switching models have been much in evidence in the macroeconomic and finance literature since the seminal work of Hamilton (1990). They are non-linear models that allow the data to be considered as being generated by two or more regimes or 'states' (e.g. 'high' and 'low' dividend–price ratio or interest rate regimes), but the regimes are unobservable. So, in the non-linear ESTAR type models, we have a constant coefficient model in which the dynamic response to the disequilibrium term is non-linear (but there is only one 'true' regime). With the Markov switching approach, the model can be linear in the parameters in each regime, but the stochastic nature of the regime shifts imparts a non-linear stochastic dynamic response as you switch between regimes. Essentially both approaches are less restrictive than the standard ECM/VECM constant parameter model, and they are simply alternative ways of providing more parameters in the model and hence giving the model more scope (loosely speaking, more 'freedom' to fit the data).

We consider only the two-regime case in our exposition (and owing to computational difficulties, the number of regimes considered in applied work is usually at most 3). The Markov property implies that the probability distribution of an *observed* variable $y_t$ lying in the interval {a, b} depends only on their state at time $t - 1$ and not on any earlier states. Suppose the *unobservable* state variable is $S_t$, then the Markov two-state process would be represented by

$$pr[S_t = 1|S_{t-1} = 1] = p_{11} \qquad pr[S_t = 2|S_{t-1} = 1] = 1 - p_{11}$$
$$pr[S_t = 2|S_{t-1} = 2] = p_{22} \qquad pr[S_t = 1|S_{t-1} = 2] = 1 - p_{22}$$

Thus, $p_{11}$ is the probability that $y_t$, which is currently in regime-1, will remain in regime-1. It can be shown that the series $y_t$ can be represented by

$$y_t = \mu_1 + \mu_2 S_t + (\sigma_1^2 + \theta S_t)^{1/2}\varepsilon_t$$

where $\varepsilon_t \sim N(0, 1)$. So, in state-1, the mean and variance are $(\mu_1, \sigma_1^2)$ and in state-2, they are $(\mu_1 + \mu_2, \sigma_1^2 + \theta)$. The unknown parameters that can be estimated using maximum likelihood are $(\mu_1, \mu_2, \sigma_1^2, \sigma_2^2, p_{11}, p_{22})$. The transition probability matrix **P** is the $2 \times 2$ matrix of the above probabilities. The *current* state probabilities are defined as $\pi_t = [\pi_{1t}, \pi_{2t}]$ where $\pi_{it}$ is the probability that $y$ is currently in state $i$. Given $\pi_t$ and the $(2 \times 2)$ probability matrix $\mathbf{P}$, then the probability that $y$ will be in a given regime next period can be obtained from $\pi_{t+1} = \pi_t P$, and it follows that $\pi_{t+k} = \pi_t P^k$.

Brooks and Persand (2001) provide an interesting example of a regime-switching model in which $y_t$ is the *GEYR* for the UK over the period January 1975 – August 1997. They note that the time series for the *GEYR* has periods of 'high' or 'low' values (as noted above), and the Hamilton filter gives statistically significant values for the parameters $(\mu_1, \mu_2, \sigma_1^2, \sigma_2^2, p_{11}, p_{22}) = (2.43, 2.07, 0.062, 0.014, 0.9547, 0.9719)$. Hence, there are different means and variances in the two regimes. Also there is less than a 10% chance of moving from a 'low' to a 'high' mean-*GEYR* regime – in the time series, this manifests itself in persistent (i.e. long) periods in which the *GEYR* either stays high or remains low.

Movements in the $GEYR = (P_t/B_t)(C/D_t)$ are dominated by $P_t$ and $B_t$, the price of stocks and bonds. A low *GEYR* essentially implies stock prices are low relative to bond prices (and relative to dividends). A trading strategy based on mean reversion would buy stocks when stock prices are low (and sell bonds). Essentially, if the *GEYR* is low (high), buy equities (bonds). (We will see this later in the value-growth stock picking strategy). Brooks and Persand (2001) use this type of trading strategy, but instead of looking at *GEYR per se* as their market timing 'signal', they use the forecast *probability* that the *GEYR* will be in a particular regime next period (see above). Hence, if the probability that *GEYR* will be in the low regime next period is greater than 0.5, this implies buying equities (otherwise hold gilts). The *forecast* probability for regime-1 (Engel and Hamilton 1990) is given by

$$p_{1,t+1|t}^f = \mu_2 + [\lambda + (p_{11} + p_{22} - 1)(p_{1,t} - \lambda)(\mu_1 - \mu_2)]$$

where $p_{1t}$ is the last *observed* probability of being in regime-1. A recursive regression and one-step ahead forecasts of $p_{1,t+1|t}^f$ are produced for 212 data points and the stock–bonds switching strategy is implemented. This is compared with a passive 'buy-and-hold' strategy for the stock index. The monthly average return for the passive and switching strategies (1980–1996) are 0.622% and 0.689%, with standard deviations of 2.14 and 1.58, and the Sharpe ratios are 0.089 (passive) and 0.16 (switching). But the switching strategy involves 16 'switches', and after taking account of transactions costs, the Sharpe ratio of the passive and switching strategies are almost identical. Results for the United States and Germany are less favourable to the switching strategy. While (as expected) Markov switching models tend to have a superior in-sample statistical performance compared to simple 'fixed parameter' time-series models (e.g. random walk, linear AR, MA(1)-GARCH), they tend to have relatively worse outside-sample forecast performance – which is due to the poor forecasts of next period's regime (Dacco and Satchell 1999).

## Markov Switching in a VECM (MS-VECM)

In principle, we can embed a Markov switching (MS) process in almost any constant parameter model, so if we augment a standard VECM linear model, we can write our

MS-VECM as

$$\Delta y_t = \mu(S_t) + \sum_{d=1}^{p-1} \psi_d(S_t)\Delta y_{t-d} + \alpha(S_t)z_{t-1} + \varepsilon_t$$

$$\varepsilon_t \sim ND(0, \Omega(S_t)) \qquad S_t = 1, 2, \ldots \text{regimes}$$

where $y_t \sim (n \times 1)$ vector of $I(1)$ variables (one of which could be the stock price, $p_t$), $S_t$ is the Markov switching variable and $z_t$ is the vector of cointegrating variables. For example, $z_t$ might be simply the log dividend–price ratio $(p_t - d_t)$ or it might be a stationary linear combination of the S&P500, the FTSE100 and the Nikkei 225 indexes or it might be the log of the futures minus spot stock indexes $f_t - s_t$ (i.e. 'the basis') for several countries (e.g. 3 cointegrating vectors $f_t - s_t$ for the spot-futures basis for the S&P500, FTSE100 and Nikkei 225). All of the above-mentioned $z_{t-1}$ variables might Granger-cause the change in the stock index $\Delta s_t$ (as well as the change in the other variables in the chosen cointegrating vectors).

Now, it is a well-established empirical fact that for most financial time series of price changes (e.g. for stock, bond and spot FX returns), the *conditional* distribution of $\Delta p_t$ (i.e. the $\varepsilon_t$ term) is non-normal and usually leptokurtic, fat-tailed and left-skewed). One way to model these non-normalities is to use time-varying conditional variances (and covariances), and these ARCH-GARCH models are discussed in Chapter 29. Alternatively, one can use non-linear functions as in ESTAR type models or the Markov Switching VECM (MS-VECM) model noted above, where the intercepts $\mu$, autoregressive dynamics $\psi_d$, the error correction coefficients $\alpha$ and the covariance matrix of errors $\Omega$ may all be regime-dependent. This more 'flexible' model might explain $\Delta y_t$ (particularly $\Delta p_t \subset \Delta y_t$) better than the standard VECM, both within sample and using out-of-sample forecasts and in predicting the shape of whole distribution (i.e. forecast density function).

A good example of the MS-VECM approach is Sarno and Valente (2004), who use weekly data 1989–2000 with $z_{it} = f_{it} - s_{it}$, where $\{s_i, f_i\} = \{$stock index, futures index$\}$ for $i =$ S&P500, Nikkei 225, FTSE100. They find that the outside-sample one-step-ahead forecasts from the MS-VECM model do not improve on the standard linear-VECM forecasts, in terms of mean absolute error (MAE) and root mean squared error. However, the proportion of correctly predicted *signs* of stock price changes in the outside sample one-step ahead forecasts are better for the MS-VECM model than for the linear-VECM model – this is a test of *relative* market timing.

Because we know the stochastic path of the covariance matrix and the regime-switching VECM parameters, we can produce the outside-sample forecast predictive density of stock price changes, week-by-week. The MS-VECM one-step ahead 'forecast densities' can be calculated analytically and are mixtures of multivariate normal distributions with weights given by the *predicted* regime probabilities – it is mainly the latter that impart skewness, kurtosis and heteroscedasticity.

Note that 'predictive' here does not imply a forecast, but the density in the chosen outside-sample period only (i.e. not the whole data period) given by the MS-VECM. The 'model' predictive density can then be compared with the true density in the data, over each forecast period. Sarno and Valente show that the MS-VECM mode gives an 'outside-sample' density, which is closer to the true density for stock price changes on the three stock indexes than does the linear-VECM. (It is good to see this confirmed, but the result is not too surprising, given that the MS-VECM is 'designed' to fit the known non-normality in the data, whereas the linear-VECM is not.)

It follows that if one is interested in the extreme tails of the distribution (i.e. at 1% level or less) for stock price changes $\Delta s_t$, then the MS-VECM model will more closely measure the change in price for this tail probability (and hence gives a better measure of the VaR at this significance level – see Chapter 28).

It is important to note what the Sarno-Valente paper does not say. There is no examination of market efficiency, only *relative* market timing (i.e. getting the sign of $\Delta s_t$ correct, more times than does an alternative model). There is no analysis of transactions costs and the riskiness of an investment strategy based on the MS-VECM approach. The $\overline{R}^2$ for the MS-VECM approach ranges from 0.08 (8%) for the Nikkei 225 index returns to 0.12 (12%) for the FTSE index returns (weekly data), and this is within sample. So outside sample, although the forecast (direction) of change improves with the MS-VECM approach *relative to* the linear-VECM, this tells us nothing about the *absolute* number of times either model forecasts the sign of $\Delta s_t$ correctly. Finally, note that the superior VaR performance of MS-VECM is for *one* asset at a 1% confidence level. In practice, financial institutions are interested in the potential loss over *many* assets, and they rely on some self-cancelling errors *across* assets in their portfolio, when calculating VaR. (Often they are also interested in the VaR at the 5% tail probability.) In practical terms, therefore, it is *portfolio* VaR that is important, not the individual asset's VaR, and we do not know if the MS-VECM model (applied to many assets) would provide an improvement over simpler approaches (e.g. a simple EWMA). What we do know is the MS-VECM model is horrendously more computer (and manpower) intensive than other methods discussed in Chapter 28, so it may remain an intellectual curiosus in the context of VaR. Of course, these models are largely a-theoretical and can be viewed as providing a relatively parsimonious description of the data. The only bit of 'finance' in the model is that riskless arbitrage ensures that $f_t = s_t$ (if we ignore the deterministic time to maturity $T-t$ in this relationship and the stochastic risk-free rate – see Cuthbertson and Nitzsche 2001b).

# 4.8 Profitable Trading Strategies?

When looking at regression equations that attempt to explain returns, an econometrician would be interested in general diagnostic tests (e.g. is the error term *iid* and the RHS variables weakly exogenous), the outside-sample forecasting performance of the equations and the temporal stability of the parameters. In many of the above studies, this useful statistical information is not always fully presented, so it becomes difficult to ascertain whether the results are as 'robust' as they seem. However, Pesaran and Timmermann (1994) provide a study of stock returns to meet such criticisms of earlier work. They run regressions of the excess return on variables known at time $t$ or earlier. They are, however, very careful about the dating of the information set. For example, in explaining annual returns from end-January to end-January (i.e. using the last trading day of the month), they use interest rates (or a term structure variable) up to the last trading day but industrial output data only up to December of the previous year (since it is published with a lag).

They looked at excess returns on the S&P 500 index and the Dow Jones Index measured over one year, one-quarter and one month for the period 1954–1971 and sub-periods. For annual excess return, a small set of independent variables, including the dividend yield, annual inflation, the change in the three-month interest rate and the term premium, explain about 60% of the variability in the excess return. For quarterly and monthly data, broadly similar variables explain about 20% and 10% of excess returns, respectively. Interestingly, for monthly and quarterly regressions, they find a non-linear effect of previous excess returns on current returns. For example, squared previous excess returns are often statistically significant, while past positive returns have a different impact than past negative returns on future returns. The authors also provide diagnostic tests for serial correlation, heteroscedasticity, normality and 'correct' functional form, and these test statistics indicate no misspecification in the equations.

To test the predictive power of these equations, they use recursive estimation (OLS) and predict the *sign* of next periods excess return (i.e. at $t + 1$) on the basis of esti- mated coefficients that only use data up to period $t$. For annual returns, 70–80% of the predicted returns have the correct sign, while for quarterly excess returns, the regres- sions still yield a (healthy) 65% correct prediction of the sign of returns. Thus, Pesaran and Timmermann (1994) reinforce the earlier results that excess returns are predictable and can be explained quite well by a relatively small number of independent variables.

Transactions costs arise from the bid-ask spread (i.e. dealers buy stock at a low price and sell to the investor at a high price), and the commission charged on a particular 'buy' or 'sell' order given to the broker. P-T use 'closing prices' that may be either 'bid' or 'ask' prices. They therefore assume that all trading costs are adequately represented by a fixed transactions cost per dollar of sales/purchases. They assume costs are higher for stocks $c_s$ than for bonds $c_b$. They consider a simple trading rule, namely,

*If the predicted excess return (from the recursive regression) is positive then hold the market portfolio of stocks, otherwise hold government bonds with a maturity equal to the length of the trading horizon (i.e. annual, quarterly, monthly).*

Note that it is the 'sign' of the return prediction that is important for this strategy, and not the overall (within sample) 'fit' of the equation (i.e. its R-squared).

The above 'switching strategy' avoids potential bankruptcy since assets are not sold short and there is no gearing (borrowing). The passive benchmark strategy is one of holding the market portfolio at all times. They assess the profitability of the switching strategy over the passive strategy for transactions costs that are 'low', 'medium' or 'high'. (The values of $c_s$ are 0, 0.5 and 1% for stocks and for bonds $c_b$ equals 0 and 0.1 percent.)

In general terms, they find that the returns from the switching strategy are higher than those for the passive strategy for annual returns (i.e. switching once per year in January) even when transactions costs are 'high' (Table 5). However, it pays to trade at quarterly or monthly intervals only if transactions costs are less than 0.5% for stocks.

**Table 5** Performance measures of the S&P500 switching portfolio relative to the market portfolio and T-bills (annual returns 1960–1990)

| | Portfolios | | | | | | | |
|---|---|---|---|---|---|---|---|---|
| | Market[1] | | | Switching[2] | | | T-Bills[3] | |
| **Transaction Costs (%)** | | | | | | | | |
| For stocks | 0.0 | 0.5 | 1.0 | 0.0 | 0.5 | 1.0 | – | – |
| For T-bills | – | – | – | 0.0 | 0.1 | 0.1 | 0.0 | 0.1 |
| **Returns and Performance** | | | | | | | | |
| Arithmetic mean return (%) | 10.780 | 10.720 | 10.670 | 12.700 | 13.430 | 12.210 | 6.750 | 6.640 |
| SD of return (%) | 13.090 | 13.090 | 13.090 | 7.240 | 7.200 | 7.160 | 2.820 | 2.820 |
| Sharpe ratio | 0.310 | 0.300 | 0.300 | 0.820 | 0.790 | 0.760 | – | – |
| Treynor ratio | 0.040 | 0.040 | 0.039 | 0.089 | 0.085 | 0.081 | – | – |
| Jensen's alpha | – | – | – | 0.045 | 0.043 | 0.041 | – | – |
| | – | – | – | (4.63) | (4.42) | (4.25) | – | – |
| Wealth at end-of-period[4] | 1,913 | 1,884 | 1,855 | 3,833 | 3,559 | 3,346 | 749 | 726 |

[1]The 'market' portfolio denotes a buy-and-hold strategy in the S&P500 index.
[2]The switching portfolio is based on recursive regressions of excess returns on the change in the three-month interest rate, the term premium, the inflation rate and the dividend yield. The switching rule assumes that portfolio selection takes place once per year on the last trading day of January.
[3]T-bills' denotes a roll-over strategy in 12 month T-bills.
[4]Starting with $100 in January 1960.
Source: Pesaran and Timmermann (1994), reproduced with permission from J. Wiley and Sons.

In addition, they find that the standard deviation of annual returns for the switching portfolio (Table 5) is below that for the passive portfolio (even under high transactions cost scenario). Hence, the switching portfolio dominates the passive portfolio on the mean-variance criterion over the whole data period 1960–1990.

The above results are found to be robust with respect to different sets of regressors in the excess return equations and over sub-periods 1960–1970, 1970–1980, 1980–1990. In Table 5, we report the Sharpe, Treynor and Jensen indices of performance for the switching and passive portfolios for the one-year horizon (see Chapter 7). For any portfolio 'p', these are given by

$$SR = (ER_p - r)/\sigma_{\mathrm{p}}$$

$$TR = (ER_p - r)/\beta_{\mathrm{p}}$$

$$(R_{\mathrm{p}} - r)_t = \alpha + \beta(R_m - r)_t + \varepsilon_t$$

The 'Jensen index' is the intercept $\alpha$ in the above regression. These three statistics are alternative measures of 'return corrected for risk'. The larger is *SR*, *TR* or $\alpha$, the more successful the investment strategy. One can calculate the *average* values of *SR* and *TR* for the switching and market portfolios. In general, except for the monthly trading strategy under the high-cost scenario, Pesaran and Timmermann find that these performance indices imply that the switching portfolio 'beats' the passive-market portfolio.

## Model Uncertainty

Pesaran and Timmermann (1995, 2000) extend the above analysis to include model uncertainty. Unlike the 1992 study, they allow the investor to choose the 'best' model at each point in time. A 'core' set of three variables (dividend–price ratio, interest rate and inflation) are always included, but a further set (change in interest rates, change in bond yield and January dummy) is tested at each point in time to obtain the best model. Also, if there is a residual 'outlier' of greater than three standard deviations, then a (0,1) dummy is added to the forecasting equation (and retained thereafter) – this applies for the 1974 and 1987 stock market crashes.

They use a number of alternative criteria to choose the 'best' model at each point in time (e.g. $\overline{R}^2$, Akaike and Schwartz criteria and 'within-sample' correct 'sign' pre-dictions). The switching strategy at $t$ is as in the earlier study, namely, buy the stock index if predicted excess returns $R_{t+1} - r_t > 0$, otherwise hold the risk-free asset. The 'passive strategy' is to hold the market index at all times.

Using recursive estimation on monthly data over 1960(11)–1992(2) for the United States and 1965(1)–1993(12) for the United Kingdom, the switching strategies (for all but the Schwartz selection criterion on US data) give higher Sharpe ratios than holding the passive market portfolio. For example, for the UK (1970–1993), the passive-market portfolio has a mean return of 20.8% p.a. and standard deviation of 36.5%, giving a Sharpe ratio of 0.33. The 'monthly' switching portfolios for 'high' transaction costs for either the Akaike or Schwartz or $R$-squared criteria give mean returns (standard deviations) of 15.8 (10.2), 18.8 (11.5) and 15.5 (10.5), implying Sharpe ratios of 0.69, 0.86 and 0.64, respectively (Pesaran and Timmermann 2000, Table 5). The Jensen's $\alpha$ (*t-stats*) for these three switching criteria are 0.061 (2.8), 0.090 (3.62) and 0.058 (2.58). In the 1980s, when markets were less volatile than the 1970s, the switching portfolios gave lower performance results but still beat the passive-market portfolio. The results are also very similar when the active strategy uses index futures rather than actual purchase of stocks. It is noteworthy that the switching portfolios did not 'lose' in the UK bear market of 1974 but neither did they 'win' in the sharp upturn of January–February 1975, since the model indicated that the investor should have been in T-bills in these periods. This may account for some of the overall success of the switching strategy.

Keen gamblers might like to note that the above results imply 'you have to earn your free lunch'. In some years, the switching strategy will lose money (e.g. for the UK data, the $R$-squared over the whole sample, without the 1974–1975 dummies, is only 0.12), and you would have had to get the crucial 1974-5 predictions correct. In years when you lose money, you would have to have enough capital (or borrowing facilities) to 'take the hit' and survive to trade another day. And of course, every month you have to perform a large number of regressions and hope that any predictability you find is genuine. For the United States, Pesaran and Timmermann (2000) find that there is no single model that performs adequately over the whole 1960–1992 period, and genuine outperformance (e.g. Sharpe ratio) based on an active (monthly) switching strategy, after taking account of transactions costs, is difficult to find.

It has been shown (Campbell and Viceira 1999, Brandt 1998, Kandel and Stamburgh 1996) that portfolio optimization in a multiperiod framework depends crucially on return predictability, where optimal portfolio weights change dramatically over time, as investors implement market timing strategies. The evidence from Pesaran and Timmermann suggests that such an 'active' portfolio strategy might be worth implementing.

## 4.9  Summary

- Univariate tests of return predictability (e.g. autocorrelation coefficients, autoregressive and ARMA models, regression-based tests, variance-ratio tests) show weak evidence of positive autocorrelation at short horizons (up to 6 months) and somewhat stronger evidence of long-horizon mean reversion (over 3–8 year horizon), for aggregate stock indexes. Results differ for different tests and in part, this is because the small sample properties of the test statistics differ but also because such univariate properties may not be constant over time. The power of univariate tests is not particularly good.

- Multivariate tests of 'market timing' indicate that (real) stock returns and excess returns are predictable. Again, this predictability is subject to much uncertainty and may sometimes 'disappear' in out-of-sample forecast tests.

- Models with non-linear dynamics or incorporating regime changes or just recursive updating of parameters indicate rather weak out-of-sample predictability, but Markov switching models pick up the non-normality in the conditional distribution of stock returns.

- There is some evidence that active trading strategies (market timing) based on the predictions from regression equations, may result in returns corrected for *(ex-post)* risk and dealing costs, which exceed those for a passive strategy but only over certain data periods.

- The key question for the validity or otherwise of the EMH is whether profits, when corrected for transactions costs and *ex-ante* risk, remain positive over a run of 'bets'. On the basis of *ex-post* outcomes, there is certainly evidence that this might well be the case, although it can always be argued that methods used to correct for the risk of the portfolio are inadequate.

- This chapter has been mainly about the statistical properties of returns – we have not really mentioned finance theory. We have found that individual and aggregate stock prices (returns) are highly volatile. In Chapters 10 and 11, we explore whether various 'rational' economic models based on 'fundamentals' can explain this high volatility – if the theories fail to explain this phenomenon, we say we have *excess volatility* or a *volatility puzzle*.

- Similarly, the high observed equity premium (and its high volatility) and the low variability in interest rates should be capable of being explained by 'economic fundamentals' – that are sources of risk which affect investors. The fact that some 'standard models' do not explain these two empirical facts has become known as the *equity premium puzzle* and the *risk-free rate puzzle* respectively, and these issues are extensively discussed in Chapters 13 and 14.

- We have also noted the positive autocorrelation in returns at short horizons and the negative autocorrelation at long horizons (i.e. mean reversion) – these phenomena will also need to be explained by our theories. It is a pretty tall order to develop a general model with rational informed investors who maximize their 'welfare' subject to constraints (e.g. you cannot consume more than your lifetime wealth), which can explain *all* of these stylized facts.

- There are also more startling 'facts' that turn up in Chapter 18, known as *anomalies*, which we would also like our theory to explain. In this, financial economists are a little like physicists, looking for a general model that can encompass all these diverse empirical findings. In future chapters, we see how successful they have been.

- The implications of return predictability and volatility for portfolio asset allocation are discussed in Chapters 5 and 6 for a static model and for intertemporal models in Chapters 15 and 16.

# 5

## MEAN-VARIANCE PORTFOLIO THEORY AND THE CAPM

## Aims

- Explain how investors who trade off expected return and risk will hold a diversified portfolio of risky assets. This gives rise to the *efficient frontier*.

- Determine how much an individual investor will borrow (or lend) at the safe rate in order to increase (decrease) her exposure to the 'bundle' of risky assets. This is, in part, determined by the *capital market line* (*CML*), which together with the efficient frontier allows us to calculate the *optimal* proportions in which to hold the risky assets. This is the *mean-variance model* of portfolio choice, and these optimal proportions constitute the *market portfolio*.

- Analyse the determinants of the equilibrium expected return on an *individual* security, so that all the risky assets are willingly held by 'mean-variance' investors. This gives rise to the *capital asset pricing model, CAPM*, where the risk premium depends on the *asset's 'beta'*.

## 5.1 An Overview

We restrict our world to one in which agents can choose a set of risky assets (stocks) and a risk-free asset (e.g. fixed-term bank deposit or a three-month Treasury Bill). Agents can borrow and lend as much as they like at the risk-free rate. We assume agents like higher expected returns but dislike risk (i.e. they are risk-averse). The expected return on an *individual* security we denote $ER_i$ and we assume that the risk on an *individual* security $i$ can be measured by the variance of its return $\sigma_i^2$. All individuals have homogeneous expectations about the expected returns, the variances and covariances (correlation) between the various returns. Transaction costs and taxes are assumed to be zero.

Consider the reason for holding a diversified portfolio consisting of a set of risky assets. Assume for the moment that funds allocated to the safe asset have already been fixed. Putting all your wealth in asset $i$, you incur an expected return $ER_i$ and a risk $\sigma_i^2$. Let us assume a two-asset world where there is a negative covariance of returns $\sigma_{12} < 0$. Hence, when the return on asset-1 rises, that on asset-2 tends to fall. (This also implies a negative correlation coefficient $\rho_{12} = \sigma_{12}/\sigma_1\sigma_2$.) Hence, if you diversify and hold both assets, this would seem to reduce the variance of the *overall* portfolio (i.e. of asset-1 plus asset-2). To simplify even further, suppose that $ER_1 = ER_2$ and $\sigma_1^2 = \sigma_2^2$ and, in addition, assume that when the return on asset-1 increases by 1%, that on asset-2 always falls by 1% (so, $\rho_{12} = -1$). Under these conditions, when you hold half your initial wealth in each of the risky assets, the expected return on the overall portfolio is $ER_1 = ER_2$. However, diversification has reduced the risk on the portfolio to zero: an above-average return on asset-1 is always matched by an equal below average return on asset-2 (since $\rho_{12} = -1$). Our example is, of course, a special case but, in general, even if the covariance of returns are zero or positive (but not perfectly positively correlated), it still pays to diversify and hold a combination of both assets.

The above simple example also points to the reason why *each* individual investor might at least hold *some* of each of *all* the available stocks in the market, if we allow him to borrow (or lend) unlimited funds at the risk-free rate $r$. To demonstrate this point, we set up a counter example. If *one* stock were initially not desired by any of the investors, then its current price would fall as investors sold it. However, a fall in the current price implies that the *expected return* over the coming period is higher, *ceteris paribus* (assuming one expected it to pay some dividends in the future). One might therefore see the current price fall until the expected return increases so that the stock is sufficiently attractive to hold.

The reader may now be thinking that the individual investor's tastes or preferences must come into the analysis at some point. However, there is a quite remarkable result, known as the *separation theorem*. The investment decision can be broken down into two separate decisions. The first decision concerns the choice of the *optimal proportions* $w_i^*$ of risky assets held, and this is *independent of the individual's preferences* concerning his subjective trade-off between risk and return. This choice only depends on the individual's views about the objective market variables, namely, expected returns, variances and covariances. If expectations about these variables are assumed to be homogeneous across investors, then *all* individuals hold the same proportions of the risky assets (e.g. all investors hold 1/20 of 'A-shares', 1/80 of 'B-shares', etc.) irrespective of their risk preferences. Hence aggregating, all individuals will hold these risky assets in the same proportions as in the *(aggregate)* market portfolio (e.g. if the share of AT&T in the total stock market index is 1/20 by value, then all investors hold 1/20 of their own risky asset portfolio in AT&T shares).

It is only after determining their optimal market portfolio that the individual's preferences enter the calculation. In the second-stage of the decision process, the individual decides how much to borrow (lend) in order to augment (reduce the amount of) his own initial wealth invested (in fixed proportions) in the market portfolio of risky assets. It is at this point that the individual's preferences enter the decision process. If the individual is *very* risk averse, she will use most of her own wealth to invest in the risk-free asset (which pays $r$) and only invest a small amount of her own wealth in the risky assets in the fixed proportions $w_i^*$. The converse applies to a less risk-averse person, who will *borrow* at the risk-free rate and use these proceeds (as well as her own initial wealth) to invest in the fixed bundle of risky assets in the optimal proportions. Note, however, this second-stage, which involves the individual's preferences, does not impinge on the *relative demands* for the risky assets (i.e. the proportions $w_i^*$). Since relative demands for the risky assets determine *equilibrium expected returns*, the latter are independent of individuals' preferences (and depend only on objective market variables as such variances and covariances of returns).

Throughout this and subsequent chapters, we shall use the following equivalent ways of expressing expected returns, variances and covariances:

$$\text{Expected return} = \mu_i \equiv ER_i$$

$$\text{Variance of returns} = \sigma_i^2 \equiv \text{var}(R_i)$$

$$\text{Covariance of returns} = \sigma_{ij} \equiv \text{cov}(R_i, R_j)$$

## CAPM and Beta

Let us turn now to some specific results about equilibrium returns that arise from the CAPM. The CAPM provides an elegant model of the determinants of the equilibrium expected return $ER_{it}$ on any *individual* risky asset in the market. It predicts that the expected excess return on an individual risky asset $(ER_i - r)_t$ is directly related to the expected excess return on the market portfolio $(ER_m - r)_t$, with the constant of proportionality given by the *beta* of the individual risky asset:

$$(ER_i - r)_t = \beta_i(ER_m - r)_t \tag{1}$$

where beta

$$\beta_i = \text{cov}(R_{it}, R_{mt}) / \text{var}(R_{mt}) \tag{2}$$

The CAPM explains the expected excess return on asset $i$, given the expected market excess return. Therefore, the CAPM does not 'explain' the market return – for this, we require a more elaborate model (see the SDF in Chapter 13). The CAPM is *not* a predictive equation for the return on asset $i$, since both the dependent and independent variables are dated at time $t$. Rather, the CAPM implies that *contemporaneous* movements in $(ER_i - r)_t$ are linked to *contemporaneous* changes in the excess market return.

$ER_{mt}$ is the expected return on the market portfolio and is the 'average' return from holding *all* assets in the optimal proportions $w_i^*$. Since actual returns on the market portfolio differ from expected returns, the variance $\text{var}(R_{mt})$ on the market portfolio is non-zero. The definition of firm $i$'s beta, $\beta_i$ indicates that equilibrium expected return of asset $i$ depends on:

(i)  the covariance between the return on security $i$ and the market portfolio, $\text{cov}(R_{it}, R_{mt})$

(ii)  is inversely related to the variance of the market portfolio, $\text{var}(R_{mt})$.

Loosely speaking, if the *ex-post* (or actual) returns *when averaged*, approximate the *ex-ante* expected return $ER_{it}$, then we can think of the CAPM as explaining the average return (over say a number of months) on security $i$.

To put the CAPM intuitively, consider the following. The standard deviation of the return on asset-A is 20% p.a. and the beta of A is 1.5. Asset-B has a return standard deviation of 60% and a beta of 0.75. You are considering holding only *one* asset, either A or B (and you have no other risky assets). Ask yourself on which asset would you want a higher average return? Well, asset-B has a much larger standard deviation of return than A, so presumably you would be happy with a higher average return on B (relative to A) because of its higher (individual) risk. Your hunch would be correct.

Now consider a slightly different question. Suppose you already hold a number of risky assets (say 25) and you are considering adding either A or B to your existing portfolio. Now, on which asset do you require the higher average return? Well, A has a beta of 1.5 and B has a beta of 0.75. Beta is proportional to the covariance (correlation) between the asset return (A or B) and the *existing* portfolio of assets you hold. The lower is beta, the lower is this correlation and therefore the less the increase in *portfolio* risk (standard deviation), if you include this asset in your portfolio. Hence, because B adds little to *portfolio* risk (compared with A), you are willing to add B to your portfolio, even if it has a relatively low average return. So, it is *incremental* portfolio risk that is important in determining average returns, not the risk of the asset in isolation (i.e. its standard deviation). This is the conceptual link between portfolio theory and the CAPM and why beta is the correct measure of security's risk, when the security is held as part of a well-diversified portfolio.

There is another intuitive point to make here. Asset-B's return has a standard deviation of 60% and a beta of 0.75 and we have agreed that when held as part of a well-diversified portfolio, asset-B will be willingly held even though it has a lower expected return than asset-A (with standard deviation of 20% p.a. and beta of 1.5). How is the very large standard deviation of asset-B influencing *portfolio* standard deviation? Well, much of the *individual* risk of this stock is 'diversified away' at almost zero cost, when you include this stock along with other stocks in a diversified portfolio. Therefore, you should receive no reward (i.e. higher average return) on the basis of stock-B's high *individual* standard deviation. The CAPM implies that you should only receive a reward, that is, an average return, on the basis of how much stock-B contributes to the risk of your *whole* portfolio – and this is given by its beta.

What does the CAPM tell us about the absolute level of equilibrium returns on individual securities in the stock market? First, note that $ER_m - r > 0$, otherwise no risk-averse agent would hold the market portfolio of risky assets when he could earn more, *for certain*, by investing all his wealth in the risk-free asset.

Returns on individual stocks (within the same country) tend to move in the same direction and hence, empirically $\text{cov}(R_{it}, R_{mt}) \geq 0$ and $\beta_i > 0$. The CAPM predicts that for those stocks that have a zero covariance with the market portfolio, they will be willingly held as long as they have an expected return equal to the risk-free rate (put $\beta_i = 0$ in (1)). Securities that have a large positive covariance with the market return ($\beta_i > 0$) will have to earn a relatively high expected return: this is because the addition of such a security to the portfolio does little to reduce *overall portfolio* variance.

The CAPM also allows one to assess the relative volatility of the expected returns on individual stocks on the basis of their $\beta_i$ values (which we assume are accurately measured). Stocks for which $\beta_i = 1$ have a return that is expected to move one-for-one with the market portfolio (i.e. $ER_i = ER_m$) and are termed *neutral stocks*. If $\beta_i > 1$, the stock is said to be an 'aggressive stock' since it moves *more* than changes in the expected market return (either up or down) and conversely 'defensive stocks' have $\beta_i < 1$. Therefore, investors can use betas to rank the relative safety of various securities. However, the latter should not detract from one of portfolio theory's key predictions, namely, that *all* investors should hold stocks in the same optimal proportions $w_i^*$. This will include neutral, aggressive and defensive stocks. An investor who wishes to 'take a position' in particular stocks may use betas to rank the stocks to include in her portfolio (i.e. she does not obey the assumptions of the CAPM and therefore does not attempt to mimic the market portfolio). The individual's portfolio beta (of $n$ assets) is $\beta_p = \sum_{i=1}^{n} w_i \beta_i$.

## 5.2   Mean-Variance Model

We assume that the investor would prefer a higher expected return $ER$ rather than a lower expected return, but she dislikes risk (i.e. is risk-averse). We choose to measure risk by the portfolio variance. Thus, if the agent is presented with a portfolio-A (of $n$ securities) and a portfolio-B (of a different set of securities), then according to the mean-variance criteria (MVC) portfolio-A is preferred to portfolio-B if

$$ER_A \geq ER_B \qquad \text{(i)}$$

and

$$\text{var}(R_A) \leq \text{var}(R_B) \text{ or } \text{SD}(R_A) \leq \text{SD}(R_B) \qquad \text{(ii)}$$

where SD = standard deviation. Of course, if, for example, $ER_A > ER_B$ but $\text{var}(R_A) > \text{var}(R_B)$, then we cannot say what portfolio the investor prefers using the MVC. Portfolios that satisfy the MVC are known as the set of *efficient portfolios*. Portfolio-A that has a lower expected return *and* a higher variance than another portfolio-B is said to be 'inefficient', and an individual would (in principle) never hold portfolio-A, if portfolio-B is available.

We wish to demonstrate in a simple fashion the gains to be made from holding a diversified portfolio of assets and initially assume only two (risky) assets. The actual return (over one period) on each of the two assets is $R_1$ and $R_2$ with *expected* returns $\mu_1 = ER_1$ and $\mu_2 = ER_2$. The variance of the returns on each security is $\sigma_i^2 = E(R_i -$

$\mu_i)^2$. Assume that the correlation coefficient between the returns is $\rho(-1 \leq \rho \leq 1)$ where

$$\rho = \sigma_{12}/\sigma_1\sigma_2 \quad \text{and} \quad \sigma_{12} = E[(R_1 - \mu_1)(R_2 - \mu_2)] \tag{3}$$

$\sigma_{12} = \text{cov}(R_1, R_2)$ is the covariance between the two returns. If $\rho = +1$, the two-asset returns are perfectly positively (linearly) related, and the asset returns *always* move in the same direction. For $\rho = -1$, the converse applies, and for $\rho = 0$, the asset returns are not (linearly) related. As we see below, the 'riskiness' of the portfolio consisting of both asset-1 and asset-2 depends crucially on the sign and size of $\rho$. If $\rho = -1$, risk can be completely eliminated by holding a specific proportion of initial wealth in *both* assets. Even if $\rho$ is positive (but less than $+1$), the riskiness of the overall portfolio is reduced by diversification (although not to zero).

## Minimum Variance 'Efficient' Portfolios

Suppose for the moment that the investor chooses the proportion of his total wealth to invest in each asset in order to *minimise portfolio risk*. He is not, at this stage, allowed to borrow or lend or place any of his wealth in a *risk-free* asset. Should the investor put 'all his eggs in one basket' and place *all* of his wealth either in asset-1 or asset-2 and incur risk of either $\sigma_1$ or $\sigma_2$ or should he hold some of his wealth in each asset, and if so, how much of each? Suppose the investor chooses to hold a proportion $w_1$ of his wealth in asset-1 and a proportion $w_2 = 1 - w_1$ in asset-2. The *actual return* on this diversified portfolio (which will not be revealed until one period later) is

$$R_p = w_1 R_1 + w_2 R_2 \tag{4}$$

The *expected return* on the portfolio (formed at the beginning of the period) is defined as

$$ER_p = w_1 ER_1 + w_2 ER_2 = w_1\mu_1 + w_2\mu_2 \tag{5}$$

The *variance of the portfolio* is given by

$$\sigma_p^2 = E(R_p - ER_p)^2 = E[w_1(R_1 - \mu_1) + w_2(R_2 - \mu_2)]^2$$
$$= w_1^2\sigma_1^2 + w_2^2\sigma_2^2 + 2w_1w_2\rho\sigma_1\sigma_2 \tag{6}$$

For the moment, we are assuming the investor is not concerned about expected return when choosing $w_i$. To minimise portfolio risk, $\sigma_p^2$, we substitute $w_2 = 1 - w_1$ and differentiate with respect to the one unknown $w_1$:

$$\frac{\partial \sigma_p^2}{\partial w_1} = 2w_1\sigma_1^2 - 2(1 - w_1)\sigma_2^2 + 2(1 - 2w_1)\rho\sigma_1\sigma_2 = 0 \tag{7}$$

Solving (7) for $w_1$, we have

$$w_1 = \frac{(\sigma_2^2 - \rho\sigma_1\sigma_2)}{(\sigma_1^2 + \sigma_2^2 - 2\rho\sigma_1\sigma_2)} = \frac{(\sigma_2^2 - \sigma_{12})}{(\sigma_1^2 + \sigma_2^2 - 2\sigma_{12})} \tag{8}$$

Note that from (8), 'portfolio variance' will be smallest when $\rho = -1$ and largest when $\rho = +1$ (assuming the $w_i$ are both positive). For illustrative purposes, assume $\sigma_1^2 = (0.4)^2$, $\sigma_2^2 = (0.5)^2$, $\rho = 0.25$ (i.e. positive correlation). Then the value of $w_1$ for minimum variance is

$$w_1 = \frac{(0.5)^2 - 0.25(0.4)(0.5)}{(0.4)^2 + (0.5)^2 - 2(0.25)(0.4)(0.5)} = \frac{20}{31} \tag{9}$$

and substituting this value of $w_1$ in (6), we have, $\sigma_p^2 = 12.1\%$, which is smaller than the variance if all his wealth had been put in asset-1 $\sigma_1^2 = (0.4)^2 = 16\%$ or all in asset-2, $\sigma_2^2 = (0.5)^2 = 25\%$. Note that, in general, the minimum variance portfolio has a positive expected return, here $ER_p = (20/31)ER_1 + (11/31)ER_2$, although $w_i$ was chosen independently of a *desired* expected return.

For the special case where $\rho = -1$, then using (8), we obtain $w_1 = 5/9$ and substituting this value in (6), we obtain $\sigma_p^2 = 0$. Thus, all risk can be diversified when the two-asset returns are perfectly negatively correlated. It follows from this analysis that an individual asset may be highly risky *taken in isolation* (i.e. its own variance of returns is high) but if it has a negative covariance with assets already held in the portfolio, then investors will be willing to add it to their existing portfolio even if its expected return is relatively low since such an asset tends to reduce *overall* portfolio risk $\sigma_p^2$. This basic intuitive notion lies behind the explanation of determination of equilibrium asset returns in the CAPM.

## Principle of Insurance

Generalising the above, from equation (6) for $n$ assets, we have

$$\sigma_p^2 = \sum_{i=1}^{n} w_i^2 \sigma_i^2 + \sum_{i=i}^{n} \sum_{\substack{j=1 \\ i \neq j}}^{n} w_i w_j \rho_{ij} \sigma_i \sigma_j$$

For the special case where asset returns are totally uncorrelated (i.e. all $n$ assets have $\rho_{ij} = 0$), the portfolio variance can be reduced to

$$\sigma_p^2 = (w_1^2 \sigma_1^2 + w_2^2 \sigma_2^2 + \cdots + w_n^2 \sigma_n^2) \tag{10}$$

Simplifying further, if all the variances are equal ($\sigma_i^2 = \sigma^2$) and all the assets are held in equal proportions ($1/n$), we have

$$\sigma_p^2 = \frac{1}{n^2} n \sigma^2 = \frac{1}{n} \sigma^2 \tag{11}$$

Hence, as $n \rightarrow \infty$, the variance of the portfolio approaches 0. Thus, if uncorrelated risks are pooled, much of the portfolio risk is diversified away. This is the 'insurance principle' and is the reason your buildings and car insurance premiums are a relatively small proportion of the value of these items. The insurer relies on these risks being largely uncorrelated across individuals when setting the premium. The total risk attached to each individual security is in part due to factors that affect all securities (e.g. interest rates, growth of the economy, etc.), and this is known as *market risk* and in part, is due to events that are specific to the individual firm (e.g. luck in gaining new orders, an unexpected fall in input costs, etc.) – this is *specific (idiosyncratic) risk*. It is this *specific risk* that can be completely eliminated when we hold many shares in a diversified portfolio. Essentially, the 'good luck' of several firms is broadly cancelled out by some other firms who are currently experiencing 'bad luck' – on average, these *specific risks* cancel out if you hold many shares. Intuitively, one is inclined to suggest that such *specific risk* should not be reflected in the average return on any stock you hold (provided you hold all stocks in a diversified portfolio). As we shall see, this intuition carries through to the CAPM.

In practice, one can reduce portfolio variance substantially even with a *random* selection of stocks, (taken from the S&P500 say), even when their returns do not have zero correlation with each other. Portfolio variance $\sigma_p^2$ falls very quickly as you increase the number of stocks held from 1 to 10, and the reduction in portfolio variance is very small after around 30 stocks in the portfolio (Figure 1). This, coupled with the brokerage fees and information costs of monitoring a large number of stocks, may explain why individuals tend to invest in only a relatively small number of stocks. Individuals may also obtain the benefits of diversification by investing in mutual funds (unit trusts) and pension funds since these institutions use funds from a large number of individuals to invest in a very wide range of financial assets, and each individual then owns a proportion of this 'large portfolio'. Note that we have not said anything about expected returns from the above 'random stock picking' strategy – although as the number of stocks approaches 30, you will tend to earn about the same average return as on the S&P500. The question is whether we can improve on this random selection procedure by choosing (*optimal*) asset proportions based on mean-variance portfolio theory.

## Portfolio Expected Return and Variance

Clearly, individuals are interested in both expected portfolio return $\mu_p \equiv ER_p$ and the risk of the portfolio $\sigma_p$. The question we now ask is how $\mu_p$ and $\sigma_p$ vary, relative to each

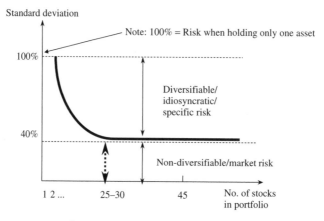

**Figure 1**   Random selection of stocks

**Table 1**  Calculation of portfolio mean and variance ($\rho = -0.5$)

| $w_1$ | $w_2 \, (= 1 - w_1)$ | Expected Portfolio Return | Portfolio Standard Deviation | Portfolio Variance |
|---|---|---|---|---|
| 0 | 1 | 20 | 30 | 900 |
| 0.2 | 0.8 | 18 | 23.07 | 532 |
| 0.4 | 0.6 | 16 | 16.37 | 268 |
| 0.6 | 0.4 | 14 | 10.39 | 108 |
| 0.8 | 0.2 | 12 | 7.21 | 52 |
| 1 | 0 | 10 | 10 | 100 |

other, as the investor *alters the proportion of her own wealth held in each of the risky assets*. Take the two-asset case. Remember that $\mu_1, \mu_2, \sigma_1, \sigma_2$ and $\sigma_{12}$ (or $\rho$) are fixed and known. As we alter $w_1$ (and $w_2 = 1 - w_1$), equation (5) and equation (6) allow us to calculate the combinations of $(\mu_p, \sigma_p)$ that ensue for each of the values of $w_1$ (and $w_2$) that we have arbitrarily chosen. (Note that there is no maximisation/minimisation problem here; it is a purely *arithmetic* calculation.) A numerical example is given in Table 1 for $\mu_1 = 10, \mu_2 = 20, \rho = -0.5, \sigma_1 = 10 \ (\sigma_1^2 = 100), \ \sigma_2 = 30 \ (\sigma_2^2 = 900)$, and is plotted in Figure 2.

We could repeat the above calculations using different values for $\rho$ (between $+1$ and $-1$). In general, as $\rho$ approaches $-1$, the $(\mu_p, \sigma_p)$ locus moves closer to the vertical axis as shown in Figure 3, indicating that a greater reduction in portfolio risk is possible for any given expected return. (Compare portfolios A and B corresponding to $\rho = 0.5$ and $\rho = -0.5$, respectively.) For $\rho = -1$, the curve hits the vertical axis, indicating there are values for $w_i$ which reduce risk to zero. For $\rho = 1$, the risk–return locus is a straight line between the $(\mu_i, \sigma_i)$ points for each individual security. In the above example, we have *arbitrarily chosen* a specific set of $w_i$ values, and there is no maximisation problem involved. Also, in the real world, there is only one value of $\rho$ (at any point in time) and hence only one risk–return locus corresponding to different values of $w_i$.

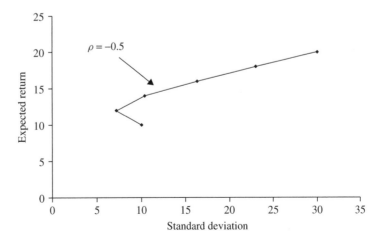

**Figure 2**  Expected return and standard deviation

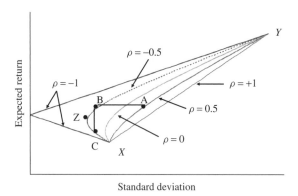

**Figure 3**   Efficient frontier and correlation

This risk–return combination is part of the *feasible set* or opportunity set available to every investor, and for two assets, it gives a graph known as the *risk–return frontier*.

## More Than Two Securities

If we allow the investor to distribute his wealth between any *two* securities A and B or B and C or A and C, we obtain three graphs, one for each 'two-asset' combination. If we now allow the agent to invest *in all three* securities, that is, we vary the proportions, $w_1, w_2, w_3$ (with $\sum_{i=1}^{3} w_i = 1$), this new 'three-asset frontier' will lie to the right of *any* of the 'two-asset frontiers'. This demonstrates that holding more securities reduces portfolio risk for *any given level of expected return*. Intuitively, more choice gives you unambiguously better outcomes in terms of $(\mu_p, \sigma_p)$ combinations. The slope of the efficient frontier is a measure of how the agent can trade off expected return against risk by altering the proportions $w_i$ held in the three assets. Note that the dashed portion of the curve below the *minimum variance point* Z (for the frontier with $\rho = -0.5$ in Figure 3) indicates mean-variance *inefficient* portfolios. An investor would never choose portfolio-C rather than B because C has a lower expected return but the same level of risk, as portfolio-B. Portfolio-B is said to *dominate* portfolio-C on the mean-variance criterion.

## Efficient Frontier

We now consider the case of $N$ assets. When we vary the proportions $w_i$ ($i = 1, 2, \ldots, N$) to form portfolios, there are a large number of possible portfolios, as we form 2, 3, $\ldots$ to $N$ asset portfolios. We can also form portfolios consisting of the same number of assets but in different proportions. Every possible portfolio is given by 'crosses' marked in Figure 4.

If we now apply the mean-variance dominance criterion, then all of the points in the interior of the portfolio opportunity set (e.g. $P_1$, $P_2$ in Figure 4) are dominated by those on the curve ABC, since the latter have a lower variance for a given level of expected return. Points on the curve AB also dominate those on BC, so the curve AB

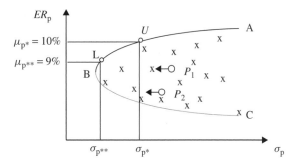

**Figure 4** Efficient and inefficient portfolios

represents the different proportions $w_i$ in the efficient set of portfolios and is referred to as the *efficient frontier*.

How does the investor *calculate* the $w_i$ values that make up the efficient frontier? The investor faces a *known* set of $n$ expected returns $\mu_i$ and variances $\sigma_i^2$ and $n(n-1)/2$ covariances $\sigma_{ij}$ (or correlation coefficients $\rho_{ij}$) and the formulae for the expected return and variance of the portfolio are

$$\mu_{\mathrm{p}} = \sum_{i=1}^{n} w_i \mu_i \tag{12}$$

$$\sigma_{\mathrm{p}}^2 = \sum_{i=1}^{n} w_i^2 \sigma_i^2 + \sum_{i=1}^{n} \sum_{\substack{j=1 \\ i \neq j}}^{n} w_i w_j \rho_{ij} \sigma_i \sigma_j \tag{13}$$

where $\sigma_{ij} = \rho_{ij}\sigma_i\sigma_j$. We assume our investor wishes to *choose* the proportions invested in each asset $w_i$ but is concerned about expected return and risk. The efficient frontier shows all the combinations of $(\mu_{\mathrm{p}}, \sigma_{\mathrm{p}})$, which *minimises portfolio* risk $\sigma_{\mathrm{p}}$ for a given level of expected portfolio return $\mu_{\mathrm{p}}$. The investor's budget constraint is $\Sigma w_i = 1$, that is, all his wealth is placed in the set of risky assets. (For the moment, he is not allowed to borrow or lend money at the riskless rate). Short sales $w_i < 0$ are permitted. A stylised way of representing how the agent seeks to map-out the efficient frontier is as follows.

1. Choose an arbitrary 'target' return on the portfolio $\mu_{\mathrm{p}}^*$ (e.g. $\mu_{\mathrm{p}}^* = 10\%$)

2. Arbitrarily choose the proportions of wealth to invest in each asset $(w_i)_1$ $(i = 1, 2, \ldots, n)$ such that $\mu_{\mathrm{p}}^*$ is achieved (using equation (12)).

3. Work out the variance or standard deviation of this portfolio $(\sigma_{\mathrm{p}})_1$ with these values of $(w_i)_1$ using (13).

4. Repeat steps (2) and (3) with a new set of $(w_i)_2$ if $\sigma_{\mathrm{p}2} < \sigma_{\mathrm{p}1}$, then discard the set $(w_i)_1$ in favour of $(w_i)_2$ and vice versa.

5. Repeat (2)–(4) until you obtain that set of asset proportions $w_i^*$ (with $\sum w_i^* = 1$) that meets the target rate of return $\mu_{\mathrm{p}}^*$ and yields the *minimum* portfolio standard

deviation denoted $\sigma_p^*$. The assets held in the proportions $w_i^*$ is an efficient portfolio and gives *one point* in $(\mu_p, \sigma_p)$ space – point U in Figure 4.

6. Choose another arbitrary 'target' rate of return $\mu_p^{**}$ ($= 9\%$ say) and repeat the above to obtain the new efficient portfolio with proportions $w_i^{**}$ and *minimum* variance $\sigma_p^{**}$ – point L.

We could repeat this exercise using alternative targets for $\mu_p$ and hence trace out the curve AULBC (Figure 4). However, only the upper portion of the curve, that is AULB, yields the *set* of efficient portfolios, and this is the efficient frontier.

It is worth noting at this stage that the general solution to the above problem could (and usually does) involve some $w_i^*$ being negative as well as positive. A positive $w_i^*$ indicates stocks that have been purchased (i.e. stocks held 'long'). Negative $w_i^*$ represent stocks held 'short', that is, stocks that are owned by someone else (e.g. a broker) that the investor borrows and then sells in the market. She therefore has a negative proportion held in these stocks (i.e. she must return the shares to the broker at some point *in the future*). She uses the proceeds from these *short sales* to augment her holding of other stocks. Overall, the efficient frontier 'involves' the following.

1. The investor chooses optimal proportions $w_i^*$, which satisfy the budget constraint $\sum w_i^* = 1$ and minimise $\sigma_p$ for any *given level* of expected return on the portfolio $\mu_p$.

2. She repeats this procedure and calculates the minimum value of $\sigma_p$ for each level of expected return $\mu_p$ and hence maps out the $(\mu_p, \sigma_p)$ points that constitute the efficient frontier. There is only *one* efficient frontier for a given set of $\mu_i, \sigma_i, \rho_{ij}$.

3. Each *point* on the efficient frontier corresponds to a different set of *optimal* proportions $w_1^*, w_2^*, w_3^*, \ldots$ in which the stocks are held.

Points 1–3 constitute the first 'decision' the investor makes in applying the separation theorem – we now turn to the second part of the decision process.

## Borrowing and Lending: Transformation Line

We now allow our agent to borrow or lend at the risk-free rate of interest, $r$. Because $r$ is fixed over the holding period, its variance and covariance (with the set of $n$ risky assets) are both zero. Thus, the agent can:

(i) invest all of her wealth in risky assets and undertake no lending or borrowing;

(ii) invest less than her total wealth in the risky assets and use the remainder to lend at the risk-free rate;

(iii) invest more than her total wealth in the risky assets by borrowing the additional funds at the risk-free rate. In this case, she is said to hold a *levered portfolio*.

The *transformation line* is a relationship between expected return and risk on a portfolio that consists of (i) a riskless asset and (ii) a portfolio of risky assets. The *transformation line* holds for *any* portfolio consisting of these two assets, and it turns out that the relationship between expected return and risk (measured by the standard deviation of the 'new' portfolio) is linear. Suppose we construct a portfolio (call it k) consisting of one risky asset with expected return $\mu_1$ and standard deviation $\sigma_1$ and the riskless asset. Then we can show that the relationship between the return on this new portfolio k and its standard deviation is

$$\mu_k = a + b\sigma_k$$

where 'a' and 'b' are constants and $\mu_k =$ expected return on the new portfolio, $\sigma_k =$ standard deviation on the new portfolio. Similarly, we can create another new portfolio 'N' consisting of (i) *a set of* $q$ risky assets held in proportions $w_i$ $(i = 1, 2, \ldots, q)$, which together constitute our one risky portfolio and (ii) the risk-free asset. Again, we have

$$\mu_N = \delta_0 + \delta_1 \sigma_N$$

To derive the equation of the transformation line, let us assume the individual has somehow already chosen a particular combination of *proportions* (i.e. the $w_i$) of $q$ risky assets (stocks) with actual return $R$, expected return $\mu_R$ and variance $\sigma_R^2$. Note that the $w_i$ are not optimal proportions but can take any values (subject to $\sum_i w_i = 1$). Now, the investor is considering what proportion of her own wealth to put in this one portfolio of $q$ assets and how much to borrow or lend at the riskless rate. She is therefore considering a 'new' portfolio, namely, combinations of the risk-free asset and her 'bundle' of risky assets. If she invests a proportion $x$ of her own wealth in the risk-free asset, then she invests $(1 - x)$ in the risky 'bundle'. Denote the actual return and expected return on this new portfolio as $R_N$ and $\mu_N$ respectively.

$$R_N = xr + (1 - x)R \tag{15}$$

$$\mu_N = xr + (1 - x)\mu_R \tag{16}$$

where $(R, \mu_R)$ is the (actual, expected) return on the risky 'bundle' of her portfolio held in stocks. When $x = 1$, all wealth is invested in the risk-free asset and $\mu_N = r$ and when $x = 0$, all wealth is invested in stocks and $\mu_N = \mu_R$. For $x < 0$, the agent borrows money at the risk-free rate $r$ to invest in the risky portfolio. For example, when $x = -0.5$ and initial wealth $= \$100$, the individual borrows $\$50$ (at an interest rate $r$) and invests $\$150$ in stocks (i.e. a levered position).

Since $r$ is known and fixed over the holding period, the standard deviation of this 'new' portfolio depends only on the standard deviation of the risky portfolio of stocks $\sigma_R$. From (15) and (16), we have

$$\sigma_N^2 = E(R_N - \mu_N)^2 = (1 - x)^2 E(R - \mu_R)^2 \tag{17}$$

$$\sigma_N = (1 - x)\sigma_R \tag{18}$$

where $\sigma_R$ is the standard deviation of the return on the set of risky assets. Equations (16) and (18) are both definitional, but it is useful to rearrange them into a single equation in terms of mean and standard deviation $(\mu_N, \sigma_N)$ of the 'new' portfolio. Rearranging (18)

$$(1 - x) = \sigma_N/\sigma_R \tag{19}$$

and substituting for $x$ and $(1 - x)$ from (19) in (16) gives the identity

$$\mu_N = r + \left[ \frac{\mu_R - r}{\sigma_R} \right] \sigma_N = \delta_0 + \delta_1 \sigma_N \qquad (20)$$

where $\delta_0 = r$ and $\delta_1 = (\mu_R - r)/\sigma_R$. Thus for *any* portfolio consisting of two assets, one of which is a risky asset (portfolio) and the other is a risk-free asset, the relationship between the expected return on this new portfolio $\mu_N$ and its standard error $\sigma_N$ is *linear* with slope given by $\delta_1$ and intercept $= r$. Equation (20) is, of course, an identity; there is no behaviour involved. Note that $(\mu_R - r)$ is always positive since otherwise no one would hold the set of risky assets.

When a portfolio consists only of $n$ risky assets, then as we have seen, the efficient opportunity set in return–standard deviation space is curved (see Figure 4). However, the opportunity set for a two-asset portfolio consisting of a risk-free asset and *any* single risky portfolio is a positive straight line. This should not be unduly confusing since the portfolios considered in the two cases are different, and in the case of the 'efficient set', the curve is derived under an optimising condition and is not just a rearrangement of (two) identities.

Equation (20) says that $\mu_N$ increases with $(\sigma_N/\sigma_R)$. This arises because from (19), an increase in $(\sigma_N/\sigma_R)$ implies an increase in the proportion of wealth held in the risky asset (i.e. $1 - x$) and since $\mu_R > r$, this raises the expected return on the new portfolio $\mu_N$. Similarly, for a given $(\sigma_N/\sigma_R) = (1 - x)$, an increase in the expected excess return on the risky asset $(\mu_R - r)$ increases the overall portfolio return $\mu_N$. This is simply because here the investor holds a fixed proportion $(1 - x)$ in the risky asset but the excess return on the latter is higher.

We can see from (20) that when all wealth is held in the set of risky assets, $x = 0$ and hence $\sigma_N = \sigma_R$, and this is designated the 100% equity portfolio (point X, Figure 5). When all wealth is invested in the risk-free asset, $x = 1$ and $\mu_N = r$ (since $\sigma_N/\sigma_R = 0$). At points between $r$ and $X$, the individual holds some of his initial wealth in the risk-free asset and some in the equity portfolio. At points like Z, the individual holds a levered portfolio (i.e. he borrows some funds at a rate $r$ and also uses all his own wealth to invest in equities).

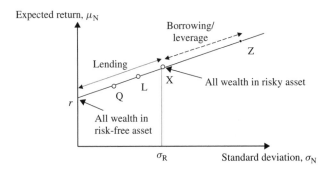

**Figure 5**   Transformation line

## Optimal 'Tangent' Portfolio

The transformation line gives us the risk−return relationship for *any* portfolio consisting of a combination of investment in the risk-free asset and any 'bundle' of stocks. There is no optimisation by agents behind the derivation of the transformation line: it is an identity. At each point on a given transformation line, the agent holds the risky assets in the *same* fixed proportions $w_i$. Suppose point X (Figure 5) represents a combination of $w_i = 20\%$, 25% and 55% in the three risky securities of firms, 'alpha', 'beta' and 'gamma'. Then points Q, L and Z also represent the same proportions of the risky assets. The only 'quantity' that varies along the transformation line is the *proportion* held in the *one* risky bundle of assets relative to that held in the risk-free asset.

The investor can borrow or lend and be anywhere along the transformation line $rZ$. (Exactly where he ends up along $rZ$ depends on his preferences for risk versus return, but, as we shall see, this consideration does not enter the analysis until much later.) For example, point Q in Figure 5 might represent 40% in the riskless asset and 60% in the bundle of risky securities. Hence, an investor with $100 would at point Q hold $40 in the risk-free asset and $60 in the risky assets made up of $0.2 \times \$60 = \$12$ in alpha and $0.25 \times \$60 = \$15$ in beta and $0.55 \times \$60 = \$33$ in the gamma securities.

Although an investor can attain any point along $rZ$, *any* investor (regardless of his preferences) would prefer to be on the transformation line $rZ'$ (see Figure 6). This is because at any point on $rZ'$, the investor has a greater expected return for any given level of risk compared to points on $rZ$. In fact, because $rZ'$ is tangent to the efficient frontier, it provides the investor with the best possible set of opportunities. Point M represents a 'bundle' of stocks held in certain *fixed* proportions. As M is on the efficient frontier, the proportions $w_i$ held in risky assets are optimal (i.e. the $w_i^*$ referred to earlier). An investor can be anywhere along $rZ'$, but M is always a fixed bundle of stocks held by *all* investors. Hence, point M is known as the *market portfolio*, and $rZ'$ is known as the *capital market line* (CML). The CML is therefore that transformation line which is tangential to the efficient frontier.

Investor preferences only determine where along the CML each *individual* investor ends up. For example, an investor with little or no risk aversion would end up at a point like K where she borrows money (at $r$) to augment her own wealth and then

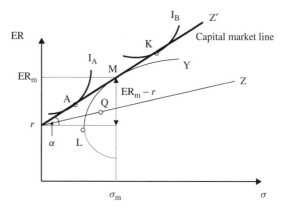

**Figure 6**   Portfolio choice

invests all of these funds in the bundle of securities represented by M (but she still holds *all* her risky stocks in the fixed proportions $w_i$).

Although each investor holds the *same proportions* in the risky assets along the CML, the *dollar amount* in each risky asset differs. If the investor borrows $50 to add to her $100 own funds, then the dollar amount in alpha, beta and gamma shares are $30, $37.50 and $82.50 respectively ($= 150w_i^*$). The risk of this levered portfolio (using (18)) is $\sigma_N = (1 - x)\sigma_m = 1.5\sigma_m$, and the expected return is $\mu_N = 1.5(\mu_R - r) + r$. Hence, the levered portfolio has to be 'north-east' of point M, such as point K (Figure 6).

### Separation principle

Thus, the investor makes two separate decisions:

(i) He uses his knowledge of expected returns, variances and covariances to calculate the set of stocks represented by the efficient frontier. He then determines point M as the *point of tangency* of the straight line from $r$ to the efficient frontier. All this is accomplished without any recourse to the individual's preferences. *All* investors, regardless of preferences (but with the same view about expected returns, etc.), will 'home in' on the portfolio proportions $w_i^*$ of the risky securities represented by M. All investors hold the *market portfolio* or, more correctly, all investors hold their risky assets in the same proportions as their relative value in the market. Put another way, if all investors hold risky assets in the same proportions, and the market is just an aggregate of all investors, then logically each investor must be holding assets in the proportions in which they are in the market. Thus, if the value of AT&T shares constitutes 10% of the total stock market valuation, then each investor holds 10% of his own risky portfolio in AT&T shares.

(ii) The investor now determines how he will combine the market portfolio of risky assets with the riskless asset. This decision does depend on his subjective risk–return preferences. At a point to the left of M, the *individual* investor is reasonably risk-averse and holds a percentage of his wealth in the market portfolio (in the fixed optimal proportions $w_i^*$) and a percentage in the risk-free asset. If the *individual* investor is less risk-averse, he ends up to the right of M, such as K, with a levered portfolio (i.e. he borrows to increase his holdings of the market portfolio in excess of his own initial wealth). At M, the individual puts all his own wealth into the market portfolio and neither borrows or lends at the risk-free rate.

The CML, $rZ'$ which is tangential at M, the market portfolio, must have the form given by (20):

$$\mu_N = r + \left[\frac{\mu_m - r}{\sigma_m}\right]\sigma_N \tag{21}$$

### The market price of risk

The amounts of the riskless asset and the bundle of risky assets held by any individual investor depends on his tastes or preferences. An investor who is relatively risk-averse, with indifference curve $I_1$, will put some of his wealth in the risk-free asset and some in the market portfolio (point A, Figure 6). A less risk averse investor will end up borrowing in order to invest more in the risky assets than allowed by his initial wealth (point K, Figure 6). However, one thing all investors have in common is that the optimal portfolio of risky assets for all investors lies on the CML and for each investor.

$$\text{slope of CML} = (\mu_m - r)/\sigma_m = \text{slope of the indifference curve} \qquad (22)$$

The slope of the CML is often referred to as the *market price of risk*. The slope of the indifference curve is referred to as the marginal rate of substitution (MRS), since it is the rate at which the individual will 'trade-off' more return for more risk.

All investor's portfolios lie on the CML, and, therefore, they all face the same market price of risk. From equation (21) and Figure 6, it is clear that for *both* investors at A and K, the market price of risk equals the MRS. Hence, *in equilibrium, all* individuals have the same trade-off between risk and return. Not only that, but at *any* point on the CML, the 'excess return per unit of risk' is maximised relative to any other portfolio along the efficient frontier, LMY (Figure 6). The introduction of a risk-free asset therefore widens the choice available to investors.

The derivation of the efficient frontier and the market portfolio has been conducted in terms of the standard deviation being used as a measure of risk. When risk is measured in terms of the variance of the portfolio,

$$\lambda_m = (\mu_m - r)/\sigma_m^2 \qquad (23)$$

then $\lambda_m$ is also frequently referred to as *the market price of risk*. Since $\sigma_m$ and $\sigma_m^2$ are conceptually very similar, this need not cause undue confusion. (See Merton 1973 for the derivation of (23) in a general equilibrium framework and Roll 1977 for a discussion of the differences in the representation of the CAPM when risk is measured in these two different ways.)

## In What Proportions Are the Assets Held?

When we allow borrowing and lending, we know that the individual will hold the set of risky assets in the optimal proportions represented by the point M. All investors choose the *proportions* in risky assets represented by M because by borrowing or lending at r, this enables them to reach the *highest* transformation line, given the efficient set or 'bundles' of risky assets. (This will ultimately allow *each* individual to be on her *own* highest indifference curve).

But a problem remains. How can we calculate the risky asset proportions $w_i^*$ represented by point M? So far, we have only shown how to calculate each set of $w_i^*$ for each point on the efficient frontier. We have not demonstrated how the proportions $w_i^*$ for the particular point M are derived. To show this, note that for *any* portfolio on the transformation line (Figure 6),

$$\tan \alpha = (ER_p - r)/\sigma_p \qquad (24)$$

where p represents *any* risky portfolio and as we have seen, $ER_p$ and $\sigma_p$ depend on $w_i$ (as well as the known values of $\mu_i$ and $\sigma_{ij}$ for the risky assets). Hence, to achieve point M, equation (24) can be maximised with respect to $w_i$, subject to the budget constraint $\sum w_i = 1$, and this yields the optimum proportions $w_i^*$. Some of the $w_i^*$ may be less than 0, indicating short selling of assets. (If short sales are not allowed, then the additional constraint $w_i^* \geq 0$ for all $i$, is required, but this would violate the assumptions used to derive the CAPM – see below).

## 5.3 Capital Asset Pricing Model

In order that the efficient frontier be the same for *all* investors, they must have homogeneous expectations about the underlying market variables $\mu_i$, $\sigma_i^2$ and $\rho_{ij}$. Hence, with homogeneous expectations, *all* investors hold *all* the risky assets in the proportions given by point M, the market portfolio. The assumption of homogeneous expectations is crucial in producing a market equilibrium where all risky assets are willingly held in the optimal proportions $w_i^*$ given by M or, in other words, in producing *market clearing*.

The mean-variance model in which agents choose optimal asset proportions also yields a model of equilibrium expected returns known as the *CAPM* (providing we assume homogeneous expectations). The equilibrium return is the 'flip side' or mirror image of the optimal asset shares held by each individual in the same *proportions*, that are independent of the individual's wealth. Here, we demonstrate how the CAPM 'drops out' of the mean-variance optimisation problem using graphical analysis (Figure 7) and simple algebra. (A more formal derivation is given in the next chapter.)

The slope of the CML is constant and represents the market price of risk, which is the same for all investors.

$$\text{Slope of CML} = (\mu_m - r)/\sigma_m \tag{25}$$

We now undertake a thought experiment whereby we 'move' from M (which contains *all* assets in fixed proportions) and create an artificial portfolio by investing some of the funds at present in the assets represented by M, in any risky security $i$. This artificial portfolio (call it p) consists of two *risky* portfolios with proportions $x_i$ in asset-i and

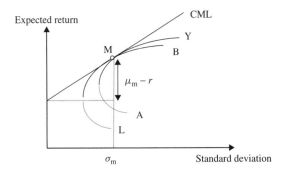

**Figure 7** Market portfolio

$(1 - x_i)$ in the portfolio at M. This portfolio $p$ has expected return $\mu_p$ and standard deviation $\sigma_p$:

$$\mu_p = x_i \mu_i + (1 - x_i)\mu_m \tag{26a}$$

$$\sigma_p = [x_i^2 \sigma_i^2 + (1 - x_i)^2 \sigma_m^2 + 2x_i(1 - x_i)\sigma_{im}]^{1/2} \tag{26b}$$

The portfolio p lies along the curve AMB and is tangent at M. It does not cross the efficient frontier since the latter by definition is the *minimum* variance portfolio for any given level of expected return. Note also that at M there is no borrowing or lending. As we alter $x_i$ and move along MA, we are 'shorting' security-$i$ and investing more than 100% of the funds in portfolio M.

The key element in this derivation is to note that at point M, the curves LMY and AMB coincide and since M is the market portfolio, $x_i = 0$. To find the slope of the efficient frontier at M, we require

$$\left[\frac{\partial \mu_p}{\partial \sigma_p}\right]_{x_i=0} = \left[\frac{\partial \mu_p}{\partial x_i}\right]\left[\frac{\partial \sigma_p}{\partial x_i}\right]^{-1} \tag{27}$$

where all the derivatives are evaluated at $x_i = 0$. From (26a) and (26b),

$$\left[\frac{\partial \mu_p}{\partial x_i}\right] = \mu_i - \mu_m$$

$$\left[\frac{\partial \sigma_p}{\partial x_i}\right] = \frac{1}{2\sigma_p}[2x_i\sigma_i^2 - 2(1 - x_i)\sigma_m^2 + 2\sigma_{im} - 4x_i\sigma_{im}] \tag{28}$$

At $x_i = 0$ (point M), we know $\sigma_p = \sigma_m$ and hence

$$\left[\frac{\partial \sigma_p}{\partial x_i}\right]_{x_i=0} = [\sigma_{im} - \sigma_m^2]/\sigma_m \tag{29}$$

Substituting (28) and (29) in (27)

$$\left[\frac{\partial \mu_p}{\partial \sigma_p}\right]_{x_i=0} = \frac{(\mu_i - \mu_m)\sigma_m}{\sigma_{im} - \sigma_m^2} \tag{30}$$

But at M, the slope of the efficient frontier (equation (30)) equals the slope of the CML (equation (25))

$$\frac{(\mu_i - \mu_m)\sigma_m}{(\sigma_{im} - \sigma_m^2)} = \frac{\mu_m - r}{\sigma_m} \tag{31}$$

From (31), we obtain the CAPM relationship

$$\mu_i = r + (\sigma_{im}/\sigma_m^2)(\mu_m - r) \tag{32}$$

Using alternative notation,

$$ER_i = r + \left[\frac{\text{cov}(R_i, R_m)}{\text{var}(R_m)}\right](ER_m - r) \tag{33}$$

When borrowing and lending in the risk-free asset is allowed, then in order for asset $i$ to be willingly held, it must command an *expected or required return* in the market given by

$$ER_i = r + \beta_i(ER_m - r) \quad \text{where} \quad \beta_i = \text{cov}(R_i, R_m)/\text{var}(R_m) \tag{34}$$

There is one further rearrangement of (34) we wish to consider. Substituting for $(ER_m - r)$ from (23) in (34) gives,

$$ER_i = r + \lambda_m \text{cov}(R_i, R_m) \tag{35}$$

## 5.4   Beta and Systematic Risk

If we define the extra return on asset $i$ over and above the risk-free rate as a risk premium,

$$ER_i = r + rp_i \tag{36}$$

then the CAPM gives the following expressions for the risk premium

$$rp_i = \beta_i(ER_m - r) = \lambda_m \text{cov}(R_i, R_m) \tag{37}$$

The CAPM predicts that only the covariance of returns between asset $i$ and the market portfolio influence the cross-section of excess returns, across assets. No additional variables such as the dividend–price ratio, the size of the firm or the earnings–price ratio should influence the cross-section of expected excess returns. All changes in the risk of asset $i$ is encapsulated in changes in $\text{cov}(R_i, R_m)$. Strictly, this covariance is a conditional covariance – the agent at each point in time forms her best view of the value for the covariance/beta.

### Security market line

The CAPM can be 'rearranged' and expressed in terms of the security market line (SML). Suppose that the historic average value of $ER_m - r$ is 8% p.a. and the risk-free rate is 5%, then the CAPM becomes

$$ER_i = r + 8\beta_i \tag{38}$$

This is a *linear* relationship between the *cross-section* of average returns $ER_i$ and the asset's beta $\beta_i$ (Figure 8) and is known as the *security market line (SML)*. If the CAPM is correct, then *all* securities should lie on the SML.

According to the CAPM/SML, the average excess monthly return (say over 60 months) on each asset $ER_i - r$ should be proportional to that asset's beta – a security with a high beta has a high risk and therefore should earn a high average return:

$$\frac{\text{Excess return on security } i}{\text{Excess return on security } j} = \frac{(ER_i - r)}{(ER_j - r)} = \frac{\beta_i}{\beta_j} \tag{39}$$

Required return = SML and actual return = ○

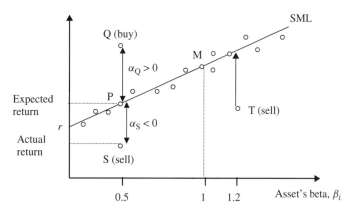

Securities that lie above (below) the SML have a positive (negative) 'alpha', indicating a positive (negative) 'abnormal return', after correcting for 'beta risk'.

**Figure 8**  Security market line, SML

The SML can be used to try to pick underpriced and overpriced stocks. To see this, consider a security S (Figure 8) with a beta of 0.5. You could replicate the beta of security S by buying a portfolio with 50% in the safe asset ($\beta = 0$) and 50% in a security with a beta of unity (i.e. $\beta_p = 0.5(0) + 0.5(1) = 0.5$). But this synthetic portfolio would lie on the SML (at P) and have a higher expected return than S. Hence, S would be sold, since its actual return is less than its equilibrium return given by its beta. If S were sold, its *current* price would fall and this would raise its *expected* return, so that S moved towards P. (Similarly, security T with $\beta_i = 1.2$ could be duplicated by borrowing 20% of your wealth at the safe rate and using your own funds plus borrowed funds to invest in a security with a $\beta_i = 1$.)

Alternatively, consider a security like Q also with $\beta_i = 0.5$ (Figure 8) but which currently has a higher average return than indicated by the SML. An investor should purchase Q. Securities like Q and S are currently mispriced (i.e. they are not on the SML), and a speculator might short sell S and use the funds to purchase Q. If the mispricing is corrected, then the price of Q will rise as everyone seeks to purchase it, because of its current high 'abnormal' average return. Conversely, everyone seeks to short sell S, so its price falls in the market. If you spotted this mispricing first and executed your trades before everyone else, then you would earn a handsome profit from this mispricing. A subtle point is that if the market return ($R_m - r$) either rises or falls unexpectedly over this period, you still make a profit. (Can you see why? Hint: note that both S and Q have the same beta.) To implement this active long–short strategy, one has 'to graph' the average historic return for a set of securities $\overline{R}_i$ (say monthly returns averaged over the past 5 years) against their $\beta_i$ estimates and look for 'big outlier securities' like Q and S. However, remember that in practice this investment strategy is risky since it assumes the CAPM is true, $\beta_i$ is measured correctly and that any mispricing will be corrected over a reasonably short time horizon.

## Systematic Risk

The *systematic risk* of a portfolio is defined as risk that cannot be diversified away by adding extra securities to the portfolio (it is also known as *non-diversifiable*, 'portfolio' or 'market risk'). There is always some risk even in a well-diversified portfolio because of the covariance of returns. We have

$$\sigma_p^2 = \sum_{i=1}^{n} w^2 \sigma_i^2 + \sum_{i=1}^{n} \sum_{\substack{j=1 \\ i \neq j}}^{n} w_i w_j \sigma_{ij} \tag{40}$$

To illustrate this dependence of portfolio variance on the covariance terms, consider a simplified portfolio where all assets are held in the same proportion ($x_i = 1/n$) and where all variances and covariances are constant (i.e. $\sigma_i^2 = \text{var}$ and $\sigma_{ij} = \text{cov}$, where 'var' and 'cov' are constant). Then, (40) becomes

$$\sigma_p^2 = \frac{n}{n^2} \text{var} + \frac{n(n-1)}{n^2} \text{cov} = \frac{1}{n} \text{var} + \left(1 - \frac{1}{n}\right) \text{cov} \tag{41}$$

It follows that as $n \to \infty$, the influence of the variance of each *individual* security on *portfolio* variance approaches zero. The portfolio variance is then determined entirely by the (constant) covariance. Thus, the variance of the returns of individual securities is 'diversified away'. However, the covariance terms cannot be diversified away, and the latter (in a loose sense) give rise to systematic risk, which is represented by the beta of the security. Hence, when assets are held as part of a well-diversified portfolio, the idiosyncratic risk of individual securities ($\sigma_i$) does not earn any return, since this risk can be diversified away. It is only the systematic risk, represented by the asset's beta, that 'earns' an expected return (i.e. 'only beta-risk is priced').

We can show the link between beta and its contribution to portfolio risk as follows. The variance of the optimal (market) portfolio is

$$\sigma_m^2 = w_1(w_1\sigma_{11} + w_2\sigma_{12} + w_3\sigma_{13} + \cdots + w_n\sigma_{1n})$$
$$+ w_2(w_1\sigma_{21} + w_2\sigma_{22} + w_3\sigma_{23} + \cdots + w_n\sigma_{2n})$$
$$+ w_3(w_1\sigma_{31} + w_2\sigma_{32} + w_3\sigma_{33} + \cdots + w_n\sigma_{3n})$$
$$+ \cdots + w_n(w_1\sigma_{n1} + w_2\sigma_{n2} + \cdots + w_n\sigma_{nn}) \tag{42}$$

where we have rewritten $\sigma_i^2$ as $\sigma_{ii}$. If the $w_i$ are those for the market portfolio, then in equilibrium, we can denote the variance as $\sigma_m^2$. For example, the contribution of security-2 to the portfolio variance may be interpreted as the bracketed term in the second line of (42), which is then 'weighted' by the proportion $w_2$ of security-2 held in the portfolio. The bracketed term contains the covariance between security-2 with *all other* securities including itself, and each covariance $\sigma_{ii}$ is weighted by the proportion of each asset in the market portfolio. It is easy to show that the term in brackets in the second line of (42) is the covariance of the return of security-2 with the return on the market portfolio $R_m$:

$$\text{cov}(R_2, R_m) = E(R_m - \mu_m)(R_2 - \mu_2) = E \sum_{i=1}^{n} w_i(R_i - \mu_i)(R_2 - \mu_2)$$

$$= w_1\sigma_{12} + w_2\sigma_{22} + w_3\sigma_{32} + \cdots + w_n\sigma_{n2} \qquad (43)$$

It is also easy to show that the contribution of security-2 to the risk of the portfolio is given by the above expression since $\partial\sigma_m^2/\partial w_2 = 2\,\text{cov}(R_2, R_m)$. In general, the variance of the market portfolio may be written

$$\sigma_m^2 = w_1\,\text{cov}(R_1, R_m) + w_2\,\text{cov}(R_2, R_m) + \cdots + w_n\,\text{cov}(R_n, R_m) \qquad (44)$$

Now, rearranging the expression for the definition of $\beta_i$,

$$\text{cov}(R_i, R_m) = \beta_i\sigma_m^2 \qquad (45)$$

and substituting (45) in (44), we have

$$\sum_{i=1}^{n} w_i\beta_i = 1 \qquad (46)$$

The $\beta_i$ of a security therefore measures the *incremental* effect of security-$i$ on the risk of the portfolio. A security with $\beta_i = 0$ when added to the portfolio has zero *additional* proportionate influence on portfolio variance, whereas $\beta_i < 0$ reduces the variance of the portfolio. Of course, the greater the amount of security-$i$ held (i.e. the larger is the absolute value of $w_i$), the more the impact of $\beta_i$ on total portfolio variance, *ceteris paribus*. Since an asset with a small value of $\beta_i$ considerably reduces the overall variance of a risky portfolio, it will be willingly held even though the security has a relatively low expected return. All investors are trading off risk, which they dislike, against expected return, which they do like. Assets that reduce overall portfolio risk therefore command relatively low returns but are, nevertheless, willingly held in equilibrium.

### The predictability of equilibrium returns

In this section, we outline how the CAPM may be consistent with returns being both variable and predictable. The CAPM applied to the *market portfolio* implies that equilibrium expected (excess) returns are given by (see (23) and Chapter 6, equation (27))

$$E_t R_{m,t+1} - r_t = \lambda E_t(\sigma_{m,t+1}^2) \qquad (47)$$

where we have added subscripts $t$ to highlight the fact that these variables will change over time. From (47), we see that equilibrium excess returns will vary over time if the *conditional* variance of the forecast error of returns is time-varying. From a theoretical standpoint, the CAPM is silent on whether this conditional variance is time-varying. For the sake of argument, suppose it is an *empirical fact* that periods of turbulence or great uncertainty in the stock market are generally followed by further periods of turbulence. Similarly, assume that periods of tranquillity are generally followed by further periods of tranquillity. A simple mathematical way of demonstrating such *persistence* in volatility is to assume *volatility* follows an autoregressive AR(1) process. A simple representation is the GARCH(1,1) model (see Chapter 2 and then Chapter 29 for a full discussion), where in the econometrics literature, the conditional variance is usually written $h_{t+1} \equiv \sigma_{t+1}^2$:

$$\sigma_{t+1}^2 = \alpha \sigma_t^2 + \beta \varepsilon_t^2 \tag{48}$$

where $\varepsilon_{t+1} \equiv R_{t+1} - E_t R_{t+1}$ is the zero mean conditional forecast error of returns (in equation (47)). The best forecast of $\sigma_{t+1}^2$ at time $t$ is $E_t \sigma_{t+1}^2 = (\alpha + \beta)\sigma_t^2$. The CAPM plus ARCH implies

$$E_t R_{m,t+1} - r_t = \lambda(\alpha + \beta)\sigma_t^2 \tag{49}$$

Hence, we have an equilibrium model in which expected returns vary and depend on information at time $t$, namely, $\sigma_t^2$. The reason expected returns vary with $\sigma_t^2$ is quite straightforward. The conditional variance $\sigma_t^2$ is the investor's best guess of next period's systematic risk in the market $E_t \sigma_{t+1}^2$. In equilibrium, such risks are rewarded with a higher expected return.

The above model may be contrasted with our simpler hypothesis, namely, that equilibrium expected returns are *constant*. Rejection of the latter model, for example, by finding that actual returns depend on information $\Omega_t$ at time $t$, or earlier (e.g. dividend–price ratio) may be because the variables in $\Omega_t$ are correlated with the omitted variable $\sigma_t^2$, which occurs in the 'true' model of expected returns (i.e. CAPM + ARCH). The above argument about the predictability of returns can be repeated for the equilibrium excess return on an *individual* asset.

$$E_t R_{it+1} = \lambda \operatorname{cov}_t(R_{i,t+1}, R_{m,t+1}) \tag{50}$$

where $\operatorname{cov}_t(R_{i,t+1}, R_{m,t+1})$ is the conditional covariance. If the covariance is, in part, predictable from information at time $t$, then equilibrium returns on asset $i$ will be non-constant and predictable. Hence, the empirical finding that returns are predictable need not necessarily imply that investors are irrational or are ignoring potentially profitable opportunities in the market.

## 5.5  Summary

- If investors have homogeneous expectations about expected returns and variances, then all 'mean-variance' investors hold risky assets in the same proportions, regardless of their preferences for risk versus return. These optimal proportions constitute the market portfolio.

- Investor's preferences enter in the second stage of the decision process, namely, the choice between the 'fixed bundle' of risky securities and the risk-free asset. The more risk averse the individual, the smaller the dollar amount of her own wealth she will place in the bundle of risky assets. But the *proportion* held in the risky assets is the same as for a less risk-averse investor.

- The CAPM (and the SML) are a consequence of mean-variance portfolio theory. The CAPM implies that in equilibrium the expected excess return on any *single* risky asset $ER_i - r$ is proportional to the excess return on the market portfolio, $ER_m - r$. The constant of proportionality is the asset's beta, where $\beta_i = \text{cov}(R_i, R_m)/\sigma_m^2$

- Relative expected excess returns on two assets $i$ and $j$ are determined solely by the betas of the two assets.

- The CAPM does not necessarily imply that equilibrium returns are constant. If the conditional covariance, $\text{cov}_t(R_i, R_m)$, varies over time, then so will equilibrium returns. In addition, equilibrium returns may be predictable from information available at time $t$. This will arise if the variances and covariances, which measure 'risk' in the CAPM model, are themselves predictable.

# 6

# INTERNATIONAL PORTFOLIO DIVERSIFICATION

## Aims

- Explain the math of calculating optimal portfolio weights when we have a large number of assets and to derive the CAPM.

- Assess the sensitivity of optimal portfolio weights to changes in estimates of mean returns, variances and covariances, and practical solutions to this issue.

- Show that by adding foreign assets we can move the *ex-ante* efficient frontier 'to the left', thus giving a better risk–return trade-off, and to investigate whether this applies in practice.

- Analyse whether an international investor should hedge currency receipts from foreign asset holdings. If she does hedge, should she use forwards, futures or options?

In this chapter, we analyse the theoretical and practical issues when mean-variance portfolio theory is applied to asset allocation. First, we know that if you *randomly* select stocks from a large set of stocks (e.g. those in the S&P500), then it is found that the risk of the portfolio (measured by the standard deviation) quickly falls to a near minimum value when only about 25 stocks are included. Some risk nevertheless remains – this is known as systematic or undiversifiable risk. A question arises as to whether this minimum level of systematic risk can be reduced by widening the choice of stocks in the portfolio to include foreign stocks (or assets).

Second, can we do better than a *random* selection of stocks? In general, we are interested in trading off 'risk against return'. The efficient frontier gives this trade-off for a given set of assets once we know the variances and covariances (correlations) of returns (and a forecast of expected returns). If we can widen the set of asset (e.g. include foreign as well as domestic assets), then it may be possible to substantially move the efficient frontier 'to the left', giving a better risk–return trade-off to the investor because of relatively low correlations between returns across different countries. A key issue for the benefits of portfolio diversification is whether these *historic* low correlations will persist in the future and whether the estimates of the volatilities and (particularly) the average returns are constant over time.

Third, if we include foreign assets in the portfolio, then the investor will usually be interested in the return (and risk) measured in terms of her 'home currency'. If the investor does not hedge these risks, then we need estimates of variances and correlations for bilateral exchange rates. If the investor hedges these risks, then exchange rate risk can be ignored and it is the 'local currency' returns and volatilities that are relevant. Of course, there is still the issue of what instruments to use for the hedge – should we use forwards, futures or options?

Fourth, if we allow the investor to borrow and lend at a risk-free rate, and we have the individual's forecasts of expected returns and covariances, then we can determine the optimal portfolio weights for this *particular* investor. We can then compare the efficiency of alternative international investment strategies (e.g. an equally weighted world portfolio) using performance indicators such as the Sharpe ratio.

Finally, the optimal portfolio weights clearly depend on our estimates of the future values of the expected returns, variances and covariances between the assets. We need to know how sensitive our optimal weights are to minor changes in these crucial inputs (since they are invariably measured with error) and whether constraining these weights (e.g. no short sales) can improve matters.

# 6.1    Mathematics of the Mean-Variance Model

The math needed to obtain optimal portfolio weights is pretty straightforward for the one-period optimisation problem, if there are no constraints put on the optimal weights (e.g. we allow a solution with some $w_i < 0$, that is, short selling). It is a standard quadratic programming problem with an analytic solution. If we want to solve the portfolio allocation problem with constraints (e.g. no short selling), then, in general, there is no analytic solution and a numerical optimisation routine is needed, but these are now commonplace (e.g. as an Excel add-on or in programs such as RATS, GAUSS(FANPAC) and Mathematica).

In this section, we demonstrate the mathematics behind various portfolio problems for an investor who is only concerned about the expected return and the variance of portfolio returns. The reader should be warned that, although the mathematics used does not go beyond simple calculus, the different models discussed have rather subtle differences, in terms of maximands and constraints. These differences should be carefully noted and are summarised at the end of the section. We cover the following:

- How to calculate the proportions $w_i$ to hold in each risky asset, so that the investor is at a point on the efficient frontier. This is the famous Markowitz problem.

- To demonstrate that any two points on the Markowitz efficient frontier can be used to map out the whole of the efficient frontier. This is often referred to as the *two-fund theorem*.

- How to combine riskless borrowing or lending, together with the choice amongst $n$ risky assets to determine the optimal proportions $w_i$ held in the market portfolio. This is the point of tangency between the capital market line (CML) and the efficient frontier.

- To demonstrate the applicability of the two-fund theorem by showing that the market portfolio is a particular combination of two efficient portfolios.

- To show that the capital asset pricing model (CAPM) is a direct consequence of mean-variance optimisation (when we also allow riskless borrowing and lending).

## The Efficient Frontier: Markowitz Model

To find a point on the efficient frontier, the investor solves the following constrained minimisation problem:

$$\min \frac{1}{2}\sigma_p^2 = \frac{1}{2}\sum_{i=1}^{n}\sum_{j=1}^{n} w_i w_j \sigma_{ij} = \frac{1}{2}(w'\Omega w) \tag{1}$$

where $w' = (w_1, w_2, \ldots, w_n)$ and $\Omega$ is the $(n \times n)$ covariance matrix $\{\sigma_{ij}\}$. The constraints are

$$\sum_{i=1}^{n} w_i ER_i = ER_p \tag{2a}$$

$$\sum_{i=1}^{n} w_i = 1 \tag{2b}$$

The use of 1/2 in (1) just makes the algebra neater. Note that the investor has estimates of $\sigma_{ij}$ and $ER_i$ and can only invest her own wealth, so that $\sum_i w_i = 1$. Note that the $w_i$ are not constrained in any way and some of the optimal values for $w_i$ may be less than zero ($w_i < 0$), so that short selling is allowed. The solution to this optimisation problem is fairly standard and involves the use of two unknown Lagrange multipliers $\lambda$ and $\Psi$ for the two constraints

$$\text{Min } L = (1/2)\sum_{i=1}^{n}\sum_{j=1}^{n} w_i w_j \sigma_{ij} - \lambda\left(\sum_{i=1}^{n} w_i ER_i - ER_p\right) - \psi\left(\sum_{i=1}^{n} w_i - 1\right) \tag{3}$$

This type of problem is most easily solved by setting it up in matrix notation (see Appendix I), but there is a pedagogic advantage in considering the algebra of the 3-variable case:

$$\begin{aligned} L = (1/2)[&w_1^2\sigma_{11} + w_1 w_2 \sigma_{12} + w_1 w_3 \sigma_{13} + w_2 w_1 \sigma_{21} + w_2^2\sigma_{22} + w_2 w_3 \sigma_{23} \\ &+ w_3 w_1 \sigma_{31} + w_3 w_2 \sigma_{32} + w_3^2\sigma_{33}] - \lambda(w_1 ER_1 + w_2 ER_2 + w_3 ER_3 - ER_p) \\ &- \psi(w_1 + w_2 + w_3 - 1) \end{aligned} \tag{4}$$

Differentiating equation (4) with respect to $w_i$, $\lambda$ and $\psi$ gives us the following first-order conditions (FOC):

$$\frac{\partial L}{\partial w_1} = (1/2)[2w_1\sigma_{11} + w_2\sigma_{12} + w_3\sigma_{13} + w_2\sigma_{21} + w_3\sigma_{31}] - \lambda ER_1 - \psi = 0 \quad (5a)$$

$$\frac{\partial L}{\partial w_2} = (1/2)[w_1\sigma_{12} + w_1\sigma_{21} + 2w_2\sigma_{22} + w_3\sigma_{23} + w_3\sigma_{32}] - \lambda ER_2 - \psi = 0 \quad (5b)$$

$$\frac{\partial L}{\partial w_3} = (1/2)[w_1\sigma_{13} + w_2\sigma_{23} + w_1\sigma_{31} + w_2\sigma_{32} + 2w_3\sigma_{33}] - \lambda ER_3 - \psi = 0 \quad (5c)$$

$$\frac{\partial L}{\partial \lambda} = \sum_{i=1}^{3} w_i ER_i - ER_p = 0 \quad (5d)$$

$$\frac{\partial L}{\partial \psi} = \sum_{i=1}^{3} w_i - 1 = 0 \quad (5e)$$

## Equations for the Minimum Variance Set

The last two equations merely reproduce the constraints. However, there is a pattern in the first three equations. Noting that $\sigma_{ij} = \sigma_{ji}$, the above equations generalised to the $n$-asset case can be written as

$$\sum_{j=1}^{n} \sigma_{ij} w_j - \lambda ER_i - \psi = 0 \quad (6a)$$

or

$$\Omega w - \lambda ER - \psi \cdot e = 0 \quad (6b)$$

$$\sum_{i=1}^{n} w_i ER_i = ER_p \quad (6c)$$

and

$$\sum_{i=1}^{n} w_i = 1 \quad (6d)$$

where $\Omega = (n \times n)$ covariance matrix, $ER$ is $(n \times 1)$ and $e$ is an $(n \times 1)$ unit vector while $\psi$ and $\lambda$ are scalars. In equation (6a), we know the $\sigma_{ij}$ and $ER' = (ER_1, ER_2, \ldots, ER_n)$ and in (6c), we arbitrarily set the scalar $ER_p$ to any fixed value. We have $(n + 2)$ linear equations and $(n + 2)$ unknowns, the $w_i$, $\lambda$ and $\psi$. These linear equations are easily solved using spreadsheet programs (e.g. in Excel) to give the optimal weights for one point on the minimum variance set once we know the basic inputs, namely, the means $ER_i$ (i.e. our forecasts of expected returns), the standard deviations and covariances $\sigma_{ij}$ for each asset return. Having obtained the optimal $w_i$ $(i = 1, 2, \ldots, n)$, these can be substituted in $\sigma_p^2 = w'\Omega w$ and $ER_p = w'ER$ to give one point on the efficient frontier. We now choose a new (arbitrary) value for $ER_p$ and repeat the exercise until we have enough points to plot out the efficient frontier (see the Excel worksheet on the web site).

Because the optimal weights are totally unconstrained, they can take on any value. A negative value indicates short selling of the stock. Any funds obtained from short selling can be used to invest in other assets and hence for some assets, $w_i$ may exceed unity (i.e. you hold more than your initial 'own wealth' in this asset). The only restriction on the optimal weights is that they sum to unity, which implies that all of your initial wealth is held in the risky assets. Clearly, the above is an instructive way of demonstrating how the efficient frontier can be constructed but it is hardly an 'efficient' computational method. However, the solution we require can be obtained in a simpler fashion by using a special property of the solution to equations (6a) to (6d) known as the two-fund theorem.

## Two-Fund Theorem

Suppose we find two optimal solutions to the Markowitz FOCs (equations (6a)–(6d)) for arbitrary values of $ER_p^{(1)}$ and $ER_p^{(2)}$.

*Solution 1:*
$$w^{(1)} = \{w_1^{(1)}, w_2^{(1)}, \ldots, w_n^{(1)}\}' \text{ and } \lambda^{(1)}, \psi^{(1)}$$

*Solution 2:*
$$w^{(2)} = \{w_1^{(2)}, w_2^{(2)}, \ldots, w_n^{(2)}\}' \text{ and } \lambda^{(2)}, \psi^{(2)}$$

where $w^{(1)}$ and $w^{(2)}$ are column vectors. Then, any linear combination of $w^{(1)}$ and $w^{(2)}$ is also a solution to the FOCs. Hence, another solution to equations (6a) to (6d) is $w^{(q)} = \alpha w^{(1)} + (1 - \alpha)w^{(2)}$ where $-\infty < \alpha < +\infty$, and it is easy to see that $\sum w_i^{(q)} = 1$. Since both solutions $w^{(1)}$ and $w^{(2)}$ make the left-hand side of equation (6a) equal to zero, their linear combination also satisfies (6a). Since we have already solved for $w^{(1)}$ and $w^{(2)}$, by altering $\alpha$ we can map out the entire minimum variance set (which will include all points on the efficient set, the upper portion of the curve). The *two-fund theorem* means that if an investor can find two 'mutual funds' (i.e. portfolios of securities which have asset proportions $w^{(1)}$ and $w^{(2)}$ which satisfy the Markowitz equations and are on the efficient set), then she can combine these two mutual funds in proportions $(\alpha, 1 - \alpha)$ to construct a portfolio that lies anywhere along the mean-variance efficient frontier. In short,

*The two-fund theorem implies that we only require two points on the efficient frontier (often referred to as two mutual funds) in order to map out the whole of the efficient frontier*

The expected return and variance of the portfolio q are

$$ER^{(q)} = \sum_{i=1}^{n} w_i^{(q)} ER_i = w^{(q)'} ER \tag{7a}$$

$$[\sigma^{(q)}]^2 = w^{(q)'} \Omega w^{(q)} = \sum_{i=1}^{n} \sum_{j=1}^{n} w_i^{(q)} w_j^{(q)} \sigma_{ij} \tag{7b}$$

As $w^{(q)}$ is a function of $\alpha$, each value chosen (arbitrarily) for $\alpha$ gives us a point on the mean-variance efficient frontier. At a purely mathematical level, the two-fund theorem allows us to simplify the solution procedure for the Markowitz equations (6a) to (6d). To solve (6a) to (6d) for *all* values of $ER_p$, we need only to find two arbitrary solutions and then form linear combinations of these two solutions. Obvious choices to simplify the problem are

(a) $\lambda = 0$ and $\psi = 1$

(b) $\psi = 0$ and $\lambda = 1$

In '(a)', the constraint $\sum_i w_i ER_i = ER_p$ is ignored, so this gives the $w^{(1)}$ corresponding to the *minimum variance portfolio*. Imposing (a) and (b) may lead to a violation of the constraint $\sum_i w_i = 1$, but the solutions can be re-scaled to allow for this. Setting $\lambda = 0$ and $\psi = 1$ in (6a) or (6b) gives $n$ equations in the $n$ unknowns $z_{(i)}^{(1)}$ (for $i = 1, 2, \ldots, n$).

$$\sum_{j=1}^{n} \sigma_{ij} z_j^{(1)} = 1 \quad \text{or} \quad \Omega z^{(1)} = e \tag{8a}$$

which is easily solved for $\mathbf{z}^{(1)} = \{z_1^{(1)}, z_2^{(1)}, \ldots, z_n^{(1)}\}$. We then normalise the $z_i$'s so they sum to one

$$w_i^{(1)} = \frac{z_i^{(1)}}{\displaystyle\sum_{j=1}^{n} z_j^{(1)}} \tag{8b}$$

The vector $w^{(1)} = \{w_1^{(1)}, w_2^{(1)}, \ldots, w_n^{(1)}\}$ is then the minimum variance point on the efficient frontier. The second (arbitrary) solution has $\psi = 0$ and $\lambda = 1$ and equation (6a) becomes

$$\sum_{j=1}^{n} \sigma_{ij} z_j^{(2)} = ER \quad \text{or} \quad \Omega z^{(2)} = ER \tag{9}$$

giving a solution $z^{(2)} = \{z_1^{(2)}, z_2^{(2)}, \ldots, z_n^{(2)}\}$ and associated $w^{(2)} = \{w_1^{(2)}, w_2^{(2)}, \ldots, w_n^{(2)}\}$. Having obtained these two solutions $w^{(1)}$ and $w^{(2)}$, we can calculate the values of

$\sum_i w_i ER_i = ER_p$ and $\sigma_p = \sum_{i,j}^n w_i w_j \sigma_{ij}$ at these *two* points on the efficient frontier. We then calculate $w^{(2)} = \alpha w^{(1)} + (1 - \alpha) w^{(2)}$ for any arbitrary $\alpha$ and alter $\alpha$ to map all the combinations of $ER^{(q)}$ and $\sigma^{(q)}$ using equation (7).

EXAMPLE    Consider a 5-assets case (see web site for Excel file). Suppose (using sample averages of historic returns data) we find the following values of $\sigma_{ij}$ and $ER$

$$\Omega_{5 \times 5} = \{\sigma_{ij}\} = \begin{bmatrix} 2.2 & 0.9 & -0.3 & 0.65 & -0.42 \\ 0.9 & 1.5 & -0.39 & 0.2 & 0.47 \\ -0.3 & -0.39 & 1.8 & 0.8 & 0.27 \\ 0.65 & 0.2 & 0.8 & 1.5 & -0.5 \\ -0.42 & 0.47 & 0.27 & -0.5 & 1.7 \end{bmatrix} \quad (10a)$$

$$ER' = (ER_1, ER_2, \ldots, ER_5) = [8.5, 18.3, 12.7, 10.8, 9.5] \quad (10b)$$

In matrix notation, the $n = 5$ equations in (8a) can be written as

$$z^{(1)} = \Omega^{-1} e \quad (11)$$

where $e$ is a $5 \times 1$ column vector of ones and hence

$$z^{(1)} = \Omega^{-1} e = \{0.3902, 0.2073, 0.3091, 0.5519, 0.7406\} \quad (12a)$$

$$\sum_{i=1}^5 z_i^{(1)} = 2.1991 \quad (12b)$$

$$w_i^{(1)} = z_i^{(1)} / \sum z_i^{(1)} = \{w_1, w_2, w_3, w_4, w_5\}$$
$$= \{0.1774, 0.0942, 0.1406, 0.2510, 0.3368\} \quad (12c)$$

The weights $w^{(1)}$ are actually the weights required to achieve the minimum variance point (since we set $\lambda = 0$ in equation (3)). The second solution using equation (9), in matrix notation is

$$\Omega z^{(2)} = ER \quad (13a)$$

$$z^{(2)} = \Omega^{-1} ER = \{-1.3839, 16.1736, 10.6532, -0.3818, 0.3368\} \quad (13b)$$

with $w^{(2)} = \{-0.0576, 0.6730, 0.4433, -0.0159, -0.0428\}$. We can then map out the whole of the mean variance set (and hence the efficient frontier) by taking linear combinations $w^{(q)} = \alpha w^{(1)} + (1 - \alpha) w^{(2)}$ with $\alpha$ varying between $\{-\infty, +\infty\}$ and each time calculating $ER^{(q)}$ and $\sigma^{(q)}$ (which are functions of $\alpha$). Unrestricted minimisation of portfolio variance often gives portfolio weights $w_i < 0$ (i.e. short selling), but some financial institutions do not allow short selling (e.g. UK pension funds). Hence, we need to derive the efficient frontier when all $w_i > 0$.

## No Short Sales

In this case, the minimisation problem is exactly the same as in (1) and (2) but with an additional constraint, namely, $w_i \geq 0$ $(i = 1, 2, \ldots, n)$. Now, we cannot use the two-fund theorem to simplify the solution procedure and indeed a special form of programming called *quadratic programming* is required in which the first-order conditions are known as the Kuhn–Tucker conditions. Some readers may be familiar with this type of solution procedure. It is usually the case that when short selling *is* allowed, nearly all of the $w_i$ are non-zero (i.e. either positive or negative) but when short sales are *not* allowed, many of the optimal $w_i$'s are set to zero, and hence only a subset of the total assets are held by the investor.

## Borrowing and Lending: Market Portfolio

When we allow the investor to borrow or lend at the risk-free rate and also to invest in $n$ risky securities, the optimal solution is the market portfolio (if all investors have the same view of expected returns, variances and covariances). The optimal proportions are determined by the tangency of the transformation line with the efficient frontier (short sales are permitted). Mathematically, to obtain the market portfolio, we choose the proportions $w_i$ to

$$\max \theta = \frac{ER_p - r}{\sigma_p} \tag{14}$$

Subject to

$$ER_p = \Sigma w_i ER_i \tag{15a}$$

$$\Sigma w_i = 1 \tag{15b}$$

$$\sigma_p = \left( \sum_{i=1}^{n} w_i^2 \sigma_i^2 + \sum_{i \neq j} \sum w_i w_j \sigma_{ij} \right)^{\frac{1}{2}} = \left( \sum_{i=1}^{n} \sum_{j=1}^{n} w_i w_j \sigma_{ij} \right)^{\frac{1}{2}} \tag{15c}$$

$ER_i$ is the *expected* return on asset-i, $ER_p$ and $\sigma_p$ are the expected return on the portfolio and its standard deviation respectively. The constraint (15b) can be directly incorporated in the maximand (14) by writing $\theta$ as

$$\theta = \frac{\Sigma w_i (ER_i - r)}{\sigma_p} \tag{16}$$

It can be shown (see Appendix II) that the FOCs are of the form

$$z_1 \sigma_{11} + z_2 \sigma_{12} + \cdots + z_n \sigma_{1n} = ER_1 - r$$

$$z_1 \sigma_{12} + z_2 \sigma_{22} + \cdots + z_n \sigma_{2n} = ER_2 - r$$

$$z_1 \sigma_{1n} + z_2 \sigma_{2n} + \cdots + z_n \sigma_{nn} = ER_n - r \tag{17}$$

where $z_i = \eta w_i$ and $\eta$ is a constant. The constant $\eta$ does not affect the solution since if $w_i$ is a solution to (16), then so is $\eta w_i$, since the $\eta$ cancels from the numerator and denominator. Having solved equation (17) for $z_i$, we can determine the optimal values for $w_i$ from

$$\sum_{i=1}^{n} w_i = 1 = \eta^{-1} \sum_{i=1}^{n} z_i \qquad (18)$$

hence

$$\eta = \sum_{i=1}^{n} z_i \quad \text{and} \quad \omega_i = \frac{z_i}{\eta} = \frac{z_i}{\displaystyle\sum_{i=1}^{n} z_i}$$

Since $ER_i, r, \sigma_i^2$ and $\sigma_{ij}$ are known, equation (17) is an $n$-equation system, which can be solved for the $n$ unknowns $z_i$ to $z_n$. Equation (17) can be written (for $k = 1, 2, \ldots, n$)

$$\sum_{i=1}^{n} \sigma_{ki} z_i = (ER_k - r) \quad \text{or} \quad \Omega z = ER - r \qquad (19)$$

where $z = (z_1, z_2, \ldots, z_n)$, $ER - r = (ER_1 - r, ER_2 - r, \ldots, ER_n - r)'$ and $\Omega$ is the $(n \times n)$ variance–covariance matrix. It follows that

$$z^* = \Omega^{-1}(ER - r) \qquad (20)$$

The above solution is easily obtained. Again, we have placed no restrictions on the values that the optimal weights can take but if short sales are prohibited, then $w_i \geq 0$ (for all $i$), and the optimisation involves the application of the Kuhn–Tucker conditions. In practice, software for a variety of optimisation procedures of this type are available as 'add-ons' to the commonly used spreadsheet programs such as Excel. As the number of assets increases or the type of restrictions on the $w_i$ become more complex, the analysis will require more flexible (and speedy) software packages such as GAUSS, Excel-Visual Basic, C++, and so on.

In the general case of $n$ assets (plus the risk-free asset), we have to solve the $n$ equations in (19). This is relatively straightforward (in Excel) once we are given the covariance matrix $\Omega$ and the forecast of expected returns $ER_i$. The solution is $z^* = \{-3.33, 15.14, 9.11, -3.14, -4.73\}$ and $w^* = \{-0.26, 1.16, 0.70, -0.24, -0.36\}$.

There is a nice connection between our earlier Markowitz mean-variance problem and that for the market portfolio weights. The set of FOCs in (17) for the market portfolio are rather similar to the FOCs in the Markowitz two-fund problem (8a) and (9), which are rewritten here with solutions $z^{(1)}$ and $z^{(2)}$:

$$\sum_{j=1}^{n} \sigma_{ij} z_j^{(1)} = 1 \quad \text{or} \quad \Omega z^{(1)} = e \qquad (8a)$$

$$\sum_{j=1}^{n} \sigma_{ij} z_j^{(2)} = ER_k \quad \text{or} \quad \Omega z^{(2)} = ER \qquad (9)$$

where $e$ is the unit vector. The right-hand side of equation (19) is $ER_k - r$ and the left-hand side is identical to that in (8a) and (9). Hence, if $z^{(1)}$ and $z^{(2)}$ are solutions to the FOCs for the Markowitz efficient frontier, then $z^* = z^{(2)} - rz^{(1)}$ is a solution for the market portfolio problem in (19). This should not be too surprising. Earlier, we found that any linear combination of the Markowitz solutions also lie on the efficient frontier. But clearly the market portfolio lies on the efficient frontier, so it too is a linear combination of $z^{(1)}$ and $z^{(2)}$. We have already calculated $z^{(1)}$ and $z^{(2)}$, so, given $r = 5\%$, the solution for the market portfolio is

$$z^* = z^{(2)} - rz^{(1)} = \{-3.33, 15.14, 9.11, -3.14, -4.73\} \qquad (21)$$

which gives the market portfolio weights of $w^* = \{-0.26, 1.16, 0.70, -0.24, -0.36\}$. The latter is, of course, the same solution as that from direct application of $z^* = \Omega^{-1}(ER - r)$ from (20). The solution $z^*$ in (20) is another consequence of the two-fund theorem.

Notice that (21) is only the market portfolio if all investors have homogeneous expectations about the $ER_i$ and the $\sigma_{ij}$'s. If the investor has her own expectations about the aforementioned variables, then $z^*$ still gives the optimum weights but only for that single investor. Different investors will then have different optimal portfolio weights. One can also introduce additional constraints such as no short selling (i.e. $w \geq 0$), but then we can no longer use the simplified solution method above and the optimal weights do not constitute the 'market portfolio'. All the above calculations require as inputs, expected returns (and the current risk free rate $r = 5\%$ say), variances and covariances (correlations), which we have assumed are constant in the above examples. In practice, we need to estimate these variables over the appropriate horizon (e.g. a day, month or year) and to recalculate the optimal portfolio proportions, as our forecasts of these variables alter.

A rather neat (and, as it turns out, intuitive) way of obtaining the optimal (unrestricted) mean variance weights from a simple regression is given in Britten-Jones (1999). You simply take a dependent variable $Y$ as a $(T \times 1)$ column of ones. The independent variable $X$ is a $(T \times k)$ matrix of $k$ asset *excess* returns, and the regression has no intercept:

$$Y = X\beta + u \qquad (22)$$

The optimum weights $w = b/\sum_{i=1}^{k} b_i$, where $b$ is the OLS estimator. This procedure also yields the standard error of $b$, so that we can test the hypotheses about these optimal weights. In particular, Britten–Jones considers an optimal (unhedged) internationally diversified portfolio (from a US investor perspective) and then tests to see if the weights $w_i$ on all the *non-US* countries are jointly statistically zero. He finds that they are, with the conclusion that a US investor should not diversify internationally. This is really an alternative manifestation of the result that the optimal weights are very sensitive to the assumptions about mean returns and the latter are measured with great uncertainty. Also, note that the 'invest at home' conclusion has only been tested for a US-based investor and the analysis only holds true if volatilities and correlations are constant (in the population). But the optimal weights (for the US investor) are found to be time-varying (e.g. that for Denmark changes from a short position of 29% to a long position of 69% when the data sample is split). Finally, the analysis does not apply if weights are restricted *a priori* (e.g. no short sales).

## The CAPM

The market portfolio is held by all investors and all assets in the market portfolio have a particular expected return. What is the relationship between these expected returns and what factors determine any particular expected return? The link between the market portfolio and expected asset returns is given by the CAPM. The CAPM assumes all investors have homogeneous expectations and decide on the proportions of risky assets to hold by maximising $\theta$ in (14) (i.e. at the point of tangency between the CML and the efficient frontier). When all assets are held, the equilibrium expected return on any asset-k is

$$ER_k = r + \beta_k(ER_m - r) \tag{23}$$

where $\beta_k = \text{cov}(R_k, R_m)/\sigma_m^2$. The above relationship must be implicit in the FOC of the market portfolio. Taking the kth equation in (17), we have

$$ER_k - r = \eta[w_1\sigma_{1k} + \cdots + w_n\sigma_{nk}] \tag{24}$$

The term in square brackets is $\text{cov}(R_k, R_m)$, since at the optimal values for $w_i$ we have

$$\text{cov}(R_k, R_m) = \text{cov}\left[R_k, \left(\sum_{j=1}^{n} w_j R_j\right)\right] = \sum_{j=1}^{n} w_j\,\text{cov}(R_j, R_k) = \sum_{j=1}^{n} w_j\sigma_{jk} \tag{25}$$

Hence equation (13) can be written as

$$ER_k - r = \eta\,\text{cov}(R_k, R_m) \tag{26}$$

Since equation (24) holds for all assets, it must also hold for the market portfolio, hence

$$ER_m - r = \eta\sigma_m^2 \tag{27}$$

Substituting for $\eta$ from (27) in (26), we obtain the CAPM

$$ER_k - r = \left[(ER_m - r)/\sigma_m^2\right]\text{cov}(R_k, R_m) = \beta_k(ER_m - r) \tag{28}$$

The expected return on any asset is determined by the assets beta and the excess market return. In a diversified portfolio, the *relative* riskiness of any two assets is determined by the relative size of their betas.

## 6.2   International Diversification

The benefits of portfolio diversification depend upon finding 'new' assets that have a 'low' correlation with existing assets in the portfolio. In an early study of international diversification, Solnik (1974) concentrated on the possible *risk-reducing benefits* of international diversification (and ignored the expected returns from the portfolio). He asked the questions:

- How many *domestic* securities must be held to ensure a reasonable level of diversification?

- Does *international* diversification lead to less risk?

Using $\sigma_p^2 = w'\Omega w$, his inputs were equal weights ($w_i = 1/n$) for each asset, and estimates of the $\sigma_{ij}$ were based on simple (arithmetic) historic sample averages (using weekly returns from 1966 to 1971). The steps in the analysis were:

1. Portfolios are generated by randomly choosing from a large set of possible stocks.

2. Form a portfolio of $n = 1$ stocks and repeat this $m$ times. Calculate the *average* standard deviation $\sigma_p^{(1)}$ for a '1-stock portfolio' (i.e. $\sigma_p^{(1)}$ is averaged over $m$, '1-asset' portfolios). This averaging prevents the calculation being dominated by 'outliers'.

3. Repeat (2) for $n = 2, n = 3, \ldots$ and so on, 'size' portfolios to obtain a sequence of average values for $\sigma_p^{(n)}$.

4. Scale each of the estimated 'size-based' standard deviations using $\sigma_p^{(1)}$:

$$V_p^{(n)} = \left[\sigma_p^{(n)}/\sigma_p^{(1)}\right]^2$$

and plot $V_p^{(n)}$ against '$n$', the number of securities in the portfolio. (Note that $V_p^{(1)} = 100\%$.)

5. Repeat steps (1) to (4) for different countries.

Solnik's key results were that about 20 randomly selected 'domestic securities' achieve the minimum level of systematic (market) risk within any one country. (Today, with increases in correlations, this would probably be achieved with about 30 stocks in a domestic US portfolio and about 40 stocks for an international portfolio.) Solnik finds, for example, that for the United States and Germany, the minimum values of $V_p^{(n)}$ are 27% and 44% respectively, implying that Germany has a higher level of systematic risk.

How effective was international diversification in reducing risk? Solnik assumes perfect hedging of foreign currency returns (at zero cost of forward cover) so that any prospective foreign currency receipts from the foreign asset are sold in the forward market (or you borrow foreign currency to purchase the shares). Note that, in practice, the above does not guarantee that you are fully hedged, since you do not know *exactly* what your shares will be worth in, say, one month's time. For a US resident (we take the United States as the 'domestic country') investing in the German all-share index, the DAX, the dollar *hedged* return is

$$Hedged\ return = R_{DAX} + Forward\ premium\ on\ the\ Euro$$

$$R_{US}^h = R_{DAX} + (F - S)/S$$

For a US-based investor, an *unhedged portfolio* in German securities provides a return in dollar terms of

$$Unhedged\ return = Return\ on\ the\ DAX + Appreciation\ of\ the\ Euro$$

$$R_{US}^u = R_{DAX} + R_S$$

where $R_{DAX}$ = return on DAX (proportionate)

$R_s$ = return on \$/Euro (i.e. proportionate change in the \$/Euro spot rate)

$(F - S)/S$ = forward premium on the Euro (exchange rates measured as \$/Euro)

Solnik (1974) takes nine countries (stock indexes) and randomly selects stocks from these countries, forming different size-based *international* portfolios. For the unhedged portfolio, the standard deviation of 'returns' and the correlation coefficients are derived using the *unhedged* returns. For the hedged returns, the forward premium is assumed to be small relative to $R_{DAX}$ and is set to zero. Therefore, unhedged returns are equal to 'local currency' returns. Solnik then calculates the statistic $V_p^{(n)}$ for the hedged and unhedged portfolios.

The hedged international diversification strategy will reduce portfolio risk $\sigma_p$ if correlations between returns in different 'local currencies' are low, relative to those within a single country. Solnik finds that for a US-based investor, the statistic $V_p^{(n)}$ falls to about 11% for the internationally diversified portfolio (whether hedged or unhedged), which is well below that for the domestic (US) portfolio of about 27%. The reason that the unhedged portfolio does nearly as well as the hedged portfolio is that, in the former, movements in the set of bilateral exchange rates (against the dollar) will be offsetting in such a well-diversified portfolio. Also, changes in most exchange rates against the dollar were not large up to 1974 (when Solnik's study ends) because the quasi-fixed exchange rate regime of Bretton Woods was in existence until about 1973. The Solnik study was pioneering in this area but has obvious limitations, namely:

• Historical averages are used for $\sigma_{ij}$.

- It takes no account of the expected returns from the portfolios.

- It assumes perfect hedging of foreign currency receipts.

## Hedging Foreign Currency Receipts

Up to now, we have largely ignored the hedging issue. Consider whether an investor who holds domestic and foreign assets should *always* fully hedge the prospective foreign currency receipts in the forward market. The answer lies in the correlations between returns on domestic and foreign stock markets and their correlation with the return on the spot currency. An unhedged position 'adds' an extra element of risk, namely, the variance of the spot rate. But it also gives rise to the possibility of low (or negative) correlations between the spot rate and either the domestic stock market or the foreign stock market or both. These correlations may offset the variance of the spot rate and hence reduce the overall portfolio variance of the *unhedged* portfolio.

It is clear from the above studies that there are many potential factors to consider in evaluating alternative portfolio allocation decisions. These include:

- How many countries to include in the study and how many assets within each country (e.g. stocks only, bonds only or both, or an even wider set of assets – such as including property).

- What will be the numeraire currency (i.e. home country) in which we measure returns and risk. Results are not invariant to the choice of 'home currency' or the time horizon (e.g. 1 month or 1 year) over which returns are measured.

- We must consider expected returns as well as risk and provide a measure of portfolio performance that includes both (e.g. Sharpe ratio, Treynor index).

- It may be just as beneficial in practice if we use some simple method of international portfolio diversification (e.g. an equally weighted allocation between alternative countries or an allocation based on a set of existing weights as in *Morgan Stanley's Capital International World Index)*.

- Whether to hedge or not hedge prospective foreign currency receipts and what instruments to use, forwards, futures or options.

- Alternative forecasts of changes in the exchange rate (e.g. historic arithmetic averages, random walk model, use of the forward rate as a predictor of next period's spot rate) give rise to different unhedged optimal portfolio weights as do different forecasts of variances and covariances (correlations).

- The different optimal portfolio weights using different forecasting schemes may not be statistically different from each other if the alternative forecasting schemes have wide margins of error.

We can only briefly deal with these issues in this chapter, but it is worth noting the results in Eun and Resnick (1997) who consider a number of these crucial issues.

They consider the home country as the United States, use a monthly return horizon for stocks (only) for six foreign country indices (Canada, France, Germany, Japan, Switzerland and the United Kingdom). They use simple historic arithmetic averages to measure the variances and covariances of returns but because the optimal portfolio weights are rather sensitive to changes in expected returns, they consider a number of alternative forecasting schemes. They measure these variables using 'in-sample' data and then calculate the optimal portfolio weights, but they then compare the outcome for the return and standard deviation of these *ex-ante* portfolios over a 12-month 'out of sample' period (using a 'bootstrapping method'). The Sharpe ratio is one measure they use to compare results from alternative methods of choosing the optimal portfolio weights. In broad terms, they find that for a US-based investor:

- For an unhedged portfolio, it is found that investing in an internationally diversified portfolio gives results that are superior (in terms of the Sharpe ratio or 'stochastic dominance analysis') to investing solely in US stocks. This result applies irrespective of whether the international portfolio comprises an equally weighted portfolio or weights equal to those in *Morgan Stanley's Capital International World Index* or the 'optimal weights' given by mean-variance analysis. However, the gains to an unhedged internationally diversified strategy are only *marginally better* than a solely domestic investment, at least for a US investor. (Clearly, this result may not hold for an investor based in a 'small' country where international diversification, even if unhedged, may be a substantial improvement on a purely domestic strategy.)

- When considering the hedging decision, fully hedging using forward contracts nearly always produces superior results than not hedging (e.g. this applies whether one uses the 'optimal' portfolio weights or the equally weighted portfolio or the weights in *Morgan Stanley's Capital International World Index*). Also, the use of the forward market is usually superior to using a protective put to hedge foreign currency receipts. Hence, there is reasonably strong evidence that for the US investor, if she diversifies internationally, then it pays to fully hedge the foreign currency receipts in some way.

- It was also found that assuming the spot rate next month equals this month's spot rate (i.e. a random walk) provides a better forecast than that based on the current forward rate. Of course, this is consistent with the 'poor' results found in testing the forward rate unbiasedness (FRU) proposition where a regression of the change in the spot rate on the lagged forward premium invariably gives a *negative* coefficient (see Chapter 25).

## Home Bias Problem

It appears from the above evidence that there is a gain to be had by investing internationally, even for a US resident. It is therefore something of a puzzle why, in practice, there is so little international diversification, particularly by US residents. This is the 'home bias puzzle'.

Portfolio theory highlights the possible gains from international diversification when domestic and foreign returns have lower correlations than those between purely domestic securities, or if exchange rate movements lower these correlations. It has been estimated that a US resident would have been 10–50% better off investing internationally (in the G7 counties) than purely domestically. However, somewhat paradoxically, US residents keep over 90% of their assets 'at home'. This also applies to investors in other countries although the figure for other countries is usually less than this 90% 'at home' – for example, UK pension funds currently have about a 70:30 split in favour of the home country. The problem is so pervasive that it is known as the *home bias problem*. It appears as if neither the risk of imposition of capital controls nor high taxes on capital can explain why these apparent gains to holding foreign equity are not exploited.

One reason for this 'home bias' may be the perceived lack of information about the detailed performance of many foreign-based companies (e.g. small 'foreign' firms). Sometimes there are legal restrictions on foreign investments. For example, currently, UK pension funds have to meet the minimum funding requirement (MFR), which is a type of solvency test that encourages investment in domestic government bonds and to a lesser extent in UK equities. Another reason for 'home bias' is that a 'proven gain' using past data does not necessarily imply a gain in the (uncertain) future.

Yet another reason why investors might not diversify internationally is that they wish to consume mainly home country goods and services with the proceeds from their investments, and this will be uncertain if the real exchange rate fluctuates. However, if *purchasing power parity* (*PPP*) holds (see Chapter 24), then the *real* return from foreign investment is the same as the real return to domestic residents of that country, so that there is no foreign exchange risk. Unfortunately, PPP only holds over very long horizons of 5–10 years, and changes in real exchange rates over a shorter time horizon can be large (e.g. plus or minus 25% over 1–5 years). This introduces uncertainty since you may wish to cash in your foreign investments just when the exchange rate is least favourable – hence this may be a reason for 'home bias'. With the cost of information flows becoming lower (e.g. the prospect of increased information on foreign companies and real-time stock price quotes and dealing over the internet), it is always possible that the home bias problem may attenuate and investors may become more willing to diversify internationally.

On the other hand, some argue that the 'home bias' problem is illusory once one takes into account the fact that the inputs to the mean-variance optimisation problem are measured with uncertainty. Although a US investor holding her stocks in the same proportions as in the S&P500 may not hold precisely the mean-variance optimum proportions, nevertheless, her S&P500 indexed portfolio may be within a 95% confidence band of this optimum position. This argument may apply with even greater force if we recognise that in the real world, we need to make a 'genuine' forecast of the inputs (i.e. forecasts of expected returns and the variance–covariance matrix) to the mean-variance optimisation problem. Under these circumstances, the S&P500 indexed portfolio may actually outperform the optimum mean-variance portfolio.

## 6.3   Mean-Variance Optimisation in Practice

It is probably true to say that a large proportion of investment funds are not allocated on the basis of mean-variance optimisation. Usually, a wide variety of criteria such as political risk, business risk and the state of the economic cycle are used in a relatively informal way, by the investment policy committee of an investment bank to determine asset allocation, across different countries. What are the problems associated with the 'pure application' of mean-variance optimisation as espoused in the textbooks and which make it difficult to apply in practice? Most obviously, it only deals with risk as measured by the variance–covariance matrix and not other forms of risk (e.g. political risk) and (in its simplest form) it only covers one specific time horizon (e.g. 1 month or 1 year etc.). However, the main reason it is not widely used is that it is somewhat of a 'black-box' and the results are subject to potentially large estimation errors.

## Estimation Errors

Consider possible estimation errors. If (continuously compounded) returns are normally, identically and independently distributed *(niid)*, with a constant population mean $\mu$ and variance $\sigma^2$, then (unbiased) estimates of the mean and standard deviation are given by

$$\overline{R} = \frac{\displaystyle\sum_{i=1}^{n} R_i}{n} \tag{29a}$$

$$\hat{\sigma} = \sqrt{\frac{\displaystyle\sum_{i=1}^{n} (R_i - \overline{R})^2}{n-1}} \tag{29b}$$

The above formulae can be applied to any chosen frequency for the data (e.g. daily, weekly, monthly) to obtain the appropriate mean return and standard deviation for any particular horizon. (We ignore complexities due to the use of overlapping data.) For example, using monthly returns data, we might find that $\overline{R} = 1\%$ p.m. and $\hat{\sigma} = 4\%$ p.m. It can be shown that the standard deviation of the estimate of $\overline{R}$ is

$$\text{stdv}(\overline{R}) = \frac{\sigma}{\sqrt{n}} \tag{30}$$

Suppose we wanted to obtain an estimate of the population mean return of 1% p.m. that was accurate to ±0.1%, given that $\sigma = 4\%$ p.m. This would require $n = 4^2/(0.1)^2 = 1600$ monthly observations, that is, 133 years of monthly data! Clearly, the accuracy of our estimate of the mean return obtained from a 'moderate sample' of, say, 60 monthly observations (i.e. 5 years) will be very poor. For example, for $n = 60$, $\text{stdv}(\overline{R}) = \sigma/\sqrt{n} = 0.52\%$, so the error is more than half of the estimated mean value for $\overline{R}$ of 1% p.m. There is an additional problem. If the population mean is not constant over time, then even using a lot of past data will not provide an accurate estimate, as data from the beginning of the period will not provide an accurate representation of the changing population mean. Hence, analysts tend to use other methods to estimate expected returns. They might use an estimate of the security market line (SML) and the asset's beta to predict expected returns or even use predictions from the APT or a more general regression model in which returns are assumed to depend on a set of 'fundamental variables' (e.g. dividend or price–earnings ratio, yield spreads, etc.). They will also combine these estimates with ancillary information on the firm or sector's company reports.

What about the accuracy of our estimate of the sample standard deviation $\hat{\sigma} = 4\%$ p.m.? The standard deviation (for normally distributed returns) of $\hat{\sigma}$ is given by

$$\text{stdv}(\hat{\sigma}) = \frac{\sqrt{2}\sigma^2}{\sqrt{n-1}} \tag{31}$$

Suppose we use 5 years ($n = 60$ monthly observations) of data to estimate $\hat{\sigma} = 4\%$ p.m. Using the above equation, we get $\text{stdv}(\hat{\sigma}) = \dfrac{\sqrt{24^2}}{\sqrt{60-1}} = 0.38\%$ p.m. Hence, the accuracy of $\hat{\sigma} = 4\%$ p.m. is relatively good at 0.38% p.m. (i.e. 9.5% of its estimated value), and estimates of variances (and covariances) using historic data is subject to much less error (relatively speaking) than estimates of the expected return.

It might be thought that the precision in estimating the expected return could be enhanced by keeping the same 'length' of data, say 5 years, but increasing the frequency of data from, say, monthly to daily. However, this does not in fact help – you cannot get something for nothing out of your fixed data set. This arises because if, say, *monthly returns* are statistically independent, then it can be shown that the expected *daily* return and standard deviation are given by $\mu_d = T\mu_m$ and $\sigma_d = \sqrt{T}\sigma_m$, where $T$ is the *fraction* of a month (and here $T = 1/30$ approximately). Hence, $\sigma_d/\mu_d = \sqrt{T}\sigma_m/T\mu_m = \sqrt{30}\sigma_m/\mu_m$, which implies that the daily standard deviation relative to the daily mean is about 5.5 times the monthly value (i.e. $\sigma_m/\mu_m$). Hence, the relative error increases as the period is shortened.

## Black Box?

The 'black-box' element in mean-variance portfolio analysis arises because the optimal weights $w_i^*$ simply 'pop out' of the maximisation procedure, and it is often difficult (especially with many assets) to undertake a sensitivity analysis that is tractable and easy to understand. Estimation error arises because the inputs, that is, the forecast of expected returns ($ER_i$) and of the elements of the variance–covariance matrix $\{\sigma_{ij}\}$ may provide poor predictions of what actually happens in the future. The 'optimiser' will significantly overweight (underweight) those securities that have large (small) forecast expected returns, negative (positive) estimated covariances and small (large) variances. Generally, it is the bias in forecasts of expected returns that are the major source of error; by comparison, forecasts of the $\sigma_{ij}$ are reasonably good.

Generally, historic averages of past returns (e.g. the sample mean return over a given 'window' of recent data) are used to measure future expected returns. These methods can be improved upon, for example, using more sophisticated recursive multivariate regressions, time-varying parameter models, or pure time series models (e.g. ARIMA and the stochastic trend model), Bayesian estimators and most recently, predictions based on neural networks. Forecasts of the variances and covariances can be based on exponentially weighted moving averages (EWMA) or even simple ARCH and

GARCH models (see Chapter 29). Essentially, these methods assume that the variance (or covariance) are a weighted average of past squared returns. Of course, they involve increased computing costs and, more importantly, costs in interpreting the results for higher management who may be somewhat sceptical and lack technical expertise. However, we have little or no evidence on how these more sophisticated alternatives might reduce the 'estimation error' in the mean-variance optimisation problem. But Simmons (1999) provides a simple yet revealing sensitivity analysis. She uses historic sample averages for $ER$ and the variance–covariances and calculates the optimal weights (from a US perspective) on the efficient frontier (with no short sales) taking US equities, US bonds, US money market assets, European stocks and Pacific stocks as the set of assets in the portfolio. She then repeats the exercise using EWMA forecasts for variances and covariances and finds a dramatic change in the optimal weights, thus showing the extreme sensitivity of mean-variance analysis to seemingly innocuous changes in the inputs.

What evidence we do have (e.g. Jobson and Korkie 1980, 1981, Frost and Savarino 1988) on the 'estimation error' from mean-variance optimisation uses simple 'historic' sample averages for forecasts of $R_i$ and $\sigma_{ij}$. As we shall see, in general, these studies suggest that the best strategy is to constrain the weight attached to any single 'security' to a relatively small value, possibly in the range 2–5% of portfolio value, and one should also disallow short sales or buying on margin.

The technique known as *Monte Carlo simulation* allows one to measure the 'estimation error' implicit in using the mean-variance optimiser. Monte Carlo simulation allows 'repeated samples' of asset returns and the variance–covariance matrix to be generated. For each 'run' of simulated data, we can calculate the estimated optimal portfolio return ($R_p$) and its standard deviation ($\sigma_p$), and hence the Sharpe ratio $(R_p - r)/\sigma_p$. We then compare these simulated outcomes with the known 'true' values given from the underlying known distribution. The procedure involves the following steps where

$n$ = number of assets in the chosen portfolio (e.g. 20)

$m$ = number of simulation runs in the Monte Carlo analysis

$q$ = length of data sample used in calculating mean returns and the variances and covariances

1. Assume returns are multivariate normal with true mean returns $\mu_i$ and variance–covariance matrix $\Sigma = \{\sigma_{ij}\}$. In the 2-asset case, the 'true values' of $\mu_1$, $\mu_2$, $\sigma_1$, $\sigma_2$ and $\sigma_{12}$ will be based on historic sample averages using $q = 60$ data points (say). But from this point on we assume these values are known *constants*. We therefore know the true 'population parameters' $\mu_i$, $\Sigma$ and can calculate the true optimal weights $w_i^*$ and the true optimal portfolio returns ($R_p^*$) and standard deviation ($\sigma_p^*$) that maximise the Sharpe ratio $S = (ER_p^* - r)/\sigma_p^*$.

2. The asset returns are generated from a multivariate normal distribution, which encapsulates the correlation structure between the asset returns:

$$R_i = \mu_i + \varepsilon_i$$

where $\varepsilon_i$ is drawn from a multivariate normal distribution, with known variance–covariance matrix $\Sigma$, calculated as noted above. Now generate $q = 60$ simulated returns ($R_i$ for each of the $i = 1, 2, \ldots, n$ assets. This is our first Monte Carlo 'run' (i.e. $m = 1$).

3. With the $q = 60$ data points for each return series, calculate the sample average returns $E\hat{R}_i^{(1)} = \sum_{i=1}^{q} R_i^{(1)}/q$ and variance–covariance matrix $\Sigma^{(1)}$. Then, use these as inputs to solve the portfolio maximisation problem to give our 'first run' values for the *simulated* optimal portfolio weights $\hat{w}_i$, portfolio return and its variance ($\hat{R}_p$, $\sigma_p)^{(1)}$.

4. Repeat step (2) and step (3) $m$-times and use the $m$-generated values of ($\hat{R}_p$, $\hat{\sigma}_p$) to obtain their average values (over '$m$-runs'), which we denote ($\overline{R}_p, \overline{\sigma}_p$) together with the average Sharpe ratio $\hat{S} = \dfrac{(\overline{R}_p - r)}{\overline{\sigma}_p}$. We can compare these averages from the Monte Carlo simulation with the known true values ($R_p^*$, $\sigma_p^*$ and $S^*$) to provide a measure of the 'bias' produced by our estimation method for expected returns and covariances.

Some empirical results from Jobson and Korkie (1980) for monthly returns on 20 stocks generated from a known multivariate distribution show that the Sharpe ratios for the simulated data ($\overline{R}_p, \overline{\sigma}_p$), the known population parameters ($R_p^*, \sigma_p^*$) and an equally weighted portfolio were vastly different at 0.08, 0.34 and 0.27 respectively. Hence, 'estimation error' can be substantial and radically alters the risk–return trade-off.

Frost and Savarino (1988) in a similar experiment found that the 'biases' $\overline{R}_p - R_p^*$ and $\overline{\sigma}_p - \sigma_p^*$ (particularly the former) fell dramatically as the portfolio weights in any one asset are restricted to a small positive value and if no short sales are allowed. In addition, for investors who are either twice or half as risk-averse as the market investor (i.e. where the latter holds the 'market portfolio' of 25 equities, say), the best outcome (in terms of certainty equivalent returns) occurs if the mean-variance optimisation is undertaken under the restriction that no more than about 3–5% is held in any one security. Also, note that either short selling or buying on margin considerably worsens performance. Thus, it appears that mean-variance optimisation can provide some improvement (albeit not large) to holding the market index as long as some restrictions are placed on the optimisation problem.

*Index tracking* in equity markets using market value weights ($w_{im}$) is fairly common-place. One constrained optimisation strategy is to maximise the Sharpe ratio subject to the optimal weights ($w_i^*$) not being more than, say, 2% from the current market weights for that stock (i.e. $\hat{w}_i^* = w_{im} \pm 0.02\, w_{im}$). Cavaglia, Melas and Miyashiuta (1994) find that the Sharpe ratio can be improved for an international equity portfolio (i.e. one which includes equity held in a large number of countries) as one moves a small amount away from the current market value weights. It is also the case in practice that no investment manager would believe in the optimal weights if these were not close to her intuitive notions of what is 'reasonable'. Indeed, UK pension funds rarely invest more than 5% of their equity portfolio in a single stock (even though an indexing strategy on the

FTSE100 would involve holding about 15% in Vodaphone-Mannesmann and a Finnish pension fund would have to hold over 50% in Nokia!).

Some constraints need to be placed on the weights obtained from the mean-variance optimiser if 'unrestricted weighting' means that the investor holds a significant percentage of any one firm or industry sector (e.g. as might be the case when holding 90% of your wealth in small-cap stocks or a large proportion of stocks in emerging markets). Unconstrained optimisation, which allows short selling, often results in weights, which imply that you should short sell large amounts of one stock and use the proceeds to invest long in another stock. Practitioners would simply not believe that such a strategy would be successful, *ex-post*.

There have been attempts to see if a given portfolio is 'close to', in a statistical sense, the mean-variance optimal portfolio (e.g. Jobson and Korkie 1980). However, such tests appear to have low power (i.e. tend not to reject mean-variance efficiency when it is false) and do not allow for inequality constraints (e.g. no short selling), so this approach is not often used in practice.

It is also worth noting that there are some technical problems in calculating the optimal weights. If the covariance matrix is large, there may be problems in inverting it and then the optimal weights may be very sensitive to slight changes in the estimated covariances.

## Learning and Bayes Theorem

A well-known result in portfolio theory is that if you add an asset with positive mis-pricing (i.e. Jensen's $\alpha > 0$) to the market portfolio, then the (squared) Sharpe ratio for this new portfolio increases by $(\alpha/\sigma_\varepsilon)^2$, where $\sigma_\varepsilon^2$ is the residual variance from the market model regression $(R_i - r) = \alpha_i + \beta_i(R_m - r) + \varepsilon_i$. A question raised by Pastor (2000) is whether this is sensible if your estimate of $\alpha$ is uncertain. In a one-period framework, Pastor assumes that we choose risky asset shares to maximise expected end-of-period wealth:

$$\max_\alpha \int U(W_{+1}) p(R_{+1}|\Lambda) \, dR_{+1}$$

where $R$ is the portfolio return and $p(.|.)$ is the probability density function (p.d.f.) given information, $\Lambda$. However, Pastor assumes that the parameters $\theta$ in the predictive equation are not known with certainty and investors use Bayes rule (see Chapter 2) to form the *predictive density* $p(R_{+1}|\Lambda)$, where

$$p(R_{+1}|\Lambda) = \int p(R_{+1}|\theta, \Lambda) p(\theta|\Lambda) \, d\theta$$

and $p(\theta|\Lambda)$ is the *posterior* distribution of $\theta$, which in turn is proportional to the *prior* distribution $p(\theta)$ and the likelihood function $L(\theta|\Lambda)$:

$$p(\theta|\Lambda) \propto p(\theta) L(\theta|\Lambda)$$

The optimal portfolio weights are given by the usual tangency condition (i.e. maximise Sharpe ratio).

$$z_t^* = \Omega^{-1}(E_t R_{+1} - r) \qquad w_i^* = z_i / \sum_i z_i$$

where $\Omega$ and $ER_{+1}$ are the first two moments of the predictive density $p(R_{+1}|\Lambda)$. The standard method to obtain $w_i^*(i = 1, 2, \ldots, n)$ would be to use *only* the sample estimates of $\Omega$ and $ER$ calculated from historic data. The Bayesian uses estimates based on the predictive distribution $p(R_{+1}|\Lambda)$, which takes into account the sample estimates and the investor's prior views about the (Jensen's) $\alpha$ and $\beta$ parameters. The posterior for $\theta = (\alpha, \beta)$ is a weighted average of the prior estimates $\theta_0$ and the sample estimates $\hat{\theta}$ (obtained using maximum likelihood). For the Bayesian, the optimal weight of any 'new' assets is proportional to $\tilde{\alpha}/\tilde{\sigma}^2$, the *posterior* means of $\alpha$ and $\sigma^2$ (the regression variance).

Pastor finds that the standard approach to determining $w_i^*$ using only sample data for $\Omega$ and $ER - r$ for US investors implies an optimal weight of foreign equities of around 40%. But because of the uncertainty in estimating (particularly) the expected returns, one cannot reject the null that the optimal tangency portfolio has a zero weight on non-US stocks (see Britten–Jones above). In a Bayesian framework, the bias towards domestic equities depends on the degree of confidence about the domestic CAPM. Pastor finds that the prior belief about mispricing in the foreign portfolio must be between $-2\%$ and $+2\%$ p.a. (i.e. $\sigma_\alpha = 1\%$) in order to explain the actual US holdings of foreign stocks (of 8% of total wealth) – so a US investor's belief in the efficiency of the domestic (US market) portfolio has to be very strong, in order to explain the observed home bias of US investors.

It remains the case, that for all its elegance, mean-variance optimisation is, in practice, merely one method of deciding on portfolio allocation. Other judgemental factors such as an assessment of political risk and the state of the economic cycle in different countries or industries play as important a role as 'pure' mean-variance analysis. Current market value proportions, as embodied in the S&P index (for example), would not be the same as those given by an unconstrained mean-variance analysis (e.g. one that uses sample averages as forecasts of the mean return and the covariance matrix). Therefore, in practice, mean-variance analysis tends to be used to see if 'new forecasts' of $R_i$ and $\sigma_{ij}$ provide some improvement in the Sharpe ratio. Sensitivity analysis of the Sharpe ratio is also usually conducted with 'user imposed' changes in key returns and covariances rather than basing them on historic averages. As the scenarios change, if the optimal weights $w_i^*$ vary greatly in the unconstrained optimisation problem, then some constraints will be placed on the $w_i^*$ (e.g. that the new optimal proportions do not vary greatly from the current market value 'index tracking' weights and also perhaps that no short selling is allowed).

In summary, our overall conclusions might be that mean-variance optimisation is useful if

- portfolio weights are constrained to a certain extent (e.g. hold less than 5% of value in any one asset or do not move more than 2% away from the 'market index weight' or do not allow short sales);

- better forecasts of returns $R_i$ and covariances $\{\sigma_{ij}\}$ are used in place of historic averages;

- a small number of assets are used (e.g. using mean-variance optimisation for allocation between say 20 country indexes) so that transparency and sensitivity analysis are possible.

## 6.4 Summary

We have discussed a wide range of practical and theoretical issues in this chapter concerning international portfolio diversification. The key elements are listed below.

- The mathematics of one-period mean-variance optimisation allows calculation of optimal portfolio weights and, under the representative agent assumption, the determination of equilibrium expected returns, that is the CAPM. It also forms the basis for other more complex portfolio optimisation techniques (e.g. those that impose constraints on the portfolio weights and intertemporal models in Chapters 15 and 16).

- There appears to be substantial gains in reducing portfolio risk by diversification with only a small number of assets (about 25). A greater risk reduction can be obtained if we diversify internationally, even if we *randomly* choose the diversified set of stocks.

- When we consider both expected return and risk, then international diversification generally improves the risk–return trade-off (i.e. pushes the efficient frontier to the left), particularly if the foreign returns are hedged either with forwards, futures or options. The improvement from international diversification is more debatable when returns are unhedged and must be examined on a case-by-case basis for a particular 'home currency' investor.

- Diversification can proceed on the basis of either random selection of stocks, or an equally weighted portfolio or tracking a broad market index (e.g. the Morgan Stanley World Index) or using a mean-variance optimiser.

- The main problem in accepting the results from a totally unconstrained mean-variance analysis is that the optimal proportions (weights) are very sensitive to forecasts of expected returns and to assets that have either very high or very low forecast variances. In practice, therefore, the optimal proportions are constrained in some way (e.g. that they must not differ from the current proportions by more than 2%).

- The home bias problem may not be as acute when we consider the uncertainties involved in actual portfolio diversification, but it is still 'a puzzle' why international diversification is as low as observed.

# Appendix I: Efficient Frontier and the CML

## Efficient Frontier

In the text, we derived the efficient frontier by exploiting the two-fund theorem. Once we have optimal weights at two points on the frontier, we can map out the whole of the frontier by forming a weighted average $w^{(q)} = \alpha w^{(1)} + (1 - \alpha)w^{(2)}$. In this appendix, we derive the optimal weights explicitly, in terms of the 'raw inputs', namely, the ($n \times n$) covariance matrix of returns $\Omega$, the expected returns on the risky assets $ER$ ($n \times 1$) and the chosen mean portfolio return $ER_p \equiv \mu_p$. The problem is to choose $w$ ($n \times 1$) to minimise *portfolio* variance $\sigma_p^2 \equiv w'\Omega w$ subject to the budget constraint $w'e = 1$ ($e$ = unit vector) and a given level of expected portfolio return $w'ER = \mu_p$. The Lagrangian is

$$\theta = \tfrac{1}{2}(w'\Omega w) - \lambda(w'ER - \mu_p) - \psi(w'e - 1) \tag{A1}$$

The first-order conditions are

$$\Omega w - \lambda ER - \psi e = 0 \tag{A2}$$

$$w'ER = \mu_p \tag{A3a}$$

$$w'e = 1 \tag{A3b}$$

from (A2)

$$w = \Omega^{-1}[\lambda ER + \psi e] \tag{A3c}$$

Hence,

$$ER'w = ER'\Omega^{-1}[\lambda ER + \psi e] = \mu_p \tag{A4}$$

$$e'w = e'\Omega^{-1}[\lambda ER + \psi e] = 1 \tag{A5}$$

(A4) and (A5) are two equations in two unknowns $\lambda$ and $\psi$, and can be written as

$$\begin{bmatrix} A & B \\ B & C \end{bmatrix} \begin{bmatrix} \lambda \\ \psi \end{bmatrix} = \begin{bmatrix} \mu_p \\ 1 \end{bmatrix} \tag{A6}$$

where

$$A = (ER')\Omega^{-1}(ER) \tag{A7a}$$

$$B = (ER')\Omega^{-1}e \tag{A7b}$$

$$C = e'\Omega^{-1}e \tag{A7c}$$

Note that $A$, $B$ and $C$ are scalars. From (A6), the (scalar) Lagrange multipliers are given by

$$\lambda = \frac{C\mu_p - B}{AC - B^2} \tag{A8a}$$

$$\psi = \frac{A - B\mu_p}{AC - B^2} \tag{A8b}$$

Substituting (A8a) and (A8b) in (A3c),

$$w^* = \Omega^{-1}\left[\frac{ER(C\mu_p - B) + e(A - B\mu_p)}{(AC - B^2)}\right] \tag{A9}$$

where $w^*$ is the $(n \times 1)$ vector of optimal proportions held in the risky assets. Using (A9), the minimum variance portfolio (for given $\mu_p$) has

$$\text{var}(R_p) = w'\Omega^{-1}w = \frac{C\mu_p^2 - 2B\mu_p + A}{AC - B^2} \tag{A10}$$

The portfolio variance is a quadratic function of the mean portfolio return. In mean-variance space this maps out a parabola, while in mean-standard deviation space, it maps out a hyperbola.

The *global* minimum variance portfolio can be obtained by minimising $w'\Omega w$ subject to $w'e = 1$ or directly from (A10) by minimising $\text{var}(R_p)$ with respect to $\mu_p$, which gives

$$\mu_p^{\text{gmv}} = B/C \tag{A11}$$

Therefore, the weights in the global minimum variance (gmv) portfolio $w^*$ (using (A9)) and the variance of this portfolio are

$$w_{\text{gmv}}^* = \Omega^{-1}e/(e'\Omega^{-1}e) \tag{A12a}$$

$$\sigma_{\text{gmv}}^2 = 1/C \tag{A12b}$$

Of course, $w_{\text{gmv}}^*$ is independent of expected returns, and the global minimum variance portfolio does earn a positive expected return $\mu_p^{\text{gmv}} > 0$, since $C$ is a quadratic form that must be positive definite.

Note also from (A9) that the portfolio weights on the efficient frontier are linear in $\mu_p$, so that for any two points on the efficient frontier, the mean return on a third portfolio is

$$\mu_p^{(3)} = \alpha\mu_p^{(1)} + (1 - \alpha)\mu_p^{(2)} \quad \text{with} \quad w_p^* = \alpha w_1^* + (1 - \alpha)w_2^*$$

This is the two-fund theorem and is sometimes expressed by saying that the mean-variance frontier is *spanned* by any two frontier returns (and this terminology is used in the allied literature when testing the CAPM).

## Capital Market Line

When we introduce a risk-free asset, the combinations of $\text{var}(R_p)$ and $\mu_p$ that minimise portfolio variance are linear. The problem is to choose $w$ to minimise $w'\Omega w$ subject to the constraint

$$R_p = w'R + w_f r \tag{A13}$$

where $w \sim (n \times 1)$ and $w'e + w_{\mathrm{f}} = 1$; hence

$$R_{\mathrm{p}} = w'(R - r.e) + r \tag{A14}$$

The Lagrangian is

$$\theta = \tfrac{1}{2}w'\Omega w + \lambda[\mu_{\mathrm{p}} - (w'ER - r.e) - r] \tag{A15}$$

and $\mu_{\mathrm{p}}$ is fixed (given). The solution is

$$w^* = k_{\mathrm{p}}z \tag{A16a}$$

$$z = \Omega^{-1}(ER - r.e) \tag{A16b}$$

$$k_{\mathrm{p}} = (\mu_{\mathrm{p}} - r)/(A - 2Br + Cr^2)$$

$$= (\mu_{\mathrm{p}} - r)/[(ER - r.e)\Omega^{-1}(ER - r.e)] \tag{A16c}$$

$$w_{\mathrm{f}}^* = 1 - e'w^* \tag{A16d}$$

$$\mathrm{var}(R_{\mathrm{p}}) = w^{*'}\Omega^{-1}w^* = \frac{(\mu_{\mathrm{p}} - r)^2}{(A - 2Br + Cr^2)} \tag{A17}$$

Note that $k_{\mathrm{p}}$ is linear in $\mu_{\mathrm{p}}$ (and so is $w^*$). The portfolio standard deviation $\sqrt{\mathrm{var}(R_{\mathrm{p}})}$ is also linear in $\mu_{\mathrm{p}}$ and, therefore, the CML (i.e. optimal weights given a choice of risk-free and risky assets) is linear in $(\sigma_{\mathrm{p}}, \mu_{\mathrm{p}})$ space. The CML is sometimes referred to as 'the efficient frontier with a riskless asset'.

There is another nice little 'nugget' we can extract from the CML, namely, the tangency portfolio. We derive the step-by-step solution for the tangency portfolio below, but we know that it lies somewhere on the CML. The solution for $w^*$, given any particular $\mu_{\mathrm{p}}$, from (A16a) consists of two elements, one $k_{\mathrm{p}}$ (a scalar) depends on the choice of $\mu_{\mathrm{p}}$ and the other $z$ is independent of the choice of $\mu_{\mathrm{p}}$. The tangency portfolio is a *specific* point on the CML, namely, the tangency point of the CML with the efficient frontier, and is independent of any arbitrarily chosen $\mu_{\mathrm{p}}$. The weights of the risky assets (only) in the tangency portfolio must therefore be *proportional* to $z$ and sum to unity. The tangency or 'market' portfolio weights $w_{\mathrm{q}}$ of the risky assets are therefore given by

$$w_{\mathrm{q}} = \frac{z}{e'z} = \frac{\Omega^{-1}(ER - r.e)}{e'\Omega^{-1}(ER - r.e)} \tag{A18}$$

where the sum of the weights $e'w_{\mathrm{q}} = 1$. The market portfolio weights $w_{\mathrm{q}}$ are the same for all investors regardless of their degree of risk aversion. The proportion held in the risk-free asset $w_{\mathrm{f}}^* = 1 - e'w^*$ is at the moment indeterminate since we have only determined $w_{\mathrm{q}}$ and not $k_{\mathrm{p}}$ and therefore not $w^*$ (see (A16a)). This should not be surprising since the choice of how much to borrow or lend at the risk-free rate *does* depend on the investor's risk preferences, and we have not introduced an objective (utility) function that 'measures' the degree of risk aversion. Only when we introduce a function that tells us how the individual trades off risk $\sigma_{\mathrm{p}}^2$ against expected portfolio return $\mu_p$ can we 'pin down' the optimal proportions to hold in the riskless asset and the risky asset bundle $w_q$.

# Appendix II: Market Portfolio

We assume short selling is permitted. Since $\sum_i w_i = 1$, we can write the maximand, incorporating this constraint:

$$\max\theta = \frac{ER_p - r}{\sigma_p} = \frac{\sum w_i(ER_i - r)}{\sigma_p} \tag{A1}$$

where

$$\sigma_p = \left( \sum_{i=1}^{n} \sum_{j=1}^{n} w_i w_j \sigma_{ij} \right)^{1/2} \tag{A2}$$

We will first illustrate the solution without using matrix algebra. Since $ER_p$ and $\sigma_p$ depend on the $w_i$, differentiating equation (A1) requires the use of the 'product rule' of differentiation (i.e. $d(uv) = u\,dv + v\,du$):

$$\frac{\partial \theta}{\partial w_i} = \Sigma w_i(ER_i - r) \left[ \frac{\partial}{\partial w_i} \left( \sum_{i=1}^{n} \sum_{j=1}^{n} w_i w_j \sigma_{ij} \right)^{-1/2} \right] + \frac{1}{\sigma_p} \frac{\partial}{\partial w_i} \left[ \sum_{i=1}^{n} w_i(ER_i - r) \right]$$

$$= \Sigma w_i(ER_i - r) \left[ \left( -\frac{1}{2} \right) (\sigma_p^{-3}) \sum_{j=1}^{n} (2w_j \sigma_{ij}) \right] + \frac{1}{\sigma_p}(ER_i - r) = 0 \tag{A3}$$

Multiplying through by $\sigma_p$ and noting $\sum_i w_i ER_i = ER_p$

$$\left[ \frac{ER_p - r}{\sigma_p^2} \right] \sum_{j=1}^{n} w_j \sigma_{ij} = (ER_i - r) \quad \text{for} \quad i = 1, 2, \ldots, n \tag{A4}$$

At the maximum, the term in square brackets is a constant, which we denote

$$\eta = \left[ \frac{ER_p - r}{\sigma_p^2} \right] \tag{A5}$$

where $\eta$ is often referred to as the *market price of risk*. Substituting equation (A5) into equation (A4), we obtain the first-order condition for the market portfolio (equation (19) in the text)

$$\sum_{j=1}^{n} \sigma_{ij} z_j = ER_i - r \quad \text{for} \quad i = 1, 2, \ldots, n \tag{19}$$

where $z_j = \eta w_j$.

## Solution: Matrix Notation

We now repeat the above solution using matrix notation:

$$\theta = \frac{w'(ER - r.e)}{(w'\Omega w)^{1/2}} = \frac{\Sigma w_i(ER - r)}{\sigma_p} \tag{A6}$$

where $w = (w_1, w_2, \ldots, w_n)$, $ER - r.e = (ER_1 - r, ER_2 - r, \ldots, ER_n - r)$, $\sigma_p = (w'\Omega w)^{1/2}$, $\Omega_{n \times n} = \{\sigma_{ij}\}$ and $e$ is the $(n \times 1)$ unit vector. Using the product rule and chain rule of differentiation,

$$\frac{d\theta}{dw} = (ER - r.e)(w'\Omega w)^{-\frac{1}{2}} - (1/2)w'(ER - r.e)(w'\Omega w)^{-\frac{3}{2}}(2\Omega w) = 0 \tag{A7}$$

where $d(w'\Omega w)/dw = 2\Omega w$. Multiplying through by the scalar $(w'\Omega w)^{1/2}$

$$ER - r = [w'(ER - r.e)/(w'\Omega w)]\Omega w \tag{A8}$$

The term in square brackets, a scalar, is the excess return on the portfolio $(ER_p - r)$ divided by the variance of the portfolio $\sigma_p^2 = (w'\Omega w)$ and is constant for any set of $w_i$'s. We denote this constant as $\eta$ (see equation (A5)) and (A8) becomes

$$ER - r.e = \Omega(\eta w) = \Omega z \tag{A9}$$

where $z = \eta w$. The solution for $z$ the $(n \times 1)$ vector is therefore given by

$$z = \Omega^{-1}(ER - r.e) \tag{A10}$$

The optimal 'market portfolio' weights are

$$w_q = \frac{z}{e'z} = \frac{\Omega^{-1}(ER - r.e)}{e'\Omega^{-1}(ER - r.e)}$$

as noted above. Since $\Sigma_i w_i = 1$, each individual weight is $w_{q,i} = z_i/\Sigma z_i$. This completes the derivation of the optimal 'tangency' or 'market portfolio' weights $z$ (or strictly $w$).

# 7

# PERFORMANCE MEASURES, CAPM AND APT

## Aims

- Define concepts that enable us to rank portfolio managers' investment performance and determine whether they can 'beat the market'.

- Relax some of the restrictive assumptions of the standard CAPM.

- Demonstrate the usefulness of the single index model, SIM.

- Examine the arbitrage pricing theory, APT, which is a multifactor model of equilibrium returns based on the principle of 'no-arbitrage'.

## 7.1 Performance Measures

It would be useful if we could assess the actual investment performance of different traders or of the same trader over time. Such performance measures would include the return *relative to* the risk of the portfolio and then rank alternative portfolios accordingly. A trader who consistently turns in a higher return than all other traders is not necessarily 'the best' trader, since his portfolio might carry a higher level of risk. An 'active' mutual fund allows the managers of that fund to invest in a wide portfolio of securities and to try and pick 'winners'. One area where a performance index would be useful is in ranking these 'active' mutual funds and seeing whether they outperform a purely 'passive' investment strategy (e.g. index trackers). The performance measures that we examine are the Sharpe, Treynor and Jensen indices.

For example, suppose the performance of fund managers is assessed every month. Over a 5-year horizon, assume two fund managers A and B have *identical* average (excess) returns of 10% p.a. from their 'active' portfolio strategies. If fund manager A has monthly returns (expressed at an annual rate) of 10.1%, 9.8%, 10.2%, 9.9%, ..., and so on, whereas the fund manager B has a sequence of returns like 20%, 2%, 25%, 0%, −39%, ..., which fund manager would you be most happy with? If you have a 1-month horizon and you like return but dislike risk (i.e. standard deviation), you would prefer manager A. This simple example demonstrates that most investors are not just concerned only with average return but also the risk associated with a particular investment strategy. There is no unambiguous measure of risk. In the above example, it is clear that the standard deviation of returns is larger for manager B than for manager A and the Sharpe ratio measures 'average return per unit of risk' and manager A has the highest Sharpe ratio.

What is causing the differential movement in the returns of manager A and manager B? It may be that manager B has a portfolio of stocks with very high betas, whereas manager A's portfolio has a rather low portfolio beta. Since both managers earned the same average return, we might conjecture that manager B is earning less average return per unit of 'beta risk' than manager A. Here we are using the beta of the portfolio as a measure of the (relative) riskiness of the two fund managers – this is the basis of Treynor's index of performance. Finally, note that according to the CAPM, the 'required return' for each manager ($i = $ A or B) is given by $RR_i = \beta_i(\overline{R}_{m,t} - \overline{r})$. Hence, the *required* CAPM risk adjusted average excess return for manager A should be lower than that for manager B, because A's stock portfolio has a lower beta. Each manager has an average excess *abnormal* return $\alpha_i = $ actual average historic excess return $- RR_i$. This is Jensen's 'alpha', which is also a widely used measure of risk adjusted performance, and the approach can be extended to multifactor models.

## Sharpe Ratio

The index suggested by Sharpe is a *reward-to-variability ratio* and is defined for any portfolio-i as

$$SR_i = \frac{ER_i - r}{\sigma_i} \tag{1a}$$

where $ER_i = $ expected return on portfolio-i, $\sigma_i = $ variance of portfolio-i and $r = $ risk-free rate. The Sharpe ratio measures the slope of the transformation line and, as we have seen, is used in mean-variance portfolio theory to choose the *optimal* weights to invest in risky assets (when borrowing and lending is permitted) – this is the 'tangent portfolio'. Used in this way, we can describe (1a) as the *ex-ante* Sharpe ratio. The ex-ante Sharpe ratio based on *forecasts* of expected returns and the portfolio variance (e.g. EWMA or GARCH models) can be used to rank alternative portfolios that you will hold over, say, the next year. In practice, the Sharpe ratio is mainly used to rank alternative portfolios, *ex-post*, that is based on their *historic* 'reward-to-variability' ratio:

$$SR_i = \frac{\overline{R}_i - \overline{r}}{\sigma_i} \tag{1b}$$

This can be calculated for any risky portfolio using a series of (say) monthly portfolio returns (together with the risk-free rate). The 'best' portfolio is then taken to be the one with the highest historic Sharpe ratio. The Sharpe ratio is widely used to compare alternative 'active' strategies (e.g. 'stock-picking' or 'market timing') with passive strategies (e.g. tracking the S&P500) and to compare the performances of different mutual funds. The Sharpe ratio is usually used to compare two (or more) well-diversified portfolios, and the assumption is that you should invest in the single 'best portfolio' with the highest Sharpe ratio.

Although widely used, the underlying assumptions behind the Sharpe ratio are rather restrictive as we see below. The 'original' Sharpe ratio is the 'correct' statistic to use when comparing the historic performance of alternative portfolios providing:

(i) We initially hold a portfolio invested solely in the riskless asset.

(ii) We then consider two (or more) mutually exclusive zero-investment strategies in either funds X or Y (or others), which are financed by borrowing.

A *zero-investment strategy* consists of taking a short position in the risk-free rate (i.e. borrowing) and investing in the fund of risky assets. (Sharpe 1966, 1975). When ranking portfolios using the Sharpe ratio, a key assumption is that any fund chosen (F = X or Y) has a zero correlation with the existing portfolio – this is assured when the existing portfolio is 'cash' (i.e. the risk-free asset), but is not the case if the original portfolio contains risky assets – as we see below.

## Case A: Existing Investment is in 'Cash'

To show why the 'original' Sharpe ratio is valid when (i) and (ii) hold, consider the following. Suppose $A$ are currently invested in your existing portfolio – which is the risk-free asset earning $r$. You now borrow $V$ to invest in any risky fund F, so the $-value of your 'new' portfolio (i.e. pre-existing 'cash' plus the zero-investment strategy in F) at $t + 1$ is

$$W_{t+1} = A(1 + r) + V[(1 + R_F) - (1 + r)] = A(1 + r) + V(R_F - r) \qquad (2)$$

The *percentage* return (with the initial $A$ as numeraire) on the 'new' portfolio is

$$R_p = r + (V/A)(R_F - r) \qquad (3)$$

where $V/A$ is the leverage ratio. It follows that

$$\sigma_p = (V/A)\sigma_F \qquad (4)$$

By definition, the Sharpe ratio of fund-F is

$$SR_F = (R_F - r)/\sigma_F.$$

where *we dispense with expectations in the notation*, for simplicity. Hence,

$$R_p = r + (V/A)\sigma_F \, SR_F \qquad (5)$$

Knowing $\sigma_F$, the investor should therefore choose $V$ to 'hit' her desired level of portfolio risk $\sigma_p^*$, hence, using (4), $V^* = A\sigma_p^*/\sigma_F$. But by now choosing that fund-F with the highest Sharpe ratio, the investor is then maximising expected return on the new portfolio (see (5)), given her risk tolerance $\sigma_p^*$. This is the basis for choosing a zero-investment strategy with any fund-F that has the highest Sharpe ratio – but this 'rule' relies on your pre-existing portfolio being the riskless asset.

For completeness, it is worth noting that a closely related concept to the Sharpe ratio is the *information ratio IR*:

$$IR_i = R_i/\sigma_i \tag{6}$$

Compared to the Sharpe ratio, the IR only 'omits' the risk-free rate from the numerator. However, it is possible for $IR_A > IR_B$ for two alternative funds A and B even though $SR_A < SR_B$, so that the two criteria can give different rankings. The Sharpe ratio is the 'correct' statistic to use since it represents the return to a *zero-investment strategy* and is just as easy to calculate.

## Case B: Initial Investment Contains Risky Assets

Now we complicate matters a little by moving away from the 'original' Sharpe ratio by assuming that your pre-existing portfolio is not 'cash' but a portfolio of risky assets E. Your pre-existing portfolio-E contains risky assets that may be correlated with the two (or more) mutually exclusive zero-investment portfolios that you are trying to add to your existing portfolio-E. Another complication is that in practice we often want to compare returns on a chosen portfolio, not with the risk-free rate but with a benchmark portfolio (e.g. S&P500). Can we still make use of a Sharpe ratio to rank alternative additions to our existing portfolio? The answer is 'yes' providing we are rather careful. The 'new' Sharpe ratio (relative to the risky benchmark portfolio) for any fund-i that we wish to add to our existing portfolio-E is

$$SR_i = \frac{R_i - R_b}{\sigma(R_i - R_b)} = \frac{R_d}{\sigma_d(R_d)} \tag{7}$$

where $R_d = R_i - R_b$ is the *difference* between the chosen portfolio-i and the benchmark portfolio. This collapses to the original Sharpe ratio for $R_b = r$. Suppose you could choose either fund-X or fund-Z to add to your existing risky portfolio-E, and $R_X > R_Z$. The *stand-alone* Sharpe ratios are

$$SR_X = \frac{R_X - R_b}{\sigma(R_X - R_b)} > SR_Z = \frac{R_Z - R_b}{\sigma(R_Z - R_b)} \tag{8}$$

Your new Sharpe ratio would be either $SR_{E+X}$ or $SR_{E+Z}$. If $SR_X > SR_Z$, does this always imply that $SR_{E+X} > SR_{E+Z}$? The answer is no! To see this intuitively, assume your existing portfolio-E is uncorrelated with the benchmark portfolio return $R_b$. Now, for simplicity, assume returns on E and X are positively correlated, while returns on E and Z are negatively correlated. Adding X to E, your new portfolio gains lots of extra return $R_X > R_Z$ but it adds to the risk of your new portfolio, since $\rho_{EX} > 0$. Adding Z to E does not provide as much extra return (as X) but it reduces risk. Hence, we cannot say for definite that $SR_{E+X} > SR_{E+Z}$. What we must do is to explicitly work out the Sharpe ratio for the two possible new portfolios.

To see how this is done assume you initially have $\$A$ invested in your pre-existing portfolio and *you short-sell the benchmark* portfolio to finance your acquisition of F (where F is either X or Z, but not a combination of both). So, again, the Sharpe ratio is defined for a zero-investment portfolio. Then,

$$W_{t+1} = A(1 + R_E) + V(R_F - R_b) \tag{9a}$$

$$R_{E+F} \equiv (W_{t+1}/A) - 1 = R_E + (V/A)(R_F - R_b) \tag{9b}$$

$$\sigma_{E+F}^2 = \sigma^2(R_E) + (V/A)^2\sigma^2(R_F - R_b)$$
$$+ 2(V/A)\sigma(R_E)\sigma(R_F - R_b)\rho(R_E, R_F - R_b) \tag{9c}$$

Hence, the standard deviation of the 'new' portfolio (i.e. E plus a long position in F and short position in the benchmark) depends on the correlation between $R_E$ and $(R_F - R_b)$, and this correlation is needed to calculate the Sharpe ratio $SR_{E+F}$ (for either F = X or Z), which is

$$SR_{E+F} = \frac{R_{E+F} - R_b}{\sigma(R_{E+F} - R_b)} \tag{10}$$

We can still follow the same procedure that we outlined for the risk-free rate benchmark portfolio. The investor chooses her level of risk tolerance $\sigma_{E+F}^*$, and (9c) can be used to calculate $V^*$, which then determines $R_{E+F}$ in (9b). Finally, the Sharpe ratio $SR_{E+F}$ is calculated. This applies for F = X and Z with $\sigma_{E+X}^* = \sigma_{E+Z}^*$, so that the level of risk tolerance is the same for both choices. Then, either X or Z is chosen to add to your existing portfolio-E, based on their respective Sharpe ratios, as calculated using (10) and providing $SR_{E+F} > SR_E > 0$.

## Case C: Old and New Portfolios

The above demonstrates that when our existing portfolio-E contains risky assets, we have to calculate the Sharpe ratio for the 'new' portfolio consisting of E *and* the additional assets that we are thinking of adding (F = X or Z). To see the intuition behind this result, we simplify the notation by renaming the new portfolio-E + F simply as 'new'. The Sharpe ratio then implies we invest in the new portfolio if (Dowd 2000)

$$SR^{new} > SR^E \quad \text{or} \quad \frac{R^{new} - R_b}{\sigma_d^{new}} > \frac{R_E - R_b}{\sigma_d^E} \tag{11a}$$

where

$$R^{new} = zR_z + (1 - z)R_E = z(R_z - R_E) + R_E \tag{11b}$$

Hence $R^{\text{new}}$ is a combination of risky candidate portfolio-Z with the existing portfolio-E. Note that $\sigma_d^E \equiv \sigma(R_E - R_b)$ already incorporates any correlation between $R_E$ and $R_b$, while $\sigma_d^{\text{new}} \equiv \sigma(R^{\text{new}} - R_b)$ incorporates any correlation between $R^{\text{new}}$ and $R_b$.

Rearranging (11a) and using (11b), it is easy to show that the Sharpe criterion implies

$$R_z - R_b > (R_E - R_b) + \frac{(R_E - R_b)}{z}\left(\frac{\sigma_d^{\text{new}}}{\sigma_d^E} - 1\right) \tag{12}$$

Some intuitively obvious conclusions from (12) are:

(a) If $\sigma_d^{\text{new}} = \sigma_d^E$, then you would include portfolio-Z in your existing portfolio as long as $R_z > R_E$.

(b) If $\sigma_d^{\text{new}} > \sigma_d^E$, then to include portfolio-Z requires $R_z > R_E$ by a sufficient amount to compensate for the higher overall *portfolio* risk when you include Z as part of your 'new' portfolio (assuming also that $R_E - R_b > 0$).

The Sharpe ratio can be linked to a limited set of utility functions in end-of-period wealth. For small symmetric risks, all utility functions behave like the quadratic (i.e. second-order Taylor series expansion). The $SR$ is closely related to the quadratic utility function, and there exists a one-to-one correspondence between portfolio choice based on maximising (expected) quadratic utility and maximising the Sharpe ratio (in the presence of a risk-free asset). However, the Sharpe ratio is not a good reward-to-risk measure if changes in wealth push the investor past the bliss point or if returns are either fat-tailed or skewed. To avoid these pitfalls, Hodges (1998) generalises the Sharpe ratio for an investor who maximises the expected utility of end-of-period wealth, assuming exponential utility (i.e. constant absolute risk aversion).

## Treynor Ratio

The Treynor ratio (1965) is

$$TR_i = \frac{ER_i - r}{\beta_i} \tag{13}$$

It is therefore a measure of the (*ex-ante*) excess return per unit of risk but this time the risk is measured by the incremental portfolio risk given by the portfolio-beta. If the CAPM holds,

$$\left(\frac{ER_i - r}{\beta_i}\right) = ER_m - r \tag{14}$$

and the value of $TR_i$ should be the same for all portfolios of securities. As with the Sharpe ratio, the Treynor ratio is used to compare the historic performance of alternative portfolios (investment strategies), and the 'best' portfolio is the one with the highest Treynor ratio.

We can calculate the average of the excess return on the market portfolio given by the right-hand side of equation (14), $\overline{R}_m - \overline{r}$, and we can also estimate the $\beta_i$ for any given portfolio using a time-series regression of $(R_i - r)_t$ on $(R_m - r)_t$. Given the portfolio average excess return $\overline{R}_i - \overline{r}$, we can compute all the elements of (13). The 'active' fund manager outperforms the chosen (passive) market portfolio (e.g. the S&P500) if her particular portfolio (denoted i) has a value of $TR_i$, which exceeds the average return on the market portfolio $\overline{R}_m - \overline{r}$. The Treynor ratio can also be used to rank alternative risky portfolios and although there are difficulties in interpreting the Treynor index if $\beta_i < 0$, this is uncommon in practice (and we do not consider it further).

A form of the Treynor ratio can also be expressed using the regression:

$$R_{i,t} - r_t = \alpha_i + \beta_i (R_m - r)_t + \varepsilon_{i,t} \tag{15}$$

The Treynor ratio is sometimes defined as $TR_i^* = \alpha_i / \beta_i$. Hence, we chose fund-A over fund-B if

$$\alpha_A / \beta_A > \alpha_B / \beta_B \tag{16}$$

Using (16) in (15), the Treynor criterion of maximising $TR_i^* = \alpha_i / \beta_i$ gives the same investment ranking as our earlier formulation based on $TR_i = (\overline{R}_i - \overline{r}) / \beta_i$. Does the Treynor ratio always give the same ranking as the Sharpe ratio? If $TR_A > TR_B$, then

$$\frac{\overline{R}_A - \overline{r}}{\beta_A} > \frac{\overline{R}_B - \overline{r}}{\beta_B}$$

Using $\beta_A = \rho_{AM} \sigma_A / \sigma_M$, it follows that

$$SR_A / \rho_{AM} > SR_B / \rho_{B,M} \tag{17}$$

where $SR_i = (\overline{R}_A - \overline{r}) / \sigma_A$. Hence, for the Treynor ratio to give the same investment decision as the Sharpe ratio requires the benchmark portfolio to be the risk-free asset and for the two alternative investments to have the same correlation with the market return. Clearly, the two criteria will not *always* imply the same investment rankings.

## Jensen's Alpha

Jensen's index ('alpha') assumes that investors hold an activity-managed portfolio-i, and performance is measured by the intercept $\alpha_i$ in the following regression:

$$R_{it+1} - r_t = \alpha_i + \beta_i (R_{mt+1} - r_t) + \varepsilon_{it+1} \tag{18}$$

The regression might use 60 or more months of time-series data on the (excess) market return and the excess return on the portfolio-i, adopted by the 'stock picker'. It is immediately apparent from equation (18) that if $\alpha_i = 0$, then we have the standard CAPM. Hence, portfolio-i earns a return in excess of that given by the CAPM/SML if $\alpha_i > 0$. The latter implies that the portfolio lies above the SML. For $\alpha_i < 0$, the active portfolio manager has underperformed relative to beta risk of her portfolio. Note that Jensen's alpha can give different portfolio rankings to the basic Sharpe ratio (which uses a risk-free benchmark). It is easily shown that if $\alpha_A > \alpha_B$, then $SR_A > SR_B$ only if $\rho_{A,M} = \rho_{B,M}$ and $\sigma_A = \sigma_B$. However, it is often the case (although clearly not always) that the Sharpe, Jensen and Treynor measures give the same rankings and usually all three are calculated for each possible portfolio.

'Jensen's-$\alpha$' is often estimated in a more complex regression than (18), where the right-hand-side variables chosen reflect many possible influences on expected returns (e.g. $\beta_i$ might be time varying, depending on a set of economic variables $z_t$ such as the dividend yield, yield gap etc.). Nevertheless, 'outperformance' is still based on $\alpha_i > 0$.

We can rearrange (18):

$$TR_i \equiv \frac{(E_t R_{it+1} - r_t)}{\beta_i} = \frac{\alpha_i}{\beta_i} + (E_t R_{m,t+1} - r_t) \tag{19}$$

The left-hand side of (19) is the Treynor' ratio $TR_i$. If beta is positive (which it is for most portfolios), then it is easy to see that when $TR_i > E_t R_{t+1}^m - r$, then $\alpha_i$ is greater than zero.

## Roll's Critique and Performance Measures

Roll's critique, which concerns the estimation of the CAPM using a sample of data, indicates that in any dataset the following relationship will always hold:

$$\overline{R}_i = \overline{r} + (\overline{R}_m - \overline{r})\hat{\beta}_i \tag{20}$$

where $\overline{R}_i$ is the sample mean of the return on portfolio-i and $\overline{R}_m$ is the sample mean of the return on the market portfolio. There is an exact linear relationship in *any* sample of data between the mean return on portfolio-i and that portfolio's beta, *if* the market portfolio is correctly measured. Hence, if the CAPM were a correct description of investor behaviour, then Treynor's index would *always* be equal to the sample excess return on the market portfolio and Jensen's index would always be zero. It follows that if the measured Treynor or Jensen indices are other than suggested by Roll, then that simply means that we have incorrectly measured the market portfolio.

Faced with Roll's critique, one can only recommend the use of these performance indices on the basis of a fairly *ad hoc* argument. If we find that our performance ranking using these three indices is largely invariant to the proxy we use for the market portfolio (e.g. S&P500, NYSE index, etc.), then Treynor, Sharpe and Jensen indices may well provide a useful summary statistic of the relative performance of alternative portfolios.

## 7.2    Extensions of the CAPM

The CAPM predicts that the expected excess return on any stock adjusted for its 'beta risk' $\beta_i$ should be the same for all stocks (and all portfolios):

$$(ER_i - r)/\beta_i = (ER_j - r)/\beta_j = \cdots \tag{21}$$

Equation (21) applies, under the somewhat restrictive assumptions of the standard CAPM, which include:

- all investors have homogeneous expectations;
- investors choose their portfolio weights to maximise the Sharpe ratio;
- investors can borrow or lend unlimited amounts at the riskless rate;
- the market is in equilibrium at all times.

It is possible to relax some of these assumptions, for example, using different borrowing and lending rates, or allowing for taxes, non-marketable assets and (price) inflation. However, these 'variants' are now, hardly discussed in the literature. There are two issues worthy of brief discussion, however; these are the 'zero-beta CAPM' and the consequences of introducing heterogeneous expectations into the mean-variance model.

## Zero-Beta CAPM: No Riskless Asset

Although investors can lend as much as they like at the riskless rate (e.g. by purchasing government bills and bonds), usually they cannot borrow unlimited amounts. In addition, if the future course of price inflation is uncertain, then there is no riskless borrowing in real terms (riskless lending is still possible in this case if government issues index-linked bonds).

In this section, we restate the CAPM under the assumption that there is no riskless borrowing or lending (although short sales are still allowed). This gives rise to the Black's (1972) *zero-beta* CAPM. Since there is no risk-free asset, the model determines *real* returns on any asset-i (or portfolio of assets):

$$ER_i = ER_z + (ER_p - ER_z)\beta_{ip} \tag{22a}$$

where $ER_z$ is the expected real return on the so-called zero-beta portfolio associated with any efficient minimum variance portfolio-p (see Figure 1). The zero-beta portfolio has the minimum variance of all portfolios *uncorrelated* with portfolio-p. (Note that portfolio-p is not the 'market portfolio' of the standard CAPM.) The beta for asset-i is

$$\beta_{ip} = \frac{\text{cov}(R_i, R_p)}{\text{var}(R_p)} \tag{22b}$$

By construction, a zero-beta portfolio has zero covariance with its corresponding efficient mean-variance portfolio-p. Note that all portfolios along ZZ' are zero-beta portfolios but Z is also that portfolio that has minimum variance (within this particular set of portfolios). It can also be shown that Z is always an inefficient portfolio (i.e. lies on the segment SS' of the efficient frontier).

Since we chose portfolio-p on the efficient frontier quite arbitrarily, it is possible to construct an infinite number of combinations of various portfolios like 'p' with their *corresponding* zero-beta counterparts. Hence, we lose a key property found in the standard CAPM, namely, that *all* investors choose the same *mix* of risky assets,

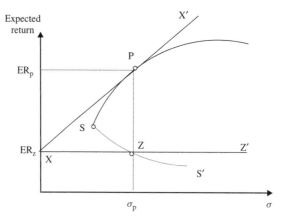

**Figure 1** Zero-beta CAPM

regardless of their preferences. This is a more realistic outcome since we know that individuals do hold different mixes of the risky assets. The equilibrium return on asset-i could equally well be represented by (22a) or by an alternative combination of portfolios $p^*$ and $z^*$ with

$$ER_i = ER_{z^*} + (ER_{p^*} - ER_{z^*})\beta^*_{ip^*} \tag{22c}$$

Of course, both (22a) and (22c) must yield the same expected return for asset-i. This result is in contrast to the standard CAPM in which the combination of the risk-free asset and the market portfolio implies a *unique* opportunity set. In addition, in the zero-beta CAPM, the line XX' does *not* represent the opportunity set available to investors.

Given any two efficient portfolios $p_i$ ($i = 1, 2$) and their corresponding orthogonal risky portfolios $Z_i$, then all investors can (without borrowing or lending) reach their desired optimum portfolio by combining these two efficient portfolios. Thus, the *two-fund property* also applies for the zero-beta CAPM.

The zero-beta CAPM provides an alternative model of equilibrium returns to the standard CAPM and its main features are:

- With no borrowing or lending at the riskless rate, an individual investor can reach her own optimal portfolio (given her preferences) by combining *any* mean-variance efficient portfolio-M with its corresponding zero-beta portfolio $Z$.

- A zero-beta portfolio is one that combines risky assets in certain proportions $w_i$ such that the return on this portfolio $ER_z = \sum_i w_i ER_i$

  (i) is uncorrelated with an efficient portfolio-p

  (ii) is the minimum variance portfolio (relative to the orthogonal portfolio-p – see Figure 1).

- The combination of the portfolios P and Z is not unique. Nevertheless, the equilibrium return on any asset-i (or portfolio of assets) is a linear function of $ER_z$ and $ER_p$, and is given by equation (22a).

## Heterogeneous Expectations

Investors may have different *subjective* expectations of expected returns, variances and covariances. This could not be the case under rational expectations where all investors are *assumed* to know the true probability distribution (model) of the stochastic returns, at all points in time. Under heterogeneous expectations, each investor will have her own *subjective* efficient frontier. For *each* investor, the problem is the standard mean-variance one of maximising the Sharpe ratio, subject to her budget constraint that gives optimum asset proportions, which differ for different investors.

In general, when we aggregate over all investors ($k = 1, 2, \ldots, p$) so that the market for each asset clears, we obtain an expression for the expected return on any asset-i, which is a complex weighted average of the investor's subjective preferences (of risk against return) and asset covariances. The marginal rate of substitution depends on the level of wealth of the individual. Hence, equilibrium returns and asset prices depend on wealth, which itself depends on prices, so there is no 'closed form' or explicit solution in the heterogeneous expectations case.

We can obtain a solution in the heterogeneous expectations case if we restrict the utility function so that the marginal rate of substitution between expected return and risk (variance) is *not* a function of wealth. Linter (1971) assumed a negative exponential utility function in wealth, which implies a constant absolute risk-aversion parameter. Even in this case, equilibrium returns, although independent of wealth, still depend on a complex weighted average of the individual's subjective expectations of the covariances and the individual's risk-aversion parameters.

# 7.3  Single Index Model

The single index model SIM is not really a 'model' in the sense that it embodies any behavioural hypotheses (e.g. about the return required to compensate for holding 'market risk') but it is merely a *statistical assumption* that the return on any security $R_{it}$ may be adequately represented as a linear function of a single (economic) variable $I_t$ (e.g. inflation or interest rates).

$$R_{it} = \theta_i + \delta_i I_t + \varepsilon_{it} \tag{23}$$

where $\varepsilon_{it}$ is a random error term, and equation (23) holds for any security (or portfolio) $i = 1, 2, \ldots, n$ and for all time periods. Hence, $I_t$ could be any variable that is found to be *correlated* with $R_{it}$, and the SIM has no specific theoretical model that seeks to explain this observed correlation.

Clearly, even if the variable chosen for $I_t$ is the excess market return $R_m - r$, the equations for the SIM and the CAPM do differ, because the CAPM uses *excess* returns on asset-i and has a zero intercept term. However, in some of the literature, the CAPM and SIM are often treated as equivalent (which they are not) and the CAPM is referred to as a 'single-factor model'. The latter is acceptable, provided $I_t$ is the *excess* market return $R_m - r$ and the dependent variable is the *excess* return on the stock ($R_i - r$). In any case, we have deliberately denoted the coefficient on $I_t$ as $\delta_i$ rather than $\beta_i$ to emphasise that, in general, the SIM differs from the CAPM.

Equation (10) can be estimated by OLS (or more sophisticated techniques such as GMM), using, say, 60 months of time-series data. This gives the estimates of the parameters $(\theta, \delta)$, the variance of the error term $\sigma^2_{\varepsilon,i}$ and other 'diagnostic output' such as the $R$-squared of the regression. Strictly speaking, the SIM also assumes that the 'unexplained element' of the return for any security-i, represented here by $\varepsilon_{it}$, is independent of that for any other security-j.

$$\text{cov}(\varepsilon_{it}, \varepsilon_{jt}) = 0 \qquad \text{for } i \neq j \text{ and for all } t \qquad (24a)$$

and $I_t$ is assumed independent of $\varepsilon_{it}$:

$$\text{cov}(I_t, \varepsilon_{it}) = 0 \qquad \text{for all } i \text{ and } t \qquad (24b)$$

Given our assumptions, it is easy to show that

$$\overline{R}_{it} = \theta_i + \delta_i \overline{I}_t \qquad (25a)$$
$$\sigma^2_i = \delta^2_i \sigma^2_I + \sigma^2_{\varepsilon,i} \qquad (25b)$$
$$\sigma_{ij} = \delta_i \delta_j \sigma^2_I \qquad (25c)$$

Equation (25a) simply says that the average return on stock-i depends on the average value of the index $\overline{I}_t$ and on the value of $\delta_i$ and $\theta_i$ for that stock. Shares that have more exposure to the index (i.e. a higher $\delta_i > 0$) will have a higher average return (for $\overline{I}_t > 0$). From (25b), we see that for any individual security, the SIM can be used to apportion the *total* volatility of its return $\sigma^2_i$ into that due to

(a) its *systematic risk* caused by changes in the index $I_t$ (which is common across all securities) and

(b) its *specific risk* $\sigma^2_{\varepsilon,i}$ caused by random events that affect only this particular security.

Hence,

Total variance of return of security-$i$ = 'delta' $\times$ variance of index $I_t$

$+$ variance of specific risk

In general, for monthly data for a particular stock, the $R$-squared of (10) is rather low, which implies that much of the variability in individual stock returns is *not* particularly well explained by the variable $I_t$. Hence, 'ball-park' figures for $\sigma_i$, $(\delta_i \sigma_I)$ and $\sigma_{\varepsilon,i}$ (expressed at an annual rate) when using the market return as the 'index' $I_t$ might be 40%, $0.9 \times 15\% = 13.4\%$ and 26.6% respectively. This simply demonstrates that much of the total monthly return variability (here 40%) for individual stocks is due to specific risk (26.6%), rather than market risk (13.4%). Of course, portfolio theory points out that this specific risk can be diversified away at near-zero cost if this security is held as part of a well-diversified portfolio. That is why the CAPM/SML predicts that the average return on any individual stock depends not on its 'own variance' but on its covariance (correlation) with the rest of the stocks in the portfolio.

Equation (25c) shows that in the SIM, the covariance between any two securities depends only on $\delta_i$, $\theta_i$ and $\sigma_I^2$, and this is useful when calculating the Value at Risk of a portfolio of stocks (see Chapter 28).

The independence assumption $\text{cov}(\varepsilon_{it}, \varepsilon_{jt}) = 0$ across different securities rarely holds exactly, in practice, for stock returns within one country. The reason for this is that it is unlikely that 'shocks' or 'news' that influence returns on firm A do not also sometimes influence the returns on firm B. When comparing returns in different countries, the SIM has a somewhat greater applicability, since macroeconomic shocks (e.g. unexpected changes in interest rates) may not be synchronised across countries. However, a violation of the assumption $E(\varepsilon_i \varepsilon_j) = 0$ does not bias the estimates of $\delta_i$, $\theta_i$ and, therefore, the SIM is quite widely used in practice (e.g. see Cuthbertson and Nitzsche 2001a). Also, it can be 'improved' by extending it to a 'multi-index' model by including more variables that are thought to influence all stock returns (to a greater or lesser extent) – for example, macroeconomic variables such as interest rates or exchange rates or 'factor mimicking' variables such as the returns on 'high minus low book-to-market value' shares (see later chapters). Such multifactor models are used in picking undervalued and overvalued stocks, in the same way that we used the SML. The APT (see the following section) is a multifactor model that incorporates some theoretical ideas on the impact of portfolio diversification on the average return on any stock.

## 7.4 Arbitrage Pricing Theory

An alternative to the CAPM in determining the expected rate of return on individual stocks and on portfolios of stocks is the arbitrage pricing theory (APT). Broadly speaking, the APT implies that the return on a security can be broken down into an expected return and an unexpected, 'surprise' or 'news' component. For any individual stock, this 'news component' can be further broken down into 'general news' that affects all stocks and specific 'news' that affects only this particular stock. For example, news that affects all stocks might be an unexpected announcement of an increase in interest rates by the Central Bank. News that affects the stocks of a specific industrial sector, for example, might be the invention of a new radar system that might be thought to influence the aerospace industry but not other industries like chemicals and service industries. The APT predicts that 'general news' will affect the rate of return on *all* stocks but by different amounts. For example, a 1% unexpected rise in interest rates might affect the return on stocks of a company that was highly geared more than that for a company that was less geared. The APT, in one sense, is more general than the CAPM in that it allows a large number of factors to affect the rate of return on a particular security. In the CAPM, there is really only one factor that influences expected returns, namely, the covariance between the return on the security and the return on the market portfolio. The APT may be represented as

$$R_{it} = R_{it}^e + u_{it}$$

where $R_{it}$ = actual rate of return on the $i$th stock, $R_{it}^e$ = the expected return on the $i$th stock and $u_{it}$ = the unexpected, surprise or news element. We can further subdivide the surprise or news element $u_{it}$ into *systematic or market risk* $m_t$, that is, the risk that affects a large number of stocks each to a greater or lesser degree. The remaining uncertainty is *unsystematic (idiosyncratic or specific) risk* $\varepsilon_{it}$, which affects a single firm or a small group of firms:

$$u_{it} = m_t + \varepsilon_{it} \tag{26}$$

As in the case of the CAPM, we shall find that systematic risk cannot be diversified away because this element of news or new information affects *all* companies. But specific risk can be diversified away and therefore is not 'priced'.

In order to make the APT operational, we need some idea of what causes the systematic risk. News about economy-wide variables are, for example, a government announcement that the GDP is higher than expected or a sudden increase in interest rates by the Central Bank. These economy-wide *factors F* (indexed by j) may have different effects on different securities, and this is reflected in the different values for the coefficients $b_{ij}$ or 'betas' given below:

$$m_t = \sum_j b_{it}(F_j - EF_j)_t = b_{11}(F_{1t} - EF_{1t}) + b_{12}(F_{2t} - EF_{2t}) + \cdots \tag{27}$$

where the expectations operator E applies to information at time $t - 1$ or earlier. For example, if for a particular firm the beta attached to the surprise in interest rates is equal to 0.5, then for every 1% that the interest rate rises above its expected level, this would increase the return on security-i by 0.5 percent (above its expected value). A crucial assumption of the APT is that the idiosyncratic or specific risk $\varepsilon_i$ is uncorrelated across different securities, $\text{cov}(\varepsilon_i, \varepsilon_j) = 0$.

## Return on the Portfolio

For simplicity, suppose there is only one systematic risk factor, $F_t$ and $n$ securities in the portfolio. The return on a portfolio $R_t^p$ of $n$-securities held in proportions $x_i$ is, by definition,

$$R_t^p = \sum_{i=1}^n x_i R_{it} = \sum_{i=1}^n x_i(R_{it}^e + b_i(F_t - EF_t) + \varepsilon_i)$$

$$= \sum_{i=1}^n x_i R_{it}^e + \left(\sum_{i=1}^n b_i x_i\right)(F_t - EF_t) + \sum_{i=1}^n x_i \varepsilon_i \tag{28}$$

The return on the portfolio is a weighted average of the expected return *plus* the *portfolio*-beta (multiplied by the 'news' about factor *F*) *plus* a weighted average of the specific risk terms $\varepsilon_i$. If the specific risk is uncorrelated across securities, then some of the $\varepsilon_i$ will be positive and some negative but their weighted sum is likely to be close to zero. In fact, as the number of securities increases, the last term on the right-hand side of (28) will approach zero – the specific risk has been diversified away. Hence, the return on the portfolio is made up of the expected returns on the individual securities and the systematic risk, as represented by the single economy-wide news term $(F_t - EF_t)$.

## A More Formal Approach

The beauty of the APT is that it does not require any assumptions about utility theory or that the mean and variance of a portfolio are the only two elements in the investor's objective function. The model is really a mechanism (an algorithm almost) that allows one to derive an expression for the expected return on a security (or a portfolio of securities) based on the idea that *riskless* arbitrage opportunities will be instantaneously eliminated. Not surprisingly, the APT does require *some* (arbitrary) assumptions. We assume that investors have homogeneous expectations and that the return $R_{it}$ on *any* stock is *linearly* related to a set of $k$-factors $F_{it}$:

$$R_{it} = a_i + \sum_{j=1}^{k} b_{ij} F_{jt} + \varepsilon_{it} \tag{29}$$

where the $b_{ij}$ are known as *factor weights*. Taking expectations of (29) and assuming $E\varepsilon_{it} = 0$, then,

$$R_{it} = ER_{it} + \sum_{j}^{k} b_{ij} (F_{jt} - EF_{jt}) + \varepsilon_{it} \tag{30}$$

Equation (30) shows that although each security is affected by all the factors, the impact of any particular $F_j$ depends on the value of $b_{ij}$ and this is different for each security. This is the source of the covariance between the returns $R_{it}$ on different securities. We assume that we can continue adding factors to (30) until the unexplained part of the return $\varepsilon_i$ is such that

$$E(\varepsilon_i \varepsilon_j) = 0 \qquad \text{for all } i \neq j \text{ and all time periods} \tag{31a}$$

$$E[\varepsilon_i (F_j - EF_j)] = 0 \qquad \text{for all stocks and factors (and all } t) \tag{31b}$$

Equation (31a) implies that unsystematic (or specific) risk is uncorrelated across securities, while (31b) implies that specific risk is independent of the factors $F$. Note that the factors $F$ are common across *all* securities and measure systematic risk. Now we perform an 'experiment' where investors form a zero-beta portfolio of $n$-assets with *zero net investment*. The zero-beta portfolio must satisfy

$$\sum_{i=1}^{n} x_i b_{ij} = 0 \text{ for all } j = 1, 2, \ldots, k \tag{32}$$

and the assumption of zero investment implies that

$$\sum_{i=1}^{n} x_i = 0 \tag{33}$$

It follows from (33) that some $x_i$ are less than zero, that is, some stocks are held short and the proceeds invested in other securities. The next part of the argument introduces the arbitrage element. If investors put up no funds and the zero-beta portfolio earns a non-zero expected return, then a risk-free arbitrage profit can be made. This arbitrage condition places a restriction on the expected return of the portfolio, so using (28), we have

$$
\begin{aligned}
R_t^p &= \sum_{i=1}^{n} x_i R_{it} = \sum_{i=1}^{n} x_i \left( ER_{it} + \sum_{j=1}^{k} b_{ij}(F_{jt} - EF_{jt}) + \varepsilon_{it} \right) \\
&= \sum_{i=1}^{n} x_i ER_{it} + \left( \sum_{i=1}^{n} x_i b_{i1} \right)(F_{1t} - EF_{1t}) + \left( \sum_{i=1}^{n} x_i b_{i2} \right)(F_{2t} - EF_{2t}) \\
&\quad + \cdots + \sum_{i=1}^{n} x_i \varepsilon_{it}
\end{aligned}
\tag{34}
$$

Using (34) and (32) plus the assumption that for a large well-diversified portfolio the last term on the right-hand-side approaches zero, we have

$$
R_t^p = \sum_{i=1}^{n} x_i ER_{it} \equiv ER_t^p
\tag{35}
$$

where the second equality holds *by definition*. Since this artificially constructed portfolio has an *actual* rate of return $R_t^p$ equal to the expected return $ER_t^p$, there is zero *variability* in its return and it is therefore riskless. Arbitrage arguments then suggest that this riskless return must be zero:

$$
ER_t^p = \sum_{i=1}^{n} x_i ER_{it} = 0
\tag{36}
$$

At first 'blush' it may seem strange that a riskless portfolio does not earn the riskless rate of interest $r_t$. This is because the riskless asset is included in the set of assets available and like other assets can be held short or long so that the net return is zero.

We now have to invoke a proof based on linear algebra. Given the conditions (31), (32), (33) and (36), which are known as orthogonality conditions, it can be shown that the expected return on any security-i may be written as a linear combination of the factor weightings $b_{ij}$. For example, for a two-factor model,

$$
ER_i = \lambda_0 + \lambda_1 b_{i1} + \lambda_2 b_{i2}
\tag{37}
$$

We noted that $b_{i1}$ and $b_{i2}$ in (30) are specific to security-i. The expected return on security-i weights these security-specific betas by a weight $\lambda_j$ that is *the same for all securities*. Hence, $\lambda_j$ may be interpreted as the extra expected return required because of a securities sensitivity to the $j$th factor (e.g. GNP or interest rates).

## Interpretation of the $\lambda_j$

Assume for the moment that we know the values of $b_{i1}$ and $b_{i2}$. We can interpret the $\lambda_j$ as follows. Consider a zero-beta portfolio (e.g. $b_{i1}$ and $b_{i2} = 0$), which has an expected return $ER_z$. If riskless borrowing and lending exist, then $ER_z = r$, the risk-free rate. Using (37), we see that

$$\lambda_0 = ER_z \quad (\text{or } r) \tag{38}$$

Next, consider a portfolio having $b_{i1} = 1$ and $b_{i2} = 0$ with an expected return $ER_1$. Substituting in (37), we obtain

$$\lambda_1 = ER_1 - \lambda_0 = E(R_1 - R_z) \tag{39}$$

Similarly,

$$\lambda_2 = E(R_2 - R_z) \tag{40}$$

Hence, an alternative to (37) is

$$ER_i = ER_z + b_{i1}E(R_1 - R_z) + b_{i2}E(R_2 - R_z) \tag{41}$$

Thus, one interpretation of the APT is that the expected return on a security-i depends on its sensitivity to the factor loadings (i.e. the $b_{ij}$). In addition, each factor loading (e.g. $b_{i1}$) is 'weighted' by the expected excess return $E(R_1 - R_z)$, that is, the (excess) return on a portfolio whose beta with respect to the first factor is one and with respect to all other factors is zero. This portfolio with a 'beta of 1' therefore mimics the unexpected movements in the factor $F_1$.

## Implementation of the APT

The APT is a factor model and may be summed up in two equations:

$$R_{it} = a_i + \sum_{j=1}^{k} b_{ij}F_{jt} + \varepsilon_{it} \tag{42a}$$

$$ER_{it} = \lambda_0 + \sum_{j=1}^{k} b_{ij}\lambda_j \tag{42b}$$

where $\lambda_0 = r_t$ or $ER_z$. Note that in (42b), the $\lambda_0$ and $\lambda_j$ are constant across all assets (in the cross-section). The time-series equation (42a) is not a prediction equation for $R_{it}$ since the factors are also measured at time $t$, the equation measures the contemporaneous risk exposure to the factors.

If there is no risk-free rate, then $\lambda_0$ must be estimated and as it is the expected return on a portfolio when all betas are zero, $\lambda_0$ is the *zero-beta rate*. The $b_{ij}$ are interpreted as the amount of exposure of asset-i to the factor $j$ and $\lambda_j$ is interpreted as the 'price' of this risk exposure. So the expected return premium on asset-i equals the *unit* exposure $\beta_{ij}$ to factor $F_j$ times $\lambda_j$, the price of this beta risk. It is the loadings or betas that determine average returns, not any characteristics of the firm. For example, 'value stocks' (i.e. stocks with high values of book-to-market) earn a high average return, not because they have high book-to-market ratios *per se* but because they have a high *loading* (i.e. high $\beta_{ij}$) on the book-to-market factor $F_j$.

The APT may be implemented in the following (stylised) way. A 'first-pass' time-series regression of $R_{it}$ on a set of factors $F_{it}$ (e.g. inflation, GDP growth, interest rates) will yield estimates of $a_i$ and the $b_{i1}, b_{i2}$, and so on. This can be repeated for $i = 1, 2, \ldots, m$ securities so that we have $m$ values for *each* of the betas, one for each of the different securities. In the 'second-pass' regression, the $b_i$ vary over the $m$ securities and are therefore the right-hand-side *variables* in (42b). Hence, in equation (42b), the $b_{ij}$ are the variables that are different across the $m$ securities. The $\lambda_j$ are the same for *all* securities and, hence, these can be estimated from the *cross-section* regression (42b) of $\overline{R}_i$ on the $b_{ij}$ (for $i = 1, 2, \ldots, m$). The risk-free rate is constant across securities and hence is the constant term in the cross-section regression.

The above estimation is a two-step procedure. There exists a superior procedure (in principle at least), whereby both equations (42a) and (42b) are estimated simultaneously. This is known as *factor analysis*. Factor analysis chooses a subset of all the factors $F_j$ so that the covariance between each equation's residuals is (close to) zero (i.e. $E(\varepsilon_i \varepsilon_j) = 0$), which is consistent with the theoretical assumption that the portfolio is fully diversified. One stops adding factors $F_j$ when the next factor adds 'little' additional explanation. Thus, we simultaneously estimate the appropriate number of $F_j$'s and their corresponding $b_{ij}$'s. The $\lambda_j$ are then estimated from the cross-section regression (42b).

There are, however, problems in interpreting the results from factor analysis. First, the signs on the $b_{ij}$ and $\lambda_j$'s are arbitrary and could be reversed. (e.g. a positive $b_{ij}$ and negative $\lambda_j$ is statistically indistinguishable from a negative $b_{ij}$ and positive $\lambda_j$). Second, there is a scaling problem in that the results still hold if the $\beta_{ij}$ are doubled and the $\lambda_j$ halved. Finally, if the regressions are repeated on different samples of data, there is no guarantee that the same factors will appear in the same order of importance. Thus, the only *a priori* constraints in the APT model are that some $\lambda_j$ and $b_{ij}$ are (statistically) non-zero: there is not a great deal of economic intuition one can impart to this result.

The reason we have spent a little time, at this point, in discussing the testing of the APT is that although the structure of the model is very general (based as it is on arbitrage arguments plus a few other minimal restrictive assumptions), nevertheless, it is difficult to implement and make operational. As well as the problems of interpretation of the $b_{ij}$ and $\lambda_j$ that we cannot 'sign' *a priori* (i.e. either could be positive or negative), we might also have problems in that the $b_{ij}$ or $\lambda_j$ may not be constant over time.

## The CAPM and the APT

It must by now be clear to the reader that these two models of equilibrium expected returns are based on rather different (behavioural) assumptions. The APT is often referred to as a *multifactor* model. The standard CAPM in this terminology, may be shown to be a very special case of the APT, namely, a single-factor version of the APT, where the single factor is the expected return on the market portfolio $ER_m$. If the return generating equation for security-i is hypothesised to depend on only one factor *and* this factor is taken to be the return on the market portfolio, then the APT gives

$$R_{it} = a_i + b_i R_{mt} + \varepsilon_{it} \tag{43}$$

This single-index APT equation (43) can be shown to imply that the expected return is given by

$$ER_{it} = r_t + b_i(ER_{mt} - r_t) \qquad (44)$$

which conforms with the equilibrium return equation for the CAPM. The APT model involves some rather subtle arguments and it is not easily interpreted at an intuitive level. The main elements are:

(i) It provides a structure for determining equilibrium returns based on constructing a portfolio that has zero risk (i.e. zero-beta portfolio) and requires no cash investment.

(ii) These conditions, plus the assumptions of linear factor weightings and a large enough number of securities to give an infinitely small (zero) specific risk, allow orthogonality restrictions to be placed on the parameters of the expected returns equation. These restrictions give rise to an expected returns equation that depends on asset-i factor loadings $b_{ij}$ and the weights $\lambda_j$'s, which are the same across different assets.

(iii) The APT does not rely on any assumptions about utility functions or that investors consider only the mean and variance of prospective portfolios. The APT does, however, require homogeneous expectations.

(iv) The APT contains some arbitrary choices when we consider its empirical implementation (e.g. what are the appropriate factors $F_j$? Are the $b_{ij}$ constant over time?). The APT is rather difficult to interpret (e.g. there are no *a priori* restrictions on the signs of the $b_{ij}$ and $\lambda_j$).

## 7.5 Summary

- The Sharpe ratio, Treynor index and Jensen index ('Jensen's alpha') are performance measures that can be used to rank alternative portfolios or investment strategies. The Jensen index can be generalised by including more 'factors' than just the market return.

- The CAPM can be generalised in several ways, although the standard CAPM and the zero-beta CAPM are often the focus in empirical work.

- The single index model SIM is a linear statistical representation of the return on any stock-i or portfolio of stocks, which assumes that only one factor has a systematic effect on returns. Accepting this model considerably simplifies the analyses of returns, optimal portfolio weights and Value at Risk calculations.

- The APT is a multifactor model of expected returns based on the no-arbitrage principle. Returns over time are influenced by several factors, and the factor betas explain the cross-section of average returns.

# 8

# EMPIRICAL EVIDENCE: CAPM AND APT

## Aims

- Demonstrate how the CAPM (and zero-beta CAPM) can be tested using time-series and cross-section approaches.

- Show that a *cross section* of average stock market returns is best explained by a multifactor model. The cross section of *stock* returns depends on the betas for book-to-market and size variables but not on the CAPM-beta.

- Demonstrate that the CAPM-beta only explains the different cross-section average returns on bonds (or T-bills) *versus* stocks.

- Outline how the APT can be viewed as an *equilibrium* multifactor model.

## 8.1 CAPM: Time-Series Tests

The 'standard' Sharpe–Lintner CAPM is a direct implication of mean-variance efficiency, under the assumption of homogeneous expectations and the existence of a (known non-stochastic) risk-free rate. The most straightforward test is that $\alpha_i = 0$, in the excess returns regression

$$ER_{it} - r_t = \alpha_i + \beta_i(ER_m - r)_t \qquad (1)$$

We assume individual returns are temporally *iid*, although we allow contemporaneous correlation across assets $E(\varepsilon_{it}\varepsilon_{jt}) \neq 0$. Then, under the assumption of joint normality of returns, (1) can be estimated by maximum likelihood using panel data ($N$ assets,

$t = 1, 2, \ldots, T$ time periods). But because we have the same (single) independent variable in all equations, maximum likelihood estimates for $(\alpha, \beta)$ are equivalent to OLS equation-by-equation: the OLS residuals can be used to form the (contemporaneous) covariance matrix for the $N$ assets $\sum = \hat{e}\hat{e}'/T$. But the asymptotic results from Wald and likelihood ratio tests may have substantial size distortions in finite samples (see Campbell, Lo and MacKinlay 1997 Chapter 5). However, there are various tests for $\alpha(N \times 1) = 0$, valid in small samples. The power (i.e. the probability of rejecting the null, given that an alternative hypothesis is true) of the exact tests is found to be increasing in $T$ (as we might expect) but is very sensitive to $N$, which should probably be kept small (i.e. less than 10). When there is conditional heteroscedasticity or serial correlation, then GMM can be used, although less is known about the small sample properties of exact tests of $\alpha = 0$. In this case, MCS can be used (e.g. with alternative distributions) or we can bootstrap the residuals, in order to obtain an empirical distribution for $\alpha$, in finite samples.

Tests of Black's *zero-beta* CAPM use *real* returns in the regression

$$R_t = \alpha + \beta R_{\mathrm{m}t} + \varepsilon_t \tag{2}$$

where $R \sim (N \times 1)$ vector of $N$-asset returns etc. and $(\alpha, \beta)$ are both $N \times 1$. The null hypothesis is

$$H_0 : \alpha = (e - \beta)\gamma$$

where $e$ is an $(N \times 1)$ unit vector and $\gamma = E(R_{0B})$ the expected return on the zero-beta portfolio, which is treated as an unobservable parameter. Panel data regression using an iterative systems estimator gives estimates of the constrained $\beta, \gamma$ (and the covariance matrix $\Sigma$) and then standard (asymptotic) Wald and likelihood ratio tests are possible.

Early studies in the 1970s find $\alpha_i = 0$ and hence tend to favour the Sharpe–Lintner CAPM but subsequent work (e.g. Campbell, Lo and MacKinlay 1997) finds against. Cochrane (1996) directly estimates a 'conditional-CAPM' where the impact of the excess market return is 'scaled' by the dividend–price ratio or the term premium. Hence, the impact of the market return on the return on assets (or portfolio of assets) depends on variables that reflect the 'state of the business cycle'. He finds that for size-sorted portfolio returns, the pricing error (i.e. Jensen's alpha) is halved compared to the standard (unconditional) CAPM.

## 8.2   CAPM: Cross-Section Tests

The CAPM states that differences in average returns in a cross section of stocks depends linearly (and solely) on asset-betas. (This is the Security Market Line, SML.) The first problem in testing this hypothesis is that *individual* stock returns are so volatile that one cannot reject the hypothesis that *average* returns across different stocks are the same. For individual stocks, $\sigma \approx 30 - 80\%$ p.a. and hence $\sigma/\sqrt{T}$ can still be very large even if $T$ is large. One answer is to sort stocks into portfolios where the sorting attempts to maximise differences in average returns – without differences in average returns, we cannot test the CAPM. In principle, any grouping is permissible, but a grouping based on, say, ticker symbols A–E, F–J, and so on, may not produce a good spread of average returns. However, grouping according to 'size' and 'book-to-market' are popular methods that produce a good spread of average returns. (Although, in early work, the grouping was based on asset-betas.)

The second major problem is that the betas are measured with error. Several methods have been used to minimise this problem. One is to assign individual stocks into a small number of 'portfolio betas'. These portfolio betas are estimated using a time-series regression of just a small number of portfolio returns (e.g. around 10) – this grouping is thought to minimise the error in estimating betas. To allow a firm to have a different beta over time, the above approach has been extended and used in rolling regressions. These issues are discussed below.

Cross-section tests take the form of a two-stage procedure (on which, more below). Under the assumption that $\beta_i$ is constant over the whole sample, a *first-pass time-series regression* for each asset $i$, taken in turn is

$$R_{it} - r_t = \alpha_i + \beta_i (ER_{\mathrm{m}} - r)_t + \varepsilon_{it} \tag{3}$$

The estimates of $\beta_i$ *for each security* may then be used in a *second-pass cross-section* regression. Here, the *sample average* monthly returns $\overline{R}_i$ (usually over the whole sample) on all $k$-securities are regressed on the $\hat{\beta}_i$'s from the first-pass regression

$$\overline{R}_i = \lambda_0 + \lambda_1 \hat{\beta}_i + v_i \tag{4}$$

Comparing (4) with the standard CAPM relation

$$R_i = r + \beta_i (R_{\mathrm{m}} - r) + \varepsilon_i \tag{5}$$

we expect $\lambda_0 = \overline{r}$, $\lambda_1 = \overline{R}_{\mathrm{m}} - \overline{r} > 0$ where a bar indicates the sample mean values. An even stronger test of the CAPM in the second-pass regression is to note that *only the betas* $\beta_i (i = 1$ to $k)$ should influence $\overline{R}_i$, so no other cross-section variables should be significant in (5) (e.g. the own variance of returns $\sigma_{\varepsilon i}^2$).

Note that in (4), the $\lambda_0$ and $\lambda_1$ are constant across all assets (in the cross section). If there is no risk-free rate, then $\lambda_0$ must be estimated and as it is the expected return on a portfolio when all betas are zero, $\lambda_0$ is the *zero-beta rate*.

An acute econometric problem is that in the first-pass time-series regression, the estimate $\hat{\beta}_i$ may be unbiased but it is measured with error. Hence, in the second-pass regression (4), we have a classic 'errors-in-variables' problem, which means that the OLS coefficient of $\lambda_1$ is downward biased. Also, if the true $\beta_i$ is positively correlated with the security's error variance $\sigma_{\varepsilon i}^2$, then the latter serves as a proxy for the true $\beta_i$ and hence if $\hat{\beta}_i$ is measured with error, then $\sigma_{\varepsilon i}^2$ may be significant in the second-pass regression. Finally, note that if the error distribution of $\varepsilon_{it}$ is non-normal (e.g. positively skewed or fat-tailed), then incorrect inferences will also ensue. In particular, positive skewness in the residuals of the cross-section regressions will show up as an association between residual risk and return, even though in the true model there is no association.

As an illustration of these early studies, consider that of Black, Jensen and Scholes (1972), who use monthly rates of return 1926–1966 in the first-pass time-series regressions. They minimised the heteroscedasticity problem and the error in estimating the betas by grouping all stocks into a set of 10 portfolios based on the size of the betas for *individual* securities (i.e. the time-series estimates of $\beta_i$ for individual securities over a rolling five-year estimation period are used to assemble the portfolios). For each of the 10 beta-sorted portfolios, the monthly return $R_{it}^p$ is regressed on $R_{mt}$ over a period of 35 years

$$R_{it}^p = \hat{\alpha}_i + \hat{\beta}_i R_{mt} \tag{6}$$

This gives the *portfolio* betas, and each individual stock is then *allocated* to one of these 10 beta values. In the second-pass cross-section regressions, the average monthly excess return $\overline{R}_i - \overline{r}$ for all *individual* stocks is regressed on their 'allocated' portfolio betas. A statistically significant positive coefficient $\lambda_1$ in (4) supports the CAPM.

Cochrane (2001) updates the above studies and provides a clear simple test of the CAPM. First, he sorts all stocks on the NYSE into 10 portfolios on the basis of size (i.e. market capitalisation) and also includes a portfolio of corporate bonds and government bonds (i.e. 12 portfolios in all). Next, he uses separate time-series regressions to estimate the 12 portfolio betas. Finally, he takes the sample average returns ($t = 1, 2, \ldots, T$) for each portfolio $\overline{R}_i$ ($i = 1, 2, \ldots, 12$) and regresses these against the 12 estimated portfolio betas $\hat{\beta}_i$. The bond portfolios have low betas and low average returns, and the size-sorted stock returns are also positively related to beta (Figure 1). Things are looking good for the CAPM. However, there are two problems. First, if we draw the SML, $\overline{R}_i = \overline{r} + (\overline{R}_m - \overline{r})\beta_i$, the points for the *stock* returns tend to lie above it rather than on it – this is perhaps not too damning. Second, the OLS regression has an average return for the smallest stock decile way above the estimated SML (Figure 1). This is the 'small firm effect' (Banz 1981) – very small firms (i.e. low market cap) earn average returns above their SML risk-adjusted value. The CAPM/SML seems to do a reasonable job of explaining bond returns *relative to* stock returns but not such a good job in explaining the cross section of average stock

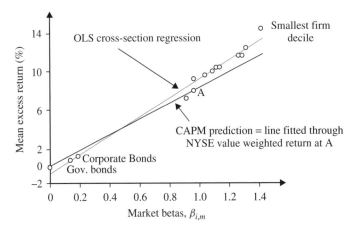

**Figure 1**  Size-sorted value-weighted decile portfolio (NYSE) : US data, post-1947

returns sorted by 'size'. As we see below, this apparent moderate 'success' of the CAPM is fragile since when stocks are sorted into deciles according to book-to-market value, these decile returns are *not* explained by market betas.

## Fama–MacBeth Rolling Regression

Fama and MacBeth (1973) provide a much-used regression methodology that involves *'rolling' cross-section regressions*. Essentially, one undertakes a separate cross-section regression for each time period, hence obtaining a time-series of the coefficient on the chosen cross-section variable (e.g. the betas), on which we can then perform various tests. To illustrate, suppose we have $N$ industry returns for any single month $t$, $R_t$ and their associated cross-section betas *are known with certainty*. The simplest test of the CAPM is to run a cross-section OLS regression *for any single month $t$*.

$$R_t = \alpha'_t e + \gamma_t \beta + \theta_t Z + \varepsilon \tag{7}$$

where $R_t = (R_1, R_2, \ldots, R_N)_t \sim N \times 1$ vector of *cross-section* excess monthly
  returns at time $t$
  $\beta = (\beta_1, \beta_2, \ldots, \beta_N) \sim N \times 1$ vector of CAPM-betas
  $\gamma_t = scalar$ cross-section coefficient for time $t$ (the 'price' of beta-risk)
  $\alpha_t = scalar$ estimate of intercept for time $t$
  $e = N \times 1$ vector of ones
  $Z =$ additional cross-section variables (e.g. book-to-market value)
  $\varepsilon = N \times 1$ vector of cross-section error terms

For any $t$, the CAPM implies $\alpha_t = \theta_t = 0$ and $\gamma_t > 0$. The Fama–MacBeth procedure 'averages' these parameter estimates of over all time periods as follows. We repeat regression (7) for each month $t = 1, 2, \ldots, T$ and obtain $T$ estimates of $\alpha_t$, $\gamma_t$ and $\theta_t$. In the second step, the time-series of these parameters are tested to see if $\alpha \equiv E(\alpha_t) = 0$, $\theta \equiv E(\theta_t) = 0$ and $\gamma \equiv E(\gamma_t) > 0$ (i.e. positive risk premium on the betas). If the returns are *iid* over time and normally distributed, then the following statistic is distributed as Student's-$t$ (with $T - 1$ degrees of freedom)

$$t_\gamma = \tilde{\gamma}/\tilde{\sigma} \tag{8}$$

where

$$\tilde{\gamma} = \sum_{t=1}^{T} \hat{\gamma}_t / T \quad \text{and} \quad \tilde{\sigma}^2 = \frac{1}{T(T-1)} \sum_{t=1}^{T} (\hat{\gamma}_t - \tilde{\gamma})^2$$

A similar procedure gives $t_\alpha$ and $t_\theta$ and hence the CAPM restrictions are easily tested. One problem with the above is that the 'true' betas are unknown, and this introduces an errors-in-variables problem. One could use instrumental variables for the betas, but the popular method of minimising this problem is to group individual returns into, say, 100 portfolios (e.g. sorted by size and book-to-market) and calculate 100 *portfolio* betas. We then assign each *individual* stock to have one of these 100 betas (see Appendix).

Fama and MacBeth (1974) used the above procedure and also included $\beta_i^2$ and $\sigma_{\varepsilon i}^2$(from the 1st-pass regression) when estimating the cross-section portfolio returns equation separately for *each month* over 1935 to 1968.

$$\overline{R}_i^p = \lambda_0 + \lambda_1 \beta_i + \lambda_2 \beta_i^2 + \lambda_3 \sigma_{\varepsilon i}^2 + \eta_i \qquad (9)$$

They find that the (time series) *average* of $\lambda_2$ and $\lambda_3$ are *not* significantly different from 0 and $\lambda_1 > 0$, thus supporting the standard CAPM.

A practical use of the CAPM is in estimating the cost of equity for a firm, which is then used in the weighted average cost of capital (WACC) to provide a discount rate in evaluating investment projects (see Cuthbertson and Nitzsche 2001a). If the firm has an estimate of beta that is biased upwards, then it will set its CAPM hurdle rate too high and may therefore forego profitable investment projects (i.e. where the internal rate of return does not exceed the upward biased hurdle rate). There are various methods in use to calculate 'beta' (Blume 1975), but Bartholdy and Peare (2003) point out that if the beta *estimated* using a proxy for the market index (e.g. S&P500) is then multiplied by a *different proxy* for the average excess market return (NYSE index), then a biased estimate of the cost of equity ensues. They then show how the Fama–MacBeth procedure can be used to obtain an unbiased estimate of the 'true' cost of equity, even if we use a proxy for the 'market index'. First, use equation (3) with a *proxy* for the market index (e.g. S&P500), on (say) 60 months of data (up to time $t$) to obtain an estimate of $\beta_i^{pr}$ for each firm. Now use monthly data for the next year $(t + 1)$ to run the cross-section regression (7) to obtain the first estimate of $\gamma_t$. Roll the regressions forward every year and calculate the average value $\tilde{\gamma}$. They show that the cost of equity capital $E_t R_{i,t+1} - r_t = \beta_i E_t(R_{m,t+1} - r_t) = \beta_i^{pr}[E(R_m^{pr} - r)/\rho_{pr,m}^2] = \beta_i^{pr}\tilde{\gamma}$ and therefore an unbiased estimate is given by $\beta_i^{pr}\tilde{\gamma}$. Hence, *any* proxy for the market portfolio can be used (e.g. S&P500, NYSE index), and we obtain an unbiased estimate of the cost of equity capital, if the above procedure is followed. Of course, the method still relies on the CAPM being the correct model of expected returns, and if the latter does not 'fit the data' well, an unbiased estimate of the cost of capital but with a large standard error may be of little comfort.

## Roll's Critique

Roll (1977) demonstrated that for *any* portfolio that is efficient *ex-post* (call it $q$), then in a *sample* of data, there is an exact linear relationship between the mean return and beta. It follows that there is really only one testable implication of the CAPM, namely, that the market portfolio is mean-variance efficient. If the market portfolio is mean-variance efficient, then the CAPM/SML *must* hold in the sample. Hence, violations of the SML in empirical work may be indicative that the portfolio chosen by the researcher is not the true 'market portfolio'. Unless the researcher is confident he has the true market portfolio (which may include land, commodities, human capital, as well as stocks and bonds), tests based on the SML are largely superfluous and provide no *additional* confirmation of the CAPM. Despite this, critique researchers have continued to explore the empirical validity of the CAPM even though their proxy for the market portfolio could be incorrect. This is because it is still of interest to see how far a particular empirical model, even if an imperfect one, can explain equilibrium returns, and we can always see if the results in the second-pass regression are robust to alternative choices for the market portfolio.

# 8.3   CAPM, Multifactor Models and APT

One direct way to test the APT is to use some form of factor analysis. Roll and Ross (1984) applied factor analysis to 42 groups of 30 stocks using daily data between 1962 and 1972. In their first-pass regressions, they find for most groups, about five 'factors' provide a sufficiently good statistical explanation of $R_{it}$. In the second-pass regression, they find that three factors are sufficient. However, Dhrymes, Friend and Gultekin (1984) show that one problem in interpreting results from factor analysis is that the number of statistically significant factors appears to increase as we include more securities in the analysis. Also, the 'factors' being linear combinations of economic variables are also impossible to interpret. Hence, research over the past 20 years has focused on multifactor regression-based approaches to explain the cross section of average returns.

As we have seen, more recent studies try to sort portfolios in such a way as to minimise the errors in measuring betas and to get as large a spread in average cross-section returns across the chosen portfolio. Indeed, since the classic Fama and French (1993) paper, attention has shifted towards models with multiple factors. To maximise the spread in the cross-section returns, individual stocks are sorted into portfolios. A frequently chosen grouping is by *quintiles* of book-to-market value (i.e. 'value') and equity market value (i.e. 'size'), giving a cross section of 25 average returns in all. The use of portfolio betas reduces measurement error and also mitigates the problem that *individual* betas may change over time because of changes in leverage, firm size, business risks, and so on.

## United States: Cross-Section Data

Fama and French (1993) find that the 25 'size and value' sorted, monthly *time-series* returns on US stocks are explained by a three-factor model where the factors are the market return, the return on a 'size' portfolio (i.e. small minus big portfolio $R_{SMB}$) and the return on a high minus low (HML) book-to-market portfolio, $R_{HML}$. The time-series and cross-section regressions are

$$R_{it} = \beta_{mi} R_{mt} + \beta_{SMB,i} R_{SMB,t} + \beta_{HML,i} R_{HML,t} \tag{10}$$

$$\overline{R}_i = \lambda_m \beta_{mi} + \lambda_{SMB} \beta_{SMB,i} + \lambda_{HML} \beta_{HML,i} \tag{11}$$

Using a time-series regression on each of the 25 portfolios in turn, we obtain estimates of the three betas in equation (10) for each of the 25 portfolios. These cross-section betas can then be used in (11) with the 25 average monthly returns $\overline{R}_i$ (averaged

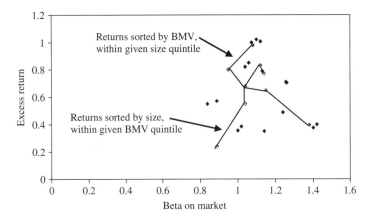

**Figure 2** Average excess returns and market beta (25 size- and BMV-sorted portfolios)

over, say, 240 months, given the noise in the data – see Cochrane (2001), Chapter 15) to estimate the λs. Fama and French (1993) find that the market betas $\beta_{mi}$ for the 25 size-value sorted portfolios are all clustered in the range 0.8 to 1.5, whereas the 25 average monthly returns have a large spread, from 0.25 to 1 (Figure 2). If the CAPM were correct, then the average returns and the market beta would be perfectly positively correlated and *all* of the points in Figure 2 would lie close to the 45° line. Hence, the CAPM-beta explains hardly any of the cross-section variability in average returns $\overline{R}_i$ across stocks (although, as we have noted above, it does help explain the different average cross-section returns on stocks versus T-bills and corporate bonds). As we see below, most of the variation in the cross-section of average stock returns is explained by the SMB and HML betas – the 'factor mimicking' portfolios and not by the CAPM-betas.

Note that if we join up points for different 'size' sorted returns (but within a given book-to-market value BMV quintile), then the positive relationship between size-sorted returns and market beta $\beta_{mi}$ reappears. (For clarity, we have done this for only one of the book-to-market quintiles in Figure 2, but this positive relationship applies to the other four quintiles with constant book-to-market values.) Hence, higher average returns of smaller firms can partly be explained by their higher market betas $\beta_{mi}$. However, it is the BMV 'sorting' that is rejecting the CAPM, since if we look at returns with size held constant but for *different* book-to-market values, then these average returns are *negatively* related to their market betas $\beta_{mi}$ (see Figure 2-this general negative relationship holds for the remaining quintiles sorted by different book-to-market value within a given size quintile – we have not 'joined up' these points in Figure 2). Hence, it matters how one sorts returns in deciding on the validity of the CAPM. But of course, the CAPM should hold for returns based on any sorting criteria, since (average) returns, whether *individual* or in *any* portfolios, should all show a linear relation between average return and market beta. So, the real anomaly (for the CAPM) is the fact that returns sorted using book-to-market 'value' cannot be explained by the CAPM-betas.

The success of the Fama–French three-factor model is demonstrated in Figure 3 where the *predicted* returns (based on equation (11)) and actual average returns for the

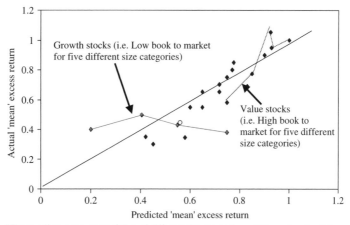

"The two lines connect portfolios of different size categories, within a given book-to-market category. We only connect the points within the highest and lowest BMV categories. If we had joined up points for the other BMV quintiles, the lines would show a positive relationship, like that for the value stocks – showing that the predicted returns from the Farna–French three-factor model broadly predict average returns on portfolios sorted by size and BMV".

**Figure 3**   Actual and predicted average returns Fama–French three-factor model

25 'size and value' sorted portfolios are graphed and are much closer to the 45° line than in Figure 2. The dotted line joining the five points in the upper right corner of Figure 3 shows stocks that have different sizes within the highest book-to-market quintile (i.e. 'low price' or 'value stocks'), and these provide a good fit to the Fama–French model. The solid line joining the five points in the lower left corner of Figure 3 are those stocks that have different sizes within the lowest book-to-market quintile (i.e. 'high price' or 'growth stocks'), and these provide the worst fit for the Fama–French model. Except for the latter 'growth stocks', we can see from Figure 3 that the predicted returns for the Fama–French three-factor model fit the actual average returns on our 25 portfolios rather well – since the points lie reasonably close to the 45° line and much closer than in Figure 2.

Also, note that the 'size effect' probably disappeared in the mid-1980s. Using data from 1979 to around 1998, Cochrane (2001) shows that for the size-sorted decile portfolios, average monthly returns are all clustered around point A in Figure 1. So, the small firm premium has disappeared as the points lie randomly around the SML, and all of the market betas of the decile portfolios are around 1.0, so there is no positive relationship between size-sorted returns and the market betas, *post*-1979 that is, after the size anomaly appeared in the literature (Banz 1981).

We can view the Fama–French model as an APT model. If the $R$-squared of the 25 time-series regressions is 100%, the three factors can perfectly mimic the 25 returns, without allowing arbitrage opportunities. Fama and French (1993) find the $R$-squareds of the time-series regressions are in excess of 90%, so the APT is a possible candidate model.

Fama and French (1996) extend their earlier analysis and find that the HML and SMB factor mimicking portfolios explain the cross-section of average returns based on sorting by 'new' categories such as price multiples (e.g. price–earnings ratios) and five-year sales growth. But the average returns on these new portfolios are not explained by their CAPM market betas. However, there is one well-known 'failure' of the Fama–French model – the HML and SMB betas do *not* explain the average returns on stocks sorted according to their recent return performance (i.e. 'momentum stocks') – see Chapter 18.

We are still left wondering about the *economic* causes of why the HML book-to-market factor is priced. There has been some progress in this area. Fama and French (1995) do find that the typical 'value firm', where price (and hence market-to-book) is low, is a generally distressed or near-bankrupt firm. Hence, HML could signal aggregate risk over the business cycle and there is weak evidence that the return on HML portfolios do help explain movements in GDP (Liew and Vassalon 1999, Heaton and Lucas 1996). It is also true that small firms tend to exhibit characteristics that indicate financial distress (e.g. high gearing or leverage), but note that this risk must be pervasive to qualify as a risk factor (since specific risk of individual firms can be diversified away at near zero cost). Also, the small-firm effect is a 'low price' phenomenon, since other measures of size, such as book value alone or the number of employees, do not predict the cross section of returns (Berk 1997). Finally, note that macro-economic factors that help predict stock returns, such as the dividend (earnings) price ratio, the term spread and the default spread, also help predict recessions, which is suggestive that a recession-type explanation may lie behind the three-factor Fama–French results using factor mimicking portfolios.

## UK: Cross-Section Data

Miles and Timmermann (1996) use the Fama–MacBeth procedure on UK monthly returns from 1979 to 1991 (12 years). For each month, the cross-section regression on 457 firms is

$$R_i = \lambda_0 + \lambda_1 \beta_i + \lambda_2 BMV_i + \lambda_3 \ln MV_i + \varepsilon_i \qquad (12)$$

where $R_i$ = monthly return and the independent variables book-to-market value $BMV_i$ and market value ('size') $\ln(MV)_i$ are lagged by one year. This regression is repeated for each month, over a 12-year period (1979–1991), so the cross-section regressions give a time-series of 144 values of each cross-section parameter $\lambda_i$. They find that BMV is the key cross-section variable in explaining average returns (average $\lambda_2 = 0.35$, average t-statistic = 2.95) and the relationship is positive – that is, high BMV companies have high average returns. They find no effect on the cross section of returns from the CAPM-beta, or betas on dividend yields, P/E ratio or leverage. They find weak evidence of 'size effect' but only for the lowest size decile.

Miles and Timmermann (1996) also report a non-parametric bootstrap test of the influence of the 'factors' on average returns. This avoids having to make the linearity and normality assumptions imposed by regression tests. In April, for each of the 12 years, they *randomly* split the sample of 457 shares into 10 equally weighted portfolios. The average mean monthly return for each of the decile portfolios is then calculated for the whole 144 months, and these are ranked, giving the maximum and minimum mean returns as well as the mean return spread (= 'max' − 'min'). The procedure is repeated 5000 times, giving three separate distributions for the 'spread' 'max' and 'min' variables and their 1%, 5% and 10% critical values under the null of random returns. When actual portfolio returns are then sorted by BMV and the 'max', 'min' and 'spread' calculated, they are significant at the 1% significance level, but this generally does not apply to other accounting variables tried.

For example, the 1% critical value for the minimum (maximum) return in the boot-strap where portfolio rankings are random is 0.83% p.m. (1.50% p.m.). When sorted by BMV, the lowest (highest) decile has a mean return of 0.75% p.m. (1.54% p.m.), which implies that sorting by BMV gives a statistically significant positive relationship (not necessarily linear) between BMV and average return at a 1% significance level. Of the other 'sorting keys', only the lowest decile by 'size' has an average return lower than the 1% critical value from the bootstrap, indicating a 'size effect' only for very small firms. The results from the non-parametric approach are therefore consistent with the regression approach, namely that BMV is a key determinant of the cross section of average returns.

### Alternative 'risk' factors

Alternative macro-economic variables (e.g. inflation, investment growth, labour income, consumption–wealth ratio) have also been used as factors in the APT interpretation (e.g. Chen, Roll and Ross 1986, Cochrane 1996, Lettau and Ludvigson 2001b) and often these macro-factors are priced (i.e. in the cross-section regression (11), the $\lambda$'s are statistically significant), thus supporting a multifactor APT model. However, in general, these macro-variables do not explain the cross section of returns sorted on value and size, as well as do the Fama–French, SMB and HML factors. The exception here is the Lettau and Ludvigson (2001a) model where the macro-variable is $z_t = (c/w)_t \Delta c_{t+1}$. For any level of consumption growth, the factor $z_t$ depends on a recession variable, the consumption–wealth ratio $c/w$, which provides a type of time-varying risk aversion. Here, the marginal utility of consumption tomorrow depends not just on consumption growth (as in the standard C-CAPM) but also on whether you are in a recession or not, that is the $c/w$ variable. The beta on the $z_t$ factor explains the cross-section returns of the 25 size-value sorted portfolios as well as do the SMB and HML, betas of the Fama–French three-factor model.

Clearly, the above empirical work suggests that more than one factor is important in determining the cross section of stock returns, and the work of Fama and French (1993, 1996) is currently the 'market leader' in explaining returns sorted by 'value' and 'size'.

## Cross-Equation Restrictions and the APT

In the original Fama and MacBeth (1973) article, their second-stage regression consists of over 2000 individual stocks that are assigned to a limited number of 100 'portfolio' betas, but there are 2000 observations on other cross-section variables such as 'size' and BMV. Hence, the larger cross-section variation in 'size' and 'value' may bias the results against the *limited* number of portfolio $\beta_i$ variables. Also, the Fama and French (1993) study uses OLS, which implicitly assumes (at any time $t$) that the cross-section idiosyncratic risks (i.e. error terms $\varepsilon_{it}$ and $\varepsilon_{jt}$) have zero correlation. The APT implies cross-equation restrictions between the time-series and cross-section parameters that are not investigated in the Fama–MacBeth and Fama–French 'single-equation' studies. The APT can be represented:

$$R_{it} = E(R_{it}) + \sum_{j=1}^{k} b_{ij} F_{ij} + \varepsilon_{it} \tag{13}$$

where $R_i$ are the asset returns and $F_j$ are the factors. Expected returns are given by

$$E(R_{it}) = \lambda_0 + \lambda_1 b_{i1} + \cdots + \lambda_k b_{ik} \tag{14}$$

Hence,

$$R_{it} = \lambda_0 + \sum_{j=1}^{k} b_{ij} \lambda_j + \sum_{j=1}^{k} b_{ij} F_{jt} + \varepsilon_{it} \tag{15}$$

A regression with an unrestricted constant term $\alpha_i$ (and setting $\lambda_0 = r$) is

$$(R_{it} - r_t) = \alpha_i + \sum b_{ij} F_{jt} + \varepsilon_{it} \tag{16}$$

Comparing (15) and (16), we see that there are non-linear cross-equation restrictions, $\alpha_i = \sum_{j=1}^{k} b_{ij} \lambda_j$ in (16), if the APT is the correct model. In the combined time-series cross-section regressions, we can use NLSUR, which takes into account the contemporaneous covariances between the error terms (and gives more efficient estimators). Hence, the $\lambda$'s and $b_{ij}$'s are jointly estimated in (15).

With US portfolio returns, McElroy, Burmeister and Wall (1985) find the APT restrictions do not hold. However, Clare et al. estimate (15) on UK data, imposing the APT parameter restrictions and allowing for the contemporaneous cross-section correlation of the error terms. The price of CAPM beta-risk (i.e. the $\lambda_\beta$ coefficient on the market return beta) is found to be positive and statistically significant. In contrast, when the variance–covariance matrix of errors is restricted to be diagonal (i.e. closer to the Fama–MacBeth procedure), $\lambda_\beta$ is not statistically significant. Also, the price of beta-risk $\lambda_\beta$ using the NLSUR estimator is reasonably stable over time, and they find no additional explanatory power from other cross-section accounting variables such as betas on 'size', book-to-market and price–earnings ratios. It is not entirely clear why these results, using NLSUR on UK data, are so very different from the Fama–MacBeth two-step approach using US data, since all NLSUR does is improve efficiency and does not correct for any bias (errors-in-variables bias is potentially present in both approaches). Maybe it is the imposition of APT restrictions that makes a difference, or returns in the United Kingdom behave differently from those in the United States. So, it seems as if the CAPM is 'alive' in the United Kingdom but 'dead' in the United States. But this conflicting evidence is extremely puzzling.

In general, the key issues in testing and finding an acceptable empirical APT model are whether the set of factors $F_{jt}$ and the resulting values of $\lambda_j$ are constant over different sample periods and across different portfolios (e.g. sorted by 'size' and by 'value'). If the $\lambda_j$ are different in different sample periods, then the price of risk for factor $j$ is time-varying (contrary to the theory). Although there has been considerable progress in estimating and testing the APT, the empirical evidence on the above issues is far from definitive.

## MCS and Bootstrap

In the previous section, there is a rather bewildering array of econometric techniques used in testing the CAPM and APT models and unfortunately space constraints limit our ability to go into these important matters in great detail – that is why we have econometrics texts, some of which do tell the truth about the limitations of these techniques in practical situations. In most econometrics texts, maximum likelihood assuming *niid* errors and a correct model specification (e.g. linear) is usually at 'the top of the tree', since it delivers asymptotically *efficient* estimates (OLS and GLS are of course special cases of ML). However, first-stage GMM with a correction to the covariance matrix of errors, for serial correlation and heteroscedasticity, (e.g. White 1980, Newey-West 1987), which does not necessarily assume a particular parameterisation of the error term or that the distribution is normal, is probably more popular in the asset pricing literature as it is thought to give estimates that are more robust to misspecification of the model. Also because many distributional results (e.g. 'the test statistic is chi-squared under the null') only apply asymptotically or exact statistics require the assumption of normality, there is increasing use of Monte Carlo simulation and bootstrapping. (The best and most accessible account of alternative estimation procedures used in asset pricing models is Cochrane (2001), Chapters 15 and 16.)

For example, to assess alternative estimation techniques when testing the CAPM, one might proceed as follows. The CAPM implies $R_{i,t}^e = \alpha_i + \beta_i R_{m,t}^e + \varepsilon_{it}$ where $R_{i,t}^e \equiv R_{i,t} - r_t$, $R_{m,t}^e \equiv R_{m,t} - r_t$ and if the CAPM is true, we expect $\alpha_i = 0$. Suppose you have results from OLS time-series regressions on 10 size-sorted portfolios using $T$ monthly observations and hence have estimates of $\alpha_i, \beta_i$ and the residuals $e_{it}$ for each of the 10 portfolios and hence the sample (contemporaneous) covariance matrix $\Sigma$. We can now generate artificial data under the assumption that the error terms are *iid* normal using the sample covariance matrix $\Sigma$. Then we generate the 10 size-portfolio returns (of length $T$) under the null that the CAPM is true: $R_{i,t}^e = 0 + \beta_i R_{m,t}^e + \varepsilon_{it}$, where the $\beta_i$ are the OLS estimates. $R_{m,t}^e$ is *assumed to be normally distributed* and $T$ values are drawn from $R_{m,t}^e \sim niid(\overline{R}_m^e, \sigma(R_m^e))$, the sample estimates, and are independent of the error term. These are the standard ML assumptions. With this artificial data, we can then estimate the CAPM, $R_{i,t}^e = \alpha_i + \beta_i R_{m,t}^e + \varepsilon_{it}$ using a variety of techniques (e.g. ML, GLS, OLS, one- or two-step GMM) and test $\alpha_i = 0$. We can repeat the above, say, 10,000 times and obtain 10,000 values of our parameters and test statistic for $\alpha_i = 0$. If the econometric technique is 'good', then we would expect to reject, the null $\alpha_i = 0$ at a 5% significance level (say) around 5% of the time (this is the 'size' of the test). Having generated artificial data on the 10 size portfolios over time (of length $T$), we can take sample averages and also run the cross-section regression $\overline{R}_i^e = \lambda_1 \hat{\beta}_i + v_i$ using OLS or cross-section GLS (= ML with covariance matrix $E(vv')$) or the Fama–MacBeth rolling regression. We can repeat this for our 10,000 simulations and test whether $\lambda_1 > 0$ and is equal to the excess market return.

We can also repeat all of the above but instead of drawing the error terms from a normal distribution, we can draw (randomly with replacement) from the original OLS *residuals* $e_{it}$ and from the original sample data on $R^e_{m,t}$ to generate the artificial data series $R^e_{i,t} = 0 + \beta_i R^e_{m,t} + e_{it}$. In addition, if we believe the residuals are serially correlated, we can use a block bootstrap (e.g. drawing the original data $\{R^e_{m,t}, e_{it}\}$ in, say, blocks of length 3, to capture MA(2) errors). Our bootstrap distributions and tests of $\alpha_i = 0$ for the alternative estimation techniques will then reflect possible serial correlation, heteroscedasticity, non-normality and non-independence of the market return and residuals found in the real data set.

Cochrane (2001) does just this for 10 size-sorted NYSE portfolios with two alternative post-WWII monthly data sets of length $T = 876$ and a shorter period $T = 240$ months. He finds that for the cross-section regressions, the results of the alternative techniques are nearly identical. Now consider the time-series tests of $\alpha_i = 0$. Under the MCS assuming *niid* residuals, although GMM (with three lags) corrects for MA errors that are not there, the rejection frequency of the null are about the same as for ML, although both reject at around 6–7% level rather than the nominal size of 5%. (It is well known that GMM assuming a long-lag *unweighted* spectral density matrix rejects the null far too often and here it rejects about 25–40% of the time, for lag length 24.) However, the bootstrap results using the real data demonstrates the usefulness of this technique when the residuals may be non-normal. The ML $\chi^2$ test has about *half* the correct size, rejecting 2.8% of the time at a 5% nominal size, while the first-stage GMM estimator (with correction for heteroscedasticity) corrects this size distortion-GMM is therefore more robust. In a later chapter, we consider further examples of the use of MCS and bootstrap techniques in examining the finite sample properties of alternative test statistics. All models are incorrect, so we should always compare the relative performance of alternative models (e.g. plausibility of assumptions, internal consistency, parsimony) as well as how they perform against the data, using a variety of techniques and tests (See *inter alia*, Cochrane 2001 and Hendry 1995 for interesting discussions of econometric testing and its relationship to economic theory, which is a much-debated topic, given that we cannot 'repeat our experiments' under (near) identical conditions, as natural scientists are able to do.)

# 8.4  Summary

- CAPM-betas explain the difference in average (cross-section) returns between stocks and bonds but not the spread of average returns *within* different portfolios of stocks.

- The Fama–French high minus low 'book-to-market returns' and 'size factor' largely explain the cross-section average returns across stock portfolios (for the United States and United Kingdom), sorted by size and book-to-market value. These 'factors' can be loosely interpreted as indicating that investors require high average returns to compensate for the risk caused by recessions – they represent 'distress premia'.

- The three-factor Fama–French model does not explain the cross section of returns where portfolios are sorted according to recent performance (i.e. momentum portfolios).

# Appendix: Fama–MacBeth Two-Step Procedure

The Fama–MacBeth cross-section regression requires an *estimate* of the stock's beta. The CAPM may be represented by

$$R_{it} = \alpha_i + \beta_i R_{mt} + \varepsilon_{it} \tag{A1}$$

where $R_i$ and $R_m$ are the *excess* returns on the stocks and the market respectively. Fama and MacBeth (1973) have around 2000 stocks but they calculate a set of 100 *portfolio* betas to which they assign the individual stocks. Allocation of the 2000 stocks to a particular portfolio beta proceeds as follows.

(i) For each stock in turn, estimate $\beta_i$ in equation (A1) using $t = 1 - 60$, monthly observations.

(ii) At $t = 61$, form 10 portfolios based on market value ('size') and then subdivide each of these portfolios into 10 further sub-samples according to the stock's estimated beta. Calculate the average monthly return on these 100 portfolios over $t = 61$ to 72 (i.e. one year). We now have 100 average returns, $\overline{R}_p$ ($p = 1, 2, \ldots, 100$) sorted by size and beta.

(iii) The above procedure is now repeated for *each year*. This gives an adequate spread in returns with which to estimate the betas. We can now either take the average betas (over time) for each of the 100 sorted portfolios or run a time-series regression for each of the 100 elements of $R_p$ taken separately, on the market return to obtain 100 portfolio betas.

(iv) In each year, *individual* stocks are then assigned a portfolio beta based on the sorted 'size-beta' *portfolio* to which they belong. This does not imply that individual company betas are constant over time. If an individual firm switches from one of the 100 'size-beta' groups to another, then the (portfolio) beta assigned to that firm will also change.

The second stage then involves using these 100 *portfolio betas* in the *cross-section* regression (A2) for the 2000 firms. This cross-section regression is repeated for all months ($t = 1, 2, \ldots$, T) of the sample giving a time-series for $\lambda_0, \lambda_1, \gamma$, which can be analysed as indicated in the text.

$$\overline{R}_i = \lambda_0 + \lambda_1 \hat{\beta}_{pi} + \gamma Z_i + v_i \tag{A2}$$

where $Z_i$ is any cross-section company variable.

# 9

# APPLICATIONS OF LINEAR FACTOR MODELS

## Aims

- Show how the market (or a factor) model can be used to quantify the impact of 'events' on stock returns.

- Explain how linear factor models are used in assessing the performance of mutual, pension and hedge funds.

- Examine the importance of luck versus skill when assessing the performance of mutual funds.

In this chapter, we utilise the factor models described in earlier chapters to examine two major areas of practical concern. The first is how to measure the impact of 'news' or 'events' on stock returns, which are the outcome of the assimilation of this 'news' by many market participants. News items might include the announcement of higher earnings than expected or the announcement of a takeover or merger of a firm. If the market is efficient and we have a 'reasonable' model of stock returns, then any *abnormal* return on stocks should reflect the impact of this 'news' on future prospects for the firm. In an efficient market, the impact of *today's* news on all future cash flows should be quickly assimilated in stock prices. The second part of the chapter looks at some of the work done in trying to see if certain mutual (and pension) funds outperform on a risk-adjusted basis and if this outperformance persists, so that it can be effectively used by investors to pick mutual fund 'stars' and avoid the mutual fund 'dogs'. We also examine the role of luck versus skill in the performance of mutual funds by utilising bootstrap techniques across the universe of mutual funds.

## 9.1    Event Studies

Event studies have been used to measure the quantitative impact of an event (or events) on the value of a firm (or firms). The event might be the announcement of a takeover bid or quarterly earnings announcements or the announcement of new share issues or an initial public offering (IPO) of shares. Event studies in the United States can be used in evidence in legal cases of insider dealing, which require a measure of abnormal share price movements. If the market is efficient, it should very quickly reflect the influence of 'the event' on all future cash flows, which is then speedily compounded in the stock price, so that there should be no *abnormal* returns in the post-event period.

For example, event studies of merger and acquisitions (M&A) announcements tend to find that the target firm's shares exhibit an abnormal rise of around 20% on average, whereas the share price effects on the acquirers are very close to zero, on average. This suggests that M&As, on average, do not reduce competition (else we would see both target and acquirer's shares rising) but the acquirers do pay a substantial bid premium in the 'market for corporate control'. Of course, there are alternatives to using the 'event study' methodology for M&As, namely studying the merged firms accounting performance (e.g. return on capital) over a longer horizon (e.g. 5 years) relative to a control group of 'similar' firms in the industry, which did not merge.

Event studies are also used to examine the effect on firm value of announcements that the firm will raise new funds by equity or bond (debt) issues. These studies generally find a (abnormal) price fall of around 2.5 to 3.5% for equity issues and a fall of around 0.2% for bond issues. This makes equity issues more costly than bond issues and is consistent with the Myers and Majluf (1984) 'pecking order' view of capital structure (see Cuthbertson and Nitzsche 2001a).

There are two models that are 'close to' the CAPM that are often used in empirical work to 'represent' stock returns – these are the *single-index model* and the *market model*.

$$R_{it} = \alpha_i + \beta_i R_{mt} + \varepsilon_{it} \qquad t = T_0, \dots, T_1$$

$$\mathbf{R}_i = \mathbf{X}_i \boldsymbol{\theta}_i + \boldsymbol{\varepsilon}_i$$

where $\mathbf{R}_i = [R_{i,T_0+1}, \dots, R_{i,T_1}]'$ is an $(T_1 - T_0) \times 1$ vector, $\mathbf{X}_i = [\mathbf{e1}, \mathbf{R}_m]$ is a $(T_1 - T_0) \times 2$ vector with $\mathbf{e1} =$ vector of ones and $\mathbf{R}_m$ is a $(T_1 - T_0) \times 1$ vector of market returns. We assume $\varepsilon_{it} \sim niid(0, \sigma_i^2)$. The market model allows $\varepsilon_i$ and $\varepsilon_j$ to be contemporaneously correlated (across firms), whereas for the single-index model, $E(\varepsilon_i, \varepsilon_j) = 0$. The single-index model is useful in portfolio theory and risk measurement ('Value at Risk'), since it allows us to calculate variances and covariances between a large number of returns using only the estimates of the $\beta_i$ and $\sigma_m^2$ (see Chapter 28). The market model only differs from the CAPM in excluding the risk-free rate, but as the latter varies much less than stock returns, the market model is a close approximation to the CAPM. Here, we illustrate the use of the market model in 'event studies'.

In principle, the event study methodology is relatively straightforward. Assume we have an event at time $\tau$ (Figure 1), which we take to be an announcement of a takeover bid. The estimation window ($T_0$ to $T_1$) is used to measure the 'normal

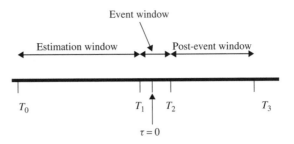

**Figure 1** Event study

return' on the target firm's stock, and the most commonly used statistical model is the *market model*. OLS gives consistent and efficient estimators, even if $\varepsilon_i$ and $\varepsilon_j$ are contemporaneously correlated. In practice, when using *daily data*, imposing $\beta_i = 0$ (i.e. constant mean return model) makes little difference to the results, since $R_{\mathrm{m}t}$ adds little to the explanatory power of the equation when using daily returns. One could also use multifactor statistical models (i.e. more right-hand side variables) such as the Fama and French (1995) three-factor model, or one could use the CAPM (i.e. $\alpha_i = 0$ and using *excess* returns) or the APT, but these also make little difference in practice. The abnormal return (AR) and cumulative abnormal return (CAR) over the event window $T_1 + 1$ to $T_2$ are

$$AR_{it} = R_{it} - \hat{R}_{it} = R_{it} - (\hat{\alpha}_i + \hat{\beta}_i R_{\mathrm{m}t}) \quad (t = T_1 + 1 \text{ to } T_2)$$

$$\boldsymbol{AR}_i = \boldsymbol{R}_i^* - \boldsymbol{X}_i^* \hat{\theta}_i$$

where $\boldsymbol{R}_i^* = [R_{i,T_1+1}, \ldots, R_{i,T_2}]'$, $\mathbf{X}_i^* = [\mathbf{e1}, \mathbf{R}_{\mathrm{m}}^*]$ with $\mathbf{R}_{\mathrm{m}}^* = [R_{\mathrm{m},T_1+1}, \ldots, R_{\mathrm{m},T_2}]'$, $\mathbf{e1}^* = (T_2 - T_1)$ column of ones, and $\hat{\theta}_i = [\hat{\alpha}_i, \hat{\beta}_i]$

$$CAR_i = \sum_{t=T_1+1}^{T_2} AR_{it} = \mathbf{e1}^{*'} \mathbf{AR}_i$$

Under the null of no abnormal returns (and assuming $\varepsilon_{it}$ is *niid*),

$$CAR_i \sim N(0, \sigma_{\mathrm{CAR}_i}^2)$$

where $\sigma_{\mathrm{CAR}_i}^2 = \boldsymbol{e1}^{*'} V_i \boldsymbol{e1}^*$ and $\mathbf{V}_i = [I - \boldsymbol{X}_i^* (\boldsymbol{X}_i' \boldsymbol{X}_i)^{-1} \boldsymbol{X}_i^{*'}] \sigma_i^2$. The standardised CAR is

$$SCAR_i = CAR_i / \hat{\sigma}_{\mathrm{CAR}_i}^2$$

$SCAR_i$ is distributed as Student's-$t$, with $(T_1 - T_0 - 2)$ degrees of freedom and can be used to test the null of zero CAR for any return $i$. The above test is easy to extend if there are $N$ firms as long as there is not any overlap of event windows (e.g. all firms have earnings announcements at $\tau = 0$). We simply sum the $AR_i$ and the variance over the $N$ firms (see Campbell, Lo and MacKinlay 1997)

$$CAR_N = N^{-1} \sum_{i=1}^{N} CAR_i \quad \text{and} \quad \mathrm{var}(CAR_N) = N^{-2} \sum_{i=1}^{N} \sigma_{\mathrm{CAR}_i}^2$$

It is worth noting at this point that for some event studies involving *several* firms, one might split the sample of firms *before* working out $AR_i$ and $CAR_i$. For example, earlier we only considered the returns on the target firm but obviously we can repeat the analysis for returns of the acquiring firm. Similarly, when measuring the impact of say earnings news on a sample of $N$ firms, one might split the firms into three different 'event samples': those experiencing 'good', 'bad' and 'no news'. The 'good', 'bad' or 'no news' firms might be those with earnings news 'greater than 2.5%', 'less than 2.5%' and 'between −2.5 and 2.5%' respectively. The 'news' in each case is the actual earnings announcement minus the *expected* earnings, where the latter is obtained either from survey evidence or some simple time-series extrapolation of past earnings.

There is now a large body of evidence that, conditional on observable *public* events, stocks experience post-event drift in the same direction as the initial event impact. These events include earnings announcements (Bernard and Thomas 1989, 1990), dividend initiations and omissions (Michaely, Thaler and Womack 1995), as well as stock issues and repurchases (Loughran and Ritter 1995, Ikenberry, Lakonishok and Vermaelen 1995) and analyst recommendations (Womack 1996). Indeed, returns over short horizons (6 months and 1 year) are predictable from both past earnings and from 'surprises' or news about earnings (i.e. public events) – Chan, Jegadeesh and Lakonishok (1996).

For example, Bernard and Thomas (1989) sort all stocks on the NYSE and AMEX on the basis of the size of their unexpected earnings (as measured by the change in earnings, assuming a random walk model). They find 'post-earnings announcement drift' or 'underreaction', since over the 60 days after the event, the decile with positive earnings surprises outperforms the decile with poor earnings surprises in 46 out of 50 quarters studied, with an average return for 'good minus bad' deciles of about 4% – which is not explained by differences in CAPM betas. Longer periods of underreaction are found for initiation and omission of dividend payments (i.e. abnormal returns over one year) for share repurchases and primary or secondary share issues (i.e. abnormal returns over four to five years). For these longer horizon abnormal returns, there are statistical problems caused by the fact that if two or more firms have an 'event' within the four- to five-year 'window', then their post-event returns are not independent – so, results are difficult to interpret using standard approaches (see, for example, Barber and Lyon 1997, Loughran and Ritter 2000, Brav 2000).

This methodology is also used to examine momentum in stock returns over short horizons. For example, Lasfer, Melnik and Thomas (2003) use the event study methodology to show that after large changes in *daily aggregate price indexes* (e.g. NYSE all-share) for 39 different countries (1989–1998), the subsequent CAR over the next five days (i.e. $t = 1$ to $5$) are positive and statistically significant. The definition of the 'event' at time $t = 0$ is that daily returns move more than two standard deviations at $t = 0$, from the average volatility over the previous $−60$ to $−11$ days. The latter are price changes of around $±2.35\%$ for developed and $±3.5\%$ for emerging markets and 'large' price changes occur about 3% of the time. For large positive price shocks, the subsequent CAR for developed and emerging market indexes over five days are 0.66% and 1.54% respectively, while after large negative shocks, the CARs are $−0.14\%$ and $−0.50\%$. Hence, there is 'momentum' over very short horizons and underreaction after large price shocks. They also find that the CARs are larger for less liquid markets (measured by market capitalisation) and are smaller in the latter part of the 1990s. However, establishing predictability and abnormal returns (relative to a 'world' market index or zero daily expected return) does not necessarily imply profits net of all transactions costs. In developed markets with futures trading, transactions costs and tracking error may be reasonably low, but this need not be the case for emerging markets where futures markets may have relatively high transactions costs or may not be available on the required indexes. In later chapters, we examine possible reasons for this pervasive result of post-event drift (e.g. learning by agents, slow diffusion of information, etc.).

### Some Practical Issues

The event day may be one single day $\tau = 0$, but if the news of the event 'leaks' (e.g. merger announcement), the event window can be extended 'backwards' towards $T_1$, and this prevents the estimation of the 'normal return' being 'contaminated' by the impact of the event. For example, in event studies of M&A, $T_1$ may be 10 days (say) before the actual official announcement.

A relatively minor problem is that daily returns generally use closing prices of the last transaction, but these do not represent the same time of day for all firms or the same time for any one firm on different days – this causes a 'non-trading' bias. The statistics we developed above assume daily returns are jointly normal and temporally *iid*. In reality, this is an approximation, so we either have to rely on the asymptotic results or perform MCS on the test statistics, using different parametric distributions or use empirical bootstrap distributions.

Non-parametric tests, notably the sign test and the rank test, are also available, which are free of distributional assumptions. Briefly, we deal with the sign test, which considers the number of cases where the *abnormal return* is positive $N^+$ out of the total number of cases $N$. Then as $N \to \infty$, we can use the asymptotically valid statistic

$$Z = \left[ \frac{N^+}{N} - 0.5 \right] \frac{N^{1/2}}{0.5} \sim N(0, 1)$$

The test assumes that abnormal returns are independent across securities and the expected proportion of abnormal returns is 0.5, under the null. In event studies, this provides a complementary test to using CAR.

## 9.2 Mutual Fund Performance

In this section, we first discuss alternative multifactor models that are used to measure the risk exposure of a mutual fund and how abnormal performance is reflected in Jensen's alpha. We then discuss recent UK and US empirical results on the performance of mutual (and pension) funds, including the persistence or otherwise of the 'top-performing' and 'bottom-performing' funds. Finally, we look at a recent study that attempts to see if any outperformance or underperformance is due to good or bad luck rather than the skill of the fund managers. That is, we look at the tails of the empirical distribution of performance.

## Unconditional Performance Measures

Clearly, an appropriate method of adjusting for risk is required when examining mutual fund performance. The most common measures that appear in the literature are presented in this section. Jensen's (1968) alpha represents abnormal performance on the basis of the market model–CAPM specification that can be stated as

$$R_{it} - r_t = \alpha_i + \beta_i(R_{mt} - r_t) + \varepsilon_{it} \tag{1}$$

where $R_{it}$ is the return on fund $i$ in period $t$, $R_{mt}$ is the return on a market proxy portfolio and $r_t$ is a risk-free rate, typically proxied in empirical work by the return on a treasury bill. If the CAPM is the correct model of equilibrium returns, the portfolio should lie on the Security Market Line and the value of alpha should be zero. Therefore, a positive and statistically significant value of alpha indicates superior risk-adjusted performance or stock-picking skills (selectivity), on the part of the fund manager. Alpha may be estimated empirically from least squares regression of equation (1) – often with a GMM correction for the standard errors.

## Carhart's Alpha Measure

The Carhart (1997) measure is the alpha estimate from a four-factor model that is an extension of (1) and includes additional risk factors for exposure to size, book-to-market value and momentum:

$$(R_{it} - r_t) = \alpha_i + \beta_{1i}(R_{mt} - r_t) + \beta_{2i}SMB_t + \beta_{3i}HML_t + \beta_{4i}PR1YR_t + \varepsilon_{it} \tag{2}$$

where $SMB_t$, $HML_t$ and $PR1YR_t$ are risk factor mimicking portfolios for size, book-to-market value and one-year momentum effects respectively in the stock holdings of the funds. Carhart's alpha is the intercept in (2).

The four-factor model is largely based on the empirical findings on US data of Fama and French (1992, 1993) and Carhart (1995). Fama and French find that a three-factor model including market returns, size and book-to-market value risk factors provides significantly greater explanatory power than using only the excess market return, when trying to explain the cross section of the average returns across funds. Fama and French (1992) report a strong negative relationship between stock returns and size: smaller firms tend to have higher average returns. They report on the basis of their size rankings a spread of 0.74% per month on average. The size factor, $SMB$ ('small minus big'), is a measure of the difference between the returns on small versus big stocks. The economic rational underpinning the specification of a size risk factor is related to relative prospects. The earnings prospects of small firms may be more sensitive to economic conditions, with a resulting higher probability of distress during economic downturns. There is also the concern that small firms embody greater informational asymmetry for investors than large firms. Both these factors imply a risk loading for size and a higher required return.

Fama and French (1992) also report a strong positive relationship between the cross section of stock returns and book-to-market value: firms with high book-to-market ratios have higher average returns than low book-to-market value stocks (i.e. the authors report a spread of 1.5% per month between the highest and lowest book-to-market stocks in their study). The book-to-market value factor, HML ('high minus low'), is a measure of the difference between the returns on high versus low book-to-market stocks. The cross section of book-to-market ratios may be the result of market overreaction to the relative prospects of firms. High (low) book-to-market ratios represent firms whose prices have 'overshot' on the downside (upside) and therefore the ratio predicts the cross section of stock returns.

The 'momentum' risk factor, *PR1YR*, captures Jegadeesh and Titman's (1993) one-year momentum anomaly. The *PR1YR* variable is the difference in returns between a portfolio of previously high-performing stocks (e.g. top quintile) and previously poor-performing stocks (e.g. bottom quintile). It captures a fund's sensitivity to following a zero-investment strategy of investing in past strong-performing 'momentum' stocks and short-selling stocks with low past returns.

## Conditional Performance Measures

The Jensen and Carhart measures described in the previous section are unconditional measures of performance. However, unconditional performance measures do not accommodate a scenario where fund managers identify changing market information about expected returns and risk and reconstitute the composition of the fund in response.

Ferson and Schadt (1996) extend the CAPM specification to a conditional performance-measurement model by allowing the factor loading on the market risk factor at time $t$ to be linearly related to a vector of instruments for the economic information set $Z_t$ as follows.

$$\beta_i = \beta_{0i} + B_i'[z_{t-1}] \qquad (3)$$

where $z_{t-1}$ is the vector of deviations of $Z_{t-1}$ from unconditional means. Therefore, $\beta_{0i}$ is the unconditional mean of the conditional beta. Substituting (3) into (1) and generalising the notation to let $R_{bt}$ denote the return on a benchmark portfolio (market portfolio in this case), the *conditional-beta* CAPM can be written as

$$(R_{it} - r_t) = \alpha_i + \beta_{0i}(R_{bt} - r_t) + B_i'[z_{t-1}(R_{b,t} - r_t)] + \varepsilon_{it} \qquad (4)$$

As $E[z_{t-1}(R_{b,t} - r_t)] = E[z_{t-1}]E[R_{bt} - r_t] + \text{cov}[z_{t-1}, (R_{b,t} - r_t)]$, the specification in (4) captures the covariance between the market-timing variables $z_{t-1}$ and the expected return on the benchmark portfolio. As before, under the null hypothesis of zero abnormal performance, $\alpha_i = 0$.

The model in (4) specifies the abnormal performance measure, $\alpha_i$, as a constant. However, it may be the case that abnormal returns are also time varying. Christopherson, Ferson and Glassman (1998) assume a linear specification for the conditional alpha as a function of the instruments in $z_{t-1}$ as

$$\alpha_i = \alpha_{0i} + A_i'[z_{t-1}] \qquad (5)$$

Using (5) in (4) yields

$$(R_{it} - r_t) = \alpha_{0i} + A_i'[z_{t-1}] + \beta_{0i}(R_{bt} - r_t) + B_i'[z_{t-1}(R_{b,t} - r_t)] + \varepsilon_{it} \qquad (6)$$

This *conditional-alpha* approach can also be applied to the Carhart four-factor model. Ferson and Schadt (1996) and Christopherson, Ferson and Glassman (1998) use instruments for economic information, $Z_t$, that previous studies have shown are useful for predicting security returns and risk over time. These include the lagged level of the one-month T-bill yield, the lagged dividend yield of the market factor, a lagged measure of the slope of the term structure, a lagged quality spread in the corporate bond market and a dummy variable to capture the January effect.

## A. UK Mutual Funds

Quigley and Sinquefield (1999) examine the performance of all UK unit trusts (i.e. open-ended mutual funds) in existence at any time between 1978 and 1997, a total of 752 funds, including non-surviving funds. They use returns calculated on a bid-price-to-bid-price basis, (i.e. gross of customer charges that are captured in the bid/offer spread), with reinvested gross dividends. This reflects the authors' objective of evaluating the performance of the fund manager and not the returns of the fund's customer/investor.

Forming an *equal-weighted* portfolio of the unit trusts (surviving and non-surviving) and estimating a Fama and French type three-factor model, the statistically significant alpha (at 5% significance level) is found to be −0.09 basis points per month. This poor performance is consistent across all four investment objectives of the funds examined (i.e. growth stocks, income stocks, general equity and smaller companies). Equal-weighted portfolios of unit trusts within each of these sectors all exhibit negative alphas. The lack of any outperformance is most notable among funds investing in small company and income stocks.

## Persistence in Performance

Historic alphas indicate past average abnormal performance. Of great interest is whether there is persistence in performance. That is to say, if we form a portfolio of stocks at time $t$ on the basis of some criteria (e.g. comprising the highest decile stock returns over the past year), hold this portfolio until $t + k$ and then rebalance, does this 'recursively formed' portfolio outperform on a risk-adjusted basis?

Quigley and Sinquefield (1999) first examine the persistence of performance by, each year, forming 10 equal-weighted portfolios of unit trusts on the basis of decile rankings of the funds' *raw returns over the previous 12 months*. Each decile of these mutual fund portfolios are held for one year and then rebalanced – these are the '*performance-portfolios*'. This strategy is repeated every year, giving a time-series of returns for each decile. The spread in the annual compound return between the best and worst fund (i.e. a zero-investment portfolio) is 3.54%. While this initially seems to point to an easy 'beat the market' strategy, in fact pursuing this strategy involves an annual turnover of 80% in the composition of the top portfolio and with a bid/offer spread of 5%, abnormal returns would be eliminated. In addition, when these performance-portfolios are adjusted for risk in a three-factor model, the alphas of the 10 portfolios do not suggest significant persistence in performance. The alphas from the top two (post-formation) 'performance portfolios', while positive, are not statistically significant (at 5% critical value). By contrast, the *negative* alphas of the bottom four portfolios are all statistically significant. This finding echoes that of a number of US studies (i.e. Carhart (1997) and Malkiel (1995)) in that, first, pursuing persistence strategies involves high turnover and, second, in risk-adjusted terms, poor performance persists but good performance does not.

Qualitatively similar results are found when Quigley and Sinquefield (1999) rank funds into deciles on the basis of their *past three-factor alphas* based (recursively) on the previous three years of data. Of the alphas of the 10 post-formation '*performance-portfolios*', only the bottom two are statistically significant and these are negative. Once again, this leads to the conclusion that poor performance persists but good performance does not. Repeating the exercise and looking at holding (rebalancing) periods greater than one year, they find that any pattern of persistence has almost entirely disappeared after three years, where the rank correlation between pre- and post-formation alphas falls to 0.12.

Blake and Timmermann (1998) is a further important contribution to the literature on UK mutual fund performance. The study examines a total of 2375 mutual funds, not all of which are restricted to investing in UK equity. Non-surviving funds constitute 973 of the total number of funds. The paper studies the sample period February 1972 to June 1995, a slightly earlier sample period than Quigley and Sinquefield (1999).

However, on the question of persistence of performance, the findings of Blake and Timmermann (1998) differ in a number of respects from those of Quigley and Sinquefield (1999). The unconditional factor model has the excess returns on the stock market index, $(R_{mt} - r_t)$, the excess return on small cap stock $R_{st}$ over the market index $R_{mt}$ and the excess returns on a five-year UK government bond $(R_{st} - r_t)$ as the independent variables:

$$(R_{it} - r_t) = \alpha_i + \beta_{mi}(R_{mt} - r_t) + \beta_{si}(R_{st} - r_t) + \beta_{si}(R_{st} - r_t) + \varepsilon_{it} \qquad (7)$$

Blake and Timmermann restrict their analysis of performance persistence to the UK equity and balanced sectors, that is, 855 funds, for which the right-hand-side variables in (7) are good benchmarks. They form two equal-weighted portfolios of funds from among the top and bottom *quartiles* on the basis of 'historic alpha' over the previous 24 months and hold these portfolios for only *one month*. The paper carries out this procedure separately for funds investing in five sectors: equity growth, equity income, general equity, smaller companies and a balanced sector. With the exception of the balanced sector, the recursive portfolios derived from the top quartile of funds in all sectors produced positive abnormal returns over the sample period. The recursively formed portfolios of the bottom quartile of funds produced negative abnormal returns over the sample period. (This finding was robust with respect to how the portfolios were weighted.) This indicates persistence in performance among both the top- and bottom-performing funds. This finding of persistence was found to be statistically significant among funds investing in growth stocks and smaller company stocks.

That there is persistence in performance among top-performing funds is in sharp contrast to the findings by Quigley and Sinquefield (1999). However, the finding of persistence among the worst-performing funds is consistent between the two studies. Direct comparisons between these two analyses is complicated by first differing measures of abnormal or risk-adjusted return and, second, differing frequencies of rebalancing. Quigley and Sinquefield (1999) recursively rebalance portfolios *annually* on the basis of abnormal return during the previous three years, while Blake and Timmermann (1998) reform portfolios *monthly*, on the basis of abnormal return over the previous two years. Blake and Timmermann (1998) rationalise the decision to revise portfolios monthly rather than annually to allow for the possibility that a fund may close during the course of a year. Notwithstanding this advantage, for an investor to exploit this apparent persistence anomaly may require considerable ongoing portfolio reconstruction, which in turn would be likely to incur significant transactions costs and management fees that may negate against earning abnormal return. As Blake and Timmermann (1998) carry out their analysis using returns on a bid-to-bid basis, the returns are gross of such transactions costs. Furthermore, the paper does not provide any information on the degree of turnover in the composition of the top and bottom performing portfolios from month to month. Therefore, inferences about the cost of attempting to exploit the persistence anomaly are made more difficult.

A difficulty with the performance persistence tests described above in Quigley and Sinquefield (1999), Blake and Timmermann (1998) and Fletcher (1997) that is, assessing persistence through a recursive portfolio formation scheme, is that it aggregates the data considerably rather than looking at persistence at the *individual* fund level. This question is picked up in Lunde, Timmermann and Blake (1999) and is also examined by Allen and Tan (1999), the latter evaluating UK investment trusts (i.e. closed-end mutual funds) rather than unit trusts. Lunde, Timmermann and Blake (1999) first sort the set of UK equity mutual fund returns into quartiles by a peer-group adjusted return measure similar to that used by Blake and Timmermann (1998) above. Funds are sorted on the basis of the previous 36 months of returns. For each quartile, the proportion of funds that fall into a given quartile based on their *subsequent* performance over the following 36 months is recorded. A contingency table of transitional probabilities is then constructed. The probability that the worst-performing (bottom quartile) funds will remain in the bottom quartile is reported as 0.332, while the probability of repeated top performance is 0.355. When surviving funds are examined in isolation, that is, a more homogeneous group, these probabilities fall to 0.284 and 0.317 respectively. Under a null hypothesis of no persistence, all of the transitional probabilities should equal 0.25. Hence, Lunde et al. report that this null is clearly rejected when looking at the full set of both surviving and non-surviving funds.

The studies described above (see Table 1) encompass most of the main issues and results that arise in the literature on performance, abnormal performance and performance persistence among UK mutual funds. There is a small number of additional studies that also examine the UK mutual fund industry using similar procedures to those already described, and these report broadly similar results. A brief description is provided below.

**Table 1** Studies of UK mutual fund performance

| Study | Period | Type of Funds | Risk-Adjusted Returns | Controls for Transactions Costs | Controls for Survivorship Bias | Performance Persistence |
|---|---|---|---|---|---|---|
| Allen and Tan (1999) | 1989–1995 | 131 investment trusts | Yes | No | Indirect test is carried out | Yes, among both top and bottom performers |
| Blake and Timmermann (1998) | 1972–1995 | 2375 unit trusts divided by 20 sectors. (855 UK equity funds used in persistence tests) | Yes | No | Yes | Yes |
| Fletcher (1997) | 1980–1989 | 101 unit trusts by growth, income and general. | Yes | No | Funds with a minimum of 2 years of returns are used | No |
| Leger(1997) | 1974–1993 | 72 investment trusts | Yes | No | No | No |
| Lunde, Timmermann and Blake (1999) | 1972–1995 | As in Blake and Timmermann (1998) | Yes | No | Yes | Yes |
| Quigley and Sinquefield (1999) | 1978–1997 | 752 unit trusts by growth, income, general equity and smaller companies | Yes | Partially | Yes | Inferior performance persists, superior performance does not |
| WM Company | 1979–1998 | UK income and growth funds | No | No | No | No |

The WM company (1999) examined surviving funds in the UK income and growth sector over the period 1979–1998. Using only raw returns, the study analysed the persistence of the top quartile of funds over five-year periods. Not surprisingly, the proportion of funds remaining in the top quartile in subsequent periods quickly declines. When there was no overlap in the sample periods, the study indicates that the proportion of funds retaining a top quartile ranking is no more than would be expected by chance alone. The conclusion is that historic relative performance is not a good guide for future performance.

In addition to unit trust and investment trust managers, the performance of other types of UK fund manager has also been examined, particularly, pension fund managers. Blake, Lehman and Timmermann (1999) examined over 306 pension funds over the period 1986–1994. An important feature to emerge from the Blake, Lehman and Timmermann (1999) study is that conclusions regarding relative performance and performance persistence are more difficult to draw, relative to studies of unit trust managers. The pensions fund market is more concentrated in terms of investment policy, and performance is determined by the asset mix of a portfolio rather than by stock selection or market-timing skills. That is, pension fund managers do not adopt much of an active trading strategy relative to other fund types, and Blake et al. report surprisingly little cross-sectional variation in returns to strategic asset allocation, security selection or market timing. Brown, Draper and McKenzie (1997) report broadly similar findings in a study of 600 pension fund managers.

Comparing and combining the results of numerous studies in an attempt to draw an overall conclusion regarding performance persistence among UK mutual fund managers is complicated by a number of factors. Different studies examine different sample periods of various lengths. Different studies also adopt different measures of risk-adjusted or abnormal return. Furthermore, different studies examine persistence using different criteria on the basis of deciles, quintiles, quartiles and median rankings. They also assess persistence using different ranking and evaluation periods, for example, one-, two-, three- and five-year return horizons. In some studies, persistence is examined by aggregating the data, see Quigley and Sinquefield (1999) and Blake and Timmermann (1998), while other studies concentrate more on the individual fund level. Finally, some studies control for survivorship bias and devote at least some discussion to performance anomalies net of transactions costs, while others do not.

Notwithstanding these caveats, it seems a reasonable characterisation of performance in the UK mutual fund industry based on the surveyed studies to say that repeat performance among top performers is small in effect and relatively short-lived. It is doubtful that a significant exploitable persistence anomaly exists at the level of the fund investor or customer net of the charges imposed by the fund. In comparison, the evidence is stronger that poor performance persists. Overall, then, an analysis of persistence may provide some modest insight for the investor into which funds to avoid but says less about which funds to select.

## B. US Mutual Funds

Studies in the literature on the performance of the US mutual fund industry are far more numerous than those for the UK and Europe. The core issues to emerge from recent studies (see Table 2) are discussed below.

**Table 2** Studies of US mutual fund performance

| Study | Period | Type of Funds | Risk-Adjusted Returns | Controls for Transactions Costs | Controls for Survivorship Bias | Performance Persistence |
|---|---|---|---|---|---|---|
| Carhart (1997) | 1963–1993 | All US equity mutual funds | Yes | Yes | Yes | Yes, among poor funds. No, among top funds |
| Chen, Jegadeesh and Wermers (2000) | 1975–1995 | All US mutual funds (predominantly equity funds) | Yes | Uses gross returns | Yes | Yes, but due to momentum rather than selectivity skills[1] |
| Christopherson, Ferson and Glassman (1998) | 1979–1990 | 273 US equity pension funds | Yes | Net of trading commissions but not of management fees | No | Yes, concentrated among poor performers |
| Elton, Gruber and Blake (1996) | 1977–1993 | 188 US equity mutual funds | Yes | Yes | Yes | Yes |
| Fletcher (1999) | 1985–1996 | 85 UK American unit trusts | Yes | Gross of load charge, net of management fee | Yes | No |
| Goetzmann and Ibbotson (1994) | 1976–1988 | 728 US mutual funds | Yes | No | No | Yes |
| Grinblatt and Titman (1992) | 1975–1984 | 279 US mutual funds | Yes | Yes | No | Yes, strongest evidence is among poor performers |
| Hendricks, Patel and Zeckhauser (1993) | 1975–1988 | No-load, growth-oriented US equity mutual funds | No in ranking period. Yes in evaluation period | Net of management fees | Yes | Yes, in short term. More evident among poor-performing funds |
| Malkiel (1995) | 1971–1991 | All US equity mutual funds | Yes | Yes | Yes | Yes during the 1970s. No during the 1980s |
| Volkman and Wohar (1995) | 1980–1989 | 332 US mutual funds | Yes | Yes | Yes | Yes |

Notes:
1. This study examines the 'buys and sells' of each fund. It finds that the stockholdings passively carried over (from one period to the next) by winning funds outperform the passively carried over holdings of losing funds. However, newly bought stocks by winning funds only marginally outperform newly bought stocks of losing funds. This suggests that momentum rather than stock-selection skills explains the persistence.

Carhart (1997) argues that many earlier findings on the performance of mutual funds were driven largely by a 'momentum effect' in the stockholdings of the funds, that may be due to luck rather than the stock-picking skills of the manager. Carhart's (1997) study is an important, comprehensive and widely cited contribution to the literature and consequently is discussed in some detail here. Carhart applies the recursive portfolio formation methodology over the 1963–1993 period. All mutual funds are sorted into deciles on the basis of *lagged one-year raw returns*, equal-weighted portfolios of funds in each decile are formed, held for one year and then rebalanced. Carhart's fund returns are net of all operating expenses and security-level transaction costs.

Carhart first applies the CAPM to the above decile 'performance-portfolios' and estimates Jensen's alpha. However, it is clear that the CAPM does not explain the cross section of mean returns on these (decile) portfolios. The CAPM betas on the top and bottom decile portfolios are almost identical and, therefore, the resulting Jensen's alphas exhibit as much dispersion as the simple returns. The Jensen's alpha estimate indicates a sizeable abnormal performance of 22 basis points per month in the top decile portfolio and a negative abnormal performance of 45 basis points per month for the bottom decile returns. A large number of the decile alphas are statistically significant (5% critical value).

In contrast to using just the excess market return (i.e. CAPM), Carhart reports that the four-factor model explains much of the spread in average decile returns amongst the post-formation '*performance-portfolios*', with size (*SMB*) and momentum (*PR1YR*) explaining most of the variation. The author reports that the momentum factor explains half of the spread between the top and bottom decile returns. However, the alpha measures from the four-factor models are negative for all portfolios and are significantly so for all 10 portfolios ranked decile 3 or lower. This leads to the conclusion that on a risk-adjusted and net-return basis, the only evidence that performance persists is concentrated in underperformance, and the results do not support the existence of skilled fund managers.

## Persistence

The same performance persistence analysis is undertaken, this time by ranking funds into deciles on the basis of 'historic' four-factor alphas (estimated recursively, using the previous three years of data) and rebalancing annually. The four-factor model is applied to these *performance-portfolios*' decile returns and, again, evidence of persistence among top-performing funds is not found to be statistically significant, while, in contrast, underperformance is found to persist.

Carhart (1997) further investigates the momentum effect. As described, the momentum variable explains almost half of the spread between the top- and bottom-performing decile portfolio returns. Funds that follow a momentum strategy in stocks may therefore consistently earn above-average raw returns, although as described above by a four-factor model, this performance may not be abnormal in risk-adjusted terms. To further examine whether momentum strategy funds do consistently outperform, the paper ranks all funds by *their loading on the momentum factor* (*PR1YR* loading). In the post-ranking period, the funds with the 'best' one-year momentum are found to underperform rather than outperform (as measured by Carhart's alpha). Carhart's analysis is conducted on returns net of security transaction costs and expenses and he explains this apparent contradiction by suggesting that funds that have high momentum factor *loadings* are not actively pursuing a momentum strategy but instead 'accidentally' [Carhart p. 73] happen to hold last year's winning stocks. By simply holding these winning stocks, the fund enjoys a higher average return without incurring the additional transactions costs that would be incurred in a rolling momentum strategy.

Carhart (1997) tries to get a handle on what determines abnormal performance (as measured by the four-factor alpha) by measuring *individual fund's* alphas using the previous three years of data and rolling the regression forward on a *monthly* basis:

$$\alpha_{it} = (\overline{R}_{it} - \overline{r}_t) - b_{1i,t-1}(\overline{R}_m - \overline{r}_t) - b_{2i,t-1}(\overline{SMB_t}) - b_{3i,t}(\overline{HML_t})$$
$$- b_{4i,t-1}(\overline{PR1YR_t}) \tag{8}$$

Each month, he then estimates the *cross-section* regression

$$\alpha_{it} = \delta_1 + \delta_2(X_{it}) + \varepsilon_{it} \tag{9}$$

where $X_{it}$ are fund characteristics: size (in logs), expenses, turnover and load fees for that month. As in Fama and MacBeth (1973), each month, Carhart (1997) estimates the cross-sectional relation in (9) and then averages the 'monthly' coefficients across all the months in the data set. His results indicate a strong negative relation between performance and all characteristics except size. Of particular interest is the coefficient on the expense ratio: for every 100 basis point increase in expense ratios, the annual abnormal return (i.e. the cross-section alpha) drops by 1.54%. Therefore, these additional fund characteristics appear to further explain abnormal performance, and the persistence therein among poor performers.

Chen, Jegadeesh and Wermers (2000) return to the question of persistence in performance due to the momentum effect as investigated in Carhart (1997). The Chen, Jegadeesh and Wermers (2000) paper is able to shed further light on whether 'winning' funds really follow momentum strategies or whether, as described by Carhart, winning funds may simply happen to *accidentally* hold the previous period's winning stocks. The data set used by Chen, Jegadeesh and Wermers (2000) includes information on the buy and sell trades of the winning and losing mutual funds between 1975 and 1995 (i.e. the top and bottom quintile of funds as ranked quarterly by raw returns).

The paper first reports that the average raw returns of winning funds during the two quarters prior to the ranking period are significantly higher than the returns of losing funds. Initially, this points to persistence in performance. In an analysis of the buy and sell trades of funds, the paper finds that the past returns of the 'buys' of winning funds are significantly higher than the past returns of the 'buys' of losing funds. This seems to point to active momentum investing by winning funds relative to losing funds and correspondingly appears to contradict the Carhart (1997) assertion that winning funds do not actively follow a momentum strategy but rather accidentally end up holding previous period winning stocks and hence benefit from a momentum effect. Nevertheless, the paper also shows that the buys of losing funds exhibit higher past returns and continue to earn higher future returns than losing funds' overall holdings, which lends some support to Carhart's argument that losing funds are accidentally stuck with past losing stocks that reduces their future overall return. However, the buys of winning funds do not significantly outperform the buys of losing funds over a one-year holding period, whether measured in risk-adjusted terms or not. These results indicate that winning funds do not possess superior stock-picking skills but may be benefiting from a momentum effect in their overall stockholdings. This effect dissipates quickly, however, as evidenced by most findings that suggest that persistence, where it exists, is relatively short-lived.

## Fund Characteristics and Performance

Wermers (2000) also picks up on the question of whether among actively managed funds there is a link between the level of trading activity or stock turnover within the fund and the level of fund performance. To address this question, Wermers (2000) applies a recursive portfolio formation methodology described previously for Carhart (1997), Blake and Timmermann (1998) and others. However, in this instance, Wermers recursively forms hypothetical portfolios of funds by ranking funds into deciles (also repeated for quintiles) by their levels of turnover during the previous year and holding these portfolios for one year. This enables an analysis of whether top decile turnover funds are also consistently the top performers.

Examining gross returns, that is, gross of transaction costs incurred and expenses imposed by the fund, Wermers reveals that the top turnover decile of funds on average outperforms the bottom decile by 4.3% p.a. over the 1975–1993 sample period. This is significant at the 10% level. Wermers also investigates the sources of this difference and reports that the difference is attributable, in descending order of importance, to funds' investment styles, stock-selection ability and market-timing ability. In terms of net returns, the difference between top and bottom turnover deciles falls to 2.1% (not significant), while the difference between top and bottom turnover quintiles is 2.7% (significant at the 5% level). In terms of risk-adjusted net returns (Carhart's alpha), there is no difference between the performance of high and low turnover funds.

Not surprisingly, Wermers reports a strong and persistent correlation between fund turnover and fund transaction costs and expense ratios. Interestingly, however, this means that on the basis of Wermers (2000), we can draw similar conclusions regarding the relationship between fund transaction costs and expenses ratios on the one hand and fund performance on the other, as that recorded between turnover and performance described above. Overall, the findings in Carhart (1997) regarding the effect on performance, at least on risk-adjusted net performance, of turnover and expenses point more strongly towards a negative relation than in Wermers (2000).

Chalmers, Edelen and Kadlec (1999) is a further comprehensive examination of the costs/performance question. This study evaluates the relationship between trading costs, expense ratio and turnover with a number of fund performance measures, during the period 1984–1991. The authors rank funds by total fund costs into quintiles each quarter and calculate the average performance of funds in each quintile over the sample. This procedure is repeated ranking by (i) trading costs, (ii) expense ratio, and (iii) turnover. In the case of all three costs ranking criteria, there is a strong negative (and significant) relationship between the costs and the performance measures tested. The relationship between turnover and performance is also found to be negative, though not significant. The findings in Chalmers, Edelen and Kadlec (1999) are broadly in line with those of Carhart (1997).

The issue of the relative performance between load and no-load funds is examined in Ippolito (1989), Elton, Gruber, Das and Hlavka (1993), Grinblatt and Titman (1994), Droms and Walker (1994), Gruber (1996), Fortin and Michelson (1995) and Morey (2003). With the exception of Ippolito (1989), who find that load funds earn rates of return that plausibly offset the load charge, generally studies find that before the effect of load charges is incorporated into return, there is no significant difference between the performance of load and no-load funds.

Morey (2003) is perhaps the most comprehensive paper to address this question as Morey is the only paper in the area to examine the load-adjusted performances of load and no-load funds. Previous papers examine only non-load-adjusted returns between the two types of funds. In addition, Morey (2003) examines relative performance within load funds between relatively high load and low load funds. The study evaluates these relative performances employing a number of both risk-adjusted and raw return measures, including a Jensen's alpha measure. Morey finds that after adjusting for loads in the return data, no-load funds outperform load funds for almost all performance measures examined, while within load funds themselves, there is little significant difference in performance between high-load funds and low-load funds.

## Investment Flows and Performance

A further area of investigation in the mutual fund performance literature is that of the relation between fund performance and the capital investment flows in and out of the fund. The direction of causation between fund flows and performance is a matter of debate. Many studies test for a positive relationship in which performance influences subsequent flows into and out of a fund, see Gruber (1996), Zheng (1999). However, Edelen (1999) examines the reverse causation.

With cash flows defined as the change in the fund's total net assets minus the appreciation in the fund's assets held at the beginning of the period, Gruber (1996) examines fund flows in period $t$ of deciles of funds ranked by performance in period $t - 1$. This is performed recursively for various values of $t$ in the post-ranking period. The study reports a strong and significant correlation between performance and subsequent capital flows.

Similarly, regressions of fund cash flows on lagged one- and two-year fund performance measures also demonstrate the significant influence of performance on subsequent fund flows. More interestingly, however, this procedure also provides insight into which performance measures investors use to evaluate managers. While many performance measures prove significant in causing capital inflows/outflows to and from funds, perhaps surprisingly, Gruber (1996) determines that a four-factor alpha measure proves particularly significant and robust. This would seem to indicate that investors are quite sophisticated in accounting for market, size, value and credit risks in choosing where to invest capital. Equally, however, it may simply reflect that fund-rating companies rank funds by this or similar criteria, and this is the cause of investors selecting such high alpha funds. DelGuercio and Tkac (2000) also find a significant relation between a fund's Jensen's alpha measure and subsequent fund flow. The authors find this to be the case for both mutual funds and pension funds, although in the latter case, tracking error is also important in influencing flows. (Tracking error is a measure of diversifiable risk and is often measured as the volatility of a portfolio's deviation from a benchmark index.)

Having found evidence that good (bad) performance gives rise to subsequent capital inflows (outflows), Gruber (1996) proceeds to evaluate whether investors improve their performance as a result of re-directing their capital. Inflows to a fund in quarter $t$ are multiplied by the risk-adjusted return of the fund in (a number of) subsequent periods. Aggregated over all funds and all time periods and expressed as a percentage of total capital inflows to all funds, the average risk-adjusted return on 'new cash' was 29 basis points per annum. A similar procedure applied to fund outflows to measure how much money an investor saves by removing their capital from a fund indicates a saving of 22 basis points per annum.

In a broadly similar study, Zheng (1999) investigates whether fund flows or 'new money flows' predict future returns and whether aggregate money flows contain information of sufficient economic significance to earn abnormal returns for an investor, that is, does fund flow information represent a smart money signal. Zheng (1999) implements a number of trading strategies on the basis of money flows and tests whether these strategies earn abnormal returns. For example, one investment strategy is to hold a portfolio of funds that exhibit positive fund flow. The portfolio is updated recursively each quarter. Another strategy is to hold funds exhibiting negative fund flow. Another portfolio holds above median cash flow funds, while yet another holds below median cash flow funds. In all cases, portfolios are reconstituted each quarter. This generates a time series of returns for each portfolio. A single-factor and multifactor performance alpha can then be estimated for these money flow-based funds. Money flow or cash flow is as defined in Gruber (1996). During the 1970–1993 sample period under investigation, Zheng (1999) reports that funds that receive new money significantly outperform those that lose money. This finding is broadly in line with that of Gruber (1996). However, the outperformance is relatively short-lived. In addition, new money funds are not found to significantly beat the market as a whole.

In the case of the Gruber (1996) and Zheng (1999) studies, one needs to be aware that an apparent relationship between fund flow and performance may simply be picking up on persistence (if it exists) in fund returns, that is, positive fund performance attracts capital or 'new money', which in turn earns a high return for investors by benefiting from performance persistence in the fund. Sirri and Tufano (1993) is a further study to look at flows into individual funds. The study broadly finds that money flows into funds with the best past performance but does not flow out of funds with the worst past performance. This is likely to reflect (i) the huge growth in the mutual fund industry generally, which means that a large proportion of fund flow is additional capital rather than capital moving between funds, and this capital is attracted to high past return funds and (ii) that there is a cost for existing investors to leave one fund to join another.

Edelen (1999) presents a rather different picture of the fund-flow fund-performance relationship. Edelen hypothesises a reverse direction of causation in this relationship to that of Gruber (1996). Specifically, that fund flow has a negative effect on subsequent fund performance. This study distinguishes between two components of a mutual fund's trading decisions, that is, between the two services provided by a mutual fund. A mutual fund manager undertakes discretionary (rational) trades on the basis of information that he anticipates will lead to a positive risk-adjusted return. In addition, however, arguably the fund's primary responsibility (and purpose) is to satisfy its investors' liquidity demands, that is, to provide a liquid equity position to its investors at low cost. Edelen (1999) argues that fund flows, or flow shocks, force the manager to engage in 'liquidity-motivated trading', which is non-discretionary. The flow shock experienced by the fund immediately alters its relative cash/equity holdings and moves the fund from its target portfolio. Sufficiently high fund flow magnitudes would increase the variability of the fund's cash position. First, this complicates the investor's task in making risk–return choices and second, it compromises the manager's objective of tracking or beating a benchmark index. Consequently, providing a liquid equity position for the investor triggers marginal trading by the mutual fund manager. Edelen argues that this liquidity component of the mutual fund manager's trading plays the role of noise trading and since noise traders face expected losses, the fund should experience negative return performance in proportion to the volume of fund flow.

Edelen (1999) partitions a mutual fund's abnormal return between return attributable to liquidity-motivated trading and that attributable to information-motivated (discretionary) trading. The paper first estimates liquidity-motivated trading as $f_{i,t} = c^{\mathrm{I}} f_{i,t}^{\mathrm{I}} + c^{0} f_{i,t}^{0}$ where $f_{i,t}^{\mathrm{I}}$ and $f_{i,t}^{0}$ denote the volumes of inflows and outflows respectively for fund-$j$ in time $t$, and $c^{\mathrm{I}}$, $c^{0}$ are the estimated coefficients in separate bivariate regressions of the volume of fund stock purchases on $f_{i,t}^{\mathrm{I}}$ and the volume of fund stock sales on $f_{i,t}^{0}$ respectively, that is, $c^{\mathrm{I}}$ and $c^{0}$ are flow-trade response coefficients. The author then constructs a regression of the form

$$AR_{i,t} = \lambda f_{i,t} + \delta d_{i,t} + \varepsilon_{i,t}$$

where $AR_{i,t}$ is the abnormal return on fund $i$ in period $t$, $f_{i,t}$ is the estimated liquidity-motivated trading and $d_{i,t}$ is the estimated information-motivated (discretionary) trading estimated as the combined volume of stock purchases and sales minus $f_{i,t}$, $\varepsilon_{i,t}$ is a random disturbance term. In order to incorporate persistence, the author supplements the right-hand side of the regression equation with lagged values of $AR_{i,t}$. Finally, in an attempt to avoid inference problems arising from the possible reverse causation between $AR_{i,t}$ and $f_{i,t}$ cited by Gruber (1996), the author instruments $f_{i,t}$ by its lagged value. Notwithstanding these difficulties, the estimation results in Edelen (1999) do provide some evidence in support of the author's hypothesis that fund flow negatively impacts on fund performance.

One overall possible conclusion from combining the findings of Gruber (1996), Zheng (1999) and Sirri and Tufano (1993) on the one hand and Edelen (1999) on the other is that high relative performance attracts capital inflow but that the fund manager, who is under pressure to provide a liquid equity investment for investors, is unable to optimally allocate funds to equity, that is, is unable to relatively quickly determine information on the basis of rational trades, and this detracts from subsequent return performance.

A further avenue of investigation in examining mutual fund capital flows is to evaluate whether fund flows in aggregate affect stock market returns. This question is taken up by Warther (1995) and is briefly addressed here. Warther (1995) divides fund flows into anticipated and unanticipated flows, using Box–Jenkins procedures to estimate anticipated flows. Monthly unanticipated fund flows are found to strongly correlate with concurrent stock market returns in a regression of the latter on the former. Anticipated fund flows are uncorrelated with stock market returns, which is consistent with informationally efficient markets where anticipated flows are 'pre-contemporaneously' discounted in returns. Warther (1995) also tests the feedback hypothesis by reversing the direction of the regression and hypothesising that fund flows are, at least in part, determined by lagged stock market returns. The author finds no empirical evidence in support of the feedback trader hypothesis, however. Remolona, Kleiman and Gruenstein (1997) also examine both directions of causality in the 'aggregate fund flow – aggregate stock market returns' relationship in order to determine if in a declining stock market, the positive feedback theory could lead to a self-sustaining decline in stock prices. However, their analysis suggests that over the 1986–1996 period, the effect of short-term stock market returns on mutual fund flows were weak.

## Mutual Fund Managers

It is also important to note that the findings relating to performance throughout this review of the literature relate to the mutual fund as the entity rather than specifically to the fund manager – the fund manager is likely to change over the return history of the fund. Therefore, it may also be important to examine the relationship between fund performance and the cross-sectional characteristics of fund managers as it is between fund performance and the characteristics of the fund, such as investment objective, expenses, and so on. This issue is pursued by Chevalier and Ellison (1999) who evaluate whether mutual fund performance is related to fund manager characteristics such as age, the average SAT score of the manager's undergraduate institution and whether the manager held an MBA. Using a sample of 492 mutual fund managers who had sole responsibility for a fund for at least some part of the 1988–1994 sample period, the authors report that managers with MBAs outperform managers without an MBA by 63 basis points per year. However, controlling for the former groups greater holdings of higher systematic risk stocks, the residual outperformance falls to zero. The study does find a small degree of residual outperformance among younger versus older fund managers (i.e. having controlled for other fund risk characteristics) and hypothesises that this is due to a harder work ethic among young mangers who are still establishing their careers and who face a higher probability of dismissal. Finally, the most robust performance difference identified is that managers from undergraduate institutions with higher SAT scores obtain higher returns, although some of this difference is attributable to risk and expense characteristics. Chevalier and Ellison (1999) suggest that the SAT score outperformance arises because of the greater natural ability, better education and better professional networks associated with having attended a higher SAT score undergraduate institution.

## Market Timing

Ideally, to test the market-timing ability of mutual fund managers, we require data on the actual asset shares to see if the manager increases her exposure to the market just before a rise in the market return. Without asset share data, we can use the Treynor and Mazuy (1996) or Merton and Henriksson (1981) regressions using conditioning variables. In the Treynor–Mazuy model, the time-varying beta is assumed to depend *linearly* on the manager's conditional forecast of the market return (i.e. $\beta_t = \bar{\beta} + \lambda(\hat{R}_{m,t+1} - ER_m)$, where $\hat{R}_{m,t+1}$ is the conditional forecast (at time $t$) of the market return). The Merton–Henriksson model assumes a similar linear relationship but beta depends on the sign of the market return forecast (i.e. $\beta_t = \bar{\beta} + \lambda(\max[0, \hat{R}^+_{m,t+1}])$

Linear parameterisations of market timing are highly restrictive (Goetzmann, Ingersoll and Ivokvich 2000) and do not separate out the fund manager's quality of information in market timing and the aggressiveness with which she reacts to this information. Jiang (2003) provides a non-parametric test of market timing that can identify the quality of the manager's market-timing ability and does not rely on linear factor models. The intuition behind the approach is that the manager should increase beta if she thinks the market will rise next period. For any two non-overlapping time periods $t_1$ and $t_2$, the statistic $x$ is greater than zero for successful market timing:

$$x = 2 \cdot \text{prob}(\beta_{t_1} > \beta_{t_2} | R_{m,t_1+1} > R_{m,t_2+1}) - 1$$

With no market-timing ability, $\beta$ has no correlation with the market return and hence prob(.) = 1/2 and $x = 0$ ($x < 0$ implies adverse market timing). Now consider the triplet observed for mutual fund $i$'s returns $\{R_{i,t_1}, R_{i,t_2}, R_{i,t_3}\}$ where $R_{m,t_3} > R_{m,t_2} > R_{m,t_1}$. A fund manager who has superior market-timing ability (regardless of her degree of aggressiveness) should have a higher average beta in the $t_2$ to $t_3$ period than in the $t_1$ to $t_2$ period. The measured value of beta in these two periods is

$$\beta_{12} = \frac{R_{i,t_2} - R_{i,t_1}}{R_{m,t_2} - R_{m,t_1}} \qquad \beta_{23} = \frac{R_{i,t_3} - R_{i,t_2}}{R_{m,t_3} - R_{m,t_2}}$$

The sample analogue to $x$ is therefore

$$\hat{\theta}_n = \binom{n}{3}^{-1} \sum_w \text{sign}(\beta_{23} > \beta_{12})$$

where $w$ represents the triplets in the data where $w \in R_{m,t_1} < R_{m,t_2} < R_{m,t_3}$ and sign(.) assumes a value of $\{1, -1, 0\}$ if the argument is {positive, negative, zero}. Jiang (2003) uses a US monthly returns database (1980–1999) of actively managed mutual funds

(1827 surviving and 110 non-surviving, excluding index trackers). There will be some funds with $\hat{\theta} > 0$ just due to luck, and the top 5% of market timers in the data have $\hat{\theta} > 8.4\%$. Therefore, we need to see whether $\hat{\theta} = 8.4\%$ would occur in the 5% right tail if $\theta = 0$ for all our funds. To evaluate this proposition, we assume a normal distribution for $\theta$ with the same standard deviation as found in our cross section of funds data. Jiang (2003) finds that the CDF of $\hat{\theta}$ for the empirical distribution is stochastically dominated by the normal distribution (under the null $\theta = 0$) and therefore, fund managers do not have market-timing ability. Hence, an investor would be better off by choosing a passive index fund rather than *randomly* choosing a fund from the universe of actively managed funds. Jiang finds some evidence that average market-timing performance is positively related to the age of the fund, the length of management tenure and negatively related to fund size – but these effects are not statistically or economically significant.

As with studies of the UK mutual fund industry, attempting to draw an overall conclusion from the body of US studies regarding performance and the persistence of performance is complicated by the fact that the studies apply a range of differing methodological approaches over various sample periods and hence are difficult to compare directly. Nevertheless, the survey of the literature above indicates that while evidence of the existence of fund managers with genuine stock-picking skills is certainly not widespread, there are some results that show managers outperforming benchmark portfolios in risk-adjusted terms. This performance is generally not found to persist beyond the short term, however. Broadly consistent with findings from studies of UK mutual funds is the evidence that poor performance has a stronger tendency to persist than good performance.

## Hedge Funds

Hedge funds, like mutual funds, are pooled investments but are subject to fewer restrictions. There are many hedge fund styles, such as long–short, short-selling, long only leveraged, emerging market funds, distressed securities, global macro and relative value arbitrage. These strategies are risky so the term *hedge fund* is rather misleading. Hedge funds require a high minimum investment, annual fees can be higher than 5% p.a., and the profit taken by the owners of the fund is as high as 20 to 25%. About 90% of hedge fund managers are based in the United States, and 9% in Europe, with a total of about 6000 funds worldwide managing around $400 billion capital. However, many funds are relatively small, and around 80% of funds have less than $100 million under management.

There has not been a great deal of work on hedge fund performance because of a lack of data. Early studies show that hedge funds have a high rate of attrition (Brown, Goetzmann and Ibbotson 1999), and there is evidence of 'positive alpha' risk-adjusted performance, with some evidence of persistence (Agarwal and Naik 2000), possibly due to style effects rather than differential manager skills (Brown, Goetzmann and Ibbotson 1999, Brown, Goetzmann and Park 2001). Fung and Hsieh (1997) find that hedge funds do not necessarily offer higher risk-adjusted returns, but hedge fund returns do have relatively low correlations with other securities, hence when around 10 to 20%

of an index tracker is supplemented with a hedge fund portfolio, this improves the risk–return profile.

Because hedge funds have a wide variety of investment styles, it is difficult to adequately characterise their returns using a linear factor model. Usually, many additional return variables are added to the Carhart four-factor model – such as a world stock index, various bond indices (including emerging market bonds and corporate bond returns) and even a commodity return index. Even then, it is very debatable whether these 'factors' can adequately mimic returns on hedge funds that contain substantial positions in options, which usually have highly non-linear payoffs.

Capocci and Hubner (2004) use a multifactor model on a large database of over 2700 hedge funds (including 801 'dead funds'), concentrating mainly on the more recent (and accurate) monthly returns over the bull market period of 1994–2000 (for which data on non-survivors is available). Funds are divided into around 20 style categories (e.g. long-short, small caps, etc.). Overall, there are around 25 to 30% of funds within any style category that have positive and statistically significant alphas, with around 5 to 10% having negative alphas and the majority of funds (i.e. around 60%) having zero alphas. The market betas of the hedge funds are lower than those for mutual funds (at around 0.3 to 0.6) and for almost all funds, the coefficient on the *SMB* factor is statistically significant. A subset of the funds also has a significant coefficient on the emerging market bond return, but only about one-third of funds show evidence of a significant HML factor, and about 15% of funds have a significant momentum factor. The *R*-squared for these multifactor regressions are mostly in the range 0.65–0.95. Hence, most hedge funds appear to have exposure to small cap stocks, while a smaller proportion are also exposed to emerging market bonds and momentum stocks.

Unfortunately, in only a few cases (i.e. long–short, convertible arbitrage, non-classified) do the positive alphas over the whole period 1994–2000 remain positive over sub-periods. When funds are sorted into deciles on the basis of their past one-year returns (Jan–Jan), held for one year and then rebalanced (equally weighted), the time series of only two of the decile portfolios (P7, P9) have statistically significant alphas, indicating a lack of persistence in performance for most deciles. Overall, the evidence is that some hedge funds show positive abnormal returns over 1994–2000 but 'picking winners' is difficult and persistence in performance seems rather weak.

## 9.3 Mutual Fund 'Stars'?

Given that there are results pointing to some mutual and hedge funds earning abnormal returns, the question then arises whether this outperformance represents stock-picking ability or whether it reflects the luck of individual fund managers. Until recently, the literature has not explicitly modelled the role of luck in fund performance. There has been some attempt to control for luck among studies of persistence by ranking funds in a period separate from the evaluation period. First, this procedure may be flawed if the model used to rank abnormal performance is mis-specified in both periods. Second, the recursive portfolio formation approach does not tell us whether *individual* fund performance persists as the identity of the funds in the various deciles or quintiles, and so on, changes over time.

As we have seen, there is considerable evidence for the United States and the United Kingdom that the *average* mutual fund underperforms its benchmark (e.g. S&P500 index, or a style benchmark return) by around 0.5 to 1.5% p.a. However, some sub-groups of managers (e.g. growth-oriented funds, Chen, Jegadeesh and Wermers 2000, Wermers 2000) do outperform their benchmarks. Can we be sure that the benchmarks we have chosen are reasonable and that 'outperformance' of some funds is not due solely to 'good luck' over several years?

Kosowski, Timmermann, White and Wermers (2003) is the first paper to explicitly control for luck in evaluating US mutual fund performance. With such a large universe of mutual funds in existence, close to 1700 in this study, one would expect that some funds will appear to exhibit abnormal performance *simply due to chance*. The question arises as to how we establish the boundaries of performance that are explicable by chance.

As we have seen, to test the performance of the average mutual fund, we require a model of expected returns for each fund (over $t = 1, 2, \ldots, T$). Here, for expositional purposes, we take the 'unconditional' CAPM (i.e. with constant parameters) as our model:

$$(R_{it} - r_t) = \alpha_i + \beta_i (R_{mt} - r_t) + \varepsilon_{it} \tag{10}$$

Then the null for no abnormal performance for any fund $i$ is $H_0 : \alpha_i = 0$. To test the performance of the *average* fund, we run (10) for each fund individually. If there are $N$ funds, the average $\alpha$ and $t_\alpha$ for the cross section of $N$ funds is

$$\alpha_{\mathrm{av}} = N^{-1} \sum_{i=1}^{N} \hat{\alpha}_i \tag{11a}$$

$$t_{\mathrm{av}} = N^{-1} \sum_{i=1}^{N} t_{\alpha_i} \tag{11b}$$

We have noted that an interesting class of alternative models to the unconditional-CAPM in (10) are *conditional models* where both $\alpha_i$ and $\beta_i$ are allowed to vary over time. If $\mathbf{z}_t$ consists of the information set known at time $t$, then the conditional model is

$$(R_{it} - r_t) = \alpha_i (\mathbf{z}_{t-1}) + \beta_i (\mathbf{z}_{t-1}) [R_{bt} - r_t] + \varepsilon_{it} \tag{12}$$

where for linear functions,

$$\alpha_i (z_t) = \alpha_{0i} + \alpha' \mathbf{z}_t \tag{13a}$$

$$\beta_i (z_t) = \beta_{0i} + \beta' \mathbf{z}_t \tag{13b}$$

The variables $\mathbf{z}_t$ control for predictable variations in factor loadings and factor risk premia. The vector $\mathbf{z}_t$ might include such variables as the dividend yield, the long–short interest rate spread, the T-bill yield and January dummies. Abnormal performance is now given by $\alpha_{0i} \neq 0$.

## US Mutual Fund 'Stars'?

Kosowski, Timmermann, White and Wermers (2003), using US monthly returns data 1962–1994 for around 1700 mutual funds, find that $\alpha_{av} = 0.003\%$ per month and $t_{av} = -0.004$, indicating the average fund does not outperform the market benchmark. But the cross-section standard deviation of these $\alpha_i$ across the 1700 funds is high at around 0.3% p.m., indicating the possibility that some funds within the sample are performing very well (and others very badly). The question they then ask is whether some of the extreme 'winner' (and 'loser') fund performance is solely due to 'luck'.

To answer this question, given the non-normality of the equation residuals, they use a bootstrap procedure. The bootstrap has the advantage that it provides a non-parametric approach to statistical inference about performance. Residuals from performance regressions are often found to be non-normal, which would make statistical inferences regarding performance based on standard $t$-tests and $F$-tests unreliable.

Here we show how to implement *one type* of bootstrap across the universe of funds. Using actual data, we have the *estimated* $\beta_i = 0.9$ (say) for a particular fund and this fund's residuals $\hat{e}_{it}$. In the bootstrap, we keep $\beta_i = 0.9$ and the $(R_{mt} - r_t)$ data series fixed. Now for this fund, with equal probability, we randomly select the $\hat{e}_{it}$ with replacement and generate a series for $(R_{it} - r_t)$ for sample size $T$, but *under the null of no outperformance*, that is, $\alpha_i = 0$:

$$R_{it} - r_t = 0 + \beta_i (R_m - r)_t + \hat{e}_{it} \tag{14}$$

Using the simulated data for $R_{it} - r_t$, we then calculate the OLS estimates $(\hat{\alpha}_i, \hat{\beta}_i)$ and the t-statistic $t_{\alpha_i}$ from (10) (using GMM standard errors). These bootstrap estimates will differ from those found using the real data because of the 'new' random draws of $\hat{e}_{it}$. For example, if the random draws with replacement by chance have a relatively large number of negative values, the bootstrap estimate of $\hat{\alpha}_i$ will be negative.

We repeat this for all funds $i = 1, 2, \ldots, N$, giving $N$ values of $\alpha_i$ and $t_{\alpha_i}$. To illustrate, suppose we are interested in whether the performance of the *best* fund is due to chance. We then choose the maximum value of $\alpha_i^{boot}(max)$ and $t_{\alpha_i}^{boot}(max)$ (i.e. the best-performing fund from the universe of all funds). This is the first run of the bootstrap (boot = 1). The above is now repeated 1000 times so we have 1000 values of each of $\alpha_i^{boot}(max)$ and $t_{\alpha_i}^{boot}(max)$, which form the empirical bootstrap distribution for the best fund (under the null of no outperformance, that is, the 'true' $\alpha_i = 0$).

We can repeat the above to obtain *separate* bootstrap distributions for $(\hat{\alpha}_i, t_{\alpha_i})$ for any percentile (e.g. 2nd, 3rd, ..., etc., best or worst funds). In fact, the bootstrap distribution for the t-statistics has 'better' properties (i.e. is a 'pivotal statistic') than those for the alphas themselves, and intuitively this is because the t-statistics are scaled by the standard error of alpha and therefore, their bootstrap distribution is less dispersed than that for the alphas themselves. Kosowski et al. record the spread in the bootstrapped alpha estimates within each percentile and show that the spread is considerably higher in the extreme tails of the distribution.

Let us consider the results for the bootstrap distribution of the fifth-best fund. Kosowski, Timmermann, White and Wermers (2003) estimate an $\hat{\alpha}$ (fifth best) using the real data for US mutual funds of about 1% per month (p.m.) with a (GMM) t-statistic of 4.0. The bootstrap has $\alpha_i = 0$ for all funds. The p-value for the t-statistic from the bootstrap distribution (for the fifth-best fund) under the null of $\alpha_i = 0$ is less than 0.001. Hence, there is a very small probability that the fifth-best fund could have generated an alpha of 1% p.m. or higher by pure chance. After controlling for luck (across all funds), we are therefore confident that the fifth-best fund has genuine stock-picking skills of around 1% p.m.

We can put this slightly differently. Kosowski, Timmermann, White and Wermers (2003) find that on the basis of the bootstrap simulated data with $\alpha_i = 0$, one should expect nine funds to have a $\alpha_i \geq 0.5\%$ p.m. (i.e. 6% p.a.) simply due to luck. But in the real data, 60 funds achieved this, so some fund managers do have genuine stock-picking skills. Active fund management lives! When repeating the analysis for different mutual fund 'styles', they find the 'stars' are most evident for the 'growth-fund' managers.

Kosowski, Timmermann, White and Wermers (2003) also find that the funds just inside the far left tail (e.g. fifth–tenth worst fund, or 1% to 10% worst fund) generally have a poor performance that cannot be attributed to bad luck – they are genuinely 'bad' stock-pickers.

It is worth noting that the results demonstrate the superior (and inferior) stock-picking skills of certain funds over an average of many months. If this performance were to persist in the future, then you would be able to pick the best fund now and beat the benchmark(s) in the future. Of course, in reality, there are many eventualities that might prevent this happening, such as a change in stock-picking technique by the fund or a change in personnel in the fund management team.

Kosowski, Timmermann, White and Wermers (2003) examine persistence *over one year* using the Carhart (1997) procedure. In January of every year, funds are sorted into fractiles on the basis of the value of alpha in the Carhart four-factor model and using the past three years of data. Equally weighted portfolios are constructed and held for one year, when the procedure is repeated and rebalancing takes place. (Hence, some or all of the mutual funds in, say, the top decile, will change every year.) The estimated alphas for various fractiles (e.g. top decile) are then computed over the period 1979 to 1993 using the real data. The bootstrap distributions for these fractiles follow a similar procedure but impose $\alpha_i = 0$ across all funds. Under the bootstrap, the top decile of funds say (with all $\alpha_i = 0$) are formed into an equally weighted portfolio, rebalanced each year and the distribution of the estimated $\hat{\alpha}$'s (and $t_\alpha$'s) for the top decile of funds is constructed. Using the whole universe of funds, they find that only the top decile of funds exhibits persistence over one year, with an alpha of 1.6% p.a. Within the aggressive growth sector, the top three deciles exhibit one-year persistence, whereas for growth funds, only the top decile shows persistence, whereas other fund styles (e.g. growth–income and balanced-income) do not exhibit persistence.

'Superior performance' is also model-specific, and the CAPM might be an incorrect model but Kosowski, Timmermann, White and Wermers (2003) use several alternative models (e.g. Fama–French three-factor model, Carhart's four-factor model that also includes a 'momentum factor' and several conditional-beta models) and find the results are broadly unchanged. Finally, there is always that bit of uncertainty around. Although there might only be, say, a 0.5% chance of your chosen 'star fund' beating the market by, say, 1% p.m. (12% p.a.), *purely due to luck* – yet nevertheless, it may have been luck!

The Kosowski, Timmermann, White and Wermers (2003) study is one of the most thorough in the area, using several alternative models to the CAPM, looking at the 'over' and 'under' performance of the top (bottom) 1%, 5%, 10%, and so on, of funds, minimising survivorship bias (e.g. by not omitting funds that only survived over part of the sample period) and much more. Overall, the conclusion that the top 5–10 funds out of 1700 or so genuinely outperform their benchmark because of skill, while the bottom 5–10 underperform because of bad stock-picking, seems to be a robust one.

Given this evidence, there seems to be something of a paradox in that there are so many 'active' mutual funds, even though many do not outperform on the basis of Jensen's alpha. Of course, a few mutual funds do outperform the passive portfolio, while others do much worse. The difficulty is in finding out who the 'winners' are and in knowing whether this relatively small group of 'winners' will continue to be winners. This is hardly a 'free lunch'.

## Bootstrap Issues

For aficionados, there are a number of issues, which arises in applying a bootstrap procedure that need to be considered. Instead of using alpha as the performance measure, one can evaluate the bootstrap distribution of the 't-statistic of alpha' under the null hypothesis of zero abnormal performance, $H_0$: $\alpha_i = 0$, and compare this bootstrap distribution to the observed t-alpha. Using t-statistics has an added bonus: funds with fewer observations may be estimated with higher variance and less precision and will in consequence tend to generate outlier alphas. There is a risk therefore that these funds will disproportionately occupy the extreme tails of the actual and bootstrapped alpha distributions. The t-statistic provides a correction by scaling alpha by its estimated precision, that is, its standard error. The distribution of bootstrapped t-statistics for extreme values is likely to have fewer problems with high variance, relative to the bootstrap distribution of alpha at the same percentile in the performance distribution. In studies of this type, the bootstrap distribution of both alpha and its t-statistic is usually constructed. (All t-statistics are usually based on Newey–West heteroscedasticity and autocorrelation adjusted standard errors.)

To further improve the precision of performance estimates, one can impose a minimum number of observations for a fund to be included in the analysis. An insufficient number of observations in the estimation is likely to increase the sampling variability of the resulting estimates. This could widen the tails of the bootstrap distribution and possibly bias the results towards the conclusion that fund performance is not outside what might be expected because of chance. For example, a minimum of 60 observations may be set as the requirement for the inclusion of funds in the analysis. The disadvantage with this approach, however, is that it imposes a certain survivor bias by restricting the examination to funds that have been skilled or lucky enough to survive for five years. To examine the significance of this issue, the sensitivity of the bootstrap results can be tested for a number of alternative minimum observations specifications.

A number of alternative bootstrap re-sampling techniques may be applied. We may re-sample residuals only, residuals and factors together, thus maintaining the same time-series pairings as observed in the underlying data or we may re-sample factors and residuals independently.

Also, it may be the case that we suspect cross-fund dependencies among fund residuals, that is, $cov(\varepsilon_i, \varepsilon_j) \neq 0$ for funds $i$ and $j$. This may well arise from a mis-specification in the performance model. To retain this correlation information in the bootstrap procedure would require using the same random draw of time observations across all funds, in each of the 1000 bootstrap simulations. Implementing this presents a difficulty, however, because the sample of funds do not all exist at the same time (i.e. some funds drop out of the sample before other funds come into being). To restrict the bootstrap analysis to contemporaneous fund histories would severely restrict the number of funds that could be selected for the analysis and could call into question the reliability of the findings. A way to mitigate this problem is to use alternative equilibrium models of performance, thus limiting the scope for misspecification and cross-fund residual correlation.

In a bootstrap procedure, randomly re-sampling residuals one at a time (with replacement) assumes the residuals are independently and identically distributed. However, if the sample of mutual funds exhibit (say) first-order serial correlation, we can allow for this dependence by bootstrapping the residuals in *blocks* of various lengths (e.g. in blocks of two for first-order MA errors, and so on).

Also of interest is whether the stock-picking skills of managers are related to the investment objective of the funds. This may be examined by applying the bootstrap procedure separately to the different investment objectives of the funds, for example, equity income, equity growth, general equity and smaller companies. In order to provide a comprehensive study of performance and to test the robustness of results, the bootstrap test should be applied to alternative performance-measurement models (i.e. both single and multifactor models with unconditional and conditional factor loadings and alphas). Kosowski, Timmermann, White and Wermers (2003) implement all of these alternative bootstrap techniques and generally they find that the results are invariant to these alternatives. This indicates that it is the non-normality of the residuals that is driving the bootstrap results in the tails of the performance distribution.

## UK Mutual Fund 'Stars'?

We now present preliminary results from a study of UK mutual funds from Cuthbertson, Nitzsche and O'Sullivan (2004), which demonstrates the use of various bootstrapping techniques across mutual funds in our attempt to find mutual fund 'stars' – that is, performance that is exceptional even after accounting for possible 'good luck' that may apply across many funds.

## Data

The mutual fund data set used comprises 1596 Unit Trusts and Open Ended Investment Companies (OEICs). Unit trusts are pooled investments that enable their investors to enjoy economies of scale in gaining access to well-diversified portfolios of securities. However, unit trusts often have different investment objectives as laid down in the trust deed. Unit trusts are 'open-ended' mutual funds in the sense that investors can purchase new units in the fund at the going market price per unit, that is, the demand for units does not increase the unit price. Unit trusts can only be traded between the investor and the trust manager; there is no secondary market. Unit trusts differ from investment trusts in that the latter may be described as a 'closed-end' fund. Although they are still pooled investments, investment trusts are, in effect, companies that are quoted on the stock exchange in their own right and whose business it is to trade in securities. Investment trusts have a fixed number of units, just as there are a fixed number of shares in a company. Unlike the case of unit trusts, demand for investment trusts may push up the price of the trust's shares. Here, it is possible for the price of the investment trust to trade at a premium (discount) where the price is higher (lower) than the value of the underlying assets of the investment trust. A premium, for example, may reflect investor demand for the skills of the investment trust manager. OEICs are constituted as companies so that investors buy shares, but the number of shares in issue varies according to demand, hence the term *open-ended*. This implies that the share price always reflects the underlying asset value and unlike investment trusts, is not affected by market sentiment towards the OEIC itself. Hence, the risk profiles of OEICs are more in line with that of unit trusts than investment trusts.

The mutual fund returns data have been obtained from Standard & Poor's Micropal. Returns are measured monthly between April 1975 and December 2002. The analysis is restricted to funds investing in UK equity. This is defined by the Investment Management Association (IMA), formerly the Association of Unit Trusts and Investment Funds (AUTIF), as having at least 80% of the fund invested in UK equity.

Among the database of 1596 funds, a total of 334 funds are referred to as *second units*. These arise because often when a fund management company first launches a new fund, it will in fact launch several very similar funds. Subsequently, the less successful funds are merged with the more successful funds. Second units are the less successful funds. They remain in the database but, post-merger, they report identical returns to that of the fund with which they were merged. Pre-merger, the returns are also very similar. Second units may also arise when a single fund splits into a number of similar funds. In this case, second units are recorded in the database for the full sample period but report identical returns pre-split. In the vast majority of cases, the split occurs late in the fund's life and, therefore, these second units report relatively few 'independent' return observations. In either case in which second units arise, they provide little new information. In this study, 334 such funds were identified and are excluded for much of the analysis. Furthermore, 128 of the funds in the database are market tracker funds. As this study is interested in examining mutual fund performance relative to the benchmark market index, the performance of tracker funds is of little interest and such funds are also excluded. Concentrating on non-tracker independent (i.e. non-second unit) funds leaves a sample of 1150 funds.

All equity funds are categorised by the investment objective of the fund. The investment objectives include equity growth (122 funds), equity income (253 funds), general equity (i.e. income and growth, 591 funds) and smaller companies (184 funds). The IMA's fund classification system specifies that equity income funds are those that aim to have a yield in excess of 110% of the yield of the FT All-Share Index, equity growth funds have a primary objective of achieving growth, general equity funds have 80% of the fund invested in UK equity and smaller company funds have at least 80% of the fund invested in UK equities that form the bottom 10% of all equities by market capitalisation. These investment styles are declared by the funds themselves but certified initially and subsequently monitored monthly by the IMA in the United Kingdom. Funds failing to remain within their stated investment objective for a period of three months are required to either rectify the situation or change their investment objective.

In order to control for survivorship bias, the data set includes both surviving funds (765) and non-surviving funds (358). In addition, funds are also categorised by the location from where the fund is operated: onshore United Kingdom (845), offshore (305). Offshore funds are mainly located in Dublin, Luxembourg and the Channel Islands.

All returns are calculated bid price to bid price with gross income reinvested. The bid/offer spread in fund returns captures the initial charge (typically 5–6%), stamp duty, dealing charges and commissions incurred by the fund and the bid/offer spreads of the underlying securities. As returns in this study are calculated bid price to bid price, they are gross of such transactions costs. The annual charge imposed by the fund on its customer is incorporated in the trust price and cannot be stripped out by Micropal in its database. Therefore, returns are net of annual charges. This may cause some concern as it implies that in the estimation of performance models, fund returns are net of annual charges, while the benchmark indices against which fund returns are measured are gross returns. This could affect the estimation of the factor loadings. However, provided the annual charge is relatively constant, which in percentage terms is the case, the estimation of factor loadings is unaffected and the alpha performance measure is simply reduced by the level of the (constant) annual charge. (Of course, the annual charge would have to be spread over 12 monthly observations.) Total Expense Ratios (TERs), which are comprised mainly of the annual charge, are available from around 1997 onwards. To address the above concern, one could add the TER to net returns as if it were constant over the life of the unit trust. As already indicated, however, such a procedure is equivalent to adding the TER to the estimate of alpha (with an appropriate monthly adjustment).

The risk-free rate is the one-month UK Treasury Bill rate and the market index is the FT All-Share Index. The factor mimicking portfolio for the size effect, $SMB_t$, is the difference between the monthly returns on the Hoare Govett Small Companies (HGSC) Index and the returns on the FTSE 100 index. The HGSC index measures the performance of the lowest 10% of stocks by market capitalisation of the main UK equity market.

The factor mimicking portfolio to model the value premium, $HML_t$, is the difference between the monthly returns of the Morgan Stanley Capital International (MSCI) UK value index and the returns on the MSCI UK growth index. To construct these indices,

Morgan Stanley ranks all the stocks in their UK national index by the book-to-market ratio. Starting with the highest book-to-market ratio, stocks are attributed to the value index until 50% of the market capitalisation of the national index is reached. The remaining stocks are attributed to the growth index. The MSCI national indices have a market representation of at least 60% (more recently, this has been increased to 85%). The national indices are designed to represent a broad range of sectors rather than simply represent the highest market capitalisation stocks.

The factor mimicking portfolio to capture the one-year momentum anomaly, $PR1YR_t$, is constructed from the FTSE 100 index. Each month, it is the equal-weighted average returns of stocks with the highest 30% of returns over the previous 11 months minus the equal-weighted average returns of stocks with the lowest 30% returns. The variable is included with a lag of one month. The instruments used in the estimation of models with conditional factor loadings and conditional performance measures are as follows. The risk-free rate is the redemption yield on a one-month UK T-bill, the dividend yield of the market factor is the dividend yield on the FT All-Share index and the slope of the term structure is the yield on the UK 10-year gilt minus the yield on the UK one-month T-bill.

## Model Selection

Estimation results of the unconditional models including the CAPM, Fama and French three-factor model and the Carhart (four-factor model), along with the unconditional Treynor–Mazuy model and Merton–Henriksson market-timing models, are broadly similar. For example, the CAPM indicates that the cross-sectional average alpha was negative at around −0.03% p.m., indicating that the average mutual fund manager underperformed the market by 0.36% p.a. However, this abnormal performance is not statistically significant at the 5% level (using the t-statistic, which is an average of absolute values across funds and is based on Newey–West heteroscedasticity and autocorrelation adjusted standard errors). The Fama and French and Carhart factor models produce similar performance results.

In terms of the factor loadings, the t-statistics across all unconditional models are consistent in showing the market-risk factor and the size-risk factor as statistically significant determinants of the cross-sectional variation in equity returns. For example, in the case of the Carhart four-factor model, the cross-sectional average t-statistic of the market-risk factor is about 25, while for the size-risk factor, the average t-statistic is 5.4. In fact, 100% and 80% of the mutual funds indicated a statistically significant t-statistic on the 'market' and 'size' risk factors respectively. The 'value' risk factor does not appear to be a significant influence in explaining fund returns, and only 24% of the sample of mutual funds produced a statistically significant t-statistic on this risk factor. The one-year momentum factor from the Carhart four-factor model also appears to be relatively unimportant where only 21% of funds registered the momentum effect as an important determinant of returns.

The findings in relation to alpha and the distribution of alpha among the *conditional-beta* and *conditional-alpha and beta* models are remarkably similar to those for the unconditional factor models. The average mutual fund manager failed to outperform the market by a statistically significant amount in nearly all models. Conditional factor model specifications permit dynamically adjusted portfolio sensitivities or generally embody market-timing activities on the part of fund managers. The above parametric tests provide evidence that fund managers collectively either do not market time or do not do so successfully. (This finding is consistent with evidence from market-timing tests among UK unit trusts in the literature (see Fletcher 1995, Leger 1997).) While parametric tests inherently involve a joint hypothesis, Jiang (2003) also finds against superior market-timing activity from non-parametric tests on US equity mutual funds.

The key model selection criterion used is the Schwartz Information Criterion (SIC), which trades off a reduction in a model's residual sum of squares for a parsimonious 'best-fit' model. This information criterion suggests that the model with the lowest SIC measure should be selected. From among the class of unconditional models, the three-factor Fama and French specification has the lowest SIC measure (on average over all mutual funds). Indeed, this model provides the best fit from among all classes of models estimated, a finding also reported in Kosowski, Timmermann, White and Wermers (2003).

For all of our alternative specifications, the normality assumption is rejected for between 60 and 80% of the mutual funds (using the Jarque–Bera test). It is this finding that largely motivates the use of the bootstrap technique, as non-normal residuals indicate that the alpha estimates themselves are also non-normally distributed, which in turn invalidates the use of standard statistical tests such as the $t$-test and F-test, which require normally distributed errors. The finding of widespread non-normally distributed fund residuals also questions the reliability of past research that draws inferences from $t$-tests regarding mutual fund abnormal performance. This strongly motivates the need to bootstrap performance estimates to determine whether significant outperformance (and underperformance) exists in the mutual fund industry.

Also, in the case of all models, over 60% of mutual funds exhibit serial correlation of order one in the residuals (using LM test statistics). This has implications for the implementation of the bootstrap analysis in which it will also be necessary to examine a bootstrap technique that now randomly draws residuals in pairs. This is necessary to preserve the information content in the serial correlation in order that the bootstrap simulations mimic the original data generation process as closely as possible.

## Bootstrap Analysis of UK Mutual Funds

As noted above, on the basis of the 'within sample' Schwartz criterion, it is found that the unconditional Fama–French three-factor model performs 'the best'. Table 3 presents bootstrap statistics for the full sample of mutual funds (i.e. for all investment objectives) for the unconditional Fama and French three-factor model. The table shows the estimated alpha and the Newey–West adjusted t-statistic of alpha using the 'real' data. The reported $p$-value is for the t-statistic of alpha, under the null of no outperformance (i.e. $\alpha_i = 0$ for all $i$). All bootstrap results reported throughout this section are based on 1000 simulations.

Take the best fund performance as an example. Table 3 reveals that the best fund ranked by alpha from the unconditional model achieved abnormal performance of

**Table 3** UK mutual fund performance

| Fund Position | Unconditional Three-Factor Model | | |
|---|---|---|---|
| | Actual Alpha | Actual t-alpha | Bootstr. $p$-value |
| **Top Funds** | | | |
| Best | 0.7853 | 4.0234 | 0.056 |
| 2nd best | 0.7239 | 3.3891 | 0.059 |
| 10th best | 0.5304 | 2.5448 | 0.022 |
| 15th best | 0.4782 | 2.4035 | 0.004 |
| **Bottom Funds** | | | |
| 15th worst | $-0.5220$ | $-3.6873$ | 0.000 |
| 10th worst | $-0.5899$ | $-4.1187$ | 0.000 |
| 2nd worst | $-0.7407$ | $-5.1664$ | 0.001 |
| Worst | $-0.9015$ | $-7.4176$ | 0.000 |

Note:
This table presents bootstrap statistics for the full sample of mutual funds, including all investment objectives for the Fama–French three-factor performance model. The first column reports the estimated alpha using the real data. The second column reports the actual t-statistics using the real data and with Newey–West heteroscedasticity and autocorrelation adjusted standard errors. The third column reports the bootstrap $p$-values of the $t_\alpha$ on the basis of 1,000 bootstrap re-samples, under the null of no outperformance (i.e. $\alpha_i = 0$). The sample period is April 1975 to December 2002.

0.785% per month. The bootstrap $p$-value of 0.056 indicates that 5.6% of the 1000 bootstrap simulations across all of the funds (under the null hypothesis of zero abnormal performance) produced a t-statistic of alpha greater than that observed for the 'best fund' in the real data. In other words, the $p$-value of 0.056 suggests, at 95% confidence, that the performance of the best fund (using the t-statistic of alpha as the performance measure) is statistically due to luck, and there is little evidence of genuine stock-picking ability on the part of the fund's manager(s).

Looking across the entire right tail of the performance distribution summarised in Table 3, the evidence indicates that there are some funds, just inside the extreme of the right tail (e.g. 10th- and 15th-best funds) that have genuine stock-picking skills, but most 'superior' fund performance is due to luck. This finding differs somewhat from Kosowski, Timmermann, White and Wermers (2003), who find stronger evidence of 'skill' amongst the best fund managers.

In the left tail of the distribution, the bootstrap $p$-value (for $t_\alpha$) at the worst performance level is $-7.4$, with a bootstrap $p$-value near to zero. That is, the 1000 lowest bootstrap $t_\alpha$-statistics across funds (under $H_0 : \alpha_i = 0$) produce a less negative t-statistic than the $-7.4$ found in using the 'real' data (from among the full sample of mutual funds). This indicates genuine poor performance rather than bad luck. It is also clear that for all of the left tail reported in Table 3, this conclusion continues to hold. The findings here for the negative performance side of the distribution are similar to those of Kosowski, Timmermann, White and Wermers (2003) US study where the evidence also suggests that poor-performing funds possess truly inferior stock-picking skills.

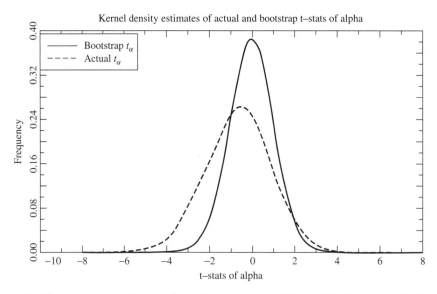

**Figure 2**   Kernel density estimates of actual t-statistics of alpha and the bootstrap distribution all UK mutual funds (unconditional three-factor model)

Figure 2 provides a graphical illustration of the comparison between the bootstrap distribution of $t_\alpha$, which is entirely due to random variation, versus the 'observed' distribution of $t_\alpha$, which uses the 'real' data from the sample of funds. This figure plots kernel density estimates of the distributions for all investment objectives, estimated by the three-factor unconditional model. It is clear from Figure 2 that the actual performance distribution of $t_\alpha$ has a much fatter left tail than the bootstrap distribution, while the right tail of the $t_\alpha$ distribution lies only just outside the right tail of the bootstrap distribution. This again indicates that there are many genuinely inferior funds, whereas the $t_\alpha$ estimates of funds in the right tail of the distribution can mainly be attributed to good luck.

Figures 3 and 4 show the bootstrap distribution of *alpha* at selected points of the performance distribution. The upper left panel of Figure 3 shows the distribution of the best alpha across funds from 1000 bootstrap re-samples under the null hypothesis of no outperformance ($H_0 : \alpha_i = 0$), while the upper right panel shows the 1000 fifth-best alphas, and so on. It is quite evident from the four panels of Figure 3 that the best bootstrap alphas are highly non-normal and have a relatively high variance but that the distribution more closely approximates normality and exhibits a lesser variance as we move even slightly closer to the centre of the performance distribution. In results not shown, this finding follows closely from the fact that the residuals from the 'best' fund regressions exhibit higher variance and a greater degree of non-normality than funds closer to the centre of the distribution. It is this high variance among the top funds' regression residuals that generates a wide dispersion among the alphas in the bootstrap procedure. In Figure 4, an almost mirror image of this is presented for the extreme lower end of the performance distribution where high variance non-normal residuals among the extremely poor funds' regressions also give rise to wide dispersion among the bootstrap alphas.

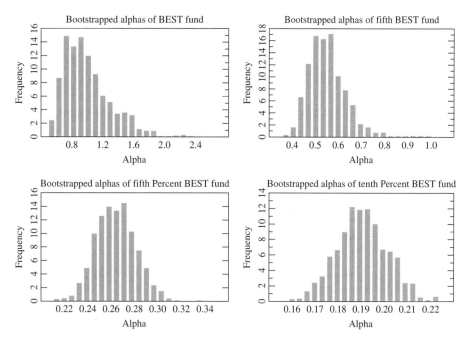

**Figure 3** Histograms of bootstrap alpha estimates: all UK mutual funds (upper end of the distribution: unconditional Fama–French three-factor model)

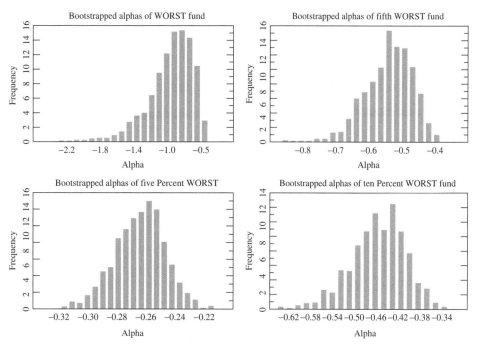

**Figure 4** Histograms of bootstrap alpha estimates: all UK mutual funds (lower end of the distribution: unconditional Fama–French three-factor model)

As an alternative interpretation, the bootstrap may be used to estimate how many funds from the sample one might expect to achieve some given level of alpha performance by random chance alone. This number can then be compared with the number of funds that actually reach this level of alpha. For example, positive alphas should be achieved by 364 funds solely on the basis of chance, whereas in fact only 240 are observed to have produced positive performance.

## Performance and Investment Styles

It is also of interest to investors to identify whether stock-picking talent is related to the investment objective of the fund. From the mutual fund performance and persistence literature, particularly among studies of the US fund industry, there is some evidence that mutual funds with a growth stock investment style tend to be among the top-performing funds (Chen, Jegadeesh and Wermers 2000).

In this study, we find that the top ten performing funds, ranked by a three-factor unconditional alpha model, comprise three growth funds, four general equity funds, three small stock funds and no income funds. Only five of the top ten funds are surviving funds as of December 2002. At the opposite end of the alpha performance scale, the worst ten funds consist of five general equity funds, two income funds and three small stock funds while there are no growth funds. At the top end of the performance spectrum, the findings here support evidence from US mutual fund studies in that growth stock funds feature highly amongst top-performing funds but are not amongst the extreme poor-performing funds.

To address the question of relative performance of mutual funds of different investment styles more rigorously, this study implements the bootstrap procedure separately within each subgroup of investment styles or objectives. These investment styles are declared by the funds themselves but certified initially and subsequently monitored monthly by the IMA in the United Kingdom. Examining the performance and skills of managers separately within each fund classification has the added advantage that in each case, one is examining a more homogeneous risk group helping to control for possible unknown cross-sectional risk characteristics that may be unspecified by the equilibrium model of returns.

A comparison between the performance results among different investment styles is provided in Figures 5 to 8. These figures present kernel density estimates of the actual and bootstrap distribution of $t_\alpha$ for equity income, equity growth, general equity and small stock funds respectively. A comparison of the figures appears to indicate that the left tails of the actual performance distributions (dashed lines) are broadly similar between sectors and indicate poor performance that cannot be attributed to bad luck. The actual performance distributions in the extreme right tail lie to the right of their zero performance bootstrap counterparts only for growth and income funds, but even here there is not much evidence of skill rather than 'good luck'.

## Length of Fund Histories

It may be advisable to restrict the bootstrap analysis to funds with a minimum number of observations. This is to exclude short-lived funds that would be likely to generate alpha

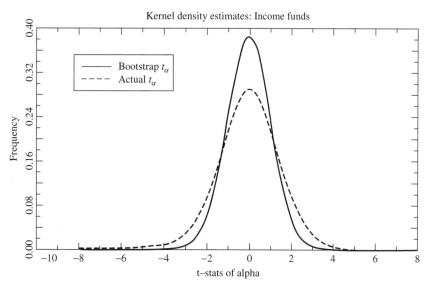

**Figure 5** Kernel density estimates of actual t-statistics of alpha and the bootstrap distribution – UK equity income funds

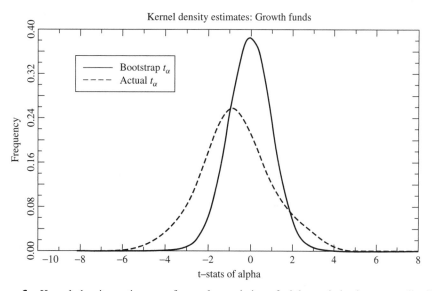

**Figure 6** Kernel density estimates of actual t-statistics of alpha and the bootstrap distribution – UK equity growth funds

performance estimates with high sampling variability making their sample estimation less reliable. These less reliably estimated funds could disproportionately occupy the extreme tails of both the actual and bootstrap distributions. Choosing instead to construct bootstrap $p$-values of the t-statistics of alpha mitigates this problem by scaling the alpha by its precision. Even so, to avoid possible problems with both the modified and unmodified performance distributions, a minimum number of observations restriction is advisable. All bootstrap $p$-values presented in this section above have

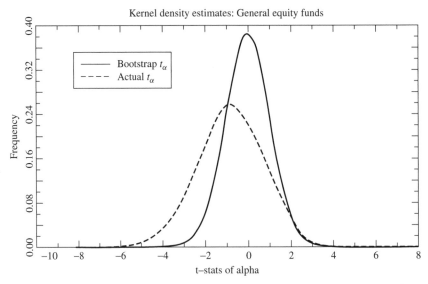

**Figure 7**   Kernel density estimates of actual t-statistics of alpha and bootstrap distribution – UK general equity funds

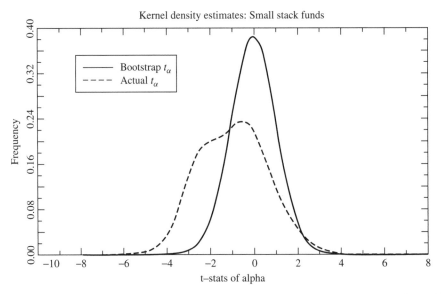

**Figure 8**   Kernel density estimates of actual t-statistic of alpha and bootstrap distribution – UK small stock funds

been calculated over funds with a minimum of 60 observations. However, a possible drawback with this approach is that it may introduce a survivorship bias because the analysis is limited to funds that have been skilled (or possibly lucky) enough to remain in existence for five years.

Owing to this possible source of bias, it is necessary to examine the sensitivity of the conclusions presented so far to this minimum number of observations restriction. In order to examine this, this study conducts the bootstrap procedure and re-estimates the empirical $p$-value for a range of alternative minimum fund histories. The unconditional three-factor model was used in all cases, and results relate to the full sample of all investment objective funds. It is found that the interpretation of the bootstrap $p$-values is unchanged in all minimum observation sample sizes. The findings already presented are not sensitive to restricting sample size (i.e. survivorship bias is not important). Specifically, performance in the left tails of the various panel distributions reject random chance as the explanation for bad performance, while in the right tails, good luck is usually the cause of 'good' performance.

## Time-Series Dependence in the Residuals

The bootstrap procedure may be modified to select residuals in blocks of size that correspond to the suspected order of serial correlation. In this study, it was shown that for a large proportion of funds, the null hypothesis of serial correlation of order one could not be rejected. The bootstrap simulation was repeated for a number of alternative block lengths in which residuals were sampled, but the $p$-values were largely invariant to this procedure. Thus, the bootstrap distributions are mainly the result of non-normality in the tails of the distribution rather than any serial correlation in the residuals.

Overall, the preliminary results of this UK study suggest that amongst the best-performing UK mutual funds, very few exhibit genuine skill in outperforming their benchmarks, while the performance of the worse funds is not due to bad luck but due to 'bad skill'. Of course, the majority of funds neither out- nor underperform their benchmarks, and the issue of persistence in performance is not addressed in this study, only the average performance over the whole data set. The reported results are for the unconditional three-factor Fama and French model, and the sensitivity of the results to alternative performance models (e.g. conditional models and market timing) needs to be carefully examined.

# 9.4 Summary

- Event studies use variants of the 'market model' to measure the abnormal response of stock returns to announcements (e.g. hostile takeover). The CAR is usually taken as the market's view of the impact of this 'news' on the value of the (equity of the) firm.

- Studies of mutual (pension) fund performance use a multifactor approach to account for the various sources of risk that may influence mutual fund portfolio returns and frequently use Jensen's alpha as a measure of abnormal return. This method can be extended to measure persistence in performance.

- Standard statistical tests on alpha indicate that there may be some 'outperformance' and some 'underperformance' for funds at either end of the distribution, but the majority of funds neither over- nor underperform. Any overperformance does not appear to be persistent even over short horizons of one or two years, but underperformance persists for slightly longer.

- After correcting for good or bad luck (using a bootstrap analysis), it has been found that some funds in both the United States and United Kingdom in the 'right tail' of the distribution genuinely outperform their benchmarks but the effect is much more pronounced for US rather than UK funds. However, amongst both US and UK funds, those in the 'left tail' underperform because of genuinely bad stock-picking skills. However, this approach is relatively novel, and hence, these preliminary results, although interesting, must be interpreted with some caution.

# 10

# VALUATION MODELS AND ASSET RETURNS

## Aims

- Show that, when expected stock returns are constant, the stock price equals the discounted present value (DPV) of future dividends, and the discount rate is constant. This is the rational valuation formula (RVF).

- A special case of the RVF, where the dividend growth rate and the discount rate are constant, gives the Gordon Growth Model.

- When equilibrium expected returns vary over time, then the discount rate in the RVF for stock prices is also time-varying.

- Show how the RVF with a time-varying discount rate and time-varying growth rate in dividends can be linearised. The link between stock price volatility and return predictability is then demonstrated.

In this chapter, we look at models that seek to determine how investors decide what is the *fundamental* or *fair* value $V_t$ for a particular stock, where the 'fundamentals' are dividends and future required returns. A key idea running through this chapter is that stock *returns* and stock *prices* are inextricably linked. Indeed, alternative models of equilibrium expected returns give rise to different expressions for the fundamental value of a stock and hence stock prices.

## 10.1 The Rational Valuation Formula (RVF)

The expected return is defined as

$$E_t R_{t+1} = \frac{E_t V_{t+1} - V_t + E_t D_{t+1}}{V_t} \tag{1}$$

where $V_t$ is the value of the stock at the end of time $t$, $D_{t+1}$ are dividends paid between $t$ and $t + 1$, $E_t$ is the expectations operator based on information $\Omega_t$ at time $t$ or earlier and

$$E(D_{t+1}|\Omega_t) \equiv E_t D_{t+1}$$

Assume investors are willing to hold the stock as long as it is expected to earn a *constant* return ($= k$). For the moment, we can think of this 'required return' $k$ as that rate of return that is just sufficient to compensate investors for the inherent riskiness of the stock, but we do not yet specify a 'model' for $k$.

$$E_t R_{t+1} = k \quad k > 0 \tag{2}$$

The stochastic behaviour of $R_{t+1} - k$ is such that no abnormal returns are made, *on average*, and excess returns are a 'fair game'.

$$E_t(R_{t+1} - k|\Omega_t) = 0 \tag{3}$$

Using (1) and (2), we obtain the Euler equation that determines the movement in 'value' over time:

$$V_t = \delta E_t(V_{t+1} + D_{t+1}) \tag{4}$$

where $\delta = $ discount factor $= 1/(1 + k)$ with $0 < \delta < 1$. Leading (4) one period:

$$V_{t+1} = \delta E_{t+1}(V_{t+2} + D_{t+2}) \tag{5}$$

Now take expectations of (5), assuming that information is only available up to time $t$:

$$E_t V_{t+1} = \delta E_t(V_{t+2} + D_{t+2}) \tag{6}$$

In deriving (6), we have used the *law of iterated expectations*:

$$E_t(E_{t+1} V_{t+2}) = E_t V_{t+2} \tag{7}$$

The expectation formed today of what one's expectation will be tomorrow at $t + 1$ for $V_{t+2}$, is the left-hand side of (7). This simply equals the expectation today of $V_{t+2}$, since under RE you cannot know *how* you will alter your expectations in the future. Equation (6) holds for all periods so that

$$E_t V_{t+2} = \delta E_t(V_{t+3} + D_{t+3}), \text{ etc.} \tag{8}$$

The next part of the solution requires substitution of (6) in (4).

$$V_t = \delta[\delta E_t(V_{t+2} + D_{t+2})] + \delta(E_t D_{t+1})$$

By successive substitution,

$$V_t = E_t[\delta D_{t+1} + \delta^2 D_{t+2} + \delta^3 D_{t+3} + \cdots + \delta^N(D_{t+N} + V_{t+N})] \tag{9}$$

Now let $N \to \infty$ and, hence, $\delta^N \to 0$. If the expected growth in $D$ is not explosive so that $E_t V_{t+N}$ is also finite, then,

$$\underbrace{\lim}_{n \to \infty} E_t \delta^N [D_{t+N} + V_{t+N}] \to 0 \tag{10}$$

Equation (10) is known as a terminal condition or *transversality condition*, and it rules out rational speculative bubbles (see Chapter 17). Equation (9) then becomes

$$V_t = E_t \sum_{i=1}^{\infty} \delta^i D_{t+i} \tag{11}$$

We have derived (11) under the assumptions that expected returns are constant, the law of iterated expectations (i.e. RE) holds for all investors and the transversality condition holds.

The *fundamental value* $V_t$ of a share is the DPV of expected future dividends. If $P_t \neq V_t$, then unexploited profit opportunities exist in the market. For example, if $P_t < V_t$, then investors would buy the share since they anticipate that they will make a capital gain as $P_t$ rises towards its 'correct value' in the future. As investors purchase the share with $P_t < V_t$, this would tend to lead to a rise in the current price as demand increases, so that it quickly moves towards its fundamental value. Now assume

- investors *at the margin* have homogeneous expectations or more precisely that their subjective view of the probability distribution of fundamental value reflects the 'true' underlying distribution;

- risky arbitrage is instantaneous, so investors set the actual market price $P_t$ equal to fundamental value $V_t$.

Then we obtain the *RVF* for stock prices with a constant discount rate:

$$P_t = E_t \left[ \sum_{i=1}^{\infty} \delta^i D_{t+i} \right] \tag{12}$$

In the above analysis, we did not distinguish between real and nominal variables, and indeed the mathematics goes through for either case: hence, (12) is true whether all variables are nominal or deflated by an aggregate goods price index. Nevertheless, intuitive reasoning and causal empiricism suggest that expected *real* returns are more likely to be constant than expected nominal returns (not least because of goods price inflation). Hence, the RVF is usually expressed in terms of real variables.

## Finite or Infinite Horizon?

If investors have a finite horizon, then they are concerned with the price that they can obtain in the near future, so does this alter our view of the determination of fundamental value? Consider the simple case of an investor with a one-period horizon:

$$P_t = \delta E_t D_{t+1} + \delta E_t P_{t+1}$$

The price today depends on the expected price at $t+1$. But how is this investor to determine the value $E_t P_{t+1}$ at which she can sell at $t+1$? If she is consistent (rational), she should determine this in exactly the same way that she does for $P_t$. That is,

$$E_t P_{t+1} = [\delta E_t D_{t+2} + \delta E_t P_{t+2}]$$

But by repeated forward induction, each investor with a one-period horizon will believe that $P_{t+j}$ is determined by the above Euler equation and hence today's price will equal the DPV of dividends in *all future periods*. Thus, even if some agents have a finite investment horizon, they will still determine the fundamental value in such a way that it is equal to that of an investor who has an infinite horizon. An alternative view, that if investors have short horizons then price cannot reflect fundamental value, is known as *short-termism*.

Later in this chapter, the assumption that equilibrium returns are constant is relaxed and we find that a version of the RVF still holds. In contrast, in Chapters 18 and 19, non-rational agents or noise traders may influence returns, and in such a model, price may not equal fundamental value.

## 10.2   Special Cases of the RVF

### A. Expected Dividends Are Constant

Suppose the best forecast of *all* future (real) dividends is the current level of dividends, so

$$D_{t+1} = D_t + w_{t+1}$$

where $w_{t+1}$ is white noise, and dividends follow a random walk. Under RE, we have $E_t(w_{t+j}|\Omega_t) = 0$ *for* $j \geq 1$ and $E_t D_{t+j} = D_t$. Hence, the growth in dividends is expected to be zero and the RVF (12) becomes

$$P_t = \delta(1 + \delta + \delta^2 + \cdots)D_t = \delta(1 - \delta)^{-1}D_t = (1/k)D_t \qquad (13)$$

Equation (13) predicts that the dividend–price (D/P) ratio or *dividend yield* is a constant equal to the required (real) return $k$. The model (13) also predicts that the percentage change in stock prices equals the percentage change in dividends. Price changes occur only when *new* information about dividends (i.e. 'fundamentals') becomes available: the model predicts that *volatility* in stock prices depends wholly on the volatility in dividends. Although an investor's best *forecast* of dividends for all future periods is $D_t$, the random element $w_{t+1}$ (i.e. news or uncertainty) may cause actual future dividends to differ from the investor's best forecast. The conditional variance of prices therefore depends on the variance in news about these fundamentals:

$$P_{t+1} - P_t = (1/k)\Delta D_{t+1} = (1/k)w_{t+1} \qquad (14)$$

and

$$\mathrm{var}(P_{t+1} - P_t|\Omega_t) = (\sigma_w/k)^2 \qquad (15)$$

Later in the book (Chapter 12), we examine the more general case where the volatility in prices depends not only on the volatility in dividends but also on the volatility in the discount rate. In fact, an attempt is made to ascertain whether the volatility in stock prices is mainly due to the volatility in dividends or the discount factor.

## B. Gordon Growth Model

A time-series model in which (real) dividends grow at a constant rate $g$ is the AR(1) model:

$$D_{t+1} = (1 + g)D_t + w_{t+1} \qquad (16)$$

where $w_{t+1}$ is white noise. *Expected* dividend growth from (16) is easily seen to be equal to $g$.

$$(E_t D_{t+1} - D_t)/D_t = g \qquad (17)$$

Note that if the *logarithm* of dividends follows a random walk with a drift parameter $g^*$, then this also gives a constant expected growth rate for dividends (i.e. $E_t(\ln D_{t+1}) = g^* + \ln D_t$). The optimal forecasts of future dividends may be found by leading (16) and by repeated substitution.

$$E_t D_{t+j} = (1 + g)^j D_t \qquad (18)$$

Substituting the forecast of future dividends from (18) in the rational valuation formula gives

$$P_t = \sum_{i=1}^{\infty} \delta^i (1 + g)^i D_t \qquad (19)$$

which after some simple algebra yields the Gordon Growth Model

$$P_t = \frac{(1 + g)}{(k - g)} D_t \quad \text{with } (k - g) > 0 \qquad (20)$$

For example, if $g = 0.03, k = 0.08$, then the price–dividend ratio is 20.6. If agents suddenly revise their expectations about $g$ or $k$, then prices will move substantially. For example, if $g$ falls to 0.02, then the new price–dividend ratio is 17, which implies an 'immediate' fall in price of 17.4%. If we assume $g$ and $k$ remain constant, then the model does not 'fit the facts' over short horizons, since prices are far more volatile than dividends over short periods (e.g. up to 5 years); although over the longer term (e.g. 25 years or more), prices and dividends tend to move broadly together (i.e. are cointegrated), as predicted by the model (i.e. $\ln P_t = \alpha + \ln D_t$ where $\alpha = \ln[(1 + g)/(k - g)]$).

## 10.3   Time-Varying Expected Returns

Suppose investors require a different expected return in each future period in order that they will willingly hold a particular stock. (Why this may be the case is investigated later.) Our model is therefore

$$E_t R_{t+1} = k_{t+1} \qquad (21)$$

where we have a time subscript on $k$ to indicate that it is time-varying. Repeating the previous steps, involving forward substitution, gives

$$P_t = E_t[\delta_{t+1}D_{t+1} + \delta_{t+1}\delta_{t+2}D_{t+2} + \cdots + \cdots \delta_{t+N-1}\delta_{t+N}(D_{t+N} + P_{t+N})] \qquad (22)$$

which can be written in a more compact form (assuming the transversality condition holds):

$$P_t = E_t\left[\sum_{j=1}^{\infty}\left[\prod_{i=1}^{j}\delta_{t+i}\right]D_{t+j}\right] \equiv E_t\sum_{j=1}^{\infty}\delta_{t,t+j}D_{t+j} \qquad (23)$$

where $\delta_{t+i} = 1/(1 + k_{t+i})$ and $\delta_{t,t+j} = \delta_{t+1}\ldots\delta_{t+j}$. The current stock price, therefore, depends on expectations of future discount rates and dividends. Note that $0 < \delta_{t+j} < 1$ for all periods and hence expected dividends \$-for-\$ have less influence on the current stock price the further they accrue in the future. However, it is possible that an event *announced* today (e.g. a merger with another company) could be expected to have a *substantial* impact on dividends starting in, say, 5 years' time. In this case, the *announcement* could have a large effect on the *current* stock price even though it is relatively heavily discounted. Note that in a well-informed ('efficient') market, one expects the stock price to respond immediately and completely to the announcement even though no dividends will actually be paid for 5 years. In contrast, if the market is inefficient (e.g. noise traders are present), then the price might rise not only in the current period but also in subsequent periods. Tests of the stock price response to announcements are known as *event studies*.

At the moment, (23) is 'non-operational' since it involves unobservable expectations terms. We cannot calculate fundamental value (i.e. the right-hand side of (23)) and hence cannot see if it corresponds to the observable current price $P_t$. We need some ancillary tractable hypotheses about investors' forecasts of dividends and the discount rate. It is relatively straightforward to develop forecasting equations for dividends, for example, on annual data, an AR(1) or AR(2) model for dividends fits the data quite well. The difficulty arises with the equilibrium rate of return $k_t$. We investigate equilibrium models of returns in a two-period and multiperiod context in later chapters and derive the implications for returns and stock prices.

For the moment, consider an *ad hoc* approach to equilibrium returns using the CAPM. This is *ad hoc* because the CAPM is based on a one-period mean-variance optimisation problem and we will use it in the multiperiod DPV formula. We are being logically inconsistent! But such *ad hoc* approaches are not unknown in applied work.

## Market Portfolio

The one-period CAPM predicts that in equilibrium, all investors will hold the market portfolio (i.e. all risky assets will be held in the same proportions in each individual's portfolio). Merton (1973) developed this idea in an intertemporal framework and showed that the *excess return* over the risk-free rate, on the market portfolio, is proportional to the expected variance of returns on the market portfolio.

$$E_t R_{m,t+1} - r_t = \lambda(E_t \sigma^2_{m,t+1}) \tag{24}$$

The expected return can be defined as comprising a risk-free return plus a risk premium $rp_t$:

$$E_t R_{m,t+1} = r_t + rp_t \quad \text{where } rp_t = \lambda E_t \sigma^2_{m,t+1} \tag{25}$$

Comparing (21) and (25), we see that according to the CAPM, the required rate of return on the market portfolio is given by

$$k_t = r_t + \lambda(E_t \sigma^2_{m,t+1}) \tag{26}$$

The equilibrium required return depends positively on the risk-free interest rate $r_t$ and on the (non-diversifiable) risk of the market portfolio, as measured by its conditional variance $E_t \sigma^2_{m,t+1}$. If either

- agents do not perceive the market as risky (i.e. $E_t \sigma^2_{m,t+1} = 0$) or
- agents are risk-neutral (i.e. $\lambda = 0$)

then the appropriate discount factor used by investors is the risk-free rate $r_t$. Note that to determine the price using the RVF, investors must determine $k_t$ and hence forecast future values of the risk-free rate and the risk premium.

## Individual Asset Returns

Consider now the price of an individual security or a portfolio of assets, which is a subset of the market portfolio (e.g. shares of either all industrial companies or all banking firms). The CAPM implies that to be willingly held as part of a diversified portfolio, the expected return on portfolio-i is given by

$$E_t R_{it+1} = r_t + \beta_{it}(E_t R_{m,t+1} - r_t) \quad \text{where } \beta_{it} = E_t(\sigma_{im}/\sigma^2_m)_{t+1} \tag{27}$$

Substituting from (24) for $E_t \sigma^2_{mt+1}$, we have

$$E_t R_{it+1} = r_t + \lambda E_t(\sigma_{im})_{t+1} \tag{28}$$

where $\sigma_{im}$ is the *covariance* between returns on asset-i and the market portfolio. Again comparing (21) and (28), the equilibrium required rate of return on asset-i is

$$k_{t+1} = r_t + \lambda E_t(\sigma_{im})_{t+1}$$

The covariance term may be time-varying and hence so might the future discount factors $\delta_{t+j}$ in the RVF for an individual security (or portfolio of securities). In the CAPM, the market only rewards investors for non-diversifiable (systematic) risk. The required (nominal) rate of return $k_t$ to willingly hold an individual stock as part of a wider portfolio is equal to the risk-free rate *plus* a reward for risk or *risk premium* $rp_t$, which depends on the (conditional) covariance.

## Linearisation of the RVF

As we shall see in Chapter 12, it is possible to linearise the RVF with a time-varying discount rate and this can prove very useful in analysing movements in stock prices. To 'get a handle on this', consider the Gordon Growth Model equation (20), which shows that a high current price–dividend ratio must be due to either high expected dividend growth or low expected future returns (discount rates). Now consider the following linearisation of the RVF (assuming no rational bubbles):

$$p_t - d_t = \text{constant} + E_t\{\sum_{j=1}^{\infty} \rho^{j-1}(\Delta d_{t+j} - h_{t+j})\} + \lim_{j\to\infty} \rho^j (p_{t+j} - d_{t+j}) \quad (29)$$

where $\rho$ is a linearisation constant with a value of around 0.95, $\Delta d_{t+j}$ is the change in log-dividends and $h_{t+j}$ is a sequence of one-period log returns. Equation (29) is a dynamic version of the Gordon Growth Model in which dividend growth and expected returns are not constant but can vary from period to period. It is consistent with the Gordon Growth Model since the price–dividend ratio depends positively on dividend growth and negatively on future expected returns. Given that the dividend–price ratio varies over time in the data, then from (29), it must forecast either future dividend growth or future returns. Put another way, a high price–dividend ratio *must* be followed (on average) by either high dividend growth or low returns $h_{t+j}$ (i.e. the discount factor) if the RVF is valid in the real world.

The above equation encapsulates many of the issues that we will discuss in future chapters. Shiller's work, discussed in detail in the next two chapters essentially shows that the volatility in the actual price (or price–dividend ratio) cannot be explained *solely* by rational agents' views of changes in expected dividend growth, since the latter does not vary enough in the data. This contradiction *cannot* be rescued by assuming that expected future stock returns $E_t h_{t+j}$ vary because of changes in interest rates, since, then a high price–dividend ratio should predict lower interest rates on average, which is not the case in the data. Hence, acceptance of the RVF must probably rely either on changes in the degree of risk aversion or on changes in the perceived level of stock market risk. Empirically, the evidence for a link between stock market volatility and expected returns (see equation (28)) is not overly strong (e.g. French, Schwert and Stambaugh 1987), and we survey this evidence in Chapter 29 concentrating on the so-called GARCH-in-mean models. Changes in the perceived level of stock market risk are discussed under the general heading of stochastic discount factor models in Chapter 13 and changing risk aversion is the subject of models of 'behavioural finance' in Chapters 18 and 19. The final term in (29) could also account for the movement in the price–dividend ratio, and this is the subject matter of Chapter 17 on rational bubbles (see Brunnermeier 2001).

Of course, one could also take the view that investors do not know the true structure of the economy (up to a set of white noise errors) and take time to learn about their environment. This would also go some way in resolving the volatility puzzle since a *random* rise in earnings over a short period might be projected into the future, thus leading to higher and hence more volatile prices than would be predicted if agents were truly rational. This idea of changing beliefs and 'incorrect' expectations formation appears throughout the book and in particular in Chapter 17.

## Volatility and Long-Horizon Forecastability

If, as is broadly the case in the data, the price–dividend ratio does *not* forecast future dividends, then it must forecast future returns. Hence, the RVF equation (29) is consistent with regression results where *long-horizon* returns can be forecast using the dividend–price ratio – the term $\sum_{j=1}^{\infty} \rho^{j-1} h_{t+j}$ is rather like a long-horizon return (for $\rho$ close to unity). Hence, in the data, high price–dividend ratios do not seem to reflect higher dividend growth but lower expected returns and hence lower expected risk premia.

An alternative representation of the linearised RVF is

$$h_t - E_{t-1} h_t = E_t - E_{t-1} \left\{ \sum_{j=0}^{\infty} \rho^j (\Delta d_{t+j} - \Delta h_{t+j+1}) \right\} \tag{30}$$

The term $E_t - E_{t-1}$ is a change in expectations or a 'surprise' event. Hence, a surprise in one-period returns must be due to either revisions in forecasts of future dividends or in future returns (or both). Campbell (1991) finds that it is revisions to future returns that mainly drive unexpected current returns – again dividends play a relatively minor role in influencing returns. Equation (30) also demonstrates the mildly counterintuitive yet logically consistent result that a rise in *expected* future returns with no change in news about dividends implies an *unexpected fall* in *current* returns. This arises because if future discount rates are expected to be higher, while dividends are unchanged, then today's price must fall.

## Expected Returns and Price Volatility

Is the empirical finding of highly volatile prices and small yet predictable changes *in expected* returns consistent? The answer is 'yes', provided expected returns are highly persistent. This is seen most easily in the Gordon Growth Model where we noted that a small *permanent* change in the required return $k$ leads to a large price change. Now, suppose *expected* returns are a persistent AR(1) process with coefficient $\phi$ close to unity:

$$h_{t+1} = \phi h_t + \varepsilon_{t+1} \tag{31}$$

Note that (31) implies $E_t h_{t+2} = \phi E_t h_{t+1}$ so that *expected* returns are persistent. Substituting in (29) for $E_t h_{t+j} = \phi^j h_t$ (and ignoring the dividend growth term),

$$(p_t - d_t) = \frac{-1}{(1 - \rho\phi)} h_t \tag{32}$$

Reasonable values are $\rho = 0.95$ and $\phi = 0.9$. Then, even a 'small' volatility in expected returns of $\sigma(E_t h_{t+1}) = 1\%$ gives $\sigma(p_t - d_t) = 6.9\%$ – a high volatility in prices. We discuss these issues further in Chapter 12.

## 10.4  Summary

- Under instantaneous arbitrage, given any model for expected *returns*, we can show that the *price* of a stock equals the PV of expected dividends and future discount factors. This is the rational valuation formula, RVF. If equilibrium expected returns are constant, then the discount rate in the RVF is constant.

- The Gordon Growth Model assumes a constant discount rate and constant growth in dividends – dividends and discount rates are persistent. Prices are very sensitive to small changes in the discount rate or the growth rate of dividends. If discount rates and dividend growth really are constant in all time periods, then (log) prices move one-for-one with the log of dividends.

- If equilibrium expected returns on an asset are given by the standard-CAPM, then the discount factor in the RVF may be time-varying. This discount factor depends on the risk-free rate and a variance term (for the market return) or a covariance term (for individual assets or a subset of the market portfolio).

- Suppose dividend growth and future discount rates are time-varying and dividend growth is *not* forecastable (e.g. (log) dividends follow a random walk). Then, even though *expected* returns are barely forecastable, yet persistent, this can lead to highly volatile prices.

# 11

# STOCK PRICE VOLATILITY

## Aims

- Explain how Shiller's variance bounds tests can be used to assess the RVF for stock prices – this results in the *volatility puzzle*.

- Analyse the statistical problems of small-sample bias and non-stationarity in the context of variance bounds tests.

- Demonstrate how the 'Peso problem' changes our interpretation of variance bounds tests.

- Show the linkages between variance bounds tests and various regression tests of the RVF.

In this chapter, we discuss whether 'fundamentals' such as changing forecasts about dividends or future returns can explain the observed volatility in stock prices. If a rational fundamentals model cannot explain such observed volatility, then we have an anomaly, which has become known as the *volatility puzzle* (Campbell 2000). In later chapters, we see that there are other stylised facts about stock returns that are difficult to rationalise in conventional models, the most prominent being the equity premium puzzle and the risk-free rate puzzle.

Volatility tests directly examine the rational valuation formula (RVF) for stock prices under a specific assumption about equilibrium expected returns. The simplest assumption is that one-period returns are constant.

$$P_t = \sum_{i=1}^{\infty} \delta^i E_t D_{t+i} \tag{1}$$

If we had a reliable measure of *expected* dividends, we could calculate the RHS of (1). A test of the RVF would then be to see if var $\left(\sum \delta^i E_t D_{t+i}\right)$ equals var($P_t$). Shiller (1981) in a seminal article obviated the need for data on expected dividends. He noted that under rational expectations (RE), actual and expected dividends only differ by a random (forecast) error and therefore so do the actual price $P_t$ and the perfect foresight price $P_t^*$, defined as $P_t^* = \sum \delta^i D_{t+i}$. Note that $P_t^*$ uses *actual* dividends. Shiller demonstrated that the RVF implies var($P_t$) $\leq$ var($P_t^*$). At the same time as Shiller, two other financial economists, LeRoy and Porter (1981), provided similar tests. However, whereas Shiller found that for US stock prices, the variance inequality was grossly violated, LeRoy and Porter found that the inequality was only marginally rejected (in a statistical sense). These two papers led to a plethora of contributions using variants of this basic methodology. Some articles emphasised the small-sample biases that might be present, whereas later work examined the robustness of the volatility tests, under the assumption that dividends are a non-stationary process.

A number of commentators often express the view that stock markets are excessively volatile – prices alter from day to day or week to week by large amounts that do not appear to reflect changes in 'news' about fundamentals. If true, this constitutes a rejection of the efficient markets hypothesis (EMH). Of course, to say that stock prices are excessively volatile requires one to have a model based on rational behaviour that provides a 'yardstick' against which one can compare volatilities. Common sense tells us, of course, that we expect stock prices to exhibit some volatility. This is because of the arrival of 'news' or new information about companies. However, the question we wish to address here is not whether stock prices are volatile but whether they are *excessively* volatile.

We now examine more formal tests of the RVF on the basis of variance bounds. Broadly speaking, variance bounds tests examine whether the variance of stock prices is consistent with the variability in fundamentals (i.e. dividends and discount rates) given by the RVF. These tests can be classified into two broad types: 'model-free' tests and 'model-based' tests. In the former, we do not have to assume a particular *statistical* model for the fundamental variables. However, as we shall see, this implies that we merely obtain a point estimate of the relevant test statistic, but we cannot derive confidence limits on this measure. Formal hypothesis testing is therefore not possible. All one can do is to try and ensure that the estimator (based on sample data) of the desired statistic is an unbiased estimate of its population value. Critics of the early variance ratio tests highlighted the problem of bias in finite samples (Flavin 1983).

A 'model-based test' assumes a particular stochastic process for dividends. This provides a test statistic with appropriate confidence limits and enables one to examine small-sample properties using Monte Carlo simulation. However, with model-based tests, rejection of the RVF is conditional on having the correct statistical model for dividends and the discount rate. We therefore have the problem of a joint null hypothesis.

A further key factor in interpreting the various tests on stock prices is whether the dividend process is assumed to be stationary or non-stationary. Under non-stationary, the usual distributional assumptions do not apply and interpretation of the results from variance bounds tests can be highly problematic. Later work in this area has been directed towards test procedures that take account of possible non-stationarity in the data.

## 11.1   Shiller Volatility Tests

Under constant (real) returns

$$P_t = \sum_{i=1}^{n} \delta^i E_t D_{t+i} + \delta^n E_t P_{t+n} \qquad (2)$$

Here, $P_{t+n}$ is the expected 'terminal price' at time $t + n$, and all investors take the same view of the future. At time $t$, we do not know what investors' forecasts of expected future dividends would have been. However, Shiller (1981) proposed a simple yet very ingenious way of getting round this problem. Suppose we have data on actual dividends in the past, say from 1900 onwards, and we have the actual price $P_{t+n}$ today, say in 2004. We assume $\delta$ is a known value, say, 0.95, for annual data, implying a required return of $k = 5.2\%$ p.a. $[\delta = 1/(1 + k)]$. Then, using (2), we can calculate what the stock price in 1900 *would have been*, if investors had forecast dividends *exactly*, in all years from 1900 onwards. We call this the perfect foresight stock price, $P_t^*$, in 1900. By moving one year forward and repeating the above, we can obtain a data series for $P_t^*$ for all years from 1900 onwards using the following formula.

$$P_t^* = \sum_{i=1}^{n} \delta^i D_{t+i} + \delta^n P_{t+n} \qquad (3)$$

When calculating $P_t^*$ for 1900, the influence of the terminal price $P_{t+n}$ is fairly minimal since $n$ is large and $\delta^n$ is relatively small. As we approach the end-point of, say, 2004, the term $\delta^n P_{t+n}$ carries more weight in our calculation of $P_t^*$. One option is therefore to truncate our sample, say, 10 years prior to the present. Alternatively, we can assume that the *actual* price at the terminal date is 'close to' its expected value $E_t P_{t+n}$ and the latter is usually done in empirical work. Comparing $P_t$ and $P_t^*$, we see that they differ by the sum of the forecast errors of dividends $w_{t+i} = D_{t+i} - E_t D_{t+i}$, weighted by the discount factor $\delta^i$.

From (2) and (3) and the definition of $w_{t+i}$:

$$P_t^* = P_t + \sum_{i=1}^{n} \delta^i w_{t+i} + \delta^n (P_{t+n} - E_t P_{t+n})$$

Assuming the final term is close to zero as $n \rightarrow \infty$ and noting that under RE, $\text{cov}(P_t, w_{t+i}) = 0$, then it follows that the RVF implies $\text{var}(P_t^*) \geq \text{var}(P_t)$.

For $x_t = P_t$ or $P_t^*$, the sample variance is given by $\text{var}(x) = \sum_{t=1}^{n} (x_t - \bar{x})^2/(n - 1)$, where $\bar{x} = $ sample mean and $n = $ number of observations. In 1900, investors did not know what future dividends were going to be, and, therefore, the actual stock price differs from the perfect foresight stock price. With hindsight, we know that investors made forecast errors $\eta_t = P_t^* - P_t$ so

$$P_t^* = P_t + \eta_t \qquad (4)$$

where $\eta_t = \sum_{i=1}^{n} w_{t+i}$. Under RE, $\eta_t$ is independent of all information at time $t$ and, in particular, $\eta_t$ will be independent of the stock price at time $t$. From (4), we obtain

$$\mathrm{var}(P_t^*) = \mathrm{var}(P_t) + \mathrm{var}(\eta_t) + 2\,\mathrm{cov}(\eta_t,\, P_t) \tag{5}$$

Informational efficiency (orthogonality) implies $\mathrm{cov}(P_t,\, \eta_t)$ is zero, hence,

$$\mathrm{var}(P_t^*) = \mathrm{var}(P_t) + \mathrm{var}(\eta_t) \tag{6}$$

Since $\mathrm{var}(\eta_t) \geq 0$,

$$\mathrm{var}(P_t^*) \geq \mathrm{var}(P_t) \tag{7a}$$

or

$$VR = \mathrm{var}(P_t^*)/\mathrm{var}(P_t) \geq 1 \quad \text{and} \quad SDR = \sigma(P_t^*)/\sigma(P_t) \geq 1 \tag{7b}$$

Hence, under EMH/RE, and a constant discount factor, we would expect the variance of the perfect foresight price $P_t^*$ to exceed that of the actual price $P_t$. For expositional reasons, we assumed that $P_t^*$ is calculated using (3). However, in much of the empirical work, an equivalent method is used. The DPV formula (3) is consistent with the Euler equation.

$$P_t^* = \delta(P_{t+1}^* + D_{t+1}) \tag{8}$$

Hence, if we assume a terminal value for $P_{t+n}^*$, we can use (8) to calculate $P_t^*$, and so on, by backward recursion. This, in fact, is the method used in Shiller (1981). One criticism of Shiller (1981) is that he uses the sample mean of prices for the terminal value $P_{t+n}^* = n^{-1} \sum_{t=1}^{n} P_t$. Marsh and Merton (1986) point out that this yields a biased estimate of $P_t^*$. However, Grossman and Shiller (1981) and Shiller's (1989) later work uses the actual stock price at $P_{t+n}$ for the unobservable $P_{t+n}^*$. The observable series, which we denote $P_{t/n}^*$, then uses (8) with $P_{t+n}$ in place of $P_{t+n}^*$. This preserves the logical structure of the model since $P_{t+n} = E(P_{t+n}^* | \Omega_{t+n})$.

Consider the results in Figure 1, which use Shiller's US data 1871–1995. The solid line is the (real) stock price $P_t$, which is clearly much more volatile than the perfect foresight stock price $P_t^*$ calculated under the assumption that the (real) discount rate is constant. 'Eyeballing' Figure 1 suggests rejecting the EMH-RVF under the constant (real) returns assumption (but, of course, we do not know the standard error surrounding our 'eyeball estimate'). Let us see what happens when we apply more rigorous tests.

## Volatility Tests

Empirical tests of the RVF generally use 'real variables'. Early work on volatility tests assume a constant real discount rate, and Shiller (1981) finds that US stock prices are excessively volatile, that is to say, inequality (7b) is grossly violated (i.e. SDR = 5.59). However, LeRoy and Porter (1981), using a slightly different formulation (see Appendix), find that although the variance bound is violated, the rejection was of borderline statistical significance.

We can rework the perfect foresight price, assuming the required real return $k_t$, and hence, $\delta_t = (1 + k_t)^{-1}$ varies over time. For example, we could set $k_t$ to equal the

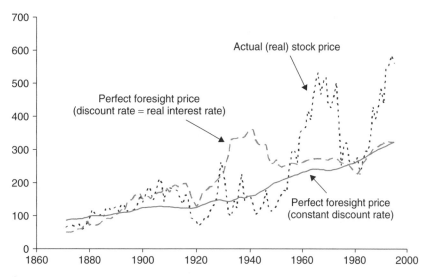

**Figure 1**    Actual stock price and perfect foresight stock price (US data 1871–1995)

actual real interest rate plus a constant risk premium, $k_t = r_t + rp$. Hence, $k_t$ varies in each year, and $P_t^*$ is calculated as

$$P_t^* = \frac{D_{t+1}}{(1+k_{t+1})} + \frac{D_{t+2}}{(1+k_{t+1})(1+k_{t+2})} + \cdots + \frac{(D_{t+n} + P_{t+n})}{(1+k_{t+1})\ldots(1+k_{t+n})} \quad (9)$$

with a terminal value equal to the end-of-sample actual price. However, even after allowing for a time-varying real interest rate, the variance bound is still violated (e.g. Mankiw, Romer and Shapiro 1991, Scott 1990). This can be seen to apply *a fortiori* when we use more recent data for the United States in Figure 1. The perfect foresight price *with a time-varying real discount rate* (equal to the real interest rate) shows more variability than if we have a constant discount rate, but even here, the actual price is far more volatile than the perfect foresight price. If we had included data between 1995 and 2004, then the volatility of the actual price series relative to the two perfect foresight price series is substantially larger even than that shown for the 1990s.

We can turn the above calculation on its head. Knowing the variability in the *actual* stock price, we can calculate the variability in real returns $k_t$ that would be necessary to equate var($P_t^*$) with var($P_t$). Shiller (1981) performs this calculation under the assumption that $P_t$ and $D_t$ have deterministic trends. Using the detrended series, he finds that the standard deviation of real returns needs to be greater than 4% p.a. However, the actual historic variability in real *interest rates* at less than 1% p.a. is much smaller than that required to 'save' the variance bounds test. Hence, the explanation for the violation of the excess volatility relationship does not appear to lie with a time-varying *ex-post* real interest rate.

Another line of attack, in order to 'rescue' the violation of the variance bound, is to use the consumption-CAPM to provide a measure of the time-varying risk premium (see Chapter 13). For power utility, the time-varying discount rate depends on the rate of growth of consumption $g$ the constant rate of time preference $\theta$ and the coefficient of relative risk aversion, $\gamma$. For simplicity, assume for the moment that dividends grow at a constant rate, $D_t = D_0 g^t$. Hence, the perfect foresight price is

$$P_t^* = D_0 g^t \left[ C_t^\gamma \sum_{s=0}^{\infty} (\theta g)^s C_{t+s}^{-\gamma} \right] \tag{10}$$

$P_t^*$ varies over time (Grossman and Shiller 1981), depending on the current level of consumption relative to a weighted harmonic average of future consumption, $C_{t+s}^{-\gamma}$. Clearly, this introduces more variability in $P_t^*$ than does the constant discount rate assumption (i.e. where the coefficient of relative risk aversion, $\gamma = 0$).

Replacing the constant growth rate of dividends by actual, *ex-post* dividends while retaining the C-CAPM formulation, Shiller (1989) recalculates the variance bounds tests for the United States for the period 1889 to 1985 using $\gamma = 4$. A graph of $P_t$ and $P_t^*$ suggests that up to about 1950, the variance bounds test is not violated. However, the relationship between the variability of actual prices and perfect foresight prices is certainly not close in the years after 1950. On balance, it does not appear that the assumption of a time-varying discount rate based on the consumption-CAPM (with CRRA utility and no market frictions) can wholly explain observed movements in stock prices.

## Statistical Issues

In this section, we demonstrate the difficulties in testing the EMH-RVF hypothesis and the ingenuity shown by researchers in tackling these problems. In a small way, these studies provide a useful 'case study' in applied econometrics of time-series data.

Flavin (1983) and Kleidon (1986) point out that there are biases in small samples in measuring var($P_t$) and var($P_t^*$), which might invalidate some of the 'first-generation' variance bounds tests. Flavin (1983) analysed these tests under the constant discount rate assumption and made two key points.

First, both var($P_t^*$) and var($P_t$) are estimated with a downward bias in small samples, the degree of bias depending on the degree of serial correlation in $P_t^*$ and $P_t$. Since $P_t^*$ is more strongly autocorrelated than $P_t$, var($P_t^*$) is estimated with greater downward bias than var($P_t$). Hence, it is possible that the sample values yield var($P_t^*$) < var($P_t$) in a finite sample, even when the null of the RVF is true. Second, Shiller's use of the sample average of prices as a proxy for terminal value of $P^*$ at $t + n$ also induces a bias towards rejection.

There is a further issue surrounding the terminal price, noted by Gilles and LeRoy (1991). The perfect foresight price is

$$P_t^* = \sum_{i=0}^{\infty} \delta^i D_{t+i} \tag{11}$$

which is unobservable. The observable series $P_{t|n}^*$ should be constructed using the actual price $P_{t+n}$ at the end of the sample. However, there is still a problem since the sample variance of $P_{t|n}^*$ understates the true (but unobservable) variance of $P_t^*$.

Intuitively, this is because $P_{t|n}^*$ is 'anchored' on $P_{t+n}$ and hence does take account of innovations in dividends that occur after the end of the sample ($P_{t|n}^*$ implicitly sets these to zero but $P_t^*$ includes these, since the summation is to infinity). Clearly, this problem is minimal if the sample is very large (infinite) but may be important in finite samples.

Flavin's (1983) criticisms of these 'first-generation tests' assumed, as did the authors of these tests, stationarity of the series being used. Later work tackled the issue of the validity of variance bounds tests when the price and dividend series are non-stationary (i.e. have a stochastic trend). Intuitively, the problem posed by non-stationary series is that the population variances are functions of time and, hence, the sample variances are not correct measures of their population values. However, it is not obvious how to 'remove' these stochastic trends from the data, in order to meaningfully apply the variance bounds tests. It is to this issue that we now turn.

## 11.2  Volatility Tests and Stationarity

Shiller's volatility inequality is a consequence purely of the assumption that the actual stock price is an unbiased and optimal predictor of the perfect foresight price $P_t^*$

$$P_t^* = P_t + u_t \tag{12}$$

where $u_t$ is a random error term, $E(u_t|\Omega_t) = 0$. Put another way, $P_t$ is a sufficient statistic to forecast $P_t^*$. No information other than $P_t$ can improve the forecast of $P_t^*$ and, in this sense, $P_t$ is 'optimal'. The latter implies that the conditional forecast error $E[(P_t^* - P_t)|\Omega_t]$ is independent of all information available at time $t$ or earlier. Since $P_t \subset \Omega_t$, then $P_t$ is independent of $u_t$ and $\text{cov}(P_t, u_t) = 0$. Using the definition of covariance for a stationary series, it follows directly from (12)

$$\text{cov}(P_t^*, P_t) = \text{cov}(P_t + u_t, P_t) = \text{cov}(P_t, P_t) + \text{cov}(P_t, u_t) = \sigma^2(P_t) \tag{13}$$

Since $\rho(P_t, P_t^*) = \text{cov}(P_t, P_t^*)/\sigma(P_t)\sigma(P_t^*)$, we obtain a 'variance equality'

$$\sigma(P_t) = \rho(P_t, P_t^*)\sigma(P_t^*) \tag{14}$$

Since the maximum value of $\rho = 1$, (14) implies the familiar variance inequality

$$\sigma(P_t) \le \sigma(P_t^*) \tag{15}$$

Stationary series have a time-invariant and constant population mean, variance (standard deviation) and autocovariance. The difficulty in applying (15) to a sample of data is knowing whether the sample is drawn from an underlying stationary series in the population.

It is also worth noting that the standard deviations in (15) are simple unconditional measures. If a time-series plot is such that it changes direction often and hence crosses its mean value frequently (i.e. is 'jagged'), then in a short sample of data, we may obtain a 'good' estimate of the population value of $\sigma(P_t)$ from its sample value. However, if the variable moves around its mean in long slow swings, then one will need a long sample of data to obtain a good estimate of the 'true' population variance (i.e. a representative series of 'cycles' in the data set are required, not just, say, one quarter or one half of a cycle). In fact, stock prices are persistent and hence move in long swings (see Figure 1) so a long data set is required to accurately measure the true standard deviation (or variance) even if the price series is actually stationary.

If a series is non-stationary, then it has a time-varying population mean or variance and hence (15) is undefined. We then need to devise an alternative variance inequality in terms of a transformation of the variables $P_t$ and $P_t^*$ into 'new' variables that are stationary. The latter has led to alternative forms of the variance inequality condition. The problem is that it is often difficult to ascertain whether a particular series is stationary or not, from statistical tests based on any finite data set. For example, the series generated as $x_t = x_{t-1} + \varepsilon_t$ is non-stationary, while $x_t = 0.98x_{t-1} + \varepsilon_t$ is stationary. However, in any finite data set (on stock prices), it is often difficult to statistically discriminate between the two, since in the regression $x_t = a + bx_{t-1} + \varepsilon_t$, the estimate of '$b$' is subject to sampling error and often one could take it as being either 1 or 0.98. Also, the distribution of the test statistic that $b = 1$ is 'non-standard' and its finite sample distribution is often unknown.

Let us return now to the issue of whether (real) dividends and therefore (for a constant $\delta$) $P_t^*$ and $P_t$ are non-stationary. How much difference does non-stationarity make in practice when estimating the sample values of $\sigma(P_t)$ and $\sigma(P_t^*)$ from a finite data set? For example, in his early work, Shiller (1981) 'detrended' the variables $P_t$ and $P_t^*$ by dividing by a simple deterministic trend $\lambda_t = e^{bt}$, where $b$ is estimated from the regression $\ln P_t = a + bt$ over the whole sample period. If $P_t$ follows a stochastic trend, then 'detrending' by assuming a deterministic trend is statistically invalid. The question then arises as to whether the violation of the variance bounds found in Shiller's (1981) study is due to this inappropriate detrending of the data.

Kleidon (1986) and LeRoy and Parke (1992) examine variance bounds using Monte Carlo simulation (MCS). For example, Kleidon (1986) assumes that expected dividend growth is a constant and dividends follow a non-stationary (geometric) random walk with drift

$$\ln D_t = \theta + \ln D_{t-1} + \varepsilon_t \tag{16}$$

where $\varepsilon_t$ is white noise. Given a generated series for $D_t$ for $m$ observations using (16), one can use the DPV formula to generate a time series of length $m$ for $P_t^*$ and for $P_t$ and establish whether $\text{var}(P_t) > \text{var}(P_t^*)$. This is the first 'run' of the MCS. Repeating this 'experiment' $m$ times, we can note how many times $\text{var}(P_t) > \text{var}(P_t^*)$. Since the RVF is 'true' by construction, one would not expect the variance bound to be violated in a large number of cases in the $m$ experiments. (Some violations will be due to chance.) In fact, Kleidon (1986) finds that when using the generated data (and detrending using $\lambda_t$), the variance bound is frequently violated. The frequency of violations is 90%, while the frequency of 'gross violations' (i.e. $VR > 5$) varied considerably, depending on the rate of interest (discount rate) assumed in the simulations. (For example, for $r = 7.5\%$, the frequency of gross violations is only about 5% but for $r = 5\%$, this figure rises dramatically to about 40%).

Shiller (1989) refined Kleidon's procedure by noting that Kleidon's combined assumptions for the growth rate of dividends and the level of interest rates implied an implausible value for the dividend–price ratio. Shiller corrects for this so that in the generated data, the dividend–price ratio equals its average historic level. Under the null of the RVF, he finds that the gross violations of the variance ratio are substantially less than those found by Kleidon.

Further, Shiller (1989) notes that in none of the above Monte Carlo studies is the violation of the variance inequality as large as that actually found by Shiller (1981) when using the 'real world' data. Shiller also points out that the 'special case' used by Kleidon (and others), namely that (the log of real) dividends follow a random walk with drift, may not be a correct time-series representation of actual data.

This debate highlights the problem in trying to discredit results, which use 'real data' by using 'specific special cases' (e.g. random walk) in a Monte Carlo analysis. These Monte Carlo studies provide a highly specific 'sensitivity test' of empirical results, but such 'statistics of interest' are conditional on a specific parametrisation of the model (e.g. random walk). One might agree with Shiller (1989) that on *a priori* economic grounds, it is hard to accept that investors believe that when faced with an unexpected increase in current dividends, of $z\%$, they expect that dividends will increase by $z\%$, in all future periods. However, the latter is implied by the random walk model of (log) dividends.

The outcome of all of the above arguments is that not only may the small-sample properties of the variance bounds tests be unreliable but also if there is non-stationarity, even tests based on large samples are incorrect. Clearly, all one can do in practice (while awaiting new time-series data as 'time' moves on!) is to assess the robustness of the volatility results under different methods of detrending. For example, Shiller (1989) reworks some of his earlier variance inequality results using $P_t/E_t^{30}$ and $P_t^*/E_t^{30}$, where the real price series are 'detrended' using a (backward) 30-year moving average of real earnings $E_t^{30}$. He also uses $P_t/D_{t-1}$ and $P_t^*/D_{t-1}$ where $D_{t-1}$ is real dividends in the previous year. Using a deterministic trend (Shiller 1981) estimated over the *whole sample period*, uses information not known at time $t$. Therefore Shiller (1989) in later work, detrends $P_t$ and $P_t^*$ using a time trend estimated only with data up to time $t$ (that is, $\lambda_t = \exp[b_t]t$, where the estimated $b_t$ changes as more data is included by using recursive least squares).

The results using these various transformations of $P_t$ and $P_t^*$ are given in Table 1. The variance inequality (15) is always violated, but the violation is not as great as in Shiller's (1981) original study using a (fixed) deterministic trend. However, the variance equality (14) is strongly violated in all of the variants.

Shiller (1989) repeats Kleidon's Monte Carlo study using the random walk model for (log) dividends. He detrends the artificially generated data on $P_t$ and $P_t^*$ by a generated real earnings series $E_t$ (generated earnings are assumed to be proportional to generated dividends). He assumes a constant real discount rate of 8.32%, (equal to the sample average annual real return on stocks). In a 1000 MCS runs, he finds that in 75.8% of cases, $\sigma(P_t/E_t^{30})$ exceeds $\sigma(P^*/E_t^{30})$. One might expect in the generated data to find about 95% of cases where $\sigma(P_t/E_t^{30}) > \sigma(P_t^*/E_t^{30})$ since the generated data 'obey' the fundamentals model by construction. Hence, when dividends are non-stationary, there is a tendency for spurious violation of the variance bounds when the series are detrended by $E_t^{30}$. However, for the generated data, the mean value of $VR = 1.443$, which although in excess of the 'true' value of 1.00, is substantially less than the 4.16

**Table 1**    Variance bounds test[1]

| | Method of Detrending | $\rho$ | $\sigma(P_t{}^*)$ | $\rho\sigma(P_t{}^*)$ | $\sigma(P_t)^2$ | VR |
|---|---|---|---|---|---|---|
| 1 | Time-varying deterministic | n.a | n.a | n.a | n.a | 2.120 |
| 2 | Using $D_{t-1}$ | | | | | |
| | (a) constant discount factor | 0.133 | 4.703 | 0.62 | 6.03 | 1.28[3] |
| | (b) time-varying discount factor | 0.06 | 7.779 | 0.47 | 6.03 | 1.29[3] |
| 3 | Using $E_t^{30}$ | | | | | |
| | (a) constant discount factor | 0.296 | 1.611 | 0.47 | 6.706 | 3.77[3] |
| | (b) time-varying discount factor | 0.048 | 4.65 | 0.22 | 6.706 | 1.44[3] |

Notes:
[1]If RVF holds, then $\sigma(P_t) = \rho(P_t, P_t{}^*)\,\sigma(P_t{}^*)$.
[2]In the second-last column, the $\sigma(P_t)$ is the standard deviation of the *actual* price.
[3]VR is mean value from MCS, where RVF holds.
Source: Figures taken from Shiller (1989, pp. 87–91).

observed in the real world data. (And in only one of the 1000 'runs' did the 'generated' variance ratio exceed 4.16.)

Clearly, since $E_t^{30}$ and $P_t{}^*$ are long moving averages, they both make long smooth swings, and one may only pick up part of the potential variability $P_t{}^*/E_t^{30}$ in small samples. The sample variance may, therefore, be biased downwards. Since $P_t$ is not smoothed, $(P_t/E_t^{30})$ may well show more variability than $P_t{}^*/E_t^{30}$ even though in a much longer sample, the converse could apply. Again, this boils down to the fact that statistical tests on such data can only be definitive if one has a long data set. The Monte Carlo evidence and the results in Table 1 do, however, place the balance of evidence against the EMH-RVF when applied to stock prices.

Mankiw, Romer and Shapiro (1991), in an update of their earlier 1985 paper (Mankiw, Romer and Shapiro 1985), tackle the non-stationarity problem by considering the variability in $P$ and $P^*$ relative to a naive forecast $P^o$. For the naive forecast, they assume dividends follow a random walk and hence $E_t D_{t+j} = D_t$ for all $j$. Using the RVF, the naive forecast gives

$$P_t^o = [\delta/(1-\delta)]D_t \qquad (17)$$

where $\delta = 1/(1+k)$ and $k$ is the constant required return on the stock. Now consider the identity

$$P_t{}^* - P_t^o = (P_t{}^* - P_t) + (P_t - P_t^o) \qquad (18)$$

The RE forecast error is $P_t{}^* - P_t$ and hence is independent of information at time $t$ and hence of $P_t - P_t^o$. Dividing (18) by $P_t$, squaring and taking expectations, we have

$$q_t = E[(P_t{}^* - P_t^o)/P_t]^2 - \{E[(P_t{}^* - P_t)/P_t]^2 + E[P_t - P_t^o)/P_t]^2\} \qquad (19)$$

and the inequalities are therefore

$$E[(P_t{}^* - P_t^o)/P_t]^2 \geq E[(P_t{}^* - P_t)/P_t]^2 \qquad (20a)$$

$$E[(P_t{}^* - P_t^o)/P_t]^2 \geq E[(P_t - P_t^o)/P_t]^2 \qquad (20b)$$

The beauty of the above relationships is that each element of the expressions is likely to be stationary, and deflating by $P_t$ is likely to minimise problems of heteroscedasticity. Equation (20a) states that the market price is a better forecast of the *ex-post* 'rational price' $P_t^*$ than is the naive forecast, and the former should have a lower mean squared error. Equation (20b) states that the *ex-post* rational price $P_t^*$ is more volatile around the naive forecast $P_t^o$ than is the market price and is analogous to Shiller's volatility inequality. An alternative test of the EMH-RVF is that $\psi = 0$ in

$$q_t = \psi + \varepsilon_t \qquad (21)$$

Using annual data 1871–1988 and an aggregate stock price index, Mankiw, Romer and Shapiro (1991) find that equation (21) is rejected at only about the 5% level for constant required real returns of $k = 6$ or 7% (although the model is strongly rejected when the required return is assumed to be 5%). When M-R-S allow the required equilibrium nominal return to equal the (nominal) risk-free rate plus a constant risk premium (i.e. $k_t = r_t + rp$), the EMH-RVF using (19) is rejected more strongly than for the constant real returns case.

In Mankiw, Romer and Shapiro (1991) just referred to, they also consider the type of regression tests used by Fama and French (1988b). More specifically, consider the following autoregression of (pseudo) returns:

$$[(P_t^{*n} - P_t)/P_t] = \alpha + \beta[(P_t - P_t^o)/P_t] + u_t \qquad (22)$$

where $P_t^{*n}$ is the perfect foresight price calculated using a specific horizon ($n = 1$, 2, ...). Mankiw, Romer and Shapiro (1991) use a Monte Carlo study to demonstrate that under plausible conditions that hold in real world data, estimates of $\beta$ and its standard error can be subject to very severe small-sample bias. These biases increase as the horizon $n$ is increased. However, when using their annual data set, under the constant real returns case (of 5, 6, or 7% p.a.), it is still the case that $H_0 : \beta = 0$ is rejected at the 1 to 5% level, for most horizons between one and ten years (see Mankiw et al). When $P_t^*$ is constructed under the assumption that equilibrium returns depend on the nominal interest rate plus a constant risk premium, then $H_0 : \beta = 0$ is only rejected at around the 5 to 10% significance levels for horizons greater than five years overall. Mankiw et al. results suggest that the evidence that long-horizon returns (i.e. $n > 5$ years) are forecastable as found by Fama–French are not necessarily clear-cut, when the small-sample properties of the test statistics are carefully examined.

The paper by Mankiw, Romer and Shapiro (1991) also tackles another problem that has caused difficulties in the interpretation of variance bounds tests, namely the importance of the terminal price $P_{t+n}$ in calculating the perfect foresight price. Merton (1987) points out that the end-of-sample price $P_{t+n}$ picks up the effect of out-of-sample events on the (within sample) stock price, since it reflects all future (unobserved) dividends. Hence, volatility tests that use a fixed end-point value for the actual price may be subject to a form of measurement error if $P_{t+n}$ is a very poor proxy for $E_t P_{t+n}^*$. Mankiw et al. and Shiller (1989) point out that Merton's criticism is of less importance if actual dividends paid out 'in sample' are sufficiently high so that the importance of out-of-sample events (measured by $P_{t+n}$) is circumscribed. Empirically, the latter case applies to the data used by Mankiw, Romer and Shapiro (1991) since they use a long sample. However, they provide another ingenious yet simple counterweight to this argument (see also Shea 1989). The perfect foresight stock price, equation (3), can be calculated for different horizons ($n = 1, 2, \ldots$) and so can $q_t$. Hence, several values of $q_t^n$ (for $n = 1, 2, \ldots$) can be calculated in which many end-of-period prices are used in a fixed sample of data. Therefore, they do not have to worry about a *single* end-of-sample price dominating their results. In general, they find that the EMH has greater support at short horizons (i.e. $n = 1$–5 years) rather than long horizons (i.e. $n > 10$ years).

In a later paper, Gilles and LeRoy (1992) assume the dividend–price ratio is stationary and their variance inequality is $\sigma^2(P_t|D_t) \leq \sigma^2(P_t^*|D_t)$. The sample estimates of the variances (1871–1988, US aggregate index as used in Shiller 1981) indicate excess volatility since $\sigma^2(P_t|D_t) = 26.4$ and $\sigma^2(P_t^*|D_t) = 19.4$. However, they note that the sample variance of $\sigma(P_t^*|D_t)$ is biased downwards for two reasons: first, because $(P_t^*|D_t)$ is positively serially correlated (Flavin 1983) and, second, because at the terminal date, the unobservable $E_t P_{t+n}^*$ is assumed to equal the actual (terminal) price $P_{t+n}$. Using Monte Carlo experiments, they find that the first source of bias is the most important and is very severe. The Monte Carlo experiment assumes a random walk for dividends; the value of $\sigma^2(P_t^*|D_t)$ in the Monte Carlo runs is 89.3 compared to 19.4 using actual sample data. On the other hand, the sample value of $\sigma^2(P_t|D_t)$ is found to be a fairly accurate measure of the population variance. Hence, Gilles–LeRoy conclude that the Shiller type variance bounds test 'is indecisive'. However, all is not lost. Gilles and LeRoy develop a test on the basis of the orthogonality of $P_t$ and $P_t^*$ (West 1988), which is more robust. This 'orthogonality test' uses the random walk assumption for (log) dividends and involves a test statistic with much less bias and less sample variability than the Shiller-type test. The orthogonality test rejects the present value model quite decisively (although note that there are some nuances involved in this procedure, which we do not document here). Thus, a reasonable summary of the Gilles–LeRoy study would be that the RVF is rejected, conditional on the random walk model of (log) dividends.

Scott (1990) follows a slightly different procedure and estimates

$$P_t^* = a + bP_t + \varepsilon_t \tag{23}$$

where the EMH-RVF implies $a = 0$ and $b = 1$. Scott deflates $P_t^*$ and $P_t$ by dividends in the previous year so that the variables are stationary and 'corrects' for serial correlation in the regression residuals. He finds that the above restrictions are violated for US stock price data so that $P_t$ is not an unbiased predictor of $P_t^*$. The $\overline{R}^2$ of the regression is very low, so that there is little (positive) correlation between $P_t$ and $P_t^*$, while $P_t$ provides a very poor forecast of the *ex-post* perfect foresight price. (Note, however, that it is the unbiasedness proposition that is important for the refutation of the EMH-RVF, not the low $R$-squared.) The EMH, however, does imply that any information $\Omega_t$ included in (23) should not be statistically significant. Scott (1990) regresses $(P_t^* - P_t)$ on the dividend–price ratio (i.e. dividend yield) and finds it is statistically significant, thus rejecting informational efficiency.

Shiller (1989) performs a similar regression deflating the prices by $E_t^{30}$:

$$(P_t^*/E_t^{30}) = a + b(P_t/E_t^{30}) + \varepsilon_t$$

He finds that $\hat{b} \ll 1$. Also, using MCS, he finds that $\hat{b}$ is downward biased but the bias is not sufficient to account for the strong rejection of the RVF using the actual data.

## 11.3 Peso Problems and Variance Bounds Tests

In the presence of a 'Peso problem', the variance bound in a sample of data may be violated even though the EMH-RVF is true. Suppose we have a sample of data in which investors think there is a small probability of a high level of dividends in the future. Investors' expectations of dividends over this sample of data is a weighted average of the 'high' dividends and the 'normal' level of dividends. However, suppose these 'high' dividends never occur. Then the out-turn for actual dividends $D_{t+j}$ are lower than investors' true expectations (i.e. $D_{t+j} < E_{t+j-1}D_{t+j}$). Investors have made systematic forecast errors within this sample period. If the sample period is extended, then we might also observe periods when investors expect lower dividends (which never occur), so $D_{t+j} > E_{t+j-1}D_{t+j}$. Hence, over the extended 'full' sample, forecast errors average zero. The Peso problem arises because we only 'observe' the first sample of data, and the observed dividends are a biased measure of expected dividends. To illustrate the Peso problem, consider an asset, which pays out a *stream* of dividend payments $D_{t+1}$, all of which are discounted at the constant rate $\delta$. For simplicity of notation, we can think of period '$t + 1$' as constituting $m$ different periods ($t = 0, 1, 2, \ldots, m$). Under the RVF, the stock price is

$$P_t = \delta E_t D_{t+1} \qquad (24)$$

where $\delta$ = constant discount factor. Suppose that $1 - \pi$ = probability being in regime-1 (i.e. 'normal dividends') so the true expectation of investors is

$$\begin{aligned} E_t D_{t+1} &= \pi E_t(D_{t+1}|Z2) + (1 - \pi)E_t(D_{t+1}|Z1) \\ &= \pi[E_t(D_{t+1}|Z2) - E_t(D_{t+1}|Z1)] + E_t(D_{t+1}|Z1) \\ &= \pi \nabla D_{t+1} + E_t(D_{t+1}|Z1) \end{aligned} \qquad (25)$$

where $E_t(D_{t+1}|Z1)$ = expected 'normal' dividends in regime-1, $E_t(D_{t+1}|Z2)$ = expected dividends in 'high' regime-2, and we assume $E_t(D_{t+1}|Z2) > E_t(D_{t+1}|Z1)$. To simplify even further, suppose that in regime-1, dividends are expected to be constant and *ex-post* are equal to $D$ so that $E_t(D_{t+1}|Z1) = D$. The key to the Peso problem is that the researcher only has data for the period over which 'high profits' do *not* materialise (i.e. over $t = 0, 1, 2, \ldots, m$) but the possibility of high profits does influence investors' 'true' expectations and hence the stock price. Rational investors set the stock price

$$\begin{aligned} P_t &= \delta E_t D_{t+1} = \delta[\pi \nabla D_{t+1} + E_t(D_{t+1}|Z1)] \\ &= \delta \pi[E_t(D_{t+1}|Z2) - D] + \delta D \end{aligned} \qquad (26)$$

where we assume high profits do not occur and dividends actually remain at their constant value $D$. Variability in the *actual* price $P_t$ given by (26) will take place either because of changing views about $\pi$ or because of changing views about future dividends, in the high profit scenario, $E_t(D_{t+1}|Z2)$. Hence, $\text{var}(P_t) > 0$. But if high profits never happen, then a constant level of dividends $D$ will be paid out, and the researcher will measure the *ex-post* perfect foresight price as the constant value $P_t^* = \delta D$ (for $t = 0, 1, 2, \ldots, m$) and hence $\text{var}(P_t^*) = 0$. Thus, we have a violation of the variance bound, that is, $\text{var}(P_t) > \text{var}(P_t^*)$, even though prices always equal fundamental value as given by (26). This is a consequence of a sample of data, which may not be representative of the (whole) population of data. If we had a longer data set, then the expected event might actually happen and hence $P_t^*$ would vary along with the actual price.

Consider the implications of the Peso problem for regression tests of $P_t^*$ on $P_t$

$$P_t^* = \alpha + \beta P_t + w_t \tag{27}$$

where, with no Peso problems, we expect $\alpha = 0$ and $\beta = 1$. Assume that 'normal dividends' $E_t(D_{t+1}|Z1)$ vary over time but high profits do not occur, so the perfect foresight price measured by the researcher is $P_t^* = \delta D_{t+1}^{(1)}$ (for $t = 0, 1, 2, \ldots, m$) where $D_{t+1}^{(1)}$ is the out-turn value in regime-1. However, the actual price is

$$P_t = \delta E_t D_{t+1} = \delta[\pi \nabla D_{t+1} + E_t(D_{t+1}|Z1)] \tag{28}$$

The regression of $P_t^*$ on $P_t$ is then

$$(\delta D_{t+1}^{(1)}) = a + b\{\delta[\pi \nabla D_{t+1} + E_t(D_{t+1}|Z1)]\} + w_t \tag{29}$$

Only if there is no expectation of a regime shift (i.e. $\nabla D_{t+1} = 0$), so that $E_t(D_{t+1}|Z1) = D_{t+1}^{(1)} - \varepsilon_{t+1}$ is an unbiased forecast of the out-turn dividends, will the coefficient $b = 1$. If $\pi$ is time-varying, this will lead to bias in estimates of $b$ as this leads to systematic changes in the actual price $P_t$ not matched by changes in the perfect foresight price $P_t^* = (\delta D_{t+1}^{(1)})$.

The Peso problem arises because of one-off 'special events' that could take place within the sample period but in actual fact do not. It considerably complicates tests of the EMH-RE hypothesis, which assume out-turn data differ from expectations by a (zero mean) random error.

## 11.4   Volatility and Regression Tests

The easiest way of seeing the relationship between the volatility tests and regression tests is to note that in the regression

$$P_t^* = a + bP_t + \varepsilon_t \tag{30}$$

the coefficient $b$ is given by

$$b = \text{cov}(P_t, P_t^*)/\sigma^2(P_t) = \rho(P_t, P_t^*)\sigma(P_t^*)/\sigma(P_t) \tag{31}$$

Substituting for $\rho$ from the variance equality (14) in (31), we see that if the variance equality holds, then $b = 1$ in the regression (30). Now consider

$$P_t^* = a + bP_t + c\Omega_t + \eta_t \tag{32}$$

Under the EMH-RVF, we expect $H_0 : a = c = 0, b = 1$. If this proves to be the case, then (31) reduces to

$$P_t^* = P_t + \eta_t \tag{33}$$

and hence the variance bounds test must also hold. The two tests are therefore equivalent under the null hypothesis. As a slight variant, consider the case where $c = 0$ but $b < 1$ (as is found in much of the empirical work above). Then, (32) reduces to

$$\mathrm{var}(P_t^*) = b^2 \, \mathrm{var}(P_t) + \mathrm{var}(\eta_t) \tag{34a}$$

$$\mathrm{var}(P_t^*) - \mathrm{var}(P_t) = (b^2 - 1) \, \mathrm{var}(P_t) + \mathrm{var}(\eta_t) \tag{34b}$$

where RE implies $\mathrm{cov}(P_t, \eta_t) = 0$. If $b^2 < 1$, then the first term on the RHS of (34b) is negative and it is possible that the whole of the RHS of (34b) is also negative. Hence, $b < 1$ may also imply a violation of the variance bounds test. Next, consider the long-horizon regressions of Fama and French (1988b)

$$h_{t,t+k} = a + bh_{t-k,t} + \eta_{t+k} \tag{35}$$

$$p_{t+k} = a + (b + 1)p_t - bp_{t-k} + \eta_{t+k} \tag{36}$$

where we have used $h_{t,t+k} \equiv p_{t+k} - p_t$. Under the null of *constant* expected returns, we expect $a \neq 0$ and $b = 0$, hence

$$p_{t+k} = a + p_t + \eta_{t+k} \tag{37}$$

For $b = 0$, the Fama–French regressions are consistent with the random walk model of stock prices.

We have shown that under the null of market efficiency, regression tests using $P_t$ and $P_t^*$ should be consistent with variance bounds inequalities and with regressions based on autoregressive models for long-horizon stock *returns*.

## 11.5  Summary

- Shiller's (1981) original seminal work using variance bounds inequalities appeared to decisively reject the RVF. Subsequent work in the 1980s pointed out deficiencies in Shiller's original approach (e.g. Kleidon 1986, Flavin 1983), but Shiller (1989) rather successfully answered his critics.

- Later work (e.g. Mankiw, Romer and Shapiro (1991) and Gilles and LeRoy (1992) has certainly demonstrated that violations of the RVF are statistically far from clear-cut and judgement is required in reaching a balanced view on this matter. To this author, the evidence cited, is on balance marginally against the EMH.

- The intuitive appeal of Shiller's volatility inequality and the simple elegance of the basic insight behind this approach have become somewhat overshadowed by the practical (statistical) issues surrounding the test procedures used, particularly problems of stationarity and small-sample bias. Recent advances in econometric methodology have allowed a more satisfactory treatment of problems of non-stationarity and the modelling of time-varying risk premia, which are discussed in the next chapter.

# Appendix: LeRoy–Porter and West Tests

The above tests do not fit neatly into the main body of this chapter but are important landmarks in the literature in this area. We therefore discuss these tests and their relationship to each other and to other material in the text.

The LeRoy and Porter (1981) variance bounds test is based on the mathematical property that the conditional expectation of any random variable is less volatile than the variable itself. Their analysis begins with a forecast of future dividends based on a limited information set $\Lambda_t = (D_t, D_{t-1})$. The forecast of future dividends based on $\Lambda_t$ is

$$\hat{P}_t = E(P_t^*|\Lambda_t) = \sum_{i=1}^{\infty} \delta^i E(D_{t+i}|\Lambda_t) \tag{A1}$$

The actual stock price $P_t$ is determined by forecasts on the basis of the full information set $\Omega_t$

$$P_t = E(P_t^*|\Omega_t) \tag{A2}$$

Applying the law of iterated expectations to (A2)

$$E(P_t|\Lambda_t) = E[E(P_t^*|\Omega_t)|\Lambda_t)] = E(P_t^*|\Lambda_t) \tag{A3}$$

Using (A1) and (A3):
$$\hat{P}_t = E(P_t|\Lambda_t) \tag{A4}$$

Since $\hat{P}_t$ is the conditional expectation of $P_t$, then from (A4), the LeRoy–Porter variance inequality is
$$\text{var}(\hat{P}_t) \leq \text{var}(P_t) \tag{A5}$$

Assuming stationarity, the sample variances of $\hat{P}_t$ and $P_t$ provide consistent estimates of their population values given in (A5). Given an ARMA model for $D_t$ and a known value for $\delta$, the series $P_t$ can be constructed using (A1). As in Shiller (1981), the procedure adopted by LeRoy–Porter yields a variance inequality. However, the LeRoy–Porter analysis also gives rise to a form of 'orthogonality test'. To see this, define the one-period forecast error of the $-return as

$$e_{t+1} \equiv (D_{t+1} + P_{t+1}) - E(D_{t+1} + P_{t+1}|\Omega_t) \tag{A6}$$

The Euler equation is
$$P_t = \delta E(P_{t+1} + D_{t+1}|\Omega_t) \tag{A7}$$

Substituting (A6) in (A7) and iterating forward,

$$P_t^* = P_t + \sum_{i=1}^{\infty} \delta^i e_{t+i} \tag{A8}$$

where $P_t^* = \sum_{i=1}^{\infty} \delta^i D_{t+i}$. If $e_t$ is stationary

$$\text{var}(P_t^*) = \text{var}(P_t) + 2\,\text{cov}\left(P_t, \sum \delta^i e_{t+i}\right) + [\delta^2/(1-\delta^2)]\,\text{var}(e_t) \tag{A9}$$

where the $e_{t+i}$ are mutually uncorrelated under RE. Under RE, the covariance term is zero, hence

$$\text{var}(P_t^*) = \text{var}(P_t) + [\delta^2/(1-\delta^2)]\,\text{var}(e_t) \tag{A10}$$

Equation (A10) is both a variance equality and an orthogonality test of the RVF. It is perhaps worth noting at this juncture that equation (A9) is consistent with Shiller's inequality. If in the data, we find a violation of Shiller's inequality, that is var$(P_t) \geq$ var$(P_t^*)$, then from (A9), this implies cov $\left(P_t, \sum \delta^i e_{t+i}\right) < 0$. Hence, a weighted average of one-period \$-forecast errors is correlated with information at time $t$, namely $P_t$. Thus, violation of Shiller's variance bound implies that (a weighted average of) one-period \$-returns is forecastable. We have therefore provided a link between Shiller's variance bounds test and the predictability of one-period \$-returns.

The West (1988) test is important because it is valid even if dividends are non-stationary (but cointegrated with the stock price) and it does not require a proxy for the unobservable $P_t^*$. Like the LeRoy–Porter variance inequality, the West test is based on a specific property of mathematical expectations – it is that the variance of the forecast error with a limited information set $\Lambda_t$ must be greater than that based on the full information set $\Omega_t$. The West inequality can be shown to be a direct implication of the LeRoy–Porter inequality. We begin with equation (A1) and note that

$$\delta(\hat{P}_{t+1} + D_{t+1}) = \delta D_{t+1} + \delta E(\delta D_{t+2} + \delta^2 D_{t+3} + \cdots | \Lambda_{t+1}) \tag{A11}$$

Applying the law of iterated expectations $E[E(.|\Lambda_{t+1})|\Lambda_t] = E(.|\Lambda_t)$ to (A11),

$$\delta E(\hat{P}_{t+1} + D_{t+1}|\Lambda_t) = \sum_{i=1}^{\infty} \delta^i E(D_{t+i}|\Lambda_t) \tag{A12}$$

Substituting for the LHS of (A12) from (A1)

$$E(\hat{P}_{t+1} + D_{t+1})|\Lambda_t) = \delta^{-1}\hat{P}_t \tag{A13}$$

Now define the forecast error of the \$-return, based on information $\Lambda_t$ as

$$\hat{e}_{t+1} \equiv \hat{P}_{t+1} + D_{t+1} - E(\hat{P}_{t+1} + D_{t+1}|\Lambda_t) \tag{A14}$$

Substituting from (A13) in (A14)

$$\hat{e}_{t+1} = P_{t+1} + D_{t+1} - \delta^{-1}\hat{P}_t \tag{A15}$$

Equation (A15) is the forecast error based on $\Lambda_t$, while (A6) is the forecast error based on $\Omega_t$ (with $\Lambda_t \subset \Omega_t$); hence, by the law of conditional mathematical expectations

$$\mathrm{var}(\hat{e}_{t+1}) > \mathrm{var}(e_{t+1}) \tag{A16}$$

Equation (A16) is the West inequality and using US data West (1988) finds (A16) is violated. Even if the level of dividends is non-stationary, the population variances in (A16) are constant (stationary) and the sample variances provide consistent estimators. However, unfortunately, the latter is only true if the level of dividends is non-stationary (e.g. $D_{t+1} = D_t + w_{t+1}$). LeRoy and Parke (1992) investigate the properties of the West test if dividends follow a geometric random walk ($\ln D_{t+1} = \ln D_t + \varepsilon_{t+1}$), and the reader should consult the original paper for further information.

The LeRoy–Porter and West inequalities are both derived by considering variances under a limited information set and under the complete information set. Hence, one might guess that these inequalities provide similar inferences on the validity of the RVF. This is indeed the case, as we can now demonstrate. The LeRoy–Porter equality (A10) holds for any information set and, therefore, it holds for $\Lambda_t$, which implies

$$\mathrm{var}(P_t^*) = \mathrm{var}(\hat{P}_t) + \frac{\delta^2}{(1-\delta^2)}\mathrm{var}(\hat{e}_t) \tag{A17}$$

The LeRoy–Porter inequality (A5) is

$$\mathrm{var}(\hat{P}_t) \leq \mathrm{var}(P_t)$$

Substituting for $\mathrm{var}(\hat{P}_t)$ from (A17) and for $\mathrm{var}(P_t)$ from (A10), we obtain the West inequality (A16).

# 12

# STOCK PRICES: THE VAR APPROACH

## Aims

- Develop a range of tests of the rational valuation formula RVF for stock prices using the VAR methodology and provide illustrative examples of these test procedures.

- Demonstrate the relationship between tests using the VAR methodology, Shiller volatility tests and tests of long-horizon returns such as Fama–French.

- Show that although one-period *returns* are hardly predictable; this may, nevertheless, imply that stock *prices* deviate significantly and for long periods from their fundamental value, resulting in excess volatility in stock prices.

- Examine the relationship between stock price volatility and the degree of persistence in one-period returns.

We have seen in Chapter 11 that a definitive interpretation of the results from several types of variance bounds test on stock prices is dogged by the stationarity issue, namely, the appropriate method of 'detrending' the series for the actual price $P_t$ and the perfect foresight price, $P_t^*$. The VAR procedure tackles this problem head-on by explicitly testing for stationarity in the variables, and it also allows several alternative metrics for assessing the validity of the RVF.

The rational valuation formula RVF is non-linear in the required rate of return (or discount factor); however, a linear approximation is possible. In applying the VAR methodology to stocks, we are able to compare a time series of the 'theoretical' (log) stock price $p_t'$ with the actual (log of the) stock price $p_t$ to ascertain whether the latter is excessively volatile. We can, therefore, compare results from the VAR methodology with Shiller volatility tests. We noted that Fama and French

(1988b) and others found that long-horizon *returns* (e.g. over 3–5 years) are 'more forecastable' than short-horizon returns (e.g. over a month or over 1–3 years). Using the linearisation of the RVF, we are able to derive a formula for long-horizon returns, and the VAR methodology then provides complementary evidence to that of Fama and French.

The RVF assumes that stock prices change only on the arrival of new information or news about 'fundamentals': that is, the future course of either dividends or discount rates. An interesting question is how much of the observed volatile movements in stock prices are due to news about returns or news about dividends. To answer this question, a key factor is whether one-period returns are *persistent*. By 'persistent', we mean that the arrival of news about *current* returns has a strong influence on all future returns and, hence, on all future discount rates. If persistence is high, we can show that news about returns can have a large effect on stock *prices* even if one-period returns are barely predictable. We also develop this theme further in the next chapter when we investigate the source of a time variation in the risk premium.

## 12.1 Linearisation of Returns and the RVF

We begin with an overview of the RVF and rearrange it in terms of the dividend–price ratio, since the latter variable is a key element in the VAR approach as applied to the stock market. We then derive the Wald restrictions implied by the RVF and the rational expectations assumption and show that these restrictions imply that one-period *excess returns* are unforecastable.

We define $P_t$ = stock price at the *end* of period $t$, $D_{t+1}$ = dividends paid *during* period $t + 1$, $H_{t+1}$ = one-period holding period return from the *end* of period $t$ to the *end* of period $t + 1$. All variables are in real terms. Define $h_{t+1}$ as

$$h_{t+1} \equiv \ln(1 + H_{t+1}) = \ln[(P_{t+1} + D_{t+1})/P_t] \tag{1}$$

The one-period return depends positively on the capital gain $(P_{t+1}/P_t)$ and the dividend yield $D_{t+1}/P_t$. Equation (1) can be linearised to give (see Appendix)

$$h_{t+1} \approx \rho p_{t+1} - p_t + (1 - \rho) d_{t+1} + k \tag{2}$$

where lower-case letters denote logarithms (e.g. $p_t = \ln P_t$), $\rho = \overline{P}/(\overline{P} + \overline{D})$ linearisation parameter and empirically is calculated to be around 0.94 for annual data, while $k$ is a linearisation constant (and for our purposes, may be largely ignored). Equation (2) is an approximation, but we will treat it as an accurate approximation. The (log) dividend–price ratio is

$$\delta_t = d_t - p_t \tag{3}$$

and equation (2) becomes

$$h_{t+1} = \delta_t - \rho \delta_{t+1} + \Delta d_{t+1} + k \tag{4}$$

Equation (4) for the one-period return undoubtedly looks a little strange and is not terribly intuitive. It is an (approximate) identity with no economic content as yet. It implies that if we wish to forecast one-period *returns*, we need to forecast the future dividend–price ratio $\delta_{t+1}$ and the growth in dividends during period $t + 1$. The observant reader might also notice that (4) is a forward difference equation in $\delta_t$ and since $\delta_t = d_t - p_t$, it can be solved forward to yield an expression for the (logarithm of the) price *level* of the stock: hence, it is a representation of the RVF in logarithms.

Solving (4) in the usual way using forward recursion (and imposing a transversality condition) (see Campbell and Shiller 1988),

$$\delta_t = \sum_{j=0}^{\infty} \rho^j (h_{t+j+1} - \Delta d_{t+j+1}) - k/(1 - \rho) \tag{5}$$

Equation (5) is also an identity (subject to the linear approximation). We now introduce an economic input to equations (4) and (5). Under the EMH, if the (log) expected (real) rate of return *required* by investors to willingly hold stocks is denoted $r^e_{t+j}$, then

$$E_t h_{t+j} = r^e_{t+j} \tag{6}$$

Then from (4),

$$\delta_t - \rho\delta^e_{t+1} + \Delta d^e_{t+1} + k = r^e_{t+1} \tag{7}$$

(note the superscript e on $\delta_{t+1}$). Solving (7) forward

$$\delta_t = \sum_{j=0}^{\infty} \rho^j (r^e_{t+j+1} - \Delta d^e_{t+j+1}) - k/(1 - \rho) \tag{8}$$

Virtually the same result is obtained if one takes expectations of the identity (4) and solves recursively to give

$$\delta_t = \sum_{j=0}^{\infty} \rho^j (h^e_{t+j+1} - \Delta d^e_{t+j+1}) - k/(1 - \rho) \tag{9}$$

where $E_t\delta_t = \delta_t$ as $\delta_t$ is known at time $t$. The only difference here is that $h^e_{t+j}$ must be interpreted as the expected one-period *required* rate of return on the stock. In the empirical work to be discussed next, much of the analysis concentrates on using VAR forecasting equations for the 'fundamentals' on the RHS of (2), namely one-period returns and dividend growth and using (9) to give *predicted values* for the dividend–price ratio, which we denote $\delta'_t$. The predicted series $\delta'_t$ can then be compared with the actual values $\delta_t$. A forecast for the (log) stock *price* is obtained using the identity $p'_t = d_t - \delta'_t$, and the latter can then be compared with movements in the actual stock price, $p_t$.

Equation (9) is a *dynamic* version of the Gordon Growth Model $D/P = r - g$ with the required rate of return and dividend growth varying period by period. So the question that we can now examine is whether the RVF holds when we allow both time-varying dividends and time-varying discount rates.

## Stock Prices and the VAR Methodology

Even when measured in real terms, stock prices and dividends are likely to be non-stationary, but the dividend–price ratio and the variable $(r_{t+1} - \Delta d_{t+1})$ are more likely to be stationary, so standard statistical results may be applied to (9). If the RVF is correct, we expect $\delta_t$ to Granger cause $(r_{t+j} - \Delta d_{t+j})$, and because the RVF (9) is linear in future variables, we can use a VAR to give forecasts of future equilibrium returns and dividend growth. The vector of variables in the agent's information set we take to be

$$z_t = (\delta_t, rd_t)' \tag{10}$$

where $rd_t \equiv r_t - \Delta d_t$. Taking a VAR lag length of one for illustrative purposes, we have

$$z_{t+1} = \begin{pmatrix} \delta_{t+1} \\ rd_{t+1} \end{pmatrix} = \begin{pmatrix} a_{11} & a_{12} \\ a_{21} & a_{22} \end{pmatrix} \begin{pmatrix} \delta_t \\ rd_t \end{pmatrix} + \begin{pmatrix} w_{1t+1} \\ w_{2t+1} \end{pmatrix} \tag{11}$$

$$\mathbf{z}_{t+1} = \mathbf{A}\mathbf{z}_t + \mathbf{w}_{t+1}$$

The $a_{ij}$ coefficients can be estimated by OLS with a GMM correction for the standard errors if there is heteroscedasticity in the error terms. Additional lags are included in the VAR to ensure the residuals are not serially correlated. A VAR with higher lags can always be written as a first-order system (the companion form), so analysis of the single-lag VAR is not restrictive. Defining $\mathbf{e1}' = (1, 0)$ and $\mathbf{e2}' = (0, 1)$, it follows that

$$\delta_t = \mathbf{e1}'\mathbf{z}_t \tag{12a}$$

$$E_t rd_{t+j} = \mathbf{e2}' E_t \mathbf{z}_{t+j} = \mathbf{e2}'(\mathbf{A}^j \mathbf{z}_t) \tag{12b}$$

Substituting (12) in (8),

$$\mathbf{e1}'\mathbf{z}_t = \sum_{j=0}^{\infty} \rho^j \mathbf{e2}'\mathbf{A}^{j+1}\mathbf{z}_t = \mathbf{e2}'\mathbf{A}(1 - \rho\mathbf{A})^{-1}\mathbf{z}_t \tag{13}$$

If (13) is to hold for all $\mathbf{z}_t$, then the non-linear restrictions (we ignore the constant term since all data is measured as deviations from the mean) are

$$f(\mathbf{a}) = \mathbf{e1}' - \mathbf{e2}'\mathbf{A}(\mathbf{I} - \rho\mathbf{A})^{-1} = 0 \tag{14}$$

Post-multiplying (14) by $(\mathbf{I} - \rho\mathbf{A})$, these become *linear* restrictions

$$\mathbf{e1}'(\mathbf{I} - \rho\mathbf{A}) - \mathbf{e2}'\mathbf{A} = 0 \tag{15}$$

These restrictions can be evaluated using a Wald test in the usual way. Thus, if the RVF is true and agents use RE, we expect the restrictions in (14)–(15) to hold. The restrictions in (15) are

$$(1, 0) = (\rho a_{11}, \rho a_{12}) + (a_{21}, a_{22}) \tag{16}$$

that is,

$$1 = \rho a_{11} + a_{21} \tag{16a}$$

$$0 = \rho a_{12} + a_{22} \tag{16b}$$

## One-Period Returns Are Not Forecastable

There is little or no direct intuition one can glean from the linear restrictions (16a), but it is easily shown that they imply that expected one-period *real excess* returns $E_t(h_{t+1} - r_{t+1})$ are unforecastable or equivalently that abnormal profit opportunities do not arise in the market. Using (4) and ignoring the constant,

$$E_t(h_{t+1} - r_{t+1}|\Omega_t) = \delta_t - \rho E_t \delta_{t+1} + E_t(\Delta d_{t+1} - r_{t+1}) = \delta_t - \rho E_t \delta_{t+1} - E_t(rd_{t+1}) \tag{17}$$

From (11),

$$E_t \delta_{t+1} = a_{11} \delta_t + a_{12} rd_t \quad \text{and} \quad E_t(rd_{t+1}) = a_{21} \delta_t + a_{22} rd_t$$

Hence,

$$E_t(h_{t+1} - r_t|\Omega_t) = \delta_t - \rho[a_{11}\delta_t + a_{12}rd_t] - (a_{21}\delta_t + a_{22}rd_t) \tag{18}$$

$$= (1 - \rho a_{11} - a_{21})\delta_t - (a_{22} + \rho a_{12})rd_t$$

Hence, given the VAR forecasting equations, the expected excess one-period return is predictable from information available at time $t$, unless the linear restrictions given in the Wald test (16) hold. The economic interpretation of the non-linear Wald test is discussed later in the chapter.

## 'Theoretical' Dividend–Price Ratio

We can define the RHS of (13) as the theoretical spread $\delta'_t$ and use our unrestricted VAR estimates to obtain a time series for $\delta'_t$

$$\delta'_t = \sum_{j=0}^{\infty} \rho^j (r^e_{t+j+1} - \Delta d^e_{t+j+1}) = \mathbf{e2}' \mathbf{A} (\mathbf{I} - \rho \mathbf{A})^{-1} \mathbf{z}_t \tag{19}$$

Under the RVF + RE, we expect movements in the actual dividend–price ratio $\delta_t$ to mirror those of $\delta'_t$, and we can evaluate this proposition by (i) time-series graphs of $\delta_t$ and $\delta'_t$ (ii) the standard deviation ratio SDR $= \sigma(\delta'_t)/\sigma(\delta_t)$ should equal unity, (iii) the correlation coefficient corr($\delta_t'$, $\delta_t$) should equal unity. Instead of working with the dividend–price ratio, we can use the identity $p_t' = d_t - \delta_t'$ to derive a series for the theoretical price *level* and compare this with the actual stock price using the metrics in (i)–(iii) above.

## Further Implications of the VAR Approach

The constructed variable $p_t'$ embodies the investor's best forecast of the DPV of future dividends and time-varying rates of return (discount rates), given the information set *assumed* in the VAR. It is, therefore, closely related to the expected value of the perfect foresight price $E_t P_t^*$ in the original Shiller volatility tests. The difference between the two is that $P_t^*$ is calculated without recourse to *specific* VAR equations to forecast the fundamental variables but merely invokes the RE unbiasedness assumption (i.e. $D_{t+1} = E_t D_{t+1} + w_{t+1}$). Put another way, $p_t'$ is *conditional* on a specific statistical model for dividends, whereas $E_t P_t^*$ is not.

It is worth briefly analysing the relationship between the (log of the) perfect foresight price $p_t^* = \ln(P_t^*)$ and the (log of the) theoretical price $p_t'$, in part so that we are clear about the distinction between these two allied concepts. In doing so, we are able to draw out some of the strengths and weaknesses of the VAR approach, compared to the Shiller variance bounds tests and regression tests on the basis of $P_t^*$. The log-linear identity (2) (with $h_{t+1}$ replaced by $r_{t+1}$) can be rearranged to give

$$p_t = \rho p_{t+1} + (1 - \rho)\, d_{t+1} - r_{t+1} + k \tag{20}$$

Equation (20) by recursive forward substitution gives a log-linear expression for the DPV of *actual* future dividends and discount rates, which we note $p_t^*$.

$$p_t^* = (1 - \rho) \sum_{j=0}^{\infty} \rho^j d_{t+j+1} - \sum_{j=0}^{\infty} \rho^j r_{t+j+1} + k/(1 - \rho) \tag{21}$$

Equation (21) uses actual (*ex-post*) values, hence, $p_t^*$ represents the (log of the) perfect foresight price. The EMH-RVF implies

$$p_t = E(p_t^* | \Omega_t) \tag{22}$$

Under RE, agents use all available information $\Omega_t$ in calculating $E_t p_t^*$, but the theoretical price $p_t'$ only uses the limited information contained in the VAR, which is chosen by the econometrician. Investors 'in reality' might use more information than is in the VAR. Does this make the VAR results rather 'weak' relative to tests based on the perfect foresight price $p_t^*$ and Shiller's variance inequalities? In one sense yes, in another sense no.

First, the VAR contains $\delta_t$ and that is why Shiller's variance bound inequality var($P_t$) $\leq$ var($P_t^*$) is transformed into an equality, namely $p_t = p_t'$ in the VAR methodology. What is more, even if we add more variables to the VAR, we still expect the coefficient on $\delta_t$ to be unity. To see this, note that from (19)

$$\delta'_t = \mathbf{e2}' f(\mathbf{a}) z_t \quad \text{where} \quad z_t = [\delta_t, rd_t] \tag{23}$$

$$f(\mathbf{a}) = \mathbf{A}(\mathbf{I} - \rho \mathbf{A})^{-1} \tag{24}$$

For VAR lag length of one, $f(\mathbf{a})$ is a $(2 \times 2)$ matrix, which is a non-linear function of the $a_{ij}$'s of the VAR. Denote the second row of $f(\mathbf{a})$ as the $2 \times 1$ vector $[f_{21}(a), f_{22}(a)] = e2' f(\mathbf{a})$ where $f_{21}$ and $f_{22}$ are scalar (non-linear) functions of the $a_{ij}$ parameters. Then from (23) we have

$$\delta'_t = f_{21}(a) \, \delta_t + f_{22}(a) \, rd_t \tag{25}$$

Since under the EMH $\delta_t = \delta'_t$, we expect the scalar coefficient $f_{21}(a) = 1$ and that for $f_{22}(a) = 0$. These restrictions hold even if we add additional variables to the VAR. All that happens if we add a variable $y_t$ to the VAR system is that we obtain an additional term $f_3(a)y_t$, and the RVF implies that $f_3(a) = 0$ (in addition to the above two restrictions).

Thus, if the VAR restrictions are rejected on a limited information set, they should also be rejected when a 'larger' information set is used in the VAR. The latter is true as a matter of logic and should be found to be true if we have a large enough sample of data. In this sense, the use of a limited information set is not a major drawback. However, in a finite data set, we know that variables incorrectly omitted from the regression by the econometrician, yet used by agents in forecasting, may result in 'incorrect' (i.e. inconsistent) parameter estimates. Therefore, in practice, using more variables in the VAR may provide a stronger test of the validity of the RVF.

Thus, while Shiller's variance bounds tests based on the perfect foresight price may suffer from problems because of non-stationarity in the data, the results based on the VAR methodology may suffer from omitted variables bias or other specification errors (e.g. wrong functional form). Although there are diagnostic tests available (e.g. tests for serial correlation in the error terms of the VAR, etc.) as a check on the statistical validity of the VAR representation, it nevertheless could yield misleading inferences in finite samples.

We are now in a position to gain some insight into the economic interpretation of the Wald test of the non-linear restrictions in (14), which are equivalent to those in (25) for our two-variable VAR. If the non-linear restrictions are rejected, then this *may* be because of $f_{22}(a) \neq 0$. If so, then $rd_t$ influences $\sum_{j=0}^{\infty} \rho^j (h^e_{t+j+1} - \Delta d^e_{t+j+1})$. To the extent that the (weighted) sum of one-period returns is a form of multi-period return, violation of the non-linear restrictions is indicative that the (weighted) return over a *long horizon* is predictable. We do not wish to push this argument further at this point since it is dealt with explicitly below, in the section on multi-period returns.

We can use the VAR methodology to provide yet another metric for assessing the validity of the EMH-RVF. This metric is based on splitting the term $r_t - \Delta d_t$ into its component elements so that $z_t = (\delta_t, \Delta d_t, r_t)'$. We can then decompose the RHS of (19) into

$$\delta_t = \delta'_{dt} + \delta'_{rt} \tag{26}$$

where

$$\delta'_{rt} = \mathbf{e3}'\mathbf{A}(1 - \rho\mathbf{A})^{-1}\mathbf{z}_t \tag{27a}$$

$$\delta'_{dt} = \mathbf{e2}'\mathbf{A}(1 - \rho\mathbf{A})^{-1}\mathbf{z}_t \tag{27b}$$

Hence, we expect $\text{corr}(\delta_t - \delta'_{dt}, \delta'_{rt}) = 1$. If this correlation coefficient is substantially less than 1, then it implies that the real expected returns $\delta'_{rt}$ are not sufficiently variable to explain the movements in the dividend–price ratio (corrected for the influence of future dividend forecasts $\delta_t - \delta'_{dt}$).

As we shall see, a variance decomposition based on (26) is also useful in examining the influence of the *persistence* in expected returns on the dividend–price ratio $\delta_t$ and hence on stock prices ($p_t = d_t - \delta_t$). The degree of persistence in expected returns is modelled by the size of certain coefficients in the $\mathbf{A}$ matrix of the VAR. We can use (26) to decompose the variability in $\delta_t$ as follows

$$\text{var}(\delta_t) = \text{var}(\delta'_{dt}) + \text{var}(\delta'_{rt}) + 2\,\text{cov}(\delta'_{dt}, \delta'_{rt}) \tag{28}$$

where the RHS terms can be shown to be functions of the $\mathbf{A}$ matrix of the VAR. However, we do not pursue this analysis here, and in this section, the covariance term does not appear since we compare $\delta_{rt}$ with $\delta_t - \delta'_{dt}$.

## Summary: RVF and VAR

We have covered rather a lot of ground but the main points in our application of the VAR methodology to stock prices and returns are as follows.

(i) The linearised RVF implies a set of cross-equation restrictions on the parameters of the VAR. These cross-equation restrictions ensure that one-period excess returns are unforecastable and that RE forecast errors are independent of information at time $t$.

(ii) From the VAR, we can calculate the 'theoretical' dividend–price ratio $\delta'_t$ and the theoretical stock price $p'_t = (d_t - \delta'_t)$. Under the null of the EMH-RVF, we expect $\delta_t = \delta'_t$ and $p_t = p'_t$. And these can be compared graphically.

(iii) The standard deviation ratio $\text{SDR} = \sigma(\delta_t)/\sigma(\delta'_t)$ and correlation $(\delta_t, \delta'_t)$ should be unity. $\delta_t$ is a sufficient statistic for future changes in $r_t - \Delta d_t$ and, hence, should at a minimum, Granger cause the latter variable.

(iv) A measure of the *relative* strength of the importance of expected dividends $(\delta'_{dt})$ and expected future returns $\delta'_{rt}$, in contributing to the variability in the dividend–price ratio $(\delta'_t)$ can be obtained from the VAR.

## 12.2  Empirical Results

The results we present are illustrative. They are, therefore, not a definitive statement of where the balance of the evidence lies. Empirical work has concentrated on the following issues.

(i) The choice of alternative models for expected one-period holding period returns.

(ii) How many variables to include in the VAR, the appropriate lag length and the temporal stability of the parameter estimates.

(iii) How to interpret any conflicting results between the alternative 'metrics' used, such as the predictability of one-period returns in a single-equation study, and the correlation, variance ratio statistics and Wald tests of the VAR methodology.

## The RVF and Predictability of Returns

The seminal work of Campbell and Shiller (1988) uses annual data on an aggregate US stock index and associated dividends for the period 1871–1986. They use four different assumptions about the one-period *required* rates of return, which are:

(a) required *real* returns are constant (i.e. $h_t = $ constant).

(b) required nominal (or real) returns equal the nominal (or real) Treasury Bill rate $h_t = r_t^c$.

(c) required real returns are proportional to consumption growth (i.e. $h_t = \gamma \Delta c_t$, where $\gamma = $ coefficient of relative risk aversion).

(d) Required real (market) returns depend on a risk premium that equals the coefficient of relative risk aversion times the (conditional) variance $V_t$ of returns on the 'market portfolio':

$$h_t = \gamma V_t$$

Hence, in the VAR, $h_t$ is replaced by one of the above alternatives. Note that (b) is the usual assumption of no risk premium, (c) is based on the consumption-CAPM, while (d) has a risk premium loosely based on the CAPM for the market portfolio (although the risk measure used, $V_t$ equals squared *ex-post* returns and is a relatively crude measure of the conditional variance of market returns).

Results are qualitatively unchanged regardless of the assumptions (a)–(d) chosen for required returns, and, therefore, we mainly comment on results under assumption (a), that is, constant real returns (Campbell and Shiller 1988, Table 4). The variables $\delta_t$, $r_t$ and $\Delta d_t$ are found to be stationary I(0) variables. In a *single-equation* regression of (approximate) log returns on the information set $\delta_t$ and $\Delta d_t$, we have

$$h_t = 0.141\delta_t - 0.012\Delta d_t \qquad (29)$$
$$\phantom{h_t = }(0.057) \qquad (0.12)$$

$$1871-1986, \ R^2 = 0.053 \ (5.3\%), \ (.) = \text{standard error}$$

Only the dividend–price ratio is statistically significant in explaining annual (one-period) real returns, but the degree of explanatory power is low ($R^2 = 5.3\%$). In the VAR (with lag length $= 1$) using $z_{t+1} = (\delta_{t+1}, \Delta d_{t+1})$ the variable $\delta_{t+1}$ is highly autoregressive, and most of the explanatory power ($R^2 = 0.515$) comes from the term $\delta_t$ (coefficient $= 0.706$, standard error $= 0.066$) and little from $\Delta d_t$. The change in real dividends $\Delta d_{t+1}$ is partly explained by $\Delta d_t$, but the dividend–price ratio $\delta_t$ is also statistically significant with the 'correct' negative sign (see (5)). Hence, $\delta_t$ Granger causes $\Delta d_t$ is a weak test of the RVF. If we take the estimated $A$ matrix of the VAR and use (23) to calculate $f_{21}(a)$ and $f_{22}(a)$ of (25), then Campbell–Shiller find

$$\delta_t' = \begin{array}{cc} 0.636 \ \delta_t - & 0.097 \ \Delta d_t \\ (0.123) & (0.109) \end{array} \tag{30}$$

Under the null of the EMH-RVF, we expect the coefficient on $\delta_t$ to be unity and that on $\Delta d_t$ to be zero: the former is rejected, although the latter is not. From our theoretical analysis, we noted that if $\delta_t' \neq \delta_t$ then *one-period returns* are predictable, and, therefore, the VAR results are consistent with *single-equation* regressions demonstrating the predictability of one-period returns (e.g. Fama and French 1988b). The Wald test of the cross-equation restrictions is rejected, as is the result that the standard deviation ratio is unity:

$$\text{SDR} = \sigma(\delta_t')/\sigma(\delta_t) = 0.637 \quad (\text{s.e.} = 0.12) \tag{31}$$

However, the correlation between $\delta_t$ and $\delta_t'$ is very high at 0.997 (s.e. = 0.006) and is not statistically different from unity. It appears, therefore, that $\delta_t$ and $\delta_t'$ move in the same direction, but the variability in actual $\delta_t$ is about 60% (i.e. $1/0.637 = 1.57$) larger than its theoretically predicted value $\delta_t'$ (under the RVF). Hence, the dividend–price ratio and, stock prices are more volatile than 'fundamentals', even when we allow dividends and the discount rate to vary over time.

Using the single-equation regression (29), the null that one-period returns are unforecastable is rejected at a 4.5% significance level, however, using the VAR methodology, the Wald test of $\delta_t = \delta_t'$ is rejected at a much higher level of 0.5%. Note that $\delta_t'$ is a weighted average of *all* future one-period returns $h_{t+1}$ and hence approximates a *long-horizon* return. The strong rejection of the Wald test is therefore consistent with the Fama–French results, where predictability is stronger for long- rather than short-horizon returns. We return to this issue below.

The results also make clear that even though one-period returns are barely predictable, nevertheless, this may imply a fairly gross violation of the equality $\delta_t = \delta_t'$ (or $p_t = p_t'$). Hence, the actual stock price is *substantially* more volatile than predicted by the RVF, even when one-period returns are largely unpredictable.

For the different expected return models, the correlation between $(\delta_t - \delta_{dt}')$ and $\delta_{rt}'$, for VAR lag lengths greater than one, is generally found to be low. Hence, a tentative conclusion would be that expected future returns are not sufficiently volatile to explain the variability in actual stock prices. In this variant of the model, variability of the stock price is mostly due to variability in expected dividends although even the latter is not sufficiently variable to 'fully' explain stock price variability (i.e. $\text{var}(\delta_t) > \text{var}(\delta_t')$ and $\text{var}(p_t) > \text{var}(p_t')$).

In a second study, Campbell and Shiller (1988, Chapter 8) extend the information set in the VAR to include the (log) earnings–price ratio $e_t$ where $e_t = \bar{e}_t - p_t$ and $\bar{e}_t = $ long moving average of the log of real earnings. The motivation for including $e_t$ is that financial analysts often use PE ratios (or earnings yield E/P) to predict future stock returns. Indeed, Campbell–Shiller find that the earnings yield is the key variable in determining returns $h_{t+1}$ and statistically it works better than the dividend–price ratio. The VAR now includes the three 'fundamental' variables $z_{t+1} = (\delta_{t+1}, \Delta d_{t+1}, e_{t+1})'$, but the basic VAR results remain broadly unchanged.

It is clear particularly after the late 1950s that there is a substantial divergence between the actual and theoretical price series, thus rejecting the RVF. There is excess volatility in stock prices, and they often diverge substantially from their 'fundamental value' $p_t'$ even though actual one-period (log) returns $h_t$ and the theoretical return $h_t'$ are highly correlated (e.g. corr$(h_t, h_t') = 0.915$, s.e. $= 0.064$, see Shiller (1988, Table 2)). The reason for the above results can be seen by using (19) and $p_t' = d_t - \delta_t'$ to calculate the theoretical price

$$p_t' = 0.256p_t + 0.776e_t + 0.046d_t - 0.078d_{t-1} \qquad (32)$$

Hence, $p_t$ only has a weight of 0.256 rather than unity in determining $p_t'$, and the *long-run* movements in $p_t'$ are dominated by the 'smooth' moving average of earnings $e_t$. However, in the short run, $p_t$ is highly volatile, and this causes $p_t'$ to be highly volatile. By definition, one-period *returns* depend heavily on price changes, hence $h_t$ and $h_t'$ are highly correlated.

The Campbell–Shiller results are largely invariant to whether required real returns or excess returns over the commercial paper rate are used as the time-varying discount rate. Results are qualitatively invariant in various sub-periods of the whole data set, 1927–86 and for different VAR lag lengths. However, Monte Carlo results (Campbell and Shiller (1989) and Shiller and Beltratti (1992)) demonstrate that the Wald test may reject too often under the null that the RVF holds when the VAR lag length is 'long' (e.g. greater than 3). Notwithstanding the Monte Carlo results, Campbell and Shiller (1989) note that in none of their 1000 simulations are the rejections of the Wald test as 'strong' or the lack of correlation between $(\delta_t$ and $\delta_t')$ or $(p_t, p_t')$ or $(h_t, h_t')$ as low as in the actual data set. This suggests that although biases exist in the VAR approach, the violations produced with the *actual* data are much worse than one would expect if the null hypothesis of the EMH-RVF were true.

Using aggregate data on UK stock prices (annual 1918–93) Cuthbertson, Hayes and Nitzsche (1997) find similar results to Campbell and Shiller (1988) for the constant excess returns model. However, the CAPM indicates that the excess *market* return depends on market volatility that is $E_t h_{t+1} - r_t = \gamma E_t V_{t+1}$. Volatility is measured as the squared market return, and the coefficient of relative risk aversion is chosen to minimise the Wald statistic ($\gamma = 2.5$ is used but variants include $\gamma$ in the range 1 to 10). It is found that volatility $V_t$ Granger causes $\Delta d_{t+j}$ and, hence, partly determines the *theoretical* dividend–price ratio $\delta_t'$. So time-varying volatility $V_t$ imparts more variability in $\delta_t'$ and, hence, it more closely matches movements in actual $\delta_t$ than does the constant returns model.

For the *constant* excess returns model (Table 1), the ratio $\sigma(\delta_t')/\sigma(\delta_t)$ is less than its theoretical value of unity, and the Wald test is rejected for all forecast horizons (see below). However, when the volatility term is included in the VAR, the point estimates of $\sigma(\delta_t')/\sigma(\delta_t)$ now exceed unity at all forecast horizons, but they are not statistically different from unity (owing to the large standard errors). Also, the Wald test is not rejected (Table 2).

**Table 1**   Constant expected excess real returns (UK annual data 1918–1993)

|  | Return Horizon (Years) | | | | | |
|---|---|---|---|---|---|---|
|  | 1 | 2 | 3.000 | 5.000 | 10.000 | Infinity |
| (i) Wald statistic | 16.137 | 24.722 | 33.227 | 43.281 | 48.484 | 48.725 |
| (p-value) | (0.001) | (0.000) | (0.000) | (0.000) | (0.000) | (0.000) |
| (ii) $\sigma(\delta'_t)/\sigma(\delta_t)$ | 0.645 | 0.447 | 0.353 | 0.291 | 0.275 | 0.275 |
| (s.e.) | (0.144) | (0.150) | (0.146) | (0.138) | (0.133) | (0.133) |
| (iii) corr($\delta_t, \delta'_t$) | 0.972 | 0.959 | 0.961 | 0.975 | 0.981 | 0.981 |
| (s.e.) | (0.020) | (0.049) | (0.052) | (0.033) | (0.021) | (0.021) |
| (iv) corr($h_{1t'}h'_{1t}$) | 0.963 | 0.929 | 0.899 | 0.866 | 0.852 | 0.852 |
| (s.e.) | (0.027) | (0.048) | (0.076) | (0.106) | (0.113) | (0.113) |

Notes:
1. The statistics in this table were derived from a three-variable VAR, where $\delta_t$, $r_t$ and $\Delta d_t$ were entered separately.
2. The raw data is from the *Equity Gilt Study by* Barclays-deZoete-Wedd (BZW), available from Barclays Capital.
3. Standard errors are heteroscedasticity corrected.

**Table 2**   CAPM volatility model ($\gamma = 2.5$)

|  | Return Horizon (Years) | | | | | |
|---|---|---|---|---|---|---|
|  | 1 | 2 | 3 | 5 | 10 | Infinity |
| (i) Wald statistic | 2.698 | 2.118 | 1.867 | 1.728 | 1.708 | 1.711 |
| (p-value) | (0.441) | (0.548) | (0.600) | (0.631) | (0.635) | (0.635) |
| (ii) $\sigma(\delta'_t)/\sigma(\delta_t)$ | 1.350 | 1.666 | 1.844 | 2.007 | 2.091 | 2.098 |
| (s.e.) | (0.331) | (0.623) | (0.803) | (0.977) | (1.067) | (1.076) |
| (iii) corr($\delta_t, \delta'_t$) | 0.945 | 0.945 | 0.945 | 0.946 | 0.946 | 0.946 |
| (s.e.) | (0.053) | (0.054) | (0.054) | (0.055) | (0.055) | (0.055) |
| (iv) corr($h_{1t}h'_{1t}$) | 0.898 | 0.884 | 0.879 | 0.875 | 0.874 | 0.873 |
| (s.e.) | (0.127) | (0.135) | (0.138) | (0.143) | (0.144) | (0.145) |

Notes:
1. The 'CAPM model' has excess returns depending on market volatility $E_t h_{t+1} - r_t = \gamma E_t V_{t+1}$ where $V_{t+1}$ = volatility (measured by the squared annual stock return).
2. The VAR contains the variables $\{\delta_t, \Delta d_t, V_t\}$.
3. Standard errors are heteroscedasticity corrected.

The CAPM volatility term does have incremental explanatory power in the VAR and $V_t$ is statistically significant in the VAR equations for $\Delta d_{t+1}$ and $\delta_{t+1}$. The dramatic change in the relationship between $\delta'_t$ and $\delta_t$ when volatility is included in the model can be seen by comparing Figures 1 and 2.

Results for France and Germany (Cuthbertson and Hyde 2002) using the CAPM volatility model (aggregate stock indices, monthly data June 73–June 96) are also superior to those for the constant excess returns model. For France (Figure 3a), the volatility model supports the RVF, while for Germany, results are less supportive (Figure 3b). Cuthbertson and Hyde interpret the latter result as being due to volatility in the German market being less than in the French market and, hence, volatility in Germany is not large enough to influence expected returns (see Chapter 29 on GARCH-in-mean models).

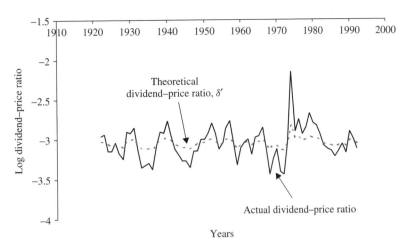

**Figure 1** Actual and 'theoretical' dividend–price ratio – constant returns model (UK data 1921–1993)

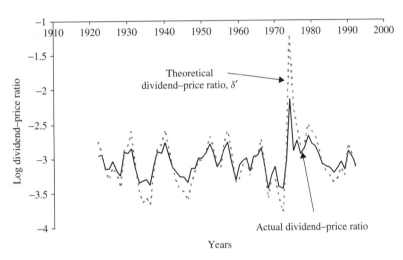

**Figure 2** Actual and theoretical dividend–price ratio – CAPM volatility model, $\gamma = 2.5$ (UK data 1921–1993)

Cuthbertson, Hayes and Nitzsche (1997) note that the 'alternative hypothesis' when using the VAR metrics is very general, namely that the market is inefficient. They, therefore, use the VAR approach to test a *specific* alternative to efficiency, namely short-termism in the UK stock market. The RVF can be written

$$\delta_t = \sum_{j=0}^{4} x^{j+1} E_t Y_{t+1+j} + x^6 \rho^5 E_t \delta_{t+5}$$

where $Y_{t+1+j} \equiv \rho^j (h_{t+1+j} - \Delta d_{t+1+j})$. Efficiency requires $x = 1$ and short-termism (i.e. future 'fundamentals' are given less weight than under the EMH) implies $x < 1$. Because the VAR methodology allows explicit time-series forecasts of $Y_{t+1+j}$ and $\delta_{t+j}$,

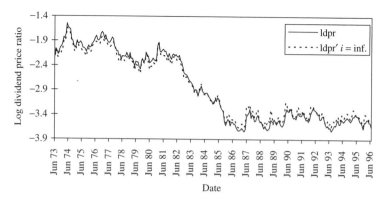

(a) Comparison of actual and theoretical log dividend–
price ratios (market volatility-CAPM model: France)

(b) Comparison of actual and theoretical log dividend–
price ratios (market volatility-CAPM model: Germany)

Notes

(i)   ldpr = actual log dividend–price ratio, ldpr' ($i$ = inf) is the theoretical log dividend–price ratio assuming an infinite forecast horizon in the RVF.

(ii)  The 'market volatility–CAPM model' assumes the expected excess market return depends on the conditional volatility of the market return (the latter is measured as squared past returns).

(iii) The coefficient of relative risk aversion used is $\gamma = 4$ for both France and Germany.

**Figure 3**

we can estimate $x$ in the above equation. Note that we can either truncate our forecast of $\delta_{t+j}$ at (say) $j = 5$ years or we can use

$$E_t \rho^5 \delta_{t+5} \equiv E_t \sum_{j=5}^{\infty} \rho^j (h_{t+1+j} - \Delta d_{t+1+j})$$

as our measure of $E_t \rho^5 \delta_{t+5}$. Using the VAR forecasts from the CAPM volatility model (with $\gamma = 2.5$), the estimate of $x$ is about 0.7 (s.e. $= 0.07$) for both of the above variants, indicating short-termism. Thus, although the RVF is not rejected when we assume excess market returns depend on market volatility, the EMH *is* rejected against the *specific* alternative of short-termism.

Cuthbertson, Hayes and Nitzsche (1999) using UK *quarterly* data (1965–92) on *aggregate* stock returns, decisively reject the C-CAPM (i.e. $E_t h_{t+1} - r_t = \gamma E_t \Delta c_{t+1}$) using the VAR approach, but the CAPM volatility model performs well for $\gamma > 3$. Next, they examine the returns on five market *sectors* (e.g. capital goods, consumer goods, etc.) where the CAPM would suggest that the expected return for any sector $i$ depends on the covariance between the return on asset $i$ and the market return:

$$E_t h_{i,t+1} - r_t = \gamma \, \text{cov}_t(h_{i,t+1}, h_{m,t+1})$$

The time-varying conditional covariance is measured by the cross product $(h_i h_m)_{t+1}$, and Cuthbertson and Galindo (1999) apply the VAR approach to sector returns. What is surprising is that the sectoral results for the VAR metrics are much improved when we assume sector returns depend on *sector volatility* rather than the *covariance* of sector returns, with the market. This suggests that investors perceive each sector as constituting 'the market'. This may be because the investors 'who make the market' actually do concentrate on only one sector (i.e. sector experts) so it is the volatility in that sector that is important to them and influences sector returns (i.e. market segmentation).

As we shall see in Chapter 18, the above result can also be interpreted with evidence from the behavioural finance literature. It has been observed (in experimental situations) that people treat the outcomes of individual gambles separately from other elements of their wealth (even given no institutional constraints). For example, when offered a gamble, people treat it as a 'stand-alone' bet and do not aggregate it with other 'bets' they may currently be involved in. This is an example of 'mental accounting' known as *narrow framing*. In our case, investors should treat all of their sectoral gambles together and realise that the risk of a bet on any *one* sector depends on the covariance of that sector's return with the market return. But if they suffer from *narrow framing*, they will perceive the risk of a bet on any one sector, in isolation. Then their *perceived* risk is correctly measured by the variance of the sectoral return.

An interesting disaggregated study by Bulkley and Taylor (1996) uses the predictions from the VAR, namely the theoretical price in an interesting way. First, a VAR is estimated recursively over 1960–1980 for each company $i$ and the predictions for the theoretical price $P'_{it}$ are obtained. For each year of the recursive sample, the gap between the theoretical value $P'_{it}$ and the actual price $P_{it}$ is used to help predict company returns $R_i$ over one- to ten-year horizons (with corrections for some company risk variables $z_k$):

$$R_i = \alpha + \gamma_o(P'_i/P_i) + \sum_{k=1}^{m} \gamma_k z_k$$

Contrary to the EMH, they find that $\gamma_o \neq 0$. They also rank firms on the basis of the top/bottom 20 (or top/bottom 10) firms, in terms of the value of $(P'_t/P_t)$ and formed portfolios of these companies. The *excess* returns over three years on holding the top 20 firms, as ranked by the $P'_i/P_i$ ratio, would have earned returns in excess of those on the S&P500 index, of over 7% p.a. They also find that excess returns cumulated over five years suggests mispricing of the top 20 shares by around 25%.

## Shiller Volatility Tests and Multi-Period Returns

In our discussion of empirical work on Shiller's volatility inequalities and the Fama–French long-horizon regressions, we noted that $P_t - P_t^*$ (where $P_t^* = $ perfect foresight price) is like a 'long-horizon' return. Hence, a regression of $P_t - P_t^*$ on the information set $\Omega_t$ should yield zero coefficients if long-horizon returns are unforecastable. Fama–French use actual long-horizon returns over $N$ periods $R_{t+N}^N$ and find that these are predictable using past returns, particularly for returns measured over a 3–5-year horizon. Fama–French use univariate-AR models in their tests.

Campbell and Shiller (1988, Chapter 8) are able to apply their linearised formula for the *one-period* return to yield *multi-period* returns, and the latter can be shown to imply cross-equation restrictions on the coefficients in the VAR. Hence, using the VAR methodology, one can examine the Fama–French 'long-horizon' results in a multivariate framework. The $i$-period return from $t$ to $t + i$ is

$$(1 + H_{i,t}) \equiv (1 + H_{1,t+1})(1 + H_{1,t+2})(1 + H_{1,t+3}) \cdots (1 + H_{1,t+i})$$

where $H_{1,t+j}$ is the *one-period* return between $t + j - 1$ and $t + j$. Hence,

$$h_{i,t}^* = \sum_{j=0}^{i-1} h_{1,t+j+1} \tag{33}$$

where $h_{i,t}^* = \ln(1 + H_{i,t})$. Equation (33) is unbounded as the horizon $i$ increases, so Campbell–Shiller prefer to work with a *weighted average* of the $i$-period log return

$$h_{i,t} = \sum_{j=0}^{i-1} \rho^j h_{1,t+j+1} \tag{34}$$

Using (34) and the identity (4) for one-period returns $h_{1,t+1}$, we have

$$h_{i,t} = \sum_{j=0}^{i-1} \rho^j (\delta_{t+j} - \rho \delta_{t+1+j} - \Delta d_{t+j+1} + k) \tag{35}$$

$$= \delta_t - \rho^i \delta_{t+i} + \sum_{j=0}^{i-1} \rho^j \Delta d_{t+j+1} + k(1 - \rho^i)/(1 - \rho)$$

Equation (35) is an (approximate) identity that defines the multi-period return $h_{i,t}$ from period $t$ to $t + i$ in terms of $\delta_t$, $\delta_{t+1}$ and $\Delta d_{t+j}$. It does not have a great deal of direct intuitive appeal but we can briefly try and interpret the first three terms (The linearisation constant, the last term, is of no consequence.) The one-period return depends on the current dividend–price ratio, and this accounts for the first term in (35). The multi-period return must depend on dividends arising from $t$ to $t + i$ and, given that we have anchored $d_t$ with the term $\delta_t$ $(= d_t - p_t)$, it must therefore depend on the *growth* in dividends – this is the third term on the RHS of (35). The second term is of decreasing importance as the return horizon increases (since $\rho^i \delta_{t+i} \to 0$ if $\delta$ is stationary and $0 < \rho < 1$). It appears because returns over a finite horizon depend on the terminal (selling) price at $t+i$ and hence on $\delta_{t+i}$.

We are now in a position to see how a multivariate forecasting equation based on a VAR may be compared with the Fama–French 'long-horizon', single-equation regressions. A VAR in $\mathbf{z}_t = (\delta_t, \Delta d_t)$ can be used to *forecast* the RHS of (35), which is the *theoretical return over i periods* denoted $h'_{i,t}$. We can then compare the actual '$i$-period' return $h_{i,t}$ with $h'_{i,t}$ using graphs, the variance ratio, and the correlation between $h_{i,t}$ and $h'_{i,t}$.

Although (35) can be used to provide a forecast of $h_{i,t}$ from a VAR on the basis of $\delta_t$ and $\Delta d_t$, equation (35) does not provide a Wald test of restrictions on the A matrix, since $h_{i,t}$ is not in the information set. However, a slight modification can yield a Wald test for multi-period returns. We introduce the behavioural hypothesis that expected *one-period excess* returns are constant

$$E_t(h_{1,t} - r_t) = c \tag{36}$$

It follows that

$$E_t(h_{i,t}|\Omega_t) = \sum_{j=0}^{i-1} \rho^j E_t r_{t+j+1} + c(1 - \rho^i)/(1 - \rho) \tag{37}$$

Taking expectations of (35) and equating the RHS of (35) with the RHS of (37), we have the familiar difference equation in $\delta_t$ that can be solved forward to give the dividend–price ratio for *i-period* returns

$$\delta_t = \sum_{j=0}^{i-1} \rho^j E_t(r_{t+j+1} - \Delta d_{t+j+1}) + \rho^i E_t \delta_{t+i} + (c-k)(1-\rho^i)/(1-\rho) \tag{38}$$

If we ignore the constant term, (38) is a similar expression to that obtained earlier, except that the summation is over $i$ periods rather than to infinity. It is the dynamic Gordon model over $i$ periods. Campbell and Shiller (1988) use (38) to form a Wald test of multi-period returns for different values of $i = 1, 2, 3, 5, 7$ and $10$ years and also for an infinite horizon. For $\mathbf{z}_t = (\delta_t, rd_t, e_t)'$, the restrictions are

$$\mathbf{e1}'(\mathbf{I} - \rho^i \mathbf{A}^i) = \mathbf{e2}' \mathbf{A}(\mathbf{I} - \rho \mathbf{A})^{-1}(\mathbf{I} - \rho^i \mathbf{A}^i) \tag{39}$$

For $i = 1$ (or $i = \infty$), the above reduces to

$$\mathbf{e1}'(\mathbf{I} - \rho \mathbf{A})' = \mathbf{e2}' \mathbf{A} \tag{40}$$

which is the case examined earlier in detail. If (40) holds, then post-multiplying by $(\mathbf{I} - \rho^i \mathbf{A}^i)$ we see that (39) also holds *algebraically* for *any* $i$. This is a manifestation of the fact that if one-period returns are unforecastable, so are $i$-period returns.

Campbell and Shiller, using the S&P index 1871–1987, find that the Wald test is rejected only at about the 2 to 4% level for $i = 1$, but these tests are rejected much more strongly for $i > 3$ (i.e. at a level of 0.2 percent or less). This mirrors the Fama–French single-equation results that multi-period returns are more forecastable than single-period returns. Again, Cuthbertson, Hayes and Nitzsche (1999) on UK data find similar results to the above for constant real and excess returns (see Table 1). But as noted above, they find evidence that *multi-period returns* are not forecastable when a measure of volatility is allowed to influence one-period returns as in the CAPM (see results from the Wald test in Table 2).

## Perfect Foresight Price and Multi-Period Returns

We now show that if the multi-period return $h_{i,t+1}$ is forecastable, this implies that the Shiller variance bound inequality is also likely to be violated. Because of the way we defined the (weighted) multi-period return, $h_{i,t+1}$ in (39), it is the case that $h_{i,t+1}$ remains finite as $i \to \infty$.

$$\lim_{i \to \infty} h_{i,t+1} = (1 - \rho) \sum_{j=0}^{\infty} \rho^j d_{t+j+1} - p_t + k/(1 - \rho) = \ln P_t^{**} - \ln P_t + k/(1 - \rho)$$

(41)

We have written the first term on the RHS of (41) as $\ln P_t^{**}$ because it is the logarithmic equivalent of the perfect foresight price $P_t^*$ in the Shiller volatility test. If $h_{i,t+1}$, the $i$-period return is predictable on the basis of information at time $t (\Omega_t)$, then it follows from (41) that in a regression of $(\ln P_t^{**} - \ln P_t)$ on $\Omega_t$, we should also find that $\Omega_t$ is statistically significant. Therefore, $\ln P_t^{**} \neq \ln P_t + \varepsilon_t$ and the Shiller variance bound could be violated. Equation (35) for $h_{i,t+1}$ for finite $i$ is a log-linear representation of $\ln P_{it}^* - \ln P_{it}$ when $P_{it}^*$ is computed under the assumption that the terminal perfect foresight price at $t + i$ equals the actual price $P_{t+i}$. The variable $\ln P_{it}^*$ is a close approximation to the variable used in the volatility inequality tests undertaken by Mankiw, Romer and Shapiro (1991) where they calculate the perfect foresight price over different investment horizons. Hence, tests on $h_{it}$ for finite $i$ are broadly equivalent to the volatility inequality of Mankiw et al. The two studies give broadly similar results but with Campbell and Shiller (1988) rejecting the EMH more strongly than Mankiw et al.

Violation of the volatility tests on the level of stock prices (from Shiller's (1981) early work), that is, $\text{var}(P_t) > \text{var}(P_t^*)$ is consistent with the view that long horizon returns are forecastable. Failure of the Wald restrictions on the VAR in the multi-period horizon case (39) and (40) can be shown to be broadly equivalent to a violation of Shiller's variance bounds tests for $j \to \infty$ and refutation of the hypothesis that multi-period returns are not predictable (as found by Fama and French (1988b) and Mankiw, Romer and Shapiro (1991)).

Overall, the empirical results show that one-period returns, $h_{1t}$ stock prices $p_t$ and the dividend–price ratio $\delta_t$ are generally too volatile (i.e. their variability exceeds that for their theoretical counterparts $h'_{1t}$, $p'_t$ and $\delta'_t$) to conform to the RVF under rational expectations. This applies under a wide variety of assumptions for expected returns.

Long-horizon returns (i.e. 3–5 years) are predictable, although returns over shorter horizons (e.g. one month, one year) are barely predictable. Nevertheless, it appears to be the case that there can be a quite large and persistent divergence between actual stock prices and their theoretical counterpart as given by the RVF. The VAR evidence, therefore, frequently rejects the EMH-RVF under several alternative models of equilibrium returns.

# 12.3 Persistence and Volatility

In this section, we wish to demonstrate how the VAR analysis can be used to examine the relationship between the predictability and persistence of one-period returns and their implications for the volatility in stock prices. We have noted that monthly returns are not very predictable and single-equation regressions have a very low $R^2$ of around 0.02. Persistence in a univariate model is measured by how close the autoregressive coefficient is to unity. In this section, we show that if expected one-period returns are largely unpredictable, yet are persistent, then news about returns can still have a large impact on stock prices. Also, by using a VAR system, we can simultaneously examine the relative contribution of news about dividends, news about future returns (discount rates) and their interaction, on the variability in stock prices.

## Persistence and News

Campbell (1991) considers the impact on stock prices of (i) changes in expected future discount rates (required returns) and (ii) changes in expected future dividends. The surprise or forecast error in the one-period expected return can be shown to be (see Appendix)

$$h_{t+1} - E_t h_{t+1} = (E_{t+1} - E_t) \sum_{j=0}^{\infty} \rho^j \Delta d_{t+j+1} - (E_{t+1} - E_t) \sum_{j=1}^{\infty} \rho^j h_{t+1+j} \quad (42)$$

which in more compact notation is

$$v_{t+1}^h = \eta_{t+1}^d - \eta_{t+1}^h \quad (43)$$

unexpected return in period $t + 1$ = news about future dividend growth

− news about future expected returns

Note that the LHS of (43) is the unexpected capital gain $p_{t+1} - E_t p_{t+1}$. The terms $\eta_{t+1}^d$ and $\eta_{t+1}^h$ on the RHS of (43) represent the DPV of 'revisions to expectations'. It simply states that a favourable out-turn for the *ex-post* return $h_{t+1}$ over and above that which had been expected $E_t h_{t+1}$ must be due to an upward revision in expectations about the growth in future dividends $\Delta d_{t+j}$ or a downward revision in future discount rates, $h_{t+j}$. If the revisions to expectations about either the growth in dividends or the discount rate are *persistent*, then any news between $t$ and $t + 1$ in either of these will have a substantial effect on unexpected returns $h_{t+1} - E_t h_{t+1}$ and, hence, on the variance of the latter. The RHS of (42) is a weighted sum of two stochastic variables $\Delta d_{t+1+j}$ and $h_{t+1+j}$. The variance of the unexpected return, can be written

$$\text{var}(v^h_{t+1}) = \text{var}(\eta^d_{t+1}) + \text{var}(\eta^h_{t+1}) - 2\,\text{cov}(\eta^d_{t+1}, \eta^h_{t+1}) \tag{44}$$

As we see below, we can decompose news about unexpected returns into the separate 'news' elements on the RHS of (44) once we assume some form of stochastic process for $h_{t+1}$ (and any other variables that influence $h_{t+1}$), that is, a VAR system. Campbell suggests a measure of the persistence in expected returns

$$P_h = \sigma(\eta^h_{t+1})/\sigma(u_{t+1}) \tag{45}$$

where $u_{t+1}$ is the innovation at time $t + 1$ in the one-period-ahead expected return, $u_{t+1} = (E_{t+1} - E_t)h_{t+2}$, so $u_{t+1}$ is a revision to expectations over *one-period* only. $P_h$ is therefore defined as

$$P_h = \frac{\text{standard error of news about the DPV of all future returns}}{\text{standard error of news about one-period-ahead expected returns}}$$

$P_h$ may be interpreted as follows. Using (45), we see that an innovation in the one-period expected return $u_{t+1}$ of 1% will lead to a $P_h$ percent change in all future discount rates $\eta^h_{t+j}$ and hence via (43) a $P_h$ percent unexpected capital loss.

## Univariate Case

It is useful to consider a simple case to demonstrate the importance of persistence in explaining the variability in stock prices. Suppose *expected* returns follow an AR(1) process

$$E_{t+1}h_{t+2} = \beta E_t h_{t+1} + u_{t+1} \tag{46}$$

The degree of persistence depends on how close $\beta$ is to unity. It can be shown (see Appendix) that

$$P_h = \rho/(1 - \rho\beta) \approx 1/(1 - \beta) \qquad (\text{for } \rho \approx 1) \tag{47}$$

$$\text{var}(\eta^h_{t+1})/\text{var}(v^h_{t+1}) \approx [(1 + \beta)/(1 - \beta)]R^2/(1 - R^2) \tag{48}$$

where $R^2 =$ the fraction of the variance of stock returns $h_{t+1}$ that is predictable. For $\beta$ close to unity, it can be seen that the $P_h$ statistic is large, indicating a high degree of persistence.

We can now use equation (48) to demonstrate that even if one-period stock returns $h_{t+1}$ are largely unpredictable (i.e. $R^2$ is low), then as long as expected returns are persistent, the impact of news about future returns on stock prices can be large. Taking $\beta = 0.9$ and a value of $R^2$ in a forecasting equation for one-period returns as 0.025, we have from (48) that

$$\text{var}(\eta^h_{t+1}) = 0.49\,\text{var}(v^h_{t+1}) \tag{49}$$

Also from (42) and (43)

$$\text{var}(p_{t+1} - E_t p_{t+1}) \equiv \text{var}(v_{t+1}^h)$$

In this case, news about future returns $\text{var}(\eta_{t+1}^h)$ explains 49% of the variance of one-period unexpected returns $v_{t+1}^h$ and hence 49% of the variability in stock prices. Hence, the predictability of stock returns can be quite low, yet if the persistence in returns is high, then news about returns can explain a large proportion of the variability in stock price movements.

Campbell is able to generalise the above univariate model by using a multivariate VAR system. The variables used are the monthly (real) return $h_{t+1}$ on the value-weighted NYSE Index, the dividend–price ratio, $\delta_t$ and the relative T-bill rate, $rr_t$. (The latter is defined as the difference between the short-term Treasury Bill rate and its one-year backward moving average: the moving average element 'detrends' the I(1) interest rate series.) The VAR for these three variables $\mathbf{z}_t = (h_t, \delta_t, rr_t)$ in companion form is:

$$\mathbf{z}_{t+1} = \mathbf{A}\mathbf{z}_t + \mathbf{w}_{t+1} \qquad (50)$$

where $\mathbf{w}_{t+1}$ is the forecast error $(\mathbf{z}_{t+1} - E_t\mathbf{z}_{t+1})$. We can now go through the usual 'VAR hoops' using (50) and (42) to decompose the variance in the unexpected stock return $v_{t+1}^h$ into that due to news about expected dividends and news about expected discount rates (returns). Using the VAR, we have (see Appendix)

$$\eta_{t+1}^h = (E_{t+1} - E_t) \sum_{j=1}^{\infty} \rho^j h_{t+1+j} = \mathbf{e1}' \sum_{j=1}^{\infty} \rho^j \mathbf{A}^j \mathbf{w}_{t+1} = \rho(\mathbf{I} - \rho\mathbf{A})^{-1}\mathbf{e1}'\mathbf{A}\mathbf{w}_{t+1} \quad (51)$$

Since $v_{t+1}^h$ is the first element of $w_{t+1}$ that is $\mathbf{e1}'\mathbf{w}_{t+1}$, we can rewrite (51) and calculate $\eta_{t+1}^d$ from the identity

$$\eta_{t+1}^d = v_{t+1}^h + \eta_{t+1}^h = (\mathbf{e1}' + \rho(1 - \rho\mathbf{A})^{-1}\mathbf{e1}'\mathbf{A})\mathbf{w}_{t+1} \qquad (52)$$

Given estimates of the $\mathbf{A}$ matrix from the VAR together with the estimates of the variance–covariance matrix of forecast errors $\Psi = E(\mathbf{w}_{t+1}\mathbf{w}_{t+1}')$, we now have all the ingredients to work out the variances and covariances in the variance decomposition. The persistence measure $P_h$ can be shown (see Appendix) to be

$$P_h = \sigma(\lambda'\mathbf{w}_{t+1})/\sigma(\mathbf{e1}'\mathbf{A}\mathbf{w}_{t+1}) = [(\lambda'\Psi\lambda)/(\mathbf{e1}'\mathbf{A}\Psi'\mathbf{A}'\mathbf{e1})]^{1/2} \qquad (53)$$

where $\lambda' = \rho(\mathbf{I} - \rho\mathbf{A})^{-1}\mathbf{e1}'\mathbf{A}$ and $\sigma(.)$ indicates the standard deviation of the terms in parentheses.

## Results

An illustrative selection of results from Campbell (1991) is given in Table 3 for monthly data over the period 1952(1)–1988(12). In the VAR equation for returns, $h_{t+1}$

**Table 3** Variance decomposition of real stock returns: US data 1952(1)–1988(12)

| $R_h^2$ | $\text{var}(\eta^d)/\text{var}(v^h)$ | $\text{var}(\eta^h)/\text{var}(v^h)$ | $-2\,\text{cov}(\eta^d, \eta^h)$ | $\text{corr}(\eta^d, \eta^h)$ |
|---------|------------|------------|------------|------------|
| 0.065   | 0.127      | 0.772      | 0.101      | −0.161     |
| [0.000] | (0.016)    | (0.164)    | (0.153)    | (−0.256)   |

Notes: $R^2$ is the fraction of the monthly real stock returns that is forecast by the VAR and [.] is the marginal significance level for the joint significance of the VAR forecasting variables. (.) = standard error. The VAR lag length is one.
Source: Campbell (1991), Table 2.

is influenced by variables other than lagged returns $h_t$, namely by the dividend–price ratio and the relative bill rate, but even then, the $R^2$ is relatively low, 0.065, compared to those for the dividend yield ($R^2 = 0.96$) and the relative bill rate ($R^2 = 0.55$). The persistence measure is calculated to be $P_h = 5.7$ (s.e. = 1.5), indicating that a 1% positive innovation in the expected return leads to a capital loss of around 6%, *ceteris paribus*. (However, persistence is smaller in the earlier 1927(1)–1951(12) period with $P_h = 3.2$, s.e. = 2.4). News about future returns $\text{var}(\eta^h)$ account for over 75% of the variance of unexpected returns, with news about dividends accounting for about 13% (Table 3). This leaves a small contribution due to the negative covariance term, of about 10%.

Campbell (1991) notes that these VAR results need further analysis, and he considers the sensitivity of the variance decomposition to the VAR lag length, possible omitted variables in the VAR, and unit roots in the dividend–price equation, which are likely to affect the small sample properties of the asymptotic test statistics used. He finds the following.

(i) The above results are largely invariant to the lag length of the VAR when using either monthly returns or returns measured over three months.

(ii) The variance of news about future returns is far less important (and that for future dividends is more important) when the dividend–price ratio is excluded from the VAR.

(iii) Performing a Monte Carlo experiment with $h_{t+1}$ *independent* of any other variables and a unit-root imposed in the dividend–price equation has 'a devastating effect' on the bias in the variance decomposition statistics. In the artificially generated series where $h_{t+1}$ is unforecastable, unexpected stock returns should only respond to news about future dividends. Hence, $\text{var}(\eta^d_{t+1})/\text{var}(v^h_{t+1})$ should equal unity and the $R$-squared for the returns equation should be zero. But in the MCS over the whole sample 1927–1980, the latter results are strongly violated (although they are not rejected for the post-war period).

Cuthbertson and Galindo (1999) repeat the Campbell analysis on UK annual data 1918–1993 for the value-weighted BZW equity index. They include a wide array of variables in the VAR, the key ones being the dividend–price ratio and a measure of volatility. There is some evidence that persistence in volatility helps explain persistence in expected returns. However, in all these variants, the contribution of the news about future returns to the movement in current returns is about four times that of news about dividends (with the covariance term being statistically insignificant). These results broadly mirror those of Campbell (1991) on US data.

The results in Campbell (1991) for the US aggregate stock market index and Cuthbertson, Hayes and Nitzsche (1997, 1999) show that there is some evidence to support the view that (in post-1950s data, in particular) stock returns in a multivariate VAR system do appear to be (weakly) predictable and reasonably persistent. Of course, this analysis does not provide an economic model of why expected returns $E_t h_{t+1}$ depend on variables like the dividend–price ratio and the relative bill rate, but merely provide a set of statistical correlations that need to be explained. The results of Campbell (1991) and Cuthbertson and Galindo (1999) also show that the variability in stock prices is likely to be mainly due to news about future returns rather than news about future dividend growth, although the *relative* importance of these two factors is difficult to pin down at all precisely. This is because results from the variance decomposition depend on the particular information set chosen (and whether dividends have a unit root).

## 12.4   Summary

- The VAR methodology and the linearisation of the RVF allows one to investigate the relationship between one-period returns, multi-period returns and the volatility of stock prices, within a common theoretical framework that also explicitly deals with the issue of stationarity of the data.

- Under a variety of assumptions about the determination of one-period returns, the evidence strongly suggests that stock prices do not satisfy the RVF and the informational efficiency assumption of RE. These rejections of the EMH-RVF seem conclusive and more robust than those found in the variance bounds literature. Stock prices appear to be excessively volatile even when we allow time-varying discount rates and dividend forecasts (using linear VAR models).

- Although monthly returns are barely predictable, the VAR approach indicates that returns at long horizons are predictable – this is consistent with results from *single-equation* return regressions.

- There is some evidence that sector returns depend on the variance of sector returns and not on the covariance between sector returns and the market (i.e. the CAPM). This can be interpreted as 'narrow framing' by investors or market segmentation by stock analysts.

- There is some persistence in one-period returns so that although the latter are hardly predictable, nevertheless, news about current returns can have quite a strong influence on future returns and hence on stock prices. Stock prices are probably influenced more by changes in expected future returns rather than changes in forecasts of dividends – but both have some influence.

# Appendix: Returns, Variance Decomposition and Persistence

In this appendix, we do three things. We show how to derive the Campbell–Shiller linearised formula for stock returns and the dividend–price ratio. We then show how these equations give rise to Campbell's variance decomposition and the importance of persistence in producing volatility in stock prices. Finally, we demonstrate how a VAR can provide empirical estimates of the degree of persistence.

## 1. Linearisation of Returns

The one-period, real holding period return is

$$H_{t+1} = \frac{P_{t+1} - P_t + D_{t+1}}{P_t} \tag{A1}$$

where $P_t$ is the *real* stock price at the end of period $t$ and $D_{t+1}$ is the *real* dividend paid during period $t + 1$. (Both the stock price and dividends are deflated by some general price level, for example, the consumer price index.) The natural logarithm of (one plus) the real holding period return we note as $h_{t+1}$ and is given by

$$h_{t+1} = \ln(1 + H_{t+1}) = \ln(P_{t+1} + D_{t+1}) - \ln(P_t) \tag{A2}$$

If lower-case letters denote logarithms, then (A2) becomes

$$h_{t+1} = \ln[\exp(p_{t+1}) + \exp(d_{t+1})] - p_t \tag{A3}$$

The first term in (A3) is a non-linear function in $p_{t+1}$ and $d_{t+1}$. We linearise it by taking a first-order Taylor series expansion around the geometric mean of $P$ and $D$:

$$\ln[\exp(p_{t+1}) + \exp(d_{t+1})] = k + \rho p_{t+1} + (1 - \rho) d_{t+1} \tag{A4}$$

where

$$\rho = \overline{P}/(\overline{P} + \overline{D}) \tag{A5}$$

and, therefore, $\rho$ is a number slightly less than unity and $k$ is a constant. Using (A3) and (A4) gives

$$h_{t+1} = k + \rho p_{t+1} + (1 - \rho) d_{t+1} - p_t \tag{A6}$$

Adding and subtracting $d_t$ in (A6) and defining $\delta_t = d_t - p_t$ as the log dividend–price ratio, we have

$$h_{t+1} = k + \delta_t - \rho \delta_{t+1} + \Delta d_{t+1} \tag{A7}$$

Equation (A7) can be interpreted as a *linear forward difference* equation in $\delta$:

$$\delta_t = -k + \rho \delta_{t+1} + h_{t+1} - \Delta d_{t+1} \tag{A8}$$

Solving (A8) by the forward recursive substitution method and assuming the transversality condition holds,

$$\delta_t = \sum_{j=0}^{\infty} \rho^j [h_{t+j+1} - \Delta d_{t+j+1}] - k/(1-\rho) \tag{A9}$$

Equation (A9) states that the log dividend–price ratio can be written as the discounted sum of all future returns minus the discounted sum of all future dividend growth rates less a constant term. If the current dividend–price ratio is high because the current price is low, then it means that in future, either required returns $h_{t+1}$ are high or dividend growth rates $\Delta d_{t+j}$ are low or both. Equation (A9) is an identity and holds almost exactly for *actual* data. However, we can treat it as an *ex-ante* relationship by taking expectations of both sides of (A9) conditional on the information available at the end of period $t$:

$$\delta_t = \sum_{j=0}^{\infty} \rho^j [E_t(h_{t+j+1}) - E_t(\Delta d_{t+j+1})] - k/(1-\rho) \tag{A10}$$

It should be noted that $\delta_t$ is known at the *end of period t* and, hence, its expectations is equal to itself.

## 2 Variance Composition

To set the ball rolling, note that we can write (A10) for period $t+1$ as

$$\delta_{t+1} = \sum_{j=0}^{\infty} \rho^j [E_{t+1}(h_{t+j+2}) - E_{t+1}(\Delta d_{t+j+2})] - k/(1-\rho) \tag{A11}$$

From (A8), we have

$$h_{t+1} - \Delta d_{t+1} - k = \delta_t - \rho \delta_{t+1} \tag{A12}$$

Substituting from (A10) and (A11) and rearranging, we obtain

$$h_{t+1} - \Delta d_{t+1} - k = E_t h_{t+1} + \sum_{j=1}^{\infty} \rho^j E_t(h_{t+j+1}) - \sum_{j=0}^{\infty} \rho^j E_t(\Delta d_{t+j+1}) - k/(1-\rho)$$

$$- \sum_{i=0}^{\infty} \rho^{i+1} E_{t+1}(h_{t+i+2}) + \sum_{i=0}^{\infty} \rho^{i+1} E_{t+1}(\Delta d_{t+i+2}) + k\rho/(1-\rho) \tag{A13}$$

The constant terms involving $k$ and $\rho$ cancel out in (A13). Substituting $j = i + 1$ in the last two summations on the RHS of (A13) and rearranging, we obtain

$$h_{t+1} - E_t h_{t+1} = \sum_{j=1}^{\infty} \rho^j E_t(h_{t+j+1}) - \sum_{j=0}^{\infty} E_t(\Delta d_{t+j+1}) - \sum_{j=1}^{\infty} \rho^j E_{t+1}(h_{t+j+1})$$

$$+ \sum_{j=1}^{\infty} \rho^j E_{t+1}(\Delta d_{t+j+1}) + \Delta d_{t+1} \qquad (A14)$$

Rearranging (A14), we obtain our key expression for unexpected or abnormal returns:

$$h_{t+1} - E_t h_{t+1} = (E_{t+1} - E_t) \sum_{j=0}^{\infty} \rho^j \Delta d_{t+1+j} - (E_{t+1} - E_t) \sum_{j=1}^{\infty} \rho^j h_{t+1+j} \qquad (A15)$$

Equation (A15) is the equation used by Campbell (1991) to analyse the impact of persistence in expected future returns on the behaviour of current unexpected returns $h_{t+1} - E_t h_{t+1}$. Each term in (A15) can be written as

$$v_{t+1}^h = \eta_{t+1}^d - \eta_{t+1}^h \qquad (A16)$$

$$\begin{pmatrix} \text{unexpected returns} \\ \text{in period } t + 1 \end{pmatrix} = \begin{pmatrix} \text{news about future} \\ \text{dividend growth} \end{pmatrix} - \begin{pmatrix} \text{news about future} \\ \text{expected returns} \end{pmatrix}$$

From (A16), we have

$$\text{var}(v_{t+1}^h) = \text{var}(\eta_{t+1}^d) + \text{var}(\eta_{t+1}^h) - 2\,\text{cov}(\eta_{t+1}^d, \eta_{t+1}^h) \qquad (A17)$$

The variance of unexpected stock returns in (A17) comprises three separate components. The variance associated with the news about cash flows (dividends), the variance associated with the news about future returns and a covariance term. Given this variance decomposition, it is possible to calculate the relative importance of these three components in contributing to the variability of stock returns. Using (A6), it is also worth noting that for $\rho \approx 1$ and no surprise in dividends,

$$h_{t+1} - E_t h_{t+1} = p_{t+1} - E_t p_{t+1}$$

where $p_t$ is the (log) stock price. Hence, the LHS of (A15) is the unexpected or 'surprise' in the stock *price*.

Campbell also presents a measure of the persistence of expected returns. This is defined as the ratio of the variability of the innovation in the expected present value of *future returns* (i.e. standard error of $\eta_{t+1}^h$) to the variability of the innovation in the *one-period-ahead* expected return. If we define $u_{t+1}$ to be the innovation at time $t + 1$ in the one-period-ahead expected return, we have

$$u_{t+1} = (E_{t+1} - E_t)h_{t+2} \qquad (A18)$$

and $P_h$ the measure of persistence of expected returns is defined as

$$P_h = \sigma(\eta_{t+1}^h)/\sigma(u_{t+1}) \tag{A19}$$

## A. Expected Returns Follow AR(1) Process

We need to be able to model the expected stock return in order to carry out the variance decomposition (A17) and to calculate the measure of persistence (A19). For exposition purposes, we follow Campbell and initially we assume that the expected stock return follows a univariate-AR(1) model. We then repeat the calculation using $h_{t+1}$ in the VAR representation. The AR(1) model for expected returns is

$$E_{t+1}h_{t+2} = \beta E_t h_{t+1} + u_{t+1} \tag{A20}$$

Using (A20), the expected value of $h_{t+2}$ at time $t$ is

$$E_t h_{t+2} = \beta E_t h_{t+1} \tag{A21}$$

where we have used $E_t E_{t+1}$ and $E_t u_{t+1} = 0$. Equation (A20) minus (A21) gives

$$(E_{t+1} - E_t)h_{t+2} = u_{t+1} \tag{A22}$$

Leading (A21) one period and taking expectations at time $t$, we have

$$E_t h_{t+3} = \beta E_t h_{t+2} = \beta^2 E_t h_{t+1} \tag{A23}$$

and similarly,

$$E_{t+1}h_{t+3} = \beta E_{t+1}h_{t+2} = \beta(\beta E_t h_{t+1} + u_{t+1}) \tag{A24}$$

Subtracting (A23) from (A24), we obtain

$$(E_{t+1} - E_t)h_{t+3} = \beta u_{t+1}$$

In general, therefore, we can write

$$(E_{t+1} - E_t)h_{t+j+1} = \beta^{i-1}u_{t+1} \tag{A25}$$

Using the definition of news about future returns, in (A15) and (A16) and using (A25), we have

$$\eta_{t+1}^h = \sum_{j=1}^{\infty} \rho^j \beta^{j-1}u_{t+1} = \rho u_{t+1}/(1 - \rho\beta) \tag{A26}$$

Hence, the variance of discounted unexpected returns is an exact function of the variance of one-period unexpected returns:

$$\text{var}(\eta_{t+1}^h) = [\rho/(1 - \rho\beta)]^2 \, \text{var}(u_{t+1}) \tag{A27}$$

Using (A27), the measure of persistence $P_h$ in (A19) is seen to be

$$P_h = \rho/(1 - \rho\beta) \approx 1/(1 - \beta)$$

Hence, if $\beta$ is close to unity, which we can interpret as a high degree of persistence in the AR(1) model, then $P_h$ will also be large. Since $p_{t+1} - E_t p_{t+1} = -\eta_{t+1}^h$ (when $\eta^d = 0$) and $\eta^h = [\rho/(1 - \rho\beta)]u_{t+1}$, then for the AR(1) case $p_{t+1} - E_t p_{t+1} = P_h u_{t+1}$. Hence, a 1% increase in $u_{t+1}$ leads to a $P_h$ percent increase in $\eta^h$ and hence a $P_h$ percent unexpected capital loss.

For the AR(1) case, we now wish to show that even if we can only explain a small proportion of the variability in one-period returns $h_{t+1}$ (i.e. returns are difficult to forecast), yet if returns are persistent, then news about returns can be very important in explaining stock price volatility. In short, the more persistent are expected returns, the more important is the variance of news about future returns $\text{var}(\eta_{t+1}^h)$ in explaining unexpected returns $h_{t+1} - E_t h_{t+1}$ (or unexpected capital gains or losses, $p_{t+1} - E_t p_{t+1}$).

Define $R^2$ to be the fraction of the variance of stock returns that is predictable,

$$R^2 = \text{var}(E_t h_{t+1})/\text{var}(h_{t+1}) \tag{A28}$$

$$1 - R^2 = \text{var}(v_{t+1}^h)/\text{var}(h_{t+1}) \tag{A29}$$

$$R^2/(1 - R^2) = \text{var}(E_t h_{t+1})/\text{var}(v_{t+1}^h) \tag{A30}$$

From (A20), the variance of $E_t h_{t+1}$ is

$$\text{var}(E_t h_{t+1}) = \text{var}(u_{t+1})/(1 - \beta^2) \tag{A31}$$

Substituting (A31) in (A30) and solving for $\text{var}(u_{t+1})$, we obtain

$$\text{var}(u_{t+1}) = (1 - \beta^2)\,\text{var}(v_{t+1}^h)R^2/(1 - R^2) \tag{A32}$$

Using (A32), equation (A27) can be written as

$$\text{var}(\eta_{t+1}^h)/\text{var}(v_{t+1}^h) = (1 - \beta^2)[\rho/(1 - \rho\beta)]^2 R^2/(1 - R^2) \tag{A33}$$

$$\approx [(1 + \beta)/(1 - \beta)]R^2/(1 - R^2)$$

The LHS of (A33) is one of the components of the variance decomposition that we are interested in and represents the importance of variance of discounted expected future returns relative to variance of unexpected returns (see equation (A17)).

For monthly returns, a forecasting equation with $R^2 \approx 0.025$ is reasonably representative. The variance ratio $VR$ in (A33) for $\beta = 0.5, 0.75$ or $0.9$ is $VR = 0.08, 0.18$ or $0.49$ respectively. Hence, for a high degree of persistence but a low degree of predictability, news about future returns can still have a large (proportionate) effect on unexpected returns $\text{var}(v_{t+1}^h)$.

## B. Multivariate Case: VAR Model

The above univariate case neglects any *interaction* between news about expected returns and news about dividends, that is, the covariance term in (A17). At a minimum, we require an equation to explain dividend growth. The covariance between the forecast errors (i.e. news) for dividend growth and those for returns can then be examined.

In this section, we assume the $(m \times 1)$ vector $\mathbf{z}_{t+1}$ contains $h_{t+1}$ as its first element. The other variables in $\mathbf{z}_{t+1}$ are known at the end of period $t + 1$ and are used to set up the following VAR model

$$\mathbf{z}_{t+1} = \mathbf{A}\mathbf{z}_t + \mathbf{w}_{t+1} \text{ and } E(\mathbf{w}_{t+1}\mathbf{w}'_{t+1}) = \mathbf{\Psi} \tag{A34}$$

where $\mathbf{A}$ is the companion matrix. The first element in $\mathbf{w}_{t+1}$ is $v^h_{t+1}$. First, note that

$$E_{t+1}\mathbf{z}_{t+j+1} = \mathbf{A}^{j+1}\mathbf{z}_t + \mathbf{A}^j\mathbf{w}_{t+1} \tag{A35}$$

$$E_t\mathbf{z}_{t+j+1} = \mathbf{A}^{j+1}\mathbf{z}_t \tag{A36}$$

Subtracting (A36) from (A35), we get

$$(E_{t+1} - E_t)\mathbf{z}_{t+j+1} = \mathbf{A}^j\mathbf{w}_{t+1} \tag{A37}$$

Since the first element of $\mathbf{z}_t$ is $h_t$, if we pre-multiply both sides of (A37) by $\mathbf{e1}'$, (where $\mathbf{e1}'$ is a $(1 \times m)$ row vector containing 1 as its first element with all other elements equal to zero), we obtain

$$(E_{t+1} - E_t)h_{t+j+1} = \mathbf{e1}'\mathbf{A}^j\mathbf{w}_{t+1} \tag{A38}$$

and hence,

$$\eta^h_{t+1} = (E_{t+1} - E_t)\sum_{j=1}^{\infty} \rho^j h_{t+1+j} = e1'\sum_{j=1}^{\infty} \rho^j \mathbf{A}^j \mathbf{w}_{t+1}$$

$$= \mathbf{e1}'\rho\mathbf{A}(\mathbf{I} - \rho\mathbf{A})^{-1}\mathbf{w}_{t+1} = \boldsymbol{\lambda}'\mathbf{w}_{t+1} \tag{A39}$$

where $\boldsymbol{\lambda}' = \mathbf{e1}'\rho\mathbf{A}(1 - \rho\mathbf{A})^{-1}$ is a non-linear function of parameters of the VAR. Since the first element of $\mathbf{w}_{t+1}$ is $v^h_{t+1}$, using (A16) and (A39), we can write

$$\eta^d_{t+1} = \mathbf{e1}'[\mathbf{I} + \rho\mathbf{A}(1 + \rho\mathbf{A})^{-1}]\mathbf{w}_{t+1} = \boldsymbol{\gamma}'\mathbf{w}_{t+1} \tag{A40}$$

It can be seen from (A39) and (A40) that both unexpected future returns and unexpected future dividends can be written as linear combinations of the VAR error terms where each error term is multiplied by a non-linear function of the VAR parameters. Setting $j = 1$ in (A38) and using (A18), we obtain

$$(E_{t+1} - E_t)h_{t+2} = u_{t+1} = \mathbf{e1}'\mathbf{A}\mathbf{w}_{t+1} \tag{A41}$$

Equations (A39) to (A41) can be used to carry out the variance decomposition and to calculate the measure of persistence $P_h$, given the VAR model. In particular, we have

$$\text{var}(\eta_{t+1}^h) = \boldsymbol{\lambda}' \boldsymbol{\Psi} \boldsymbol{\lambda} \tag{A42}$$

$$\text{var}(\eta_{t+1}^d) = \boldsymbol{\gamma}' \boldsymbol{\Psi} \boldsymbol{\gamma} \tag{A43}$$

$$\text{var}(v_{t+1}^h) = \mathbf{e1}' \boldsymbol{\Psi} \mathbf{e1} \tag{A44}$$

$$\text{cov}(\eta_{t+1}^h, \eta_{t+1}^d) = \boldsymbol{\lambda}' \boldsymbol{\Psi} \boldsymbol{\gamma} \tag{A45}$$

$$\text{var}(u_{t+1}) = \mathbf{e1}' \mathbf{A} \boldsymbol{\psi} \mathbf{A}' \mathbf{e1} \tag{A46}$$

$$P_h = [(\boldsymbol{\lambda}' \boldsymbol{\Psi} \boldsymbol{\lambda}) / (\mathbf{e1}' \mathbf{A} \boldsymbol{\Psi} \mathbf{A}' \mathbf{e1})]^{1/2} \tag{A47}$$

Once the 'A' parameters of the VAR and the covariance matrix $\boldsymbol{\Psi}$ have been estimated, the required variances and covariances can easily be calculated. One can use OLS to estimate each equation in the VAR individually, but Campbell suggests the use of the Generalised Method of Moments (GMM) estimator (Hansen 1982) to correct for any heteroscedasticity that may be present in the error terms. The GMM point estimates of parameters are identical to the ones obtained by OLS, although the GMM variance–covariance matrix of all the parameters in the model will be 'corrected' for the presence of heteroscedasticity (White 1984).

The standard errors of the variance statistics in (A42)–(A47) can be calculated as follows. Denote the vector of all parameters in the model by $\boldsymbol{\theta}$ (comprising the non-redundant elements of $\mathbf{A}$ and $\boldsymbol{\Psi}$) and the heteroscedasticity adjusted variance–covariance matrix of the estimate of these parameters by $\mathbf{V}$. Suppose, for example, we are interested in calculating the *standard error* of $P_h$. Since $P_h$ is a non-linear function of $\boldsymbol{\theta}$, its variance can be calculated as

$$\text{var}(P_h) = \left( \frac{\partial P_h}{\partial \boldsymbol{\theta}} \right)' \mathbf{V} \left( \frac{\partial P_h}{\partial \boldsymbol{\theta}} \right) \tag{A48}$$

The derivatives of $P_h$ with respect to the parameters $\boldsymbol{\theta}$ can be calculated numerically. The standard error of $P_h$ is then the square root of $\text{var}(P_h)$.

# 13

# SDF MODEL AND THE C-CAPM

## Aims

- Present a class of models known as (stochastic discount factor) SDF models.

- Show that the consumption-CAPM (C-CAPM) is a SDF model in which the discount factor depends on the marginal utility of current and next periods consumption.

- Show the relationship between the C-CAPM and the 'standard' Sharpe–Lintner CAPM from mean-variance portfolio theory.

- Demonstrate how interest rates, risky-asset returns and asset prices are interrelated in the C-CAPM.

In the following, we discuss the consumption-CAPM (or C-CAPM), a more general asset-pricing framework than the 'standard' mean-variance CAPM discussed in earlier chapters. In this model, investors do not base their behaviour on the one-period mean and standard deviation of returns as in the standard-CAPM, but the model is intertemporal, in that investors are assumed to maximise expected utility of current and future consumption.

In the C-CAPM, financial assets allow the consumer to smooth her consumption pattern over time, selling assets to finance consumption in 'bad' times and saving in 'good' times. Assets whose returns have a high negative conditional covariance *with consumption* will be willingly held even though they have low expected returns. This is because they can be 'cashed in' at a time when they are most needed, namely when consumption is low, and, therefore, extra consumption yields high marginal utility. This model associates an asset's systematic risk with the state of the economy (i.e. consumption).

The SDF model is a generic model whereby asset returns $R_{i,t+1}$ or prices $P_{it}$ can be expressed as $E_t\{R_{i,t+1}M_{t+1}\} = 1$ or $P_{it} = E_t\{M_{t+1}X_{i,t+1}\}$, where $M_{t+1}$ is the stochastic discount factor (or pricing kernel) and $X_{i,t+1}$ is the asset's next period's pay-off. Specific SDF models arise because of different formulations of $M_{t+1}$ and in this chapter we deal mainly with the C-CAPM. A key element of SDF models is that $M_{t+1}$ is the same for all assets.

The C-CAPM is a SDF model in which, under power utility, the discount rate is determined by consumption growth. Indeed, consumption, the risk-free rate, the expected *equilibrium* return on risky assets and asset prices are all simultaneously determined in the SDF model. In the SDF model, $M_{t+1}$ may be time-varying, giving rise to a time-varying risk premium.

# 13.1 Consumption-CAPM

In the one-period standard-CAPM, the investor's objective function is assumed to be fully determined by the (one-period) standard deviation and expected return on the portfolio. All investors choose risky-asset shares to maximise the Sharpe ratio. Equilibrium returns then arise as a consequence that all agents have the same expectations and all assets must be willingly held.

An alternative view of the determination of equilibrium returns is provided by the C-CAPM. Here, the investor maximises expected utility that depends only on current and future consumption (see Lucas 1978, Mankiw and Shapiro 1986, Cochrane 2001). Financial assets play a role in this model in that they help to smooth consumption over time. Securities are held to transfer purchasing power from one period to another. If an agent had no assets and was not allowed to accumulate assets, then her consumption would be determined by her current income. If she holds assets, she can sell some of these to finance consumption when her current income is low. An individual asset is therefore more 'desirable' if its return is expected to be high when consumption is expected to be low. Thus, the systematic risk of the asset is determined by the covariance of the asset's return with respect to consumption (rather than its covariance with respect to the return on the market portfolio as in the 'standard' CAPM).

As we shall see, the C-CAPM can be presented in a large number of equivalent ways – some more intuitive than others. In short, it is subject to more costume changes than a successful 1930s Hollywood musical, choreographed by Busby Berkeey. It is a colourful, well-established model that appears regularly throughout the asset-pricing and portfolio literature. The model has seen some intriguing developments (from *Gold Diggers of 1933* to *Cabaret* to *Phantom of the Opera*, to continue the tenuous metaphor) in order that it more closely explains the empirical facts. At the end of the next few chapters, you will be in a position to judge whether it is a mere entertaining theoretical diversion or whether it also explains the 'real world' sufficiently well to make it useful for analysis of asset returns and risk premia.

### Notation

The dollar pay-off next period to holding an asset is $X_{t+1} \equiv P_{t+1} + D_{t+1}$, where $P_{t+1}$ is the (end-of-period) price and $D_{t+1}$ are dividends paid between $t$ and $t + 1$. The *gross* return on an asset is defined as $R^*_{t+1} = X_{t+1}/P_t \equiv R_{t+1} + 1$. Hence, a gross return of $R^* = 1.10$ represents a 'return' (as normally expressed) of $R = 0.10$ (10%).

## First-Order Condition

First, we present an intuitive argument to derive the FOC for an investor who is concerned about maximising her lifetime utility from (real) consumption. (Utility is time-separable – see Chapter 1.) Because investors care about *real* consumption, asset returns are also in real terms. The first-order condition (FOC) for maximising expected utility has the agent equating the utility loss from a reduction in *current* consumption, with the additional expected gain in (discounted) consumption *next period*. Lower consumption expenditure at time $t$ allows investment in an asset that has an expected positive return and therefore yields extra resources for future consumption. More formally, a \$1 reduction in (real) consumption today reduces utility by $U'(C_t)$ but results in an expected payout of $E_t R^*_{it+1}$ next period. When spent on next period's consumption, the discounted extra utility per (real) dollar is $\theta U'(C_{t+1})$. The discount rate $\theta = 1/(1 + t_\mathrm{p})$, where $t_\mathrm{p}$ is the subjective time preference rate and in annual data $\theta \approx 0.97$. Hence, the present value of *total extra* utility expected next period is $E_t\{R^*_{it+1}\theta U'(C_{t+1})\}$. In equilibrium, we have

$$U'(C_t) = E_t\{R^*_{it+1}\theta U'(C_{t+1})\} \tag{1a}$$

or

$$E_t\{R^*_{it+1}M_{t+1}\} = 1 \tag{1b}$$

where

$$M_{t+1} = \theta U'(C_{t+1})/U'(C_t) \tag{1c}$$

$M_{t+1}$ is the marginal rate of substitution of current for future (discounted) consumption and depends on agents' preferences ('tastes') between consumption today and consumption tomorrow. Equation (1b) holds for *any* two assets $i$ and $j$, hence, we can immediately derive the *excess* return version of the FOC

$$E_t\{(R^*_{it+1} - R^*_{jt+1})M_{t+1}\} = 0 \tag{1d}$$

where for a risk-free asset $R^*_{jt+1} = R^*_{ft}$. Note that (1d) is unchanged if we measure returns as real or nominal, since real returns equal nominal returns less the expected inflation rate and the latter 'cancels' in (1d).

### *Two-period model*

A slightly more formal derivation based on 'peturbation' ideas is as follows (Cochrane 2001). Consider the two-period case for simplicity, with a *time-separable* utility

$$\max U = U(C_t) + E_t[\theta U(C_{t+1})] \tag{2}$$

(Somewhat cavalierly, we have used $U$ on the left-hand side to represent 'total utility' – we could have introduced another symbol here to avoid any confusion with the time $t$ and $t + 1$ utility functions $U(C_t)$ and $U(C_{t+1})$ – but we think no confusion will arise from this.) The constraints are

$$C_t = \tilde{C}_t - P_t N \tag{3a}$$

$$C_{t+1} = \tilde{C}_{t+1} + X_{t+1} N \tag{3b}$$

where $C_t$ = real non-durable consumption plus service consumption from durables
$\quad\ \tilde{C}_t$ = consumption levels before purchase of the asset
$\quad\ P_t$ = price of (any) asset
$\quad\ N$ = number of units of asset purchased
$X_{t+1} \equiv P_{t+1} + D_{t+1} = pay\text{-}off$ at $t + 1$
$\quad\ \theta$ = subjective *discount* factor $(0 < \theta < 1)$

Time separability implies that *marginal* utility in any period does not depend on consumption in other periods. For example, $U = (C_t \cdot C_{t+1})^\delta$ would *not* be time separable-since $\partial U / \partial C_t = \delta C_t^{\delta-1} C_{t+1}^\delta$, marginal utility at $t$ depends on $C_t$ and $C_{t+1}$. Additive separability (over time) implies $U = f(C_t) + \theta f(C_{t+1})$, and this ensures that $\partial U / \partial C_t$ depends only on $C_t$ and not on $C_{t+1}$.

Assume your consumption is optimal and there are no financial assets. We now 'perturb' you so you may now choose some of these assets. This enables us to establish the first-order conditions for equilibrium returns for any asset and any individual. Any asset purchase of $N$ units reduces current consumption by $P_t N$. However, if these $N$ units of the asset each pay-off \$$X_{t+1}$ at $t + 1$, then these additional funds can be used to increase consumption in $t + 1$ from its original level of $\tilde{C}_t$ to $\tilde{C}_{t+1} + X_{t+1} N$.

Using the constraints (3a) and (3b) and maximising (2) with respect to $N$

$$P_t U'(C_t) = E_t[\theta U'(C_{t+1}) X_{t+1}] \tag{4}$$

which can be rearranged to give the key *pricing* relationship for any asset:

$$P_t = E_t(M_{t+1} X_{t+1}) \tag{5}$$

where for the C-CAPM, the *stochastic discount factor* is

$$M_{t+1} = \theta U'(C_{t+1}) / U'(C_t) \tag{6}$$

$M_{t+1}$ is also referred to as the *pricing kernel* and in the C-CAPM it is the *marginal rate of substitution* (MRS) between current and future consumption. The latter is easily seen by taking the total differential of (2) and setting it to zero:

$$dU = U'(C_t) dC_t + \theta U'(C_{t+1}) dC_{t+1} = 0 \tag{7}$$

If lifetime utility $U$ is held constant, this implies

$$\left( \frac{dC_t}{dC_{t+1}} \right) = -\frac{\theta U'(C_{t+1})}{U'(C_t)} \tag{8}$$

The gross return $R^*$ and (net) return $R$ are

$$R^*_{t+1} \equiv 1 + R_{t+1} \equiv X_{t+1}/P_t \tag{9}$$

Hence, from (5), we deduce that returns are determined as

$$1 = E_t[M_{t+1}R^*_{t+1}] \tag{10}$$

which is the result obtained earlier. Note that (5) and (10) apply to any individual, and do not require any special assumptions about utility (apart from additivitive separability and concavity) or any distributional assumptions about returns. Only when we come to implement the model do we then use some of these additional assumptions.

## Risk-Free Rate

What determines changes in the 'risk-free' rate? If a risk-free security is traded, then we can take '$R$' outside of the expectation in (10) so that

$$R^*_{ft} = 1/E_t(M_{t+1}) \tag{11}$$

If a risk-free security is not traded, then $R_f$ in (11) is the 'shadow' risk-free rate (or 'zero-beta' rate). Equation (11) is not particularly intuitive – we need to 'replace' the unobservable SDF in terms of some observable(s). One way to do this is to choose an explicit form for the utility function, and we also assume consumption growth is lognormally distributed.

### *Power utility and lognormal consumption growth*

With power utility, we have

$$U(C_t) = \frac{1}{(1-\gamma)}C_t^{1-\gamma} \tag{12}$$

and note that as $\gamma \to 1$ we have 'log utility', $U(C_t) = \ln(C_t)$. From (6) and (12),

$$M_{t+1} = \theta(C_{t+1}/C_t)^{-\gamma} \tag{13}$$

A standard statistical result is that if $Z$ is lognormal, then $\ln Z \sim N(\mu_{\ln Z}, \sigma^2_{\ln Z})$ and

$$E[kZ] = \exp[k\mu_{\ln Z} + (1/2)k^2\sigma^2_{\ln Z}] \tag{14}$$

where $k$ is a constant. Using (11), (13) and (14), the risk-free rate is given by (see Appendix)

$$R^*_{ft} = \left[\theta\left\{\exp\left[-\gamma E_t \Delta c_{t+1} + \frac{\gamma^2}{2}\sigma_t^2(\Delta c_{t+1})\right]\right\}\right]^{-1} \tag{15}$$

where $\Delta c_{t+1} \equiv \ln(C_{t+1}/C_t)$. Taking logarithms

$$\ln R_{ft}^* = -\ln\theta + \gamma E_t \Delta c_{t+1} - \frac{\gamma^2}{2}\sigma_t^2(\Delta c_{t+1}) \tag{16}$$

Note that $\ln R_{ft}^* = \ln(1 + R_f) \approx R_f$. (In continuous time where $\Delta c \equiv dC/C$, the last term in (16), disappears.) From (16), we can deduce the following relationship between consumption growth and the risk-free rate:

(a) Real interest rates are high when expected consumption growth is high. High real interest rates are required to lower consumption today in order to save today and then increase consumption tomorrow.

(b) Real interest rates are high when $\theta$ is low (for given $E_t \Delta c_{t+1}$). When people are impatient and discount future consumption heavily, high real interest rates are required to encourage saving (and hence additional consumption tomorrow, $E_t \Delta c_{t+1}$).

(c) Suppose consumption growth is expected to be highly volatile (for any given *expected* level of consumption growth). Then you lose more utility as consumption falls than you gain utility, from an equal rise in consumption. (This is the curvature of the utility function and diminishing marginal utility.) Hence, with higher volatility of consumption, people want to save more and real interest rates are driven lower. This is a form of precautionary saving.

(d) If $\gamma = 0$ (i.e. linear utility function and hence no risk aversion), then the real rate is constant and equal to the subjective discount factor, $\theta$.

(e) As the curvature $\gamma$ of the (power) utility function increases, the real rate is more responsive to consumption growth. For example, higher expected consumption growth now requires a higher real interest rate, because a high $\gamma$ implies less willingness to deviate from a smooth consumption path over time.

Note that in equation (16), consumption is endogenous, so we could also interpret our 'correlations' in the opposite direction. For example, high interest rates lead to high saving at $t$ and hence higher consumption at $t + 1$ and hence high consumption growth.

## Returns on Risky Assets

We now turn to the return and price of *risky* assets in the stochastic discount factor model. What determines the movement in asset returns over time and what determines the average return on risky asset $i$, relative to that on risky asset $j$? The key determinant of both these effects is the size of the *covariance* between the stochastic discount factor $M_{t+1}$ and the asset return. The C-CAPM in terms of returns for any risky asset $i$ is (where we drop some time subscripts for notational ease):

$$1 = E_t(MR_i^*) \tag{17}$$

For any two random variables $x$ and $y$,

$$E(xy) = \text{cov}(x, y) + (Ex)(Ey) \tag{18}$$

hence using (17) and (18):

$$1 = E_t(M)E_t(R_i^*) + \text{cov}_t(M, R_i^*) \tag{19}$$

$$E_t(R_i^*) = \frac{1}{E_t(M)}[1 - \text{cov}_t(R_i^*, M)] \tag{20}$$

Using $R_f^* = 1/E_t(M) = U'(C_t)/\theta E_t U'(C_{t+1})$ in (20) and noting that $\text{cov}_t(M, R_i^*) = \theta \, \text{cov}_t[U'(C_{t+1}), R_i^*]/U'(C_t)$, we obtain a key equation that determines the *excess* return on any risky asset $i$:

$$(E_t R_i^* - R_f^*)_{t+1} = -R_f^* \text{cov}_t(M, R_i^*) = -\frac{\text{cov}_t[U'(C_{t+1}), R_{i,t+1}^*]}{E_t[U'(C_{t+1})]} \tag{21}$$

Note that '$C_{t+1}$' now appears in the numerator and denominator. The relative (expected excess) return of two assets $i$ and $j$ differ only because the covariance of $R_i$ or $R_j$ with (the marginal utility of) consumption is different. An asset whose return has a negative covariance with $U'(C_{t+1})$ and hence a positive covariance with $C_{t+1}$ will have to offer a high expected return, in order that investors are willing to hold the asset. This is because the asset pays off when consumption is high, and consumers are already 'feeling good' and so the higher return gives them little additional utility. Conversely, asset returns that co-vary negatively with consumption (i.e. positively with $U'(C_{t+1})$) provide insurance and will be willingly held, even if they promise a low expected return.

If we assume joint lognormality of consumption growth and asset returns, it can be shown (see Appendix) that excess returns are given by

$$E_t(r_{i,t+1}^* - r_{ft}^*) + (1/2)\sigma_t^2(r_{i,t+1}^*) = -\text{cov}_t(m_{t+1}, r_{i,t+1}^*)$$

where $r_{i,t+1}^* = \ln R_{i,t+1}^*$, and so on. The second term is the Jensen effect and the covariance term is the risk premium.

## 13.2 C-CAPM and the 'Standard' CAPM

The FOCs (5) or (10) of the SDF model hold for *any individual* with any utility function that is time-separable and depends only on consumption. If we now assume a representative agent (i.e. agents all have the same utility function), then the FOC can be interpreted as an equation that determines *equilibrium* expected returns, and the FOCs represent the *consumption-CAPM* (C-CAPM). Using $R^* = 1 + R$ in (21), we have

$$E_t R_{i,t+1} - R_{f,t} = \frac{-\text{cov}_t\{U'(C_{t+1}), R_{i,t+1}\}}{E_t\{U'(C_{t+1})\}} \tag{22}$$

What is the relationship between the standard-CAPM and the C-CAPM? The standard-CAPM can be derived from the C-CAPM, if the return on the market portfolio $R_{m,t+1}$ of all risky assets is *perfectly correlated* with the marginal utility of consumption at $t+1$, $U'(C_{t+1})$ (which implies perfect conditional correlation with $M_{t+1}$). The market portfolio is also sometimes referred to as the *wealth portfolio*, since with no labour income, it comprises all your wealth. A perfect *linear* relationship between $U'_{t+1}$ *and* $R_m$ which, simplifying the notation a little, is:

$$U'_{t+1} = a + bR_m \tag{23}$$

where we have used the subscript m to denote the optimal portfolio from the mean-variance model. It follows from (23) that

$$\text{cov}_t\{U'_{t+1}, R_i\} = b\,\text{cov}(R_i, R_m) \tag{24a}$$

$$\text{cov}_t\{U'_{t+1}, R_m\} = b\,\text{var}(R_m) \tag{24b}$$

$$\text{var}_t(U'_{t+1}) = b^2\,\text{var}(R_m) \tag{24c}$$

therefore

$$\rho(U'_{t+1}, R_m) = \frac{\text{cov}_t(U'_{t+1}, R_m)}{\sqrt{\text{var}(U'_{t+1})}\sqrt{\text{var}(R_m)}} = 1 \tag{24d}$$

Applying (22) to the market portfolio (i.e. replacing $R_i$ by $R_m$) and rearranging,

$$\frac{1}{E_t\{U'(C_{t+1})\}} = \frac{-(E_t R_m - R_f)}{\text{cov}_t\{U'_{t+1}, R_m\}} \tag{25}$$

Substituting for $E_t[U'(C_{t+1})]$ from (25) in (22), then using (24a) and (24b), we obtain the standard-CAPM

$$E_t(R_i - R_f) = \beta_t E_t(R_m - R_f) \tag{26a}$$

where

$$\beta_t = \frac{\text{cov}_t(R_i, R_m)}{\text{var}_t(R_m)} \tag{26b}$$

Hence, the standard-CAPM can be derived from the C-CAPM and we have not had to assume any particular distribution of asset returns. However, we have had to make the possibly unrealistic assumption that the marginal utility of consumption is perfectly negatively (conditionally) correlated with the return on the market portfolio – so we have gained a somewhat Pyrrhic victory here. All we have demonstrated is the link between the C-CAPM and the standard-CAPM and shown that they are unlikely in general to be consistent with each other. For example, if utility is quadratic, then marginal utility *is* linear in consumption, and our assumption then implies a perfect conditional correlation between $C_{t+1}$ and $R_{m,t+1}$, but this is unlikely to hold in the data! Finally, note that all of the above results hold if we had assumed that the SDF $M_{t+1} = a_t + b_t R_{m,t+1}$. This is the case since the denominator in $M_{t+1}$ is $U'(C_t)$, and this is non-stochastic (conditional on expectations formed at time $t$), and the time-varying $\{a_t, b_t\}$ are also known at time $t$.

It can be shown that the linear relationship $M_{t+1} = a_t + b_t R_{m,t+1}$ can be derived under the following assumptions (Cochrane 2001):

1. two-period *quadratic* utility in $C_t$ and $C_{t+1}$

2. one-period exponential utility and multivariate normal returns

3. log utility and normally distributed returns

4. infinite-horizon time-separable quadratic utility and *iid* returns

Note that none of the above allow for any labour income in the maximisation problem, and cases (1) and (2) result in a *conditional*-CAPM since $a_t$ and $b_t$ depend on variables at time $t$ (e.g. $C_t$, $R_{m,t}$).

## Two-Period Problem

Take the simplest case of two-period quadratic utility

$$\max\{-\tfrac{1}{2}(C_t - C)^2 - \tfrac{1}{2}\theta E_t(C_{t+1} - C)^2\}$$

Subject to

$$C_{t+1} = W_{t+1} = R_{m,t+1}(W_t - C_t)$$

$$R_{m,t+1} = \sum_{i=1}^{n} \alpha_i R_{i,t+1} \qquad \sum_{i=1}^{n} \alpha_i = 1$$

where $R_{m,t+1}$ represents the *gross* return (for compatibility with Chapter 15), $C = $ a constant and the budget constraint indicates that the 'market portfolio' is the return on wealth $W_t$ (which is exogenously given). The investor chooses $C_t$, $C_{t+1}$ and $\alpha_i$, the portfolio weights in $n$ assets. The SDF is

$$M_{t+1} = \frac{\theta U'(C_{t+1})}{U'(C_t)} = \frac{\theta(C_{t+1} - C)}{(C_t - C)}$$

Substituting from the budget constraint for $C_{t+1}$ gives

$$M_{t+1} = \frac{-\theta C}{(C_t - C)} + \frac{\theta(W_t - C_t)}{(C_t - C)} R_{m,t+1}$$

So, $M_{t+1}$ is a linear function of $R_{m,t+1}$ (conditional on $W_t$ and $C_t$).

Take the second case above. We have already derived asset demand functions assuming one-period negative exponential utility and multivariate normality in Chapter 1 and here $C_{t+1} = W_{t+1}$ so $U(W_{t+1}) = -e^{-bW_{t+1}} = e^{-bC_{t+1}}$. The budget constraint is $W_{t+1} = C_{t+1} = A_f R_f + A'R_{t+1}$, where $R_{t+1}$ is the vector of risky-asset returns and $W_t = A_f + A'e$. The optimal *dollar* amount held in the risky assets $A = (A_1, A_2, \ldots, A_n)$ is given by

$$A = b^{-1}\Sigma^{-1}[E(R) - R_f e]$$

where $\Sigma$ = (conditional) variance–covariance matrix of the $n$ risky asset returns, $R$, $b$ is the CARA coefficient and $e$ is a vector of ones. Notice that $A$ are the *dollar* amounts held in the risky assets, which are independent of wealth. (The dollar demand for the risk-free asset is $A_f = W_t - \sum_{i=1}^{n} A_i$.) If all investors are 'identical', then

$$ER - R_f e = b\Sigma A = b\operatorname{cov}(R, R_m)$$

where $\Sigma A$ gives the covariance of each return with $R_m = A'R + A_f R_f$ and hence the covariance with the investors overall *portfolio* return. Therefore, with negative exponential utility in end-of-period wealth $W_{t+1}$ (or $C_{t+1}$), the C-CAPM gives the standard-CAPM because consumption is again replaced by the market (wealth) portfolio.

## Multi-Period Problem

Case 'three' above assumes log utility, $U(C) = \ln C$. In Chapter 15, we show that in an intertemporal consumption-portfolio model, log utility gives optimal consumption proportional to wealth (assuming no stochastic labour income). Therefore, the return on the wealth portfolio is proportional to consumption growth and the SDF, $M$ is linear in the return on the wealth portfolio. Log utility is another special case, where income and substitution effects of a change in expected returns just offset each other, so that $C/W$ is independent of returns.

Finally, let us consider the fourth case above. As we shall see in the next few chapters, the concept of a value function $V(\cdot)$ allows you to reformulate a multi-period optimisation problem as a two-period problem since

$$V(W_t) = \max_{(C_t,\alpha_t)} \left\{ U(C_t) + \theta E_t \left[ \max_{C_{t+1},C_{t+2}\dots}^{\alpha_{t+1},\alpha_{t+2}\dots} E_{t+1} \sum_{j=0}^{\infty} \theta^j U(C_{t+j+1}) \right] \right\}$$

can be written

$$V(W_t) = \max_{(C_t,\alpha_t)} \{U(C_t) + \theta E_t V(W_{t+1})\}$$

where $V(\cdot)$ is the value function and 'represents' the utility to be derived from the *optimal* consumption $(C_{t+1}, C_{t+2}, \ldots)$ in all future periods. To emphasise this point, note that the value function $V(W_{t+1}) = V[R_{m,t+1}(W_t - \tilde{C}_t)]$, where $\tilde{C}_t$ is the *optimum* level of consumption (from solving the FOC). So, the value function $V(W_t)$ is the achieved level of expected utility, if you invest your wealth optimally, and is a function of wealth because the higher the wealth, the more happiness you can potentially achieve. $V(\cdot)$ may also be a function of other variables, and we discuss this possibility below and in later chapters.

These equations 'tell the same story' mathematically. The first says you maximise discounted lifetime utility and have to consider (for example) the marginal utility gain from an extra pizza today against the loss in utility from not being able to consume an extra bottle of wine in, say, 10 years time. But the interpretation of the second equation is more appealing. You evaluate the increase in marginal utility from, say, a holiday *today* in terms of its expected impact on the marginal utility you expect to lose from the fall in *wealth* next period $V'(W_{t+1})$ (rather than the effect on, say, $U'(C_{t+j})$, $j =$

1, 2, 3, ... which is the marginal utility loss from lower consumption in all future periods – for example, not going to the cinema every week for the next four years or more). It can be shown that if returns are *iid*, then maximising intertemporal *quadratic utility* in consumption subject to the budget constraint $W_{t+1} = R_{m,t+1}(W_t - C_t)$ gives a FOC similar to that for the two-period case

$$P_t U'(C_t) = \theta E_t[V'(W_{t+1})X_{t+1}] \quad \text{or} \quad E_t(M_{t+1}R_{m,t+1}) = 1$$

where

$$M_{t+1} = \theta \frac{V'(W_{t+1})}{U'(C_t)} = \theta \frac{V'(W_{t+1})}{V'(W_t)}$$

$V(.)$ is the value function and $U'(C_t) = V'(W_t)$ is the envelope condition. Note that $U'(C_t) = V'(W_t)$ because *at the optimum*, the extra marginal utility from consumption today must equal the marginal utility from any change in wealth. We discuss the value function extensively in Chapter 15, but for now note that if the intertemporal utility function in *consumption* is quadratic (i.e. depends on $(C_{t+j} - C)^2$ terms), then the *value function* is quadratic in *wealth*, given the budget constraint (with no labour income) and assuming *iid* returns. However, in general, it is *not true* that any (acceptable) functional form for utility (e.g. power) gives rise to the value function $V(W_t)$ having the same functional form. Hence, if this 'mysterious' value function is *quadratic* in wealth,

$$V(W_{t+1}) = -(\phi/2)(W_{t+1} - W)^2$$
$$M_{t+1} = \frac{-\theta\phi(W_{t+1} - W)}{U'(C_t)} = -\theta\phi \frac{R_{m,t+1}(W_t - C_t) - W}{U'(C_t)}$$

So $M_{t+1}$ is linear in $R_{m,t+1}$ (conditional on $C_t$ and $W_t$). Notice that in order to obtain $M_{t+1}$ linearly related to $R_{m,t+1}$, the value function must only contain the wealth variable. If the *marginal* value of wealth depends on other variables (e.g. $Z$ = cumulative recent losses on risky assets), then we have $V'(W_{t+1}, Z_{t+1})$ and $M_{t+1} = f(R_{m,t+1}, Z_{t+1})$, and the one-factor 'standard-CAPM' would no longer hold. We investigate value functions that contain wealth and other variables in Chapters 14 and 15.

Note that in the above multi-period problem we assumed quadratic utility, which is restrictive but, nevertheless, may be a reasonable *approximation* for small changes (i.e. second-order Taylor series expansion). Why do we need the *iid* assumption to be able to write $V(W_{t+1})$ as a function of wealth only? At time $t = 0$, the investor chooses $(C_0, C_1, C_2, \ldots, C_t, \ldots)$ and asset shares $(\alpha_0, \alpha_1, \ldots, \alpha_t, \ldots)$ in order to maximise

$$V(W_t) \equiv E_t \sum_{j=0}^{\infty} \theta^j U(C_{t+j})$$

subject to

$$W_{t+1} = R_{m,t+1}(W_t - C_t) \qquad R_{m,t+1} = \alpha_t' R_{t+1} \qquad \alpha' e = 1$$

where $e$ = vector of ones, $\boldsymbol{R}_t = (R_1, R_2, \ldots R_N, R_f)'$. Note that there is no labour income in the budget constraint. If risky-asset returns are not *iid* (and the risk-free rate is not constant), then the optimal portfolio shares in risky assets $\alpha_{0t} = (\alpha_{01}, \alpha_{02}, \ldots, \alpha_{0n})$ may depend on some variable that helps forecast future returns, $R_{t+1}, R_{t+2}, \ldots$. For example, if a low dividend–price ratio $(D/P)$ *today* has predictive power for future returns, then the value function depends not only on wealth but also on the dividend–price ratio $V(W_t, (D/P)_t)$. This is why we need the *iid* assumption as well as quadratic utility in order that $M_{t+1}$ is linearly related to $R_{m,t+1}$. Then, the SDF intertemporal consumption-portfolio model collapses to the standard-CAPM. In Chapters 14 to 16, we analyse portfolio problems in which there are 'state variables' other than wealth, in the value function.

It is now possible to see the limitations of the standard–CAPM. The CAPM assumes that investors are only concerned about their investment portfolio *in isolation* and not how the returns on that portfolio might be linked with the wider economy, such as income levels. For example, other things equal, one might expect that investors would hold an asset with a low expected return if it paid off in recession periods (i.e. the asset return and output were negatively correlated). The C-CAPM picks up such a negative correlation via consumption growth. However, there may be variables other than consumption that influence the individual's utility, and this gives rise to factor models (see below). That is enough of a 'trailer' for what is to come in later chapters, so let us now return to the further implications of the SDF model for prices and then move on to factor models.

## 13.3  Prices and Covariance

An equivalent analysis to the above can be conducted in terms of prices rather than returns. We then find that prices depend on the expected pay-off plus a 'risk premium', which is determined by the covariance between $M_{t+1}$ and the random pay-off $X_{t+1}$.

Using (18) in $P_t = E_t(MX)$ and substituting $R_f^* = 1/E(M)$

$$P_t = \frac{E_t(X_{t+1})}{R_f^*} + \text{cov}_t(M_{t+1}, X_{t+1}) \tag{27a}$$

which after incorporating the definition of $M_{t+1}$ gives

$$P_t = \frac{E_t(X_{t+1})}{R_f^*} + \frac{\text{cov}_t[\theta U'(C_{t+1}), X_{t+1}]}{U'(C_t)} \tag{27b}$$

If there is no risk aversion (i.e. utility is linear in consumption) or if consumption is constant, then the usual 'risk-neutral' formula applies:

$$P_t = \frac{E_t(X_{t+1})}{R_f^*} \tag{28}$$

So under risk-neutrality, the price of a risky asset is the expected present value of its pay-off $X_{t+1}$ discounted using the *risk-free* rate. Under risk aversion, (27) applies, and the second term in (27a) or (27b) is a *risk adjustment*. For example, this is positive for a positive covariance. If the pay-off $X_{t+1}$ is high when marginal utility is high (i.e. consumption is low), then the asset will have a high *current* price. The latter implies, *for a given* $E_t(X_{t+1})$, a low expected return (between $t$ and $t + 1$). So, (27b) is consistent with (28). Basically, you are willing to pay more for an asset than the expected pay-off discounted at the risk-free rate, if the asset has a high pay-off $X_{t+1}$ when marginal utility is high. This is the insurance principle again.

The relationship between returns and prices used above sometimes appears paradoxical. But think about it. Since $R^*_{t+1} \equiv X_{t+1}/P_t$, then a low price *today*, with a fixed cash flow $X_{t+1}$ payable at $t + 1$, must imply a high return $R^*_{t+1}$.

## 13.4    Rational Valuation Formula and SDF

We can derive the Rational Valuation Formula for any asset, using the SDF equilibrium condition

$$E_t(R^*_{t+1}M_{t+1}) = 1 \tag{29}$$

and the definition

$$R^*_{t+1} \equiv (V_{t+1} + D_{t+1})/V_t \tag{30}$$

We then obtain

$$V_t = E_t(M_{t+1}[V_{t+1} + D_{t+1}]) \tag{31}$$

Repeated forward substitution then yields (assuming the transversality condition holds)

$$V_t = E_t \sum_{j=1}^{\infty} M_{t,t+j}D_{t+j} \quad \text{where} \quad M_{t,t+j} = M_{t+1} \, M_{t+2} \cdots M_{t+j} \tag{32}$$

$M_{t,t+j}$ is a possibly time-varying *stochastic discount factor*. Again, using (18), we can replace the $E(xy)$ term in (32) to give

$$P_t = \sum_{j=1}^{\infty} \frac{E_t D_{t+1}}{R^*_{f,t+j}} + \sum_{j=1}^{\infty} \text{cov}_t(D_{t+j}, M_{t,t+j}) \tag{33}$$

where $1/R^*_{f,t+j} \equiv E_t(M_{t,t+j})$ is the $j$-period risk-free interest rate. Again, those assets whose dividends have a negative covariance with marginal utility (and positive covariance with consumption) have lower prices – and hence command a higher return (for a given expected dividend stream).

## 13.5    Factor Models

Factor models assume that the SDF depends linearly on a set of $n$ factors $f_{i,t}$.

$$M_{t+1} = \sum_{i=1}^{n} b_{i,t} f_{i,t+1}$$

The linearity assumption could be explicitly derived (e.g. from two-period quadratic utility in consumption, where consumption is the factor) or can be viewed as a Taylor series approximation of a non-linear relationship. Also, if marginal utility contains other state variables $U_c(C_t, Z_t)$, then the $Z_t$ may also be related to the factors.

## Conditional and Unconditional Models

We have seen above that, in general, the coefficients $\{a_t, b_t\}$ may be time-varying, and for the standard-CAPM (i.e. one-factor model with the factor $f_{t+1} = R_{m,t+1}$)

$$M_{t+1} = a_t + b_t R^*_{m,t+1}$$

where $R^*_{m,t+1}$ is the gross return on the 'market' or 'wealth' portfolio (of all assets). Using $E_t[R^*_{i,t+1} M_{t+1}] = 1$, the *conditional* model is

$$1 = E_t[(a_t + b_t R^*_{m,t+1}) R^*_{i,t+1}]$$

Taking *unconditional* expectations

$$1 = E(a_t R^*_{i,t+1}) + E[b_t(R^*_{m,t+1} R^*_{i,t+1})]$$

Using $E(xy) = (Ex)(Ey) + \text{cov}(x, y)$, we have

$$1 = E(a_t)E(R^*_{i,t+1}) + \text{cov}(a_t, R^*_{i,t+1}) + E(b_t)E(R^*_{m,t+1} R^*_{i,t+1}) + \text{cov}(b_t, R^*_{m,t+1} R^*_{i,t+1})$$

Hence, the *conditional*-CAPM does not imply an unconditional-CAPM, that is,

$$1 \neq E[\{E(a_t) + E(b_t)R^*_{m,t+1}\}R^*_{i,t+1}]$$

unless the covariance terms are zero, which, in general, they are not (e.g. for quadratic utility $a_t$ and $b_t$ depend on $C_t$, and the latter may not be uncorrelated with $R^*_{i,t+1}$ or $R^*_{m,t+1}$). Of course, if $a$ and $b$ are constant over time, then the *conditional* model *does* imply that the *unconditional* model holds, since

$$1 = E_t[(a + bR^*_{m,t+1}) R^*_{i,t+1}]$$

implies

$$1 = E[(a + bR^*_{m,t+1}) R^*_{i,t+1}]$$

One problem in implementing the factor model is that we would like the coefficients $a_t$ and $b_t$ to be constant because then the Euler equation can be estimated using a constant coefficient GMM approach

$$E[(a + bf_{t+1})R^*_{i,t+1}] = 1$$

One 'trick' to mitigate this problem is to assume that $\{a_t, b_t\}$ depend on a set of variables $z_t$ observable at time $t$, (e.g. dividend–price ratio) so that

$$M_{t+1} = a(z_t) + b(z_t) f_{t+1}$$

If $a$ and $b$ are *linear* in $z_t$, then

$$M_{t+1} = a_0 + a_1 z_t + b_0 f_{t+1} + b_1 (z_t f_{t+1})$$

and instead of a one-factor model with time-varying coefficients, we now have a three-factor model, but with fixed (constant) coefficients, and we can apply standard GMM regression techniques. In practice, we might include several $z$ variables, and the model would then have cross-product terms between all the $z$'s and all the factors $f_{jt}$.

The so-called latent factor literature assumes that unobserved processes can be specified for the factors, while a more common approach is to choose a small number of explicit variables that are thought to influence future consumption (e.g. output growth, inflation). Another strand in this literature assumes that $f_i$ are 'factor mimicking portfolios' that pick up systematic sources of risk (e.g. the Fama–French three-factor model can be interpreted in this way). One rationale for using factor mimicking portfolios is the fact that consumption (the 'correct' variable in the C-CAPM) is measured with error, and the chosen factors might better measure variables that influence current and future consumption. However, the scope for 'fishing' expeditions and data mining are considerable in this area. Also, if investors use conditioning information that is omitted by the econometrician, then it is obvious that testing the underlying C-CAPM is fraught with difficulties of interpretation and one can always claim that rejection of the conditional C-CAPM is due to 'unobservable' factors (Hansen and Richard 1987).

If we view these factor models as special cases of the C-CAPM, then excess returns on risky assets are determined by all the covariances of the factors with the asset return. They are also *common* factors – any factor that determines the return on asset $i$ should also influence the expected return of asset $j$. Of course, the standard-CAPM can be viewed as a factor model, where the single factor is the return on the market portfolio.

## 13.6  Summary

- In the SDF model, the key equations for the risk-free return, the return on any risky asset $i$ and the price of any risky asset, which apply for *any individual*, are

$$R_{ft}^* = 1 / E_t(M_{t+1})$$

$$1 = E_t(R_{i,t+1}^* M_{t+1})$$

$$P_{it} = E_t(X_{i,t+1} M_{t+1})$$

where $M_{t+1}$ is the stochastic discount factor. For the C-CAPM, $M_{t+1} = \theta U'(C_{t+1})/U(C_t)$. Adding the representative agent assumption implies the above equations determine *equilibrium* returns.

- In the C-CAPM, the risk premium depends on the (conditional) *covariance* between the asset return $i$ and the SDF. The risk premium may be time-varying.

- In the C-CAPM, with power utility and under joint lognormality of consumption growth and asset returns, the risk premium for asset $i$ depends on the conditional *covariance* between observable consumption *growth* and the return on asset $i$. Also the (real) rate of interest is negatively related to the conditional variance of consumption (the precautionary savings effect) and positively related to the expected growth in consumption.

- The C-CAPM implies that asset *prices* depend on expected dividends and future stochastic discount factors, $M_{t,t+j}$.

- The standard-CAPM can be viewed as a special case of the C-CAPM, where there is perfect correlation between the SDF, $M_{t+1}$ and the market return $R_m$. However, there is no reason why this assumption should hold in general, although it could be seen as a first-order Taylor series approximation of a non-linear relationship or explicitly derived under restrictive assumptions (e.g. two-period quadratic utility).

- Factor models assume that the MRS, $M_{t+1}$ depends linearly on a set of factors (which may be more accurately measured than consumption). This allows expected returns to depend on all the *conditional* covariances between the factors and the asset return.

- As Cochrane (2001) makes clear, the C-CAPM *as represented in the above three equations* does *not* assume normally distributed returns, *iid* returns, two-period investors, quadratic utility or the absence of labour income. Of course, to make the model more tractable or interesting, we may invoke some of these latter assumptions.

# Appendix: Joint Lognormality and Power Utility

Joint lognormality is a frequently used simplifying assumption in SDF models. Here, we show how it can be used to obtain more tractable and intuitive results for risky-asset returns and the risk-free rate.

## A. Joint Lognormality

**To show:**
When the stochastic discount factor $M_{t+1}$ and the gross return on *any* asset $R^*_{t+1}$ are *jointly lognormal*, then

$$E_t(M_{t+1}R^*_{t+1}) = 1 \tag{A1}$$

implies the equilibrium no-arbitrage condition

$$E_t(\ln R^*_{t+1} - \ln R^*_{ft}) + \tfrac{1}{2}\sigma_t^2(\ln R^*_{t+1}) = -\operatorname{cov}_t(\ln M_{t+1}, \ln R^*_{t+1}) \tag{A2a}$$

or

$$E_t(r^*_{t+1} - r^*_{ft}) + (1/2)\sigma_t^2(r^*_{t+1}) = -\operatorname{cov}_t(m_{t+1}, r^*_{t+1}) \tag{A2b}$$

where lower-case letters are logarithms and $\sigma^2(r_{t+1}^*)$ is the Jensen effect and the covariance term is the risk premium. Thus, the expected excess return on any risky asset depends (negatively) on the *covariance* between the stochastic discount factor and the asset's return.

**Proof :**

Let $\ln X \sim N(\mu, \sigma^2)$, where $\mu = E(\ln X)$ and $\sigma^2$ is the variance of '$\ln X$'. Hence, $X$ is lognormal and a standard result is

$$E(X) = e^{(\mu + \sigma^2/2)} \equiv e^{E(\ln X) + \sigma^2(\ln X)/2} \tag{A3}$$

where $\sigma^2(\ln X)$ is the variance of '$\ln X$'. From (A3), taking logarithms,

$$\ln E(X) = E(\ln X) + \sigma^2(\ln X)/2 \tag{A4}$$

Let $X = (M_{t+1} R_{t+1}^*)$, then from (A4) and (A1), taking conditional expectations,

$$\ln E_t[M_{t+1} R_{t+1}^*] = E_t[\ln(M_{t+1} R_{t+1}^*)] + \sigma_t^2(\ln[M_{t+1} R_{t+1}^*])/2 = 0 \tag{A5a}$$

hence

$$E_t(m_{t+1}) + E_t(r_{t+1}^*) + \sigma_t^2(m_{t+1})/2 + \sigma_t^2(r_{t+1}^*)/2 + \text{cov}_t(m_{t+1}, r_{t+1}^*) = 0 \tag{A5b}$$

When $R^*$ is the non-stochastic risk-free rate,

$$E_t(r_{t+1}^*) = r_{ft}^*$$

$$\sigma_t^2(r_{ft}^*) = \text{cov}(m_{t+1}, r_{ft}^*) = 0$$

Equation (A5b) gives an equation for the risk-free rate:

$$E_t(m_{t+1}) + r_{ft}^* + \tfrac{1}{2}\sigma_t^2(m_{t+1}) = 0 \tag{A6}$$

or,

$$r_{ft}^* = -E_t(m_{t+1}) - (1/2)\sigma_t^2(m_{t+1})$$

Subtracting (A6) from (A5b) then gives the required equilibrium no-arbitrage condition (A2a) or (A2b) for any risky asset $i$ under the lognormality assumption:

$$E_t(r_{t+1}^* - r_{ft}^*) + (1/2)\sigma_t^2(r_{t+1}^*) = -\text{cov}_t(m_{t+1}, r_{t+1}^*) \tag{A2b}$$

Note that if $m_{t+1}$ and $r_{t+1}^*$ are conditionally homoscedastic so that $\text{var}_t(x) = E_t(x - E_t x)^2 = \text{var}(x - E_t x)^2$, we can drop the $t$ subscripts on the variance and covariance terms (but not on $E_t(r_{t+1}^* - r_{ft}^*)$). Comparing (A2) with the no-arbitrage equation *without* assuming lognormality (see equation (21)), that is,

$$E_t R_{t+1}^* - R_{ft}^* = -R_{ft}^* \text{cov}_t(M_{t+1}, R_{t+1}^*) \tag{A7}$$

the key qualitative difference is the additional term in (A2) of $(1/2)\sigma^2(r^*_{t+1})$, which is the Jensen inequality term (JIT). It arises from taking expectations of a non-linear function since $E[f(x)] \neq f[E(x)]$ unless $f(x)$ is linear.

## B. Lognormality Plus Power Utility

We now incorporate the assumption of power utility and derive equations for the expected return on the risk-free asset and for any risky asset. With power utility, we have

$$M_{t+1} = \theta(C_{t+1}/C_t)^{-\gamma} \tag{A8}$$

$$m_{t+1} = \ln\theta - \gamma\Delta c_{t+1} \tag{A9}$$

The condition variance is

$$\sigma_t^2(m_{t+1}) = \gamma^2\sigma_t^2(\Delta c_{t+1}) \tag{A10}$$

Substituting (A9) and (A10) in (A6), the equilibrium *risk-free rate* under lognormality and power utility is

$$r_{ft}^* = -\ln\theta + \gamma E_t(\Delta c_{t+1}) - \frac{\gamma^2}{2}\sigma_t^2(\Delta c_{t+1}) \tag{A11}$$

which is equation (16) in the text. Turning now to the *risky-asset return*, from the definition of conditional covariance and using (A9), we have

$$\text{cov}_t(m_{t+1}, r^*_{t+1}) \equiv E_t[(m_{t+1} - E_t m_{t+1})(r^*_{t+1} - E_t r^*_{t+1})] = -\gamma\,\text{cov}_t(\Delta c_{t+1}, r^*_{t+1}) \tag{A12}$$

The *unobservable* covariance in the left-hand side of (A12) is now represented by the *observable* covariance between consumption *growth* and the asset return (scaled by $\gamma$, the coefficient of relative risk aversion or inverse of the intertemporal elasticity of substitution). We are nearly there. Taking (A2b)

$$E_t(r^*_{t+1} - r_{ft}^*) + (1/2)\sigma_t^2(r^*_{t+1}) = -\text{cov}_t(m_{t+1}, r^*_{t+1}) = \gamma\,\text{cov}_t(\Delta c_{t+1}, r^*_{t+1}) \tag{A2b}$$

and using the approximations $r^*_{t+1} \equiv \ln R^*_{t+1} \approx R_{t+1}$ and $\sigma_t^2(r^*_{t+1}) \approx \sigma_t^2(R_{t+1})$ and $\text{cov}_t(\Delta c_{t+1}, r^*_{t+1}) \approx \text{cov}_t(\Delta C_{t+1}/C_t, R_{t+1})$, we have the *approximation* that under lognormality and power utility

$$E_t(R_{t+1} - R_{f,t}) + \tfrac{1}{2}\sigma_t^2(R_{t+1}) = \gamma\,\text{cov}_t(\Delta C_{t+1}/C_t, R_{t+1}) \tag{A13}$$

The second term is the Jensen effect, and the risk premium depends on the conditional covariance between consumption *growth* and the return on the risky asset. The higher the covariance between consumption growth and the return on the risky asset, the higher the expected return on the risky asset will be, if agents are willingly to hold this asset. But if we consider the log of the expected ratio of gross returns, we eliminate the need for the Jensen inequality term since

$$\ln\{E_t(R^*_{t+1}/R^*_{f,t})\} = \gamma \operatorname{cov}_t(\Delta c_{t+1}, R_{t+1}) \qquad (A14)$$

Covariances are 'king' in stochastic discount factor models, since they determine conditional expected returns on risky assets or portfolios of risky assets.

# 14

# C-CAPM: EVIDENCE AND EXTENSIONS

## Aims

- Determine whether the C-CAPM fits the stylised facts of near non-predictability of stock returns over short horizons, yet stronger predictability over longer horizons.

- Examine whether the C-CAPM fits the stylised facts of a high average equity risk premium for aggregate stock returns and a low mean value and volatility of the risk-free rate. These two stylised facts constitute the so-called *equity premium puzzle* and the *risk-free rate puzzle.*

- To see if estimates of the Euler equations/FOCs of the C-CAPM give 'reasonable' parameter estimates for the degree of risk aversion.

- Analyse whether more general (i.e. non-separable) utility functions that contain additional state variables such as wealth, or past consumption, improve the empirical performance of the stochastic discount factor (SDF) model.

## 14.1  Should Returns be Predictable in the C-CAPM?

Is the stochastic discount factor (SDF) model consistent with the stylised fact that returns over short horizons (e.g. intraday, over one day, or one week) are virtually unpredictable and hence price follows a martingale process? Remember that $P_t$ is a *martingale*, if

$$P_t = E_t P_{t+1} \quad \text{or} \quad P_{t+1} = P_t + \varepsilon_{t+1} \tag{1}$$

where $E_t \varepsilon_{t+1} = 0$ and $\varepsilon_{t+1}$ is independent of $P_t$. For a martingale, the return (with zero dividends) is $E_t P_{t+1}/P_t = 1$, a constant, and if in addition $\varepsilon_t$ is *iid*, then prices follow a *random walk*. The first-order condition for the SDF model is

$$P_t U'(C_t) = E_t[\theta U'(C_{t+1})(P_{t+1} + D_{t+1})] \tag{2}$$

Hence, the SDF model implies $P$ is a martingale if

(a) investors are risk-neutral (i.e. $U(C)$ is linear so $U'(C) = $ constant) *and*

(b) no dividends are paid between $t$ and $t+1$ *and*

(c) $\theta$ is close to 1

The C-CAPM is consistent with the stylised facts of near unpredictability of intra-day and daily stock, bond and spot-FX price changes, since the above assumptions (a)–(c) are not unreasonable over short horizons. Of course, if daily price changes are definitely unpredictable, this would invalidate 'technical analysis' (e.g. chartism, candlesticks, neural networks) as a method of making money (corrected for risk and transactions costs).

## Longer Horizons

Long-horizon stock returns (e.g. over one- to five-year horizons) appear to exhibit some predictability (although the relationships uncovered are not necessarily stable over different time periods). Is the C-CAPM consistent with this stylised fact? In terms of returns, the C-CAPM for any risky-asset return $R$ gives

$$E_t R_{t+1}^* - R_{f,t}^* = \frac{-\operatorname{cov}_t(M_{t+1}, R_{t+1}^*)}{E_t(M_{t+1})} = -\left[\frac{\sigma_t(M_{t+1})}{E_t(M_{t+1})}\right]\sigma_t(R_{t+1}^*)\rho_t(M_{t+1}, R_{t+1}^*) \tag{3}$$

where $R_{t+1}^* \equiv (1 + R_{t+1})$, and so on. If we now assume (for simplicity) power utility and lognormal consumption growth, then

$$E_t R_{t+1}^* - R_{f,t}^* \approx [\gamma_t \sigma_t(\Delta c_{t+1})]\sigma_t(R_{t+1}^*)\rho_t(M_{t+1}, R_{t+1}^*) \tag{4}$$

Both of the above equations hold when $R_{t+1}^*$ is replaced by $R_{t+1}$. There is no reason why any of the conditional moments on the right-hand side of (4) might not vary over time. However, variables that forecast return volatility do not seem to also forecast expected returns (e.g. Schwert 1989), and interpreting $\rho_t$ is a little fraught. Hence, key contenders for explaining changes in equilibrium excess returns over time include either time-varying risk aversion $\gamma_t$ or time-varying volatility of consumption. As we shall see, time-varying risk aversion has been widely used to 'explain' observed time-varying excess returns within the framework of the SDF approach.

However, note that all those 'kitchen sink' time-series regression equations that claim 'returns are predictable' cannot be mapped one-to-one into changes in $\gamma_t$ or

$\sigma_t(\Delta c_t)$. The best one can say is that the variables used in these return predictability equations (e.g. dividend–price ratio, price inflation, yield spreads, etc.) are 'indicative' of changes in $\gamma_t$ or $\sigma_t(\Delta c_{t+1})$. But this is not very reassuring or scientific!

## Hansen–Jagannathan Bounds and the Sharpe Ratio

The SDF model implies a lower bound for the discount factor, which can be compared with the observed Sharpe ratio, to provide a test of the SDF model, with a specific utility function. The 'flexibility' of this approach is that the bound can be calculated for a wide variety of possible utility functions and for various values for the risk-aversion parameter. For example, this enables us to see what alternative values of the risk-aversion parameter are consistent with a given utility function. If for a given utility function, no values of the risk-aversion parameter are 'intuitively acceptable', we can discard this particular utility function from further consideration – anyway, that is the purists' version of this approach. In this section, we drop the time subscripts for convenience (i.e. $E \equiv E_t$, $M \equiv M_{t+1}$).

Using $\mathrm{cov}(R_i^*, M) \equiv \rho_{iM}\sigma(R_i^*)\sigma(M)$ and substituting in $1 = E(MR_i^*)$,

$$1 = E(MR_i^*) = E(M)E(R_i^*) + \rho_{iM}\sigma(R_i^*)\sigma(M) \tag{5}$$

Rearranging and using $E(M) = 1/R_\mathrm{f}$,

$$\frac{ER_i^* - R_\mathrm{f}^*}{\sigma(R_i^*)} \equiv \frac{E(R_i^{*e})}{\sigma(R_i^{*e})} = -\rho_{iM}\frac{\sigma(M)}{E(M)} \tag{6}$$

where $R_i^{*e}$ is the excess return. The term on the left is the Sharpe ratio for an asset or portfolio of risky assets. For any portfolio $i$, equation (6) gives the Hansen and Jagannathan (1991) bound for the discount factor. Since $\rho_{iM}$ has an *absolute* maximum value of 1,

$$\frac{\sigma(M)}{E(M)} \geq \frac{|E(R_i^{*e})|}{\sigma(R_i^{*e})} \tag{7}$$

Given that the right-hand side is measurable, then equation (7) provides a lower bound for the behaviour of the SDF for any asset $i$ (and is a simple version of the 'Hansen–Jagannathan bound' – see below). We can also see what (7) implies for those 'special' portfolios that lie on the 'efficient frontier' where the latter now applies to the case where we have a riskless asset – this is the wedge-shaped region in Figure 1 (the upper portion of which is the equivalent of the CML). We can now connect our SDF approach with the standard-CAPM, mean-variance model.

First, all asset returns lie within the wedge-shaped region. By combining risky assets into a portfolio with minimum variance for any given level of expected return, we obtain mean-variance efficient portfolios (when we have a riskless asset). All returns *on* the wedge-shaped frontier are perfectly correlated with the SDF, $M$ so that $|\rho_{iM}| = 1$. Returns on the upper portion (i.e. equivalent of the CML) are perfectly negatively correlated with $M$ and hence positively correlated with consumption and from (6) command

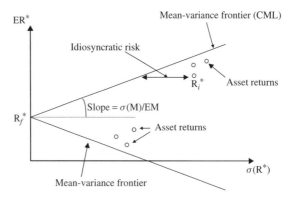

**Figure 1** Mean-variance frontier (with risk-free asset)

the highest expected return. Conversely, those assets (or portfolios) on the lower portion of the wedge have $\rho_{iM} = +1$ and hence have lower expected returns because $R_i$ and *consumption* are perfectly *negatively* correlated, and these assets provide insurance against changes in consumption.

Any two returns on the wedge-shaped mean-variance frontier $(R_{mv,1}, R_{mv,2})$ are perfectly correlated with each other (because each is perfectly correlated with $M$) and hence

$$R_{\mathrm{mv},1} = R_{\mathrm{f}} + \delta(R_{\mathrm{mv},2} - R_{\mathrm{f}})$$

$$M = a + bR_{\mathrm{mv},j} \quad \text{and} \quad R_{\mathrm{mv},j} = c + dM$$

where $j$ = any portfolio on the mean-variance efficient frontier. The last two equations demonstrate that any return on the frontier (i.e. $R_{\mathrm{mv},j}$) contains all the pricing information in the pricing kernel or SDF, $M$. Finally, it can be shown that the expected excess return on any asset $i$ is proportional to its beta with any return on the efficient frontier $\beta_{i,\mathrm{mv}}$

$$ER_i - R_{\mathrm{f}} = \beta_{i,\mathrm{mv}}(ER_{\mathrm{mv}} - R_{\mathrm{f}})$$

A graph of the cross section of (average) returns $ER_i$ $(i = 1, 2, \ldots, N)$ is linearly related to $\beta_{i,\mathrm{mv}}$. Since the above equation also applies to $R_{\mathrm{mv}}$, which has a beta of unity, the factor risk premium $\lambda_M = ER_{\mathrm{mv}} - R_{\mathrm{f}}$. From (3), for any asset $i$, we have

$$E_t R_{i,t+1} - R_{\mathrm{f}} = \frac{-\mathrm{cov}_t(M_{t+1}, R_{i,t+1})}{E_t(M_{t+1})} = \frac{\mathrm{cov}_t(M_{t+1}, R_{i,t+1})}{\mathrm{var}_t(M_{t+1})} \left( \frac{-\mathrm{var}_t(M_{t+1})}{E_t(M_{t+1})} \right)$$

$$= \beta_{i,M} \lambda_M$$

where $\beta_{i,M}$ is the coefficient of $R_i$ regressed on $M$, while $\lambda_M$ is independent of any asset $i$ and can be interpreted as the market price of risk. For power utility $M_{t+1} = \beta(C_{t+1}/C_t)^{-\gamma}$, it can be shown (by taking a Taylor series expansion of the above equation):

$$E_t R_{i,t+1} - R_{\mathrm{f}} \approx \beta_{i,\Delta C_{t+1}}[\gamma \, \mathrm{var}_t(\Delta C_{t+1})]$$

So the SDF model with power utility implies that the market price of risk depends positively on $\gamma$ and the riskiness of consumption. The direct parallels between the standard-CAPM (mean-variance model) and the SDF model should be apparent in the above equations. The SDF model has $M_{t+1}$ as a generic variable, for which the market return $R_{mv}$ is a special case. (Note that in all of the above equations, we can replace $R$ by $R^*$.)

Let us now return to the implications for the Sharpe ratio for any portfolio that lies on the efficient frontier (CML). From (6), with $|\rho_{iM}| = 1$, we have

$$SR_{mv} = \left| \frac{E(R^*_{mv}) - R^*_f}{\sigma(R^*_{mv})} \right| = \frac{\sigma(M)}{E(M)} = \sigma(M)R^*_f \qquad (8)$$

Hence, all portfolios on the efficient frontier have the *same* Sharpe ratio and the 'fundamentals' that determine the *size* of the Sharpe ratio are the risk-free rate and the volatility of the SDF. Since both of these variables may move over time, we also expect the measured Sharpe ratio to vary. Using power utility where $U'(C) = C^{-\gamma}$ and assuming consumption growth is lognormal,

$$\frac{\sigma(M)}{E(M)} = \frac{\sigma\{(C_{t+1}/C_t)^{-\gamma}\}}{E\{(C_{t+1}/C_t)^{-\gamma}\}} = [\exp\{\gamma^2\sigma^2(\Delta c_{t+1})\} - 1]^{1/2} \approx \gamma\sigma(\Delta c) \qquad (9a)$$

Hence, from (8) and (9a), a high observed Sharpe ratio for assets or portfolios on the efficient frontier is consistent with the C-CAPM if consumption growth is volatile or $\gamma$ is large. Both of these are indicators of 'riskiness' in the economy. Also, the Sharpe ratio moves over time with the changing conditional volatility of consumption growth. For any asset $i$ that is *not on* the efficient frontier (CML), the Sharpe ratio (from (6)) under power utility and lognormality should equal

$$SR_i \approx -\rho_{iM}\gamma\sigma(\Delta c) \qquad (9b)$$

## 14.2   Equity Premium Puzzle

The Mehra and Prescott (1985) seminal article on the equity premium puzzle is based on the SDF model and requires the following assumptions.

(i)  Standard preferences (e.g. power utility) over consumption.

(ii)  Agents maximise lifetime utility that depends only on consumption and utility is time-separable.

(iii)  Asset markets are complete – agents can write insurance contracts against any contingency (e.g. spells of unemployment).

(iv)  Trading in assets takes place in a frictionless market and therefore is costless (i.e. brokerage fees, taxes, etc., are insignificant).

It can be shown that assumptions (iii) and (iv) *imply* a 'representative agent' so that individual consumption moves the same as per capita consumption (on non-durables and services). Note that a sufficient condition for a representative agent model is that *all* individuals have identical preferences (utility functions) and ownership of production possibilities, so they then have identical consumption. But this is not a necessary assumption – the key is that asset markets are complete and markets frictionless (Constantinides 1982).

Let us assume the S&P500 index $R_m$ is always on the upper portion of the efficient frontier, so that $\rho_{iM} = -1$. Over the last 50 years (i.e. post-WWII), the average real return was around 9% p.a. with a standard deviation of 16% p.a. and the average real risk-free rate was 1% p.a., giving $SR = 0.5$. The standard deviation of the growth in consumption is about 1% p.a. For the C-CAPM in (9a) to 'fit' these stylised facts requires a risk-aversion coefficient of $\gamma = 50$. From experiments on gambles, $\gamma$ is thought to be in the range 3–10, so the prediction of the C-CAPM for the equity premium is way off the mark. This is known as the *equity premium puzzle*.

## How Risk-Averse Are You?

It is rather difficult to pin down an acceptable range for the degree of risk aversion either by introspection or from experimental economies where people are presented with a range of 'bets' under laboratory conditions. One way to investigate the plausibility of different values of $\gamma$, the coefficient of relative risk aversion, is to examine the certainty equivalent amount (as outlined in Chapter 1) for various bets. Suppose we assume power utility and an initial level of annual consumption (or income) of $C_0 = \$50,000$. How much would you pay per annum to *avoid* a fair bet that gave you plus or minus $\$y$ p.a. (for the rest of your life)? For power utility, the answer is the value $\$z$, which satisfies

$$(C_0 - z)^{1-\gamma} = \tfrac{1}{2}(C_0 + y)^{1-\gamma} + \tfrac{1}{2}(C_0 - y)^{1-\gamma}$$

which gives

$$z = C_0 \left\{ 1 - \left[ \frac{1}{2}\left(1 + \frac{y}{C_0}\right)^{1-\gamma} + \frac{1}{2}\left(1 - \frac{y}{C_0}\right)^{1-\gamma} \right]^{\frac{1}{1-\gamma}} \right\}$$

It can be shown that for *small* bets, this can be approximated by

$$\frac{z}{y} = \frac{\gamma}{2}\left(\frac{y}{C_0}\right)$$

$$\left(\frac{amount\ to\ avoid\ bet}{size\ of\ the\ bet}\right) = \frac{\gamma}{2}\left(\frac{size\ of\ the\ bet}{C_0}\right)$$

where $\gamma$ is the *local* curvature, $\gamma = -CU''(C)/U'(C)$. Hence, for small bets, power utility is not unreasonable, since if the size of the bet $y$ is small in relation to the initial consumption level $C_0$, then the amount you would pay to avoid the bet is also small (relative to the size of the bet).

This is shown in Table 1 where we use the above equation for $z$ and find that even with $\gamma = 50$, you would pay a relatively small amount of $5 to avoid a fair bet that

**Table 1**  Dollar amount you would pay to avoid a fair bet

| Amount of Bet ($) | Risk Aversion $\gamma$ | | | | |
|---|---|---|---|---|---|
| | 2 | 10 | 50 | 100 | 250 |
| 10 | 0.002 | 0.01 | 0.05 | 0.1 | 0.25 |
| 100 | 0.2 | 1.0 | 5.0 | 9.9 | 24.0 |
| 1,000 | 20 | 99 | 435 | 655 | 863 |
| 10,000 | 2000 | 6,920 | 9,430 | 9,718 | 9,888 |
| 20,000 | 8,000 | 17,600 | 19,573 | 19,789 | 19,916 |

Notes:

(i) The initial level of consumption (income) is $50,000 p.a., and we assume power utility (i.e. constant coefficient of relative risk aversion, $\gamma$).

(ii) The GAUSS program can be found on the web site for the book.

could change your initial consumption (wealth) of $50,000 by plus or minus $100. This is because for *small* bets, the local curvature of the utility function is close to being linear (i.e. risk-neutral). However, if the bet were plus or minus $10,000 (or larger), then with $\gamma = 50$, you would pay nearly the full $10,000 (i.e. $9430) to avoid the bet. You are very risk-averse to large bets (this is the basis of the Rabin (2000) paradox). Note that even if you have a high initial level of consumption (income) of $300,000, then with $\gamma = 50$, you are still willing to pay a hefty $6092 to avoid the $10,000 fair bet. You are willing to pay less than the consumer who starts off with $C_0 = \$50,000$ because the utility function is 'flatter' at higher initial levels of consumption (i.e. diminishing marginal utility). The numbers generated in Table 1 using probabilities of, say, car theft or your house burning down could be compared with insurance premiums actually paid and $\gamma$ adjusted to match these premia. It is found that people are willing to pay substantially more than actuarially fair values to insure against these risks, implying low values for $\gamma$. So we are still left with the puzzle of why people are so risk-averse when it comes to stocks.

The above results do not crucially depend on the functional form of the utility function. As long as utility is an increasing concave function of wealth (consumption), expected utility appears reasonable for small bets but absurd for large bets. To see this in a slightly different way, consider the following proposal. Suppose we know that Mr Monty Casino will *always* turn down a 50:50 gamble of losing $10 or gaining $11 and he is a risk-averse expected utility maximiser (i.e. utility is an increasing concave function of wealth). Now we offer Mr Monty Casino a 50:50 bet where he could lose $100 and gain $Y. What is the maximum $Y we can offer so that we *know* he will take this bet? Well, $2000 for a 'win' seems not unreasonable. Certainly, casual introspection would suggest Mr Casino would take the bet for $20,000 to win and certainly for $1 million or $1 billion to win (remember he can only lose $100). In fact, as an expected utility maximiser, if he rejects the 50:50, lose $10/gain $11, then he will *always* refuse a 50:50, lose $100/gain *any* amount. This is the Rabin paradox (Rabin 1998, 2000, Rabin and Thaler 2001), and the result seems absurd and makes one very uneasy about using expected utility on the basis of only the *level* of wealth as a criterion when considering large bets.

The latter conclusion cannot be overturned by considering repeated bets of the same type. If a person turns down one fair bet to lose $X$ or gain $Y$, then expected utility implies the person will turn down an offer to play many of these same gambles (Samuelson 1963). Neither can the Rabin paradox be (qualitatively) overturned by considering different initial wealth levels. For example, if an expected utility maximising 'rich person' turns down a 50-50 bet of lose $10,000/gain $11,000, then she will also turn down at 50:50 bet of lose $100,000/gain $\infty$. The above conceptual difficulties with risk-averse expected utility maximisation as a description of behaviour has led to alternative utility functions where utility depends on *changes* in wealth, where losses are much more 'painful' than gains (e.g. loss aversion or disappointment aversion) and where individuals consider gains and losses in isolation (i.e. 'narrow framing'). We discuss these in later chapters.

The problem with evidence from 'experiments' in the laboratory is that individual's choices violate the axioms of expected utility (an issue we take up later) and 'bets' that are far outside one's usual experience are hard to evaluate. (This applies *a fortiori* when individuals are asked how much they would pay to reduce the probability of avoiding particular types of risk such as a car accident or a crash in a metro system or aircraft.)

If we accept the axioms of expected utility, then high values for risk aversion are not totally at variance with introspection and this would help resolve the equity premium puzzle. But as we see below, a high $\gamma$ can introduce other problems, namely reconciling the low level and variability of the risk-free rate (as observed in nearly all developed economies). An alternative to a high $\gamma$ with respect to wealth bets is to assume that investors also worry about variables other than just consumption and this is explored further below.

Finally, note that the S&P500 may not lie on the efficient frontier of *all* assets, since it comprises only a subset of possible investments, and the data indicates a correlation coefficient of about 0.2 (rather than the 'theoretical' unity) between the S&P500 and aggregate consumption, hence $\rho_{im} = 0.2$. But using (9b) (with power utility), this would imply a value of $\gamma = 250$ to 'fit the facts'. This makes the puzzle even more difficult to explain.

## Using Individual Consumption

If the C-CAPM applies to every investor, the representative agent assumption allows us to use *aggregate* consumption in testing the model. But only a small proportion of US citizens hold stocks and it is the correlation between consumption growth of these *active traders* with asset returns that determines the risk premium. Empirically, the correlation between the consumption of active traders and stock returns is higher than that for aggregate consumption, but it is still not high enough to solve the equity premium puzzle (Mankiw and Zeldes 1991). Indeed, moving to *individual* (non-durable) consumption does not solve the equity premium problem because

(a) although *individual* consumption is more subject to idiosyncratic shocks, it is hard to believe that it varies by around $\sigma(\Delta c_{i,t+1}) = 50\%$ p.a.;

(b) individual consumption growth will be less correlated with the market return than is aggregate consumption growth (where $\rho_{iM} \approx 0.2$) and makes it even more difficult to satisfy (9b).

## Risk-Free Rate Puzzle: Is $\gamma = 50$ Acceptable?

The so-called 'equity premium puzzle' is now really considered as two puzzles. One is the fact that the observed (real) equity premium of around 8% p.a. is too high to be explained by a model with 'standard preferences' unless the risk-aversion parameter $\gamma$ is 'unacceptably' high. The second is the *risk-free rate puzzle* (Weil 1992): when risk aversion is high, the standard C-CAPM model gives an equilibrium risk-free rate that is higher and more volatile than that found in the data (where the mean real T-bill rate is around 1% p.a.). So, even if a high risk aversion coefficient is accepted, so that the observed equity premium is explained by the model, it then does not fit the facts concerning movements in the risk-free rate. To see this, note that with power utility, lognormality and $\theta = 0.99$:

$$\ln R_{\mathrm{ft}}^* \approx R_{\mathrm{ft}} = \ln \theta + \gamma E_t(\Delta c_{t+1}) - \frac{\gamma^2}{2}\sigma_t^2(\Delta c_{t+1}) \qquad (10)$$

where $R_{\mathrm{ft}}$ is the risk-free rate (expressed as a decimal). What does the C-CAPM imply for the risk-free rate for $\gamma = 50$? (We ignore the final term that disappears in the continuous-time version of the model and is an inappropriate approximation when $\gamma$ is large.) For $\gamma = 50$,

$$R_{\mathrm{ft}} = -0.01 + 50(0.01) = 0.49 \qquad (49\% \text{ p.a.}) \qquad (11)$$

Annual consumption growth is approximately *iid*, so we have used the unconditional expectations, $E(\Delta c) = 0.01$ and $\sigma(\Delta c) = 0.01$. Here, the real interest rate predicted by the C-CAPM (with power utility and lognormality) is about 50% p.a. and clearly does not resemble the average real interest rate of around 1% p.a. found in the data for many developed economies (if we include the last term, then the model predicted interest rate is 36.5%).

Also if $\gamma = 50$, then when consumption growth is 1% above or below its average level, the model predicts real interest rates will move about plus or minus 50% points (e.g. a situation could arise whereby *you pay* someone else 50% p.a. in real terms to borrow from you!). Hence, $\gamma = 50$ implies that aversion to intertemporal substitution of consumption is so high that massive swings in interest rates are required to induce additional saving today (and hence higher consumption tomorrow).

Cochrane (2001) has a nice example to illustrate what $\gamma = 50$ implies for real interest rates. If you earn \$50,000 p.a. and you normally spend 5% (\$2500) on an annual vacation, then you will voluntarily skip this year's vacation only if interest rates rise to about

$$R_{\mathrm{ft}} \approx (52,500/47,500)^{50} - 1 = 14,800\% \text{ p.a.} \qquad (12)$$

In reality, you might be willing to postpone your vacation for a somewhat lower interest rate than this! Thus, with time-separable power or logarithmic or exponential utility functions, the equity premium puzzle arises because the C-CAPM cannot explain both the observed high average return (and Sharpe ratio) for risky assets *together with* relatively low real interest rates that also exhibit low volatility.

## 14.3 Testing the Euler Equations of the C-CAPM

### Cross-Section Evidence

The C-CAPM can be tested using either cross-section or time-series data. A cross-section test of the C-CAPM is based on

$$ER_i = a_0 + a_1 \beta_{c,i} \tag{13}$$

where $a_0 = (1 - EM)/EM$, $a_1 = \alpha\theta \operatorname{cov}(R_m, \Delta c)/EM$, $\beta_{c,i} = \operatorname{cov}(R_i, \Delta c)/\operatorname{var}(\Delta c)$. Equation (13) is the security market line (SML) for the C-CAPM. Average returns are linear in $\beta_{c,i}$. In cross-section data, $EM$ and $\operatorname{cov}(R_m, \Delta c)$ are constant, hence $a_1$ should be the same for all stocks $i$. We use the sample mean for $ER_i$ and the sample estimate for $\beta_{ci}$, for each stock $i$ or portfolio $i$. Mankiw and Shapiro (1986) test the CAPM and C-CAPM using cross-section data on 464 US companies over the period 1959–1982. They find that the standard-CAPM clearly outperforms the C-CAPM, since when $\overline{R}_i$ is regressed on both $\beta_{mi}$ and $\beta_{ci}$, the former is statistically significant, while the latter is not. Breeden, Gibbons and Litzenberger (1989) find similar results for industry and bond portfolios, while Cochrane (1996) finds that the C-CAPM performs worse than the standard-CAPM, using a cross section of size-sorted portfolio returns. However, it is worth remembering that the CAPM 'prices' assets assuming the market return is given – the CAPM does not proffer any economic explanation of the return on the *market*, whereas the C-CAPM does, since it assumes the latter depends on the volatility of consumption growth. Put another way, in principle, the C-CAPM or SDF model tries to explain *all* asset returns in terms of the underlying sources of *economic* risk (such as consumption), and not in terms of other asset returns – a rather tall order.

### Time-Series Evidence

With power utility, the Euler equations/FOCs for the risky and risk-free asset in the C-CAPM are

$$e_{it+1} \equiv \theta E_t\{(C_{t+1}/C_t)^{-\gamma}(R^*_{it+1} - R^*_{ft})\} = 0 \tag{14a}$$

$$e_{ft+1} \equiv \theta E_t\{(C_{t+1}/C_t)^{-\gamma} R^*_{ft}\} = 1 \tag{14b}$$

After invoking the law of iterated expectations to give *unconditional* expectations, the simplest test of the FOCs is to take sample averages (over time) of $e_i$ and $e_f$ (and their standard errors), for different values of $\gamma$. Kocherlakota (1996) reports that for an aggregate stock index, a value of $\gamma \geq 8.5$ (given $\theta = 0.99$) is required for the first sample moment to be statistically zero – this is the 'equity bit' of the equity premium puzzle. Unfortunately, for $\gamma = 8.5$ (and $\theta = 0.99$), then $e_f$ is statistically different from 1, so the representative consumer can gain by shifting consumption from the future to the present (i.e. increasing savings) – this is the risk-free rate puzzle.

Direct tests of (14) using *conditional* expectations in a non-linear time-series regression provide estimates of $\gamma$ (with $\theta$ often imposed). Using only risky-asset returns, the FOC is

$$\{(C_{t+1}/C_t)^{-\gamma}\theta R^*_{it+1} - 1\} = \varepsilon_{it+1} \tag{15a}$$

Since (15a) holds for all risky assets (or portfolios), it implies a set of cross-equation restrictions, since the parameters $(\theta, \alpha)$ appear in all equations. This model does not perform well for a wide range of alternative assets included in the portfolio (e.g. portfolios comprising just US equities or US equities plus US bonds, or portfolios consisting of equities and bonds in different countries; see, *inter alia*, Hodrick 1987, Cumby 1990, Smith 1993). In Smith's (1993) study, which uses an 'international' basket of assets, the parameter restrictions in (15a) are often found to hold, but the parameters themselves are not constant over time.

We can also apply equation (15a) to the *aggregate* stock market return $R_m$ and noting that (15a) applies for any return horizon $t + j$, we have, for $j = 1, 2, \ldots$

$$\{(C_{t+j}/C_t)^{-\gamma} R^*_{m,t+j} - 1\} = \varepsilon_{t+j} \tag{15b}$$

Equation (15b) can be estimated on time-series data and because it holds for horizons, $j = 1, 2, \ldots$ and so on, we again have a system of equations with 'common' parameters $(\theta, \alpha)$. Equation (15b) for $j = 1, 2, \ldots$ are similar to the Fama and French (1988b) regressions using returns over different horizons, except here we implicitly incorporate a time-varying expected return. Flood, Hodrick and Kaplan (1986) find that the performance of the C-CAPM model deteriorates, in statistical terms, as the time horizon is extended. Hence, they find against (this version of) the C-CAPM. Overall, the conditional C-CAPM with power utility is a poor representation of the time-series behaviour of asset returns in terms of formal statistical tests on $\gamma$ and cross-equation restrictions.

## Hansen–Jagannathan Bounds

For the S&P500, the Hansen–Jagannathan (H–J) bound implies

$$\frac{\sigma(M)}{E(M)} \geq \frac{|E(R^{*e}_i)|}{\sigma(R^{*e}_i)} \approx 0.5$$

With $E(M) = 1/R^*_f \approx 0.99$, then the above implies that $\sigma(M) \approx \gamma\sigma(\Delta c) > 50\%$ p.a. and with $\sigma(\Delta c) \approx 1\%$ p.a., this implies $\gamma = 50$. As noted above, if we recognise that the correlation between aggregate consumption growth and the return on the S&P500 is around 0.2, then this implies $\gamma = 250$.

### Value function

The equity premium puzzle is about the smoothness or absence of volatility in real consumption. You may be tempted to think of utility depending on wealth rather than consumption and 'the wealth portfolio' is undoubtedly more volatile than consumption, given investment in the stock market. In the previous chapter, we noted that the value function $V(W)$ is a key element of the FOCs in an intertemporal model, and the H–J bound becomes

$$\frac{ER - R_\text{f}}{\sigma(R)} \leq \frac{-WV_{ww}}{V_w}\sigma(\Delta w)$$

where $\sigma(\Delta w) = \sigma(R_m) \approx 16\%$ p.a. for an investor who holds the market portfolio of stocks. If we wish to explain the market Sharpe ratio of 0.5, then the lower bound on the local risk-aversion parameter over wealth has to be

$$\frac{-WV_{ww}}{V_w} = \frac{0.5}{0.16} = 3.125$$

which seems much more plausible than the value of 50 or more discussed above. However, as we see in Chapter 15, if returns are *iid* and $V$ depends only on wealth (e.g. no labour 'income'), then in an intertemporal consumption model, consumption is proportional to wealth, hence $\sigma(\Delta c) = \sigma(\Delta w)$. Hence, explaining the high Sharpe ratio by invoking the high volatility in stock market wealth and low (local) risk aversion over wealth, requires the volatility of consumption growth to be 16% p.a. – clearly not supported by the data. Hence, using wealth in place of consumption does not solve the equity premium puzzle – the puzzle reappears as implying an implausible volatility for real consumption.

A test of the C-CAPM is possible by extending the H–J bound to *several assets* taken together. When we have several assets, the H–J bound can be used to put limits on the values of the SDF and, in particular, the risk-aversion coefficient (for a particular utility function) that are acceptable, given the empirical variance–covariance matrix of returns. The H–J bound for several assets can be shown to be (see Appendix)

$$\sigma^2(M) \geq [\boldsymbol{P} - (EM)(EX)]'\Sigma^{-1}[\boldsymbol{P} - (EM)(EX)] \qquad (16)$$

where $\boldsymbol{P} = N \times 1$ vector of asset prices, $\boldsymbol{X} = N \times 1$ vector of asset pay-offs, $\Sigma = (N \times N)$ variance–covariance matrix of pay-offs. By dividing through by the initial price, the $\boldsymbol{P}$ vector becomes a vector of ones $\boldsymbol{e}1$ and $\boldsymbol{X}$ is replaced by $\boldsymbol{R}^*$, a vector of gross asset returns, so that

$$\sigma^2(M) \geq [\boldsymbol{e}1 - (EM)(E\boldsymbol{R}^*)]'\sum\nolimits_R^{-1}[\boldsymbol{e}1 - (EM)(E\boldsymbol{R}^*)] \qquad (17)$$

It is easily seen that (17) collapses to the single risky-asset case in (7) – see Appendix. To illustrate how the H–J bound can reveal information on possible values for the risk-aversion coefficient that are acceptable, given the empirical variance–covariance

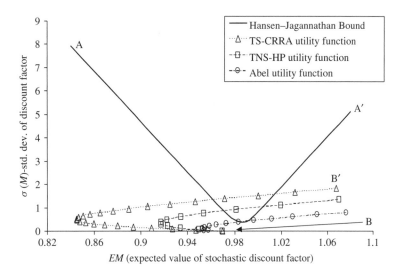

**Figure 2**   Hansen–Jagannathan bounds (German data)

of returns, we proceed as follows. Suppose we have time-series data on the real return on a stock index and the real risk-free rate, so that $ER^*$ is a $(2 \times 1)$ vector.

If we substitute the sample average return $\overline{R}^*$ for $ER^*$ and the sample variance–covariance matrix of returns $\Sigma_R$ in the right-hand side of (17), we have a scalar that is quadratic in $EM$ (i.e. RHS $= a_0 + a_1 E(M) + a_2[E(M)]^2 = f(EM, (EM)^2)$, where the $a_i$ depend on the estimates $\overline{R}^*, \Sigma_R$. We now calculate $\sigma(M) = [a_0 + a_1 E(M) + a_2(EM)^2]^{1/2}$ and plot $EM$ versus $\sigma(M)$ for alternative values of $EM$, which is shown as the U-shaped parabola A–A′ (Figure 2). This provides the admissible lower bound for $\sigma(M)$, $EM$ combinations.

Now let us see if the H–J lower bound holds for a particular utility function over consumption and reasonable values of the risk-aversion parameter. First, consider time-separable power utility (which has a constant coefficient of relative risk aversion $\gamma$) where $M_{t+1} = \theta(C_{t+1}/C_t)^{-\gamma}$. Assume $\theta = 0.97$ is known, which on annual data implies a real discount rate of 3%. Use sample data on consumption growth to calculate $\overline{M}$ and standard deviation $\sigma(M)$ for any given $\gamma$. So, we have $\overline{M} = f_1(\gamma)$ and $\sigma(M) = \dfrac{\sum (M_t - \overline{M})^2}{T-1} = f_2(\gamma)$. We can plot points in $\{\sigma(M), EM\}$ – space for alternative values of $\gamma$ (Figure 2, curve B–B′, indicated by 'triangles'). The curve B–B′ shows combinations of $\overline{M}$ and $\sigma(M)$ for different values of $\gamma$ (given the TS-CRRA power utility function). Values of $\gamma$ for curve B–B′ that satisfy the bound are points above and within the U-shaped curve A–A′. As an example, consider results for Germany using aggregate annual (real) stock returns and the (real) risk-free rate as our two assets (see Figure 2), for three alternative utility specifications (Cuthbertson and Hyde 2004). For the familiar time-separable power utility function (TS-CRRA), Figure 2 shows that the values of $\gamma$ for which the curve B–B′ lies within the H–J lower bound of the curve A–A′ are $\gamma = 31$ to $34$ – very high coefficients of risk aversion.

Figure 2 also includes results for two alternative time *non*-separable habit-persistence utility functions denoted by 'TNS-HP' and 'Abel' (Abel 1990). Even for these utility functions, it is found that curves such as B–B′ lie above and within the 'lower bound' (i.e. curve A–A′) for values of $\gamma > 8$ and less than 10 for the two habit specifications – these values of $\gamma$ are also rather high. Several studies on US and UK data have found that for power utility, the values of $\gamma$ that are in the admissible region, are large and in the 10–25 range. Even with alternative utility functions such as 'habit persistence', the bound is often violated for 'reasonable' values of $\gamma$ (e.g. 2 to 4) – see Engsted (1998). Hence, the C-CAPM fails to lie within the H–J bound, for reasonable risk–aversion parameters and various utility functions, which depend on consumption growth or habit persistence in consumption (Burnside 1994, Engsted 1998, Hansen and Jagannathan 1991). This is a further manifestation of the equity premium puzzle and the failure of variants of the C-CAPM.

The above results can be formally tested, and the relevant distribution theory for the H–J bounds, including allowance for short-sale constraints, bid/ask spreads and other market frictions can be found in Cochrane and Hansen (1992) and Hansen, Heaton and Luttmer (1995), with an excellent account in Cochrane (2001).

## 14.4 Extensions of the SDF Model

The standard (power utility) SDF model does not *simultaneously* explain the high equity premium and the risk-free rate puzzle. Possible avenues out of this impasse are as follows.

(a) Power utility is OK, but we need to introduce non-separabilities where the marginal utility of consumption (at time $t$) depends on other state variables (e.g. wealth, past consumption).

(b) The basic SDF model is correct and utility just depends on consumption, but the power utility function is incorrect. So, we need to try other functional forms.

(c) The last 50 years of US stock returns were largely 'good luck' rather than a payment for risk. This is a kind of 'Pesoproblem' since we are arguing that the out-turn data does not reflect 'true' *ex-ante* risk, as viewed by investors over the period from about 1950 to 1999.

(d) Individual consumption is poorly measured by aggregate per capita consumption.

### Luck and Mismeasurement of the Sharpe Ratio

Given the data we have, an estimate of the equity premium is subject to wide margins of error. Taking the *excess* return to be 8% p.a. and $\sigma = 16\%$ for the S&P500 and using a reasonable ('ball-park') approximation that returns are *iid*, the standard error of the expected (average) return $\overline{R}$ is $\sigma/\sqrt{T}$. Hence with $T = 50$ years of data, a two-standard deviation confidence band for expected excess returns is $8\% \pm 2(2.3\%)$, that is, about 3.5 to 12.5%, a considerable range. For 20 years of data, the standard deviation of expected returns is 3.6% ($= 16/\sqrt{20}$), so a mean return of 8% at the lower two-standard deviation bound is close to zero. However, relatively large uncertainty in *measuring* expected returns could go either way for the equity premium puzzle, since we could take either the upper or lower limit as being the 'true' mean return.

Maybe the US data is atypical and really the United States just got lucky over the last 50 years. After 1945, the United States has had a few major and debilitating wars (e.g. the Cold War from 1945 to 1989, including the blockade of Berlin, the Korean War in the 1950s, the Cuban missile crisis of 1962, Vietnam in the 1970s and the very short Gulf War of 1992 and the Afghan and Iraq wars of 2001 and 2003). None of these resulted in the use of nuclear weapons, and other countries that have obtained 'the bomb', such as Russia, China, Israel, Pakistan and India, have not used it. There have been no major natural disasters, or nationwide political upheavals (e.g. race riots) in the United States. There has been no foreign occupying force in the United States since independence, and only two major acts of terrorism on US soil, the Oklahoma bombing in 1995, for which Timothy McVeigh was convicted, and the attack on the Twin Towers in New York on 9/11 in 2001.

The above 'lucky' scenario has not applied to many other countries around the world. When measuring the equity premium from a 'world investor' point of view in 1900, perhaps we should also include average returns from Germany, Japan, China, Russia and its satellite countries, all of whom suffered major wars/insurrection and stock prices that never recovered. Also, post-WWII, returns from newly industrialised economies of South America and the Far East should be included. The US figures may therefore suffer from survivorship bias. Unfortunately, high-quality continuous data on 'other markets' are often not available over a long run of years.

Jorion and Goetzmann (1999) have attempted to measure expected returns and the standard deviation of returns across many countries for a long time series of data (1920–1996). Although it is difficult to generalise, they find that the real return in the United States is 4.3% p.a., whereas in all other markets (some of which ceased trading for some periods), it was a mere 0.8% p.a. However, holding a hypothetical world index gives a real return of around 4.3% p.a. because it is dominated by the United States. Dimson, Marsh and Staunton (2002) rework the historic data over 1900–2000 for 16 countries and find an equity risk premium of 5.8% p.a. for the United States and of 4.8% for the United Kingdom (geometric averages), while it is 5% for all 16 countries – so, over this period, the United States is not particularly atypical, and survivorship bias appears to be relatively small. The relatively low figures found for the US equity premium by Dimson et al. are due to slightly different index construction and use of a longer time period.

Suppose we assume a 'true' expected excess return as low as 3% p.a. (rather than around 8% p.a.) so the Sharpe ratio is 0.2 $(= 3/16)$. Then the C-CAPM (with power utility) and given $\sigma(\Delta c) = 0.01$ still requires a risk-aversion parameter of around 20 (or 100 if we consider the correlation $\rho_{iM} = 0.2$). So, even if the 50-year historic average excess return of 8% p.a. in the United States is a 'Pesoproblem' (i.e. good luck), we still need a risk-aversion coefficient in excess of 20. But the high and volatile interest rates that this implies for the C-CAPM with power utility are not found in the data. Hence, the risk-free rate puzzle still remains.

The crux of the problem is that we need a model where the mean of the SDF $R_f^* = 1/E(M)$ does not vary very much over time, in order to 'explain' the low volatility of interest rates, while we require a high $\sigma(M)$ to explain the observed Sharpe ratios (see equation (7)). In effect, we lack one degree of freedom since the one-state variable in the model, namely consumption, cannot explain these two contradictory facts. We need another state variable in the utility function that can co-vary with the stochastic discount factor. There are a number of candidates for an additional state variable such as leisure, foreign consumption, past levels of consumption and financial wealth.

In addition, we require our model to explain the stylised fact of long-horizon predictability. For example, returns are higher following a low value for the price–dividend ratio. Also, stock prices are low in recessions and empirically are followed by high future returns, hence the Sharpe ratio varies counter-cyclically (i.e. SR is high in recessions and low in booms) – our chosen model needs to explain these stylised facts.

## Non-Separability

If the *marginal* utility of consumption depends on another variable $Z$ as well as consumption $U_c(C, Z)$, then expected returns will depend on the covariances between $Z_t$ and $R_{i,t}$, as well as the consumption covariance. However, note that this would *not* happen if $U(C, Z)$ was separable, that is, $U(C, Z) = f(C) + g(Z)$. There are various forms of non-separability to consider:

  (i) additional *state* variables like leisure or wealth in the utility function.

 (ii) habit-persistence effects – so past values as well as current values of consumption appear in the utility function.

(iii) so-called *non-state separable* utility functions, where marginal utility of consumption in one state ('hot') is affected by the level of consumption in another state ('cold') – Epstein and Zin (1989).

## Wealth in the Utility Function

Bakshi and Chen (1996) provide an intertemporal model, where utility also depends on a social wealth index $S_t = W_t/V_t$, where $W_t$ = individual's wealth, $V_t$ = social wealth index (i.e. being middle class). They call this the 'spirit of capitalism' model since utility depends not only on consumption but also independently on your 'wealth status', relative to that of others (a kind of 'keeping up with the Jones's'). One form of (non-separable) utility function they use is

$$U(C_t, W_t, V_t) = \frac{C_t^{1-\gamma}}{(1-\gamma)} \left(\frac{W_t}{V_t}\right)^{-\lambda} \tag{18}$$

which reduces to the standard case for $\lambda = 0$. The solution for expected returns from the intertemporal problem is

$$ER_i - R_f = \gamma \sigma_{ic} + \lambda \sigma_{iw} - \lambda \sigma_{iv} \tag{19}$$

Because of the difficulty in measuring the appropriate social wealth index $V_t$, tests of the Euler equation assume $V$ is constant and the last term in (19) disappears. The FOCs are

$$E_t\{M_{t+1}, R_{i,t+1}\} = 1 \tag{20}$$

where

$$M_{t+1} = \theta \left(\frac{C_{t+1}}{C_t}\right)^{-\gamma} R_{W,t+1}^{-\lambda} \left[1 + \frac{\lambda}{\gamma - 1}\left(\frac{C_{t+1}}{W_{t+1}}\right)\right]$$

The wealth portfolio is taken to be an aggregate stock market index, and $R_i$ are different size-based portfolios. The estimates of $\gamma$ for the different portfolios are in the range 2.3–3.08 (with $\lambda$ in the range of 0.75–1.27), and the over-identifying restrictions are not rejected when more than two risky portfolios are simultaneously included in the test (see Bakshi and Chen 1996, Table 3). In addition (for $\lambda = 2$), the model does not violate the H–J bounds, when the coefficient of relative risk aversion $\gamma$ is between 6 and 8.

Clearly, it is the high covariance between $R_W$ and $R_i$ that allows the model to give a low estimate of $\gamma$, while still explaining 'volatile' movements in $R_i$. Also, there is some leeway in 'acceptable' values of $\lambda$, which is not really pinned down *a priori* (apart from $\lambda > 0$). The model solves the equity premium bit of the 'puzzle' with low $\gamma$, but there does not seem to be any tests of the risk-free rate Euler equation presented – so we do not know about the other half of the puzzle.

## Separating 'States' and 'Time': Epstein–Zin

In the standard power utility function, the 'curvature parameter' $\gamma$ plays a dual role. First, increasing $\gamma$ makes individuals want to smooth consumption over different *dates* – they dislike volatile growth in consumption and want to smooth their consumption path. But, second, a higher $\gamma$ also makes individuals want consumption in different *states of the world* to be similar – they dislike risk. The parameter $\gamma$ is both the coefficient of relative risk aversion and also equals the reciprocal of the intertemporal elasticity of substitution.

Epstein and Zin (1989, 1991) propose a generalised expected utility (GEU) function, $U_t = U[C_t, E_t(U_{t+1})]$, a special case of which is a constant elasticity function of current consumption and *future utility*.

$$U_t = \left[(1 - \delta)C_t^{1-1/\psi} + \delta E_t\{U_{t+1}^{1-\gamma}\}^{1/\lambda}\right]^{1/(1-1/\psi)} \tag{21}$$

where $\lambda = (1 - \gamma)/(1 - 1/\psi)$. The degree of risk aversion is determined by $\gamma$, while the elasticity of intertemporal substitution is $\psi$, so these can now be different. In principle, one parameter $\gamma$ can be used to explain the equity premium and the other $\psi$ to explain the low level and variability in the risk-free rate. If $\gamma = 1/\psi$, we have the standard power utility. The budget constraint in real terms (with no labour income) is $W_{t+1} = (1 + R_{m,t+1})(W_t - C_t)$ with $R_{m,t+1} = \sum_{j=1}^{n} \alpha_{j,t} R_{j,t+1}$ and $\sum_{j=1}^{n} \alpha_{j,t} = 1$. All invested real wealth $W_t$ consists of equity, bonds, real estate, and so on. Unfortunately, the FOCs contain the unobservable $E_t U_{t+1}$ but if consumption growth is *iid*, the FOCs can be written

$$\delta E\{(C_{t+1}/C_t)^{-\gamma}(R_{i,t+1} - R_{f,t})\} = 0 \tag{22a}$$

$$\delta[E(C_{t+1}/C_t)^{1-\gamma}]^{(\gamma-1/\psi)/(1-\gamma)} E\{(C_{t+1}/C_t)^{-\gamma} R_{f,t}^*\} = 1 \tag{22b}$$

which avoids the use of the unobservable market return, where the latter includes human capital, housing wealth as well as stock market wealth – Kocherlakota (1996). Equation (22a) is the same as the standard FOC (with power utility), so risk aversion $\gamma$ *still has to be high* to explain the equity premium. But given $\gamma$, we can choose $\psi$ in (22b) to exactly match the sample moments, so there is no risk-free rate puzzle with these GEU preferences.

We can explore recursive utility a little further, which will give us some insights into intertemporal models we meet in the next chapter. If we are willing to accept that only the market return enters the budget constraint $W_{t+1} = (1 + R_{m,t+1})(W_t - C_t)$, then Campbell, Lo and MacKinlay (1997) show that the recursive utility function with lognormality in consumption and asset returns gives:

$$\ln M_{t+1} = \frac{(1-\gamma)}{(1-\psi)}\Delta c_{t+1} - \frac{(1-\gamma\psi)}{(1-\psi)} r_{m,t+1}^* \tag{22c}$$

$$r_{f,t}^* = -\ln\delta + \frac{(\lambda-1)}{2}\sigma_m^2 - \frac{\lambda}{2\psi^2}\sigma^2(\Delta c) + \frac{1}{\psi}E_t\Delta c_{t+1} \tag{22d}$$

$$E_t(r_{i,t+1}^* - r_{f,t}^*) + \frac{\sigma_t^2(r_i^*)}{2} = (\lambda/\psi)\sigma_t(r_i^*, \Delta c) + (1-\lambda)\sigma_t(r_i^*, r_m^*) \tag{22e}$$

where $\lambda = (1-\gamma)/(1-1/\psi)$ and lower-case letters indicate logs (i.e. $\ln R^* \equiv r^*$). These equations show that the recursive utility model nests the C-CAPM with power utility (i.e. when $\gamma = 1/\psi$ and hence $\lambda = 1$) and the standard static CAPM with power utility $\lambda = 0$ (i.e. $\gamma = 1$, so consumption is proportional to wealth and $\lambda = 0$, so the only term in the above equation is $\lambda\sigma_t(r_i^*, \Delta c) = \lambda\sigma_t(r_i^*, r_m^*)$, where $r_m^*$ is the return on the total wealth portfolio). However, in general, the average excess return on any risky asset $i$ depends on the covariance between consumption growth and the asset return (C-CAPM) and on the covariance between the market return and the asset return.

## Time-Varying Risk Premium

Estimation of the Euler equations (22a) and (22b) provide a test of these SDF models, but it does not give a time series of the risk premium – for this, we need an explicit reduced form solution in terms of observable variables and a model of time-varying conditional covariances. Let us see how we might do this using GARCH models to mimic the time-varying risk premium. The SDF model can be expressed as above in real terms (equations 22d and 22e) or in nominal terms. The nominal budget constraint is

$$W_{t+1}^{\text{nom}} = (1 + R_{m,t+1}^{\text{nom}})(W_t^{\text{nom}} - P_t C_t)$$

$$\text{or} \quad W_{t+1} = \frac{(1 + R_{m,t+1}^{\text{nom}})}{(1 + \pi_{t+1})}(W_t - C_t)$$

where $P$ = consumer price index, $W^{\text{nom}}$ is nominal wealth, $W$ is real wealth, $(1 + R_{t+1}) = (1 + R_{t+1}^{\text{nom}})/(1 + \pi_{t+1})$ and $(1 + \pi_{t+1}) = P_{t+1}/P_t$. Using nominal returns, the Epstein–Zin utility function and joint lognormality (Campbell, Lo and MacKinlay 1997, Smith, Sorensen and Wickens 2003) gives

$$E_t(R_{i,t+1}^{\text{nom}} - R_{f,t}^{\text{nom}}) + \frac{1}{2}\sigma_t^2(R_i^{\text{nom}}) = -\frac{(1-\gamma)}{(1-\psi)}\text{cov}_t(\Delta c_{t+1}, R_{i,t+1}^{\text{nom}})$$

$$-\frac{\psi(1-\gamma)}{1-\psi}\text{cov}_t(\pi_{t+1}, R_{i,t+1}^{\text{nom}})$$

$$+\frac{(1-\psi\gamma)}{(1-\psi)}\text{cov}_t(R_{m,t+1}^{\text{nom}}, R_{i,t+1}^{\text{nom}})$$

In trying to implement the above, the problem is in finding an adequate measure of the market return on *all* assets. If we make the (rather heroic) assumption that the market portfolio consists of a *fixed* weighted average of the return on equity and the risk-free rate, then

$$R_{m,t+1}^{\text{nom}} = \theta R_{i,t+1}^{\text{nom}} + (1 - \theta)R_{f,t}^{\text{nom}}$$

and

$$E_t(R_{i,t+1}^{\text{nom}} - R_{f,t}^{\text{nom}}) + \left[\frac{1}{2} - \frac{\theta(1-\psi\gamma)}{1-\psi}\right]\sigma_t^2(R_{i,t+1}^{\text{nom}}) = -\frac{(1-\gamma)}{(1-\psi)}\text{cov}_t(\Delta c_{t+1}, R_{i,t+1}^{\text{nom}})$$

$$-\frac{\psi(1-\gamma)}{1-\psi}\text{cov}_t(\pi_{t+1}, R_{i,t+1}^{\text{nom}})$$

Note that $c_t \equiv \ln C_t$ is real consumption but all the other variables are in nominal terms. Let $\beta_2 = -(1-\gamma)/(1-\psi)$ and $\beta_3 = -\psi(1-\gamma)/(1-\psi)$, then estimation of the above equation gives estimates for $\gamma = \beta_2 - \beta_3 + 1$ and $\psi = \beta_3/\beta_2$ and there are no restrictions on the coefficient for $\sigma_t(R_{i,t+1}^{\text{nom}})$.

## Factor Models

Factor models assume that the SDF depends linearly on a set of $k$ factors $f_{i,t}$.

$$\ln M_{t+1} = \sum_{j=1}^{k} \beta_j f_{j,t+1}$$

If the factors are jointly lognormally distributed with equity returns (denoted $i$), then the SDF approach gives the no-arbitrage condition

$$E_t(r^*_{i,t+1} - r^*_{f,t}) + \frac{\sigma^2_t(r^*_i)}{2} = \sum_{j=1}^{k} \beta_j \sigma_t(r^*_i, f_j) \tag{22f}$$

This is the most general SDF model since the $b_j$ are unrestricted, but we have the practical problem of deciding on the factors to use. The C-CAPM with power or Epstein–Zin (recursive CES utility) give specific coefficients on the covariance terms (for example, as in equation 22e). The 'static' CAPM can be interpreted as a very restrictive SDF model to explain the expected excess return on asset $i$, where we have only one factor, the market return and the covariance term $\gamma \sigma_t(r^*_i, r_m)$. If we are trying to explain the excess return on some *aggregate equity index* $E_t(r^*_{i,t+1} - r^*_{f,t})$ and, in addition, we assume the market portfolio consists of a *fixed* weighted average of the return on *equity* and the risk-free rate, then the covariance term $\gamma \sigma_t(r^*_i, r^*_m)$ becomes a variance term $\gamma \sigma_t(r^*_m, r^*_m)$. These restrictive assumptions allow us to interpret the static CAPM of Chapter 5 (Section 5.4) as an SDF model.

In general, the key result of the SDF model is that expected excess returns depend on one or more covariance terms (which may be time-varying). This is also true of the C-CAPM and static CAPM models. Since the advent of ARCH and GARCH models in the 1990s (see Chapter 29), there are voluminous empirical studies that look at the relationship between asset returns (particularly on some aggregate equity index) and the *variance* of the returns, but, in general, these would be inconsistent with the no-arbitrage conditions of the SDF model, which implies the use of covariances. Empirically, the use of the conditional variance to explain expected returns was popular because it only required the use of univariate ARCH/GARCH processes, whereas implementing the SDF approach requires the use of multivariate processes. Of course, if the SDF model is empirically poorly determined, then as a *data description*, the use of the variance term is defensible.

The Euler equation approach does not give a time series for the risk premium, since the latter is implicit in the FOCs of the Euler equation rather than explicit as in the 'reduced form' results of the SDF model given above. In both the Euler equation and reduced form approaches, ancillary simplifying assumptions (e.g. power utility) have to be made. A time series for the risk premia covariance terms in SDF models can be obtained using multivariate ARCH/GARCH models, although there are difficulties of 'convergence' if there are a large number of parameters to estimate. According to the SDF model, the conditional covariances from the GARCH processes should be statistically significant in the mean equation for expected returns (e.g. see (22e)), hence these are referred to as *multivariate GARCH in mean* MGM models.

Smith, Sorensen and Wickens (2003), using monthly data 1975(6)–2001(12) for both the United Kingdom and United States, estimate the mean return equation for aggregate equity returns $E_t(R^{nom}_{i,t+1} - R^{nom}_{f,t})$ along with the multivariate GARCH process for a vector of variables $x = \{R^{nom}_{i,t+1} - R^{nom}_{f,t}, \pi_{t+1}, \Delta c_{t+1}, \Delta y_{t+1}\}'$, where $y_t$ (the log of aggregate output) is included as an additional 'factor'. The MGM model for the expected returns equation can be written

$$x_{t+1} = \alpha + \Gamma x_t + B g_t + \varepsilon_{t+1}$$

where $\varepsilon_{t+1}|\Omega_t \sim D(0, H_t)$ and $g_t = vec(H_{t+1})$. The *vec* operator converts the lower triangle of a symmetric matrix into a vector and '*D*' stands for 'distribution' and usually either normal or Student's *t*-distribution (to incorporate fat tails) are used (see Chapter 29). The mean return equation also contains a dummy variable for the crash of October 1987. In the general SDF model, the first row of $\Gamma$ should be zero and the first row of $B$ is $(-1/2, \beta_{11}, \beta_{12}, \beta_{13}, \ldots)$, which then represents equation (22f).

The covariance terms $H_{t+1}$ can be estimated using a multivariate GARCH model (see Chapter 29) and Smith, Sorensen and Wickens (2003) use a restricted VECM (1,1)-BEKK model (Engle and Kroner 1995):

$$H_{t+1} = V'V + A'(H_t - V'V)A + F'(\varepsilon_t \varepsilon_t' - V'V)F$$

In the most general SDF model, the covariances terms are between $R_{i,t+1}^{\text{nom}}$, the market return on equity, and the $\{\pi_{t+1}, \Delta c_{t+1}, \Delta y_{t+1}\}$ variables. The time-varying risk premia as modelled in the GARCH covariance terms explain some of the movement in excess equity returns, but the estimate of $\gamma = \beta_2 - \beta_3 + 1$ and $\psi = \beta_2/\beta_1$ in the Epstein–Zin C-CAPM model are both unacceptable. For example, for the United States, $\hat{\gamma} = 783$ and $\hat{\psi} = -118$ and for the United Kingdom $\hat{\gamma} = 844$ and $\hat{\psi} = -4.5$. The power utility model gives similar results to the Epstein–Zin formulation, and, therefore, both variants of the C-CAPM are not supported by the data. In the general SDF model (with no restrictions on the size or sign of the covariance terms in the mean return equation), Smith, Sorensen and Wickens (2003) find that in the mean return equation, the time-varying covariance terms on consumption (t-statistic $\approx 2.9$ for US and 1.57 for UK) and inflation (t-statistic $\approx 1.7$ for US and 2.8 for UK) are just statistically significant, but those on output and the variance of the market return are not (the latter rules out the static CAPM). The proportion of movements in excess returns explained by the SDF risk premia is around 4%.

Overall, modelling the time-varying covariance terms with observable factors (i.e. inflation, consumption and output) and a (restricted) GARCH model using UK or US monthly data is extremely difficult, and even with a fairly general 'data-based' SDF model, it is difficult to find statistically significant covariance effects on expected equity returns.

## SDF Model without Consumption Data

Campbell (1993) demonstrates how the above excess return equation can be represented *without using consumption data* and only using returns. The idea is based on a log-linearisation of the wealth constraint

$$\Delta w_{t+1} \approx r_{m,t+1}^* + k + (1 - 1/\rho)(c_t - w_t)$$

where $r_{m,t+1}^* = \ln R_{m,t+1}^*$, and so on, $\rho = 1 - \exp(\overline{c - w})$ and $k$ is a linearisation constant. (Note we have defined $\rho$ here to be compatible with Campbell's notation.)

Iterating the above equation forward and using the above log-linear equations for $r_{f,t}^*$ and $r_{i,t+1}^*$, Campbell shows that

$$c_t - w_t = (1 - \psi)E_t \left[ \sum_{j=1}^{\infty} \rho^j r_{m,t+j}^* \right] + k^*$$

where $k^*$ depends on $\text{cov}_t(r_m^*, \Delta c)$. Clearly, $\psi > 1$ implies the substitution effect of expected returns dominates the income effect and the consumption–wealth ratio falls as $Er_{m,t+j}^*$ increases (and vice versa for $\psi < 1$). If $\psi = 1$, the consumption–wealth ratio is independent of expected returns. If we push on a little further, we obtain a nice 'intuitive' equation for excess returns. From the above equation, it is straightforward to derive

$$c_{t+1} - E_t c_{t+1} = (w_{t+1} - E_t w_{t+1}) + (1 - \psi)(E_{t+1} - E_t) \left[ \sum_{j=1}^{\infty} \rho^j r_{m,t+j+1}^* \right]$$

$$= (r_{m,t+1}^* - E_t r_{m,t+1}^*) + (1 - \psi)(E_{t+1} - E_t) \left[ \sum_{j=1}^{\infty} \rho^j r_{m,t+j+1}^* \right]$$

where the last substitution comes from the log-linear budget constraint. Again, $\psi > 1$ or $\psi < 1$ is crucial in determining the impact of *revisions* in expected future returns $(E_{t+1} - E_t)$ on the variability in consumption. More importantly, however, the above equation indicates that the covariance of any asset return $i$ with consumption can be represented by the covariance between the return $i$ and the market return (i.e. the wealth portfolio), and it can be shown that

$$E_t(r_{i,t+1}^* - r_{f,t}^*) + \frac{\sigma_t^2(r_i^*)}{2} = \gamma\, \sigma_t(r_i^*, r_m^*) + (\gamma - 1)\sigma_t(r_i^*, h_m)$$

where

$$\sigma(r_i^*, h_m) \equiv \text{cov}_t \left( r_{i,t+1}^*, E_{t+1} \left[ \sum_{j=1}^{\infty} \rho^j r_{m,t+1+j}^* \right] - E_t \left[ \sum_{j=1}^{\infty} \rho^j r_{m,t+1+j} \right] \right)$$

We have replaced covariances of $r_i^*$ with consumption growth, with (i) covariances with the market return and (ii) covariances with news about *future* market returns, while $\psi$ disappears from the excess return equation.

The above equation is a discrete time version of Merton's (1973) continuous-time model where asset expected returns depend on 'hedge portfolios' that represent changes in the investment opportunity set (i.e. the covariance term $\sigma_t(r_i^*, h_m)$). Also, it is clear from the previous equation what special circumstances are required for the covariance of the asset's return with the market to be a sufficient statistic to price the asset (i.e. the model reduces to the static CAPM). These conditions are:

(i) the investment opportunity set is constant, $\sigma_t(r_i^*, h_m) = 0$ or

(ii) the coefficient of relative risk aversion, $\gamma = 1$ or

(iii) $r_m$ follows a univariate stochastic process, then news about future returns is perfectly correlated with *current* returns – hence $\sigma_t(r_i^*, r_m)$ contains all information about $\sigma_t(r_i^*, h_m)$.

As we shall see in the next chapter, the assumption that the investment opportunity set is constant (i.e. returns are *iid*) or that $\gamma = 1$ (log utility) are important 'special cases' in intertemporal models.

For the market return, the above equation becomes

$$E_t(r_{m,t+1}^* - r_{f,t}^*) + \frac{\sigma_t^2(r_m^*)}{2} = \gamma\sigma_t^2(r_m^*) + (\gamma - 1)\sigma_t(r_m^*, h_m)$$

Note that if (i) $\gamma = 1$ or (ii) $\gamma \neq 1$ and the market return is unforecastable (i.e. $\sigma_t(r_m^*, h_m) = 0$), then the risk premium can be measured using the historic Sharpe ratio. If $\gamma > 1$ and $\sigma_t(r_m^*, h_m) < 0$ (i.e. long-run mean reversion), then the Sharpe ratio overstates the risk premium.

## International CAPM

If we apply Campbell's model to investment in foreign assets, the *real* return in local currency depends on the local price level and the change in the real exchange rate. If returns are nominal, then (local currency) inflation is an additional variable to be considered. If we take country-1 as the numeraire currency, then the *real* return to country-$j$'s investor is (see Chapter 1)

$$R_{p,t+1}^* = R_{p,t+1}^{\mathrm{nom},1} \frac{P_t^1}{P_{t+1}^1} \frac{Q_t}{Q_{t+1}}$$

where $R_{p,t+1}^{\mathrm{nom},1}$ = nominal return of country-$j$ investor's portfolio expressed in country-1's currency, $P_t^1$ = price level in currency 1 and $Q_t$ = real exchange rate (good-1/good-$j$). It follows, after taking logs,

$$r_{p,t+1}^* = r_{p,t+1}^{\mathrm{nom},1} - \pi_{t+1}^1 - \Delta q_{t+1}$$

where $\pi \equiv \ln(P_{t+1}^1/P_t^1)$. If purchasing power parity (PPP) holds, then the real return to investor-$j$ is simply the nominal return in currency-1 less the inflation rate in currency-1. But if PPP does not hold, the real return depends on the real exchange rate. The (real) budget constraint for an international investor is

$$W_{t+1} = R_{p,t+1}^*(W_t - C_t)$$

This can be linearised as indicated above (Campbell 1993) and consumption substituted out of the equation for expected returns. With recursive utility, the expected returns equation for asset-$i$ (Ng 2004) is

$$E_t(r_{i,t+1}^{\mathrm{nom}} - r_{f,t}^{\mathrm{nom}}) + \frac{\sigma_t^2(r_i^{\mathrm{nom}})}{2} = \gamma V_{i,m} + (1 - \gamma)V_{i,q} + V_{i,\pi} + (\gamma - 1)(V_{i,hm} - V_{i,hq})$$

where $V_{i,m} = \mathrm{cov}_t(r_{i,t+1}^{\mathrm{nom},1}, r_{m,t+1}^{\mathrm{nom},1} - \pi_{t+1}^1)$ is the covariance between the asset-$i$ return and the real market return. Also, $V_{i,q} = \mathrm{cov}_t(r_{i,t+1}^{\mathrm{nom},1}, \Delta q_{t+1})$, and $V_{i,hm} = \mathrm{cov}(r_{i,t+1}^{\mathrm{nom},1}, h_m)$, where $h_m$ is news about future real market returns (i.e. $h_m = (E_{t+1} - E_t) \sum_{k=1}^{\infty} \rho^k (r_{m,t+k+1}^{\mathrm{nom},1} - \pi_{t+k+1}^1)$ and finally, $V_{i,hq} = \mathrm{cov}(r_{i,t+1}^{\mathrm{nom},1}, h_q)$ where $h_q$ is defined analogously to $h_m$ but is 'news' about future values of $\Delta q_{t+k+1}$.

It is clear from the above equation that this 'international-CAPM' is similar in structure to Campbell's (1993) 'domestic-CAPM', but there are additional covariance terms due to the international variable ($\Delta q_{t+1}$) and the inflation rate $\pi_{t+1}$, because returns are in nominal terms. The coefficient restrictions on the '$V$' terms are also obvious. $V_{i,hm}$ and $V_{i,hq}$ are intertemporal hedging terms, but if 'domestic' equity returns and real exchange rates are *not* predictable, these variables equal zero and the model is a 'static' ICAPM (where returns depend only on covariances with the market return, real exchange rate changes and inflation). Of course, when PPP holds, $V_{i,q} = V_{i,hq} = 0$, and the model reduces to Campbell's (1993) 'domestic-CAPM'. Finally, if $\gamma = 1$, the standard (static) CAPM applies. Ng (2004) attempts to implement this international-CAPM (without consumption) for local equity returns and foreign exchange returns for the United States, United Kingdom, Japan and Germany (July 1978–April 1998). The market return is a world equity index. Surprises in $h_m$ and $h_q$ can be measured by estimating a VAR in these (and other) variables, $z_t$ and future surprises then depend on the estimated covariance matrix from the VAR (see Chapter 12). The expected equity and FX returns $r_{i,t+1}^{\mathrm{nom}}$ are also assumed to depend on the $z$ variables.

Ng (2004) finds that the intertemporal hedging terms $V_{i,hm}$ and $V_{i,hq}$ are (statistically) important in determining the cross section of asset returns. However, Ng also finds that the $\gamma(V_{i,hm} - V_{i,hq})$ term is proportional to the $\gamma V_{i,m} + (1-\gamma)V_{i,q} + V_{i,\pi}$ term so the latter terms are sufficient to explain the cross section of returns and the model collapses to a 'static' international CAPM. Therefore, the dynamic hedging terms add little from an empirical perspective, and the model also cannot explain average returns on the high book-to-market *country* portfolios of Fama and French (1998).

## 14.5  Habit Formation

We now turn to another form of non-separability, namely, habit persistence, which has proved very useful in analysing the equity premium and risk-free rate puzzles. In habit-formation models, it is not the absolute level of consumption that is important but consumption relative to some previous benchmark level. This seems a reasonable starting point since casual introspection suggests people worry about a fall in consumption relative to its past level, even though after the fall, the absolute level of consumption may be the second or third highest for the past 20 years. Also, social insurance contracts (e.g. payouts from car, personal accident and unemployment insurance) rarely insure the full value and therefore protect against a fall in value.

Habit-persistence models are usually representative agent models where the non-separable utility function is of the form $U(C_t, Z_t)$ with $Z_t = f(C_{t-1}, C_{t-2}, \ldots)$. The exact form of $U(C_t, Z_t)$ can vary, for example, as follows.

*Individual habit persistence*

$$U = \frac{(C_{i,t} - \lambda C_{i,t-1})^{1-\gamma}}{1 - \gamma} \qquad \lambda > 0 \tag{23}$$

*'Keeping up with the Jones's'*

$$U = \frac{C_{i,t}^{1-\gamma} C_t^{\lambda} C_{t-1}^{\lambda}}{(1 - \gamma)} \tag{24}$$

where $C_{i,t}$ is an individual's consumption and $C_t$ is aggregate consumption (Constantinides 1990, Heaton 1995, Abel 1990, Gali 1994). In implementing these models, the problem is that the FOCs contain terms of the form $\theta E\{(U'_{t+1}/U'_t)(R_{i,t+1} - R_{f,t})\} = 0$. But $U'_{t+1}$ depends on the investor's ability to predict future consumption growth, which is unobservable unless we make the ancillary assumption that consumption growth is *iid*. Neither of these models simultaneously explains *both* the equity premium and the risk-free rate puzzles.

The habit-persistence model of Campbell and Cochrane (1999) we examine in further detail to gain an insight into why some of these models can explain a high equity premium with standard preferences and a low 'power coefficient' $\gamma$, while still predicting the low level and volatility of interest rates. The reason is that the local curvature $- CU''(C)/U'(C)$ depends not only on $\gamma$ but also on how far consumption is above (or below) its habit level – local curvature or 'risk aversion' can, therefore, be high in recessions (i.e. current consumption below habit level). The low-power coefficient gives a low level and variability of interest rates (i.e. a low intertemporal elasticity of substitution). But investors still find stocks risky, not because of low consumption but because they dislike recessions, which give high local curvature and hence high risk aversion. Put another way, investors dislike stocks because they pay off poorly in recessions.

## Campbell–Cochrane: Habit-Persistence C-CAPM

As noted above, a key factor in the Campbell–Cochrane model is that the (local) curvature of the power utility function depends on the *current* level of consumption *relative* to its habit level of the recent past. What determines utility is not a high or low *absolute level* of consumption but high or low current consumption *relative to its recent average value*. The 'new' state variable is, therefore, a 'weighted average of past consumption' or 'habit', $X_t$, and the power utility function is non-separable in $C_t$ and $X_t$ (so that it *cannot* be written $U_t(C_t, X_t) = U(C_t) + U(X_t)$):

$$U_t = \sum_{t=0}^{\infty} \theta^t \frac{(C_t - X_t)^{1-\gamma} - 1}{1 - \gamma} \tag{25}$$

where $U_t(C_t, X_t) = [(C_t - X_t)^{1-\gamma} - 1]/(1 - \gamma)$. This utility function embodies 'keeping up with the Jones's' since each *individual's* habit is determined by *everyone else's* past consumption (Abel 1990). Also,

$$U_c(C_t, X_t) = (C_t - X_t)^{-\gamma} = (S_t C_t)^{-\gamma} \tag{26}$$

where $S_t \equiv (C_t - X_t)/C_t = 1 - X_t/C_t$ and $S_t$ is the 'surplus consumption ratio'. $S_t$ is a recession indicator: as $C_t$ falls towards its previous average level, $S_t$ rises. The curvature (i.e. loosely risk aversion) of the utility function is

$$\eta_t = -\frac{C_t U_{cc}(C_t, X_t)}{U_c(C_t, X_t)} = \frac{\gamma}{S_t} \tag{27}$$

Hence, even if the 'power coefficient' $\gamma$ is small (e.g. $\gamma = 2$), $\eta_t$ will be large when current consumption is close to previous 'habit levels', $X_t$. Not only that, but as we move into a recession, $S_t$ falls and $\eta_t$ rises, implying increased risk aversion in a recession. The Sharpe ratio for this model (see equation (4)) is

$$\frac{E_t R_{t+1} - r}{\sigma_t(R_{t+1})} = \eta_t \sigma_t(\Delta c_{t+1})\rho_t(\Delta c_{t+1}, R_{t+1}) \tag{28}$$

where $r = \ln R_f^*$. A high average $\eta_t$ implies we can explain a high average Sharpe ratio. Also, even if $\sigma_t$ and $\rho_t$ are constant, since $\eta_t$ rises in a recession, the model explains the counter-cyclical pattern in the Sharpe ratio. The SDF is

$$M_{t+1} \equiv \theta \frac{U_c(C_{t+1}, X_{t+1})}{U_c(C_t, X_t)} = \theta \left(\frac{C_{t+1} - X_{t+1}}{C_t - X_t}\right)^{-\gamma} = \theta \left(\frac{S_{t+1}C_{t+1}}{S_t C_t}\right)^{-\gamma} \tag{29}$$

With 'small' $\gamma = 2$, we can have low 'aversion' to intertemporal substitution so consumers will be willing to switch consumption between $t$ and $t + 1$, with small changes in interest rates (while the 'large' $\eta_t$ 'gives the high equity premium'). Indeed, in this model,

$$r_t = -\ln E_t(M_{t+1}) = -\ln\theta + \gamma g - \frac{1}{2}\left(\frac{\gamma}{\bar{S}}\right)^2 \sigma_t^2(\Delta c) \tag{30a}$$

$$\bar{S} = \sigma(\Delta c)\sqrt{\frac{\gamma}{(1-\phi)}} \quad \text{and} \quad g = E_t(\Delta c_{t+1}) \tag{30b}$$

The parameter $\phi$ (= 0.87) is the degree of persistence in $s = \ln S$. Directly from (30a), 'small' $\gamma = 2$ implies a small responsiveness of $r$ to changes in consumption growth, $g$.

There are two opposing forces at work in keeping interest rates relatively stable. As we enter a recession, $C_t$ falls towards $X_t$ and marginal utility $U_c = (C - X)_t^{-\gamma}$ rises. In our earlier model, this led to increased borrowing (so you could consume more when $U_c$ was high) and interest rates were driven up. The countervailing force in this model is that in a recession, risk aversion $\eta_t$ is high and this leads to an increase in *precautionary saving*, which tends to lower interest rates. These two effects tend to cancel each other out, leading to near-constant interest rates.

Essentially, what Campbell–Cochrane have cleverly done is to introduce non-linearities in the response of $M_{t+1}$ to consumption growth (see (29)). The log of the surplus consumption ratio $s_{t+1}$ follows a slow mean reverting AR(1) process with a non-linear response $\lambda(s_t)$ to *shocks* in consumption growth $v_{t+1}$:

$$\Delta c_{t+1} = g + v_{t+1} \quad v_{t+1} \sim niid\,(0, \sigma^2) \tag{31}$$

$$s_{t+1} = (1 - \phi)\bar{s} + \phi s_t + \lambda(s_t)v_{t+1} \tag{32a}$$

where

$$\lambda(s_t) = \frac{1}{S}\sqrt{1 - 2(s_t - \bar{s})} - 1 \tag{32b}$$

The rather complex process in (32) ensures that consumption is always above habit since $S = e^s > 0$. The process for $s_{t+1}$ in (32) when substituted in (29) for $\ln M_{t+1}$ gives

$$m_{t+1} = a + b(s_t) + d(s_t)\Delta c_{t+1} \tag{33}$$

where $b(s_t)$ and $d(s_t)$ are non-linear functions of $s_t$ and the parameters $\theta, \gamma, \phi$. Hence, $m_{t+1}$ responds not only to consumption growth $\Delta c_{t+1}$ (as in the non-habit C-CAPM) but the sensitivity of $m_{t+1}$ to $\Delta c_{t+1}$ depends on the state of the economy, $s_t$.

What about relative returns $(ER_i/ER_j)$ in this model? With $\gamma = 2$, then from the definition of $M_{t+1}$ in (29), a large value for $ER_i/ER_j$ must come from the $(S_{t+1}/S_t)^{-\gamma}$ term, that is the covariance of $R_i$ or $R_j$, with consumption relative to habit – a kind of 'recession' variable. In the non-habit C-CAPM, relative returns are determined by assets' return covariances with consumption growth, *per se*, and *not* consumption relative to its recent average level. This subtle distinction makes a major difference to the predictions of the model.

## Calibration and Simulation

There are no formal statistical tests since this is a calibration model. It is assessed by simulation and then checking the model output with the stylised facts found in real world data. Using past data, values for the underlying 'fundamental values' are taken to be $g = 1.89$, $\sigma = 1.9$, $r = 0.94$. The parameter $\phi = 0.87$ is chosen so the model produces the autocorrelation of the price–dividend ratio found in the data. Also $\gamma = 2$ is used and $\bar{S} = 0.57$ follows. The model is then simulated 10,000 times using $v_{t+1} \sim niid\,(0, \sigma^2)$ and various statistics calculated. A reasonable value of $\theta = 0.89$ is used, which generates a (mean) interest rate of 0.94% and a Sharpe ratio of 0.5. From simulations of the model, we can obtain a generated data series for stock prices $P_t$ and returns. A regression of the return over different horizons on the price–dividend ratio shows a negative coefficient and $R$-squared that both increase (in absolute terms) with horizon and is close to those found in the real world data. So the model 'simulates' the return predictability, the high Sharpe ratio and low level and volatility of real interest rates found in real world data. But note that the equity premium is explained by assuming high risk aversion (i.e. $\eta_t$ is high when $C_t$ is close to habit $X_t$). However, the risk-free rate is decoupled from $\eta_t$ and depends on $\gamma$, which can be small, so it gives low variability in the risk-free rate.

The marginal utility of consumption is given by

$$U_c = C_t^{-\gamma} \left( \frac{C_t - X_t}{C_t} \right)^{-\gamma}$$

so consumers dislike low consumption (as in the standard model) but they also dislike recessions (i.e. when consumption is low relative to its recent past level). Stocks are risky partly because consumption is volatile (but not very much) but mainly because bad stock returns tend to happen in recessions (i.e. are correlated with the habit variable).

Campbell and Cochrane (1999) use the above model to throw light on why the C-CAPM performs so badly relative to the standard-CAPM or the conditional-CAPM – that is where forecasting variables like the dividend-price ratio also affect asset returns (Cochrane 1996). They generate returns and consumption data from the habit-formation model at high frequency so with only one shock in the model, consumption growth, returns and the SDF are perfectly positively *conditionally* correlated by construction. This is because over small time horizons, the non-linearities in the model virtually disappear. However, as the time interval is extended the response of consumption growth, returns and the discount factor respond differently to the 'shock' and are therefore imperfectly *unconditionally* correlated and, for example, the dividend–price ratio predicts future returns. The standard-CAPM and the conditional-CAPM predict the cross section of returns better than the habit C-CAPM, even though the latter is the true model. This is because the market return is better *unconditionally* correlated with the true SDF as it is affected when the dividend–price ratio changes, whereas consumption growth is not. Of course, this establishes a prima facie case for the habit–consumption model but does not demonstrate it is the correct model of asset returns.

## 14.6   Equity Premium: Further Explanations

### Incomplete Markets

General equilibrium incomplete markets models are rather complex and are often solved numerically, and it is often difficult to extract the intuitive aspects of the models. Nevertheless, in this section, we compare the complete markets SDF model with two-period and infinite horizon *incomplete* markets models. The latter focus on *individual* consumption, whereas SDF models usually invoke the 'representative agent', and hence it is *aggregate* consumption and its correlation with asset returns that is the key driving variable for expected returns.

Suppose individuals can insure themselves and hence offset any individual idiosyncratic shocks. For example, faced with unemployment, the individual either has an insurance contract that pays off in this 'bad' state or has sufficient financial assets (savings) to 'weather the storm'. Then an individual's consumption will be similar to aggregate per capita consumption. But then with standard preferences, we have the equity premium puzzle again.

The incomplete markets literature keeps the standard preferences but notes that when markets are incomplete, individual consumption may vary more than per capita consumption. Hence, *individual* consumption may be more highly correlated with stock returns, thus requiring lower risk aversion to explain the observed equity premium. The additional consumption variability in incomplete markets also implies that individuals save more to self-insure against consumption shocks. This increased saving then lowers the average risk-free rate. Hence, such models might be capable of explaining both parts of the equity premium puzzle (Weil 1992).

Two-period general equilibrium models with incomplete markets are not sufficient to capture the 'self-insurance', which is possible over long horizons. For example, if I live for only two periods (and have zero bequests), then a negative income shock in the second year will be fully reflected in lower individual consumption, thus increasing the variability of one's consumption. But if I expect to live for many years, then I can smooth out my consumption by saving less in the 'shock period' and saving more in the future when my income is high. This *dynamic* self-insurance reduces the impact of idiosyncratic risk on individual consumption.

Kocherlakota (1996) provides a 'neat' intuitive example of dynamic self-insurance in an incomplete markets infinite horizon model. This leads to smaller savings than in the two-period incomplete markets case and hence is much *less successful* in generating the low risk-free rate we require.

In this 'model', there is a continuum of identical infinitely lived agents with random incomes that are independent of each other (so the variability in per capita income is zero). Individuals cannot write insurance contracts against the variability in their individual income. They can make risk-free loans to each other but cannot borrow more than $B from each other. Assume initially that $B is not binding because (permanent) income $y_{min}/r$ never falls below $B. For every lender, there must be a borrower so $y_{min} > 0$, if there is to be trade in equilibrium.

The probability of an uninsurable fall in consumption is smaller in the infinite horizon case than the two-period case. Although aggregate net saving is zero, the individual has a line of credit of $y_{min}/r$ to 'buffer' a fall in consumption and only a long sequence of negative income shocks could make this constraint binding. Hence, most individuals will not face a binding constraint and, therefore, the extra saving required for self-insurance, even with incomplete markets, will be less than in the two-period model. Hence, the incomplete markets model with an infinite horizon give savings levels that approach those found in the complete markets model and hence do not 'fit' the 'low' observed risk-free rate.

In the above model, shocks to income are stationary and eventually die out. In the incomplete markets model of Constantinides and Duffie (1996) shocks to individual labour income are permanent. Dynamic self-insurance over an infinite horizon is then impossible because the permanent income shock must be fully reflected in consumption. If permanent income falls by $x$, then to keep a smooth profile of consumption, the latter must also fall by $x$ in every period. Hence, in this model, the risk-free rate may be much lower than in the complete markets case.

The Constantinides and Duffie (1996) model is ingenious and is 'reverse engineered' to generate *any* equity premium, together with low and relatively constant interest rates and requires no transactions costs or borrowing constraints. As we have seen, idiosyncratic risk, which is uncorrelated with asset returns, has no effect on equilibrium returns. If we make idiosyncratic risk correlated with the market, individuals can trade financial assets with each other to 'remove' the correlation. For example, if A gets more labour income in a stock market boom and B gets more labour income when the market is low, then A will sell assets to B, and such trades will remove the correlation between the individual income shocks and asset returns and therefore will have no effect on prices.

The way the C–D model generates 'high risk' (with low risk aversion) is very subtle and basically depends on the non-linearity of marginal utility. Income shocks are uncorrelated with returns so they cannot be traded away. But *non-linear* marginal utility transforms these shocks into marginal utility shocks that *are* correlated with asset returns and hence affect equilibrium returns. The C–D model is 'engineered' so that when the market declines, the *variance* of idiosyncratic shocks rises.

The basic intuition (Cochrane 2000) can be seen by summing the usual FOC over all $N$ individuals ($j = 1, 2, \ldots, N$)

$$0 = E\{S_N[(C_{t+1}^{(j)}/C_t^{(j)})^{-\gamma}](R_{t+1} - R_{ft})\} \tag{34}$$

where $S_N = (1/N) \sum_{j=1}^{N} [(C_{t+1}^{(j)}/C_t^{(j)})^{-\gamma}]$ is the sum over $j$ individuals and $C^{(j)}$ is the consumption of individual $j$. If the *cross-section* variation in consumption growth is lognormal,

$$0 = E\left\{\exp\left[-\gamma(S_N \Delta c_{t+1}^{(j)}) + \frac{\gamma^2}{2}\sigma_N^2(\Delta c_{t+1}^{(j)})\right](R_{t+1} - R_{ft})\right\} \tag{35}$$

where $\sigma_N^2(.)$ represents the variance of consumption growth *across* all individuals. The $\sigma_N^2(.)$ term introduces additional 'priced' risk, if it is correlated with asset returns. Since the C–D model can be engineered to fit the stylised facts, its validity hinges on the key assumptions that (i) shocks to individual labour income are permanent (ii) whether cross-section uncertainty about individual income is higher when the market is lower – that is, do you require a high equity premium because stock returns are low, when income shocks are also 'bad'. Evidence in Heaton and Lucas (1996) and Deaton and Paxson (1994) on US cross-section data suggest that C–D's assumptions do not hold (e.g. the autocorrelation of undiversifiable income shocks may be around 0.5 rather than 1).

The C–D model and the various habit-persistence models, although very different in structure, have one thing in common. Consumers do not fear a fall in returns and wealth *per se* but a fall in wealth when they are already feeling 'bad'. In the habit-persistence models, bad times are when consumption is low *relative to its recent past*, while in C–D, 'bad' is when individual labour market risk is high. Broadly speaking, the additional state variable in both models could be described as a 'recession variable'.

## Trading Costs

It is possible that the additional *cost of trading stocks* over (risk-free) bonds drives a wedge between these two returns. Suppose trading bonds is costless. Over an infinite horizon, with constant dividends, the return on stocks is $R_S = D/P$. It can be shown that if you hold stocks for ever, then the upper bound on the equity premium (Kocherlakota 1996) is

$$R_S - R_f = \tau R_f$$

where $\tau$ is the proportionate cost of trading stocks (relative to the zero cost assumed for trading bonds). Thus, for $R_f = 1\%$, the additional transactions cost would have to be 600% to explain an equity premium of 6%. Clearly if an individual has a binding borrowing constraint, you cannot smooth your consumption after a negative income shock, without selling stocks (i.e. you cannot hold stocks for ever). If this happens frequently and it is expensive to trade stocks, you may demand a higher equity premium, but it is unlikely that this effect can account for the large observed equity premium.

Borrowing constraints can potentially lower the risk-free rate (compared with a situation of no borrowing constraints). If people have a negative income shock and their borrowing constraint is binding then they cannot borrow any further. Hence, given that demand must equal supply in the bond (loan) market there are now more lenders than borrowers and the interest rate must be lower (than in a model with no borrowing constraints). But those facing a borrowing constraint could sell stocks and use the funds to smooth their consumption. However, if they are also constrained in the stock market (i.e. have no stocks), then the supply of stocks exceeds the demand (compared to a no-constraints model) and the equity return would fall – hence, the equity *premium* might be much the same in these models where some agents are constrained as it is in the 'no-constraints' standard model (Kocherlakota 1996).

## 14.7 Summary

- The C-CAPM is consistent with near-zero predictability in stock, bond and FX returns over very short horizons (e.g. up to 1 month). The C-CAPM allows predictability of returns over longer horizons as conditional forecasts of consumption and return volatility change over time (and possibly the coefficient of risk aversion also changes). However, variables used in empirical return predictability regressions are often not directly related to the moments of the C-CAPM.

- The C-CAPM with power utility (over the level of consumption) cannot explain the observed high risk premium on stocks (i.e. the *equity premium puzzle*) together with the low mean level and variability in the risk-free rate (i.e. the *risk-free rate puzzle*).

- The equity premium puzzle also manifests itself in the failure of the C-CAPM to explain the observed Sharpe ratio (for, say, the S&P500), the multi-asset H–J bound and the cross-section and time-series behaviour implied by the C-CAPM Euler equation.

- Attempts to 'solve' the equity premium puzzle using the SDF model have met with some but not complete success, most notably by introducing additional state variables (e.g. wealth, habit consumption) into the utility function.

- Similarly, 'solving' the equity premium puzzle using an incomplete markets approach is possible, but the required assumption of permanent shocks to individual income would not be widely accepted.

# Appendix: Hansen–Jagannathan Bound

Consider a regression projection of $M_t$ on a set of $N$ asset pay-offs $X_t$ $(N \times 1)$:

$$M_t - E(M) = (X_t - E(X))'\boldsymbol{\beta} + \varepsilon_t \tag{A1}$$

where $M_t$ is a scalar, whilst $X$ and $\boldsymbol{\beta}$ are both $(N \times 1)$. Using (A1), and the fact that $E(\varepsilon_t) = E(\varepsilon_t X) = 0$,

$$(M_t - E(M))(X_t - E(X)) = (X_t - E(X))(X_t - E(X))'\boldsymbol{\beta} + (X_t - E(X))\varepsilon_t \tag{A2}$$

Hence:

$$E(M_t X) = E(M)E(X) + \Sigma\boldsymbol{\beta} \tag{A3}$$

where $\Sigma = \text{cov}(X, X')$. Since $M$ correctly prices all the assets $P = E(M_t X)$ and from (A3), we solve for $\boldsymbol{\beta}$:

$$\boldsymbol{\beta} = \Sigma^{-1}[P - E(M)E(X)] \tag{A4}$$

From (A1) and noting that in a regression $\varepsilon_t$ is uncorrelated with $X_t$ by construction, then

$$\sigma^2(M) = \sigma^2\{(X_t - E(X))'\boldsymbol{\beta}\} + \sigma^2(\varepsilon) = \sigma^2(z) + \sigma^2(\varepsilon) \tag{A5}$$

where $z = X_t - E(X)'\boldsymbol{\beta}$, hence $Ez = 0$ and

$$\sigma^2(z) \equiv E(z'z) = \boldsymbol{\beta}'\Sigma\boldsymbol{\beta} \tag{A6}$$

Substituting for $\boldsymbol{\beta}$ from (A4):

$$\sigma^2(z) = [P - E(M)E(X)]'\Sigma^{-1}[P - E(M)E(X)] \tag{A7}$$

Substituting (A7) in (A4) and noting that $\sigma^2(\varepsilon) > 0$, we obtain the inequality found in the text

$$\sigma^2(M) \geq [P - E(M)E(X)]'\Sigma^{-1}[P - E(M)E(X)] \tag{A8}$$

Dividing through by $P$ (element-by-element), the $P$ vector becomes a vector of ones $= \mathbf{e1}$ and the $X$ vector, a vector of gross returns $R^*$, hence:

$$\sigma^2(M) \geq [\mathbf{e1} - E(M)E(R^*)]'\Sigma_R^{-1}[\mathbf{e1} - E(M)E(R^*)] \tag{A9}$$

where $\Sigma_R$ is now the variance–covariance matrix of *returns*. When we have only one risky asset, we set $\mathbf{e1} = 1$, $\Sigma_R = \sigma^2(R^*)$, and given $E(M) = 1/R_f^*$, (A9) reduces to the Sharpe ratio version of the Hansen–Jagannathan bound, equation (7) in the text:

$$\sigma(M)/E(M) \geq E(R^* - R_f^*)/\sigma(R^*) \tag{A10}$$

# 15

# INTERTEMPORAL ASSET ALLOCATION: THEORY

## Aims

- Solve a two-period consumption-portfolio model in which agent's utility is time-separable and depends only on consumption. Assets are used to carry over wealth from one period to the next (and labour income does not enter the budget constraint). Agents simultaneously choose desired consumption and the desired amounts to hold in risky and risk-free assets.

- Show that in the two-period model, the general solution has consumption and asset shares, depending on current wealth and a forecast of next period's expected returns on the risky assets (as well as the risk-free rate and a measure of risk aversion).

- Extend the model to the multi-period case where agents at time $t$ decide on their optimal consumption path $(C_t, C_{t+1}, \ldots, C_T)$ and their optimal asset proportions $(\alpha_t, \alpha_{t+1}, \ldots, \alpha_T)$ for all future periods. The general form of the solution (for time-separable utility) is the same as for the two-period case, and consumption and asset shares depend on current wealth and all future expected returns.

- For the special case of power utility and *iid* returns, the solutions for consumption and asset shares are the same in the two-period case as in the multi-period case (i.e. independent of horizon). The consumption–wealth ratio and asset shares are both independent of wealth but depend on expected asset returns. For log utility, the consumption–wealth ratio is independent of wealth (as for power utility) but now is also independent of expected returns.

- To show how the FOCs of the SDF model, $E\{R_{i,t+1}M_{t+1}\} = 1$ can be derived from the multi-period portfolio-consumption optimisation problem.

# 15.1  Two-Period Model

The model assumes individuals wish to maximise utility that depends only on consumption today and tomorrow. Individuals choose the optimal amounts of consumption $C_t$ and $C_{t+1}$ and the amounts to hold in a set of risky assets and a risk-free asset.

We present this two-period model in some detail because it turns out that the solution technique used is also applicable in a multi-period model (with some minor modifications). The solution technique involves a backward recursion, that is, we first solve the model for the final period ($t + 1$) and only then do we proceed to solve for period $t$ (i.e. today). This will allow us to see the role played by the *value function* and the *Bellman equation*, which are used in the multi-period framework. As we shall see, even in a two-period model, a simple closed form solution for consumption and asset holdings is often difficult to obtain. This is why portfolio-consumption models are often tested using some form of Euler equation or first-order conditions (FOC), as we saw in Chapter 14 on the C-CAPM. Of course, one can always solve these FOCs for consumption and asset holdings using numerical techniques, although such results are not immediately interpretable. But, given a numerical solution technique, we can always change an exogenous or state variable (e.g. the level of wealth) and measure its effect on equilibrium consumption and asset holdings.

Although our two-period model is an equilibrium model, it is not a *general* equilibrium model because the fundamental sources of changes in asset returns (e.g. productivity and physical investment), that is, the supply side of the economy, are not explicitly modelled.

To aid economic interpretation of the model, we assume power utility (and for $\gamma = 1$, logarithmic utility). Two key results using this particular class of utility functions are that consumption is proportional to wealth and asset shares are independent of wealth.

## The Model

Individuals choose consumption ($C_t$, $C_{t+1}$) and asset shares $\alpha_i$ to maximise two-period (time-separable) utility:

$$\max U = U(C_t) + \theta E_t U(C_{t+1}) \quad 0 < \theta < 1 \tag{1}$$

where $E_t$ is the expectations operator. (Somewhat cavalierly, we have used $U$ on the left-hand side to represent 'total utility' – we could have introduced another symbol here to avoid any confusion with the time $t$ and $t + 1$ utility functions $U(C_t)$ and $U(C_{t+1})$–but we think no confusion will arise from this.) There is no labour income, so the budget constraint is

$$W_{t+1} = R_{t+1}(W_t - C_t) \tag{2}$$

where $W_t$ is the initial endowment of real wealth and $R_{t+1}$ is the *gross (real) return* on the asset *portfolio* (we cease using $R_{t+1}^*$ for the gross return, for notational ease). Hence,

$$R = \sum_{i=1}^{n} \alpha_i R_i \quad \text{where} \sum_{i=1}^{n} \alpha_i = 1 \tag{3}$$

and $\alpha_i$ = proportion of wealth held in asset $i$. Assume a risk-free asset with return $R_f$ (the $n$th asset) then take $m = n - 1$ and $\alpha_n = 1 - \sum_{i=1}^{m} \alpha_i$. So, once we have solved for the optimal values of $\alpha_i$ $(i = 1, 2, \ldots, m)$, the optimal value for the share of the risk-free asset follows from the above identity. Portfolio returns are

$$R = \alpha_n R_f + \sum_{i=1}^{m} \alpha_i R_i = \left(1 - \sum_{i=1}^{m} \alpha_i\right) R_f + \sum_{i=1}^{m} \alpha_i R_i$$

$$= R_f + \sum_{i=1}^{m} \alpha_i (R_i - R_f) \tag{4}$$

We have incorporated the constraint $\sum_{i=1}^{n} \alpha_i = 1$ into equation (4) so that the coefficients on $\alpha_i$ $(i = 1, 2, \ldots, m)$ are now unconstrained. To solve the *dynamic programming* problem, we require an end-point condition that (without loss of generality) is taken to be a zero bequest, so that

$$W_{t+2} = 0 \text{ and hence } C_{t+1} = W_{t+1} \tag{5}$$

The maximand (1) can be written

$$\max U = U(C_t) + \theta U(W_{t+1}) = U(C_t) + \theta E_t U(R_{t+1}[W_t - C_t]) \tag{6}$$

We have now incorporated the budget constraint (2) in (6), and this little 'trick' implies we do not need to use Lagrange multipliers in solving the model. Note that the portfolio return $R_{t+1}$ is a function of the $\alpha_i$. Assuming power utility,

$$U(C) = C^{1-\gamma}/(1-\gamma) \qquad 0 < \gamma < 1 \tag{7a}$$

$$U'(C) = C^{-\gamma} \tag{7b}$$

Since $C_{t+1} = W_{t+1}$, note that

$$U'(C_{t+1}) = U'(W_{t+1}) = W_{t+1}^{-\gamma} \tag{7c}$$

We already know the general form of the solution to the maximisation problem, which is that the 'choice variables' for the individual $C_t$ and $\alpha_{it}$ $(i = 1, 2, \ldots, m)$ must depend on the exogenous or state variables, that is, $W_t$ and $E_t R_{i,t+1}$ plus of course any parameters such as $\gamma$ and $\theta$. Hence, the general closed-form solutions will be of the form

$$C_t = h(W_t, E_t f(R_{i,t+1}), R_f, \theta, \gamma)$$

$$\alpha_{it} = g(W_t, E_t f(R_{i,t+1}), R_f, \theta, \gamma)$$

where $f$ and $g$ are (possibly) non-linear functions (which are often difficult or impossible to derive analytically).

### Optimal consumption: power utility

The FOC for $C_t$ from (6) is

$$\frac{\partial U}{\partial C_t} = 0 = U'(C_t) + \theta E_t \left( \frac{\partial U}{\partial W_{t+1}} \right) \left( \frac{\partial W_{t+1}}{\partial C_t} \right) \tag{8a}$$

assuming power utility using (7b) and (2)

$$0 = C_t^{-\gamma} + \theta E_t \{ W_{t+1}^{-\gamma} (-R_{t+1}) \} \tag{8b}$$

Substituting for $W_{t+1}$ from (2) and rearranging

$$\left( \frac{W_t - C_t}{C_t} \right) = [\theta E_t \{ R_{t+1}^{(1-\gamma)} \}]^{1/\gamma} = E_t[f(R_{t+1}(\alpha_i), \gamma, \theta)] \tag{9}$$

where $f(.)$ is a non-linear function of $R_{t+1}$, which is itself a function of the asset shares $\alpha_i$ and the individual asset returns $(R_{it+1}, R_{ft})$. Rearranging,

$$C_t^* = \frac{1}{[1 + E_t f(R_{t+1}(\alpha_{it}), \theta \gamma)]} W_t \tag{10}$$

Hence, optimal consumption is proportional to wealth and depends on the *investment opportunity set*, that is, expected returns on all the non-risky assets and the risk-free asset. The consumption–wealth ratio depends on $E_t[f(R_{t+1}, R_f, \theta, \gamma)]$ so the impact of the *expected* portfolio return, $R_{t+1}$, on *current* consumption depends on income and substitution effects (see below) – a higher expected return tends to reduce current consumption (substitution effect) but it also increases next period's wealth (income effect), which tends to lower current consumption. As we shall see, for the special case of $\gamma = 1$, these two effects just cancel each other, and consumption is independent of expected returns. Note that (10) is not the 'full' closed form solution for $C_t$ because $R_{t+1}$ depends on the $\alpha_i$ decision variables.

### Optimal asset shares

The FOC for $\alpha_i$ is

$$\frac{\partial U}{\partial \alpha_i} = 0 = \theta E_t \left( \frac{\partial U}{\partial W_{t+1}} \right) \left( \frac{\partial W_{t+1}}{\partial \alpha_i} \right) \equiv \theta E_t \left\{ U_w \frac{\partial W_{t+1}}{\partial \alpha_i} \right\} \quad i = 1, 2, \dots, n \tag{11}$$

Using (2) and (4) and the power utility function for $U(W_{t+1})$,

$$0 = \theta E_t \{ W_{t+1}^{-\gamma} (W_t - C_t)(R_i - R_f) \} \tag{12}$$

Substituting for $W_{t+1}$ from (2)

$$0 = \theta E_t \{ [(W_t - C_t) R_{t+1}]^{-\gamma} [(W_t - C_t)(R_{i,t+1} - R_f)] \}$$

$$0 = E_t \{ R_{t+1}^{-\gamma} (R_{it+1} - R_f) \} \tag{13}$$

since the $\theta(W_t - C_t)^{1-\gamma}$ can be taken out of the expectation (as it is known at time $t$) and then it 'cancels out'. Remember that $R_{t+1}$ depends on $\alpha_i$, so substituting from (4),

$$0 = E_t \left\{ \left[ R_f + \sum_{i=1}^{m} \alpha_{it}(R_{it+1} - R_f) \right]^{-\gamma} (R_{it+1} - R_f) \right\} \qquad (14a)$$

There are $m$ equations of the form (14a) that can be solved to give the optimal values for $\alpha_{it}$. Schematically, the solution to (14a) can be represented

$$\alpha_{it}^* = g(E_t[f(R_{k,t+1})], R_{ft}, \gamma) \quad \text{for } k = 1, 2, \ldots, m \qquad (14b)$$

Equation (14) is more exciting than it looks at first sight. Suppose there is only *one* risky asset $i$, so that (14) is the conditional expectation of a non-linear function of the *single* random variable $R_i$. Once we know the probability density function for $R_i$, we can calculate the expected value and obtain the solution for $\alpha_{it}$. When we have $m$ risky assets, the optimal solution for any $\alpha_{it}$ depends on the conditional expected (one-period) returns on *all* of the $m$ risky assets. We therefore need to know the multivariate distribution of one-period returns. Heuristically, equation (14) can be directly solved for $\alpha_{it} = g(f(E_t R_k), R_f, \gamma)$ for $k = 1, 2, \ldots, m$. A key result from (14) is that the *proportion* held in risky asset $i$ is independent of current wealth (and hence of previous savings-consumption decisions). So, once we have the solutions $\alpha_{it}^*$, we can use these in (10) to immediately solve for $(C_t^*/W_t)$ as a non-linear function of expected returns on all assets. This 'separability' property arises for any isoelastic utility function such as power utility (and hence logarithmic utility, $\gamma = 1$). The fact that $\alpha_{it}^*$ is independent of current wealth is useful when seeking to aggregate over individuals' assets holdings – although this need not detain us here. Note, however, that, *in general*, the FOCs imply that the $\alpha_i^*$ depend on both wealth and expected returns $ER_i$ and hence (10) and (14b) have to be solved simultaneously (e.g. this is the case for quadratic utility).

### Solution: power utility

- Asset *shares* depend only on expected returns (and $\gamma$) and are independent of wealth.

- The consumption–wealth ratio depends only on expected returns and is also independent of wealth (since the $\alpha_i$'s are independent of wealth – see (14b)).

It is worth noting that in equation (6), the maximand

$$U(W_t) = U(C_t) + \theta E_t U(W_{t+1}) \qquad (6)$$

can be interpreted as implying that at $t$, total utility $U(W_t)$ depends on the exogenous *state variable* $W_t$. Also (6) is a recursive equation. By solving backwards from $t + 1$, we have found the optimal $C_t^*$ and $\alpha_{it}^*$ and, hence, using (2), $W_{t+1} = R_{t+1}(W_t - C_t)$ can be obtained. Hence, one could also calculate the optimal value of utility $U(W_t)$ in (6). This recursive relationship is very important in the multi-period framework since the latter can be viewed as a series of one-period problems like (6). In a multi-period context, having obtained $U(W_t)$, we substitute this value in the right-hand side for $E_{t-1}(W_t)$ and proceed to choose the optimal $C_{t-1}$ and $\alpha_{t-1}$ on the basis of similar FOCs and then obtain a value for $U(W_{t-1})$. We continue the backward recursion until we determine the optimal values $C_o$, $\alpha_{0i}$ at $t = 0$ for the multi-period case. This is Bellman's recursive optimal solution method in stochastic dynamic programming.

### Solution: logarithmic utility, $\gamma = 1$

- Note that the general form of the FOCs for the $\alpha_i$ in equation (14) are unchanged when $\gamma = 1$, so the optimal $\alpha_i^*$ remains independent of the level of wealth.

- Consumption is not only proportional to wealth but is also *independent of the investment opportunity* set (i.e. expected returns). From the FOC (9), with $\gamma = 1$,

$$C_t = \frac{W_t}{1 + \theta} \tag{15}$$

Here, the income and substitution effects of a change in expected returns just cancel so that consumption remains unchanged.

## Evaluating Expectations

Some readers might be a little perplexed about evaluating expectations terms in the above non-linear functions. In principle, this is easy since for any continuous function $g(x)$ with probability distribution function $f(x)$, the expected value of $g(x)$ (e.g. $g(x) = x^2$) is

$$E_t[g(x)] = \int_o^\infty g(x) f(x_t | x_{t-1}, x_{t-2}, \ldots) \, dx \tag{16}$$

where $x = R_i$ the gross return, so the integral is from 0 to $\infty$. The value of the integral is obtained either analytically or (more usually) numerically. For example, $f(x)$ might be assumed to be the normal density function. The density function $f(.)$ is the conditional density, since returns at $t$ might depend on returns at $t-1$ or earlier (i.e. time-varying or predictable returns). In the special case of *iid* returns, the conditional distribution is the same as the unconditional one.

To see that (16) just results in a known 'number', consider a simple discrete case with only two possible outcomes for the gross return, namely, $\lambda$ and $1/\lambda$ (with $\lambda$ known, e.g. $\lambda = 1.1$) and

$$\text{Prob}\{R_i = \lambda\} = 1/2 = \text{Prob}(R_i = 1/\lambda) \quad \lambda > 1 \tag{17}$$

Then for $g(R) = R$, for example,

$$E[g(R)] = ER = (1/2)\lambda + (1/2)\lambda^{-1} = 1.0045 \tag{18a}$$

and for $g(R) = R^2$,

$$E[g(R)] = ER^2 = \frac{\lambda^2}{2} + \frac{\lambda^{-2}}{2} = 1.0182 \qquad (18b)$$

So, now we know the solution technique for a consumption-portfolio problem over two periods. These FOCs apply for every individual, and we have obtained optimal values for $C_t^*$ and $\alpha_{it}^*$ for each individual.

## Hunt the C-CAPM/SDF Model of Equilibrium Returns

To move from FOCs for the *individual* to those for the market as a whole, we have to make some assumptions about asset supplies and invoke the 'representative agent' assumption (i.e. identical utility functions). Then we can analyse the behaviour of *equilibrium* asset returns.

In the previous section, we concentrated on getting closed-form solutions for consumption and asset shares, but this model must have the FOCs for the C-CAPM/SDF model 'hidden away' somewhere. Indeed, it does, as we can see by setting up the maximisation problem using Lagrange multipliers. We have

$$\max U = U(C_t) + \theta E_t \{U(C_{t+1})\} \qquad (19)$$

where the budget constraint is

$$C_{t+1} = W_{t+1} = R_{t+1}(W_t - C_t) \quad \text{with} \quad R_{t+1} = \sum_{i=1}^{n} \alpha_i R_{i,t+1} \qquad (20)$$

One asset may be risk free and the constraint is:

$$\sum_{i=1}^{n} \alpha_i = 1 \qquad (21)$$

The Lagrangian is

$$U(C_t) + \theta E_t \{U(C_{t+1})\} + \lambda \left(1 - \sum_{i=1}^{n} \alpha_i\right) \qquad (22)$$

Using (20) and differentiating (22) in turn with respect to $C_t$, then $\alpha_i$, the FOCs are

$$U'(C_t) = \theta E_t \{U'(C_{t+1}) R_{t+1}\} \equiv \theta E_t \left\{U'(C_{t+1}) \sum_{i=1}^{n} \alpha_i R_{i,t+1}\right\} \qquad (23)$$

$$\theta E_t \{U'(C_{t+1}) R_{i,t+1}\} - \lambda/(W_t - C_t) = 0 \quad i = 1, 2, \ldots, n \qquad (24)$$

From (24), we see that the investor chooses between assets $i$ and $j$ to equalise expected marginal utilities at $t + 1$

$$E_t \{U'(C_{t+1}) R_{i,t+1}\} = E_t \{U'(C_{t+1}) R_{j,t+1}\} \qquad (25)$$

Multiplying (24) by $\alpha_i$, summing from 1 to $n$ and then substituting in (23) gives

$$U'(C_t) = \sum_{i=1}^{n} \alpha_i [\lambda/(W_t - C_t)] = \lambda/(W_t - C_t) \tag{26}$$

Substituting (26) in (24) gives the FOC as represented in the SDF model

$$\theta E_t \left\{ \frac{U'(C_{t+1})}{U'(C_t)} R_{i,t+1} \right\} = E_t \{ M_{t+1} R_{i,t+1} \} = 1 \quad i = 1, 2, \ldots, n$$

The above equation subsumes the FOC for the risk-free rate $R_f E_t(M_{t+1}) = 1$. The only difference between this and our previous 'perturbation approach' (see Chapter 11) is that we have introduced an explicit budget constraint and explicitly solved the constrained maximisation problem. Hence, all the results in Chapter 11 hold for this consumption-portfolio model.

It is perhaps worth noting that introducing (non-stochastic) *exogenous* labour income $Y_t$ would have implied a budget constraint

$$C_{t+1} \equiv W_{t+1} = R_{t+1}(W_t + Y_t - C_t)$$

and the key FOCs remain unchanged (but $W_t + Y_t$ replaces $W_t$).

## 15.2  Multi-Period Model

The agent acts as a price-taker in asset markets and then chooses today's consumption and asset shares to maximise *lifetime* utility. As we shall see, this multi-period problem can be transformed into a sequence of two-period problems by invoking the concept of a *value function*. The value function is a recursive relationship that can be 'solved backwards' from the terminal date and is often referred to as the *Bellman equation* in the stochastic dynamic programming literature. So, at $t$, to calculate today's optimal values, you have to calculate all the optimal values 'backwards' from $T$ to $t$. However, having chosen the optimal $C_t^*$, $C_{t+1}^*$, and so on, *at time $t$*, there will be new information that arrives between $t$ and $t + 1$. Hence, *at $t + 1$*, we recalculate the new optimal value, $\tilde{C}_{t+1}^*$, which will not usually be equal to that chosen at time $t$, for period $t + 1$ (i.e. $C_{t+1}^* \neq \tilde{C}_{t+1}^*$). The general closed-form solution at $t$ to the intertemporal problem will be of the form

$$C_t = f(W_t, E_t R_{t+j}, \gamma, \theta, T - t) \tag{27a}$$

$$\alpha_{it} = g(W_t, E_t R_{t+j}, \gamma, \theta, T - t) \tag{27b}$$

where $\gamma$ represents parameter(s) from an intertemporal utility function. Closed-form solutions are often not possible, but for power and logarithmic ($\gamma = 1$) time-separable utility functions, we can make some progress in this direction. These intertemporal models are *sometimes* easier to deal with in continuous time, but for consistency (and perhaps added realism), we will only use discrete time.

## Preferences and Budget Constraint

The individual is assumed to maximise a time-separable utility function that depends (only) on current consumption $C_o$ and all future consumption $(C_1, C_2, \ldots)$ and the current period is $t = 0$

$$U = E_0 \sum_{t=0}^{T-1} U(C_t, t) + B(W_T, T) \tag{28}$$

where $B(.)$ is the bequest function at time $T$. We are going to use power utility since although this is a very special case, it does save 'miles' (kilometres) of algebra and allows us to see inside the 'black box' of the FOCs. For power utility, we have

$$U(C_t, t) = \theta^t C_t^{1-\gamma}/(1-\gamma) \tag{29a}$$

$$B(W_T, T) = \theta^T W_T^{1-\gamma}/(1-\gamma) \tag{29b}$$

To simplify the notation, we will drop the separate time variable $t$, so, for example, $U(C_t, t) \equiv U(C_t)$. The budget constraint is

$$W_{t+1} = R_{t+1}(W_t - C_t) \tag{30}$$

and the *portfolio* return is

$$R_{t+1} = \sum_{i=1}^{m} \alpha_{it}(R_{i,t+1} - R_{ft}) + R_{ft} \tag{31}$$

with $\alpha_{it}$ being the asset shares to be determined and $R_i$ are the $m = n - 1$ risky asset returns. The risk-free asset share is given by $\alpha_n = 1 - \Sigma_{i=1}^m \alpha_i$. The solution technique closely follows that for the two-period case analysed above, although the algebra does get a little detailed and involved – 'so hold on to your summation and expectations operators'. Note that although we present the solution for $m$ values of $\alpha_{it}$, the math would go through (a little neater) if we had just one risky asset (and one risk-free asset).

## The Value Function

To solve these multi-period problems, we introduce the value function $J(W_t)$ (sometimes called the *derived utility of wealth function*) defined as

$$J(W_t) = \max E_t \left\{ \sum_{s=t}^{T-1} U(C_s) + B(W_T) \right\} \tag{32}$$

Note that $J(W_t)$ is the *maximised value* of the utility function at *time t*. Hence, optimal decisions are taken from any time $t \geq 0$ onwards. The value function will allow us to express the multi-period problem as a sequence of two-period problems. It follows that

$$J(W_T) = B(W_T) \tag{33}$$

At $T-1$, the individual chooses $C_{T-1}, \alpha_{T-1}$ to maximise

$$J(W_{T-1}) = \underbrace{\max}_{C_{T-1}, \alpha_{T-1}} \{U(C_{T-1}) + E_{T-1}B(W_T)\} \tag{34}$$

Substituting from (30) and noting from (31) that $R_{t+1}$ is a function of $\alpha_{it}$, (34) becomes

$$J(W_{T-1}) = \max_{C_{T-1}, \alpha_{T-1}} \{U(C_{T-1}) + E_{T-1}\{B(R_T(\alpha_{i,T-1})(W_{T-1} - C_{T-1}))\}\} \tag{35}$$

and we have a familiar two-period problem. The FOC for $C_{T-1}$ gives

$$0 = U'(C_{T-1}) + E_{T-1}\{B_W(W_T)(\partial W_T/\partial C_{T-1})\} \tag{36}$$

where $B_W = \partial B/\partial W_T = \theta^T W_T^{-\gamma}$ for power utility and from (30)

$$\partial W_T/\partial C_{T-1} = -R_T \tag{37}$$

Hence, (36) can, in general, be written

$$0 = U'(C_{T-1}) - E_{T-1}\{B_W(W_T)R_T(\alpha_i)\} \tag{38a}$$

$$= U'(C_{T-1}) - E_{T-1}\left\{B_W(W_T)\left[\sum_{i=1}^{m} \alpha_{i,T-1}(R_{i,T} - R_f) + R_f\right]\right\} \tag{38b}$$

The FOC for $\alpha_i$ after differentiating (34) and using (30) and (31) is

$$0 = E_{T-1}\{B_W(W_T)(R_{i,T} - R_f)\} \quad (i = 1, 2, 3, \ldots, m) \tag{39}$$

Multiplying (39) by $\alpha_i$ and summing over $i = 1, 2, \ldots, m$

$$E_{T-1}\{\sum_{i=1}^{m} \alpha_i R_{i,T} B_W(W_T)\} = R_f E_{T-1}\{B_W(W_T)\} \tag{40}$$

or

$$0 = E_{T-1}\{B_W(W_T) \sum_{i=1}^{m} \alpha_i(R_{i,T} - R_f)\} \tag{41}$$

Substituting from (41) in the FOC for consumption (38b), an alternative expression is

$$U'(C_{T-1}) = R_f E_{T-1}\{B_W(W_T)\} \tag{42}$$

In principle, the single FOC (38b) and the $m$ FOCs (39) are $m+1$ equations in $m+1$ unknowns, namely, $C_{T-1}$ and the $m$ values $\alpha_{i,T-1}$. These can be solved for the optimal asset shares and consumption at $T-1$. Let us do this for the special case of power utility where

$$B_W(W_T) = \frac{\partial}{\partial W_T}\theta^T W_T^{1-\alpha}/(1-\alpha) = \theta^T W_T^{-\gamma} \tag{43a}$$

$$U'(C_{T-1}) = \theta^{T-1}C_{T-1}^{-\gamma} \tag{43b}$$

Substituting (43a) and (43b) in the FOC, (38a) and using (30) and (31) to 'substitute out' $W_T$, we obtain after some manipulation

$$\theta^{T-1}C_{T-1}^{-\gamma} = \theta^T (W_{T-1} - C_{T-1})^{-\gamma} E_{T-1}\{R_T^{1-\gamma}(\alpha_i)\} \tag{44}$$

or

$$\frac{C_{T-1}^*}{W_{T-1}} = \frac{1}{1 + [\theta E_{T-1}\{R_T^{1-\gamma}(\alpha_i)\}]^{1/\gamma}} \tag{45}$$

Where $R_T(\alpha_i)$ indicates that $R_T$ is a function of the asset shares. As in the two-period case, with power utility, we find that optimal consumption is proportional to wealth and also depends on expected returns. Note that for log utility $\gamma = 1$, consumption is proportional to wealth but *independent of changing investment opportunities* (i.e. the expected return on assets) – as in the two-period model. Using power utility, let us turn to the FOC for asset shares, equation (40), reproduced here:

$$E_{T-1}\{R_{i,T} B_W(W_T)\} = E_{T-1}\{R_f B_W(W_T)\} \tag{46a}$$

Using (43a)

$$E_{T-1}\{R_{i,T} W_T^{-\gamma}\} = E_{T-1}\{R_f W_T^{-\gamma}\} \tag{46b}$$

Now substitute $W_T = (W_{T-1} - C_{T-1})R_T$ from (30) and for $R_T$ from (31) and after cancelling terms in $(W_{T-1} - C_{T-1})$, we obtain

$$E_{T-1}\left[ (R_i - R_f)\left( \sum_{i=1}^{m} \alpha_{i,T-1}(R_{iT} - R_f) + R_f \right)^{-\gamma} \right] = 0 \quad i = 1, 2, \ldots, m \tag{47}$$

Equations (47) are $m$ equations in the $m$ unknowns $\alpha_i$ and can be solved for

$$\alpha_{i,T-1}^* = g(E_{T-1}R_i, E_{T-1}R_j, \ldots, R_f) \tag{48}$$

once we have the density function for returns. As in the two-period problem, $\alpha_i^*$ are independent of wealth – therefore, *all* power utility investors hold the same asset *proportions*. Of course, power utility is a very special case and, in general, $\alpha_{i,T-1}$ would also be a function of wealth. Asset proportions also depend on expected returns but if returns are *iid*, then $\alpha_{i,t}$ is the same regardless of the planning horizon of the investor, $T - t$. This special case is often referred to as *myopic behaviour*, because in a multi-period model, optimal asset proportions are identical to those of a one-period investor.

Having solved for $\alpha_{i,T-1}^*$ from (47), these can be substituted in (45) to solve for $C_{T-1}^*/W_{T-1}$. Again, as with the two-period case, with power utility, we do not need to solve for $\alpha_{T-1}^*$ and $C_{T-1}^*$ simultaneously.

## Recursions Unlimited

Since we have optimal values for $C_{T-1}^*$ and $\alpha_{i,T-1}^*$, we have an optimal value for $J(W_{T-1})$ from (34). Using the value function (34), we can set out the optimisation problem for $T-2$

$$J(W_{T-2}) = \max_{C_{T-2}, \alpha_{T-2}} E_{T-2}\{U(C_{T-2}) + U(C_{T-1}^*) + B(W_T)\} \tag{49}$$

At $T-2$, $W_{T-2}$ is known, and the *principle of optimality* states that at $T-2$, we can choose $C_{T-2}, \alpha_{iT-2}$ and given this outcome at $T-2$, the remaining decisions for $T-1$ must be optimal. Furthermore, using iterated expectations, $E_{T-2}E_{T-1}(X) = E_{T-2}(X)$, we can write (49) as

$$J(W_{T-2}) = \max \left\{ U(C_{T-2}) + E_{T-2}\left( \max_{C_{T-1}, \alpha_{i,T-1}} E_{T-1}\left[ U(C_{T-1}^*) + B(W_T) \right] \right) \right\} \tag{50}$$

$$J(W_{T-2}) = \max\{U(C_{T-2}) + E_{T-2}[J(W_{T-1})]\} \tag{51}$$

where $J(W_{T-1})$ is calculated using the *optimal* values $C_{T-1}^*$, $W_{i,T-1}^*$ found at $T-1$. Intuitively, (51) has the utility function dependent on this period's consumption $C_{T-2}$ and next period's wealth $W_{T-1}$. If I consume more at $T-2$, then wealth next period will be lower and hence there is a trade-off.

Equation (51) is a recursion for $J(.)$, and the solution to (51) will be of the same form as that for (34), which we have already noted. Hence, in general, for any $t = 0, 1, 2, \ldots, T-1$, the optimality conditions by analogy with (42) and (39) with $J_W$ replacing $B_W$ are

$$U'(C_t) = R_{ft} E_t J_W(W_{t+1}) = J_W(W_t) \tag{52a}$$

$$E_t\{R_{it+1} J_W(W_{t+1})\} = R_{ft} E_t\{J_W(W_{t+1})\} \quad \text{for } i = 1, 2, 3, \ldots, m, \text{ assets} \tag{52b}$$

The only part of the above results we have not explicitly derived is the *envelope condition* in (52a), namely

$$U'(C_t) = J_W(W_t) \tag{52c}$$

This representation of the FOC for consumption implies that along the optimum path, a dollar saved that adds to wealth should give the same marginal utility as a dollar spent on consumption. The envelope condition is obtained by totally differentiating the value function (51) and then substituting using the FOCs, and this is done in Appendix I.

The FOCs in (52a) and (52b) look rather 'neat' and succinct, but for any given utility function, the solution still has to be worked out, and a closed-form solution is generally only possible for a small subset of admissible utility functions. In general, optimal asset proportions and consumption at any time $t$ will *both* depend on wealth, expected returns from $t$ to $T-1$ and the parameters of the utility function. A complete closed-form solution is often difficult or impossible to derive. Therefore, the model is often empirically tested using regression techniques based only on the FOC/Euler equation, as we have seen in earlier chapters.

Even in the case of log utility, the solution for the optimal weights $\alpha_i$ in (47) or (52b) is not straightforward even with only one risky asset, since we have to evaluate the expectation of the non-linear function of returns. However, the solution for optimal $C_t$ (see Appendix II) can be shown to be

$$C_t = \frac{1-\theta}{(1-\theta^{T-t+1})} W_t \tag{53}$$

Hence, log utility individuals plan to consume their wealth 'smoothly' throughout their remaining lifetime ($t$ to T).

Also if returns are *iid*, then with power utility, asset demands are independent of the horizon of the investor – this is referred to as *myopic behaviour*, because in a multi-period model where the investor is forward looking, optimal asset proportions are identical to those of a one-period investor.

After having conscientiously followed the above derivation, the reader might be a little deflated to learn that the above was worked out by Samuelson (1969) – some time ago. But the general ideas behind the solution technique of stochastic dynamic programming and the value function are still used to help find admissible trial solutions in many intertemporal stochastic models. However, in many cases, at the end of the day, a numerical solution is often all that can be obtained (see Barberis, Huang and Santos 2001). For example, with log utility, we know the explicit solution for consumption is (53). In contrast, a numerical solution would give a single value for $C_t$, given that $W_t$ is a known input. Then, by numerically re-solving for $C_t$, given different input values for $W_t$, we could deduce the linear relationship given by (53) (i.e. we would plot alternative input values for $W_t$ against the resulting numerical optimum values for $C_t$). Hence, in more complex cases, we have a *computable* equilibrium model on which we can perform 'what if' numerical simulations. Indeed, we can obtain the optimal consumption path $C_t, C_{t+1}, \ldots, C_T$ and the optimal asset proportions in the current and all future periods once we have the state variable $W_t$ and a 'forecast' of expected returns (in all future periods). Knowing the optimal $C_t^*$ and $\alpha_{it}^*$ for all $t$, we also know the lifetime utility from (28) or recursive use of the Bellman equation.

These types of model are very prevalent in economics, usually where there is an intertemporal element and constraints on behaviour. For example, the design of 'optimal' tax, pensions and welfare benefits packages requires the government to set tax and benefit rates for those in work and for retirees. Constraints might include a lifetime budget constraint (including benefit income and state pension payments), a minimum level of benefit (i.e. in any period), together with assumptions about labour supply and the return on assets. The tax-benefit rates that maximise some lifetime utility function (of consumption and leisure) can then be calculated and lifetime utility compared under alternative policy scenarios (e.g. different income tax rates, or degree of risk aversion). Hence, it is important to understand the intuitive and technical issues behind this class of models, and we have made a start with our consumption-portfolio model and in the following section, we discuss these issues further.

The 'expectations' must be calculated numerically. In the above model, the only 'exogenous' stochastic variables are asset returns. If we add 'uncertain' labour income into the budget constraint, we have to deal with any correlation between returns and labour income when calculating expectations – this considerably complicates the numerical solution procedure (Campbell and Vicera 1999).

## 15.3  SDF Model of Expected Returns

As with our two-period model, we can examine the FOCs of our intertemporal consumption-portfolio choice model and derive FOCs of the equations representing the SDF formulation. It is here that the 'succinct forms' of the FOCs in terms of the value function are useful and give us the solution we require almost immediately (so perhaps it was worth the effort in deriving them). The FOCs for consumption and asset shares are

$$U'(C_t) = J_W(W_t) = R_{\mathrm{ft}} E_t\{J_W(W_{t+1})\} \tag{54}$$

$$E_t\{R_{i,t+1} J_W(W_{t+1})\} = R_{\mathrm{ft}} E_t\{J_W(W_{t+1})\} \quad i = 1, 2, \ldots, m \tag{55}$$

The envelope condition in (54) holds for all $t$, hence

$$U'(C_{t+1}) = J_W(W_{t+1}) \tag{56}$$

Substituting (56) in (54) and rearranging, we obtain the SDF equation for the *risk-free* rate

$$R_{\mathrm{ft}} E_t(M_{t+1}) = 1 \tag{57}$$

where $M_{t+1} = U'(C_{t+1})/U'(C_t)$ is the SDF or pricing kernel. (Note that here we have 'absorbed' $\theta$ in $M_{t+1}$ since $U(C_t) = \theta^t f(C_t)$, where $f(C_t)$ is the 'usual' utility function, for example, $f(C_t) = \ln C_t$.)

For the *risky assets*, we make the same substitution of (56) in (55) and then use (54) to give

$$E_t\{R_{i,t+1} U'(C_{t+1})\} = U'(C_t) \quad i = 1, 2, \ldots, m \tag{58}$$

$$E\{R_{i,t+1} M_{t+1}\} = 1 \tag{59}$$

Hence, unbeknown to us, the SDF model that we have been discussing at length in Chapters 10 and 11 is consistent with our intertemporal consumption-portfolio model. It is also worth noting that (58) is itself a recursion and it holds for any investment horizon, since

$$U'(C_t) = E_t\{R_{i,t+1} U'(C_{t+1})\} = E_t\{R_{i,t+1} R_{i,t+2} U'(C_{t+2})\} \tag{60}$$

hence

$$1 = E_t\{R_{i,t,t+2} M_{t,t+2}\} \tag{61}$$

where $X_{t,t+2} = X_{t,t+1} X_{t+1,t+2}$ and $X = R_i \text{ or } M$.

## 15.4  Summary

- The multi-period consumption-portfolio problem with time-separable utility and one state variable (wealth) can be solved recursively working 'backwards' from time $T$, using the value function/Bellman equation.

- In general, the optimal asset shares (for the risky and riskless assets) and optimal consumption–wealth ratio depend on wealth, expected returns and the degree of risk aversion.

- For the special case of isoelastic marginal utility (i.e. power and log utility), the optimal FOCs can be solved independently of each other, first for asset shares and then for the consumption–wealth ratio. But, in general, these two sets of FOCs must be solved simultaneously (at each point in time).

- For power utility, optimal asset shares and the consumption–wealth ratio are both independent of wealth but depend on expected returns. For logarithmic utility $\gamma = 1$, the consumption–wealth ratio is also independent of expected returns (and just depends on $\theta$ and time, $T - t$).

- The FOCs or Euler equations for the SDF model (i.e. C-CAPM) can be derived from the FOCs of the consumption-portfolio problem.

# Appendix I: Envelope Condition for Consumption-Portfolio Problem

We derive the envelope condition as follows. The value function (also called the *Bellman equation*) at $T - 1$ is

$$J(W_{T-1}) = \underbrace{\max}_{C_{T-1}, \alpha_{iT-1}} \{U(C_{T-1}) + E_{T-1}B(W_T)\} \tag{A1a}$$

Now assume we have solved for the optimal values of $\{C_{T-1}, \alpha_{T-1}\}$ and substituted these values back into the value function. Using these *optimal values* in (A1a), the Bellman equation at $T - 1$ is

$$J(W_{T-1}) = U(C_{T-1}) + E_{T-1}\{B(W_T)\}$$

$$= U(C_{T-1}) + E_{T-1}B\left\{\left[\sum_{i=1}^{m}\alpha_i(R_i - R_f) + R_f\right](W_{T-1} - C_{T-1})\right\} \tag{A1b}$$

where the 'max' can now be dispensed with as $\{C_{T-1}, \alpha_{T-1}\}$ now represent the optimal values. Take the total differential of $J(W_{T-1})$ with respect to $W_{T-1}$, noting that $dB(W_T) = (\partial B / \partial W_T)dW_T$ and $dW_T$ depends on $W_{T-1}, \alpha_{i,T-1}$ and $C_{T-1}$ since

$$W_T = (W_{T-1} - C_{T-1})R_T(\alpha_{t,T-1}) \tag{A2}$$

$$J_{W(T-1)} = U'(C_{T-1})\frac{\partial C_{T-1}}{\partial W_{T-1}} + E_{T-1}\left\{B_{W(T)}\right.$$

$$\left. \times \left[\frac{\partial W_T}{\partial W_{T-1}} + \frac{\partial W_T}{\partial C_{T-1}}\frac{\partial C_{T-1}}{\partial W_{T-1}} + \sum_{i=1}^{m}\frac{\partial W_T}{\partial \alpha_i}\frac{\partial \alpha_i}{\partial W_{T-1}}\right]\right\} \tag{A3}$$

where $J_{W(T-1)} \equiv \dfrac{\partial J(W_{T-1})}{\partial W_{T-1}}$. Using the definition

$$W_T = \left[ \sum_{i=1}^{m} \alpha_i (R_{i,T} - R_f) + R_f \right] (W_{T-1} - C_{T-1}) \equiv R_T (W_{T-1} - C_{T-1}) \qquad (A4)$$

to calculate the partial derivatives, we have

$$J_{W(T-1)} = U'(C_{T-1}) \frac{\partial C_{T-1}}{\partial W_{T-1}} + E_{T-1} \left\{ B_{W(T)} \left[ R_T \left( 1 - \frac{\partial C_{T-1}}{\partial W_{T-1}} \right) \right] \right.$$

$$\left. + B_{W(T)}(W_{T-1} - C_{T-1}) \sum_{i=1}^{m} (R_{i,T} - R_f) \frac{\partial \alpha_i}{\partial W_{T-1}} \right\} \qquad (A5)$$

This really looks a mess but note that the FOCs (38a) and (39) for the optimal values of $\{C_{T-1}, \alpha_{T-1}\}$ derived in the text are

$$E_{T-1}\{B_W R_T\} = U'(C_{T-1}) \qquad (A6a)$$

$$E_{T-1}\{B_W (R_{i,T} - R_f)\} = 0 \qquad (A6b)$$

Also note that anything dated at $T - 1$ is known and can be taken out of the expectations sign. Hence, we obtain

$$J_{W(T-1)} \equiv U'(C_{T-1}) \frac{\partial C_{T-1}}{\partial W_{T-1}} + E_{T-1} \left\{ U'(C_{T-1}) \left( 1 - \frac{\partial C_{T-1}}{\partial W_{T-1}} \right) + 0 \right\} \qquad (A7)$$

simplifying

$$J_{W(T-1)} = U'(C_{T-1}) \qquad (A8)$$

This is the envelope condition we require, which is discussed in the text. Also from (42) in the text, another version of the FOC is that $U'(C_{T-1}) = R_f E_{T-1}(B_W)$ and hence we also note that

$$J_{W(T-1)} = R_f E_{T-1}\{B_{W(T)}\} \qquad (A9)$$

A full proof would require that we show that (A8) and (A9) hold for a general value of $t$ and not just for $T - 1$, but we do not pursue that here.

# Appendix II: Solution for Log Utility

It is instructive to solve the multi-period problem for optimal consumption and asset shares to see how the value function (Bellman equation) plays a pivotal role. We do this for the most tractable case, namely log utility. We know from the text that the FOCs for optimal $C$ and $\alpha_i$ can be solved independently and that $C/W$ is independent of *expected* returns and hence of $\alpha_i^*$ – the latter considerably simplifies the solution for $C/W$ since we do not have to know the explicit optimal solution for $\alpha_i$.

The steps we require are:

(i) solve the FOCs for $C_{T-1}^*, \alpha_{T-1}^*$.

(ii) substitute solutions $(C_{T-1}^*, \alpha_{T-1}^*)$ into the Bellman value function and calculate the optimal $J(W_{T-1})$.

(iii) use the FOCs at $T-1$, which include terms in $J_W(W_{T-1})$, to solve for optimal $(C_{T-2}^*, \alpha_{T-2}^*)$ and continue this recursion.

We have

$$B(W_T) = \theta^T \ln W_T \tag{A1}$$

$$U(C_{T-1}) = \theta^{T-1} \ln C_{T-1} \tag{A2}$$

$$R_T = \sum_{i=1}^{m} \alpha_i (R_{i,T} - R_f) + R_f \tag{A3}$$

$$W_T = (W_{T-1} - C_{T-1}) R_T \tag{A4}$$

The FOCs (A6a) at $T-1$ for consumption is

$$U_c(C_{T-1}^*) = \theta^{T-1} C_{T-1}^{-1} = \theta^T E_{T-1}\{B_W(W_T) R_T\} = \theta^T (W_{T-1} - C_{T-1})^{-1} \tag{A5}$$

which implies

$$C_{T-1}^* = W_{T-1}/(1+\theta) \tag{A6}$$

For log utility, $C_{T-1}^*$ is independent of $E_{T-1}[R_T(\alpha_i)]$, which means we do not have to solve for $\alpha_i^*$ to find $C_{T-1}^*$. However, the FOCs (A6b) for the asset shares are

$$0 = E_{T-1}\{(R_{i,T} - R_f) B_W(W_T)\} = E_{T-1}\{(R_{i,T} - R_f)/R_T(\alpha_i^*)\} \quad i = 1, 2, \ldots, m \tag{A7}$$

where we have used (A1) and (A4) and cancelled the non-stochastic term in $\theta^T/(W_{T-1} - C_{T-1})$.

After evaluating the expectation in (A7), these $m$ equations can be solved for the $m$ unknowns $\alpha_i^*(T-1)$, and the solution is independent of wealth.

### Solving for $J(W_{T-1})$ at optimal $\{C_{T-1}^*, \alpha_{T-1}^*\}$

Now we calculate the value function at $T-1$

$$J(W_{T-1}) = \underset{\{C_{T-1}, w_{T-1}\}}{\max} \quad \{U(C_{T-1}) + E_{T-1}[B(W_T)]\}$$

$$= \underset{\{C_{T-1}, w_{T-1}\}}{\max} \quad \{\theta^{T-1} \ln C_{T-1} + E_{T-1}(\theta^T \ln W_T)\} \tag{A8}$$

Now substitute for $C_{T-1}^*, \alpha_{i,T-1}^*$, and, hence, we can 'remove' the 'max' in the previous expression

$$J(W_{T-1}) = \theta^{T-1} \ln[W_{T-1}/(1+\theta)] + \theta^T E_{T-1}\{\ln[(W_{T-1} - C_{T-1}^*) R_T]\} \tag{A9}$$

Substitute again for $C_{T-1}^* = W_{T-1}/(1+\theta)$ in (A9)

$$J(W_{T-1}) = \theta^{T-1}(1+\theta)\ln W_{T-1} + k(\theta) + \theta^T E_{T-1}[\ln R_T(\alpha_{i,T-1}^*)] \tag{A10}$$

where $k(\theta) = -\theta^{T-1}\ln(1+\theta) + \theta^T \ln(\theta/(1+\theta))$.

The important aspect to bear in mind is that we know from the FOCs that $R_T(\alpha_{i,T-1}^*)$ is independent of $W_{T-1}$ and therefore

$$J_W(W_{T-1}) = \theta^{T-1}(1+\theta)/W_{T-1} \tag{A11}$$

### First-order conditions at T − 2

At $T-2$, the FOC for consumption is

$$U_c(C_{T-2}^*) = R_f E_{T-2} J_W(W_{T-1}) \tag{A12}$$

$$\theta^{T-2}/C_{T-2}^* = E_{T-2}\{\theta^{T-1}(1+\theta)R_f/W_{T-1}\}$$

$$= E_{T-2}\left\{ \frac{\theta^{T-1}(1+\theta)R_f}{(W_{T-2} - C_{T-2}^*)R_{T-1}} \right\} \tag{A13}$$

It looks from (A13) as if $C_{T-2}^*$ depends on $R_{T-1}$ and, hence, on $\alpha_{i,T-1}^*$. However, we can show that for log utility $R_f E_{T-2}\{1/R_{T-1}\} = 1$ and assume for the moment this is true. Then, (A13) solves for

$$C_{T-2}^* = \frac{W_{T-2}}{(1+\theta+\theta^2)} \tag{A14}$$

Generalising this recursion for any $t < T-1$,

$$C_t = \frac{W_t}{(1+\theta+\theta^2+\theta^{T-t})} = \left[\frac{(1-\theta)}{1-\theta^{T-t+1}}\right] W_t \tag{A15}$$

It remains to prove our assertion that for log utility

$$R_f E_{T-2}\{1/R_{T-1}\} = 1 \tag{A16}$$

One expression for the FOC for consumption (see equation (42)) at $T-1$ is

$$U_c(C_{T-1}^*) = E_{T-1}\{B_W(W_T)R_f\} \tag{A17a}$$

$$\theta^{T-1}/C_{T-1}^* = \theta^T R_f E_{T-1}\{1/(W_{T-1} - C_{T-1}^*)R_T\} \tag{A17b}$$

Substituting $C_{T-1}^* = W_{T-1}/(1+\theta)$ and rearranging, we obtain

$$R_f E_{T-1}\{1/R_T(\alpha_i^*)\} = 1 \tag{A18}$$

This will also hold for $E_{T-2}\{1/R_{T-1}\}$ since the form of the FOC is the same as at $T - 1$. This completes the last part of the proof.

Note that we have not explicitly solved for $\alpha_{it}^*$ ($t = T - 1$, $T - 2$, ...) as this requires evaluating the expectations terms. Also, for power utility ($\gamma \neq 1$), the solution for $C_t^*$ depends on expected returns and hence $\alpha_{i,t}^*$. Therefore, although a solution is still possible in closed form, it is a little more complex.

# 16

# INTERTEMPORAL ASSET ALLOCATION: EMPIRICS

## Aims

- Introduce stochastic labour income into the intertemporal consumption-portfolio model. This gives rise to a hedging demand for risky assets, which depends on the correlation between shocks to returns and shocks to labour income.

- Investigate conditions whereby risky-asset shares depend on the horizon of the investor.

- Analyse the implications of allowing social security contributions to be invested in the stock market.

- Examine the quantitative impact of predictability in returns for optimal asset allocation.

- Show how uncertainty about the parameters of the prediction equation for stock returns influences optimal asset shares.

- Investigate the implications of alternative preference specifications on the demand for assets.

## 16.1 Retirement and Stochastic Income

Intertemporal portfolio-consumption models are becoming extremely popular in analysing consumption and asset choices in a variety of settings, for example, when in work and when retired and also in the design of state and private pension systems. In this section, we give no more than a summary of these models, which illustrates their relationship with the relatively simple approaches discussed so far and the sensitivity of their conclusions to slight changes in assumption about key parameters – in particular, the introduction of stochastic labour income, which introduces a hedging demand for risky assets.

An interesting issue is whether portfolio-consumption models are consistent with the standard advice given in the popular press that people in employment should invest more in risky assets (and less in safe assets) than people who are retired. Also, for people in work, a 60–40 split between risky and the riskless asset is often cited as a useful 'rule of thumb'.

Our simple intertemporal model with time-separable power utility (and no labour income) has risky asset shares ($\alpha$), depending on (conditional) expected returns. Samuelson (1969) and Merton (1969, 1971) demonstrate that for the horizon of the investor (i.e. $T - t$) to have no effect on risky-asset shares in an intertemporal consumption-portfolio choice model, requires rather special circumstances. These include power utility, *iid* returns on assets and the absence of labour income. This equivalence between the single-period and multi-period solutions is often referred to as the *myopic* portfolio choice solution. Hence, under these assumptions, asset shares do not differ between working and retirement years.

Bodie, Merton and Samuelson (1992) include *certain* labour income in the intertemporal consumption-portfolio model (with power utility and *iid* returns). Labour income is a non-tradeable asset (i.e. you cannot borrow against future labour income, and human capital is the value today of this future income). In this model, certain labour income acts like a risk-free asset and 'crowds out' the latter, leading to an increased share held in the risky assets. Hence, $\alpha^e > \alpha^r$, where e = 'in employment' and r = 'in retirement'. The certain labour income in employment implies that more will be invested in the risky asset (than in retirement, when labour income is assumed to be zero).

If labour income is *uncertain* but *uncorrelated* with risky returns, the tilt towards risky assets is less than in the certain income case (Viceira 2001). But when stochastic income is uncorrelated with returns, households with high human capital (i.e. high expected future income) will hold more risky assets than those with low human capital.

Viceira (2001) addresses the portfolio-consumption problem when income is stochastic and may be *contemporaneously correlated* with risky-asset returns. We now have an additional state variable, labour income, and this can give rise to a hedging demand for risky assets (first noted by Merton (1971) in an intertemporal model with time-varying expected returns). Hedging demand arises from the desire to reduce lifetime consumption risk, and here this risk arises from the correlation between returns and income. If shocks to income are negatively related to shocks to returns, then stocks are 'desirable' since they provide a return when income is low and hence help smooth out consumption.

In Viceira's model, agents maximise expected intertemporal power utility subject to a budget constraint

$$\max_{\{c_t, \alpha_t\}_0^\infty} E \sum_{t=0}^{\infty} \theta^t U(C_t) \tag{1a}$$

$$W_{t+1} = (W_t + Y_t - C_t) R_{p,t+1} \tag{1b}$$

$0 < \theta < 1$ is the discount factor and $Y_t$ is employment (labour) income, which is zero in the retirement state. Labour income is uninsurable – you cannot write claims against your future income. There are no labour supply decisions, so income is exogenous. The portfolio return is

$$R_{p,t+1} = \alpha_t (R_{1,t+1} - R_f) + R_f \tag{2}$$

where $R_{1,t+1} = \exp(r_{1,t+1})$ is the return on the *single* risky asset, $R_f = \exp(r_f)$ is the risk-free rate and $\alpha_t$ the risky-asset share. The share held in the riskless asset is $(1 - \alpha_t)$. The natural logarithm of income is a random walk with drift $g$, and expected excess (log) returns $(r_{1,t+1} - r_f)$ are assumed constant

$$Y_{t+1} = Y_t \exp(g + \varepsilon_t) \tag{3a}$$

$$r_{1,t+1} - r_f = \mu + u_{t+1} \tag{3b}$$

$$\text{var}_t(u_{t+1}) = \sigma_u^2, \quad \text{var}_t(Y_{t+1}) = \sigma_\varepsilon^2, \quad \text{cov}_t(u_{t+1}, \varepsilon_{t+1}) = \sigma_{\varepsilon u} \tag{3c}$$

The error term $u_{t+1}$ is independent of the employment/retirement state. In addition, consumption growth and asset returns are assumed jointly lognormal.

The employment–retirement state is random. Employment occurs with a probability $\pi^e$ and retirement with probability $\pi^r = 1 - \pi^e$ $(0 < \pi^r < 1)$, with retirement being irreversible, and labour income in retirement is zero. After retirement, there is a constant probability of death $\pi^d$, so people live $1/\pi^d$ years after retirement, while the expected number of years to retirement is $1/(1 - \pi^e)$.

Because there is zero income in the retirement state (denoted by superscript r), we have our standard model with Euler equation

$$1 = E_t \{ \theta^r (C_{t+1}^r / C_t^r)^{-\gamma} R_{i,t+1} \} \tag{4}$$

where $\theta^r = (1 - \pi^r)\theta$ and $R_{i,t+1}$ can be either $i = 1$, $f$ or $p$, that is, the risky asset, the risk-free asset or the portfolio return. Viceira provides approximate solutions on the basis of a second-order Taylor series expansion, so that precautionary savings effects (i.e. volatility terms) are included (Campbell and Viceira 1999). This provides some useful intuitive insights and allows a closed-form solution for both consumption and asset shares. For the retirement state, optimal (log) consumption and portfolio shares are

$$c_t^r = b_0^r + b_1^r w_t \tag{5a}$$

$$\alpha_t^r = \frac{\mu + \sigma_u^2/2}{\gamma b_1^r \sigma_u^2} \tag{5b}$$

where

$$b_1^r = 1 \tag{5c}$$

$$b_0^r = \ln \left\{ 1 - \exp \left[ \left( \frac{1}{\gamma} - b_1^r \right) E_t r_{p,t+1}^r + \frac{1}{\gamma} \ln \theta^r + \frac{1}{2\gamma} (1 - b_1^r \gamma)^2 \, \text{var}_t(r_{p,t+1}^r) \right] \right\} \tag{5d}$$

We can relate (5a) to our earlier result (see Samuelson (1969) and equation (45) in Chapter 15)

$$\left(\frac{C}{W}\right)_t = \frac{1}{1 + [\theta^r E_t(R_{p,t+1}^{1-\gamma})]^{1/\gamma}}$$

It can be shown that when $R_{p,t+1}$ is lognormal, the above reduces to Viceira's solution $c_t - w_t = b_0^r$ (see Viceira 2001, Appendix B). The constant term $b_0$ depends on $\gamma$, $\theta$, expected returns and the conditional variance of returns. But if $\gamma = 1$ (log utility), then from (5d), the (log) consumption–wealth ratio depends only on $\theta$ and is independent of expected returns and the variance of returns. This mirrors our earlier result for log utility where we found $(C/W)_t = [(1 - \theta)/(1 - \theta^{T-t+1})]$.

From (5d), consumption–wealth ratio is increasing in the time preference rate, $-\ln \theta \approx t_p$, and the relationship between the consumption–wealth ratio and expected portfolio returns depends on the 'dividing line' for constant CRRA investors of whether $\gamma$ is greater than or less than unity (i.e. log utility). For log utility investors, $(C/W)_t$ is independent of returns. For more risk-averse (retired) investors (i.e. $\gamma > 1$), the $(C/W)_t$ ratio is increasing in expected portfolio returns (see (5a) and (5d)), because the income effect of an increase in $Er_p$ on wealth outweighs the substitution effect (i.e. save more today). The impact of $\text{var}_t(r_{p,t+1})$ on $(C/W)_t$ is zero for $\gamma = 1$ but otherwise has a negative impact – the greater the uncertainty about $r_p$, the lower is $(C/W)$ and the higher is today's saving (i.e. precautionary savings).

Since returns are *iid* (and labour income is zero), the risky-asset share $\alpha_t^r$ is the same in all *retirement* periods (i.e. the usual myopic result). But $\alpha_t^r$ is higher, the higher is the expected return $\mu$ and the lower is volatility in returns $\sigma_u^2$.

## Hedging Demand

So far so good, as this reproduces our earlier results. But what about consumption and asset shares in the employment state? In the employment state, there is a probability you will stay employed and receive labour income and a probability you will enter retirement, hence the Euler equation is

$$1 = E_t\{[\pi^e \theta^e (C_{t+1}^e/C_t^e)^{-\gamma} + (1 - \pi^e)\theta^e (C_{t+1}^r/C_t^r)^{-\gamma}]R_{it+1}\} \tag{6}$$

for $i = 1$, f or p and $\theta^e = \theta$, while $\theta^r = (1 - \pi^r)\theta$. The solution for (log) consumption and the risky-asset share is

$$c_t^e - y_t = b_0^e + b_1^e(w_t - y_t) \tag{7a}$$

$$\alpha^e = \frac{\mu + \sigma_u^2/2}{\gamma \bar{b}_1 \sigma_u^2} - \frac{\pi^e(1 - b_1^e)}{\bar{b}_1}\frac{\sigma_{\varepsilon u}}{\sigma_u^2} \tag{7b}$$

where $0 < b_1^e < 1$, $\bar{b}_1 = \pi^e b_1^e + (1 - \pi^e)$ and $b_1^e$ is a constant that is an increasing function of $g$ (income growth) and also depends on the variance of income growth, the variance of portfolio returns and the covariance between these two. The dependence of $\alpha^e$ on the expected number of years until retirement, that is, $(1 - \pi^e)^{-1}$, implies that asset shares (of the employed) do depend on the 'horizon' considered.

Consider the special case $\sigma_{\varepsilon u} = 0$ so income shocks are uncorrelated with shocks to asset returns. Then it can be shown that $\alpha^e > \alpha^r$. Also it can be shown that the longer are expected years to retirement, the larger is $\alpha^e$, even when returns are *iid* (see Viceira 2001, Table 1). Illustrative results for $\gamma = 2$ and 5 are shown in Table 1. For $\gamma = 5$, as years to retirement increase from 5 to 35, then $\alpha^e$ increases from 42 to 76%, whereas $\alpha^r$ (for $\gamma = 2$) is 34%. For any given fixed number of years to retirement, an increase in risk aversion ($\gamma$) leads to a lower value for $\alpha^e$ (and $\alpha^r$).

The optimal solution is therefore consistent with our rule of thumb that those in work should hold more in risky assets than those who are retired. But is this rule of thumb robust? No, it is not if we consider the hedging demand, that is the second term on the RHS of (7b). The 'hedging term' is $\beta = \sigma_{\varepsilon u}/\sigma_u^2$, which is the regression slope of labour income shocks on unexpected stock returns. As shocks to income and returns become more positively correlated, $\alpha^e$ falls – you hold less risky assets because when income is low, asset returns are also low, so the latter are less useful in smoothing consumption. Comparing panel A with panel B in Table 1 demonstrates how a positive correlation between labour income and stock returns reduces $\alpha^e$ (for any given time to retirement and any $\gamma$).

Conversely, if $\sigma_{\varepsilon u} < 0$, then risky assets are a good hedge against unfavourable income shocks, so the hedging demand is positive (and then $\alpha^e > \alpha^r$). This hedging demand, which did not appear in our earlier simpler model with no stochastic labour income, can have a powerful impact on $\alpha^e$, and these hedging effects are larger, the longer the expected time to retirement. However, for a correlation of *plus* 25% between income and asset return shocks (and $\gamma$ between 2 and 12), it is the case that $\alpha^e > \alpha^r$ (but $\alpha^e - \alpha^r$ is much smaller than for the zero correlation case) – see Viceira 2001, Table 1, Panel B. There are other interesting results for this model based on numerical simulations. But we now turn to another variant of the model, which addresses the question of whether to allow social security contributions to be invested in stocks as well as risk-free assets.

**Table 1** Percentage portfolio shares $\alpha^e$ as $\gamma$ and expected time to retirement vary

| CRRA ($\gamma$) | Expected Time to Retirement (Years) | | | | $\alpha^r$ |
| --- | --- | --- | --- | --- | --- |
| | 35 | 20 | 10 | 5 | |
| **Panel A: Corr$(r_{1,t+1}, \Delta y_{t+1}) = 0\%$** | | | | | |
| 2 | 294 | 190 | 140 | 115 | 90 |
| 5 | 76 | 61 | 49 | 42 | 36 |
| **Panel B: Corr$(r_{1,t+1}, \Delta y_{t+1}) = 25\%$** | | | | | |
| 2 | 255 | 175 | 133 | 111 | 89 |
| 5 | 63 | 52 | 44 | 39 | 36 |

Source: Adapted from Viceira 2001, Table 1.

## Social Security and Pensions

The US social security fund is currently invested in risk-free bonds. However, if individuals can borrow to invest in equities, they can achieve a portfolio that is just as risky as if the retirement account were invested in equities. Hence, a shift to social security contributions being invested in equities will only add to welfare if some (poor) people are unable to borrow or face high fixed costs of equity market participation.

The idea in Campbell and Viceira (1999) is to measure the *ex-ante* lifetime welfare gains from a system in which $\psi\%$ of social security contributions are invested in stocks and $1 - \psi$ in the riskless asset, where $\psi$ can vary between 0 and 100%. Returns are *iid*, and shocks to returns may be contemporaneously correlated with income shocks. The income process is more complex than that in Viceira with deterministic life-cycle effects (e.g. humped-shaped earnings with age) and permanent and transitory shocks. The investor cannot borrow against future labour income or retirement wealth and cannot short stocks. Disposable income after forced saving in social security contributions of $\psi Y_{it}$ is

$$Y_{it}^{d} = (1 - \psi) Y_{it} \tag{8}$$

Retirement contributions $\psi Y_{it}$ can be invested in stocks $R_1$ or in the risk-free asset, as can liquid wealth $W_{it}^{L}$ for each individual $i$:

$$W_{i,t+1}^{R} = R_{p,i,t+1}^{R}(W_{it}^{R} + \psi Y_{it}) \tag{8a}$$

$$W_{i,t+1}^{L} = R_{p,t,t+1}^{L}[W_{it}^{L} + (1 - \psi) Y_{it} - C_{it}] \tag{8b}$$

$$R_{p,i,t+1}^{k} = \alpha_{it}^{k} R_{1,t+1} + (1 - \alpha_{it}^{k}) R_{f} \tag{8c}$$

where $k = L$ (liquid wealth) or $R$ (retirement wealth). Intertemporal power utility (weighted by the conditional probability of being alive) over consumption is the maximand, and the individual chooses $\alpha_{it}^{L}$, which depends on the state variables $[W_{it}^{L} + (1 - \psi) Y_{it}]$ and $W_{it}^{R}$. We can obtain numerical optimal solutions for $\alpha_{it}^{L}$ and $C_{it}$ for alternative values of both $\psi$, which determines the social security contributions, and for $\alpha_{it}^{R}$, the proportion of these contributions that are invested in equities. The fixed 'end point' is to ensure that the average (across individuals) of the replacement ratio of income in retirement is 60%. Hence, more investment of social security retirement funds in equities with mean return $\mu = 6\%$ p.a. with the real rate of interest at 2% p.a. (i.e. equity premium of 4% p.a.), implies that a cut in social security contributions is possible (given the fixed replacement ratio of 60%). In fact, changing $\alpha^{R}$ from 0 to 50% allows $\psi$ to fall from 10 to 6%.

Campbell et al. find a modest welfare gain equivalent to 3.7% of consumption if half (rather than zero) of the social security contributions are invested in equities, but this falls to 0.5% if the social security tax rate is held constant. The authors recognise the limitations of even this rather complex model. First, the equity premium is held constant even when more of retirement wealth is invested in stocks. In fact, the effect of a lower equity premium on welfare depends on whether this arises from a fall in the return on risky assets $R_1$ or a higher risk-free rate $r$. Quite obviously, a fall in $R$

or rise in $r$ reduces any welfare gains from the switch of social security contributions from bonds to equities.

The model embodies a 'self-financing' social security retirement system, so there is no redistribution between households. Some cohorts suffer rather low terminal values of social security retirement wealth, which would yield only a very low annuity value on retirement. This might induce others to speculate on possible bail-outs of such people, which might in turn impact on their consumption–savings pattern. Returns are *iid*, so there are no market-timing possibilities (see the following section), and housing wealth is excluded. Also, idiosyncratic labour income shocks are uncorrelated with returns, and labour supply is exogenous. Nevertheless, the model provides a useful first step in evaluating and thinking about a key policy area.

## 16.2  Many Risky Assets

We have seen that the introduction of an additional stochastic variable (i.e. labour income) gives rise to hedging demands for risky assets. Now we allow the investor to hold more than one risky asset (Campbell and Viceira 1999) so that hedging demand arises because of the conditional correlation between different asset returns. Our model also allows predictability in asset returns on the basis of a VAR system. Campbell, Chan and Viceira (2003) assume an infinitely level investor with Epstein–Zin recursive preferences, no labour income and no portfolio constraints (e.g. short-selling is allowed, and there are no borrowing constraints). The beauty of the approach is that Campbell et al. provide approximate analytic solutions so we can get some intuitive feel for what is going on. The utility function is

$$U(C_t, E_t(U_{t+1})) = \left[ (1-\delta)C_t^{\frac{1-\gamma}{\theta}} + \delta(E_t(U_{t+1}^{1-\gamma}))^{\frac{1}{\theta}} \right]^{\frac{\theta}{1-\gamma}} \tag{9}$$

where $\gamma > 0$ is the coefficient of relative risk aversion, $\psi > 0$ is the elasticity of intertemporal substitution, $0 < \delta < 1$ is the discount factor and $\theta = (1-\gamma)/(1-\psi^{-1})$. For time-separable power utility, $\gamma = \psi^{-1}$ so $\theta = 1$. Log utility has $\gamma = \psi^{-1} = 1$.

The budget constraint and portfolio real return are

$$W_{t+1} = (W_t - C_t)R_{p,t+1} \tag{10a}$$

$$R_{p,t+1} \equiv \sum_{i=1}^{k-1} \alpha_{i,t}(R_{i,t+1} - R_{k,t+1}) + R_{k,t+1} \tag{10b}$$

where the $k$th asset is the benchmark asset (e.g. nominal T-bill), but it may not be riskless in real terms (i.e. there is inflation risk). The portfolio return and budget constraint are log-linearised, and the Euler equation for asset $i = 1, 2, \ldots, k-1$ is

$$E_t(r_{i,t+1} - r_{k,t+1}) + \frac{1}{2}\text{var}_t(r_{i,t+1} - r_{k,t+1})$$
$$= \frac{\theta}{\psi}(\sigma_{i,c-w,t} - \sigma_{k,c-w,t}) + \gamma(\sigma_{i,p,t} - \sigma_{k,p,t}) - (\sigma_{i,k,t} - \sigma_{k,k,t}) \tag{11}$$

where lower-case letters are logarithms. The expected excess return on asset $i$ therefore depends upon *conditional covariances* between the return on asset $i$ and (i) the (log) consumption-wealth ratio c-w, (ii) the portfolio return and (iii) the benchmark asset $k$. The variance term in (11) is the Jensen inequality term, and (11) is exact if consumption and asset returns are jointly lognormally distributed, which is the case when $\psi = 1$. It can be shown that when asset returns (and any forcing variables such as the dividend–price ratio) are driven by a linear VAR system with homoscedastic errors, that the covariances just referred to are linear functions of the state variables $z_t$ in the VAR. The homoscedasticity implies that the state variables only predict changes in expected returns and do not predict changes in risk (but the risk, mean return link may not be very strong empirically – Chacko and Viceira 1999). Solving the Euler equation gives optimal risky-asset shares:

$$\alpha_t = \frac{1}{\gamma} \sum_{xx}^{-1} \left[ E_t(x_{t+1}) + \frac{1}{2} \text{var}_t(x_{t+1}) + (1 - \gamma)\sigma_{k,x} \right]$$
$$+ \frac{1}{\gamma} \sum_{xx}^{-1} \left[ -\left(\frac{\theta}{\psi}\right)(\sigma_{i,c-w,t} - \sigma_{k,c-w,t}) \right] \tag{12}$$

where $x_{t+1}$ is the vector of excess returns $r_i - r_k$ (for $i = 1, 2, \ldots, k - 1$) with covariance matrix $\sum_{xx}$. The terms in square brackets are linear functions of the $z_t$ variables for the VAR, where $z_t = [r_{k,t}, x_t, s_t]$ and $s_t$ are the 'non-returns' variables in the VAR (e.g. dividend–price ratio). Hence, asset shares vary over time as the variables in the VAR signal predictability.

The first term on the RHS of (12) is the *myopic component* of asset demands since it only depends on *next* period's (excess) return $x_{t+1}$ and also does not depend on $\psi$, the elasticity of intertemporal substitution. For a logarithmic investor, $\gamma = 1$ and $\theta = 0$, hence the second bracketed term, the *hedging demand*, equals zero, leaving only the myopic demand. Also, if investment opportunities are constant, then over time, the hedging component is zero for any value of $\gamma$. If, in addition, the benchmark asset is not risky, then $\sigma_{k,x} = 0$, and we obtain the familiar static solution (with the Jensen term) for asset shares, $\alpha_t = \gamma^{-1} \sum_{xx}^{-1} [E_t x_{t+1} + (1/2) \text{var}_t(x_{t+1})]$. In general, however, asset returns vary because of changing forecasts of both $E_t(x_{t+1})$ and the covariance terms (which depend linearly on $z_t$). The consumption growth equation is

$$E_t \Delta c_{t+1} = \psi \ln(\delta) + \frac{1}{2}\frac{\theta}{\psi} \text{var}_t(\Delta c_{t+1} - \psi r_{p,t+1}) + \psi E_t(r_{p,t+1}) \tag{13}$$

In (13), consumption growth is higher, (i) the higher is $\delta$ (i.e. the less weight given to current consumption) (ii) the higher is the expected return on the portfolio and (iii) the lower is $\text{var}_t(\Delta c_{t+1} - \psi r_{p,t+1})$ for $\theta > 0$ – which holds for power utility since $\theta = 1$.

With recursive preferences, only in special cases (Giovannini and Weil 1989) can we obtain closed-form solutions, and these are listed below for comparison with our earlier results.

- For constant *iid* returns (i.e. the VAR only contains a constant), the investor consumes a fixed proportion of her wealth, which depends on her own rate of time preference, relative risk aversion and intertemporal substitution $\psi$ and the investment horizon, $T - t$ (Bhamra and Uppal 2002). Also there is a myopic portfolio rule – that is, the investor chooses $\alpha_t$ as if her investment horizon were just one period (and $\alpha_t$ is independent of $\psi$).

- If expected returns are time varying but $\gamma = 1$, then the myopic portfolio rule applies but the consumption–wealth ratio is time varying. If $\gamma = 1$ and $\psi = 1$, then the consumption–wealth ratio is also constant.

- If $\psi = 1$ but $\gamma \neq 1$, then the consumption–wealth ratio is constant ($=1 - \delta$), but the optimal portfolio rule is not myopic.

Campbell, Chan and Viceira (2003) solve the model numerically, first using three risky assets: stocks, nominal bonds and bills. If the VAR only contains a constant term (i.e. returns are *iid*) and we set $\gamma = 1$, then optimal portfolio shares are myopic and only depend on the variance–covariance matrix $\sum_{xx}$, and the (constant) expected excess returns on each asset. In this case, investors are long in stocks and bonds with more being held in stocks because of their higher unconditional expected return (i.e. high *ex-post* equity premium). Moving from this baseline case, they include several variables in the VAR and consider cases where $\gamma \neq 1$. Here, hedging demand influences both the mean value of $\alpha_t$ and the sensitivity of $\alpha_t$ to changes in the state variables $z_t$. For conservative investors with risk aversion $\gamma > 1$ (i.e. risk tolerance $= 1/\gamma < 1$), stock demand is always greater than the myopic portfolio demand, so the hedging demand is positive (and is a humped-shaped function of $1/\gamma$). In fact, stocks are a good hedge for their own future returns since (in the VAR) the shocks to the dividend–price ratio are negatively correlated with shocks to stock returns, and this increases the hedging demands for stocks (when $\gamma > 1$). They also find that shocks to nominal bonds returns are positively correlated with shocks to stock returns, and this encourages investors (with intermediate levels of risk aversion) to short bonds in order to hedge their long stock positions. When an additional asset, namely inflation linked bonds, is added to the list of assets, these are held long in large amounts by *extremely* conservative investors, in order to hedge real interest rate risk and because they provide a good hedge for stocks (i.e. negative correlation between shocks to indexed bonds and shocks to stock returns). A summary of some of the main intertemporal consumption–portfolio models is provided in Table 2.

## 16.3 Different Preferences

We noted in a previous chapter that loss aversion (LA) preferences, when added to a power utility function (over multiperiod consumption – Barberis and Huang 2001), can help in explaining the equity premium puzzle with a 'reasonable' value of the risk aversion parameter. One of the reasons for introducing loss aversion is that a constant

**Table 2** Asset demands: intertemporal consumption-portfolio choice

| | | Labour Income | Returns IID | Predictable Returns | Consumption |
|---|---|---|---|---|---|
| Samuelson (1969) | Rebalancing Discrete time Power utility | No | $\alpha^* = (ER - r)/\gamma\sigma^2$ $\alpha^*$ independent of horizon (myopic) | No | $C/W = (ER, \gamma, T-t)$ $C/W = f(\gamma, T-t)$ – for log utility |
| Merton (1969, 1971) | Rebalancing Continuous time Power utility | No | As Samuelson (1969) | Additional hedging demand – covariance between expected returns and shocks to returns | As Samuelson (1969) |
| Campbell and Viceira (1999) Bhamra and Uppal (2002) | Rebalancing Discrete time Recursive utility Loglinear approxns. | No | For many risky assets $\alpha^* = f(\Sigma^{-1}, ER, \gamma, \psi)$ Myopic for $\gamma = 1$ | Additional hedging demand – covariances between shocks to different asset returns and the C/W ratio | As Samuelson (1969) But for $\psi = 1$, C/W is constant |
| Brodie, Merton and Samuelson (1992) | As Samuelson (1969) | Deterministic | Myopic – but with $\alpha^*$ with labour income) > $\alpha^*$ (no labour income) Labour income acts like a risk-free asset, so hold more of *risky* asset | No | As Samuelson (1969) |
| Viceira (2001) | Rebalancing Discrete time Utility Loglinear approxn. | Stochastic labour income | Myopic plus hedging demand (covariance between shocks to returns and shocks to labour income) Horizon effects even when returns are *iid* | No | As Samuelson (1969) -plus Jensen inequality term in var(R). C/W independent of ER for log utility investors |

Notes: This table gives a summary of the broad key results from a non-exhaustive set of research papers in this area – for details, see text.

relative risk aversion (CRRA) utility function (e.g. power utility) in the level of consumption has a number of problems.

First, it gives low values for the equity premium. Second, if the expected return on stocks is positive, then *all* investors hold stocks – yet in most countries, relatively few people invest in the stock market. The only way we can produce low stock market participation for CRRA investors is to assume very large fixed entry costs for investors (Campbell and Viceira 1999, Liu and Loewenstein 2002). Third, CRRA and the expected utility framework are at odds with the 'Rabin puzzle' (Rabin 2000). The latter arises because expected utility investors, if they turn down a 'small' gamble where they could lose $100 or gain $110 with equal probability (and for any initial wealth level), they will also turn down 50:50 bets of losing $1000 or gaining *any* amount of money – this is known as a *Rabin gamble* (Rabin 2000). For example, with CRRA preferences and $\gamma = 10$, an investor would turn down the 111/110 gamble. However, her willingness to pay (i.e. difference between the certain wealth from not gambling minus the certainty equivalent of the gamble) to avoid a gamble of losing $1000 or gaining over $1m (with equal probability), is only about $280. The marginal utility of additional wealth for CRRA utility asymptotes as wealth increases and becomes virtually zero very fast – hence the CRRA investor would reject the Rabin gamble for a very small payment.

Unlike standard expected utility investors, LA utility investors do not necessarily have to have a highly concave utility function in order to dislike the 100/110 gamble. This is because the utility function is discontinuous at the reference point. Loss aversion means they can hate to lose the $100, but for gains, the utility function need not have high curvature. Although, as we have seen, LA helps explain the equity premium puzzle, Ang and Bekaert (2001) point out some drawbacks of LA preferences. These include the arbitrary nature of the 'reference point' (against which we measure gains and losses) and how we choose to update it. They also show that when applied to portfolio theory, it is *possible* to obtain some 'strange' results for the share of risky assets (e.g. there may be no finite optimal weight, $\alpha^*$ and $\alpha^*$ may be less than zero for a zero risk premium).

Ang and Bekaert (2001) suggest using *disappointment-aversion* (DA) preferences (Gul 1991), which imply aversion to losses, but the reference point is endogenous, being defined as outcomes above or below the certainty equivalent. The CRRA utility function is a special case of DA preferences. Because DA preferences embody loss aversion, they avoid the Rabin puzzle. For example, a DA investor with $\gamma = 2$, who weights utility losses 1.18 more than for an equal gain, will reject the 100/110 gamble but will be willing to take on the large Rabin gamble (i.e. will pay as much as $3664 to bet on a 50:50 chance of a gain of $25,000 or a loss of $2000).

In a model where investors maximise utility of terminal wealth and have DA preferences, we can explain why participation in the stock market may be low – people dislike losses more than an equal gain and, hence, many choose not to hold stocks at all (if they have a reasonable degree of loss aversion of around 1.66). In contrast, CRRA utility never gives a zero allocation to stocks (for $ER - r > 0$) and for $\alpha^* = 5\%$, $\gamma$ must be as high as 36. Disappointment aversion is also consistent with home bias if bear markets across countries are positively correlated, since DA investors dislike negative skewness and would tend to reduce international holdings of stocks. DA investors would also want to insure against downturns and hence would purchase put-protected products. The application of DA utility to practical issues in portfolio allocation is relatively new and it remains to be seen if such preferences can explain a wide range of phenomena.

# 16.4  Horizon Effects and Uncertainty

So far, we have said only a little about how the investor's horizon might influence her choice between stocks and bonds (i.e. the risk-free asset). In the static mean-variance model, the optimal risky-asset proportions are determined by conditional expected returns relative to the variance of portfolio returns, but the horizon is chosen exogenously by the investor. It is a one-period maximisation problem. Each period, the investor can form new forecasts, and this will result in 'new' asset proportions. In the special case that returns are *iid* (and, hence, expected portfolio returns and the covariance of returns are constant), risky-asset proportions will not change from period to period. Hence, optimal asset proportions will also be the same for two investors with different horizons. Intuitively, this arises because *iid* (log) asset returns imply that expected returns and portfolio variance both increase in proportion to the investment horizon (i.e. $ER_T = T\mu$ and $\sigma_T^2 = T\sigma^2$). In any case, the mean-variance model is not intertemporal, so it is not particularly useful for investigating horizon effects in a coherent way.

Barberis and Huang (2001) investigates horizon effects in a model with power utility (we take $\gamma = 10$) where agents at time $T$ choose asset proportions to maximise utility of end-of-period wealth $EU(W_{T+H})$ and so the portfolio is not rebalanced between $T$ and $T + H$. (Also, there is no labour income in the model.)

## Buy and Hold, IID Returns

With power utility, *iid* returns and *continuous* rebalancing, optimal asset shares are independent of horizon $H$ (Samuelson 1969). In part, this is due to the fact that for *iid* returns, long-horizon mean returns $H\mu$ and variance $H\sigma^2$ both scale linearly with horizon $H$. With a *buy-and-hold* strategy and no parameter uncertainty, this result continues to hold, and for $\gamma = 10$, we find $\alpha^* \approx 40\%$ (see Figure 1). If we now introduce parameter uncertainty, $\alpha^*$ depends negatively on horizon $H$, with $\alpha^*(H = 1) \approx 35\%$ and falls monotonically to $\alpha^*(H = 10) \approx 20\%$ (Barberis and Huang 2001, Figure 1). The reason for this is that if $R_t = \mu + \varepsilon_t$ but $\mu$ is uncertain and is updated using Bayes rule, this introduces additional risk at long horizons and returns no longer appear to be *iid* from the investor's perspective. For example, if there are a few good (bad) returns, Bayesian updating increases (decreases) the agents' estimate of $\mu$ and, hence, introduces *positive* autocorrelation in returns. The latter implies $\sigma_T^2 > T\sigma^2$ and, hence, the share held in stocks $\alpha$ falls as the investor's horizon lengthens.

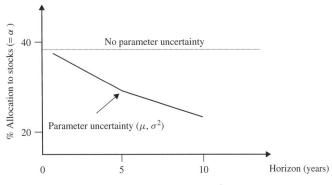

Notes:   1. Returns model is $r_{t+1} = \mu + \varepsilon_{t+1}$,     $\varepsilon_{t+1} \sim N(0, \sigma^2)$.
2. Data for estimates of $(\mu, \sigma^2)$ from 1986–95.

**Figure 1**   'Buy and hold': no predictability ($\gamma = 10$)

## Buy-and-Hold: Predictability in Returns

The prediction equations for stock returns and the dividend–price ratio are

$$r_{t+1} = \mu + \beta z_t + \varepsilon_{r,t+1}$$

$$z_{t+1} = \delta + \phi z_t + \varepsilon_{z,t+1}$$

The distributions we require depend on the value of the dividend yield $z_T$ at time $T$, the beginning of the buy-and-hold period. The variance of returns over multi-period horizons now depends on the contemporaneous covariance between the errors in the returns equation and the dividend yield, since, for example,

$$\mathrm{var}_T\,(r_{T+1} + r_{T+2}) = 2\sigma_r^2 + (\beta^2\sigma_z^2 + 2\beta\sigma_{r,z})$$

Empirically, on US data, $(\beta, \phi) > 0$ and $\sigma_{r,z} < 0$, and the term in parentheses is found to be negative. Hence, predictability, but with no *parameter* uncertainty, implies that long-horizon conditional variance grows slower than linearly with the investor's horizon (i.e. $\sigma_H^2 < H\sigma^2$).

Remember we saw above that with no parameter uncertainty and no predictability (i.e. *iid* returns), $\alpha^*$ is independent of horizon. However, with *no parameter uncertainty but with predictability* (and $\gamma = 10$), optimal $\alpha^*$ rises rapidly with horizon from $\alpha^*(H = 1) \approx 40\%$ to $\alpha^*(H = 10) \approx 90\%$ (see Figure 2). This result arises for two reasons. First, the dividend–price ratio at $T$ predicts high returns in the future and, second, because $\sigma_H^2 < H\sigma^2$, stocks look less risky to a long-horizon investor. Both of these tend to increase stock holdings for a long-horizon investor.

However, if we now account for *parameter uncertainty*, the optimal $\alpha^*$ (see Appendix) still rises with horizon (up to year 7), then falls a little and asymptotes at a much lower value, $\alpha^*(H = 10) \approx 55\%$, compared to the 'no uncertainty' case, where $\alpha^*(H = 10) \approx 90\%$ (Figure 2). The reasons for this drop in the optimal $\alpha^*(H = 10)$

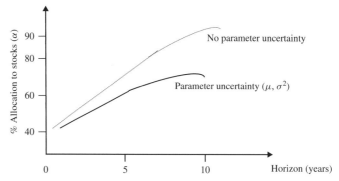

Notes:    1. A bivariate VAR model (1952–1995) for returns and the dividend–price
          ratio is used.
          2. Dividend yield at $T = 0$ is set at its sample mean value.

**Figure 2**    'Buy and hold': predictability in returns ($\gamma = 10$)

**Table 3**    Horizon effects and uncertainty: buy-and-hold

| | Risky-Asset Demands | Reason |
|---|---|---|
| **Panel 1: IID Returns** | | |
| 1A No parameter uncertainty | $\alpha$ independent of horizon | $\mu_H = H\mu$, $\sigma_H^2 = H\sigma^2$ Expected return and variance both scale with horizon |
| 1B Parameter uncertainty $(\mu, \sigma^2)$ | $\alpha$ falls with horizon | $\sigma_H^2$ increases faster than horizon because of estimation risk |
| **Panel 2: Predictability** $(r_{t+1} = \mu + \beta z_{t+1} + \varepsilon_{t+1}$ **and** $z_{t+1} = \delta + \phi z_t + v_{t+1})$ | | |
| 2A No parameter uncertainty | $\alpha$ increases strongly with horizon | (i) High $z_t$ signals high future returns (ii) $\sigma_{r,z} < 0$ then $\sigma_H^2 < H\sigma^2$ |
| 2B Parameter uncertainty | $\alpha$ tends to increase with horizon but less strongly than for no uncertainty case | (i) Uncertainty about $\mu$ makes $\sigma_H^2 > H\sigma^2$ – tends to reduce $\alpha$ (ii) True predictive power of $z_t$ is uncertain – tends to reduce $\alpha$ at longer horizon (compared to no uncertainty case) |

Note: Investor at $t = 0$ chooses $\alpha$ to maximise $U(W_H)$ with power utility and $\gamma = 10$.

at long horizons are twofold. With no uncertainty, $\sigma_H^2$ grows less than linearly with horizon, which tends to increase the demand for stocks. But with parameter uncertainty and concave utility (i.e. risk aversion), any possible 'downside' effect of uncertainty about returns has a greater effect than the (equally likely) upside. The investor is, therefore, uncertain whether the dividend yield does 'slow down' the conditional variance over long horizons. The second effect is that uncertainty about the *mean* return makes the conditional variance grow more quickly with horizon – hence making stocks look more risky and reducing $\alpha^*$ relative to the no uncertainty case. These results are summarised in Table 3.

## Dynamic Asset Allocation: Rebalancing Every Year

When returns are predictable and mean-reverting but there is no uncertainty, an investor (with $\gamma > 1$) who rebalances her portfolio will allocate more to stocks at longer horizons, as a *hedge* against changes in expected returns (Merton 1973). Barberis and Huang (2001) shows that with predictability *and* parameter uncertainty (but no learning between the rebalancing periods), asset shares $\alpha^*$ usually increase with horizon, but at a much slower rate than for the certainty case.

Barberis' model assumes the investor knows the functional form of the returns and dividend process and that their underlying true parameters are constant. In practice, this is unlikely to hold, and this additional uncertainty may further reduce the optimal allocation to stocks, at long horizons, for an investor who takes account of parameter uncertainty.

Overall, estimation risk can substantially alter optimal asset allocations compared to the no uncertainty case – hence, results from the latter may not adequately explain actual portfolio behaviour and must be interpreted with due caution.

# 16.5  Market Timing and Uncertainty

In the previous section, we answered the question 'what proportions are held in the risky asset by two investors with different investment horizons' (when both investors either do or do not take into account parameter uncertainty). In contrast, market timing is about altering one's portfolio at each point in time, on the basis of an observed signal (e.g. dividend–price ratio) at time $T$.

Campbell and Viceira (1999) directly address the market-timing issue in the intertemporal (consumption) utility model with continuous rebalancing (and with no labour income). A VAR in returns and the dividend–price ratio provides 'predictability'. The Campbell–Viceira model results in very strong market timing, with the allocation to stocks moving from $-50$ to $220\%$, as the dividend–price ratio moves from minus two to plus one standard deviation from its mean. This strong market timing is also a feature of other forecasting schemes (Brennan, Schwartz and Lagnado 1997) and different methodologies (Gallant, Hansen and Tauchen 1990, Brandt 1998).

Clearly, the major omission in these market-timing results is the uncertainty surrounding the prediction of expected returns. Barberis and Huang (2001) also looks at this problem, where agents maximise $EU(W_{T+H})$ (rather than intertemporal consumption) and there is no intermediate trading (i.e. buy-and-hold strategy).

With no parameter uncertainty, the higher the initial dividend yield (i.e. the lower are current prices), the higher the allocation to stocks *at any given horizon*, and $\alpha^*$ continues to rise monotonically with horizon. However, *with parameter uncertainty* (and $\gamma = 10$), the higher dividend yield at $T$ has hardly any effect on $\alpha^*(H = 10)$, that is, at long horizons (but it does have an effect at shorter horizons). This insensitivity is because the true forecasting power of the dividend yield is uncertain, and the 'signal' cannot be relied upon over long horizons. Hence, with no parameter uncertainty, $\alpha^*(H = 10)$ is very sensitive to the initial value of the dividend yield but is very insensitive when the investor takes account of parameter uncertainty. (Also, with uncertainty, the risky-asset share can be negatively related to horizon if the initial dividend–price ratio is very high – so long-horizon investors hold *less* stocks than short horizon investors.)

Put another way, incorporating parameter uncertainty greatly reduces the optimal proportion allocated to stocks, *for any given deviation of the dividend–price ratio from its mean*. With 'uncertainty', the optimal allocations (for $\gamma = 10$) are in the relatively narrow range of 30–50% over different horizons, compared to 30–100% (maximum) with no parameter uncertainty.

Market timing in these models also implies that you will often miss upturns in the market (e.g. 1995–2000), which would be picked up by a passive index-tracking fund. So another risk here, which is not factored into the market-timing model, is that you may lose your job before your market-timing strategy is seen to pay off!

So, although predictability suggests strong market-timing effects on portfolio allocation, this appears to be substantially reduced when parameter uncertainty is incorporated into the decision problem.

## 16.6   Stochastic Parameters

If returns are *iid* and the investor has power utility, then asset demands $\alpha_t$ from optimising over intertemporal (additive) utility from consumption, are independent of the investor's horizon (Samuelson 1969). If future returns are predictable (e.g. from the dividend–price ratio) so investment opportunities are time-varying, then there is an intertemporal hedging demand (Merton 1971). As we have seen, Barberis and Huang (2000) uses utility of end-of-period wealth and introduces uncertainty about the parameters of the prediction equation, but there is no time variation in the unknown parameters themselves (e.g. the mean return is unknown by the investor, but its *true value* never changes). Xia (2001), using a continuous-time intertemporal consumption model, allows the *parameters* $\delta_t$ and $\beta_t$ of the prediction equation (e.g. $R_{t+1} = \delta_t + \beta_t z_t$) to vary over time (the dynamics of both parameters are mean-reverting diffusion processes) and then calculates the optimal asset shares – which contain a hedging demand. Xia (2001) shows that the hedging demand is very complex under learning, with stochastic parameters. Asset shares depend on the usual myopic term $(ER - r)/\gamma \sigma_R^2$ plus the hedging demand, which consists of three elements (which are additive). The first part of the hedging demand depends upon $(z_t - \bar{z})$, where $z_t$ is the predictor variable – this disappears when there is no uncertainty about the unknown parameter $\beta$. The second hedging component depends on $\sigma_{z,R}$ and is zero if there is no correlation between the predictor variable $z$ and the risky-asset return. Finally, the third component depends on $\sigma_{\beta,R}$, which is the need to hedge against *stochastic* variation in the (unknown) parameter $\beta$.

It can be shown that $\sigma_{\beta,R}$ may increase or decrease with horizon, depending on the current value of $z_t$. Hence, the conventional advice that young investors should hold more in equities is not generally valid (Xia 2001).

As we have seen, when there is *no* parameter uncertainty, an investor maximising intertemporal utility of consumption over a long horizon $(T - t)$, will aggressively market time and move into stocks, with a response that is monotonic in the current

predictor variable $z_t$. With learning, this response is attenuated and is no longer mono-
tone in the $z_t$ variable. This is because with learning, the hedging demand from the
parameter uncertainty is negative and may eventually dominate the expression for
$\partial \alpha_t / \partial z_t$.

Therefore, in this stochastic parameter environment, the hedging effect depends on
the current estimate of the unknown parameters, the degree of uncertainty about this
estimate, the current value of the predictive variable $z_t$ and the investor's horizon
$(T - t)$. The Xia (2001) model provides a good example of the sensitivity of results
in this area to the model of learning used. Even here, the investor knows quite a lot,
namely, the functional form of the prediction equation $R_{t+1} = f(z_t)$ and the dynamic
process for $z_t$ (taken to be mean-reverting, that is, an Ornstein–Uhlenbeck process
in continuous time). Also the investor envisages no regime changes in the prediction
equation. So there is still some way to go in modelling a 'reasonable' learning process
and embedding it in an intertemporal consumption-portfolio choice model.

# 16.7    Robustness

In the previous section, we have concentrated on parameter or estimation uncertainty.
Another type of uncertainty is when an investor uses a particular model of asset returns
(e.g. mean-reverting process) but is aware that an alternative model may also explain
returns. Robustness refers to the fact that investors then choose their asset allocations to
insure against the worst-case *alternative model*. They want their chosen model to deliver
a good outcome, assuming it holds exactly but also to deliver a reasonable outcome if
an alternative model is the correct description of reality. The investor is worried about a
worst-case outcome (across alternative models), and this can be interpreted as a form of
maxmin expected utility – you minimise the possibility of undesirable outcomes (Roy
1952). Thus, the investor suffers from *uncertainty aversion* across models yet could
still have a low value for the CRRA parameter $\gamma$.

Maenhout (2001) addresses this robustness issue in a model where the investor
chooses consumption and asset shares to maximise intertemporal (power) utility of
consumption (and there is no labour income). However, the investor considers alternative models for stock returns (that are 'similar' or 'close' to each other) where a
parameter $\theta$ measures the strength of preference for robustness ($\theta = 0$ gives standard
expected utility maximisation). For power utility and *iid* returns, a 'robust investor'
holds optimal risky-asset shares

$$ \alpha^* = \frac{1}{(\gamma + \theta)} \left( \frac{ER - r}{\sigma^2} \right) $$

Therefore, a desire for robustness reduces the demand for the risky asset (compared to
the expected utility case). Also, the consumption–wealth ratio depends on $\theta$ as well as
$(ER - \mu)/\sigma^2$ and $\gamma$. If returns are predictable (e.g. mean-reverting), then robustness
gives rise to a positive hedging demand for the risky asset (even for logarithmic
investors, $\gamma = 1$) whereas a hedging demand usually only occurs in the expected utility
framework for $\gamma \neq 1$. Note that 'robust investors' do not learn about their environment,

they merely insure against worst-case outcomes. Again, the idea of robustness, which made a prominent, if somewhat short, appearance in the context of maxmin outcomes for choosing alternative *macroeconomic* models, has yet to prove its usefulness in the area of portfolio selection.

## Conclusions

The above analysis indicates the complexities of intertemporal models and the sensitivity of optimal asset shares to the predictability in returns and to their hedging components (i.e. covariances between shocks to different state variables). If results are very sensitive to particular assumptions, the practical value of such models may be questioned. Put another way, all models are stylised descriptions of reality and, therefore, sometimes, relatively innocuous assumptions may be crucial to the key results. However, it is only through careful analysis of alternative models that we can get some idea of the limitations of the analysis, and recent work is providing much information on these issues. Perhaps a key feature of this complex and challenging area is the many different possibilities one has to consider, most of which we have discussed in this chapter. These include the following.

- Using a finite or infinite horizon model in discrete or continuous time.

- Simplification to obtain interpretable closed form solutions (e.g. Merton 1971, Kim and Omberg 1996, Campbell and Viceira 1999, 2000) or more complex models that often require intensive numerical solution techniques or approximate solutions (which may not be valid if we move far from the initial conditions).

- Choice of utility function (e.g. power versus Epstein–Zin recursive utility or loss-aversion preferences) and its arguments (e.g. consumption, losses and gains or end-of-period wealth (e.g. Brennan, Schwartz and Lagnado 1997).

- Imposition of constraints (e.g. no short sales, borrowing limits, bankruptcy, and so on – Brennan, Schwartz and Lagnado 1997), which generally implies 'complex' numerical solutions.

- Choice of the number of state variables (e.g. how many assets, inclusion of stochastic labour income, or stochastic parameter uncertainty).

- Whether to allow predictable asset returns and whether to assume agents know the parameters of the prediction equations or they have to learn about these parameters, which may also be time-varying. What form of updating of parameters to use – purely data-based schemes (e.g. recursive OLS, Kalman Filter), regime switches or Bayesian learning?

## 16.8    Summary

- The introduction of a state variable other than returns, such as stochastic labour income, considerably complicates the solutions of the intertemporal consumption-portfolio model and introduces a hedging demand. If shocks to returns and labour income are negatively (positively) correlated, this increases (reduces) the demand for the risky asset. With a negative correlation, the risky-asset acts as a hedge against unexpected falls in labour income, allowing a smoother path for consumption and, hence, the demand for the risky asset is higher. Hedging demands also arise when returns ('the investment opportunity set') are time-varying.

- Loss aversion (e.g. disappointment aversion preferences) can explain why many investors do not participate in the stock market at all – their fear of losses makes it rational for them to avoid such risky bets, with high utility losses when the market falls. This result can only be obtained in standard power utility models if there are very high fixed entry costs to participation. Also loss-aversion utility avoids the Rabin paradox, whereby if investors avoid a small (50–50) gamble, they will not enter a gamble where they could lose relatively little but gain an *infinite* amount of money.

- Parameter uncertainty considerably reduces the demand for risky assets at any horizon, compared to the 'no uncertainty' case. This also appears to be the case when 'model uncertainty' and a robust maxmin criterion is used in asset-allocation decisions. Also, where returns are predictable, parameter uncertainty implies asset shares do not rise at a very *fast rate* and to very high levels as the investor's horizon lengthens – as is the case with predictability but no parameter uncertainty.

- If there is predictability in stock returns, the value of the predictor variable (e.g. dividend–price ratio) can have very strong positive (market-timing) effects on the demand for stocks. However, this seems to be considerably attenuated when there is parameter uncertainty.

# Appendix: Parameter Uncertainty and Bayes Theorem

Barberis and Huang (2001) very clearly sets out the issues in determining the optimal asset share in an intertemporal model under estimation uncertainty, using Bayes rule. Several aspects of this methodology are widely used, so we outline the key features of this approach. In order to determine the optimal asset allocation today (e.g. between one risky stock and one riskless asset), we have to forecast assets returns one or more periods ahead. Suppose initial wealth at time $T$ is $W_T$ and we wish to invest to maximise utility from terminal wealth with a horizon $H$ periods ahead. If $W_T = \$1$ and $\alpha$ is allocated to stocks, then

$$W_{T+H} = (1 - \alpha) \exp(r_f H) + \alpha \exp(r_f H + r_{T+1} + r_{T+2} + \cdots + r_{T+H})$$

where $r_f = $ *real* risk-free rate, $r_T$ is the (per period) *real* stock return (both continuously compounded). With CRRA utility,

$$U(W_{T+H}) = \frac{(W_{T+H})^{1-\gamma}}{1 - \gamma} \tag{A1}$$

The simplest case is a buy-and-hold strategy where the investor chooses $\alpha$ (at time $T$ and holds this portfolio to time $T + H$) and maximises $E_T U(W_{T+H})$, which can be written

$$\max_{\alpha} E_T \frac{[(1 - \alpha)\exp(r_f H) + \alpha \exp(r_f H + R_{T+H})]^{1-\gamma}}{1 - \gamma} \tag{A2}$$

where $R_{T+H} = r_{T+1} + r_{T+2} + \cdots + r_{T+H}$. Suppose we believe that stock returns are generated by

$$r_{t+1} = \mu + \beta z_t + \varepsilon_{t+1} \tag{A3}$$

where $z_t = $ dividend–price ratio (and is AR(1) say) and $\varepsilon_t$ is $iid$ $(0, \sigma^2)$ and $\theta = (\mu, \beta)$. If we assume the investor believes the OLS coefficients $\theta$ are estimated without error so that $\hat{\theta} = \theta$), then the investor's problem is

$$\max_{\alpha} \int U(W_{T+H}) p(R_{T+H}|z, \hat{\theta}) \, dR_{T+H} \tag{A4}$$

where $p(R_{T+H}|z, \hat{\theta})$ is the probability density function, given $z = (z_1, z_2, \ldots, z_T)$, the observed values of $z$ up to today ($= T$) and assuming $\theta$ is precisely given by $\hat{\theta}$. But (A4) does not take into account the uncertainty surrounding the estimate of $\theta$ and, hence, the uncertainty in future forecasts of $R_{T+H}$ arising from this source. A useful way of taking account of the uncertainty about $\theta$ is to use Bayes concept of a posterior distribution $p(\theta|z)$ that summarises the uncertainty about $\theta$, given the data observed so far. The *predictive distribution* is the probability distribution based only on the data sample observed and not on any fixed value of $\theta$

$$p(R_{T+H}|z) = \int p(R_{T+H}|\theta, z) p(\theta|z) \, d\theta \tag{A5}$$

Notice that the integration is over possible values of $\theta$. The investor then solves

$$\max_{\alpha} \int U(W_{T+H}) p(R_{T+H}|z) \, dR_{T+H} \tag{A6}$$

The posterior distribution $p(\theta|z)$ is proportional to the prior distribution $p(\theta)$ and the likelihood function for $\theta$

$$p(\theta|z) \propto p(\theta) L(\theta; z) \tag{A7}$$

The likelihood reflects the best estimate of $\theta$ using only the data on $z$, while the prior distribution is the investor's view of $\theta$ before examining the data (e.g. from theoretical considerations, such that it would be 'unreasonable' if $\theta$ lay outside a certain range).

## No Parameter Uncertainty: Returns IID

To illustrate the calculation of these alternative distributions, consider the simplest case where stock returns are *iid*

$$r_t = \mu + \varepsilon_t \qquad \varepsilon_t \sim iid(\mu, \sigma^2)$$

How can we evaluate the integral in (A4)? The p.d.f. conditional on fixed (known) parameters is $p(R_{T+H}|z, \theta) \equiv p(R_{T+H}|r, \mu, \sigma)$, where $r_{T+j} = \mu + \varepsilon_{T+j}$ for $(j = 1, 2, \ldots, H)$. Hence, $R_{T+H} = r_{T+1} + r_{T+2} + \cdots + r_{T+H}$ is normally distributed with mean $H\mu$ and variance $H\sigma^2$. The integral in (A4) is evaluated numerically by simulation. Suppose we have some function $g(y)$ and wish to evaluate

$$\int g(y)p(y)\,dy$$

where $p(y)$ is the p.d.f. The integral is approximated by

$$(1/m)\sum_{i=1}^{m} g(y^{(i)})$$

where $y^{(1)}, \ldots, y^{(m)}$ are independent draws from the probability density function $p(y)$. Given empirical values for $\mu$ and $\sigma^2$, we, therefore, draw $m = 1$ million values (say) from $N(\mu, \sigma^2)$ to give $R_{T+H}^{(i)} \sim N(\mu H, H\sigma^2)$ and evaluate the sum in (A4) as

$$EU(W_{T+H}) = \frac{1}{m}\sum_{i=1}^{m} \frac{\{(1-\alpha)\exp(r_f H) + \alpha\exp(r_f H + R_{T+H}^{(i)})\}^{1-\gamma}}{(1-\gamma)} \qquad \text{(A8)}$$

for a given $\alpha$. We then search over a grid of values for $\alpha^{(j)} = \{0, 0.01, 0.02, \ldots, 0.98, 0.99\}$ to determine the optimal $\alpha^{(j)}$ that maximises $EU(W_{T+H})$. Note that we constrain our solutions for $\alpha$ to exclude the possibility of short-selling ($\alpha < 0$) or buying on margin ($\alpha > 1$). (Barberis and Huang (2001) uses the posterior means of $\mu$ and $\sigma^2$ and as the 'fixed values' for these variables – see below). The above can be repeated for different horizons $H$ to see how the optimal $\alpha$ varies with horizon (although for *iid* returns and no parameter uncertainty, we expect $\alpha$ to be independent of horizon-but this will not necessarily be the case with uncertain parameters). Similarly, we can solve for $\alpha^*$ for different values of the risk-aversion parameter $\gamma$.

## Parameter Uncertainty: Returns are IID

We have to evaluate (A6), which requires the predictive distribution in (A5). To evaluate the latter, we first require the posterior distribution $p(\theta|z) = p(\mu, \sigma^2|r)$. In constructing the posterior distribution, we can use either an informed prior (i.e. some initial guess for $\mu = \mu_0$) or a diffuse (uninformative) prior such as

$$p(\mu, \sigma^2) \propto 1/\sigma^2 \qquad \text{(A9)}$$

For this diffuse prior, it can be shown that the posterior distribution $p(\mu, \sigma^2|r)$ is

$$\sigma^2|r \sim IG\left(\frac{T-1}{2}, \frac{1}{2}\sum_{t=1}^{T}(r_t - \bar{r}^2)\right) \qquad \text{(A10a)}$$

$$\mu|\sigma^2, r \sim N(\bar{r}, \sigma^2/T) \qquad \text{where } \bar{r} = \sum_{t=1}^{T} r_t \qquad \text{(A10b)}$$

The posterior distribution for $\mu$ is the maximum likelihood estimate when we have a diffuse prior. Equation (A10b) says that the best estimate of $\mu$ is the sample mean, and this estimate has a variance $(\sigma^2/T)$. If $\sigma^2$ is known by the investor, this would be the end of the story. But if $\sigma^2$ is not known, it too must be estimated from available data $(t = 1, 2, \ldots, T)$ and this is given in (A10a) where the posterior distribution of $\sigma^2$ is an inverse gamma (IG) distribution. If one were sampling from the posterior distribution at any time $T$ (so $T$ and $\bar{r}$ are known), then we would first make a draw from the inverse gamma distribution (A10a) to obtain $\sigma^{(i)}$ (for $i = 1$) and then use this value to draw from the normal distribution for $\mu^{(i)}$ in (A10b). If this is repeated many times, $i = 1, 2, \ldots, m$ (where $m$ may have to be as high as one million for the required degree of accuracy), we obtain an accurate representation of the posterior distribution.

Given that the 'true' $\mu$ is constant, then from (A10b), we see that the posterior delivers an accurate value for $\mu$ as $T \to \infty$ (since the variance $\sigma^2/T$ approaches zero), although in our case $T$ is fixed by the length of data available to the investor when she makes her buy-and-hold decision. In the case of an informative prior, the posterior distribution becomes more complex. However, intuition suggests that the posterior distribution of $\theta$ should be a weighted average of the prior values $\theta_0$ and the sample data estimates $\hat{\theta}$ and this is the case.

We now have $m = 1$ million values of $(\mu, \sigma^2)$ drawn from the posterior $p(\mu, \sigma^2|r)$ where $r = (r_1, r_2, \ldots, r_T)$ and now we sample *one point* from $N(H\mu, H\sigma^2)$ for each of these 1 million pairs $(\mu, \sigma^2)$. This gives us 1 million values from the predictive distribution for the uncertainty case, $p(R_{T+H}|z)$ in (A5), which are then averaged to give $EU(W_{T+H})$ in (A8) for a given $\alpha$. Equation (A8) is again maximised with a grid search over $\alpha^{(j)}$.

The 1 million values of $(\mu, \sigma^2)$ from the *posterior distribution* for monthly returns when averaged give $\hat{\mu} = 0.0065$ (std. dev. = 0.0039) and a mean estimate of $\sigma^2$ of 0.0019 (std. dev. = 0.0003). The mean is estimated with considerable error, while the estimate of $\sigma^2$ is more precise, as we might expect. (These values are used for the *known 'true'* $\mu$ and $\sigma^2$ when drawing from $N(\mu, \sigma)$ for the 'no parameter uncertainty case' described earlier).

## Rebalancing

Barberis and Huang (2001) also repeats the above analysis when investors rebalance their portfolio annually, so they maximise

$$\max_{\alpha} E_{t_0} \left( \frac{W_k^{1-\gamma}}{1-\gamma} \right)$$

where $t_0$ is the decision period that moves forward every $k = 12$ months. The investor now has different degrees of uncertainty about the parameters at each rebalancing period, as well as different 'initial values' for the dividend yield. Solving this problem is far more complex and requires dynamic programming using the Bellman equation, which is solved by backward induction (Barberis and Huang 2001).

# 17

# RATIONAL BUBBLES AND LEARNING

## Aims

- Show how explosive rational bubbles and periodically collapsing bubbles arise as solutions to the Euler equation and how one tests for the presence of these 'exogenous' bubbles.

- Demonstrate how bubbles may also depend on fundamentals such as dividends and how one might test for the presence of these 'intrinsic bubbles'.

- Show how models with 'recursive learning' about either the dividend or the returns process can lead to more volatility in prices (than under RE) and also give returns that are predictable, even if the RVF holds.

- Demonstrate how 'self-referential' models of learning converge to a rational expectations equilibrium and how such models can generate prices that are more volatile than those in a 'pure' RE model (i.e. where agents know the parameter values).

## 17.1 Rational Bubbles

The idea of self-fulfilling 'bubbles' or 'sunspots' in asset prices has been discussed almost since organised markets began. Famous documented 'first' bubbles (Garber 1990) include the South Sea share price bubble of the 1720s and the Tulipomania bubble in the seventeenth century. In the latter case, the price of tulip bulbs rocketed between November 1636 and January 1637 only to suddenly collapse in February 1637 and by 1639, the price had fallen to around 1/200th of 1% of its peak value. The increase in stock prices in the 1920s and subsequent 'crash' in 1929, the US/UK stock market rises of 1994–2000 and subsequent crash of 2000–2003 and the rise of the dollar spot FX-rate between 1982 and 1985 and its subsequent fall over the next few years have also been interpreted in terms of self-fulfilling bubbles. Keynes (1936) of course is noted for his observation that stock prices may not be governed by an objective view of 'fundamentals' but by what 'average opinion expects average opinion to be'. His analogy for the forecasting of stock prices was that of trying to forecast the winner of a beauty contest. Objective beauty is not necessarily the issue, what is important is how one thinks the other judges' perceptions of beauty will be reflected in their voting patterns.

Rational bubbles arise because of the indeterminate aspect of solutions to rational expectations models, where the process governing stock prices is encapsulated in the Euler equation. The price you are prepared to pay today for a stock depends on the price you think you can obtain at some point in the future. But the latter depends on the expected price even further in the future. The Euler equation determines a sequence of prices but does not 'pin down' a unique price *level* unless somewhat arbitrarily, we impose a terminal condition (i.e. the transversality condition) to obtain the unique solution. However, in general, the Euler equation does not rule out the possibility that the price may contain an explosive bubble. (There are some subtle qualifications to the last statement and, in particular, in the representative agent model of Tirole (1985), he demonstrates uniqueness for an economy with a finite number of rational, infinitely lived traders, and Tirole (1985b) demonstrates that bubbles are only possible when the rate of growth of the economy is higher than the steady-state return on capital.)

While one can certainly try and explain prolonged rises or falls in stock prices as being due to some kind of irrational behaviour such as 'herding' or 'market psychology', nevertheless, recent work emphasises that such sharp movements or 'bubbles' may be consistent with the assumption of rational behaviour. Even if traders are perfectly rational, the actual stock price may contain a 'bubble element', and, therefore, there can be a divergence between the stock price and its fundamental value.

## Euler Equation and the Rational Valuation Formula

We investigate how the market price of stocks may deviate, possibly substantially, from their fundamental value even when agents are homogeneous and rational and the market is informationally efficient. To do so, we show that the market price may equal its fundamental value plus a 'bubble term' and yet the stock is still willingly held by rational agents and no excess profits can be made. To simplify the exposition, assume (i) agents are risk-neutral and have rational expectations and (ii) investors require a constant (real) rate of return on the asset $E_t R_{t+i} = k$. The Euler equation is

$$P_t = \delta(E_t P_{t+1} + E_t D_{t+1}) \tag{1}$$

where $\delta = 1/(1 + k)$. This may be solved under RE by repeated forward substitution

$$P_t = P_t^f = \sum_{i=1}^{\infty} \delta^i E_t D_{t+i} \tag{2}$$

where we assume the transversality condition holds (i.e. $\lim(\delta^n E_t D_{t+n}) = 0$, as $n \to \infty$). The transversality condition ensures a unique price given by (2) which we denote as the fundamental value $P_t^f$. The basic idea behind a rational bubble is that there is another mathematical expression for $P_t$ that satisfies the Euler equation, namely

$$P_t = \sum_{i=1}^{\infty} \delta^i E_t D_{t+i} + B_t = P_t^f + B_t \tag{3}$$

and $B_t$ is the 'rational bubble'. Thus, the actual market price $P_t$ deviates from its fundamental value $P_t^f$ by the amount of the rational bubble $B_t$. So far, we have not indicated any properties of $B_t$: clearly, if $B_t$ is large relative to fundamental value, then *actual* prices can deviate substantially from their fundamental value.

In order that (3) should satisfy (1), we have to place some restrictions on the dynamic behaviour of $B_t$ and we determine these restrictions by establishing a potential contradiction. We do so by assuming (3) is a valid solution to (1), and this then restricts the dynamics of $B_t$. Start by leading (3) by one period and taking expectations at time $t$

$$E_t P_{t+1} = E_t[\delta E_{t+1} D_{t+2} + \delta^2 E_{t+1} D_{t+3} + \cdots + B_{t+1}]$$
$$= [\delta E_t D_{t+2} + \delta^2 E_t D_{t+3} + \cdots + E_t B_{t+1}] \tag{4}$$

where we have used the law of iterated expectations $E_t(E_{t+1} D_{t+j}) = E_t D_{t+j}$. The RHS of the Euler equation (1) contains the term $\delta(E_t P_{t+1} + E_t D_{t+1})$, and using (4), we can see that this is given by

$$\delta[E_t D_{t+1} + E_t P_{t+1}] = \delta E_t D_{t+1} + [\delta^2 E_t D_{t+2} + \delta^3 E_t D_{t+3} + \cdots + \delta E_t B_{t+1}] \tag{5}$$

Substituting the definition of $P_t^f$ from (2) in the RHS of (5), we have

$$\delta[E_t D_{t+1} + E_t P_{t+1}] = P_t^f + \delta E_t B_{t+1} \tag{6}$$

Substituting from (6) into (1),

$$P_t = P_t^f + \delta E_t B_{t+1} \tag{7}$$

But we now seem to have a contradiction since (3) and (7) cannot, *in general*, both be solutions to (1). We can make these two solutions (3) and (7) equivalent if

$$E_t B_{t+1} = B_t/\delta = (1 + k)B_t \tag{8}$$

Then, (3) and (7) collapse to the same expression and satisfy (1). An alternative approach to showing the bubble must be a martingale is to note that from (1), we can write $P_t + B_t = \delta(E_t P_{t+1} + E_t D_{t+1} + E_t B_{t+1})$, *providing* $B_t = E_t B_{t+1}$. More generally, (8) implies

$$E_t B_{t+m} = B_t/\delta^m \tag{9}$$

Hence (apart from the known discount factor), $B_t$ must behave as a martingale: the best forecast of all future values of the bubble depends only on its current value. While the bubble solution satisfies the Euler equation, it violates the transversality condition (for $B_t \neq 0$) and because $B_t$ is arbitrary, the stock price in (3) is non-unique.

What kind of bubble is this mathematical entity? Note that the bubble is a valid solution, providing it is expected to grow at the rate of return required for investors to willingly hold the stock, from (8), we have $E(B_{t+1}/B_t) - 1 = k$. Investors do not care if they are paying for the bubble (rather than fundamental value) because the bubble element of the actual market price pays the *required* rate of return, $k$. The bubble is a self-fulfilling expectation.

Consider a simple case where expected dividends are constant and the value of the bubble at time $t$, $B_t = b$ ($> 0$) a constant. The bubble is deterministic and grows at the rate $k$, so that $E_t B_{t+m} = (1+k)^m b$. Thus, once the bubble exists, the actual stock price at $t + m$, even *if dividends are constant*, is from (3)

$$P_{t+m} = \frac{\delta D}{(1 - \delta)} + b(1+k)^m \qquad (10)$$

Even though fundamentals (i.e. dividends) indicate that the actual price should be constant, the presence of the bubble means that the actual price can rise continuously, since $(1 + k) > 1$.

In the above example, the bubble becomes an increasing proportion of the actual price since the bubble grows but the fundamental value is constant. In fact, even when dividends are not constant, the stock price always grows at a rate that is less than the rate of growth of the bubble ($= k$) because of the payment of dividends

$$(E_t P_{t+1}/P_t) - 1 = k - E_t D_{t+1}/P_t \qquad (11)$$

In the presence of a bubble, the investor still uses all available information to forecast prices and rates of return. Hence, forecast errors are independent of information at time $t$ and excess returns are unforecastable. Tests of informational efficiency are, therefore, useless in detecting bubbles. However, the bubble does not allow (supernormal) profits, since all information on the future course of dividends and the bubble is incorporated in the current price: the bubble satisfies the fair game property.

Our bubbles model can be extended (Blanchard 1979) to include the case where the bubble collapses with probability $(1 - \pi)$ and continues with probability $\pi$

$$B_{t+1} = B_t(\delta\pi)^{-1} \quad \text{with probability } \pi \qquad (12a)$$

$$= 0 \qquad\qquad \text{with probability } 1 - \pi \qquad (12b)$$

This structure also satisfies the martingale property. These models of rational bubbles, it should be noted, tell us nothing about how bubbles start or end; they merely tell us about the time-series properties of the bubble once it is under way. The bubble is 'exogenous' to the 'fundamentals model' and the usual RVF for prices.

As noted above, investors cannot distinguish between a price rise that is due solely to fundamentals or because of the bubble. Individuals do not mind paying a price over the fundamental's price as long as the bubble element yields them the required rate of return next period *and is expected to persist*. One implication of rational bubbles is that they cannot be negative (i.e. $B_t < 0$). This is because the bubble element falls at a faster rate than the stock price. Hence, a negative rational bubble ultimately ends in a zero price. Rational agents realise this and they, therefore, know that the bubble will eventually burst. But by backward induction, the bubble must burst immediately, since no one will pay the 'bubble premium' in the earlier periods. Thus, if the actual price $P_t$ is below fundamental value $P_t^f$, it cannot be because of a rational bubble. If negative bubbles are not possible, then if the bubble is ever zero, it cannot restart. This arises because the innovation $(B_{t+1} - E_t B_{t+1})$ in a rational bubble must have a zero mean. If the bubble started again, the innovation could not be mean zero since the bubble would have to go in one direction only, that is, increase, in order to start up again.

In principle, a positive bubble is possible since there is no upper limit on stock prices. However, in this case, we have the rather implausible state of affairs where the bubble element $B_t$ becomes an increasing proportion of the actual price and the fundamental part of the price becomes relatively small. One might conjecture that this implies that individuals will feel that at some time in the future, the bubble must burst. Again, if investors think that the bubble must burst at some time in the future (for whatever reason), then it will burst now. To see this, suppose individuals think the bubble will burst in the year 2030. They must realise that the market price in the year 2029 will reflect only the fundamental value because the bubble is expected to burst over the coming year. But if the price in 2029 reflects only the fundamental value, then by backward induction, this must be true of the price in all earlier years. Therefore, the price *now* will reflect only fundamentals. Thus, it seems that in the real world, rational bubbles can really only exist if each individual's horizon is shorter than the time period when the bubble is expected to burst. The idea here is that one would pay a price above the fundamental value because one believes that someone else will pay an even greater price in the future. Here, investors are myopic, and the price at some future time $t + N$ depends on what they think, and other investors think, the price will be.

# 17.2 Tests of Rational Bubbles

It is relatively easy to demonstrate that violation of Shiller's variance-bound inequality cannot be taken to imply the presence of rational bubbles. Intuitively, this is because the terminal price $P_N$ used in the test will contain any bubble element. More formally, note that in calculating the perfect foresight price, an approximation to the infinite horizon discounting in the RVF is used, and the *calculated* perfect foresight price is $P_t^*$

$$P_t^* = \sum_{i=1}^{N} \delta^i D_{t+i} + \delta^N P_{t+N} \tag{13}$$

where $P_N$ is the *actual* market price at the end of the data set. The variance bound under the null of constant (real) required returns is $\text{var}(P_t) \leqslant \text{var}(P_t^*)$. However, a bubble is incorporated in this null hypothesis. To see this, note that with a rational bubble,

$$P_t = P_t^{\text{f}} + B_t \tag{14}$$

and $E_t(B_{t+N}) = (1+k)^N B_t = \delta^{-N} B_t$. If we now replace $P_N$ in (13) by a term containing the bubble $P_{t+N} = P_{t+N}^{\text{f}} + B_{t+N}$, then

$$E_t P_t^* = P_t^{\text{f}} + \delta^N E_t B_{t+N} = P_t^{\text{f}} + B_t \tag{15}$$

Hence, even in the presence of a bubble, we have from (14) and (15) that $P_t = E_t P_t^*$. An early test for bubbles (Flood and Garber 1980) assumed a non-stochastic bubble that is $P_t = P_t^{\text{f}} + (B_o/\delta^t)$, where $B_o$ is the value of the bubble at the beginning of the sample period. Hence, in a regression context, there is an additional term of the form $(B_o/\delta)^t$. Knowing $\delta$, a test for the presence of a bubble is then $H_0 : B_o \neq 0$. Unfortunately, because $(1/\delta) > 1$, the regressor $(1/\delta)^t$ is exploding, and this implies that tests on $B_o$ depend on non-standard distributions, and correct inferences are therefore problematic. (For further details, see Flood, Garber and Scott 1984.)

An ingenious test for bubbles is provided by West (1987a). The test involves calculating a particular parameter by two alternative methods. Under the assumption of no bubbles, the two parameter estimates should be equal within the limits of statistical accuracy, while in the presence of rational bubbles, the two estimates should differ. A strength of this approach (in contrast to Flood and Garber 1980, Flood, Garber and Scott 1984) is that it does not require a specific parameterisation of the bubble process: *any* bubble that is correlated with dividends can in principle be detected. To illustrate the approach, note first that $\delta$ can be estimated using (instrumental variables) estimation of the 'observable' Euler equation

$$P_t = \delta(P_{t+1} + D_{t+1}) + u_{t+1} \tag{16}$$

where $u_{t+1} = -\delta[(P_{t+1} + D_{t+1}) - E_t(P_{t+1} + D_{t+1})]$. Now assume an AR(1) process for dividends

$$D_t = \alpha D_{t-1} + v_t \qquad |\alpha| < 1 \tag{17}$$

Under the no-bubbles hypothesis, the RVF and (17) give

$$P_t = \Psi D_t + \varepsilon_t \tag{18}$$

where $\Psi = \delta\alpha/(1 - \delta\alpha)$ and $\varepsilon_t$ arises because the econometrician has a subset of the true information set. An *indirect* estimate of $\Psi$, denoted $\hat{\Psi}$, can be obtained from the regression estimates of $\delta$ from (16) and $\alpha$ from (17). However, a *direct* estimate of $\Psi$ denoted $\hat{\Psi}^*$ can be obtained from the regression of $P_t$ on $D_t$ in (18). Under the null of no bubbles, the indirect and direct estimates of $\Psi$ should be equal.

Consider the case where bubbles are present and hence $P_t = P_t^{\text{f}} + B_t = \Psi D_t + B_t$. The regression of $P_t$ on $D_t$ now contains an omitted variable, namely, the bubble and the estimate of $\Psi$, denoted $\hat{\Psi}^\tau$, will be inconsistent:

$$\text{plim}\hat{\Psi}^\tau = \Psi + \text{plim}\left(T^{-1}\sum D_t^2\right)^{-1}\text{plim}\left(T^{-1}\sum D_t B_t\right) \tag{19}$$

If the bubble $B_t$ is correlated with dividends, then $\hat{\Psi}^\tau$ will be biased (upwards if $\text{cov}(D_t, B_t) > 0$) and inconsistent. But the Euler equation and the dividend forecasting equations still provide consistent estimators of the parameters and hence of $\hat{\Psi}$. Therefore, in the presence of bubbles, $\hat{\Psi} \neq \hat{\Psi}^\tau$ (and a Hausman (1978) test can be used to detect any possible change in the coefficients).

The above test procedure is used by West (1987a) whose data consists of the Shiller (1981) S&P index 1871–1980 (and the Dow Jones index 1928–78). West finds a substantive difference between the two sets of estimates, thus rejecting the null of no bubbles. However, this result could be due to an incorrect model of equilibrium returns or dividend behaviour. Indeed, West recognises this and finds the results are reasonably robust to alternative ARMA processes for dividends but in contrast, under a time-varying discount rate, there is no evidence against the null of no bubbles. Flood, Hodrick and Kaplan (1994) point out that if one iterates the Euler equation for a second period, the estimated ('two-period') Euler equation is not well specified, and estimates of $\delta$ may, therefore, be biased. Since the derivation of the RVF requires an infinite number of iterations of the Euler equation, this casts some doubt on the estimate of $\delta$ and, hence, on West's (1987a) results.

West (1988a) develops a further test for bubbles, which again involves comparing the difference between two estimators, on the basis of two different information sets. One limited information set $\Lambda_t$ consists of current and past dividends, and the other information set is the optimal predictor of future dividends, namely the market price $P_t$. Under the null of no bubbles, forecasting with the limited information set $\Lambda_t$ ought to yield a larger forecast error (strictly, innovation variance), but West finds the opposite. This evidence refutes the no bubbles hypothesis, but, of course, it is also not necessarily inconsistent with the presence of fads.

Some tests for the presence of rational bubbles are based on investigating the stationarity properties of price and dividend data. An exogenous bubble introduces an explosive element into prices, which is not (necessarily) present in the fundamentals (i.e. dividends or discount rates). Hence, if the stock price $P_t$ 'grows' faster than $D_t$, this could be due to the presence of a bubble term $B_t$. These intuitive notions can be expressed in terms of the literature on unit roots and cointegration. Using the RVF (under the assumption of a constant discount rate), if $P_t$ and $D_t$ are unit root processes, then they should be cointegrated.

If dividends (or log dividends) are integrated of order one I(1) and $P_t = [\delta/(1 - \delta)]D_t$, then $P_t$ must be I(1) and cointegrated with $D_t$ and $z_t = P_t - \delta/(1 - \delta)D_t$ is stationary I(0). Using aggregate stock price and dividend indexes, Diba and Grossman (1988) find that $\Delta P_t$ and $\Delta D_t$ are stationary and $P_t$ and $D_t$ are cointegrated, thus rejecting the presence of explosive bubbles of the type represented by equation (8).

Unfortunately, the interpretation of the above tests has been shown to be potentially misleading in the presence of what Evans (1991) calls *periodically collapsing bubbles*. The type of rational bubble that Evans examines is one that is always positive but can 'erupt' and grow at a fast rate before collapsing to a positive mean value, when the process begins again. The path of the periodically collapsing bubble (see Figure 1) can be seen to be different from a bubble that grows continuously.

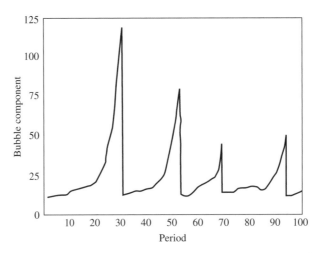

**Figure 1** Bubble component. Source: Evans (1991). Reproduced by permission of the American Economic Association

Intuitively, one can see why testing to see if $P_t$ is non-stationarity I(1) might not detect a bubble component like that in Figure 1. The (Dickey–Fuller) test for stationarity essentially tries to measure whether a series has a strong trend or an unconditional variance that is non-constant. Clearly, there is no strong upward trend in Figure 1, and although the variance alters over time, this may be difficult to detect particularly if the bubbles have a high probability of collapsing (within any given time period). If the bubbles have a very low probability of collapsing, we are close to the case of 'explosive bubbles' (i.e. $E_t B_{t+1} = B_t / \delta$) examined by Diba and Grossman, and here one might expect standard tests for stationarity to be more conclusive.

Heuristically (and simplifying somewhat), Evans proceeds by using MCS to generate a series for a periodically collapsing bubble. Adding the bubble to the fundamentals $P_t^f$ (e.g. under the assumption that $D_t$ is a random walk with drift) gives the generated stock price series, which is then subject to standard tests for the presence of unit roots. He finds that the results of his unit root tests depend crucially on $\pi$, the probability (per period) that the bubble does *not* collapse. For values of $\pi < 0.75$, more than 90% of the simulations erroneously indicate that $\Delta P_t$ is stationary and $P_t$ and $D_t$ are cointegrated. Hence, 'periodically collapsing bubbles' are often not detectable using standard unit root tests. (The reason for this is that 'standard tests' assume a *linear* autoregressive process, whereas Evans' simulations involve a complex non-linear bubble process.) Thus, the failure of Diba and Grossman to detect continuously explosive bubbles in stock prices does not necessarily rule out other types of rational bubble. Clearly, more sophisticated statistical tests of non-stationarity are required to detect periodically collapsing bubbles (see, for example, Hamilton 1994).

## 17.3 Intrinsic Bubbles

One of the problems with the type of bubble discussed so far is that the bubble is a *deus exmachina* and is exogenous to fundamentals such as dividends. The bubble term arises as an alternative solution (strictly the homogeneous part of the solution) to the Euler equation for stock prices. Froot and Obstfeld (1991) suggest a different type of bubble phenomenon, which they term an *intrinsic bubble*. 'Intrinsic' is used because the bubble depends (in a non-linear deterministic way) on fundamentals, namely the level of (real) dividends. The bubble element, therefore, remains constant if 'fundamentals' remain constant but increases (decreases) along with the level of dividends. For this form of intrinsic bubble, if dividends are persistent, so is the bubble term, and stock prices will exhibit persistent deviations from fundamental value. In addition, the intrinsic bubble can cause stock prices to overreact to changes in dividends (fundamentals), which is consistent with empirical evidence.

To analyse this form of intrinsic bubble, assume a constant real required rate of return $r$ (in continuous time). The Euler equation is

$$P_t = e^{-r} E_t(D_{t+1} + P_{t+1}) \tag{20}$$

which implies a fundamentals price $P_t^f$ (assuming the transversality condition holds) given by

$$P_t^f = \sum_{k=1}^{\infty} e^{-r(k)} E_t(D_{t+k}) \tag{21}$$

However, $P_t = P_t^f + B_t$ is also a solution to the Euler equation if $B_t$ is a martingale, $B_t = e^{-r}[E_t B_{t+1}]$ The 'intrinsic bubble' is constructed by finding a non-linear function of dividends such that $B_t$ is a martingale and hence satisfies the Euler equation, where

$$B(D_t) = cD_t^{\lambda} \qquad c > 0, \lambda > 1 \tag{22}$$

If log dividends follow a random walk with drift parameter $\mu$ and conditional variance $\sigma^2$, that is, $\ln(D_{t+1}) = \mu + \ln(D_t) + \varepsilon_{t+1}$, then the bubble solution $\hat{P}_t$ is

$$\hat{P}_t = P_t^f + B(D_t) = \alpha D_t + cD_t^{\lambda} \tag{23}$$

where $\alpha = (e^r - e^{\mu + \sigma^2/2})^{-1}$. The fundamentals solution $P_t^f = \alpha D_t$ is a stochastic version of Gordon's (1962) growth model, which gives $P_t^f = (e^r - e^{\mu})^{-1} D_t$ under certainty. It is clear from (23) that stock prices overreact to current dividends compared to the 'fundamentals only' solution (i.e. $\partial P_t^f / \partial D_t = \alpha$) because of the bubble term (i.e. $\partial P_t / \partial D_t = \alpha + c\lambda D_t^{\lambda-1}$). Froot and Obstfeld simulate the intrinsic bubble in (22) assuming reasonable values for $(r, \mu, \sigma^2)$, estimated values for $c$ and $\lambda$ (see below) and with $\varepsilon_{t+i}$ being *iid*. They compare the pure fundamentals path, the intrinsic stochastic bubble path $\hat{P}_t$ given by (23) and, in addition, an intrinsic bubble that depends on time as well as dividends, which gives rise to a path for prices denoted $\tilde{P}_t$

$$\tilde{P}_t = aD_t + bD_t e^{(r-\mu-\sigma^2/2)t} \tag{24}$$

The intrinsic bubble in (24) depends on time and allows a comparison with parametric bubble tests, which often invoke a deterministic exponential time trend (Flood and Garber 1990, Blanchard and Watson 1982, Flood and Garber 1994). The simulated values of these three price series are shown in Figure 2, and it is clear that the intrinsic bubble

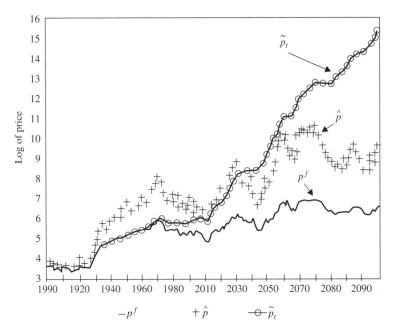

**Figure 2** Simulated stock price paths. Source: Froot and Obstfeld (1991). Reproduced by permission of the American Economic Association

can produce a plausible-looking path for stock prices $\hat{P}_t$ and one that is persistently above the fundamentals path $P_t^f$ (although, in other simulations, the intrinsic bubble $\hat{P}_t$ can be above the fundamentals path $P_t^f$ and then 'collapse' towards $P_t^f$). From Figure 2, we see that in a *finite* sample, the intrinsic bubble may not look explosive and, therefore, it may be difficult to detect using statistical tests. (The time-dependent intrinsic bubble $\tilde{P}_t$, on the other hand, yields a path that looks explosive, and this is more likely to be revealed by standard tests.)

Froot and Obstfeld test for the presence of intrinsic bubbles using a simple transformation of (23).

$$P_t/D_t = c_0 + cD_t^{\lambda-1} + \eta_t \tag{25}$$

where the null of no bubble implies $H_0 : c_0 = \alpha$ and $c = 0$ (where $\alpha = e^r - e^{\mu+\sigma^2/2}$). Using representative values of $e^r = 1.09$ (p.a.) for the real S&P index, while for real dividends process, $\mu = 0.011$, $\sigma = 0.122$, then the sample average value for $\alpha$ equals 14. Under the null of no bubbles, $P_t$ and $D_t$ should be cointegrated with cointegration parameter $c_0 = \alpha$, of about 14. In a simple OLS cointegrating regression of $P_t$ on $D_t$, Froot and Obstfeld find that $P_t = \Psi + 37D_t$ and hence $P_t$ overreacts to dividends. In addition, $P_t - 14D_t$ is not stationary and, therefore, $P_t$ and $D_t$ are not cointegrated. The 'fundamentals only' solution $P_t = \alpha D_t$ also implies that $\ln P_t$ and $\ln D_t$ are cointegrated with a cointegration parameter of unity. However, estimates reveal this parameter to be in the range 1.6–1.8 and that $(\ln P_t - \ln D_t)$ may not be stationary. Hence, taken at face value, these tests tend to reject the (no-bubble) fundamentals model. However, Froot and Obstfeld note that the OLS cointegrating parameter could be heavily biased (Banerjee, Dolado, Galbraith and Hendry 1993) and that the power and size of these tests are problematic.

Froot and Obstfeld then consider a direct test for the presence of intrinsic bubbles on the basis of estimation of (25). A representative result is

$$(P/D)_t = \underset{(2.28)}{14.6} + \underset{(0.12)}{0.04} \; D_t^{1.6(1.1)} \tag{26}$$

Annual data: 1900–1988, $R$-squared = 0.57, (.) = Newy–West standard errors.

Although there are some subtle small sample econometric issues involved in testing for $c = 0$ and $\lambda - 1 = 0$ in (25), the evidence above is, in part, supportive of the existence of an intrinsic bubble. The *joint* null, that $c$ and $\lambda - 1$ equal zero is strongly rejected. However, the empirical evidence is not decisive since we do not reject the null that $c = 0$. One can simulate values for the fundamentals price $P_t^f = 14.6D_t$, and the price with an intrinsic bubble $\hat{P}_t$ given by (23) and compare these two series with the actual price $P_t$. The path of the intrinsic bubble (Figure 3) is much closer to the actual path of stock prices than is $P_t^f$. The size of the bubble can also be very large as in the post-World War II period. Indeed, at the end of the period, the bubble element of the S&P index appears to be large.

Finally, Froot and Obstfeld assess the sensitivity of their results to different dividend models (using Monte Carlo methods) and to the addition of various alternative functions

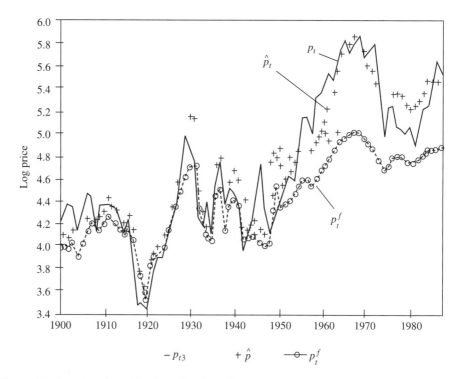

$$- p_{t3} \qquad + \hat{p} \qquad \multimap p_t^f$$

**Figure 3** Actual and predicted stock prices. Source: Froot and Obstfeld (1991). Reproduced by permission of the American Economic Association

for $D_t$ or other deterministic time trends in the regression (22). The estimates of the basic intrinsic bubble formulation in (23) are quite robust.

Driffell and Sola (1998) repeat the Froot–Obstfeld model assuming dividend growth undergoes regime shifts, in particular, that the (conditional) variance of dividend growth varies over the sample. A graph of (real) dividend growth for the United States shows relatively low variance between 1900 and 1920, followed by periods of fairly rapid 'switches' in variance over 1920–1950 and then relatively low and constant variance post-1950. Driffell and Sola use the two-state Markov switching model of Hamilton (1989) to model dividend growth, and this confirms the results given by 'eyeballing' the graph. They then have two equations of the form (23) corresponding to each of the two states, of 'high' and 'low' variance. However, their graph of the price with an intrinsic bubble is very similar to that of Froot and Obstfeld (see $\hat{p}_t$, Figure 3), so this particular variant does not appear to make a major difference.

There are a number of statistical assumptions required for valid inference in the approach of Froot and Obstfeld (some of which we have mentioned). For this reason, they are content to state that 'the results above merely show that there is a coherent case to be made for bubbles'. They would probably agree that the evidence is also consistent with other hypotheses.

## Econometric Issues

There are severe econometric problems in testing for rational bubbles, and the interpretation of the results is problematic. Econometric problems that arise include the analysis of potentially non-stationary series using finite data sets, the behaviour of asymptotic test statistics in the presence of explosive regressors as well as the standard problems of obtaining precise estimates of non-linear parameters (for the intrinsic bubbles) and corrections for heteroscedasticity and moving average errors. Tests for rational bubbles are often contingent on having the correct equilibrium model of expected returns: we are, therefore, testing a joint hypothesis. Rejection of the no-bubbles hypothesis may simply be a manifestation of an incorrect model based on fundamentals.

Another difficulty in interpreting results from tests of rational bubbles arises from the Peso problem, which is really a form of 'omitted variables' problem. Suppose investors in the market had information, within the sample period studied by the researcher, that dividends might increase rapidly in the future, but in the actual data, the event did not occur and dividends increased at their 'normal' rate. In the *sample* of data, the stock price would rise substantially (because of the RVF), but there would only be a moderate increase in dividends. Stock prices would look as if they have overreacted to (current) dividends and, more importantly, such a rise in price might be erroneously interpreted as a bubble. This problem of interpretation is probably most acute when there are very large price *changes* such as the long bull run of the 1990s (the 'new economy' idea) followed by the crash of 2000–2003. When we turn to periodically collapsing bubbles, it appears unlikely that standard tests will detect such phenomena.

# 17.4 Learning

In this section, we do not cover the extensive literature on dynamic learning and convergence to RE equilibrium (see Evans and Honkapohja 2001) but instead concentrate on approaches to learning that directly address the question of excess volatility and return predictability. Our 'baseline model' is still the 'pure' RE approach where agents know the 'true' structure of the economy (up to a white noise error process). However, we contrast results from the standard RE model with those from simple learning processes. In these learning models, agents are 'rational' but unlike RE, they do not know the true parameters of the equations for dividends or returns and have to estimate them from limited data. We assume agents optimally update their estimates of the true population parameters as more data arrives. They then use these weakly rational forecasts (based on a limited information set) in the RVF to obtain an estimate of the 'price under learning'. The latter can then be compared with the observed price (and stock returns), to see if the 'learning model' mimics the real data better than the 'pure' RE approach. We discuss the complementary issue of the impact of learning on portfolio choice in a later chapter.

## Gordon Growth Model

A simple but intuitive learning model is that of Barsky and DeLong (1993), who use the simple Gordon (1962) growth model, where (real) stock prices $P_t = D_{t+1}/(R - g_t)$, where $R$ is the (known) required real rate of return and $g_t$ is the expected 'steady state' growth rate of dividends based on information up to time $t$. Barsky and DeLong (1993) use this model to calculate fundamental value $V_t = D_{t+1}/(R - g_t)$, assuming that agents have to continually update their estimate of the future growth in dividends. They then compare $V_t$ with the actual S&P500 stock price index $P_t$ over the period 1880–1988.

For the simplest case of a constant value of $(R - g)^{-1} = 20$, which equals the average P/D ratio, then $V_t = 20D_{t+1}$. Even here, the broad movements in $V_t$ over a *long horizon* of 10 years are as high as 67% of the variability in $P_t$ (see Barsky–DeLong 1993, Table III, p. 302), with the pre-World War II movements in the two data series being even closer.

The simple exogenous learning process for dividend *growth* they propose is the familiar 'adaptive expectations'

$$E_t \Delta d_{t+1} = \theta E_{t-1} \Delta d_t + (1 - \theta)\Delta d_t \quad 0 < \theta < 1 \tag{27}$$

or

$$E_t \Delta d_{t+1} - E_{t-1}\Delta d_t = (1 - \theta)[\Delta d_t - E_{t-1}\Delta d_t] \tag{28}$$

The change in expectations between $t - 1$ and $t$ depends on the previous periods forecast error, with adjustment parameter $(1 - \theta)$. If $\theta$ is large (e.g. 0.95), new information on dividend growth has little impact on the change in expectations. The adaptive expectations forecasting scheme can be shown to be rational if dividend growth $\Delta d_{t+1}$ follows an IMA(1,1) process

$$\Delta d_{t+1} = \Delta d_t + (\varepsilon_{t+1} - \theta\varepsilon_t) \tag{29}$$

To see this, take expectations of (29) and also lag one period

$$E_t\Delta d_{t+1} = \Delta d_t - \theta\varepsilon_t \tag{30a}$$

$$E_{t-1}\Delta d_t = \Delta d_{t-1} - \theta\varepsilon_{t-1} \tag{30b}$$

From (30a) and (30b)

$$E_t\Delta d_{t+1} - \theta E_{t-1}\Delta d_t = \Delta d_t - \theta\Delta d_{t-1} - \theta(1-\theta L)\varepsilon_t \tag{31}$$

From (29), we have $\Delta d_t - \Delta d_{t-1} = (1 - \theta L)\varepsilon_t$, and using this in (31), we obtain (28) as required

$$E_t\Delta d_{t+1} - \theta E_{t-1}\Delta d_t = (1 - \theta)\Delta d_t \tag{32}$$

By backward substitution, (27) can also be written

$$E_t\Delta d_{t+1} = (1 - \theta)\sum_{i=0}^{t-1}\theta^i\Delta d_{t-i} + \theta^t\Delta d_0 \tag{33}$$

Subtracting (30b) from (30a) and using the IMA process (29), we obtain another formulation of adaptive expectations

$$E_t\Delta d_{t+1} = E_{t-1}\Delta d_t + (1 - \theta)\varepsilon_t \tag{34}$$

Equations (27), (32), (33) and (34) are all equivalent expressions. Equation (33) demonstrates that the one-period-ahead forecast of $\Delta d_{t+1}$ depends on a long (geometric) distributed lag of past dividend growth – hence, forecasts change only slowly. Equation (34) tells a similar story since for $\theta \approx 0.95$, *revisions* to forecasts of dividend growth depend very little on new information $\varepsilon_t$ – ditto for equation (28). Barsky – DeLong 1993, note that estimates of the IMA(1,1) process (29) give values of $\theta$ in the range 0.95–1, and even in large samples, it is impossible to say whether $(1 - \theta)$ is a small positive number or zero.

They use (28) to update forecasts of $E_t\Delta d_{t+1}$ each time period and assume this mimics agents' views of the 'steady-state' growth rate $g_t$. These changing values of $g_t$ then give a series for $V_t = D_{t+1}/(R - g_t)$, which is more volatile than assuming a constant $g$. They find the volatility of 10-year changes in $V_t$ is as high as 76% of the volatility in $P_t$ (see Barsky–DeLong 1993, Table III, p. 302). However, it should also be noted that although long swings in $P_t$ are in part explained by this model, changes over shorter horizons such as one year or even five years are not well explained, and movements in the (stationary) price–dividend ratio are also not well explained. Hence, at best, the above evidence is broadly consistent with the view that real dividends and real prices move together in the long run (and hence are likely to be cointegrated), but price and fundamental value can diverge quite substantially over a number of years even when the model incorporates an elementary learning process for dividend growth.

## Constant Discount Rate

Timmermann (1993) investigates the impact of learning on price volatility and predictability using a MCS and compares these results with the RE model (both models have a constant discount rate). The learning model is very similar to that of Barsky – DeLong, but the MCS allows us to judge the possible distribution of outcomes rather than giving just a point estimate. Constant expected dividend growth is assumed

$$\ln D_t = \mu + \ln D_{t-1} + \varepsilon_t \quad \varepsilon_t \sim niid(0, \sigma^2) \tag{35}$$

Hence, in the standard constant returns (discount rate) model with rational expectations, the stock price is

$$P_t^{\text{RE}} = \frac{(1+g)}{(R-g)} D_t = kD_t \tag{36}$$

where $(1 + g) = \exp(\mu + \sigma^2/2)$. Under RE, the volatility in prices is proportional to the volatility in dividends, and expected returns (being constant) are not forecastable using the dividend–price ratio. However, in the data, we know that prices are more volatile than dividends, and the dividend–price ratio forecasts future returns. Can a simple adaptive learning model for dividends 'fit the facts', even in a model with constant expected returns? To analyse this issue, consider a standard adaptive learning process for $\mu$ and $\sigma^2$ for sample size $n$

$$\hat{\mu}_t = \frac{(n-1)}{n}\hat{\mu}_{t-1} + \frac{\Delta \ln D_t}{n} \tag{37a}$$

$$\hat{\sigma}_t^2 = \frac{(n-1)}{n^2}\left[n\hat{\sigma}_{t-1}^2 + (\hat{\mu}_{t-1} - \Delta \ln D_t)^2\right] \tag{37b}$$

Conditional forecasts for dividends are

$$\hat{E}_t D_{t+i} = D_t \exp(i\hat{\mu}_t + i\hat{\sigma}_t^2/2) \tag{38}$$

which substituted in the RVF gives a non-linear function for 'prices under learning'

$$\hat{P}_t = \left\{ \frac{\exp(\hat{\mu}_t + \hat{\sigma}_t^2/2)}{1 + R - \exp(\hat{\mu}_t + \hat{\sigma}_t^2/2)} \right\} D_t \quad \text{for} \quad \hat{\mu}_t + \hat{\sigma}_t^2/2 < \ln(1+R) \tag{39}$$

With estimates of $\mu$, $\sigma$ from the regression (35), together with an estimate of $R$, we can *simulate* the dividend series under RE and compute $P_t^{\text{RE}}$.

Similarly, given starting values $\hat{\mu}_1$ and $\hat{\sigma}_1$, (37), (38) and (39) give *simulated* values 'under learning' for $\hat{P}_t$ and hence $\hat{P}_t/\hat{D}_t$ and the asset return $(1 + \hat{R}_t) \equiv (\hat{P}_t + \hat{D}_t)/\hat{P}_{t-1}$. In the MCS, the following rule was adopted for (39) to rule out non-finite stock prices: if $\hat{\mu}_t + \hat{\sigma}_t^2/2 \geqslant \ln(1 + R)$, use $\hat{\mu}_{t-1}$ and $\hat{\sigma}_{t-1}^2$ in place of $[\hat{\mu}_t, \hat{\sigma}_t^2]$. These simulations are repeated 1000 times, and the empirical distribution of the regression coefficient of $\hat{R}_{t+1}$ on $(\hat{D}/\hat{P})_t$ obtained. Of course, as $n$ increases, $\hat{P}_t$ approaches the time series for $P_t^{\text{RE}}$ since $\hat{\mu}_t$ and $\hat{\sigma}_t^2$ converge on their population values $\mu$ and $\sigma$.

Timmermann (1993) finds that learning increases the volatility of stock prices (relative to the simulated RE prices) and even in a 'large' sample of 100 (years), the *gross* violation of Shiller's variance ratio (i.e. of five or more) with learning still exceeds 10% – even though the model has a constant discount rate and is 'rational under the learning rule'. For sample sizes of 40, the gross violation of Shiller's volatility ratio is as high as 30–50%. For the learning model, the proportion of return regressions with a statistically significant coefficient on (D/P) is around 40–60% for sample sizes $n = 40 - 500$, and these simulated returns are also serially correlated – a feature of the actual data.

Hence, observed 'excess volatility' and return predictability may not be the result of a time-varying risk premium (i.e. changing *expected* returns) but are capable of being explained with a constant discount rate, if one allows agents to learn about the population parameters (of the dividend process).

Why does learning generate predictability? Suppose agents' current forecast of dividend growth $\hat{\mu}_t$ is below its true level $\mu$. Prices will be below their 'RE level' and, hence, measured D/P will be high. As $\hat{\mu}_t$ rises towards $\mu$, then via (39), prices will rise (faster than under RE) and this generates positive future returns, which are correlated with today's D/P ratio. Intuitively, to see how learning generates 'extra' volatility in prices is not so straightforward (see Timmermann 1993) but clearly there may be more movement in $\hat{\mu}_t, \hat{\sigma}_t^2$ than in their fixed population values $\mu, \sigma^2$. Also, under RE, a dividend innovation will lead to a proportionate adjustment in prices, but under learning, the estimate of the growth rate $\hat{\mu}_t$ will also increase, giving 'extra' volatility to prices.

Timmermann (1996) repeats the above approach, this time assuming dividends are trend stationary (in either levels or logs)

$$D_{t+1} = \mu + \gamma t + \rho D_t + \varepsilon_{t+1} \qquad \varepsilon_{t+1} \sim niid(0, \sigma^2) \tag{40}$$

This is important because Shiller's (1981, 1989) empirical results show a *gross* violation of the variance ratio under the assumption of stationary dividends, whereas Kleiden (1986) shows that *gross* violations are more likely if dividends are non-stationary, even if RE holds. Using recursive OLS on (40) Timmermann generates stock prices under learning $\hat{P}_t$ for different sample lengths, so that eventually the learning parameters converge on their true values $(\mu, \rho, \gamma, \sigma^2)$. He finds that under learning and a stationary dividend process, the MCS produces a large number of *gross* violations of Shiller's variance ratio, even in large samples. Returns are also predictable from the (D/P) ratio and are autocorrelated. Hence, once again, Shiller's gross violation using real data may reflect learning in an otherwise rational model (with a constant discount rate).

Veronesi (2003) extends the above approach by combining learning about the drift rate of dividends with a Peso problem. In the sample of data $\{0, T\}$, there is actually no change in the drift (growth) rate of dividends but there is a very small *ex-ante* probability ($\lambda = 0.005$), that is, once in 200 years, that the growth rate would fall

5% for the duration of 20 years (e.g. as might have been the case around the 1930s recession). There is also a small probability $\mu = 0.05$ that once in a 'recession', the economy would revert back to its normal growth rate. Agents must learn about the growth rate by observing past realisations. There is, therefore, uncertainty about the drift and about whether the economy has entered a long recession. If they observe some negative dividend innovations, the conditional probability of being in the 'normal state' falls from $\pi(t)$ close to unity towards $\pi(t) = 0.5$, the point of maximum uncertainty. As investors become more uncertain, they react more strongly to news, hence, they expect returns to be more volatile and, therefore, raise their discount rate. Investors are assumed to maximise expected intertemporal utility using a constant absolute risk aversion (CARA) function over consumption ($U(C) = e^{-\gamma C}$), so that demand for the risky asset is independent of wealth. The RE equilibrium price is a convex function of $\pi(t)$, which is very steep when $\pi(t)$ is close to unity and flat for $\pi(t)$ close to zero. Hence, there is an asymmetric effect of the stock price, namely a very large reaction to bad news in good times and a smaller reaction to good news in bad times. Dividends are assumed to follow a Brownian motion (i.e. the continuous-time equivalent of a random walk) and, therefore, it can be shown that the posterior probability $\pi(t)$ also follows a Brownian motion where the drift rate depends on $\lambda$ and $\mu$.

The qualitative results of the model are consistent with a number of stylised facts about stock returns and volatility, which can be reproduced by a Monte Carlo simulation after calibrating the model (e.g. risk-free real rate of 3% p.a. and an *implied* coefficient of *relative* risk aversion $= \gamma w$, of around 3). Relative to the baseline 'no-learning, no Peso problem case' that is a constant and known dividend growth, the model delivers a relatively high equity premium (from 0.77 to 3%), a GARCH(1,1) model with high persistence and with an asymmetric effect to positive and negative news (i.e. leverage effect). There is also an overreaction of prices to dividends because of changes in $\pi(t)$, providing an additional impact of dividends on prices, which implies the elasticity exceeds unity. In the 'baseline case', prices move proportionately to dividends (with volatility of 6.5%) but with learning, the volatility of stock prices rises relative to the volatility of dividends, from 6.5% p.a. to around 21%. Hence, Peso problems where investors have to learn about the dividend growth rate can reproduce many of the stylised facts of stock returns even though the probability of a regime shift is very small (but it must be relatively large and persist for many years).

## Learning in an Equilibrium Model

Timmermann (1993, 1996) above shows that parameter uncertainty and learning can produce predictability and excess volatility. Lewellen and Shanken (2002) extend this approach in an equilibrium model with fully rational agents, who update parameter estimates using Bayes rule. As well as reproducing Timmermann's earlier results, the model shows that even though returns are predictable using *past data* and profits can be earned using 'outside-sample' predictions (on past data) nevertheless, when *looking forward*, regressions estimated from past data do not help forecast *ex-ante* future returns. This is because predictability is actually *caused* by learning (and is not assumed as part of the model). So the predictability in the data is not perceived by the fully rational investors, who believe expected returns are constant, nor can it be exploited by investors to earn abnormal profits. This is a profound conclusion since it implies that perhaps the most crucial type of tests of the EMH we examine, namely the presence of exploitable risk-adjusted profit opportunities based on past data, are uninformative. This paradoxical result arises in part because of the difference between results from repeated gambles (i.e. a *frequentist interpretation* of past profits) and the conditional nature of investment decisions that depend on observed dividends *at a point in time*.

The structure of the model closely resembles that of DeLong, Shleifer, Summers and Waldmann (1990a), and the reader might first like to review this model in Chapter 19, before proceeding further. Our learning model has individuals living for two periods, with overlapping generations. The investor has one-period constant absolute risk aversion (CARA) utility function in end-of-period (second period) wealth $U(w) = -\mathrm{e}^{-2\gamma w}$, which gives rise to optimal asset *shares*, $\alpha_t^*$:

$$\alpha_t^* = \frac{1}{2\gamma}[\mathrm{var}_t^s(p_{t+1} + d_{t+1})]^{-1}[E_t^s(p_{t+1} + d_{t+1}) - (1+r)p_t] \tag{41}$$

where $\gamma > 0$ is the risk-aversion parameter, superscript s indicates the subjective distribution of investors using whatever information they view as relevant, $p_t = $ price of the risky asset (*not* the log of the price) and $d_t = $ the level of dividends. The risk-free rate is $r$, and the risk-free asset is in perfectly elastic supply, whereas the supply of each risky asset is (normalised) to unity. The *true* distribution (unknown to investors) of dividends $d_t$ is *niid* over time, with constant mean $\delta$ and variance $\sigma^2$

$$d_t \sim N^{\mathrm{true}}(\delta, \sigma^2) \tag{42}$$

so estimation risk goes to zero as $t \to \infty$. In the first-period, individuals decide on their allocation of exogenously given wealth. We assume only one risky asset (as we do not discuss the implications of the model for the CAPM and the cross-sectional behaviour of asset returns – for this, see Lewellen and Shanken 2002). Since the supply of the risky asset is unity, from (41), the equilibrium price in terms of next period's price is

$$p_t = \frac{1}{(1+r)}[E_t^s(p_{t+1} + d_{t+1}) - 2\gamma\, \mathrm{var}_t^s(p_{t+1} + d_{t+1})] \tag{43}$$

Under perfect information (i.e. no uncertainty), the equilibrium price ($p_t = p$, a constant) is

$$p = \frac{\delta}{r} - \frac{2\gamma\sigma^2}{r} \tag{44}$$

The simplest assumption about parameter uncertainty is that investors have no prior view about $\delta$ (i.e. 'diffuse prior') so that their estimate of $\delta$ depends solely on past data. (We also assume $\sigma^2$ is known.) Using Bayes rule, the posterior distribution of $\delta$ at time $t$ is $N(\overline{d}_t, (1/t)\sigma^2)$ and the subjective '*predictive* distribution' is

$$d_{t+1} \sim N^s\left(\overline{d}_t, \left(\frac{t+1}{t}\right)\sigma^2\right) \tag{45}$$

The investor's best forecast of $\delta$ is the average dividend $\overline{d}_t$ (using data up to time $t$). The uncertainty about the mean of $d_t$ is reflected in the forecast of its variance. Rational investors are Bayesian but also forward looking, so solving the price equation forward gives the closed form solution for current prices

$$p_t = \frac{\overline{d}_t}{r} - 2\gamma \, f(t)\sigma^2 \tag{46}$$

where $f(t)$ is a deterministic function of time, which converges to $1/r$ as $t \rightarrow \infty$. Hence, the parameter uncertainty case, (46), collapses to the certainty case, (44), as $t \rightarrow \infty$ (because the true $\delta$ and $\sigma^2$ are constant).

We are now in a position to analyse the subjective distribution and the true distribution of returns, under Bayesian learning. Actual price changes that are determined by actions of our Bayesian investors are

$$p_{t+1} - p_t = \frac{1}{r}(\overline{d}_{t+1} - \overline{d}_t) + 2\gamma[f(t) - f(t+1)] \tag{47}$$

Ignoring the deterministic term, investors believe prices follow a martingale

$$E_t^s(p_{t+1} - p_t) = 0 \tag{48}$$

since investors cannot predict changes in (subjective) expected dividends. However, actual prices are time-varying as investors update their view about $\overline{d}_t$ as new data arrives.

If we assume the true mean level of dividends is $\delta = 0.05$ (5% p.a.) with $\sigma^2 = 0.10$ (10% p.a.), then we can generate a price series under learning using (47), where $\overline{d}_t$ is determined from random draws from an $N(0.05, 0.10)$ distribution. The perfect information case has equilibrium $p_t = 1$ (for all $t$), whereas we find that the imperfect information case has prices wandering around '1' in long swings. But as $t \rightarrow \infty$, the price approaches its fundamental value of unity (since Bayesian learning with constant parameters converges on the true parameters). These simulated prices do not 'look like' a random walk because they depend on $\overline{d}_t = d_0 + d_1 + \cdots + d_t$ (where $d_t \sim N(\delta, \sigma^2)$, which moves in long swings but with the price eventually converging to the constant true mean value $\delta$. Hence, excess volatility is observable in the data. However, changes in prices are completely unpredictable by our Bayesian investors. Given the realisation of prices (under learning), it can be shown that we would observe negative serial correlation in 'absolute' returns $\text{cov}(R_t, R_{t+1}) < 0$ where $R_{t+1} = d_{t+1} + p_{t+1} - p_t$. Also, a high dividend today predicts lower future returns next period (i.e. $\text{cov}(d_t, R_{t+1}) < 0$), and there is mean reversion over long horizons (because price eventually equals fundamental value). The econometrician would, therefore, 'discover' these properties in the data even though all investors are rational and perceive no predictability in prices.

Let us now turn to the question of why we might find a profitable trading rule using 'outside-sample' tests on past data, even though a Bayesian investor always perceives zero expected profits. Suppose the trading rule is to hold the risky (riskless) asset if $\overline{d}_t < K (> K)$, for some arbitrary constant $K$ for the filter rule. On the basis of *repeated sampling* (i.e. frequentist view) using past data, if $\overline{d}_t < K$, then *on average* $\overline{d}_t$ will also be less than the *true* mean $\delta$ and, hence, realised dividends and, thus, prices next period, will on average be higher. But the Bayesian investor has to base her decisions, conditional on past dividends that are a *single draw* from the dividend process. The investor's view of $\delta$ is always centred on $\overline{d}_t$, and $\overline{d}_t$ is equally likely to be above or below $\delta$. Repeated sampling is irrelevant to the Bayesian.

The above is the simplest version of the Lewellen and Shaken model, and they also allow informative priors, known regime changes for $\delta$ and they investigate the implications of the model for tests of cross-section variation in returns (where the CAPM can be rejected even though investors are mean-variance efficient). Thus, a model with rational investors and parameter uncertainty is consistent with the stylised facts, although this does not prove that learning is responsible for these outcomes. Parameter uncertainty therefore makes the interpretation of tests of market efficiency extremely hazardous. More rigorous tests of the EMH on 'real data' requires not only a model of equilibrium returns but also a model which mimics Bayesian updating and a reasonable 'prior' – a daunting task.

Although we do not pursue it here, it is worth noting that when asset demands are derived from an *intertemporal* model with learning, the parameter uncertainty acts like another state variable (e.g. like stochastic labour income) and gives rise to an intertemporal hedging demand (which is not present in the asset demand functions of the Lewellen–Shanken model). We briefly discuss this rather complex issue in our later chapter on intertemporal portfolio models.

## Self-Referential Learning

In the above models, dividends follow an *exogenous* time-invariant process and agent's estimates of the dividend process and, hence, prices (via the RVF) eventually converge to their true values. Suppose now that there is some feedback from prices to dividends – the convergence of the learning process is no longer guaranteed, and there may be multiple RE equilibria. Self-referential learning models deal with this problem (Marcet and Sargent 1989).

We can think of agents having a recursive estimate of a set of parameters $\hat{\rho}_t$, so the data is generated by some function $T(\hat{\rho}_t)$. If $z_t$ are the observable state variables used by agents, then a general representation of the dynamics of $z_t$ is

$$z_t = T(\rho_t)z_{t-1} + V(\rho_t)u_t \qquad (49)$$

where $u_t$ is a 'shock' whose impact on $z_t$ may depend on agents' parameter estimates $V(\rho_t)$. The RE solution is a fixed point $\rho$ of $T(\rho)$ where $T(\rho) = \rho$. Stability of convergence to RE depends on the stability of the differential equation

$$\frac{\partial \rho_t}{\partial t} = T(\rho_t) - \rho_t \qquad (50)$$

*Local* stability can be found by linearising round the fixed point

$$\frac{\partial \rho_t}{\partial t} = T'_\rho(\rho)(\rho_t - \rho) \qquad (51)$$

and depends on the real parts of the eigenvalues of $T'_\rho(\rho)$. Intuitively, the estimated parameters $\rho_t$ must lie 'close to' the equilibrium parameters, and agents' prior views must, therefore, rule out estimates that would not move them towards equilibrium. Clearly, self-referential learning requires more sophisticated agents than does simple (OLS) adaptive learning, where feedback is ignored.

In the context of stock prices, stability of self-referential learning imposes restrictions on the parameters in the reduced form for prices given by the RVF. To sketch this, suppose we estimate a VAR for dividends and prices (Timmermann 1994) and use the forecasts

$$\hat{D}_{t+1} = \hat{\phi}_{1t} D_t + \hat{\lambda}_{1t} P_t \tag{52a}$$

$$\hat{P}_{t+1} = \hat{c}_{1t} P_t + \hat{c}_{3t} D_t \tag{52b}$$

Suppose the underlying *true* dividend process with *constant* parameters is

$$D_t = \phi_1 D_{t-1} + \lambda_1 P_{t-1} + u_t \tag{52c}$$

The Euler equation is

$$P_t = \theta E_t[P_{t+1} + D_{t+1}] \quad 0 < \theta < 1 \tag{53}$$

Substituting (52a) and (52b) in (53) and using (52c) to eliminate $D_t$,

$$P_t = \frac{\theta}{1 - \theta\hat{c}_{1t} - \theta\hat{\lambda}_{1t}}\{[\lambda_1(\hat{c}_{3t} + \hat{\phi}_{1t})]P_{t-1} + [\phi_1(\hat{c}_{3t} + \hat{\phi}_{1t})]D_{t-1} + (\hat{c}_{3t} + \hat{\phi}_{1t})u_t\} \tag{54}$$

Note that (54) contains a mixture of the true (constant) underlying coefficients $(\phi_1, \lambda_1)$ and the estimated values from (52a) and (52b). The RE price depends on $(P_{t-1}, D_{t-1})$ but because of agents incomplete knowledge of the parameters, $P_t$ depends on *all* lagged values of $P$ and $D$, as the parameters are sequentially updated. With learning (as opposed to RE), 'history matters' for the dynamics. The state 'vector' is $z_t = (P_t, D_t)$ and $\rho_t = (\hat{\phi}_{1t}, \hat{\lambda}_{1t}, \hat{c}_{1t}, \hat{c}_{3t})$, which can be estimated using OLS in the bivariate VAR. Rational expectations imply that agents' forecasts, given *their* information as encapsulated in (52a) and (52b), should equal the coefficients of the true data generation process represented by (52c) and (54) By comparing (54) with (52b), the fixed points for the price equation are the solutions to

$$T_{11}(\rho) = \frac{\theta\lambda_1(c_3 + \phi_1)}{1 - \theta c_1 - \theta\lambda_1} = c_1 \tag{55a}$$

$$T_{12}(\rho) = \frac{\theta\phi_1(c_3 + \phi_1)}{1 - \theta c_1 - \theta\lambda_1} = c_3 \tag{55b}$$

For the dividend equation, we simply have

$$\phi_{1t} = \phi_1 \quad \text{and} \quad \lambda_{1t} = \lambda_1 \tag{55c}$$

and these parameters are not influenced by learning and converge to their true values. The 'fixed point' equations (55) embody the usual RE non-linear cross equation restrictions. Convergence to RE then depends on the eigenvalues of the derivatives of the price equation at the fixed points in (55a) and (55b). Timmermann (1994) estimates the VAR represented by (52a) and (52b) using UK aggregate stock price data (1926–1986) and evaluates the eigenvalues of the linearised differential equations. He finds that for the system in levels (52), the eigenvalues indicate a non-convergent learning process but when estimated in first differences, one of the fixed points is stable, so agents could 'learn' and approach the RE equilibrium. Clearly, these two contradictory results may be a manifestation of the non-stationarity of the variables in the levels equations.

In a later paper (Timmermann 1996), the VAR is estimated *recursively* on US data (S&P500) and (54) used to generate $P_t$ under self-referential learning (using a MCS). It is found that compared to exogenous adaptive learning (i.e. recursive OLS on the dividend equation only), the self-referential learning price series is not much more volatile than the RE price series, in a finite sample of data. Perhaps this is not too surprising, given that the self-referential learning model has to lie 'close to' the RE model, if convergence is ultimately to arise. So, the 'exogenous' OLS learning model 'fits' more closely the empirical stylised fact of excess volatility than does the self-referential model.

## Regime Changes and Learning

We now turn to a study of US stock prices using the Campbell–Shiller VAR methodology, which deals with regime changes and how forecasts of dividends and future expected returns might differ, depending on what regime the agent believes she is in. The causes of excess volatility and the relative importance of future dividends and expected returns in explaining movements in stock prices can be contrasted with the 'single-regime' fixed coefficient VAR approach.

We have already noted that (log) dividends are borderline non-stationary and there may be regime changes (e.g. periods of 'high' and 'low' dividend growth) in the observed data series. Agents, therefore, have to learn about what regime they are in, and this may influence their future forecasts of dividend growth. This is the idea in Evans (1998), who examines the Campbell–Shiller linearised RVF assuming the VAR used for forecasting the change in 'fundamentals' $(r_t - \Delta d_t)$ and the dividend–price ratio $\delta_t$ have a two-state Hamilton (1989) regime switching representation. For the US annual data 1871–1991, forecasts from the switching VAR are very different from those in a standard (constant parameter) VAR. Simplifying considerably, the switching VAR allows more volatility in the forecasts of the fundamentals (because of the regime switches) and, hence, explains more of the observed variability in the (log) dividend–price ratio, $\delta_t$, where

$$\delta_t = \tilde{E}_t \sum_{i=1}^{\infty} \rho^{i-1}(r_{t+i} - \Delta d_{t+i}) + \text{constant} \tag{56}$$

and $r_t = $ interest rate, $\rho = $ constant and the expectation $\tilde{E}_t$ depends on the expected future regime. An individual's forecast error will depend on the RE forecast error *and* the error in forecasting the future regime – the latter will not be zero in small samples. Since switching induces a *small* sample correlation between investors' forecast errors and the dividend–price ratio $\delta_t$, it is, therefore, possible in this framework that Shiller's variance bound is violated, even though the RVF holds. The regime-switching VAR model implies that over 60% of the variability in $\delta_t$ is due to variability in the fundamentals $(r - \Delta d)$, (compared to 35% for the standard VAR), and only 14% is due to changes in expected returns. (An extended version of the model allows agents to learn which regime they are currently in, but this does not greatly affect the empirical results.) Hence, as an explanation of movements in stock prices (i.e. $\delta_t$), 'cash flows' are relatively more important and time-varying expected returns less so in the switching model (compared to a model with no regime switches). This illustrates the difficulty in reaching a consensus on what are the 'stylised facts' (i.e. the importance of cash flows versus time-varying expected returns) when different models are used. In the regime-switching model, there can also be predictability in *ex-post* stock returns over long horizons.

## Non-Recurring Structural Breaks

In the Barsky and DeLong (1993) and early models incorporating learning, the underlying or *population* parameters (e.g. dividend growth rate) are constant. In Evans (1998), dividends switch between two *recurring* states, and the only problem investors face is to solve the filtering problem of identifying the current but unknown state. The latter seems reasonable when thinking in terms of stages of the business cycle for example, but there may be rare occasions (e.g. 1929–32, the two World Wars) when the dividend process undergoes large one-off 'breaks' that herald a new regime that does not recur. Timmermann (2001) argues that after such 'breaks', investors are subject to considerable uncertainty and because historical data is of little use, these breaks are likely to cause large revisions to expectations. If investors have full information about the break (e.g. higher growth rate in dividends), this will result in a single outlier in the returns process at the time of the break. Timmermann, therefore, proposes that agents slowly learn about the break (i.e. incomplete information), and this has important implications for the distribution of returns (e.g. skewness, kurtosis, autocorrelation, volatility clustering).

Timmermann's approach is to set up a model where the low frequency breaks in dividends are governed by a Markov switching process with an expanding set of *non-recurring* states. The model is then solved for the stock price under full information, Bayesian learning (i.e. conditional on knowing the underlying state) and a 'filtering model' where *state probabilities* are updated through Bayes rule. A constant coefficient of relative risk aversion, power utility function is used so that the Euler equation for stock prices is (with $C_{t+1} = D_{t+1}$)

$$P_t = \delta E_t[(P_{t+1} + D_{t+1})(D_{t+1}/D_t)^{-\gamma}] \tag{57}$$

with real dividends given by

$$\ln D_{t+1} = \ln D_t + \mu_{t+1} + \sigma_{t+1}\varepsilon_{t+1} \tag{58}$$

where $\mu_{t+1}, \sigma_{t+1}$ can change at break points and $\varepsilon_{t+1} \sim N(0, 1)$ so the growth rate of dividends is $g_{t+1} \equiv \exp(\mu_{t+1} + \sigma_{t+1}^2/2) - 1$.

After a break, the new mean growth rate $g_{t+1}$ is drawn from a uniform density function G(.) with upper and lower limits $[g, \overline{g}]$. In the simulations, the minimum and maximum (real) dividend growth rates are $-4\%$ p.a. and 6% p.a. respectively, giving an average growth rate of 1% p.a. with (fixed) monthly volatility $\sigma = 1.5\%$ p.m. (5.2% p.a.), which matches that in the data (1871–1999). The real discount rate $\delta = 7.5\%$ p.a. and the (fixed) probability of switching between regimes is $\pi = 0.997$, which implies that the drift of the dividend process changes about once every 30 years (giving an average of about 4–5 switches over the 1871–1999 simulation period).

We know that monthly stock returns (S&P500) are subject to high volatility, skewness, fat tails, first-order serial correlation and volatility clustering (ARCH) effects. In the simulated model with no breaks ($\pi = 1$), none of these features ensues – since $P_t$ is then governed by a stationary fixed parameter stochastic process. With breaks, but with full information (and $\gamma = 0$) volatility, skewness and kurtosis increase because of outliers in returns caused by the breaks, but there is no volatility clustering.

Under Bayesian learning, the model gives average volatility of 3.3%, close to the sample estimate of 4.1% and the skewness, kurtosis and volatility clustering (for $\gamma < 0.5$) are also similar to that found in the data, but there is not much serial correlation in returns. Timmermann also uses the simulated data to test the one over-identifying restriction of the Euler equation (49) using $Z = $ (constant, dividend yield, lagged return) as instruments in the GMM estimator. He finds that with 'breaks' and learning, the rejection frequency for Hansen's J-test at the 5% critical value is nearer 10% in most cases.

Once again, we find that numerous 'stylised facts' about returns are consistent with a model where breaks in the dividend process occur, and agents have to slowly update their forecasts of future dividends.

## 17.5 Summary

- Mathematically, rational bubbles arise because, in the absence of a transversality condition, the Euler equation yields a solution for stock prices that equals fundamental value plus a 'bubble term', where the latter follows as a martingale process.

- In the presence of a bubble, stock returns are unpredictable and, therefore, RE orthogonality tests cannot be used to detect rational bubbles.

- In the early literature, bubbles were exogenous to fundamentals (i.e. dividends). The 'origin' of the bubble cannot be explained, and only the time path of the bubble is given by these models.

- Standard unit root and cointegration tests may be able to detect continuously exploding bubbles but are unlikely to detect periodically collapsing bubbles.

- *Intrinsic bubbles* depend, in a non-linear deterministic way, on economic fundamentals (e.g. dividends) yet still satisfy the Euler equation. Evidence for intrinsic bubbles is based, in part, on direct estimation of bubble solutions, where price depends on specific non-linear parametric function of dividends. Evidence for intrinsic bubbles is somewhat inconclusive.

- If prices are determined by the RVF, but agents recursively update their estimates of the true (fixed) parameters of the dividend process, then 'prices under learning' will be more volatile than prices under 'pure' RE, even if expected returns are constant. Also, with recursive updating of parameters, simulated returns are autocorrelated and can be predicted from the dividend–price ratio – this mimics the real data.

- Models in which there are rare but extreme 'structural breaks' and where agents have to learn about the new parameters after these *non-recurring* regime changes can also mimic the stylised facts of high volatility, skewness, kurtosis, autocorrelation and volatility clustering of returns found in the real data.

- If agents are rational and use Bayesian updating of the parameters, then an equilibrium model can also reproduce the stylised facts noted above and, in particular, one may find profitable trading rules in past data, even though investors could not have detected these *ex-ante*.

- Under 'self-referential' learning, convergence to a 'pure' RE equilibrium for prices depends on the size of parameters in the learning model. US data (S&P500) do not give much additional volatility in the stock price series than a pure RE model and, hence, self-referential learning does not appear to explain the 'stylised fact' of high volatility in actual stock prices (under a constant discount rate).

- Models that incorporate different switching regimes for the fundamental variables present agents with a 'filtering problem' – agents have to ascertain the probability of being in a particular regime in order to forecast future dividends. In the Campbell–Shiller VAR methodology, this can give rise to different forecasts (e.g. for dividend growth) to the 'fixed coefficient' VAR and, hence, different conclusions about the relative importance of dividend growth versus time-varying expected returns in explaining stock price movements.

# 18

# BEHAVIOURAL FINANCE AND ANOMALIES

## Aims

- Show how behavioural finance differs from the standard efficient markets approach.
- Demonstrate how risk aversion, finite investment horizons and systematic risk can lead to mis-pricing.
- Show how noise traders survive in the market.
- Assess the evidence from psychological experiments on individual and group behaviour.
- Outline the main anomalies found in stock markets and how behavioural finance might 'explain' such potential profitable opportunities.

## 18.1  Key Ideas

A particular market can only be declared inefficient relative to a specific chosen model, usually based on 'fundamentals'. Efficiency is a joint hypothesis of the correct model and immediate elimination of any discrepancy between the actual price and the fundamentals (or model determined) price. A model is not a perfect description of reality and, therefore, there is always a 'residual' – some element of the complete data set that is not explained by the model. If these 'residuals' have a systematic pattern, we would classify them as anomalies or puzzles. Behavioural finance seeks to explain these anomalies either by some kind of non-standard behaviour (e.g. irrationality or non-standard preferences) or the inability of the rational investors to equate fair value (i.e. fundamentals price) with the actual price. 'Noise traders' is the generic term given to any 'non-fundamentals' traders.

In many behavioural finance models, investors may still maximise expected utility (say) subject to budget and other constrains (e.g. no short-selling), but the utility function chosen and the way investors form expectations may be non-standard. In other types of behavioural model, there are two distinct groups, the rational fundamentals traders and the 'irrational' noise traders.

There is a vigorous debate on how far either the rational fundamentals approach (with incorporation of transactions costs) or the alternative behavioural approach can 'explain' the empirical facts, using assumptions that can be generally accepted as 'reasonable'. For example, when considering the performance of a soccer player (e.g. David Beckham), the 'fundamentals supporters' might say, 'Well, he didn't score quite as many goals as predicted by my individual profit maximising model, because the playing field is not *perfectly* smooth.' The behavioural modeller might say, 'He didn't score many goals because he experiences a much greater loss in self-esteem when the other side scores than when he himself scores.' (That is, he has an additional variable in his utility function than just *his* goals scored and he suffers from 'loss-aversion'.) Alternatively, the behavioural modeller might say that the objective function of maximising goals scored and, hence, individual profits, is correct. But the opposition are irrational (e.g. jealous of his celebrity glamour status, off the field) and, hence, act as 'noise footballers' and want to unfairly injure him, so he 'goes forward' less than in a completely rational world where all teams 'play by the rules'. This approach recognises that the outcome of the soccer match depends on the interaction between 'rational' (intertemporal profit maximising) soccer players and the irrational 'noise footballers' and whether the former then begin to imitate the latter. (You may have noticed a certain amount of 'tit-for-tat' behaviour on the soccer field in that when one side begin to commit offences, the other side get rattled and also commit crazy offences directly in front of the referee – for example, when Beckham was sent off in the 1998 England–Argentina World Cup game.)

Because of the possibility of model error, much of the evidence against the efficient market hypothesis (EMH) is based on so-called 'anomalies' rather than evaluating sophisticated statistical tests of models based on fundamentals (e.g. regression tests of the CAPM, Shiller volatility tests, etc.). To minimise model error, one element of the literature looks for situations where there are price anomalies between *very close substitutes* (e.g. twin shares, ADRs, closed-end funds) that should have been arbitraged away. Another part of the anomalies literature looks for trading rules that earn money corrected for risk and transactions costs – this requires statistical measures of risk that may be contentious and, hence, still involve some 'model error'. Two key questions that behavioural models need to answer are:

- why does mis-pricing persist in the market?
- how do noise traders survive in the market?

In behavioural models, there are 'no free lunches' (i.e. excess profits corrected for risk and transactions costs). But this does not imply that 'the price is right' (i.e. price equals discounted expected cash flows, in which the expectation is over the correct distribution and the discount rate is based on an acceptable preference specification). Essentially, 'the price is right' is a shorthand for the EMH. But in some behavioural models, prices do not equal fundamental value because the rational traders are inhibited in some way from arbitraging away any mis-pricing caused by the noise traders.

Note that the EMH does not require that *all* participants in the market are 'efficient' and well informed. There can be a set of irrational or 'noise' traders in the market who do not quote prices equal to fundamental value. All the EMH requires is that there are sufficient 'smart money' traders around, who recognise that $P_t$ will eventually equal fundamental value $V_t$. So, if some irrational traders quote $P_t < V_t$, the smart money will quickly move in and purchase stocks from the irrational traders, thus pushing $P_t$ quickly towards $V_t$.

Take a simple case in which all soccer clubs are financed by share issues (readers who are interested in other sports can substitute their own teams and players). Assume that noise traders initially purchase Real Madrid shares at a fair price of €25. Now assume that after a few hours, consuming alcohol in numerous bars, the noise traders, as a group, *irrationally* feel unduly pessimistic about the ability of Real Madrid's manager. Hence, they sell shares and push down the price of Real Madrid with the final price settling at $P = €20$, below the unchanged fundamental value of $V = €25$. The noise traders have sold at below €25 and, hence, lose money. Fully informed rational traders (e.g. Mrs. Victoria Beckham?) should now step in and buy Real's shares while simultaneously hedging their bets by *short*-selling a (correctly priced) close substitute security that has similar cash flows to Real Madrid, in future states of the world. Let this substitute security be shares in Barcelona F.C. (their historic rivals). If the general market for soccer shares falls (e.g. loss of lucrative TV deals), then the 'long-short' rational trader still makes a profit when the mis-pricing is corrected. The *general market* fall implies a loss on Real Madrid of, say, €1 but a gain of around €1 on the short position in Barcelona. But when the *mis-pricing* of Real Madrid is corrected, the 'long-short' trader will gain her €5 per share. This is because if rational traders enter the market and buy at €20, they begin to push the price up towards the fair value of $V = €25$ and, in the process, make a profit. (This profit is at the expense of the noise traders.) The noise traders' initially purchased at a fair price of €25 but sold at below €25 (to the rational traders) and, hence, they should be 'forced out' of the market by the rational guys (i.e. Darwinian survival of the fittest). The price of Real Madrid will rise to its fundamental value very quickly if there are enough rational traders with sufficient funds willing to enter the market. However, the above scenario may not ensue for the following reasons.

## Fundamental Risk

Short-selling of the substitute security may protect the rational trader from most of the (football) industry (systematic) risk but specific risk (e.g. news that Beckham, who currently plays for Real Madrid, has broken his leg) still remains. So the 'arbitrage' is not riskless.

## Noise-Trader Risk and Finite Horizon

Even if Barcelona F.C. is a *perfect* substitute for Real Madrid, it is still possible for noise traders to become *even more pessimistic* about the abilities of Real Madrid's manager and, hence, for Real's price to fall further (below €20). This is the *noise-trader risk* faced by the rational traders. If rational traders have long horizons *and* prices eventually do converge to fundamental value, then they will not worry about noise traders' risk, they just have to wait longer for their arbitrage profits and ride out any short-term losses. But, professional portfolio managers generally have relatively short horizons and manage other people's money, so there is a separation of 'brains and capital' (Shleifer and Vishny 1997), and, hence, arbitrage opportunities may not be eliminated.

## Short-Selling

Most pension and some mutual fund managers are not allowed to short-sell. Hedge funds can short-sell, but they would need access to a plentiful supply of (Barcelona) shares from their broker. Also, they need to be able to borrow Barcelona shares for as long as it takes the mis-pricing to be corrected. If not, they may have to repurchase Barcelona shares in the market at an unfavourable price – known as being 'bought-in'. Also, if foreign shares are involved, shorting these (e.g. shares in Inter Milan) may be difficult, and brokerage fees and bid-ask spreads need to be factored in to the arbitrage calculation. (As well as the possibility that the Italian football 'market' is not a close substitute for the market risk of Real Madrid shares.)

## Model Risk

The rational traders cannot be sure that Real Madrid is underpriced at €20 because their estimate of the fundamentals price of €25 (e.g. using the Gordon growth model) may be incorrect. This 'model risk' may limit the positions taken by the rational arbitrageurs.

## Beauty Contest

If rational investors have finite horizons, then they will be concerned about the price at some future time $N$. But, if they base their expectations of $E_t P_{t+N}$ on expected future dividends from $t + N$ onwards, then we are back to the infinite horizon assumption of the rational investor (see Chapter 4). However, if we allow heterogeneous agents in our model, then if agents believe the world is not dominated by rational investors, the price at $t + N$ will depend in part on what the rational investor feels the irrational investors' views of $P_{t+N}$ will be (i.e. Keynes' beauty contest). This general argument also applies if rational investors know that other rational investors use different models of equilibrium asset returns. Here, we are rejecting the EMH assumption that all investors instantaneously know the true model. In these cases, rational investors may take the view that the actual price is a weighted average of the rational valuation (or alternative rational valuations) and the effect on price of the irrational traders (e.g. technical traders, such as chartists and those who use candlestick charts or neutral networks – see Cuthbertson and Nitzsche 2001a). Hence, price might not always equal fundamental value.

## Learning Costs

If there are learning costs in finding the true model or in obtaining all the information, this may limit the *number* of rational traders who are in a position to spot and hence eliminate the mis-pricing of Real Madrid shares. It may be that there are enough arbitrageurs, with sufficient funds in the aggregate, so that even over a finite horizon, risky profitable opportunities are arbitraged away. The force of the latter argument is weakened, however, if we recognise that any single arbitrageur is unlikely to know either the fundamental value of a security or to realise when observed price changes are due to deviations from the fundamental's price. Arbitrageurs as a group are also likely to disagree amongst themselves about fundamental value (i.e. they have heterogeneous expectations), and this could increase the general uncertainty they perceive about profitable opportunities, even in the long term. The smart money may, therefore, have difficulty in *identifying* any mis-pricing in the market. Hence, if funds are limited (i.e. a less than perfectly elastic demand for the underpriced securities by arbitrageurs) or horizons are finite, it is possible that profitable *risky* arbitrage opportunities can persist in the market for some time.

If one recognises that 'information costs' (e.g. man-hours, machines, buildings) may be substantial and that marginal costs rise with the breadth and quantity of trading, then this also might provide some limit on arbitrage activity in some areas of the market. For example, to take an extreme case, if information costs are so high that dealers either concentrate solely on bonds or solely on stocks (i.e. complete market segmentation), then differences in expected returns between bonds and stocks (corrected for risk) might not be immediately arbitraged away.

## Necessary and Sufficient Conditions

A great deal of the analysis of financial markets relies on the principle of arbitrage (e.g. see Shleifer and Summers 1990). Arbitrageurs (or smart money or rational speculators) continually watch the market and quickly eliminate any divergence between the actual price and fundamental value and, hence, immediately eliminate any profitable opportunities. If a security has a perfect substitute, then arbitrage is riskless. Riskless arbitrage ensures that *relative* prices are equalised. However, if there are no close substitutes so that arbitrage is risky, then arbitrage may not pin down the *absolute* price levels of stocks (or bonds) *as a whole*.

The risk in taking an arbitrage position only occurs if the smart money has a finite horizon. The smart money may believe that prices will *ultimately* move to their fundamental value and, hence, in the long term, profits will be made. However, if arbitrageurs have to either borrow cash or securities (for short sales) to implement their trades and, hence, pay *per period fees* or report their profit position on their 'book' to their superiors at frequent intervals (e.g. monthly, quarterly), then an infinite horizon certainly cannot apply to all or even most trades undertaken by the smart money.

First, consider the case in which there is *no* close substitute security and, hence, the arbitrageur is exposed to fundamental risk. Then mis-pricing can persist if (see Barberis and Thaler 2003):

(i) arbitrageurs are risk averse *and*

(ii) fundamental risk is systematic.

Condition (i) ensures that no *one* arbitrageur will be willing to wipe out the mis-pricing by taking a large position and (ii) ensures mis-pricing is not wiped out by a large number of investors, each taking a *small* position in the mis-priced security.

If a perfect substitute security exists (i.e. identical cash flows in all states of the world) and the two securities have different prices, then there is no fundamental or model risk but only noise-trader risk. The arbitrageur can be completely sure of the mis-pricing. For this mis-pricing to persist, we require:

(i) arbitrageurs are risk averse and *have short horizons*

(ii) noise-trader risk is systematic.

In (i), we require a 'short horizon' to prevent a single (wealthy!) arbitrageur from waiting for the *certain* mis-pricing to be corrected. Again, condition (ii) is required so that lots of small investors cannot diversify away the risk of the mis-priced security.

## 18.2  Beliefs and Preferences

Above, we have explained why risky arbitrage may be limited and insufficient to keep actual prices of stocks in line with their fundamental value. We now discuss the experimental evidence on individual's beliefs and preferences (see Barberis and Thaler 2003, Shleifer and Summers 1990 and Shiller 1989 for a summary).

Psychological experiments tend to show that individuals make systematic (i.e. non-random) mistakes. Subjects are found to overreact to new information (news), and they tend to extrapolate past price trends. They are *over-confident*, which makes them take on excessive risk.

Behavioural psychology provides experimental evidence that people are not rational in forming their forecasts. A Bayesian approach in which the individual weights her prior beliefs and recent information to produce a best forecast is often optimal. But, in practice, individuals seem to attach too much weight to recent data and can be *over-confident* about their forecasting ability.

When agents do *not* know the true data-generating process, they often believe that small samples reflect the 'population' (i.e. the 'law of small numbers' or '*sample size neglect*'). For example, if David Beckham scores in three consecutive soccer matches, he is on a 'hot streak' and people erroneously increase their subjective probability that he will score in the next game. But this estimate may not be at all representative of his average scoring rate for the whole of the previous season to date, and in reality, there may be no serial correlation in his scoring pattern. Even when they *know* the true data generation process (e.g. coin toss), after five heads in a row, they might place a probability greater than 1/2 that the next play will result in 'tails' (e.g. see the opening scene of Tom Stoppard's play *Rosencrantz & Guildenstern are Dead*). This is referred to as the *gambler's fallacy*.

People also *anchor* too much on an initial position. When asked to estimate the percent of African countries there are in the United Nations, people's responses were influenced by the initial random number $x$ (where $0 < x < 100$) they were given. Those who were asked to compare their estimate with $x = 10\%$ replied '25%', while those who were asked to compare with $x = 60\%$ estimated 45% (on average). There are also *memory biases* whereby a more recent or more salient event will influence people's views on probable outcomes. For example, people who have recently experienced a car theft will overestimate the probability of car theft in their city (compared to someone who has not experienced a car theft).

## Ellsberg Paradox

There are a large number of experiments that show that individuals often do not follow the basic axioms of expected utility theory when deciding between alternative gambles even when they know the true probability distribution of outcomes. Even allowing the use of *subjective* probabilities rather than objective probabilities does not appear to rescue expected utility, when describing rational choice under uncertainty (Savage 1964). Ellsberg (1961) provides an experiment that demonstrates that individuals do not behave rationally according to the axioms of expected utility. There are two urns, each containing a mix of red and blue balls. Urn 1 contains 100 balls but with an unknown number of red and blue balls. Urn 2 contains 50 red and 50 blue balls, so the probability of either a red or blue ball drawn at random is 1/2. The subjects are aware of the above and are asked to choose between one of two gambles, with a payment of $100 for guessing correctly. The first choice is:

(a)  ball drawn at random from Urn 1: $100 if red, $0 if blue

(b)  ball drawn at random from Urn 2: $100 if red, $0 if blue.

Subjects tend to choose B, where the probabilities are known and equal to 1/2. Choice of B rather than A implies they think $p$ (*red in Urn 1*) $< 1/2$.

The next choice subjects are presented with is:

(c)  ball drawn at random from Urn 1: $100 if blue, $0 if red

(d)  ball drawn at random from Urn 2: $100 if blue, $0 if red.

Subjects tend to choose D over C, where the probabilities are known. But this implies that they believe $p(blue\ in\ Urn1) < 1/2$, which in turn implies $p(red\ in\ Urn1) > 1/2$.

The latter contradicts the choice of B over A, which we found implies $p(redinUrn1) < 1/2$. This is the Ellsberg paradox. The experiment also suggests that people particularly dislike situations where they do not know the probability distribution of possible outcomes. The latter is referred to as *ambiguity aversion* and has been observed in a wide variety of experimental situations, particularly when participants are made aware of their lack of knowledge before choosing between alternative bets – for example, bets on sporting events by non-sports fans (Fox and Tversky 1995).

## Mental Accounting

How can we encapsulate how people might assess the utility of particular outcomes in the stock market? There are several possibilities. Suppose you begin with financial wealth of $1000 and take two bets, the first results in a gain of $200 and the second a loss of $50. The standard lifetime utility approach (ignoring discounting) would imply that $U = U(1000) + U(1200) + U(1150)$ where $U(.)$ is a non-linear concave function over the wealth outcomes in each period (e.g. power utility). The *change* in utility for each bet is then $U(1200) - U(1000)$ and $U(1150) - U(1200)$ respectively. Alternatively, the investor might only be concerned about terminal wealth $U(1150)$ at retirement, say, in which case the utility of intermediate positions is irrelevant, only $U(1150)$ matters. Another possibility is that the investor has a baseline utility level $U_0$ and is concerned only about *gains* and *losses* relative to this baseline starting point. This is a form of *mental accounting*, known as *narrow framing*, since the investor is only concerned about outcomes from the stock market and does not aggregate these with other elements of wealth (e.g. changes in income or in the value of her housing wealth). Here, lifetime utility is measured as $U_0 + U(+100) + U(-50)$. This also raises the possibility that $U(-50)$ may be given a higher *weighting* than, say, $U(+50)$ so that the utility from a gain followed by an equal loss is $U(+50) + \lambda U(-50)$ with $\lambda > 1$ – this is *loss-aversion*. The impact of loss-aversion on lifetime utility clearly depends on the frequency with which investors monitor their portfolios – if you evaluate your portfolio frequently (e.g. once per month), you will note more periods of negative stock returns than if you evaluate your portfolio every, say, five years (see Rabin and Thaler 2001).

Yet another alternative is that any gains or losses are measured not in absolute terms but relative to an initial level of utility that the investor *slowly adjusts* as their wealth either rises or falls – the idea is that gains or losses are measured relative to 'habit levels' of wealth – this idea appears in the Campbell–Cochrane consumption habit persistence model (Chapter 14) and is applied to wealth bets by Barberis, Shleifer and Wurgler (2001) – see Chapter 19. Indeed, all of the above formulations have been used in the literature, sometimes in conjunction with the usual power utility function.

# 18.3 Survival of Noise Traders

If we envisage a market where there are smart speculators who tend to set prices equal to fundamental value and noise traders who operate on rules of thumb, a question arises as to how the noise traders can survive in this market. If noise traders hold stocks when the price is above the fundamental value, then the smart money should sell these assets to the noise traders, thus pushing down the price. As the price falls towards its fundamental value, the noise traders lose money and tend towards bankruptcy, while the smart money can, if they wish, buy back the stocks at the lower price. On the other hand, if the noise traders hold assets whose price is below the fundamental value, then the smart money should purchase such assets from the noise traders, and they will then make a profit as the price rises towards the fundamental value. Hence, the net effect is that the noise traders lose money and, therefore, should disappear from the market, leaving only the smart money. When this happens, prices should then reflect fundamentals.

Of course, if there were an army of noise traders who *continually entered* the market (and continually went bankrupt), it would be possible for prices to diverge from fundamental value for some significant time. But one might argue that it is hardly likely that noise traders would enter a market where previous noise traders have gone bankrupt in large numbers. However, entrepreneurs often believe they can succeed where others have failed. To put the reverse argument, some noise traders will be successful over a finite horizon, and this may encourage others to attempt to imitate them and enter the market, ignoring the fact that the successful noise traders had in fact taken on more risk and just happened to get lucky – this is survivorship bias.

Can we explain why an *existing cohort* of noise traders can still make profits in a market that contains smart money? The answer really has to do with the potential for herding behaviour. No individual smart money trader can know that all other smart money traders will force the market price towards its fundamental value in the period of time for which he is contemplating trading the stock. Thus, any strategy that the sophisticated traders adopt, given the presence of noise traders in the market, is certainly not riskless. There is always the possibility that the noise traders will push the price even further away from fundamental value, and this may result in a loss for the smart money. Thus, risk-averse smart money may not fully arbitrage away the influence of the noise traders. If there are enough noise traders who follow *common* fads, then noise-trader risk will be pervasive (systematic). It cannot be diversified away and must, therefore, earn a reward or risk premium in equilibrium. Noise trading is, therefore, consistent with an average return that is greater than that given by the fundamental's model. If noise traders hold a large share of assets subject to noise-trader risk, they *may* earn above average returns and survive in the market. For example, if noise traders are more active in dealing in shares of 'distressed firms', this may explain why such firms earn an above average return corrected only for CAPM-beta risk. It is because the noise-trader risk is greater for such stocks, and this is reflected in their higher return.

The impact of noise traders on prices may well be greater when most investors follow the advice given in finance textbooks and *passively* hold the market portfolio. If noise traders move into a particular group of shares on the basis of 'hunch', the holders of the market portfolio will do nothing (unless the movement is so great as to require a change in the 'market value' proportions held in each asset). The actions of the noise traders need to be countered by a set of genuine arbitrageurs who are active in the market. In the extreme, if *all* investors hold the market portfolio but *one* noise trader enters the market wishing to purchase shares of a particular firm, then its price will be driven to infinity.

Arbitrageurs may not only predict fundamentals but may also divert their energies to anticipating changes in demand by the noise traders. If noise traders are optimistic about particular securities, it will pay arbitrageurs to create more of them (e.g. junk bonds, dot-coms, telecom firms, mutual funds, oil stocks) via, for example, the expansion of the activities the securities business of investment banks. Suppose a conglomerate has interests in the oil market and noise traders are temporally attracted by 'oil'. Then it may pay the conglomerate to split off its oil division and issue new oil shares that are currently in vogue with noise traders at abnormally high prices.

Arbitrageurs will also behave like noise traders in that they attempt to *pick stocks* that noise-trader sentiment is likely to favour: the arbitrageurs do not necessarily counter shifts in demand by noise traders. Just as entrepreneurs invest in casinos to exploit gamblers, it pays the smart money to spend considerable resources in gathering information on possible future noise-trader demand shifts (e.g. for dot-coms in the 1990s). Hence, some arbitrageurs may have an incentive to behave like noise traders. For example, if noise traders are perceived by arbitrageurs to be positive feedback traders, then as prices are pushed above fundamental value, arbitrageurs get in on the bandwagon themselves in the hope that they can sell out 'near the top'. They, therefore, 'amplify the fad'. Arbitrageurs may expect prices in the longer term to return to fundamentals (perhaps aided by arbitrage sales) but in the short term arbitrageurs will 'follow the trend'. This evidence is consistent with findings of positive autocorrelation in returns at short horizons (e.g. weeks or months) as arbitrageurs and noise traders follow the short-term trend and negative correlation at longer horizons (e.g. over three or more years) as some arbitrageurs take the 'long view' and sell the overpriced shares. Also, if 'news' triggers off noise-trader demand, then this is consistent with prices over-reacting to 'news'.

## Group Behaviour

We examine why a market might contain *a substantial number* of noise traders who follow simple 'rules of thumb' and follow waves of investor sentiment (herding behaviour) rather than act on the basis of fundamentals. In order that noise traders as a group are capable of influencing market prices, their demand shifts must broadly move in unison (i.e. be correlated across noise traders).

Experiments on *group behaviour* (Shiller 1989) include Sherif's (1937) 'autokinetic experiment', where individuals in total darkness were asked to predict the movement of a pencil of light. In the experiment with *individuals*, there was no consensus about the degree of movement (which in fact was zero). When a group of individuals performed the same experiment but this time each individual could hear the views of the others, then a consensus emerged (which differed across groups) about the degree of movement. In an experiment by Asch (1952), individuals acting alone compare lengths of line segments. The experiment is then repeated with a group in which all other members of the group are primed to give the *same wrong answers*. The individual, when alone, usually gave objectively correct answers but when faced with group pressure, the 'individual' frequently gave 'wrong' answers. After the experiment, it was ascertained that the individual usually knew the correct answer but was afraid to contradict the group. If there is no generally accepted view of what is the correct or fundamental price of a given stock, then investors may face uncertainty rather than risk (i.e. they do not know the true conditional distribution of returns). This is likely to make them more susceptible to investor sentiment.

Models of the *diffusion of opinions* are often rather imprecise. There is evidence that ideas can remain dormant for long periods and then be triggered by some seemingly trivial event. The news media obviously play a role here, but research on persuasion often finds that informal face-to-face communication amongst family, friends and co-workers is of greater importance in the diffusion of views than is the media. There are mathematical theories of the diffusion of information based on models of epidemics. In such models, there are 'carriers' who meet 'susceptibles' and create 'new carriers'. Carriers die off at a 'removal rate'. The epidemic can give rise to a humped-shaped pattern if the infection 'takes off'. If the infection does not take off (i.e. because of either a low infection rate or a low number of susceptibles or a high removal rate), then the number of new carriers declines monotonically. The difficulty in applying such a model to investor sentiment is that one cannot accurately quantify the behavioural determinants of the various variables (e.g. the infection rate) in the model, which are likely to differ from case to case.

Shiller (1989) uses the above ideas to suggest that the bull market of the 1950s and 1960s may have something to do with the speed with which general information about how to invest in stocks and shares (e.g. investment clubs) spread amongst individuals. He also notes the growth in institutional demand (e.g. pension funds) for stocks over this period, which could not be offset by individuals selling their own holdings to keep their *total* savings constant. This is because individuals' holdings of stocks were not large or evenly distributed (most being held by wealthy individuals): some people in occupational pension funds simply had no shares to sell.

Herding behaviour or 'following the trend' has frequently been observed in the housing market, in the stock market crash of 1987 (see Shiller 1990) and in the foreign exchange market (Frankel and Foot 1986 and Allen and Taylor 1989). Summers (1986) and Shleifer and Summers (1990) show that a time series for share prices that is *artificially generated* from a model in which price deviates from fundamentals in a *persistent way* does produce a time series that mimics actual price behaviour (i.e. close to a random walk), so that some kind of persistent noise-trader behaviour is broadly consistent with the observed data.

Of course, it is always possible that as people learn through repetition, they will adjust their 'rule of thumb' biases. Also, experts may be less (or more) prone to biases than 'Joe Public', and large incentives may also reduce such biases. However, it appears that biases do remain, and in a world that has a structure that changes over time, such biases certainly may persist as learning is then a continuing process.

# 18.4  Anomalies

## Calendar Effects

The weekend effect refers to the fact that there appears to be a systematic fall in stock prices between the Friday closing and Monday opening. One explanation of the weekend effect is that firms and governments release 'good news' between Monday and Friday but wait until the weekend to release bad news. The bad news is then reflected in 'low' stock prices on Monday. However, in an efficient market, some agents should recognise this and should (short) sell on Friday (price is 'high') and buy on Monday (price is 'low'), assuming that the expected profit more than covers transactions costs and a payment for risk. This action should lead to a 'removal' of the anomaly.

The so-called January effect is a similar phenomenon. The daily rate of return on common stocks appears to be unusually high during the early days of the month of January. For the United States, one explanation is due to year-end selling of stock in order to generate capital losses, which can then be offset against capital gains to reduce tax liability. (This is known as 'bed and breakfasting' in the UK.) In January, investors purchase stock to return to their original portfolio holdings. Again, if the EMH holds, this predictable pattern of price changes should lead to purchases by non-tax payers (e.g. pension funds) in December when the price is low and selling in January when the price is high, thus eliminating the profitable arbitrage opportunity. The January effect seems to take place in the first five trading days of January (Keane 1983) and also appears to be concentrated in the stocks of small firms (Reinganum 1983). There are numerous other calendar effects in the anomalies literature (e.g. turn of the year, holiday effects, week of the month effects). The question is whether these statistically significant effects, when taken in isolation, remain when dependencies operating across different calendar effects are accounted for.

## Data-Snooping Bias

In a salutary paper, Sullivan, Timmermann and White (2001) note the vast number of studies that find calendar effects in stock returns and address the problem of whether this is due to 'chance' (data mining). They use over 100 years of daily returns data (on the S&P500 and its futures index) to examine a huge set of up to 9500 possible calendar rules, including some that were not reported in the literature. (Those reported in the literature tend to be only the 'successful' ones and, hence, bias the results.) The basic idea is to take account of the problem that the size of a test, based on a search for the largest possible t-statistic for predictability, can be very different from its nominal value. They use White's (2000) 'bootstrap snooper', which provides $p$-values for the 'success' of a calendar effect, once the effects of data mining have been accounted for. They find that the best calendar rule (from either the 'large' or 'small' set considered) does not yield a statistically significant ('reality check') $p$-value for 'predictability', where the latter is taken to be either the mean return or the Sharpe ratio.

Also, the performance of the best in-sample calendar rule gives an inferior out-of-sample performance. Hence, after accounting for data snooping, they find no significant calendar effects. Broadly speaking, the data-snooping idea is an attempt to get around a type of survivorship bias problem because researchers that fail to find predictability may not get published (or even submit their research). So, in the journals, we may see a disproportionate number of articles that demonstrate predictability.

## The Small-Firm Effect

Between 1960 and the middle of the 1980s, small-capitalized companies earned on average a higher rate of return than the overall stock market index in many industrialised countries (Dimson, Marsh and Staunton 2002). Of course, according to the CAPM, this could be due to the higher risks attached to these small firms that should be reflected in their higher CAPM-beta values. However, we noted in Chapter 8 that small-firm stocks *do not* lie on the CAPM-security market line (Reinganum 1982, 1983, Cochrane 2001). The small-firm effect seemed to disappear in the late 1980s after the anomaly had been documented in the academic and professional literature – so, eventually, the market 'removed' this anomaly (Cochrane 2001, Dimson, Marsh and Staunton 2002).

## Winner's Curse: 'Buy the Dogs, Sell the Stars'

We have noted that there is evidence of *mean reversion* in stock returns over long horizons (3–5 years). A key issue for the validity of the EMH is whether such predictability can lead to excess profits net of transactions costs and risk. A seminal example of this approach is DeBondt and Thaler (1985). They take 35 of the most extreme 'winners' and 35 of the extreme 'losers' over the five years from January 1928 to December 1932 (based on monthly return data from the universe of stocks on the NYSE) and form two distinct portfolios of these companies' shares. They follow these companies for the next five years, which constitutes 'the test period'. They repeat the exercise 46 times by advancing the start date by one year each time. Finally, they calculate the average 'test period' performance (in excess of the return on the *whole* NYSE index), giving equal weight (rather than value weights) to each of the 35 companies. They find (Figure 1) the following.

(i) Five-year returns for the 'loser portfolio' are about 30%, while losses for the 'winner portfolio' are around 10%.

(ii) Excess returns on the 'loser portfolio' tend to occur in January (i.e. 'January effect').

(iii) There is long horizon mean reversion (i.e. a price fall is followed by a price rise and vice versa).

It is worth emphasising that the so-called 'loser portfolio' (i.e. one where prices have fallen dramatically *in the past*) is in fact the one that makes high returns *in the future*: a somewhat paradoxical definition of 'loser'. An arbitrage strategy of buying the 'loser portfolio' and short-selling the 'winner portfolio' (i.e. 'buy the dogs' and 'sell the stars') beats the passive strategy of holding the S&P500 (see DeBondt and Thaler 1987).

Bremer and Sweeney (1991) find that the above results also hold for very short time periods. For example, for a 'loser portfolio' comprising stocks where the *one-day* price fall has been greater than 10%, the subsequent returns are 3.95% *after five days*.

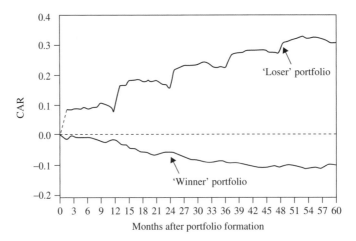

**Figure 1** Cumulative excess returns for 'winner' and 'loser' portfolios. *Source*: DeBondt and Thaler (1989). Reproduced by permission of the American Economic Association

They use stocks of *large firms only*. Therefore, they have no problem that the bid-ask spread is a large percentage of the price (which could distort the results). Also, they avoid problems with 'the small-firm effect' (i.e. smaller firms are more 'risky' and, hence, require a greater than average equilibrium excess return). Hence, Bremer and Sweeney also seem to find evidence of supernormal profits.

Other studies that demonstrate profits to 'contrarian strategies' over long horizons include Chopra, Lakonishok and Ritter (1992) for the United States, Richards (1995, 1997) who uses national stock market indexes, and Lakonishok, Shleifer and Vishny (1994).

One explanation of the above results is that 'perceived risk' of the 'loser portfolio' is judged to be 'high', hence requiring a high average excess return in the future if one is to hold them. The measurement of risk in early studies is sometimes relatively crude or non-existent and is often measured using Jensen's alpha or the Sharpe ratio in later studies.

## Twin Shares

Froot and Dabora (1999) analyse the case of *Royal Dutch* and *Shell*, who agreed to merge cash flows on a 60:40 basis but remained as separate companies. If price equals fundamental value, then the price ratio of these two shares should be *Royal Dutch/Shell* = 1.5. But underpricing and overpricing are found to have been as large as 35% and 15% respectively, and the mis-pricing is persistent. Here, there is little or no fundamental risk, and short-selling is not difficult. Of course, noise-trader risk remains, and this (plus the short horizon of rational traders) could be the cause of the persistent mis-pricing. Hence, there is 'no free lunch' but 'prices are not right'. However, they were 'right' by 2001 when the shares sold at a ratio of 1.5, so the mis-pricing did eventually disappear. It is also the case that *Royal Dutch*, which is traded in the United States, and Shell, which is traded in the United Kingdom, co-move closely with the S&P500 and the FTSE index respectively, thus de-linking 'fundamental' cash flows from prices and suggesting systematic noise-trader risk in the two markets or, put slightly differently, a 'preferred habitat' in specific stocks. (We meet this idea again when discussing 'style investing' in stocks and the expectations hypothesis of the term structure.)

## ADRs

ADRs are *foreign* shares held in trust by US financial institutions and traded in New York. The shares also trade in their 'home' stock market, where their price often differs from their New York price. There is a near perfect substitute, so if the ADR in New York is at a premium to the actual share in the home stock market, then arbitrageurs should short-sell the ADR and purchase in the domestic stock market. But persistent price deviations are observed even where there are no restrictions to US ownership of the shares on the 'home' market. Presumably, this anomaly is due to noise-trader risk, limiting such arbitrage.

## Index Effect

When stocks are included (excluded) from the S&P500 index, there is often a large increase (decrease) in their price. Here, there is a price change that is *independent* of any (observed) change in fundamental value. In other words, 'no news moves prices', which violates the RVF and the EMH. Wurgler and Zhuravkaya (2002) shows that the price jump is largest for those stocks with the worst substitute securities (i.e. stocks for which arbitrage is the most risky). Indeed, 'good' substitute securities are hard to find since Zhuravkaya finds that the R-squared of returns with the 'best' substitute security are usually below 25%. Hence, the anomaly may be due to the presence of systematic fundamental risk (plus risk aversion).

## Closed-End Funds

Closed-end funds issue a *fixed number* of shares, and trading in the shares of the closed-end fund then takes place between investors. The cash raised by the fund is used to purchase a 'basket' of investments, usually in stocks and bonds. The shares that comprise the 'basket' in the closed-end fund are generally also traded openly on the stock market. The value of the fund, the net asset value (NAV), ought, therefore, to equal the market value of the individual shares in the fund. But this is often not the case.

Closed-end fund share prices often differ from NAV. When initially created, closed-end funds sell at above NAV; when they are terminated, they sell at NAV, and during their life, they usually trade at a discount to NAV, which on average is about 10% but varies over time. Also, the discounts on very different types of closed-end funds tend to move together. This violates the EMH, because investors could buy the closed-end fund's shares at the discount price (say) and at the same time short-sell a portfolio of stocks that are identical to that held by the fund. The investor would thereby ensure she eventually earned a riskless profit equal to the discount.

Several reasons have been offered for such closed-end fund discounts. First, closed-end fund members face a tax liability (in the form of capital gains tax) if the fund should sell securities after they have appreciated. This potential tax liability justifies paying a lower price than the market value of the underlying securities. Second, some of the assets in the closed-end fund are less marketable (i.e. trade in 'thin' markets). Third, agency costs in the form of management fees might also explain the discounts. However, Malkiel (1977) found that the discounts were substantially in excess of what could be explained by the above reasons, while Lee, Shleifer and Thaler (1990) find that the discounts on closed-end funds are primarily determined by the stocks of small firms.

There is a further anomaly. At the initial public offering, the closed-end fund shares incur underwriting costs, and the shares in the fund are, therefore, priced at a premium over their true market value. The value of the closed-end fund then generally moves to a discount within six months. The anomaly is why any investors purchase the initial public offering and thereby pay the underwriting costs via the future capital loss. Why do investors not just wait six months before purchasing the fund at the lower price?

Ideas from behavioural finance are consistent with many of these facts. If noise-trader risk is systematic, then it will be 'priced' and, hence, the closed-end fund price will be below NAV (see the DeLong, Shleifer, Summers and Waldmann (1990b) model in the next chapter). At liquidation of the fund, any noise-trader risk will disappear and, hence, price will equal NAV. Initial overpricing of the funds may be due to entrepreneurs creating additional funds when noise traders 'favour' this type of investment. The strong co-movement of the discount across diverse funds (given that the funds' underlying cash flow 'fundamentals' are not highly correlated) may be due to general movements in noise-trader sentiment about all such funds. Bodurtha, Kim and Lee (1993) find that closed-end funds containing German equities but traded in the United States co-move more with the United States than the German stock market, again demonstrating a de-linking of cash flows and value, which tells against the EMH.

Lee, Shleifer and Thaler (1991) also show that closed-end funds and small stocks are both largely held by individual (US) investors and the closed-end fund discount and returns on small stocks are strongly positively correlated, which is suggestive of systematic noise-trader behaviour. More recently, Gemmill and Thomas (2002) run a bivariate VECM where investor flows and the discount are cointegrated (so the two are related in the long run), and this disequilibrium error correction term affects (i.e. Granger causes) 'flows' rather than changes in the discount. The results are from a monthly time series (1991–97) of 158 UK equity funds and provides further evidence of the influence of investor sentiment on the discount – across many different funds.

## Co-Movement in Stock Returns

In the efficient markets approach, co-movement in returns is because of co-movement in cash flows (or in the discount rate), caused by a common factor influencing news about future earnings (e.g. sale of TV rights for Spanish league soccer, causing co-movement in returns of Real Madrid and Barcelona soccer clubs) or the discount rate. However, as we have seen with returns on Royal Dutch and Shell, according to the EMH, these should be perfectly positively correlated, but they are not.

To counter the efficient markets view, Barberis and Shleifer (2003) note that 'noise-trader' investors may have 'preferred habitats' of stocks such as small-cap, banking, and so on, whose cash flows happen to be largely uncorrelated. However, if noise-trader sentiment is systematic, then such 'categories' should exhibit high co-movement of returns, and new stocks included in these categories should begin to move more with that category than before. Barberis, Shleifer and Wurgler (2001) show that this is the case when stocks are added to the S&P500 since their beta with the S&P500 increases, while their beta with stocks *outside* the S&P500 falls. These observed changes seem to have little to do with a change in cash flow co-movement, since inclusion in the S&P500 signifies no information about correlation between cash flows.

## Optimal Diversification?

Assuming mean-variance portfolio theory is the 'correct' method (or model) for investors' portfolio choices, it is found that US and Japanese investors place too great a proportion (usually in excess of 90%) in domestic assets and not enough in foreign assets. Indeed, portfolio choice models that include human capital often imply that investors should *short* domestic stocks because they are highly correlated with their human capital. This is the home-bias problem.

Grinblatt and Keloharju (2001) and Huberman (2001) also find there is a home-bias problem *within* countries, whereby investors place too much of their stock market wealth in firms that are located close to them geographically. Grinblatt and Keloharju (2001) find that Finnish investors hold and trade mainly Finnish stocks, while Huberman (2001) finds that investors hold many more shares in their local Regional Bell Operating Company (RBOC) shares than in out-of-state RBOC shares.

It has been found that 401(K) pension plans have a strong bias towards holding *own-company* stock (Benartzi 2001) even though 'own-company' returns are highly correlated with the individual's own labour income. This became widespread knowledge when it was revealed after the collapse of Enron that a large number of its employees held their defined contribution pension plans mainly in Enron shares and who unfortunately lost substantial amounts of money. Benartzi and Thaler (2001) find that diversification by individuals often follows a simple 1/*n* rule. Individuals allocate 1/*n* of their savings to each investment choice offered and appear to disregard the different effective allocations to stocks and bonds that this entails. An example will clarify this process. When offered a choice between (A) a 'stock plus bond fund' and (B) a 'stock plus balanced fund' (where the latter has 50% stocks and 50% bonds) and (C) a 'bond and balanced fund', they choose a 50:50 split from within each separate fund offered. Applying the 1/*n* rule exactly to choice 'A' gives an *effective* stock-bonds allocation (S, B) = (50%, 50%), for choice 'B' gives (S, B) = (67%, 33%) and for choice 'C' (S, B) = (33%, 67%). When participants are actually offered choices 'A' or 'B' or 'C', they follow the 50:50 rule fairly closely, resulting in an average allocation to stocks for 'A', 'B' and 'C' of 54%, 73% and 35% respectively.

It follows from the 1/*n* rule that in 401(K) funds that predominantly offer stock funds, individuals will end up mechanically allocating more to stocks. Benartzi and Thaler (2001) examine 170 retirement savings plans, which are divided into three groups: 'low', 'medium' and 'high' categories, depending on the *fraction* of funds that are stock funds. For example, if the 1/*n* rule is used, then we expect to see the 'low' category, which contains funds with relatively few stock funds (and a large number of bond funds) to result in an effective allocation to stocks, which is rather low. In the 'low', 'medium' and 'high' categories, they find the actual allocation to stocks is 36%, 65% and 85% respectively, which broadly follows the 1/*n* rule (i.e. the more stock relative to bond funds in your 'plan', the more you end up holding stocks, even though in principle any allocation to stocks is possible).

In terms of 'rational behaviour' with full information, the above is difficult to explain. From psychological experiments, we know that people do not like situations in which they feel they do not know the objective probability distribution of possible outcomes and they may, therefore, feel more 'familiar' with domestic stocks or stocks of the company where they work. This is an example of 'ambiguity aversion' – you avoid situations where you have little confidence in the probability distribution of outcomes.

## Buying and Selling

One direct way of assessing the EMH is to see if 'active' investors do make 'good' investment decisions over repeated trades. Odean (1999) and Barber and Odean (2000) find that the average return of investors (of a large brokerage firm) underperform a set of standard benchmarks. In addition, across all investors, the average *annual* return on stocks that they buy performs worse than those that they sell, and investors are more likely to sell stocks that have risen rather than those that have fallen relative to their initial purchase price. (Whereas the latter should be more prevalent given tax offsets for losses.) Also, those that trade often (i.e. relatively more men than women) earn lower average returns. In short, investors trade too often and are bad stock-pickers – they would be better holding a diversified passive benchmark portfolio. It may be that active stock-pickers and frequent traders are simply overconfident and a cohort of new overconfident people continually enter the market. Their reluctance to sell 'losers' (sometimes called the *disposition effect*) may be because of the fact that they do not like to admit to having made an error. (This can be rationalised in terms of a 'kinked' utility function over gains and losses – see Barberis and Thaler 2003.)

This disposition effect has also been observed in the housing market, where people in a 'bear market' who are selling at a loss relative to their purchase price, set their price about 30% higher than vendors of similar properties who are not selling at a loss (since they purchased some time ago). What is more, the loss-averse sellers actually do obtain higher prices than the other vendors (Genesove and Mayer 2001).

## Investment Styles

There are many investment styles advocated by gurus in the financial press and by investment houses. Two of the most popular styles over the past ten years have been 'value stocks' (also referred to as a 'value-growth' strategy) and a 'momentum strategy' – but how are these defined? A crucial difference between these two strategies lies in the time period over which you decide to form your portfolio and the length of time you hold the portfolio. A 'value-growth' investment scenario buys *long-term* losers ('the dogs') and short-sells *long-term* winners ('the stars') – it is, therefore, a contrarian or reversal strategy and relies for its success on long horizon mean reversion in stock returns (noted in the statistical tests of Chapter 4). The evidence for mean reversion could be based on univariate autoregressions or Fama–French's long horizon returns or variance ratio statistics. Alternatively, mean reversion could be due to long horizon return predictability where the predictor variable itself is mean reverting (e.g. D/P ratio or book-to-market).

## Value-Growth Strategy

DeBondt and Thaler's (1985) 'buy the dogs' strategy, where 'the dogs' are (say) the decile portfolio that have fallen the most over the last four years and then sell after *at least* one year is an example of a 'value strategy' consistent with univariate statistical tests. Jegadeesh and Titman (1993) and Fama and French (1996) also provide similar examples but with different definitions of 'value stocks'. For example, an alternative definition of 'the dogs' are stocks with high book-to-market value (BMV). Of course, if 'the dogs' have high CAPM-betas, this would be fine for the EMH, but unfortunately this is not so. As we have seen, using average (cross-section) returns, Fama and French (1996) find that the average return from 'the dogs' portfolio (and the average returns on the other deciles) can be explained by their relative (high-minus-low) HML-betas (i.e. Fama–French's 'dogs' have high 'HML-betas'). Fama and French (1996) show that going long 'the dogs' and short-selling 'the stars' gives an average *monthly* return of 0.75–1.6%. But 'buying the dogs' can also yield higher Sharpe ratios than holding the market portfolio, although the extra 'bang' per unit of risk varies over different years.

Lakonishok, Shleifer and Vishny (1994) and Ali, Hwang and Trombley (2003) find that short-selling in July of each year, the bottom quintile of US stocks sorted by BMV (after correcting for size) and buying the top quintile (and rebalancing each year), gives average returns of around 8%, 21% and 30% over the subsequent one-, two- and three-year horizons. To implement this strategy, you have to have funds or credit lines to sustain losses and also the ability to short-sell. It remains a risky strategy. One explanation of the book-to-market effect is that it is due to mis-pricing caused by market participants underestimating future earnings for high BMV stocks and overestimating earnings for low BMV stocks (La Porta, Lakonishok, Shleifer and Vishny 1997, Skinner and Sloan 2002). But why do arbitrageurs not move in and exploit this opportunity and eliminate the mis-pricing?

## Risk and Mis-pricing

So, are the predictable 'long horizon' returns from the BMV effect due to the high *ex-ante* risk of the strategy or due to mis-pricing over long horizons? This is a difficult question to answer as it requires an acceptable model of risk and an assessment of transactions costs (which should not be high as this is a 'long horizon' investment strategy). Ali, Hwang and Trombley (2003) seek to throw some light on this question by looking at the cross section of three-year average BMV quintile returns for the United States, with various measures of transactions costs and the risk of the portfolio, over the period 1976–97. (They repeat these annual cross-section regressions every year and use the Fama and MacBeth (1973) procedure to test the statistical significance of the independent variables, with a Newy–West correction for non white noise errors.)

The proxy variables for transactions costs are the average trading volume, the (average) percent bid-ask spread ($=$ (bid $-$ ask)$/0.5$(bid $+$ ask)) and the frequency of zero daily returns (i.e. illiquid stocks). Short-selling costs (i.e. the possibility of a 'short squeeze' if brokers request immediate return of stocks) are picked up by the proportion of common stock held by institutional investors. The less a stock is held by institutional investors, the less likely a short squeeze can be met from alternative lenders of the stocks and the higher the perceived cost of arbitrage. Measures of investor sophistication include the number of analysts covering the stock and the number of institutional owners of the stock.

An explicit variable is used to measure the risk of arbitrage, namely, the variance of the residuals from the market model estimated using daily returns over the previous 250 days. The idea here is that stocks with relatively high specific risk are unlikely to be correctly priced because arbitrageurs generally have poorly diversified portfolios, since they 'follow' only a small number of stocks. Hence, specific risk is important to arbitrageurs since it cannot be hedged (unlike systematic risk), and arbitrageurs with finite horizons are less likely to take positions in stocks with high specific risk and hence remove any pricing 'anomalies' (Shleifer and Vishny 1997). The 'variance variable' is found to be statistically significant (even when all other variables are included in the cross-section regression), indicating some role for 'limited arbitrage'. Put slightly differently, Ali, Hwang and Trombley (2003) find that the 10% of stocks with the greatest return volatility produce a three-year return of 51.3%, for a portfolio long in the highest BMV quintile and short in the lowest BMV quintile. The corresponding return for the lowest volatility decile is only 1.7%, and this pattern appears in 20 of the 22 separate years of the study. Of course, this risky arbitrage explanation cannot be definitive since if the high BMV variable does capture increased risk of financial distress, the latter could be stronger for firms with high volatility of returns.

The composition of any portfolio of 'value stocks' will overlap considerably for most definitions of 'value'. For example, for low price, low P/E ratios, high BMV and low market value ('size'), the set of firms might substantially overlap in each decile (particularly the lowest and highest), since it is mainly 'price' that drives movements in *all* these variables. In other words, the *additional explanatory* power or extra predictability in using one rather than another definition of value may be quite small, although book-to-market does particularly well across a wide range of studies. Of course, within the APT framework, you may be willing to accept that the HML-beta is a valid measure of risk. Hence, the fact that 'buying the dogs' gives higher returns than the market is not a problem, since these stocks have high betas for the BMV 'risk factor'. In other words, the Fama–French three-factor model (i.e. market beta, SMB-beta and HML-beta) explains the cross section of returns sorted on the basis of book-to-market. Indeed, we noted earlier that it is the HML-beta that provides most of the cross-section explanatory power.

What is certain is that trying to 'beat the market' over any return horizon with any strategy seems highly risky. With value stocks, you have to buy firms whose price has been falling for some years, and many of these firms are 'distressed' and close to bankruptcy. At the same time, you have to short-sell stocks that have been increasing in price over several years and are the current paragons of corporate virtue and virility. In addition, you may be 'buying the dogs' in a recession period and you will have to hold your position for between say one and four years and in the intervening period, your position might make losses. This strategy takes a very brave individual and if that individual is employed by an investment bank, he may get fired before the strategy is seen to yield good positive returns (e.g. after the bursting of the 'dot.com bubble' in 2000, some analysts who had sold stock in 1998 or 1999 were vindicated, but by then they had also lost their jobs). Maybe, in such circumstances, there is more *perceived* risk around than is picked up by our *ex-post* measures (i.e. betas), so that, in reality, the excess return to value investing was a just reward for the additional risk taken, not to mention transactions costs and possible high costs associated with short-selling.

## Bull Run

To underscore the possibility of limited arbitrage, ask yourself what you might have done in 1999 after observing the bull run in the United States and United Kingdom from 1995. Suppose your analysis of 'fundamentals' implied the S&P500 was currently overpriced (Shiller 1999). You would need to short the S&P500 and buy a 'similar' correctly priced index (e.g. the 'Russell 2000' of small stocks) and wait. You would have faced fundamental risk if any 'news' about large companies in the S&P500 was not highly correlated with 'news' about small companies. You face noise-trader risk (i.e. the S&P500 could rise even more) and model risk (i.e. are you really sure the S&P500 is overpriced relative to fundamentals?). If you had held your position for six months or even a year, its value may have fallen dramatically. Of course, if you had been able to 'hang on' to 2002–2003, your strategy would have been vindicated, but by that time, you may have had a nervous breakdown or lost your job, or both! Alternatively, you could have taken the bold decision of John Ralfe, the manager of the pension fund of Boots (the UK drug store/chemists) who, by 2001, had moved all funds out of equities into bonds – which *ex-post*, can be viewed as possibly the best 'one-off' market timing 'call' of the last 50 years. (In fact, the move into long-term bonds, including index-linked bonds, may have been more a desire to match the time profile of pension liabilities with the fund's cash flows.)

## Momentum Strategy

Here, the portfolio formation time period is small, usually based on the return over the previous year (or less), and the holding period is also 'short', usually one year. The momentum strategy is to buy short-term 'winners' and sell (short) the short-term 'losers'. You buy the 'top decile' of stocks that have risen the most over the past year and finance your purchases by selling the bottom decile that has risen the least. (This is also called a *relative strength* strategy.) The strategy is repeated each month, and each 'portfolio' is held for the subsequent year. Fama and French (1996) report the average monthly US returns from this momentum strategy of 1.3% p.m. (15.6% p.a.) for the July 1963 to December 1993 period and 0.38% p.m. (4.56% p.a.) over the January 1931 to February 1963 period. Clearly, a successful momentum strategy in beating the market return only occurred in the 1963–93 period, perhaps demonstrating some fragility for this strategy.

Recently, Jegadeesh and Titman (2001) re-examine the momentum strategy, initially cited in their 1993 paper. They use all stocks from the NYSE/AMEX but exclude NAS-DAQ stocks (and stocks priced below $5). At the end of each month, stocks are ranked into decile portfolios on the basis of their returns over the previous six months (i.e. month 5 to month 0) and these portfolios are then equally weighted. Each portfolio is held for six months (i.e. month 1 to month 6) following the ranking month. The ranking based on the 'previous six months' needs a little clarification by way of an example. The December 'winner' portfolio consists of 10% of the stocks with the highest returns over the previous June to November, the previous May to October, and so on, ending with the previous January to June period. These are 'overlapping' portfolios, and the maximum 'look back' time is actually one year. The momentum portfolio is self-financing since the loser portfolio P10 (i.e. lowest returns over the past six months) is short sold and the winner portfolio P1 is purchased. The portfolios are rebalanced every month. The average return of the past winners P1 over 1965–97 is 1.67% p.m. and of the past losers P10 is 0.58% p.m., hence, the winners outperform the losers by 1.09% p.m. (t-stat = 5.65) and this holds over the sub-periods 1965–89 and 1990–97.

To assess the performance of the actual momentum returns relative to their expected return, they undertake a time-series regression of the monthly returns of each of the P1 to P10 decile portfolios on either the excess market return $R_M$ (only) or the Fama–French 'three-factor' returns $R_M$, $R_{SMB}$, $R_{HML}$, which then gives a 'Jensen's alpha'. For the market return factor (only), the alphas are largest for P1 (0.54% p.m.) and smallest for P10 (−0.57 p.m.), and the difference in alphas at 1.1% p.m. ($t = 4.59$) is statistically significant. Similarly, for the Fama–French three-factor model, the difference in alphas is 1.29% p.m. ($t = 7.8$). Hence, the P1–P10 momentum strategy appears to generate statistically significant abnormal returns.

Jegadeesh and Titman (2001) also examine the returns to the momentum portfolios over a 'post-holding period' (i.e. months 13 to 60). The *cumulative* momentum returns for all of the P1 to P10 portfolios peaks at around 12% p.a. after one year (i.e. an average of 1% p.m.) and subsequent returns are nearly always negative, so that cumulative returns after month 60 are only about 1% per annum – this is long horizon mean reversion.

The above result is consistent with the Barberis, Shleifer and Vishny (1998) model of 'conservatism bias' where individual's underweight new information when updating their priors, so prices adjust slowly to new information. Once the information is fully incorporated, stock returns are no longer predictable, so the post-holding period excess returns are zero. The evidence is also consistent with models incorporating 'self-attribution bias' (Daniel, Hirshleifer and Subrahmanyam 1998), where informed traders attribute the *ex-post* short-term 'winners' to superior skill and *ex-post* 'losers' to bad luck. This overconfidence means they purchase more 'winners' and slowly push prices above fundamental value. Rational traders then eventually step in, and the gains of the winner portfolio are eventually reversed. Hong and Stein (1999) in their model to explain short-term momentum and long horizon return reversal, have two groups of investors. Noise traders base their decisions on past returns, while rational traders use 'fundamentals news' about cash flows. But information is transmitted with a delay, so prices initially under-react to news, and this produces momentum returns. The noise traders then observe the momentum returns and push the price of past winners above fundamental value, which eventually leads to price reversals. Each set of agents uses information rationally, but the information flow to the noise traders arrives with a lag, and each type of trader uses separate information sets (i.e. 'news about dividends' and past returns) – we discuss these models in more detail in the next chapter.

Although the data is consistent with these behavioural models, Jegadeesh–Titman note that the *negative* returns in the post-holding period occur mainly in the fourth year after portfolio formation, and this appears to be a rather 'long lag'. Also, most of the return reversal occurs in the month of January while the momentum profits in the six-month holding period all occur *outside* the month of January. This is a peculiar asymmetry.

Overall, the fact that the successful momentum strategy outlined in Jegadeesh and Titman (1993) is found to hold on new data from the 1990–97 period weakens the argument that the original 1993 results are due to data-snooping biases. Whether these profits continued in the 2000–2002 stock market meltdown remains to be seen.

Daniel and Titman (2000) extend the above approach by using a three-way sort of US returns (1963:07–1997:12). All stocks on NYSE, AMEX and NASDAQ are sorted into *quintiles* on the basis of market capitalisation ('size'), book-to-market ('value') and prior one-year returns ('momentum'), which gives 125 ($5 \times 5 \times 5$) portfolios. Each of the 125 portfolios is value weighted and rebalanced once per year. This is an obvious extension of the Fama and French (1993) two-way sort on 'size' and 'value'.

The strategy adopted then involves buying the {high-value, high-momentum} portfolio and selling the {low-value, low-momentum} portfolio, which we denoted as the 'HH–LL' strategy. This 'sorting' produces stunning results of positive returns in 31 out of the 34 years, with an average return of 1.04% p.m. (12.64% p.a.), which is statistically different from zero ($t = 5.66$). The CAPM-market beta of HH–LL is $-0.258$ and Jensen's $\alpha$ is 1.17% p.m. ($t = 6.6$). Hence, the HH–LL portfolio produces significant abnormal returns and provides insurance against the market return.

Also, when the monthly returns $R_{HH-LL}$ are regressed on a mutual fund (excess) return index $R_{MF}$ or on ($R_{MF} - R_M$), the (Jensen) alphas are both positive at around 1.1 (and statistically significant). The former indicates that if the HH–LL portfolio is added to the mutual fund, the Sharpe ratio can be increased, while the latter indicates that adding the HH–LL portfolio would increase expected return without increasing the tracking error of the mutual fund (relative to the market portfolio of all stocks). The increase in the (squared) Sharpe ratio depends on the size of $\alpha_i^2/\sigma_i$ where $\alpha_i$ is the intercept and $\sigma_i$ is the residual standard deviation of the regression of the 'new' excess return $R_i$ on the chosen excess (market) return (Jobson and Korkie 1984). They also show that if the HH–LL portfolio comprises 2% of the mutual fund portfolio, the average Sharpe ratio of this 'augmented' mutual fund portfolio $\{SR_{aug} = (\overline{R}_p - \overline{R}_f)/\sigma(R_p - R_f)\}$ increases from 4 to 12% (i.e. by a factor of 3) – although this may require short positions in some securities in the HH–LL portfolio. Also, the 'Sharpe ratio' for the tracking error $\{SR_{trk} = (\overline{R}_p - \overline{R}_m)/\sigma(R_p - R_m)\}$ increases from 0.12 to 1, indicating a better return-risk performance when a '2% tilt' towards the HH–LL portfolio is added to the mutual fund. Again, it will be interesting to see if this HH–LL strategy continued to be successful in the crash period of 2000–2002.

The momentum strategy is based on the small positive autocorrelations found in short horizon returns that manifest themselves in *monthly* return autoregressions with Rsq $\approx 0.0025$ (1/4%). Cochrane (2001) notes that *individual* stock returns have $\sigma = 40\%$ p.a. and, therefore, the top decile *average* return is $E(R|R > x) = \int_x^\infty r f(r)dr / \int_x^\infty f(r)dr$. From the normal distribution, $\int_x^\infty f(r)dr = 0.10$ implies $x = 1.2816\sigma$. The average return of the top decile therefore works out at $E(R|R > x) = 1.76$ standard deviations above the mean. Taking a mean return of 10% p.a. and $\sigma = 40\%$ p.a. implies that the top and bottom decile portfolios have average annual returns of around 80% and *minus* 60% p.a. He then shows that only a small amount of continuation in momentum will give the 1% monthly return of the above studies. To see this, note that the *monthly* standard deviation of *individual* returns is around $\sigma_{mth} = 40\%/\sqrt{12} = 11.55\%$, and the standard deviation of *predictable* monthly returns is $\sigma(\hat{R}) = \sqrt{Rsq}\sigma_{mth} = \sqrt{0.0025}(11.55\%) = 0.58\%$ p.m. Hence, under normality, the highest decile will earn $1.76 \times 0.58\% \approx 1\%$ p.m. above the mean return of all stocks. Hence, the 'buy-winners, short-losers' momentum strategy should earn about 2% p.m. yet it only earns at best around 1.5% p.m. (see above). Put another way, the highest decile momentum portfolio has typically increased in price by about 80% in the previous year, and the loser portfolio declined by 60%. It, therefore, only takes a small amount of positive autocorrelation for this to result in (say) a 1% *monthly average* return over the *next* year, but that 1% is not exceptional (Cochrane 2001).

## Transactions Costs

On investigating momentum stocks, it is found that the gains primarily come from shorting small illiquid stocks between November and December (i.e. tax loss selling) and transactions costs are therefore likely to be high, which may outweigh the gains noted (Carhart 1997, Moskowitz and Grinblatt 1999). In Jegadeesh and Titman (1993), profits from momentum trading are adjusted for average trading costs because of mean commission rates and market impact effects (Berkowitz, Logue and Noser 1988). But this average does not take account of the cross-section differences in transactions costs (e.g. small stocks have higher transactions costs) and their time variation. The figures used also exclude bid-ask spreads, taxes and short-sale costs. The momentum strategy is trading-intensive, requiring four trades (buy-sell and sell-buy) every six months, so with average abnormal returns (i.e. alpha estimate) over six months of around 6%, this profit could be wiped out if costs per trade exceeded 1.5%.

Lesmond, Schill and Chunsheng (2004) undertake a detailed assessment of the above trading costs (including the fact that not all of the momentum portfolio is 'turned over' every six months) and find that momentum strategies on US stocks do not earn profits after correcting for all transactions costs. They investigate the performance of Jegadeesh and Titman (1993, 2001) and Hong, Lim and Stein (2000), P1 (best performers) and P3 (worst performers) portfolios, using the 30–70 percentile break points. Transactions costs for the P1 (best performers) and P3 (worst performers) portfolios are found to be around 4.5% and 5% respectively (every six months), whereas the average figure used by Jegadeesh and Titman (1993, 2001) was 0.5%. These 'new' transactions costs imply that the average six-month momentum abnormal returns for the P1–P3 strategy of about 6% (per six months) barely cover transactions costs (and returns net of transactions costs are usually not statistically significant). It remains to be seen whether a more detailed look at transactions costs for other documented successful momentum strategies (e.g. in non-US markets, bond markets and other sectors – see Rouwenhorst 1998, Gebhart, Hvidkjaer and Swaminathan 2001, Lewellen 2002) also imply near zero (net) momentum returns.

The empirical anomalies that have been documented certainly cast doubt on the EMH – it may be possible to make supernormal profits because of some predictability in stock returns. However, it must be noted that many of the above anomalies are most prominent amongst small and 'distressed' firms (e.g. January and 'size' effects, 'value-growth' and momentum strategies, discounts on closed-end funds). It may be that *ex-ante* perceived risk is higher than that measured *ex-post*, so these anomalies may not yield excess returns corrected for *perceived* risk. While some anomalies do persist, others disappear (e.g. small-firm effect). Certainly, the anomalies literature has given the EMH a 'bit of a hard time'. If you look hard and are willing to take on substantial risk over repeated gambles (i.e. lose some cash on the way to your financial nirvana), it is possible to find profitable opportunities in the stock market over specific time periods. This may result in excess profits even after correction for risk (and transactions costs), but there still appear to be no blindingly obvious 'free lunches' around. It is difficult to 'beat the market' by stock picking and although my MBA students did not believe this in the bull run of the 1990s, they tend to believe it a little more since 2000.

# 18.5 Corporate Finance

When should managers issue new shares? Under the EMH, there is no advantage in 'market timing' share issues. Market price always equals the present value (PV) of future profits from existing and planned investment projects of the firm. But if there is systematic noise-trader optimism about the PV of possible future investments, this will be reflected in a high share price. Managers should then take advantage of this irrational overpricing and issue new shares at this time. However, managers should not use these funds for fixed investment since the 'true' NPV of new fixed investment projects is zero (in equilibrium). The funds should be invested either in other firms that have positive NPV projects or in cash. Conversely, 'irrationally' undervalued shares should be repurchased by the managers, but again fixed investment should remain unchanged. The above argument can be tempered by real-world considerations, however, since if new funds raised are not used for new investment, the noise traders may try to remove the managers. Also, the managers may invest more in order to empire build rather than maximising shareholder value.

Baker and Wurgler (2000) find evidence that firms with high market-to-book ratios do not use new equity funds to increase investment but to add to cash balances. Also, the share of *new* equity issues (amongst total equity plus new bond-issues) is higher when the stock market is high – reflecting the market timing view. Finally, market-to-book is also a good predictor of new equity issues in a *cross section* of firms. Firms with high market-to-book issue more equity, while those with low market-to-book repurchase their shares.

Over time, if two (otherwise) identical firms (e.g. size, industry, fraction of tangible assets, etc.) have different degrees of noise-trader sentiment so their average market-to-book values are different, then the market timing idea would imply different equity-to-debt ratios (i.e. a different capital structure). Consistent with this, Baker and Wurgler (2002) find that a firm's maximal historic market-to-book ratio is a good predictor of the 'equity to total capital' ratio in a cross section of firms. It is also the case that survey evidence points to a market timing view of equity issues since over 65% of CFOs say they make equity issues on the basis of their view of overvaluation in their share price.

While the above evidence is consistent with the noise-trader idea, it is also broadly consistent with a pecking-order rule for capital structure with *no* irrationality. Suppose managers think a 'high' stock price is due to rational investors marking the price up because of genuine positive NPV investment opportunities. Then if internal funds (and bond finance) are exhausted, the manager will rationally issue more equity when the stock is 'high' – as in the noise-trader case. However, the crucial difference between the two scenarios is that in the rational case, more fixed investment will *definitely* take place, whereas in the noise-trader model (but with rational managers) extra investment will not take place (since NPV < 0) *unless* of course, the managers engage in a 'game' with the noise traders. Hence, there is no clear-cut difference in predictions here, and discrimination between these two stories is likely to be highly problematic and contentious.

## Irrational Managers

Let us relax the assumption that managers are rational but instead assume that they are overconfident about their own abilities. Roll's (1986) 'hubris hypothesis' of takeover activity assumes takeovers have no intrinsic synergy gains but occur because bidders are overconfident and overestimate the synergies available. It follows that the price of the target will rise and that of the bidder will fall by a similar amount. So there will be much takeover activity but no overall synergy gains – there is some evidence to suggest this may be correct (see Demodoran 2000).

Managerial optimism also explains the pecking-order view of financing investment projects. If an optimistic manager thinks the equity market persistently undervalues her firm, then she will use internal funds and debt markets before resorting to equity markets to finance expansion. So, fixed investment should be more closely linked to cash flows rather than say Tobin's Q and there is some evidence for this (e.g. Cuthbertson and Gasparro 1993).

## 18.6   Summary

- Behavioural finance is consistent with the 'no free lunch' proposition but argues that this may not imply 'the price is right'.

- Persistent mis-pricing can occur when there are *no close substitutes* (for a stock), if arbitrageurs are risk averse and fundamental risk is systematic. Alternatively, mis-pricing is possible when there is *no fundamentals risk* as long as arbitrageurs are risk averse, have short horizons and there is systematic noise-trader risk.

- Evidence from psychological studies can be adduced in favour of the behavioural finance approach.

- The anomalies literature has unearthed many potential cases where abnormal profits may be made. In many cases, strategies for beating the market (e.g. weekend and January effects, value-growth and momentum strategies) require the investor to hold risky positions, and it is still much debated whether such profits would survive transactions costs and adjustments for *ex-ante* risks.

- Other anomalies (e.g. ADRs, twin shares, index effect, closed-end funds) seem to persist and involve little risk, so here the empirics give stronger support to the behavioural finance view.

# 19

# BEHAVIOURAL MODELS

## Aims

- Show how rational traders and noise traders interact to give equilibrium prices that diverge from fundamental value and how rational traders may cause excess volatility.

- Examine how short-termism could lead to mispricing.

- Show how investors' misperceptions about either available public or private information about earnings can lead to post-earning announcement drift, momentum and overreaction of stock prices.

- Analyse how noise traders (e.g. momentum traders, style investors) and fundamentals traders interact to produce underreaction followed by overreaction in stock prices and cross-correlations between different classes of stocks.

- Demonstrate how a non-standard utility function incorporating both consumption and 'other variables', in an intertemporal optimising model where investors suffer from loss aversion, can explain the 'stylised facts' of stock returns (such as excess volatility, predictability and the equity premium puzzle).

So far, we have been discussing the implications of noise traders in fairly general terms, and now it is time to examine more formal models. One set of models assumes noise traders and rational traders interact to give equilibrium prices that clear the market. A second broad approach assumes all agents are identical but have non-standard preferences – here, utility depends on the change in wealth as well as the level of consumption, and agents may fear losses more than gains. These models often assume intertemporal utility maximisation as in the 'standard approach'.

# 19.1   Simple Model

Shiller (1989) provides a simple piece of analysis in which stylised empirical results can be explained by the presence of noise traders. The proportionate demand for shares by the smart money is $Q$ and is based (loosely) on the mean-variance model

$$Q_t = (E_t R_{t+1} - \rho)/\theta \tag{1}$$

If $E_t R_{t+1} = \rho$, demand by the smart money equals zero. If $Q_t = 1$, the smart money holds all the outstanding stock, and this requires an expected return $E_t R_{t+1} = \rho + \theta$. Hence, $\theta$ is a kind of risk premium to induce the smart money to hold all the stock.

We now let $(Y_t/P_t)$ equal the *proportion* of stock held by noise traders. In equilibrium, the proportions held by the smart money and the noise traders must sum to unity

$$Q_t + (Y_t/P_t) = 1 \tag{2}$$

substituting (1) in (2)

$$E_t R_{t+1} = \theta[1 - (Y_t/P_t)] + \rho \tag{3}$$

Hence, the expected return as perceived by the smart money depends on what they think is the current and future demand by noise traders: the higher is noise trader demand, the higher are current prices and the lower is the expected return perceived by the smart money. Using (3) and the definition

$$E_t R_{t+1} = E_t[(P_{t+1} + D_{t+1})/P_t - 1] \tag{4}$$

we obtain

$$P_t = \delta E_t(P_{t+1} + D_{t+1} + \theta Y_t) \tag{5}$$

where $\delta = 1/(1 + \rho + \theta)$. Hence, by repeated forward substitution,

$$P_t = \sum_{t=0}^{\infty} \delta^t (E_t D_{t+1} + \theta E_t Y_{t+1}) \tag{6}$$

If the smart money is *rational* and recognises demand by noise traders, then the smart money will calculate that the market clearing price is a weighted average of fundamentals (i.e. $E_t D_{t+1}$) and future noise trader demand $E_t Y_{t+1}$. The weakness of this 'illustrative model' is that noise trader demand is completely exogenous. However, as we see below, we can still draw some useful insights.

If $E_t Y_{t+1}$ and, hence, aggregate noise trader demand is random around zero, then the moving average of $E_t Y_{t+1}$ in (6) will have little influence on $P_t$, which will be governed primarily by fundamentals. Prices will deviate from fundamentals but only randomly. On the other hand, if demand by noise traders is expected to be persistent (i.e. 'large' values of $Y_t$ are expected to be followed by further large values), then small changes in current noise trader demand can have a powerful effect on current price, which might deviate substantially from fundamentals over a considerable period of time.

Shiller (1989) uses the above model to illustrate how tests of market efficiency based on regressions of *returns* on information variables known at time $t$ have low power to reject the EMH when it is false. Suppose dividends (and the discount rate) are constant and hence the EMH (without noise traders) predicts that the stock price is constant. Now suppose that the market is actually driven *entirely* by noise traders. Let noise trader demand be characterised by

$$Y_t = u_{t-1} + u_{t-2} + u_{t-3} + \cdots + u_{t-n} \tag{7}$$

where $u_t$ is white noise. Equation (7) has the property that a unit increase in $u_t$ at time $t$ generates changes in $Y$ in future periods that follow a 'square hump' that dies away after $n$ periods. Using (6), price *changes* $(P_{t+1} - P_t)$ only arise because of *revisions* to expectations about future noise trader demand that are weighted by $\delta, \delta^2, \delta^3$, and so on. Because $0 < \delta < 1$, price changes are heavily dominated by $u_t$ (rather than by past $u_{t-j}$). However, as $u_t$ is random, price changes in this model, which by construction is dominated by noise traders, are nevertheless largely unforecastable.

Shiller generates a $\Delta P_{t+1}$ series using (6) for various values of the persistence in $Y_t$ (given by the lag length $n$) and for alternative values of $\rho$ and $\theta$. The generated data for $\Delta P_{t+1}$ is regressed on the information set consisting only of $P_t$. Under the EMH, we expect the R-squared of this regression to be zero. For $\rho = 0, \theta = 0.2$ and $n = 20$, Shiller finds $R^2 = 0.015$. The low R-squared supports the constant returns EMH, but it results from a model where price changes are *wholly determined* by noise traders. In addition, the price *level* can deviate substantially from fundamentals even though price *changes* are hardly forecastable. He also calculates that if the generated data includes a constant dividend price ratio of 4%, then the 'theoretical R-squared' of a regression of the return $R_{t+1}$ on the dividend price ratio $(D/P)_t$ is 0.079. Hence, empirical evidence that returns are only weakly related to information at time $t$ is not necessarily inconsistent with prices being determined by noise traders (rather than by fundamentals). Overall, Shiller makes an important point about empirical evidence. The evidence using real world data is not that stock returns are unpredictable (as suggested by the EMH) but that stock returns are not *very* predictable. However, the latter evidence is also not inconsistent with possible models in which noise traders play a part.

If the behaviour of $Y_t$ is exogenous (i.e. independent of dividends) but is stationary and mean reverting, then we might expect *returns* to be predictable. An above-average level of $Y$ will eventually be followed by a fall in $Y$ (to its mean long-run level). Hence, prices are mean reverting, and current returns are predictable from previous period's returns.

In addition, this simple noise trader model can explain the positive association between the dividend–price ratio and next period's return on stocks. If dividends vary very little over time, a price rise caused by an increase in $E_t Y_{t+1}$ will produce a fall in the dividend price ratio. If $Y_t$ is mean reverting, then prices will fall *in the future*, so returns $R_{t+1}$ also fall. Hence, $(D/P)_t$ is positively related to returns $R_{t+1}$ as found in empirical studies. Shiller also notes that if noise trader demand $Y_{t+1}$ is influenced either by past returns (i.e. bandwagon effect) or past dividends, then the share price might overreact to current dividends compared to that given by the first term in (6), that is, the fundamentals part of the price response.

# 19.2   Optimising Model of Noise Trader Behaviour

In the 'neat' model of DeLong, Shleifer, Summers and Waldmann (1990b), both smart money and noise traders are risk averse and maximise utility of terminal wealth. There is a finite horizon, so that arbitrage is risky. The (basic) model is constructed so that there is no fundamental risk (i.e. dividends are known with certainty) but only noise trader risk. The noise traders create risk for themselves and the smart money by generating fads in the demand for the risky asset. The smart money forms optimal forecasts of the future price on the basis of the correct distribution of price changes, but noise traders have biased forecasts. The degree of *price misperception* of noise traders $\rho_t$ represents the *difference* between the noise trader forecasts and optimal forecasts

$$\rho_t \sim N(\rho^*, \sigma^2) \tag{8}$$

If $\rho^* = 0$, noise traders' forecasts agree with those of the smart money (on average). If noise traders are on average pessimistic (e.g. bear market), then $\rho^* < 0$, and the stock price will be below fundamental value and vice versa. As well as having this long-run view $\rho^*$ of the divergence of their forecasts from the optimal forecasts, 'news' also arises so there can be *abnormal* but *temporary* variations in optimism and pessimism, given by a term $(\rho_t - \rho^*)$. The specification of $\rho_t$ is ad hoc but does have an intuitive appeal based on introspection and evidence from behavioural/group experiments.

In the DeLong et al model, the *fundamental value* of the stock is a constant and is arbitrarily set at unity. The market consists of two types of asset: a risky asset and a safe asset. Both noise traders and smart money are risk averse and have mean-variance preferences, so their demand for the risky asset depends positively on expected return and inversely on the noise trader risk (see Appendix I). The noise trader demand also depends on whether they feel bullish or bearish about stock prices (i.e. the variable $\rho_t$). The risky asset is in fixed supply (set equal to unity), and the market clears to give an equilibrium price $P_t$. The equation that determines $P_t$ looks rather complicated, but we can break it down into its component parts and give some intuitive feel for what is going on:

$$P_t = 1 + \frac{\mu}{r}\rho^* + \frac{\mu}{(1+r)}[\rho_t - \rho^*] - \frac{2\gamma\mu^2\sigma^2}{r(1+r)^2} \tag{9}$$

where $\mu$ = the proportion of investors who are noise traders, $r$ = the riskless real rate of interest, $\gamma$ = the degree of (absolute) risk aversion, $\sigma^2$ = the variance of noise trader misperceptions. If there are no noise traders, $\mu = 0$ and (9) predicts that market price equals fundamental value (of unity). Now let us suppose that at a particular point in time, noise traders have the same long-run view of the stock price as does the smart money (i.e. $\rho^* = 0$) and that there are no 'surprises' (i.e. no abnormal bullishness or bearishness), so that $(\rho_t - \rho^*) = 0$.

We now have a position in which the noise traders have the same view about future prices as does the smart money. However, the equilibrium market price still *does not solely reflect fundamentals*, and the market price is less than the fundamental price – given by the last term on the RHS of equation (9). This is because of the presence of noise trader risk, since their potential actions may influence future prices. The price is below fundamental value so the smart money (and noise traders) may obtain a positive expected return (i.e. capital gain) as compensation for the noise trader risk. This mispricing is probably the key result of the model and involves a *permanent* deviation of prices from fundamentals. We refer to the effect of the third term in (9) as the amount of 'basic mispricing'.

Turning now to the second term in equation (9), we see, for example, that the noise traders will push the price above fundamental value if they take a *long-term view* that the market is bullish ($\rho^* > 0$). The third term reflects *abnormal* short-term bullishness or bearishness. These terms imply that at particular time periods, the price may be above or below fundamentals.

If $\rho_t - \rho^*$ is random around zero, then the actual price would deviate randomly around its 'basic mispricing' level. In this case, stock prices would be 'excessively volatile' (relative to fundamentals where volatility is zero). From (9), the variance of prices is

$$E_t(P_t - E_t P_t)^2 = \frac{\mu^2 \, \text{var}_t(\rho_t - \rho^*)}{(1+r)^2} = \frac{\mu^2 \sigma^2}{(1+r)^2} \tag{10}$$

Hence, excess volatility is more severe, the greater is the variability in the misperceptions of noise traders $\sigma^2$, the more noise traders there are in the market $\mu$ and the lower is the cost of borrowing funds $r$. To enable the model to reproduce *persistence* in price movements and, hence, the broad bull and bear movements in stock prices that we observe, we need to introduce 'fads' and 'fashions'. Broadly speaking, this implies, for example, that periods of bullishness are followed by further periods of bullishness, which can be represented by a random walk in $\rho_t^*$

$$\rho_t^* = \rho_{t-1}^* + \omega_t \tag{11}$$

where $\omega_t \sim N(0, \sigma_w^2)$. (Note that $\sigma_\omega^2$ is different from $\sigma^2$, in the previous equation.) At any point in time, the investor's optimal forecast of $\rho^*$ is its current value. However, as 'news' $\omega_t$ arrives, noise traders alter their views about $\rho_t^*$, and this 'change in perceptions' persists over future periods. It should be clear from the second term in (9) that the random walk in $\rho_t^*$ implies $P_t$ will move in long swings, and, hence, there will be 'bull and bear' patterns in $P_t$.

Fortune (1991) assumes for illustrative purposes that $\omega_t$ and $(\rho_t - \rho^*)$ are *niid* and uses representative values for $r, \mu, \gamma$, in (9). He then generates a time series for $P_t$ shown in Figure 1. The graph indicates that for this *one* simulation, price falls to 85% of fundamental value (which itself may be rising) with some dramatic rises and falls in the short run.

An additional source of *persistence* in prices could be introduced into the model by assuming that $\sigma^2$ is also autoregressive (e.g. ARCH and GARCH processes). It is also not unreasonable to assume that the 'conversion rate' from being a smart money trader to being a noise trader may well take time and move in cycles. This will make $\mu$ (i.e. the proportion of noise traders) exhibit persistence and, hence, so might $P_t$. It

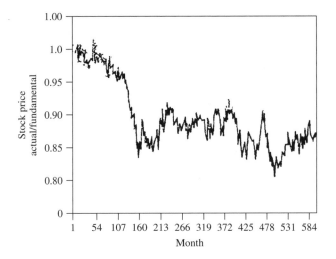

**Figure 1** Simulated 50-year stock price history. Source: Fortune (1991), Fig. 6, p. 34. Reproduced by permission of *The Federal Reserve Bank of Boston*

follows that in this model, prices may differ from fundamentals for substantial periods of time because arbitrage is incomplete. Also, persistence in $\rho_t - \rho^*$ could be mean reverting. This would imply that prices are mean reverting and that *returns* on the stock market are partly predictable from past returns or from variables such as the dividend–price ratio.

## Can Noise Traders Survive?

DeLong et al show that where the proportion of noise traders is fixed in each period (i.e. $\mu$ is constant), it is possible (although not guaranteed) that noise traders do survive, even though they tend to buy high and sell low (and vice versa). This is because they are over-optimistic and underestimate the true riskiness of their portfolio. As a consequence, they tend to 'hold more' of the assets subject to bullish sentiment. In addition, if noise trader risk $\sigma^2$ is large, the smart money will not step in with great vigour to buy underpriced assets because of the risk involved.

The idea of imitation can be included in the model by assuming that the conversion rate from smart money (s) to noise traders (n) depends on the excess returns earned by noise traders over the smart money $(R^n - R^s)$

$$\mu_{t+1} = \mu_t + \psi(R^n - R^s)_t \tag{12}$$

where $\mu$ is bounded between 0 and 1. DeLong et al also introduce fundamental risk into the model. The per period return on the risky asset becomes a random variable, $r + \varepsilon_t$ where $\varepsilon_t \sim N(0, \sigma_\varepsilon^2)$. In this version of the model, the probability of noise trader survival is always greater than zero. This is because of what they call the 'create space' effect, whereby risk is increased to such an extent that it further inhibits risk-averse smart money from arbitraging any potential gains. (The latter result requires $\psi$ to be 'small', since otherwise the newly converted noise traders may influence price, and this would need to be predicted by the 'old' noise traders who retire.)

## Closed-End Funds

We have noted that closed-end funds often tend to sell at a discount and this discount varies over time, usually across *all* funds. Sometimes, such funds sell at a premium. Using our noise trader model, we can get a handle on reasons for these 'anomalies'. Let the risky asset be the closed-end fund itself and the safe asset the actual underlying stocks. The smart money will try to arbitrage between the fund and the underlying stocks (e.g. buy the fund and sell the stocks short, if the fund is at a discount). However, even if $\rho_t = \rho^* = 0$, the fund (risky asset) will sell at a discount because of inherent noise trader risk (see (9)). Changes in noise trader sentiment (i.e. in $\rho^*$ and $\rho_t - \rho^*$) will cause the discounts to vary over time and as noise trader risk is systematic, we expect discounts on most funds to move together.

In the noise trader model, a number of closed-end funds should also tend to be started at the same time, namely when noise trader sentiment for closed-end funds is high (i.e. $\rho^* > 0$, $\rho_t > 0$). When existing closed-end funds are at a premium, it pays the smart money to purchase shares (at a relatively low price), bundle them together into a closed-end fund and sell them at a premium to optimistic noise traders.

## Changes in Bond Prices

Empirically, when the long-short spread $(R - r)$ on bonds is positive, then long rates tend to fall, and the *prices* of long bonds increase. This is the opposite of the pure expectations hypothesis of the term structure. The stylised facts of this anomaly are consistent with our noise trader model, with the long bond being the risky asset (and the short bond the safe asset). When $R_t > r_t$, then the *price* of long bonds as viewed by noise traders may be viewed as abnormally low. If noise trader fads are mean reverting, they will expect bond prices to rise in the future and, hence, long rates $R$ to fall. This is what we observe in the empirical work. Of course, even though the noise trader model explains the stylised facts, this leaves us a long way from a formal test of the noise trader model in the bond market.

Overall, the key feature of the DeLong et al model is to demonstrate the possibility of underpricing in *equilibrium*. The other effects mentioned above depend on one's adherence to the possibility of *changes* in noise trader sentiment, which are persistent. However, 'persistence' is not the outcome of an optimising process in the model, although it is an intuitively appealing one.

## Short-Termism

In a world of only smart money, the fact that some of these investors take a 'short-term' view of returns should not lead to a deviation of price from fundamentals. The argument is based on the implicit forward recursion of the rational valuation formula.

If you buy today at time $t$, in order to sell tomorrow, your return depends (in part) on the expected capital gain and, hence, on the price you can get tomorrow. But the latter depends on what the person you sell to at $t+1$ thinks the price will be at $t+2$, and so on. Hence, a linked chain of short-term 'rational fundamental' investors performs the same calculation as an investor with an infinite horizon.

With a finite investment horizon and the presence of noise traders, the above argument does not hold. True, the longer the horizon of the smart money, the more willing she may be to undertake risky arbitrage based on divergences between price and fundamental value, the reason being that in the meantime, she receives the insurance of dividend payments each period and she has a number of periods over which she can wait for the price to rise to fundamental value. However, even with a 'long' but finite horizon, there is some price resale risk. The share in the total return from dividend payments over a 'long' holding period is large but there is still substantial risk present from uncertainty about price in the 'final period'.

We note from the noise trader model that if a firm can make its equity appear less subject to noise trader sentiment (i.e. to reduce $\sigma^2$), then its underpricing will be less severe and its price will rise. This reduction in uncertainty might be accomplished by:

(a) raising current dividends (rather than investing profits in an uncertain long-term investment project. For example, R&D expenditures)

(b) swapping into debt and out of equity

(c) share buybacks.

Empirical work by Jensen (1986) and many others has shown that items (a)–(c) do tend to lead to an increase in the firm's share price, and this is consistent with our interpretation of the influence of noise traders just described. It follows that in the presence of noise traders, one might expect changes in capital structure to affect the value of the firm (contrary to the Modigliani–Miller hypothesis).

## Destabilising Rational Traders

In the DeLong, Shleifer, Summers and Waldmann (1990b) model in the previous section, the rational traders always move prices back towards fundamentals but not sufficiently to eliminate the mispricing of the 'momentum' noise traders. Suppose we accept the presence of momentum traders who buy (sell) after a price rise (fall). The anecdotal evidence for this is quite strong. Some chartists are known to chase 'trends', while stop-loss orders lead to selling after a price fall, as does forced liquidation of your short position if you face increased margin calls that you cannot meet. Portfolio insurance can also lead to selling (buying) after a price fall (rise). For example, if you have sold (written) a call option (to a customer), then you hedge the position by buying stocks (i.e. delta hedging). If stock prices subsequently fall, the delta of the written call also falls and your new hedge position requires that you sell some of your stocks. (Strictly, portfolio insurance applies to replication of a 'stock plus put' portfolio with a 'stock plus futures' portfolio, but our delta hedge example gives a similar result.) So, portfolio insurance *logically* implies that you sell stocks after a price fall (and buy stocks after a price rise) – see Cuthbertson and Nitzsche (2001b). There is also experimental evidence (Andreassen and Kraus 1990) where economics students, when faced with actual stock price data, tend to sell after a *small* price rise (and vice versa) but buy after a *run* of price rises (i.e. momentum).

DeLong, Shleifer, Summers and Waldmann (1990a) use the analytic framework developed above but now allow the rational traders (who are aware of momentum buying by noise traders) to *anticipate* momentum behaviour. Hence, rational traders also buy after a price rise. The rational traders hope to 'ride the wave' caused by the momentum traders but to sell before price begins to fall back to its fundamental value. The short-run behaviour of arbitrageurs is, therefore, *destabilising* and creates even larger *short-run* positive autocorrelation in returns (after the arrival of new fundamental's news), but returns are mean-reverting over long horizons (i.e. negative autocorrelation).

Space constraints dictate that we cannot develop the model fully here but merely sketch out the salient features. The model has four time periods (0, 1, 2, 3) and three types of trader. Rational traders maximise end-of-period wealth (consumption) and have mean-variance asset demands (i.e. proportional to next period's expected return and inversely related to the variance of returns). Momentum traders' demand depends on the previous period's price *change*, while the 'passive investors' demand for the risky asset depends on last period's price (i.e. a mechanical buy low–sell high strategy). The market clears in each period and there is a noisy signal about fundamentals (i.e. dividends) that influences the demand of the rational traders and, hence, their view of future actions by momentum traders. Good public news at time $t = 1$ about (end-of-period-3) dividends leads to a rise in prices due to the fundamentals traders. In turn, this causes an increase in demand by momentum traders at $t = 2$ and, finally, a fall in prices in period-3, back to their fundamental level. There can be overshooting even if rational traders do not anticipate future increased momentum traders' demand, but the overshooting is exacerbated if rational traders 'jump on the bandwagon'. So, an increase in the *number* of forward-looking rational traders entering the model can increase the 'overshooting'.

The model is consistent with anecdotal evidence about the 'players' in the market. Investment banks have 'insider' information about customer order flow and may use this to anticipate future demands by momentum traders (see Chapter 29 on market microstructure). A stronger variant of this is 'front running', where market makers purchase (sell) on *their own account* before executing the buy (sell) orders given to them by their customers. (This attracted the attention of the New York Attorney General, Eliot Spitzer, in 2003.) In the United States, 'Investment Pools' often generate interest in 'hot-stocks', so as to attract momentum investors. Soros' (1987) investment strategy in the 1960s and 1970s could also be viewed as betting on future crowd behaviour when he took (successful) long horizon bets on stocks involved in conglomerate mergers throughout the 1960 and in Real Estate Investment Trust stocks throughout the 1970s. In September 1992, he also successfully implemented a short horizon strategy of selling the pound sterling, from which he is reputed to have made $1 billion over a few weeks (although whether this was 'chasing trends' or a fundamental misalignment is debatable).

Evidence from survey data on FX forecasting services (Frankel and Froot 1988) indicates that during the mid 1980s the 'inexorable' rise of the USD (with unchanged interest differentials) led forecasters to predict both a rise in the US dollar over one month and a depreciation by the end of the year. Their recommendation to investors was to buy today, *even though they thought the USD was overpriced relative to fundamentals*. The DeLong, Shleifer, Summers and Waldmann (1990a) model demonstrates that this is a perfectly rational statement.

Is it the case that momentum traders are really dumb, should lose money and, hence, be forced out of the market? This criticism can be answered by assuming that additional momentum traders (e.g. using new techniques such as neutral networks and genetic algorithms) enter the market or existing momentum traders return with new backers. (If you read the *Financial Times* or *Wall Street Journal*, you will have noted this occurs quite frequently, although with the recent tougher environment on Wall Street, this may occur less often in the future.) Also, if lots of momentum traders lose money over the same period, they can claim 'everybody did badly', and they may retain their investment mandates. There is evidence to suggest that pension fund mandates are not altered because of absolute losses but because of *worse* losses than your competitors – so some momentum traders may remain in the market. Also, such mandates are decided by a wide variety of factors other than 'return' (e.g. management costs, provision of analysts' research and investment 'style'). The earlier model of DeLong, Shleifer, Summers and Waldmann (1990b) shows that noise traders may carry more market risk than the rational traders, so even if they make judgement errors, they can earn positive returns.

# 19.3  Shleifer–Vishny Model: Short-Termism

The underpricing of an *individual* firm's stock is not a direct result of the formal noise trader model of DeLong et al since this formal model requires noise trader behaviour to be systematic across all stocks. However, the impact of high borrowing costs on the *degree* of mispricing in individual shares has been examined in a formal model by Shleifer and Vishny (1990). They find that current mispricing is most severe for those stocks where mispricing is *revealed* at a date in the distant future (rather than, say, next period). Suppose physical investment projects with uncertain long horizon payoffs are financed with shares whose true value is only revealed to the market after some time. In the Shleifer–Vishny model, these shares will be severely underpriced. It follows that the firm might be less willing to undertake such long horizon, yet profitable projects and short-termism on the part of the firm's managers might ensue. That is, they choose less profitable short-term investment projects rather than long-term projects since this involves less current undervaluation of the share price and less risk of them losing their jobs from a hostile takeover or management reorganisation by the Board of Directors. This is a misallocation of real resources. We begin our description of this model by considering the infinite horizon case where the smart money is indifferent as to *when* the actual price moves to its fundamental value.

## Timing of Arbitrage Profits in a Perfect Capital Market

If the smart money can borrow and lend unlimited amounts, then she does not care how long it takes a mispriced security to move to its fundamental value. In Table 1, we consider a simple case of underpricing where the cost of borrowing, $r$, and the fundamentals return on the security (i.e. dividend return, $q$) are identical at 10%. If the mispriced security moves from \$5 to its fundamental value of \$6 after only one period, the price including the dividend payout is $\$6(1 + q) = \$6.60$ in period-1. At the end of period-1, the arbitrageur has to pay back the loan plus interest, that is $\$5(1 + r) = \$5.50$. If the price only achieves its fundamental value in period-2, the arbitrageur receives $\$6(1 + q)^2 = \$7.26$ at $t + 2$ but has to pay out additional interest charges between $t + 1$ and $t + 2$. However, in *present value terms*, the arbitrageur has an equal gain of \$1 regardless of when the mispricing is irradicated. Also, with a perfect capital market, she can take advantage of any further arbitrage possibilities that arise since she can always borrow more money at any time.

In the case of a *finite horizon*, fundamentals and noise trader risk can lead to losses from arbitrage. If suppliers of funds (e.g. banks) find it difficult to assess the ability of arbitrageurs to pick genuinely underpriced stocks, they may limit the amount of funds to the arbitrageur. Also, they may charge a higher interest rate to the arbitrageur because they have less information on her true performance than she herself does (i.e. the interest charge under asymmetric information is higher than that which would occur under symmetric information).

If $r = 12\%$ in the above example, while the fundamentals return on the stock remains at 10%, then the arbitrageur gains more if the mispricing is eliminated *sooner* rather than *later* (Appendix II). If a strict credit limit is imposed, then there is an additional cost to the arbitrageur, namely that if money is tied up in a long horizon arbitrage position, then she cannot take advantage of other potentially profitable arbitrage opportunities.

An arbitrageur earns more potential dollar profits the more she borrows and takes a position in undervalued stocks. She is, therefore, likely to try and convince (signal to) the suppliers of funds that she really is 'smart' by engaging in repeated short-term arbitrage opportunities since long horizon positions are expensive and risky. Hence, smart money may have an incentive to invest over short horizons rather than eliminating long horizon arbitrage possibilities.

**Table 1**  Arbitrage returns: perfect capital market

**Assumptions:**
Fundamental value = \$6
Current price = \$5
Interest rate, $r$ = 10% per period
Return on risky asset, $q$ = 10% per period (on fundamental value)
Smart money borrows \$5 at 10% and purchases stock at $t = 0$.

|  | Selling Price (including dividends) | Repayment of Loan | Net Gain | DPV of Gain (at r = 10%) |
|---|---|---|---|---|
| Period-1 | $6(1 + q) = \$6.60$ | $5(1 + r) = \$5.50$ | \$1.10 | \$1 |
| Period-2 | $6(1 + q)^2 = \$7.26$ | $5(1 + r)^2 = \$6.05$ | \$1.21 | \$1 |

The formal model of Shleifer and Vishny (1990) has both noise traders and smart money (see Appendix II). Both 'short' and 'long' assets have a payout at the *same time* in the future but the *true value* of the short asset is *revealed* earlier than that for the 'long' asset. In equilibrium, arbitrageurs' rational behaviour results in greater *current* mispricing of 'long assets', where the mispricing is revealed at long horizons. The terms 'long' and 'short', therefore, refer to the date at which the mispricing is revealed (and not to the actual cash payout of the two assets). Both types of asset are mispriced, but the long-term asset suffers from *greater mispricing* than the short asset.

In essence, the model relies on the cost of funds to the arbitrageur being greater than the fundamentals return on the mispriced securities. Hence, the longer the arbitrageur has to *wait* before she can liquidate her position (i.e. sell the underpriced security), the more it costs. The sooner she can realise her capital gain and pay off 'expensive' debts, the better. Hence, it is the 'carrying cost' or per period cost of borrowed funds that is important in the model. The demand for the long-term mispriced asset is lower than that for the short-term mispriced asset and, hence, the *current price* of the long-term mispriced asset is lower than that for the short-term asset.

Investment *projects* that have uncertain payoffs (profits) that accrue in the distant future may be funded with assets whose true fundamental value will not be revealed until the distant future (e.g. the Channel Tunnel between England and France, where passenger revenues were to accrue many years after the finance for the project had been raised). In this model, these assets will be (relatively) strongly undervalued.

The second element of the Shleifer and Vishny (1990) argument that yields adverse outcomes from short-termism concerns the behaviour of the managers of the firm. They conjecture that managers of a firm have an asymmetric weighting of mispricing. *Underpricing* is perceived as being relatively worse than an equal amount of overpricing. This is because either underpricing encourages the Board of Directors to change its managers or managers could be removed after a hostile takeover on the basis of the underpricing. *Overpricing*, on the other hand, gives little benefit to managers who usually do not hold large amounts of stock or whose earnings are not strongly linked to the stock price. Hence, incumbent managers might underinvest in long-term physical investment projects.

A hostile acquirer could abandon the long-term investment project, hence improving short-term cash flow and current dividends, all of which reduce uncertainty and the likely duration of mispricing. She could then sell the acquired firm at a higher price, since the degree of underpricing is reduced when she cancels the long-term project. The above scenario implies that some profitable (in DPV terms) long-term investment projects are sacrificed because of (the rational) short-termism of arbitrageurs, who face 'high' borrowing costs or outright borrowing constraints. This is contrary to the view that hostile takeovers involve the replacement of inefficient (i.e. non-value maximising) managers by more efficient acquirers. Thus, if smart money cannot wait for long-term arbitrage possibilities to unfold, they will support hostile takeovers that reduce the mispricing and allow them to close out their arbitrage position more quickly.

# 19.4 Contagion

Kirman's (1993a) 'cute' model is very different to that of DeLong et al in that it explicitly deals with the interaction between individuals, the rate at which individuals' opinions are altered by recruitment and hence the phenomenon of 'herding' and 'epidemics'. The basic phenomenon of 'herding' was noted by entomologists. It was noted that ants, when 'placed' equidistant from two identical food sources that were constantly replenished, were observed to distribute themselves between each source in an asymmetric fashion. After a time, 80% of the ants ate from one source and 20% from the other. Sometimes a 'flip' occurred, which resulted in the opposite concentrations at the two food sources. The experiment was repeated with one food source and two symmetric bridges leading to the food. Again, initially, 80% of the ants used one bridge and only 20% used the other, whereas intuitively one might have expected that the ants would be split 50–50 between the bridges. One type of recruitment process in an ant colony is 'tandem recruiting', whereby the ant that finds the food returns to the nest and recruits by contact or chemical secretion. Kirman notes that Becker (1991) documents similar herding behaviour when people are faced with very similar restaurants in terms of price, food, service, and so on, on either side of the road. A large majority choose one restaurant rather than the other even though they have to 'wait in line'. Note that here, there may be externalities in being 'part of the crowd', which we assume does not apply to ants.

We have already noted that stock prices may deviate for long periods from fundamental value. A model that explains 'recruitment' and results in a concentration at one source for a considerable time period and then a possibility of a 'flip' clearly has relevance to the observed behaviour of speculative asset prices. Kirman makes the point that although economists (unlike entomologists) tend to prefer models based on optimising behaviour, optimisation is not necessary for survival (e.g. plants survive because they have evolved a system whereby their leaves follow the sun but they might have done much better to develop feet, which would have enabled them to walk into the sunlight). Kirman's model of recruitment has the following assumptions.

(i) There are two views of the world, 'black' and 'white', and each agent holds one (and only one) of them at any one time.

(ii) There are a total of $N$ agents, and the system is defined by the number ($= k$) of agents holding the 'black' view of the world.

(iii) The evolution of the system is determined by individuals who meet at random and there is a probability $(1 - \delta)$ that a person is converted ($\delta$ = probability not converted) from black to white or vice versa. There is also a small probability $\varepsilon$ that an agent changes his 'colour' independently before meeting anyone (e.g. due to exogenous 'news' or the replacement of an existing trader by a new trader with a different view).

(iv) The above probabilities evolve according to a statistical process known as a *Markov chain*, and the probabilities of a conversion from $k$ to $k + 1, k - 1$ or 'no change' is given by

$$k \rightarrow \begin{cases} k+1 & \text{with probability } p_1 = p(k, k+1) \\ \text{no change} & \text{with probability } = 1 - p_1 - p_2 \\ k-1 & \text{with probability } p_2 = p(k, k-1) \end{cases}$$

where

$$p_1 = \left[ \frac{1-k}{N} \right] \left[ \varepsilon + \frac{(1+\delta)k)}{N-1} \right]$$

$$p_2 = \frac{k}{N} \left[ \varepsilon + \frac{(1-\delta)(N-k)}{N-1} \right]$$

In the special case $\varepsilon = \delta = 0$, the first person always gets recruited to the second person's viewpoint, and the dynamic process is a martingale with a final position at $k = 0$ or $k = N$. Also, when the probability of being converted $(1 - \delta)$ is relatively low and the probability of self-conversion $\varepsilon$ is high, then a 50–50 split between the two ensues. Kirman works out what proportion *of time* the system will spend in each state (i.e. the equilibrium distribution). The result is that the smaller the probability of spontaneous conversion $\varepsilon$ relative to the probability of not being converted $\delta$, the more time the system spends at the extremes, that is, 100% of people believing the system is in one or other of the two states. (The required condition is that $\varepsilon < (1 - \delta)/(N - 1)$, see Figure 2.) The *absolute* level of $\delta$, that is, how 'persuasive' individuals are, is not important here but only that $\varepsilon$ is small *relative to* $(1 - \delta)$. Although persuasiveness is independent of the number in each group, a majority once established will tend to persist. Hence, individuals are more likely to be converted to the *majority* opinion of their colleagues in the market, and the latter is the major force in the evolution of the

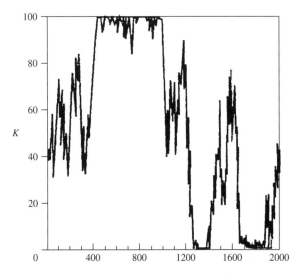

**Figure 2** 100,000 meetings every fiftieth plotted: $\varepsilon = 0.002$, $\delta = 0.8$. Source: A. Kirman (1993a). *The Quarterly Journal of Economics.* ©1993 by the President and Fellows of Harvard College and the Massachusetts Institute of Technology. Reproduced by permission

system (i.e. the probability that any single meeting will result in an increase in the majority view is higher than that for the minority view).

Kirman (1991) uses this type of model to examine the possible behaviour of an asset price such as the exchange rate, which is determined by a *weighted average* of fundamentalists' and noise traders' views. The proportion of each type of trader $w_t$ depends on the above evolutionary process of conversion via the Markov chain process. He simulates the model and finds that the asset price (exchange rate) may exhibit periods of tranquillity followed by bubbles and crashes as in Figure 3. In a later paper, Kirman (1993a) assumes the fundamentals price $p_{ft}$ follows a random walk and hence is non-stationary, while the noise traders forecast by simple extrapolation. The change in the *market* price $\Delta p_{t+1}$ is

$$\Delta p_{t+1} = w_t \Delta p_{f,t+1} + (1 - w_t)\Delta p_{n,t+1} \qquad (13)$$

where the noise trader forecast is extrapolative

$$\Delta p_{n,t+1} = p_t - p_{t-1} \qquad (14a)$$

and the fundamentals forecast

$$\Delta p_{f,t+1} = \upsilon(\overline{p}_t - p_t) \qquad (14b)$$

is an error correction model around the long-run equilibrium $\overline{p}_t$. The weights $w_t$ depend on the parameters governing the rate of conversion of market participants. The weights are endogenous and incorporate Keynes' beauty queen idea. Individuals meet each other and are either converted or not. They then try and assess which opinion is in the majority and base their forecasts on who they think is in the majority, fundamentalists or noise traders. Thus, the agent does not base her forecast on her own beliefs but on

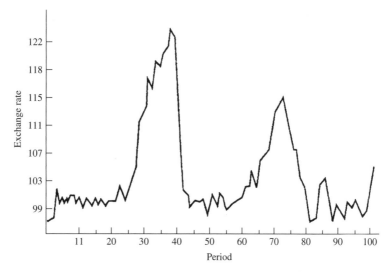

**Figure 3** Simulated exchange rate for 100 periods with $S = 100$. Source: Kirman (1991) in Taylor, M.P. (ed.) money and financial markets, Figure 17.3, p. 364. Reproduced by permission of Blackwell Publishers

what she perceives is the majority view. The model is then simulated and exhibits a pattern that resembles a periodically collapsing bubble. When the noise traders totally dominate, prices are constant, and when the fundamentalists totally dominate, prices follow a random walk. Standard tests for unit roots are then applied (e.g. Dickey and Fuller 1979, Phillips and Perron 1988) and cointegration tests between $p_t$ and $\overline{p}_t$ tend (erroneously) to suggest there are no bubbles present. A modification of the test by Hamilton, which is designed to detect points at which the system switches from one process to another, was only moderately successful. Thus, as in the cases studied by Evans (1991), when a periodically collapsing bubble is present, it is very difficult to detect.

Of course, none of the models discussed in this chapter are able to explain what is a crucial fact, as far as public policy implications are concerned. That is to say, they do not tell us how far away from the fundamental price a portfolio of particular stocks might be. For example, if the deviation from fundamental value is only 5% for a portfolio of stocks, then even though this persists for some time, it may not represent a substantial misallocation of investment funds, given other uncertainties that abound in the economy. Noise trader behaviour may provide an *a priori* case for public policy in the form of trading halts, during specific periods of turbulence or of insisting on higher margin requirements. The presence of noise traders also suggests that hostile takeovers may not always be beneficial for the predators since the actual price they pay for the stock of the target firm may be substantially above its fundamental value. However, establishing a *prima facie* argument for intervention is a long way short of saying that a specific government action in the market is beneficial.

## 19.5  Beliefs and Expectations

Investors might have mistaken beliefs about their forecasts of earnings, and Barberis, Shleifer and Vishby (1998) show how this can produce post-earnings announcement drift, short-run momentum, long-run mean reversion and price–earnings ratios that help forecast future returns. It is a more elaborate model than that of Barsky and DeLong (1993), who simply assume that dividend *growth* is forecast using an IMA(1,1) model (i.e. adaptive expectations), and this implies prices move more than proportionately to changes in current dividends (see Chapter 17).

Systematic errors following announcements of *public* information are made, because investors sometimes think earnings are in a 'mean-reverting' regime and sometimes in a 'trending' regime, when, in fact, earnings follow a random walk. The investor has to work out in what earnings regime she thinks the economy is operating and then determine her investment decisions.

The model assumes risk-neutral investors and a form of 'representativeness', that is, when an investor sees a *small run* of positive earnings, she (erroneously) applies the 'law of small numbers' and forecasts high earnings growth in the future. After all, earnings do not *appear* to be 'average' since investors mistakenly believe this would manifest itself in some periods of bad and good earnings news, even in a short sample.

However, when there is a *single* positive earnings announcement, conservatism dominates, and investors believe earnings will partly fall back to normal (i.e. some mean reversion) and, therefore, prices underreact to positive news. Further positive news will lead to a diminution of 'conservatism', and the law of small numbers will then apply, and there will be post-earnings price drift and momentum. The investor may then believe she is in the trending regime, and the P–E ratio increases above its equilibrium value, given by the random walk model of earnings. Prices are now too high (relative to fundamentals) as the growth in earnings does not materialise (since true earnings follow a random walk). Hence, there is long-term mean reversion in prices, future returns are lower and predictable from the previous high level of the P–E ratio.

## Dispersion of Opinions

The Barberis, Shleifer and Vishny (1998) model deals with misperceptions about public information. What about the assimilation of private information? Suppose individual investors undertake private research on a company and they all hold diverse views, which are known by all. Investors who are bullish will buy the share, while those who are bearish will want to short-sell the stock. If the latter are not allowed to short-sell (e.g. pension funds and most mutual funds), then those stocks that have the greatest diversity of views will have 'greater optimism' reflected in their price (Miller 1977). Therefore, price–earnings ratios will be too high and will result in low subsequent returns, when the sellers finally enter the market. Here, predictability from the P–E ratio does not require systematic bullishness or bearishness (as in DeLong, Shleifer, Summers and Waldmann 1990a), merely dispersion of opinions.

Tests of the above require some measure of dispersion of opinion. Diether, Malloy and Scherbina (2002) uses dispersion of analysts forecasts of current earnings and groups stocks into quintiles on the basis of this measure. Then the high dispersion quintile is followed by subsequently lower average returns than for the low dispersion quintile of stocks. Chen, Hong and Stein (2001) use the fraction of mutual funds that hold a particular stock as a measure of dispersion of opinion and find lower subsequent returns for stocks with high dispersion.

## Overconfidence

What if investors are overconfident about their own *private* information about a firm? If the private information is 'good', then prices will be above fundamentals (earnings) and P–E ratios will be high. Subsequent *public* information will 'reveal' this overpricing and future returns will be low and predictable from the P–E ratio. Daniel, Hirshleifer and Subrahmanyan (1998) combine this overconfidence idea with 'self attribution bias' in order to explain post-earnings announcement drift and momentum effects. The investor treats public information in an asymmetric way. If overconfidence on positive *private* news is then followed by positive *public* news, the investor 'attributes' this to her skill, and she becomes even more overconfident and pushes prices up even further. If positive private news is followed by bad public news, the investor retains her private views for the moment. The net effect is greater overconfidence and momentum. In the Barberis, Shleifer and Vishny (1998) 'mistaken expectations' model and the above 'overconfidence model', most of the correction to stock prices should come when investors find out their private information really is incorrect – that is, at earnings announcement dates. This is consistent with the evidence in Chopra, Lakonishok and Ritter (1992) and La Porta, Lakonishok and Shleifer (1997), who find that certain stock portfolios (e.g. value or growth stocks) earn low average returns on days of the year close to earnings announcements.

## 19.6   Momentum and Newswatchers

An interesting model involving the interaction of heterogeneous agents is that of Hong and Stein (1999). Momentum traders base their investment decisions only on past price changes while 'newswatchers' only observe *private* information which diffuses gradually across the newswatcher population. Both sets of agents are boundedly rational since they do not use all information available. If there are only newswatchers then prices respond monotonically and there is underreaction as news slowly becomes assimilated into prices, but there is no overreaction until we introduce momentum traders. After some good news at time $t$, prices slowly rise due to the increased demand of newswatchers. This leads to increased demand by some momentum traders at $t + 1$, which causes an acceleration in prices and further momentum purchases. Momentum traders make most of their profits early in the 'momentum cycle'. Momentum traders who buy later (at $t + i$ for some $i > 1$) lose money because prices overshoot their long-run equilibrium and, therefore, some momentum traders buy after the peak (i.e. there is a negative externality imposed on the 'late' momentum traders). The dynamics are the outcome of a market clearing equilibrium model, but the bounded rationality assumption (e.g. momentum traders only use univariate forecasts and do not know when the 'news' arrives) is crucial in establishing both short horizon positive autocorrelation and long horizon price reversals (i.e. overshooting).

If we allow the introduction of *fully informed* 'smart money' traders into the model, the above conclusions continue to hold as long as the risk tolerance of the smart money traders is finite. (When the risk tolerance of the smart money is infinite, then prices follow a random walk.)

The model, therefore, yields predictions that are consistent with observed profits from momentum trading (Jegadeesh and Titman 1993, 2001), which may be due to the slow diffusion of initially *private* information. The 'events literature' demonstrates that observed *public* events (e.g. unexpectedly good earnings, new stock issues or repurchases, analysts recommendations) lead to post-event price drift (in the same direction as the initial event) over horizons of 6–12 months. The Hong–Stein model can only generate this price drift if newswatchers after observing *public* news require additional *private* information before they are able to translate public news into views about future valuation. Otherwise, newswatchers would be able to immediately incorporate the public news into prices.

The basic structure of the model is rather complex, and we can only highlight the main features here. The newswatchers purchase a risky asset that pays a single liquidating dividend $D_T$, some time later at $T$, where

$$D_T = D_O + \sum_{j=0}^{T} \varepsilon_j$$

where the $\varepsilon_j$s are $iid(0, \sigma^2)$. So that private information moves slowly through the newswatcher population, we assume there are $z$ groups of newswatchers so that each dividend innovation $\varepsilon_j = \varepsilon_j^1 + \varepsilon_j^2 + \cdots + \varepsilon_j^z$ (with each sub-innovation having a variance of $\sigma^2/z$). As we shall see, if there are $z$ newswatchers, then each dividend innovation at time $t$ takes until time $t + z - 1$ for every newswatcher to have assimilated this news. So private information takes $t + z - 1$ time periods to become fully public. The way this is modelled is as follows. At time $t$, newswatcher group-1 observes $\varepsilon_{t+z-1}^1$, group-2 observes $\varepsilon_{t+z-1}^2$, and so on, so each group observes a fraction $1/z$ of the innovation $\varepsilon_j$. Then at $t+1$, group-1 observes $\varepsilon_{t+z-1}^2$, group-2 observes $\varepsilon_{t+z-1}^3$, and so on, through to group $z$, which now observes $\varepsilon_{t+z-1}^z$. At time $t+1$, each sub-innovation of $\varepsilon_{t+z-1}$ has now been seen by a fraction $2/z$ of newswatchers, and the information has spread further. Hence, $\varepsilon_{t+z-1}$ becomes totally public by time $t + z - 1$, but the diffusion of information is slow (and depends on $z$ the number of newswatchers, which is a proxy for the rate of information flow). On average, all the newswatchers are equally well informed.

Each newswatcher has constant $(= \gamma)$ absolute risk aversion (CARA) utility and at time $t$, their asset demands are based on a static optimisation (i.e. buy and hold until $T$) and, *most importantly*, they do not condition on past prices (they are, therefore, boundedly rational). Without loss, the riskless rate is assumed to be zero, and the newswatchers have an infinite horizon.

Momentum traders also have CARA utility but have *finite* horizons. At each time $t$, a new group of momentum traders enters the market and holds their position until $t + j$. Momentum traders base their demand on predictions of $P_{t+j} - P_t$ and make forecasts on the basis of $\Delta P_{t-1}$ only (i.e. univariate forecast). If momentum traders are allowed to forecast prices on the basis of a distributed lag of past prices (with different weights on each lag), then the results from the model would not go through – this is the bounded rationality assumption again. The order flow demand $F_t$ from generation $t$ momentum traders is

$$F_t = A + \phi \Delta P_{t-1}$$

There are $j$ momentum traders at $t$, and their demand is assumed to be absorbed by the newswatchers (who act as market makers). So if $Q =$ fixed supply of risky assets, then the newswatchers must absorb $S_t$, where

$$S_t = Q - \sum_{i=1}^{j} F_{t+1-i} = Q - jA - \sum_{i=1}^{j} \phi \Delta P_{t-i}$$

It can then be shown that equilibrium prices (which clear the market) are given by

$$P_t = [D_t + \{(z - 1)\varepsilon_{t+1} + (z - 2)\varepsilon_{t+2} + \ldots \varepsilon_{t+z-1}\}/z] - Q + jA + \sum_{i=1}^{j} \phi \Delta P_{t-i}$$

where $\phi$ in equilibrium can be shown to depend on the coefficient of risk tolerance $1/\gamma$ of the momentum traders. The term in square brackets indicates that prices are autocorrelated. The model is solved numerically, and sensitivity analysis provides the following qualitative results.

(i) Overshooting is greatest for the holding period horizon $j = 12$ months, where the overshooting is around 34%.

(ii) As risk tolerance increases, momentum traders respond more aggressively to past price changes, equilibrium $\phi$ increases, and there is greater overshooting.

(iii) As the information diffusion parameter $z$ increases (so that private news travels 'slower'), then momentum traders are more aggressive (i.e. $\phi$ increases) and their profits higher, as short-run continuation is more pronounced. Also overshooting increases, leading to larger negative autocorrelations in the reversal phase

The result in (i) is consistent with the findings of Jegadeesh and Titman (1993, 2001), where momentum profits occur up to horizons of around 12 months. The last result (iii) provides a further test of the model, providing we can isolate stocks where information diffusion is likely to be relatively slow. Hong, Lim and Stein (2000) use 'firm size' and 'analysts' (residual) coverage' (i.e. coverage after correcting for firm size) as proxies for slow information dissemination. They find that six-month momentum profits decline with market cap and with increased analysts' coverage. Also, in low analyst coverage stocks, momentum profits persist for horizons of about two years as opposed to less than one year in high coverage stocks.

The above model gets one a long way with a minimum of assumptions, but there are some limitations of the model. The newswatchers are time inconsistent in that they decide their asset demands in a static framework at $t$, but they then change their demands as they absorb the demands of the momentum traders. The newswatchers are not allowed to participate in 'frontrunning'. If newswatchers were to condition their demand on past prices, then they would know that good news would lead to increased momentum demand and they would buy more aggressively at time $t$ to benefit from the forecast momentum demand. This would mitigate any underreaction (but it would not entirely eliminate it).

The model has underreaction to private news but this does not necessarily imply underreaction to public news (e.g. earnings announcements) found in the data. However, if the assimilation of this public news takes time as private agents undertake their respective calculations of its implications for prices, then the model can deliver post-event drift. Of course, if momentum traders are allowed to observe this public news, they may trade more quickly, in which case there may be no eventual over-reaction to public news and, hence, no price reversals. However, it should be noted that representative agent models cannot yield predictions of the type (i)–(iii) above as they only condition on public news that is immediately available.

## 19.7   Style Investing

In the previous chapter, we noted the prevalence of 'style investing'. Casual empiricism suggests that many mutual funds are based on styles (e.g. value-growth, momentum, small cap, tech stocks, real estate, etc.). It may be the case that investors allocate their wealth across a limited number of styles and are not particularly concerned about the allocation to *individual* stocks within any given style category. Certainly, there are economies of monitoring and transactions cost to style investing, compared to building a portfolio on the basis of the analysis of *individual* stocks (Bernstein 1995, Swensen 2000). We have already encountered models that rely on the interaction of momentum traders and some form of rational traders or arbitrageurs as in DeLong, Shleifer, Summers and Waldmann (1990a) and Hong and Stein (1999), where the demands for stocks by momentum (noise) traders depend on their *absolute past* performance. Barberis and Shleifer (2003), in their model of style investing, assume that momentum investors' demand for stocks of a particular style $X$ depend on past returns on $X$ *relative to* past returns on the alternative style $Y$ (e.g. $X = $ old economy stocks, $Y = $ new economy stocks). Hence, momentum investors move into stocks in style-$X$ and out of style-$Y$, if past returns on $X$ exceed those on $Y$. This increases the returns on assets in style-$X$ and decreases the returns on assets in style-$Y$. There is negative autocorrelation across asset returns in the two different styles, at short lags. But $Y$ eventually rises back towards its fundamental value and, hence, at long lags, the autocorrelation between $\Delta P_{x,t}$ and $\Delta P_{y,t-k}$ (for large $k$) will be positive.

There are arbitrageurs or fundamental traders in the model whose demand depends on their estimate of expected returns based on fundamentals (i.e. final dividends). The arbitrageurs also act as market makers for the 'switchers', absorbing their changing demands. The model delivers a market clearing price for all assets but because the fundamental traders are boundedly rational and do not know the time-series properties of the change in demand of the switchers, the market clearing price differs from that when there are only fundamentals traders.

From this description, one can see that the broad set-up of the equilibrium model has features in common with Hong and Stein (1999), but the different behavioural assumptions of the switchers and fundamental traders does lead to some different predictions. Before we examine the latter, we briefly present the main elements of the model, and we derive the equilibrium market price for assets in style-$X$ and style-$Y$.

There are $2n(= 100, \text{say})$ risky assets in fixed supply (and the risk-free asset has infinitely elastic supply and a zero return). Each risky asset is a claim to a single liquidating dividend to be paid at a future time

$$D_{i,T} = D_{i,0} + \varepsilon_{i,1} + \varepsilon_{i,2} + \ldots + \varepsilon_{i,T}$$

where $\varepsilon_{it}$ are announced at time $t$ and $\varepsilon_t = (\varepsilon_{1,t}, \varepsilon_{2,t} \ldots \varepsilon_{2n,t})' \sim N\left(0, \sum_D\right)$ and *iid* over time. There are two styles $X$ and $Y$ with assets 1 to $n$ in style-$X$ and $n + 1$ through $2n$ in style-$Y$. The return (= price change) to style-$X$ is

$$\Delta P_{x,t} = P_{x,t} - P_{x,t-1} \quad \text{where} \quad P_{x,t} = n^{-1} \sum_{i \in X} P_{i,t}$$

Each asset's shock $\varepsilon_{it}$ depends on a market factor ($= m$, common to both styles), one style factor ($s = $ either $X$ or $Y$) and an idiosyncratic cash flow shock, specific to a single asset $i$.

Each of these factors has a unit variance and is orthogonal to the other factors so that

$$
\sum_{D}^{ij} = \text{cov}(\varepsilon_{it}, \varepsilon_{jt}) = \begin{cases} 1 & i = j \\ \psi_m^2 + \psi_s^2 & i, j \quad \text{in the same style } i \neq j \\ \psi_m^2 & i, j \qquad \text{in different styles} \end{cases}
$$

The demand by switchers depends on the relative past performance of the two styles. For assets $i$ in style-$X$, the number of shares demanded is

$$
N_{i,t}^S = \frac{1}{n} \sum_{k=1}^{t-1} \theta^{k-1} \left( \frac{\Delta P_{x,t-k} - \Delta P_{y,t-k}}{2} \right) = \frac{N_{x,t}^S}{n}
$$

with $0 < \theta < 1$ giving declining weights on past relative performance. Symmetrically, for assets $j$ in style-$Y$

$$
N_{j,t}^S = \frac{1}{n} \sum_{k=1}^{t-1} \theta^{k-1} \left( \frac{\Delta P_{y,t-k} - \Delta P_{x,t-k}}{2} \right) = \frac{N_{y,t}^S}{n}
$$

The above assumes that style investors move their demand from one style to another (e.g. value to growth stocks) within the same asset class (i.e. stocks) and do not move funds out of other asset classes (e.g. cash, bonds, FX) when they wish to switch styles. This may be largely true of institutional investors who have fairly constant 'strategic' asset allocations across alternative asset classes. Also, transactions costs might imply that a favoured style is financed from sales of one (or a few) badly performing 'style' rather than many. There may also be 'rules of thumb' that result in natural *twin styles* (e.g. value versus growth), so when one style is doing well, the 'twin style' nearly always does badly.

The fundamental traders maximise expected end-of-period utility of wealth using a CARA utility function. Hence, when returns are normally distributed, optimal asset demands are linear in expected returns.

$$
N_t^F = (1/\gamma)(V_t^F)^{-1}[E_t^F(P_{t+1}) - P_t]
$$

where $V_t^F \equiv \text{var}_t^F(P_{t+1} - P_t)$, $N_t^F = (N_1, N_2, \dots N_{2n})'$, $P_t = (P_1, P_2 \dots P_{2n})'$ and $\gamma$ is the degree of absolute risk aversion. If the fixed supply of the $2n$ assets is given by the vector $Q = N_t^F + N_t^S$, then substituting $N_t^F = Q - N_t^S$ in the above equation gives

$$
P_t = E_t^F(P_{t+1}) - \gamma V_t^F(Q - N_t^S)
$$

Iterating forward and noting that $E_{T-1}^F P_T = E_{T-1}^F(D_T) = D_{T-1}$, then

$$
P_t = D_t - \gamma V_t^F(Q - N_t^S) - E_t^F \sum_{k=1}^{T-t-1} \gamma V_{t+k}^F(Q - N_{t+k}^S)
$$

where $D_t = (D_{1,t}, \ldots, D_{2n,t})'$. The covariance matrix $V^F$ is assumed to be time-invariant ($= V$) and has the same structure as the cash flow covariance matrix $\sum_D$. The term $E_t^F(N_{t+k}^S)$ is assumed to be constant so that fundamental traders are boundedly rational and do not calculate the time-series properties of $N_{t+k}^S$ but merely absorb some of the demands by the switchers. Dropping all the non-stochastic terms gives

$$P_t = D_t + \gamma V N_t^S$$

with the price of asset $i$ in style-$X$

$$P_{it} = D_{it} + \left(\frac{\psi}{n}\right) \sum_{k=1}^{t-1} \theta^{k-1} \left(\frac{\Delta P_{x,t-k} - \Delta P_{y,t-k}}{2}\right)$$

where $\psi$ depends directly on $\gamma$ and on the parameters of the covariance structure of $\sum_D = V$. The price of asset $j$ in style-$Y$ is the same form as the above equation but with the sign on $(\Delta P_x - \Delta P_y)$ reversed (i.e. symmetry). With only fundamental traders $P_t = D_t$ but with switchers, price deviates from fundamentals, and the deviation is persistent if $\theta$ is close to 1.

The model is calibrated with $\psi_m = 0.25$, $\psi_s = 0.5$, $\theta = 0.95$ and $\lambda = 0.093$ (so that equilibrium return volatility broadly matches US data) and, in turn, this gives $\phi = (\psi/n)^{-1} = 1.25$. They take $n = 50$ so there are 50 assets in each style ($X$ and $Y$) and $D_{io} = 50$ for all $i$.

## Predictions and Co-Movement

First, consider the co-movement of style returns. If there is a one-time cash flow shock to style-$X$ (i.e. $\varepsilon_{i,1} = 1$, $\varepsilon_{i,t} = 0$ for $t > 1$, $\forall i \in X$), then $P_x$ follows a long damped oscillation around its (new higher) fundamental value, with $P_x$ initially overshooting its long-run equilibrium and then slowly mean reverting. This positive autocorrelation at short horizons and negative autocorrelation at long lags is also predicted by other momentum models (e.g. Hong and Stein 1999, DeLong, Shleifer, Summers and Waldmann 1990a). The reason for this is straightforward. Good news about cash flows in assets of style-$X$ lead to price rises, which stimulate the demand of switchers, pushing prices above fundamental value. A new 'feature' of this style approach is that the prices of assets in style-$Y$ initially fall as they are sold to help finance purchases of assets in style-$X$ (i.e. symmetry effect). This makes style-$Y$ look even worse *relative to* style-$X$ returns, so there is increased momentum sales of style-$Y$ assets and, hence, $Y$'s prices also overshoot. Note that the price of $Y$ moves without any cash flow news about the stocks in $Y$ and the autocorrelation *across styles* is negative at short horizons. Eventually, fundamental traders sell the overpriced stocks in style-$X$ and price moves to its long-run fundamental level. Bad news about stocks in style-$X$ or good news about style-$Y$ would accelerate this process.

So, style-$X$ imposes a negative externality on assets in style-$Y$, the magnitude of which depends on how investors finance purchases in $X$. If they sell small amounts from many other different style portfolios, then the externality will be less than if they just sell from the single *twin-style* assets in $Y$.

It follows from the above analysis that if (say) only *one* asset in style-$X$ experiences a one-time positive cash flow, then the price of other assets in style-$X$ will also experience increases (unrelated to cash flows), while stocks in style-$Y$ will again experience a fall in price (again unrelated to cash flows). In the Hong and Stein (1999) and DeLong, Shleifer, Summers and Waldmann (1990a) models, good news about asset $i (i \in X)$ only affects the price of asset $i$ and not the prices of other assets in the *same* style $(i \in X)$, nor assets belonging to style-$Y$. The predictions of these models differ in this respect.

The above results are consistent with the success of investing in small caps between 1979 (Banz 1981) and around 1983, after which returns on small caps were poor. Data snooping could also set off changes in returns unrelated to cash flow news, while the poor returns on some styles (e.g. value stocks in the US in 1998 and 1999), even though cash flows were good (Chan, Karceski and Lakonishok 2000), may have been due to an increased demand for stocks viewed as being in *alternative* styles (e.g. large growth stocks).

Investors move into *all* securities in a particular style category, if the past style return has been relatively good. Hence, there may be positive co-movement in individual asset returns within a particular style category, which is unrelated to common sources of cash flows. This is consistent with the co-movement in prices of closed-end funds, even when their net asset values are only weakly correlated (Lee, Shleifer and Thaler 1991) – this would not be predicted by DeLong, Shleifer, Summers and Waldmann (1990a) and Hong and Stein (2003) where *individual* asset returns are driven by underlying cash flows, nor in certain learning models (Veronesi 1999, Lewellen and Shanken 2002). Of course, other models are capable of explaining some co-movement that is unrelated to cash flows. For example, in Kyle and Xiong (2001), after banks suffer trading losses, they may sell stocks to restore their capital base. This is consistent with the financial crisis of 1998 where aggregate stock prices in different countries fell simultaneously (even though different countries had different economic fundamentals), but it is not a strong candidate to explain co-movement in sub-categories of stocks (e.g. small caps).

According to the fundamentals approach, prices of Royal Dutch and Shell, which are claims to the same cash flow stream, should move very closely together. But Froot and Dabora (1999) show that Royal Dutch moves closely with the US market, while Shell moves mainly with the UK market. Royal Dutch is traded mostly in the United States and Shell mostly in London and, hence, they may 'belong to' these two 'styles'. Similarly, if a stock is added to the S&P500 index (i.e. 'a style'), then in the future, one might expect it to co-vary more with the S&P500 and its correlation with stocks outside the S&P500 to fall (Barberis Shleifer and Wurgler 2001).

Finally, Barberis and Shleifer show that a momentum strategy based on style, that is, buy into styles that have good recent performance, should offer Sharpe ratios that are at least as good as momentum strategies based on the momentum performance of *individual* assets. This is consistent with the momentum strategies based on industry portfolios (Moskowitz and Grinblatt 1999) and on size-sorted and book-to-market sorted momentum portfolios (Lewellen 2002).

Even when more sophisticated arbitrageurs are introduced into the model so they understand the time-variation in the momentum traders' demands $N_t^S$, this does not necessarily reduce the size and persistence in the mispricing. This arises because as in the model of DeLong, Shleifer, Summers and Waldmann (1990a), the arbitrageurs do not sell when the price is above fundamental value – they *buy*, knowing that the increasing demand by feedback traders will raise the price even further, after which the arbitrageurs exit at a profit. In other words, the arbitrageurs mimic the behaviour of the momentum traders after a price rise (or fall).

The style model we have discussed above provides an analytic framework in which boundedly rational arbitrageurs and momentum style investors inter-react and gives new predictions compared to models based purely on momentum in *individual* stocks.

# 19.8  Prospect Theory

Prospect theory is a descriptive model of decisions under risk, based on the psychological experiments of Kahneman and Tversky (1979). They noted that individuals take gambles that violate the axioms of expected utility theory. Their experiments indicate that individuals are concerned about *changes* in wealth (rather than the absolute level of wealth) and they are much more sensitive to losses than to gains – known as *loss aversion*. Note, however, that although prospect theory moves away from the standard expected utility function that just depends on consumption, there are many other alternative objective functions one could use, which do not invoke expected utility. These include disappointment aversion (Gul 1991), maximising the minimum expected utility when using alternative distributions for returns (Gilboa and Schmeidler 1989, Camerer and Weber 1992), using weighted utility (Chew 1989) or rank-dependent utility (Segal 1989) and using robust rules (Anderson, Hansen and Sargent 2000).

In the models below, which incorporate the prospect theory approach, there are no exogenous noise traders interacting with the smart money. Instead, it is a fully optimising approach, but agents have a non-standard utility function: lifetime utility depends not only on consumption but also on recent gains and losses on risky assets (i.e. the change in stock market wealth). This is the 'narrow framing' assumption since gains and losses on other assets are ignored and even though investors have long horizons, they are worried by *annual* gains and losses. There is experimental evidence to back up the idea that losses influence people's asset allocation. Thaler, Tversky, Kahneman and Schwartz (1997) show stock and bond returns (generated from two normal distributions calibrated, to mimic actual returns) to three groups of investors; the first is shown monthly observations, the second, annual observations and the third group, returns only over (non-overlapping) five-year periods. At the end of each of their respective horizons, they are asked to allocate their funds between stocks and bonds and told whether they made gains or losses. After 200 months worth of observations, each group is asked to make a final allocation, which is to apply over the next 400 months (i.e. about 33 years). Subjects who were given monthly observations would have observed more losses than those shown annual or five-year returns, and they find that this group allocates proportionately less of their funds to stocks in the final allocation.

In a one-period model, Benartzi and Thaler (1995) show that loss aversion can produce a high equity premium but in their *intertemporal* model Barberis, Ming and Tano (2001) find that they need an additional effect, a form of integral control that they refer to as *prior losses* (Thaler and Johnson 1990). The idea is very straightforward and intuitively plausible, namely that if you have suffered losses over *several* previous periods (i.e. cumulatively), then a loss in the current period will be relatively more painful so that your risk aversion increases. The converse also applies, so that after a series of gains (e.g. in a casino), individuals become more willing to gamble, since they are now 'playing with the house money' – that is, the casino's money, not their 'own'. Barberis, Ming and Tano (2001) show that loss aversion plus 'prior losses' can explain the stylised facts of a high equity premium and high volatility of stock returns, the low level and volatility of interest rates and the predictability in stock returns (e.g. a low price–dividend ratio leads to higher future returns).

Clearly, the idea of time-varying risk aversion is similar to that in the Campbell–Cochrane habit persistence model, but it is cumulative changes in wealth rather than cumulative levels of past consumption that lead to changing risk aversion. As we shall see, Barberis et al use the calibration approach and show that with 'reasonable' parameter values, the model yields time-series behaviour for stock returns and the interest rate that are consistent with the stylised facts.

Empirical evidence indicates a tendency for investors to sell winning rather than losing stocks (Shefrin and Statman 1985, Odean 1998), and this is broadly consistent with prior loss and loss aversion, although these studies assume utility gains, and losses only occur when they are *realised* via a sale of stock. In Barberis et al, utility gains and losses occur even when gains and losses are not realised.

## The Model

There are two assets, a risk-free rate in zero net supply paying a gross rate of $R_{f,t}^*$ and a risky asset paying $R_{t+1}^*$ (between $t$ and $t+1$). The risky asset has a total supply of one unit and is a claim on a dividend sequence $\{D_t\}$. There is a continuum of infinitely lived agents, each endowed with one unit of the risky asset at $t = 0$, which they hold at all times. In 'Economy I', agents consume the dividend stream (Lucas 1978), and aggregate consumption $C_t$ equals aggregate dividends $D_t$, which, therefore, have the same stochastic process (i.e. *iid* lognormal)

$$c_{t+1} - c_t = g_c + \sigma_c \varepsilon_{t+1} \qquad \varepsilon_{t+1} \sim niid(0, 1) \qquad (15)$$

In 'Economy II', consumption and dividends are separate stochastic processes that are still *individually iid* but with different means and standard deviation and non-zero correlation between their respective errors – see below.

Utility is a power function of consumption, with an additional function $v(.)$ reflecting the dollar gain or loss $X_{t+1}$ experienced between $t$ and $t+1$.

$$U = E_t \left[ \sum_{t=0}^{\infty} \theta^t \frac{C_t^{1-\gamma}}{1 - \gamma} + b_t \theta^{t+1} v(X_{t+1}, z_t) \right] \qquad (16)$$

where $\gamma > 0$ is the coefficient of relative risk aversion over consumption, $v(X_{t+1}, z_t)$ is the utility from gains and losses and $z_t$ represents prior gains or losses. If there are no prior gains or losses, $z_t = 1$ (which is further explained below). The term $b_t$ is an exogenous scaling factor. An annual horizon is chosen. If $S_t = \$100$ is the reference level, then

$$X_{t+1} = S_t(R^*_{t+1} - R^*_{f,t}) \tag{17}$$

so for $R^*_{t+1} = 1.20$ and $R^*_f = 1.05$, then $X_{t+1} = \$15$. The Kahneman and Tversky (1979) loss aversion utility function chosen is a piecewise linear function

$$v(X_{t+1}, z_t = 1) = \begin{cases} X_{t+1} & X_{t+1} \geq 0 \\ \lambda X_{t+1} & X_{t+1} < 0 \end{cases} \tag{18}$$

where $\lambda > 1$ to reflect loss aversion and here there are no prior gains or losses. This utility function is consistent with the experimentally observed risk aversion for small wealth bets. The usual smooth utility functions (e.g. power) calibrated to match individuals' risk aversion over small bets lead to absurd results over larger gambles. For example, Rabin (2000) shows that an expected utility maximiser who turns down a 50:50 bet of losing \$100 or gaining \$110 will also turn down a 50:50 bet of losing \$1000 and gaining *any* (including an infinite) amount of money. Loss aversion avoids this 'Rabin paradox'.

In Barberis et al, it is the expected utility of $v(X_{t+1})$ that is important, and they assume equal subjective probabilities of gains and losses (rather than Kahneman and Tversky's (1979) non-linear transformation of these probabilities). From (17) and (18), utility depends on returns

$$v(X_{t+1}, z_t = 1) = v[S_t(R^*_{t+1} - R^*_{f,t})] = S_t \hat{v}(R^*_{t+1}) \tag{19}$$

where

$$\hat{v}(R^*_{t+1}, z_t = 1) = \begin{cases} R^*_{t+1} - R^*_{f,t} & for \quad R^*_{t+1} \geq R^*_{f,t} \\ \lambda(R^*_{t+1} - R^*_{f,t}) & R^*_{t+1} < R^*_{f,t} \end{cases} \tag{20}$$

The scaling term $b_t$ in (16) is required so that as wealth $S_t$ increases over time, it does not dominate the utility function. We can use either *aggregate* consumption or wealth as the scaling factor, and Barberis et al choose the former (which is exogenous to the individual investor).

$$b_t = b_0 \overline{C}_t^{-\gamma} \quad b_0 > 0 \tag{21}$$

For $b_0 = 0$, utility in (16) reverts to the familiar power function over consumption only, while the larger is $b_0$, the greater the weight given to utility from wealth changes (i.e. returns) rather than to consumption.

## Prior Outcomes

The idea that risk aversion is lower (higher) after a sequence of gains (losses) comes from responses to survey questions (Thaler and Johnson 1990) such as the following.

1. You have just won \$30. Choose between:
   (a) a 50% chance to gain \$9 and a 50% chance to lose \$9 [8%]

   (b) no further gain or loss [1%]

2. You have just lost $30. Choose between:
   (a) a 50% chance to gain $9 and a 50% chance to lose $9 [3%]

   (b) No further gain or loss [6%]

The percentage of respondents choosing each option is shown in parenthesis and, therefore, you are much less willing to gamble after you have lost $30.

Gertner (1993) also shows that this 'playing with the house money' effect also works for larger bets, where the participants in a TV game show have to place bets on whether the next card drawn at random will be higher or lower than the card currently showing. Linville and Fisher, using survey evidence, find that people prefer unpleasant events to occur far apart rather than close together and they also prefer a 'bad' followed by a 'pleasant' event to occur close together so one cushions the other.

To implement the descriptive notion of prior outcomes, we require a *historic benchmark level* $Z_t$ for the risky asset and then $S_t - Z_t$ measures how much you are 'up' or 'down'. When $S_t > Z_t$, the investor becomes less risk averse than usual. The state variable measuring prior outcomes is $z_t = Z_t/S_t$, and a value of $z_t < 1$ represents substantial prior gains and, hence, less risk aversion. Utility is determined by $X_{t+1}$ and $z_t$, so we now have $v(X_{t+1}, z_t)$. The functional form for $v(X_{t+1}, z_t)$ is simple but ingenious and incorporates (a) utility loss depends on the size of *prior* gains or losses and (b) prior gains are penalised less (in utility terms) than prior losses. We set $R_f^* = 1$ for simplicity (see Barberis, Ming and Tano 2001 for the case of $R_f^* \neq 1$) and we split returns into two parts, relative to a benchmark level.

Suppose we begin with a benchmark level of $Z_t = \$90$ and $S_t = \$100$, so $z_t = 0.9$ and we have prior gains. If stock prices fall in $t+1$ to $S_t R_{t+1}^* = \$80$, we do not penalise all of the loss of $20 by $\lambda = 2.0$, say. The loss from $100 to the benchmark $Z_t = \$90$ is only penalised with a weight of 1 and the loss below the benchmark (i.e. from $90 to $S_{t+1} = \$80$) is penalised at $\lambda = 2.0$. Hence, the overall disutility of the $20 loss is

$$\text{Change in utility} = (90 - 100)(1) + (80 - 90)2.0 = -30 \tag{22}$$

$$\text{Change in utility} = (Z_t - S_t)(1) + (S_t R_{t+1}^* - Z_t)\lambda = S_t(z_t - 1)(1) + S_t(R_{t+1}^* - z_t)\lambda \tag{23}$$

If losses are small enough, $S_t R_{t+1}^* > Z_t$ or, equivalently, $R_{t+1}^* > z_t$, then the entire loss is only penalised at the lower rate of 1. Consider the impact on utility in two cases: prior losses and prior gains.

### Case A: prior gains: $z_t \leq 1$

$$v(X_{t+1}, z_t) = \begin{cases} S_t(R_{t+1}^* - 1) & R_{t+1}^* \geq z_t \\ S_t(z_t - 1) + \lambda S_t(R_{t+1}^* - z_t) & R_{t+1}^* < z_t \end{cases} \tag{24}$$

Hence, if $S_t = \$100$, $Z_t = \$90$ and $S_t R_{t+1}^* = \$90$, then $R_{t+1}^* = z_t = 0.9$ and current returns of $R_{t+1}^* - 1 = -10\%$ just offset the historic prior gains of 10% and receive a utility loss weight of 1. But if $S_t R_{t+1}^* = \$80$, then $R_{t+1}^* = 0.8 < z_t = 0.9$, and the current loss of 20% implies the value of $S_t R_{t+1}^* = \$80$ is below its historic reference level of $Z_t = \$90$, and the 'pain' in terms of utility loss is greater (i.e. $\lambda$ comes into play in (24)).

### Case B: prior losses $z_t > 1$

A similar scenario applies when we begin from a situation of prior losses, except we assume that any further loss inflicts even greater pain so that here we make $\lambda$ an increasing function of prior losses

$$\lambda(z_t) = \lambda + k(z_t - 1) \quad \text{for } z_t > 1 \text{ and } k > 0 \tag{25}$$

and

$$v(X_{t+1}, z_t) = \begin{cases} X_{t+1} & X_{t+1} \geq 0 \\ \lambda(z_t) X_{t+1} & X_{t+1} < 0 \end{cases} \tag{26}$$

Let $\lambda = 2$ and suppose $k$ is set at 10. Let $Z_t = \$110$ and $S_t = \$100$, which implies prior losses of $\$10$ and $z_t = 1.1$. So when $z_t$ increases from 1.0 to 1.1 (i.e. higher prior losses), the pain of *additional* losses is now penalised at $\lambda(z_t) = 2.0 + 10(0.1) = 3$ rather than $\lambda = 2.0$. The only further 'realistic' requirement is that $z_t$ should move sluggishly relative to $S_t$ so that when $S_t$ rises (falls), $Z_t$ rises (falls) *but by less than* $S_t$.

$$z_{t+1} = \eta \left( z_t \frac{R}{R_{t+1}^*} \right) + (1 - \eta) \quad 1 > \eta > 0 \tag{27}$$

where $R = $ constant and $\eta$ measures the degree of sluggishness. Now $\eta$ can be varied, so that $\eta = 0$ implies $z_{t+1} = 1$ so that $Z_t$ tracks $S_t$ one-for-one, while $\eta = 1$ implies $z_{t+1}$ responds sluggishly. For $\eta \neq 1$, when $R_{t+1}^* > R$, then $z_{t+1}$ falls relative to $z_t$.

### Optimisation

The intertemporal optimisation problem is

$$\max E_t \left\{ \sum_{t=0}^{\infty} \left[ \theta^t \left( \frac{C_t^{1-\gamma}}{1-\gamma} \right) + b_0 \theta^{t+1} \overline{C}_t^{-\gamma} v(X_{t+1}, z_t) \right] \right\} \tag{28}$$

where $X_{t+1} = S_t(R_{t+1}^* - R_{f,t}^*)$ and the 'wealth' constraint (with no labour income) is

$$W_{t+1} = (W_t - C_t) R_{f,t}^* + S_t(R_{t+1}^* - R_{f,t}^*) \tag{29}$$

The model is calibrated and then simulated to see if it produces the stylised facts in the real world data, with particular reference to the equity premium puzzle. Some of the parameters are chosen using historic average values, some based on behavioural studies, while others are chosen to 'match' certain properties found of the data. The 'base-line' solution is obtained numerically, using consumption growth $g_c = 1.84\%$ p.a. with $\sigma_c = 3.79\%$, risk aversion (over consumption) $\gamma = 1.0$ and the time preference rate $\theta = 0.98$. These parameters ensure that the equilibrium risk-free rate $R_f^* - 1 = 3.86$

(see (31)) equals that found in the data and, hence, ensures there is no 'risk-free rate puzzle'.

A range of values for $k$ are used, with increasing values of $k$ indicating the increased pain of a loss when it follows earlier losses. For example, $k = 3$ allows average loss aversion to remain around 2.25. Suppose $z_t$ is initially equal to one and the stock market falls by 10%. Then, with $\eta = 1$, for example, $z_t$ moves to 1.1, and any additional losses are penalised at $2.25 + 3(0.1) = 2.55$ – only a slight increase in 'pain' (see (25)). But with the pain of a loss $k = 50$, the above implies that if the stock market falls by 10%, then (with $\eta = 1$) any additional losses are penalised with a weight of $2.25 + 5 = 7.25$. As we see below, increasing $k$ tends to increase the simulated equity premium and bring it closer to that observed in the data. The constant $R$ is set at a level to ensure the unconditional mean of $z_t = 1$. Simulation results are given for various values of $b_0$, since we have no priors on the likely value for this parameter.

The loss aversion parameter $\lambda$ is taken to be 2.25. The parameter $\eta$ controls the persistence in $z_t$ and, hence, the persistence in the price–dividend ratio: $\eta = 0.9$ (i.e. sluggish response) is chosen so that the simulated price–dividend ratio has autocorrelation properties close to that found in the data.

The numerical solution procedure is complex and uses an iterative technique since the state variable $z_{t+1}$ is a function of both the dividend–price ratio and $\varepsilon_{t+1}$ and is of the form $z_{t+1} = h(z_t, \varepsilon_{t+1})$. Using Monte Carlo simulation, 10,000 draws of $\varepsilon_{t+1}$ give a series for $z_{t+1}$, which in turn can be used to simulate returns and the dividend–price ratio.

### Results: 'Economy I'

When dividends have exactly the same stochastic process as consumption, results on the average equity premium and its volatility are not very impressive. For $b_0 = 2, k = 3$, the simulated equity premium is 0.88% p.a. (s.d. = 5.17% p.a.), while in the real data, these are 6.03% p.a. (s.d. = 20.02). Even when $b_0$ is increased to 100 (giving the prior loss part of the utility function more weight) and $k$ to 50 (i.e. higher loss aversion for any given prior losses), the simulated mean equity premium only rises to 3.28% p.a. (s.d. = 9.35).

### Results: 'Economy II'

We now turn to 'Economy II' where dividends follow

$$d_{t+1} - d_t = g_d + \sigma_d \varepsilon_{t+1} \quad \text{with } g_d = 1.84\% \text{p.a. and } \sigma_d = 12\% \text{p.a.}$$

and the correlation between shocks to consumption and dividend growth is taken to be 0.15. The model-generated 'statistics of interest' are shown in Table 2 along with their empirical counterparts.

For $b_0 = 2, k = 3$, the model generates an equity premium of 2.62% p.a. (s.d. = 20.87), which is better than for 'Economy I' but still less than the empirically observed 6.03% p.a. (s.d. = 20.02). If we increase the pain due to prior losses so that $b_0 = 2$

**Table 2** Model-generated statistics and empirical values Economy II (Barberis, Ming and Tano 2001)

| | Model Values | | Empirical Values |
|---|---|---|---|
| | $b_0 = 2$ $k = 3$ | $b_0 = 2$ $k = 10$ | |
| **Excess Stock Return (Equity Premium)** | | | |
| Mean | 2.62 | 5.02 | 6.03 |
| Standard deviation | 20.87 | 23.84 | 20.02 |
| Sharpe ratio | 0.13 | 0.21 | 0.30 |
| Average loss aversion | 2.25 | 3.5 | – |
| **Price–Dividend Ratio** | | | |
| Mean | 22.1 | 14.6 | 25.5 |
| Std. Dev. | 2.25 | 2.5 | 7.1 |
| **Return Autocorrelations** | | | |
| Lag-1 | −0.07 | −0.12 | 0.07 |
| -2 | −0.03 | −0.09 | −0.17 |
| -3 | −0.04 | −0.06 | −0.05 |
| -4 | −0.04 | −0.04 | −0.11 |
| -5 | −0.02 | −0.03 | −0.04 |
| **Corr $\{(P/D)\}_t$, $(P/D)_{t-k}$** | | | |
| $k = 1$ | 0.81 | 0.72 | 0.70 |
| $k = 3$ | 0.53 | 0.38 | 0.45 |
| $k = 5$ | 0.35 | 0.20 | 0.40 |
| **Regression** | | | |
| $R_{t,t+k} = \alpha_k + \beta_k (D/S)_t$ | | | |
| $\beta_1$ | 4.6(2%) | 4.4(6%) | 4.2(7%) |
| $\beta_2$ | 8.3(4%) | 7.5(10%) | 8.7(16%) |
| $\beta_3$ | 11.6(5%) | 9.7(12%) | 12.3(22%) |
| $\beta_4$ | 13.7(6%) | 11.5(14%) | 15.9(30%) |
| (%) =% R-squared of regression | | | |

but now $k = 10$, the model delivers an equity premium of 5.02% p.a. (s.d. = 23.84) much closer to that in the real data but accompanied by only a modest increase in the average level of loss aversion from 2.25 to 3.5.

The solution for the stock return can be written

$$R_{t+1} = \frac{1 + f(z_{t+1})}{f(z_t)} e^{g_d + \sigma_d \varepsilon_{t+1}}$$

so allowing a separate process for dividends with $\sigma_d = 12\%$ (whereas $\sigma_c = 3.79\%$) provides the extra volatility in stock returns. Intuitively, the higher volatility arises because if there is a positive dividend innovation, this leads to higher stock prices and a higher return. But this increases prior gains so the investor is less risk averse, which lowers the rate at which future dividends are discounted, thus leading to even higher prices and greater movement (volatility) in returns. (The reverse applies for a negative dividend innovation, with the added 'kicker' if there are prior losses.) Since returns are more volatile on average and the investor experiences more losses, the loss aversion requires a higher equity premium. Note that without the assumption of prior outcomes (i.e. set $z_t$ to zero), the model with $b_0 = 2$ generates a very small equity premium of around 2% (s.d. = 12%), and this only rises to 2.88% (s.d. = 12%) for $b_0 = 100$.

The model uses as one input a low correlation of innovations in dividends and consumption growth of 0.15 – close to that in the actual data of around 0.1. The model then generates a low correlation between consumption and *stock returns*. This is because returns respond to dividend news and any change in risk aversion due to changes in returns. In the model, both of the latter are largely driven by shocks to dividends that have a low correlation with consumption – hence, returns and consumption are only weakly correlated in the model (and in the real world data). This low correlation between consumption growth and stock returns is not present in the Campbell and Cochrane (2000) habit persistence model where changes in risk aversion and, hence, returns, are driven by consumption, implying a high correlation between these variables.

Long horizon predictability also arises from the slowly changing degree of risk aversion, due to the sluggish response to prior gains or losses (see Table 2). A positive dividend innovation leads to rising prices, hence lower risk aversion and even higher prices. The price–dividend ratio will now be high. The investor is now less risk averse and, therefore, subsequent desired returns will be lower. Hence, the price–dividend ratio helps predict future returns, which is consistent with the empirical work of Campbell and Shiller (1988). Hence, investor's risk aversion changes over time because of prior losses or gains, so expected returns also vary over time in the model, which leads to predictability. The price–dividend ratio in the model is also highly persistent and autocorrelated (Table 2).

The model also produces negatively autocorrelated returns since high prices (returns) lead to lower risk aversion and, hence, lower returns in the future (Table 2). Negatively autocorrelated returns imply long horizon mean reversion (e.g. Poterba and Summers 1988, Fama and French 1988a, Cochrane 2001 – as noted in earlier chapters).

What about the risk-free rate? In this model, the risk-free rate is decoupled from the prospect theory portion of the utility function and is given by the standard Euler equation

$$1 = \theta R_{\mathrm{f}}^* E_t [(\overline{C}_{t+1}/\overline{C}_t)^{-\gamma}] \tag{30}$$

where $\overline{C}_t$ is aggregate consumption and in equilibrium

$$\ln R_{\mathrm{f}}^* = -\ln \theta + \gamma g_{\mathrm{c}} - (\gamma^2/2)\sigma_{\mathrm{c}}^2 \tag{31}$$

The mean of the risk-free rate and its volatility are primarily determined by $(\gamma g_{\mathrm{c}})$ and the volatility of consumption growth, where $g_{\mathrm{c}} = 1.84\%$ and $\sigma_{\mathrm{c}} = 3.79\%$. Hence, the model implies a low value for the mean of the risk-free rate, with relatively low volatility. Although the Euler equation for $R_{\mathrm{f}}$ is decoupled from the prospect theory utility function, it is the latter that allows more volatility in the return on the risky asset. The Euler equation is

$$1 = \theta E_t [R_{t+1}^* (\overline{C}_{t+1}/\overline{C}_t)^{-\gamma}] + b_0 \theta E_t [\hat{v}(R_{t+1}^*, z_t)] \tag{32}$$

and the average return on the risky asset depends on changes in wealth relative to prior losses, as well as the 'standard' *aggregate* consumption growth term.

Note in Table 2 that the model explains the average price–dividend ratio but not its volatility, which has a standard deviation of 2.25–2.5% in the model but 7.1% in the data. Additional state variables (e.g. consumption relative to habit) would increase the volatility of the models' price–dividend ratio, but this is left for further work.

Is it the loss aversion parameter $\lambda$ or the prior loss parameter $z_t$ that generates the key results in 'Economy II'? The solution for returns (given $z_t = 0$) is

$$R^*_{t+1} = \frac{P_{t+1} + D_{t+1}}{P_t} = \frac{1 + f_{t+1}}{f_t} e^{g_\mathrm{d} + \sigma_\mathrm{d} \varepsilon_{t+1}}$$

where $f_t$ is the dividend–price ratio, which does not now depend on $z_t$. The volatility in $R_{t+1}$ now depends only on the volatility of log dividend growth $\sigma_\mathrm{d}$ of 12%, which is not sufficient to match the data. Hence, prior losses are needed in the utility function, in order to change the degree of loss aversion and, hence, move expected returns more than cash flows by allowing changes in the discount rate. So the key factor in this model is that returns must move more than cash flows. Note, however, that changes in loss aversion are not the only possible reason for this result. One could also have changing perceptions of risk or 'overreaction' to dividend news or perhaps, learning about some key parameters in the model (e.g. the mean rate or volatility of dividend growth) – these are issues for future research.

The basic conceptual ideas behind this prospect theory model are rather similar (but not identical) to those in the Campbell–Cochrane (2000) habit persistence model. Both models require utility to depend on a state variable relative to its recent past. For Campbell–Cochrane, this is excess consumption $S_t = (C_t - X_t)/X_t$, and changing risk aversion is most sensitive when $C_t$ is close to $X_t$ (i.e. close to habit consumption). In Barberis et al, it is current stock returns relative to recent prior gains or losses (i.e. the $z_t$ variable) that is important. In both models, the variables $S_t$ and $z_t$ are assumed to be sluggish, since some 'sluggishness' is required to 'fit' the observed persistence in the dividend–price ratio, which gives rise to long horizon predictability.

In both models, risk aversion changes over time, depending on their respective state variables. Campbell–Cochrane use only consumption (relative to habit) in the utility function, while Barberis et al have utility depending on consumption and (prior) returns (i.e. changes in wealth). The Barberis et al model has a low value for $\gamma = 1.0$, but you need the additional (prior) loss aversion term in the maximand to fit the stylised facts found in the data. The Campbell–Cochrane model requires a high degree of risk aversion (which depends on consumption relative to habit), but the utility function is 'more conventional' and parsimonious. Broadly speaking, since these are calibration models and both broadly mimic the stylised facts, which model you favour depends in part on how realistic you find the assumptions of each model. But that takes us outside the realms of positive economics. These are both interesting models and maybe they can be usefully extended to include other elements such as learning behaviour and even the addition of some non-rational traders.

The reader should be aware that there are now a plethora of behavioural models incorporating, for example, systematic forecasting errors for earnings using public information (Barberis, Shleifer and Vishny 1998), initial overconfidence about one's forecasts based on private information, which is tempered by the arrival of public information (Daniel, Hirshleifer and Subrahmanyan 1998) as well as the models described above. A key debate is how 'unifying' these models are, since their assumptions are often tailored to explain a particular phenomenon (e.g. underreaction followed by price reversals) to the exclusion of other phenomena (e.g. covariation). On the other hand, standard intertemporal expected utility maximisation models are also 'amended' to more closely explain particular 'anomalies' (e.g. the equity premium puzzle). The debate is also clouded by the different techniques used to test the models (e.g. standard hypothesis tests on parameters versus calibration and simulation). An excellent overview of these issues can be found in Barberis and Thaler (2003).

# 19.9   Summary

- There has been an explosion in the behavioural finance literature in recent years, resulting in a wide variety of models that attempt to explain observed anomalies (e.g. closed-end fund discounts, momentum profits) and the 'stylised facts' (e.g. equity premium, predictability in stock returns). The explicit models are usually not tested by using regression techniques and formal hypothesis tests but by some form of calibration and simulation.

- Some behavioural models amend the standard utility function to include variables other than consumption, for example changes in wealth due to stock market fluctuations, and where investors may suffer from 'loss aversion'.

- Other behavioural models concentrate on the interaction between rational or smart money traders and noise traders who (often) are assumed to base investment decisions on past price movements. The timing of private and public information on future cash flows between 'newswatchers' and momentum traders is often crucial in producing short-term momentum profits and long-term price reversals and, hence, predictability. Cross correlations amongst stock returns (whose cash flows are not correlated) can be rationalised in a model of *style investing*.

- The DeLong et al model has rational agents and noise traders maximising expected end-of-period wealth, but the noise traders can be irrationally optimistic or pessimistic about future returns. This noise trader risk implies that equilibrium price can be permanently below the fundamentals price (even when the noise traders have the same expectations as the rational traders).

- The Shleifer–Vishny model highlights the interaction between the costs of borrowing (to purchase shares) and the time information about a firm's future prospects is revealed. Mispricing is greater, the longer the time it takes to reveal to the market the success of the firm's investment decisions. This might encourage short-termism by managers in their choice of investment project.

- Some noise trader models such a Kirman (1993a) rely on contagion and conversion of opinion to generate rapid and large price movements, which are broadly consistent with the observed data.

- Prospect theory assumes individuals care about gains and losses, as well as the level of consumption and investors suffer from loss aversion. In Barberis, Ming and Tano (2001), individuals maximise lifetime utility from consumption and changes in wealth. The model is then calibrated (from observed consumption and dividend data) and simulated. The predictions of the model 'fit' a number of stylised facts, which include a low level and volatility in the risk-free rate, long horizon predictability of stock returns and a relatively high equity premium (but lower than that observed in the real data).

- There has been tremendous progress in producing a wide variety of 'behavioural models', which will continue to influence our views of the underlying causes of observed phenomena such as excess volatility, the equity risk premium, stock return predictability and the anomalies literature.

# Appendix I: The DeLong et al Model of Noise Traders

The basic model of DeLong, Shleifer, Summers and Waldmann (1990b) is a two-period overlapping generations model. There are no first-period consumption or labour supply decisions: the resources agents have to invest are, therefore, exogenous. The only decision is to choose a portfolio in the first period (i.e. when young) to maximise the expected utility of end-of-period wealth. The 'old' then sell their risky assets to the 'new young' cohort and use the receipts from the safe asset to purchase the consumption good. The safe asset '$s$' is in perfectly elastic supply. The supply of the uncertain/risky asset is fixed and normalised at unity. Both assets pay a known real dividend $r$ ($=$ riskless rate) so there is no fundamental risk. One unit of the safe asset buys one unit of the consumption good and, hence, the real price of the safe asset is unity.

The proportion of noise traders NT is $\mu$, with $(1 - \mu)$ smart money SM operators in the market. The SM correctly perceives the distribution of returns on the risky asset at $t+1$. NT can be 'bullish' or 'bearish' and misperceive the true price distribution. The NT *average misperception* of the expected price is denoted $\rho^*$ and at any point in time, the actual misperception $\rho_t$ is

$$\rho_t \sim N(\rho^*, \sigma^2) \tag{A1}$$

Each agent maximises a constant absolute risk aversion utility function in end-of-period wealth, $W$

$$U = -\exp(-2\gamma W) \tag{A2}$$

If returns on the risky asset are normally distributed, then maximising (A2) is equivalent to maximising

$$EW - \gamma \sigma_w^2 \tag{A3}$$

where $EW =$ expected final wealth, $\gamma =$ coefficient of absolute risk aversion. The SM, therefore, chooses the amount of the risky asset to hold, $\lambda_t^s$, by maximising

$$E(U) = c_0 + \lambda_t^s[r + {}_tP_{t+1}^e - P_t(1+r)] - \gamma(\lambda_t^s)^2 {}_t\sigma_{pt+1}^2 \tag{A4}$$

where $c_0$ is a constant and ${}_t\sigma^2_{\mathrm{p}t+1}$ is the one period ahead conditional expected variance of price

$$
{}_t\sigma^2_{\mathrm{p}t+1} = E_t(P_{t+1} - E_t P_{t+1})^2 \tag{A5}
$$

The NT have the same objective function as the SM but her expected return has an additional term $\lambda^n_t \rho_t$ (and, of course, $\lambda^n_t$ replaces $\lambda^s_t$ in (A4)). These objective functions are of the same form as those found in a simple two-asset, mean-variance model (where one asset is a safe asset). Setting $\partial E(U)/\partial \lambda_t = 0$ in (A4), gives the familiar mean-variance asset demand functions for the risky asset for the SM and the NTs

$$
\lambda^s_t = E_t R_{t+1}/2\gamma({}_t\sigma^2_{\mathrm{p}t+1}) \tag{A6}
$$

$$
\lambda^n_t = \frac{E_t R_{t+1}}{2\gamma({}_t\sigma^2_{\mathrm{p}t+1})} + \frac{\rho_t}{2\gamma({}_t\sigma^2_{\mathrm{p}t+1})} \tag{A7}
$$

where $E_t R_{t+1} = r + {}_t P^e_{t+1} - (1+r)P_t$. The demand by NTs depends in part on their abnormal view of expected returns as reflected in $\rho_t$. Since the 'old' sell their risky assets to the young and the fixed supply of risky assets is 1, we have

$$
(1-\mu)\lambda^s_t + \mu\lambda^n_t = 1 \tag{A8}
$$

Hence, using (A6) and (A7), the equilibrium pricing equation is

$$
P_t = \frac{1}{(1+r)}(r + {}_t P_{t+1} - 2\gamma_t \sigma^2_{\mathrm{p}t+1} + \mu\rho_t) \tag{A9}
$$

The equilibrium in the model is a steady state where the unconditional distribution of $P_{t+1}$ equals that for $P_t$. Hence, solving (A9) recursively,

$$
P_t = 1 + \frac{\mu(\rho_t - \rho^*)}{(1+r)} + \frac{\mu\rho^*}{r} - \frac{2\gamma_t\sigma^2_{\mathrm{p}t+1}}{r} \tag{A10}
$$

Only $\rho_t$ is a variable in (A10), hence

$$
{}_t\sigma^2_{\mathrm{p}t+1} = \sigma^2_{\mathrm{p}t+1} = \mu^2\sigma^2/(1+r)^2 \tag{A11}
$$

where from (A1), $\rho_t - \rho^* = N(0, \sigma^2)$. Substituting (A11) in (A10), we obtain the equation for the price level given in the text

$$
P_t = 1 + \frac{\mu(\rho_t - \rho^*)}{(1+r)} + \frac{\mu\rho^*}{r} - \frac{2\gamma\mu^2\sigma^2}{r(1+r)^2} \tag{A12}
$$

# Appendix II: The Shleifer–Vishny Model of Short-Termism

This appendix formally sets out the Shleifer and Vishny (1990) model whereby long-term assets are subject to greater mispricing than short-term assets. As explained in the text, this may lead managers of firms to pursue investment projects with short horizon cash flows in order to avoid severe mispricing and the risk of a takeover.

There are three periods 0, 1, 2, and firms can invest either in a 'short-term' investment project with a \$ payout of $V_s$ in period-2 or a 'long-term' project also with a payout only in period-2 of $V_g$. The key distinction between the projects is that the true value of the short-term project becomes known in period-1, but the true value of the long-term project does not become known until period-2. Thus arbitrageurs are concerned not with the timing of the cash flows from the project but with the timing of the mispricing and in particular, the point at which such mispricing is revealed. The riskless interest rate is zero, and all investors are risk neutral.

There are two types of trader, noise traders NT and smart money SM (arbitrageurs). Noise traders can either be pessimistic ($S_i > 0$) or optimistic at time $t = 0$ about the payoffs $V_i$ from both types of project ($i = $ s or g). Hence, both projects suffer from systematic optimism or pessimism. We deal only with the pessimistic case (i.e. 'bearish' or pessimistic views by NTs). The demand by noise traders for the equity of a firm engaged in project $i$ ($= $ s or g) is

$$q(NT, i) = (V_i - S_i)/P_i \qquad (A1)$$

For the bullishness case, $q$ would equal $(V_i + S_i)/P_i$. Smart money (arbitrageurs) face a borrowing constraint of \$b at a gross interest rate $R > 1$ (i.e. greater than one plus the riskless rate). The SM traders are risk neutral so they are indifferent between investing all \$b in either of the assets $i$. Their demand curve is

$$q(SM, i) = n_i b/P_i \qquad (A2)$$

where $n_i = $ number of SM traders who invest in asset $i$ ($= $ s or g). There is a unit supply of each asset $i$ so equilibrium is given by

$$1 = q(SM, i) + q(NT, i) \qquad (A3)$$

and, hence, using (A1) and (A2), the equilibrium price for each asset is given by

$$P_i^e = V_i - S_i + n_i b \qquad (A4)$$

It is assumed that $n_i b_i < S_i$ so that both assets are mispriced at time $t = 0$. If the SM invests \$b, at $t = 0$, she can obtain $b/P_s^e$ shares of the short-term asset. At $t = 1$, the payoff per share of the short-term asset $V_s$ is revealed. There is a total \$ payoff in period-1 of $V_s(b/P_s^e)$. The net return $NR_s$ in period-1 over the borrowing cost of $bR$ is

$$NR_s = \frac{V_s b}{P_s^e} - bR = \frac{bV_s}{(V_s - S_s + n_s b)} - bR \qquad (A5)$$

where we have used equation (A4). Investing at $t = 0$ in the long-term asset, the SM purchases $b/P_g^e$ shares. In period $t = 1$, she does nothing. In period $t = 2$, the true value $V_g$ per share is revealed, which discounted to $t + 1$ at the rate $R$, implies a \$

payoff of $bV_g/P_g R$. The amount owed at $t = 2$ is $bR^2$, which when discounted to $t + 1$, is $bR$. Hence, the net return in period-1 $NR_g$ is

$$NR_g = \frac{bV_g}{P_g R} - bR = \frac{bV_g}{R(V_g - S_g + n_g b)} - bR \qquad (A6)$$

The only difference between (A5) and (A6) is that in (A6) the return to holding the (mispriced) long-term share is discounted back to $t = 1$ since its true value is not revealed until $t = 2$. In equilibrium, the returns to arbitrage over one period, on the long and short assets, must be equal ($NR_g = NR_s$) and, hence, from (A5) and (A6)

$$\frac{(V_g/R)}{P_g^e} = \frac{V_s}{P_s^e} \qquad (A7)$$

Since $R < 1$, then in equilibrium, the long-term asset is more underpriced (in percentage terms) than the short-term asset (when the noise traders are pessimistic, $S_i > 0$). The differential in the mispricing occurs because payoff uncertainty is resolved for the short-term asset in period-1 but for the long-term asset, this does not occur until period-2. Price moves to fundamental value $V_s$ for the short asset in period-1 but for the long asset not until period-2. Hence, the long-term fundamental value $V_g$ has to be discounted back to period-1, and this 'cost of borrowing' reduces the return to holding the long asset.

# 20

# THEORIES OF THE TERM STRUCTURE

## Aims

- Analyse zero coupon and coupon paying bonds, spot yields, continuously compounded spot yields, the holding period yield and the yield to maturity.

- Show how the rational valuation formula may be applied to the determination of bond prices.

- Examine various models of the term structure, including the (pure) expectations hypothesis, liquidity preference hypothesis, market segmentation hypothesis and preferred habitat models.

- Explain the shape of the yield curve.

One reason for interest in the relationship between long rates and short rates is that most central banks at some time or another attempt to influence short-term interest rates as a lever on the real economy, in an attempt to ultimately influence the rate of inflation. This is usually accomplished by the monetary authority either engaging in open market operations (i.e. buying or selling bills) or threatening to do so. Changes in *short rates* (with unchanged inflationary expectations) may influence real inventory holdings and consumers' expenditure (particularly on durable goods). Short-term interest rates may have an effect on interest rates on long maturity government bonds; this is the yield curve or term structure relationship. If government loan rates influence corporate bond rates, then the latter may affect real investment in plant and machinery. Hence, monetary policy can influence real economic activity both directly and indirectly (see Cuthbertson and Nitzsche (2001a)).

If the central bank's interest rate policy is seen as a credible anti-inflation strategy, then a rise in short rates is likely to lead to lower expectations of future inflation and lower *future* short-term interest rates and, hence, lower *long* rates – this may produce a downward sloping yield curve. On the other hand, if nominal short rates are increased in response to a higher level of inflation, then long rates might rise as people expect higher inflation in the future – this may produce an upward sloping yield curve. Unexpected changes in domestic short rates may also influence capital flows and the exchange rate – this link is subject to much uncertainty – but if operative, interest rate policy can then influence price competitiveness, the volume of net trade (exports minus imports) and the level of output and employment. We deal with the link between short rates and the exchange rate in Chapter 24.

Financial economists are interested in the behaviour of bond prices and interest rates as a test-bed for various behavioural hypotheses about market participants and market efficiency. Bond prices may shed light on the validity of the EMH, the results of which may be compared with tests based on stock returns and stock prices (as discussed in earlier chapters). The nominal stock price under the EMH is equal to the DPV of expected dividend payments. Similarly, the nominal price of a government bond may be viewed as the DPV of future nominal coupon payments. However, since the nominal coupon payments are known with certainty, the only source of variability in bond prices under rational expectations is news about future one-period interest rates (i.e. the discount factors). In the bond market, tests of the EMH tend to concentrate on the behaviour of 'yields' rather than prices. For example, Shiller's variance bounds tests compare $P_t$ and the perfect foresight stock price $P_t^*$, while the VAR methodology compares $P_t$ and the theoretical price $P_t'$. Similarly, in the bond market, we can compare the perfect foresight yield $R_t^*$ or the perfect foresight yield spread $S_t^*$ with their actual values $R_t$ and $S_t$, respectively. These issues are discussed in the next chapter, after dealing here with some basic concepts and developing theories of the term structure.

## 20.1    Prices, Yields and the RVF

The investment opportunities provided by bonds can be summarised not only by the holding period yield but also by spot yields and the yield to maturity. Hence, the 'return' on a bond can be defined in a number of different ways, and in this section, we clarify the relationship between these alternative measures. We then look at various hypotheses about the behaviour of participants in the bond market on the basis of the EMH, under alternative assumptions about expected 'returns'.

'Plain vanilla' coupon paying bonds provide a stream of income called *coupon payments* $C_{t+i}$, which are known (in nominal terms) for all future periods, at the time the bond is purchased. In most cases, $C_{t+i}$ is constant for all time periods, but it is sometimes useful to retain the subscript for expositional purposes. Most bonds, unlike stocks, are redeemable at a fixed date in the future ($= t + n$) for a known price, namely, the par value, redemption price or maturity value, $M_n$. There are some bonds that, although they pay coupons, are never redeemed, and these are known as *perpetuities* (e.g. $2\frac{1}{2}\%$ Consols, issued by the UK government).

A bill (e.g. Treasury Bill) has no coupon payments but its redemption price is fixed and known at the time of issue. The return on the bill is, therefore, the difference between its issue price (or market price when purchased) and its redemption price (expressed as a percentage). A bill is always issued at a *discount* (i.e. the issue price is less than the redemption price) so that a positive return is earned over the life of the bill. Bills are, therefore, often referred to as *pure discount bonds* or *zero coupon bonds*. Most bills that are traded in the market are for short maturities (i.e. they have a maturity at issue of three months, six months or a year). Coupon paying bonds, on the other hand, are usually for maturities in excess of one year with very active markets in the 5–15 year band. In this chapter, we shall be concerned only with (non-callable) government 'fixed coupon' bonds and bills and we shall assume that these carry no risk of default (i.e. corporate bonds are not considered).

Because coupon paying bonds and stocks are similar in a number of respects, we can apply many of the analytical ideas, theories and formulae we derived for the stock market to the bond market.

## Spot Yields/Rates

The spot yield (or spot rate) is that rate of return that applies to funds that are borrowed or lent at a known risk-free interest rate *over a given horizon*. For example, suppose you can lend funds (to a bank, say) at a rate of interest $r^{(1)}$, which applies to a one-year loan between $t = 0$ and $t = 1$. For an investment of $\$P$, the bank will pay out $M_1 = \$P(1 + r^{(1)})$ after one year. Suppose the bank's rate of interest on 'two-year money' is $r^{(2)}$, expressed at an *annual* compound rate. Then, $\$P$ invested will accrue to $M_2 = \$P(1 + r^{(2)})^2$ after two years. Thus, *today's* quoted spot rate for year$-n$, therefore, assumes that the $\$P$s invested *today* are 'locked-in' for $n$ years.

In principle, a sequence of spot rates can be calculated from the observed market price *of pure discount bonds* of different maturities. If the observed market price of bonds of maturity $n = 1, 2, \ldots$ are $P_t^{(1)}, P_t^{(2)} \ldots$ and so on, then each spot yield can be derived from $(1 + r_t^{(n)})^n = M/P_t^{(n)}$.

An equivalent way of viewing spot yields is to note that they provide a discount rate applicable to money accruing at *specific* future dates, with no risk of default. If you are offered $\$M = \$1$ payable in $n$ years, then the DPV of this sum is $M/(1 + r^{(n)})^n$ – indeed, this is today's 'fair price' of a zero coupon bond that matures in $n$ years

$$p_t^{(n)} = \ln P_t^{(n)} = \ln M - n \ln(1 + r_t^{(n)}) \tag{1}$$

We can also express the price in terms of a continuously compounded rate (see Chapter 1), which is defined as $rc_t = \ln(1 + r_t)$, hence

$$p_t^{(n)} = \ln P_t^{(n)} = \ln M - n[rc_t] \quad \text{or} \quad P_t^{(n)} = M \exp(-rc_t n) \tag{2}$$

In practice, (discount) bills or pure discount bonds often do not exist at the long end of the maturity spectrum (e.g. over one year). However, spot yields at longer maturities can be *approximated* using data on coupon paying bonds (although the details need not concern us here; see McCulloch 1971, 1990).

If we have an *n*-period *coupon paying bond* and market-determined spot rates exist for all maturities, then the market price of the bond is determined as

$$P_t^{(n)} = \frac{C_{t+1}}{(1 + r_t^{(1)})} + \frac{C_{t+2}}{(1 + r_t^{(2)})^2} + \cdots + \frac{C_{t+n} + M_{t+n}}{(1 + r_t^{(n)})^n} = \sum_{i=1}^{n} V_i \qquad (3)$$

where $M$ = maturity (redemption) value and $V_i = C_{t+i}/(1 + r_t^{(i)})^i$ for $i = 1, 2, \ldots,$ $n - 1$ and $V_n = (C_{t+n} + M_n)/(1 + r_{t+n}^{(n)})^n$. The market price is the DPV of future coupons (and maturity value) where the discount rates are spot yields. If the above formula does not hold, then riskless arbitrage profits can be made by *coupon stripping*. To illustrate this point, consider a two-period coupon bond and assume its market price $P_t^{(2)}$ is *less than* $V_1 + V_2$. But the current market price of two *zero coupon* bonds with payouts of $C_{t+1}$ and $(C_{t+2} + M_{t+2})$ will be $V_1$ and $V_2$, respectively. The coupon paying bond can be viewed as two zero coupon bonds. If $P_t^{(2)} < V_1 + V_2$, then one could purchase the two-year coupon bond and sell a claim on the 'coupon payments' in years 1 and 2, that is $C_{t+1}$ and $(C_{t+2} + M_{t+2})$, to other market participants. If zero coupon bonds are correctly priced, then these claims could be sold *today* for $V_1$ and $V_2$, respectively. Hence, an instantaneous riskless profit of $(V_1 + V_2 - P_t^{(2)})$ can be made. In an efficient market, the increased demand for the two-year coupon paying bond would raise $P_t^{(2)}$, while sales of the coupons would depress prices of one- and two-year zero coupon bonds. Hence, this riskless arbitrage would lead to the restoration of the equality in (3). Finally, note that as a matter of definition, the 'flat yield' is $C/P_t$ and the coupon *rate* on the bond is $C/M$.

## Holding Period Return, HPR

If one holds a coupon paying bond between $t$ and $t + 1$, the return is made up of the capital gain plus any coupon payment. For bonds, this measure of 'return' is known as the (one-period) *holding period return (or yield)*:

$$H_{t+1}^{(n)} = \frac{P_{t+1}^{(n-1)} - P_t^{(n)} + C_t}{P_t^{(n)}} \qquad (4)$$

where for a 'zero', $C_t = 0$ and the HPR is just the capital gain. Note that in the above formula, the *n*-period bond becomes an $(n - 1)$-period bond after one period. (In empirical work on long-term bonds (e.g. with $n > 10$ years), researchers often use $P_{t+1}^{(n)}$ in place of $P_{t+1}^{(n-1)}$ since for data collected weekly, monthly or quarterly, they are approximately the same.)

The definition of $H_{t+1}$ in (4) is the *ex post* (or actual) HPR. As investors at time $t$ do not know $P_{t+1}$, they will have to form *expectations* of $P_{t+1}$ and, hence, of the expected HPR. (Note that future coupon payments are usually known at time $t$ for all future periods.)

## Yield to Maturity (Redemption Yield)

For coupon paying bonds, the rate that is quoted in the market is the yield to maturity YTM. Investors know the current market price of the bond $P_t$, the stream of (annual) coupon payments, $C$, the redemption (or maturity) value of the bond ($= M$) and its maturity date, $n$. Now *assume* that the coupon payments at different horizons are discounted using a *constant* discount rate at time $t$, $1/(1 + y_t)$. Note that $y_t$, the YTM, has a subscript $t$ because it may vary over time (but it does not vary in each period in the DPV formula). If we now equate the DPV of the coupon payments with the current market price, we have

$$P_t = \frac{C}{(1 + y_t)} + \frac{C}{(1 + y_t)^2} + \cdots + \frac{C + M}{(1 + y_t)^n} \tag{5}$$

The bond may be viewed as an investment for which a capital sum $P_t$ is paid out today, and the investment pays the known stream of dollar receipts ($C$ and $M$) in the future. The *constant* value of $y_t$, which *equates* the LHS and RHS of (5), is the 'internal rate of return' on this investment, and for a bond, $y_t$ is referred to as the *yield to maturity* or *redemption yield* on the ($n$-period) bond. Clearly, one has to calculate $y_t$ each time the market price changes. The financial press generally report bond prices, coupon rates and yield to maturity. It is worth noting that the yield to maturity is *derived from* the market variables ($P_t$, $C$, $M$, $n$), and it does not *determine* the price in any economic sense. In fact, equation (3), using spot rates $r_{t+i}$, determines the bond price, and $P_t$ is then used by the financial community to calculate $y_t$ using (5). The reason for quoting the YTM in the market is that it provides a 'single number' for each bond of a given maturity (whereas (3) involves a *sequence* of spot rates). The yield to maturity on an $n$-period bond and another bond with $m$ periods to maturity will generally be different at any point in time, since each bond may have different coupon payments $C$, which are discounted over different time horizons (i.e. $n$ and $m$). It is easy to see from (5) that bond prices and redemption yields move in opposite directions and that for any given change in the redemption yield $y_t$, the percentage change in price of a long-bond is greater than that for a short-bond. Also, the yield to maturity formula (5) reduces *to* $P_t = C/y_t$ *for* a *perpetuity* (i.e. as $n \to \infty$).

Although redemption yields are widely quoted in the financial press, they are a somewhat ambiguous measure of the 'return' on a bond. When calculating the yield to maturity, it is implicitly assumed that agents are able to reinvest the coupon payments at the *constant rate* $y_t$ in all future periods, over the life of the bond. To see this, consider the yield to maturity for a two-period bond given by (5), rearranged

$$(1 + y_t)^2 P_t = C(1 + y_t) + (C + M) \tag{6}$$

The LHS is the terminal value (in two years' time) of $\$P_t$ invested at the constant annualised rate $y_t$. The RHS consists of the amount ($C + M$) paid at $t + 2$ and an amount $C(1 + y_t)$ that accrues at $t + 2$, after the first year's coupon payments have been reinvested at the rate $y_t$. Since (5) and (6) are equivalent, the DPV formula assumes that the first coupon payment is reinvested after year-1 at a rate $y_t$. However, there is little reason to argue that investors believe that they will be able to reinvest *all* future coupon payments at the constant rate $y_t$. Note that the issue here is not that investors have to form a view of future reinvestment rates for their coupon payments but that they choose to assume, for example, that the reinvestment rate applicable on a 20-year bond, between, say, years 9 and 10, will equal the *current* yield to maturity $y_t$ on the 20-year bond.

There is another way to examine the problem of using the yield to maturity as a measure of the return on a coupon paying bond. Consider two bonds with different coupon payment *streams* $C_{t+i}^{(1)}$, $C_{t+i}^{(2)}$ but the same price, maturity date and maturity value. Using (5), this will imply two different yields to maturity $y_{1t}$ and $y_{2t}$. If an investor holds both of these bonds in his portfolio and he believes equation (5), then he must be implicitly assuming that he can reinvest coupon payments for bond-1 between time $t + j$ and $t + j + 1$ at the rate $y_{1t}$ and at the *different* rate $y_{2t}$ for bond-2. But in reality, the reinvestment rate between $t + j$ and $t + j + 1$ will be the same for both bonds and will equal the one-period spot rate applicable between these years (which is unknown at time $t$).

Notwithstanding the above, the YTM is usually considered a useful approximation of the average annual percentage return on the bond, if it is held to maturity. However, because of the above defects in the concept of the yield to maturity, *yield curves* based on this measure are usually difficult to interpret in an unambiguous fashion.

# 20.2 Theories of the Term Structure

We examine theories of the term structure in terms of the one-period HPR and then using spot yields. In the next chapter, we show more formally how the HPR equation can be linked to spot yields on long- and short-bonds.

## Expectations Hypothesis

If all agents are risk neutral and concerned only with expected return, then the expected one-period HPR (over, say, one month or one quarter) on *all* bonds, no matter what their maturity, would be equalised and would be equal to the known (safe) return $r_t$ on a one-period asset (e.g. 1-month Treasury Bill).

$$E_t H_{t+1}^{(n)} = r_t \quad \text{(for all } n\text{)} \tag{7}$$

This is the *pure expectations hypothesis* (PEH) where the 'term' or risk premium is zero for all maturities. All agents at the margin are 'plungers'. For example, suppose a bond with three years to maturity has an unexpected HPR in excess of that on a bond with two years to maturity. Agents would sell the two-year bond and purchase the three-year bond, thus pushing up the *current* price of the three-year bond and reducing its one-period HPR. The opposite would occur for the two-period bond and, hence, all holding period returns would be equalised. If we now add the assumption of rational expectations,

$$H_{t+1}^{(n)} - r_t = \eta_{t+1}^{(n)} \quad \text{(for all } n\text{)} \tag{8}$$

Hence, one test of the PEH (+ RE) is that the *ex post excess* holding period yield should have a zero mean, be independent of all information at time $t$ ($\Omega_t$) and, hence, the residual $\eta_{t+1}^{(n)}$ should be serially uncorrelated (but can be heteroscedastic).

It seems reasonable to assert that because the return on holding a long-bond (for one period) is uncertain (because its price at the end of the period is unknown at $t$), the excess HPR ought to depend on some form of 'reward for risk' or term premium $T_t^{(n)}$.

$$E_t H_{t+1}^{(n)} = r_t + T_t^{(n)} \qquad (9)$$

Without a model of the term premium, equation (9) is a tautology. The simplest (non-trivial) assumption to make about the term premium is that it is (i) constant over time and (ii) independent of the term to maturity of the bond (i.e. $T_t^{(n)} = T$). This constitutes the *expectations hypothesis* (EH) (Table 1). Obviously, this gives similar predictions as the PEH, namely, no serial correlation in the excess HPR and that the latter should be independent of $\Omega_t$. Note that the excess HPR is now equal to a constant for all maturities. For the EH + RE and a *time invariant* term premium, we obtain the variance inequality

$$\text{var}(H_{t+1}^{(n)}) \geq \text{var}(r_t) \qquad (10)$$

Thus, the variance of the one-period HPR on an $n$-period bond should be greater than or equal to the variance of the one-period safe rate. Equivalently, the variance of the *excess* HPR should be the same for different maturity bonds.

## Liquidity Preference Hypothesis, LPH

Here, the assumption is that the term premium does not vary over time but it does depend on the term to maturity of the bond (i.e. $T_t^{(n)} = T^{(n)}$). For example, bonds with longer periods to maturity may be viewed as being more 'risky' than those with a short period to maturity, even though we are considering a fixed holding period for both bonds. This might arise because the price change is larger for any given change in the yield, for bonds with longer maturities. Consider the case where the *one-month* HPR on 20-year bonds is more *volatile* than that on ten-year bonds. Here, one might require a higher expected return on the 20-year bond in order that it is willingly held in the portfolio, alongside the ten-year bond. If this difference in price volatility depends only on the difference in the term to maturity, then this could give rise to a liquidity premium that depends only on $n$.

The liquidity preference hypothesis asserts that the expected excess HPR is a constant for any given maturity, but for those bonds that have a longer period to maturity, the term premium will increase. That is to say the expected excess HPR on a ten-year bond would exceed the expected excess HPR on a five-year bond, but this gap would remain constant over time. Thus, for example, ten-year bonds might have *expected* excess returns 1% above those on five-year bonds, for all time periods. Of course, in the data, *actual* ten-year excess returns will vary randomly around their expected HPR because of (zero mean) forecast errors in each time period. Under the liquidity

**Table 1**   The term structure: A summary

All yields are continuously compounded spot yields

1. **Pure Expectations Hypothesis, PEH**
   (a) *Expected excess return is zero*
   (b) *The term premium is zero for all maturities*

$$E_t H_{t+1}^{(n)} - r_t = 0 \quad R_t^{(n)} - E_t(r_{t+j}'s) = 0$$

2. **Expectations Hypothesis or Constant Term Premium**
   (a) *Expected excess return equals a constant that is the same for all maturities*
   (b) *The term premium is constant and the same for all maturities*

$$E_t H_{t+1}^{(n)} - r_t = T \quad R_t^{(n)} - E_t(r_{t+j}'s) = \Phi^{(n)}$$

   where $T$ and $\Phi^{(n)}$ are the one-period and $n$-period term premia.

3. **Liquidity Preference Hypothesis**
   (a) *Expected excess return on a bond of maturity n is a constant but the value of the constant is larger the longer the period to maturity*
   (b) *The term premium increases with n, the time period to maturity*

$$E_t H_{t+1}^{(n)} - r_t = T^{(n)} \quad R_t^{(n)} - E_t(r_{t+j}'s) = \Phi^{(n)}$$

   where $T^{(n)} > T^{(n-1)} \ldots$ and so on.

4. **Time-Varying Risk**
   (a) *Expected excess return on a bond of maturity n varies both with n and over time*
   (b) *The term premium depends on maturity n and varies over time*

$$E_t H_{t+1}^{(n)} - r_t = T(n, z_t) \quad R_t^{(n)} - E_t(r_{t+j}'s) = \Phi(n, z_t)$$

   where $T(.)$ is some function of $n$ and a set of variables $z_t$.

5. **Market Segmentation Hypothesis**
   (a) *Excess returns are influenced at least in part by the outstanding stock of assets of different maturities*
   (b) *The term premium depends in part on the outstanding stock of assets of different maturities*

$$E_t H_{t+1}^{(n)} - r_t = T(z_t^{(n)}) \quad R_t^{(n)} - E_t(r_{t+j}'s) = \Phi(z_t^{(n)})$$

   where $z_t^{(n)}$ is some measure of the *relative* holdings of assets of maturity '$n$' as a proportion of total assets held.

6. **Preferred Habitat Theory**
   *Bonds that mature at dates that are close together should be reasonably close substitutes and, hence, have similar term premia.*

preference hypothesis,

$$E_t H_{t+1}^{(n)} - r_t = T^{(n)} \quad T^{(n)} > T^{(n-1)} > \cdots \tag{11}$$

Again, under RE, the liquidity preference hypothesis predicts that excess HPRs are serially uncorrelated and independent of information at time $t$. Thus, apart from a fairly innocuous constant term, then using regression analysis, the main testable implications of the PEH, EH and the liquidity preference hypothesis (LPH) are identical. For the PEH, we have a zero constant term, for the EH, we have $T = $ constant and for the LPH, we have a different constant for each bond of maturity $n$. Because the PEH, EH and the LPH are so similar, we may often refer to them simply as the EH. As we shall see in the next section, the key distinction is between the EH (with a zero or constant term premium over time) and a model that allows the term premium *to vary over time*.

## Market Segmentation Hypothesis

The market segmentation hypothesis may be viewed as a reduced form or market equilibrium solution of a set of standard asset demand equations. To simplify, suppose we have only two risky assets, that is, bonds $B_x$ and $B_y$ with their respective demand functions

$$(B_x/W)^{\mathrm{d}} = f_1(E_t H_{x,t+1} - r_t, E_t H_{y,t+1} - r_t, Z) \tag{12a}$$

$$(B_y/W)^{\mathrm{d}} = f_2(E_t H_{x,t+1} - r_t, E_t H_{y,t+1} - r_t, Z) \tag{12b}$$

where $W = $ financial wealth, $Z = $ any other variables that influence demand, $r = $ the safe return on Treasury Bills and $E_t H_{x,t+1} = $ expected holding period return on bonds of maturity $x$. The demand function for T-Bills is given as a residual from the budget constraint

$$(TB/W) = 1 - (B_x + B_y)/W \tag{13}$$

and need not concern us. If we now assume that the supply of $B_x$ and $B_y$ are exogenous, then market equilibrium rates are given by solving (13)

$$E_t H_{x,t+1} - r_t = g_1[B_x/W, B_y/W, Z] \tag{14a}$$

$$E_t H_{y,t+1} - r_t = g_2[B_x/W, B_y/W, Z] \tag{14b}$$

Hence, the expected excess HPRs on two bonds of different maturities depend on the proportion of wealth held in each of these assets. This is the basis of the market segmentation hypothesis. In general, the demand functions (12) contain many independent variables $Z$; for example, the variance of returns, real wealth, price inflation and lagged values of these variables.

## Preferred Habitat Hypothesis

The preferred habitat theory is, in effect, agnostic about the determinants of the term premium. It suggests that we should only compare 'returns' on government bonds of similar maturities, and one might then expect excess holding period yields to move closely together.

## 20.3    Expectations Hypothesis

The EH can also be derived in terms of spot yields where $R_t^{(n)}$ and $r_t$ are per-period rates. Consider investing $\$A$ in a (zero coupon) bond with $n$ years to maturity. The terminal value of the investment is

$$TV = \$A(1 + R_t^{(n)})^n \tag{15}$$

where $R_t^{(n)}$ is the annual (compound) rate on the $n$-period long-bond. Next, consider the alternative strategy of reinvesting $\$A$ and any interest earned in a series of 'rolled-over' *one-period* investments, for $n$ years. Ignoring transactions costs, the *expected* terminal value $E_t(TV)$ of this series of one-period investments is

$$E_t(TV) = \$A(1 + r_t)(1 + E_t r_{t+1})(1 + E_t r_{t+2}) \ldots (1 + E_t r_{t+n-1}) \tag{16}$$

where $r_{t+i}$ is the rate applicable between periods $t + i$ and $t + i + 1$. The investment in the long-bond gives a known terminal value since this bond is held to maturity. Investing in a series of one-year investments gives a terminal value that is subject to uncertainty, since the investor must guess the future values of the one-period spot yields, $r_{t+j}$. However, under risk neutrality, the terminal values of these two alternative strategies will be equalised:

$$(1 + R_t^{(n)})^n = (1 + r_t)(1 + E_t r_{t+1})(1 + E_t r_{t+2}) \ldots (1 + E_t r_{t+n-1}) \tag{17}$$

The equality holds because if the terminal value corresponding to investment in the long-bond exceeds the *expected* terminal value of that on the sequence of one-year investments, then investors would at time $t$ buy long-bonds and sell the short-bond. This would result in a rise in the current market price of the long-bond and, given a fixed maturity value, a fall in the long (spot) yield $R_t^{(n)}$. Simultaneously, sales of the short-bond would cause a fall in its current price and a rise in $r_t$. Hence, the equality in (17) would be quickly (instantaneously) restored.

We could *define* the expected 'excess' or 'abnormal' profit on a $\$1$ investment in the long-bond over the sequence of rolled-over short investments as

$$E_t(AP_t) \equiv R_t^{(n)} - E_t(r_{t+j}{'}s) \tag{18}$$

where $E_t(r_{t+j}{'}s)$ represents the RHS of (17). The PEH applied to *spot yields*, therefore, implies that the *expected* excess or abnormal profit is zero. We can go through the whole taxonomy of models in terms of $E_t(AP_t)$ in the same way as we did for holding period yields. These are summarised in Table 1 and need no further comment here.

Taking logarithms of (17) and using the approximation $\ln(1 + z) \approx z$ for $z$ close to zero, we obtain the *approximate* linear relationship

$$R_t^{(n)} = (1/n)[r_t + E_t r_{t+1} + E_t r_{t+2} + \cdots E_t r_{t+n-1}] \tag{19}$$

In terms of *continuously compounded* rates, the same analysis yields

$$A \exp(R_t^{(n)} n) = E_t[A \exp(r_t) \exp(r_{t+1}) \ldots \exp(r_{t+n-1})] \tag{20}$$

where $R_t^{(n)}$ and $r_{t+i}$ are now continuously compounded rates. Taking logarithms, we obtain

$$R_t^{(n)} = (1/n)E_t[r_t + r_{t+1} + r_{t+2} + \cdots + r_{t+n-1}] \tag{21}$$

which is an *exact* relationship, only if we ignore Jensen's inequality, which states $E[f(x)] \neq f(Ex)$. So, in fact, (21) is not exact since we are taking expectations of $E_t(\exp r_{t+j}) \neq \exp(E_t r_{t+j})$. However, Campbell (1986) shows that for all practical purposes, we can ignore Jensen's inequality.

## Forward Rates

Forward rates can be calculated from the appropriate spot rates. For example, a two-year investment at $R_t^{(2)}$ must give the same return as a one-year spot investment at $r_t$ followed by a forward investment between $t$ and $t + 1$, at a forward rate $f_{12,t}$ (see Cuthbertson and Nitzsche 2001a). Since the forward rate is known at time $t$, it is a riskless investment. Using continuously compounded (annual) rates,

$$2R_t^{(2)} = r_t + f_{12,t} \tag{22}$$

$$f_{12,t} = 2R_t^{(2)} - r_t \tag{23}$$

Comparing (23) with (21), the EH implies

$$E_t r_{t+1} = f_{12,t} \quad \text{or, equivalently,} \quad E_t r_{t+1} - r_t = (f_{12,t} - r_t) \tag{24}$$

so the forward rate is an unbiased predictor of the future spot rate. Forward rates can be calculated for all horizons. Under RE, tests of the EH can be based on forward rate regressions for different maturities, $(m, n)$:

$$r_{t+m}^{(n-m)} - r_t = \alpha + \beta(f_{mn,t} - r_t) + \varepsilon_{t+m} \quad (n > m) \tag{25}$$

Under the null of the EH, $\alpha = 0$, $\beta = 1$.

## Yield Curve

The PEH forms the basis for an analysis of the (spot) yield curve. For example, viewed from time $t$, if short rates are expected to rise (i.e. $E_t r_{t+j} > E_t r_{t+j-1}$ for all $j$), then from (19), the long rate $R_t^{(n)}$ will be above the current short rate, $r_t$. The yield curve – a graph of $R_t^{(n)}$ against time to maturity, $n$ – will be upward sloping since $R_t^{(n)} > R_t^{(n-1)} > \cdots > r_t$. The converse applies, so the yield curve is downward sloping for $E_t r_{t+j} < E_t r_{t+j-1}$ (for all $j$). Since expected future short rates are influenced by expectations of inflation (i.e. Fisher effect), the yield curve is likely to be upward sloping when inflation is expected to increase in future years and downward sloping if the central bank has a credible anti-inflation strategy. If there is a *small* monotonic liquidity premium that depends only on the term to maturity $n$, where $T^{(n)} > T^{(n-1)} > \cdots$, then the basic qualitative shape of the yield curve will remain as described above (see Cuthbertson and Nitzsche 2001a). The yield curve can also be analysed within the context of the stochastic discount factor (SDF) model – where an explicit risk premium influences the shape of the yield curve (see chapter 23).

## 20.4  Summary

- The yield to maturity, although widely quoted in the financial press, is a somewhat misleading measure of the average annual 'return' on a bond over its life, since it assumes coupons can be reinvested at the *current* YTM.

- The one-period HPR on coupon paying bonds consists of a capital gain plus a coupon payment. In an efficient market, the bond price can be viewed as the present value of known future coupon payments (plus the redemption value) discounted using spot rates.

- The EH (plus RE) implies that the *expected excess* holding period return $(E_t H_{t+1}^{(n)} - r_t)$ is constant and, hence, independent of information at time $t$, $\Omega_t$.

- Alternative theories of the term structure are, in the main, concerned with whether term premia are (a) zero, (b) constant over time and for all maturities, (c) constant over time but differ for different maturities, (d) depend on the proportion of wealth held in 'long debt'. These assumptions give rise to the pure expectations hypothesis PEH, the expectations hypothesis EH, the liquidity preference hypothesis LPH and the market segmentation hypothesis, respectively. Time-varying term premia can be introduced into the EH equations in an ad hoc way and more formally in the SDF approach.

- The expectations hypothesis EH applied to spot yields implies that the long rate is a weighted average of expected future short rates. Agents are risk neutral and equalise expected returns over all investment horizons. Hence, no abnormal profits can be made by switching between 'longs' and 'shorts' and the EMH under risk neutrality holds.

- The yield curve is a graph (at a point in time) of (spot) yields on bonds $R_t^{(n)}$ against their time to maturity, $n$. The *shape* of the yield curve is determined primarily by investors' expectations of future short rates. If future short rates are expected to rise (or fall), then the yield curve will be upward (or downward) sloping.

# 21

# THE EH – FROM THEORY TO TESTING

## Aims

- Analyse several tests of the expectations hypothesis (EH) of the term structure (i.e. assuming a time invariant or zero term premium).

- Show that under the EH, the expected excess *one-period HPR* (for a bond of any maturity) is independent of any information available when the forecast was made. (The latter is sometimes referred to as the local expectations hypothesis, but we will not use this term.)

- Demonstrate that under the EH, the *long-rate equation* implies that the current yield spread (between the long rates and short rates) is an optimal predictor of *next period's change-in-long rates*.

- Show that the EH can be written in terms of the *future-short-rate equation*, which implies that the spread is an optimal predictor of future changes in *short* rates, over the life of the 'long-bond'. If the *actual* spread moves more than the expected future change in short rates, this is referred to as the *over-reaction hypothesis*.

- Derive tests of the EH on the basis of an explicit VAR forecasting scheme.

- Show how the EH implies variance bounds test on yields (or the spread).

There has been much debate about whether the tests of the EH are consistent with each other and with the absence of arbitrage opportunities (Cox, Ingersoll and Ross 1981, McCulloch 1993, Fisher and Gilles 1998). Campbell (1986) shows that any differences are likely to be empirically irrelevant, while Longstaff (2000b) shows that these forms of the EH can hold generally without arbitrage opportunities, when markets are not complete. We, therefore, refer to all our tests as versions of the EH, noting that a constant term premium makes little difference to the theoretical model or the tests employed. A key distinction is whether we allow for a *time-varying term premium*, and this is examined at a later point.

# 21.1    Alternative Representations of the EH

The EH implies that the *expected* return on different maturity bonds, over any holding period, should be equalised. For example, the return (i.e. capital gain) on holding *any* *n*-year zero coupon bond over a one-year horizon should equal the known yield on a riskless one-year bond. An equivalent formulation is possible in terms of *spot yields* on different maturity bonds. For example, if yields on ten-year bonds are *currently* above those on one-year bonds, this does not imply that ten-year bonds earn more over a ten-year horizon. In such circumstances, the PEH implies that one-year yields are expected to rise in the future (i.e. over the next one to nine years) so that expected returns on a *series* of one-year investments equal the higher yield on the ten-year bond. So, the EH can be represented in a large number of equivalent ways, and one of our tasks is to point out these interrelationships.

For completeness, in the derivation that follows, we include a risk premium. We show how the EH can be represented in a variety of ways, all of which are derived from the version of the EH in which the (*continuously compounded*) expected HPR equals the risk-free one-period rate plus a risk premium:

$$E_t h_{t+1}^{(n)} \equiv E_t[\ln P_{t+1}^{(n-1)} - \ln P_t^{(n)}] = r_t + T_t^{(n)} \tag{1}$$

The log bond price is

$$\ln P_t^{(n)} = -R_t^{(n)} n \tag{2}$$

Using (1) and (2), we immediately obtain the following:

### Change-in-long-rate equation

$$(n-1)\{E_t R_{t+1}^{(n-1)} - R_t^{(n)}\} = \beta_L S_t^{(n)} + T_t^{(n)} \tag{3}$$

where under the EH, $\beta_L = 1$ and under the PEH, $T_t^{(n)}$ is zero. Equation (1), although based on the HPR, implies a term structure relationship in terms of future short rates. Substituting $S_t^{(n)} = R_t^{(n)} - r_t$ in (3), the EH gives the forward difference equation

$$n R_t^{(n)} = (n-1) E_t R_{t+1}^{(n-1)} + r_t + T_t^{(n)} \tag{4}$$

Leading (4) one period,

$$(n-1) R_{t+1}^{(n-1)} = (n-2) E_{t+1} R_{t+2}^{(n-2)} + r_{t+1} + T_{t+1}^{(n-1)} \tag{5}$$

Taking expectations of (5) using $E_t E_{t+1} = E_t$ and substituting in (4),

$$nR_t^{(n)} = (n-2)E_t R_{t+2}^{(n-2)} + E_t(r_{t+1} + r_t) + E_t(T_{t+1}^{(n-1)} + T_t^{(n)}) \qquad (6)$$

Continually substituting for the first term on the RHS of (6) and noting that $(n-j)E_t R_{t+j}^{(n-j)} = 0$ for $j = n$, we obtain the following:

### Long rates are a weighted average of future short rates

$$R_t^{(n)} = E_t R_t^{*(n)} + E_t \Phi_t^{(n)} \qquad (7)$$

where

$$R_t^{*(n)} = (1/n) \sum_{i=0}^{n-1} r_{t+i} \qquad \text{perfect foresight long rate} \qquad (8a)$$

$$\Phi_t^{(n)} = (1/n) \sum_{i=0}^{n-1} T_{t+i}^{(n-i)} \qquad \text{average risk premium} \qquad (8b)$$

Hence, the $n$-period long rate equals a weighted average of expected future short rates $r_{t+i}$ plus the average risk premium on the $n$-period bond, $\Phi_t^{(n)}$. This formulation was introduced earlier, and we now see that it is an alternative representation of the HPR equation (1), as is the change in the long-rate equation (3). The variable $R_t^{*(n)}$ is referred to as the *perfect foresight long rate* since it is a weighted average of the *out-turn* values for one-period short rates, $r_{t+i}$. Subtracting $r_t$ from both sides of (7), we obtain an equivalent expression as follows.

### Future-short-rate equation

$$E_t S_t^{*(n,1)} = S_t^{(n,1)} + E_t \Phi_t^{(n)} \qquad (9)$$

where

$$S_t^{(n,1)} = R_t^{(n)} - r_t \qquad \text{actual spread} \qquad (10a)$$

$$S_t^{*(n,1)} = \sum_{i=1}^{n-1} (1 - i/n) E_t \Delta r_{t+i} \qquad \text{perfect foresight spread} \qquad (10b)$$

Invoking rational expectation (RE), a test of the EH is the regression

$$S_t^{*(n,1)} = \alpha + \beta_S S_t^{(n,1)} + \gamma \Omega_t + \upsilon_{t+n-1} \qquad (11)$$

where $\Omega_t$ is a vector of variables known at time $t$ and $\upsilon_{t+n-1}$ is a weighted average of the $n-1$, RE forecast errors for the future short rates $(r_{t+j} = E_t r_{t+j} + \eta_{t+j})$. Under the EH, we expect $\beta_S = 1$ and $\gamma = 0$. Equation (9) states that the actual spread

$S_t^{(n,1)}$ between the $n$ period and one-period rate equals a weighted average of expected *changes* in future short rates plus a term premium. The variable $S_t^{*(n,1)}$ is known as the perfect foresight *spread*. As we shall see, the variables in (7), namely, $R_t^{(n)}$ and $r_{t+i}$, are usually found to be non-stationary, whereas $\Delta r_{t+i}$ and $S_t^{(n,1)}$ are found to be stationary I(0) variables. Hence, econometric tests on (9) can be based on standard distributions (whereas those on (7) cannot). Equations (7) and (9) are general expressions for the term structure relationship, but they are non-operational unless we assume a specific form for the term premium.

It is perhaps worth bearing in mind that for $n = 2m$ (e.g. six-month and three-month bonds), the long-rate and short-rate regressions (3) and (9) are equivalent. Also, if (3) holds *for all* $(n, m)$, then so will (9). However, if (3) is rejected for some subset of values of $(n, m)$, then equation (9) does not necessarily hold, and, hence, it provides independent information on the validity of the EH. In early empirical work, the above two formulations were mainly undertaken for $n = 2m$, in fact, usually for three- and six-month pure discount bonds (e.g. Treasury Bills) on which data is readily available. Hence, the two regressions are statistically equivalent. Results are, however, available for other maturities (i.e. $n \neq 2m$), and we report some of these in the next chapter.

## Variance Bounds Tests

The 'future-short-rate' equation (9) provides a variance bounds test, which is equivalent to the regression (11) under the null of the EH (with a constant term premium). We can calculate the perfect foresight spread $S_t^{*(n,1)} = \sum_{i=1}^{n-1} (1 - i/n) \Delta r_{t+i}$ using past data and compare it with the actual spread $S_t^{(n,1)}$. Indeed, the EH (with constant term premium) implies

$$\text{var}(S_t^{*(n,1)}) \geq \text{var}(S_t^{(n,1)}) \tag{12}$$

since $\text{var}(\upsilon_{t+n-1}) \geq 0$ and under RE, $\text{cov}(S_t^{(n,1)}, \upsilon_{t+n-1}) = 0$. Standard tests on the variance bound using spreads will be valid if the *change* in interest rates and the spread are both stationary I(0) variables, which is thought to be the case. On a historic note, this type of volatility test was originally done on the *levels* of interest rates (Shiller 1989). The *perfect foresight long rate* is

$$R_t^* = \frac{1}{n}[r_t + r_{t+1} + r_{t+2} + \cdots + r_{t+n-1}] \tag{13}$$

Under the EH + RE (i.e. $r_{t+i} = E_t r_{t+i} + \eta_{t+i}$), we have

$$R_t^* = R_t + w_t \tag{14}$$

where $w_t = (1/n) \sum_{i=1}^{n-1} \eta_{t+i}$ and $E_t(\eta_{t+i}|\Omega_t) = 0$. Using past data, we can construct a time series for $R_t^*$. Under RE, agents' forecasts are unbiased and, hence, the *sum* of the forecast errors $w_t$ should be close to zero for large $n$. Hence, for long-term bonds, we expect the perfect foresight rate $R_t^*$ to track the broad swings in the *actual* long-rate $R_t$. Clearly, under the RE, the forecast error $w_t$ is independent of $\Omega_t$ and, hence, it is independent of $R_t$. Hence, from (14), we have

$$\text{var}(R_t^*) \geq \text{var}(R_t) \qquad (15)$$

since by RE, $\text{cov}(R_t, w_t) = 0$ and $\text{var}(w_t) \geq 0$. Also, under the null of the EH,

$$R_t^* = a + bR_t + c\Omega_t + \varepsilon_t \qquad (16)$$

we expect $b = 1$ and $c = 0$. These 'early' volatility tests were certainly innovative at the time, but if 'raw' data on the levels of interest rates are used and these are non-stationary (which is likely), then the variances are undefined and the tests suspect. Then the same tests can be undertaken with the spread $S_t$ and the perfect foresight spread $S_t^*$, where we expect $\text{var}(S_t^*) \geq \text{var}(S_t)$.

It is obvious from equations (3) and (11) that the OLS regression coefficient on the spread will be inconsistent if we ignore a time-varying term premium (and it is correlated with the spread). This inconsistency will be greater, the greater the variance of the term premium relative to the variance of the spread and the greater is the correlation between these two variables. It has also been shown (Walsh 1998) that even if the EH is true but the monetary authorities alter the short rate in response to changes in the spread, the regression coefficient on the spread will be inconsistent.

Equation (11) indicates that the actual spread $S_t^{(n)}$ is an optimal predictor of expected future changes in short rates $E_t S_t^{*(n)}$, but only if the term premium is time invariant. The distinction between the expected *one-period* term premium $E_t T_t^{(n)}$ and the *average* of future term premia $E_t \Phi_t^{(n)}$ will be important in some of the arguments presented below.

The EH applied to spot yields assumes investors are risk neutral and base their investment decision only on *expected* returns. The inherent variability or uncertainty concerning returns is of no consequence to their investment decisions. In terms of our equations, the EH implies $T^{(n)} = \Phi^{(n)} = 0$ for all $n$.

Instead of 'replacing' $E_t r_{t+j}$ by the out-turn values $r_{t+j}$ to form the perfect foresight spread $S_t^*$, we could use an *explicit equation* to forecast the $r_{t+j}$'s. As we shall see, this forecast is known as the *theoretical spread* denoted $S_t'$. We now have several methods for testing the EH, as follows, which are equivalent under the null.

- The excess HPR regression

- The change-in-long-rate regression

- The change-in-future short-rate regression using out-turn values – the perfect foresight spread

- The change-in-future short-rate regression using an explicit forecasting equation – the theoretical spread

- Variance bounds tests

## 21.2   VAR Approach

In this section, we discuss the following.

- How the EH gives rise to cross-equation parameter restrictions in the VAR forecasting equation(s).

- How the VAR equations can be used to provide a time-series forecast of future short rates – the theoretical spread $S_t'$ – which can then be compared with the actual spread $S_t$ using a variance ratio statistic and correlation coefficient.

When multiperiod forecasts of future short rates are required, we can use the Campbell–Shiller (C–S) vector autoregression (VAR) approach. We illustrate the approach using a simple example. The EH applied to a three-period horizon gives

$$R_t = \tfrac{1}{3}(r_t + E_t r_{t+1} + E_t r_{t+2}) \tag{17}$$

which may be re-parameterised to give

$$S_t = \tfrac{2}{3}\Delta E_t r_{t+1} + \tfrac{1}{3}\Delta E_t r_{t+2} \tag{18}$$

where $S_t = R_t - r_t$ is the long-short spread, $E_t \Delta r_{t+1} = (E_t r_{t+1} - r_t)$ and $E_t \Delta r_{t+2} = (E_t r_{t+2} - E_t r_{t+1})$. Now assume that both $S_t$ and $\Delta r_t$ may be represented as a bivariate vector autoregression (VAR) of order one (for simplicity):

$$S_{t+1} = a_{11} S_t + a_{12}\Delta r_t + \omega_{1t+1} \tag{19a}$$

$$\Delta r_{t+1} = a_{21} S_t + a_{22}\Delta r_t + \omega_{2t+1} \tag{19b}$$

or in vector notation,

$$\mathbf{z}_{t+1} = \mathbf{A}\mathbf{z}_t + \boldsymbol{\omega}_{t+1} \tag{20}$$

where $\mathbf{z}_{t+1} = (S_{t+1}, \Delta r_{t+1})'$, $\mathbf{A}$ is the $(2 \times 2)$ matrix of coefficients $a_{ij}$, and $\boldsymbol{\omega}_{t+1} = (\omega_{1t+1}, \omega_{2t+1})'$. From (20), the optimal prediction of future $z$'s using the chain rule of forecasting is:

$$E_t \mathbf{z}_{t+1} = \mathbf{A}\mathbf{z}_t \tag{21a}$$

$$E_t \mathbf{z}_{t+2} = E_t \mathbf{A}\mathbf{z}_{t+1} = \mathbf{A}^2 \mathbf{z}_t \tag{21b}$$

Now let $\mathbf{e1}' = (1, 0)$ and $\mathbf{e2}' = (0, 1)$ be $2 \times 1$ selection vectors. It follows that

$$S_t = \mathbf{e1}'\mathbf{z}_t \tag{22a}$$

$$E_t \Delta r_{t+1} = \mathbf{e2}' E_t \mathbf{z}_{t+1} = \mathbf{e2}'\mathbf{A}\mathbf{z}_t \tag{22b}$$

$$E_t \Delta r_{t+2} = \mathbf{e2}' E_t \mathbf{z}_{t+2} = \mathbf{e2}'\mathbf{A}^2 \mathbf{z}_t \tag{22c}$$

Substituting the above in the PEH equation (18),

$$S_t = \mathbf{e1}'\mathbf{z}_t = \left(\tfrac{2}{3}\mathbf{e2}'\mathbf{A} + \tfrac{1}{3}\mathbf{e2}'\mathbf{A}^2\right)\mathbf{z}_t \tag{23}$$

## Cross-Equation Restrictions in the VAR

If (23) is to hold for all values of $\mathbf{z}_t$, then the following non-linear restrictions between the coefficients $a_{ij}$ must hold.

$$f(\mathbf{a}) = \mathbf{e1}' - \mathbf{e2}'[(2/3)\mathbf{A} + (1/3)\mathbf{A}^2] = 0 \tag{24}$$

where $f(\mathbf{a})$ is defined as the set of restrictions. A test of the EH plus the forecasting scheme represented by the VAR simply requires one to estimate the unrestricted VAR equations and apply a test statistic on the basis of the restrictions in (24).

## Wald and Likelihood Ratio Tests

It is worth giving a brief account of the form of the Wald test at this point. After estimating our $(2 \times 2)$ VAR, we have an estimate of the variance–covariance matrix of the *unrestricted* VAR system:

$$\Sigma = \begin{bmatrix} \sigma_1^2 & \sigma_{12} \\ \sigma_{21} & \sigma_2^2 \end{bmatrix} \tag{25}$$

If there is no heteroscedasticity, the variances and covariances of the error terms are calculated from the residuals from each equation (e.g. $\sigma_1^2 = \sum_t \hat{w}_{1t}^2/n$, $\sigma_{12} = \sum_t \hat{w}_{1t}\hat{w}_{2t}/n$) – otherwise we use a GMM correction for heteroscedasticity. The variance–covariance matrix of the non-linear function $f(\mathbf{a})$ in (24) is given by

$$\text{var}[f(\mathbf{a})] = f_a(\mathbf{a})' \sum f_a(\mathbf{a}) \tag{26a}$$

where $f_a(\mathbf{a})$ is the first derivative of the restrictions with respect to the $a_{ij}$ parameters. The Wald statistic is

$$W = f(\mathbf{a})\{\text{var}[f(\mathbf{a})]\}^{-1} f(\mathbf{a})' \tag{26b}$$

There is little intuitive insight one can obtain from the general form of the Wald test (but see Buse 1982). However, the larger is the variance of $f(\mathbf{a})$, the smaller is the value of $W$. Hence, the more imprecise the estimates of the A-matrix, the smaller is $W$ and the more likely one is 'to pass' the Wald test (i.e. not reject the null). In addition, if the restrictions hold exactly, then $f(\mathbf{a}) \approx 0$ and $W \approx 0$. It may be shown that under the standard conditions for the error terms, $W$ is distributed asymptotically as central $\chi^2$ under the null with $r$ degrees of freedom, where $r = $ number of restrictions. If $W$ is less than the critical value $\chi_c^2$, then we do not reject the null $f(\mathbf{a}) = 0$.

In principle, we can also use a likelihood ratio test. This compares the 'fit' of the unrestricted two-equation system with that of the restricted system. Denote the variance–covariance matrix of the unrestricted VAR as $\sum_u$ and the restricted system $\sum_r$, where the restrictions (24) are imposed. The likelihood ratio test is computed as

$$LR = n . \ln\left[\left(\det\sum\nolimits_r\right) \Big/ \left(\det\sum\nolimits_u\right)\right] \tag{27}$$

where $n$ = number of observations and 'det' indicates the determinant of the covariance matrix $\det \sum = \sigma_1^2 \sigma_2^2 - (\sigma_{12})^2$. If the restrictions hold in the data, then we do not expect much change in the residuals and, hence, $\det \sum_r \approx \det \sum_u$ so that $LR \approx 0$. Conversely, if the data do not comply with the restrictions, we expect the 'fit' to be worse and the restricted residuals to be larger (on average) than their equivalent unrestricted counterparts and $\det \sum_r / \det \sum_u$ and, hence, $LR$ will be large. $LR$ is distributed asymptotically as (central) chi-squared under the null, with $q$ degrees of freedom (where $q$ = number of parameter restrictions). Thus, we reject the null if $LR > \chi_c^2(q)$ where $\chi_c^2(q)$ is the critical value. Unfortunately, the $LR$ test requires us to estimate the VAR under the rather complex cross-equation restrictions in (23). Clearly, this is not straightforward here (but see Bekaert, Hodrick and Marshall 1997) and, therefore, in this literature, the Wald test is usually used, even given its deficiencies.

The VAR–Wald test procedure is very general. It can be applied to more complex term structure relationships and can be implemented with high-order lags in the VAR. Campbell and Shiller (1991) show that under the EH, the spread between $n$-period and $m$-period bond yields ($n > m$) denoted $S_t^{(n,m)}$ may be represented

$$S_t^{(n,m)} = E_t \sum_{i=1}^{k-1} (1 - i/k)\Delta^m r_{t+im}^{(m)} \tag{28}$$

where $\Delta^m r_t = r_t - r_{r-m}$ and $k = n/m$ (an integer). For example, for $n = 4$, $m = 1$, $S_t^{(4,1)} = R_t^{(4)} - r_t^{(1)}$ and

$$S^{(4,1)} = E_t \left(\tfrac{3}{4}\Delta r_{t+1}^{(1)} + \tfrac{2}{4}\Delta r_{t+2}^{(1)} + \tfrac{1}{4}\Delta r_{t+3}^{(1)}\right) \tag{29}$$

A VAR of higher order is of the form

$$S_{t+1} = (a_{11}S_t + a_{12}\Delta r_t) + (a_{13}S_{t-1} + a_{14}\Delta r_{t-1})$$
$$+ (a_{15}S_{t-2} + a_{16}\Delta r_{t-2}) + \cdots + \omega_{1t+1} \tag{30a}$$

$$\Delta r_{t+1} = (a_{21}S_t + a_{22}\Delta r_t) + (a_{23}S_{t-1} + a_{24}\Delta r_{t-1})$$
$$+ (a_{25}S_{t-2} + a_{26}\Delta r_{t-2}) + \cdots + \omega_{2t+1} \tag{30b}$$

However, having obtained estimates of the $a_{ij}$ in the usual way, we can rearrange the above 'high lag' system into a first-order system. For example, suppose we have a VAR of order $p = 2$, then in matrix notation, this is equivalent to

$$\begin{bmatrix} S_{t+1} \\ \Delta r_{t+1} \\ S_t \\ \Delta r_t \end{bmatrix} = \begin{bmatrix} a_{11} & a_{12} & a_{13} & a_{14} \\ a_{21} & a_{22} & a_{23} & a_{24} \\ 1 & 0 & 0 & 0 \\ 0 & 1 & 0 & 0 \end{bmatrix} \begin{bmatrix} S_t \\ \Delta r_t \\ S_{t-1} \\ \Delta r_{t-1} \end{bmatrix} \begin{bmatrix} \omega_{1t+1} \\ \omega_{2t+1} \\ 0 \\ 0 \end{bmatrix} \tag{31}$$

Equation (31) is known as the *companion form* of the VAR and may be compactly written as

$$\mathbf{Z}_t = \mathbf{A}\mathbf{Z}_{t-1} + \omega_{t+1} \tag{32}$$

where $Z'_{t+1} = [S_{t+1}, \Delta r_{t+1}, S_t, \Delta r_t]$. Given the $(2p \times 1)$ selection vectors $e\mathbf{1}' = [1, 0, 0, 0]$, $e\mathbf{2}' = [0, 1, 0, 0]$, we have

$$S_t^{(n,m)} = \mathbf{e1}'\mathbf{Z}_t \tag{33a}$$

$$\Delta r_t^{(m)} = \mathbf{e2}'\mathbf{Z}_t \tag{33b}$$

$$E_t \Delta r_{t+j}^{(m)} = \mathbf{e2}'\mathbf{A}^j\mathbf{Z}_t \tag{33c}$$

where, in our example, $n = 4$, $m = 1$, $p = 2$. If (33) is substituted into the general short-rate equation (9), the VAR non-linear restrictions can be shown to be

$$f(\mathbf{a}) = \mathbf{e1}' - \mathbf{e2}'\mathbf{A}[\mathbf{I} - (m/n)(\mathbf{I} - \mathbf{A}^n)(\mathbf{I} - \mathbf{A}^m)^{-1}](\mathbf{I} - \mathbf{A})^{-1} = 0 \tag{34}$$

For our example, this gives

$$f^*(\mathbf{a}) = \mathbf{e1}' - \mathbf{e2}'\mathbf{A}[\mathbf{I} - (1/4)(\mathbf{I} - \mathbf{A}^4)(\mathbf{I} - \mathbf{A})^{-1}](\mathbf{I} - \mathbf{A})^{-1} = 0 \tag{35}$$

## Interpretation of Cross-Equation Restrictions

Let us return to the three-period horizon EH to see if we can gain some insight behind the non-linear restrictions of the $(2 \times 2)$ VAR. We have from (19b) and (19a),

$$E_t S_{t+1} = a_{11} S_t + a_{12} \Delta r_t \tag{36a}$$

$$E_t(\Delta r_{t+2}) = a_{21} E_t S_{t+1} + a_{22} E_t \Delta r_{t+1} \tag{36b}$$

Using the above equations and (19b),

$$E_t(\Delta r_{t+2}) = a_{21}(a_{11} S_t + a_{12}\Delta r_t) + a_{22}(a_{21} S_t + a_{22}\Delta r_t)$$
$$= (a_{21}a_{12} + a_{22}^2)\Delta r_t + a_{21}(a_{11} + a_{22})S_t \tag{37}$$

Using (19b) and (37) in the EH equation (18),

$$S_t = \tfrac{2}{3}(a_{21}S_t + a_{22}\Delta r_t) + \tfrac{1}{3}[(a_{21}a_{12} + a_{22}^2)\Delta r_t + a_{21}(a_{11} + a_{22})S_t]$$
$$= \left[\tfrac{2}{3}a_{22} + \tfrac{1}{3}(a_{21}a_{12} + a_{22}^2)\right]\Delta r_t + \left[\tfrac{2}{3}a_{21} + \tfrac{1}{3}a_{21}(a_{11} + a_{22})\right]S_t$$
$$= f_1(\mathbf{a})\Delta r_t + f_2(\mathbf{a})S_t \tag{38}$$

Equating coefficients on both sides of (38), the non-linear restrictions are

$$0 = f_1(\mathbf{a}) = \tfrac{2}{3}a_{21} + \tfrac{1}{3}(a_{21}^2 + a_{22}a_{11}) \tag{39a}$$

$$1 = f_2(\mathbf{a}) = \tfrac{2}{3}a_{22} + \tfrac{1}{3}a_{22}(a_{21} + a_{12}) \tag{39b}$$

It has been rather tedious to derive these conditions by the long-hand method of substitution and it is far easier to do so in matrix form. The matrix restrictions in (34) for $n = 3, m = 1$ must be equivalent to those in (39), and this is left as a simple exercise for the reader. As before, the non-linear cross-equation restrictions (39) ensure that

(i) expected (abnormal) profits based on information $\Lambda_t$ in the VAR are zero

(ii) the EH equation (18) holds

(iii) the error in forecasting $\Delta r_{t+1}, \Delta r_{t+2}$ using the VAR is independent of information at time $t$ or earlier. The latter is the orthogonality property of RE.

## Theoretical Spread, $S'_t$ and the Actual Spread, $S_t$

Campbell and Shiller (1991) suggest some additional 'metrics' for measuring the empirical success of the EH, and we outline these for the three-period case (i.e. $n = 3$, $m = 1$)

$$S_t = \tfrac{2}{3}E_t\Delta r_{t+1} + \tfrac{1}{3}E_t\Delta r_{t+2} \qquad (40)$$

The RHS of (40) may be measured as a linear prediction from the VAR, the theoretical spread $S'_t$:

$$S'_t = \mathbf{e2}'[(2/3)\mathbf{A} + (1/3)\mathbf{A}^2]\mathbf{z}_t = f(\mathbf{A})\mathbf{z}_t = f_1(\mathbf{a})\Delta r_t + f_2(\mathbf{a})S_t \qquad (41)$$

The theoretical spread is the econometricians' 'best shot' at what the true (RE) forecast of (the weighted average of) future changes in short-term interest rates will be. If the EH (40) is correct, then $f_2(\mathbf{a}) = 1$ and $f_1(\mathbf{a}) = 0$ and, hence, $S'_t = S_t$, and the *actual* spread $S_t$ should be highly correlated with the theoretical spread. In the data set, the latter restrictions will (usually) not hold exactly and, hence, we expect $S'_t$ from (41) to broadly move with the actual spread $S_t$. Hence, under the null hypothesis of the PEH + RE, the following 'statistics' provide useful metrics against which we can measure the success of the PEH (see Engsted 2002).

- In a graph of $S_t$ and $S'_t$ against time, the two series should broadly move in unison but with 'spikes' in $S_t$ larger than those in $S'_t$.

- In the regression, $S'_t = \alpha + \beta S_t + v_t$, we expect $\alpha = 0$ and $\beta = 1$.

- Either the variance ratio VR or the standard deviation ratio (SDR) should be unity as should the correlation between $S_t$ and $S'_t$:

$$\text{VR} = \text{var}(S_t)/\text{var}(S'_t) \quad \text{or} \quad \text{SDR} = \sigma(S_t)/\sigma(S'_t) \quad \text{and} \quad \text{corr}(S_t, S'_t) = 1 \quad (42)$$

Sometimes, we will refer to SDR rather loosely as the 'variance ratio' since both give similar inferences. The *over-reaction hypothesis* implies SDR $> 1$ or $\beta > 1$, since then the actual spread moves more than the (weight average) of expected future short rates (i.e. the theoretical spread $S'_t$).

The EH equation (40) implies that $S_t$ is a sufficient statistic for future changes in short rates and, hence, $S_t$ should 'Granger cause' changes in interest rates. This implies that in the VAR equation, (19b) for $\Delta r_{t+1}$, lagged values of $S_t$ should (as a group), contribute in part to the explanation of $\Delta r_{t+1}$ (so-called block exogeneity tests can be used here).

Suppose $R_t$ and $r_t$ are I(1) variables and, hence, $\Delta r_{t+j}$ is I(0). If the EH is correct, then from (18), the spread $S_t = R_t - r_t$ must also be I(0). Hence, $R_t$ and $r_t$ must be cointegrated, with a cointegration parameter of unity.

It is worth noting that if the econometrician believes that the 'exact' RE model (40) is correct then $S_t$ and $S_t'$ would be equal in all time periods. The latter statement does not imply that rational agents do not make forecasting errors – they do. However, $S_t$ is set in the market with reference to the *expected* value of future interest rates. But, if we have a 'non-exact' RE equation then $S_t - S_t'$ is a measure of this stochastic deviation (i.e. an error term in (40)).

An advantage of the VAR approach over the perfect foresight spread is that it avoids using overlapping data, in which corrections to standard errors (using GMM) can be problematic in small samples. One disadvantage of the VAR is that an explicit forecasting scheme for $(S_t, \Delta r_t)$ is required and if misspecified, our statistical results are biased. Also, the Wald test has poor small-sample properties, and it is not invariant to the precise way the non-linear restrictions are formed (e.g. Gregory and Veall 1985). Also, the Wald test may reject the null hypothesis of the EH + RE because of only 'slight deviations' in the data from the null hypothesis. For example, if $f_1(\mathbf{a}) = 1.03$ in (39) but the standard error on $f_1(\mathbf{a})$ is 0.003, one would reject $H_0 : f_1(\mathbf{a}) = 1$ (on a $t$-test) but an economist would still say that the data largely supported the EH.

One word of warning. Do not confuse the perfect foresight spread $S_t^*$ with the theoretical spread $S_t'$ used in the VAR methodology. The perfect foresight spread $S_t^*$ is a constructed variable that 'replaces' the expectations variables by their actual values. It is the spread that would ensue *if* agents forecast with 100% accuracy. On the other hand, the theoretical spread is an *explicit* forecast of future interest rates based on the econometricians' best guess of the variables investors might actually use in forecasting future short rates.

## 21.3 Time-Varying Term Premium – VAR Methodology

Testing the EH while allowing for a time-varying risk premium requires a three-variable VAR that not only contains the spread and the change in short rates (as used above) but also includes the excess holding period return. The latter variable (see equation (1)) may capture (with error) some of the movements in the (stationary) term premium (Tzavalis and Wickens 1997). Consider the three-variable VAR system comprising

$$\mathbf{Z}_t = [S_t, \Delta r_t, h_t - r_{t-1}] \tag{43}$$

which contains stationary variables. It follows that there exists a trivariate Wold representation (Hannan 1970), which may be approximated by a VAR of order $p$, which in companion form is

$$\mathbf{Z}_{t+1} = \mathbf{A}\mathbf{Z}_t + \mathbf{v}_{t+1} \tag{44}$$

Equation (1) implies that the expected excess holding period return $E_t h_{t+1} - r_t$ is a constant, only if the term premium is time invariant, and in terms of the VAR, this implies (since all variables are expressed as deviations from means):

$$\mathbf{e3'A} = 0 \tag{45}$$

This is the only *additional* restriction compared to our two-variable VAR, and the other restrictions (34), (39a)–(39b) implied by the short-rate equation still hold in the three-variable case. If any of (39a)–(39b) are rejected, this is indicative that expectations about future *average* term premia, $\Phi_t^{(n)} = (1/n) \sum T_{t-i}^{(n-i)}$ are time varying (see (9)).

### Surprises in future short rates and term premia

We are now in a position to assess how far 'surprises' or 'news' in the one-period holding period return $eh_{t+1} = h_{t+1} - E_t h_{t+1}$ are due to 'news' about future interest rates or 'news' about future changes in the term premium $T_t^{(n)}$ and, hence, how important the latter may be in accounting for any empirical rejections of the PEH (i.e. which assumes a constant or zero term premium).

An unanticipated change in the holding period return must be due to an unanticipated change in the long rate (see (1) and (2)). The long rate changes either because of a revision to expectations about future short rates or revisions to the future (one-period) term premia (see (7)). From equations (1)–(3), we obtain (see Tzavalis and Wickens 1997)

$$
\begin{array}{ccc}
\text{'Surprise' in the} & = \text{'News' about} + \text{'News' about} \\
\text{holding period return} & \text{future rates} & \text{future term premia}
\end{array}
$$

$$eh(n, t+1) = -er(n, t+1) - eT(n, t+1) \tag{46}$$

where

$$eh_{t+1}^{(n)} \equiv h_{t+1}^{(n)} - E_t h_{t+1}^{(n)} = [h_{t+1}^{(n)} - r_t] - [E_t h_{t+1}^{(n)} - r_t] \tag{47a}$$

$$er_{t+1}^{(n)} = (E_{t+1} - E_t) \sum_{i=1}^{n-1} \sum_{j=1}^{i} \Delta r_{t+j} \tag{47b}$$

$$eT_{t+1}^{(n)} = (E_{t+1} - E_t) \sum_{i=1}^{n-1} T_{t+i}^{(n-i)} \tag{47c}$$

The intuition behind equation (46) is as follows. For an $n$-period bond, if there is an unexpected rise in its one-period return $(h_{t+1} - E_t h_{t+1})$, this must be due to an unexpected fall in long rates $R_t^{(n)}$, which in turn may be due to an unexpected fall in current or future short rates (i.e. the $er_{t+1}^{(n)}$ term in equation (47b)). Alternatively, the unexpected rise in $h_{t+1}$ could be caused by an unexpected fall in agents' perceptions of the *average* of future risk premia (i.e. the term $eT_{t+1}^{(n)}$ in equation (47c)).

Empirically, how can we assess the relative importance of variations in expectations about future term premia? From equations (47a) to (47c) and using the VAR equation (44), we see that 'surprises' depend on the residuals from the VAR. In particular, the term $\mathbf{v}_{3,t+1} = \mathbf{e3}'\mathbf{v}_{t+1}$ is the error term in the third equation of the VAR and represents the surprise in the excess holding period return $h_{t+1} - E_t h_{t+1}$. Also,

$$eT_{t+1}^{(n)} = -er_{t+1}^{(n)} - eh_{t+1}^{(n)}$$
$$= \mathbf{e2}'[(n-1)\mathbf{I} + (n-2)\mathbf{A} + (n-3)\mathbf{A}^2 + \cdots + (n-(n-1))\mathbf{A}^{n-2}]$$
$$\times \mathbf{v}_{2,t+1} - \mathbf{v}_{3,t+1} \tag{48}$$

The first term is merely the weighted sum of the surprises in future short rates [i.e. $(E_{t+1} - E_t) \sum_{i=1}^{n-1} \sum_{j=1}^{i} \Delta r_{t+j}$] where $\mathbf{e2}'$ 'picks out' the second element in the error term $\mathbf{v}_{t+1}$, which corresponds to the surprise in short rates. The $\mathbf{A}$-matrix represents the degree of persistence in news about future short rates. From (46), if news about future term premia are very small (i.e. $eT_{t+1}^{(n)} \approx 0$), then the surprise in the one-period return $eh_{t+1}^{(n)}$ wholly reflects 'news' about future short rates so, $eh_{t+1} = -er_{t+1}$ and the following metrics should apply.

$$\sigma(er, eh) = 1 \tag{49a}$$
$$\rho(er, eh) = -1 \tag{49b}$$

In addition, from equations (46), (47a) and (1), we obtain

$$h_{t+1}^{(n)} - r_t = T_t^{(n)} - er_{t+1}^{(n)} - eT_{t+1}^{(n)} \tag{50}$$

To the extent that the variables in the VAR adequately proxy the term premium $T_t^{(n)}$, the residual from the one-period holding period regression equation (1) picks up the influence of news about short rates and news about the term premium. If $eT_{t+1}^{(n)} \approx 0$, then '(1 − R-squared)' of the excess return equation in the VAR (i.e. the third equation) indicates the proportion of the excess holding period return that is due to variation in news about future short rates.

## 21.4  Summary

- The EH implies that the spread $S_t^{(n,m)}$ between the $n$-period (spot) yield $R_t^{(n)}$ and the $m$-period spot yield $R_t^{(m)}$ is an optimal predictor of both the *expected* future change in the long rate (over one period) and expected future changes in short rates and gives rise to the following regression tests.

### Long-rate equation

$$((n-m)/m)[R_{t+m}^{(n-m)} - R_t^{(n)}] = \alpha + \beta_L S_t^{(n,m)} + \gamma \Omega_t + \varepsilon_{t+m}$$

### Future-short-rate equation

$$S_t^{(n,m)*} = \alpha + \beta_S S_t^{(n,m)} + \gamma \Omega_t + \eta_t$$

where the perfect foresight spread $S_t^{(n,m)*} = (1/k) \sum_{i=0}^{k-1} \Delta^m R_{t+im}^{(m)}$, for $k = n/m$, an integer. Under the EH + RE, we expect $\beta_S = \beta_L = 1$ and $\gamma = 0$. A constant, non-zero term premium implies $\alpha \neq 0$.

- The future-short-rate equation can be tested by using out-turn values for $\Delta r_{t+j}$ and forming the perfect foresight spread $S_t^*$ in a single-equation regression or by invoking an explicit forecasting equation for the $\Delta r_{t+j}$ and using the theoretical spread $S_t'$ – the latter is the VAR approach.

- In the VAR approach, the EH implies $S_t' = S_t$ and, hence, $\sigma(S_t') = \sigma(S_t)$ and $\text{corr}(S_t', S_t) = 1$. The EH also implies cross-equation restrictions between the parameters of the VAR.

- Using the excess HPR in the VAR, we can gain some insight into the behaviour of the time-varying term premium.

- Variance bounds *inequalities* were originally used to test the EH, but these have now largely been superseded by the above regression-based tests.

# 22

# EMPIRICAL EVIDENCE ON THE TERM STRUCTURE

## Aims

- Examine the type and quality of data used in testing term structure models.

- Examine properties of long and short rates and issues of cointegration.

- Analyse early work on variance bounds tests, comparing the time-series behaviour of the long rate and the perfect foresight spread.

- Present evidence on whether the forward rate provides an unbiased forecast of future spot rates.

- Present results from single-equation tests of the expectations hypothesis EH using the 'change-in-long-rate' and the 'change-in-short-rate' equations.

- Provide a detailed case study of various tests of the EH, using the VAR methodology, including the possibility of a time-varying term premium.

- Analyse why the various tests of the EH, which are equivalent under the null, give different inferences in practice.

In this chapter, we examine tests of the EH using variance bounds, single-equation regressions and the VAR methodology. For the most part, we concentrate on the EH with a time-invariant term premium, but towards the end of the chapter, we look at models that try to explicitly account for a time-varying term premium – but these are not based on the no-arbitrage SDF approach – an issue we take up in Chapter 23.

# 22.1    Data and Cointegration

The 'quality' of the data used in empirical studies varies considerably. This can make comparisons between different studies somewhat hazardous. The yield data used by researchers might represent either opening or closing rates (on a particular day of the month) and may be 'bid' or 'offer' rates or an average of the two rates. The next issue concerns 'timing'. If we are trying to compare the return on a three-year bond with the rolled-over investment on three one-year bonds, then the yield data on the long-bond for time $t$ must be measured at exactly the same time as that for the short rate and the investment horizons should coincide exactly. In other words, the rates should represent actual (spot) dealing rates on which one could undertake each investment strategy.

As we noted in the previous chapter, tests of the expectations hypothesis, in principle, require data on spot yields. The latter are usually not available for maturities greater than about two years and have to be estimated from data on the prices of coupon paying bonds: this can introduce further approximations.

## Cointegration Properties of Interest Rates

Given that long rates $R_t$ and short rates $r_t$ are found to be I(1), $\Delta R$ and $\Delta r$ are I(0) by construction. A weak test of the PEH + RE implied by the 'future-short-rate' or 'long-rate' equations (see previous chapter) is that $R_t$ and $r_t$ are cointegrated with a cointegration parameter of unity. Alternatively, the EH implies that the spreads $S_t = R_t - r_t$ should be I(0). While it is often found to be the case that, *taken as a pair*, any two interest rates are cointegrated and each spread $S_t^{(n,m)}$ is stationary, this cointegration procedure can be undertaken in a more comprehensive fashion. If we have $q$ interest rates that are I(1), then the EH implies that there are $(q-1)$ linearly independent spreads that are cointegrated. We can arbitrary normalise on the one-period rate $R^{(1)} \equiv r$ so that for $X_t = \{r, R^{(2)}, \ldots R^{(q)}\}$, the EH implies restricted cointegrating vectors of the form $\{1, -1, 0, \ldots 0\}, \{1, 0, -1, 0, \ldots 0\}$, and so on. Also, some of the $(q-1)$ spreads should enter the vector ECM that explains the change in the set of interest rates $\Delta X_t$. The Johansen (1988) procedure allows one to test for these cointegrating vectors simultaneously in a vector error correction model VECM of the form

$$\Delta X_t = \theta(L)\Delta X_{t-1} + \gamma' X_{t-1} + \varepsilon_t \tag{1}$$

where $\gamma$ is a $(q \times q)$ matrix of parameters and (below) $\mathbf{R} = \{R^{(2)}, \ldots R^{(q)}\}$

$$\Delta X_t = \theta(L)\Delta X_{t-1} + \alpha_1'(R^{(1)} - \beta_1'\mathbf{R})_{t-1} + \alpha_2'(R^{(1)} - \beta_2'\mathbf{R})_{t-1}$$
$$+ \cdots + \alpha_{q-1}'(R^{(1)} - \beta_q'\mathbf{R})_{t-1} + \varepsilon_t$$

First, we test to see if the number of cointegrating vectors in the system equals $q - 1$ and then test the joint null for the cointegrating parameter restrictions implied by the EH. Both are somewhat 'minimal' tests of the validity of the EH. Shea (1992) and Hall,

Anderson and Granger (1992) find that although we cannot reject the presence of $q - 1$ cointegrating vectors on US data, nevertheless, it is frequently the case that some of the $\{1, -1, 0, \ldots 0\}$, $\{1, 0, -1, 0, \ldots 0\}$, and so on, type restrictions are rejected by the data. Putting subtle statistical issues aside (of which there are many, not least small sample properties), a key consideration in interpreting these results is whether the VECM is an adequate representation of the data generation process for interest rates (e.g. are the parameters constant over the whole sample period?). If the VAR is acceptable but some of the restrictions are numerically (and statistically) far from the form $\{1, -1, 0, \ldots 0\}$, $\{1, 0, -1, 0, \ldots 0\}$, etc, then the EH is rejected for the *whole* maturity spectrum. However, the EH may still hold for some subset of yields (e.g. at the very short end – see Cuthbertson 1996, Cuthbertson, Hayes and Nitzsche 1998) or for particular subsets of the data set (see Hall, Anderson and Granger 1992).

Recently, Hansen (2002) tests the cointegration restrictions implied by the EH on US data but assuming there are structural changes at known times. He finds a structural break in the 1979–1982 period of monetary base control when interest rates rose dramatically and were extremely volatile. After taking account of this structural break in the *dynamics* of the VECM, he finds *constant* cointegrating vectors that satisfy the EH. Rather than posit a structural break, Seo (2003) can be interpreted as 'getting rid of the 1979–1982 data problem' by abandoning the linear VECM and using a non-linear target threshold model TAR. In the linear VECM, the cointegrating parameters are already very close to their EH values of $\{1, -1, 0, \ldots 0\}$, $\{1, 0, -1, 0, \ldots 0\}$, and so on, and in the TAR model, this is still the case, but the latter allows the dynamic response of changes in $R_t$ or $r_t$ to differ, depending on whether the spread $R_{t-1} - r_{t-1}$ is above an upper threshold, below a lower threshold or between the two thresholds. The TAR model for the US provides some incremental explanatory power for the cointegration VECM compared with the linear VECM over the period 1973–1995. Sarno and Thornton (2003) undertake a similar study to Seo (2003) on daily US data 1974–1999 in a bivariate non-linear asymmetric VECM using the Federal Funds (FF) rate and the Treasury Bill (TB) rate. The cointegrating vector (over the whole sample) is $z = FF - 1.15TB + 0.5$, and this disequilibrium term appears separately for positive and negative deviations. In addition, there is an ESTAR term in $z$, to account for any symmetric non-linear effects on $\Delta F$ or $\Delta TB$. These non-linear effects reduce the residual variance by about 20% (i.e. about a 10% reduction in the standard error of the regression, compared to the linear VECM). Most of the adjustment takes place via the FF rate and as the authors note, this is a little surprising because the FF rate is targeted by the Federal Reserve and, therefore, one might expect the TB rate to adjust more to the disequilibrium in $z$. If agents can accurately forecast policy changes in the FF rate and move the TB rate ahead of changes in FF, then this would show up in the data as a strong lagged response of the FF rate to the disequilibrium – but this would require the market to accurately forecast policy changes and that seems unlikely. It would be interesting to examine how far these non-linear effects are due to the volatile movements in interest rates in the monetary targeting period of 1979–1982. (In the following, we will see that the 1979–1982 period in the United States affects many different types of test of the EH but is also relatively easily and satisfactorily dealt with using simple dummy variables.) The above results may be summarised as follows.

(i) For the most part, long and short rates are cointegrated, with a cointegration parameter close to or equal to unity.

(ii) Spreads do tend to Granger cause future changes in interest rates for most maturities (i.e. some of the $\alpha_i$ in (1) are statistically significant).

(iii) There are dynamic non-linearities in the relationship between US interest rates, but it remains to be seen how robust these are to different sample periods and how far they bias the estimates in linear models. These models do not provide detailed tests of the EH except for the somewhat weak test that interest rates are cointegrated and that the cointegrating vectors are of the form $\{1, -1, 0, \ldots 0\}$, $\{1, 0, -1, 0, \ldots 0\}$, and so on (Balke and Fomby 1997).

Whatever the results from cointegration tests in finite samples, the implication of not taking the spread to be stationary implies that its (unconditional) variance approaches infinity as the time horizon lengthens or equivalently that long rates and short rates eventually permanently drift apart over time – it would be a brave economist who would posit such behaviour, since it implies that the risk premium is also non-stationary and is, therefore, unbounded.

## 22.2    Variance Bounds Tests

If the EH + RE holds and the term premium depends only on $n$ (i.e. is time invariant), then the variance of the actual long rate should be less than the variability in the perfect foresight long rate, $\text{var}(R_t^{(n)*})$. Hence, the variance ratio

$$VR = \text{var}(R_t^{(n)}) / \text{var}(R_t^{(n)*}) \tag{2}$$

should be less than unity. However, in initial variance bounds tests by Shiller (1979) using US and UK data on *yields to maturity* 1966–1977 and by Pesando (1983) on Canadian bonds, these researchers find that the VR exceeds unity. This result was confirmed by Singleton (1980), who provided a formal *statistical* test of (2) (i.e. he computed appropriate standard errors for VR).

If we assume that a *time-varying* term premium $T_t^{(n)}$ can be added to the EH, then the violation of the variance bounds test could be due to variability in $T_t^{(n)}$. If this is the case, the variability in the term premium would have to be large in order to reverse the empirical results from these variance bounds tests.

However, there are some severe econometric problems with the early variance bounds tests discussed above. First, if the interest rate series have stochastic trends (i.e. are non-stationary), then their variances are not defined and the usual test statistics are inappropriate. Second, even assuming stationarity, Flavin (1983) demonstrates that there may be substantial small-sample bias in the usual test statistics used. To overcome the latter problem, Shiller (1989, Chapter 13) used two very long data sets for the United States (1857–1988) and United Kingdom (1824–1987) to compare $R_t$ and the long moving average of short rates, namely the perfect foresight long rate $R_t^*$. To mitigate problems of non-stationarity in the level of interest rates, Shiller (1989) performs the following regression.

$$R_t^* - R_{t-1} = \alpha + \beta(R_t - R_{t-1}) + v_t \qquad (3)$$

Shiller finds for the United States, $\hat{\beta} = 1.156$ ($s.e. = 0.253$) and for the United Kingdom, $\hat{\beta} = 0.347$ ($s.e. = 0.178$). For the United States, we can accept the EH, since $\hat{\beta}$ is not statistically different from unity but for the United Kingdom, the EH is rejected at conventional significance levels. Overall, for this long data set using the yields to maturity, the EH (with constant term premium) holds up quite well for the United States but not for the United Kingdom.

Using more recent data, we have graphed $R_t$ and $R_t^*$ for the United States and United Kingdom in Figures 1a and 1b. 'By eye', it would appear that the variability in $R_t$ and $R_t^*$ for the United States (Figure 1a) is broadly comparable up to 1979. In 1979, the United States introduced monetary base control, which lasted until 1982, after which inflation, and hence interest rates, followed a downward trend. Clearly, the 1979–1982 period is problematic for the EH, although even after 1982, the variability in $R_t$ appears greater than that of $R_t^*$.

For the United Kingdom (Figure 1b), it is clear that the 1970–1985 period appears very problematic for the EH as actual long rates $R_t$ move much more than the perfect foresight long rate $R_t^*$, and this pattern persists (although it is attenuated somewhat) up until the last few years of (historically) low and fairly stable interest rates. Of course, the level of long rates is very close to a random walk and the two figures contain a

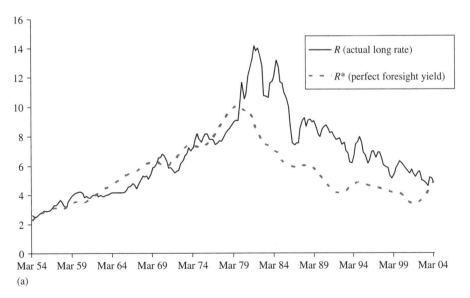

(a)

**Figure 1** (a) Actual and perfect foresight yield (USA: 1954–2004). (b) Actual and perfect foresight yield (UK: 1964–2004)

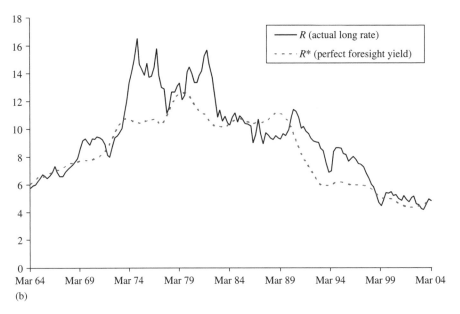

(b)

**Figure 1**   (*continued*)

relatively short data set so our 'casual empiricism' provides only a 'ball park' estimate of what is going on.

## 22.3   Single-Equation Tests

### Excess Holding Period Return

Under the EH, the excess holding period return (EHPR) should be independent of all information at time $t$, and any liquidity premium should depend only on maturity and increase with time to maturity. If we take an *unconditional* average of the HPR on US bonds (1953–1997) of 1 to 5 years' maturity, it is found (Cochrane 2000) that the $HPR^{(1)} = 5.8$ ($\sigma_1 = 2.83$), whereas for $HPR^{(5)} = 6.4$ ($\sigma_5 = 6.6$). Given an average short rate of around 5% over this period, the *excess* HPR does not increase appreciably and by much less than the standard deviation of the HPR. The Sharpe ratio $(SR) = \mathrm{EHPR}/\sigma(\mathrm{EHPR})$ for bonds is, therefore, much less than for stocks and is relatively constant over different maturities. Broadly similar results hold for other G10 countries. Thus, at 'first blush', the EH appears reasonable. However, the picture becomes less favourable after examination of tests based on *conditional* (rather than unconditional) expectations.

### Forward Rate Regressions

Under the EH, the *one-period* forward rate at time $t$, applicable to period $n$ to $n + 1$, should be an unbiased predictor of the *one-period* out-turn spot rate at $t + n$:

$$R_{t+n}^{(1)} = \alpha^* + \beta^* f_t^{(n)} + \eta_{t+n} \tag{4a}$$

where $\beta^* = 1$. Running regressions like (4a) for different forward rates $n = 2, 3, \ldots$ gives $\beta^*$ and R-squared very close to unity. But, unfortunately, this does not validate the EH because $r$ and $f$ are non-stationary so we may have a spurious regression problem. It is more sensible and statistically valid to see if the current forward-spot *spread* forecasts *changes* in interest rates, since these variables are stationary:

$$R^{(1)}_{t+n} - R^{(1)}_t = \alpha + \beta(f^{(n)}_t - R^{(1)}_t) + \eta_{t+n} \qquad (4b)$$

where $R^{(1)}_t = r_t$ is the current short rate. Regressions like (4b) give dramatically different results. The R-squared drops to around 0.005 (1/2%) for $n = 1$ year and to about 0.10 (10%) for $n = 4$ years. The $\beta$ coefficient in (4b) is around 0.3 ($s.e. = 0.30$) for $n = 1$ year, rising to 0.75 ($s.e. = 0.30$) for $n = 4$ years.

One of the problems with (4b) is the 'loss of data' when using long maturities. For example, if $n = 15$ years, we lose 180 months of observations at the end of the sample. Equation (5) also has serially correlated disturbances. Backus, Foresi, Mozumdar and Wu (2001) suggests an alternative to (5). The EH implies

$$f^{(n)}_t = E_t R^{(1)}_{t+n} + rp^{(n)}_t \qquad (5a)$$

$$f^{(n-1)}_{t+1} = E_{t+1} R^{(1)}_{t+n} + rp^{(n-1)}_{t+1} \qquad (5b)$$

where $rp^{(n)}_t$ is the risk premium for period $t + n$ and $f^{(n)}_t$ is the *one-period* forward rate for $n$ periods ahead, which should be an unbiased forecast of the *one-period* spot rate at $t + n$. Note that the forward rate in (5b), beginning at $t + 1$ and for a horizon of $n - 1$, 'coincides in time' with $R^{(1)}_{t+n}$. From (5a) and (5b), using the law of iterated expectations (i.e. $E_t E_{t+1} = E_t$) and assuming a time-invariant term premium gives a regression test of the EH on the basis of the term premia of forwards rates:

$$f^{(n-1)}_{t+1} - R^{(1)}_t = \delta^{(n)}_0 + \delta^{(n)}_1 (f^{(n)}_t - R^{(1)}_t) + \varepsilon^{(n)}_t \qquad (6)$$

$R^{(1)}_t$ is included so that the regression variables are stationary and under the EH, we expect $\delta^{(n)}_1 = 1$. The advantage of (6) is that using say a ten-year horizon, the one-period forward rate in the dependent variable is observable at month 119 ahead and there is no truncation of the data (i.e. loss of data). Also we avoid the use of overlapping data in (6), whereas in (5a), this tends to 'distort' the (GMM) standard errors, in small samples.

Using US data 1976–1998, Backus, Foresi, Mozumdar and Wu (2001) and Christiansen (2003) find $\delta^{(n)}_1$ is around 0.95 for maturities $n = 1$ to 25 years, but statistically different from unity. However, when the 1979–1982 period of US monetary base control is excluded and the data period is 1987–1998 then $\delta^{(n)}_1$ is around 0.98–1.0 for $n = 1$ to 25 and is not statistically different from unity, thus supporting the EH.

Hence, on US data, for maturities in excess of one year, the EH works rather well on the basis of these forward rate regressions once we exclude the period of very volatile interest rates in the 1979–1982 monetary base control experiment.

## Pure Discount Bonds/T-Bills

A great deal of the early empirical work on the EH was undertaken using three- and six-month T-Bills (i.e. pure discount (zero coupon) bonds). The long-rate, short-rate and the EHPR equations are very simple. Using *quarterly* data, we have the following.

### *Change-in-long-rate*

$$(R_{t+1}^{(3)} - R_t^{(6)}) = \alpha_L + \beta_L S_t^{(6,3)} + \varepsilon_{t+1} \tag{7}$$

where $S_t^{(6,3)} = R_t^{(6)} - R_t^{(3)}$ and $\alpha_L$ is the constant term premium. (Note that the six-month bond becomes a three-month bond after three months.)

### *Change-in-short-rate*

$$(1/2)\Delta R_{t+1}^{(3)} = \alpha_S + \beta_S S_t^{(6,3)} + \varepsilon_{t+1} \tag{8}$$

This is the regression of the perfect foresight spread, $S_t^{(6,3)*} = (1/2)\Delta R_{t+1}^{(3)}$ on the actual spread, $S_t^{(6,3)}$.

### *HPR regression*

$$H_{t+1} - R_t^{(3)} = c_o + c_1 \Omega_t + \varepsilon_{t+1} \tag{9}$$

Since the variables on the RHS of all three equations are dated at time $t$, they are uncorrelated with the RE forecast error $\varepsilon_{t+1}$ and, hence, OLS on these regression equations yields consistent parameter estimates (but a GMM correction to the covariance matrix may be required). Under the EH, we should find

$$H_0 : \beta_L = \beta_S = 1 \text{ and } c_1 = 0$$

Regressions using either of the above three equations give similar inferences as the estimated parameters are exact *linear* transformations of each other (for $n = 2\,\text{m}$). On US quarterly data, 1963(1)–1983(4) Mankiw and Summers (1984) finds $\beta_L = -0.407$ ($s.e. = 0.4$), which has the wrong sign. Simon (1989), using US weekly data on Treasury Bills, 1961–1988, finds $\beta_S = 0.04$ ($s.e. = 0.43$), although for one of the sub-periods chosen, namely the 1972–1979 period, he finds $\beta_S = 0.8$ ($s.e. = 0.34$), which is not statistically different from 1. Both studies find that the expectations hypothesis is rather strongly rejected.

Mankiw and Summers (1984) seeks to explain the failings of the EH by considering the possibility that the expectations of $r_{t+1}$ by market participants as a whole consists of a weighted average of the rationally expected rate ($E_t r_{t+1}$) of the 'smart money' traders and a simple naive myopic forecasting scheme (i.e. noise traders) based simply on the current short rate. If $\tilde{r}_{t+1}^e$ denotes the market's average expectation, then Mankiw assumes

$$\tilde{r}_{t+1}^e = w r_t + (1 - w)(E_t r_{t+1}) \tag{10}$$

where $0 < w < 1$. The EH then becomes

$$R_t = (1/2)r_t + (1/2)\tilde{r}_{t+1}^e + \phi \tag{11}$$

Substituting (10) in (11) and rearranging gives an equation similar to (8) but where $\beta_s = (1 + w)/(1 - w) > 1$. However, incorporating this 'mixed' expectations scheme does not rescue the expectations hypothesis, since Mankiw finds $\beta_s$ is negative. In a later paper, Mankiw and Miron (1986) investigate why the EH using three- and six-month bills fails so abysmally post-1915 but appears to perform much better in the period 1890–1914. Estimating over four sub-periods between 1915 and 1979, Mankiw–Miron find $\beta_S$ is approximately zero and the R-squared is very low (<0.06). For 1890–1914 (quarterly data), they find some improvement

$$\Delta r_{t+1} = -0.57 + 1.51(R_t - r_t) \tag{12}$$
$$\phantom{\Delta r_{t+1} = } (0.14) \qquad (0.18)$$

The R-squared $= 0.40$ and although $\beta_S$ is positive, one still cannot accept the null that $\beta_s = 2$. They suggest that the reason for the improvement in the performance of the EH in the pre-1915 period, which is prior to the setting up of the Federal Reserve, is that $E_t \Delta r_{t+1}$ is more variable. After 1915, the Fed attempted to smooth interest rates, which can be represented as $E_t \Delta r_{t+1} = 0$, that is, $r_{t+1}$ follows a random walk (strictly speaking, a martingale). Hence, post-1915, the spread would have no predictive power for future changes in interest rates. If there is a time-varying term premium that is correlated with the spread, then the OLS $\hat{\beta}_S$ is inconsistent, that is, plim$\hat{\beta}_s \neq \beta_s$. This 'bias' is smaller, the greater the *variance* of $E_t(\Delta r_{t+1})$. When $\Delta r_{t+1}$ is unpredictable, $\sigma^2(E_t \Delta r_{t+1}) = 0$ and plim$\hat{\beta} = 0$. The estimated value of $\hat{\beta}$ approaches its true value as the variance of $E_t \Delta r_{t+1}$ increases. Mankiw–Miron show that in a simple predictive equation for $\Delta r_{t+1}$

$$\Delta r_{t+1} = \theta_1(L)r_t + \theta_2(L)R_t + \varepsilon_{t+1}$$

The R-squared decreases from 0.4 for the 1890–1914 period to around zero for the post-1915 period, thus confirming the above conjecture that the EH performs better in the pre-1915 period because interest rates are more predictable.

Another possible reason for the poor performance of the EH at short maturities is that the monetary authorities may increase short rates in response to the size of the long-short spread – where the latter signals a higher expected future inflation and, hence, the need for contractionary monetary policy. Kugler (2002) finds evidence that there is a change in the parameter of this reaction function in the United States in the 1979–1982 period, and he attributes the poor performance of the EH to this effect.

## 22.4 Expectations Hypothesis: Case Study

For pedagogic purposes, we first consider in some detail the study of Cuthbertson and Nitzsche (2003) on UK spot rates (recently constructed by the Bank of England – Anderson, Breedon and Deacon 1996, Anderson and Sleath 1999). The spot rates are calculated from coupon bonds whose prices are collected contemporaneously and represent rates on which actual trades could take place (except for brokerage fees, which are small). The maturities considered are for 2, 3, ..., 10 years inclusive and also for 15, 20 and 25 years. The data set runs from February 1975 and is sampled monthly. Unless stated otherwise, hypothesis tests are assessed using a 5% significance level.

The data set also allows us to avoid the approximation made in much of the earlier work using long rates, namely, to approximate $h_{t+1}^{(n)} = [\ln P_{t+1}^{(n-1)} - \ln P_t^{(n)}]$ by $[\ln P_{t+1}^{(n)} - \ln P_t^{(n)}]$, when we do not have data on $\ln P_{t+1}^{(n-1)}$. It has been shown by Bekaert, Hodrick and Marshall (1997) that this approximation can cause bias in regression tests of the EH, particularly for the 'change in the long-rate equation' (6). As with all studies of the EH at the long end of the market (where observed zero coupon yields are not available), there is some approximation error in our data, since the yield curve is fitted, although this does of course minimise the influence of 'outliers' in the raw data itself.

The analysis is undertaken using both the one-month and the three-month rate as a representative short rate, but as qualitative results did not differ for these two rates, we only report results using the one-month short rate. Graphs of the two-year rate and the 25-year rate relative to the one-month T-Bill rate are shown in Figures 2 and 3 and clearly each of the two series moves together in the long run, and there is considerable variability in the spread.

The key equations are

$$(n-1)\{E_t R_{t+1}^{(n-1)} - R_t^{(n)}\} = \beta_L S_t^{(n)} + T_t^{(n)} \tag{13}$$

$$S_t^{*(n,1)} \equiv \sum_{i=1}^{n-1} (1 - k/n) E_t \Delta r_{t+i} = \beta_s S_t^{(n,1)} + \Phi_t^{(n)} \tag{14}$$

where $\beta_L = \beta_s = 1$ under the EH with constant term premia.

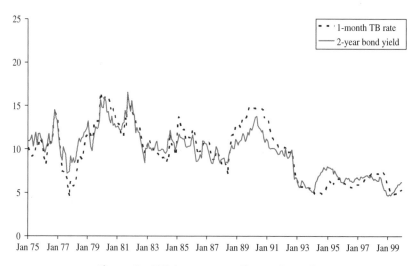

**Figure 2**    UK interest rates (2 year, 1 month)

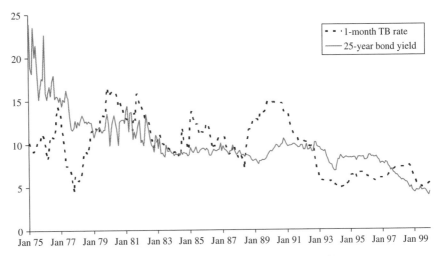

**Figure 3**   UK interest rates (25 year, 1 month)

**Table 1**   'Long-rate equation': $(n-1)R_{t+1}^{(n-1)} - R_t^{(n)} = \alpha + \beta_L(R_t^{(n)} - r_t) + \varepsilon_{t+1}$

| Interest Rate Maturities | $\alpha$ | | $\beta$ | | $R^2$-Statistic |
|---|---|---|---|---|---|
| | Coeff. | s.e. | Coeff. | s.e. | |
| (2 year, 1 month) | −0.5352 | 0.9189 | 0.4506 | 0.7136 | 0.0013 |
| (3 year, 1 month) | −0.9921 | 1.3083 | 0.9113 | 0.8619 | 0.0038 |
| (4 year, 1 month) | −1.4752 | 1.6742 | 1.1470 | 0.9934 | 0.0045 |
| (5 year, 1 month) | −1.9116 | 2.0365 | 1.1502 | 1.1172 | 0.0036 |
| (6 year, 1 month) | −2.2625 | 2.4053 | 0.9562 | 1.2374 | 0.0020 |
| (7 year, 1 month) | −2.5293 | 2.7808 | 0.6229 | 1.3540 | 0.0007 |
| (8 year, 1 month) | −2.7351 | 3.1601 | 0.2027 | 1.4660 | 0.0001 |
| (9 year, 1 month) | −2.9152 | 3.5407 | −0.2666 | 1.5730 | 0.0001 |
| (10 year, 1 month) | −3.0958 | 3.9218 | −0.7610 | 1.6751 | 0.0007 |
| (15 year, 1 month) | −4.4868 | 6.0238 | −3.4832 | 2.1930 | 0.0085 |
| (20 year, 1 month) | −6.7220 | 9.6725 | −7.5456 | 3.0920 | 0.0197 |
| (25 year, 1 month) | −9.7165 | 16.4440 | −14.4373 | 4.6790 | 0.0312 |

Notes:
Equations are estimated over the period January 1976 to November 1999 by GMM with White (1980) correction to the standard errors, due to the presence of heteroscedasticity. Asymptotic standard errors are reported.

## Single-Equation Regression

For the coefficient on the spread $\beta_L$ in the long-rate regressions (Table 1), we cannot reject the EH that this coefficient is unity for $n = 2$ to 10 years but the null is rejected for $n = 15$, 20 and 25. The $\beta_L$ coefficients are positive and close to unity for $n = 3$ to 6, but then decline, becoming negative at longer maturities. The above is consistent with the presence of bias in the OLS results, caused by a time-varying term premium (see the VAR results below) for $n = 15$, 20, 25. However, the most striking aspect of these results is the relatively large standard errors for $\beta$ and the low R-squared of the regressions. Except for $n = 15$, 20, 25, we could also accept the null that the spread

**Table 2**   'Future-short-rate equation': $\sum (1 - i/n)\Delta r_{t+i} = \alpha + \beta_S(R_t^{(n)} - r_t) + \varepsilon_t$

| Sample Period | Maturity of Long Rates (in Months) | $\alpha$ | | $\beta$ | | $R^2$-Statistic |
|---|---|---|---|---|---|---|
| | | Coeff. | s.e. | Coeff. | s.e. | |
| Feb. 75–Dec. 99 | $n = 24$ | −0.1559 | 0.3418 | 0.8794 | 0.1995 | 0.3032 |
| Feb. 75–Dec. 98 | $n = 36$ | −0.3722 | 0.4382 | 0.9791 | 0.2123 | 0.3749 |
| Feb. 75–Dec. 97 | $n = 48$ | −0.5959 | 0.4944 | 1.0746 | 0.2086 | 0.4676 |
| Feb. 75–Dec. 96 | $n = 60$ | −0.8110 | 0.5193 | 1.1158 | 0.1937 | 0.5442 |
| Feb. 75–Dec. 95 | $n = 72$ | −1.0175 | 0.4901 | 1.1251 | 0.1496 | 0.6097 |
| Feb. 75–Dec. 94 | $n = 84$ | −1.1999 | 0.4222 | 1.1391 | 0.1038 | 0.6698 |
| Feb. 75–Dec. 93 | $n = 96$ | −1.3703 | 0.3491 | 1.1816 | 0.0816 | 0.7360 |
| Feb. 75–Dec. 92 | $n = 108$ | −1.5519 | 0.3047 | 1.1533 | 0.0699 | 0.7810 |
| Feb. 75–Dec. 91 | $n = 120$ | −1.6416 | 0.2457 | 1.0978 | 0.0696 | 0.8105 |

Notes:

Equations are estimated over sample period stated in column 1 by GMM with Newey-West (1987) correction to the standard errors, due to the presence of heteroscedasticity and a moving-average error of order $n - 1$. Asymptotic standard errors are reported. Equations are only reported for $n_{max} = 120$ (10 years) because of the lack of degrees of freedom caused by having to truncate the data to accommodate future changed in the short rate, given our finite data set.

has *no* predictive power for next period's change in long rates. The small-sample results in Bekaert, Hodrick and Marshall (1997, Table 6) indicate that the OLS $\beta_L$ is biased upwards with a mean value from the empirical distribution of $\beta_L \approx 2$ when the true $\beta_L = 1$, implying a stronger rejection of the EH for $n = 15, 20, 25$ if these bias corrections broadly apply in our data.

Results using the perfect foresight spread (14) in the future-short-rate equation (Table 2) are much more favourable to the EH. Indeed, the $\beta_S$ coefficients for $n = 2$–10 years are all close to unity, with reasonably small (asymptotic) standard errors. (Note that we cannot estimate this equation for maturities longer than 10 years because of the loss of data as we model future changes in short rates over long horizons. This problem is not present in the VAR results below.) The above qualitative results would not alter if we applied the bias corrections in Bekaert, Hodrick and Marshall (1997, Table 6 – see below) since the finite sample upward bias for $\beta_S$ is quite small (and Bekaert et al also find that empirical distribution for $\beta_S$ is a little more dispersed than the asymptotic distribution).

## VAR Analysis

The unit root/cointegration properties of UK interest rates have been extensively examined (see for example, Taylor 1992, MacDonald and Speight 1991, Cuthbertson 1996, Cuthbertson, Hayes and Nitzsche 1996), and each element of $\mathbf{z} = [S_t, \Delta r_t, h_t - r_{t-1}]$ used in the VAR analysis is stationary. Also the A-matrix of VAR coefficients has the largest eigenvalue in the range of 0.92–0.97 (for our sample of maturities), indicating a dynamically stable VAR for forecasting future short rates.

The three-variable VAR has $\mathbf{z}_t = [S_t, \Delta r_t, h_t - r_{t-1}]$. The restriction that the excess holding period return $E_t h_{t+1} - r_t$ is not time varying, namely $\mathbf{e3'A} = 0$ is rejected only for the very long maturities $n = 15, 20$ and 25 years, at the 5% level of significance or

**Table 3**   Are excess one-period returns time varying?

| Interest Rate Maturities | Wald Test | |
| --- | --- | --- |
| | $H_0 : \mathbf{e3}'\mathbf{A} = 0$ | |
| | Statistic | p-value |
| (2 year, 1 month) | 2.41 | 0.49 |
| (3 year, 1 month) | 3.42 | 0.33 |
| (4 year, 1 month) | 5.57 | 0.13 |
| (5 year, 1 month) | 6.69 | 0.08 |
| (6 year, 1 month) | 5.89 | 0.12 |
| (7 year, 1 month) | 4.30 | 0.23 |
| (8 year, 1 month) | 3.03 | 0.39 |
| (9 year, 1 month) | 2.39 | 0.50 |
| (10 year, 1 month) | 2.31 | 0.51 |
| (15 year, 1 month) | 7.83 | 0.05 |
| (20 year, 1 month) | 8.37 | 0.04 |
| (25 year, 1 month) | 8.06 | 0.04 |

Notes:
The sample period is from January 1976 to November 1999. The standard errors are heteroscedastic-robust (White, 1980). The null hypothesis for a non-time varying (one-period) term premium is $H_0 : \mathbf{e3}'\mathbf{A} = 0$. The test statistic is asymptotically distributed as $\chi^2$ with 3 degrees of freedom (critical values at the 5% and 10% level of significance are 7.815 and 6.25, respectively).

better (Table 3). This implies that the variables in the VAR may provide a noisy proxy for a time-varying term premium for these longer maturities.

Turning now to the VAR-metrics. The theoretical spread $S_t'$ is the prediction of future short rates using the VAR: $S_t' = f(\mathbf{A})\mathbf{z_t}$. A graph of the actual spread $S_t$ and the theoretical spread $S_t'$ for $n = 2$ years shows a reasonably close correspondence (Figure 4), but that

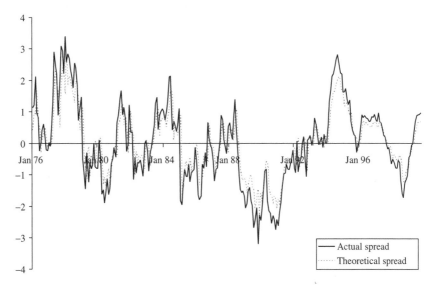

**Figure 4**   UK actual and theoretical spread (2 year, 1 month)

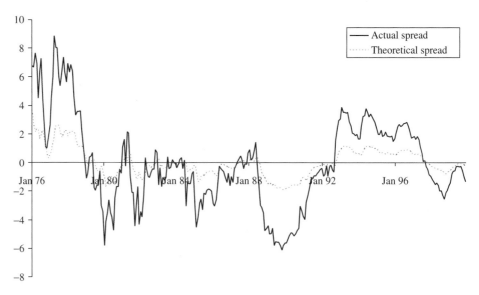

**Figure 5**   UK actual and theoretical spread (25 year, 1 month)

for $n = 25$ years does not (Figure 5), with clear visual evidence of 'overreaction' of the spread relative to expected changes in future short rates.

The results in Table 4 that provide metrics for the relationship between the actual spread $S_t$ and the theoretical spread $S_t'$ indicate that for $n = 2$ to 10 years, the VAR restrictions are not rejected (using a Wald test), the correlation coefficients between the actual and theoretical spread are very close to unity and the standard deviation ratios are not statistically different from unity. Technically, the correlation coefficients are significantly different from unity, given their asymptotic standard errors are so small. But in Bekaert, Hodrick and Marshall (1997, Table 6), the small sample empirical standard deviation of $\rho(S_t', S)$ is around 0.10, and this would lead to non-rejection of the EH on our data.

For $n = 2$ to 10, our results stand in sharp contrast to the 'clear' rejections of the EH on US data at the long (and short) end of the maturity spectrum (Campbell and Shiller 1991, Bekaert, Hodrick and Marshall 1997). However, for $n = 15, 20, 25$, the VAR-metrics on the UK data also indicate rejection of the EH, and this is consistent with the presence of a time-varying term premium for these maturities (i.e. the restriction $\mathbf{e3'A} = 0$ is rejected).

## News and the Term Premium

The rejection of the restriction $\mathbf{e3'A} = 0$ (for $n = 15, 20, 25$ years, Table 3) suggests that the *one-period* risk premium $T_t^{(n)}$ is time varying. However, results from Table 4 in which we compare the actual spread $S_t$ and the theoretical spread $S_t'$ suggests that the variation in *average* future premia $\Phi_t^{(n)} = (1/n) \sum T_{t+i}^{(n)}$ is relatively small. Can we reconcile these two pieces of evidence?

**Table 4**  Actual spread $S_t$ and theoretical spread $S_t'$

| Interest Rate Maturities | Wald Test | | $\rho(S_t, S_t')$ | | $\sigma(S_t')/\sigma(S_t)$ | |
| --- | --- | --- | --- | --- | --- | --- |
| | $H_0 : S_t = S_t'$ | | | | | |
| | Value | p-value | Value | Std. error | Value | p-value |
| (2 year, 1 month) | 2.43 | 0.49 | 0.9043 | 0.0092 | 0.7527 | 0.2116 |
| (3 year, 1 month) | 3.25 | 0.35 | 0.9276 | 0.0074 | 0.8059 | 0.2321 |
| (4 year, 1 month) | 4.88 | 0.18 | 0.9385 | 0.0068 | 0.8236 | 0.2519 |
| (5 year, 1 month) | 5.67 | 0.13 | 0.9442 | 0.0063 | 0.8213 | 0.2666 |
| (6 year, 1 month) | 5.04 | 0.17 | 0.9474 | 0.0058 | 0.8099 | 0.2772 |
| (7 year, 1 month) | 3.80 | 0.28 | 0.9494 | 0.0053 | 0.7936 | 0.2862 |
| (8 year, 1 month) | 2.76 | 0.43 | 0.9508 | 0.0050 | 0.7736 | 0.2946 |
| (9 year, 1 month) | 2.22 | 0.53 | 0.9508 | 0.0048 | 0.7496 | 0.3015 |
| (10 year, 1 month) | 2.22 | 0.53 | 0.9532 | 0.0047 | 0.7242 | 0.3062 |
| (15 year, 1 month) | 8.20 | 0.04 | 0.9595 | 0.0049 | 0.5865 | 0.2885 |
| (20 year, 1 month) | 10.63 | 0.01 | 0.9608 | 0.0054 | 0.4445 | 0.2403 |
| (25 year, 1 month) | 22.55 | 0.00 | 0.9507 | 0.0094 | 0.3268 | 0.2015 |

Notes:
The sample period is from January 1976 to November 1999. The null that the actual spread $S_t$ is a sufficient statistic for future changes in short rates (i.e. the theoretical spread, $S_t'$) is denoted $H_0 : S_t = S_t'$ and implies cross-equation restrictions on the A-matrix of the VAR that are tested using the Wald statistic. The variables in the VAR are $Z = [S_t, \Delta r_t, h_t - r_{t-1}]$. The test is asymptotically $\chi^2$ distributed with 3 degrees of freedom (critical values at the 5% and 10% level of significance are 7.815 and 6.25, respectively).

In Table 5, we compare the time-series behaviour of the unexpected return $eh_{t+1} \equiv h_{t+1} - E_t h_{t+1}$ with 'news' about future changes in interest rates $er_{t+1}$. For all maturities up to 10 years, the standard deviation ratio $\sigma(er)/\sigma(eh)$ and the correlation coefficient $\rho(er, eh)$ are very close to $+1$ and $-1$ respectively, which indicates that nearly all of the variation in the unexpected return $eh_{t+1}$ is due to news about future short rates $er_{t+1}$ and very little is due to 'news' about the future *average* term premium $\Phi_t^{(n)}$. For maturities of 15, 20 and 25 years, the correlation coefficient declines somewhat, but except for the 25-year maturity, we still do not reject that this metric is $-1$, while its standard deviation ratio is 0.8128 (asymptotic standard error of 0.14).

If $eT_{t+1}^{(n)} \approx 0$, then '(1 – R-squared)' of the excess return equation in the VAR (i.e. the third equation) indicates the proportion of the excess holding period return that is due to variation in news about future short rates. The 'R-squared' for the $(h_{t+1} - r_t)$ equation in the VAR (Table 6) is in the range 0.01–0.05 (except for $n = 20, 25$ when it

**Table 5**   'News' about future short rates ($er_{t+1}$) and one-period returns ($eh_{t+1}$)

| Interest Rate Maturities | $\rho(er_{t+1}, eh_{t+1})$ | | $\sigma(er_{t+1})/\sigma(eh_{t+1})$ | |
|---|---|---|---|---|
| | Statistic | Std. Error | Statistic | Std. Error |
| (2 year, 1 month) | −0.9931 | 0.0186 | 0.9512 | 0.0742 |
| (3 year, 1 month) | −0.9982 | 0.0101 | 1.0072 | 0.0797 |
| (4 year, 1 month) | −0.9994 | 0.0066 | 1.0509 | 0.0808 |
| (5 year, 1 month) | −0.9993 | 0.0083 | 1.0704 | 0.0795 |
| (6 year, 1 month) | −0.9979 | 0.0166 | 1.0656 | 0.0777 |
| (7 year, 1 month) | −0.9941 | 0.0314 | 1.0444 | 0.0765 |
| (8 year, 1 month) | −0.9870 | 0.0521 | 1.0164 | 0.0772 |
| (9 year, 1 month) | −0.9759 | 0.0773 | 0.9892 | 0.0827 |
| (10 year, 1 month) | −0.9607 | 0.1049 | 0.9673 | 0.0952 |
| (15 year, 1 month) | −0.8300 | 0.2070 | 0.9680 | 0.2051 |
| (20 year, 1 month) | −0.6492 | 0.2292 | 0.9831 | 0.2114 |
| (25 year, 1 month) | −0.4971 | 0.2288 | 0.8128 | 0.1416 |

Notes:
The sample period is from January 1976 to November 1999. The null hypothesis is that unexpected one-period excess returns $eh = h_{t+1} - E_t h_{t+1}$ are solely due to news about future short rates ($er$). The null implies: $\rho(er, eh) = -1$ and $\sigma(er)/\sigma(eh) = 1$. The variables in the VAR are $\mathbf{Z} = [S_t, \Delta r_t, h_t - r_{t-1}]$.

rises to 0.11 and 0.14 respectively). This indicates that variations in news about future short rates account for nearly all (i.e. about 95–99%) of the variation in *ex-post* excess returns, and there is relatively little variation in *expected* excess returns. The latter is of course subject to the major qualification that the variables in the VAR adequately mimic changes in expected returns. Table 6 also shows the Ljung–Box statistics for the VAR equations for the spread, change in short rate and excess holding period return and indicate that serial correlation is only a problem for the latter equation for maturities of 20 and 25 years – this may imply some variation in the term premium that is not adequately modelled by the included variables.

Variations in the *one-period* term premium $T_t^{(n)}$ do have a statistically significant effect on *one-period* returns for $n = 10, 15, 25$ since we do not reject $\mathbf{e3'A} = 0$ (Table 3) and, hence, could lead to biased estimates of $\beta_L$ at these maturities and a rejection of the EH. However, future changes in short rates over a long horizon (Table 2) depend on the average of all future expectations of $T_{t+i}^{(n)}$ ($i = 1, 2, \ldots, n$), of which the current value $T_{t+1}^{(n)}$ only has a weight of $(1/n)$. Our results suggest that there is no strong persistence in $T_{t+i}^{(n)}$ and, hence, the variability in the *average* future risk premium $\Phi_t^{(n)} = (1/n)E_t \sum T_{t+i}^{(n)}$ is small, relative to changes in expectations about future short rates. Hence, changes in future short rates over many periods dominate changes in future *average* risk premia $\Phi^{(n)}$ *even at long maturities* and this is why the metrics comparing $S_t$ and $S_t'$ (see Table 4) broadly support the EH under the null of a negligible average time-varying risk premium.

## Summary: UK Data

For 'short' maturity bonds ($n = 2$ to 10 years), the EH with a constant term premium is supported by the UK data and it, therefore, follows that for these maturities, unexpected

**Table 6**  Summary statistics VAR: $Z = [S_t, \Delta r_t, h_t - r_{t-1}]$

| Interest Rates | Q-statistics | | | | | | R-squared | | |
|---|---|---|---|---|---|---|---|---|---|
| | $S_t$ – eqn | | $\Delta r_t$ – eqn | | $(h_t - r_{t-1})$ – eqn | | $S_t$ | $\Delta r_t$ | $(h_t - r_{t-1})$ |
| | Q(1) | Q(6) | Q(1) | Q(6) | Q(1) | Q(6) | | | |
| (2 year, 1 month) | 0.49 | 4.38 | 0.63 | 10.3 | 0.02 | 8.09 | 0.8378 | 0.1127 | 0.0097 |
| (3 year, 1 month) | 0.34 | 3.93 | 0.73 | 10.5 | 0.07 | 10.4 | 0.8758 | 0.1160 | 0.0165 |
| (4 year, 1 month) | 0.34 | 4.10 | 0.79 | 10.9 | 0.12 | 10.2 | 0.8940 | 0.1121 | 0.0274 |
| (5 year, 1 month) | 0.40 | 3.89 | 0.82 | 11.3 | 0.13 | 8.08 | 0.9036 | 0.1064 | 0.0321 |
| (6 year, 1 month) | 0.50 | 3.89 | 0.82 | 11.5 | 0.11 | 6.33 | 0.9087 | 0.1003 | 0.0283 |
| (7 year, 1 month) | 0.65 | 4.22 | 0.80 | 11.6 | 0.08 | 5.48 | 0.9117 | 0.0948 | 0.0200 |
| (8 year, 1 month) | 0.82 | 4.57 | 0.78 | 11.6 | 0.06 | 5.14 | 0.9139 | 0.0900 | 0.0121 |
| (9 year, 1 month) | 0.97 | 4.64 | 0.74 | 11.5 | 0.04 | 5.00 | 0.9161 | 0.0860 | 0.0076 |
| (10 year, 1 month) | 1.08 | 4.32 | 0.71 | 11.4 | 0.02 | 5.00 | 0.9186 | 0.0825 | 0.0075 |
| (15 year, 1 month) | 0.98 | 1.84 | 0.43 | 9.59 | 0.81 | 10.6 | 0.9318 | 0.0631 | 0.0547 |
| (20 year, 1 month) | 0.12 | 1.54 | 0.12 | 6.90 | 3.72 | 20.2 | 0.9332 | 0.0344 | 0.1118 |
| (25 year, 1 month) | 0.08 | 6.68 | 0.05 | 5.99 | 2.14 | 35.6 | 0.9163 | 0.0251 | 0.1413 |

Notes:

The sample period is from January 1976 to November 1999. The lag length of the VAR has been chosen to be $p = 1$ for all maturities. The Ljung–Box Q-statistics are reported for lag lengths of 1 and 6 months, with critical values (at 5% significance level) of 3.84, 12.59 respectively.

changes in holding period returns depend solely on revisions to forecasts about future short rates.

Testing the EH while allowing for a time-varying risk premium requires a three-variable VAR, which not only contains the spread and the change in short rates (as used in earlier work) but also includes the excess holding period return, where the latter variable may capture movements in the (stationary) term premium. With this modification (as suggested by Tzavalis and Wickens 1997), our results support the presence of a (stationary) time-varying term premium that influences the *one-period* excess holding period return, but only for long maturity bonds ($n = 15, 20, 25$ years).

However, the one-period term premium $T_t^{(n)}$ is *not* persistent and, hence, has a relatively small impact on the *average* term premium $\Phi_t^{(n)} = (1/n)E_t \sum T_{t+i}^{(n)}$, relative to changes in expectations about future short rates. This time-varying *average* term premium, therefore, does not cause severe bias in the OLS estimate of $\beta_S$ and in the VAR-metrics. The latter results are also consistent, with the spread being an optimal predictor of future short rates as suggested by the EH (i.e. with a near time-invariant *average* term premium).

Nevertheless, the presence of a time-varying term premium for $n = 10, 15, 20$ is sufficient to lead to a rejection of the EH for the change-in-long-rate equation (Table 2) because the *one-period* term premium $T_t^{(n)}$ has a direct impact on the change in long rates and, hence, may severely bias the OLS coefficient $\beta_L$ on the spread. Thus, by invoking the possibility of a time-varying term premium at very long maturities, we are able to go some way to reconciling the results from various tests of the EH on UK data.

## 22.5    Previous Studies

At the short end of the maturity spectrum, Cuthbertson (1996), using a two-variable VAR [$\mathbf{z} = (S_t, \Delta r_t)$] investigates the EH for maturities up to one year, using UK spot rate data, while Cuthbertson, Hayes and Nitzsche (1998, 2000) for German data and Cuthbertson and Bredin (2000, 2001) for Ireland at the short and long end broadly find in favour of the EH. (The occasional failure of the Wald test of cross-equation restrictions is the only downside in these results – but see the following for possible biases here.)

Taylor (1992) uses UK data on fairly long maturities of 5, 10 and 15 years over the period January 1985 to November 1989. Taylor reports strong rejections of the Wald restrictions (p-values of 0.00), a rejection of the restriction that the variance ratios equal unity, the smallest value being 1.5 (with an $s.e. = 0.14$). These results are in sharp contrast to those reported by Cuthbertson and Nitzsche (2003) above for the 2–10-year maturities. The difference in results may be due to Taylor's use of the yield to maturity rather than spot yields.

### US and Other Countries

There is a great deal of evidence on the EH for the United States. Campbell and Shiller (1991) and Bekaert, Hodrick and Marshall (1997) provide an overview based on applying the VAR methodology to monthly data on spot rates (derived from a cubic spline-fitting technique on coupon paying bonds). In general, for a wide variety of maturities from 1 to 12 months and for 2-, 3-, 4-, ..., 10-year maturities, they find evidence against the EH. Although the spread predicts future changes in short rates in the right direction, actual movements in the spread are greater than that required under the null that the EH is the correct model. This is *the over-reaction hypothesis* and implies that the actual spread is not an unbiased predictor of future changes in short rates. For example, Campbell and Shiller (1991) use *monthly* data on US government bonds for maturities of up to five years, including maturities for 1, 2, 3, 4, 6, 9, 12, 14, 36, 48 and 60 months for the period 1946–1987. Their data are, therefore, towards the short end of the maturity spectrum. Generally speaking, they find little or no support for the EH at maturities of less than one year from the regressions of the perfect foresight spread $S_t^*$ on the actual spread $S_t$, their $\beta$ values being in the region 0 to 0.5 rather than close to unity. Similarly, the values of $corr(S_t, S_t')$ are relatively low, being in the range $0-0.7$, and the values of the $\text{VR} = \sigma^2(S_t)/\sigma^2(S_t')$ are in the range $2-10$, for maturities of less than one year. At maturities of four and five years, Campbell and Shiller (1991) find more support for the EH since the variance ratio VR and the correlation between $S_t$ and $S_t'$ are close to unity. However, Campbell and Shiller do not directly test the VAR cross-equation restrictions, but this has been done subsequently by Shea (1992), who, in general, finds they are rejected.

Updating Campbell and Shiller's (1991) work, Bekaert, Hodrick and Marshall (1997) for US data report estimates of the spread coefficient in the long-rate equation of $-0.8$ (one-year maturity) to $-2.3$ (five-year maturity) and for the future-short-rate equation of $0.33$ (one-year maturity) to $0.57$ (five-year maturity). On the basis of *asymptotic* p-values, the EH (for $n = 1, 3, 5$ years) is rejected at better than a 4% significance level. While the VAR-metric that the correlation between $S'$ and $S$ is unity is not rejected, that for the standard deviation ratio between $S'$ and $S$ being unity is clearly rejected (at better than a 3% significance level for the asymptotic test), with this ratio for all three maturities being around 0.4.

Bekaert, Hodrick and Marshall (1997) also undertake a MCS study of the small-sample properties of the above tests, under the null that the EH is true (and using a VAR-GARCH data generation process for the short rate). They find severe upward bias in the coefficients on the spread in the long-rate regressions (e.g. an OLS value of $+2.6$ is obtained for the five-year maturity, when the true-$\beta_L = 1$), a moderate upward bias on the spread coefficient of the future-short-rate regression (e.g. a value of $\beta_s = 1.4$ rather than unity at the five-year maturity). Although the dispersion of the small-sample empirical distributions is higher than their asymptotic values, nevertheless, the above small-sample results *strengthen* the rejection of the EH on the basis of the 'long-rate' and 'short-rate' equations. Interestingly, they find that the VAR-metrics $\rho(S_t', S_t) = 1$ and $\text{SDR} = \sigma(S_t')/\sigma(S_t) = 1$ suffer virtually no bias (although the empirical standard deviations for the SDRs are slightly smaller, compared to their asymptotic values). However, again, they find that these small-sample Monte Carlo results strengthen the *rejection* of the EH on US data.

In a later paper, Bekaert, Hodrick and Marshall (2001) use a Monte Carlo simulation to investigate the small-sample properties of the coefficients on the spreads in the 'change in long rates' and 'future change in short rates' equations, under the null that the EH is true but incorporating *regime switches* in the data generation process for the short rate. This model mimics 'Peso problems' that might bias the regression coefficients. They find that Peso effects cause substantial upward bias in the regression coefficients and, not surprisingly perhaps, also increase the dispersion of the small-sample distributions (compared to the asymptotic distributions). But now, the evidence against the EH weakens considerably. When they also add a small time-varying term premium into the model (which is correctly priced), the small-sample distributions for $\beta_s$ and $\beta_L$ become even more dispersed, skewed and biased in the direction of explaining the data (e.g. some negative values for $\beta_L$ in the long-rate equations emerge in the 2.5% tail). However, these Monte Carlo simulation results cannot explain the observed regression results for the longer five-year maturity rates used.

Harris (2001) uses a panel data approach on US data to account for the possibility of a time-varying term premium TVP causing bias in the OLS estimate of the spread coefficient $\beta_L$ in the long-rate equation (13). Using a one-factor model of the term premium, which is captured by time-specific fixed effects in the panel data regression, enables an unbiased estimate of the OLS coefficient. Without accounting for a TVP, the average value of the coefficient on the spread in (13) is $\beta_L = -3.2$ (averaged over 1–13-year maturities), while in the panel regression, its value is $-1.98$ ($s.e. = 0.213$). While this is indicative of the presence of a TVP leading to biased OLS estimates in (13), the incorporation of a TVP does not rescue the EH because the $\beta_L$ coefficient is still statistically significantly different from unity.

Mankiw and Miron (1986) argue that the EH is likely to perform better empirically under a policy of monetary targeting rather than interest-rate smoothing. Kugler (1988), using US, German and Swiss monthly data on one- and three-month Euromarket deposit rates, found support for the EH only on German data (for the period of March 1974 to August 1986), which he interprets as broadly consistent with the Mankiw–Miron hypothesis. Similarly, Engsted (1996), using Danish money market rates and for longer maturity bonds (Engsted and Tanggaard 1995), finds considerable support for the EH providing the variation in interest rates is relatively large (i.e. in the post-1992 ERM 'crisis period'). This is to be expected, given the analysis of Mankiw and Miron (1986): if interest-rate stabilisation results in random walk behaviour for short rates, then the expected change in short rates is zero, and the spread has no predictive power for future short rates, contrary to the EH (see also Rudebusch 1995).

Although it is clear from Mankiw and Miron (1986) that econometric tests of the EH require sufficient variability in expected changes in short rates, it is also the case that very large (unpredictable) changes may increase agents' perceptions of the riskiness in holding bonds and thus invalidate the EH because of the presence of a time-varying term premium (see Engle, Lilien and Robins 1987, Hall, Anderson and Granger 1992, Tzavalis and Wickens 1995). The presence of a time-varying term premium (modelled using the HPR in a three-variable VAR) seems to assist in explaining results using US data, where term premium effects at long horizons appear to be 'stronger' than in the UK data (see Tzavalis and Wickens 1997).

In contrast to results at the long end of the maturity spectrum, Tzavalis and Wickens (1997), using monthly US data (1970–1986) on maturities of 3-, 6- and 12-month T-Bills, find considerable support for the EH using the VAR methodology (as long as the period of monetary base control 1979–1982 is omitted), as does Longstaff (2000a) using US repo rates at the very short end of the maturity spectrum (i.e. overnight to three months). When testing the validity of the EH on US data, the modelling of the 1979–1982 period when interest rates were highly volatile and, therefore, one might expect to observe time-varying term premia, is clearly important. Driffell and Sola (1994) use the VAR framework (using only three- and six-month US rates) with Hamilton (1988) Markov switching between two regimes. They also include a white noise error term in the future-short-rate equation $S_t = (1/2)E_t \Delta r_{t+1} + u_t$, which results in less restrictive cross-equation VAR restrictions (than if $u_t = 0$). After finding that by including the period 1979–1982 the EH fails, they repeat the VAR procedure, assuming 1979–1982 is a different regime. Now the EH cross-equation restrictions are accepted, and the Hamilton procedure gives a probability of 1 that all of the 1979–1982 period is a different regime (to the rest of the data). Hence, the

Hamilton filter is almost equivalent to including a $\{\ldots 0, 0, 1, 1, 1, \ldots 0, 0 \ldots\}$ dummy for this period.

Investigating the 1979–1982 period along slightly different lines, Tzavalis and Wickens (1995) show that a GARCH model adequately picks up the conditional volatility of excess HPR over this period. However, when a dummy variable taking the value 1 in the 1979–1982 period is included in the GARCH (1,1) specification, the conditional volatility no longer has a 'mean' effect on $(h_{t+1} - r_t)$, although GARCH effects in the residuals of this equation are still in evidence (but with less persistence). Thus, any tests of the EH on US data must be wary of the influence of the 1979–1982 period. The propensity for the EH to 'fail' when interest rates are highly volatile is also seen in other countries, such as Hong Kong (1992–2000), at the short end of the maturity spectrum (i.e. 3–12-month maturities). Gerlach (2003) finds that a GARCH variance term, when added to the change-in-short-rate equation, is statistically significant, implying a time-varying term premium may be present in the Hong Kong market, which allows a move to non-rejection for $\beta_s = 1$ (although $\beta_s$ is measured with considerable error and has a large standard deviation).

## Why Such Divergent Results?

Can we account for those divergent results for the EH across different maturities and even across different countries? Usually, stronger support for the EH is given by the perfect foresight regressions in comparison with those from the VAR approach (particularly the rejection of the VAR cross-equation restrictions). One reason for this is that the perfect foresight regressions that use (14) implicitly allow potential *future* events (known to agents but not to the econometrician) to influence expectations, whereas the VAR approach requires an *explicit* information set known both to agents *and* the econometrician at time $t$ or earlier. The market for short-term instruments is often heavily influenced by the government's monetary policy stance and in 'second guessing' the timing of interest rate changes by central banks. In periods of government intervention (influence), any purely 'backward-looking' regressions might be thought to provide poor predictors of future changes in interest rates: however, the rational expectations assumption $r_{t+j} = E_t r_{t+j} + \omega_{t+j}$ only requires unbiasedness and may suffer less from this effect. Hence, on this count, one might expect the perfect foresight regressions to perform better than the VAR approach and to yield relatively greater support for the EH (if it is indeed true).

The frequency of the data collection, the extent to which rates are recorded contemporaneously (i.e. are they recorded at the same time of day?) and any approximations used in calculating yields or changes in bond prices might explain the conflicting results in each of the above studies. Most importantly, Bekaert, Hodrick and Marshall (1997) show that small-sample biases in test statistics could account for different inferences, particularly for the Wald test and for the long-rate equation, but less so with the variance ratio and correlation statistics of the VAR methodology. So, MCS and bootstrapping of 'test statistics' also go some way in explaining divergent empirical results.

Kozicki and Tinsley (2001) raise the possibility that standard *univariate* time-series representations of the short rate (as in a random walk representation) are biased because they fail to take account of shifts in market perceptions of the policy targets for inflation, which provide a bound on long horizon forecasts of possible future short rates. They, therefore, impose this 'end-point' restriction on forecasts of the short rate at long horizons, and agents slowly learn about the new monetary policy regime. With these forecasts plus the EH, they can predict long rates at each point in time. There is a close relationship between the predicted long rate and the actual long rate for US data for 1960–1995 (see their Figures 2–4). The VECM forecasts of the short rate have an error correction term that keeps long rates and short rates from continually diverging, so it is not clear if the Kozicki and Tinsley (2001) critique carries as much weight when using the VECM method.

Empirical results on a wide set of data tend to be 'mixed'. However, overall, if we had to draw conclusions from this vast array of evidence, we would argue that the EH generally does pretty well for maturities up to five years, except in periods of extreme turbulence (e.g. US monetary base control 1979–1982), which might constitute a regime change and cause severe Peso problems. Of course, in the past, changes in nominal yields (and spreads) have been quite large. In a period of low and fairly stable yields, a time-varying term premium may provide a *relatively* large contribution to changes in yields. We will have to wait and see.

## 22.6  Summary

- Variance bounds tests using the *level* of long rates and the perfect foresight long rate suffer from non-stationarity problems that can be overcome by using the perfect foresight *spread* and the actual spread – because spreads are stationary variables.

- If long rates and short rates are I(1), then the EH implies that (long-short) spreads are stationary and spreads should Granger cause changes in future rates. Using stationary variables means standard test procedures can be used, although small sample problems may still be present.

- The VAR methodology provides statistical tests of the EH based on a comparison of the actual spread $S_t$ and perfect foresight spread, $S_t'$ (i.e. a forecast of future changes in short rates).

- Under the null that the EH is true, the 'metrics' provided by the VAR approach include correlation and variance ratio tests, $\rho(S_t', S_t) = 1$ and SDR $= \sigma(S_t')/\sigma(S_t) = 1$ and a test of cross-equation restrictions on the parameters of the VAR.

- MCS and bootstrapping the empirical distribution of the various statistics used to test the EH indicate that the asymptotic test statistics are often misleading in finite samples.

- Empirical results on the validity of the EH, using the change in long rates and change in short rates (single equation) regressions and results from the VAR approach are somewhat mixed. Except for US data, the majority of these tests generally support the EH, although there may be some turbulent periods when a time-varying term premium seems important (e.g. USA 1979–1982).

# 23

# SDF AND AFFINE TERM STRUCTURE MODELS

## Aims

- Show how the stochastic discount factor SDF approach gives rise to term structure equations that contain explicit risk premia, depending on conditional covariances.

- Demonstrate how affine models can be used to explain the shape and movements in the yield curve.

A bond is a risky asset when the holding period is less than the maturity of the bond, since its resale value is uncertain. Unlike a stock, a bond (usually) has a terminal date that fixes its redemption value at par, so no transversality condition applies. This fixed terminal value is useful when using the SDF approach to determine the price of a long-bond or its (spot) yield.

## 23.1 SDF Model

As we shall see, the SDF approach introduces a specific risk premium on long-bonds. The long rate depends not just on expected future short rates as in the EH but also on a risk premium, which varies with the conditional covariances between the SDF and a sequence of long rates of differing maturities. In principle, these conditional covariances can be estimated using a GARCH-in-mean approach, with observable factors (e.g. consumption growth), but this methodology has not been widely applied in empirical work.

To make the SDF model tractable, an *affine* or linear structure is often assumed, whereby the price of the bond depends *linearly* on a single latent factor $z_t$ or multiple factors $z_{it}$. In the single-factor model, although $z_t$ is initially an unobservable factor, under certain assumptions it can be shown to depend linearly on the observable short rate. This enables an explicit form for the shape and position of the yield curve to be derived and, hence, provides an *SDF-affine model* of the term structure of interest rates. These affine models are discussed below in discrete time, but they can also be derived in continuous time or using a lattice approach (see Cuthbertson and Nitzsche 2001b for an introduction). The key difference between the EH and the SDF-affine approach is that the latter incorporates a risk premium that is consistent with no-arbitrage opportunities along the yield curve.

To develop the SDF model of interest rates, we begin with the usual equilibrium condition (FOC)

$$E_t[M_{t+1}(1 + H_{n,t+1})] = 1 \qquad (1)$$

where

$$(1 + H_{n,t+1}) \equiv P_{n-1,t+1}/P_{n,t} \qquad (2)$$

$$P_{n,t} = e^{-n.R_{n,t}} \text{ and } R_{n,t} = (-1/n)p_{n,t} \qquad (3)$$

$(1 + H_{n,t+1})$ is the holding period yield on an $n$-period zero coupon bond and $R_{n,t}$ is the spot yield on this bond, paying \$1 at maturity. Taking logarithms and using $h_{n,t+1} = \ln(P_{n-1,t+1}/P_{n,t})$,

$$h_{n,t+1} = p_{n-1,t+1} - p_{n,t} = nR_{n,t} - (n-1)R_{n-1,t+1} \qquad (4)$$

where $p_{n,t} = \ln P_{n,t}$. When $n = 1$, the bond is risk-free and from (1),

$$(1 + r_t)E_t M_{t+1} = 1$$

In Appendix I, we show that the FOC (1), under the assumption that $P_{n,t}$ and $M_{t+1}$ are jointly lognormal, gives the by now familiar equilibrium no-arbitrage condition.

$$E_t(h_{n,t+1} - r_t) + \tfrac{1}{2}V_t(h_{n,t+1}) = -\text{cov}_t(m_{t+1}, h_{n,t+1}) \qquad (5)$$

where $m_{t+1} = \ln M_{t+1}$ and $V_t(.)$ is the conditional volatility. The second term on the left-hand side is the Jensen effect and 'cov$_t$' is the term (risk) premium. In Appendix I, the equilibrium yield for the $n$-period bond is shown to be

$$R_{n,t} = \frac{1}{n}\sum_{i=0}^{n-1} E_t r_{t+i} - \frac{1}{2n}\sum_{i=0}^{n-1}(n-i-1)^2 V_t(R_{n-i-1,t+i+1})$$

$$- \frac{1}{n}\sum_{i=0}^{n-1}(n-i-1)\,\text{cov}_t(m_{t+i+1}, R_{n-i-1,t+i+1}) \qquad (6)$$

The first term on the right-hand side is the (risk neutral) 'expectation hypothesis', but in the SDF model, the long rate also depends on a conditional variance term (i.e. a Jensen effect) and covariance terms, which constitute the risk premium. The SDF model embodies the no-arbitrage condition but even under risk neutrality $\text{cov}_t(.,.) = 0$, the 'EH' does not hold because of the Jensen effect. However, the latter is found to be empirically negligible. Hence, the EH (and tests discussed in previous chapters) assumes the covariance terms are negligible relative to expected movements in the short rate.

Nominal rates $r_t$ are determined by the real rate $rr_t$ and expected inflation $E_t\pi_{t+1}$, so the shape of the yield curve given by (6) is influenced by the latter two variables as well as the term premium (and Jensen effect). Note, however, that (5) and (6) are currently of little use since we have not yet defined the determinants of the SDF.

## Testing the SDF Model: Observable Factors

A direct way of testing the SDF model (under lognormality) for $h_{n,t+1}$ in (5) is to assume a *linear* relationship between $m_{t+1}$ and a set of observable factors $z_{it}$:

$$m_{t+1} = a + \sum_{i=1}^{m} b_i z_{i,t+1} \qquad (7)$$

and the no-arbitrage condition for the log holding period return (HPR) becomes

$$E_t(h_{n,t+1} - r_t) + (1/2)V_t(h_{n,t+1}) = -\Sigma_{i=1}^{m} b_i \text{cov}_t(z_{i,t+1}, h_{n,t+1}) \qquad (8)$$

The choice of the observable factors is rather arbitrary, but they might include consumption growth (C-CAPM), inflation and the change in the short rate and the long-short spread. Other variables that might influence bond risk might include the 'usual suspects' such as the change in the exchange rate, money supply and real output growth. The difficulty is in modelling the conditional covariances. One could attempt to use a multivariate GARCH model, for example using two long rates ($n = 1, 2$), we have

$$\mathbf{x}_{t+1} = (h_{1,t+1} - r_t, h_{2,t+1} - r_t, z_{1t}, z_{2t} \ldots)'$$
$$\mathbf{x}_{t+1} = \boldsymbol{\alpha} + \mathbf{B}\mathbf{x}_t + \mathbf{D}vech(\mathbf{H}_{t+1}) + \boldsymbol{\varepsilon}_{t+1} \qquad \boldsymbol{\varepsilon}_{t+1}|\Omega_t \sim N(O, \mathbf{H}_{t+1})$$

Consider $n = 1, 2$, then the HPR equation (8) implies the restrictions $\mathbf{e1'B} = \mathbf{e2'B} = 0$, where $(\mathbf{e1}, \mathbf{e2})$ are vectors with unity in the (first, second) position and zeros elsewhere. This ensures that $h_{n,t+1} - r_t$ does not depend on its own lagged values. In addition, the first row of $\mathbf{D}$ is $\{-1/2, 0, -d_{13}\}$ and the second row is $\{0, -1/2, -d_{23}\}$. This ensures only the variance term enters the equations for $h_{j,t+1} - r_t (j = 1, 2)$, and $d_{13}$ and $d_{23}$ pick up the conditional covariance terms. In general, the difficulty is in restricting the 'size' of $\mathbf{D}$ since, in principle, it contains variances and covariances between all the variables in $x_{t+1}$. Although ad hoc restrictions can be placed on $\mathbf{D}$ (e.g. constant correlations across the $\varepsilon_i, \varepsilon_j$'s), the large number of parameters to be estimated (particularly if the number of maturities is more than three) means the model is not usually attempted. This is one of the problems of multi-factor SDF models – how to simultaneously estimate all the conditional covariances. This problem would be compounded if one tried to use stochastic volatility models (which allows an error term to be added to the volatility process).

Note that with power utility over consumption and using nominal returns, we have

$$m_{t+1} = \psi - (crra)\Delta c_{t+1} - \pi_{t+1} \tag{9}$$

where $\pi_{t+1} = $ inflation and only these two variables could appear in the analysis. In the literature, there is little direct testing with observable factors, possibly because of the difficulties of estimation, possibly because consumption and HPRs are known to have a very low conditional covariance. However, an important exception is Balfoussia and Wickens (2003), who apply the above multivariate GARCH-in-mean (MGM) model using US monthly data 1970–1998. The GARCH equations are 'diagonal' so that each conditional covariance only depends on its *own* past values and on its *own* past surprises. For the C-CAPM, we have $z_{1t} = \Delta c_{t+1}$ and $z_{2t} = \pi_{t+1}$ (see equation (9)), and the HPR for maturity $n$ is:

$$E_t(h_{n,t+1} - r_t) + (1/2)V_t(h_{n,t+1}) = (crra)\,\mathrm{cov}_t(h_{n,t+1}, \Delta c_{t+1}) + \mathrm{cov}_t(h_{n,t+1}, \pi_{t+1})$$

Hence, the parameter on $\mathrm{cov}_t(h_{n,t+1}, \Delta c_{t+1})$ is the coefficient of relative risk aversion, and the coefficient on $\mathrm{cov}_t(h_{n,t+1}, \pi_{t+1})$ should be unity. The constancy of these coefficients *across maturities* (i.e. across the equations for $h_{n,t+1} - r_t$ for different $n$) provides a further test of the model. Note that although $crra$ is constant across equations, the term premia differ across maturities (and over time) because the 'size' of the estimated conditional covariance terms (from the GARCH processes) differ for different maturities. Unfortunately, the C-CAPM does not perform well on the US data, with the estimated value of $crra$ equal to 36 (but not statistically significant in any of the HPR equations). Also, the coefficients on the $\mathrm{cov}_t(h_{n,t+1}, \pi_{t+1})$ term do not equal unity and are not constant across equations. When adding additional macro-economic factors to give a more general SDF model (see equations (7a) and (8)), the coefficients on the conditional covariance terms are then unrestricted. Now the term $\mathrm{cov}_t(h_{n,t+1}, \pi_{t+1})$ is statistically significant in the equations for the conditional mean returns, $E_t h_{n,t+1} - r_t$, but the coefficients on these covariance terms are not constant across different maturities. The latter results also apply to the consumption covariance terms (in the model using the HPRs on five different maturity bonds).

Using equation (8) and estimates of the time-varying covariance terms from the MGM model, we can estimate

$$h_{n,t+1} = \alpha + \beta r_t + \gamma \phi_{n,t} + \varepsilon_{n,t+1}$$

or equivalently, the change-in-long-rate equation,

$$(n-1)(R_{t+1}^{(n-1)} - R_t^{(n)}) = \delta + \mu(R_t^{(n)} - r_t) + \upsilon \phi_{n,t} - \varepsilon_{n,t+1}$$

where $\phi_{n,t}$ is the sum of the covariance terms in (8). According to the EH, $\alpha = 0, \beta = 1$ or $\delta = 0, \mu = 1$. If the MGM model provides a good estimate of the time-varying risk premium, then we would also expect $\gamma = 1$ or $\upsilon = -1$. Because $h_{n,t+1}$ and $r_t$ are near unit root processes, omission of the term premium $\phi_{n,t}$ in the HPR equation should not bias $\hat{\beta}$ by very much, providing $\phi_{n,t}$ is I(0) (i.e. $\hat{\beta}$ is super consistent). On the other hand, the variables in the change-in-long-rate equation are I(0) and, therefore, omitting $\phi_{n,t}$ might cause substantial bias in $\mu$. Unfortunately, including the MGM estimate of $\phi_{n,t}$ in the latter equation leads to $\mu$ moving further away from $+1$ (for most maturities) and, hence, the failure of the EH on US data is not rescued by using an MGM model and the SDF approach. Balfoussia and Wickens (2003) have established that the relationship between excess HPRs and conditional covariances (modelled using a specific parameterisation of a MGM model) is not sufficiently statistically well determined and stable to explain time-varying term premia in US HPRs of different maturities. As noted in the previous chapter, the inclusion of the 1979–1982 period when interest rates were highly volatile may be problematic in MGM models, which are known to be sensitive to 'outliers'. In the above SDF approach, we used observable factors, and one of the problems is knowing which factors to use in the empirical model, since our analysis gives little guidance on this (only the inflation factor is a fairly obvious choice). An alternative is to use unobservable factors that can be incorporated in latent affine factor models.

## 23.2 Single-Factor Affine Models

An alternative method of obtaining measures of term premia is the use of affine models of the term structure. The Vasicek (1977) and Cox, Ingersoll and Ross (1985) are special cases of the SDF model where the conditional covariances of the HPR with the factors are linear functions of the factors themselves. The single-factor Vasicek model implies that the shape of the yield curve and the risk premium depend only on the time to maturity and the *shape* of the yield curve is fixed through time. The single-factor Cox, Ingersoll and Ross model also fixes the shape of the yield curve but allows the risk premium to move over time due to changes in the short rate. Greater flexibility in the shape of the yield curve requires multi-factor affine models (see the survey by Piazzesi 2002).

The most tractable and simple assumption to adopt (so let us adopt it!) for the functional form for the bond price is that it is a linear function of some (as yet undefined) factor $z_t$

$$p_{n,t} = -[A_n + B_n z_t] \qquad (10)$$

For the moment, equation (10) is completely arbitrary. It states that bonds of all maturities ($n$) only move over time when the single-factor $z_t$ changes and the quantitative impact of any change in $z_t$ on $p_{n,t}$ depends only on the maturity of the bond.

What we hope to show is that our affine (linear) assumption plus the no-arbitrage SDF conditions (1) are consistent with predicting the stylised facts about the observed yield curve. These include the following.

(i) The yield curve is usually observed to be an upward sloping, smooth curve that 'flattens' out at long maturities.

(ii) When it moves up or down, the yield curve mostly preserves its upward sloping shape and yields of different maturities move by broadly (but not exactly) the same amount (i.e. near parallel shifts in the yield curve).

(iii) Occasionally, the yield curve is observed to be downward sloping.

(iv) Occasionally, the upward sloping yield curve has a 'humped shape' at medium-term maturities.

Solution of these *affine models* proceeds via the following steps.

(a) Begin with the assumption that $p_{n,t}$ is linear in $z_t$ with coefficients $A_n$, $B_n$.

(b) Assume a 'plausible' linear time-series model (TSM) for the relationship between $m_{t+1}$ and $z_t$ that can be estimated (usually by Kalman filter methods).

(c) Deduce the restrictions on $A_n$, $B_n$ as functions of the parameters, which are implied by the no-arbitrage SDF model.

(d) Substitute these expressions for $A_n$, $B_n$ into the linear equation for $p_{n,t}$. We now have the no-arbitrage equilibrium relationship for $p_{n,t}$ and that for $R_{n,t}$ follows from $R_{n,t} = (-1/n)p_{n,t}$ (for all maturities $n$).

(e) Investigate whether the equilibrium 'theoretical' yield curve is consistent with the stylised facts noted above.

There are two popular ad hoc TSMs to explain the joint behaviour of $m_{t+1}$ and $z_t$, and these are given below.

### A. Cox–Ingersoll–Ross model (CIR)

$$-m_{t+1} = z_t + \lambda e_{t+1} \tag{11a}$$

$$(z_{t+1} - \mu) = \theta(z_t - \mu) + e_{t+1}. \tag{11b}$$

where $e_{t+1} = \sigma\sqrt{z_t}\varepsilon_{t+1}$ with $\varepsilon_{t+1} \sim iid(0, 1)$ and, hence, $V_t(e_{t+1}) = \sigma^2 z_t$.

### B. Vasicek model

Equations in (11a) + (11b) apply but $e_t$ is homoscedastic, that is, $e_{t+1} = \sigma\varepsilon_{t+1}$.

### Solution: CIR model

Using either of the above TSM in the no-arbitrage equation (1) gives, after much tedious manipulation (see Appendix II), solutions for $A_n$ and $B_n$ and, hence, for $p_{n,t}, R_{n,t}$ and the risk premium. $A_n$ and $B_n$ are functions of the parameters, namely $(\mu, \phi, \lambda, \sigma^2, n)$. The short rate $r_t$ is found to be an exact linear function of $z_t$, which enables us at any point to substitute the unobservable $z_t$ with the observable $r_t$. In general, this substitution of $z_t$ by $r_t$ is not usually possible. In Appendix II, we demonstrate that for the Cox–Ingersoll–Ross (CIR) model,

$$r_t = (1 - \tfrac{1}{2}\lambda^2\sigma^2)z_t \tag{12}$$

$$E_t(h_{n,t+1} - r_t) = (\tfrac{1}{2}B_{n-1}^2\sigma^2 + \lambda B_{n-1}\sigma^2)z_t \tag{13}$$

where the first term on the right in (13) is the Jensen effect, the second term is the risk premium

$$rp_t = -\text{cov}_t(m_{t+1}, p_{n-1,t+1}) = \lambda B_{n-1}\sigma^2 z_t \tag{14}$$

Finally, long rates for different maturities can be shown to depend linearly on the single-factor $z_t$ and, hence, on the short rate $r_t$:

$$R_{n,t} = (-1/n)p_{n,t} = \tfrac{1}{n}[A_n + B_n z_t] = \frac{A_n}{n} + \frac{B_n}{n\left(1 - \frac{1}{2}\lambda^2\sigma^2\right)} r_t \tag{15}$$

### Solution: Vasicek model

We only give the solution for the yield curve and the term (risk) premium

$$R_{n,t} = \tfrac{1}{n}\left[A_n - \tfrac{1}{2}\lambda^2\sigma^2 B_n\right] + \left(\frac{B_n}{n}\right)r_t \tag{16}$$

$$rp = \lambda\frac{(1 - \theta^{n-1})\sigma^2}{(1 - \theta)} \tag{17}$$

where the $A_n$ and $B_n$ again depend on the parameters $(\lambda, \mu, \theta, n, \sigma^2)$. It is easily seen from (15) and (16) that the shape of the yield curve in the CIR and Vasicek models depends on $n$, and the curve moves up and down with changes in the short rate, $r_t$. The CIR and Vasicek models both imply that the *shape* of the yield curve over time is constant, but in practice, we know that it changes shape (e.g. sometimes upward and sometimes downward) sloping. Hence, these 'single-factor' affine models do not fit the facts. In addition, in the Vasicek model, the risk premium does not change over time, but only with maturity – a somewhat restrictive result.

There have been two broad approaches to provide tractable SDF models that 'fit' more of the 'stylised facts'. The most obvious generalisation is to extend the affine approach to include multiple factors. Even with just two factors, the shape of the yield curve can alter as the two factors move differently. The second broad development is to take a multi-factor model (usually for tractability limited to three factors) and to add observable macroeconomic factors such as inflation and real activity.

## 23.3  Multi-Factor Affine Models

There are now several factors $z_i$ and the above equations hold with $z$ as a vector (with parameters now in matrix form). The complexity of these models and the number of parameters to be estimated can increase rapidly, so simplifications are often imposed. For example, if the adjustment matrix $\theta$ in (11b) is taken to be diagonal and the vector error term $e_{t+1} = \Sigma\sqrt{S_t}\varepsilon_{t+1}$ has $\Sigma$ independent of $\theta$ and $S_t$ $(= \text{diag } z_{it})$ is diagonal, then equation (10) is additive in $z_{it}$:

$$E_t h_{n,t+1} - r_t = (1/2)\sum_{i=1}^{m} B_{i,n-1}^2\sigma_i^2 z_{it} + \sum_{i=1}^{m}\lambda_i B_{i,n-1}\sigma_i^2 z_{it} \tag{18}$$

where the risk premium is the final term. However, the short rate now depends on a linear combination of the $z_{it}$, and we can no longer 'replace' the $z_{it}$ by the observable $r_t$. If there are more than $n$ yields (including the short rate), then the $n$ factors are not a unique linear combination of the $m$ yields, and some form of principal components is needed to 'assign' the observable $m$ yields ($m < n$) amongst the $n$-unobservable factors. However, because there are more factors, the shape of the yield curve can be more flexible and, usually, two or three factors are sufficient to approximate the different observed shapes of the yield curve. If there are fewer yields than factors, then the model is not an *observable* factor model.

## Empirical Results

Gong and Remolona (1997) and Dai and Singleton (2003) have estimated two- and three-factor CIR affine models, while Jagadeesh and Pennacchi (1996) estimate a single-factor and a two-factor Vasicek model (using Eurodollar futures contracts – a highly liquid market). In models with more than one factor, the 'short rate' cannot 'replace' the factor, so estimation is complex. Two- and three-factor models generally reject the one-factor model in hypothesis tests, but they often retain some implausible effects (e.g. state variables with an exceptionally long half life and sometimes negative short rates). Ang and Piazzesi (2003) add macro-factors 'inflation' and 'real output' that are formed as principal components from a larger set of macro-variables. These two macro-factors are included in the unobservable three-factor model, which is applied to bond yields of 1, 6, 12, 36 and 60 months. All the factors are assumed independent of each other. These observable macro-factors as well as the $z_{it}$ ($i = 1, 2, 3$) influence the short rate and the shape of the yield curve. It still remains to be seen whether the affine approach can adequately model *all* the 'stylised facts'.

The affine approach can also be applied to index bonds that give a linear term structure equation for both the nominal long rate $R_{n,t}^{(Nom)}$ and real long rate $R_{n,t}^{(real)}$ of the form

$$R_{n,t}^{(j)} = 1/n \left[ \sum_{i=0}^{n-1} (E_t r_{t+i}^{(j)} + E_t \phi_{t+i}^{(j)}) \right] \tag{19}$$

where $j = Nom$ or $real$ and $\phi$ represents the term premium and the Jensen term. Using the Fisher equation $r_t^{Nom} = r_t^{real} + E_t \pi_{t+1}$, where $\pi_{t+1}$ is the rate of inflation, we obtain

$$(1/n) \sum_{i=0}^{n-1} E_t \pi_{t+i} = R_{n,t}^{(Nom)} - R_{n,t}^{(real)} - (1/n) \sum_{i=0}^{n-1} E_t \phi_{t+i}^{\pi} \tag{20}$$

Expected (average) inflation is determined by the difference between nominal and real yields less the inflation risk premium $\phi^{\pi} \cong \phi^{Nom} - \phi^{real}$. For example, Remolona, Wickens and Gong (1998) find the inflation risk premium is time varying with an average level of around 1% p.a. in the United Kingdom for the 1990s.

## 23.4  Summary

- The SDF model (under lognormality) implies that the excess HPR is not constant but depends on a (possibly) time-varying conditional covariance term (and a Jensen effect).

- The SDF model is more general than the EH (which assumes risk neutrality). In the SDF model, the long rate depends not only on expected future short rates but also on the covariance terms between the SDF and the $n$-bond yields. Empirical tests of the EH assume these covariances (and the Jensen effect) are negligible relative to changes in expected future short rates.

- Affine models of the term structure are a particular form of SDF model, where the (log) of the SDF ($m_{t+1}$) is assumed to be linear in a set of factors, $z_{it}$. Affine models usually give explicit closed-form solutions for long-bond yields $R_{n,t}$ from which we may infer the shape and changing position of the yield curve. Except in some simple cases, affine models contain unobservable factors that require complex estimation techniques.

- Empirically, the SDF model of the excess HPR using *observable* covariances has not been widely examined, probably because of the difficulty in estimating 'large' GARCH-in-mean models. Empirically, affine models, usually with two or three factors, have been able to explain some aspects, but not all, of the shape of the yield curve.

# Appendix I: Math of SDF Model of Term Structure

The discrete time versions of the SDF model presented below rely heavily on Smith and Wickens (2002). In this section, we establish the no-arbitrage equation for prices and yields of different maturities and for the holding period return. The risk premia in these equations depend on the covariance between the SDF and the appropriate price or return under consideration. For the SDF model, the no-arbitrage condition is

$$E_t[M_{t+1}(1 + h_{n,t+1})] = 1 \tag{A1}$$

or

$$P_{n,t} = E_t[M_{t+1}P_{n-1,t+1}] \tag{A2}$$

For $n = 1$, the bond is risk-free, hence,

$$(1 + r_t)E_t[M_{t+1}] = 1 \tag{A3}$$

This defines $E_t(M_{t+1}) = 1/(1 + r_t)$ in terms of the risk-free rate. If $P_{n,t}$ and $M_{t+1}$ are *jointly lognormal*, then from (A2),

$$
\begin{aligned}
p_{n,t} &= E_t(m_{t+1} + p_{n-1,t+1}) + \tfrac{1}{2}V_t(m_{t+1} + p_{n-1,t+1}) \\
&= E_t m_{t+1} + E_t p_{n-1,t+1} + \tfrac{1}{2}[V_t(m_{t+1}) + V_t(p_{n-1,t+1}) \\
&\quad + 2\operatorname{cov}_t(m_{t+1}, p_{n-1,t+1})]
\end{aligned} \tag{A4}
$$

Using $p_{o,t} = 0$ in (A4), the price of a one-period bond is

$$p_{1t} = E_t(m_{t+1}) + \tfrac{1}{2}V_t(m_{t+1}) \tag{A5}$$

Subtracting (A3) from (A4), the no-arbitrage equation for prices, which is also the excess HPR, is

$$E_t(p_{n-1,t+1}) - p_{n,t} + p_{1,t} + \tfrac{1}{2}V_t(p_{n-1,t+1}) = -\operatorname{cov}_t(m_{t+1}, p_{n-1,t+1}) \quad (A6a)$$

$$E_t(h_{n,t+1} - r_t) + (1/2)V_t(p_{n-1,t+1}) = -\operatorname{cov}_t(m_{t+1}, p_{n-1,t+1}) \quad (A6b)$$

Using $\ln P_{n,t} = -n\ln(1 + R_{n,t}) \approx -nR_{n,t}$, (A6) can be expressed in terms of yields.

$$-(n-1)E_t(R_{n-1,t+1}) + nR_{n,t} - r_t + \frac{(n-1)^2}{2}V_t(R_{n-1,t+1})$$
$$= (n-1)\operatorname{cov}_t(m_{t+1}, R_{n-1,t+1}) \quad (A7)$$

Equation (A7) is the 'change-in-long-rate' equation we noted for the EH. The EH assumes a constant risk premium, whereas the SDF model has a risk premium given by the $\operatorname{cov}_t(., .)$ term, and the $V_t(.)$ term is a Jensen inequality term (JIT).

A further substitution in (A7) for $h_{n,t} = -(n-1)R_{n-1,t+1} + nR_{n,t}$ gives the no-arbitrage expected excess holding period return:

$$E_t(h_{n,t+1} - r_t) + \tfrac{1}{2}V_t(h_{n,t+1}) = -\operatorname{cov}_t(m_{t+1}, h_{n,t+1}) \quad (A8)$$

Equations (A6)–(A8) are alternative representations of the no-arbitrage condition (A1) under joint lognormality. The covariance term is the risk premium, and variance terms appear because of the Jensen effect. Finally, forward recursion on (A7) gives the familiar expression for the long rate in terms of expected future short rates, plus the term premium (and Jensen effects).

$$R_{n,t} = \frac{1}{n}\sum_{i=0}^{n-1}E_t r_{t+i} - \frac{1}{2n}\sum_{i=0}^{n-1}(n-i-1)^2 V_t(R_{n-i-1,t+i+1})$$
$$- \frac{1}{n}\sum_{i=0}^{n-1}(n-i-1)\operatorname{cov}_t(m_{t+i+1}, R_{n-i-1,t+i+1}) \quad (A9)$$

Equation (A9) points to the rather obvious fact that the pure expectations hypothesis is a special case of the SDF model (under lognormality), where the risk premium $\operatorname{cov}_t(.)$ is zero and Jensen effects are inconsequential. Of course, until we can model the stochastic discount factor $m_{t+i+1}$ and, hence, the covariance terms, the model remains non-testable.

# Appendix II: Single-Factor Affine Models

One way of deriving explicit equations for the shape of the yield curve is to assume $m_{t+1}$ is linearly related to a single-factor $z_t$ (which we see below can sometimes be measured by the observable short rate). In these affine models, $p_{n,t}$ is assumed to be a linear function of the factor $z_t$.

$$p_{n,t} = -[A_n + B_n z_t] \quad (A10)$$

hence

$$R_{n,t} = -\frac{1}{n}p_{n,t} = \frac{A_n}{n} + \frac{B_n}{n}z_t \tag{A11}$$

and

$$r_t = -p_{1,t} = A_1 + B_1 z_t \tag{A12}$$

We now derive the (recursive) restrictions on $A_n$ and $B_n$ in order to satisfy the no-arbitrage condition (A1) of the SDF model. We then compare the resulting equation for the excess HPR, $E_t h_{n,t+1} - r_t$ with (A6b), to obtain an explicit expression for the risk premium in terms of $A_n$ and $B_n$. We assume an arbitrary yet reasonable and tractable TSM for $m_{t+1}$ and $z_t$ – the well-known Cox, Ingersoll and Ross (1985) CIR model.

$$-m_{t+1} = z_t + \lambda e_{t+1} \tag{A13a}$$

$$(z_{t+1} - \mu) = \theta(z_t - \mu) + e_{t+1} \tag{A13b}$$

where $e_{t+1} = \sigma \sqrt{z_t}\varepsilon_{t+1}$, with $\varepsilon_{t+1} \sim iid(0, 1)$ and $V_t(e_{t+1}) = \sigma^2 z_t$. In this model, the conditional mean of $m_{t+1}$ is equal to $z_t$ [see (A13a)]. The factor $z_t$ is assumed to be autoregressive around a long run mean value of $\mu$ [see (A13b)], and the speed of mean reversion is determined by $\theta$. We now proceed to derive the formula for $p_{n,t}$ by considering the right-hand side terms in (A4). Substituting from (A13a), (A13b) and (A10),

$$E_t(m_{t+1} + p_{n-1,t+1}) = -[z_t + A_{n-1} + B_{n-1}E_t z_{t+1}]$$

$$= -[z_t + A_{n-1} + B_{n-1}(\mu(1-\theta) + \theta z_t)] \tag{A14}$$

and

$$V_t(m_{t+1} + p_{n-1,t+1}) = V_t(\lambda e_{t+1} + B_{n-1}e_{t+1}) = (\lambda + B_{n-1})^2 \sigma^2 z_t \tag{A15}$$

Substituting (A14) and (A15) in the no-arbitrage equation (A4) and using the 'affine equation' (A10) for $p_{n,t}$, we have the rather complex equation

$$p_{n,t} = -[A_n + B_n z_t] = -[(1 + \theta B_{n-1})z_t + A_{n-1} + B_{n-1}\mu(1-\theta)]$$

$$+ \tfrac{1}{2}(\lambda + B_{n-1})^2 \sigma^2 z_t \tag{A16}$$

Equating the constant term and the terms in $z_t$ on the right- and left-hand sides gives the recursive formulae for $A_n$ and $B_n$:

$$A_n = A_{n-1} + B_{n-1}\mu(1-\theta) \tag{A17a}$$

$$B_n = 1 + \theta B_{n-1} - \tfrac{1}{2}(\lambda + B_{n-1})^2 \sigma^2 \tag{A17b}$$

Since $\ln P_{o,t} = p_{o,t} = 0$, $A_o, B_o = 0$, and these are starting values to use in the recursions (A17). For $n = 1$, we have

$$B_1 = 1 - \tfrac{1}{2}\lambda^2\sigma^2 \quad \text{and} \quad A_1 = 0 \tag{A18}$$

so that

$$r_t = -p_{1,t} = A_1 + B_1 z_t = (1 - \tfrac{1}{2}\lambda^2 \sigma^2) z_t \tag{A19}$$

Hence, the short rate is linearly related to $z_t$ and we can 'replace' the unobservable $z_t$ in the above expressions (A10) and (A11) for $p_{n,t}$, $R_{n,t}$ with the observable short rate, $r_t$. The holding period yield is defined in terms of (log) prices, and substituting from (A16), (A19),

$$
\begin{aligned}
E_t(h_{n,t+1} - r_t) &\equiv E_t(p_{n-1,t+1}) - p_{n,t} - p_{1,t} \\
&= \tfrac{1}{2} B_{n-1}^2 \sigma^2 z_t + \lambda B_{n-1} \sigma^2 z_t
\end{aligned}
\tag{A20}
$$

From (A6b),

$$E_t h_{n,t+1} - r_t = -\tfrac{1}{2} V_t(p_{n-1,t+1}) - \text{cov}_t(m_{t+1}, p_{n-1,t+1}) \tag{A6b}$$

Comparing (A20) with (A6b), we see that the first term is the Jensen effect and the second term is the risk premium $-\text{cov}_t(m_{t+1}, p_{n-1,t+1})$, both of which depend on $z_t$. It is worth noting that if $m_{t+1}$ is non-stochastic (i.e. $\lambda = 0$), then the risk premium is zero. Again in (A2), we can 'replace' $z_t$ with $r_t$, using (A19) so the excess HPR depends linearly on $r_t$, as does the risk premium. It should not be too surprising that in a 'linear world' driven by one factor, the latter is the temporal driving variable for (log) prices, long rates and the term premium (only the latter result should not be entirely intuitive). The Vasicek model can be solved in exactly the same fashion as above, but we do not pursue that here.

# 24

## THE FOREIGN EXCHANGE MARKET

## Aims

- Provide a brief overview of alternative exchange rate regimes.

- Show how price competitiveness can be represented in terms of purchasing power parity, PPP, and the law of one price, LOOP.

- Demonstrate how riskless arbitrage determines the forward rate – this is covered-interest parity, CIP.

- Show that if *risky* arbitrage opportunities are eliminated (by risk-neutral speculators), this gives rise to uncovered interest parity, UIP.

- Analyse the relationship between CIP, UIP and forward rate unbiasedness FRU and that between UIP, PPP and real interest parity, RIP.

## 24.1 Exchange Rate Regimes

The behaviour of the exchange rate, particularly for small open economies that undertake a substantial amount of international trade, has been at the centre of macroeconomic policy debates for many years. There is no doubt that economists' views about the best exchange rate system to adopt have changed over the years. It is worthwhile briefly outlining the main issues.

After World War II, the Bretton Woods arrangement of 'fixed but adjustable exchange rates' applied to most major currencies. As capital flows were small and often subject to government restrictions, the emphasis was on price competitiveness.

Countries that had faster rates of inflation than their trading partners were initially allowed to borrow from the International Monetary Fund (IMF) to finance their trade deficit. If a 'fundamental disequilibrium' in the trade account developed, then after consultation, the deficit country was allowed to fix its exchange rate at a new lower parity. After a devaluation, the IMF would also usually insist on a set of austerity measures, such as cuts in public expenditure, to ensure that real resources (i.e. labour and capital) were available to switch into export growth and import substitution. The system worked relatively well for a number of years and succeeded in avoiding the re-emergence of high tariffs and quotas that had been a feature of 1930s protectionism.

The US dollar was the anchor currency of the Bretton Woods system, and it was initially linked to gold at a fixed price of $35 per ounce. The system began to come under strain in the middle of the 1960s. Deficit countries could not persuade surplus countries to mitigate the competitiveness problem by a revaluation of the surplus countries currency. There was an asymmetric adjustment process that invariably meant the deficit country had to devalue. The possibility of a large-step devaluation allowed speculators a 'one-way bet' and encouraged speculative attacks on those countries that were perceived to have poor current account imbalances, even if it could be reasonably argued that these imbalances were temporary. The United States ran large current account deficits which increased the amount of dollars held by third countries. (The US extracted 'seniorage' by this means). Eventually, the amount of externally held dollars exceeded the value of gold in Fort Knox when valued at the 'official price' of $35 an ounce. At the official price, free convertibility of the dollars into gold became impossible. A two-tier gold market developed (with the free market price of gold very much higher than the official price) and eventually, convertibility of the dollar into gold was suspended by the US authorities. By the early 1970s, the pressures on the system were increasing as international capital became more mobile and differential inflation rates between countries increased and caused large deficits and surpluses on current accounts. By 1972, most major industrial countries had de facto left the Bretton Woods system and floated their currencies.

In part, the switch to a floating exchange rate regime had been influenced by monetary economists. They argued that control of the domestic money supply would ensure a desired inflation and exchange rate path. In addition, stabilising speculation by rational agents would ensure that large, persistent swings in the real exchange rate, and hence in price competitiveness, could be avoided by an announced credible monetary policy (usually in the form of money supply targets).

Towards the end of the 1970s, a seminal paper by Dornbusch (1976) showed that if FOREX dealers are rational yet goods prices are 'sticky', then exchange-rate overshooting could occur. A contractionary monetary policy could result in a loss of price competitiveness over a substantial period with obvious deflationary consequences for real trade, output and employment. Although in long-run equilibrium the economy would move to full employment and lower inflation, the loss of output in the transition period could be more substantial in the Dornbusch model than in earlier monetary models, which assume that prices are 'flexible'. (We examine monetary models of exchange rate determination in Chapter 27).

The volatile movement in nominal and real exchange rates in the 1970s led some European countries to consider a move back towards more managed exchange rates, which was eventually reflected in the workings of the Exchange Rate Mechanism (ERM) from the early 1980s. European countries that joined the ERM agreed to try to keep their bilateral exchange rates within announced bands around a central parity. The bands could be either wide ($\pm 6\%$) or narrow ($\pm 2.25\%$). Unofficially, the Deutsch Mark (DM) became the anchor currency. In part, the ERM was a device to replace national monetary targets with German monetary policy as a means to combat domestic inflation. Faced with a fixed exchange rate against the DM, a high-inflation country has a clear signal that it must quickly reduce its rate of inflation to that pertaining in Germany. Otherwise, unemployment would ensue in the high-inflation country, which is a 'painful mechanism' for reducing inflation. The ERM allowed countries to realign their (central) exchange rates in the case of a fundamental misalignment. However, when a currency hits the bottom of its band because of a random speculative attack, all the central banks in the system may try to support the weak currency by coordinated intervention in the FOREX market.

The perceived success of the ERM in reducing inflation and exchange rate volatility in the 1980s led the G10 countries to consider a policy of coordinated intervention (i.e. the Plaza and Louvre accords) to mitigate 'adverse' persistent movements in their own currencies. The latter was epitomised by the 'inexorable' rise of the US dollar in 1983–1985, which seemed to be totally unrelated to changes in economic fundamentals. Recently, some economists have suggested a more formal arrangement for currency zones and currency bands for the major currencies along the lines of the rules in the ERM.

In the early 1990s, the ERM came under considerable strain. Increasing capital mobility and the removal of all exchange controls in the ERM countries facilitated a speculative attack on the Italian lira, sterling and the franc around 16 September 1992 (known as *Black Wednesday*). Sterling and the lira left the ERM and allowed their currencies to float. About one year later, faced with further currency turmoil, most ERM bands were widened to $\pm 15\%$. The reasons for a move to monetary union in Europe are complex, but one is undoubtedly the desire to 'remove' the problem of floating or quasi-managed exchange rates. The move to monetary union was formally started at a meeting of EU leaders on 10 December 1991 at Maastricht in the Netherlands, where 'convergence criteria' were set out for entry into the common currency as well as the timetable.

In January 1999, 11 EU countries formed a Monetary Union and irrevocably locked their exchange rates against the Euro, and full implementation of euro 'notes and coins' in retail transactions began in January 2002. The EU countries that entered 'Euroland' in 1999 were Austria, Belgium, Finland, France, Germany, Ireland, Italy, Luxemborg, Netherlands, Portugal and Spain, with Greece joining in 2002. By and large, these countries met the 'Maastricht' inflation and interest rate targets, but meeting the maximum 3% budget deficit criterion took some 'creative accounting'. A large number of countries also failed the debt ratio criterion (e.g. Belgium and Italy had debt–GDP ratios in excess of 100%). So, the Maastricht criteria were in the end merely 'guidelines' for entry. The EU countries that initially stayed out were the United Kingdom, Denmark, Greece (joined 2002) and Sweden.

The euro started life as the currency used by the initial 11 participating European countries. It is used for invoicing commercial transactions and there are many financial assets (e.g. loans, stocks, bonds, futures, swaps and derivatives) that are now denominated in euros. The euro is a rival to the US dollar, and it may eventually become an important vehicle and reserve currency. However, it has experienced a continuous fall against the US dollar from 1.17 USD per euro in January 1999 to around 0.83 USD per euro in October 2000, a fall of around 30% in under two years. Since then, it has reversed and in 2003, was back around its initial level of 1.1. Nominal and real exchange rates of major 'economies' certainly move around considerably.

Outside of Europe, the years 1997–1999 saw great currency turmoil in the Far East, where banking crises in Thailand, Indonesia, Malaysia and Japan have resulted in depreciations of around 30–40% of some of these currencies against the US dollar. The immediate reason for the withdrawal of foreign capital appears to be the 'excess' foreign currency borrowing by domestic banks. This foreign currency was then switched into local currency loans (many of which were used in property speculation), and these became 'non-performing'. Hence, it was (correctly) thought that the banks that were unhedged could not pay back the interest and capital on the foreign currency loans, and this triggered a general capital outflow.

Also, in 1998, the Russian rouble depreciated sharply against the US dollar, again because bank loans to Russia denominated in foreign currency seemed to be liable to default. Growth in the Russian economy was virtually non-existent, there were massive falls in tax receipts (and a disintegration of the tax collecting system) and, hence, many public sector workers had wage arrears in excess of six months. The Brazilian 'real' became the next victim in 1999, when Brazil too had to devalue in the face of speculative pressure, which the IMF and the granting of loans from the United States were unable to stem. This set of events has led to calls in the G10 for a 'new economic order' or a *new financial architecture* that involves a more proactive role for the IMF in trying to avert currency crises or at least mitigating their adverse impact on countries.

One of our main tasks in this part of the book is to examine why there is such confusion and widespread debate about the desirability of fixed versus floating exchange rates and the move to common currency areas. It is something of a paradox that economists are usually in favour of 'the unfettered market' in setting 'prices' but in the case of the exchange rate, perhaps the key 'price' in the economy, there are widely divergent views.

## 24.2   PPP and LOOP

Law of one price (LOOP) is an equilibrium condition in the market for individual homogeneous tradeable goods and forms a basic building block for several models of the exchange rate on the basis of economic fundamentals. It is a 'goods arbitrage' relationship. For example, if applied solely to the domestic economy, it implies that a 'Lincoln Continental' should sell for the same price in New York City as in Washington DC (ignoring transport costs between the two cities). If prices are lower in New York, then demand would be relatively high in New York and low in Washington DC. This would cause prices to rise in New York and fall in Washington DC, hence equalising prices. In fact, the threat of switch in demand would be sufficient for well-informed traders to make sure that prices in the two cities are equal. The LOOP applies the same arbitrage argument across countries, the only difference being that one must convert one of the prices to a 'common currency' for comparative purposes. Purchasing power parity (PPP) assumes that the LOOP applies using some aggregate price index (e.g. wholesale goods price index or the consumer price index, CPI) but because we spend little time discussing index number problems, then in what follows, you can think of LOOP and PPP as equivalent.

## Absolute PPP

If domestic tradeable goods are perfect substitutes for foreign goods and the goods market is 'efficient' (i.e. there are low transactions costs, perfect information, perfectly flexible prices, no artificial or government restrictions on trading, etc.), then 'middlemen' or arbitrageurs will act to ensure that the price is equalised in a common currency. If the foreign currency price is $P^*$ dollars and $S$ is the exchange rate (domestic currency per unit of foreign currency, say, sterling per dollar), then the price of a foreign import in domestic currency (sterling) is $SP^*$. Domestic producers of a close (perfect) substitute for the foreign good and arbitrageurs in the market will ensure that domestic (sterling) prices $P$ equal the import price in the domestic currency, $SP^*$:

$$P = SP^* \quad \text{or} \quad p = s + p^* \tag{1}$$

where $p = \ln P$, and so on. Here is a simple example. Harrods, the department store in London, sells 'hampers', that is, a 'fixed' basket of goods (e.g. containing paté, champagne, etc.), and so does Saks in New York. If the Saks' hamper costs \$200 and the spot rate is £0.6667 per \$ (1.5 \$ per £), then the price of the Saks' hamper to a UK resident is £133.34. PPP implies that the price of the Harrods' hamper will also be set at £133.34 by arbitrageurs, otherwise a near riskless profit could be made by shipping hampers (e.g. after purchasing on the World Wide Web) between the two countries. If the LOOP always holds and the price of the Saks' hamper rises to \$210, then the price of the Harrods' hamper will rise to £140 (if $S$ remains at 0.6667 £s per \$).

## Relative PPP

Relative PPP assumes $P$ and $SP^*$ may not be equal but $P$ moves proportionately with $SP^*$ so $P = k\,(SP^*)$ and, hence,

$$\Delta p = \Delta s + \Delta p^* \tag{2}$$

PPP may also be viewed as an equilibrium condition for the current account of the balance of payments (for given levels of domestic demand and world trade). This is simply because if PPP holds over time, then it means that there is no incentive for domestic residents to switch demand from tradeable goods of the foreign country (i.e. imports) to domestically produced substitutes (or vice versa).

The *real exchange rate* is a measure of price competitiveness and is the price of domestic, relative to foreign goods (in a common currency).

$$S^r = P^* S / P \tag{3}$$

Given our earlier analogy, the real exchange rate is initially $S_o^r = (P^* S)/P = (\$200)$ $(0.6667)/£133.34 = 1$ implying that a Harrods' hamper and Saks' hamper cost the same in sterling for a UK resident (and the same in USD for a US resident). It follows from the definition of the real exchange rate that if PPP holds, then the real exchange rate or price competitiveness remains constant. But in reality, the real exchange rate is far from constant and moves in very long 'mean reverting' swings, indicating that price competitiveness does *not* hold over substantial periods of time.

If goods arbitrage were the only factor influencing the exchange rate, then the exchange rate would obey PPP

$$s = p - p^* \tag{4a}$$

or

$$\Delta s = \Delta p - \Delta p^* \tag{4b}$$

Hence, movements in the exchange rate would *immediately* reflect differential rates of inflation, and the latter is often found to be the case in countries suffering from hyper-inflation (e.g. Germany in the 1920s, some Latin American countries in the 1980s, economies in transition in Eastern Europe and Russia after 1990). However, one might expect goods arbitrage to work rather imperfectly in complex industrial economies with moderate inflation and a wide variety of heterogeneous tradeable goods. Hence, PPP may hold only in the very long run in such economies.

## Evidence on PPP

*Absolute* PPP implies that prices of the same goods should sell for the same price in different countries. For example, the price of gold in USD should be the same if the gold is sold in the United Kingdom, the Euro area or the United States. Of course, absolute PPP might not hold for some tradeable goods because of tariff barriers, differential tax rates on goods and because profit margins vary depending on the degree of competition. The latter underlies the 'pricing to market' (PTM) hypothesis (Krugman 1978) where some goods, when sold in foreign markets, are set equal to the local price and, hence, are immune to exchange rate changes. Knetter (1989, 1993) finds this is particularly true for German and Japanese firms (e.g. German beer exported to the United Kingdom has a different price to that exported to the United States). Persistent price differentials could also be due to menu costs of changing prices by firms or because consumers face fixed costs when switching between products. There is also the problem of classifying what are similar goods. Even the 'eating experience' of

McDonald's 'Big Mac Hamburgers' vary depending on restaurant space, queuing time, whether the ketchup is free and how the burger is bundled with other items (e.g. milk shakes, Cola, etc.). Also, some goods (viz. cars and electrical goods) have different national standards (e.g. 110 volts versus 250 volts), different information gathering costs, non-tariff barriers, environmental standards and different warranty or after-sales service. For example, insurance and transport costs have been estimated to be of the order of 10% but with large variations across countries. Finally, when producers can price discriminate, exporters may 'price-to-market' in the exporting country.

There does seem to be a lack of goods arbitrage because *absolute* prices are not equalised across countries. Engel and Rogers (1996), using 14 disaggregated price indices for 23 cities in the United States and Canada, show:

(i) within one country, the relative price of the *same* goods between two cities is a positive function of the distance between them.

(ii) when comparing across countries for the same goods, the price differential is much greater than in (i) and the 'border effect' on price differentials is equivalent to adding between 2,500 and 23,000 miles between domestic cities.

(iii) the cross-border price differentials are much more persistent than their within country equivalents.

Parsely and Wei (1996) and Rogers and Jenkins (1995) find similar results to Engel and Rogers (1996) and, also find that the *persistence* of price differentials is much greater across borders than within the same country. Engel (1993) demonstrates the absence of absolute PPP. He notes that for 2000 pairwise comparisons, the (conditional) variances of the relative prices of *similar* goods in the United States and Canada are much more volatile than the relative prices of very *different* goods *within* either country. Also, studies of fairly homogeneous products (e.g. screws, nuts and bolts, paper and glass, German beer exported to the United States and United Kingdom) show an absence of absolute PPP.

## Aggregate Price Indices

Absolute PPP is usually tested with aggregate price indices, but there are difficulties here. The indices often do not cover the same bundle of goods in each country, and the bundle changes over time as new goods are added. When using time-series data, one also has to assume that absolute PPP holds in the base year. Strictly, only tradeable goods (e.g. at wholesale manufacturers' prices) should be included in the PPP index (unless one has a theory connecting tradeables and non-tradeables prices, when an index like the CPI can then be used).

One way to test absolute PPP is to undertake a test for cointegration between the spot rate and relative prices

$$s_t = \alpha p_t - \alpha^* p_t^* + \varepsilon_t$$

An ADF test of the OLS residuals from the above equation can be used to test the null of no cointegration, $\gamma \geq 0$:

$$\Delta \hat{\varepsilon}_t = \gamma \hat{\varepsilon}_{t-1} + \sum_{i=1}^{m} \delta_i \Delta \hat{\varepsilon}_{t-i} + u_t$$

against the alternative $\gamma < 0$. (The above equation may include a constant term – critical values for $\gamma$ vary, depending on the precise form of this equation.) We cannot test the $\{1, -1\}$ restrictions on the parameters in a single-equation framework, given the bias in the OLS standard errors. Using the Johansen (1988) procedure in a trivariate VAR system or using the Phillips and Hansen (1990) modified OLS estimator allows test of the restrictions. In general, such tests are favourable to the existence of a cointegrating vector and, hence, for mean reversion in the interwar or earlier periods (for industrialised countries) but less favourable for the post-1973 float period (see Sarno and Taylor 2002 for an overview).

## Random Walk

The problem of univariate unit-root tests is their low power (particularly if the root is as large as 0.95) in rejecting the false null. For example, using MCS with a root $(1 - \gamma) = 0.95$, then even with $T = 100$ annual observations, the power of the Dickey–Fuller $t$-test $\hat{\tau} = \hat{\gamma}/s.e.(\hat{\gamma})$ is only around 12%. This means that the probability of *never* being able to reject the unit root is around 88%, even though we have a stationary process. Therefore, it is not hard to see why early tests of PPP using standard univariate unit-root tests on aggregate price indices and post-1973 data found it difficult to reject the null of a random walk for the *real* exchange rate except for hyper-inflation countries.

Power can be increased by increasing the *span* of data (although not by increasing the frequency of observation, for example, from annually to monthly, within a given time span – Shiller and Perron 1985). Studies, therefore, extend the data set. Using over a century of data and employing unit-root tests, the consensus has moved towards the view that for moderate inflation countries, the real exchange rate is probably mean reverting over the long run (Cheung and Lai 1994, Lothian and Taylor 1996) even after taking account of the possibility of structural breaks and different exchange rate regimes over such a long period of data (e.g. periods of 'fixed', floating and managed floating regimes).

However, the above studies find that the real exchange rate is also very persistent at around 15% p.a., implying a half-life of 3–5 years (i.e. it takes 3–5 years for a shock to the real exchange rate to move halfway to its final long-run value) – see Rogoff (1996) for a summary. Recent studies show that even for the post-WWII period, mean reversion in the real exchange rate is found in *panel data* (i.e. testing PPP using more than 100 countries) and again the half-life is around four years (Frankel and Rose 1995). Panel data increases the power of the unit-root test, but it still remains possible that *some* countries in the panel do not exhibit mean reversion, since the portmanteau test may be dominated by a few countries where PPP does hold in the long run. Of course, the opposite is also possible, that is, we do not reject the null of non-stationarity, but this may be because of only one non-stationary real exchange rate, with the rest being stationary. Taylor and Sarno (1998) and Sarno and Taylor (1998) address these problems and find that G5 real exchange rates against the US dollar are mean reverting (using the Johansen procedure) in the post-1973 floating period. Although standard unit-root tests are far from infallible, the conclusion around the mid-1990s was that real exchange rates are very persistent but probably mean reverting (see Ardeni and Lubian 1991, Grilli and Kaminsky 1991, Rogoff 1996).

The above empirical results may be put into context when one considers an alternative approach to PPP working via the wage–price inflationary spiral. We show in the appendix that a rise in foreign (import) prices or a depreciation of the domestic currency raises production costs for the domestic industry and, hence, domestic prices and wages. The resulting equation that explains domestic inflation is

$$\Delta p = \frac{b_1}{1 - b_1}[f + b_1(\chi_w - \chi_p) + a_2(y - \overline{y})] + \Delta(p + s) \tag{5}$$

where $y - \overline{y} = $ deviation of output from its natural rate, $f = $ 'wage push' factors, $\chi_w = $ exogenous growth in real wages, $\chi_p = $ growth in labour productivity. It follows that PPP holds if

$$f + b_1(\chi_w - \chi_p) + a_2(y - \overline{y}) = 0 \tag{6}$$

Hence, PPP holds when output is at its natural rate, 'wage push' factors '$f$' are zero and real wages grow at the rate of labour productivity. One can see that the factors in (6) involve rather complex, slowly varying long-term economic and socio-political forces, and this may account for the difficulty in empirically establishing PPP even in a very long span of data.

Pricing to market PTM for some goods (e.g. automobiles, electronics) will also lead to deviations from PPP (Krugman 1978). If some producers invoice their exported goods in foreign currency, then any change in the exchange rate will initially leave relative prices unchanged and, hence, the LOOP will be violated, and real and nominal exchange rates will move together. However, PTM, although it occurs for some goods, does not seem to be widely adopted (except for the United States) – Goldberg and Knetter (1997).

## Unit Roots and Non-Linearities

There are some approaches that suggest that the real exchange rate will not be mean reverting. Rogoff (1996) notes that the Harrod, Samuelson and Balassa (HSB) effect predicts that PPP might not always hold, since fast-growing countries should have appreciating *real* exchange rates. In its simplest form, the HSB effect assumes productivity growth is faster in the tradeables relative to the non-tradeables sector. The LOOP holds in the tradeables sector but faster productivity growth raises wages in the tradeables sector in line with productivity (but tradeables prices stay constant since unit costs have not changed). A competitive labour market then leads to wage rises in the non-tradeables sector and because productivity here is unchanged, non-tradeables prices rise. The latter leads to a rise in the aggregate price index (e.g. CPI) and, given an unchanged exchange rate (since tradeables prices are unchanged), PPP using aggregate prices is violated and the domestic real exchange rate increases. This fits some countries like Japan and the yen–USD exchange rate (1945–1996) but not for many other industrialised countries and, overall, the evidence on the HSB effect is very mixed (e.g. deGregorio, Giovannini, Wolf, Gordon and deMenil 1994).

Others (e.g. Krugman 1990) argue that *cumulative* current account deficits should influence real exchange rates as they represent a kind of portfolio balance effect, redistributing wealth across countries. Another strand in the literature (Froot and Rogoff 1991) suggests that because government expenditure is mainly in non-traded goods, this would lead to a change in the relative price of services to tradeables and, hence, an increase in the real exchange rate.

Models of PPP that incorporate transactions costs (Dumas 1992, Sercu, Uppal and vanHulle 1995) emphasise that *within* a no-arbitrage 'transactions cost band', the real exchange rate may follow a random walk but *outside* this band, potential profits to arbitrage are large enough to induce mean reverting behaviour. Overall, the real exchange rate follows a non-linear process that is mean reverting. Time aggregation will tend to smooth any discontinuous adjustment between the two regimes for individual goods and if we aggregate over goods with different arbitrage costs, it seems likely that aggregate price indices used in testing PPP will exhibit a *smooth* non-linear process.

An alternative view giving rise to non-linearities (Kilian and Taylor 2003) is that there are heterogeneous expectations about the 'correct' level for the exchange rate. Hence, when the rate is close to equilibrium and opinions are diffuse, the fundamentals traders will be influenced by noise traders (e.g. charts and technical analysis), and this causes unit-root behaviour in the exchange rate. When the exchange rate moves substantially from equilibrium, then more fundamentalists recognise the disequilibrium and move the exchange rate back towards equilibrium (see also DeGrauwe, Dewachter and Embrechts (1993) for a similar model that gives non-linear 'chaotic' behaviour for the exchange rate).

Nevertheless, although long-run PPP based on standard unit-root tests is now largely accepted as an empirical fact, there is still a PPP puzzle. The puzzle is that the volatility of both real and nominal exchange rates is about the same over short horizons, suggesting that all 'the action' is in the nominal exchange rate rather than relative prices. This implies that money and financial shocks (i.e. nominal shocks) should be important here rather than real shocks (e.g. to productivity and preferences, which are thought to be not particularly volatile). But we would expect these nominal shocks to die out completely after about two to three years as sticky wages and prices adjust – but, in fact, the real deviations from PPP exist for over five years. This is the puzzle, that is, what is causing these large and long swings in the real exchange rate?

One way out of the above predicament is to assume that the exchange rate follows a mean reverting *non-linear* process, generates simulated data using a Monte Carlo experiment and examines the power (i.e. the ability to reject a false null) of conventional unit-root tests. Taylor (2001) shows that under these circumstances there is substantial upward bias in the estimated half-life. He also shows that when the true model is AR(1) but the data used in the unit-root test is time aggregated (e.g. the true AR(1) model is monthly but the data is sampled annually), the half-life again increases substantially.

Recent empirical work uses explicit non-linear models for the real exchange rate (e.g. Obstfeld and Taylor 1997, Michael, Nobay and Peel 1997 – for the interwar period). For example, Taylor, Peel and Sarno (2001) use the ESTAR model (outlined in Chapter 4) on four bilateral exchange rates against the US dollar for the post-1973 period. A simplified version of the ESTAR model (assuming an AR(1) process) is

$$z_t = (\pi_0 + \pi_1 z_{t-1}) + (\pi_1^* z_{t-1}) F(z_{t-j}) + \varepsilon_t$$

where $F(z_{t-j}) = 1 - \exp[-\gamma(z_{t-j} - c)^2/\sigma_z^2]$. $F(z_{t-1})$ is U-shaped and bounded between zero and unity. If $z_{t-j} = c$, then $F = 0$, and the equation for $z_t$ becomes a linear AR(1) model. As $(z_{t-1} - c) \to \infty$, the disequilibrium is very large and $F = 1$, so we have a different AR(1) model with the coefficient on $z_{t-1}$ being $(\pi_1 + \pi_1^*)$. In the model, $\pi_1 \geq 0$ is admissible, but we must have $(\pi_1 + \pi_1^*) < 0$. For small deviations, $z_t$ could follow a unit root (or even explosive) process but for large deviations, the process is mean reverting. One can immediately see why conventional (linear) univariate unit-root tests might give misleading inferences if the ESTAR model is the true model. Somewhat paradoxically, non-rejection of a unit root, *when the ESTAR model is true*, may indicate that the real exchange rate has been close to equilibrium. Not surprisingly, it can be shown using MCS that the power of univariate tests is low when the alternative of the ESTAR model is true, but panel unit-root tests do have more power (against the false null of a unit root).

In non-linear models, the half-life after a shock to the real exchange rate depends on the initial disequilibrium position and on the size of the shock. Using MCS, Taylor, Peel and Sarno (2001) show that when shocks are small, the ESTAR model delivers a half-life of around three to five years but for largest shocks, the half-life is below three years. This goes some way to resolving the puzzle of the 'glacial' (Rogoff 1996) half-life found in linear models of adjustment to PPP.

Over the years, there has been increased 'technical firepower' applied to testing PPP, and this has undoubtedly nudged the evidence in favour of mean reversion and long-run PPP. However, given index number problems and low power of unit-root tests, most economists and policy makers would have taken the view that real exchange rates were probably mean reverting even before the latest developments outlined above. The policy problem has always been the persistent and substantial rises in the real exchange rate that can mean devastation for industries in the tradeable's sector, even though their productivity and unit labour costs (in the domestic currency) are unchanged – coupled with the fact that this situation may not be symmetric when the real exchange rate falls and market share cannot be completely recaptured (i.e. hysteresis). What is certainly true is that international goods markets appear to be far less integrated than national goods markets – the latter is one reason often cited for joining a common currency area like EMU, where 'price transparency' encourages intra-country trade and generates less price dispersion because of increased competition.

## 24.3 Covered-Interest Parity, CIP

There are two main types of 'deal' on the foreign exchange (FX) market. The first is the 'spot' rate, which is the exchange rate quoted for immediate delivery of the currency to the buyer (actually, delivery is two working days later). The second is the forward rate, which is the guaranteed price agreed today at which the buyer will take delivery of currency at some future period. You can hedge future receipts or payments of foreign currency by using the forward market today to 'lock in' a known exchange rate, for some future date. For most major currencies, highly traded forward maturities are for one to six months ahead and, in exceptional circumstances, three to five years ahead. The market-makers in the FX market are mainly the large banks, and they are over-the-counter (OTC) trades.

The relationship between spot and forward rates can be derived as follows. Assume that a UK Corporate Treasurer has a sum of money, £$A$, that he can invest in the United Kingdom or the United States for one year, at which time, the returns must be paid to his firm's shareholders. We assume the forward transaction carries no default risk. Therefore, for the treasurer to be indifferent as to where the money is invested, it has to be the case that returns from investing in the United Kingdom equal the returns in sterling from investing in the United States. The return from investing in the United Kingdom will be $A(1 + r)$ where $r$ is the UK rate of interest. The return in sterling from investing in the United States can be evaluated using the spot exchange rate, $S(£/\$)$ and the forward exchange rate, $F$ for one year ahead. Converting the $A$ pounds into dollars will give us $A/S$ dollars that will increase to $(A/S)(1 + r^*)$ dollars in one year's time if $r^*$ *is* the US rate of interest. If the forward rate for delivery in one year's time is $F(£/\$)$, then the UK Corporate Treasurer can 'lock-in' an exchange rate today and receive, with certainty, £$(A/S)(1 + r^*)F$ in one year's time. Equalising returns, we have

$$A(1 + r) = (A/S)(1 + r^*)F \qquad (7)$$

which becomes

$$F/S = (1 + r)/(1 + r^*) \qquad (8)$$

or

$$f - s = r - r^* \qquad (9)$$

where $f = \ln F$ and $s = \ln S$ and we have used the approximation $\ln(1 + r) = r$, where $r$ is measured as a decimal. The above equations represent the 'covered-interest parity' (CIP) condition, which is an equilibrium condition based on riskless arbitrage. If CIP does not hold, then there are forces that will quickly restore equilibrium. For example, if $r > r^*$ and $f = s$, there is a riskless arbitrage profit to be made. Today, US residents would purchase UK T-Bills, pushing their price up and interest rates down. US residents would also have to buy sterling spot and sell dollars forward today, hence, spot sterling would appreciate (i.e. $s$ falls) and $f$ would rise, thus tending to restore equality in (9). In fact, because the transactions are riskless, arbitrageurs ensure the quoted forward rate equals $s + r - r^*$.

Using continuously compounded interest rates $F = Se^{(r-r^*)T}$ where $T = $ time to maturity (in years) of the forward contract. Hence, (9) then becomes an exact relationship (rather than an approximation).

# 24.4 Uncovered Interest Parity, UIP

We can repeat the scenario in the previous section but this time assuming the UK Corporate Treasurer is willing to make a forecast for the exchange rate that will prevail in one year's time $S_{t+1}^e$, when she converts her dollar investment back into sterling. If the Corporate Treasurer is risk neutral, she is concerned only with the expected return from the two alternative investments. Hence, she will continue to invest in the United States rather than the United Kingdom until *expected returns* are equalised.

$$S_{t+1}^e / S_t = (1 + r_t)/(1 + r_t^*) \tag{10}$$

$$s_{t+1}^e - s_t = r_t - r_t^* \tag{11}$$

where $s_{t+1} = \ln S_{t+1}$. (Equation (11) is exact if continuously compounded rates are used). Uncovered Interest Parity (UIP) can be interpreted as the condition for equilibrium on the capital account under the assumption of risk neutrality, since if UIP holds, there is no incentive to switch speculative funds between the two countries. The UK Corporate Treasurer knows that she is taking a risk because the value of the exchange rate in one year's time is uncertain; however, she ignores this risk when undertaking her portfolio allocation decision.

Let us now relax the risk neutrality assumption by invoking the CAPM. For the UK Treasurer, the risk-free rate is $r$, and the expected return on a 'round trip' risky investment in the United States is

$$1 + E_t R_{t+1}(\text{UK} \longrightarrow \text{US}) \equiv S_{t+1}^e (1 + r_t^*)/S_t \tag{12}$$

From the CAPM,

$$E_t R_{t+1} - r_t = \beta_i (E_t R_{m,t+1} - r_t) \tag{13}$$

where $\beta_i$ is the beta of the foreign investment (which depends on the covariance between the market portfolio and the US portfolio). $E_t R_{m,t+1} - r_t$ is the expected return on the market portfolio of assets held in *all* the different currencies and assets (i.e. the world portfolio). The RHS of (13) is a measure of the risk premium as given by the CAPM. For the moment notice that, if we assume $\beta_i = 0$, then (13) reduces to UIP. The CAPM is a special case of the SDF model applied to domestic and foreign asset returns (see Chapter 13).

Returning to the UIP equation (11), it is obvious that if this does not hold, there is an incentive for risk-neutral speculators to switch funds between countries. If the latter happens very quickly (or the threat of it happening is prevalent), then UIP will be maintained at all times. Clearly, the UIP condition assumes that the market is dominated by risk-neutral speculators and that neither risk-averse 'rational speculators' nor noise traders have a powerful influence on market prices.

## 24.5   Forward Rate Unbiasedness, FRU

From (9) and (11), if CIP and UIP hold simultaneously, the forward rate is an unbiased predictor of the future spot rate

$$f_t = E_t s_{t+1} \tag{14}$$

Note that unbiasedness holds regardless of the expectations formation process for $Es_{t+1}$ (i.e. one need not assume rational expectations) but it does require risk neutrality (so that UIP holds). If any two of the relationships from the set UIP, CIP and forward rate unbiasedness (FRU) are true, then the third will also be true.

Under risk neutrality, if FRU does not hold, there would be (risky) profitable opportunities available by speculating in the forward market. Whether (14) holds because there is active speculation in the forward market or because CIP holds *and* all speculation occurs in the spot market so that UIP holds, does not matter for the EMH. The key feature is that there are no unexploited profitable opportunities.

## 24.6   Real Interest Rate Parity

If UIP and PPP hold, then

$$\Delta s_{t+1}^{e} = s_{t+1}^{e} - s_t = (r - r^*)_t \tag{15}$$

$$\Delta s_{t+1}^{e} = \Delta p_{t+1}^{e} - \Delta p_{t+1}^{*e} \tag{16}$$

It follows that

$$r_t - \Delta p_{t+1}^{e} = r_t^* - \Delta p_{t+1}^{*e} \tag{17}$$

and, hence,

$$\text{PPP} + \text{UIP} \Rightarrow \text{Real Interest Rate Parity, RIP}$$

Again, if any two conditions from the set of UIP, PPP and real interest parity (RIP) are true, then the third is also true. Given relatively high information and adjustment costs in goods markets, it is not too surprising that PPP only holds over a relatively long time period (say, 5–10 years). Indeed, we know that in the short run, movements in the real exchange rate are substantial. Hence, even under risk neutrality (i.e. UIP holds), one might take the view that *expected* real interest rate parity would only hold over a rather long horizon. Note that it is *expected* real interest rates that are equalised. However, if over a run of years, agents are assumed *not* to make systematic errors when forecasting inflation and exchange rate changes, then *actual* average real interest rates would be equalised.

The RIP condition also goes under the name of the international Fisher hypothesis. It may be considered as an arbitrage relationship based on the view that 'capital' (i.e. investment funds) will flow between countries to equalise the expected real return in each country. One assumes that a representative basket of goods (with prices $p$ and $p^*$) in each country gives equality utility to the international investor (e.g. a 'Harrods' hamper' in the United Kingdom is perceived as equivalent to a 'Saks' hamper' from New York). International investors then switch funds via purchases of financial assets or by direct investment to where they yield the highest expected return in real terms. This arbitrage leads to an equalisation of expected real rates of return. Note that the investor's returns accrue in terms of the consumption goods of one particular country. Hence, if real returns are earned in the United Kingdom, say, but you wish to consume US goods (e.g. a Saks' hamper produced in the United States), you have to exchange sterling for dollars at the end of the investment period. However, under RIP, price competitiveness holds so you can obtain the same purchasing power (or set of goods) in the United States as in the United Kingdom.

It is worth emphasising that all the relationships discussed above are equilibrium conditions. There is no direction of causality implicit in any of these relationships. Thus, in the case of UIP, we cannot say that interest differentials 'cause' expectations of changes in the exchange rate (or vice versa). Of course, we can expand our model to include other equations where we explicitly assume some causal chain. For example, suppose we assert (on the basis of economic theory and evidence about government behaviour) that exogenous changes in the money supply by the central bank 'cause' changes in domestic interest rates. Then, given the UIP condition, the money supply also 'causes' a change in the expected rate of appreciation or depreciation in the exchange rate. The exogenous change in the money supply influences both domestic interest rates and the expected change in the exchange rate. Here, 'money' is causal (by assumption) and the variables in the UIP relationship are jointly and simultaneously determined.

In principle, when testing the validity of the three relationships UIP, CIP and FRU or the three conditions UIP, PPP and RIP, we need only test any two (out of three), since if any two hold, the third will also hold. However, because of data availability and the different quality of data for the alternative variables, evidence on all three relationships in each set has been investigated.

# 24.7   Summary

- If PPP holds, then price competitiveness and the real exchange rate are constant over time. Also, goods cost the same whether they are purchased in the domestic economy or in the foreign country.

- Evidence suggests that the real exchange rate moves in long swings, which implies that price competitiveness is restored only after 5–10 years.

- If the forward rate is given by $F_t = S_t(1 + r_t)/(1 + r_t^*)$, then no riskless arbitrage profits can be made. This is the CIP condition.

- UIP implies that the *expected* rate of depreciation of the domestic currency equals the interest differential between the domestic and foreign country.

- CIP and UIP imply that the forward rate is an unbiased forecast of the future spot rate (i.e. FRU holds).

- UIP and PPP imply that real interest rates are equalised across different countries.

# Appendix: PPP and the Wage–Price Spiral

In the wages version of the expectations augmented Phillips curve, wage inflation, $\Delta w$, is determined by price inflation, $\Delta p$, and excess demand $(y - \overline{y})$. To this, we can add the possibility that workers may push for a particular growth in real wages $\chi_w$ on the basis of their perceptions of their productivity. There may also be other forces $f$ (e.g. minimum wage laws, socio-economic forces) that may influence wages. It is often assumed that prices are determined by a mark-up on unit wage costs and domestic import prices of raw materials. Hence, our wage–price model is

$$\Delta w = \chi_w + a_1 \Delta p + a_2(y - \overline{y}) + f \tag{A1}$$

$$\Delta p = b_1(\Delta w - \chi_p) + b_2 \Delta pm \tag{A2}$$

where $\chi_p$ is the trend growth rate of labour productivity. Imports are assumed to be predominantly homogeneous tradeable goods (e.g. agricultural produce, oil, iron ore, coal) or imported capital goods. Their foreign price is set in world markets and converted into domestic import prices as follows.

$$\Delta pm = \Delta p^* + \Delta s \tag{A3}$$

Substituting (A1) into (A2), we obtain

$$\Delta p = (1 - a_1 b_1)^{-1}[b_1(\chi_w - \chi_p) + b_2 \Delta pm + a_2 b_1(y - \overline{y}) + b_1 f] \tag{A4}$$

Equation (A4) is the price expectations augmented Phillips curve (PEAPC) that relates price inflation to excess demand $(y - \overline{y})$ and other variables. If we make the reasonable assumptions that in the long run there is no money illusion $(a_1 = 1)$, that is, a vertical long-run PEAPC, and there is homogeneity with respect to total costs $(b_1 + b_2 = 1)$, then (A4) becomes

$$\Delta p = [b_1/(1 - b_1)][f + b_1(\chi_w - \chi_p) + a_2(y - \overline{y})] + \Delta(p^* + s) \tag{A5}$$

Assume that the terms in square brackets are zero. Then the long-run secular influences on domestic prices are $p^*$ and $s$, and PPP will hold, that is,

$$\Delta p = \Delta p^* + \Delta s \tag{A6}$$

A rise in foreign prices $p^*$ or a depreciation of the domestic currency (i.e. $s$ rises) leads to a rise in domestic prices (via (A2)), which in turn leads to higher wage inflation (via (A1)). The strength of the wage–price feedback, as wage rises lead to further price rises, and so on, depends on the size of $a_1$ and $b_1$. Under the homogeneity assumptions

$a_1 = 1$ and $b_1 + b_2 = 1$, the strength of the feedback is such that PPP holds in the long run. That is to say, a 1% depreciation of the domestic currency (or rise in foreign prices) eventually leads to a 1% rise in the aggregate domestic price index, ceteris paribus. Of course, PPP will usually not hold in the short run in this model either because of money illusion $a_1 < 1$ or less than full mark-up of costs $b_1 + b_2 < 1$ or because of the influence of the terms in square brackets in equation (A5).

# 25

# TESTING CIP, UIP AND FRU

## Aims

- Show how tests of covered interest parity (CIP) require careful attention to data, as covered arbitrage is (virtually) riskless.

- Examine tests of forward rate unbiasness (FRU) and uncovered interest parity (UIP) both in a single-equation and VAR framework.

- Analyse how 'Peso problems' complicate the 'interpretation' of tests of FRU.

In this chapter, we discuss the methods used to test covered and uncovered interest parity and the forward rate unbiasedness proposition. We find that there is strong evidence in favour of covered interest parity for most maturities and time periods studied. Tests of forward rate unbiasness, FRU (or uncovered interest parity, UIP) generally find against the hypothesis and we explore some tests using survey data to ascertain whether this is due to a failure of risk neutrality or RE. In this chapter, we discuss both 'single-equation tests' of FRU over a one-period horizon and tests over multi-period horizons using the VAR framework.

## 25.1 Covered Interest Arbitrage

Let us consider whether it is possible, in practice, to earn riskless profits via covered interest arbitrage. In the real world, the distinction between bid and offer rates both for interest rates and for forward and FX-spot rates is important when assessing potential riskless profit opportunities. In the strictest definition, an arbitrage transaction requires no capital: the agent borrows the funds. Consider a *UK investor* who borrows £$A$ in the Euro-sterling market at an offer rate $r_£^o$. At the end of the period, the amount owing will be

$$Z_1 = A \left( 1 + r_£^o \frac{D}{365} \right) \tag{1}$$

where $A$ = amount of borrowed (£), $Z_1$ = amount owed at end of period (£), $r_£^o$ = offer rate (proportionate) on Euro-sterling loan, and $D$ = number of days funds are borrowed.

Now consider the following set of transactions. The investor takes his £$A$ and exchanges sterling for dollars at the bid rate, $S^b$ (US dollars per pound sterling) in the spot market. So $S^b$ is the spot market bid for sterling. He invests these dollars in a Euro-dollar deposit that pays the bid rate, $r_\$^b$. He simultaneously switches these dollars into sterling at the forward rate $F^o$ (on the offer side). All these transactions take place instantaneously. The amount of sterling he will receive *with certainty* at the end of $D$ days is given by

$$Z_2(UK \rightarrow US) = \frac{A \cdot S^b [1 + r_\$^b (D/360)]}{F^o} \tag{2}$$

Note that the day count convention in the United States and followed in (2) is to define 'one year' as 360 days. The *percentage excess return ER* to investing £$A$ in US assets and switching back into sterling on the forward market is therefore given by

$$ER(£ \rightarrow \$) = 100 \left( \frac{Z_2 - Z_1}{A} \right) = 100 \left[ \frac{S^b}{F^o} \left( 1 + r_\$^b \frac{D}{360} \right) - \left( 1 + r_£^o \frac{D}{365} \right) \right] \tag{3}$$

Hence, if you arbitrage from sterling to US dollars using £$M$, then you will earn a sterling profit of £$(M \cdot ER/100)$ with certainty at the end of the period. Looking at the covered arbitrage transaction from the point of view of a US resident, we can consider the covered arbitrage return from moving out of dollars into sterling assets at the spot rate, investing in the United Kingdom and switching back into dollars at the current forward rate. This must be compared with the cost of borrowing in dollar-denominated assets in the United States. A similar formula to that given in (3) ensues:

$$ER(\$ \rightarrow £) = 100 \left[ \frac{F^b}{S^o} \left( 1 + r_£^b \frac{D}{365} \right) - \left( 1 + r_\$^o \frac{D}{360} \right) \right] \tag{4}$$

Given riskless arbitrage, one would expect that $ER(£ \rightarrow \$)$ and $ER(\$ \rightarrow £)$ are both zero. Covered arbitrage involves no 'price risk', the only risk is credit risk due to failure of the counterparty to provide either the interest income or deliver the forward currency. If we are to adequately test the CIP hypothesis, we need to obtain simultaneous 'dealing' quotes on the spot and forward rates and the two interest rates. There have been many studies looking at possible profitable opportunities due to covered interest arbitrage but not all use simultaneous dealing rates. However, Taylor (1987, 1989a) has looked at the CIP relationship in periods of 'tranquillity' and 'turbulence' in the foreign exchange market and he uses simultaneous quotes provided by foreign exchange and money market brokers. We will, therefore, focus on this study. The rates used by Taylor represent firm offers to buy and sell and as such they ought to represent the best rates (highest bid, lowest offer) available in the market, at any point in time. In contrast, rates quoted on the Reuters screen are normally 'for information only' and may not be actual trading rates. Taylor uses Eurocurrency rates and these have very little credit counterparty risk and, therefore, differ only in respect of their currency of denomination.

Taylor also considers brokerage fees and recalculates the above returns under the assumption that brokerage fees on Eurocurrency transactions represent about 1/50th of 1%. For example, the interest cost in borrowing Euro-dollars taking account of brokerage charges is $r_\$^o + 1/50$, while the rate earned on any Euro-dollar deposits is reduced by a similar amount, $r_\$^b - 1/50$.

He estimates that brokerage fees on spot and forward transactions are so small that they can be ignored. In his 1987 study, Taylor looked at data collected every 10 minutes on the trading days of the 11th, 12th and 13th November 1985. This yielded 3500 potential arbitrage opportunities, and he found that after allowing for brokerage costs, there were no profitable covered arbitrage opportunities. The results, therefore, strongly support covered interest parity and the efficient markets hypothesis. In a second study, Taylor (1989a) re-examined the same covered interest arbitrage relationships but this time in periods of 'market turbulence' in the FOREX market. The historic periods chosen were the 1967 devaluation of sterling in November of that year, the 1972 flotation of sterling in June of that year as well as some periods around the General Elections in both the United Kingdom and the United States in the 1980s. The covered interest arbitrage returns were calculated for maturities of 1, 2, 3, 6 and 12 months. The general thrust of the results is as follows.

- In periods of 'turbulence', there were some profitable opportunities to be made.

- The size of the profits tend to be smaller in the floating rate period than in the fixed rate period of the 1960s and became smaller as participants gained experience of floating rates, post-1972.

- The frequency, size and persistence over successive time periods of profitable arbitrage opportunities increase as the time to maturity of the contract is lengthened. Hence, there are larger and more frequent profit opportunities at a 12-month rather than a one-month forward transaction.

Let us take a specific example. In November 1967, a £1 million arbitrage into dollars would have produced only £473 profit, but just after the devaluation of sterling (i.e. a period of turbulence), there were sizeable riskless returns of about £4000 and £8000 on riskless arbitrage at the three-month and six-month maturities respectively. Capital controls (on UK sterling outflows) that were in force in the 1960s cannot account for these results since Euro-sterling deposits/loans were not subject to such controls. In periods of turbulence, returns sometimes persist over a number of days at the long end of the maturity spectrum, while at the short end of the maturity spectrum, profits are much smaller.

The reason for small yet persistent returns over a one-month horizon may well be due to the fact that the opportunity cost of traders' time is positive. There may not be enough traders in the market who think it is worth their time and effort to take advantage of *very small* profitable opportunities. Given the constraint of how much time they can devote to one particular segment of the market, they may prefer to execute trades with larger expected returns, even if the latter are risky (e.g. speculation on the *future* spot rate). It may even be more worthwhile for them to fill in their dealers' pads and communicate with other traders rather than take advantage of very small profitable opportunities. The riskless returns available at the longer end of the market are quite large and represent a clear violation of market efficiency. Taylor puts forward several hypotheses as to why this may occur, all of which are basically due to limitations on the credit positions dealers can take in the foreign exchange market.

Market makers are generally not free to deal in any amount with any counterparty that they choose. Usually, the management of a bank will stipulate which other banks it is willing to trade with (i.e. take on credit risk), together with the maximum size of liabilities that the management of the bank consider it is prudent to have outstanding with any other bank, at any point in time. Hence, there is a kind of liquidity constraint on covered arbitrage. Once the credit lines are 'full', no further business can be conducted with that bank (until outstanding liabilities have been unwound). This tends to create a preference for covered arbitrage at the short end of the market, since funds are 'freed up' relatively frequently.

Banks are also often unwilling to allow their foreign exchange dealers to borrow substantial amounts from other banks at long maturities (e.g. one year). For example, consider a UK foreign exchange dealer who borrows a large amount of dollars from a New York bank for covered arbitrage transactions over a one-year horizon. If the UK bank wants dollar loans from this same New York bank *for its business customers*, it may be thwarted from doing so because it has reached its credit limits. If so, foreign exchange dealers will retain a certain degree of slackness in their credit limits with other banks, and this may limit covered arbitrage at the longer end of the maturity spectrum. Another reason for self-imposed credit limits on dealers is that central banks often require periodic financial statements from banks, and the central bank may consider the short-term gearing position of the commercial bank when assessing its 'soundness'. If foreign exchange dealers have borrowed a large amount of funds for covered arbitrage transactions, this will show up in higher short-term gearing.

Taylor notes that some of the larger banks are willing to pay up to 1/16th of 1% above the market rate for Euro-dollar deposits as long as these are in blocks of over $100 million. Hence, Taylor recognises that there may be some mismeasurement in the Euro-dollar rates he uses and, hence, profitable opportunities may be more or less than found in his study.

Taylor finds relatively large covered arbitrage returns in the fixed exchange rate period of the 1960s; however, in the floating exchange rate period, these were far less frequent and much smaller. For example, in Table 1, we see that in 1987 there were effectively no profitable opportunities in the one-month maturities from sterling to dollars. However, at the one-year maturity, there are riskless arbitrage opportunities from dollars into sterling on both the Monday and Tuesday. Here, $1 million would yield a profit of around $1500 at the one-year maturity.

**Table 1**  Covered arbitrage: percentage excess returns (1987)

|  | 1 Month | | 6 Month | | 1 Year | |
|---|---|---|---|---|---|---|
|  | ($£ \to \$$) | ($\$ \to £$) | ($£ \to \$$) | ($\$ \to £$) | ($£ \to \$$) | ($\$ \to £$) |
| Monday<br>8th June 1987–12 noon | −0.043 | −0.016 | −0.097 | −0.035 | −0.117 | −0.162 |
| Tuesday<br>9th June 1987–12 noon | −0.075 | −0.064 | −0.247 | +0.032 | −0.192 | 0.150 |

Source: Data summary from Taylor 1989a, Table 3.

Taylor's study does not take account of any differential taxation on interest receipts from domestic and foreign investments, and this may also account for the existence of persistent profitable covered arbitrage at maturities of one year. It is unlikely that market participants are influenced by the perceived relative risks of default between, say, Euro-sterling and Euro-dollar investments, and hence this is unlikely to account for arbitrage profits even at the one-year maturities. Note that one cannot adequately test CIP between assets with different credit risk characteristics (either 'market price risk' or credit risk). For example, studies that compare covered transactions between Euro-sterling deposits and US corporate bonds are unlikely to be very informative about forward market efficiency and CIP.

Note that CIP can hold even if no trades actually take place. It is the *threat* of riskless arbitrage that ensures CIP. This is in part reflected in the fact that if you go to a bank for a forward quote, it calculates the forward rate it will offer you by using the CIP relationship. That is to say it checks on the values of $r_£$, $r_\$$ and $S_t$ and then quotes you a rate $F_t$ calculated using

$$F_t = S_t \frac{(1 + r_\$)}{(1 + r_£)} \tag{5}$$

where we have ignored the bid-offer distinction. It would clearly be irrational or down right stupid if a bank quoted a rate for $F_t$ different from that given by the CIP equation. Looking at potentially profitable trades using data on which market makers may have undertaken actual trades is clearly a useful way of testing CIP. However, many early studies of CIP run the regression

$$(f - s)_t = a + b(r_\$ - r_£)_t + \varepsilon_t \tag{6}$$

The null of CIP is $H_0 : a = 0, b = 1$, and if there are transactions costs, these may show up as $a \neq 0$. Since $(r_\$ - r_£)_t$ is endogenous then 2SLS or IV rather than OLS should be used when estimating (6). However, these regression tests of CIP have a number of acute problems. The regressions generally do not distinguish between bid and offer rates, do not *explicitly* (or carefully) take account of transactions costs and often the rates are not sampled contemporaneously. Also, even if you do not reject the null $a = 0, b = 1$, this merely implies that CIP holds *on average*, but this does not imply that it holds *continuously*. For these reasons, we do not report these regression tests.

Clinton (1988) points out that deviations from CIP should be no greater than the minimum transactions costs in the two deposit markets and the foreign exchange swap market (i.e. the practical implementation of a forward transaction – see Cuthbertson and Nitzsche 2001b). This neutral band he estimates as +0.06% p.a. from parity over the 1985–1986 period.

Balke and Wohar (1998) and Peel and Taylor (2002) examine the dynamic behaviour of *deviations* from CIP using non-linear TAR models. Peel and Taylor (2002) use weekly inter-war data and estimate a neutral bandwidth of 50 basis points (on an annual basis) and some moderate persistence outside of the bands. Balke and Wohar (1998) for United States–United Kingdom, January 1974–September 1993 find (asymmetric) mean reversion outside the neutral band, which also has less persistence than inside the band. Overall, the evidence suggests that for the recent data periods, arbitrage profits from CIP seem to be relatively infrequent or small.

## 25.2  Uncovered Interest Parity

The actual (*ex-post*) return to a domestic investor (e.g. 'Euro resident') investing €1 in a foreign risk-free (US) bond at an annual interest rate $r^*$ and converting the proceeds back to domestic currency one year later is $(1 + r^*)(S_{t+1}/S_t)$, where $S$ = domestic price of one unit of foreign exchange (e.g. € per \$). When investing in the United States, the *excess* return for a domestic investor (over a risk-free investment in domestic assets) is

$$1 + R_{t+1} = \frac{(1 + r^*)S_{t+1}}{(1 + r)S_t}$$

$$\ln(1 + R_{t+1}) \approx R_{t+1} = (r^* + \Delta s_{t+1}) - r \qquad (7)$$

using $\ln(1 + x) \approx x$ and $\ln S_t = s_t$. The return to *foreign* investment is the *foreign* interest rate plus the expected appreciation of the *foreign* currency. *Ex-ante*, the (approximate) *expected* excess return to foreign investment is

$$E_t R_{t+1} = (r^* + E_t \Delta s_{t+1}) - r \qquad (8)$$

where $E_t \Delta s_{t+1} \equiv E_t s_{t+1} - s_t$ and $s_{t+1}$ is the only stochastic variable. Note that $\Delta s_{t+1} > 0$, that is, a rise in $s$ implies an appreciation of the *foreign* currency (a depreciation in the domestic currency). The investment in the foreign asset is risky because the future foreign currency receipts are not 'covered' in the forward market. If investors are risk neutral and care only about expected returns, then arbitrage ensures that expected *excess* returns $E_t R_{t+1} = 0$ and we have the UIP condition

$$r - r^* = E_t \Delta s_{t+1} \qquad (9)$$

UIP implies that you cannot make money on average by switching funds between, say, the United States and Europe. You will win some 'bets', but these will be matched by bets that make losses, and the net gains average out to zero. Consider now a US resident investing in 'Euroland'. To the US resident, the foreign interest rate is the Euro-rate, and let $r^* = 6\%$ with domestic US rates $r = 2\%$. Then if UIP holds, the extra return in Euros the *US investor* makes (relative to US interest rates) will be offset (on average) by a depreciation of 4% in the Euro against the USD. Put another way, high interest rates in a foreign country (i.e. in Europe relative to the US) should not imply high *returns* to foreign investment but should signal an equal expected depreciation of the foreign currency.

Certainly, for high-inflation countries (e.g. South America in the 1980s, South East Asia in the late 1990s, Eastern European economies in the early 1990s) the broad predictions of the *unconditional* UIP relationship were borne out. Countries with relatively high interest rates also had depreciating currencies. The UIP relationship also broadly holds unconditionally (i.e. taking averages over many years) for moderate inflation countries such as the United Kingdom, Germany, Switzerland and Japan (Engel 1996). However, the latter is a very weak test of UIP since what is important is a test involving *conditional* expectations, that is, whether there are *temporary* periods when profits can be made by switching, based on *known interest differentials at a point in time*. A suitable regression is

$$\Delta s_{t+1} = \alpha + \beta (r - r^*)_t + \gamma \Lambda_t + \varepsilon_{t+1} \tag{10}$$

where $\Lambda_t$ are any variables known at time $t$. If UIP + RE holds, we expect $\alpha = \gamma = 0$, $\beta = 1$ and $\varepsilon_{t+1}$ to be serially uncorrelated. It is generally found that $\beta \neq +1$ and in fact $\beta$ is usually negative and of the order of $-1.0$ to $-4.0$ for various currencies (when the USD is the numeraire currency), time periods and different horizons for $\Delta s_{t+1}$ (e.g. monthly, quarterly, annual). As we shall see below, (10) is the FRU equation, since under CIP, we can replace $(r - r^*)_t$ with the forward premium $fp_t$.

Empirically, $\beta < 0$, and this implies that in periods when the interest *differential* in favour of the foreign country is high, the foreign currency tends to *appreciate*, $(\Delta s_{t+1} > 0)$ giving a positive dollar return to the US investor who borrows in dollars and lends in foreign currency. Hence, UIP is rejected. However, the R-squared in these annual regressions is usually quite low (i.e. of the order of 0.035) so such 'bets' are highly risky, although they do 'pay off' (in terms of positive returns) over a run of 'bets'.

Note that the above regression (10) with $\beta < 0$ does not imply that you make money on average by holding bank deposits in countries that simply have interest rates that are higher than in the United States (e.g. highly risky countries like Russia, Indonesia, Brazil, Argentina and Turkey in the 1990s). This is because the 'intercept' may offset the impact of the interest differential term. Equation (10) says you make money by holding bank deposits in countries that have higher interest rates *than normal*, relative to the United States (i.e. the regression $Y = \hat{\alpha} + \hat{\beta}X$ can be written $(Y - \overline{Y}) = \hat{\beta}(X - \overline{X})$, and it is $X - \overline{X} = (r - \overline{r}) - (r^* - \overline{r}^*)$ that *wholly* determines movements in $Y$ around its mean value). Under RE and risk neutrality, the above results are inexplicable. Of course, if we believe that countries with above-average interest rates are countries that also tend to have monetary instability, political unrest, a weak and non-diversified export base (e.g. only a few different agricultural exports), then the high expected return to investing in these countries may be a payment for this systematic risk – however, we still have to measure this risk, an issue we return to in later chapters (unfortunately with not much success).

Note that, in general, UIP does *not* imply that the exchange rate is a martingale and, therefore, unforecastable. UIP only implies the spot rate is a martingale ($E_t s_{t+1} = s_t$) *if* relative interest rates $r_t^* - r_t$ are zero in all time periods. Clearly, this is nonsense, since relative interest rates do vary over time. Also, studies that demonstrate cointegration amongst either a set of exchange rates or exchange rates and other macro-variables do imply that *exchange rates* are predictable (Granger–Engle theorem) – but this does not necessarily violate market efficiency. As we noted above, UIP implies that by observing today's relative interest rates, we can predict changes in the spot rate, but this does not imply we earn excess *returns*. (Since $E_t R_{t+1} = 0$, under UIP.)

Early empirical work tested equation (10) by regressing $\Delta s_{t+1} - (r_t - r_t^*)$ on a wide variety of economic variables available at time $t$ or earlier. Frankel (1979) found that for the DM/$ rate on quarterly data over the 1970s, all additional variables tried were insignificant. Haache and Townend (1981), using monthly data on the sterling effective rate (July 1972–February 1980), found that relative interest rates have unit coefficient but lagged values of the change in the exchange rate and a measure of credit expansion are also significant. (Similar results were obtained for the £/$ rate.) Cumby and Obstfeld (1981), using weekly data (July 1974–June 1978) on six major currencies against the dollar, also found that lagged values of the dependent variable $\Delta s_{t+1} - (r_t - r_t^*)$ of up to 16 weeks are statistically significant for six bilateral currencies against the USD. Hence, UIP is rejected.

If we accept CIP, then the above regressions for UIP are equivalent to regressing $\Delta s_{t+1} - fp_t \equiv s_{t+1} - f_t$ on known variables at time $t$ – this is FRU, which is discussed in the next section.

## 25.3 Forward Rate Unbiasedness, FRU

Using covered interest parity $r_t - r_t^* = f_t - s_t$ in (9) and rational expectations $s_{t+1} = E_t s_{t+1} + \varepsilon_{t+1}$, we obtain *forward rate unbiasedness*, *FRU*:

$$s_{t+1} = f_t + \varepsilon_{t+1} \quad \text{or,} \quad E_t \Delta s_{t+1} = fp_t \qquad (11)$$

where $fp_t = (f - s)_t$ is the forward premium. FRU + RE is usually tested in an equation of the form

$$E_t R_{t+1} = \alpha + \delta fp_t + \gamma \Lambda_t + \varepsilon_{t+1} \qquad (12)$$

or, equivalently,

$$E_t \Delta s_{t+1} = \alpha + \beta fp_t + \gamma \Lambda_t + \varepsilon_{t+1} \qquad (13a)$$

where $\Lambda_t$ are any variables known at time $t$. FRU implies $\alpha = \delta = \gamma = 0$ and $\beta = 1$, while RE implies $E_t(\varepsilon_{t+1} | \Omega_t) = 0$, which includes the assumption that $\varepsilon_{t+1}$ is serially uncorrelated. Hence, FRU + RE implies

$$E_t \Delta s_{t+1} = fp_t \qquad (13b)$$

Note that all of the previous equations and the next could be equally represented for the forward rate for any maturity $k$, so that (13b) becomes

$$E_t \Delta s_{t+k} = fp_t^k$$

where $E_t \Delta s_{t+k} \equiv E_t s_{t+k} - s_t$ is the $k$-period change in the exchange rate and $fp_t^k = f_t^k - s_t$ is the forward premium for currency delivery in the contract $k$ periods from today. To simplify the notation, we consider only the 'one-period' ahead case wherever possible.

## Simple Risk Premium

We can *define* the risk premium as

$$rp_t \equiv f_t - E_t s_{t+1} = fp_t - E_t \Delta s_{t+1} \tag{14}$$

The forward premium now consists of two parts – the expected depreciation and the risk premium. Under risk neutrality, $f_t = E_t s_{t+1}$, so the expected profit from forward market speculation is zero. But if $f_t > E_t s_{t+1}$, then the investor has to pay a premium (above its expected price $E_t s_{t+1}$) to buy the foreign currency in the forward market – this is a payment for incurring risk and allows the dealer providing the foreign currency to earn an *expected* profit. Risk neutrality implies $rp_t = 0$. Note that $rp_t$ is a definition of the risk premium, but we have not associated it with any 'fundamental' economic variables – we do this later. Assuming CIP, the above can also be written

$$\textit{Return to foreign investment } R = (r_t^* + E_t \Delta s_{t+1}) - r_t + rp_t = 0$$

Arbitrage by borrowing the domestic currency at $r_t$ and investing in foreign assets now requires an additional payment of $rp_t$ before arbitrage ceases.

Let us examine how a time-varying risk premium could lead to bias and inconsistency in OLS estimates of $\beta$. Rearranging (14) and assuming RE, the regression to test FRU is now

$$E_t \Delta s_{t+1} = \alpha + \beta fp_t + \gamma \Lambda_t + (\varepsilon_{t+1} - rp_t) \tag{15}$$

If $rp_t$ and $fp_t$ in equation (15) are correlated, then the OLS estimator is inconsistent. This is the standard 'errors in variables' problem in econometrics. 'Correct' (i.e. asymptotically unbiased) estimates may be obtained using an instrumental variables technique, with the covariance matrix estimated using GMM if heteroscedasticity is present.

## Time-Series Properties

Empirically, the spot rate is a non-stationary I(1) variable, and hence $\Delta s_{t+1}$ is I(0). The RE forecast error must be stationary I(0) – if it were not, it would be forecastable from past information. It follows that under FRU + RE, the forward premium must be stationary and the cointegrating vector between $s_{t+1}$ and $f_t$ should be $\{1, -1\}$. Note that

FRU + RE implies the cointegrating vector $\{1, -1\}$, but a finding of cointegration *per se* between $f_t$ and $s_{t+1}$ does not necessarily imply FRU + RE. To see this, rearrange $\Delta s_{t+1} = \alpha + \beta(f - s)_t + \varepsilon_{t+1}$, when $\beta \neq 1$ so the null of FRU + RE is *not* true.

$$(s_{t+1} - f_t) = \alpha + (\beta - 1)(f - s)_t + \varepsilon_{t+1} \qquad (16)$$

If $(f - s)_t$ and $\varepsilon_{t+1}$ are stationary, then $s_{t+1} - f_t$ must be stationary and, hence, co-integrated. But equation (16) holds for $\beta \neq 1$, so cointegration does not imply FRU.

There have been hundreds (if not thousands) of stationarity/cointegration tests on spot and forward rates both as single equations and where the forward-spot relationships for different currencies (usually against the USD) are stacked in a VAR-ECM, Johansen system and tests for multiple cointegrating $\{1, -1\}$ vectors undertaken – see Engel (1996) for a summary. The results of these tests are not unambiguous. Some studies find $fp_t$ is not stationary, particularly using the univariate test, while others do reject non-stationarity – particularly those employing panel unit-root tests where forward premia at, say, 1-, 3-, 6-, and 12-month maturities appear in a Johansen VECM system (e.g. Barkoulas, Baum and Chakraborty 2003). In fact, $fp_t$ is highly persistent with a 'near' unit root. Generally, $(s_{t+1} - \beta f_t)$ is found to be I(0), so $s_{t+1}$ and $f_t$ are cointe-grated, but the cointegrating vector is not always found to be $\{1, -1\}$. Those who are familiar with the myriad of cointegration and stationarity tests will be aware that such tests in small samples can be rather sensitive to the specific test statistics employed, and the power of such tests against 'reasonable' alternative hypotheses is often very low (although better for panel unit-root tests). This author finds it hard to believe that the forward premium is non-stationary, since it is hard to believe that $f$ and $s$ would eventually drift infinitely far apart. Of course, if we abandon FRU + RE and incor-porate a risk premium, then $fp_t$ could be non-stationary if $rp_t$ is also non-stationary (see equation 15) – but the latter seems equally implausible, based on introspection (but see Lewis and Evans 1999). The only sensible way forward is to concentrate on equations like (13) and use MCS or bootstrapping when testing $\beta = 1$, to obtain the empirical distribution of $\beta$. This can be done under alternative views about stationarity or otherwise of $fp_t$.

## Tests

The finding of a negative $\beta$ in (13a) is a robust result across many time periods from the 1920s to the present, across many currencies (usually against the USD) and for alternative horizons for the forward rate (e.g. one-month, three-months, one-year). The average value across many studies is about *minus one*, with values usually in the range $-0.8$ to $-4.1$. This is the *forward premium puzzle*. These results apply in single-equation studies (e.g. Fama 1984, Meese and Rogoff 1983, McCallum 1994), when several exchange rates are included (using a SURE estimator) and when a bivariate VAR with $z = \{\Delta s_{t+1}, fp_t\}$ is used (Baillie and McMahon 1989, Bekaert and Hodrick 1993). Flood and Rose (1996) find that under fixed exchange rates, $\beta$ is positive $(= 0.58)$ but significantly less than one, while floating exchange rate countries have $\beta$ significantly less than one. Bekaert and Hodrick (1992) find that $(s_{t+1} - f_t)$ is predictable using the forward premium, and the degree of predictability increases with the (forward rate) horizon, reaching an R-squared of 30–40% at the one-year horizon. This refutes FRU + RE.

Note that if the spot rate follows a random walk, then the estimated value of $\beta$ will be close to zero regardless of whether the market is efficient. Also, if the spot rate is a random walk, then $f_t = E_t s_{t+1} = s_t$, the forward premium is zero and susceptible to measurement errors in the regression (13). Hence, when the spot rate is *close to* a random walk, there will be difficulties in obtaining precise estimates of $\beta$. To mitigate this problem, we could regress $(s_{t+1} - f_t)$ on $\Lambda_t$ – but empirically the coefficient on $\Lambda_t$ is found to be non-zero (using GMM standard errors) for most currencies, again refuting FRU (Hansen and Hodrick 1980).

The forward rate $f_t$ and $s_{t+1}$, which are both $I(1)$, are usually found to be co-integrated, but this does not imply FRU, that is, $\beta = 1$ (e.g. McFarland, McMahon and Ngama 1994), neither does refutation of FRU imply that forward premia do not help in forecasting future changes in the exchange rate. Given cointegration between $f_t$ and $s_t$, the Engle–Granger theorem implies that the *term structure* of forward premia (i.e. $f_t^k - s_t$ for forward horizons $k = 1, 2, 3 \ldots$) should help predict changes in spot rate $\Delta_k s_{t+k}$ (over horizons $k$) and Clarida and Taylor (1997) demonstrate this in a Johansen VECM framework. Sarno and Valente (2004a,b) extend this approach by including a three-state Markov switching process for the parameters of the VECM and the covariance matrix of error terms. This is an MS-VECM model – see Chapter 4. The one-step ahead 'predictive densities' for the weekly change in each of eight bilateral spot-USD exchange rates (1985–2003) for the MS-VECM model are closer to the *actual* realisations of the change in spot rates than the 'predictive densities' for the linear-VECM or random walk models. (No other forecast diagnostics such as outside sample sign tests and MAE and RMSE for the competing models are given.) As noted in Chapter 4, we know that the conditional distribution of the change in exchange rates is non-normal so it is not too surprising that a model that allows non-normality is an improvement on models that do not have this property. Note also that these 'cointegration' results, while interesting as a relatively parsimonious representation of the dynamics, have little direct bearing on the validity or otherwise of FRU.

## Jensen Inequality Terms (JIT)

It is worth noting that FRU + RE is slightly different if we consider *real* returns (profits) to forward market speculation

$$E_t \left[ \frac{F_t - S_{t+1}}{P_{t+1}^\$} \right] = 0 \qquad (17)$$

where $P^\$$ is the dollar price level for US consumers (and $F$ is measured as dollars per unit of foreign currency). Assuming conditional lognormality, (17) becomes

$$E_t s_{t+1} = f_t - 0.5 \, \text{var}_t(s_{t+1}) + \text{cov}_t(s_{t+1}, p_{t+1}^\$) \qquad (18)$$

The last two terms are Jensen inequality terms (JIT). So, even for a risk-neutral US investor, FRU does not hold when we incorporate the JIT. It also follows that risk neutrality does not imply UIP unless we again ignore the JIT terms. If we ignore the covariance term, which empirically is very small, one could estimate (18) using a GARCH-in-mean model for $\text{var}_t(s_{t+1})$. Bekaert and Hodrick (1993) and Baillie and Bollerslev (1989) have found that the coefficient on $\text{var}_t(s_{t+1})$ is not statistically different from zero and omitting it from (18) does not affect estimates of $\beta$ which remain negative. In general, JIT in the FX market are thought to be small and can be ignored in practice.

## FRU: RE Versus Risk

The rejection of FRU + RE could be due to a failure of rational expectations or of risk neutrality. If the estimate of $\beta$ is $-1$, $E_t \Delta s_{t+1} = (-1)fp_t$ and $sd(E_t \Delta s_{t+1}) = sd(fp_t)$. Using $rp_t \equiv fp_t - E_t \Delta s_{t+1}$ and the RE assumption that expectations are independent of information at time $t$ (i.e. $fp_t$), then

$$sd(rp_t) = 2\, sd(E_t \Delta s_{t+1}) \quad \text{and} \quad sd(f_t - E_t s_{t+1}) = 2\, sd(E_t \Delta s_{t+1})$$

Given that $\Delta s_{t+1}$ is highly volatile, this implies, that a highly volatile risk premium is required to explain the forward premium puzzle. Also, the *predictable* component of the excess return has a greater variation than the *expected* depreciation itself. These two 'stylised facts' become important when assessing the validity of certain general equilibrium models of the forward market, which we undertake in later chapters. It can also be shown that, given the following two regressions,

$$s_{t+1} - s_t = \alpha + \beta(f_t - s_t) + \varepsilon_{t+1}$$

$$f_t - s_{t+1} = \gamma + \delta(f_t - s_t) + v_{t+1}$$

and using (14),

$$\beta = \frac{\text{var}(E_t \Delta s_{t+1}) + \text{cov}(rp_t, E_t \Delta s_{t+1})}{\text{var}(rp_t) + \text{var}(E_t \Delta s_{t+1}) + 2\,\text{cov}(rp_t, E_t \Delta s_{t+1})}$$

$$\delta = \frac{\text{var}(rp_t) + \text{cov}(rp_t, E_t \Delta s_{t+1})}{\text{var}(rp_t) + \text{var}(E_t \Delta s_{t+1}) + 2\,\text{cov}(rp_t, E_t \Delta s_{t+1})}$$

$$\delta - \beta = [\text{var}(rp_t) - \text{var}(E_t \Delta s_{t+1})]/\,\text{var}(fp_t)$$

Note that, given the estimated $\beta$ is negative, this implies that the risk premium and the expected depreciation must be negatively correlated. Following Fama (1984), if $rp_t$ is highly variable, then the forward premium will be a poor predictor of the expected change in the spot rate. A positive value for $\delta - \beta$ indicates that the variance of the risk premium is greater than the variance of expectations about $E_t \Delta s_{t+1}$, and $\delta - \beta$ provides a quantitative guide to the relative importance of the time variation in the risk premium under the maintained hypothesis that RE holds.

Studies (e.g. Fama 1984, Koedijk and Ott 1987) usually find that $\delta - \beta > 0$ with $\beta < 0$ and $\delta > 0$. Fama (1984) finds a range for $\delta - \beta$ of 1.6 (for Japanese yen) to

4.2 (for the Belgian franc). Hence, under the null of RE, the FRU proposition fails because the (linear additive) risk premium is time varying.

It is worth repeating that a limitation of the above analysis is that the potentially time-varying risk premium $rp_t$ is assumed to depend linearly only on the time-varying forward premium $fp_t$ and is not based on any well-founded economic theory. Also, the results *assume* that RE holds so that any violation of the null hypothesis is attributed to a time-varying risk premium. What we require is a method that allows the failure of FRU to be apportioned between a violation of RE and variations in the risk premium.

## Survey Data

By using survey data on agents' expectations of the future spot rate, Frankel and Froot (1987), Froot and Frankel 1989 show how one can apportion the rejection of the null of FRU, between that due to a failure of RE and that due to a failure of risk neutrality. Consider the usual forward premium regression

$$\Delta s_{t+1} = \alpha + \beta fp_t + \varepsilon_{t+1} \tag{19}$$

where $\varepsilon_{t+1} = E_t s_{t+1} - s_{t+1} \equiv E_t \Delta s_{t+1} - \Delta s_{t+1}$ is the RE forecast error. The OLS regression coefficient $\beta$ is given by

$$\beta = \text{cov}(\Delta s_{t+1}, fp_t) / \text{var}(fp_t) \tag{20}$$

It is easy to show by substituting for $\Delta s_{t+1}$ from (19) in (20) that

$$\beta = 1 - \beta_{RE} - \beta_{RN} \tag{21}$$

where

$$\beta_{RE} = -\text{cov}(\varepsilon_{t+1}, fp_t) / \text{var}(fp_t) \tag{22}$$

$$\beta_{RN} = 1 - \text{cov}(E_t \Delta s_{t+1}, fp_t) / \text{var}(fp_t) \tag{23}$$

Under the assumption of RE, the forecast error $\varepsilon_{t+1}$ is independent of the information set $\Omega_t$ and, hence, $fp_t$ so that $\beta_{RE} = 0$. Also, regardless of how expectations are formed under FRU, the expected rate of appreciation $E_t \Delta s_{t+1}$ will equal the forward premium $fp_t$ so that $\text{cov}(E_t \Delta s_{t+1}, fp_t) = 1$ and, hence, $\beta_{RN} = 0$ (i.e. risk neutrality holds). If RE *and* risk neutrality hold, then $\beta_{RE}$ and $\beta_{RN} = 0$ and, hence, from (21), $\beta = 1$, as one would expect.

If we have survey data on $E_t s_{t+1}$, we can construct a data series for $\varepsilon_{t+1} = s_{t+1} - E_t s_{t+1}$ along with the sample analogues of $\beta_{RE}$ and $\beta_{RN}$ or equivalently run the regressions

$$E_t s_{t+1} - s_t = \alpha + \beta_{RE}(f_t - s_t) + \omega_{t+1}$$

$$f_t - s_{t+1} = \gamma + \beta_{RN}(f_t - s_t) + v_{t+1}$$

These equations provide evidence on the importance of the breakdown of either RE or risk neutrality in producing the result $\beta \neq 1$.

Let us remind ourselves of some problems that arise in using survey data. The first question is whether the data is qualitative (e.g. respondents answer 'up', 'down', or 'same') or quantitative (e.g. respondents answer 'my forecast of the exchange rate for sterling in 91 days is 1.4 Euro/£'). If qualitative data is used, then different methods used to transform the data generally give different *quantitative* results for $E_t s_{t+1}$. Hence, we can have different sets of quantitative data purporting to measure the same expectations. Also, our quantitative data may be either for individuals or for averages (or median value) over a *group* of individuals. In principle, RE applies to an individual's expectations and not to an average taken over a set of individuals.

There is also the question of whether the respondents are likely to give correct, thoughtful answers and whether the individuals surveyed remain as a fixed cohort or change over time. Also, when dealing with the FRU proposition, the individual's estimate of $E_t s_{t+1}$ must be taken at the same time as $f_t$ (and $s_t$). Finally, there is the problem of whether the horizon of the survey data (on $E_t s_{t+1}$) exactly matches the out-turn figure for $s_{t+1}$. These problems bedevil attempts to draw very firm conclusions from studies on the basis of survey data. Different conclusions by different researchers may be due to such 'quality differences' in the survey data used.

Let us return to the study by Frankel and Froot (1986, 1987), Froot and Frankel (1989) who use quantitative survey data on US respondents. They calculate $\beta_{RE}$ and $\beta_{RN}$ and using (21), they find that $\beta \neq 1$ (in fact, $\beta$ is negative) and that this is primarily attributed to a failure of RE (i.e. $\beta_{RE}$ is non-zero). This broad conclusion holds over five (main) currencies and over horizons of one, three and six months, for data from the mid-1970s and 1980s. In fact, $\beta_{RE}$ is usually not statistically different from unity, although Bekaert and Hodrick (1992) notes that the R-squared in this regression is far from unity, as it should be if risk factors are inconsequential. MacDonald and Torrance (1988), using quantitative survey data on UK respondents in 1985/86, also obtain similar results to Frankel–Froot.

Taylor (1989b) uses *qualitative* survey data on UK respondents, which he transforms into quantitative data for the period 1981–1985. He finds the opposite of the above results, namely that the failure of $\beta \neq 1$ is mainly due to $\beta_{RN} \neq 0$. However, this evidence is fairly weak since for three out of the four exchange rates studied, $\beta_{RE} = \beta_{RN} = 0$ and in only one case is $\beta_{RN} > 0$. In fact, $\beta_{RN} = 1.4(t = 0.15)$ for the sterling effective rate, but it is difficult to interpret results using the effective rate since this is a 'basket' of currencies (each of which has a set of bilateral forward rates). On balance, the evidence based on regressions using survey data (in particular, see Froot and Frankel (1989)) indicate that the FRU puzzle may be mainly due to systematic forecast errors but there is also *some variation* in the risk premium.

The failure of FRU may be due to the fact that agents are not (Muth) rational and, therefore, *do* make systematic forecast errors. However, it could equally be due to the fact that agents take time to learn about new exchange rate processes and while they are learning, they make systematic errors because they do not know the true model. This learning could persist for some time if either the fundamentals affecting the exchange rate are continually changing or the influence of noise traders on the market varies over time. Alternatively, there may also be a 'Peso problem', and a failure of FRU may occur even when agents are rational, because the econometrician does not measure these expectations correctly, in a specific finite sample – these issues are discussed in the following section.

# 25.4 Testing FRU: VAR Methodology

We can test FRU over multi-period horizons by invoking RE and replacing $E_t \Delta s_{t+m}$ with the out-turn value $\Delta s_{t+m}$ and regressing it on the forward premium where $f_t^{(m)}$ is the forward rate for horizon $m$. However, in this section, we use the VAR methodology to give an explicit forecast of $E_t \Delta s_{t+m}$. We have discussed single-equation tests of FRU and we now wish to 'extend' these tests for forward rates over multi-period horizons. Consider

$$\Delta s_{t+1} = a_{11} \Delta s_t + a_{12} fp_t + w_{1t+1} \tag{24}$$

In the *one-period case* when the forward rate refers to delivery at time $t + 1$, then FRU implies $H_0 : a_{11} = 0, a_{12} = 1$. Note that the EMH also implies that the forecast error is independent of the limited information set $\Lambda_t = (\Delta s_t, fp_t)$

$$\Delta s_{t+1} - E_t \Delta s_{t+1} = a_{11} \Delta s_t + (a_{12} - 1)(f - s)_t + w_{1t+1} \tag{25}$$

where $E_t \Delta s_{t+1} = fp_t$ under the null. In the *one-step* ahead case, we require only equation (24) to test FRU. However, we now consider a two-step ahead prediction (which is easily generalised).

### Two-period case

Suppose we have quarterly data but we are considering forward rates $f_t$ for six months ahead, hence FRU is

$$E_t s_{t+2} - s_t = E_t \Delta_2 s_{t+2} = fp_t \tag{26}$$

The forecast two periods ahead is

$$E_t \Delta_2 s_{t+2} \equiv E_t \Delta s_{t+2} + E_t \Delta s_{t+1} \tag{27}$$

Leading (24) one-period forward, we see that to forecast $E_t \Delta s_{t+2}$, we require a forecast of $E_t(fp_{t+1})$. Hence, we require an equation to determine $fp$, which we take to be

$$fp_{t+1} = a_{21} \Delta s_t + a_{22} fp_t + w_{2t+1} \tag{28}$$

Equations (24) and (28) are a simple bivariate vector autoregression VAR. If $(s_t, f_t)$ are I(1) variables but $(s_t, f_t)$ have a cointegrating parameter $(1, -1)$, then $fp_t = f_t - s_t$ is I(0) and all the variables in the VAR are stationary. Such stationary variables may be represented by a unique infinite moving average (vector) process, which may be inverted to yield an autoregressive process.

The FRU hypothesis (26) implies a set of non-linear cross-equation restrictions amongst the parameters of the VAR, and these restrictions ensure that the two-period forecast error implicit in (26) is independent of information $\Lambda_t = (\Delta s_t, fp_t)$. Using (27), (24) and (28),

$$E_t \Delta_2 s_{t+2} = E_t \Delta s_{t+2} + E_t \Delta s_{t+1}$$

$$= a_{11}(a_{11} \Delta s_t + a_{12} fp_t) + a_{12}(a_{21} \Delta s_t + a_{22} fp_t) + (a_{11} \Delta s_t + a_{12} fp_t) \tag{29}$$

Collecting terms and equating the resulting expression for $E_t \Delta_2 s_{t+2}$ with $fp_t$

$$E_t \Delta_2 s_{t+2} = \theta_1 \Delta s_t + \theta_2 fp_t = fp_t \tag{30}$$

where

$$\theta_1 = a_{11}^2 + a_{12} a_{21} + a_{11} \tag{31a}$$

$$\theta_2 = a_{11} a_{12} + a_{12} a_{22} + a_{12} \tag{31b}$$

It is clear that (30) can only hold for all values of $\Delta s_t$ and $fp_t$ if

$$\theta_1 = 0 \quad \text{and} \quad \theta_2 = 1 \tag{32}$$

The forecast error for the spot rate between $t$ and $t + 2$, under FRU, is

$$\Delta_2 s_{t+2} - E_t \Delta_2 s_{t+2} = [\theta_1 \Delta s_t + \theta_2 fp_t + \eta_{t+1}] - fp_t \tag{33}$$

where the term in parenthesis is derived from the VAR and $\eta_{t+1}$ depends on $w_{t+1}$ (for $i = 1, 2$). If $\theta_1$ and $\theta_2$ are *unrestricted*, then the *expected value* of the forecast error will, in general, depend on $(\Delta s_t, fp_t)$, that is, information at time $t$. It is only if $\theta_1 = 0$ and $\theta_2 = 1$ that the orthogonality property of RE holds. In a previous chapter, we noted that these restrictions can be tested using either a Wald or a likelihood ratio statistic. Considering the latter (which is tractable here), the restrictions can be rearranged to give

$$a_{21} = -a_{11}(1 + a_{11})/a_{12} \tag{34a}$$

$$a_{22} = [1 - a_{12}(1 + a_{11})]/a_{12} \tag{34b}$$

Substituting for $a_{21}$ and $a_{22}$ in (28), the *restricted* VAR equations are

$$\Delta s_{t+1} = a_{11} \Delta s_t + a_{12} fp_t \tag{35a}$$

$$fp_{t+1} = \left[ \frac{-a_{11}(1 + a_{11})}{a_{12}} \right] \Delta s_t + \left[ \frac{1 - a_{12}(1 + a_{11})}{a_{12}} \right] fp_t \tag{35b}$$

The log-likelihood value from the restricted system (35a + 35b) can be compared with that from the unrestricted system (24) + (28). If the difference in log-likelihoods is large (or small), then the restrictions are rejected (or not rejected).

We will quickly demonstrate how the above problem (with VAR lag length $p = 1$) can be represented in matrix form and how it can be generalised. The matrix form of the unrestricted VAR is

$$z_{t+1} = A z_t + w_{t+1} \tag{36}$$

where $z_{t+1} = (\Delta s_{t+1}, fp_{t+1})$ and $A(2 \times 2) = \{a_{ij}\}$. Let $e\mathbf{1} = (1, 0)$ and $e\mathbf{2} = (0, 1)$ so that

$$\Delta s_t = e\mathbf{1}' z_t \tag{37a}$$

$$fp_t = e\mathbf{2}' z_t \tag{37b}$$

It follows that

$$E_t z_{t+2} = E_t A z_{t+1} = A^2 z_t \tag{38}$$

$$E_t(\Delta_2 s_{t+1}) = E_t(\Delta s_{t+2} + \Delta s_{t+1}) = e\mathbf{1}'(A^2 + A)z_t \tag{39}$$

From (26), FRU implies

$$e\mathbf{1}'(A + A^2)z_t = e\mathbf{2}'z_t \quad \text{hence} \quad e\mathbf{2}' - e\mathbf{1}'(A + A^2) = 0 \tag{40}$$

where

$$A^2 = \begin{pmatrix} a_{11}^2 + a_{12}a_{21}, & a_{11}a_{12} + a_{12}a_{22} \\ a_{21}a_{11} + a_{22}a_{21}, & a_{21}a_{12} + a_{22}^2 \end{pmatrix} \tag{41}$$

It is easy to see that (40) are the same restrictions as we worked out earlier in (31), 'by substitution'. Generalising, a forward prediction of $\Delta s_{t+m}$ for any horizon $m$ is given by

$$E_t \Delta_m s_{t+m} = \sum_{i=1}^{m} E_t \Delta s_{t+i} \tag{42}$$

and, hence, FRU for an $m$-period forward rate $fp_t^{(m)}$ is

$$E_t \Delta_m s_{t+m} = \sum_{i=1}^{m} e\mathbf{1}' A^i z_t = fp_t^{(m)} \tag{43}$$

The FRU restrictions for an $m$-period horizon are

$$f(A) = e\mathbf{2}' - e\mathbf{1}' \sum_{i=1}^{m} A^i = 0 \tag{44}$$

The VAR predictions $E_t \Delta_m s_{t+m}$ in (43) give a time series for the 'theoretical forward premium' (over $m$ periods), which can be compared with the actual forward premium (using graphs, variance ratios and correlation coefficients), as with our earlier VAR expositions.

## Uncovered Interest Parity

The uncovered interest parity (UIP) condition can also be applied over a multi-period horizon, and the VAR approach used in exactly the same way as described above. The multi-period UIP condition is

$$E_t \Delta_m s_{t+m} \equiv E_t(s_{t+m} - s_t) = (r - r^*)_t$$

For example, if we have quarterly data, the interest differential on *one-year* bonds should equal the expected change in the exchange rate over the subsequent four quarters (i.e. $m = 4$). The above UIP equation is similar to the FRU equation except we have $(r_t - r_t^*)$ on the RHS and not $fp_t^{(m)}$. However, it should be obvious that the analysis for a VAR in $\Delta s_t$ and $(r_t - r_t^*)$ goes through in exactly the same fashion as for FRU. Of course, if CIP holds, then using $r_t - r_t^*$ is equivalent to using $fp_t$ and testing FRU.

## Recent Empirical Results

Recent studies are virtually unanimous in finding rejection of the VAR restrictions when testing FRU (or the equivalent UIP hypothesis) – assuming a time-invariant risk premium. The rejection of FRU is found to hold at several horizons (e.g. three, six, nine and 12 months) over a wide variety of alternative information sets, across different currencies and over several time spans of data (see, for example, Hakkio 1981, Baillie and McMahon 1989, Levy and Nobay 1986, Taylor 1989c).

## Term Structure of Forward Premia

Some studies have combined tests of *covered* interest parity CIP, with the EH of the term structure of interest rates applied to *both* domestic and foreign interest rates. Of course, if you believe (from other evidence) that CIP always holds (and we do!), then this is a test of the EH holding simultaneously in two (or more) countries. By way of illustration, consider the *covered* interest parity CIP relationships (in logarithms) for three- and six-month interest rates and forward rates but using *monthly* data

$$fp_t^{(3)} = f_t^{(3)} - s_t = d_t^{(3)} \tag{45a}$$

$$fp_t^{(6)} = f_t^{(6)} - s_t = d_t^{(6)} \tag{45b}$$

where $d_t^{(i)} = r_t^{(i)} - r_t^{*(i)}$ $(i = 3, 6)$. If the EH holds in *both* the domestic and foreign country,

$$d_t^{(6)} = (d_t^{(3)} + E_t d_{t+3}^{(3)})/2 \tag{46}$$

where the subscript $t + 3$ applies because we use monthly data. The above equations imply a term structure of forward premia:

$$fp_t^{(6)} = (fp_t^{(3)} + E_t fp_{t+3}^{(3)})/2 \tag{47}$$

Equation (47) is conceptually the same as that for the term structure of spot yields on zero coupon bonds, discussed in Chapter 22. Clearly, given any VAR involving $fp_t^{(6)}$ and $fp_t^{(3)}$ (and any other relevant information variables), (47) will imply the by now familiar set of cross-equation restrictions.

There have been a number of VAR studies applied to (47), and they usually resoundingly reject the expectations hypothesis of the term premia in forward rates (e.g. see Sarno and Taylor 2002). Since we have strong independent evidence that *covered* interest parity holds for most time periods and most maturities, rejection of the restrictions implicit in the VAR parameters applied to (47) is most likely due to a failure of the EH of the term structure to hold in both the domestic and foreign countries.

## Testing UIP and the EH

A similar analysis to the above can be used to simultaneously test the expectations hypothesis of the term structure of interest rates in two countries and the UIP relationship between these two countries. (Again note that if CIP holds, then testing UIP is equivalent to testing FRU.) The EH for any two countries is

$$E_t \sum_{i=1}^{n-1} (1 - i/n) \Delta r_{t+i}^j = (R_{t,n}^j - r_t^j) \qquad j = 1, 2$$

where $r^j$ = short (one-period continuously compounded) rate for country $j$, $R_{t,n}^j$ is the long rate for country $j$. The UIP relationship is

$$E_t s_{t+1} - s_t = r_t^k - r_t^j$$

where $s_t$ = (log) currency $j$ per unit of currency $k$. All we now require is a vector $z_t \equiv (\Delta s_t, \Delta r_t^k, \Delta r_t^j, R_{t,n}^j - r_t^j, R_{t,n}^k - r_t^k)$ in the VAR, and we can undertake separate tests of the implied cross-equation restrictions for each of the above three equations separately or any combination of the three. Note that the VAR, even if it has only one lag, involves estimating 25 parameters – these parameters are consistent but biased.

Bekaert and Hodrick (2001) undertook the above tests using a bilateral USD exchange rate with either UK pound sterling (GBP) or the Deutsche Mark (DM) together with one-month and 12-month interest rates (monthly data, January 1975–July 1997). They used single-equation regressions tests, the Wald test of the non-linear VAR parameter restrictions, and they also develop a Lagrange multiplier (LM) test, which requires constrained estimates of the VAR under the null. The latter is not easy, but Newey and McFadden (1994) show how (approximate) values for the constrained parameters can be obtained from the unconstrained estimates. In addition, Bekaert and Hodrick find the empirical distribution of the test statistics by bootstrapping the residuals.

They confirm earlier results that the Wald test suffers from extreme size distortions, whereas the LM test does not. For example, when simultaneously testing the VAR restrictions for all three arbitrage relationships for German–US data, the Wald and LM test statistics are 47.7 and 21.34, hence one test decisively rejects the null, and the other does not (based on the asymptotic 5% critical value of 25). But the empirical 5% critical values from the bootstrap where the joint null of the EH and UIP is true are 47.5 and 22.1, so the joint restrictions are now just about acceptable at a 5% significance level. This very careful study emphasises the need to use empirical bootstrap distributions and when one does, any rejections of the EH of the term structure or the UIP condition are found to be much less dramatic than when using the asymptotic results.

## Frictions and Data

The FRU proposition assumes investors have sufficient funds to bring $f_t$ in line with $E_t s_{t+1}$. But in the real world, it may be that restrictions on borrowing, short-sales and transactions costs prevent this happening. There is some evidence (He and Modest

1995, Luttmer and Nishiotis 1995, Goodhart and Taylor 1992) that these effects could be substantial, but the general consensus appears to be that they are unlikely to be large enough to 'explain' the FRU observed in the data, where $\hat{\beta} < -1$.

Recently, Breuer and Wohar (1996) carefully examined the data issues surrounding tests of FRU. They ensure the spot rate at $t + 1$ (i.e. the spot value date) exactly matches the delivery date in the forward contract (i.e. the 'forward value date'). They also examine whether using 'bid forward/ask spot' (and vice versa) affects the results, compared to using averages of bid and ask. For example, they find that after implementing these refinements, the FRU hypothesis is still decisively rejected. Using one-month forward rates for Germany, the United Kingdom, Switzerland and Japan (against the USD) over 1974–1993, the estimates of $\beta$ are mostly in the range from $-0.6$ to $-2.0$ and the null that $\beta = 1$ is rejected with $p$-values around 0.001 (0.1 of 1%).

## 25.5  Peso Problems and Learning

In previous sections, we have noted that the simplifying assumptions of risk neutrality and RE are not consistent with the empirical results on FRU. In this section, we examine two reasons for the apparent empirical failure of FRU. First, we analyse how the Peso problem can complicate the interpretation of tests of the EMH and then move on to discuss learning.

### Peso Problem

The failure of the FRU in empirical tests may be due to the Peso problem. The Peso problem leads the researcher to measure expectations incorrectly, hence forecasts may appear biased and not independent of information at time $t$.

In the mid-1970s, the Mexican Peso was on a notionally fixed exchange rate against the US dollar. But it traded consistently at a forward discount for many years, in anticipation of a devaluation (which eventually occurred in 1976). Prima facie, the fact that the forward rate for the Peso was persistently below the out-turn value for the spot rate (in, say, three months' time) implies persistent profitable arbitrage opportunities for risk-neutral speculators.

The Peso problem arises from the fact that there could be unobservable (and hence unquantifiable) events that *may* occur in the future but in our sample of data never actually do occur. It is completely rational for an investor in forming her expectations to take account of factors that are unobservable to the econometrician. However, if the event never occurs in the sample of data examined by the econometrician, then we could erroneously infer that the agent's expectations are biased. Hence, the econometrician may believe that she has unearthed a refutation of RE but in fact she has not.

To illustrate the problem further, let us consider the Peso problem in a fairly simple way. If the Mexican government's fixed exchange rate policy is entirely credible (call this 'regime-1') and has been adhered to for a number of years, then for time periods $\{t = 0, 1 \ldots t_1\}$ *in regime-$t_1$*.

$$E_t s_{t+1} = s_t \tag{48}$$

Hence, under 'complete credibility' survey data on expectations, $E_t s_{t+1}$ would be unbiased forecasts of future spot rates $s_{t+1}$ $\{t = 0, 1, \ldots t_1\}$.

Now suppose that foreign investors begin to think the government's commitment to a fixed exchange rate has weakened and that there is a non-zero probability $\pi$ that the Peso will be devalued and a probability $(1 - \pi)$ that it will remain 'fixed'. This new regime we denote as 'partial' credibility. A rational investor would then form expectations

$$E_t s_{t+1} = \pi E_t(s_{t+1}|Z2) + (1 - \pi) E_t(s_{t+1}|Z1)$$

$$= \pi[E_t(s_{t+1}|Z2) - E_t(s_{t+1}|Z1)] + E_t(s_{t+1}|Z1)$$

$$= \pi \nabla s_{t+1} + E_t(s_{t+1}|Z1) \tag{49}$$

for periods $t = \{t_1 + 1, t_1 + 2, \ldots, T\}$, where $E_t(s_{t+1}|Z1) =$ exchange rate under the fixed exchange rate, regime-1, $E_t(s_{t+1}|Z2) =$ exchange rate under the devaluation possibility and $\nabla s_{t+1} \equiv [E_t(s_{t+1}|Z2) - E_t(s_{t+1}|Z1)]$. Since a devaluation is expected in the partial credibility regime, $E_t(s_{t+1}|Z2) > E_t(s_{t+1}|Z1)$. Suppose, however, that during the partial credibility regime the Mexican government does *not* alter the exchange rate. The out-turn data in the partial credibility regime will, therefore, be $s_t$, the existing fixed parity. Hence, even *survey data* collected over this partial credibility period (which accurately measures $E_t s_{t+1}$) will not equal the (constant) out-turn value $s_t$, since from (41), using $E_t(s_{t+1}|Z1) = s_t$,

$$E_t s_{t+1} = \pi[E_t(s_{t+1}|Z2) - s_t] + s_t \neq s_t \tag{50}$$

Now suppose the regime shift *does* occur, then even here the *ex-post* forecast error does not equal its value under RE:

$$\tilde{w}_{t+1} = s_{t+1}^{(2)} - E_t s_{t+1} = [s_{t+1}^{(2)} - E_t(s_{t+1}|Z2)] - (1 - \pi)\nabla s_{t+1}$$

$$= \varepsilon_{t+1} + (1 - \pi)\nabla s_{t+1}$$

where $\varepsilon_{t+1}$ is the RE forecast error if agents know for certain the regime shift has occurred. Hence, the *ex-post* forecast error, which is observable if we have survey data on expectations, is non-zero and biased. Also, if $\pi$ varies over time (e.g. due to changing economic information), then a regression of $\tilde{w}_{t+1}$ on information at time $t$ will, in general, yield a non-zero coefficient. Hence, we have an apparent refutation of the informational efficiency assumption of RE because the forecast error is not independent of information at time $t$. Notice that even if $\pi$, the probability of the unobserved event is small, the 'bias' in the forecast error $\tilde{w}_{t+1}$ can still appear large if the potential change in the spot rate under the new regime is thought to be large – that is, $\nabla s_{t+1}$ is large.

Now let us consider the problems caused when we try to test for FRU. In the partial credibility regime, investors think a devaluation of the Peso is likely so $E_t(s_{t+1}|Z2) > E_t(s_{t+1}|Z1)$ (remember that $s_t$ is in units of Pesos per US dollar and hence an increase in $s_t$ is a devaluation of the Peso). Under FRU, speculation in the forward market ensures

$$f_t = E_t s_{t+1} \tag{51}$$

But from (50), if we remain in regime-1 so $E_t(s_{t+1}|Z1) = s_t$ then $f_t > s_t$ and $fp_t = (f - s)_t \neq 0$. In the partial credibility regime, $fp_t$ will change if $\pi$ changes but if the devaluation never occurs, then $\Delta s_{t+1} = 0$ and a regression test of FRU would fail even though (51) holds.

The Peso problem, therefore, arises because one is testing a hypothesis with a finite data set, in which there are unobservable events that could potentially occur but do not. If there is instantaneous learning, then when the regime shift *actually occurs* and is widely known, the term $\nabla s_{t+1} = 0$, and forecast errors equal the RE forecast error from this period onward – hence, the Peso problem is a small-sample problem. Of course, it could be a 'repeating' small-sample problem if potential 'new' regimes occur.

In *principle*, we can get around the Peso problem by using accurate survey data on expectations when testing $E_t s_{t+1} = f_t$. But using survey data has its own problems (see above). It is possible that Peso problems are fairly prevalent. Clearly, a longer data set is likely to mitigate the Peso problem but perhaps not irradicate it entirely. Hence, the apparent rejection of FRU can always be attributed to 'hidden' Peso problems.

## Learning

If agents take time to learn about their new environment, this can also generate forecast errors displaying serial correlation and with a non-zero mean, even when agents use rational expectations. Suppose there are two possible regimes $Z1$ and $Z2$ (Lewis 1989a, 1995), then the expected exchange rate is

$$E_t s_{t+1} = \pi_t E_t(s_{t+1}|Z1) + (1 - \pi_t)(E_t s_{t+1}|Z2)$$

If there has been a regime shift at $m < t$, then agents will slowly update their probabilities using a Bayesian updating rule

$$\pi_t = \frac{\pi_{t-1} L(\Delta s_t, \Delta s_{t-1}, \dots \Delta s_{m+1}|Z1)}{\pi_{t-1} L(\Delta s_t, \Delta s_{t-1}, \dots \Delta s_{m+1}|Z1) + (1 - \pi_{t-1}) L(\Delta s_t, \Delta s_{t-1}, \dots \Delta s_{m+1}|Z2)}$$

where $L(.|.)$ are the likelihoods of the observed data, given the old or new regimes are in force and $\pi_t$ is the *posterior* probability of no regime shift. If the data are from the new regime, then the likelihood $L(.|Z1)$ will fall as additional data from the new regime are assimilated and $\pi_t$ approaches zero. However, while agents are learning about the new regime, they will attach non-zero probabilities to each regime, even though in reality only one of the regimes is in force – this gives rise to non-zero forecast errors. Suppose in reality the economy has switched to regime-$Z2$, then the forecast error is

$$s_{t+1}^{(2)} - E_t s_{t+1} = [s_{t+1}^{(2)} - E_t(s_{t+1}|Z2)] - \pi_t[E_t(s_{t+1}|Z1) - E_t(s_{t+1}|Z2)]$$

$$= \varepsilon_{t+1} - \pi \nabla s_{t+1}$$

and the *ex-post* forecast error is non-zero. Lewis (1989b) attributes about half of the rise in the US dollar in the early 1980s to agents using Bayesian learning.

Studies examining Peso problems (Lewis 1988, 1991) and regime shifts in exchange rates (e.g. Engel and Hamilton 1990, Kaminsky 1993) certainly establish the possibility that the US dollar during the 1980s could be due to such phenomena. The problem is that the FRU result $\beta < -1$ applies across many data periods and currencies and it is difficult to believe that there are so many potential regime shifts that agents do not eventually learn or that Peso problems are endemic.

## 25.6 Summary

- Riskless arbitrage opportunities in the FX market sometimes do appear at relatively long horizons (one year) but for the most part, there are no large *persistent* profitable opportunities and CIP holds.

- Single-equation regressions, panel data regressions and the VAR approach suggest that FRU (and UIP) do not hold, but one cannot conclusively apportion this rejection of FRU between a 'failure' of risk neutrality and of RE.

- Because of a presumption of frequent and possibly substantial central bank intervention in forward and spot markets, Peso problems are likely to be present. However, they are virtually impossible to quantify, and this makes it difficult to interpret whether the fairly decisive rejection of FRU imply a rejection of the EMH.

# 26

# MODELLING THE FX RISK PREMIUM

## Aims

- Show from the empirical result in the FRU regression that $\beta < -1$ (rather than $\beta = +1$) implies several inequalities between variables that any model of the risk premium must satisfy in order to 'fit the facts'.

- Present empirical tests of the C-CAPM-SDF model, the latent variable and affine models of the relationship between FX returns for different currencies.

- To demonstrate how cash-in-advance models of FX returns can be solved and calibrated so that 'statistics of interest' from this 'artificial economy' approach can be compared with real world data.

Just because investors hold foreign currency assets, it does not imply they require a risk premium, because most of this risk might be diversifiable. It is only when the risk on an asset covaries with some underlying pervasive source of variation (e.g. the market portfolio, the marginal rate of substitution in consumption) that the risk becomes undiversifiable and, therefore, commands an additional return. In any case, there is a paradox when considering two assets, foreign and domestic. If a US resident views holding Euro bonds as having exchange rate risk, then the expected return (in USD) on Euro bonds would exceed the return on safe domestic US bonds. But from the Euro residents' viewpoint, they would then be getting a lower return on their domestic assets than on (risky) US assets. Hence, the risk premium on foreign assets must be negative for Euro residents, if it is positive for US investors (ignoring Jensen inequality terms). It follows that the risk premium must depend on the *relative* riskiness of domestic and foreign assets. We look at various models that attempt to measure this time-varying risk premium.

## 26.1   Implications of $\beta < 1$ in FRU Regressions

We show that the strong empirical finding that $\text{plim}(\hat{\beta}) < 0$ in the FRU regression can be used to infer certain relationships between variables, which *any* theory of the risk premium must satisfy (Fama 1984). These empirical results are useful in assessing the validity of SDF, affine and cash-in-advance models of the FX risk premium later in this chapter. FRU + RE requires $\alpha = 0$, $\beta = 1$, and $E(\varepsilon_{t+1}|\Omega_t) = 0$ in the regression

$$\Delta s_{t+1} = \alpha + \beta \, fp_t + \varepsilon_{t+1} \tag{1a}$$

$$\beta = \text{cov}(\Delta s_{t+1}, fp_t)/\text{var}(fp_t) \tag{1b}$$

where $s_t = $ log of spot rate (domestic per unit of foreign currency), $fp_t \equiv f_t - s_t$ and $f_t = $ log of the forward rate. We *define* the risk premium as

$$rp_t \equiv f_t - E_t s_{t+1} = fp_t - E_t \Delta s_{t+1} \tag{2}$$

Under RE,

$$\Delta s_{t+1} = E_t \Delta s_{t+1} + \varepsilon_{t+1} \tag{3}$$

and $\varepsilon_{t+1}$ is independent of information at time $t$, hence

$$\text{cov}\{fp_t, \Delta s_{t+1}\} = \text{cov}\{fp_t, E_t \Delta s_{t+1}\} \tag{4a}$$

Using (4a) and substituting for $E_t \Delta s_{t+1}$ from (2),

$$\text{cov}\{fp_t, \Delta s_{t+1}\} = \text{var}(fp_t) - \text{cov}\{fp_t, rp_t\}$$

Substitute for $fp_t$ from (2) in the covariance term

$$\text{cov}\{fp_t, \Delta s_{t+1}\} = \text{var}(fp_t) - \text{cov}\{E_t \Delta s_{t+1}, rp_t\} - \text{var}(rp_t) \tag{4b}$$

Using (4b) in (1b),

$$\text{plim}(\hat{\beta}) = 1 - \beta_{rp} \tag{5}$$

where

$$\beta_{rp} = \frac{\text{cov}\{E_t \Delta s_{t+1}, rp_t\} + \text{var}(rp_t)}{\text{var}(fp_t)} \tag{6}$$

Empirically, we find that $\text{plim}(\hat{\beta}) < 0$, hence, $\beta_{rp} > 1$, which from (6) gives

$$\text{cov}\{E_t \Delta s_{t+1}, rp_t\} + \text{var}(rp_t) > \text{var}(fp_t) \tag{7}$$

But from (2),

$$\text{var}(fp_t) = \text{var}(E_t \Delta s_{t+1} + rp_t) = \text{var}(E_t \Delta s_{t+1}) + \text{var}(rp_t) + 2\,\text{cov}\{E_t \Delta s_{t+1}, rp_t\} \tag{8}$$

Using (7) and (8), $\beta_{rp} > 1$ implies

$$\text{cov}\{E_t \Delta s_{t+1}, rp_t\} + \text{var}(E_t \Delta s_{t+1}) < 0 \tag{9}$$

Since $\text{var}(E_t \Delta s_{t+1}) > 0$, then (9) implies our *first inequality*, namely the expected change in the spot rate is negatively related to movements in the risk premium (i.e. the speculative forward profit $f_t - E_t s_{t+1}$):

$$\text{cov}\{E_t \Delta s_{t+1}, rp_t\} < 0 \tag{10}$$

where $rp_t \equiv f_t - E_t s_{t+1}$. From (9), we also require

$$|\text{var}(E_t \Delta s_{t+1})| < |\text{cov}\{E_t \Delta s_{t+1}, rp_t\}| = |\rho \sigma (E_t \Delta s_{t+1}) \sigma (rp_t)| \tag{11}$$

Since $|\rho_{\max}| = 1$, the above implies the *second inequality*, namely the variance of the risk premium must exceed the variance of the *expected* change in the spot rate:

$$\text{var}(rp_t) \equiv \text{var}(f_t - E_t s_{t+1}) > \text{var}(E_t \Delta s_{t+1}) \tag{12}$$

We will revisit these two inequalities in what follows.

## 26.2 Consumption-CAPM

The C-CAPM can be used to model speculative returns in the FX market. Note that the excess nominal return to foreign investment using the spot market is $R_{s,t+1} \equiv (\Delta s_{t+1} + r^* - r)$, where $r_t^* = $ foreign interest rate and $r = $ domestic interest rate. It is also possible to *speculate* in the forward market with return $R_{F,t+1} = s_{t+1} - f_t$. But if CIP holds, then $f_t = s_t + r_t - r_t^*$ and $R_{s,t+1} = R_{F,t+1}$. When testing the CAPM, these two different ways of measuring the speculative return are used. The FOC/Euler equation for any two assets $i$ and $j$ is

$$U'(C_t) = \theta E_t\{R_{i,t+1} \; U'(C_{t+1})\} = \theta E_t\{R_{j,t+1} \; U'(C_{t+1})\} \tag{13a}$$

Rearranging (13a) and using US dollar and Euro returns,

$$0 = E_t\{(R_{t+1}^{\$} - R_{t+1}^{\euro})M_{t+1}\} \tag{13b}$$

where $R^{\$} = $ *real* return on \$-assets

$R^{\euro} = $ *real* return on Euro-assets

$M_{t+1} = \theta U'(C_{t+1})/U'(C_t) = \theta(C_{t+1}/C_t)^{-\gamma}$ for power utility

$S = $ exchange rate (= domestic per unit of foreign currency, \$ per €)

$C_t = $ *domestic (US) real consumption*

The C-CAPM uses real returns and, hence, equation (13b) can be written for any currency $j$:

$$0 = E_t\left\{\left(\frac{(F_{jt} - S_{j,t+1})P_t^{\$}}{S_{j,t} P_{t+1}^{\$}}\right) M_{t+1}\right\} \tag{14}$$

where here $P_t^\$$ is the *dollar* price level. The intuition behind (14) is that the forward contract requires no investment at $t$, hence $(F_t - S_{t+1})/S_t$ is the return from forward speculation. Note that $U'(C_{t+1})/P_{t+1}^\$$ is the marginal utility per USD. The representative investor's preferences in (13a) do not depend on her location. Under joint lognormality and power utility, (14) gives for any currency $j$ (see Kaminsky and Periga 1990, p. 54),

$$E_t \Delta s_{j,t+1} - fp_{j,t} = -0.5 \operatorname{var}_t(\Delta s_{j,t+1}) - \operatorname{cov}_t(\Delta s_{j,t+1}, \pi_{t+1}^\$) + \gamma \operatorname{cov}_t(\Delta s_{j,t+1}, \Delta c_{t+1})$$
(15)

where $\pi_{t+1} = \ln(P_{t+1}/P_t)$. Note that it is only the exchange rate terms that have the $j$ subscript because prices and consumption refer solely to the domestic economy (investor). Since $rp_t \equiv fp_t - E_t \Delta s_{t+1}$, the 'risk premium' depends on the first two Jensen inequality terms, while the 'true' risk premium is the $+\gamma \operatorname{cov}(\Delta s_{j,t+1}, \Delta c_{t+1})$ term (which is zero for $\gamma = 0$).

Tests of the C-CAPM are based on the FOCs such as (14) or on an explicit solution (under lognormality) like (15). The difficulty with the latter is the need to measure time-varying conditional covariances – a notoriously difficult task if the number of covariance terms is greater than around two (see below).

Mark (1985), Hodrick (1989) and Modjtahedi (1991) have estimated equation (14) jointly on a number of currencies (against the USD) with monthly, three-monthly and six-monthly forward rates, assuming power utility and using aggregate per capita US (non-durables and services) consumption. The (overidentifying) cross-equation restrictions on $\gamma$ are rejected, and $\hat{\gamma}$ is of the order of 40–70, way outside an acceptable range. Similar results apply when the pound sterling is the numeraire currency and UK consumption data is used.

Kaminsky and Periga (1990) estimate equation (15) for the German mark, yen and pound sterling (against the USD). The 'RE residuals' are assumed to follow a multivariate GARCH model (BEKK (see Engle and Kroner (1995))). The five variables used were

$$z'_{t+1} = [\Delta c_{t+1}^\$, \pi_{t+1}^\$, (s_{t+1} - f_t)^j, (s_{t+1} - f_t)^k, (s_{t+1} - f_t)^m]$$
(16)

where $j, k, m =$ yen, pound, mark (against the USD) and the five-equation system is

$$\mathbf{z}_{t+1} = \mathbf{A}_0 + \mathbf{A}_1(L)\mathbf{z}_t + \mathbf{D}vec(\mathbf{H}_{t+1}) + \boldsymbol{v}_{t+1}$$
(17)

$H_{t+1}$ is the covariance matrix of errors and $vec(H_{t+1})$ stacks the *lower* portion of $H$, the error covariances in a vector $vec\{H_{t+1}\} = \{h(1, 1), h(1, 2) \ldots h(1, 5), h(2, 2), h(2, 3) \ldots h(2, 5), h(3, 3), h(3, 2) \ldots h(3, 5), h(4, 4), h(4, 5), h(5, 5)\} - 15$ conditional variance–covariances in all. The restrictions imposed by (15) on the $(15 \times 15)$ matrix $\mathbf{D}$ are $d(3, 3) = d(4, 4) = d(5, 5) = \gamma$; $d(3, 10) = d(4, 13) = d(5, 15) = -1$; $d(3, 7) = d(4, 8) = d(5, 9) = -0.5$, with all other $d(i, j) = 0$. The non-zero values of $\{d_{ij}\}$ 'pick out' the effect of the conditional variance and covariance terms in (15) on the mean values of $(\Delta s_{t+1} - fp_t)$ for the three currencies (against the USD). They do not reject the joint hypothesis that the three coefficients on $\operatorname{var}_t(\Delta s_{j,t+1})$ are $-0.5$, and those on $\operatorname{cov}(\Delta s_{t+1}, \pi_{t+1}^\$)$ are $-1$. The coefficient of relative risk aversion is found to be constant across the three currencies. However, the residuals $v_{t+1}$ should not be forecastable from information at time $t$. But they find that for the yen and British pound sterling (but not for Germany), the residuals are predictable using the forward discount and, therefore, the model does not explain all of the 'risk premium' $f_t - E_t s_{t+1}$. Most damning is the result that the estimate of $\gamma$ is in excess of 350. Hence, the *ex-ante* returns from forward market speculation $f_t - E_t s_{t+1}$ are too volatile to be explained by $\text{cov}(\Delta s_{t+1}, \Delta c_{t+1})$ unless $\gamma$ is very large – a result similar to that for the C-CAPM applied to the equity premium. Backus, Gregory and Telmer (1993) use habit consumption $c_t - \lambda c_{t-1}$ in the utility function, which then 'appears' in $M_{t+1}$, but this also fails to rescue the model.

## SDF Model of FX Returns (C-CAPM)

Smith and Wickens (2002) estimate the C-CAPM of the excess return to foreign investment along the lines of Kaminsky and Periga (1990) but they use a simpler form of GARCH process, which has constant correlations. Essentially, this allows them to estimate the GARCH processes as univariate equations rather than using maximum likelihood in a multivariate model (which is always difficult in a highly parameterised system). The covariances are then given by $\rho_{ij}\sigma_{i,t}\sigma_{j,t}$, where the time-varying standard deviations are from the univariate GARCH processes. These covariances are then used in the returns equation, which again is estimated by single-equation techniques.

The C-CAPM for the excess return to foreign investment for US domestic investors is of the form

$$E_t R_{t+1} + 0.5 V_t(R_{t+1}) = k_{us} \text{cov}_t(\Delta c_{t+1}^{US}, R_{t+1}) + \text{cov}_t(\Delta p_{t+1}^{US}, R_{t+1}) \quad (18)$$

where $R_{t+1} = (\Delta s_{t+1} + r_t^* - r_t)$. The spot rate $s_t$ is measured as domestic per unit of foreign currency (here \$ per £). Hence, the larger the conditional covariance of the *depreciation* of the USD with the growth of US consumption and with US inflation, the greater the risk premium for US investors in foreign bonds. A similar equation holds for UK domestic investors:

$$E_t R_{t+1} - 0.5 V_t(R_{t+1}) = -k_{uk} \text{cov}_t(\Delta c_{t+1}^{uk}, R_{t+1}) - \text{cov}_t(\Delta p_{t+1}^{uk}, \Delta c_{t+1}^{uk}) \quad (19)$$

Adding these two equations, the $V_t(.)$ term disappears and $ER_{t+1}$ depends on the covariances for both the United Kingdom and United States consumption and inflation:

$$E_t R_{t+1} = 0.5\{k_{us} \text{cov}_t(\Delta c_{t+1}^{US}, R_{t+1}) + \text{cov}_t(\Delta p_{t+1}^{us}, R_{t+1}) - k_{uk} \text{cov}_t(\Delta c_{t+1}^{uk}, R_{t+1})$$
$$- \text{cov}_t(\Delta p_{t+1}^{uk}, \Delta c_{t+1}^{uk})\} \quad (20)$$

Using USD-pound sterling and monthly data 1975(1)–1997(12), none of the covariance terms of the C-CAPM is statistically significant, and the coefficient of relative risk aversion is of the wrong sign and very large. Smith and Wickens (2002) then generalise the model by assuming the SDF may be influenced (linearly) by variables in the monetary model. Additional covariances between returns and the following variables, namely, consumption, output and money growth, now appear in the expected returns equation, which becomes

$$R_{t+1} = \gamma_1 R_t + \gamma_2 fp_t + \gamma_3 V_t(R_{t+1}) + \phi^{us} Z^{us}_{t+1} + \phi^{uk} Z^{uk}_{t+1} + \varepsilon_{t+1} \qquad (21)$$

where $R_t$ and $fp_t$ and $V_t(R_{t+1})$ have been added to create a general model, but we expect $\gamma_i = 0$ $(i = 1, 2, 3)$ if the SDF model holds and $Z^{us}_{t+1}$, $Z^{uk}_{t+1}$ represent the covariance terms for the US and UK variables. Some support is found for the conditional covariance terms entering the equation for mean (expected) returns, but the evidence is not strong. Also, contrary to the model, the lagged return and forward premium remain statistically significant. Hence, the 'monetary factors' in the SDF model have little support, and the forward premium puzzle remains (Mark and Wu (1998) and Engel (1996) reach similar conclusions).

Conditional covariances are often modelled in a multivariate GARCH framework. But the number of parameters to estimate can be large even with just a few covariance terms (see Chapter 29), unless some arbitrary restrictions are placed in the GARCH parameters. This would seem to limit the usefulness of the GARCH approach in SDF asset-pricing models.

## Latent Variables and the Intertemporal C-CAPM

Latent variable models 'substitute out' the conditional covariance terms of the C-CAPM by assuming they are linear functions of a set of observable variables, $z_t$. The C-CAPM for any asset $j$ can be expressed

$$E_t(R_{j,t+1} - R_{0,t+1}) = \frac{-\text{cov}_t(M_{t+1}, R_{j,t+1})}{E(M_{t+1})} \qquad (22)$$

where $R_0$ is the return on an asset with a zero covariance with $M_{t+1}$ ($R_0$ plays the same role as the risk-free rate in the 'domestic' C-CAPM). Now take $R_{b,t+1}$ as the return on the mean-variance frontier, which is a weighted average of $R_{0,t+1}$ and the minimum variance return. Then, it can be shown (Hodrick 1987)

$$E_t(R_{j,t+1} - R_{0,t+1}) = \beta_{j,t} E_t(R_{b,t+1} - R_{0,t+1}) \qquad (23)$$

where $\beta_{j,t} = \text{cov}_t(R_{b,t+1}, R_{j,t+1})/\text{var}_t(R_{b,t+1})$.

Although $\beta_{j,t}$ can be time varying, it is reasonable that $\beta_{j,t}/\beta_{i,t}$ is constant $(= \lambda)$, so that expected relative returns $E_t(R_{i,t+1} - R_{0,t+1})/E_t(R_{j,t+1} - R_{0,t+1}) = \lambda$, a constant. (This is broadly equivalent to the 'domestic' CAPM where relative returns on assets $i$ and $j$ depend on their relative betas.)

We are now in a position to demonstrate the restrictions implicit in this model, if we assume relative returns for assets $i$ and $j$ depend *linearly* on a set of observable variables $z_{kt}$

$$R_{i,t+1} - R_{0,t+1} = \sum_{k=1}^{n} \alpha_k z_{kt} + u_{i,t+1} \qquad (24a)$$

$$R_{j,t+1} - R_{0,t+1} = \sum_{k=1}^{n} \delta_k z_{kt} + u_{j,t+1} \qquad (24b)$$

The latent variable model implies the restrictions $\alpha_k/\delta_k = \lambda$ for $k = 1, 2, \ldots n$. Tests often use $(S_{j,t+m} - F_{j,t+m})/S_{j,t}$ as the return to speculation in the forward market on currency $j$ (over any future horizon, e.g. $m = 1$ or 3 months) as the dependent variable. The $z$ variables might include the forward discount and past forecast errors. Several studies (e.g. Hansen and Hodrick 1983, Campbell and Clarida 1987, Huang 1989, Lewis 1990) find conflicting evidence on the validity of the cross-equation restrictions, but the model tends to perform better at the three-month than the one-month horizon. Cumby and Huizinga (1992) provide a further test of the model that predicts that fitted values from the regressions (18) using different currencies should be highly correlated (perfectly correlated if there were no estimation error). They find these correlations are in the range 0.33–0.65 and statistically different from unity – thus rejecting the model.

Giovanni and Jorion (1987), Mark (1988) and Cumby (1988) all try various statistical models of the time variation in the beta of equation (17) and, in general, they fail to reject the restrictions, which suggests support for these models. However, Engel (1996, p. 163) argues that this failure to reject the null is due to the low power of the tests. That is, the 'alternative' and the 'model' are both pretty awful (i.e. 'explain' very little), so imposing the restrictions does not reduce the 'fit' too much.

## 26.3 Affine Models of FX Returns

As with affine models of the term structure, we can apply the affine (linear) structure to provide forcing variables $z_{1t}$, $z_{2t}$ for the domestic and foreign economies. These are used in the FOCs to generate equations for the variables of interest, namely, the change in the spot rate and the forward premium. To get the general idea, consider a one-factor model where the factors are independent and country specific and are linearly related to the SDF, $m_{t+1}$. In a CIR structure,

$$-m_{t+1} = z_{1t} + \lambda\sigma\sqrt{z_{1t}}\varepsilon_{1,t+1} \tag{25}$$

$$-m_{t+1}^* = z_{2t} + \lambda\sigma\sqrt{z_{2t}}\varepsilon_{2,t+1} \tag{26}$$

$$z_{it+1} - \mu = \theta(z_{it} - \mu) + \sigma\sqrt{z_{it}}\varepsilon_{i,t+1} \quad \text{for } i = 1, 2 \tag{27}$$

Above, for simplicity, we assume the parameters $\lambda, \sigma, \theta$ are the same for both countries. For this case, it can be shown that the short rate for each country is linear in $z$:

$$r_{i,t} = (1 - 0.5(\lambda\sigma)^2)z_{it} \quad \text{for } i = 1, 2 \tag{28}$$

and the FX variables are given by

$$fp_t = \left[1 - 0.5(\lambda\sigma)^2\right](z_{1t} - z_{2t}) \tag{29a}$$

$$E_t\Delta s_{t+1} = (z_{1t} - z_{2t}) \tag{29b}$$

$$f_t - E_t s_{t+1} = -0.5(\lambda\sigma)^2(z_{1t} - z_{2t}) \tag{29c}$$

Given $\beta < 1$ in the FRU equation, we know this requires that the risk premium and the expected depreciation of the spot rate are negatively correlated. But it is easy to see from (29b) and (29c) that the risk premium $rp_t \equiv f_t - E_t s_{t+1}$ and the expected rate of depreciation are negatively correlated in our affine model. However, our model predicts that the beta value in the FRU regression of $E_t \Delta s_{t+1}$ on $fp_t$ is $1/[1 - 0.5(\lambda\sigma)^2]$, which is positive and greater than one – see (29a) and (29b). But this contradicts the empirical evidence that $\beta < 1$ and, hence, our CIR one-factor affine model is rejected. Backus, Foresi and Telmer (2001) try a two-factor model with interdependent factors and for some parameterisations, this can be made to give a negative $\beta$, but only at the expense of some unacceptable distributional properties for the unobserved factors and the forward premium. In short, affine models of the SDF have not so far explained the forward premium puzzle.

# 26.4 FRU and Cash-in-Advance Models

Cash-in-Advance (CIA) models take the standard FOCs of the C-CAPM plus purchasing power parity (PPP) relationship but impose the inequality restrictions that agents must have sufficient domestic or foreign currency to purchase their desired consumption levels in each country. It is an endowment economy. Standard cash-in-advance models with time-separable preferences over consumption seek to explain all the stylised facts of forward-spot behaviour, which are:

(i) the forward discount is persistent but with a relatively low volatility.

(ii) the expected forward speculative profit $f_t - E_t s_{t+1}$ has a higher volatility than the forward premium.

(iii) the spot rate has a higher volatility than either $(f_t - E_t s_{t+1})$ of $fp_t$, and is close to a martingale process.

(iv) FRU is violated since in $\Delta s_{t+1} = \alpha + \beta fp_t + \varepsilon_{t+1}$, we find $\hat{\beta} \approx -1$, whereas it should be *plus* 1.

Note that the *expected* forward speculative profit $f_t - E_t s_{t+1}$ is usually measured by the fitted values from a regression of $f_t - s_{t+1}$ on the forward premium. Remember, we earlier found that the coefficient $\beta$ can be written

$$\beta = \frac{\text{cov}_t\{E_t \Delta s_{t+1}, f_t - E_t s_{t+1}\} + \text{var}_t(E_t \Delta s_{t+1})}{\text{var}_t(fp_t)} \tag{30}$$

It can be shown that a negative beta requires

(a) $\text{cov}_t\{.\} < 0$           (see equation 10)

and

(b) $\text{var}_t(f_t - E_t s_{t+1}) > \text{var}_t(E_t \Delta s_{t+1})$    (see equation 12)

## Standard Cash-in-Advance Models

In the standard CIA model, agents maximise intertemporal *separable* utility that depends on consumption in two countries by two households. Agents must hold money (cash) of each country, in order to purchase consumption goods in that country. The first-order conditions are

$$S_t = \frac{U'_{2t}/P_t^2}{U'_{1t}/P_t^1}$$

$$q_t^j = \theta E_t \left[ \frac{(U'_{j,t+1}/P_{t+1}^j)}{(U'_{j,t}/P_t^j)} \right] \quad (j = 1, 2 \text{ countries})$$

$$\frac{F_t}{S_t} = \frac{q_t^2}{q_t^1}$$

where $U'$ is marginal utility, $P^j$ = goods price in country, $j = (1, 2)$, $q_t^j$ = bond price, $S_t$ = spot rate, $F_t$ = forward rate and $\theta$ = discount factor. The first equation is the PPP condition, where the real exchange rate equals the marginal rate of substitution of home and foreign goods. The second equation gives the nominal price $q_t^j$ of home and foreign bonds for $j = 1, 2$ countries and the third equation is the CIP relationship. Since the quantity theory of money holds, prices are proportional to that country's money supply so the change in the spot exchange rate depends on *relative* money supply growth in the two countries. Via the bond pricing equation (and the assumption that real and nominal shocks have zero covariance), the forward discount $\ln(F_t/S_t)$ also depends on relative monetary growth. However, relative monetary growth is persistent and, hence, the standard CIA model predicts the change in the spot rate and the forward discount are both persistent. But in the data, the change in the spot rate is approximately white noise and, therefore, the standard CIA model cannot explain the stylised facts.

Moore and Roche (2002) extend the standard CIA model by assuming that all portfolio decisions are made *before* the realisation of monetary shocks. This allows the ratio of bond prices to affect the real exchange rate (together with the marginal rate of substitution):

$$S_t = E_t \left( \frac{U'_{2,t+1}/P_{t+1}^2}{U'_{1,t+1}/P_{t+1}^1} \right) \left( \frac{q_t^1}{q_t^2} \right)$$

This allows the model to predict both a higher volatility for the spot rate and less persistence since the influence of (persistent) relative money supplies can be attenuated by the volatile changes in bond prices. When the model is calibrated assuming an AR(1) process for money and consumption growth, it does reduce the autocorrelation in the spot rate and increase its volatility compared to the 'standard' model, but the predictions of the simulated calibrated model are still largely at odds with the data.

The standard cash-in-advance model can explain either (i) or (ii) above but not both, and it does not explain the failure of FRU with $\beta < 0$ (Bekaert 1996).

## Habit Persistence

Moore and Roche (2002) then examine whether the 'stylised facts' can be reproduced by a standard CIA model that is modified by incorporating habit persistence *á la* Campbell and Cochrane (2000), and they are able to explain (i) and (ii) but

unfortunately not (iii). It is worth examining this approach in more detail because it provides a 'case study' of these types of 'calibration' or 'artificial economy' models. We will not derive the model 'line-by-line' as many of the results are two-country versions of the Campbell and Cochrane (1999) type model, which we have already discussed.
Broadly speaking, this approach proceeds as follows.

(a) Set up the constrained optimisation problem and derive the FOCs of the relationship between the endogenous variables in the system (e.g. consumption growth, asset returns, money supply).

(b) Choose some variables as exogenous and model them as simple stochastic processes that broadly mimic the time-series properties found in the data. For example, in an endowment economy, assume consumption growth is *niid* with constant mean. This is the 'calibration'.

(c) Simulate the exogenous variables in this artificial economy and derive the time path of the endogenous variables (e.g. spot rate, forward rate, interest rates) using the FOCs and calculate 'statistics of interest'. Usually, the latter are 'moments' like means, variances and correlations between key variables, but this could be extended to skewness, kurtosis and regression relationships (e.g. regression of the change in the spot rate on forward premium).

(d) Repeat '(c)' for $m = 1000$ times and calculate the average values of the statistics of interest and compare them with those found in the real world data. If, in the 'artificial economy', the statistics of interest are close to those in the real data, then the model is deemed a success.

One can also change the time-series properties of the forcing variables (e.g. model consumption growth as a stationary AR(1) process) and repeat the whole procedure to determine how sensitive are the statistics of interest to such 'reasonable' alternatives.
The model has two countries, two goods and, hence, two monies. The habit-intertemporal, power utility function of the representative agent is

$$\sum_{t=0}^{\infty} \theta^t U(C_{it}^1, C_{it}^2) = \sum_{t=0}^{\infty} \frac{\theta^t (X_{it}^1)^{1-\gamma}}{1-\gamma} + \frac{\theta^t (X_{it}^2)^{1-\gamma}}{1-\gamma} \tag{31}$$

where $X_{it}^j = (C_{it}^j - H_{it}^j)/C_{it}^j$ for superscript $j = 1, 2$ countries and $i = 1, 2$ households. $C_{it}^j$ is the consumption of goods of country-$j$ by households of country-$i$, $H_{it}^j$ is habit consumption, $X_{it}^j$ is surplus consumption where $X_{it}^j = 0$ is the worst possible state. The cash-in-advance constraint is that money $N^j$ of country-$j$ is needed to buy country-$j$'s goods (either by residents or foreigners).

$$N_{it}^j \geq P_t^j C_{it}^j \quad i = 1, 2 \text{ and } j = 1, 2 \tag{32}$$

$P_t^j$ is country-$j$'s prices in country-$j$'s money. For positive interest rates, (32) is an equality. At end of period $t$ (beginning of $t + 1$), *domestic* households' holdings of *domestic* currency are

$$N^1_{1t+1} \geq P^1_t C^1_t + B^1_{1t} - F_t G^1_t \tag{33}$$

The first term is the receipts from the consumption endowment, the second term arises from redemption of nominal bonds and the third term is the number of contracts of foreign currency held long ($G^1_t > 0$) and $F_t$ is the one-period forward rate (domestic per unit of foreign currency). Domestic holdings of foreign currency are

$$N^2_{1t+1} \geq B^2_{1t} + G^1_t \tag{34}$$

There are similar equations for *foreign* households' holdings of domestic and foreign currency

$$N^1_{2t+1} \geq B^1_{2t} + F_t G^2_t \quad \text{(domestic currency)} \tag{35}$$

$$N^2_{2t+1} \geq P^2_t C^2_t + B^2_{2t} - G^2_t \quad \text{(foreign currency)} \tag{36}$$

where $G^2_t > 0$ is a short position in forward foreign exchange for the foreign country. Equilibrium in the goods, money and forward markets is

$$C^j_t = C^j_{1t} + C^j_{2t} \quad j = 1, 2 \tag{37a}$$

$$N^j_t = N^j_{1t} + N^j_{2t} \quad j = 1, 2 \tag{37b}$$

$$G^1_t = G^2_t \tag{37c}$$

There is perfect international risk pooling, so equilibrium consumption is half of the current endowment, $C^i_{jt} = 0.5 Y^i_t$, where $Y^i_t$ is the endowment of the $i$th country at time $t$. The usual FOCs are

$$E_t \left[ \theta(1 + r^j_t) \frac{U'(C^j_{t+1}) P^j_t}{U'(C^j_t) P^j_{t+1}} - 1 \right] = 0 \quad j = 1, 2 \tag{38}$$

where for $j = (1, 2)$ we have $U'(C^j) = (C^j X^j)^{-\gamma}$ and $r^j_t$ ($j = 1, 2$) are the nominal rates of interest in the two countries. A further FOC is PPP:

$$\frac{S_t P^2_t}{P^1_t} = \frac{U'(C^2_t)}{U'(C^1_t)} = \frac{(C^2_t X^2_t)^{-\gamma}}{(C^1_t X^1_t)^{-\gamma}} \tag{39}$$

where $S_t$ is the spot rate, and the forward rate is given by

$$\frac{F_t}{S_t} = \frac{(1 + r^1_t)}{(1 + r^2_t)} \tag{40}$$

The forcing variables in the model are consumption growth, which is *niid*

$$\frac{C^j_{t+1}}{C^j_t} = (1 + \mu^j_{t+1}) \tag{41}$$

$$\mu^j_{t+1} = \overline{\mu}^j + \upsilon^j_{t+1} \quad \upsilon^j_{t+1} = N(0, \sigma^2_{\upsilon j}) \quad j = 1, 2 \tag{42}$$

and monetary growth whose mean growth follows an AR(1) process

$$\frac{N_{t+1}^j}{N_t^j} = (1 + \pi_{t+1}^j) \quad j = 1, 2 \tag{43}$$

$$\pi_{t+1}^j = (1 - \rho)\overline{\pi}^j + \rho\pi_t^j + u_{t+1}^j \quad u_{t+1}^j = N(0, \sigma_{uj}^2) \tag{44}$$

The correlation between real shocks $\upsilon_t$ and monetary shocks $u_t$ is assumed to be zero (in the baseline model), and parameters are the same across countries. Surplus consumption, as in Campbell and Cochrane (1999), is a 'persistent' AR(1) process with adjustment parameter $\phi$, and $\lambda(x)$ is a non-linear function of the surplus consumption ratio

$$x_{t+1}^j = (1 - \phi)\overline{x}^j + \phi x_t^j + \lambda(x_t^j)\upsilon_{t+1}^j \quad j = 1, 2 \tag{45}$$

It is this relationship that is crucial for the models' 'new' predictions compared to the standard cash-in-advance model. The non-linear function $\lambda(x_t^j)$ can magnify any shocks $\upsilon_{t+1}$ to real consumption growth, and $\phi > 0.9$ imparts persistence.

It can be shown (basically from (38)) that the real rate $rr$ is constant (in both countries) and that the nominal rate is given (for each country) by

$$r_t^j = rr^j + [(1 - \rho)\overline{\pi} + \rho\pi_t^j - \mu^j] - [0.5(\sigma_n^2 + (1 - 2\gamma[1 - 2\lambda(x_t^j)]\sigma_\upsilon^2))] \tag{46}$$

Using $f_t - s_t = r_t^1 - r_t^2$ in (46), the forward premium is

$$\begin{aligned} fp_t &= [\rho(\pi_t^1 - \pi_t^2)] + [\gamma\sigma_\upsilon^2\{\lambda(x_t^1) - \lambda(x_t^2)\}] \\ &\approx [\rho(\pi_1^1 - \pi_t^2)] - [\gamma(1 - \phi)(\overline{X}/\gamma)(x_t^1 - x_t^2)] \end{aligned} \tag{47}$$

where the last term in (47) is a linearisation of $\lambda(x_t)$. By substituting the cash-in-advance equality from (32) in the PPP equation (39) and taking logs and substituting in the exogenous processes for consumption, money and surplus consumption, we obtain

$$\Delta s_{t+1} = [\rho(\pi_t^1 - \pi_t^2) + (u_{t+1}^1 - u_{t+2}^2) + (1 - \gamma)\upsilon_{t+1}^2] + [\gamma(\Delta x_{t+1}^1 - \Delta x_{t+2}^2)] \tag{48}$$

The expected forward profit is given by '(47) minus the *expected* value of (48)' and this can be shown to be

$$f_t - Es_{t+1} = \gamma(1 - \phi)\left(1 - \frac{\overline{X}}{\gamma}\right)(x_t^1 - x_t^2) \tag{49}$$

In equations (46), (47) and (48), if we set $\lambda(x_t^j) = 0$, then the model collapses to the standard cash-in-advance model (with no habit), so essentially $\lambda(x_t)$ provides an additional 'risk premium'.

In (46), the first term in square brackets is monetary growth less real consumption growth and can be viewed as expected inflation. When surplus consumption is low, $\lambda(x_t)$ is high, and the nominal rate is high to compensate for the increased inflation risk. In (47), the $\rho(\pi_t^1 - \pi_t^2)$ term is the differential inflation rate (i.e. money growth) and the influence of habit $(x_t^1 - x_t^2)$ on $fp$ depends crucially on the initial level of the home country's surplus consumption ratio, relative to the foreign surplus consumption ratio. The 'new' element in equation (48) for $\Delta s_{t+1}$ is that it depends on the differential *growth* in surplus consumption, and this is why the spot rate may be highly volatile in this model. Note that in the standard model, $E_t \Delta s_{t+1}$ is determined solely by differential inflation rates $(\pi_t^1 - \pi_t^2)$.

We are in a position to calculate the variances and covariances for the key variables of the model, given that the steady state value of surplus consumption is

$$\overline{X}^j = \sigma_{vj}\sqrt{\gamma/(1-\phi)} \tag{50}$$

The unconditional variance of the forward discount, change in spot rate and expected forward profit using (40) with (47), (48) and (49) are:

$$\text{var}(fp_t) = 2\left(\frac{\rho^2\sigma_u^2}{1-\rho^2} + \gamma(1-\phi)\sigma_v^2\sigma_x^2\right) \tag{51a}$$

$$\text{var}(\Delta s_{t+1}) = 2\left(\frac{\sigma_u^2}{1-\rho^2} + (1-\phi)^2\gamma^2\sigma_x^2 + \sigma_v^2\left(1-\frac{\gamma}{\overline{X}}\right)^2\right) \tag{51b}$$

$$\text{var}(f_t - E_t s_{t+1}) = 2(1+\phi)^2\gamma^2\left(1-\frac{\overline{X}}{\gamma}\right)^2\sigma_x^2 \tag{51c}$$

where $\sigma_x^2$ is the unconditional variance of $x_t^j$ ($j = 1, 2$). The habit model adds terms in $\sigma_x$ and $\gamma/\overline{X}$ to the standard model and can be seen to increase the absolute volatilities of the spot rate return, forward discount and expected forward profit (for $\overline{X} < 1$, $\gamma/\overline{X} > 2$). The *relative* volatilities are such that the spot return volatility (51b) increases more than *either* the forward discount volatility (51a) or the volatility of the expected forward profit (51c). But the volatility of the expected forward profit increases more than the volatility of the forward discount. All these qualitative volatility inequalities conform to those found in the real world data, but it remains to show whether they match the size of the actual moments in the real data. It can also be shown that 'habits' increase the *persistence* of the forward discount and decrease the persistence of the spot return (for $\phi > \rho$ and $\sigma_v^2$ terms relatively small).

Now let us turn to the $\beta$ coefficient in the FRU regression (1a).

$$\beta = \frac{\text{cov}(E_t s_{t+1} - s_t, f_t - E_t s_{t+1}) + \text{var}(E_t \Delta s_{t+1})}{\text{var}(fp_t)}$$

For $\beta$ to be negative, we require the covariance term to be (i) negative and (ii) larger in absolute value than $\text{var}(E_t \Delta s_{t+1})$. The second condition (Fama 1984) is equivalent to $\text{var}(f_t - E_t s_{t+1}) > \text{var}(E_t \Delta s_{t+1})$.

In the cash-in-advance model, both $E_t \Delta s_{t+1}$ and $f_t - E_t s_{t+1}$ depend on $x_t^1 - x_t^2$, the difference between home and foreign log surplus consumption ratios. But $\Delta s_{t+1}$ is more sensitive to habits than $f_t - E s_{t+1}$, and movements in the latter are, there-fore, dominated by $E_t s_{t+1}$, and this creates the negative correlation $\text{cov}(E_t \Delta s_{t+1}, f_t -$

$s_{t+1}) < 0$, a necessary condition for $\beta < 0$. But unfortunately, the model also predicts that $\text{var}(E_t \Delta s_{t+1}) > \text{var}(f_t - E_t s_{t+1})$, and this implies that $\beta > 1$ in the habit model – which is completely at odds with the empirical data. The model increases the volatility of the spot return $\Delta s_{t+1}$, and much of this is due to an increased volatility of the *expected* spot return. To enable $\beta < 0$, we require $\text{var}(\Delta s_{t+1}) > \text{var}(f_t - E_t s_{t+1}) > \text{var}(E_t \Delta s_{t+1})$, and the last inequality is violated by the habit model.

The above are analytic results, but one can simulate the exogenous stochastic processes in a multivariate model and numerically calculate the moments and compare them with those from real world data. Moore and Roche (2002) find considerable correspondence between the Monte Carlo 'moments' and the empirical moments for the UK, US and Japanese bilateral rates. For example, for the US–UK, the artificial economy model gives a volatility of the spot return, the expected forward profit and the forward discount as 9.5%, 1.09% and 1.04% respectively. Also, for the artificial economy, the persistence (i.e. AR(1) coefficient) in the spot return is −0.01 and for the forward premium 0.66, while the value of $\beta$ in the FRU regression is 1.79 (Moore and Roche 2002, Table 6). The estimated beta for the FRU regression using the calibrated model for the alternative bilateral rates lies in the range 0.96–2.1, but this is far from its real world value of around minus 1 or lower. Therefore, what the model requires to 'fit' the data is a mechanism that delivers a high *unconditional* $\text{var}(\Delta s_{t+1})$ but a moderate volatility in $E_t \Delta s_{t+1}$ – in other words, a high volatility of surprises in the spot return. Unfortunately, the model as it currently stands does not resolve the FRU puzzle, even allowing for a time-varying risk premium.

## Real and Nominal Exchange Rates

Although CIA models have to date not 'solved' the forward premium puzzle, they can broadly mimic the stylised facts of (i) the high volatility in real and nominal exchange rates and the high correlation between them, as well as and (ii) the persistence in *real* exchange rates and near random walk behaviour of *nominal* exchange rates.

Standard CIA models (i.e. utility depends on the level of consumption in the two countries) with the assumption of sticky prices can explain the above stylised facts (Chari, Kehoe and McGrattan 2001, Bergin and Feenstra 2001). The sticky price assumption allows persistence in the real exchange rate while also allowing the near random walk behaviour of nominal exchange rates (which is driven in part by relative monetary growth). These models require a large value for $\gamma$ (i.e. a low value for the elasticity of intertemporal substitution) in order to generate high volatility in the nominal exchange rate (see equation (31) with $X_t^j = 1$, that is a standard utility specification).

Even if we assume perfectly flexible prices, the above stylised facts can be explained by a CIA model if we allow the persistence in the real exchange rate to arise from persistence in habit formation as in equation (45). To see this, note that the real $S^r$ and nominal exchange rate $S$ are given by

$$S_t^r = \frac{U_t'(C_t^2)}{U_t'(C_t^1)} = \frac{(C_t^2 X_t^2)^{-\gamma}}{(C_t^1 X_t^1)^{-\gamma}} \quad \text{and} \quad S_t = \frac{S_t^r P_t^1}{P_t^2}$$

Taking logarithms and using $p_t^1 - p_t^2 = (n^1 - n^2) - (y^1 - y^2)$,

$$S_t^r = (y_t^1 - y_t^2) + \gamma(x_t^1 - x_t^2)$$
$$S_t = (\gamma - 1)(y_t^1 - y_t^2) + \gamma(x_t^1 - x_t^2) + (n_t^1 - n_t^2)$$

There is perfect international risk pooling, so equilibrium consumption is half of the current endowment, $C_{jt}^i = 0.5Y_t^i$, where $Y_t^i$ is the endowment of the $i$th country at time $t$. Compared to the standard utility function, the habit persistence model introduces the (log of the) surplus consumption ratio $x_t$ into the determination of real and nominal exchange rate (Moore and Roche 2002). Without the habit persistence term $x_t$, the $\gamma$ needs to be greater than unity to generate a positive correlation between the real and nominal exchange rate and to generate large volatility in the nominal spot rate (Chari, Kehoe and McGrattan 2001). By including the habit term $x_t$, which is highly persistent ($\phi \approx 0.97$), we can obtain the stylised facts without price stickiness or a large value for $\gamma$ (Moore and Roche 2002). The near random walk behaviour of the nominal rate is in part due to the near random walk behaviour of relative consumption (i.e. endowment) and relative money supply growth (which has a low persistence as a series for the monetary base is used and not, say, broad money, which would be highly autoregressive).

The CIA approach using either sticky prices and a standard utility function over consumption or flexible prices and a habit persistence utility function has had some success in mimicking the stylised facts of the time-series properties (i.e. first two moments) of real and nominal exchange rates. Note, however, that these models take the time-series process for consumption (and money) as given and infer the properties of exchange rates – they are endowment models and not general equilibrium models. There is also some flexibility in what they choose to be 'money' in their calibration exercise that gives the researcher some degree of flexibility in 'fitting the facts', since there are few formal tests possible (e.g. parameter restrictions). But as noted above, no CIA model explains the forward premium puzzle but neither do other approaches.

## 26.5 Summary

- The C-CAPM model, when tested using either the FOCs or explicitly modelling conditional covariances or using a latent variable approach, performs poorly across a number of currencies and time periods.

- CIA models have the usual FOCs for the C-CAPM, but domestic and foreign currency is needed prior to consumption purchases. Data on FX returns, and so on, are generated for this 'artificial' economy. To 'test' the model, the 'artificial data' is used to generate 'statistics of interest' (e.g. variances and covariances) that are then compared with actual 'statistics' using the real data.

- CIA models explain some of the stylised facts on forward and spot rates, but they do not explain the FRU result that $\beta < 0$. Indeed, the habit persistence CIA model generates an artificial economy in which $\beta > 1$.

# 27

# EXCHANGE RATE AND FUNDAMENTALS

## Aims

- Show how relative money supplies influence the spot rate via the PPP relationship. This is the basis of the flex-price monetary model, FPMM.

- Analyse how exchange rate overshooting arises from a model with 'sticky' goods prices and 'smart' speculators. These are sticky-price monetary models, SPMM.

- Show how the uncovered interest parity (UIP) relationship can give rise to a forward-looking monetary model.

- Examine illustrative empirical tests of monetary models of the exchange rate using cointegration techniques, dynamic error correction models, ECM, and including outside-sample forecasting performance.

- Outline the key features of the 'new open-economy macroeconomics'.

## 27.1 Monetary Models

There are a large number of alternative models based on 'economic fundamentals' that have been used to analyse movements in the spot exchange rate. We can do no more than sketch the main ideas in this chapter. It is probably correct to say that monetary models in their various forms have dominated the theoretical and empirical exchange rate literature, and we discuss a number of these such as the flex-price and sticky-price monetary models and the Frankel real interest rate model. As we shall see, these models have been far from successful in explaining movements in exchange rates. Indeed, there is no consensus amongst economists on the appropriate set of economic fundamentals that influence exchange rates and this, in part, is why policy makers have sought to limit exchange rate movements by cooperative arrangements such as Bretton Woods and the ERM in Europe and in the latter case, a move to full currency union, EMU. The flex-price monetary model (FPMM) concentrates on the current rather than the capital account and assumes prices are flexible and output is exogenously determined by the supply side of the economy. Under floating rates, the FPMM predicts a close relationship between rapid monetary growth and a depreciating exchange rate (and vice versa) – which, for example, is broadly consistent with events in Italy, the United Kingdom, Germany and Japan in the first half of the 1970s and in some Latin American countries in the 1970s and 1980s. In fact, in terms of its predictions, the textbook Mundell–Fleming model under the assumption of a full-employment level of output yields similar results to the FPMM.

Unfortunately, the FPMM failed to adequately explain the large swings in the *real* exchange rate (i.e. price competitiveness) that occurred in a number of small open economies, such as those of the United Kingdom, the Netherlands and Italy in the second half of the 1970s and early 1980s. The FPMM takes 'money' as the only asset of importance and, hence, ignores other asset flows in the capital account of the balance of payments. Once we recognise the importance of capital flows, which have obviously increased due to the gradual dismantling of exchange controls, we have to address the question of expectations. Speculative short-term capital flows respond to relative interest rates between the domestic and foreign country but also depend upon expectations about exchange rate movements. The sticky-price monetary model (SPMM) invokes the rational-expectations hypothesis to deal with exchange rate expectations, and it is usually assumed that uncovered interest parity (UIP) holds. Price adjustment in the goods market is slow and is determined by excess demand working via the price expectations augmented Phillips curve (PEAPC). The combination of sticky prices and high capital mobility implies that changes in monetary (and fiscal) policy can cause 'large' swings in the nominal and real exchange rate and possibly lead to exchange rate overshooting.

A recurring theme in the exchange rate literature concerns the response of the exchange rate to a change in domestic interest rates. The FPMM predicts that a depreciation ensues after a *rise* in domestic interest rates, while the SPMM yields the opposite conclusion. The real interest rate monetary model (RIMM) clarifies this exchange rate–interest rate nexus.

Finally, a defect of the SPMM is its implicit assumption of the perfect substitutability of domestic and foreign assets and failure to analyse explicitly the stock flow interactions arising from current account imbalances. This is remedied in the portfolio balance model of exchange rates (PBM).

## Flex-Price Monetary Model

The FPMM relies on the PPP condition and a stable demand for money function. The (logarithm) of the demand for money is assumed to depend on (the logarithm of) real income, $y$, the price level, $p$, and the level of the (bond) interest rate, $r$. We assume a similar 'foreign' demand for money function. Monetary equilibria in the domestic and foreign country are given by

$$m^s = p + \phi y - \lambda r \tag{1a}$$

$$m^{s^*} = p^* + \phi^* y^* - \lambda^* r^* \tag{1b}$$

where foreign variables are starred. In the FPMM, the domestic interest rate is exogenous – a rather peculiar property. This assumption implies that the domestic interest rate is rigidly linked to the exogenous world interest rate because of the assumption of 'perfect capital mobility' and a *zero* expected change in the exchange rate. Given that output is also assumed fixed at the full-employment level (i.e. the neoclassical supply curve), then any excess money can only influence the 'perfectly flexible' domestic price level one for one: hence the 'neutrality of money' holds.

Equilibrium in the traded goods 'market' (i.e. the current account) ensues when prices in a common currency are equalised, in short, when PPP holds:

$$s = p - p^* \tag{2}$$

The world price, $p^*$, is exogenous to the domestic economy, being determined by the world money supply, and $s$ is the (logarithm) of the spot exchange rate (domestic per unit of foreign currency). The domestic money supply determines the domestic price level and, hence, the exchange rate is determined by *relative* money supplies. Algebraically, substituting (1) in (2) and rearranging,

$$s = (m^s - m^{s^*}) - \phi y + \phi^* y^* + \lambda r - \lambda^* r^* \tag{3}$$

Possible transmission mechanisms underlying (3) are (i) an increase in the domestic money supply leads to an increased demand for *foreign* goods (and assets), an excess demand for foreign currency and a depreciation in the domestic exchange rate; producers then 'arbitrage' domestic prices upwards to match the new level of import prices of tradeable goods. Alternatively, (ii) excess money balances cause an excess demand for *domestic* goods, followed by a rise in domestic prices via the Phillips curve. This is followed by a switch to relatively cheap foreign goods, causing downward pressure on the domestic exchange rate.

It is worth noting that the effect of either a change in output or the domestic interest rate on the exchange rate in the FPMM is contrary to that found in a Keynesian model. A higher level of output or lower domestic interest rates in the FPMM causes an increase in the domestic demand for money. The latter allows a lower domestic price level to achieve money market equilibrium and, hence, results in an *appreciation* in the exchange rate (see, for example, Frenkel, Gylfason and Helliwell 1980, Gylfason and Helliwell 1983). Now, a rise in nominal interest rates may ensue either because of a tight monetary policy or because of an increase in the expected rate of inflation, $\pi$ (Fisher hypothesis):

$$r = \psi + \pi \tag{4}$$

where $\psi$ is the real interest rate. Adding this relationship to the FPMM (3), we see that a high expected rate of domestic inflation is associated with a high nominal interest rate and a depreciation in the domestic exchange rate (i.e. $s$ has a 'high' value). Thus, the interest rate–exchange rate relationship appears somewhat less perverse when the Fisher hypothesis is added to the FPMM to yield what one might term the *hyperinflation* – FPMM. The latter terminology arises because $r$ is dominated by changes in $\pi$ in hyperinflations (e.g. as in Germany in the 1920s). This is all very well, but one might be more disposed to view that the *change* in $s$, rather than its *level*, depends on the expected rate of inflation, as in the Frankel (1979) 'real-interest' model discussed below.

The FPMM may be tested by estimating equations of the form (3) for the exchange rate or by investigating the stability of the PPP relationship and the demand for money functions. As far as equation (3) is concerned, it worked reasonably well empirically in the early 1970s floating period for a number of bilateral exchange rates (see Bilson 1978), but in the late 1970s, the relationship performed badly other than for countries with high inflation (e.g. Argentina and Brazil). The increase in *capital* mobility in the 1970s may account for the failure of the FPMM where the exchange rate is determined solely by relative prices (PPP). Although there are difficulties in testing the PPP relationship, we have noted that it only holds in the long run. Also, the instability in money demand functions in the 1970s–1990s in the G10 economics is well documented (see Cuthbertson 1991a,b, 1997), and this would imply a failure of the FPMM.

In the latter half of the 1970s, the FPMM ceased to provide an accurate description of the behaviour of exchange rates for a number of small open economies. For example, in the United Kingdom over the period 1979–1981, the sterling *nominal* effective exchange rate (i.e. the rate against a basket of currencies) *appreciated* substantially even though the UK money supply grew rapidly relative to the growth in the 'world' money supply. However, more startling, the *real* exchange rate (i.e. price competitiveness or the terms of trade) appreciated by about 40% over this period, and this was followed by an equally sharp fall over the 1981–1984 period. The FPMM can only explain changes in the real exchange rate by *differential short-run* lags in the response of domestic (and foreign) price levels to changes in relative money supplies. Faced with the kind of evidence cited above, these lags appeared to be highly variable or, in other words, the FPMM failed to explain this phenomenon adequately.

## SPMM: Dornbusch Overshooting

The SPMM provides an explanation of exchange rate overshooting (Dornbusch 1976) and short-run changes in real output. The model is able to resolve the conundrum found in the FPMM where one obtains the counter-intuitive result that a rise in domestic interest rates leads to a depreciation in the domestic currency. In the SPMM, if the rise in nominal rates is unexpected and, hence, constitutes a rise in *real* interest rates, the conventional result, namely an appreciation in the exchange rate, ensues.

Like the FPMM, the SPMM is 'monetarist' in the sense that the neutrality of money is preserved in the long run by invoking a vertical neoclassical supply curve for output (or equivalently a vertical long-run Phillips curve). However, PPP holds only in the long run and, hence, short-run changes in the real net trade balance are allowed.

Key elements in the SPMM are the assumption of a conventional, stable demand for money function and UIP. Agents in the foreign exchange market are assumed to form rational expectations about the future path of the exchange rate: they immediately act on any new information, and this is what makes the exchange rate 'jump' and undergo frequent changes. In addition, in the SPMM, the capital account and the money market 'clear' in all periods but the goods market, where prices are sticky, does not. It is this combination of 'flex-price' and 'fix-price' markets that can produce exchange rate overshooting.

We present a simplified account of the Dornbusch (1976) model, beginning with a description of the main behavioural assumptions, followed by an analysis of the impact of a tight monetary stance on the economy.

The UIP relationship expresses the condition for equilibrium on the capital account. Foreign exchange speculators investing abroad *expect* a return of $r^* + \mu$ percent, where $r^* =$ foreign interest rate, $\mu =$ expected *appreciation* of the *foreign* currency (depreciation in the domestic currency). With perfect capital mobility and risk neutrality, equilibrium requires

$$r = r^* + \mu \tag{5}$$

Suppose we begin with $r = r^* = 10\%$ and hence $\mu = 0$. *Expectations* about the exchange rate are assumed to be regressive. If the actual rate lies below the long-run equilibrium rate, $\bar{s}$, then agents expect the actual rate to rise towards the long-run rate, that is, for the spot rate of the domestic currency to *depreciate*, in the future:

$$\mu = \theta(\bar{s} - s) \qquad 0 < \theta < 1 \tag{6}$$

This 'expectations equation' may be made fully consistent with rational expectations in that this regressive formula allows expectations to be correct *ex post*, given the other equations in the Dornbusch model. Equilibrium in the money market implies

$$m^s = m^d = -\lambda r + \phi y + p \tag{7}$$

In the goods market, aggregate demand AD is given by

$$AD = \delta(s - p + p^*) - \sigma r + \gamma y + \gamma' \tag{8}$$

The first term represents the impact of the real exchange rate on *net* trade volumes (i.e. exports minus imports), the second is interest elastic real (investment) expenditures $(-\sigma r)$, the third, the consumption function $(\gamma y)$ net of expenditure effects on imports and the final term, exogenous demand factors such as government expenditure $(\gamma')$. The 'supply side' is represented by a vertical long-run Phillips curve. The rate of inflation responds to excess demand in the goods market; prices adjust slowly to equilibrium $(0 < \Pi < 1)$:

$$\Delta p = \Pi(AD - \bar{y}) = \Pi[\delta(s - p + p^*) - \sigma r + \gamma y + \gamma' - \bar{y}] \tag{9}$$

where $\bar{y}$ is the full-employment level of output.

### Flexible prices: long run

We begin in equilibrium in the goods and money markets and assume UIP holds (i.e. $r = r^*$ and $\mu = 0$). Consider a reduction of 1% in the money supply. If prices are perfectly flexible, a fall of 1% in the price level will restore money market equilibrium (with an unchanged level of interest rates in the long run). In addition, if the exchange rate *appreciates* by 1%, the *real* exchange rate remains constant, and real aggregate demand continues to match aggregate supply. In the long run, the interest rate is unchanged and, therefore, real investment is unchanged. With unchanged interest rates, the exchange rate is *expected* to remain constant in the future and UIP holds. After a monetary contraction of 1%, prices fall by 1% and the exchange rate will appreciate by 1% in order to maintain price competitiveness (PPP). This is the 'long-run' outcome.

### Fixed prices: short-run overshooting

In contrast, now assume prices and output are sticky in the short run. With $y$ and $p$ 'sticky', a decrease in the money supply requires a rise in $r$ to 'clear' the money market $(dr = -(1/\lambda)dm^s)$, equation (7). The rise in $r$ causes a potential capital inflow that can be stopped only if the domestic exchange rate is *expected* to depreciate, thus re-establishing UIP. But according to equation (6), an *expected* depreciation of the domestic currency requires the *actual* spot rate immediately to appreciate above its long equilibrium value. Hence, the exchange rate 'overshoots' its long-run value.

The economics behind this actual appreciation today is as follows. If $m^s$ falls by 1% and $\lambda = 1/2$, then the interest rate $r$ rises by 2% to clear the money market (with $y$ and $p$ fixed in the short run). The higher interest rate, with unchanged expectations about the spot rate, leads to a capital inflow into the domestic economy (i.e. UIP does not hold at the moment). The increased demand for domestic currency pushes up the actual spot rate today. How far will the spot rate rise until foreign speculators stop purchasing the domestic currency? The interest differential in favour of the domestic economy is 2%. Therefore, the spot rate rises *today* until it is 2% above its known long-run value, since rational speculators will then believe that it will fall by 2% over the coming year. This *expected* 2% fall in the domestic currency just offsets the 2% higher domestic interest rates they receive, and now UIP holds. Hence, if the spot rate was initially 100, then after the rise in domestic interest rates of 2%, it would immediately jump to 103, before slowly falling to its long-run value of 101 by the end of the year (i.e. a long run appreciation of 1%). Hence, the exchange rate overshoots its long-run value, since it immediately moves from 100 to 103 before ending up at 101. It does *not* rise monotonically from 100 to 101. It is all beautifully consistent, which it has to be, since agents are rational and know the true model of the economy (up to a set of white noise errors).

It is useful to present a simplified account of the mathematics behind this result. Because of the vertical Phillips curve, output is fixed in the long run, and the neutrality of money implies $d\bar{p} = dm^s$. As PPP also holds in the long run, $d\bar{s} = d\bar{p} = dm^s$ (where a bar over a variable indicates its long-run value). Turning to the short run, assume $p$ and $y$ are fixed, so that any short-run disequilibrium in the money market is taken up by adjustments in $r$:

$$dr = -dm^s/\lambda \tag{10}$$

To preserve UIP in the short run, the *expected* appreciation in the exchange rate $\mu$ must equal the interest differential $dr$ (note that $dr^* = 0$):

$$d\mu = dr = -dm^s/\lambda \tag{11}$$

From the expectations equation (6) and using (11) above, the *short-run* change in the exchange rate is

$$ds = d\bar{s} - d\mu/\theta = [1 + (\theta\lambda)^{-1}]dm^s \tag{12}$$

Since $\theta\lambda > 0$, the initial change in the spot rate of $[1 + (\theta\lambda)^{-1}]dm^s$ exceeds the 'unit' long-run change: $d\bar{s} = dm^s$. It is clear that 'overshooting' is in part due to the restrictive channels through which monetary policy is forced to operate. Initially, all adjustment in the money market is via the interest rate, only in the long run does the price level equilibrate the money market and the interest rate return to its original level. Although it may not be immediately apparent from the above analysis, the assumption of risk neutrality is of crucial importance for overshooting. Note that, in contrast to the prediction of the FPMM, the response of the exchange rate to the interest rate is as one might intuitively expect: an unanticipated jump in the interest rate (consequent on a fall in the money supply) leads to an *appreciation* of the domestic currency.

## Frankel Real Interest Monetary Model, RIMM

Frankel (1979) provides a general model for analysing the impact of changes in the interest rate on the exchange rate and we refer to this as the 'real interest monetary model'. It provides a Dornbusch relationship with respect to the nominal interest rate ($\partial s/\partial r < 0$) and a hyperinflation FPMM with respect to the expected rate of inflation ($\partial s/\partial \pi > 0$). Also, the exchange rate may overshoot its long-run equilibrium value.

Frankel's model assumes uncovered arbitrage but modifies the Dornbusch expectations equation for the exchange rate by adding a term reflecting relative expected secular inflation ($\pi - \pi^*$). The 'expectations equation' is

$$s^e - s = \theta(\bar{s} - s) + (\pi - \pi^*) \tag{13}$$

and UIP yields

$$s^e - s = r - r^* \tag{14}$$

The expected rate of depreciation ($s^e - s$) depends upon the deviation of the exchange rate from its equilibrium value, which as we know, gives Dornbusch-type results. In addition, if $s = \bar{s}$, the expected rate of depreciation is given by the expected inflation differential between the domestic and foreign currency: as we shall see, this term generates hyperinflation FPMM results. Frankel shows that the expectations equation is consistent with *rational* expectations. (We do not deal with this aspect.) Combining (13) and (14) and rearranging, we have

$$\bar{s} - s = (1/\theta)[(r - \pi) - (r^* - \pi^*)] \tag{15}$$

The movement in the spot rate around its equilibrium value is determined by the relative *real* interest differential. In long-run equilibrium, $s = \bar{s}$, which implies $\bar{r} - \bar{r}^* = \pi - \pi^*$; and the term in square brackets may be rewritten as $[(r - r^* - (\bar{r} - \bar{r}^*)]$. It is only when a tight monetary policy raises the nominal interest differential $(r - r^*)$ above its long-run level $(\bar{r} - \bar{r}^*)$ given by relative expected inflation that the 'current' exchange rate appreciates above its long-run equilibrium level $(\bar{s} - s > 0)$.

We now assume that PPP holds in the long run, and with the usual demand for money functions (with $\phi = \phi^*, \lambda = \lambda^*$ for simplicity), we obtain an expression for the *long-run* exchange rate (as in the FPMM):

$$\bar{s} = \bar{p} - \bar{p}^* = \bar{m} - \bar{m}^* - \phi(\bar{y} - \bar{y}^*) + \lambda(\bar{r} - \bar{r}^*)$$
$$= (\bar{m} - \bar{m}^*) - \phi(\bar{y} - \bar{y}^*) + \lambda(\pi - \pi^*) \tag{16}$$

where we have used $\bar{r} - \bar{r}^* = \pi - \pi^*$ (the 'international Fisher effect' that is implicit in the hyperinflation FPMM). The crucial elements in the Frankel model are the expectations equation (13) and the distinction between the short-run and long-run determinants of the exchange rate. Substituting for $\bar{s}$ from (15) in (16), we obtain Frankel's ('reduced-form') exchange rate equation

$$s = \bar{m} - \bar{m}^* - \phi(\bar{y} - \bar{y}^*) - (1/\theta)(r - r^*) + [(1/\theta) + \lambda](\pi - \pi^*)$$
$$= \bar{m} - \bar{m}^* - \phi(\bar{y} - \bar{y}^*) + \alpha(r - r^*) + \beta(\pi - \pi^*) \tag{17}$$

where $\alpha = -(1/\theta)$ and $\beta = (1/\theta) + \lambda$. We can now characterise our three competing models in terms of the parameters $\alpha$ and $\beta$.

It is evident from Table 1 that in the Frankel model, we obtain a Dornbusch-type result $(\partial s/\partial r < 0)$ if interest rates increase while inflation expectations remain constant. This situation is likely to correspond to an *unanticipated* change in the money supply, which has an immediate impact on interest rates (to 'clear' the money market) but is not immediately perceived as permanent and, hence, does not influence $\pi$. On the other hand, an *equal* increase in the nominal interest rate, $r$, and inflationary expectations $\pi$ cause a depreciation in the exchange rate $(\beta + \alpha > 0)$ – an FPMM-type result. Hence, by adding an ancillary assumption to the Dornbusch-type model, namely (13),

**Table 1**   The Frankel real interest rate model

| Model | Parameters |
|---|---|
| Frankel | $\alpha < 0, \beta > 0; |\beta| > |\alpha|$ |
| FPMM | $\alpha > 0, \beta = 0$ |
| FPMM-hyperinflation | $\alpha = 0, \beta > 0$ |
| Dornbusch-SPMM | $\alpha < 0, \beta = 0$ |

an *anticipated* increase in the money supply becomes likely to lead to an expected and actual depreciation of the domestic currency. Implicitly, the Frankel model highlights the possible differential response of the exchange rate to anticipated and unanticipated changes in the money supply and interest rates.

## Portfolio Balance Model

The FPMM and SPMMs make two important simplifying assumptions: all domestic and foreign assets are perfect substitutes and any wealth effects of a current account surplus or deficit can be ignored. The portfolio balance model of exchange rates explores the consequences of explicitly relaxing these assumptions (see e.g. Branson 1977, Isard 1978, Dornbusch and Fischer 1980). The level of the exchange rate in the portfolio balance model (PBM) is determined, at least in the short run, by supply and demand in the markets for all financial assets (e.g. money, domestic and foreign bonds). In the PBM, a surplus (deficit) on the current account represents a rise (fall) in net domestic holdings of foreign assets. The latter affects the level of domestic wealth and, hence, the desired demand for assets, which then affects the exchange rate. Thus, the PBM is an inherently dynamic model of exchange rate adjustment that includes interactions between the current account, the rate of asset accumulation, asset demands and the price level. In the simplest PBM, there are conventional demand functions for domestic money $M$, domestic bonds $B$ and foreign bonds held by domestic residents $B^*$:

$$M/W = m(r, r^* + E_t \Delta s_{t+1})$$

$$B/W = B(r, r^* + E_t \Delta s_{t+1})$$

$$SB^*/W = B^*(r, r^* + E_t \Delta s_{t+1})$$

where $r$ = domestic interest rate, $r^*$ = foreign interest rate and $E_t \Delta s_{t+1}$ = expected depreciation of the domestic currency. Domestic money and bonds and foreign bonds are gross substitutes. Domestic wealth consists of domestic money and bonds and foreign bonds, and the change in foreign bonds is governed by the current account surplus $T(S/P)$ since the capital account must equal the current balance in equilibrium:

$$W = M + B + SB^*$$

$$\dot{B}^* = T(S/P) + r^* B^*$$

A devaluation improves the trade balance $T' > 0$. The model can be solved either assuming static or rational expectations, and overshooting of the exchange rate is possible. Note that goods prices are indeterminate in the model (and long-run neutrality is usually assumed). The 'theoretical' PBM ignores the demand for equity, but it is useful in analysing the impact of open market operations on the exchange rate.

Testing the PBM is difficult because of data limitations. Direct tests involve estimating the asset demand functions (e.g. Lewis 1988, Cuthbertson and Galindo 1999). An alternative is to solve the PBM, which gives a reduced form equation for the exchange rate that depends on assets other than money, namely domestic and net foreign bonds (usually measured by the cumulative current account position). Both of these approaches have achieved only moderate success and are not particularly robust over different currencies and time periods (Frankel 1982a, Rogoff 1984).

## Forward-Looking Models

Including UIP in the FPMM, we have

$$E_t s_{t+1} - s_t = r_t - r_t^* \tag{18}$$

$$s_t = p_t - p_t^* = (m - m^*)_t - \phi(y - y^*)_t + \lambda(r - r^*)_t \tag{19}$$

substituting for $r - r^*$ from the UIP condition and rearranging, we have

$$s_t = [1/(1+\lambda)]z_t + [\lambda/(1+\lambda)]E_t s_{t+1} \tag{20}$$

where $z_t = (m - m^*)_t - \phi(y - y^*)_t$. By repeated forward substitution,

$$s_t = [1/(1+\lambda)] \sum_{i=0}^{\infty} [\lambda/(1+\lambda)]^i E_t z_{t+i} \tag{21}$$

where we have imposed a transversality condition. From (21), the spot rate only changes if there is new information or news about the future path of $z_{t+i}$. In the Dornbusch-SPMM, we can introduce inertia into the system if prices respond with a lag to excess demand $X_t$ in the goods market.

$$p_t - p_{t-1} = \delta X_t \tag{22}$$

Excess demand is high when the real exchange rate depreciates (i.e. $s_t$ increases)

$$X_t = q_1(s_t + p_t^* - p_t) \tag{23}$$

Using UIP and the money demand equations, this gives rise to a similar form to (21) except that there is now inertia in the exchange rate

$$s_t = \theta_1 s_{t-1} + \lambda \sum_{j=0}^{\infty} \theta_2^j E_t z_{t+j} \qquad 0 < (\theta_1, \theta_2) < 1 \tag{24}$$

where $z_t$ depends on relative money supplies and real output. The portfolio balance model PBM may also be represented in the form (24) by noting that here we can amend the UIP condition to incorporate a risk premium that depends on relative asset holdings in domestic $B_t$ and foreign bonds $B_t^*$.

$$r_t - r_t^* = E_t s_{t+1} - s_t + f(B_t/B_t^*) \tag{25}$$

The resulting equation (25) for the exchange rate now has relative bond holdings in the vector of fundamentals, $z_t$.

Forecasts of the future values of the fundamentals $z_{t+j}$ depend on information at time $t$ and, hence, equation (25) can be reduced to a purely backward-looking equation in terms of the fundamentals (if we ignore any implicit cross-equation RE restrictions), and this is often how such models are empirically tested in the literature. However, one can also exploit the full potential of the forward terms in (24), which imply cross-equation restrictions, if one is willing to posit an explicit set of VAR forecasting equations for the fundamental variables.

## 27.2   Testing the Models

As one can see from the analysis in the previous section, tests of SPMM involve regressions of the spot rate on relative money stocks, interest rates, and so on, while tests of the PBM also include other asset stocks. If we ignore hyperinflation periods, then these models have not proved successful in predicting movements in bilateral spot rates, particularly in post-1945 data. Some of the models do work reasonably well over short sub-periods but not over the whole period. Meese (1990) provides an early study of the performance of such models. He estimates a general equation that, in the main, subsumes all of the above theories:

$$s_t = a_0 + a_1(L)(m - m^*)_t + a_2(L)(y - y^*)_t + a_3(L)(r - r^*)_t$$

$$+ a_4(L)(\pi - \pi^*)_t + a_5(L)(F - F^*)_t + \varepsilon_t \tag{26}$$

where $F =$ stock of foreign assets held by domestic residents and $F^* =$ stock of domestic assets held by foreign residents. Meese (1990) repeats the earlier tests of Meese and Rogoff (1983) by running equation (26) up to time period $t$ and then using it to forecast out-of-sample for horizons of one, six and 12 months. New data is then added, and the estimation and forecasting process is repeated. The forecasts use actual future values of the RHS variables. He then compares the root mean square forecast errors from (26) with those from a benchmark provided by the 'no change' prediction of the random walk model of the exchange rate. Meese finds that the forecasts using economic fundamentals in (26) are in all cases worse than those of the random-walk hypothesis.

Meese (1990) dismisses the reasons for the failure of these models based on fundamentals as mismeasurement of variables, inappropriate estimation techniques or even omitted variables (since so many alternatives have been tried). He suggests that the failure of such models may be due to weakness in their underlying relationships such as the PPP condition, and the instability found in money demand functions and the mounting evidence from survey data on expectations that agents' forecasts do not obey the axioms of rational expectations.

### PPP-LOOP

Some of the variables in (26) are likely to be I(1) and, hence (to avoid statistical problems), more recent studies examine the cointegration properties of the data and establish cointegration between $s_t$ and relative prices (PPP) and between $s_t$ and 'fundamentals' such as money supply and output. Using data from the post-Bretton Woods float, single-equation tests of PPP have generally found that relative prices and nominal exchange rates are not cointegrated (Rogoff 1996). It is well known that standard tests take the null hypothesis as 'no cointegration', and the power to reject the null is extremely low in a short data span (the power of unit-root tests depends on the span of data and not its frequency, so one cannot increase 'power' by using quarterly data, say, rather than annual data). One way of overcoming this problem is to use longer spans of data, and studies that use about a century of data do find considerable support for long-run PPP (e.g. Lothian and Taylor 2000, Taylor 2001).

Other studies of PPP use panel data, since it has been found that this increases the power of cointegration tests and many panel studies using only the post-Bretton Woods data find support for long-run PPP (e.g. Frankel and Rose 1996, Taylor and Sarno 1998). One difficulty in interpreting these panel results is that when the null of no cointegration is rejected, we do not know whether PPP applies to all countries in the panel or only to a few. However, even given the somewhat conflicting evidence from alternative cointegration tests, most economists would accept that PPP holds in the long run (5–10 years), although deviations from PPP can be very large and persistent.

## Monetary Fundamentals

Mark (1995) examines the usefulness of 'fundamentals' in explaining changes in the (log) exchange rate over short and long horizons. Mark (1995) takes the monetary model as determining fundamentals $z_t = (m - m^*) - \alpha(y - y^*)$, and the exchange rate adjusts slowly to disequilibrium in the fundamentals:

$$s_{t+k} - s_t = \delta_k + \beta_k(s_t - z_t) + \varepsilon_{t+k}$$

Mark uses quarterly data on the US Dollar against the Canadian Dollar, Deutsche Mark, Yen and Swiss Franc, 1973–1991. The above exchange rate equation is a simple form of *error correction model*, with an error correction term $(s - z)_t$. Mark finds that the $R^2$ in the above regression and the value of $\beta_k$ increase as the horizon $k$ increases from 1 to 16 quarters. This is the same phenomenon we noted for long horizon stock returns. Mark finds that out-of-sample forecasts at long horizons ($k = 16$) outperform the random-walk model for DM, Yen and Swiss Franc. The above analysis is not a test of a 'fully specified' monetary model but demonstrates that 'monetary fundamentals' may provide a useful predictor of the exchange rate over long horizons (although not necessarily over short horizons).

Mark (1995) recognises that OLS estimates of $\beta_k$ are biased (Stamburgh 1999). To assess the degree of bias, he undertakes a MCS in a model where $s_t$ follows a random walk, while fundamentals $z_t$ (e.g. money supply) are a persistent AR(1) process.

$$\Delta s_t = \alpha_0 + \varepsilon_{1t}$$

$$z_t = \gamma_0 + \gamma_1 z_{t-1} + \varepsilon_{2t}$$

Using representative values for the parameters, he generates a series for $s_t$ and $z_t$ and performs the above error correction model on this 'artificial data'. He finds that the mean value of the OLS estimates $\beta_k$ in the artificial data are positive when they should be zero, since $\Delta s_t$ is a random walk by construction. This gives him a measure of the bias in the real data (see Chapter 2). For example, if the mean value of $\beta_k$ in the MCS is 0.20, while in the real data it is 0.205, then the bias adjusted beta, adj-$\beta_k = 0.205 - 0.20 = 0.005$. Hence, the seemingly large $\hat{\beta}_k = 0.205$ in the real data is misleading because it is biased, and a bias corrected value would be 0.005. The above would then indicate that fundamentals in the real data have hardly any effect on future changes in the spot rate. After bias-adjusting the betas obtained using the real data (and using empirical standard errors), Mark finds that fundamentals have some explanatory power at long horizons ($> 4$ years) but not at short horizons ($< 4$ years).

Cointegration tests can be applied to monetary models of the exchange rate, where in the long run,

$$s_t = (m - m^*)_t - \phi(y - y^*)_t + \lambda(r - r^*)_t \qquad (27)$$

and UIP implies

$$(r - r^*)_t = E_t \Delta s_{t+1} \qquad (28)$$

Under RE, the forecast error is I(0) (otherwise it is predictable from information known at $t$) and empirically $s_{t+1}$ is I(1), hence (28) implies $r - r^*$ is I(0). In (28), if $r - r^*$ is I(0), then it cannot cointegrate with $s_t$, which is I(1), hence the *statistical long-run* relationship between $s_t$ and monetary fundamentals is

$$s_t = (m - m^*)_t - \phi(y - y^*)_t \qquad (29)$$

where we expect the coefficient on $(m - m^*)$ to be unity. The coefficient on $(y - y^*)$ will be unity only if the income elasticity of the demand for money is unity in both countries. Of course, it is possible that for some countries, $s_t$, $(m - m^*)$ and $(y - y^*)$ are all I(0), in which case the issue of cointegration does not arise.

Groen (2000) and Mark and Sul (2001), using post-Bretton Woods data in a *panel* of countries, find cointegration in (27) with $\phi = 1$ and forecasts based on an error correction model (ECM) generally outperform the random-walk model. Clearly, the *panel* results of Mark and Sul (2001) supporting cointegration across the whole panel of countries, may, nevertheless, 'contain' *some* countries where the monetary model does not hold.

In contrast, Rapach and Wohar (2002) use over a century of annual data for 14 exchange rates (against the USD) and test for cointegration in (29). Results using a battery of tests are mixed, with cointegration holding for France, Italy, Netherlands and Spain and moderate support for Belgium, Finland, Portugal and Switzerland and no support for Australia, Canada, Denmark, Sweden and the United Kingdom. Where cointegration has been established, Rapach and Wohar then run a bivariate VECM:

$$\Delta s_t = \{\Delta s_{t-j}, \Delta fdm_{t-j}\} + \alpha_{11} z_{t-1} + \varepsilon_{1t} \qquad (30a)$$

$$\Delta fdm_t = \{\Delta s_{t-j}, \Delta fdm_{t-j}\} + \alpha_{21} z_{t-1} + \varepsilon_{2t} \qquad (30b)$$

where 'fundamentals' $fdm_t = (m - m^*)_t - (y - y^*)_t$ and $z_t = (s - fdm)_t$. For Belgium, Italy and Finland, $\alpha_{11} \neq 0$ and $\alpha_{21} = 0$, so the fundamentals are weakly exogenous for these three countries (but not for others), and the disequilibrium in the 'fundamentals' drives changes in the exchange rate (and not vice versa). In fact, it is $(m - m^*)_{t-1}$ that is doing all the work here because if $(y - y^*)$, which is I(0), is included separately, it is not statistically significant.

Rapach and Wohar (2002) then use (30a) to provide 'outside sample' forecasts for $\Delta s_t$, updating the parameters each year, using data up to $t - 1$ and forecasting one year ahead. These forecasts are undertaken only for those countries for which $z_t$ is I(0) (i.e. $s$, $m$ and $y$ cointegrate). The forecasts using fundamentals are compared to the 'no change' random-walk prediction using a variety of metrics (e.g. mean square error, MSE). They find that the monetary model outperforms the random-walk model for some of the countries (Belgium, Italy and possibly Switzerland) where the ECM term is statistically significant in the $\Delta s_t$ equation. In contrast, when the ECM term is statistically insignificant (e.g. France, Portugal, Spain), the forecast performance of (30a) is inferior to the random walk 'no change' prediction. Also note that Rapach and Wohar's (2002) forecasting results allow the coefficients on the dynamics to alter every period (i.e. they are not be constant) and we do not know the contribution of these short-run 'delta' terms relative to that of the ECM term, to the overall forecast performance. It is not saying a lot if $\Delta s_t = f(\Delta s_{t-j}, \Delta fdm_{t-j})$ provides a better forecast than simply $\Delta s_t = 0$. It is the ECM term that embodies the long-run economic theory so it would be interesting to know whether excluding this term leads to a major deterioration in the forecast performance. Indeed, the Theil U statistics, $U = RMSE_{fdm}/RMSE_{RW}$, lie mainly between 0.98 and 1.02, so the forecast improvement for the fundamentals model over the random-walk model is rather marginal.

Overall, even this technically proficient 're-run' of the monetary model gives far from satisfactory results, and one cannot imagine a central banker using this model when deciding on the monetary policy stance for the 'moderate inflation' countries considered in the study.

Since PPP holds, it appears that the weakness of the monetary model lies with the stability of the money demand relationship, and difficulties here have been well documented (e.g. see Cuthbertson 1997 and other articles therein). The above 'tests' assume linearity, and it is possible that the effect of disequilibrium in the fundamentals on $\Delta s_t$ is non-linear. Indeed, Taylor and Peel (2000) find that $z_t = (s - fdm)_t$ is stationary and model these residuals from the cointegrating regression as a non-linear ESTAR model and find (as with the dividend–price ratio for stocks) that 'close to equilibrium', the exchange rate behaves as a random walk but well away from equilibrium, it is mean reverting (around the monetary fundamentals).

## Forward-Looking Models: The VAR Approach

In our analysis of the FPMM, we saw that the spot rate may be represented as a forward convolution of fundamental variables

$$s_t = (1 + \lambda)^{-1} \sum_{i=0}^{\infty} [\lambda/(1 + \lambda)]^i E(x_{t+i}|\Omega_t) \tag{31}$$

where

$$x_t = (m_t - m_t^*) - (\phi y_t - \phi^* y_t^*) \tag{32}$$

Subtracting $x_t$ from both sides of (31),

$$q_t = s_t - x_t = \sum_{i=1}^{\infty} \psi^i E_t(\Delta x_{t+i} | \Omega_t) \tag{33}$$

where $\psi = \lambda/(1 + \lambda)$, $E_t \Delta x_{t+1} = x_{t+1} - x_t$ and $E_t \Delta x_{t+i} = E_t(x_{t+i} - x_{t+i-1})$ for $i > 1$. We may somewhat loosely refer to $q_t = s_t - x_t$ as the actual 'exchange rate spread'. If the economic fundamentals in $x_t$ are I(1), then $\Delta x_{t+i}$ in (33) is I(0) and, hence, $s_t$ and $x_t$ should be cointegrated and $q_t \sim$ I(0). If we form a VAR in $z_t = (q_t, \Delta x_t)'$, then it is easy to see that (33) implies

$$\mathbf{e1}'\mathbf{z}_t = \sum_{i=1}^{\infty} \psi^i \mathbf{e2}'\mathbf{A}^i\mathbf{z}_t = \mathbf{e2}'\psi\mathbf{A}(\mathbf{I} - \psi\mathbf{A})^{-1}\mathbf{z}_t \tag{34}$$

The Wald restrictions implied by this version of the FPMM are

$$\mathbf{e1}' - \mathbf{e2}'\psi\mathbf{A}(\mathbf{I} - \psi\mathbf{A})^{-1} = 0 \tag{35a}$$

or

$$\mathbf{e1}'(\mathbf{I} - \psi\mathbf{A}) - \mathbf{e2}'\psi\mathbf{A} = 0 \tag{35b}$$

Equation (35b) is a set of linear restrictions that imply that the RE forecast error for the spot rate is independent of any information available at time $t$ other than that given by the variables in $x_t$. We can also define the *'theoretic exchange rate spread'* $q_t'$ as

$$q_t' = \mathbf{e2}'\psi\mathbf{A}(\mathbf{1} - \psi\mathbf{A})^{-1}\mathbf{z}_t \tag{36}$$

and compare this with the actual 'spread' $q_t$. To implement the VAR methodology, we need to have estimates of $\{\phi, \phi^*\}$ to form the variable $q_t = s_t - x_t$ and estimates of $\lambda$ to calculate $\psi$. An implication of the FPMM is that

$$s_t = (m_t - m_t^*) - (\phi y_t - \phi^* y_t^*) + (\lambda r_t - \lambda^* r_t^*) \tag{37}$$

is a cointegrating relationship, given that all the variables are I(1). Estimates of $(\phi, \phi^*, \lambda, \lambda^*)$ can be obtained from cointegration regressions either single equation or using the Johansen procedure. The variables $q_t = s_t - x_t$ and $\Delta x_t$ can then be constructed and used in the VAR.

MacDonald and Taylor (M–T) (1993) provide a good illustration of the implementation of this procedure. They use monthly data January 1976 to December 1990 on the DM/Dollar rate. From the Johansen procedure, they find they do not reject the null that the coefficients on relative money supplies and relative income are unity for the 'home' (Germany) and 'foreign' (USA) variables and that the interest rate coefficients are nearly equal and opposite:

$$s_t = (m - m^*)_t + (y_t - y_t^*) + 0.049r_t - 0.050r_t^*$$

They take $\lambda = \lambda^* = 0.05$ and, hence, $x_t = (m - m^*)_t - (y_t - y_t^*)$. M–T find that the Wald tests decisively reject the RE cross-equation restrictions. The variance of the actual 'spread' $q_t$ exceeds the variance of the theoretical spread $q_t'$ given by (36) by a factor greater than 100, and the forward-looking FPMM, therefore, performs abysmally.

As in the Rapach–Wohar approach, M–T note that the presence of a cointegrating vector (32) implies that the spot rate may be represented as a dynamic ECM, and they run a second-stage regression to estimate the short-run dynamic response of $s_t$. Their preferred ECM is

$$
\begin{aligned}
\Delta s_t = \quad &0.005 \quad + \quad 0.24\Delta s_{t-2} \quad - \quad 0.42\Delta_2\Delta m_t \quad - \quad 0.79\Delta y_t \quad - \quad 0.008\Delta^2 r_t^* \\
&(0.003) \quad\;\; (0.07) \qquad\qquad (0.23) \qquad\qquad (0.34) \qquad\qquad (0.003) \\
&- \quad 0.025q_{t-1} \\
&\quad\;\; (0.013)
\end{aligned}
\tag{38}
$$

where $R^2 = 0.14$, SE = 3.2%, (.) = standard error. The equation passes all the usual diagnostic tests, although note that the $R^2$ of 14% indicates that little of the variation in $\Delta s_t$ is explained by the equation. They then perform a 'rolling regression' and use (38) to forecast over different horizons as the estimated parameters are updated. They find that the RMSEs for the ECM are *slightly* less than those from the random walk, 'no change' forecasts, for horizons of one, two, three, six, nine and 12 months. Again, note that most of the statistical explanation in (38) appears to be due to the ad hoc dynamic terms, and little of the statistical explanation seems due to the long-run error correction term. The forecasts are likely to be dominated by the difference terms, which probably approximate a random walk themselves, hence, the reason why the reported RMSEs are approximately the same as those for the random-walk model. The M–T study is a valiant attempt to correctly test a sophisticated version of the FPMM but the model is clearly rejected for DM/$ spot rate.

## Volatility of Spot Rate and Fundamentals

A novel approach to testing monetary models of the exchange rate is provided by Flood and Rose (1995). They compare the volatility of the spot rate with the volatility in 'economic fundamentals' for periods of 'fixed rates' (e.g. Bretton Woods) and floating rates. Not surprisingly, exchange rates are far more volatile in the floating rate periods. If monetary models are correct, then one should observe a dramatic increase in volatility in some of the economic fundamentals (e.g. relative money supplies) when a previously 'fixed' exchange rate is allowed to float. For nine industrialised (OECD) countries, Flood and Rose find that although the conditional volatility of bilateral exchange rates against the dollar alters dramatically across these exchange rate regimes, none of the economic fundamentals experience a marked change in volatility. Hence, one can legitimately conclude that the economic fundamentals in the monetary models (e.g. money supply, interest rates, inflation rates, output) do not explain the volatility in exchange rates.

A more formal exposition of the Flood–Rose methodology in testing the FPMM may be obtained from (3) with $\phi = \phi^*$, $\lambda = \lambda^*$ and substituting for $r - r^*$ from the UIP condition

$$s_t = TF_t + \lambda(s_{t+1}^e - s_t) \tag{39}$$

where $TF_t = (m - m^*)_t - \phi(y - y^*)_t$ stands for 'traditional fundamentals'. We define 'virtual fundamentals' as $VF_t = s_t - \lambda(r - r^*)_t$. Under the FPMM, equation (3), we expect the variability in virtual fundamentals $VF_t$ to equal the variability in traditional fundamentals $TF_t$. To obtain a time series for $TF_t$ and $VF_t$, all one requires is a representative value for the structural parameters of the demand for money function $\lambda$ and $\phi$. As reported above, Flood and Rose find that while the volatility of $VF_t$ increases dramatically in the floating rate period, the volatility of traditional fundamentals $TF_t$ changes very little. (This result is invariant to reasonable values of $\lambda$ and $\phi$ and also holds when they consider the SPMM.) Flood and Rose suggest that since few macroeconomic variables undergo dramatic changes in volatility, which coincide with changes in exchange rate regimes, it is unlikely that *any* exchange rate model based only on economic fundamentals will prove adequate. For nine OECD countries, they also correlate the average monthly variance of the exchange rate over successive two-year horizons $\sigma^2(S)$ against the variance of various macroeconomic variables. They find that there is no correlation between $\sigma^2(S)$ and either the variability in the money supply or interest rates or FOREX reserves or stock prices and only a rather weak negative correlation with the variance of output.

## Rational Bubbles

Rational bubbles are possible in the forward-looking model, and we briefly discuss these issues below. There are severe econometric difficulties in testing for rational bubbles, and such tests are contingent on having the correct equilibrium model of asset returns. Rejection of the no-bubbles hypothesis may be due to misspecification of the underlying model involving fundamentals. The latter is particularly acute for monetary models of the exchange rate since these provide a rather poor statistical representation of movements in the spot exchange rate. The FPMM with a deterministic bubble term results in an equation for the spot rate of the form

$$s_t = (1 + \lambda)^{-1} \sum_{i=0}^{\infty} [\lambda/(1 + \lambda)]^i E_t x_{t+i} + B_0 [(\lambda + 1)/\lambda)]^t \tag{40}$$

where $x_t$ = set of monetary variables, $B_0$ = value of bubble at $t = 0$. The null of no-bubbles is $H_0 : B_0 = 0$. However, if the $x_t$ variables are a poor representation of the true fundamentals, then the estimate of $B_0$ may be different from zero, as it is the only other candidate left to help explain the dependent variable. Testing $B_0 = 0$ in (40) is also problematic because of the 'exploding regressor' problem. However, the test due to West (1987a) avoids the latter problem and provides a test for any form of bubble, whether stochastic or deterministic.

Meese (1986) uses the FPMM as his maintained fundamentals model for the $/DM exchange rate (1973–1982) and rejects the no-bubbles hypotheses. West (1987b) uses a second type of West (1987a) test and augments the FPMM of Meese to include money demand errors that may pick up other potential 'fundamentals'. He finds against the presence of bubbles for the $/DM rate (1974–1984). Because of the poor empirical performance of exchange rate models based on fundamentals, there is little one can say with any degree of certainty about the presence or otherwise of rational bubbles in FX rates.

## 27.3 New Open-Economy Macroeconomics

There has been a concerted effort over the last 10 years or so to embed macroeconomic models with 'sound' microfoundations (Woodford 2003, Clarida, Gali and Gertler 1999), and this has had an impact on open-economy models (Obstfeld and Rogoff 2000). The basis for 'rigorous microfoundations' is usually interpreted by assuming agents maximise an intertemporal utility function subject to a budget constraint. We noted that this type of model has also come to the fore in the SDF approach, which seeks to explain risky asset demands and the equity premium. Also, because we have an explicit intertemporal utility function, this implies we can analyse alternative solutions in terms of their impact on overall welfare.

In the following, we give a flavour of these open-economy models. As empirical testing of such models and their use in policy analysis is as yet not widely established, the interested reader is referred to Lane (2001) and Sarno and Taylor (2002) for more information.

Like intertemporal consumption portfolio models, the new open-economy models (NOEM) are stochastic general equilibrium models, which are usually calibrated and simulated rather than estimated. In Obstfeld and Rogoff, 'producer-consumer' agents maximise lifetime utility:

$$U = \sum_{t=0}^{\infty} \delta^t \left[ \frac{\sigma}{\sigma - 1} \ln C_t^{(\sigma-1)/\sigma} + \frac{\kappa}{1 - \varepsilon} \ln \left( \frac{M_t}{P_t} \right)^{1-\varepsilon} - \frac{k}{\mu} y_t(z)^\mu \right]$$

Subject to the dynamic budget constraint (for all $t$),

$$B_{t+1} - B_t + rB_t + \frac{M_t - M_{t-1}}{P_t} = \frac{p_t(z)}{P_t} - C_t - T_t$$

where $C_t$ = aggregate consumption, $M_t$ = money balances, $B_t$ = internationally traded riskless bond, $r$ = *real* interest rate, $T_t$ = tax receipts and $y$ = real output. The term in $-y(z)$ in square brackets represents the fact that higher output implies less leisure, hence, lower utility. The parameter $z$ indexes the continuum of agents in the model.

In the model, the LOOP holds for *individual* goods with price $p_t(z)$, and PPP holds for the *aggregate* price level (i.e. $P = SP^*$). *Real* interest rate parity is assumed to hold, which links the real rate to the nominal rate.

With sticky prices in the short run, an increase in the money supply has real effects in the short run, and in the long run, money is not neutral because there is wealth accumulation via the current account. For example, with sticky prices, an increase in the money supply leads to a fall in *nominal* interest rates and via UIP, a depreciation in the exchange rate. The latter leads to higher exports (fewer imports), generating an increased *demand* for output. Monopolistic competition implies with price above marginal cost, producers supply the extra output demanded at unchanged prices. The 'home' current account moves into surplus in the short run, and this leads to a higher level of long-run wealth. The latter implies that money is not neutral in the long run (i.e. even after all price adjustments). There is no exchange rate overshooting in the model, and in the *long run*, the exchange rate does not necessarily depreciate. It can be shown that a monetary expansion is unambiguously welfare enhancing as it mitigates the monopoly price distortion. We hope this very brief account of this general equilibrium model demonstrates its versatility and the possibility of generating results that may differ from those of the 'standard' monetary models discussed earlier.

A number of key issues have arisen in this literature, which include the question of whether prices should be sticky in the currency of the buyer (local currency) or of the seller (producer currency pricing) or whether stickiness should apply to wages or prices (Betts and Devereux 2000). A statistical test (as opposed to calibration) of an NOEM applied to 'small' open economies of Australia, Canada and the United Kingdom has been undertaken by Bergin (2003) with mixed results. The model seeks to explain the nominal exchange rate, the current account, prices, money and the real interest rate, with shocks to technology, the foreign interest rate, foreign demand and changing tastes. A restricted and unrestricted model are estimated and compared using a likelihood ratio test (after estimation by maximum likelihood). Although the restricted model is not rejected for two of the three countries considered, the model cannot beat a random walk when forecasting the exchange rate or the current account for any of the three countries. Price rigidities are important for the model since a version with flexible prices is rejected – but this is hardly a major insight given what we know about the empirics of PPP.

At a theoretical level, this class of dynamic general equilibrium model has now been extended in a number of directions, with more elaborate price stickiness mechanisms (e.g. pricing-to-market versus staggered price setting), more elaborate preferences (e.g. non-separability of consumption and leisure, changing the degree of substitution of home and foreign goods), introducing capital goods and a time-varying risk premium. Not surprisingly, changing the assumptions (including the parameters of the utility function) changes some of the predictions of the model and, hence, 'agreeing on a particular new open-economy model is hardly possible at this stage' (Sarno and Taylor 2002, p. 165). The usual refrain here is 'more research is needed in this area', and that is certainly true before this class of model is deemed acceptable for real world policy analysis.

## 27.4 Summary

It is important that the reader is aware of the alternative models used to try to explain movements in spot exchange rates in terms of economic fundamentals, not least because these models have to some extent helped shape key economic policy decisions as we noted in our opening remarks.

- It seems unlikely that any minor refinements to the traditional monetary models would lead to dramatic improvements in their statistical performance. At present, it would appear to be the case that *formal* tests of the various models lead one to reject them.

- Over short horizons, say up to about one year, monetary fundamentals generally do not help predict changes in the spot rate. Over longer horizons of four years, fundamentals do provide some (but not much) predictive power for some currencies (Mark 1995, Rapach and Wohar 2002) and the relationship may be non-linear (Taylor and Peel 2000, Taylor, Peel and Sarno 2001).

- On balance, we must recognise that we are still very unsure of the underlying determinants of the spot exchange rate in industrialised countries with moderate inflation. But the concepts and ideas that underlie these models (e.g. PPP, UIP relative money supplies) do still play a role in *guiding* policy makers – although many factors other than the models discussed in this chapter are taken into account by policy makers when setting interest rates.

- The new open-economy models provide a mechanism for analysing monetary policy in an intertemporal equilibrium framework with imperfect competition and allow welfare analysis of alternative policies. This is an interesting development but there is as yet little consensus on the most appropriate model and little empirical verification. Hence, policy conclusions remain extremely tentative.

- The absence of clear-cut policy implications on exchange rates arise because of the statistical inadequacy of all of the 'structural' monetary models we have discussed in this and previous chapters. To use an analogy, note that as far as explaining the behaviour of the exchange rate is concerned, it is not that 'the emperor has no clothes', it is that he has too many but none of them appear to fit very well. This has resulted in policy makers trying to mitigate the severity of wide swings in the real exchange rate either by coordinated central bank intervention or a move towards currency zones or moving towards a common currency such as in the Euro zone.

# 28

# MARKET RISK

## Aims

- Define the concept of Value at Risk (VaR) and demonstrate how we measure the VaR of a single asset and a portfolio of assets for which the portfolio return is a linear function of the individual asset returns and the returns are (multivariate) normal. This method is known as the *delta–normal* or *variance–covariance (VCV)* approach.

- Outline the limitations of calculating the VaR of option positions in terms of the delta and delta + gamma approximations.

- Show how 'mapping' can reduce the number of inputs into the calculation for VaR and how we can 'map' some non-linear instruments (e.g. bonds) into an approximate linear framework and hence continue to use the VCV approach.

- Examine non-parametric methods of estimating portfolio-VaR, such as the historical simulation approach and its extension using bootstrapping procedures.

- Demonstrate how the VaR for portfolios containing options can be calculated using the delta method (i.e. linear approximation), the delta-gamma approximation and Monte Carlo simulation.

- Analyse variants on the traditional VaR approach such as 'stress testing', 'worse case scenario analysis' and 'extreme value theory'.

In this chapter, we discuss market risk, that is, risk arising from price changes on marketable assets such as stocks, bonds, foreign exchange, futures and options. A large number of financial institutions (and some large industrial and commercial companies) hold net positions in a wide variety of assets. For their own prudential reasons, financial intermediaries need to measure the overall 'dollar' market risk of their portfolio, which is usually referred to as the *Value at Risk* (VaR). In addition, the regulatory authorities use VaR to set minimum capital adequacy requirements to cover market risk. The investment bank J.P. Morgan played a key role in developing the VaR approach, and its material is published under the title *Risk Metrics*™. If your knowledge of options is rather poor, then you should consult Cuthbertson and Nitzsche (2001b) at this point.

# 28.1 Measuring VaR

What is VaR? If the *daily* VaR is found to be $100 m at a 5% critical value, this implies that in only 1 day out of 20 will the financial institution lose more than $100 m. It is worth noting at the outset that VaR can be measured in several different ways: the variance–covariance method, historical simulation-bootstrapping techniques, Monte Carlo simulation (MCS), stress testing and extreme value theory. Much of the material discussed is based on the risk measurement methodology as set out in *RiskMetrics*™ (1996), which emanates from J.P. Morgan.

The riskiness of a single asset is summarised in the probability distribution of its returns. Often, there is no *single* acceptable measure of the riskiness of a particular distribution, although for the normal distribution, the standard deviation is frequently used. The risk of a single asset whose returns are identically, independently and normally distributed (i.e. *niid*) can be (unambiguously) measured by its variance (or standard deviation). For normally distributed returns, we can be 90% certain that the actual return will equal the expected return plus or minus $1.65\sigma$, where $\sigma$ is the standard deviation of the returns. Put another way, we expect the actual return to be *less than* $\mu - 1.65\sigma$ or greater than $\mu + 1.65\sigma$ only 1 time in 20 (i.e. 5% of the time).

Further, if we assume the mean return is zero, we could take $(1.65\sigma)$ as a measure of 'downside risk' (with 5% probability). Hence, if we hold a net position of $V_0$ in one asset, then the $-downside 'Value at Risk' is

$$\text{VaR} = \$V_0(1.65\sigma) \tag{1}$$

Suppose the calculated VaR of a portfolio of assets is $100 m over a 1-day horizon. Then equivalent expressions for the VaR would be

> **The maximum amount I *expect* to lose in 19 out of 20 days is $100 m, or I *expect* to lose more than $100 m only 1 day in every 20 days.**

If asset returns are non-normal, then the 90% confidence region is not $\pm 1.65\sigma$. However, as we shall see, for many asset returns, the normality assumption is a reasonable approximation.

## VaR: Portfolio of Assets

For many asset portfolios, it is reasonable to assume a *linear* relationship between the dollar change in the value of the portfolio $dV_p$ and the asset returns:

$$dV_p = \sum_{i=1}^{n} N_{0,i} dP_i = \sum_{i=1}^{n} V_{0,i} R_i = \sum_{i=1}^{n} V_{0,i}(dP_i/P_i) \tag{2}$$

where $N_{0i}$ is the number of assets $i$, $V_{0,i} = N_{0,i} : P_{0,i}$ is the \$-(present) value held in asset $i$ and $R_i$ is the return on asset $i$. The above holds exactly for equities and is a reasonable approximation for several other securities (e.g. coupon paying bonds, FRAs, FRNs, forwards, futures and swaps). It follows directly from equation (2) that the \$-standard deviation of the portfolio is given by the usual formula

$$\sigma_{dV_p} = \left[ \sum_{i=1}^{n} V_{0,i}^2 \sigma_i^2 + \sum_{i \neq j} \sum V_{0,i} V_{0,j} \rho_{i,j} \sigma_i \sigma_j \right]^{1/2} \tag{3}$$

Equation (3) can be used to calculate the standard deviation of the portfolio regardless of the form of the distribution of asset returns. But the standard deviation alone does not allow us to determine the 5% lower 'cut-off' value unless we assume a specific distribution for asset returns. In particular, if we add the assumption of (multivariate) normally distributed asset returns, then the diversified VaR at the 5th percentile is $VaR_p = 1.65\sigma_{dV_p}$, which can be more compactly written

$$\textbf{Diversified } VaR_p = \sqrt{ZCZ'} \tag{4}$$

where $\mathbf{Z} = [VaR_1, VaR_2, \ldots, VaR_n]$, the VaR of each asset taken separately is $VaR_i = V_{0,i}(1.65\sigma_i)$ and $\mathbf{C}$ is the correlation matrix. For example, the correlation matrix for $n = 3$ assets would be

$$\mathbf{C} = \begin{bmatrix} 1 & \rho_{12} & \rho_{13} \\ \rho_{12} & 1 & \rho_{23} \\ \rho_{13} & \rho_{23} & 1 \end{bmatrix}$$

The linearity and normality assumptions are crucial here. The change in asset values is sometimes perfectly consistent with linearity (e.g. stocks) and where it is not, we often impose linearity as an approximation (i.e. we use a first-order Taylor series expansion). Note that if the relationship between portfolio value $dV_p$ and asset returns is highly non-linear (e.g. for stock options), then even if the returns of the underlying assets (e.g. stocks) are themselves normally distributed, the distribution of the portfolio's value will *not be normally distributed*. Hence, for example, for a portfolio of options, the complete distribution may be needed to accurately calculate the VaR (for any given percentile) and we cannot simply use the '1.65$\sigma$' rule.

Providing we can use the linearity and (multivariate) normality assumptions, all we need to calculated for the diversified VaR is the correlation matrix, the (present) value of each asset holding $V_{0,i}$ and the return volatilities. This is known as the 'variance–covariance' (VCV) method.

The worse case VaR occurs when all the assets are assumed to be held long (i.e. all $V_{0,i} > 0$) and all asset returns are perfectly positively correlated (hence $C =$ the unit matrix where all elements $= 1$). Thus, from (4),

$$\textbf{Worse case VaR} = VaR_1 + VaR_2 + \cdots + VaR_n$$

Table 1 shows how the above formulae can be easily applied in matrix form. There are three assets (stocks) with \$10,000 held in each asset, but asset-2 has been sold short.

**Table 1** VaR for portfolio of 3 'spot' assets

| Assets | Value of Asset | Std. Dev. | VaR | Abs. VaR | | Correlation Matrix | | |
|--------|---------------|-----------|------|----------|---|------|------|------|
| 1 | 10,000 | 5.41% | 894 | 894 | | 1 | 0.962 | 0.403 |
| 2 | −10,000 | 3.04% | −502 | 502 | | 0.962 | 1 | 0.610 |
| 3 | 10,000 | 3.64% | 600 | 600 | | 0.403 | 0.610 | 1 |
| | | | | | Individual VaRs | 894 | −502 | 600 |
| | | Worse case VaR | | 1996 | Div. VaR | 783 | | |

The correlations are all positive and quite high. The 'worse case' or undiversified VaR is \$1996 but the diversified VaR is much less at \$783. This is because although asset-2 has a positive correlation with the other assets, it has been sold short, which effectively creates a negative correlation in the portfolio.

## Forecasting Volatility

The VCV method is a parametric method since we require forecasts of volatilities and correlations. Many practitioners (e.g. *RiskMetrics*[TM]) use an exponentially weighted moving average (EWMA) forecast for daily volatility:

$$\sigma_{t+1|t}^2 = \lambda \sigma_{t|t-1}^2 + (1 - \lambda) R_t^2 \tag{5}$$

where $R_t^2$ is the daily squared return. The parameter $\lambda = 0.94$, which minimises the past forecast errors (over a given horizon of, say, 100 days and across several asset classes). Similarly, the forecast of covariance is

$$\sigma_{xy,t+1|t}^2 = \lambda \sigma_{xy,t|t-1}^2 + (1 - \lambda) X_t Y_t \tag{6}$$

where $X_t$, $Y_t$ are the daily returns on two assets $X$ and $Y$. Hence, the forecast of correlations is

$$\rho_{xy} = \sigma_{xy}/\sigma_x \sigma_y \tag{7}$$

The above equations are recursions and can be updated daily as new data arrives on $X_t$ and $Y_t$.

### *Longer horizons*

What about forecasting volatility over horizons longer than one day? First and most obvious, we could recalculate the standard deviation with 'returns' measured over the required horizon – the direct method. For example, we would use monthly stock returns over, say, the previous 36 months in equation (5) to calculate the monthly standard deviation. A more widely used method is the 'root $T$-rule' ($\sqrt{T}$-rule). This is based on the fact that if daily (log) price changes are identically and independently distributed (over time), then

$$\sigma_T = \sqrt{T}\sigma \tag{8}$$

where $\sigma$ is the forecast of the *daily* standard deviation (we have suppressed the time subscripts) and $T$ is the number of trading days in the forecast horizon. For example, over 25 business days (i.e. approximately 1 month), the standard deviation is $\sigma_{25} = \sqrt{25}\sigma = 5\sigma$. The direct method requires one to recompute all the variance measures for all assets over any chosen 'new' horizon, so the square root rule is computationally much less burdensome (and can be accurately used for volatilities up to a horizon of about 1 month).

## Delta and Full Valuation Methods

The Black and Scholes (1973) option price formulae apply to European options (i.e. no early exercise). We consider only stock options, where the underlying asset in the option contract is a stock of a particular company (which pays no dividends). The option pricing formulae can be derived (using stochastic calculus) by assuming a lognormal process for the stock price (see Cuthbertson and Nitzsche 2001b). The Black–Scholes formula for the price of a European call option looks rather formidable:

$$C = SN(d_1) - N(d_2)PV = SN(d_1) - N(d_2)Ke^{-rT} \tag{9}$$

where $d_1 = \dfrac{\ln(S/PV)}{\sigma\sqrt{T}} + \dfrac{\sigma\sqrt{T}}{2} = \dfrac{\ln(S/K) + (r + \sigma^2/2)T}{\sigma\sqrt{T}}$

$d_2 = d_1 - \sigma\sqrt{T} = \dfrac{\ln(S/K) + (r - \sigma^2/2)T}{\sigma\sqrt{T}}$

- $C$  is the price of call option (call premium)
- $r$  is the safe rate of interest for horizon $T$ (continuously compounded)
- $S$  is the current share price
- $T$  is the time to expiry (as proportion of a year)
- $PV$  is the present value of the strike price $(= Ke^{-rT})$
- $\sigma$  is the annual standard deviation of the (continuously compounded) return on the stock
- $N(\cdot)$  is the cumulative normal distribution

A similar formula applies for a put option. For our purposes, all we need to note is that the call (or put) premium is a non-linear function of the underlying stock price, $S$ (see Figure 1)

For a call, the call premium increases with $S$ and the 'delta' of the call option is defined as

$$\Delta_c = \partial C/\partial S = N(d_1) > 0$$

In Figure 1, we see that the true change in the option's price when $S$ moves from 50 to 51 is 0.4. The option's delta is the slope of the line $X - Y$, and this provides a first-order approximation to the true change in the option's price (i.e. $dC = \Delta_c\, dS$), which is an underestimate of the true change. However, if we are willing to use this first-order approximation, then $dC/C_0 = (S_0/C_0)\Delta_c(dS/S_0)$ so that the *return* on the option is linear in the *return* on the stock $dS/S_0$ and, hence, we can apply the variance–covariance method to calculating VaR. Of course, this approximation will be

Call premium and stock price are positively related

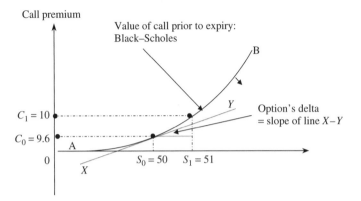

**Figure 1**   Black–Scholes option price: long call

a poor one if the change in $S$ is large, and this is why we require alternative techniques, such as Monte Carlo simulation (MCS), to obtain a more accurate VaR estimate for portfolios containing options (see the following).

For a put option, the relationship between the put premium $P$ and $S$ is negative

$$\Delta_p = \partial P / \partial S = N(d_1) - 1 < 0$$

Note from Figure 1 that the value of the call option's delta varies between zero (for low values of $S$, that is, when the option is 'well out-of-the-money') to unity (for high values of $S$ – that is when the option is 'well in-the-money'). Therefore, the value of delta changes as $S$ changes. This is known as the option's *gamma* (see Figure 2), which is the same for long calls and puts:

$$\Gamma(\text{call or put}) = \frac{\partial \Delta}{\partial S} = \frac{\partial^2 f}{\partial S^2} = \frac{N'(d_1)}{S\sigma\sqrt{T}} \geq 0 \tag{10}$$

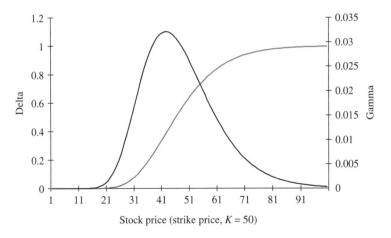

**Figure 2**   Delta and gamma: long call

where $N'(x) = \dfrac{e^{-x^2/2}}{\sqrt{2\pi}} \geqslant 0$ and $f = C$ or $P$. The explicit formulae for the option's delta and gamma are directly calculated from the Black–Scholes formulae. The 'gamma' represents the change in the curvature (that is the *change* in delta, at different values of $S$). Clearly, $\Gamma$ is fairly constant when the call is either very-in-the-money or ($S \gg K$) or very-out-of-the-money ($S \ll K$) but can vary a great deal for a near-the-money option (see Figure 2). To obtain a negative gamma, one must hold a short call or put.

Where portfolio value depends non-linearly on asset returns (e.g. options), a key issue is whether one uses a linear (or second-order) approximation or one uses a 'complete' or 'full' valuation method. A second main issue is whether the underlying asset returns are (multivariate) normally distributed.

To demonstrate the variance–covariance approach to measuring portfolio-VaR for 'non-linear' assets, consider the following. Let $N_i$ be the number of assets of type $i$, each with value of $V_i$. These assets $V_i$ could be options where there is a non-linear relationship between $V_i$ and the underlying asset price $S$ (e.g. stock price)

$$V_p = \sum_{i=1}^{n} N_i V_i \tag{11}$$

If the value of each asset $V_i$ depends on an underlying asset $S_i$ (e.g. an option on a stock), then a *first-order approximation* to the change in portfolio value is

*Change in value = (sensitivity to price changes)(change in prices)*

$$dV_p = \sum_{i=1}^{n} N_i S_i (\partial V_i / \partial S_i)(dS_i / S_i) \equiv \sum_{i=1}^{n} (V_{0,i} \Delta_i) R_i \tag{12}$$

where $V_{0,i} \equiv N_i S_i$, $\partial V_i / \partial S_i = \Delta_i$ and the 'return' on the underlying asset is $R_i \equiv dS_i / S_i$. This is known as the *delta valuation method*, since any first derivative is loosely referred to as *the delta* of the asset (e.g. for options). For example, if $V_i$ is the option premium, then $\partial V_i / \partial S_i = \Delta_i$ is the option's delta. If we make the additional assumption that asset returns $dS_i / S_i$ are (multivariate) normally distributed, then we can use the quantiles of the (standard) normal distribution to determine the VaR. Hence the term delta–normal method. Note that the delta–normal method requires a forecast of the variances and covariances of the returns on the *underlying* assets in the options contracts. If we define the VaR of a single option position as $VaR_i \equiv 1.65(V_{0,i} \Delta_i)\sigma_i$, where $\sigma_i$ is the standard deviation of the stock return, then (4) can be applied in the usual way to give the diversified VaR. (Also note that (12) is a generalisation of (2) since if $V_i$ is the stock price, then $\partial V_i / \partial S_i = 1$ and $N_i S_i = V_{0,i}$ is the initial wealth held in stock.)

However, the delta–normal method could be extremely inaccurate for options (particularly those which are 'at-the-money'), since the option's delta is only a first-order approximation to the non-linear price response. So, for options, we could go one step further and approximate the change in value of a portfolio of options using a second-order (Taylor series) approximation

$$dV_p = \sum_{i=1}^{n} N_i S_i \Delta_i (dS_i / S_i) + (1/2)\Gamma_i S_i^2 (dS_i / S_i)^2 \tag{13}$$

where $\Gamma_i$ is the gamma of an individual option. Calculating the change in value using the above equation (not surprisingly) is called the *delta–gamma method*. However, there is a problem in that the 'appearance' of the $(dS_i/S_i)^2$ term implies that the change in value is no longer linear in returns and, hence, we cannot apply the known 'cut-off' points of the normal distribution (e.g. $-1.65$ for the 5% lower tail). As we shall see, equation (13) can also be used to calculate the (approximate) change in the value of an option portfolio, where the stock returns are generated using MCS.

Again, we can make some further approximations to 'force' non-linear pay-offs like options into the variance–covariance approach. For expositional purposes, consider a *single* option with Black–Scholes price $P = f(S, r, y, \sigma, T - t)$. A second-order Taylor series expansion gives

$$dP = df = \frac{\partial f}{\partial S} dS + \frac{1}{2} \frac{\partial^2 f}{\partial S^2} (dS)^2 = \Delta S \frac{dS}{S} + \frac{1}{2} \Gamma S^2 \left[ \frac{dS}{S} \right]^2 \qquad (14)$$

To apply our delta–gamma approximation properly, we need to fit a distribution that matches that for $df$. Assuming $dS/S$ is normal with mean zero and standard deviation $\sigma$, it can be shown that the first three moments of $df$ are

$$\mu_{df} \equiv \mathrm{E}(df) = (1/2)S^2 \Gamma \sigma^2$$

$$\mathrm{E}(df^2) = S^2 \Delta^2 \sigma^2 + (3/4)S^4 \Gamma^2 \sigma^4$$

$$\mathrm{E}(df^3) = (9/2)S^4 \Delta^2 \Gamma^2 \sigma^4 + (15/8)S^6 \Gamma^3 \sigma^6 \qquad (15)$$

Knowing the right-hand side values for $\Delta$, $\Gamma$ (from Black–Scholes), the current stock price $S$ and an estimate of $\sigma$ (e.g. implied volatility or an EWMA or GARCH measure of volatility), we can calculate $\mu_{df}$, $\mathrm{E}(df^2)$ and $\mathrm{E}(df^3)$. If we ignore $\mathrm{E}(df^3)$, then the first two moments can be fitted to a normal distribution with mean $\mu_{df}$ and variance $\sigma_{df}^2 \equiv \mathrm{E}(df^2) - [\mathrm{E}(df)]^2$ and then we immediately know the VaR at the 5th percentile is $1.65\sigma_{df}$. However, it is sometimes dangerous to ignore the $\mathrm{E}(df^3)$ term. But even here, there are procedures available that allow one to take the first *three* moments and obtain an explicit formula for the *percentiles* of the (unknown) distribution, using the so-called Cornish–Fisher expansion (see Cuthbertson and Nitzsche 2001b). This approach can be extended to apply to a portfolio of options.

But we still have problems, since the option portfolio's values depend on changes in other variables, since European call and put premia on a dividend-paying stock (or on foreign currency or on futures options) under the Black–Scholes assumptions are $P = f(S, r, y, \sigma, T - t)$ where $P$ is the option premium. So a Taylor series expansion gives

$$dP = df = \frac{\partial f}{\partial S} dS + \frac{1}{2} \frac{\partial^2 f}{\partial S^2} (dS)^2 + \frac{\partial f}{\partial \sigma} d\sigma + \frac{\partial f}{\partial r} dr + \frac{\partial f}{\partial y} dy + \frac{\partial f}{\partial t} dt$$

$$= \Delta \, dS + \tfrac{1}{2} \Gamma (dS)^2 + \Lambda \, d\sigma + \rho_r \, dr + \rho_y \, dy + \theta \, dt \qquad (16)$$

Including the additional *linear* terms in $r$, $y$ and $\sigma$ in the calculation of the VaR is not a problem providing the assumption of multivariate normality holds. However, the latter assumption is not realistic particularly for $r$ and for volatility $\sigma$. Hence, if we want to assess the VaR of the option due to changes in volatility or if we require a more accurate measure of VaR (e.g. under alternative distributions to the normal for the underlying asset, $S$), then we must eschew the delta–gamma methodology and use other methods such as Monte Carlo simulation from which we can obtain the VaR from the complete distribution for the option premia outcomes (see the following).

So, if the value of an asset or portfolio of assets is highly non-linear in asset returns, then we have to use the *full valuation method*:

*Change in value = value at 'new' prices − value at initial prices*

Generally speaking, the full valuation method is often used in conjunction with Monte Carlo simulation to calculate the VaR of positions containing options.

## 28.2 Mapping Assets: Simplifications

### Domestic Equity

Estimation of the variances and particularly the $n(n-1)/2$ correlations for *all n stocks* in a particular country in order to measure their VaR would be computationally extremely burdensome. To simplify matters, one can make use of the single index model (SIM), since this allows all of the variances and covariances between returns to be subsumed into the $n$-asset betas. The individual asset returns are therefore 'mapped' into the market return. The SIM assumes the return on asset $i$ is solely determined by the market return (see Appendix II).

$$R_i = \alpha_i + \beta_i R_{\mathrm{m}} + \varepsilon_i \tag{17}$$

where $R_i$ is the return on asset $i$, $R_{\mathrm{m}}$ is the market return, $\beta_i$ is the beta of stock $i$. The $\varepsilon_i$ are assumed to be temporarily *niid*. In addition, we make the crucial assumption that there is no contemporaneous correlation across error terms, $E(\varepsilon_i \varepsilon_j) = 0$. (Also, $R_{\mathrm{m}}$ is independent of $\varepsilon_i$.) An estimate of $\beta_i$ can be obtained from a 'risk measurement service' or by running a time-series regression of $R_i$ on $R_{\mathrm{m}}$ (using, say, the last six months of daily data). The return on the stock portfolio of $n$ assets (with proportionate weights $w_i$) is

$$R_{\mathrm{p}} = \sum_{i=1}^{n} w_i R_i = \alpha_{\mathrm{p}} + \beta_{\mathrm{p}} R_{\mathrm{m}} + \sum w_i \varepsilon_i \tag{18}$$

where $\alpha_{\mathrm{p}} = \sum w_i \alpha_i$ and $\beta_{\mathrm{p}} = \sum w_i \beta_i$ is the beta of the equity portfolio. Hence, the return on the stock portfolio depends *linearly* on the market return and the portfolio beta $\beta_{\mathrm{p}}$. It can be shown that the standard deviation of the portfolio of equities is given by

$$\sigma_{\mathrm{p}} = \beta_{\mathrm{p}} \sigma_{\mathrm{m}} \tag{19}$$

The specific risk of each stock $\varepsilon_i$ is diversified away when held as part of a portfolio. Hence, the terms $\sum w_i^2 \sigma_{\varepsilon_i}^2$ are small and can be ignored. Thus, to calculate $\sigma_{\mathrm{p}}$, we only require estimates of $\beta_i$ for the $n$ assets and an estimate of $\sigma_m$. We, therefore, dispense with the need to estimate $n$ values for $\sigma_i$ and, more importantly, $n(n-1)/2$ values for the $\rho_{ij}$. What we have done is 'mapped' the stock returns into their local (market) index. This considerably reduces the computational burden of estimating the portfolio's VaR, which is given by

$$VaR_p = V_{0,p}1.65\sigma_p = V_{0,p}\beta_p(1.65\sigma_m) \tag{20}$$

where $V_{0,p}$ is the dollar-total held in the portfolio. Noting that $w_i = (V_{0,i}/V_{0,p})$, the above equation can be represented in matrix form as

$$\textbf{Diversified } VaR_p = \sqrt{ZCZ'} = \sum_{i=1}^{n} VaR_i \tag{21}$$

where $VaR_i = V_{0,i}(\beta_i 1.65\sigma_i)$, $\mathbf{Z} = [VaR_1, VaR_2, \ldots, VaR_n]$ and here for the SIM, the correlation matrix $\mathbf{C} =$ the unit matrix. This is because in the SIM, the only source of *systematic* movement in each of the individual returns is the market return ($R_m$) since $E(\varepsilon_{it}, \varepsilon_{jt}) = 0$ and, hence, all asset returns move up and down together (albeit not by the same amount).

The SIM is a factor model with only one factor, $R_m$. However, this approach could be extended within the VaR 'mapping' framework by assuming several factors (e.g. the three Fama-French factors) influence all $n$-asset returns. Then the correlations between *all* the $n$-asset returns will only depend on the ($3\times3$) correlation matrix of these underlying 'risk factors' (and their betas).

## VaR: Foreign Equities

If some stocks are held overseas, how do we calculate portfolio-VaR? This is done by assuming the SIM holds *within* any single country and then applying the usual variance–covariance approach to the foreign (local currency) return and the exchange rate. Suppose a US-based investor holds a *portfolio* of German equities with a standard deviation given by the SIM

$$\sigma_G = \beta_p \sigma_{DAX} \tag{22}$$

where $\sigma_{DAX}$ is the standard deviation of the DAX (i.e. a market index for German stocks) and $\beta_p$ is the beta of the German portfolio. Clearly, this portfolio is subject to changes in the DAX and foreign exchange risk from changes in the Dollar–Euro exchange rate. If the Euro value of the portfolio is $V_{0,E}$, then the dollar value is $V_{0,\$} = S_0 V_{0,E}$ where $S_0$ is the current exchange rate (\$ per Euro). The change in the *dollar* value of the portfolio is (approximately linear and) equal to

$$\Delta V_p = V_{0,\$}(R_G + R_{FX}) \tag{23}$$

where $V_{0,\$}$ is the initial \$ value of German equity portfolio

$R_G$ is the return on German portfolio

$R_{FX}$ is the change in \$–Euro exchange rate (measured in (\$/Euro))

The variance of the portfolio therefore depends on the correlation $\rho$ between $R_G$ and $R_{FX}$ (as well as their variances) and the Dollar–VaR is

$$VaR_p = (1.65)\sigma_{dV_p} = V_{0,\$}(1.65)(\sigma_G^2 + \sigma_{FX}^2 + 2\rho\sigma_G\sigma_{FX})^{1/2} \tag{24}$$

Again, this may be expressed in matrix form as

$$VaR_p = \sqrt{ZCZ'} \tag{25}$$

where $\mathbf{Z} = [V_{0,\$}(1.65)\sigma_G, V_{0,\$}(1.65)\sigma_{FX}]$, $\mathbf{C} = (2{\times}2)$ correlation matrix, with $\rho_{12} = \rho_{G,FX}$. We can extend this approach to a two-asset portfolio consisting of domestic and foreign assets. For example, if a US investor held $V_{0,\$}^{US}$ in *US equities* and $V_{0,\$}^G$ in *German equities*, then the appropriate $Z$ vector would be

$$Z = [V_{0,\$}^{US}(1.65)\sigma_{US}, V_{0,\$}^G(1.65)\sigma_G, V_{0,\$}^G 1.65\sigma_{FX}] \tag{26}$$

The variable $\sigma_{us}$ is the volatility of the US equity position that is calculated from $\sigma_{us} = \beta_p^{us}\sigma_{sp}$ where $\beta_p^{us}$ is the portfolio beta of the US equities and $\sigma_{sp}$ is the volatility of the S&P equity index. In this case, the $(3 \times 3)$ correlation matrix would be

$$C = \begin{bmatrix} 1 & \rho_{US,G} & \rho_{US,FX} \\ \rho_{US,G} & 1 & \rho_{G,FX} \\ \rho_{US,FX} & \rho_{FX,G} & 1 \end{bmatrix}$$

Using (26) puts the problem in exactly the same framework as the 'domestic only' case since each individual asset has $VaR_i = V_{0,i}(1.65)\sigma_i$ and $Z = [VaR_1, VaR_2, \ldots VaR_n]$, where for *each* foreign portfolio, there is also a corresponding bilateral exchange rate $\sigma_{FX}$ (against the US Dollar for a US resident).

If foreign portfolios are unhedged, then there can still be some risk reduction (and hence a low VaR) if some of the spot-FX rates have low (or negative) correlations with either the US Dollar or with stock market returns in different countries. If the investor hedges the FX positions (using the forward market), then, clearly, any spot-FX volatilities and correlations do not enter the calculation of VaR. Hence, it is not *always* the case that hedging foreign currency assets gives a lower *portfolio* volatility than not hedging.

## Bonds

Bond prices and yields are non-linearly related. For a zero coupon bond,

$$P_{it} = M_i e^{-y_i t_i}$$

where $P_{it}$ = price of the bond at $t$, $M_i$ = payment on the bond at time $t_i$, $y_i$ = (continuously compounded) spot yield at time $t$ for period $t_i$. A first-order approximation is

$$\frac{dP_i}{P_i} = -t_i\, dy_i \tag{27a}$$

and

$$\sigma_i(dP/P) = t_i\sigma(dy_i) \tag{27b}$$

where $t_i$ is the duration of a zero. Suppose at *each time* $t_i$, we have total coupon payments from $k$ bonds of $TC_i = \Sigma_{j=1}^{k}C_j$. A set of coupon paying bonds is just a series of zero coupon bonds and the *value* of a portfolio of coupon bonds with total coupons $TC_i$ at each time $t_i$ is

$$V_{P,t} = \sum_{i=1}^{n} TC_i e^{-y_i t_i} = \sum_{i=1}^{n} V_{0,i} \tag{28a}$$

where $V_{0,i} \equiv TC_i e^{-y_i t_i}$ is the present value (price) of the total coupon payments at $t_i$. Hence,

$$dV_{P,t} = \sum_{i=1}^{n} V_{0,i}(-t_i\,dy_i) = \sum V_{0,i}(dP_i/P_i) \tag{28b}$$

The change in value of the bond portfolio is *linear* in the change in prices of the zeros. From (27b), we can calculate the standard deviation of bond returns $\sigma_i(dP/P)$, given $\sigma(dy_i)$, on the basis of an EWMA forecast. In addition, if we assume yield changes are normally distributed and accept the duration approximation, we can use (28b) in the usual way to calculate the VaR of a bond portfolio using the VCV method. We have 'mapped' the non-linear yield-bond price relationship into a linear framework (see Cuthbertson and Nitzsche 2001b for further discussion). The VaR of the bond portfolio is

$$VaR_p = 1.65\sigma(dV_p) = \sqrt{ZCZ'}$$

where $Z = \{VaR_1, VaR_2, \ldots VaR_n\}$ and $VaR_i = 1.65V_{0,i}\sigma_i$, with $\sigma_i = \sigma(dP_i/P_i)$ the standard deviation of the *price* of the zeros and $C$ is the correlation matrix of zero coupon bond returns $(dP_i/P_i)$.

## 28.3 Non-Parametric Measures

The approaches in the previous section in estimating variances and correlations assume a specific parametric model for the volatility of returns (e.g. EWMA, ARCH and GARCH) and when using the 'delta method' to calculate portfolio-VaR, normality is also usually invoked. If returns are actually non-normal, this will produce biased estimates/forecasts. If we do not wish to assume a particular distribution for returns, we can instead use a non-parametric approach to estimate VaR, a popular one being historical simulation. The *actual* daily profit (loss) figures $\Delta V_{pt}$ for an $n$-asset *portfolio* at time $t$ are

$$\$\Delta V_{pt} = \sum_{i=1}^{n} V_i R_{it} \tag{29}$$

where $V_i$ is the *fixed* \$-value of asset $i$ held by the investor *today* and $R_{it}$ is the (proportionate) historic daily return on asset $i$. The historic simulation method to estimate the portfolio-VaR is extremely straightforward. It assumes that recent history will be representative of what might happen tomorrow. We take the $n$-asset returns and calculate the change in portfolio value for each of, say, 1000 days of historic data, assuming the amounts $V_i$ remain unchanged. These 1000 values of $\$\Delta V_{pt}$ are then arranged from low to high. That value of $\$\Delta V_{pt}$ which just has 1% of the 'lower returns' in the tail is then taken to be the forecast VaR for the next day (at the 99% confidence level). If the 10 lowest returns of the 1000 days are $-\$10\,\text{m}$, $-\$9.1\,\text{m}\ldots -\$2.2\,\text{m}$, then the forecast VaR for the next day for the 1% tail would be $\$2.2\,\text{m}$. One could also produce a histogram for $\$\Delta V_{pt}$ and hence obtain measures of skewness and excess kurtosis (these allow us to assess any deviations from the normality assumption).

The historic simulation approach is non-parametric since variances and covariances (between the $n$-asset) returns do not have to be explicitly estimated, they are implicit in the historic asset returns and hence in the estimated portfolio-VaR. There is, therefore, no model risk or parameter estimation risk. Any fat tails or autocorrelation (since the revaluation is taken sequentially day 1, day 2, etc.) in the historic data are incorporated in the portfolio-VaR and because we construct the empirical histogram, we do not need to assume normality to find the lower tail cut-off point. The method can also be used to estimate the VaR of non-linear positions either by invoking the 'delta approximation' (with the historic $R_i$ as inputs for the underlying) or more satisfactorily, by revaluing the options portfolio using the actual historic series for option prices, if these are available. It is also possible to calculate a measure of the precision of the portfolio-VaR estimate on the basis of the historic simulation method (e.g. using the historic kernel approach of Butler and Schachter 1996).

A drawback of the historic simulation method is that accurate percentile estimates of the VaR using this method (e.g. 1st percentile) require a long time series of data to be accurate. Since tail events are 'unusual', we need quite a lot of data to reliably estimate the tail. For example, if we are interested in the 1% lower tail, then in our historic data set, this will only occur 1 in every 100 observations. On the other hand, the longer is our historic data set, the more the 'old' data rather than the more recent data, will influence our forecast of tomorrow's VaR. Butler and Schachter (1996) indicate the possibility of quite large standard errors on VaRs based on the historic simulation method (e.g. between 6% and over 20%). There is also a certain lack of flexibility. For example, one cannot easily answer the question as to how the estimated VaR changes if volatility of one of the assets increases by 10% more than that observed in the 'historic' data window. However, the non-parametric approach (e.g. using a 1000-day data window) has been found for some cases to be more accurate than parametric approaches (e.g. EWMA with the VCV method). For example, Mohoney (1996), using a portfolio of equities and FX, finds that forecasts (one day ahead) using non-parametric estimates yield out-turn values for portfolio-VaR that are very close to the 1% and even the 0.1% tail probabilities. (In contrast, the parametric EWMA and GARCH models tend to understate the number of forecasts falling in the 'extreme tails' below the 5% level.)

An obvious key defect of the historic simulation approach is the complete dependence of the results on the *particular* data set used. The data set used may contain 'unusual events' that are not thought to be likely to happen again in the immediate future (e.g. Sterling leaving the ERM in 1992, the Asian crisis of 1997/1998, the events of 9/11 in the United States). If so, the historic simulation estimate of VaR in the forecast period may be biased. Indeed, if we use, say, a 1000-day historic moving data window, these 'unusual events' will remain in the VaR forecast for 1000 days. To mitigate this problem, we could arbitrarily choose to use declining weights on returns further in the past when calculating the historic simulation VaR for the portfolio. Of course, such problems, to a greater or lesser extent, plague almost any method that relies on past data to forecast the future, including the usual 'variance–covariance' VaR method (and also to a large extent in the Monte Carlo method described below). As we shall see, stress testing can, in principle, explicitly limit any direct dependence on past events/data (since the 'scenario' is chosen by the investigator). However, even here, past events usually provide a guide as to which 'scenarios' to investigate.

A variant of the 'pure' historic simulation approach is the *bootstrapping technique*. As described above, the historical simulation approach consists of 'one draw' from the historic data set, in which the 1000 daily observations are sampled only once to obtain the portfolio-VaR. The drawings are, therefore, without replacement and taken in chronological order, day-1, day-2, and so on (thereby retaining any serial correlation properties of the actual returns data). In the bootstrap approach, the $T = 1000$ returns (on the $n$ assets) are drawn with equal probability in *random order* and replaced.

We can think of each batch of $n$-asset returns for a *specific day* as being written on a single sheet of paper corresponding to the $n$-vector $R$. Each day of historic data provides $n$ different numbers on separate sheets, each page being numbered from 1 to 1000, corresponding to the 1000 days of historic data. We then draw $m$-numbers ($m > n$) randomly from a uniform distribution of 1000 numbers, *with replacement*. For example, suppose the $m$-uniform random numbers drawn (rounded up to whole numbers) are $\{27, 700, 1, 990, 700, 43, 1 \ldots 999\}$. Then we turn to pages $27, 700, 1, 990, 700 \ldots 999$ and write down the $n$-asset returns $R^k$, for pages $k = 27, 700, 1, 990, 700, 43 \ldots 999$, that appear on each of these pages. This would give a total of $m$ vectors, each containing $n$ asset returns. We then revalue the portfolio using equation (27) for each of these $m$ days and complete the histogram and calculate the 1st percentile VaR. Hence, we can 'reproduce' our 1000 returns on the $n$ assets as many times as we like (in our case, a total of $m > n$ times). This mitigates the 'lack of data' problem of the historic simulation method and hence, in principle, we can estimate the portfolio-VaR more accurately (although in practice this may not always be the case – see Butler and Schachter 1996).

If we thought that only the last 100 days of data is representative of what might happen tomorrow, it would be very dangerous to take the *single* most negative value of $\$\Delta V_p$ as the forecast of the VaR for tomorrow, at the first percentile. However, we could bootstrap $m$ times from this 100 days of data (with replacement) and obtain a more representative estimate of the 1% tail value.

The bootstrapping technique has similar advantages to the historical simulation approach but still has the key defect that the original $T = 100$ historic observations (say) still need to be 'representative' of what might happen tomorrow. Also, the 'larger simulated' set of data comes at a price. Since bootstrapping 'picks out' each set of daily returns at random (from the 100 historic 'days' of data), the simulated returns will 'lose' any of the serial correlation that happens to be in the historic returns (i.e. the bootstrap method implicitly assumes returns are independent over time). However, the latter can be solved by using a block-bootstrap whereby if day $x$ is chosen (at random), then the returns on days $x - j$ to $x + j$ are used to revalue the portfolio, for this 'draw' of the bootstrap.

As the regulators allow financial institutions to choose their own 'internal models', then the historic simulation approach may gain adherents, since although the raw data input requirements are greater than the parametric-VaR approach, the computational burden is somewhat smaller. However, the non-parametric approach is likely to be complementary, rather than a substitute, for the parametric-VaR approach, which does retain greater flexibility and ease of interpretation.

# 28.4 Monte Carlo Simulation

Monte Carlo simulation (MCS) is a very flexible parametric method that allows one to generate the whole distribution of portfolio returns and hence 'read off' the VaR at any desired percentile level. It is particularly useful for calculating the VaR for portfolios that contain assets with non-linear pay-offs, such as options. It is a parametric method because we assume a specific distribution for the underlying asset returns (e.g. returns on stocks, bonds, interest rates and spot-FX) and, therefore, the variances and correlations between these returns need to be estimated, before being used as inputs to the MCS. However, one need not assume that the distribution is multivariate normal (although this is often assumed in practice) and, for example, one could choose to generate the underlying asset returns from a fat-tailed distribution (e.g. Student's $t$-distribution) or one that has a skewed left tail (e.g. jump diffusion process). However, note that even if the underlying asset returns have a multivariate normal distribution, the distribution of the change in value of a portfolio of options will, in general, not be multivariate normal because of the non-linear relationship between the underlying asset return and the option premia (e.g. as with the Black–Scholes formula). Within the MCS framework applied to options, we can also choose whether to calculate the change in value of the portfolio of options by using the full valuation method (e.g. Black–Scholes), the 'delta' or 'delta + gamma' approximation or, indeed, other methods of calculating option premia (e.g. finite difference methods). Of course, measuring VaR using the linear or 'delta method' may not be accurate when options that are near the money are included in the portfolio, because in reality these have a non-linear pay-off.

Stress testing (see the following) and MCS have common elements. Indeed, stress testing is a bit like a 'one-off' or 'limited' MCS where the analyst decides on the path of the underlying assets rather than this being wholly dictated by (an average of) past data. Often, a stress test would consider 'extreme' values for the 'underlying assets' (e.g. very large falls in the exchange rate when holding a currency option) and then we would work out the change in the value of the portfolio of options for these 'new' extreme values for the underlying. Of course, at best, this provides only a small number of 'extreme' scenarios. In one sense, MCS improves on this by generating a whole sequence of possible values for the underlying asset returns, which are then used to calculate possible changes in a portfolio of options. In the following section, we begin by showing how to measure the VaR of a single option using MCS and then move on to consider the VaR for a portfolio that contains several options.

## Single Asset: Long Call

Suppose you hold a long call on a stock option with $S_0 = 100$, $K = 100$, $r = 0.05$, $\sigma = 0.6$ (60%) and with $T - t = 1$ year to maturity. The initial value of the call using Black–Scholes ($BS_0$) is 25.5. What is the VaR of this call over a 30-day horizon? Using MCS, we simulate the stock price over 30 days assuming it follows a geometric Brownian motion (GBM) with drift ($\mu = 0.05$) – see Appendix I.

After 30 days, if the simulated stock price is $S_{30}$, then the 'new' call premium is given by the Black–Scholes equation $V^{(1)} = BS(S_{30}, T - 30/365, \ldots)$, where we have assumed that the other inputs $r = 0.05$ and $\sigma = 0.6$ remain constant over the 30-day horizon. The change in value for this first 'run' of the MCS is $\Delta V^{(1)} = BS_{30} - BS_0$. We now repeat the above for, say, $m = 10{,}000$ runs and obtain $\Delta V^{(i)}$ for $i = 1, 2, 3, \ldots, 10{,}000$. Finally, we order the values of $\Delta V$ from lowest to highest (or plot them in a histogram – see Figure 3) and the 5% (1%) lower cut-off point gives the VaR, which here is 14.5 (17.9), that is, about 57% (70%) of the initial call premium $C_0 = 25.5$. Even though stock returns are assumed to be normally distributed, the histogram of the call premium is non-normal because of the curvature of the relationship between the call premium and the stock price (see Figure 3). We chose to value the option using a closed form solution, namely Black–Scholes (i.e. the full valuation method). We could instead have approximated the change in the option premium using either the linear 'delta approximation' or the 'delta–gamma' approximation. The choice depends on the degree of accuracy versus the tractability of a particular valuation approach. We discuss this further in the following section.

## Multiple Assets

Consider a two-asset portfolio consisting of $N_i$ assets with prices $V_i$. To make the algebra simple, assume we hold $N_1$ options on an underlying (stock) with price $P_1$ and

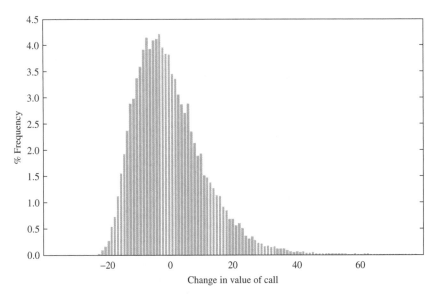

**Figure 3**   Market risk: VaR

$N_2$ options *on a different* stock, with price $P_2$. Both stocks are 'domestic'. If $N_i > 0$ ($< 0$), then the options are held long (short). Using MCS, what is the VaR over, say, a five-day horizon? The Monte Carlo methodology to calculate the five-day VaR at the 5th percentile involves the following steps.

The *initial value* of the portfolio is

$$\$V_0 = N_1 V_1 + N_2 V_2 \tag{30}$$

where $V_1$, $V_2$ are the initial prices of the options at $t = 0$. Let us assume we value the options using the full valuation method and the appropriate Black–Scholes formula. We can denote the initial option premia as $V_i = BS_0(P_i, K_i, T_i)$, where $K$ is the strike price, $T_i$ = time to maturity. We have suppressed the volatility of the option $\sigma$ and the domestic interest rate in this notation since we assume these remain unchanged over the five-day horizon.

Using *estimates* of daily volatility and correlation, we take random drawings from a (multivariate normal) distribution and generate a large number of paths (for illustrative purposes, we choose 1000) for the two stock *returns*, which have the same correlation structure as the historic data. This is the Monte Carlo simulation. If asset prices follow a GBM with zero drift, then the *one-day* return on asset-1 and asset-2 (continuously compounded) with measured daily standard deviations $\sigma_1$ and $\sigma_2$ respectively is

$$R_{1t} = \ln(P_{1t}/P_{1t-1}) = \sigma_1 z_1 \quad z_1 \sim niid(0, 1) \tag{31a}$$

$$R_{2t} = \ln(P_{2t}/P_{2t-1}) = \sigma_2 z_2 \quad z_2 \sim niid(0, 1) \tag{31b}$$

where $P_{it}$ are the underlying stock prices. The random variables $z_1$ and $z_2$ have mean zero, standard deviation of unity but with the correlation between $z_1$ and $z_2$ equal to $\rho$ (i.e. the one-day ahead forecast of the correlation coefficient between the two stock returns). The expected return on each asset is assumed to be zero (since $E(z_i) = 0, i = 1, 2$) and the variance of the return is $\sigma_i$ since $\sigma(z_i) = 1$. The random variables $z_i$ are assumed to be (multivariate) normally distributed, which implies returns are (conditionally) normally distributed. The return over a $t$ = five-day horizon is given by

$$R_{it+5} = \ln(P_{it+5}/P_{it}) = \sigma_i \sqrt{t} z_i \quad i = 1, 2 \tag{32}$$

Translate the ($1000 \times 2$) *returns* into ($1000 \times 2$), 'five-day ahead' *prices* for the two stocks using the above $\sqrt{T}$-rule:

$$P_{i,t+5} = P_{i,0} \exp(\sigma_i \sqrt{5} z_i) \tag{33}$$

Using the appropriate Black–Scholes formula, calculate the 10,000 'new' simulated *portfolio values* and change in portfolio values.

$$\$V_{t+5}^{(1+2)} = N_1 V_{1,t+5} + N_2 V_{2,t+5} \quad \text{and} \quad \$\Delta V_{t+5}^{(1+2)} = \$V_{t+5}^{(1+2)} - \$V_0^{(1+2)} \tag{34}$$

where $V_{i,t+5} = BS_i(P_{i,t+5}, T_i - 5/365)$. Plot a histogram of the 10,000 simulated values for the change in the \$-value of the portfolio $\Delta V_{t+5}^{(1+2)}$ and find the 5th percentile cut-off point of the distribution.

## Approximations: Delta and 'Delta + Gamma'

In the previous section, we used the full valuation method for the options. Alternatively, one can approximate the change in value using the option's delta $\Delta_i$ (evaluated at the initial stock price at $t = 0$). Let us compare the VaR over 30 days for our long call using the full valuation method (Black–Scholes) with the VaR given by the delta and 'delta + gamma' approximations. For the delta approximation,

$$\Delta V_{i,t+30} = \Delta_i (P_{i,t+30} - P_i) \tag{35}$$

where $P_{i,t+30}$ is the simulated value of the stock price at $t = 30$. Using $\Delta_i$ provides a (linear) first-order approximation to the change in the call premium. The second-order *approximation* incorporating the option's gamma is

$$\Delta V_{i,t+30} = \Delta_i (P_{i,t+30} - P_i) + 0.5\Gamma (P_{i,t+30} - P_i)^2 \tag{36}$$

This comparison is given in Table 2. At the 1% percentile, the full valuation method gives a VaR of 17.9 (a fall of 70%), the delta approximation gives 21.1 (a fall of 83%), which implies a substantial error, whereas the 'delta + gamma' method gives −17.8 (a fall of 69.9%), which is very close to that for the full valuation method.

In the above Monte Carlo simulation, we assume (conditional) normality of stock returns. But if these distributions in reality have fat tails (or are not symmetric), then the estimated VaR is likely to be an underestimate of the true VaR. We then need to repeat the MCS, sampling from return distributions that are more representative of the actual empirical data. When the option pay-off is 'complex' (e.g. path dependent) and a closed form solution is not available, we have to use an alternative valuation method within the MCS methodology (see Cuthbertson and Nitzsche 2001b).

Because of the limitations in the VaR calculations just discussed, they are often supplemented by stress testing. Stress testing estimates the sensitivity of a portfolio to 'extreme movements' in certain key returns. It, therefore, tells you how much you will lose in a particular state of the world but gives no indication of how likely it is that this state of the world will actually occur. Choice of 'extreme movements' may

**Table 2**   VaR delta and delta + gamma approximation

| Inputs | | | |
|---|---|---|---|
| Current stock price | $100 | Call premium ($t = 0$) | $25.5 |
| Volatility of stock | 60% p.a. | Strike price, $K$ | $100 |
| Mean return of stock | 5% p.a. | Interest rate, $r$ | 5% p.a. |
| | | VaR horizon | 30 days |
| **Value at Risk** | | | |
| **Percentile** | **Full Valuation** | **Delta Approximation** | **Delta and Gamma** |
| 1% | 17.9 (70.4%) | 21.1 (82.7%) | 17.8 (69.9%) |
| 5% | 14.5 (57.0%) | 15.7 (61.8%) | 13.9 (54.7%) |

Notes:
Figures for the VaR are in $s and in parentheses is the percentage loss in value (i.e. $VaR/initial value of call).

be based on those that occurred in particular crisis periods (e.g. 1987 stock market crash, the 1992 'crisis' when sterling left the ERM, the 1997–1998 Asian currency crisis, and the 2000–2003 stock market meltdown). The covariances and movement in asset prices are based on these crisis periods – when correlations tend to increase dramatically. The choice of inputs for the stress test(s) will depend on the financial institution's assessment of the likely source of the key sensitivities in the portfolio. Clearly, stress testing can only be done for relatively simple portfolios since otherwise the implicit correlations in the chosen scenario may be widely at variance with those in the historic data or even for any conceivable future event. Note another danger of stress testing, namely that a portfolio might actually benefit from 'extreme' movements yet be vulnerable to 'small' movements (e.g. long straddle).

In general, stress testing has some limitations. The same stress-testing scenario is unlikely to be informative for all institutions (portfolios). For example, a commodities dealer is unlikely to find a stress test of a rise in all interest rates of 300 bp informative. One can also usefully turn the scenario approach 'on its head' and ask, 'Given my portfolio, what set of *plausible* scenarios (for interest rates, exchange rates, etc.) will yield the worst outcome?' Stress testing is, therefore, a useful complement to the usual VaR calculations but both require considerable judgement in their practical implementation.

# 28.5    Alternative Methods

Put somewhat simplistically, VaR is an attempt to encapsulate the market risk of a portfolio of assets in a single figure with a given probability. This 'single figure' can be calculated in a number of ways, depending on the modelling process chosen. For example, in the so-called parametric approach, one often assumes normally distributed returns, specific forecasts of volatilities and correlations and we also allow for certain diversification effects. When the portfolio contains options, then the 'parametric' Monte Carlo simulation method is often used. Clearly, these approaches are subject to 'model error' since the estimated variances and covariances may be incorrect. In contrast, in the 'non-parametric' historic simulation method, we 'observe' how the portfolio's value would have changed, given the actual historic data on returns. This often results in a single VaR figure being reported, although the method can easily give the whole distribution of portfolio returns. The method requires a substantial amount of data, and the results can sometimes be highly dependent on the sample of historic data chosen.

Let us examine some of the problems of the above approaches, which are based in some way on 'averaging' over a sample of recent data. For example, a portfolio with market value $V_0 = \$606$ m and $\sigma = 1\%$ (per day) has a VaR of $10 m over one day at the 5th percentile ($= V_0 1.65\sigma$). This indicates that for 19 days out of 20, losses are not expected to exceed $10 m, while losses could exceed $10 m in about one day out of every 20. However, the VaR figure gives no indication of what the *actual losses* on this one day will be. If returns are (conditionally) normal, then the cut-off point for the 0.5% left tail is $3.2\sigma$, giving a VaR of $19.4 m. So we can be 'pretty sure' losses will not exceed $20 m. But even then, we cannot be absolutely sure of the *actual* dollar loss because

- even with the normal distribution, there is a small probability of a very large loss.

- actual returns have fatter tails than those of the normal distribution, so larger, more frequent dollar losses (on average) will occur (relative to those calculated assuming normality).

- correlations and volatilities can change very sharply. For example, in the first quarter of 1993, the daily correlation between returns on the Nikkei-225 and the FTSE-100 varied from $+0.9$ to $-0.9$ (Jackson, Maude and Perraudin 1997), and the daily volatility on the Nikkei-225 in the first quarter of 1995 varied between 0.7 and 1.8%.

## Worse Case Scenario

One way of handling (or at least mitigating) the aforementioned 'size of loss problem' is to use worse case scenario (WCS) analysis. Here, we do not simply calculate the VaR at the 5th percentile cut-off point. Instead, we examine *only* the lower tail outcomes and use these to calculate the worst case that we *expect* to occur in the tail (Boudoukh, Richardson and Whitelaw 1995). The method, therefore, attempts to answer the question 'What is the average *size* of the maximum loss over the next H-trading days, given that we end up in the tail?', whereas VaR concentrates on the *frequency* of a particular loss (e.g. a 1% VaR of $1 m implies in only 1 out of every 100 days will losses exceed $1 m). WCS is based on Monte Carlo simulation and gives a higher figure for 'risk' than does VaR since it is based on the distribution of extreme returns in the lower tail.

For example, Boudoukh, Richardson and Whitelaw (1995) report a 1% VaR of $-2.33\%$ (standard deviations) but an average WCS loss of $-2.51\%$ and with a 1% tail value for these 'worse case' outcomes of $-3.72\%$. The key problems in using WCS analysis are the increased computational costs of the Monte Carlo simulations and the assumption (in a multi-asset portfolio) that correlations estimated from historic data are applicable to extreme movements in returns, as represented in the tail.

## Extreme Value Theory

Yet another method that concentrates on the tails of the distribution is the extreme value (EV) approach. This method is used in the natural sciences for estimating maximum extreme losses with a specific degree of confidence (e.g. for the failure of a dam or nuclear power plant). In a very broad sense, the EV approach is a mixture of the historical simulation approach together with estimation of the shape of the tail of the distribution. Unlike the historic simulation approach, it uses data only from the lower tail. It uses this data to estimate the shape of the tail, without imposing any specific assumptions concerning the (rest of the) distribution. Danielsson and deVries (1997) report that for percentiles below 5%, the VCV–VaR approach tends to underpredict the occurrence of tail events, the historical simulation approach tends to overpredict, while the EV approach performs well. Hence, the EV approach appears to be more accurate the 'smaller' is the tail probability one is interested in.

All of the methods discussed (e.g. the variance–covariance parametric approach, historic simulation approach, stress tests, Monte Carlo simulation, EV theory) generally assume the portfolio is held fixed over the holding period considered. This limitation becomes more unrealistic the longer the time horizon over which VaR is calculated. For example, while one may not be able to liquidate a position within a day (particularly in crisis periods), this is not necessarily true over periods longer than, say, 10 days. Another crucial dimension that is missing in all the approaches is the 'bounce-back period'. On a mark-to-market basis, estimated cumulative 10-day losses might be large, but if markets fully recover over the next 20 days, the cumulative actual losses over 30 days could be near zero. It may, therefore, be worthwhile to examine the VaR without using the $\sqrt{T}$ scaling factor, but instead trying to get an explicit estimate of volatilities over longer horizons (e.g. where returns might exhibit more mean reversion). However, it requires a substantial amount of data to estimate, say, monthly return volatility directly.

All in all, the statistical methods and the real time computational aspects used to calculate VaR are impressive. However, it should by now be obvious that even when measuring market risk (i.e. excluding credit risk, operational risk, etc.), a large element of judgement is required for any of the chosen methodologies.

## 28.6 Summary

- If we assume returns are (multivariate) normally distributed and that portfolio value is linearly related to asset returns, then the VaR (at any chosen percentile) is easily calculated using the delta–normal or variance–covariance (VCV) method.

- If returns are independently (and identically) distributed, then we can use the $\sqrt{T}$-rule for scaling up volatility forecasts over different horizons (i.e. $\sigma_T = \sqrt{T}\sigma$, where $\sigma$ is the one-day forecast of volatility).

- Mapping ameliorates the 'large data storage and measurement' problem and allows the VCV method to be used with some non-linear instruments (e.g. bonds). The single index model (SIM) is used to simplify calculations of VaR for equities held in a particular country. The VCV method can be usefully applied to stocks, bonds, FX, swaps and futures.

- The VaR for portfolios containing 'plain vanilla' European options can be accurately measured using Monte Carlo simulation (MCS), and this is usually supplemented by stress testing.

- The historical simulation method is pretty accurate in predicting even the lower tail cut-off points (e.g. between the 1st and 5th percentiles) but it requires a substantial time series of data and is a little inflexible (e.g. difficult to do sensitivity analysis), compared to the standard parametric variance–covariance method.

- Examination of the tails of the distributions as in WCS analysis and the EV approach probably does not yield a great deal of 'value added' to compensate for their increased complexity.

- Some form of stress testing provides a complementary view of market risk to that provided by the parametric and non-parametric VaR approaches. But all methods require considerable judgement when trying to ascertain the 'true' market risk.

# Appendix I: Monte Carlo Analysis and VaR

Call and put premia are non-linear functions of the underlying asset price. Monte Carlo simulation can be used to obtain the VaR for a portfolio that contains options (as well as other assets). If we want to assess the $-value of a portfolio consisting of two or more assets, we must take into account the correlation between the *returns* on each asset. We assume the (continuously compounded) returns on the underlying assets (i.e. the change in prices) are multivariate normal and, therefore, the price levels are multivariate lognormal. We will demonstrate the technique using a two-asset case, but this can easily be generalised to the $n$-asset case and programmed into the appropriate statistical software.

We assume asset returns $R_i$ are multivariate normal, that is, $R \sim N(0, \Sigma)$. Assume we have estimates/forecasts of the variance–covariance matrix of returns from which we can construct the correlation matrix, $C$. For the $(2 \times 2)$ case, we have

$$\Sigma = \begin{bmatrix} \sigma_{11} & \sigma_{12} \\ \sigma_{21} & \sigma_{22} \end{bmatrix} \tag{A1}$$

and

$$C = \begin{bmatrix} 1 & \rho \\ \rho & 1 \end{bmatrix} \tag{A2}$$

where $\sigma_{12} = \sigma_{21}$ and the correlation coefficient $\rho = \sigma_{12}/\sigma_1\sigma_2$. A simple piece of matrix algebra allows us to map the $C$-matrix into two $(2 \times 2)$ matrices 'A', such that

$$\mathbf{C} = \mathbf{AA'} \tag{A3}$$

and '$\mathbf{A}$' is the lower triangular matrix:

$$A = \begin{bmatrix} 1 & 0 \\ \rho & \sqrt{1 - \rho^2} \end{bmatrix} \tag{A4}$$

The A-matrix is the Choleski factorisation of $\mathbf{C}$. It is easy to check that $\mathbf{C} = \mathbf{AA'}$. The reason for the Choleski factorisation is that if $\boldsymbol{\varepsilon}(2 \times 1)$ consists of two *independent* $N(0, 1)$ variables (i.e. mean zero, unit variance and zero covariance, $\boldsymbol{\varepsilon} \sim N(0, \mathbf{I})$), then we can generate a set of standard normal variables $\mathbf{Z}$:

$$\mathbf{Z} = \mathbf{A}\boldsymbol{\varepsilon} \tag{A5}$$

The constructed variables in $\mathbf{Z}$ will then have zero mean, unit variance but have a correlation of $\rho$. Thus, $\mathbf{Z}$ has a correlation structure the same as that given by the correlation matrix $\mathbf{C}$. Once we have generated the $z_i$, we can derive our two-asset returns and prices levels over a $t$-period horizon using

$$P_t^{(i)} = P_0^{(i)} \exp(\sigma_i \sqrt{t} z_i) \tag{A6a}$$

$$R_{i,t} = \ln(P_t^{(i)}/P_0^{(i)}) \tag{A6b}$$

It is now easy to show that the asset returns (equation (A6b)) over the horizon from $t = 0$ to $t$ have standard deviations of $\sigma_i \sqrt{t}$ and a correlation coefficient of $\rho$. To see this, note that from equation (A4) and equation (A5), we have

$$z_1 = \varepsilon_1 \quad \text{and} \tag{A7a}$$

$$z_2 = \rho \varepsilon_1 + \sqrt{1 - \rho^2} \, \varepsilon_2 \tag{A7b}$$

The variables $z_1$ and $z_2$ have $\varepsilon_1$ in common. This is the source of the correlation between $z_1$ and $z_2$ and, hence, between the two-asset returns. From equations (A6a) and (A6b),

$$R_{1t} = \sigma_1 \sqrt{T} z_1 \tag{A8a}$$

and

$$R_{2t} = \sigma_2 \sqrt{T} z_2 \tag{A8b}$$

To see that the simulated returns will have zero mean and correlation $\rho$, note that $Ez_1 = Ez_2 = 0$, since $E(\varepsilon_1) = E(\varepsilon_2) = 0$. Hence,

$$\text{var}(z_1) = \text{var}(\varepsilon_1) = 1 \tag{A9a}$$

$$\text{var}(z_2) = \rho^2 \, \text{var}(\varepsilon_2) + (1 - \rho^2) \, \text{var}(\varepsilon_2) = 1 \tag{A9b}$$

$$\text{cov}(z_1, z_2) = E(z_1 z_2) = \rho E(\varepsilon_1^2) + \sqrt{1 - \rho^2} E(\varepsilon_1 \varepsilon_2) = \rho \tag{A9c}$$

Since $\text{cov}(\varepsilon_1, \varepsilon_2) = 0$, the variance of returns *over a T-day horizon* are $\text{var}(R_i) = \sigma_i^2 T \, \text{var}(z_i) = \sigma_i^2 T$. The correlation between *returns* (over a $T$-day horizon) using equations (A8a) and (A8b) is the same as the one-day correlation coefficient

$$\rho_T = \text{cov}(R_{1,t}, R_{2,t})/\sigma_1 \sqrt{T} \sigma_2 \sqrt{T} = \rho \tag{A9d}$$

One final nuance is worth mentioning. Above, we used the MCS to generate the *one-period* return and then used the $\sqrt{T}$-rule to calculate the price at $t + 5$. Alternatively, we can generate $P_{t+5}$ using either of the following recursions (which are discrete approximations to a GBM).

$$P_t = [1 + \mu \Delta t + \sigma \varepsilon_t \sqrt{\Delta t}] P_{t-1} \tag{A10a}$$

and

$$P_t = P_{t-1} \exp[(\mu - \sigma^2/2)\Delta t + \sigma \varepsilon_t \sqrt{\Delta t}] \tag{A10b}$$

We usually take $\sigma$ to be the annual standard deviation, $\mu$ is the annual mean return and $\Delta t$ is the time step (denoted as a fraction of a year (e.g. 1 day = 1/365)). In our simplified example above, we used the second equation with $\sigma = 1$-*day* volatility, $\Delta t = 1$ *day* and $\mu = 0$. The first equation, 'the multiplicative form', has a random term that is $N(0, 1)$ and only produces an approximation to a *lognormal* distribution for $P$, whereas the second equation gives an exact lognormal for *any* size of step $\Delta t$.

In fact, if we are only interested in the value of $P$ at a specific time $T$, we can obtain $P_T$ in 'one-step' using

$$P_T = P_0 \exp[(\mu - \sigma^2/2)T + \sigma \varepsilon_t \sqrt{T}] \qquad \text{(A11)}$$

## Practical Issues

Most statistic software produces *uniform* pseudo-random numbers, that is, numbers that lie between 0 and 1 that occur with *equal* probability. These can then be 'transformed' into standard normal variables in a variety of ways. For example, if $\varepsilon_i$ is a uniform random number, then $Z_i = \sum_{i=1}^{12} \varepsilon_i - 6$ will give a standard normal variable. The latter method, however, gives too many values close to the mean, but this problem can be mitigated by other 'transformations' (e.g. Box–Muller transformation).

Two key 'numerical' problems in our MCS are either, the simulated 'pseudo'-random numbers are not in fact random or, the Choleski decomposition fails numerically. Random number generators actually use a deterministic algorithm. They take a particular 'seed number' as a starting point and generate numbers that appear random (and pass tests for independence, etc.). For a given 'seed number', the set of random numbers will be repeated. The problem is that as you increase the number of 'runs', the random number generator may 'choose' a seed it has already used. This leads to repetitions or cycles in your 'random' numbers and a spurious increase in accuracy of your Monte Carlo results. Another problem is that standard MCS tends to produce numbers that 'cluster', so additional observations do not provide new information and for a 'small' number of runs, this tends to bias the results. However, so-called quasi-Monte Carlo (QMC) techniques or low discrepancy sequences are designed to appear random but avoid producing 'clusters', so the MCS becomes much more efficient and can produce accurate results with substantially fewer 'runs'. The idea is that the 'quasi-random' sample 'remembers' the previous sample and tries to position itself away from any previous samples, thus 'filling' the sample space without any clustering. There are many ways to generate quasi-random samples, and the reader is referred to the excellent book by Clewlow and Strickland (1998).

The second problem is that in order to undertake the Choleski decomposition, the estimated variance–covariance matrix $\Sigma$ must be positive semi-definite. This requires that the number of observations is greater than the dimension of the covariance matrix $\Sigma$ and there is no perfect collinearity amongst the returns. If $\Sigma$ is large, then near perfect collinearity is a strong possibility and this is why we try to reduce the number of returns by some form of 'mapping'.

# Appendix II: Single Index Model (SIM)

We wish to show how the variance of a portfolio using the SIM is

$$\sigma_p = \left[ \sum_{i=1}^{n} \omega_i \beta_i \right] \sigma_m = \beta_p \sigma_m \qquad \text{(A1)}$$

where $\sigma_p$ = portfolio standard deviation, $\sigma_m$ = standard deviation of the market port-folio and $\beta_p = \sum_i w_i \beta_i$ is the 'beta' of the portfolio. The SIM is represented by equation (A2) together with the additional assumptions in (A3):

$$R_i = \alpha_i + \beta_i R_m + \varepsilon_i \tag{A2}$$

$$E(\varepsilon_i) = 0 \tag{A3a}$$

$$E(\varepsilon_i \varepsilon_j) = \sigma_{\varepsilon i}^2 \{= 0\} \quad \text{for } i = j \{i \neq j\} \tag{A3b}$$

$$\text{cov}(R_m, \varepsilon_i) = 0 \tag{A3c}$$

Hence, it follows that

$$ER_i = \alpha_i + \beta_i ER_m \tag{A4a}$$

$$\sigma_i^2 = \beta_i^2 \sigma_m^2 + \sigma_{\varepsilon i}^2 \tag{A4b}$$

$$\sigma_{ij} = \beta_i \beta_j \sigma_m^2 \quad (i \neq j) \tag{A4c}$$

The portfolio expected return and standard deviation (variance) are defined as:

$$ER_p = \sum_i w_i ER_i \tag{A5a}$$

$$\sigma_p^2 = \sum_{\substack{i=1 \\ i \neq j}}^{n} \sum_{j=1}^{n} \omega_i \omega_j \sigma_{ij} \tag{A5b}$$

The above formula for portfolio variance requires $n$-variances and $n(n-1)/2$ covari-ances. For $n = 150$, this amounts to 11,325 'inputs'. To calculate $ER_i$, we also require an additional $n = 150$ values of $\alpha_i$, making a grand total of 11,475 inputs. To reduce the number of inputs required, we utilise the SIM. Substituting from equation (A4a) in (A5a), we get

$$ER_p = \sum_i (w_i \alpha_i + w_i \beta_i ER_m) = \alpha_p + \beta_p ER_m \tag{A6}$$

where $\alpha_p = \sum_i w_i \alpha_i$ and $\beta_p = \sum_i w_i \beta_i$. Substituting for $\sigma_i^2$ and $\sigma_{ij}$ from equation (A4) in (A5b) gives

$$\sigma_p^2 = \left[ \sum_{i,j}^{n} \omega_i \omega_j \beta_i \beta_j \right] \sigma_m^2 + \sum_{i=1}^{n} \omega_i^2 \sigma_{\varepsilon i}^2 = (\Sigma \omega_i \beta_i)(\Sigma \omega_j \beta_j) \sigma_m^2 + \Sigma \omega_i^2 \sigma_{\varepsilon i}^2 \tag{A7}$$

$$\sigma_p^2 = \beta_p^2 \sigma_m^2 + \Sigma \omega_i^2 \sigma_{\varepsilon i}^2 \tag{A8}$$

Equation (A8) may be interpreted as

**Total portfolio risk = market risk + specific risk** (A9)

Calculation of $ER_p$ and $\sigma_p^2$ under the SIM requires $3n$ estimates of $\alpha_i$, $\beta_i$, $\sigma_{\varepsilon i}$ plus estimates of $\sigma_m^2$ and $ER_m$, a total of $3n + 2$ inputs (which for $n = 150$ assets $= 452$ inputs). This is a considerable saving on the general model equations (A5a) and (A5b).

Specific risk is simply the (weighted) residual sum of squares from the regression (A2). If we do not have a diversified portfolio, then the final term in (A8) is non-zero and must be included to calculate $\sigma_p^2$. However, assume for the moment that $\omega_i = 1/n$ for all stocks in the portfolio, then

$$\sigma_p^2 = \beta_p^2 \sigma_m^2 + n^{-1}(\Sigma \sigma_{\varepsilon i}^2 / n) \tag{A10}$$

The final term in brackets is the *average* specific risk $\overline{\sigma}_{\varepsilon i}$. Hence, the last term is $(1/n)\overline{\sigma}_{\varepsilon i}$ and as $n \to \infty$ this term goes to zero ($n = 25$ randomly selected shares is enough to ensure this last term is small). Hence, in a well-diversified portfolio,

$$\sigma_p = \left[ \sum_{i=1}^{n} \omega_i \beta_i \right] \sigma_m = \beta_p \sigma_m \tag{A11}$$

If $V_i$ is the position in asset $i$, then the portfolio value is $V_p = \Sigma_{i=1}^{n} V_i$ and $w_i = V_i / V_p$. The VaR for the portfolio can be expressed in two equivalent ways:

$$VaR_p = V_p(1.65)\sigma_p = \sum_i V_i(1.65\beta_i)\sigma_m = \sum_{i=1}^{n} VaR_i \tag{A12}$$

where $VaR_i \equiv V_i \beta_i (1.65\sigma_m)$. Or, equivalently,

$$VaR_p = \sum_{i=1}^{n} VaR_i = (\mathbf{ZCZ'})^{1/2} \tag{A13}$$

where $\mathbf{Z} = [VaR_1, VaR_2, \dots, VaR_n]$ and $\mathbf{C}$ is the *unit* matrix. *RiskMetrics*[TM] provides estimates of $\sigma_m$, and the user provides values of $V_i$ and estimates of the betas. A crucial assumption in the SIM is $E(\varepsilon_i \varepsilon_j) = 0$ that is the covariance of shocks to company $i$ (or industry $i$) and company $j$ are contemporaneously uncorrelated. However, for small positive correlations of $\varepsilon_i$ and $\varepsilon_j$ as found in practice in daily returns, specific risk still falls quite rapidly as $n$ increases.

Somewhat as a side issue, it is worth noting that *under the assumptions of the SIM*, the correlations between stocks can be calculated from estimates of betas (and variances).

$$\rho_{ij} = \frac{\sigma_{ij}}{\sigma_i \sigma_j} = \frac{\beta_i \beta_j \sigma_m^2}{\sigma_i \sigma_j} \tag{A14}$$

where $\sigma_i$ and $\sigma_j$ are given by (A4b). Note that if the SIM fitted perfectly so that $\sigma_{\varepsilon i} = 0$, then $\rho = 1$ because each asset return is uniquely determined by $R_m$. However, in *RiskMetrics*[TM], the correlation coefficients $\rho_{ij}$ are calculated directly because *RiskMetrics*[TM] seeks to provide a *common* method of forecasting correlations for stocks, bonds, FOREX, and so on, and the SIM may not be applicable for all asset classes. Note that the so-called *market model* relaxes the assumption of the SIM that $\text{cov}(\varepsilon_i, \varepsilon_j) = E(\varepsilon_i \varepsilon_j) = 0$. But in doing so, our simplified expression for portfolio risk (A11) does not hold. Once $E(\varepsilon_i \varepsilon_j) \neq 0$, then *all* the covariances are required to calculate $\sigma_p$.

# 29

# VOLATILITY AND MARKET MICROSTRUCTURE

## Aims

- Measure asset return volatility and examine the economic variables that might influence it.

- Ascertain the importance of time-varying risk premia, as modelled by ARCH and GARCH processes, in determining expected asset returns – for stock, bond and spot-FX returns.

- Examine the structure of the FX market, which might influence bid-ask spreads and spot exchange rates.

- Show how survey data can be used to assess the rational expectations hypothesis and the influence of different types of trader on price changes.

- Assess the ability of technical trading rules to earn 'abnormal profits' based on trades using high frequency data.

As we have noted in previous chapters, ARCH and GARCH processes can be used to model asset returns that depend on *time-varying* variances and covariances (e.g. standard-CAPM, SDF models). In this chapter, we summarise some of these approaches applied to stock, bond and FX returns. We show how persistence in the risk premium can, in principle, lead to large swings in stock *prices* – as observed in the data. Estimates of persistence in the risk premium may be sensitive to the inclusion of other economic variables in the prediction equation for expected stock returns, such as the dividend–price ratio, the risk-free interest rate and the volume of trading in the market. Hence, we examine the robustness of the relationship between expected returns, time-varying variances and covariances. We provide examples of how *multivariate* ARCH-GARCH are used in dynamic hedging using stock index futures, in measuring time-varying risk premia across different maturity bonds and in measuring covariances between stock and bond returns.

The rest of the chapter is devoted to market microstructure issues. Traditionally, this area has concerned itself with the influence of different types of trading structure on the behaviour of prices and returns over short horizons. Volatility is clearly part of the story here, but this area also examines the determinants of the bid-ask spread and whether 'trading variables' (e.g. order flow, size of trades) influence prices. We also include a discussion of survey data under this heading since how agents forecast future prices has a direct bearing on the assumption of rational expectations and the possibility of destabilising speculation. Finally, technical trading rules (e.g. chartists, filter rules, genetic algorithms) are usually applied to high frequency data and, therefore, we examine whether these earn 'abnormal profits' over a run of bets.

# 29.1 Volatility

Let us remind ourselves of the 'stylised facts' concerning return volatility over horizons of up to one month (i.e. intraday, daily, weekly and monthly returns). Return volatility for stocks and spot FX appear to go through periods where changes (in either direction) are large and other periods when changes are small. Also, when changes in returns are small (large), they tend to remain small (large) for some time. There are also 'outliers', that is, particularly large positive or negative returns, which occur more frequently than would be the case if returns were normally distributed. Hence, the volatility of stock returns over short horizons (e.g. up to 1 month) has the following properties.

(i) Volatility is time varying (i.e. periods of tranquillity and turbulence).

(ii) There is volatility clustering: large (small) changes in returns tend to be followed by large (small) changes of either sign, for some considerable time – volatility is autoregressive and persistent.

(iii) The unconditional distribution of returns has 'fat tails'.

(iv) The (conditional) correlation between returns on different assets appears to vary over time.

We require models to 'explain' these stylised facts, since time-varying variances and covariances are crucial in implementing portfolio allocation and in measuring 'riskiness' (e.g. Value at Risk).

Measurement of volatility is not straightforward. A measure of the markets' view of volatility can be 'extracted' from the Black–Scholes equation (or other closed form solutions) for options prices. The observed option's price is $P_t = f(S_t, \sigma_t, r_t, T - t, K)$, where $f$ is a non-linear function. All variables except $\sigma_t$ are known at $t$, so we can 'back-out' the markets forecast of volatility (known as implied volatility), over the life of the option. A time series for implied volatility can be obtained for any underlying asset on which there are traded options in liquid markets for which there is a closed form solution (e.g. stock options, stock index options, futures options). Usually, implied volatilities are used as a benchmark to compare against statistical measures of volatility, which is the subject of this chapter.

One measure of volatility, the *range estimator* is defined as

$$h_t = \ln(high_t/low_t) \tag{1}$$

where 'high' and 'low' are the observed prices over the interval considered (e.g. over one trading day). If there is autocorrelation in volatility, the following equation can be estimated.

$$h_t = \alpha_0 + \sum_{j=1}^{p} \alpha_j h_{t-j} + \varepsilon_t \tag{2}$$

Alternatively, the squared (daily) return $h_t = (R_t - \mu)^2$ could be used as an estimate of volatility, where for monthly frequency or less, a reasonable approximation is to set $\mu = 0$. Clearly, $h_t$ in (1) uses only two data points within the day. As an alternative, one might choose to measure (daily) volatility as the sample average of squared *hourly* returns.

Another simple but popular measure of the volatility in stock returns is to use *exponentially weighted moving average*, EWMA. Here, volatility is time varying and can be forecast using a moving window of past data. For example, when forecasting daily volatility, the EWMA model is widely used in Value at Risk calculations:

$$h_{t+1} = \lambda h_t + (1 - \lambda)R_t^2 \tag{3}$$

The coefficient $\lambda$ can be estimated or a value of $\lambda$ chosen to minimise outside-sample forecast errors across a range of asset returns (e.g. as in *RiskMetrics*™ who choose $\lambda = 0.94$ for daily data). By backward recursion, (3) implies that the forecast of volatility is a long weighted average of past squared returns – so volatility is persistent.

## Arch-GARCH

The simplest GARCH model is

$$R_{t+1} = \mu + \varepsilon_{t+1} \tag{4a}$$

$$h_{t+1} = \alpha_0 + \alpha_1 h_t + \alpha_2 \varepsilon_t^2 \tag{4b}$$

$$h_{t+1} \equiv E_t(R_{t+1} - E_t R_{t+1})^2 = E(\varepsilon_{t+1}^2 | \Omega_t) \tag{4c}$$

$h_{t+1}$ is the conditional variance of returns $R_{t+1}$ and equals $E(\varepsilon_{t+1}^2 | \Omega_t)$, where $\Omega_t$ is information at time $t$. The GARCH(1,1) model (4b) assumes that the conditional variance is autoregressive – this gives rise to volatility clustering. The unconditional variance is constant and is given by

$$var(\varepsilon_{t+1}) = \alpha_0/[1 - (\alpha_1 + \alpha_2)] \quad \text{for } (\alpha_1 + \alpha_2) < 1 \tag{5}$$

For $(\alpha_1 + \alpha_2) = 1$, the unconditional variance is undefined, and this model is known as *integrated* or IGARCH(1,1). Note that the EWMA model is IGARCH if $\mu = 0$. An equivalent representation of the error term in (4a) is $\varepsilon_{t+1} = \sqrt{h_{t+1}}u_{t+1}$, where $u_{t+1}$ is *iid* with a zero mean and unit variance. The 'standardised' residuals $\hat{v}_t = (\hat{\varepsilon}_{t+1}/\sqrt{\hat{h}_{t+1}})$ should be random and can be tested for normality (e.g. Bera-Jarque test). In practice, when using stock returns, it is usually found that $\hat{v}_t$ still exhibits some leptokurtosis (i.e. fat tails) but less so than the $\varepsilon_t$. Estimation of GARCH($p, q$) models by maximum likelihood is now relatively standard and available in many econometric software packages (e.g. TSP, EVIEWS, PCGIVE, MFIT, RATS, GAUSS-FanPac).

## 29.2   What Influences Volatility?

Schwert (1989) looks at possible sources for time-varying volatility. He examined how far the conditional volatility in *stock* returns depends on its own past volatility and also on the volatility in other economic variables (fundamentals) such as bond volatility and the volatility in real output. If perceptions of risk are persistent, then an increase in risk today will increase perceptions of risk in many future periods. Stock prices depend on the risk premium via the rational valuation formula, RVF. Hence, if risk is persistent, a small increase in perceived risk might cause a large fall in current stock prices.

Schwert (1989) examines *conditional* volatilities, namely, the volatility in stock returns, conditional on having obtained the best forecast for stock returns. If the best forecast for stock returns is denoted $E(R_{t+1}|\Omega_t)$, then $\varepsilon_{t+1} = (R_{t+1} - E_t R_{t+1})$ is the conditional forecast error. Since $E_t \varepsilon_{t+1} = 0$, the conditional variance of the forecast error of returns is $\mathrm{var}(\varepsilon_{t+1}|\Omega_t) \equiv E_t (R_{t+1} - E_t R_{t+1})^2$. Schwert uses a simple measure of conditional volatility. He assumes the best forecast of *monthly* stock returns $R_{t+1}$ is provided by an AR model (we exclude monthly dummies):

$$R_{t+1} = \alpha_0 + \sum_{j=0}^{m} \alpha_j R_{t-j} + \varepsilon_{t+1} \tag{6}$$

Schwert finds that the (absolute value) of the residuals $\hat{\varepsilon}_{t+1}$ from (6) exhibit serial correlation, which he also models as an AR process:

$$|\hat{\varepsilon}_{t+1}| = \sum_{j=1}^{s} \rho_j |\hat{\varepsilon}_{t-j+1}| + u_{t+1} \tag{7}$$

This is a (simple) form of autoregressive conditional heteroscedasticity ARCH, in the forecast errors. From the ARCH regression, we obtain estimates of the $\rho_j$. The *predictions* from (7), $\varepsilon_{t+1}^* = \sum_{j=1}^{s} \hat{\rho}_j |\hat{\varepsilon}_{t-j+1}|$, then provide a time-varying estimate of the *conditional* standard deviation of the forecast errors for stock returns. The above method is used by Schwert to obtain the conditional volatility of other economic time series. He uses equations (6) and (7) on monthly data for stock returns (an aggregate index), for bond returns, inflation, short-term interest rates, the growth in industrial production (output) and monetary growth.

The *sum* of the $\rho_j$ in (7) is a measure of *persistence* in volatility. For example, for $\rho = 0.95$, a unit shock at time $t$ (i.e. $u_t = 1$) has an impact on $\varepsilon_{t+12}$ of 0.54 after 12 months and an impact on $\varepsilon_{t+24}$ of 0.3 after 24 months. However, if $\rho = 0.5$, the impact of $u_t$ on $\varepsilon_{t+12}$ is nearly zero. A high value of $\rho$ therefore implies a 'long memory'. All the series examined by Schwert for the United States are found to exhibit persistence in volatility over the period 1859–1987 with the sum of the $\rho$ in the region of 0.8 to 0.85. Hence, in principle, the persistence in stock return volatility is mirrored by persistence in volatility for other fundamental variables.

Now consider the possible relationship between the conditional volatility of stock returns $\hat{\varepsilon}_{t+1}$ and the conditional volatility of the economic fundamentals, $\varepsilon_{it}$ where $i = $ conditional volatility of output, bond rates, inflation, and so on. Schwert runs a regression of stock return volatility $|\hat{\varepsilon}_t|$ on its own lagged values and also on lagged values of the $|\varepsilon_{it}|$ for the fundamental variables. Any 'reverse influence', that is, from stock volatility to the volatility in fundamentals such as output, can be obtained from an equation with output volatility as the dependent variable. In fact, Schwert generally estimates the stock return volatility equation together with the 'reverse regressions' in a vector autoregressive VAR system.

Schwert's results are mixed. He finds little evidence that volatility in economic fundamentals (e.g. output, inflation) has a discernible influence on stock return volatility (and the impact is not stable over time). However, there is a statistically significant effect from interest rate and corporate bond rate volatility on stock volatility. Also, some other 'non-volatility' economic variables do influence the monthly conditional stock return volatility. These include the debt-equity ratio (leverage), which has a positive impact, as does trading activity in the month. The latter is measured by the growth rate in the number of trades or buy/sell orders and the number of trading days in the month. Stock volatility is also shown to be higher during recessions than in economic booms. Examination of the results from the 'reverse regressions' reveals that there is some weak evidence that volatility in stock returns has incremental explanatory power for the volatility in output. In Schwert's study, much of the movement in stock return volatility is *not* explained by the economic variables examined – the R-squared values in the reported regressions are usually in the region of 0 to 0.3. Hence, much of the monthly conditional volatility in stock returns is due to 'news'.

## Returns and Volatility

If the perceived risk premium on an aggregate stock index is adequately measured by an ARCH model in conditional variance, then it follows that the future risk premium is, in part, predictable. Persistence in variance implies an increase in variance today will increase the perceived riskiness of stocks in all future periods and via the RVF, could lead to a large change in the level of stock prices. Poterba and Summers (P–S) (1988) is one of the first studies to investigate whether changes in investor's perceptions of risk are large enough to account for the very sharp movements in stock *prices* that are actually observed. If their model can explain the actual movements in stock prices, then as it is based on rational behaviour, stock prices cannot be *excessively* volatile.

P–S use a linearised approximation to the RVF, and they are able to show exactly how the stock price responds to a surprise increase in the perceived riskiness of stocks. The response depends crucially on the degree of persistence in conditional volatility. If the degree of persistence in volatility is 0.5, then P–S calculate that a 1% increase in volatility leads to only a 1.2% fall in stock prices. However, if the degree of persistence is 0.99, then the stock price would fall by over 38% for every 1% increase in volatility: a sizeable effect. Given that stock prices often do undergo sharp changes over a very short period of time, then for the P–S model to 'fit the facts', we need to find a high degree of persistence in volatility.

P–S treat all variables in the RVF in real terms, and $P_t$ is the real S&P index over the period 1928–1984. As P–S wish to focus on the impact of the risk premium on $P_t$, they assume real dividends grow at a constant rate $g$, and the real risk-free rate is constant. The intertemporal CAPM (Merton 1973, 1980) suggests that the risk premium on the market portfolio is proportional to the conditional variance of forecast errors on equity returns $h_{t+1} \equiv E_t \sigma_{t+1}^2$, hence

$$E_t R_{t+1} = r_t + \lambda h_{t+1} = r_t + rp_t \qquad (8)$$

where $\lambda$ is the market price of risk and $rp_t = \lambda h_{t+1}$. In Merton's intertemporal CAPM, $\lambda$ depends on a weighted average of different consumers' relative risk aversion parameters, which are assumed to be constant. P–S assume that conditional volatility can be represented by ARMA model(s), and here we assume an AR(1) process:

$$h_{t+1} = \alpha_0 + \alpha_1 h_t + v_{t+1} \qquad 0 > \alpha_1 > 1 \qquad (9)$$

where $v_{t+1}$ is a white noise error. The $v_{t+1}$ term provides the mechanism by which we may (randomly) switch from a period of high volatility to one of low volatility as $v_{t+1}$ moves from positive to negative. A large value for $\alpha_1$ implies a high degree of persistence in volatility. If $h_t$ follows an AR(1) process, then so will the risk premium: $rp_t = \lambda \alpha_0 + \lambda \alpha_1 rp_{t-1}$. To make the problem tractable, P–S linearise the RVF around the mean value of the risk premium $\overline{rp}$, which gives

$$\frac{\partial[\ln P_t]}{\partial[\ln(h_t)]} = \frac{\overline{rp}}{[1 + \overline{r} + \overline{rp} - \alpha_1(1 + g)]} \qquad (10)$$

Thus, the response of $P_t$ to a change in volatility $h_t$ increases with the degree of persistence $\alpha_1$. P–S compute an *unconditional* volatility measure for the variance of *monthly* stock returns based on the average *daily* change in the S&P Composite Index over a particular month. Hence, for month $t$,

$$h_t = \sum_{i=1}^{m} s_{ti}^2 / m \qquad (11)$$

where $s_{ti} = $ *daily change* in the stock index in month $t$ and $m = $ number of trading days in the month. For example, an AR(1) model gives a value of $\alpha_1$ in the range 0.6–0.7. They also use estimates of implied volatility from options prices, which measure *ex-ante* or forward-looking volatilities and here they also find that there is little persistence in volatility. P–S find that a 50% increase in volatility depresses the share price by only a minuscule 0.7% (and the largest effect they find empirically is a fall of 11%). Hence, within the P–S framework, persistence in volatility is too low to explain the observed sharp movements in stock prices.

## GARCH-in-Mean

Chou (1988) repeats the P–S analysis using an explicit model of *conditional* variances based on a GARCH(1,1) model. This avoids the use of the P–S two-step estimation technique that gives inconsistent estimates of the parameters (Pagan and Ullah 1988). Chou assumes expected returns on the market portfolio are given by the CAPM

$$R_{t+1} - r_t = \lambda h_{t+1} + \varepsilon_{t+1} \tag{12}$$

where $R_{t+1}$ = return on the market portfolio, $r_t$ = risk-free rate and $h_{t+1}$ is the conditional variance:

$$E_t(R_{t+1} - E_t R_{t+1})^2 = E_t(\varepsilon_{t+1}^2) = h_{t+1} \tag{13}$$

where $\varepsilon_{t+1}|\Omega_t \sim N(0, h_{t+1})$. According to the CAPM, the expected excess market return varies directly with the conditional variance: large forecast errors (i.e. more risk) require compensation in the form of higher expected returns. The GARCH(1,1) model is

$$h_{t+1} = \alpha_0 + \alpha_1 \varepsilon_t^2 + \alpha_2 h_t \tag{14}$$

The GARCH(1,1) model is a form of adaptive expectations in the second moment of the distribution. The forecast of the conditional variance at $t + 1$ is $h_{t+1} = \alpha_0 + (\alpha_1 + \alpha_2)h_t$. By recursive substitution and the law of iterated expectations, the conditional variance for all future periods $t + s$ is

$$h_{t+s} = \frac{\alpha_0[1 - (\alpha_1 + \alpha_2)^{s+1}]}{1 - (\alpha_1 + \alpha_2)} + (\alpha_1 + \alpha_2)^s h_t \tag{15}$$

The $\alpha_i$ are constrained to be non-negative so that the conditional variance is always non-negative. If $(\alpha_1 + \alpha_2) = 1$, then a change in the current variance $h_t$ has a one-for-one effect on *all* future expectations. If $(\alpha_1 + \alpha_2) < 1$, then the influence of $h_t$ on $h_{t+s}$ dies away exponentially. Thus, $(\alpha_1 + \alpha_2)$ measures the degree of *persistence* in the conditional variance. If $(\alpha_1 + \alpha_2) \geq 1$, then the *un*conditional variance $\alpha_0/[1 - (\alpha_1 + \alpha_2)]$ is not defined (and we have a non-stationary (explosive) series in the conditional variance). Equations (12) + (14) constitute a 'GARCH-in-mean' or GARCH-M model. Chou (1988) estimates these two equations simultaneously, using maximum likelihood. The data is for *weekly* returns (Tuesday–Tuesday closing prices) on the NYSE value weighted stock price index (with dividends reinvested) over the period 1962 to 1985 (1225 observations).

Chou finds that the estimate of the market price of risk $\lambda$ over various sub-periods is not well determined statistically and borders on being statistically insignificant. However, it has plausible point estimates in the range 3–6 (P–S obtain a value of

3.5 and Merton 1973 finds a value of 3.2). The value of $(\alpha_1 + \alpha_2)$ is very stable over sub-periods and is around 0.98, indicating substantial persistence. It follows from our previous discussion that observed sharp falls in stock *prices* can now be explained using the RVF. Indeed, when $(\alpha_1 + \alpha_2) = 1$ (which is found to be largely acceptable on statistical grounds by Chou), stock prices move tremendously and the elasticity $d(\ln P_t)/d(\ln h_t)$ can be as high as (minus) 60.

Chou re-estimates his GARCH(1,1) model for different 'return horizons' using returns over $N = 5$, 20, 50 and 250 trading days. He finds the estimates $(\alpha_1 + \alpha_2)$ are very stable at around 0.95 in all of these variants. As a point of comparison, Chou calculates the P–S measure of variance (see equation (11)) using different values of $N$. He then estimates $h_{Nt+1} = a_0 + a_1 h_{Nt} + v_{t+1}$ for various values of $N$. He finds that $\alpha_1$, the degree of persistence, varies tremendously, increasing from near zero for $N = 5$ (working) days, to $\alpha_1 = 0.6$ for $N = 20$ days (i.e. 1 month) and to $\alpha_1 = 0.9$ for $N = 250$ days (i.e. 1 year). This suggests that the P–S method may not have correctly captured the true degree of persistence.

As a counterweight to the above, consider a slight modification of Chou's model as used by Lamoureux and Lastrapes (1990a). They assume that conditional volatility is influenced both by past forecast errors (GARCH) and by the volume of trading, VOL (i.e. number of buy/sell orders undertaken during the day):

$$h_{t+1} = \alpha_0 + \alpha_1 \varepsilon_t^2 + \alpha_2 h_t + \gamma VOL_t$$

They model *daily* returns and, hence, feel it is realistic to assume constant expected returns $\mu$:

$$R_{t+1} = \mu + \varepsilon_{t+1} \quad \varepsilon_{t+1} \sim N(0, h_{t+1})$$

They estimate the equations for 20 actively traded companies using about one year of daily data (for 1981 or 1982). When $\gamma$ is set to zero, they generally find a similar result to Chou, namely, strong, persistent GARCH effects (i.e. $(\alpha_1 + \alpha_2) \approx 0.8$ to 0.95). When $VOL_t$ is added, they find that $\alpha_1 = \alpha_2 = 0$ but $\gamma \neq 0$ and the residuals are now normally distributed. Hence, conditional volatility $h_{t+1}$ is not determined by past forecast errors but by the volume of trading (i.e. the persistence in VOL accounts for the persistence in $h_{t+1}$). They interpret VOL as measuring the arrival of new information and therefore conjecture that, in general, GARCH effects in other studies are really measuring the persistence in the arrival of new information (see the discussion on market microstructure, in the following). Thus, on this data set, the Chou model is shown to be very sensitive introducing $VOL_t$ into the GARCH process. However, Brooks (1998) demonstrates that market volume does not improve outside-sample *forecasts* of volatility in a simple GARCH model. The sensitivity of the GARCH-M model to specification changes is examined further in the following section, as is the importance of VOL in the market microstructure models.

## The CAPM and Dividends

The study by Attanasio and Wadhwani (1990) starts with the empirical observation that, from previous work, we know that the expected excess return on an aggregate stock market index (which is assumed to proxy the market portfolio), depends on the previous periods dividend–price ratio. The latter violates the EMH under constant expected excess returns. Previous work in this area often assumed *a constant* risk premium but then sometimes interpreted the presence of the dividend yield as *indicative* of a time-varying risk premium. Attanasio and Wadhwani suggest that if we explicitly model the time-varying risk premium, we may find that the dividend yield ($= Z_t$) does *not* influence expected returns. If so, this would support the CAPM

$$(R_{m,t+1} - r_t) = \lambda h_t + \delta Z_t + \varepsilon_{t+1}$$

where we expect $\lambda > 0$ and $\delta = 0$. The time-varying conditional variance is assumed to be determined by a GARCH(1,2) model (with the dividend yield added)

$$h_{t+1} = \alpha_0 + \alpha_1 h_t + \alpha_2 \varepsilon_t^2 + \alpha_3 \varepsilon_{t-1}^2 + \pi Z_t$$

where $\alpha_1$ and $\pi$ are constrained to be non-negative. Hence, the dividend yield affects the conditional variance – this is not a violation of the CAPM. Using monthly data from January 1953 to November 1988 on an aggregate US stock price series, a representative result is (Attanasio and Wadhwani 1990, Table 2)

$$(R_{m,t+1} - r_t) = - \underset{(0.025)}{0.035} + \underset{(0.39)}{0.55 Z_t} - \underset{(1.05)}{4.05 r_t} + \underset{(11.3)}{22.3 h_{t+1}} \qquad (16)$$

$$1953(1)-1988(11), \ R^2 = 0.059, \ (.) = \text{standard error}$$

$$h_{t+1} = \alpha_0 + \underset{(0.03)}{0.015 \varepsilon_t^2} + \underset{(0.04)}{0.022 \varepsilon_{t-1}^2} + \underset{(0.06)}{0.87 h_t} + \underset{(0.024)}{0.053 Z_t} \qquad (17)$$

In the CAPM equation (16), the conditional variance is found to be (just) statistically significant and the dividend yield $Z_t$ is not, thus supporting the CAPM. However, in (16), we report results when Attanasio–Wadhwani also include the short rate which is statistically significant, and this rejects the CAPM. In the GARCH equation (17), the dividend yield $Z_t$ has a statistically significant effect on the conditional variance, and this would explain why previous researchers who assumed a constant risk premium found $Z_t$ significant in the returns equation of the CAPM. Note that there is also considerable persistence in the conditional variance since $(\alpha_1 + \alpha_2 + \alpha_3) = 0.91$.

## Noise Trader Risk and Serial Correlation

Positive feedback (momentum) traders buy after a price rise and sell after a price fall (e.g. use of 'stop-loss' orders or 'portfolio insurers'). This gives rise to *positive* serial correlation in returns. Negative feedback traders pursue the opposite strategy; they 'buy low' and 'sell high'. Hence, a price fall would be followed by a price rise if these traders dominated the market. (The latter would also be true for investors who assign a *constant share* of market value wealth to each asset, since a price fall on asset $i$ will lead to a fall in its 'value share' in the portfolio and hence lead to additional purchases and a subsequent price rise.) The demand for stocks by noise traders $N_t$ (as a proportion of the total market value of stocks) may be represented

$$N_t = \gamma R_{t-1} \qquad (18)$$

with $\gamma > 0$ indicating positive feedback traders and $\gamma < 0$ indicating negative feedback traders and $R_{t-1}$ is the holding-period return in the previous period. Let us assume that the demand for shares by the smart money is determined by a (simple) mean-variance model:

$$S_t = (E_t R_{t+1} - \mu)/\psi_t \qquad (19)$$

where $S_t$ = proportion of stock held by 'smart money', $\mu$ = expected rate of return (for which demand by the 'smart money' is zero), $\psi_t$ = measure of the perceived riskiness of shares. We assume $\psi_t$ is a positive function of the conditional variance $h_t$ of stock prices: $\psi = \psi(h_t)$. Thus, the smart money holds more stock, the higher the expected return and the smaller is the riskiness of stocks. If the smart money holds all the stocks, then $S_t = 1$ and rearranging (19), we have the CAPM for the market portfolio where the excess return $E_t R_{t+1} - \mu$ depends on a risk premium, which is proportional to the conditional variance of stock prices, $\psi_t = \psi(h_t)$. Equilibrium in the market requires all shares to be held:

$$S_t + N_t = 1 \qquad (20)$$

Substituting (18) and (19) in (20), rearranging and using the RE assumption,

$$R_t = \mu + \psi(h_t) - \gamma \psi(h_t) R_{t-1} + \varepsilon_t \qquad (21)$$

Thus in a market with smart money and noise traders, the serial correlation in $R_t$ will depend on the type of noise trader. Somewhat paradoxically, a positive feedback trader (i.e. $\gamma > 0$) results in *negative* serial correlation in $R_t$ (for any given constant level of risk $h_t$) and vice versa. A linear form for $\psi(h_t)$ in equation (21) gives

$$R_t = \mu + \theta h_t + (\gamma_0 + \gamma_1 h_t) R_{t-1} + \varepsilon_t \qquad (22)$$

The direct impact of feedback traders at a constant level of risk is given by the sign of $\gamma_0$. However, suppose $\gamma_0$ is positive (i.e. positive serial correlation in $R_t$) but $\gamma_1$ is negative. Then as risk $h_t$ increases, the coefficient on $R_{t-1}$, namely, $\gamma_0 + \gamma_1 h_t$, could change sign, and the serial correlation in stock returns would move from positive to negative as risk increases. This would suggest that as volatility increases, the market becomes more dominated by positive feedback traders who, when they interact in the market with the smart money, result in overall negative serial correlation in returns.

Sentana and Wadhwani (1992) estimate the above model using US *daily* data from 1855 to 1988, together with a complex GARCH model of the time-varying conditional variance. Their GARCH model allows the number of non-trading days to influence conditional variance (French and Roll 1986), although in practice, this is not found to be statistically significant. The conditional variance is found to be influenced differentially by positive and negative forecast errors (i.e. asymmetric GARCH). Ceteris paribus, a unit negative shock, $\varepsilon_t$, leads to a larger change in conditional variance than does a positive forecast error.

The switch point for the change from positive serial correlation in returns to negative serial correlation is $h_t > (-\gamma_0/\gamma_1)$, and they find $\gamma_0 = 0.09$, $\gamma_1 = -0.01$ and the switch point is $h_t > 5.8$. Hence, when volatility is low, stock returns at very short horizons (i.e. daily) exhibit *positive* serial correlation but when volatility is high returns exhibit negative autocorrelation. This model, therefore, provides some statistical support for the view that the relative influence of positive and negative feedback traders may vary with the degree of risk (but it does not explain why this might happen). As is familiar in such studies of aggregate stock returns, Sentana–Wadhwani also find that the conditional variance exhibits substantial persistence (with the sum of coefficients on the GARCH parameters being close to unity). In the empirical results, $\theta$ is not statistically different from zero, so that the influence of volatility on the mean return on stocks only works through the non-linear variable, $\gamma_1 h_t R_{t-1}$.

Lee, Jiang and Indro (2002) use weekly US data 1973 to 1995 to see if a 'change in investor sentiment index' has a *direct* effect in an equation for expected returns (for either the S&P500, NASDAQ or the DJIA index), and there is also a GARCH-in-mean effect on expected returns. They also allow the change in sentiment index to directly appear in the GARCH volatility model. They find that an increase in bearish sentiment leads to an increase in volatility with the largest effect being on the NASDAQ (i.e. on small stocks) and this then leads to a fall in expected returns, working via the volatility term in the expected returns regression. There is also a *direct* impact of the change in sentiment index on expected returns. These results are broadly consistent, with noise traders influencing expected returns and their volatility (as in the DeLong et al model).

## Bond Market

In a pioneering study, Engle, Lilien and Robins (1987) use a simple ARCH-in-mean model to determine the excess holding period return (HPR) on US long-bills over short-bills. The excess HPR is found to depend positively on the conditional variance (coefficient = 0.687, t-stat = 5.2), and the ARCH volatility process is statistically significant (although the sum of the coefficients at 1.6 is somewhat greater than unity). Engle et al then include the yield spread $(R_t - r_t)$ in the excess returns equation and find it is statistically significant, so the CAPM is violated.

Although the results of Engle et al appear to demonstrate strong effects of the conditional variance on expected equilibrium returns, Tzavalis and Wickens (1995) demonstrate that this result is sensitive to the data period chosen and, in particular, whether the period of extreme volatility in interest rates in 1979 to 1982 is included (i.e. when monetary base targeting was in operation in the United States). Broadly speaking, Tzavalis and Wickens (using monthly data) reproduce Engle et al's results using a GARCH(1,1) model but then include a dummy variable $DV_t$ taking the value unity over the months 1979(10) and 1982(9) and zero elsewhere. They find that when $DV_t$ is included, the degree of persistence in volatility falls, that is, $(\alpha_1 + \alpha_2)$ in the GARCH process is of the order of 0.3 rather than 0.9 (and the dummy variable is highly significant and positive). In addition, the expected HPR is no longer influenced by the conditional variance so there is no GARCH-in-mean effect on expected returns. Of course, the dummy variable merely increases the average level of volatility in the 1979–1982 period, and the reasons for such an exogenous shift remain unexplained. Therefore, on the basis of intuitive economic arguments, one might still favour the model without the dummy variable and take the view that persistence in volatility is high only when the level of volatility is high. There may be a threshold effect so that in periods of high volatility, volatility is highly persistent and influences equilibrium expected returns. In contrast, in periods of low volatility, persistence is much lower, and the relatively low value of the conditional variance does not have a perceptible impact on equilibrium returns. Intuitively, the above seems plausible but clearly this asymmetric threshold effect requires further investigation.

## GARCH: Some Variants

There are probably more variants on the simple GARCH(1,1) process than there are varieties of breakfast cereal. A number of variants introduce asymmetries into the volatility process. The intuition is that after a surprise fall of $x\%$ in stock returns, perceived volatility will increase more than after a surprise rise in stock returns of an equal amount. Such asymmetries can be introduced either by adding 'new' economic variables to the GARCH equation (e.g. gearing or leverage, that is, the debt to equity ratio) or more usually by amending the GARCH process itself. For example, the Glosten, Jagannathan and Runkle (GJR) (1993) model adds an indicator variable:

$$h_t = \alpha_0 + \alpha_1 \varepsilon_{t-1}^2 + \alpha_2 h_{t-1} + \gamma (\varepsilon_{t-1}^2 D_{t-1}) \tag{23}$$

where $D_{t-1} = \begin{cases} 1 & \text{if } \varepsilon_{t-1} < 0 \\ 0 & \text{otherwise} \end{cases}$

A more complex asymmetric model is the EGARCH approach of Nelson (1991), for example,

$$\ln h_t = \alpha_0 + \alpha_1 \ln h_{t-1} + \gamma \frac{\varepsilon_{t-1}}{\sqrt{h_{t-1}}} + \left[ \frac{|\varepsilon_{t-1}|}{\sqrt{h_{t-1}}} - \sqrt{\frac{2}{\pi}} \right] \tag{24}$$

Here, $h_t$ can never be negative (even if the parameters are negative) and the model can be applied to a very general distribution (i.e. the GED) for $\varepsilon_t$, although conditional normality is often used in practice. If $\gamma < 0$, then negative surprises in returns lead to higher conditional volatility than equal positive surprises. These models applied to daily, weekly and monthly stock returns generally find empirical evidence of some asymmetries, but such effects are not particularly strong.

## Forecasting Performance

How do the various GARCH models perform relative to other volatility models? Day and Lewis (1992) estimate a GARCH-in-mean model

$$(R_{t+1} - r_t) = \lambda_0 + \lambda \sqrt{h_t} + \varepsilon_{t+1} \tag{25}$$

for the S&P100 returns using weekly data from March 1983 to December 1989. They consider the GARCH(1,1) and EGARCH process. Within sample, they find little difference between GARCH(1,1) and EGARCH and for both, the 'mean effect' is not statistically significant (i.e. $\lambda = 0$). However, a series for implied volatility (from options prices) does add additional explanatory power when added to the GARCH and EGARCH models – although the GARCH and EGARCH models themselves also perform reasonably well 'in-sample'.

A more stringent test of the models is provided by their outside-sample forecasting performance. Using a rolling window, they update the models each week and then use them to forecast volatility one week ahead. They choose two *ex-post* measures for weekly volatility, either squared weekly returns ($V_t^w = R_{w,t}^2$) or the variance of the week's daily returns (i.e. $V_t^d = \sum_{i=1}^{5} (R_i - \mu)^2$ where $R_i$ = daily return, $\mu$ = mean of daily returns). These measures of *ex-post* weekly volatility are used as the dependent variable in a regression on the one-week ahead *forecasts*. The alternative forecasts are provided by either the two GARCH models or by the implied volatility (from options) or from a simple historic moving average of volatility (i.e. $V_t^{ma} = \sum_{i=1}^{m} R_{t-i}^2 / m$). The results are disappointing since the implied volatility series and the two GARCH models provide no statistical explanatory power for (the two) *ex-post* volatility series $V_t^w$ and $V_t^d$ (R-squared $\approx 0.025$). In fact, historic volatility $V_t^{ma}$ is the only variable to help predict the two measures of *ex-post* (out-turn) volatility. Although, even here, the R-squared is still low at around 0.038 – so volatility is extremely difficult to predict using any method. This should not be too surprising, given that volatility is highly variable. However, it does perhaps explain why in forecasting daily Value at Risk (VaR), by the VCV method, financial institutions tend to stick with a simple forecasting equation like EWMA.

It is perhaps worth mentioning stochastic volatility models at this point. These include an additional stochastic term in the conditional variance equation that (most simply) gives

$$y_{t+1} = \mu + \sqrt{h_t}\varepsilon_{t+1} \quad \varepsilon_{t+1} \sim N(0, 1) \tag{26}$$

$$\ln h_{t+1} = \alpha_0 + \alpha_1 \ln h_t + \sigma_u u_{t+1}^2 \tag{27}$$

where $u_t \sim N(0,1)$. Stochastic volatility models can be used with MCS to price options where volatility (as well as the underlying asset) is assumed to be stochastic. Stochastic volatility models can be estimated using Kalman filter techniques, but we do not discuss this further (see Cuthbertson and Nitzsche 2001b, Ruiz and Shephard 1994).

## 29.3  Multivariate GARCH

In earlier chapters, we noted the use of multivariate GARCH in testing SDF models. The simplest multivariate GARCH model consists of *two* asset return equations and, therefore, two conditional variances and one conditional covariance. The simplest equation for the two mean returns is

$$R_{t+1} - r_t = \mu + \varepsilon_{t+1}$$

where $R_{t+1} - r_t$, $\mu$ and $\varepsilon_{t+1}$ are $(2 \times 1)$ vectors. Turning now to the GARCH process for the conditional covariances of the $(2 \times 1)$ error term $\varepsilon_{t+1} = \{\varepsilon_{1,t+1}, \varepsilon_{2,t+1}\}'$, even here, there are a large number of parameters to estimate for the unrestricted model. So, in practice, *a priori* (yet relatively ad hoc) restrictions are imposed to reduce the number of parameters to a manageable level. The 'VECH' notation is usually used for the multivariate GARCH process (Bollerslev, Engle and Wooldridge 1988) and here continuing with the two-asset return case (with only one lag in the GARCH process), we have

$$VECH\,(\mathbf{H}_{t+1}) = \mathbf{C} + \mathbf{A}\left[VECH\left(\sum_t \sum_t'\right)\right] + \mathbf{B}[VECH\,(\mathbf{H}_t)]$$

$$\sum_t |\Omega_{t-1} \sim N(0,\,H_t) \qquad\qquad (28)$$

where $\mathbf{H}_t = \begin{bmatrix} h_{11,t} & h_{12,t} \\ h_{21,t} & h_{22,t} \end{bmatrix}$ $\quad \sum_t = \begin{bmatrix} \varepsilon_{11,t} & \varepsilon_{12,t} \\ \varepsilon_{21,t} & \varepsilon_{22,t} \end{bmatrix}$

The VECH operator takes the upper (or lower) triangular portion of the matrix and creates a single-column vector, for example, we could take

$$VECH\,(\mathbf{H}_t) = [h_{11}, h_{22}, h_{12}]_t'$$

$$VECH\left(\sum_t \sum_t'\right) = VECH\begin{bmatrix} \varepsilon_{11}^2 + \varepsilon_{12}^2 & \varepsilon_{11}\varepsilon_{21} + \varepsilon_{12}\varepsilon_{22} \\ \varepsilon_{21}\varepsilon_{11} + \varepsilon_{22}\varepsilon_{12} & \varepsilon_{21}^2 + \varepsilon_{22}^2 \end{bmatrix}_t$$

$$= \left[\varepsilon_{11}^2 + \varepsilon_{12}^2,\quad \varepsilon_{21}^2 + \varepsilon_{22}^2,\quad \varepsilon_{11}\varepsilon_{21} + \varepsilon_{12}\varepsilon_{22}\right]_t'$$

$VECH\,(\mathbf{H}_t)$ and $VECH\left(\sum_t \sum_t'\right)$ are $(3 \times 1)$ vectors, $\mathbf{A}$ and $\mathbf{B}$ are $(3 \times 3)$ matrices of coefficients and $\mathbf{C}$ is a $(3 \times 1)$ column vector. Without any restrictions, the VECH model has, for example, $h_{11}$, depending on lagged values of each of $(h_{11}, h_{22}, h_{12})$ and the three distinct error terms in $VECH\,(\sum \sum')$ above, making seven parameters in all (including the constant $c_{11}$). For example, the first equation for $h_{11,t+1}$ is

$$h_{11,t+1} = c_{11} + a_{11}(\varepsilon_{11,t}^2 + \varepsilon_{12,t}^2) + a_{12}(\varepsilon_{21,t}^2 + \varepsilon_{22,t}^2) + a_{13}(\varepsilon_{11,t}\varepsilon_{21,t} + \varepsilon_{12,t}\varepsilon_{22,t})$$

$$+ b_{11}h_{11,t} + b_{12}h_{22,t} + b_{13}h_{12,t}$$

The two-asset system, therefore, has $3 \times 7 = 21$ parameters in the three GARCH-type equations for $(h_{11}, h_{22}, h_{12})_t$, quite a number to try to estimate (even for this simple two-asset case). To simplify the model, we can impose the (arbitrary) restriction that $\mathbf{A}$ and $\mathbf{B}$ are diagonal, so each conditional variance (covariance) is

$$h_{ij,t} = \alpha_{ij} + \beta_{ij}(\varepsilon_i \varepsilon_j)_{t-1} + \gamma_{ij} h_{ij,t-1} \qquad\qquad (29)$$

and this reduces the number of parameters to estimate to nine (in the two-asset model). We have to ensure that the estimated parameters give a positive semi-definite covariance matrix, which is not guaranteed. 'Positive definite' implies the diagonal terms are positive and the off-diagonal elements are symmetric – desirable properties for variances and covariances. A positive semi-definite covariance matrix also implies that for any portfolio weights, the portfolio variance will be greater or equal to zero – again a desirable property.

A slightly different model ensures the **H** matrix is always positive definite, and this gives the 'BEKK model' (see Engle and Kroner 1995):

$$H_{t+1} = C'C + A'H_t A + B' \left( \sum_t \sum_t' \right) B \tag{30}$$

where for $n = 3$ assets (say) then **C, A** and **B** are ($3 \times 3$) matrices and the quadratic terms ensure positive definiteness. For $n = 3$ (assets), which would not be unusual when implementing the SDF model and a single lag in the GARCH process on $h_t$ and $\varepsilon_t^2$ (i.e. GARCH($p = 1, q = 1$) or GARCH(1,1) as it is usually stated in this literature), then the BEKK model requires estimation of $n(n + 1)/2 + (p + q)n^2 (n + 1)^2/4 = 78$ parameters. The vector error correction model formulation VECM(1,1)-BEKK of this model is

$$H_{t+1} = V'V + A'(H_t - V'V)A + B'(\varepsilon_t \varepsilon_t' - V'V)B$$

where $V$ is the 'long run' or unconditional covariance matrix (which can be initialised from sample averages). The other terms represent deviations around this long-run equilibrium. (This equation is an error correction model ECM that we met in Chapter 2 but here applied to second moments.) For $n = 3$, the number of parameters to estimate in the VECM-BEKK model is $3n^2 = 27$. We can further restrict this model so that $V$ is lower triangular and $A$ and $B$ to be lower triangular so the *restricted* VECM-BEKK has $3n(n+1)/2 = 18$ parameters to estimate. Finally, we can simplify the estimation by imposing a *constant* correlation between $\varepsilon_{i,t+1}$ and $\varepsilon_{j,t+1}$

$$h_{ij,t+1} = \rho_{ij}[h_{ii,t+1}h_{jj,t+1}]^{1/2} \quad \text{and} \quad h_{ii,t+1} = c_i + \alpha_i h_{ii,t} + \beta_i \varepsilon_{it}^2$$

which has $3n + n(n - 1)/2 = 12$ parameters to estimate. But as we are trying to model time-varying variances and covariances, this is a somewhat restrictive version of a multivariate GARCH process – it only allows covariances to vary over time if the variances are time varying ($\sigma_{ij,t} = \rho_{ij}\sigma_{i,t}\sigma_{j,t}$). Clearly, there is a major trade-off between the number of covariances one can practically include in the multivariate GARCH approach and the flexibility of the GARCH processes employed, and this has been noted in various earlier chapters when modelling stock, bond and FX returns.

## Futures Hedge

We can demonstrate the use of multivariate GARCH by considering a dynamic hedge using stock index futures. It is easy to show (Cuthbertson and Nitzsche 2001b) that the optimal number of stock index futures contracts to minimise the hedging error of a well-diversified stock portfolio is

$$N_{f,t} = - \left( \frac{TVS_0}{zF_0} \right) \beta_t \quad \text{(i.e. short } N_{f,t} \text{ futures contracts)} \tag{31}$$

where $TVS_0$ = cash value of your stock portfolio, $F_0$ = current futures price, $z$ = value of an index point (e.g. \$250 for the S&P500 futures contract) and

$$\beta_t = h_{12,t+1}/h_{22,t+1} \tag{32}$$

$h_{22}$ is the conditional variance of the change in futures price and $h_{12}$ is the conditional covariance between the change in stock price of the portfolio and the change in the futures price. If the hedge was 'perfect', the change in value of the stock-futures portfolio would be zero. The simplest hedge ratio is a static hedge where $\beta$ is fixed and is given by the OLS regression coefficient where $\Delta S_t/S_{t-1}$ (i.e. stock index return) is regressed on $\Delta F_t/F_{t-1}$ (the futures index). Alternatively, one can estimate a multivariate GARCH model for $(h_{11}, h_{22}, h_{12})_t$ with a rolling window, use it to forecast one period ahead and then use the minimum variance hedge ratio $\beta_t$ each period. Results in Brooks, Henry and Persand (2002) using daily hedging suggest that the static hedge reduces the variance of the out-of-sample hedging error by about 90%. Using the BEKK-GARCH(1,1)-type model reduces the hedging error by a further 2% or so, but adding GJR asymmetry effects provides no further improvement (Brooks, Henry and Persand 2002, see also Cumby, Huizinga and Obstfeld 1983, Franses and vanDijk 1996). These studies demonstrate that GARCH-type models provide a modicum of improvement when used for dynamic futures hedging over the conventional static (OLS) hedge ratio.

## Bond Returns

Implementation of multivariate GARCH models often involves estimating a large number of parameters, and the estimation is highly non-linear, which can create additional (convergence) problems. Because of these technical difficulties, particularly given a finite data set, researchers usually place some limitation on the number of assets considered, and second, the parameters of the GARCH process are usually restricted in some way.

The theoretical model of the bond market we outline in the following incorporates bonds of varying maturities and also allows for time-varying risk premia. The basic model used is the CAPM and, hence, time-varying premia are modelled via time-varying covariances, using multivariate GARCH. Let us start with the returns equations. For the *market portfolio*, the excess HPR ($= y_{m,t+1}$) is proportional to the market price of risk $\lambda$ and the *conditional variance* of the market return:

$$y_{m,t+1} = \lambda \, \text{var}_t(y_{m,t+1}) + \varepsilon_{m,t+1} \tag{33}$$

where we assume $\varepsilon_{m,t+1} \sim N(0, h_{m,t+1})$. For a bond of maturity $n$, the excess HPR ($= y_{n,t+1}$) depends on the conditional covariance:

$$y_{n,t+1} = \lambda \, \text{cov}_t(y_{n,t+1}, y_{m,t+1}) + \varepsilon_{n,t+1} \tag{34}$$

where

$$\text{cov}_t(y_{n,t+1}, y_{m,t+1}) = E_t(\varepsilon_{m,t+1}\varepsilon_{n,t+1}) = h_{mn,t+1} \tag{35}$$

We can, therefore, rewrite (34) as

$$y_{n,t+1} = \lambda h_{mn,t+1} + \varepsilon_{n,t+1} \tag{36}$$

For an $n$-period bond, its *own* conditional variance and its conditional covariance with the market are modelled using GARCH(1,1) equations

$$h_{n,t+1} = \alpha_0 + \alpha_1 h_{n,t} + \alpha_2 \varepsilon_{n,t}^2 \tag{37a}$$

$$h_{nm,t+1} = \delta_0 + \delta_1 h_{nm,t} + \delta_2 \varepsilon_{n,t} \varepsilon_{m,t} \tag{37b}$$

The GARCH conditional variance for the *market* is

$$h_{m,t+1} = \gamma_0 + \gamma_1 h_{m,t} + \gamma_2 \varepsilon_{m,t}^2 \tag{38}$$

If we have only *one* $n$-period bond and returns for the market portfolio, we already have nine GARCH parameters to estimate plus the $\lambda$ in the expected returns equation. As we add more bonds of different maturities, the number of GARCH parameters increases rapidly. Hence, Hall, Miles and Taylor (1989), who estimate the above model for bonds of several maturities, assume the GARCH parameters for each maturity bond are the same. Also, although they have bond data for several different countries, they assume that the market portfolio consists *only* of domestic bonds (i.e. does not contain any foreign bonds) – so this also cuts down on the number of GARCH covariance terms. Data used is monthly. For the *market portfolio* of bonds, there is evidence of a GARCH effect in variance as $\gamma_1$, $\gamma_2$ are non-zero. However, the conditional variance does not appear to explain, statistically at least, much of the variation in the excess market HPRs, $y_{m,t+1}$, since in equation (33), $\lambda$ is only statistically different from zero for Japan and France (and we can accept $\lambda = 0$ for the United Kingdom, Canada, United States and Germany). In general, Hall et al also find that the conditional *covariance* terms do not influence HPRs on bonds of maturity $n$ (for $n = 1$–3, 3–5, 5–7, 7–9, 10–15, and greater than 15 years) in a number of countries (e.g. United Kingdom, Japan, United States and Germany).

Hall et al also test to see whether information at time $t$, namely, *lagged* excess HPRs and the yield spread, influence the excess HPR. In the majority of cases, they reject the hypothesis that these two variables are statistically significant. However, particularly at the short end of the market (e.g. 1–3 year bonds), they find that the time-varying *own-variance* $h_t$ is quantitatively and statistically far more important than the time-varying covariance term $h_{nm,t}$, thus rejecting the CAPM.

There are many potential candidates to explain the rather mixed results across maturities and countries found in the Hall et al study. First, the market portfolio is taken to be all domestic bonds (e.g. no foreign bonds and no domestic or foreign equities are included). Second, there are a large number of parameters to estimate, so Hall et al assume that the parameters in the different GARCH equations for variances and covariances are equal (i.e. $\alpha_i = \delta_i = \gamma_i$, for $i = 1, 2$). This saves on degrees of freedom and mitigates possible difficulties in maximising a highly non-linear likelihood function but may impose invalid restrictions.

Despite some restrictive assumptions in the Hall et al study, it does suggest that time-varying risk premia (which exhibit persistence) do exist in bond markets but they are rather difficult to pin down empirically and the effects are not uniform across bonds of different maturities and different countries. The study does highlight the difficulties in using the multivariate GARCH-in-mean approach to model the CAPM with time-varying variances and covariances. The number of parameters to be estimated and the non-linearity of the maximisation procedure on a limited (and perhaps somewhat poor) data set imply that any results are likely to involve wide margins of error and they may not be terribly robust to slight specification changes.

## Interaction: Stock and Bond Markets

In the CAPM, all agents hold the market portfolio of *all* assets in proportion to market value weights. However, we know that most gains from diversification may be obtained by holding around 25 assets. Given transactions cost, costs of collecting and monitoring information, as well as the need to hedge projected outflows of cash against maturing assets, holding a subset of the market portfolio makes sense for some individuals and institutions. An investor might, therefore, focus his attention on the choice between *groups* of assets and be relatively unconcerned about the specific set of assets within a particular 'block'. Thus, the investor might focus his decision on the returns from holding of six-month bills, a group of long-bonds and a group of stocks. The latter simplification is used by Bollerslev, Engle and Wooldridge (1988) when simultaneously modelling the three-month HPR on these three broad classes of asset using the CAPM. It is easily shown that if we have three broad assets categories that constitute the market portfolio, then

$$\text{cov}(y_1, y_n) = \text{cov}\left(y_1, \sum_1^3 w_j y_j\right) = w_1 \sigma_{11t} + w_2 \sigma_{12t} + w_3 \sigma_{13t} \qquad (39)$$

where $w$ = value-weight of each asset in the market portfolio. Thus, we can split the 'single' CAPM covariance term into the above three components. The *excess* return equations for the three assets are

$$y_{i,t+1} = \alpha_1 + \lambda \left[ \sum_{j=1}^3 w_j h_{ij,t} \right] \qquad (40)$$

where the $w$ are known and $\lambda$ is the market price of risk, which according to the CAPM, should be the same across all assets. Bollerslev et al estimate three excess HPR equations of the form (40): one for six-month bills, another for 20-year bonds and one for a stock market index. They model the three time-varying variance and covariance terms using a multivariate diagonal VECH-GARCH(1,1) model, with the terms $(h_{11}, h_{12}, h_{22}, h_{13}, h_{23}, h_{33})$ of the form

$$h_{ij,t+1} = \alpha_{ij} + \beta_{ij} h_{ij,t} + \gamma_{ij} \varepsilon_{it} \varepsilon_{jt} \qquad (41)$$

The broad thrust of the results on US data 1959(1)–84(2) is

(i) The excess holding period yield on the three assets does depend on the time-varying conditional covariances since $\lambda = 0.499$ (s.e. $= 0.16$).

(ii) Conditional variances and covariances are time varying and are adequately modelled using the diagonal VECH-GARCH(1,1) model.

(iii) Persistence in conditional *variance* is greatest for bills, then for bonds and finally for stocks ($\beta_{ii} + \gamma_{ii}$ equals 0.91, 0.62 and 0.55 respectively).

When the *own variance* from the GARCH equations is added to (40), it is statistically insignificant (as one would expect under the CAPM). However, the CAPM does not provide a 'complete' explanation of excess HPRs since when the lagged excess HPR for asset $i$ is added to (40), it is found to be statistically highly significant – this rejects the standard-CAPM.

## Volatility in Spot-FX Markets

There has been an enormous amount of work in modelling time-varying volatility in the spot-FX market using ARCH and GARCH models. Early work using univariate models (e.g. Engle and Bollerslev 1986, Diebold 1988, Baillie and Bollerslev 1989, Bollerslev, Chou and Kroner 1992) established strong ARCH effects using intraday, daily and weekly data with much weaker effects at a monthly horizon and with ARCH effects largely disappearing at horizons over one month. We discussed in Chapter 23 the role of multivariate GARCH models where conditional *covariances* affect expected returns to foreign exchange speculation. These GARCH effects represent time-varying risk premia. Although the persistence in volatility (and covariances) is established in these models, the statistical significance of GARCH-*in-mean* effects (i.e. the risk premium) is not particularly robust across alternative currencies and time periods.

## Volatility Contagion

Prevalent in the literature, which looks at persistence in volatility, is the idea that news or new information in one market can affect volatility in another market. This is tested by including the error terms $\varepsilon_{j,t-1}^2$ (for markets $j = 1, 2, \ldots m$) dated at $t - 1$, in the GARCH(1,1) equation for volatility in market $i$, $h_{it} (i \neq j)$. Engle, Ito and Lin (1990) and Ito, Engle and Lin (1992) use the analogy of a meteor shower versus a heat wave. A hot day in New York may be followed by another hot day in New York but not usually by a hot day in Tokyo – this is the idea of 'news' as a heat wave. Alternatively, a meteor shower in New York will almost certainly be followed by a meteor shower in Tokyo – that is, news in one market 'spills over' into other markets (after a short lag). Using intraday data in the USD-Yen exchange rate, Engle Ito and Lin find that news is like a meteor shower and moves across different markets as they open around the world.

# 29.4 Market Microstructure – FX Trading

A great deal of the empirical work on market microstructure has concentrated on the foreign exchange market. In part, this is because of availability of high quality, high frequency data. Until very recently, the FX market was highly 'decentralised'. Unlike centralised markets (e.g. London Stock Exchange LSE, New York Stock Exchange NYSE) where trades are made public within minutes, in the FX market, many deals take place over the telephone, telex or computer network between two (or more) counterparties and are not made public. The participants are market makers, brokers and customers. About 100 market makers worldwide (typically large banks) stand ready to buy and sell currencies (i.e. 'two-way price') at indicative screen prices up to certain limits (limit orders). The market maker receiving a telephone call quotes bid-ask prices, and the spread enables the market maker to earn a profit on a round trip trade. The average time span for the inventory cycles of a trader may be around 10–15 minutes, and inventory risk is a crucial determinant of FX spread quotations (Lyons 1995, 1996). Lyons (1998b) finds that a dealer might average around $100,000 in profits per day on a volume of $1 billion. 'Customers' are non-dealers who may be in other banks, central banks or pension and mutual funds (including hedge funds). While market makers may trade on their own account, brokers do not and make money by keeping a 'book' of the market makers' limit orders for buying and selling, from which they quote the *inside spread* (i.e. best bid and ask prices for a particular limit order). Brokers charge a fee for bringing market makers together and preserve the anonymity of the two sides to the trade.

Customer trades in the spot market are relatively small (e.g. around 5% in the US) and *direct* inter-dealer trades comprise about 40% of transactions, with brokered inter-dealer trades around 55% of all spot trades. Credit risk is an issue in these trades, and dealers will have prudential credit exposure levels with counterparties, and this is why most FX trades are inter-dealer. The two main inter-dealer broking systems are Reuters Dealing 2002-2 and Electronic Broking Services (EBS)-Spot Dealing System. These systems keep track of net credit lines with correspondent banks, so traders know deals can go ahead at posted prices (although the counterparty is anonymous).

There has been an explosion of interest in the microstructure approach to analysing the foreign exchange market in recent years. The novelty of this approach being that it analyses the actual trading process in the market – focusing on factors such as order flow and bid-ask spreads. The attractions of this approach in the case of FX markets are three-fold. First, the growth of electronic trading in the inter-bank market means that high-quality microstructure data is now becoming available, whereas the informal telephone-based market made it very difficult to track the trading process. Second, the failure of more traditional models to predict or even explain FX movements (within sample) makes the attraction of a new approach obvious – applied economists used to calling an R-squared of 4% a success when it came to modelling FX rates are now staggered by an R-squared of 60% or more achieved by microstructure models (though the extent to which these R-squared values reflect a true explanation of FX movements is a moot point). Third, one of the puzzles of FX markets is the staggering amount of order flow it generates and so the microstructure approach holds out the hope of explaining this, as well as the more traditional FX market puzzles such as the forward premium.

The growth of electronic trading in the FX market means that – for the inter-bank (inter-dealer) community at least – the market is almost unrecognisable compared to that described as recently as 1999 by Richard Lyons (1999). Whereas the market used to be decentralised and opaque in the sense that telephone transactions were private to the counterparties involved and no firm bid-ask prices were available before transactions took place, now almost all trading in the major currencies takes place through one of two electronic trading systems (EBS and Reuters-2002). The electronic systems are effectively order books where market participants can either post prices and quantities, which they are prepared to trade (limit orders), or 'hit' an existing limit order (a market order). As a result, participants in this market can see firm bid and ask prices on their trading screen (pre-trade transparency) and can see what transactions have recently taken place and at what price (post-trade transparency). Unfortunately, final customers are still left in the dark as only the inter-dealer community is allowed access to these trading screens. Thus, for corporate customers, institutional investors and even hedge funds, the market remains opaque since they can only access *indicative* bid and ask prices (through systems such as Reuters' FXFX) and have to phone a dealer to transact.

In 2001 (BIS 2001), *daily* global turnover in FX was around $1.2 trillion, with forward transactions (outright forwards and FX swaps) covering about 65% of trades. The US dollar is involved in around 90% of all transactions worldwide as it provides the vehicle currency for cross trades between other currencies. The German Mark (now the Euro) is the second most used currency, followed by the Yen and then Sterling. The UK market takes around 31% of all trades, followed by the United States (16%), Japan (9%) and Singapore (6%). Market makers provide 'double auction' prices (i.e. they quote bid and ask prices) but the brokered market is a 'single auction' market (i.e. quotes for either buy or sell but not both).

Although total turnover has declined somewhat since the 1998 survey (mainly due to the introduction of the Euro), it is still the case that trading activity in the FX market dwarfs that in the other major markets (i.e. bonds and equities). This high turnover, coupled with the failure of many traditional FX models to explain either movements in or the high volatility of FX rates, has led many to wonder if the act of trading itself explains most of the movements in FX rates (rather than the more traditional view that assumes that trading is simply a conduit for new information). Research on this idea has been the most eye-catching area of the FX microstructure literature. The determination of the size of the bid-ask spread, market volume and volatility has been examined in the light of the market microstructure in FX described above.

## Bid-Ask Spread

A low degree of transparency facilitated by inter-dealer trades may help *reduce* bid-ask spreads. This arises because a large customer order (to buy or sell) can be dissipated across a number of (uninformed) dealers prior to any information revelation about the large imbalances of the dealer that undertook the initial trade with the customer. Hence, low transparency leads to a high level of inter-dealer inventory risk sharing (before any price impact is felt) and hence lower spreads. Hau, Killeen and Moore (2002) believe that this mechanism applied in the first year after the introduction of the Euro on 1 January 1999. The 'removal' of currencies increased information about currency imbalances amongst Euro dealers, and the increased inventory risk (i.e. prices move against you while holding the currency) led to a widening of spreads. For example, the switch from the German Mark to the Euro led to an increase in mean spreads against the USD from 3.76 to 5.26 b.p., against the Yen from 5.1 to 8.3 b.p. and against Sterling from 3.1 to 9.2 b.p (compared to the 'former' spreads against the DM vehicle currency, in the pre-Euro period). It is also well known from other microstructure studies that spreads and the volume of trading are inversely related (Hau, Killeen and Moore 2002 confirm this for the first year of the Euro), while spreads are proportional to exchange rate volatility (Glosten and Milgrom 1985, Admati and Pfleiderer 1998) and to forecasts of inventory price risk (Bessembinder 1994).

## Order Flow

The empirical importance of order flow as a proximate determinant of very short-run movements in exchange rates has been recently established (Lyons 1999, Evans and Lyons 1999). 'Order flow' is the net value of buyer-initiated orders less seller-initiated orders, and changes represent the net demand for a currency. One interpretation is that 'order flow' captures both private and public information available to market participants and so gives a better picture of how prices are updated. In essence, this approach assumes that some traders are better informed than others, so the market attempts to infer the private information available to these traders by monitoring and responding to order flow. Evans and Lyons (1999) show that order flow is a significant determinant of changes in a number of bilateral daily exchange rates (over periods of 4 months or less), and their out-of-sample forecasts over short horizons beat the random walk model. Lyons (1995) and Bessembinder (1994) establish a link between (proxies for) increased inventory carrying costs and a widening of spreads.

## 29.5    Survey Data and Expectations

We examine the use of survey data in assessing whether changing expectations might cause destabilising exchange rate movements. If one were to read the popular press, then one would think that foreign exchange dealers were speculators, par excellence. Young men in striped shirts, wearing 'sharp-suits', are frequently seen on television, shouting simultaneously into two telephones in order to quickly execute buy and sell orders for foreign currencies. The obvious question that arises is, are these individuals purchasing and selling foreign exchange on the basis of news about fundamentals or do they in fact 'chase trends'? If it is the latter, the question then arises as to whether they can have a pervasive influence on the price of foreign exchange. As we have seen, there has been a large number of technically sophisticated tests of market efficiency using FRU. However, there has been remarkably little work done on the techniques used by actual foreign exchange dealers and whether these might cause movements in exchange rates, which are *not* related to news about fundamentals. A useful representative study by Allen and Taylor (1989) looks at a particular small segment of the foreign exchange market, and they undertake a survey of chartists' behaviour. Chartists study only the price movements in the market and base their view of the future solely on past price changes. Chartists believe that they can recognise patterns in past price movements, which can be used to predict future movements and hence generate profitable trading strategies. This of course would not be the case in an efficient market.

Individual chartists use a variety of methods to predict future price changes. For example, they might use moving averages of past prices to try to predict future prices. They may have very high frequency graphs of, say, minute-by-minute price movements and they attempt to infer systematic patterns in these graphs. Consider, for example, the idealised pattern given in Figure 1, which is known as 'the head and shoulders reversal pattern'. On this graph is drawn a horizontal line called *the shoulder*. Once the pattern reaches point D, that is, a peak below the neckline, the chartist would assume this signals a full trend reversal. He would then sell the currency, believing that it would fall in the future and he could buy it back at a lower price. As another example, consider Figure 2, the so-called 'symmetric triangle' indicated by the oscillations converging on the point at A. To some chartists, this would signal a future upward movement. Figure 3 shows the short moving average of the price series crossing the longer moving average from below at point A and this is taken as a 'buy signal' (with the opposite case at point B).

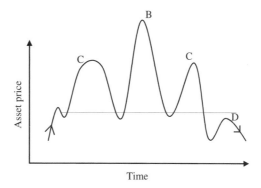

**Figure 1**    Head and shoulder

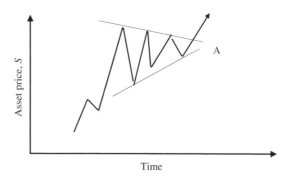

**Figure 2**    Symmetric triangle

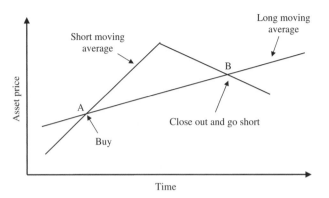

**Figure 3**   Cross-over strategy

Clearly, the interpretation of such graphs is subjective. As a group to influence the market, most chartists must interpret the charts in roughly the same way, otherwise all the chartists would do would be to introduce some random noise into prices but no trends. It is well known that chartists also use survey data on 'market sentiment'. For example, if 'sentiment' is reported to be optimistic about the European economy, the chartists may well try to step in early and buy Euros – this could also lead to bandwagon effects.

## Modelling Expectations Formation

We need to examine the *heterogeneity* in forecasts of the exchange rate in order to get a handle on whether such forecasts might be destabilising. Heterogeneity in expectations can be tested using

$$S_{j,t}^e - S_{A,t}^e = g_j + \varepsilon_{j,t} \tag{42}$$

where $S_{j,t}^e$ is the individual's expectation and $S_{A,t}^e$ is the cross-section average forecast. Ito (1990) and Elliot and Ito (1999) find considerable heterogeneity (i.e. $g_j \neq 0$) for Japanese-based exchange rate forecasts, and similar results for other currencies are found by MacDonald and Marsh (1996).

Next, we need to examine what type of forecasting process agents use, since this determines whether bandwagon effects apply or expectations are mean reverting. The *extrapolative model* gives a bandwagon effect (for $\beta_{j,h} > 0$):

$$S_{j,t,h}^e - S_t = \alpha_{j,h} + \beta_{j,h}(S_t - S_{t-1}) + \delta_{j,h}Z_t + \varepsilon_{j,t,h} \tag{43}$$

where $S_{j,t,h}^e$ is the expected exchange rate for individual $j$ at time $t$ for horizon $h$ (e.g. 3 months). $Z_t$ may contain additional variables (e.g. time trend, crisis dummies) and there may be additional lags, $S_{t-k} - S_{t-k-1}$, in the equation.

The *regressive model* is

$$S_{j,t,h}^e - S_t = \alpha_{j,h} + d_{j,h}(\overline{S}_t - S_t) + \delta_{j,h}Z_t + \varepsilon_{j,t,h} \tag{44}$$

with $0 < d_{j,h} < 1$ and $\overline{S}_t$ is a measure of the equilibrium exchange rate, which could be a moving average of past rates or based on economic fundamentals (e.g. PPP).

The *adaptive model* is

$$S_{j,t,h}^e - S_{j,t-h,h}^e = \alpha_{j,h} + (1 + f_{j,h})(S_t - S_{j,t-h,h}^e) + \delta_{j,h} Z_t + \varepsilon_{j,t,h} \qquad (45)$$

where $0 < (1 + f) < 1$. 'Random effects' models allow the 'slope' and intercept coefficients to vary across individuals, while the 'fixed effects' models impose equal slope coefficients *across individuals*.

Bénassy–Quérér, Larribeau and MacDonald (2002) use data on around 35 forecasters for three currencies (DM/\$, Yen/\$, £/\$) for $h = 3$- and 12-month horizons where participants are surveyed weekly over the period from January 1990 to December 1994. It is found that most forecasters use extrapolative forecasts but there is heterogeneity as the parameters $\beta_{j,h}$ differ across different forecasters, although they are all negative and around $-0.3$ to $-0.41$ at the 3- and 12-month horizons. The latter implies that a rise in the exchange rate is followed by an expectation of a fall next period, and this result is generally found in earlier studies (Cavaglia, Verschoor and Wolff 1993a,b, Prat and Uctum 1994). Some forecasters do use the regressive and adaptive models, so there is also heterogeneity in the models used. Apart from establishing some prima facie evidence for heterogeneity of models used and of different parameter estimates (for the same model across different forecasters), it is impossible to gauge the *economic* significance of such heterogeneity.

When all three models are (additively) subsumed in a single equation, this indicates that some individuals use different models at the two different horizons (i.e. 3 and 12 months) and no single model dominates across all forecasters (although the regressive model now has most adherents).

The data set on which the Allen–Taylor study is based was conducted on a small panel of chartists (between 10 and 20 responded every week) over the period June 1988–March 1989. They were telephoned every Thursday and asked for their expectations with respect to the sterling–dollar, dollar–mark and dollar–yen exchange rates for one and four weeks ahead, yielding about 36 observations per chartist per currency. The survey also asked the chartist about the kind of information they used in making their forecasts and to whom the information was passed (e.g. actual traders).

It was found that at the shortest horizons, say, intraday to one week, as much as 90% of the respondents used some chartist input in forming their exchange rate expectations. As the time horizon lengthens to three months, six months or one year, the weight given to fundamentals increases, and 85% of the respondents judged that over these longer horizons, 'fundamentals' were more important than chart analysis. However, chart analysis was always seen as complementary to the analysis based on fundamentals and, therefore, it is possible that chart analysis influences exchange rates even at these longer horizons.

If one looks *ex-post* at the accuracy of the chartists' forecasts taken as a whole, then, in general, Allen and Taylor find the following.

- There is a tendency for the forecasts to miss turning points. On a rising or falling market, the chartists' expectations underestimate the extent of the rise or fall.
- Prediction errors are noticeably greater at the four-week horizon than at the one-week horizon. Individual chartist's forecasts for four-week ahead predictions are generally unbiased, but they are biased for the one-week ahead predictions.

- For all the chartists taken as a whole, they correctly predict the change in the exchange rate over one-week and four-week horizons approximately 50% of the time. This is what one would accept if their forecasts were purely due to chance.

However, the above results for *all* chartists neglect the possibility that *individual* chartists might in fact do well and do consistently well over time. In fact, there are differences in forecasting accuracy among the chartists and there are some chartists who are systematically 'good'. However, one cannot read too much into the last result since the time period of the survey is fairly short and in a random sample of individuals, one would always expect that a certain percentage would do 'better than average'.

Again taking chartists as a whole, Allen and Taylor assess whether they outperform alternative methods of forecasting (e.g. forecasts based on the random walk, ARIMA or a VAR model using exchange rates, the interest rate differential and the relative stock market performance). The results here are mixed. However, few individual forecasters (apart from forecaster 'M') beat the random walk model. In most cases, the ARIMA and VAR forecasts were worse than predictions of 'no change' based on the random walk, and most chartists failed to beat any of these statistical forecasting models. However, overall there is not much in it. All of the statistical forecasting methods and the chartists' forecasts had approximately the same root mean squared errors for one-week and four-week ahead forecasts with, on balance, the random walk probably doing best. However, there were some chartists (e.g. chartist 'M') who consistently outperformed all other forecasting methods.

Since Allen and Taylor have data on expectations, they can correlate changes in expectations with changes in the actual exchange rate. We are particularly interested in whether chartists have bandwagon expectations. That is to say, when the exchange rate increases between $t-1$ and $t$, does this lead all chartists to revise their expectations upwards? Allen and Taylor tested this hypothesis but found that for all chartists as a group, bandwagon expectations did not apply. Thus, chartist advice does not appear to be intrinsically destabilising in that they do not overreact to recent changes in the exchange rate. Allen and Taylor also investigate whether chartists have adaptive or regressive expectations. These are essentially mean-reverting expectations, and there were some chartists who approximated this behaviour. Overall, the results seem to suggest there are agents in the market who make systematic forecasting errors, but there appears to be no 'bandwagon' effect from this behaviour and, at most, chartists might influence short-run deviations of the exchange rate from fundamentals.

The Allen–Taylor study did not examine whether chartists' forecasts actually resulted in profitable trades, they merely looked at the accuracy of chartists' forecasts. However, a number of studies have been done (Goodman 1979, 1980, Levich 1980, Bilson 1981) that have looked at *ex-post* evaluations of forecasting services, *some* of which were provided by technical analysts (e.g. chartists). A major finding of these studies is that certain foreign exchange advisory services do consistently outperform the forward rate as a predictor of the future spot rate.

Surveys of participants in other FX markets generally point to the use of technical analysis at shorter horizons, with fundamentals playing an increasing role as the forecast horizon lengthens (e.g. Lui and Mole 1998 for Hong Kong-based FX dealers,

Cheung and Wong (1999, 2000) for FX markets in Hong Kong, Tokyo and Singapore, and Menkhoff (1998) for German FX dealers).

Overall, survey data on FX traders points to the heterogeneity of expectations with little evidence of strong bandwagon effects, which would lead to major destabilising movements in spot rates over short horizons. This evidence makes any interpretation of observed short-run changes in spot rates even more perplexing (e.g. is it risk or Peso effects or just unexplained non-linear responses?).

Surveys are clearly useful in establishing how far technical trading is applied in various markets, while quantitative and qualitative survey data on expectations can be used to gauge the applicability of the rational expectations assumption. However, such evidence does not establish how important such factors are in price determination, but they do underpin other models that assume different types of trader, learning and some form of bounded rationality.

# 29.6    Technical Trading Rules

Filter rules are also used to predict exchange rates. A simple filter rule is to buy the currency when it rises $k\%$ above its most recent trough and selling whenever the currency falls $k\%$ below its most recent peak. If the market is efficient and UIP holds, then the interest cost of implementing this strategy should just equal any profits made on changes in the spot rate. Early studies (e.g. Dooley and Shafer 1983, Levich and Thomas 1993) do indicate profitable trades using filter rules over days or weeks and more recently Engel and Hamilton (1990) show that the USD over the 1970s and 1980s exhibited long trend-like swings, which could be exploited using 'trend following' filter rules. Of course, substantial losses could be incurred in various sub-periods and such profits are not riskless. So, using daily or weekly data, there is evidence that technical trading rules can be profitable in the spot-FX market even after transactions costs, and it is difficult to see how this might be compensation for risk (e.g. Levich and Thomas 1993, Neely, Weller and Dittmar 1997). However, the trading frequency in these studies is around three to 26 trades *per annum*. But survey evidence (Allen and Taylor 1990, Cheung and Chinn 2001) indicates that technical analysis is widely used over very short horizons, that is, over a few days and mainly for intraday trades (where technical traders aim to have a net open position of zero at the end of the day). So is it possible to make profits (ideally corrected for risk) over very short horizons?

Goodhart and Curcio (1992) use analysts' support and resistance levels published by Reuters, while Curcio, Goodhart, Guillaume and Payne (1997) examine filter rules using intraday data but do not find profitable opportunities. Olsen & Associates of Zurich claim their proprietary (unpublished) trading models, using five-minute data, do earn profits.

A recent study by Neely and Weller (2003) uses spot FX bid-ask data sampled at half-hourly intervals (to avoid microstructure problems such as bid-ask bounce, Lyons 2001) for four currencies against the dollar (i.e. GBP, DEM, JPY and CHF). One forecasting model uses a genetic algorithm based on (i) $S_t/\overline{S}_t$, where $\overline{S}$ = moving average over previous two weeks, (ii) difference in nearby futures prices (US minus foreign contract) and (iii) time of day, although the last two are found to be uninformative. The cumulative excess return for a signal $z_t$ at time $t$ over the period from $t = 0$ to $T$ is

$$r = \sum_{t=0}^{T-1} z_t r_t + n \ln(1 - 2c)$$

where $z_t = +1(-1)$ for a long (short) position at $t$, $r_t$ is the continuously compound return from holding a long position in foreign currency from $t$ to $t + 1$ and $n =$ number of trades from $t = 0$ to $t = T$. The constant $c =$ one-way transactions cost (i.e. between one and five basis points). The genetic algorithm is estimated (i.e. 'trained') and 'selected' over two data periods (ending at 31 May 1996) to yield the highest value for $r$. The 'outside-sample' forecasting period is then from 1 June 1996 to 31 December 1996.

An alternative model used by Neely and Weller is a linear autoregressive process, together with a filter rule. For example, if you have a long position at $t - 1$, then you only switch to a short position at $t$ if the model predicts a fall greater than the size of the filter $f (= 1, 2, \ldots$ or 5 basis points). If the genetic algorithm is trained assuming zero transactions costs, then the 'outside-sample' predictions generate significant returns of over 100% per annum. But this involves trading about every hour and implies a *breakeven* transactions cost of around one basis point for a one-way trade – but the actual cost is around 2 to 2.5 basis points for large FX trades, hence the forecasting algorithm does not make profits after transactions costs. When the genetic algorithm is 'trained' using $c = 1$ or 2 b.p., then trading frequency in the out-of-sample period falls sharply and again trading is not profitable after transactions costs. Similar results are found when using the autoregressive filter rule, partly because the genetic algorithm works mainly due to the lagged exchange rates (and not the other two variables) and, therefore, closely mimics the autoregressive model. The evidence above, therefore, points to there being 'no free lunches' to FX trading over short horizons.

## Data-Snooping Bias

Sullivan, Timmermann and White (1999) note that a number of studies find that technical trading rules earn profits and address the problem of whether this is due to 'chance' (data mining). Results reported in the literature tend to be only the 'successful' ones and, hence, bias the results. The basic idea is to take account of the problem that the size of a test, based on a search for the largest possible t-statistic for predictability, can be very different from its nominal value. They use White's (2000) 'bootstrap snooper', which provides p-values for the 'success' of a particular trading rule, once the effects of data mining have been accounted for. Broadly speaking, the data-snooping idea is an attempt to get around a type of survivorship bias problem (i.e. in the journals, we see a disproportionate number of articles that demonstrate predictability).

Sullivan, Timmermann and White (1999) examine technical trading rules (e.g. filter rules, moving averages, support and resistance levels) applied to *daily* data on the Dow Jones Industrial Average DJIA over the last 100-year period and for the S&P500 futures contract over the 1984–96 period. They consider over 8000 variants of these trading rules.

There is evidence that over the 1976 to 1986 period, certain trading rules outperformed the benchmark portfolio (i.e. holding cash) even after adjustment for data snooping. But the probability that the *best*-performing trading rules outperformed the benchmark over the out-of-sample 1987 to 1996 period is only 12% and is not statistically significant using standard critical values. Hence, the market appears to have become more efficient over the last 10 years, possibly due to cheaper and faster information processing. (We discussed data-snooping biases for calendar rules on stock returns in the chapter on anomalies.)

An idea of the difference made by considering data snooping is the result that for the S&P500 futures index, superior performance (over holding cash) of a particular trading rule of 10% p.a. for 1984 to 1996 has a p-value of 0.04 when considered in isolation. But given that this trading rule is chosen from a large universe of possible trading rules, its data-snooping p-value is actually 0.90. This is a powerful illustration of the possible influence of data mining (and why you should read Sullivan et al if you think you have discovered a statistically significant trading rule that you think will make you millions of dollars).

## 29.7 Summary

- The past 10 years have seen exponential growth in the number of empirical studies examining the conditional volatility (covariances) of asset returns using ARCH and GARCH processes. Empirically, for US data, only a small part of the conditional volatility in stock returns is explained by past volatility and the volatility in economic fundamentals (e.g. output, gearing).

- There is considerable evidence that the conditional variance of stock and FX returns (for intraday, daily, weekly and monthly horizons) are persistent. At longer return horizons, GARCH effects are usually not found.

- The high degree of persistence in conditional volatility of stock returns implies that observed movements in stock prices may be consistent with the RVF with a time-varying risk premium. However, the impact of conditional *variances* on expected market returns has been difficult to establish at all precisely using *GARCH-in-mean* models. This applies *a fortiori* for the effect of conditional *covariances* on returns (for subsets of the market portfolio).

- It is possible that noise traders as well as smart money influence the expected return on an aggregate stock market index, and the impact of noise traders may depend on whether we are in a 'high' or 'low' volatility regime.

- Using GARCH-in-mean models, there appears to be only very weak evidence of a time-varying term premium on the HPR for short-term zero-coupon bonds (bills). As the variability in the price of bills is in most periods smaller than that of long-term bonds (or equities), this result is perhaps not too surprising. When the short-term bill markets experience severe volatility (e.g. United States, 1979–1982), the evidence of persistence in time-varying term premia and the impact of the conditional variance on expected return is much stronger.

- Holding-period returns on long-term bonds do seem to be influenced by time-varying conditional variances and covariances, but the stability of such relationships is open to question.

- While ARCH and GARCH models provide a useful statistical basis for modelling time-varying second moments, the complexity of some of the parameterisations, particularly in multivariate models, is such that precise estimates are often not obtained in empirical work.

- Market microstructure studies, particularly in FX markets, have demonstrated the importance of order flow as a proximate determinant of changes in spot-FX rates and inventory holdings as a key determinant of bid-ask spreads.

- Noise traders (chartists) probably do influence spot-FX rates over short horizons but survey evidence suggests that chartists and other FX-forecasters are unlikely to form expectations that lead to destabilising movements in the exchange rate. However, since survey data cannot measure the 'market influence' of forecasters (i.e. how much are their forecasts backed with 'real money'), any inferences can at best be qualitative.

- The evidence that technical trading rules applied to high frequency data (e.g. intraday, daily returns) in the stock and spot-FX markets yield excess returns (after transactions costs and an adjustment for risk) does not seem particularly strong. You have to look very hard to find such potentially profitable 'strategies', and the repeated gambles are often subject to high transactions costs and high risk.

# REFERENCES

Abel, A.B. (1990) 'Asset Prices under Habit Formation and Catching up with the Joneses', *American Economic Review*, **80**, 38–42.

Admati, A. and Pfleiderer, P. (1988) 'A Theory of Intraday Patterns: Volume and Price Variability', *Review of Financial Studies*, **1**, 3–40.

Agarwal, V. and Naik, N.Y. (2000) 'Multi-period Performance Persistence Analysis of Hedge Funds', *Journal of Financial and Quantitative Analysis*, **35**, 327–342.

Ali, A., Hwang L.-S. and Trombley, M.A. (2003) 'Arbitrage Risk and the Book-to-market Anomaly', *Journal of Financial Economics*, **69**, 355–373.

Allen, D. and Tan, M. (1999) 'A Test of the Persistence in the Performance of UK Managed Funds', *Journal of Business Finance and Accounting*, **26**(5), 559–593.

Allen, H. and Taylor, M.P. (1989) 'Chart Analysis and the Foreign Exchange Market', *Bank of England Quarterly Bulletin*, **29**(4), 548–551.

Allen, H. and Taylor, M.P. (1990) 'Charts, Noise and Fundamentals in the Foreign Exchange Market', *Economic Journal*, **100**(400), 49–59.

Anderson, E., Hansen, L. and Sargent, T. (2000) 'Robustness, Detection and the Price of Risk', Working Paper, NYU.

Anderson, N., Breedon, F. and Deacon, M. (1996) *Estimating and Interpreting the Yield Curve*, John Wiley, Chichester.

Anderson, N. and Sleath, J. (1999) 'New Estimates of the UK Nominal and Real Yield Curves', *Bank of England Quarterly Bulletin*, **39**(4), 384–392.

Andreassen, P.B. and Kraus, S.J. (1990) 'Judgmental Extrapolation and the Salience of Change', *Journal of Forecasting*, **9**(4), 347–372.

Ang, A. and Bekaert, G. (2001) 'Stock Return Predictability – Is it There?' Working Paper, Columbia University, New York.

Ang, A. and Piazzesi, M. (2003) 'A No-arbitrage Vector Autoregression of Term Structure Dynamics with Macroeconomic and Latent Variables', *Journal of Monetary Economics*, **50**(4), 745–787.

Ardeni, P.G. and Lubian, D. (1991) 'Is There Trend Reversion in Purchasing Power Parity', *European Economic Review*, **35**(5), 1035–1055.

Arrow, K.J (1970) *Essays in the Theory of Risk Bearing*, North Holland, Amsterdam, The Netherlands.

Asch, S.E. (1952) *Social Psychology*, Prentice Hall.

Attanasio, O. and Wadhwani, S. (1990) 'Does the CAPM Explain Why the Dividend Yield Helps Predict Returns?', London School of Economics, Financial Markets Group Discussion Paper No. 04.

Backus, D., Foresi, S. and Telmer, C. (2001) 'Affine Term Structure Models and the Forward Premium Anomaly', *Journal of Finance*, **56**, 279–304.

Backus, D., Foresi, S., Mozumdar, A. and Wu, L. (2001) 'Predictable Changes in Yields and Forward Rates', *Journal of Financial Economics*, **59**, 281–311.

Backus, D., Gregory, A. and Telmer, C. (1993) 'Accounting for Forward Rates in Markets for Foreign Currency', *Journal of Finance*, **48**(5), 1887–1908.

Baillie, R.T. and Bollerslev, T. (1989) 'Common Stochastic Trends in a System of Exchange Rates', *Journal of Finance*, **44**(1), 167–181.

Baillie, R.T. and McMahon, P.C. (1989) *The Foreign Exchange Market: Theory and Evidence*, Cambridge University Press, Cambridge, Mass.

Baker, M. and Wurgler, J. (2000) 'The Equity Share in New Issues and Aggregate Stock Returns', *Journal of Finance*, **55**(5), 2219–2257.

Baker, M. and Wurgler, J. (2002) 'Market Timing and Capital Structure', *Journal of Finance*, **LVII**, 1–32.

Bakshi, G.S. and Chen, Z. (1996) 'The Spirit of Capitalism and Stock Market Prices', *American Economic Review*, **86**(1), 133–157.

Balfoussia, C. and Wickens, M. (2003) 'Macroeconomic Sources of Risk in the Term Structure', mimeo, Department of Economics, University of York, February.

Balke, N.S. and Fomby, T.B. (1997) 'Threshold Cointegration', *International Economic Review*, **38**, 627–645.

Balke, N.S. and Wohar, M.E. (1998) 'Nonlinear Dynamics and Covered Interest Parity', *Empirical Economics*, **23**, 535–559.

Banerjee, A., Dolado, J.J., Galbraith, J.W. and Hendry, D.F. (1993) *Co-integration, Error-correction, and the Econometric Analysis of Non-stationary Data*, Oxford University Press.

Bank for International Settlements. (2001) '*Central Bank Survey of Foreign Exchange and Derivatives Market Activity*', Basle.

Banz, R.W. (1981) 'The Relationship Between Return and Market Value of Common Stock', *Journal of Financial Economics*, **9**(1), 3–18.

Barber, B. and Lyon, J. (1997) 'Detecting Long-run Abnormal Stock Returns: The Empirical Power and Specification of Test Statistics', *Journal of Financial Economics*, **43**, 341–372.

Barber, B.M. and Odean, T. (2000) 'Trading is Hazardous to Your Wealth: The Common Stock Investment Performance of Individual Investors', *Journal of Finance*, **55**, 773–806.

Barberis, N. (2000) 'Investing for the Long Run when Returns are Predictable', *Journal of Finance*, **55**, 225–264.

Barberis, N. and Huang, M. (2001) 'Mental Accounting, Loss Aversion, and Individual Stock Returns', *Journal of Finance*, **56**, 1247–1292.

Barberis, N. and Shleifer, A. (2003) 'Style Investing', *Journal of Financial Economics*, **68**, 161–199.

Barberis, N. and Thaler, R. (2003) 'A Survey of Behavioural Finance', in G.M. Constantinides, M. Harris and R. Stulz (eds.), *Handbook of the Economics of Finance*, Elsevier Science B.V.

Barberis, N., Huang, M. and Santos, T. (2001) 'Prospect Theory and Asset Pricing', *Quarterly Journal of Economics*, **CXVI**(1), 1–53.

Barberis, N., Shleifer, A. and Wurgler, J. (2001) 'Comovement', Unpublished Working Paper, University of Chicago.

Barberis, N., Shleifer, A. and Vishny, R. (1998) 'A Model of Investor Sentiment', *Journal of Financial Economics*, **49**, 307–345.

Barclays Capital. (2003) *Equity Gilt Study*, Barclays Capital, London.

Barkoulas, J., Baum, C.F. and Chakraborty, A. (2003) 'Forward Premiums and Market Efficiency: Panel Unit-root Evidence from the Term Structure of Forward Premiums', *Journal of Macroeconomics*, **25**, 109–122.

Barsky, R.B. and DeLong, J.B. (1993) 'Why Does the Stock Market Fluctuate?', *Quarterly Journal of Economics*, **108**(2), 291–311.

Bartholdy, J. and Peare, P. (2003) 'Unbiased Estimation of Expected Return Using CAPM', *International Review of Financial Analysis*, **12**, 69–81.

Batchelor, R.A. and Dua, P. (1987) 'The Accuracy and Rationality of UK Inflation Expectations: Some Qualitative Evidence', *Applied Economics*, **19**(6), 819.

Becker, G.S. (1991) 'A Note on Restaurant Pricing and Other Examples of Social Influences on Price', *Journal of Political Economy*, **99**(5), 1109–1116.

Bekaert, G. and Hodrick, R.J. (1993) 'On Biases in the Measurement of FX Risk Premiums', *Journal of International Money and Finance*, **12**, 115–138.

Bekaert, G. (1996) 'The Time-variation of Risk and Return in Foreign Exchange Markets: A General Equilibrium Perspective', *Review of Financial Studies*, **9**, 427–470.

Bekaert, G. and Hodrick, R.J. (1992) 'Characterising Predictable Components in Excess Returns on Equity and Foreign Exchange Markets', *Journal of Finance*, **47**(2), 467–509.

Bekaert, G. and Hodrick, R.J. (2001) 'Expectations Hypothesis Tests', *Journal of Finance*, **56**, 1357–1394.

Bekaert, G., Hodrick, R.J. and Marshall, D.A. (1997) 'On Biases in Tests of the Expectations Hypothesis of the Term Structure of Interest Rates', *Journal of Financial Economics*, **44**(3), 309–348.

Bekaert, G., Hodrick, R.J. and Marshall, D.A. (2001) 'Peso Problem Explanations for Term Structure Anomalies', *Journal of Monetary Economics*, **48**(2), 241–270.

Benartzi, S. (2001) 'Excessive Extrapolation and the Allocation of 401(k) Accounts to Company Stock', *Journal of Finance*, **56**(5), 1747–1764.

Benartzi, S. and Thaler, R.H. (1995) 'Myopic Loss Aversion and the Equity Premium Puzzle', *Quarterly Journal of Economics*, **CX**(1), 73–92.

Benartzi, S. and Thaler, R.H. (2001) 'Naïve Diversification Strategies in Defined Contribution Saving Plans', *American Economic Review*, **91**(1), 79–98.

Bénassy-Quérér, A., Larribeau, S. and MacDonald, R. (2002) 'Models of Exchange Rate Expectations: How Much Heterogeneity?' *International Financial Markets, Institutions and Money*, **13**, 113–136.

Bergin, P.R. (2003) 'Putting the 'New Open Macroeconomics' to a Test', *Journal of International Economics*, **60**, 3–34.

Bergin, P.R. and Feenstra, R.C. (2001) 'Pricing-to-market, Staggered Contracts and Real Exchange Rate Persistence', *Journal of International Economics*, **54**, 333–359.

Berk, J. (1997) 'Does Size Really Matter?' *Financial Analyst Journal*, Sept./Oct., 12–18.

Berkowitz, S.A., Logue, D.E. and Noser, E.A. (1988) 'The Total Costs of Trading in the NYSE', *Journal of Finance*, **43**, 97–112.

Bernard, V.L. and Thomas, J. (1989) 'Post-earnings Announcement Drift: Delayed Price Response or Risk Premium?', *Journal of Accounting Research*, **27**, 1–48.

Bernard, V.L. and Thomas, J. (1990) 'Evidence that Stock Prices do not Fully Reflect the Implications of Current Earnings for Future Earnings', *Journal of Accounting and Economics*, **13**, 305–340.

Bernstein, R. (1995) *Style Investing*, John Wiley, New York.

Bessembinder, H. (1994) 'Bid-ask Spreads in the Interbank Foreign Exchange Markets', *Journal of Financial Economics*, **35**, 317–348.

Betts, C. and Devereux, M.B. (2000) 'Exchange Rate Dynamics in a Model of Pricing-to-Market', *Journal of International Economics*, **50**(1), 215–244.

Bhamra, H. and Uppal, R. (2002) Non-Redundant Derivatives in a Dynamic General Equilibrium Economy', mimeo, London Business School.

Bilson, J.F.O. (1978) 'The Monetary Approach to the Exchange Rate: Some Empirical Evidence', *IMF Staff Papers*, **25**, 48–77.

Bilson, J.F.O. (1981) 'The "Speculative Efficiency" Hypothesis', *Journal of Business*, **54**, 435–451.

Black, F. (1972) 'Capital Market Equilibrium with Restricted Borrowing', *Journal of Business*, **45**(3), 444–455.

Black, F. and Scholes, M. (1973) 'The Pricing of Options and Corporate Liabilities', *Journal of Political Economy*, **81**(3), 637–654.

Black, F., Jensen, M.C. and Scholes, M. (1972) 'The Capital Asset Pricing Model: Some Empirical Tests', in M.C. Jensen (ed.), *Studies in the Theory of Capital Markets*, Praeger, New York.

Blake, D. and Timmermann, A. (1998) 'Mutual Fund Performance: Evidence from the UK', *European Finance Review*, **2**, 57–77.

Blake, D., Lehman, B. and Timmermann, A. (1999) 'Asset Allocation Dynamics and Pension Fund Performance', *Journal of Business*, **72**, 429–461.

Blanchard, O.J. (1979) 'Speculative Bubbles, Crashes and Rational Expectations', *Economic Letters*, **3**, 387–389.

Blanchard, O.J. and Watson, M.W. (1982) 'Bubbles, Rational Expectations and Financial Markets', in P. Wachtel (ed.), *Crises in the Economic and Financial System*, Lexington Books, Lexington, Mass., pp. 295–315.

Blume, M. (1975) 'Betas and their Regression Tendencies', *Journal of Finance*, **30**(3), 785–795.

Bodie, Z., Merton, R.C. and Samuelson P. (1992) 'Labour Supply Flexibility and Portfolio Choice in a Life-cycle Model', *Journal of Economic Dynamics and Control*, **6**(3/4), 725–.

Bodurtha, J., Kim, D. and Lee, C.M. (1993) 'Closed-end Country Funds and US Market Sentiment', *Review of Financial Studies*, **8**, 879–918.

Bollerslev, T., Chou, R.Y. and Kroner, K.F. (1992) 'ARCH Modeling in Finance: A Review of the Theory and Empirical Evidence', *Journal of Econometrics*, **52**, 5–59.

Bollerslev, T., Engle, R.F. and Wooldridge, J.M. (1988) 'A Capital Asset Pricing Model with Time-varying Covariances', *Journal of Political Economy*, **96**(1), 116–131.

Boudoukh, J., Richardson, M. and Whitelaw, R. (1995) 'Expect the Worst', *Risk*, **8**, 100–101.

Brandt, M.W. (1998) 'Estimating Portfolio Consumption Choice: A Conditional Euler Equations Approach?', Wharton School W.P.

Branson, W.H. (1977) 'Asset Markets and Relative Prices in Exchange Rate Determination', *Sozial Wissenschaftliche Annalen*, **1**.

Brav, A. (2000) 'Inference in Long-Horizon Event Studies', *Journal of Finance*, **55**, 1979–2016.

Breeden, D.T., Gibbons, M.R. and Litzenberger, R.H. (1989) 'Empirical Tests of the Consumption-oriented CAPM', *Journal of Finance*, **44**(2), 231–262.

Bremer, M.A. and Sweeney, R.J. (1991) 'The Reversal of Large Stock Price Decreases', *Journal of Finance*, **46**(2), 747–754.

Brennan, M.J., Schwartz, E.S. and Lagnado, R. (1997) 'Strategic Asset Allocation', *Journal of Economic Dynamics and Control*, **21**, 1377–1403.

Breuer, J.B. and Wohar, M.E. (1996) 'The Road Less Travelled: Institutional Aspects of Data and their Influence on Empirical Estimates with an Application to Tests of Forward Rate Unbiasedness', *Economic Journal*, **106**(434), 26–38.

Britten-Jones, M. (1999) 'The Sampling Error in Estimates of Mean-variance Efficient Portfolio Weights', *Journal of Finance*, **52**(2), 637–659.

Brooks, C. (1998) 'Forecasting Stock Return Volatility: Does Volume Help?', *Journal of Forecasting*, **17**, 59–80.

Brooks, C. and Persand, G. (2001) 'The Trading Profitability of Forecasts of the Gilt-equity Yield Rates', *International Journal of Forecasting*, **17**, 11–29.

Brooks, C., Henry, O.T. and Persand, G. (2002) 'Optimal Hedging and the Value of News', *Journal of Business*, **75**(2), 3330–3352.

Brown, G., Draper, P. and McKenzie, E. (1997) 'Consistency of UK Pension Fund Investment Performance', *Journal of Business Finance and Accounting*, **24**(2), 155–178.

Brown, S.J., Goetzmann, W.N. and Ibbotson, R.G. (1999) 'Offshore Hedge Funds Survival and Performance 1989–1995', *Journal of Business*, **72**, 91–118.

Brown, S.J., Goetzmann, W.N. and Park, J. (2001) 'Careers and Survival Competition and Risk in the Hedge Fund and CTA Industry', *Journal of Finance*, **56**, 1869–1886.

Brunnermeier, M.K. (2001) *Asset Pricing Under Asymmetric Information: Bubbles, Crashes, Technical Analysis and Herding*, Oxford University Press, Oxford.

Buhlmann, P. (1997) 'Sure Bootstrap for Time Series', *Benoulli*, **3**, 123–148.

Bulkley, G. and Taylor, N. (1996) 'A Cross-section Test of the Present Value Model', *Journal of Empirical Finance*, **2**(4), 295–306.

Burnside, C. (1994) 'Hansen-Jagannathan Bounds as Classical Tests of Asset Pricing Models', *Journal of Business and Economic Statistics*, **12**, 57–79.

Buse, A. (1982) 'The Likelihood Ratio, Wald and Lagrange Multiplier Test: An Expository Note', *American Statistician*, **36**(3), 153–157.

Butler, J.S. and Schachter, B. (1996) 'Improving Value-at-Risk Estimates by Combining Kernel Estimation with Historical Simulation', *Proceedings of the 32nd Conference on Bank Structure and Competition*, Federal Reserve Bank of Chicago, Chicago, pp. 363–380.

Camerer, C. and Weber, M. (1992) 'Recent Developments in Modelling Preferences: Uncertainty and Ambiguity', *Journal of Risk and Uncertainty*, **5**, 325–370.

Campbell, J. and Clarida, R.H. (1987) 'The Term Structure of Euromarket Rates: An Empirical Investigation', *Journal of Monetary Economics*, **19**, 25–44.

Campbell, J.Y. (1986) 'A Defense of Traditional Hypothesis About the Term Structure of Interest Rates', *Journal of Finance*, **41**, 183–193.

Campbell, J.Y. (1991) 'A Variance Decomposition for Stock Returns', *Economic Journal*, **101**(405), 157–179.

Campbell, J.Y. (1993) 'Intertemporal Asset Pricing Without Consumption Data', *American Economic Review*, **83**, 487–512.

Campbell, J.Y. (2000) 'Asset Pricing at the Millennium', *Journal of Finance*, **55**, 1515–1567.

Campbell, J.Y. (2001) 'Forecasting US Equity Returns in the 21st Century', Harvard University, mimeo.

Campbell, J.Y. and Cochrane, J.H. (2000) 'Explaining the Poor Performance of Consumption-based Asset Pricing Models', *Journal of Finance*, **55**, 2863–2878.

Campbell, J.Y. and Shiller, R.J. (1988) 'Stock Prices, Earnings, and Expected Dividends', *Journal of Finance*, **43**(3), 661–676.

Campbell, J.Y. and Shiller, R.J. (1989) 'The Dividend Ratio Model and Small Sample Bias – A Monte Carlo Study', *Economic Letters*, **29**, 325–331.

Campbell, J.Y. and Shiller, R.J. (1991) 'Yield Spreads and Interest Rate Movements: A Bird's Eye View', *Review of Economic Studies*, **58**, 495–514.

Campbell, J.Y. and Viceira, L.M. (1999) 'Consumption and Portfolio Decisions When Expected Returns are Time Varying', *Quarterly Journal of Economics*, **114**(2), 433–496.

Campbell, J.Y. and Viceira, L.M. (2000) 'Consumption and Portfolio Decisions When Expected Returns are Time Varying: Erratum', Unpublished Paper, Harvard University.

Campbell, J.Y., Chan, Y.L. and Viceira, L.M. (2003) 'A Multivariate Model of Strategic Asset Allocation', *Journal of Financial Economics*, **67**(1), 41–80.

Campbell, J.Y., Lo, A.W. and MacKinlay, A.C. (1997) *The Econometrics of Financial Markets*, Princeton University Press.

Capocci, D. and Hubner, G. (2004) 'Analysis of Hedge Fund Performance', *Journal of Empirical Finance*, **11**, 55–89.

Carhart, M. (1995) 'Survivor Bias and Mutul Fund Performance', Working Paper, School of Business Administration, University of Southern California, Los Angeles, Calif.

Carhart, M. (1997) 'On Persistence in Mutual Fund Performance', *Journal of Finance*, **52**(1), 57–82.

Cavaglia S., Melas, D. and Miyashiuta, O. (1994) 'Efficiency Across Frontiers', *Risk*, **7**(10), 56–61.

Cavaglia, S., Verschoor, W.F.C. and Wolff, C.P. (1993a) 'Further Evidence on Exchange Rate Expectations', *Journal of International Money and Finance*, **12**, 78–98.

Cavaglia, S., Verschoor, W.F.C. and Wolff, C.P. (1993b) 'On the Biasedness of Forward Foreign Exchange Rates: Irrationality or Risk Premium', *Journal of Business*, **67**, 321–343.

Cecchetti, S.G., Lam, P.-S. and Mark, N.C. (1990) 'Mean Reversion in Equilibrium Asset Prices', *American Economic Review*, **80**(3), 398–418.

Cerny, A. (2004) *Mathematical Techniques in Finance: Tools for Incomplete Markets*, Princeton University Press.

Chacko, G. and Viceira, L.M. (1999) 'Dynamic Consumption and Portfolio Choice with Stochastic Volatility in Incomplete Markets', NBER Working Paper No. 7377.

Chalmers, J., Edelen, R. and Kadlec, G. (1999) 'Transaction Cost Expenditures and the Relative Performance of Mutual Funds', Working Paper, University of Oregon.

Chan, L.K.C., Jegadeesh, N. and Lakonishok, J. (1996) 'Momentum Strategies', *Journal of Finance*, **51**, 1681–1713.

Chan, L.K.C., Karceski, J. and Lakonishok, J. (2000) 'New Paradigm or Same Old Hype in Equity Investing?', *Financial Analysis Journal*, **56**, 23–26.

Chari, V.V., Kehoe, P.J. and McGrattan, E.R. (2001) 'Can Sticky Price Models Generate Volatile and Persistent Real Exchange Rates?', Federal Reserve Bank of Minneapolis Staff Report, No. 277.

Chen, H.L., Jegadeesh, N. and Wermers, R. (2000) 'The Value of Active Mutual Fund Management: An Examination of the Stockholdings and Trades of Fund Managers', *Journal Financial Quantitative Analysis*, **35**(3), 343–368.

Chen, N., Roll, R. and Ross, S.A. (1986) 'Economic Forces and the Stock Market', *Journal of Business*, **59**, 383–403.

Chen, Y. (2003) 'Discriminating Between Competing STAR Models', *Economics Letters*, **79**, 161–167.

Cheung, Y.W. and Chinn, M.D. (2001) 'Currency Traders and Exchange Rate Dynamics: A Survey of the US Market', *Journal of International Money and Finance*, **20**(4), 439–471.

Cheung, Y.W. and Lai, K.S. (1994) 'Mean Reversion in Real Exchange Rates', *Economics Letters*, **46**(3), 251–256.

Cheung, Y.W. and Wong, C.Y.P. (1999) 'Foreign Exchange Traders in Hong Kong, Tokyo and Singapore: A Survey Study', *Advances in Pacific Basin Financial Markets*, **5**, 111–134.

Cheung, Y.W. and Wong, C.Y.P. (2000) 'Survey of Market Practitioners' View on Exchange Rate Dynamics', *Journal of International Economics*, **51**(2), 401–419.

Chevalier, J. and Ellison, G. (1999) 'Are Some Mutual Fund Managers Better Than Others? Cross Sectional Patterns in Behaviour and Performance', *Journal of Finance*, **54**(3), 875–899.

Chew, S. (1989) 'Axiomatic Utility Theories with Betweeness Property', *Annals of Operations Research*, **19**, 273–298.

Chiang, R., Davidson, I. and Okunev, J. (1997) 'Some Further Theoretical & Empirical Implications Regarding the Relationship Between Earnings Dividends & Stock Prices', *Journal of Banking and Finance*, **21**, 17–35.

Chopra, N., Lakenishok, J. and Ritter, J. (1992) 'Measuring Abnormal Performance: Do Stocks Overreact?' *Journal of Financial Economics*, **31**, 235–268.

Chou, R.Y. (1988) 'Volatility Persistence and Stock Valuations: Some Empirical Evidence Using GARCH', *Journal of Applied Econometrics*, **3**, 279–294.

Christiansen, C. (2003) 'Testing the Expectations Hypothesis Using Long-maturity Forward Rates', *Economics Letters*, **78**, 175–180.

Christopherson, J., Ferson, W. and Glassman, D. (1998) 'Conditioning Manager Alphas on Economic Information: Another Look at the Persistence of Performance', *Review of Financial Studies*, **11**(1), 111–142.

Clare, A., O'Brien, R., Thomas, S. and Wickens, M. (1993) 'Macroeconomic Shocks and the Domestic CAPM: Evidence from the UK Stock Market', Discussion Paper 93-02, Department of Economics, Brunel University, UK.

Clare, A., Priestly, R. and Thomas, S. (1997) 'Stock Return Predictability or Mismeasured Risk?', *Applied Financial Economics*, **7**(6), 679–688.

Clarida, R. and Taylor, M.P. (1997) 'The Term Structure of Forward Exchange Premiums and the Forecastability of Spot Exchange Rates: Correcting the Errors', *Review of Economics and Statistics*, **79**, 353–361.

Clarida, R., Gali, J. and Gertler, M. (1999) 'The Science of Monetary Policy: A New Keynesian Perspective', *Journal of Economic Literature*, **XXXVII**(4), 661–1734.

Clewlow, L. and Strickland, C. (1998) *Implementing Derivatives Models*, John Wiley, Chichester.

Clinton, K. (1988) 'Transactions Costs and Covered Interest Arbitrage: Theory and Evidence', *Journal of Political Economy*, **96**, 358–370.

Cochrane, J.H. (1996) 'A Cross-sectional Test of an Investment-based Asset Pricing Model', *Journal of Political Economy*, **104**, 572–621.

Cochrane, J.H. (1997) 'Where is the market Going?', *Economic Perspectives*, (Federal Reserve Bank of Chicago) **21**(6).

Cochrane, J.H. (2001) *'Asset Pricing'*, Princeton University Press, Princeton, N.J.

Cochrane, J.H. and Hansen, L.P. (1997) 'Asset Pricing Explorations for Macroeconomics' in O. Blanchard and S. Fisher (eds), *NBER Macroeconomics Annual 1997*, MIT Press, Cambridge, Mass., pp. 115–165.

Constantinides, G.M. (1982) 'Intertemporal Asset Pricing with Heterogeneous Consumers and without Demand Aggregation', *Journal of Business*, **55**(2), 253–267.

Constantinides, G.M. (1990) 'Habit Formation – A Resolution of the Equity Premium Puzzle', *Journal of Political Economy*, **98**(3), 519–543.

Constantinides, G.M. and Duffie, D. (1996) 'Asset Pricing with Heterogeneous Consumers', *Journal of Political Economy*, **104**(2), 219–240.

Corradi, V., Swanson, N.R. and White, H. (2000) 'Testing for Stationarity-ergodicity and for Co-movements Between Non-linear Discrete Markov Processes', *Journal of Econometrics*, **96**(1), 1.

Cox, J.C., Ingersoll Jr, J.E. and Ross, S.A. (1981) 'A Re-examination of Traditional Hypotheses about the Term Structure of Interest Rates', *Journal of Finance*, **36**(4), 769–799.

Cox, J.C., Ingersoll, J.E. and Ross, S.A. (1985) 'A Theory of the Term structure of Interest Rates', *Econometrica*, **53**, 385–407.

Cumby, R. (1990) 'Consumption Risk and International Equity Returns: Some Empirical Evidence', *Journal of International Money and Finance*, **9**, 182–192.

Cumby, R.E. (1988) 'Is it Risk? Explaining Deviations from Uncovered Interest Parity', *Journal of Monetary Economics*, **22**, 279–299.

Cumby, R.E. and Huizinga, J. (1992) 'Investing the Correlation of Unobserved Expectations: Expected Returns on Equity and Foreign Exchange Markets and Other Examples', *Journal of Monetary Economics*, **30**, 217–253.

Cumby, R.E. and Obstfeld, M. (1981) 'A Note on Exchange-rate Expectations and Nominal Interest Differentials: A Test of the Fisher Hypothesis', *Journal of Finance*, **36**(3), 697–703.

Cumby, R.E., Huizinga, J. and Obstfeld, M. (1983) 'Two-step Two-stage Least Squares Estimation in Models with Rational Expectations', *Journal of Econometrics*, **21**, 333–355.

Curcio, R., Goodhart, C., Guillaume, D. and Payne, R. (1997) 'Do Technical Trading Rules Generate Profits. Conclusions from the Intra-day Foreign Exchange Market', *International Journal of Finance and Economics*, **2**(4), 267–280.

Cuthbertson, K. (1991a) 'Modelling the Demand for Money' in C.J. Green and D.T. Llewellyn (eds.), *Surveys in Monetary Economics, Volume I, Monetary Theory and Policy*, Blackwell, Oxford.

Cuthbertson, K. (1991b) 'The Encompassing Implications of Feedforward Versus Feedback Mechanisms: A Reply to Hendry', *Oxford Economic Papers*, **43**(2), 344–350.

Cuthbertson, K. (1996) 'The Expectations Hypothesis of the Term Structure: The UK Interbank Market', *Economic Journal*, **106**(436), 578–592.

Cuthbertson, K. (1997) 'Microfoundations and the Demand for Money', *Economic Journal*, **107**(443), 1186–1201.

Cuthbertson, K. and Bredin, D. (2000) 'The Expectations Hypothesis of the Term Structure: The Case of Ireland', *Economic and Social Review*, **31**(3), 267–281.

Cuthbertson, K. and Bredin, D. (2001) 'Risk Premia and Long Rates in Ireland', *Journal of Forecasting*, **20**, 391–403.

Cuthbertson, K. and Galindo, L. (1999) 'The Demand for Money in Mexico', *Manchester School*, **67**(2), 154–166.

Cuthbertson, K. and Gasparro, D. (1993) 'The Determinants of Manufacturing Inventories in the UK', *Economic Journal*, **103**(421), 1479.

Cuthbertson, K. and Hyde, S. (2002) 'Excess Volatility and Efficiency in French and German Stock Markets', *Economic Modelling*, **19**(3), 3.

Cuthbertson, K. and Hyde, S. (2004) 'Resurrecting the C-CAPM: Empirical Evidence from France and Germany', Working Paper, School of Accounting and Finance, University of Manchester.

Cuthbertson, K. and Nitzsche, D. (2001a) *Investments: Spot and Derivatives Markets*, John Wiley, Chichester.

Cuthbertson, K. and Nitzsche, D. (2001b) *Financial Engineering: Derivatives and Risk Management*, John Wiley, Chichester.

Cuthbertson, K. and Nitzsche, D. (2003) 'Long Rates, Risk Premia and the Over-reaction Hypothesis', *Economic Modelling*, **20**(2), 417–435.

Cuthbertson, K., Hayes, S. and Nitzsche, D. (1996) 'The Behaviour of Certificate of Deposit Rates in the UK', *Oxford Economic Papers*, **48**, 397–414.

Cuthbertson, K., Hayes, S. and Nitzsche, D. (1997) 'The Behaviour of UK Stock Prices and Returns: Is the Market Efficient?' *Economic Journal*, **107**(443), 986–1008.

Cuthbertson, K., Hayes, S. and Nitzsche, D. (1999) 'Market Segmentation and Stock Price Behaviour', *Oxford Bulletin of Economics and Statistics*, **61**(2), 217–236.

Cuthbertson, K., Hayes, S. and Nitzsche, D. (2000) 'Are German Money Market Rates Well Behaved?' *Journal of Economics, Dynamics and Control*, **34**, 347–380.

Cuthbertson, K., Nitzsche, D. and O'Sullivan, N. (2004) 'UK Mutual Fund Performance: Skill or Luck?', Cass Business School Working Paper, mimeo.

Dacco, R. and Satchell, S.E. (1999) 'Why Do Regime Switching Models Forecast So Badly?' *Journal of Forecasting*, **18**, 1–16.

Dai, Q. and Singleton, K. (2003) 'Term Structure Dynamics in Theory and Reality', *Review of Financial Studies*, **16**(3), 631–678.

Daniel, K., Hirshleifer, D. and Subrahmanyam, A. (1998) 'Investor Psychology and Security Market Under and Overreactions', *Journal of Finance*, **53**(6), 1839–1885.

Danielsson, J. and deVries, C.G. (1997) 'Extreme Returns, Tail Estimation and Value at Risk', *Journal of Empirical Finance*, **4**, 241–257.

Day, T.E. and Lewis, C.M. (1992) 'Stock Market Volatility and the Information Content of Stock Index Options', *Journal of Econometrics*, **52**, 267–287.

Deaton, A. and Paxson, C. (1994) 'Intertemporal Choice and Inequality', *Journal of Political Economy*, **102**(3), 437–467.

DeBondt, W.F.M. and Thaler, R.H. (1985) 'Does the Stock Market Overreact?' *Journal of Finance*, **40**(3), 793–805.

DeBondt, W.F.M. and Thaler, R.H. (1987) 'Further Evidence on Investors Overreaction and Stock Market Seasonally', *Journal of Finance*, **42**, 557–581.

DeBondt, W.F.M. and Thaler, R.H. (1989) 'Anomalies: A Mean-reverting Walk Down Wall Street', *Journal of Economic Perspectives*, **3**(1), 189–202.

DeGrauwe, P., Dewachter, H. and Embrechts, M. (1993) *Exchange Rate Theory: Chaotic Models of Foreign Exchange Markets*, Blackwell, Oxford.

deGregorio, J., Giovanni, F. and Wolf, H.C., Gordon, R.J. and deMenil, G. (1994) 'International Evidence on Tradables and Nontradables Inflation', *European Economic Review*, **38**(6), 1225–1256.

DelGuercio, D. and Tkac, P.A. (2000) 'The Determinants of Flow of Funds of Managed Portfolios: Mutual Funds versus Pension Funds', Working paper, Lundquist College of Business, University of Oregon.

DeLong, B.J., Shleifer, A., Summers, L.H. and Waldmann, R.J. (1990a) 'Positive Feedback Investment Strategies and Destabilizing Rational Speculation', *Journal of Finance*, **45**(2), 379–395.

DeLong, J.B., Shleifer, A., Summers, L.H. and Waldmann, R.J. (1990b) 'Noise Trader Risk in Financial Markets', *Journal of Political Economy*, **98**(4), 703–738.

Dhrymes, P.T., Friend, I. and Gultekin, N.B. (1984) 'A Critical Re-examination of the Empirical Evidence on the APT', *Journal of Finance*, **39**(2), 323–346.

Diba, B.T. and Grossman, H.L. (1988) 'Explosive Rational Bubbles in Stock Prices?' *American Economic Review*, **78**(3), 520–530.

Dickey, D.A. and Fuller, W.A. (1979) 'Distribution of the Estimators for Autoregressive Time Series with a Unit Root', *Journal of the American Statistical Association*, **74**(366), 427–431.

Diebold, F.X. (1988) 'Serial Correlation and the combination of forecasts', *Journal of Business and Economic Statistics*, **6**, 105–111.

Diether, K., Malloy, C. and Scherbina, A. (2002) 'Stock Prices and Differences of Opinion: Empirical Evidence that Stock Prices Reflect Optimism', *Journal of Finance*, **57**, 2113–2141.

Dimson, E., Marsh, P. and Staunton, M. (2002) *Triumph of the Optimists: 101 Years of Global Investment Returns*, Princeton University Press, Princeton, N.J.

Dooley, M.P. and Shafer, J.R. (1983) 'Analysis of Short-run Exchange Rate Behavior: March 1973 to November 1981', in T. Bigman and T. Taya (eds.), *Exchange Rate and Trade Instability: Causes, Consequences and Remedies*, Harper Business, pp. 43–69.

Dornbusch, R. (1976) 'Expectations and Exchange Rate Dynamics', *Journal of Political Economy*, **84**(6), 1161–1176.

Dornbusch, R. and Fischer, S. (1980) 'Exchange Rates and the Current Account', *American Economic Review*, **70**(5), 960–971.

Dowd, K. (2000) 'Adjusting for Risk: An Improved Sharpe Ratio', *International Review of Economics and Finance*, **9**, 209–220.

Driffell, J. and Sola, M. (1994) 'Testing the Term Structure of Interest-rates Using Stationary Vector Autoregression with Regime Switching', *Journal of Economic Dynamics and Control*, **18**(3/4), 601–628.

Driffell, J. and Sola, M. (1998) 'Intrinsic Bubbles and Regime Switching', *Journal of Monetary Economics*, **42**(2), 357–374.

Droms, W. and Walker, D. (1994) 'Investment Performance of International Mutual Funds', *Journal of Financial Research*, **17**(1), 1–11.

Dumas, B. (1992) 'Dynamic Equilibrium and the Rural Exchange Rate in a Separated World', *Review of Financial Studies*, **5**(2), 153–180.

Edelen, R.M. (1999) 'Investor Flows and the Assessed Performance of Open-end Mutual Funds', *Journal of Financial Economics*, **53**, 439–466.

Elliott, G. and Ito, T. (1999) 'Heterogeneous Expectations and Tests of Efficiency in the Yen/Dollar Forward Exchange Rate Market', *Journal of Monetary Economics*, **43**(2), 435–456.

Ellsberg, D. (1961) 'The Crude Analysis of Strategic Choice', *American Economic Review*, **51**(2), 472–478.

Elton, E., Gruber, M. and Blake, C. (1996) 'The Persistence of Risk Adjusted Mutual Fund Performance', *Journal of Business*, **69**(2), 133–157.

Elton, E., Gruber, M., Das, S. and Hlavka, M. (1993) 'Efficiency with Costly Information: A Reinterpretation of Evidence from Managed Portfolios', *Review of Financial Studies*, **6**, 1–21.

Engle, C. (1993) 'Real Exchange Rates and Relative Prices? An Empirical Investigation', *Journal of Monetary Economics*, **32**(1), 35–50.

Engle, C. (1996) 'The Forward Discount Anomaly and the Risk Premium: A Survey of Recent Evidence', *Journal of Empirical Finance*, **3**(2), 123–192.

Engle, C. and Hamilton, J.D. (1990) 'Long Swings in the Dollar: Are They in the Data and Do Market Know it', *American Economic Review*, **80**(1), 689–713.

Engle, C. and Rogers, J.H. (1996) 'How Wide is the Border', *American Economic Review*, **86**, 1112–1125.

Engle, R.F. and Bollerslev, T. (1986) 'Modelling the Persistence of Conditional Variances', *Econometric Review*, **5**(1), 1–50.

Engle, R.F. and Granger, C.W.J. (1987) 'Co-integration and Error Correction: Representation, Estimation, and Testing', *Econometrica*, **55**(2), 251–276.

Engle, R.F. and Kroner, K.K. (1995) 'Multivariate Simultaneous Generalized ARCH', *Econometric Theory*, **11**(1), 122–150.

Engle, R.F., Ito, T. and Lin, W.L. (1990) 'Meteor Showers or Heat Waves? Heteroscedastic Intra-daily Volatility in the Foreign Exchange Market', *Econometrica*, **58**, 525–542.

Engle, R.F., Lilien, D.M. and Robins, R.P. (1987) 'Estimating Time Varying Risk Premia in the Term Structure: The ARCH-M Model', *Econometrica*, **55**(2), 391–407.

Engsted, T. (1996) 'The Predictive Power of the Money Market Term Structure', *International Journal of forecasting*, **12**, 289–295.

Engsted, T. (1998) 'Evaluating the Consumption-capital Asset Pricing Model Using Hansen-Jagannathan Bounds: Evidence from the UK', *International Journal of Finance and Economics*, **3**, 291–302.

Engsted, T. and Tanggaard, C. (1995) 'The Predictive Power of Yield Spreads for Future Interest Rates: Evidence from the Danish Term Structure', *Scandinavian Journal of Economics*, **97**(1), 145–159.

Engsted, T. C. (2002) 'Measures of Fit for Rational Expectations Models', *Journal of Economic Surveys*, **16**(3), 301–356.

Epstein, L.G. and Zin, S.E. (1989) 'Substitution, Risk Aversion and the Temporal Behavior of Consumption Growth and Asset Returns: A Theoretical Framework', *Econometrica*, **57**(4), 937–969.

Epstein, L.G. and Zin, S.E. (1991) 'Substitution, Risk Aversion and the Temporal Behavior of Consumption and Asset Returns – An Empirical Analysis', *Journal of Political Economy*, **99**(2), 263–286.

Eun, C.S. and Resnick, B.G. (1997) 'International Equity Investment with Selective Hedging Strategies', *Journal of International Financial Markets, Institutions and Money*, **7**(1), 21–42.

Evans, G.W. (1991) 'Pitfalls in Testing for Explosive Bubbles in Asset Prices', *American Economic Review*, **81**(4), 922–930.

Evans, G.W. and Honkapohja, S. (2001) *'Learning and Expectations Macroeconomics*, Princeton University Press, Princeton, N.J.

Evans, M.D. (1998) 'Dividend Variability and Stock Market Swings', *Review of Economic Studies*, **65**, 711–740.

Evans, M.D. and Lyons, R.K. (2002) 'Order Flow and Exchange Rate Dynamics', *Journal of Political Economy*, **110**(1), 170–180.

Fama, E.F. (1984) 'Forward and Spot Exchange Rates', *Journal of Monetary Economics*, **14**, 319–338.

Fama, E.F. and French, K.R. (1988b) 'Dividend Yields and Expected Stock Returns', *Journal of Financial Economics*, **22**, 3–25.

Fama, E.F. and French, K.R. (1993) 'Common Risk Factors in the Returns on Stocks and Bonds', *Journal of Financial Economics*, **33**, 3–56.

Fama, E.F. and French, K.R. (1998) 'Value Versus Growth: The International Evidence', *Journal of Finance*, **51**, 55–84.

Fama, E.F. and French, K.R. (1988a) 'Permanent and Temporary Components of Stock Prices', *Journal of Political Economy*, **96**, 246–273.

Fama, E.F. and French, K.R. (1995) 'Size and Book-to-market Factors in Earnings and Returns', *Journal of Finance*, **50**(1), 131–155.

Fama, E.F. and French, K.R. (1996) 'Multifactor Explanations of Asset Pricing Anomalies', *Journal of Finance*, **47**, 426–465.

Fama, E.F. and MacBeth, J. (1973) 'Risk, Return and Equilibrium: Empirical Tests', *Journal of Political Economy*, **81**(3), 607–636.

Fama, E.F. and MacBeth, J.D. (1974) 'Tests of the Multiperiod Two-parameter Model', *Journal of Financial Economics*, **1**(1), 43–66.

Fama, E.F. and French, K.R. (2002) 'The Equity Premium', *Journal of Finance*, **57**(2), 637–659.

Ferson, W. and Schadt, R. (1996) 'Measuring Fund Strategy and Performance in Changing Economic Conditions', *Journal of Finance*, **51**(2), 425–462.

Fisher, M. and Gilles, C. (1998) 'Around and Around: The Expectations Hypothesis', *Journal of Finance*, **53**(1), 365–386.

Flavin, M.A. (1983) 'Excess Volatility in the Financial Markets: A Reassessment of the Empirical Evidence', *Journal of Political Economy*, **91**(6), 929–956.

Fletcher, J. (1995) 'An Examination of the Selectivity and Market Timing Performance of UK Unit Trusts', *Journal of Business Finance and Accounting*, **22**(1), 143–156.

Fletcher, J. (1997) 'An Examination of UK Unit Trust Performance Within the Arbitrage Pricing Framework', *Review of Quantitative Finance and Accounting*, **8**, 91–107.

Fletcher, J. (1999) 'The Evaluation of the Performance of UK American Unit Trusts', *International Review of Economics and Finance*, **8**(4), 455–466.

Flood, R.P. and Garber, P.M. (1980) 'Market Fundamentals Versus Price Level Bubbles: The First Tests', *Journal of Political Economy*, **88**(4), 745–770.

Flood, R.P. and Garber, P.M. (1994) *Speculative Bubbles, Speculative Attacks and Policy Switching*, MIT Press, Cambridge, Mass.

Flood, R.P. and Rose, A.K. (1995) 'Fixing Exchange Rates: A Virtual Quest for Fundamentals', *Journal of Monetary Economics*, **36**(1), 3–38.

Flood, R.P. and Rose, A.K. (1996) 'Fixes of the Forward Discount Puzzle', *Review of Economic Studies*, **40**(1–2), 209–224.

Flood, R.P., Garber, P.M. and Scott, L.O. (1984) 'Multi-country Tests for Price-level Bubbles', *Journal of Economic Dynamics and Control*, **84**(3), 329–340.

Flood, R.P., Hodrick, R.J. and Kaplan, P. (1994) 'An Evaluation of Recent Evidence on Stock Price Bubbles', in R.P. Flood and P.M. Garber (eds.), *Speculative Bubbles, Speculative Attacks and Policy Switching*, MIT Press, Cambridge, Mass., pp. 105–133.

Fortin, R. and Michelson, S.E. (1995) 'Are Load Mutual Funds Worth the Price', *Journal of Investing*, **4**(3), 89–94.

Fortune, P. (1991) 'Stock Market Efficiency: An Autopsy?' *New England Economic Review, Federal Reserve Bank of Boston*, March/April, 17–40.

Fox, C. and Tversky, A. (1995) 'Ambiguity Aversion and Comparative Ignorance', *Quarterly Journal of Economics*, **110**(3), 585–604.

Frankel, J.A. (1979) 'On the Mark: A Theory of Floating Exchange Rates Based on Real Interest Differentials', *American Economic Review*, **69**(4), 610–622.

Frankel, J.A. (1982a) 'A Test of Perfect Substitutability in the Foreign Exchange Market', *Southern Economic Review*, **49**(2), 406–416.

Frankel, J.A. (1982b) 'In Search of the Exchange Risk Premium: A Six Currency Test Assuming Mean-variance Optimization', *Journal of International Money and Finance*, **1**, 255–274.

Frankel, J.A. and Froot, K.A. (1986) 'The Dollar as an Irrational Speculative Bubble: The Tale of Fundamentalists and Chartists', *Marcus Wallenberg Papers on International Finance*, **1**, 27–55.

Frankel, J.A. and Froot, K.A. (1987) 'Using Survey Data to Test Standard Propositions Regarding Exchange Rate Expectations', *American Economic Review*, **77**(1), 133–153.

Frankel, J.A. and Froot, K.A. (1988) 'Chartist, Fundamentalists and the Demand for Dollars', *Greek Economic Review*, **10**, 49–102.

Frankel, J.A. and Rose, A.K. (1995) 'Empirical Research on Nominal Exchange Rates', in G. Grossman and K. Rogoff (eds.), *Handbook of International Economics*, **III**, North Holland, Amsterdam, pp. 1689–1729.

Frankel, J.A. and Rose, A.K. (1996) 'A Panel Project on Purchasing Power Parity: Mean Reversion within and between Countries', *Journal of International Economics*, **40**, 209–224.

Franses, P.H. and vanDijk, D. (1996) 'Forecasting Stock Market Volatility Using non-linear GARCH Models', *Journal of Forecasting*, **15**, 229–235.

French, K.R. and Roll, R. (1986) 'Stock Return Variances: The Arrival of Information and the Reaction of Traders', *Journal of Financial Economics*, **17**, 5–26.

French, K.R., Schwert, G.W. and Stamburgh, R.F. (1987) 'Expected Stock Returns and Volatility', *Journal of Financial Economics*, **19**, 3–29.

Frenkel, J.A., Gylfason, T. and Helliwell, J.F. (1980) 'A Synthesis of Monetary and Keynesian Approaches to Short-run Balance-of-payments Theory', *Economic Journal*, **90**, 582–592.

Frino, A. and Gallagher, D. (2001) 'Tracking S&P500 Index Funds', *Journal of Portfolio Management*, **28**, 44–55.

Froot, K. and Rogoff, K. (1991) 'The EMS, the EMU and the Transition to a Common Currency', *NBER Macroeconomics Annual*, **6**, 269–317.

Froot, K.A. and Dabora, E. (1999) 'How are Stock Prices Affected by the Location of Trade?' *Journal of Financial Economics*, **53**, 189–216.

Froot, K.A. and Frankel, J.A. (1989) 'Forward Discount Bias: Is it an Exchange Risk Premium?' *Quarterly Journal of Economics*, **104**(1), 139–161.

Froot, K.A. and Obstfeld, M. (1991) 'Intrinsic Bubbles: The Case of Stock Prices', *American Economic Review*, **81**(5), 1189–1214.

Frost, P. and Savarino, J. (1988) 'For Better Performance Constrain Portfolio Weights', *Journal of Portfolio Management*, **14**, 29–34.

Fung, W. and Hsieh, D.A. (1997) 'Empirical Characteristics of Dynamic Trading Strategies: The Case of Hedge Funds', *Review of Financial Studies*, **10**, 275–302.

Gali, J. (1994) 'Keeping up with the Joneses: Consumption Externalities, Portfolio Choice, and Asset Pricing', *Journal of Money, Credit and Banking*, **26**(1), 1–8.

Gallagher, L.A. and Taylor, M.P. (2001) 'Risky Arbitrage, Limits of Arbitrage and Non-linear Adjustment in the Dividend Price Ratio', *Economic Enquiry*, **39**(4), 524–537.

Gallant, A.R., Hansen, L.P. and Tauchen, G.E. (1990) 'Using Conditional Moments of Asset Payoffs to Infer the Volatility of Intertemporal Marginal Rates of Substitution', *Journal of Econometrics*, **45**, 141–180.

Garber, P.M. (1990) 'Famous First Bubbles', *Journal of Economic Perspectives*, **4**(2), 35–54.

Gebhardt, W.R., Hvidkjaer, S. and Swaminathan, B. (2001) 'Stock and Bond Market Interaction: Does Momentum Spillover?', Unpublished Working Paper, Cornel University.

Gemmill, G. and Thomas, D.C. (2002) 'Noise Trading, Costly Arbitrage and Asset Prices: Evidence from Closed End Funds', *Journal of Finance*, **LVII**(6), 2571–2594.

Genesove, D. and Mayer, C. (2001) 'Loss Aversion and Seller Behavior: Evidence from the Housing Market', *Quarterly Journal of Economics*, **116**, 1233–1260.

Geotzmann, W., Ingersoll Jr, J. and Ivokvich, Z. (2000) 'Monthly Measurement of Daily Timers', *Journal of Financial and Quantitative Analysis*', **35**, 257–290.

Gerlach, S. (2003) 'Interpreting the Term Structure of Interbank Rates in Hong Kong', *Pacific-Basin Finance Journal*, **11**, 593–609.

Gertner, R. (1993) 'Game Shows and Economic Behaviour–Risk Taking on "Card Sharks"', *Quarterly Journal of Economics*, **108**(2), 507.

Gilboa, I. and Schmeidler, D. (1989) 'Maximum Expected Utility with Non-unique Prior', *Journal of Mathematical Economics*, **18**, 141–153.

Gilles, C. and LeRoy, S.F. (1991) 'Econometric Aspects of the Variance-bounds Tests: A Survey', *Review of Financial Studies*, **4**(4), 753–791.

Gilles, C. and LeRoy, S.F. (1992) 'Bubbles and Changes', *International Economic Review*, **33**(2), 323–339.

Giovanni, A. and Jorion, P. (1987) 'Interest Rates and Risk Premia in the Stock Market and in the Foreign Exchange Market', *Journal of International Money and Finance*, **6**, 107–124.

Giovannini, A. and Weil, P. (1989) 'Risk Aversion and Intertemporal Substitution in the Capital Asset Pricing Model', NBER Working Paper No. 2824.

Glosten, L.R. and Milgrom, P.R. (1985) 'Bid, Ask and Transaction Prices in a Specialist Market with Heterogeneously Informed Traders', *Journal of Financial Economics*, **14**, 71–100.

Glosten, R., Jagannathan, R. and Runkle, D.E. (1993) 'On the Relation Between Expected Value and the Volatility of the Normal Excess Return on Stocks', *Journal of Finance*, **48**(5), 1779–1801.

Goetzmann, W.N. and Ibbotson, R. (1994) 'Do Winners Repeat', *Journal of Portfolio Management*, **20**(2), 9–18.

Goetzmann, W.N. and Jorion, P. (1999) 'Re-emerging Markets', *Journal of Financial and Quantitative Analysis*, **34**(1), 1–32.

Goldberg, P.K. and Knetter, M.M. (1997) 'Goods Prices and Exchange Rates: What Have We Learned?' *Journal of Economic Literature*, **XXXV**(3), 1243–1272.

Gong, F. and Remolona, E.M. (1997) 'Two Factors Along the Yield Curve', *Manchester School*, **75**, 1–31.

Goodhart, C. and Curcio, R. (1992). 'When Support/Resistance Levels are Broken, Can Profits be Made? Evidence From the Foreign Exchange Market', Discussion Paper 142, London School of Economics, Financial Markets Group.

Goodhart, C.E. and Taylor, M.P. (1992) 'Why Don't Individuals Speculate in Forward Foreign Exchange?' *Scottish Journal of Political Economy*, **39**, 1–13.

Goodman, S.H. (1979) 'Foreign Exchange Rate Forecasting Techniques: Implications for Business and Policy', *Journal of Finance*, **34**(2), 415–427.

Goodman, S.H. (1980) 'Who's Better than the Toss of a Coin?' *Euromoney*, 80–84.

Gordon, M.J. (1962) *The Investment, Financing and Valuation of the Corporation.*, Irwin, Homewood, Ill.

Goyal, A. and Welch, I. (1999) 'The Myth of Predictability: Does the Dividend Yield Forecast the Equity Premium?' Working Paper, UCLA, Calif.

Granger, C.W.J. and Terasvirta, T. (1993) *Modelling Non-linear Economic Relationships*, Oxford University Press, Oxford.

Gregory, A.W. and Veall, M.R. (1985) 'Formulating Wald Tests of Nonlinear Restrictions', *Econometrica*, **53**(6), 1465–1468.

Grilli, V. and Kaminsky, G. (1991) 'Nominal Exchange Rate Regimes and the Real Exchange Rate: Evidence from the United States and Great Britain, 1885–1986', *Journal of Monetary Economics*, **27**(2), 191–212.

Grinblatt, M. and Titman, S. (1992) 'The Persistence of Mutual Fund Performance', *Journal of Finance*, **47**(5), 1977–1984.

Grinblatt, M. and Titman, S. (1994) 'A Study of Monthly Mutual Fund Returns and Performance Evaluation Techniques', *Journal of Financial and Quantitative Analysis*, **29**(3), 419–444.

Groen, J.J. (2000) 'Long Horizon Predictability of Exchange Rates: Is It for Real?' *Empirical Economics*, **24**(3), 451–469.

Grinblatt, M. and Keloharju, M. (2001) 'How Distance, Language, and Culture Influence Stockholdings and Trades', *Journal of Finance*, **56**, 1053–1073.

Grossman, S.J. and Shiller, R.J. (1981) 'The Determinants of the Variability of Stock Market Prices', *American Economic Review*, **71**, 222–227.

Grossman, S.J. and Stiglitz, J.E. (1980) 'The Impossibility of Informationally Efficient Markets', *American Economic Review*, **66**, 246–253.

Gruber, M. (1996) 'Another Puzzle: The Growth in Actively Managed Mutual Funds', *Journal of Finance*, **51**(3), 783–810.

Gul, F. (1991) 'A Theory of Disappointment Aversion', *Econometrica*, **59**(3), 667–686.

Gylfason, T. and Helliwell, J.F. (1983) 'A Synthesis of Keynesian, Monetary and Portfolio Approaches to Flexible Exchange Rates', *Economic Journal*, **93**(372), 820–831.

Haache, G. and Townend, J. (1981) 'Exchange Rates and Monetary Policy: Modelling Sterling's Effective Exchange Rate, 1972–80', in W.A. Eltis and P.J.N. Sinclair (eds.), *The Money Supply and the Exchange Rate*, Oxford University Press, Oxford, pp. 201–247.

Hakkio, C.S. (1981) 'Expectations and the Forward Exchange Rate', *International Economic Review*, **22**, 383–417.

Hall, A.D., Anderson, H.M. and Granger, C.W.J. (1992) 'A Cointegration Analysis of Treasury Bill Yields', *Review of Economic and Statistics*, **74**, 116–126.

Hall, S.G., Miles, D.K. and Taylor, M.P. (1989) 'Modelling Asset Prices with Time Varying Betas: Some Evidence from the London Stock Exchange', *Manchester School*, **LVII**(4), 340–356.

Hamilton, J.D. (1988) 'Rational-expectations Econometric Analysis of Changes in Regime', *Journal of Economic Dynamics and Control*, **12**(3), 385–423.

Hamilton, J.D. (1990) 'Analysis of Time Series Subject to Changes in Regimes', *Journal of Econometrics*, **45**(1/2), 39–70.

Hamilton, J.D. (1994) *Time Series Analysis*, Princeton University Press, Princeton, N.J.

Hannan, E.J. (1970) *Multiple Time Series*, John Wiley, New York.

Hansen, L.P. (1982) 'Large Sample Properties of Generalized Method of Moments Estimators', *Econometrica*, **50**(4), 1029–1054.

Hansen, L.P. and Hodrick, R.J. (1980) 'Forward Exchange Rates as Optimal Predictors of Future Spot Rates: An Econometric Analysis', *Journal of Political Economy*, **88**(5), 829–853.

Hansen, L.P. and Hodrick, R.J. (1983) 'Risk Averse Speculation in the Forward Foreign Exchange Market: An Econometric Analysis of Linear Models', in J.A. Frenkel (ed.), *Exchange Rates and International Macroeconomics*, University of Chicago Press, pp. 113–142.

Hansen, L.P. and Jagannathan, R. (1991) 'Restrictions on Intertemporal Marginal Rates of Substitution Implied by Asset Returns', *Journal of Political Economy*, **99**, 225–262.

Hansen, L.P. and Richard, S.F. (1987) 'The Role of Conditioning Information in Deducing Testable Restrictions Implied by Dynamic Asset Pricing Models', *Econometrica*, **55**(3), 687–613.

Hansen, L.P., Heaton, J. and Luttmer, E. (1995) 'Econometric Evaluation of Asset Pricing Models', *The Review of Financial Studies*, **8**, 237–274.

Hansen, P.R. (2002) 'Structural Changes in the Cointegrated Vector Autoregressive Model', *Journal of Econometrics*, **114**, 195–295.

Harris, R.D. (2001) 'The Expectations Hypothesis of the Term Structure and Time-varying Risk Premia: A Panel Data Approach', *Oxford Bulletin of Economics and Statistics*, **63**(2), 233–246.

Harris, R.D. and Sanchez-Valle, R. (2000a) 'The Information Content of Lagged Equity and Bond Yields', *Economic Letters*, **68**, 179–184.

Harris, R.D. and Sanchez-Valle, R. (2000b) 'The Gilt-equity Yield Rates and the Predictability of UK and US Equity Returns', *Journal of Business Finance and Accounting*, **27**(3), 333–357.

Hau, H., Killeen, W. and Moore, M. (2002) 'The Euro as an International Currency: Explaining Puzzling First Evidence from the Foreign Exchange Markets', *Journal of International Money and Finance*, **21**, 351–383.

Hausman, J.A. (1978) 'Specification Tests in Econometrics', *Econometrica*, **46**, 1251–1272.

He, H. and Modest, D. (1995) 'Market Frictions and Consumption Based Asset Pricing', *Journal of Political Economy*, **103**, 94–117.

Heaton, J. (1995) 'An Empirical Investigation of Asset Pricing with Temporally Dependent Preference Specifications', *Econometrica*, **63**(3), 681–717.

Heaton, J. and Lucas, D. (1996) 'Evaluating the Effects of Incomplete Markets on Risk-sharing and asset Pricing', *Journal of Political Economy*, **103**, 94–117.

Hendricks, D., Patel, J. and Zeckhauser, R. (1993) 'Hot Hands in Mutual Funds: Short Run Persistence of Performance', *Journal of Finance*, **48**, 93–130.

Hendry, D.F. (1995) *Dynamic Econometrics*, Oxford University Press, Oxford.

Hensen, L.P. and Richard, S.F. (1987) 'The Role of Conditioning Information in Deducing Testable Restrictions Implied by Dynamic Asset Pricing Models', *Econometrica*, **55**, 587–613.

Hoare Govett (1991) 'UK Market Prospects for the Year Ahead', Equity Market Strategy.

Hodges, S. (1998) 'A Generalization of the Sharpe Ratio and its Application to Valuation Bounds and Risk Measures', FORC Preprint 98/88, April, University of Warwick.

Hodrick, R.J. (1987) *The Empirical Evidence of the Efficiency of Forward and Future Foreign Exchange Markets*, Harwood, Chur.

Hodrick, R.J. (1989) 'Risk Uncertainty and Exchange Rates', *Journal of Monetary Economics*, **23**, 433–459.

Hogg, R.V. and Tanis, E.A. (1993) *Probability and Statistical Inference*, Macmillan, London.

Hong, H. and Stein, J.C. (1999) 'A Unified Theory of Underreaction, Momentum Trading, and Overreaction in Asset Markets', *Journal of Finance*, **54**(6), 2143–2184.

Hong, H., Lim, T. and Stein, J.C. (2000) 'Bad News Travels Slowly: Size, Analyst Coverage and the Profitability of Momentum Strategies', *Journal of Finance*, **55**(1), 265–295.

Huang, R.D. (1989) 'An Analysis of Intertemporal Pricing for Forward Exchange Contracts', *Journal of Finance*, **44**, 181–194.

Huberman, G. (2001) 'Familiarity Breeds Investments', *Review of Financial Studies*, **14**, 659–680.

Ibbotson Associates (2001) *Stocks, Bonds, Bills and Inflation Year book*, Ibbotson Associates, Chicago.

Ikenberry, D., Lakonishok, J. and Vermaelen, T. (1995) 'Market Underreaction to Open Market Share Repurchases', *Journal of Financial Economics*, **48**, 181–208.

Ippolito, R.A. (1989) 'Efficiency with Costly Information: A Study of Mutual Fund Performance 1965–1984', *Quarterly Journal of Economics*, **104**(1), 1–23.

Isard, P. (1978) 'Exchange Rate Determination: A Survey of Popular Views and Recent Models', Princeton Studies in International Finance, No. 42.

Ito, T. (1990) 'Foreign Exchange Rate Expectations: Micro Survey Data', *American Economic Review*, **80**(3), 434–449.

Ito, T., Engle, R.F. and Lin, W.L. (1992) 'Where Does the Meteor Shower Come From? The Role of Stochastic Policy Coordination', *Journal of International Economics*, **32**, 221–240.

Jackson, P., Maude, D.J. and Perraudin, W. (1997) 'Bank Capital and Value-at-risk', *Journal of Derivatives*, **4**, 73–90.

Jagannathan, R., McGatten, E.R. and Scherbina, A. (2001) 'The Declining US Equity Premium', NBER Working Paper No. 8172.

Jegadeesh, N. and Pennacchi, G. (1996) 'The Behaviour of Interest Rates Implied by the Term Structure of Eurodollar Futures', *Journal of Money, Credit and Banking*, **28**(3), 47–70.

Jegadeesh, N. and Titman, S. (1993) 'Returns to Buying Winners and Selling Losers: Implications for Stock Market Efficiency', *Journal of Finance*, **48**(1), 56–91.

Jegadeesh, N. and Titman, S. (2001) 'Profitability of Momentum Strategies and Evaluation of Alternative Explanations', *Journal of Finance*, **56**, 699–720.

Jensen, M. (1968) 'The Performance of Mutual Funds in the Period 1945–1964', *Journal of Finance*, **23**, 389–416.

Jensen, M.C. (1978) 'Some Anomalous Evidence Regarding Market Efficiency', *Journal of Financial Economics*, **6**(2), 95–101.

Jensen, M.C. (1986) 'Agency Costs of Free Cash Flow, Corporate Finance, and Takeovers', *American Economic Review*, **76**(2), 323–332.

Jiang, W. (2003) 'A Nonparametric Test of Market Timing', *Journal of Empirical Finance*, **10**, 399–425.

Jobson, J.D. and Korkie, B. (1984) 'On the Jensen Measure and Marginal Improvements in Portfolio Performance: A Note', *Journal of Finance*, **39**, 245–252.

Jobson, J.D. and Korkie, B.M. (1980) 'Estimation for Markowitz Efficient Portfolios', *Journal of the American Statistical Association*, **75**, 544–554.

Jobson, J.D. and Korkie, B.M. (1981) 'Putting Markowitz Theory to Work', *Journal of Portfolio Management*, **7**, 70–74.

Johansen, S. (1988) 'Statistical Analysis of Cointegration Vectors', *Journal of Economic Dynamics and Control*, **12**, 231–254.

Jorion, P. (2003) 'The Long-term Risks of Global Stock Markets', Graduate School of Management, University of California at Irvine, mimeo.

Kahneman, D. and Tversky, A. (1979) 'Prospect Theory: An Analysis of Decision under Risk', *Econometrica*, **47**, 263–291.

Kaminsky, G. (1993) 'Is there a Peso Problem? Evidence from the Dollar/Pound Exchange Rate, 1976–1987', *American Economic Review*, **83**(3), 450–472.

Kaminsky, G. and Peruga, R. (1990) 'Can a Time Varying Risk Premium Explain Excess Returns in the Forward Market for Foreign Exchange?' *Journal of International Economics*, **28**, 47–70.

Kandel, S. and Stamburgh, R.F. (1996) 'On the Predictability of Stock Returns: An Asset Allocation Perspective', *Journal of Finance*, **51**, 385–424.

Keane, S.M. (1983) *Stock Market Efficiency: Theory, Evidence and Implications*, Philip Allan, Oxford.

Keim, D.B. and Stamburgh, R.F. (1986) 'Predicting Returns in the Stock and Bond Markets', *Journal of Financial Economics*, **17**, 357–390.

Keynes, J.M. (1936) *The General Theory of Employment, Interest, and Money*, Harcourt, Brace and World, New York.

Kilian, L. and Taylor, M.P. (2003) 'Why is it so Difficult to Beat the Random Walk Forecast of Exchange Rates?' *Journal of International Economics*, **60**(1), 85–107.

Kim, T.S. and Omberg, E. (1996) 'Dynamic Nonmyopic Portfolio Behavior', *Review of Economic Studies*, **9**(1), 141–161.

Kirman, A.P. (1991) 'Epidemics of Opinion and Speculative Bubbles in Financial Markets', in M. Taylor (ed.), *Money and Financial Markets*, Macmillan, London.

Kirman, A.P. (1993a) 'Ants, Rationality, and Recruitment', *Quarterly Journal of Economics*, **108**(1), 137–156.

Kirman, A.P. (1993b) *'Testing for Bubbles'*, European University Institute, Florence, Ala.

Kleidon, A.W. (1986) 'Variance Bounds Tests and Stock Price Valuation Models', *Journal of Political Economy*, **94**, 953–1001.

Knetter, M.M. (1989) 'Price Discrimination by US and German Exporters', *American Economic Review*, **79**, 198–210.

Knetter, M.M. (1993) 'International Comparisons of Price-to-market Behaviour', *American Economic Review*, **83**, 374–486.

Kocherlakota, N.R. (1996) 'The Equity Premium: It's Still a Puzzle', *Journal of Economic Literature*, **XXXIV**, 42–71.

Koedijk, K.G. and Ott, M. (1987) 'Risk Aversion, Efficient Markets and the Forward Exchange Rate', *Review, Federal Reserve Bank of St. Louis*, **69**(10), 5–13.

Kosowski, R., Timmermann, A., Wermers, R. and White, H. (2003) 'Can Mutual Fund Stars Really Pick Stocks? New Evidence from a Boostrap Analysis', Discussion Paper, University of Southern California, San Diego, Calif.

Krugman, P.R. (1978) 'Pricing to Market When the Exchange Rate Changes', in S.W. Arndt and J.D. Richardson (eds.), *Real-financial Linkages Among Open Economies*, MIT Press, Cambridge, Mass, pp. 49–70.

Krugman, P.R. (1990), 'Equilibrium Exchange Rates in International Monetary Policy Co-ordination and Exchange Rate Fluctuations', in W.H. Branson, J.A. Frankel and M. Goldstein (eds.), *University of Chicago Press*, Chicago, pp. 159–187.

Kugler, P. (1988) 'An Empirical Note on the Term Structure and Interest Rate Stabilization Policies', *Quarterly Journal of Economics*, **103**(4), 789–792.

Kugler, P. (2002) 'The Term Premium, Time Varying Interest Rate Volatility and Central Bank Policy Reaction', *Economics Letters*, **76**, 311–316.

Kyle, A. and Xiong, W. (2001) 'Contagion as a Wealth Effect', *Journal of Finance*, **56**, 1401–1443.

La Porta, R., Lakonishok, J., Shleifer, A. and Vishny, R. (1997) 'Good News for Value Stocks: Further Evidence on Market Efficiency', *Journal of Finance*, **52**(2), 2.

Lakonishok, J., Shleifer, A. and Vishny, R.W. (1994) 'Contrarian Investment, Extrapolation and Risk', *Journal of Finance*, **49**(5), 5.

Lamoureux, C.G. and Lastrapes, W.D. (1990a) 'Heteroscedasticity in Stock Return Data: Volume Versus GARCH Effects', *Journal of Finance*, **45**(1), 221–229.

Lamoureux, C.G. and Lastrapes, W.D. (1990b) 'Persistence in Variance, Structural Change and the GARCH Model', *Journal of Business and Economic Statistics*, **8**, 225–234.

Lane, P.R. (2001) 'The New Open Economy Macroeconomics: A Survey', *Journal of International Economics*, **54**(2), 235–266.

Lasfer, M.A., Melnik, A. and Thomas, D.C. (2003) 'Short-term Reaction of Stock Markets in Stressful Circumstances', *Journal of Banking and Finance*, **27**, 1959–1977.

Lee, C.M.C., Shleifer, A. and Thaler, R. (1991) 'Investor Sentiment and the Closed-end Fund Puzzle', *Journal of Finance*, **46**(1), 75–110.

Lee, C.M.C., Shleifer, A. and Thaler, R.H. (1990) 'Closed-end Mutual Funds', *Journal of Economic Perspectives*, **4**(4), 153–164.

Lee, T.H., White, H. and Granger, C.W.J. (1993) 'Testing for Neglected Nonlinearity in Time Series Models – A comparison of Neutral Network Methods and Alternative Tests', *Journal of Econometrics*, **56**(3), 269–290.

Lee, W.Y., Jiang, C.X. and Indro, D.C. (2002) 'Stock Market Volatility, Excess Returns and the Role of Investor Sentiment', *Journal of Banking and Finance*, **26**, 2277–2299.

Leger, L. (1997) 'UK Investment Trusts: Performance, Timing and Selectivity', *Applied Economics Letters*, **4**, 207–210.

LeRoy, S.F. and Parke, W.R. (1992) 'Stock Market Volatility: Tests Based on the Geometric Random Walk', *American Economic Review*, **82**(4), 981–992.

LeRoy, S.F. and Porter, R.D. (1981) 'The Present-value Relation: Tests Based on Implied Variance Bounds', *Econometrica*, **49**, 555–574.

Lesmond, D.A., Schill, M.J. and Chunsheng, Z. (2004) 'The Illusory Nature of Momentum Profits', *Journal of Financial Economics*, **71**, 349–380.

Lettau, M. and Ludvigson, S. (2001a) 'Consumption, Aggregate Wealth and Expected Stock Returns', *Journal of Finance*, **56**, 815–847.

Lettau, M. and Ludvigson, S. (2001b) 'Resurrecting the (C)CAPM: A Cross-sectional Test When Risk Premia are Time-varying', *Journal of Political Economy*, **109**(6), 1238–1287.

Levich, R.M. (1980) 'Analysing the Accuracy of Foreign Exchange Advisory Services: Theory and Evidence', Chapter 5 in R.M. Levich and Wihlborg (eds.), *Exchange Risk and Exposure*, Lexington Books.

Levich, R.M. and Thomas, L.R. (1993) 'The Significance of Technical Trading Rule Profits in the Foreign Exchange Market: A Bootstrap Approach', *Journal of International Money and Finance*, **12**, 451–474.

Levy, E. and Nobay, R. (1986) 'The Speculative Efficiency Hypothesis: A Bivariate Analysis', *Economic Journal*, **96**, 109–121, Conference Supplement.

Lewellen, J.W. (2002) 'Momentum and Autocorrelation in Stock Returns', *Review of Financial Studies*, **15**, 533–563.

Lewellen, J. and Shanken, J. (2002) 'Learning, Asset-pricing Tests and Market Efficiency', *Journal of Finance*, **57**(3), 1113–1145.

Lewis, K.K. (1988) 'Testing the Portfolio Balance Model: A Multi-lateral Approach', *Journal of International Economics*, **24**, 109–127.

Lewis, K.K. (1989a) 'Can Learning Affect Exchange Rate Behaviour? The Case of the Dollar in the Early 1980's', *Journal of Monetary Economics*, **23**(1), 79–100.

Lewis, K.K. (1989b) 'Changing Beliefs and Systematic Rational Forecast Errors with Evidence from Foreign Exchange', *American Economic Review*, **79**(4), 621–636.

Lewis, K.K. (1990) 'The Behaviour of Eurocurrency Returns Across Different Holding Periods and Regimes', *Journal of Finance*, **45**, 1211–1236.

Lewis, K.K. (1991) 'Was There a "Peso Problem" in the U.S. Term Structure of Interest Rates – 1979–1983', *International Economic Review*, **32**(1), 159–173.

Lewis, K.K. (1995) 'Are Foreign Exchange Rate Intervention and Monetary Policy Related, and Does it Really Matter?' *Journal of Business*, **68**(2), 185–214.

Li, H. and Maddala, G.S. (1997) 'Bootstrapping Cointegration Regressions', *Journal of Econometrics*, **80**, 297–318.

Lin, C.F.J. and Terasvirta, T. (1994) 'Testing the constancy of Regression Parameters Against Continuous Structural Change', *Journal of Econometrics*, **62**(2), 211–228.

Lintner, J. (1971) 'The Aggregation of Investors' Diverse Judgements and Preferences in Purely Competitive Security Markets', *Journal of Finance and Quantitative Analysis*, **4**(4), 347–450.

Liu, H. and Loewenstein, M. (2002) 'Optimal Portfolio Selection with Transaction Costs and Finite Horizons', *Review of Financial Studies*, **15**, 805–835.

Lo, A.W. and MacKinlay, A.C. (1988) 'Stock Market Prices do not Follow Random Walks: Evidence from a Simple Specification Test', *Review of Financial Studies*, **1**, 41–66.

Longstaff, F.A. (2000a) 'The Term Structure of Very Short-term Rates: New Evidence for the Expectations Hypothesis', *Journal of Financial Economics*, **58**, 397–415.

Longstaff, F.A. (2000b) 'Arbitrage and the Expectations Hypothesis', *Journal of Finance*, **55**, 989–994.

Lothian, J.R. and Taylor, M.P. (1996) 'Real Exchange Rate Behaviour: The Recent Float from the Perspective of the Past Two Centuries', *Journal of Political Economy*, **104**, 488–510.

Lothian, J.R. and Taylor, M.P. (2000) 'Purchasing Power Parity over Two Centuries: Strengthening the Case for Real Exchange Rate Stability: A Reply to Coddington and Liang', *Journal of International Money and Finance*, **19**, 759–764.

Loughran, T. and Ritter, J.R. (1995) 'The New Issues Puzzle', *Journal of Finance*, **50**, 23–51.

Loughran, T. and Ritter, J.R. (2000) 'Uniformly Least Powerful Tests of Market Efficiency', *Journal of Financial Economics*, **55**(3), 361–389.

Lucas, R.E. (1978) 'Asset Prices in an Exchange Economy', *Econometrica*, **46**, 1426–1446.

Lunde, A., Timmermann, A. and Blake, D. (1999) 'The Hazards of Mutual Fund Underperformance: A Cox Regression Analysis', *Journal of Empirical Finance*, **6**, 121–152.

Luttmer, E. and Nishiotis, G. (1995) 'Joint Restrictions on Preferences with Non-traded Goods and Partially Integrated Financial Markets', *Kellogg Graduate School of Management*, Northwestern University, Evanston, Ill.

Lyons, R.K. (1995) 'Tests of Microstructural Hypotheses in the Foreign Exchange Market', *Journal of Financial Economics*, **39**, 321–351.

Lyons, R.K. (1996) 'Foreign Exchange Volume: Sound and Fury Signifying Nothing?', in J.A. Frankel, G. Giampaolo, and G. Alberto, (eds.), *The Microstructure of Foreign Exchange Markets*, University of Chicago Press, Chicago, pp 183–205.

Lyons, R.K. (1998) 'Profits and Position Control: A Week of FX Dealing', *Journal of International Money and Finance*, **17**, 97–115.

Lyons, R.K. (2001) *The Microstructure Approach to Exchange Rates*, MIT Press, Cambridge, Mass.

MacDonald, R. and Marsh, I.W. (1996) 'Foreign Exchange Forecasters are Heterogeneous: Confirmation and Consequences', *Journal of International Money and Finance*, **15**, 665–685.

MacDonald, R. and Power, D. (1995) 'Stock Prices, Dividends and Retention: Long-Run Relationships and Short-Run Dynamics', *Journal of Empirical Finance*, **2**, 135–151.

MacDonald, R. and Speight, A.E.H. (1991) 'The Term Structure of Interest Rates under Rational Expectations: Some International Evidence', *Applied Financial Economics*, **1**, 211–221.

MacDonald, R. and Taylor, M.P. (1993) 'The Monetary Approach to the Exchange Rate: Rational Expectations, Long Run Equilibrium and Forecasting', *IMF Staff Papers*, **40**(1), 89–107.

MacDonald, R. and Torrance, T.S. (1988) 'On Risk, Rationality and Excessive Speculation in the Deutschemark United States Dollar Exchange Market: Some Evidence Using Survey Data', *Oxford Bulletin of Economics and Statistics*, **50**(2), 107–123.

Maenhout, P.J. (2001) 'Robust Portfolio Rules, Hedging and Asset Pricing', Working Paper, Finance Department, INSEAD, France.

Mahoney, J. (1996) 'Forecasting Biases in Value-at-risk Estimations: Evidence from Foreign Exchange and Global Equity Portfolios', Working Paper, Federal Reserve Bank of New York, September.

Malkiel, B.G. (1977) 'The Valuation of Closed-end Investment-company Shares', *Journal of Finance*, **32**(3), 847–859.

Malkiel, B.G. (1995) 'Returns from Investing in Equity Mutual Funds 1971 to 1991', *Journal of Finance*, **50**(2), 549–572.

Mankiw, N.G. and Miron, J.A. (1986) 'The Changing Behavior of the Term Structure of Interest Rates', *Quarterly Journal of Economics*, **101**(2), 211–228.

Mankiw, N.G. and Shapiro, M.D. (1986) 'Risk and Return: Consumption Beta Versus Market Beta', *Review of Economics and Statistics*, **68**(3), 452–459.

Mankiw, N.G. and Summers, L.H. (1984) 'Do Long-term Interest Rates Overreact to Short Term Interest Rates', *Brookings Papers on Economic Activity*, **1**, 223–242.

Mankiw, N.G. and Zeldes, S.P. (1991) 'The Consumption of Stockholders and Non-stockholders', *Journal of Financial Economics*, **29**(1), 97–112.

Mankiw, N.G., Romer, D. and Shapiro, M.D. (1985) 'An Unbiased Reexamination of Stock Market Volatility', *Journal of Finance*, **40**, 677–687.

Mankiw, N.G., Romer, D. and Shapiro, M.D. (1991) 'Stock Market Forecastability and Volatility: A Statistical Appraisal', *Review of Economic Studies*, **58**, 455–477.

Marcet, A. and Sargent, T.J. (1989) 'Convergence of Least Squares Learning Mechanisms in Self-referential Linear Stochastic Models', *Journal of Economic Theory*, **48**(2), 337–368.

Mark, N.C. (1985) 'On Time Varying Risk Premia in the Foreign Exchange Market: An Econometric Analysis', *Journal of Monetary Economics*, **16**, 3–18.

Mark, N.C. (1988) 'Time Varying Betas and Risk Premia in the Pricing of Forward Foreign Exchange Contracts', *Journal of Financial Economics*, **22**, 335–354.

Mark, N.C. (1995) 'Exchange Rates and Fundamentals: Evidence on Long Horizon Predictability', *American Economic Review*, **85**(1), 201–218.

Mark, N.C. and Sul, D. (2001) 'Nominal Exchange Rates and Monetary Fundamentals: Evidence from a Small Post Bretton Woods Panel', *Journal of International Economics*, **53**, 29–52.

Mark, N.C. and Wu, Y. (1998) 'Rethinking Deviations from Uncovered Interest Parity: The Role of Covariance Risk and Noise', *Economic Journal*, **108**(451), 1686–1706.

Marsh, T.A. and Merton, R.C. (1986) 'Dividend Variability and Variance Bounds Tests for the Rationality of Stock Market Prices', *American Economic Review*, **76**, 483–498.

McCallum, B.T. (1994) 'A Reconsideration of the Uncovered Interest Parity Relationship', *Journal of Monetary Economics*, **33**, 105–132.

McCulloch, J.H. (1971) 'Measuring the Term Structure of Interest Rates', *Journal of Business*, **44**, 19–31.

McCulloch, J.H. (1990) 'U.S. Government Term Structure Data', in B. Friedman and F. Hahn (eds.), *The Handbook of Monetary Economics*, North Holland, Amsterdam, The Netherlands.

McCulloch, J.H. (1993) 'A Reexamination of Traditional Hypotheses about the Term Structure – A Comment', *Journal of Finance*, **48**(2), 779.

McElroy, M.B., Burmeister, E. and Wall, K.D. (1985) 'Two Estimators for the APT Model When Factors are Measured', *Economic Letters*, **19**, 271–275.

McFarland, J.W., McMahon, P.C. and Ngama, Y. (1994) 'Forward Exchange Rates and Expectations during the 1920s: A Re-examination of the Evidence', *Journal of International Money and Finance*, **13**, 627–636.

Meese, E. (1990) 'Currency Fluctuation in the Post-Bretton Woods Era', *Journal of Economic Perspectives*, **4**(1), 117–134.

Meese, R.A. (1986) 'Testing for Bubbles in Exchange Markets: A Case of Sparkling Rates', *Journal of Political Economy*, **94**(2), 345–373.

Meese, R.A. and Rogoff, K. (1983) 'Empirical Exchange Rate Models of the Seventies: Do they Fit Out of Sample?' *Journal of International Economics*, **14**, 3–24.

Mehra, R. and Prescott, E.C. (1985) 'The Equity Premium: A Puzzle', *Journal of Monetary Economics*, **15**, 145–161.

Menkhoff, L. (1998) 'The Noise Trading Approach – Questionnaire Evidence from Foreign Exchange', *Journal of International Money and Finance*, **17**, 547–564.

Merton, R.C. and Henriksson, R. (1981) 'On Market Timing and Investment Performance II: Statistical Procedures for Evaluating Forecasting Skills', *Journal of Business*, **54**, 513–533.

Merton, R.C. (1969) 'Lifetime Portfolio Selection under Uncertainty. The Continuous-time Case', *Review of Economics and Statistics*, **51**, 247–257.

Merton, R.C. (1971) 'Optimum Consumption and Portfolio Rules in a Continuous Time Model', *Journal of Economic Theory*, **3**, 373–413.

Merton, R.C. (1973) 'An Intertemporal Capital Asset Pricing Model', *Econometrica*, **41**, 867–887.

Merton, R.C. (1980) 'On Estimating the Expected Return on the Market', *Journal of Financial Economics*, **8**, 323–361.

Merton, R.C. (1987) 'On the Current State of the Stock Market Rationality Hypothesis', in S. Fischer (ed.), *Macroeconomics and Finance: Essays in Honor of Franco Modigliani*, MIT Press, Cambridge, Mass.

Michael, P., Nobay, A.R. and Peel, D.A. (1997) 'Transactions Costs and Non-Linear Adjustment in Real Exchange Rates: An Empirical Investigation', *Journal of Political Economy*, **105**, 862–879.

Michaely, R., Thaler, R.H. and Womack, K.L. (1995) 'Price Reactions to Dividend Initiations and Omissions: Overreaction or Draft?', *Journal of Finance*, **50**, 573–608.

Miles, D. and Timmermann, A. (1996) 'Variation in Expected Stock Returns: Evidence on the Pricing of Equities from a Cross-section of UK Companies', *Economica*, **63**(251), 369–382.

Modjtahedi, B. (1991) 'Multiple Maturities & Time Varying Risk Premia in Forward Exchange Markets: An Econometric Analysis', *Journal of International Economics*, **30**, 69–86.

Moore, M.J. and Roche, M.J. (2002) 'Volatility and Persistent Real Exchange Rates without Sticky Prices', *Quarterly Financial Economics*.

Moore, M.J. and Roche, M.J. (2002) 'Less of a Puzzle: A New Look at the Forward Forex Market', *Journal of International Economics*, **58**(2), 387–411.

Morey, M.R. (2003) 'Should You Carry the Load? A Comprehensive Analysis of Load and No-load Mutual Fund Out-of-sample Performance', *Journal of Banking and Finance*, **27**, 1245–1271.

Moskowitz, T. and Grinblatt, M. (1999) 'Do Industries Explain Momentum?' *Journal of Finance*, **54**, 1249–1290.

Muth, J.F. (1961) 'Rational Expectations and the Theory of Price Movements', *Econometrica*, **29**(3), 315–335.

Myers, S. and Majluf, N. (1984) 'Corporate Financing and Investment Decisions When Firms Have Information Investors Do Not Have', *Journal of Financial Economics*, 187–221.

Neely, C.J. and Weller, P.A. (2003) 'Intraday Technical Trading in the Foreign Exchange Market', *Journal of International Money and Finance*, **22**, 223–237.

Neely, C.J., Weller, P.A. and Dittmar, R. (1997) 'Is Technical Analysis in the Foreign Exchange Market Profitable? A Genetic Programming Approach', *Journal of Financial and Quantitative Analysis*, **32**, 405–426.

Nelson, D.B. (1991) 'Conditional Heteroscedasticity in Asset Returns', *Econometrica*, **59**(2), 343–370.

Newey, W.K. and McFadden, D.L. (1994) 'Large Sample Estimation and Hypothesis Testing', in R.F. Engle and D.L. McFadden (eds.), *Handbook of Econometrics: Volume 4*, Elsevier Science, Amsterdam, The Netherlands, pp. 2111–2245.

Newey, W.K. and West, K.D. (1987) 'A Simple, Positive Semi-definite, Heteroskedasticity and Auto-correlation Consistent Covariance Matrix', *Econometrica*, **55**(3), 703–708.

Ng, D.T. (2004) 'The International CAPM When Expected Returns are Time Varying', *Journal of International Money and Finance*, **23**, 189–230.

Obstfeld, M. and Rogoff, K. (2000) 'New Directions for Stochastic Open Economy Models', *Journal of International Economics*, **20**(1), 1.

Obstfeld, M. and Taylor, A.M. (1997) 'Nonlinear Aspects of Goods-market Arbitrage and Adjustment: Heckscher's Commodity Points Revisited', *Journal of the Japanese and International Economies*, **11**, 441–479.

Odean, T. (1998) 'Are Investors Reluctant to Realize their Losses?' *Journal of Finance*, **53**, 1775–1798.

Odean, T. (1999) 'Do Investors Trade Too Much?' *American Economic Review*, **89**, 1279–1298.

Pagan, A.R. and Ullah, A. (1988) 'The Econometric Analysis of Models with Risk Terms', *Journal of Applied Econometrics*, **3**, 87–105.

Parsley, D.C. and Wei, S.J. (1996) 'Convergence to the Law of One Price without Trade Barriers or Currency Fluctuations', *Quarterly Journal of Economics*, **111**, 1211–1136.

Pastor, L. (2000) 'Portfolio Selection and Asset Pricing Models', *Journal of Finance*, **LV**(1), 179–223.

Patterson, K. (2000) *An Introduction to Applied Econometrics*, Palgrave.

Peel, D.A. and Taylor, M.P. (2002) 'Covered Interest Arbitrage in the Inter-war Period and the Keynes-Einzig Conjecture', *Journal of Money, Banking and Credit*, **34**(1), 51–75.

Pesando, J.E. (1983) 'On Expectations, Term Premiums and the Volatility of Long-term Interest Rates', *Journal of Monetary Economics*, **12**(3), 467–474.

Pesaran, M.H. (1987) *The Limits to Rational Expectations*, Blackwell, Oxford.

Pesaran, M.H. and Timmermann, A. (1994) 'Forecasting Stock Returns: An Examination of Stock Market Trading in the Presence of Transaction Costs', *Journal of Forecasting*, **13**(4), 335–367.

Pesaran, M.H. and Timmermann, A. (1995) 'Predictability of Stock Returns: Robustness and Economic Significance', *Journal of Finance*, **50**(4), 1201–1228.

Pesaran, M.H. and Timmermann, A. (2000) 'A Recursive Modelling Approach to Predicting UK Stock Returns', *Economic Journal*, **110**(460), 159–191.

Phillips, P.C.B. and Hansen, B.E. (1990) 'Statistical Inference in Instrumental Variables Regression with I(1) Processes', *Review of Economic Studies*, **57**, 99–125.

Phillips, P.C.B. and Perron, P. (1988) 'Testing for a Unit Root in Time Series Regression', *Biometrika*, **75**(2), 335–346.

Piazzesi, M. (2002) 'Affine Term Structure Models', *Handbook of Financial Econometrics*, North Holland.

Politis, D.N. and Romano, J.P. (1994) 'The Stationary Bootstrap', *Journal of the American Statistical Association*, **89**, 1303–1313.

Poterba, J.M. and Summers, L.H. (1986) 'The Persistence of Volatility and Stock Market Fluctuations', *American Economic Review*, **76**(5), 1142–1151.

Poterba, J.M. and Summers, L.H. (1988) 'Mean Reversion in Stock Prices: Evidence and Implications', *Journal of Financial Economics*, **22**, 26–59.

Prat, G. and Uctum, R. (1994) 'Formation des Anticipations de Change: les Enseigneres des Enqueteres du Consensus Forecasts', *AFFI 16th Annual Meeting*, Paris, December.

Psaradakis, Z. (2001) 'On Bootstrap Inference in Cointegrating Regressions', *Economics Letters*, **72**, 1–10.

Quigley, G. and Sinquefield, R. (1999) 'The Performance of UK Equity Unit Trusts', Report by Dimensional Fund Advisors for Institute for Fiduciary Education.

Rabin, M. (1998) 'Psychology and Economics', *Journal of Economic Literature*, **XXXVI**(1), 11–46.

Rabin, M. (2000) 'Risk Aversion and Expected Utility Theory: A Calibration Theorem', *Econometrica*, **68**(5), 5.

Rabin, M. and Thaler, R.H. (2001) 'Anomalies: Risk Aversion', *Journal of Economic Perspectives*, **15**(1), 219–232.

Rapach, D.E. and Wohar, M.E. (2002) 'Testing the Monetary Model of Exchange Rate Determination: New Evidence from a Century of Data', *Journal of International Economics*, **58**(1), 359–386.

Reinganum, M.R. (1982) 'A Direct Test of Roll's Conjecture on the Firm Size Effect', *Journal of Finance*, **37**(1), 27–35.

Reinganum, M.R. (1983) 'The Anomalous Stock Market Behavior of Small Firms in January: Empirical Tests for Tax-loss Selling Effects', *Journal of Financial Economics*, **12**(1), 89–104.

Remola, E.M., Kleiman, P. and Gruenstein, D. (1997) 'Market Returns and Mutual Fund Flows', *Economic Policy Review, Federal Reserve Bank of New York*, July.

Remolona, E.M., Wickens, M.R. and Gong, F.F. (1998) 'What was the Market's View of UK Monetary Policy? Estimating Inflation Risk and Expected Inflation with Indexed Bonds', Federal Reserve Bank of New York Discussion Paper.

Richards, A. (1995) 'Comovements in National Stock Market Returns: Evidence of Predictability but Not Cointegration', *Journal of Monetary Economics*, **36**, 631–654.

Richards, A. (1997) 'Winner-loser Reversals in National Stock Market Indices: Can They Be Explained?' *Journal of Finance*, **51**, 2129–2144.

Robinson, P.M. (1994) 'Efficient Tests of Nonstationary Hypothesis', *Journal of the American Statistical Association*, **89**, 1420–1437.

Rogers, J.H. and Jenkins, M. (1995) 'Haircuts or Hysteresis? Sources of Movements in Real Exchange Rates', *Journal of International Economics*, **38**, 339–360.

Rogoff, K. (1984) 'On the Effects of Sterilized Intervention: An Analysis of Weekly Data', *Journal of Monetary Economics*, **14**, 133–150.

Rogoff, K. (1996) 'The Purchasing Power Parity Puzzle', *Journal of Economic Literature*, **XXXIV**(June), 647–668.

Roll, R. (1977) 'A Critique of Asset Pricing Theory's Tests', *Journal of Financial Economics*, **4**, 1073–1103.

Roll, R. (1986) 'The Hubris Hypothesis of Corporate Takeovers', *Journal of Business*, **59**(2), 541–566.

Roll, R. and Ross, S.A. (1980) 'An Empirical Investigation of the APT', *Journal of Finance*, **35**(5), 1073–1103.

Roll, R. and Ross, S.A. (1984) 'A Critical Re-examination of the Empirical Evidence on the APT: A Reply', *Journal of Finance*, **39**(2), 347–350.

Rouwenhorst, K.G. (1998) 'International Momentum Strategies', *Journal of Finance*, **53**, 267–284.

Roy, A.D. (1952) 'Safety First and the Holding of Assets', *Econometrica*, **20**, 431–449.

Rudebusch, G.D. (1995) 'Federal-Reserve Interest-rate Targeting, Rational Expectations, and the Term Structure', *Journal of Monetary Economics*, **35**(2), 245–274.

Samuelson, P. (1963) 'Risk and Uncertainty: A Falacy of Large Numbers', *Scienta*, **98**, 108–113.

Samuelson, P. (1965) 'Proof that Properly Anticipated Prices Fluctuate Randomly', *Industrial Management Review*, **6**, 41–49.

Samuelson, P.A. (1969) 'Lifetime Portfolio Choice Selection by Dynamic Stochastic Programming', *Review of Economics and Statistics*, **51**(3), 239–246.

Sarno, L. and Taylor, M.P. (1998) 'Real Exchange Rates under the Recent Float: Unequivocal Evidence of Mean Reversion', *Economics Letters*, **60**, 131–137.

Sarno, L. and Taylor, M.P. (2002) *The Economics of Exchange Rates*, Cambridge University Press, Cambridge.

Sarno, L. and Thornton, D.L. (2003) 'The Dynamic Relationship between the Federal Funds Rate and the Treasury Bill Rate: An Empirical Investigation', *Journal of Banking and Finance*, **27**, 1079–1110.

Sarno, L. and Valente, G. (2004a) 'Empirical Exchange Rate Models and Currency Risk: Some Evidence from Density Forecasts', Discussion Paper, University of Warwick.

Sarno, L. and Valente, G. (2004b) 'Modeling and Forecasting Stock Returns: Exploiting the Futures Market, Regime Shifts and International Spillovers', *Journal of Applied Econometrics*.

Savage, L. (1964) *The Foundations of Statistics*, John Wiley, New York.

Schwert, G.W. (1989) 'Why Does Stock Market Volatility Change Over Time?' *Journal of Finance*, **44**(5), 1115–1153.

Scott, L.O. (1990) 'Asset Prices, Market Fundamentals, and Long-term Expectations: Some New Tests of Present Value Models', Unpublished, University of Georgia, Athens, Ga.

Segal, U. (1989) 'Anticipated Utility: A Measure Representation Approach', *Annals of Operations Research*, **19**, 359–373.

Sentana, E. and Wadhwani, S. (1992) 'Feedback Traders and Stock Return Autocorrelations: Evidence From a Century of Daily Data', *Economic Journal*, **102**(411), 415–425.

Seo, B. (2003) 'Nonlinear Mean Reversion in the Term Structure of Interest Rates', *Journal of Economic Dynamics and Control*, **27**(11/12), 2243–2265.

Sercu, P., Uppal, R. and vanHulle, C. (1995) 'The Exchange Rate in the Presence of Transaction Costs: Implications for Tests of Purchasing Power Parity', *Journal of Finance*, **50**(4), pp. 1309–1319.

Sharpe, W.F. (1966) 'Mutual Fund Performance', *Journal of Business*, **39**(1), 119–138.

Sharpe, W.F. (1975) 'Adjusting for Risk in Portfolio Performance Measurement', *Journal of Portfolio Management*, **Winter**, 29–34.

Shea, G.S. (1989) 'Ex-post Rational Price Approximations and the Empirical Reliability of the Present-value Relation', *Journal of Applied Econometrics*, **4**(2), 139–159.

Shea, G.S. (1992) 'Benchmarking the Expectations Hypothesis of the Term Structure: An Analysis of Cointegration Vectors', *Journal of Business and Economic Statistics*, **10**(3), 347–365.

Sheffrin, S.M. (1983) *Rational Expectations*, Cambridge University Press, Cambridge, Mass.

Sherif, M. (1937) 'An Experimental Approach to the Study of Attitudes', *Sociometry*, **1**, 90–98.

Shiller, R.J. (1979) 'The Volatility of Long-term Interest Rates and Expectations Models of the Term Structure', *Journal of Political Economy*, **87**(6), 1190–1219.

Shiller, R.J. (1981) 'Do Stock Prices Move too Much to be Justified by Subsequent Changes in Dividends?' *American Economic Review*, **71**, 421–436.

Shiller, R.J. (1989) *Market Volatility*, MIT Press, Cambridge, Mass.

Shiller, R.J. (1990) 'Speculative Prices and Popular Models', *Journal of Economic Perspectives*, **4**(2), 55–65.

Shiller, R.J. (1999) 'Human Behavior and the Efficiency of Financial Markets', *Handbook of Macroeconomics*, **1**, 1305–1340.

Shiller, R.J. and Beltratti, A.E. (1992) 'Stock Prices and Bond Yields', *Journal of Monetary Economics*, **30**, 25–46.

Shiller, R.J. and Perron, P. (1985) 'Testing the Random Walk Hypothesis: Power Versus Frequency of Observation', *Economics Letters*, **18**, 381–386.

Shleifer, A. and Summers, L.H. (1990) 'The Noise Trader Approach to Finance', *Journal of Economic Perspectives*, **4**(2), 19–33.

Shleifer, A. and Vishny, R.W. (1990) 'Equilibrium Short Horizons of Investors and Firms', *American Economic Review*, **80**(2), 148–153.

Shleifer, A. and Vishny, R.W. (1997) 'The Limits of Arbitrage', *Journal of Finance*, **52**(1), 35–55.

Siegel, J. (1998) *Stocks for the Long Run*, 2nd edition, McGraw-Hill, New York.

Simon, D.P. (1989) 'Expectations and Risk in the Treasury Bill Market: An Instrumental Variables Approach', *Journal of Financial and Quantitative Analysis*, **24**(3), 357–365.

Simons, K. (1999) 'Should US Investors Invest Overseas?' *New England Economic Review (Federal Reserve Bank of Boston)*, Nov./Dec., 29–39.

Singleton, K.J. (1980) 'Expectations Models of the Term Structure and Implied Variance Bounds', *Journal of Political Economy*, **88**(6), 1159–1176.

Sirri, E.R. and Tufano, P. (1993) 'Buying and Selling Mutual Funds: Flows, Performance, Fees and Services', Working Paper, Harvard Business School, Cambridge, Mass.

Skinner, D. and Sloan, R. (2002) 'Earnings Surprises, Growth Expectations and Stock Returns, or, Don't Let an Earnings Torpedo Sink Your Portfolio', *Review of Accounting Studies*, **7**, 289–312.

Smith, P.N. (1993) 'Modeling Risk Premia in International Asset Markets', *European Economic Review*, **37**(1), 159–176.

Smith, P.N. and Wickens, M.R. (2002) 'Asset Pricing with Observable Stochastic Discount Factors', *Journal of Economic Surveys*, **16**, 397–446.

Smith, P.N., Sorensen, S. and Wickens, M.R. (2003) 'Macroeconomic Sources of Equity Risk', Working Paper, University of York.

Solnik, B. (1974) 'Why not Diversify Internationally Rather than Domestically', *Financial Analysts Journal*, Jul./Aug., 48–54.

Soros, G. (1987) *The Alchemy of Finance*, Simon and Schuster, New York.

Stamburgh, R.F. (1999) 'Predictive Regressions', *Journal of Financial Economics*, **54**, 375–421.

Sullivan, R., Timmermann, A. and White, H. (1999) 'Data-snooping, Technical Trading Rule Performance, and the Bootstrap', *Journal of Finance*, **65**(5), 1647

Sullivan, R., Timmermann, A. and White, H. (2001) 'Dangers of Data Mining: The Case of Calendar Effects in Stock Returns', *Journal of Econometrics*, **105**(1), 249–286.

Summers, L.H. (1986) 'Does the Stock Market Rationally Reflect Fundamental Values?' *Journal of Finance*, **41**(3), 591–601.

Swensen, D. (2000) *Pioneering Portfolio Management*, The Free Press, New York.

Taylor, A.M. (2001) 'Potential Pitfalls for the Purchasing Power Parity Puzzle? Sampling and Specification Biases in Mean Reversion Tests of the Law of One Price', *Econometrica*, **69**(2), 473–498.

Taylor, M.P. (1987) 'Covered Interest Parity: A High-frequency, High Quality Data Survey', *Economica*, **54**, 429–438.

Taylor, M.P. (1988) 'What Do Investment Managers Know? An Empirical Study of Practitioners Predictions', *Economica*, **55**, 185–202.

Taylor, M.P. (1989a) 'Covered Interest Arbitrage and Market Turbulence', *Economic Journal*, **99**(396), 376–391.

Taylor, M.P. (1989b) 'Expectations, Risk and Uncertainty in the Foreign Exchange Market: Some Results Based on Survey Data', *Manchester School*, **57**(2), 142–153.

Taylor, M.P. (1989c) 'Vector Autoregressive Tests of Uncovered Interest Rate Parity with Allowance for Conditional Heteroscedasticity', *Scottish Journal of Political Economy*, **36**(3), 238–252.

Taylor, M.P. (1992) 'Modelling the Yield Curve', *Economic Journal*, **102**(412), 524–537.

Taylor, M.P. and Peel, D.A. (2000) 'Nonlinear Adjustment, Long-run Equilibrium and Exchange Rate Fundamentals', *Journal of International Money and Finance*, **19**, 33–53.

Taylor, M.P. and Sarno, L. (1998) 'The Behaviour of Real Exchange Rates During the Post-Bretton Woods Period', *Journal of International Economics*, **46**, 281–312.

Taylor, M.P., Peel, D.A. and Sarno, L. (2001) 'Nonlinear Mean-reversion in Real Exchange Rates: Towards a Solution to the Purchasing Power Parity Puzzles', *International Economic Review*, **42**, 1015–1042.

Thaler, R.H. and Johnson, E.J. (1990) 'Gambling with the House Money and Trying to Breakeven – The Effects of Prior Outcomes on Risky Choice', *Management Science*, **36**(6), 643–660.

Thaler, R.H., Tversky, A., Kahneman, D. and Schwartz, A. (1997) 'The Effect of Myopia and Loss Aversion on Risk Taking: An Experimental Test', *Quarterly Journal of Economics*, **112**, 647–661.

Timmermann, A. (1993) 'How Learning in Financial Markets Generates Excess Volatility and Predictability in Stock Prices', *Quarterly Journal of Economics*, **108**, 1135–1145

Timmermann, A. (1994) 'Why do Dividend Yields Forecast Stock Returns?' *Economic Letters*, **46**, 146–158.

Timmermann, A. (1996) 'Excess Volatility and Predictability of Stock Returns in Autoregressive Dividend Models with Learning', *Review of Economic Studies*, **63**(3), 523–558.

Timmermann, A. (2001) 'Structural Breaks, Incomplete Information and Stock Prices', *Journal of Business and Economic Statistics*, **19**(3), 299–314.

Tirole, J. (1985) 'Asset Bubbles and Overlapping Generations', *Econometrica*, **53**(5), 1071–1100.

Tobin, J. (1956) 'The Interest-elasticity of Transactions Demand for Cash', *Review of Economics and Statistics*, **38**(3), 241–247.

Treynor, J.L. and Mazuy, K. (1996) 'Can Mutual Funds Outguess the Market?' *Harvard Business Review*, **44**, 131–136.

Treynor, J.L. (1965) 'How to Rate Management of Investment Funds', *Harward Business Review*, **43**(1), 63–75.

Tzavalis, E. and Wickens, M. (1995) 'The Persistence of Volatility in the US Term Premium 1970–1986', *Economic Letters*, **49**(4), 381–389.

Tzavalis, E. and Wickens, M.R. (1997) 'Explaining the Failure of the Term Spread Models of the Rational Expectations Hypothesis of the Term Structure', *Journal of Money, Credit and Banking*, **29**(3), 364–380.

Vasicek, O.A. (1977) 'An Equilibrium Characterization of the Term Structure', *Journal of Financial Economics*, **5**(2), 177–188.

Veronesi, P. (1999) 'Stock Market Overreaction to Bad News in Good Times: A Rational Expectations Equilibrium Model', *Review of Financial Studies*, **12**, 975–1007.

Veronesi, P. (2003) 'The Peso Problem Hypothesis and Stock Market Returns', *Journal of Economic Dynamics and Control*, **28**, 707–725.

Viceira, L.M. (2001) 'Optimal Portfolio Choice for Long-horizon Investors with Nontradable Labor Income', *Journal of Finance*, **56**(2), 433–470.

Volkman, D. and Wohar, M. (1995) 'Determinants of Persistence in Relative Performance of Mutual Funds', *Journal of Financial Research*, **XVIII**, 415–430.

Walsh, C.E (1998) *Monetary Theory and Policy*, Princeton University Press.

Warther, V.A. (1995) 'Aggregate Mutual Fund Flows and Security Returns', *Journal of Financial Economics*, **39**, 209–235.

Weil, P. (1992) 'Equilibrium Asset Prices with Undiversifiable Labour Income Risk', *Journal of Economic Dynamics and Control*, **16**(3/4), 769.

Welch, I. (2000) 'Views of Financial Economists on the Equity Risk Premium and Other Issues', *Journal of Business*, **73**, 501–537.

Welch, I. (2001) 'The Equity Premium Consensus Forecast Revisited', Working Paper, Yale School of Management.

Wermers, R. (2000) 'Mutual Fund Performance: An Empirical Decomposition into Stock-picking Talent, Style, Transactions Costs and Expenses', *Journal of Finance*, **55**(2), 1655–1695.

West, K.D. (1987a) 'A Specification Test for Speculative Bubbles', *Quarterly Journal of Economics*, **102**(3), 553–580.

West, K.D. (1987b) 'A Standard Monetary Model and the Variability of the Deutschemark-dollar Exchange Rate', *Journal of International Economics*, **23**, 57–76.

West, K.D. (1988a) 'Asymptotic Normality, When Regressors have a Unit Root', *Econometrica*, **56**(6), 1397–1417.

West, K.D. (1988b) 'Dividend Innovations and Stock Price Volatility', *Econometrica*, **56**, 37–61.

White, H. (1980) 'A Heteroscedasticity-consistent Covariance Matrix Estimator and a Direct Test for Heteroscedasticity', *Econometrica*, **48**, 55–68.

White, H. (1984) *Asymptotic Theory for Econometricians*, Academic Press, New York.

WM Company. (1999) 'Comparison of Active and Passive Management of Unit Trusts for Virgin Direct Financial Services'.

Womack, K.L. (1996) 'Do Brokerage Analysts' Recommendations Have Investment Value?' *Journal of Finance*, **51**(1), 137–167.

Woodford, M. (2003) *Interest and Prices: Foundations of a Theory of Monetary Policy*, Princeton University Press, Princeton, N.J.

Wurgler, J. and Zhuravskaya, K. (2002) 'Does Arbitrage Flatten Demand Curves for Stocks?', *Journal of Business*, **75**, 583–608.

Xia, T. (2001) 'Learning about Predictability: The Effects of Parameter Uncertainty on Dynamic Asset Allocation', *Journal of Finance*, **56**(1), 205–246.

Zheng, L. (1999) 'Is Money Smart? A Study of Mutual Fund Investors' Fund Selection Ability', *Journal of Finance*, **54**(3), 901–933.

# Recommended Reading

Here is a highly selective list of texts for 'recommended reading'. These are our 'desirable dozen' books in the finance-economics area that we think complement QFE-II and which our M.Sc./Ph.D. students have also found useful. Some are financial economics, some econometrics and others lead you on to derivatives and financial engineering – all are worth dipping into.

Campbell, J.Y., Lo, A.W. and MacKinlay, A.C. (1997) *The Econometrics of Financial Markets*, Princeton University Press.

– still a classic reference in this area.

Cochrane, J.H. (2001) *Asset Pricing*, Princeton University Press.

– a classic on the theoretical basis of asset pricing, expertly interwoven with relevant econometric techniques.

Cerny, A. (2004) *Mathematical Techniques in Finance*, Princeton University Press.

– clear, practical approach to the math of derivatives and hedging.

Cuthbertson, K. and Nitzsche, D. (2001) *Investments Spot and Derivative Markets*, John Wiley.

– useful and accessible introduction to financial markets.

Cuthbertson, K. and Nitzsche, D. (2001) *Financial Engineering: Derivatives & Risk Management*, John Wiley.

– concentrates on pricing of derivatives and their use in risk management

– both the above texts have a website (www.wiley.co.uk/cuthbertson), with Powerpoint, Excel and Gauss files and other student material.

Hamilton, J.D. (1994) *Time Series Analysis*, Princeton University Press.
– 'The Bible' – but weighs in a few pounds heavier.

Hull, J.C. (2003) *Options, Futures and Other Derivatives*, Prentice Hall.
– concise, accessible text on derivatives.

Luenberger, D.G. (1998) *Investment Science*, Oxford University Press.
 – nice mix of intuitive ideas and math examples of theory of spot and derivative assets.

Patterson, K. (2000) *An Introduction to Applied Econometrics*, Palgrave.
 – a very clear introduction to modern time series econometrics.

Sarno, L. and Taylor M.P.T. (2002) *The Economics of Exchange Rates*, Cambridge University Press.
 – concise, comprehensive and up-to-date coverage.

Shiller, R.J. (2001) *Irrational Exhuberance*, Princeton University Press.
 – classic, popular account of stock market investment.

 – quite simply, read anything he writes (www.econ.yale.edu).

Sydsaeter, K. and Hammond, P. (2002) *Essential Mathematics for Economic Analysis*, Prentice Hall.
 – very well presented introduction to basic math.